SCOREBOARD & BROADCASTING

Senior Director, Scoreboard & Broadcasting ... Michael Bonner
Senior Producer, Scoreboard & Video Production ... Nima Ghandforoush
Producer, Scoreboard & Video Production ... Gregory Colello
Assistant Manager, Scoreboard & Broadcasting ... Brett Moldoff
Senior Producer, Yankees on Demand ... Pete Gergely
Producer, Yankees on Demand ... Brandon Mihm
Public Address Announcer ... Paul Olden
Public Address Announcer Emeritus ... Bob Sheppard
Organists ... Paul Cartier, Ed Alstrom

SECURITY

Executive Director, Team Security ... Edward Fastook
Executive Director, Stadium/Event Security ... Todd Letcher
Manager, Security Systems Administration ... Matthew Deane
Team Security ... Mark Kafalas
Stadium Security ... Joe Flannino, Jerry Laveroni
Executive Security ... Mike Fitzgerald, George Olynyk, George Redding, Robert Schnebly

STADIUM OPERATIONS

Senior Director, Stadium Operations ... Doug Behar
Stadium Superintendent ... Pete Pullara
Assistant Director, Stadium Operations ... Robert Passaro
Head Groundskeeper ... Dan Cunningham
Manager, ADA ... Carol Laurenzano
Manager, Stadium Operations ... Anthony Odierno
Systems Manager, Stadium Operations ... Megan Manfred
Coordinator, ADA ... Aaron Pickus
Administrative Assistant ... Josephine Doring

TECHNOLOGY

Senior Director, Technology ... Mike Lane
Systems Administrator, Technology ... Ryan Vilar de Queiros
Systems Engineer, Technology ... Frank Valletutti
Systems Developer, Technology ... Eddie Coblentz
Technical Services Coordinator, Technology ... John Klippel

TICKET OPERATIONS

Senior Director, Ticket Operations ... Irfan Kirimca
Executive Director, Ticket Operations ... Kevin Dart
Manager, Ticket Operations ... James Traynor
Ticket Office Representatives ... Andrew Deutsch, Hank Grazioso, Dan Hansbury, Scott Liller, Edwin Ruiz, Kate Scanlon
Group Sales Representatives ... Frank Costa, Carlos Gomez, Rosa Muniz, Ronald Stasko
Phonebank ... Betsy Colon, Simone Moragne, Stuart Powell, John Terhune

TOURS & HISTORY

Director, Stadium Tours ... Tony Morante
Tour Coordinators ... Lindsey Spierer, Nick True Palmer

YANKEES FAN CLUB

Director, Yankees Fan Club ... Christy Lee

BASEBALL OPERATIONS (TAMPA)

Vice President, Amateur Scouting ... Damon Oppenheimer
Vice President, Player Personnel ... Billy Connors
Director of Player Development ... Pat Roessler
Coordinator of International Player Development ... Pat McMahon
Assistant Director, Baseball Operations ... Eric Schmitt
Assistant Director, International Operations ... Alex Cotto
Assistant Director, Amateur Scouting ... John Kremer
Equipment Manager, Player Development ... David Hays
Clubhouse Manager, Player Development ... Chris Root
Clubhouse Assistant, Player Development ... Eddie Rivera
Director of Information Systems ... Rob Owens
Pitching Coordinator ... Nardi Contreras
Hitting Coordinator ... James Rowson
Defensive Coordinator ... Jody Reed
Catching Coordinator ... Julio Mosquera
Outfield Instructor ... Jack Hubbard
Video Coordinator ... Adam Czajkowski
Assistant, Player Development ... Yunior Tabares
Coordinator, Mental Conditioning ... Hector Gonzalez
Coordinator, Mental Conditioning ... Chris Passarella
Chinese Interpreter ... Tim Wei Ting Lin
Administrative Assistant ... Jackie Williams
Receptionist ... Linda Cotney

INTERNATIONAL BASEBALL OPERATIONS

Director, International Scouting ... Donny Rowland
Director, Latin American Scouting ... Victor Mata
Director, Latin Baseball Academy ... Joel Lithgow
Manager, Latin Baseball Academy ... Aniuska Sanchez
Latin American Scouting Coordinator ... Ricardo Finol
Clubhouse/Equipment Manager ... Raudo Baez
Clubhouse Attendants ... Jose Guillen, Ambiorix Ozuna

MEDICAL AND TRAINING STAFF (TAMPA)

Team Physician, Tampa ... Andrew Boyer, M.D.
Team Orthopedic Surgeon, Tampa ... Allen Miller, M.D.
Team Chiropractor, Tampa ... Scott Hegseth, D.C.
Head Athletic Trainer, Player Development ... Mark Littlefield
Strength & Conditioning Coordinator ... Mike Wickland
Asst. Strength & Conditioning Coordinator ... Javier Alvidrez

ADMINISTRATION (TAMPA)

Executive Vice President ... Philip A. McNiff
Senior Vice President, General Counsel ... Norman Stallings
Vice President, Marketing ... Howard Grosswirth
Vice President, Community Relations ... John Szponar
Vice President, Administration ... Diann Blanco
Vice President, Operations ... Dean Holbert
Vice President, Risk Management ... Therese Jenkins
Vice President, Spring Training Operations ... Richard Kraft
Vice President, Security ... Randy Baker
Assistant, Director Security ... Bill Navarra
Stadium Supervisor ... Ronnie Kaufman
Controller ... Derrick Baio
Director, Payroll ... Newton Linebaugh
Director, Accounting ... Kevin Adler
Director of Information Technology ... Rudy Ramirez
Head Groundskeeper ... Ritchie Anderson
Assistant Head Groundskeeper ... Jeff Eckert
Grounds Supervisor, Player Development ... Chris Connell
Director, Ticket Operations ... Brian Valdez
Assistant Director, Ticket Operations ... Jennifer Magliocchetti
Manager, Stadium Services ... John Sibayan
Director, Florida Operations, General Manager, Tampa Yankees ... C. Vance Smith
Director, Fantasy Camp, Asst. General Manager, Tampa Yankees ... Julie Ko Kremer
Community Relations Consultant ... Ray Negron

PLAYER DEVELOPMENT AND SCOUTING

Yankees Complex • 3102 N. Himes Ave. • Tampa, FL 33607
PHONE: (813) 875-7569
FAX: (813) 873-2302

MAJOR LEAGUE SPRING TRAINING FACILITY

George M. Steinbrenner Field
1 Steinbrenner Dr. • Tampa, FL 33614
PHONES: (813) 879-2244 • (800) 96-YANKS
FAX: (813) 879-0247

TAMPA STAFF

Miguel Amezquita, Steven Ansaldi, Mike Ansotegui, Eric Baio, Gabriel Baker, Jose Gonzalez Batista, Benjamin Beiro, Brett Boggs, Michael Breden, Kevin Brown, Aaron Butler, Christine Carey, Rolando Chavez, Kimberly Diaz, Brad Delaosa, Allison Ennis, Matthew Farrar, Dawn Galuska, Laurie Gaydos, Matthew Gess, Timothy Guidry, Francisco Hernandez, Juan Hernandez, Milagro Hernandez, John Johnson, Holly Kelley, William King, Bryant Leonard, AmySue Manzione, Ralph Martinez, Dennise Maurer, Joanne Nastal, George Narvaez, Matt Nixon, Gonzalo Noy, Charles Poole, John Quilleon, Josh Roach, Johanna Scanio, Jenette Sibayan, Joe Sigismondi, Tony Sustaita, Matt Szponar, Robert Testo, Jason Valentin, Jamie Ventura, Charles Vissicchio, Robert Vliet, Neil Walter, Katie Woytisek, Krystal Woytisek.

LEGENDS HOSPITALITY, LLC

Corporate Mailing Address
614 Frelinghuysen Avenue • Newark, NJ • 07114
PHONE: (862)-902-5450
FAX: (862) 902-5475

Yankee Stadium Mailing Address
Yankee Stadium • One East 161st Street • Bronx, NY 10451

LEGENDS STAFF

Chief Executive Officer ... Michael Rawlings
Chief Operating Officer ... Dan Smith
President and Chief Customer Officer ... Marty Greenspun
Chief Financial Officer ... David Hammer
Vice President of Finance ... Jim Sheppard
Senior Vice President ... Michael Phillips
Executive Assistant to the Senior Vice President ... Kathleen Kincel
General Manager, Merchandise ... Michael Loparo
Assistant Manager, Merchandise ... Bradley Wilton
Buyer ... Saeed Ramsaroop
Merchandise Supervisor ... Timothy Anziano
Manager, Yankees Team Store ... Anthony Bergamo
General Manager, Concessions ... Anthony Parnagian
Administrative Assistant ... Erin Nargi
Warehouse Manager ... Shiv Ally
Concessions Manager ... Chris Buffa
Vending Manager ... Chris Gallo
Assistant Warehouse Manager ... Leonard Middleton
Utility Manager ... Chabbilall Robert
Concessions Manager ... Joseph Slomski
In-Seat Manager ... Michael Drummond
General Manager, Premium Services ... Don Muszalski
Executive Sous Chef, Legends Suite Club ... R. Christian Hipszer
Manager, Audi Yankees Club/Mohegan Sun Sports Bar ... Max Resomardono
Catering Manager ... Jaisun Ihm
Suite Manager ... Amanda Wood
Assistant Suite Manager ... Ann Marie New
Manager, Legends Suite Club ... Margaret Ann Quinlan
Director, Human Resources ... Robert Brooks
Assistant Manager, Human Resources ... Kevin O'Connor
Manager, Customer Service ... Kimberly Lyons
Controller ... Mark Garramone
Assistant Controller ... Don Croce
Accounts Payable ... Kenya Kendricks
Payroll ... Michael Zagorski
IT Specialists ... Joseph Goerlitz, Matthew Block
Accountants ... Richard DeJesus, David Maul

George M. Steinbrenner III

Principal Owner / Chairperson

Currently the longest-tenured owner in Major League Baseball, George M. Steinbrenner III, celebrates his 37th anniversary as Principal Owner of the New York Yankees in 2010. Under his leadership, the Yankees have become the leading sports franchise and the most highly recognized sports brand in the world.

On January 3, 1973, a group of businessmen formed and led by Mr. Steinbrenner purchased the New York Yankees from CBS for a net price of $8.7 million. It took just five years for his aggressive leadership to turn the organization back into World Champions. In the 37 years he has been Principal Owner of the club, the Yankees have posted a Major League-best .565 winning percentage (3,308-2,551-3 record) while winning 11 American League pennants and seven World Championships (also the most in the Majors).

In addition to the team's on-field success, the New York Yankees have consistently shattered franchise and league attendance records at home and on the road. In 2009, they drew 3,719,358 fans in their first season of play in Yankee Stadium, topping the American League in attendance for the seventh straight season (2003-09). Currently, the Yankees remain the only franchise in baseball history to draw more than 4 million fans at home in four consecutive seasons (2005-08).

Away from Yankee Stadium, the Yankees continue to be one of the most sought after attractions in all of sports. They drew 6,502,416 combined fans in home and road games during the 2009 regular season, topping the AL for the 11th consecutive year (1999-2009). For seven straight seasons from 2002-08, the Yankees led all 30 Major League clubs in combined attendance, drawing at least 7 million total fans in each of the final five years of that stretch (2004-08) to mark five of the six largest single-season attendance totals in professional sports history, including the all-time mark of 7,325,051 fans in 2006.

In recent years, Mr. Steinbrenner's foresight into both sports and business has continued to build the value and prominence of the franchise, positioning it for the future. In 2002, the *Sporting News* named him the No. 1 "Most Powerful Man in Sports." *Forbes Magazine* has consistently listed the Yankees as the most valuable franchise in all of Baseball. Mr. Steinbrenner's vision led to the creation of YankeeNets, which owned the New Jersey Nets and New Jersey Devils and ultimately led to the launch of the YES Network, a trailblazing enterprise that has been the nation's most watched regional sports network for the past seven years. Most recently, Mr. Steinbrenner teamed with long-time friend and Dallas Cowboys owner Jerry Jones, creating Legends Hospitality, LLC, a new concession and merchandising company which currently operates at the Yankees' and Cowboys' new stadiums.

In 2006, his participation in the groundbreaking ceremony for the new Yankee Stadium underscored his role as the principal impetus in moving the much-anticipated facility towards its opening in 2009.

During the nationally broadcast pregame ceremony prior to the 2008 All-Star Game at the original Yankee Stadium, Major League Baseball and the Yankees organization paid tribute to the Baseball legend. On a field lined with the 2008 All-Stars and the largest gathering of Hall of Famers ever assembled, Mr. Steinbrenner was given the honor of delivering the ceremonial first-pitch baseball to the pitcher's mound at the center of the infield.

Baseball Commissioner Allan H. (Bud) Selig may have best described Mr. Steinbrenner's legacy by saying, "Without a doubt, George Steinbrenner is one of the most accomplished owners in the history of Major League Baseball. His stewardship of the New York Yankees has produced seven World Championships, continuing the remarkable tradition of a franchise that is as proud as any in all of sports. George has been a trusted friend since he entered baseball in 1973. Time and again, he has been a source for sound advice and great support. George Steinbrenner is more than just a legendary baseball man. He is simply a great man."

With 37 seasons of ownership now completed, Mr. Steinbrenner's tenure has exceeded that of any other New York Yankees owner by 13 years (Colonel Jacob Ruppert purchased the Yankees with Tillinghast L'Hommedieu Huston in January 1915, bought out Huston in 1922, and maintained sole ownership in the club until his death in January 1939—a total of 24 years). Since Mr. Steinbrenner became Principal Owner, the other 29 Major League clubs have had over 100 owners or ownership groups while the Yankees have had just one.

Mr. Steinbrenner's success in the sports world began at an early age. He was a multi-sport athlete at Culver Military Academy (where he is in the Athletic Hall of Fame) and at Williams College. He began his successful coaching career as an assistant football coach at two Big Ten universities, Northwestern and Purdue. Then he assembled championship basketball teams in the National Industrial and American Basketball Leagues. In 2002, he was honored with the highly prestigious Gold Medal Award from the National Football Foundation and College Hall of Fame for a lifetime of "outstanding commitment, dedication and dynamic leadership in his business, as well as his personal life."

Mr. Steinbrenner has devoted as much time and effort to the U.S. Olympic Committee as he has to his many other sporting endeavors. He was Chairman of the U.S. Olympic Committee Foundation (1997-2002) and the Olympic Overview Commission (1988-89) that was created to evaluate the structure and efforts of the U.S. Olympic program. He also served as Vice President of the USOC (1989-96) and has been honored with the General Douglas MacArthur USOC Foremost Award and the F. Don Miller United States Olympic Award.

Mr. Steinbrenner is a member of the Baseball Hall of Fame's Board of Directors and has served on the NCAA Foundation Board of Trustees since 1990.

Most of Mr. Steinbrenner's philanthropic endeavors are performed without fanfare. However, he has been repeatedly recognized by the communities in which he immerses himself. In 1993, he earned the Tampa Civitan Club's "Outstanding Citizen" Award, and in 1998, Tampa Law Enforcement named him "Citizen of the Year" for founding a scholarship fund for the children of slain law enforcement officers. In addition, Mr. Steinbrenner was honored as an "Outstanding New Yorker" by the New York Society of Association Executives in 1997 and credited in 2009 by the Museum of the City of New York as one of the "New York City 400," recognizing "people who have helped create the world's greatest city since its founding in 1609."

In February 2008, the Tampa City Council and the Board of the Hillsborough County Commissioner's Office both passed resolutions endorsing the renaming of Legends Field after Mr. Steinbrenner to pay tribute to his numerous contributions to the area. On March 27, 2008, Mr. Steinbrenner—joined by his family—pulled down a curtain draped above the outfield scoreboard to unveil the new name for the Yankees' spring training home: George M. Steinbrenner Field.

In the fall of 2009, George M. Steinbrenner High School was opened in Lutz, Fla. The school was named after Mr. Steinbrenner by the Hillsborough County School Board in recognition of his philanthropic involvement in the community, particularly with the school system.

Chronology of Yankees Ownership

January 9, 1903: Frank Ferrell and Bill Devery purchase the Baltimore franchise of the American League for $18,000 and move the team to New York.
January 11, 1915: Col. Jacob Ruppert and Col. Tillinghast L'Hommedieu Huston purchase the Yankees for $460,000.
May 21, 1922: Col. Ruppert buys out Col. Huston for $1,500,000.
January 13, 1939: Col. Ruppert dies.
January 25, 1945: Dan Topping, Del Webb and Larry MacPhail purchase the Yankees for $2,800,000 from the estate of the late Col. Ruppert.
November 2, 1964: CBS purchases 80 percent of the Yankees for $11,200,000, later buys the remaining 20 percent.
January 3, 1973: A limited partnership, headed by George M. Steinbrenner as its Managing General Partner, purchases the Yankees from CBS for a net price of $8.7 million.

Harold Z. (Hal) Steinbrenner

Managing General Partner / Co-Chairperson

Hal Steinbrenner begins his 20th season with the New York Yankees organization in 2010 and his second as Managing General Partner / Co-Chairperson. On November 20, 2008, Major League Baseball formalized Mr. Steinbrenner's role as the New York Yankees' managing partner.

In his first full year as Managing General Partner in 2009, the Yankees capped their historic inaugural season in Yankee Stadium with their 27th World Championship.

The 41-year-old son of Principal Owner George Steinbrenner was elected General Partner by the New York Yankees Partnership in 1996, and he held that title for 13 seasons. In 2007, Mr. Steinbrenner was also named Chairman of Yankee Global Enterprises, LLC.

Along with General Partner / Co-Chairperson Hank Steinbrenner, his responsibilities include overseeing all areas of the club's business and baseball operations, and directing financial aspects of the New York Yankees, Yankee Global Enterprises and affiliates. In addition, he serves on the Board of Directors for Legends Hospitality, LLC, a concession and merchandising company developed with the Dallas Cowboys which operates at the Yankees' and Cowboys' new stadiums.

Mr. Steinbrenner is also Chairman and CEO of Steinbrenner Hotel Properties and holds a seat on both the Board of Directors of the Boys & Girls Club of Tampa Bay and the Special Operations Warrior Foundation.

Mr. Steinbrenner attended Culver Military Academy and graduated from Williams College in 1991 with a Bachelor of Arts degree. He earned a Master's degree in Business Administration from the University of Florida in 1994. Mr. Steinbrenner and his wife, Christina, currently reside in Tampa, Fla.

Henry G. (Hank) Steinbrenner

General Partner / Co-Chairperson

Hank Steinbrenner begins his third season as General Partner and second season as Co-Chairperson of the New York Yankees. Along with Managing General Partner / Co-Chairperson Hal Steinbrenner, the 52-year-old son of Principal Owner George Steinbrenner is responsible for overseeing all areas of the club's business and baseball operations.

Prior to the 2008 season, Mr. Steinbrenner was directly involved in the delicate negotiations and eventual re-signings of Yankees All-Stars Jorge Posada, Mariano Rivera and Alex Rodriguez, while guiding the managerial search that concluded with the hiring of former Yankees catcher and bench coach Joe Girardi, who led the club to the 2009 World Series title. Mr. Steinbrenner was also part of the collaborative front office effort of the 2008-09 offseason, which led to the signings of free agent first baseman Mark Teixeira and pitchers CC Sabathia and A.J. Burnett, who helped propel the club to the 27th championship in franchise history.

Mr. Steinbrenner has served as Chairman and Director of Minch Transit Company, Vice President and Director of Bay Farms Corporation, Vice President and Director of Mid-Florida Hotels Corporation, and has been a member of the board of the Ocala Breeders Sales Company. In the Tampa Bay community, he has been involved in a number of children's charities.

Mr. Steinbrenner attended Culver Military Academy and Central Methodist College. He is the father of four children and resides in Tampa, Fla.

Hot Ticket

The Yankees drew 3,719,358 fans in their first season of play in Yankee Stadium in 2009, topping the American League in attendance for the seventh straight season (2003-09). They drew a combined 6,502,416 fans in home and road games in 2009, topping the AL for the 11th consecutive year (1999-2009). The Yankees currently own five of the six largest single-season attendance totals in professional sports history, including the all-time mark of 7,325,051 fans in 2006. In addition, the Yankees are the only Major League franchise to reach the four-million mark in home attendance in four straight seasons, accomplishing the feat from 2005-08.

HIGHEST SINGLE-SEASON HOME AND ROAD ATTENDANCE

Attendance	Club	Year	Total Attendance (Home, Road)
7,325,051	**New York Yankees**	**2006**	**(4,243,780 – home; 3,081,271 – road)**
7,249,285	**New York Yankees**	**2007**	**(4,271,083 – home; 2,978,202 – road)**
7,178,421	Colorado Rockies	1993	(4,483,350 – home; 2,695,071 – road)
7,149,137	**New York Yankees**	**2008**	**(4,298,543 – home; 2,850,594 – road)**
7,088,291	**New York Yankees**	**2005**	**(4,090,692 – home; 2,997,599 – road)**
7,083,958	**New York Yankees**	**2004**	**(3,775,292 – home; 3,308,666 – road)**

Jennifer Steinbrenner Swindal

General Partner / Vice Chairperson

Jennifer Steinbrenner Swindal begins her second full season in the role of General Partner / Vice Chairperson of the New York Yankees. In 2008, Ms. Steinbrenner held the title of Senior Vice President of New Stadium Public Affairs. The elder daughter of Principal Owner George Steinbrenner previously served in the Yankees Public Affairs Department in 1984-85 prior to spending 23 years actively participating in the philanthropic community.

Her present responsibilities include the implementation and integration of various community programs relating to Yankee Stadium. In addition, she serves in a supervisory role for the New York Yankees and Tampa Yankees Foundations, overseeing numerous local, regional and national outreach efforts.

Ms. Steinbrenner has a distinguished record of contributing to community projects and initiatives, including current commitments on the Florida State Fair Authority (Executive Committee, Agricultural Committee, and Chairwoman of the Marketing Committee), Board of Directors of Mary Lee's House (a child protection and advocacy center in Tampa), Board of Directors and Executive Committee of the H.B. Plant Museum, Board of Directors of the New York Pops, and Advisory Committee for the Tampa Salvation Army. She has also held prior board positions with the Children's Cancer Center of Tampa, Boys & Girls Clubs of Tampa Bay, Florida Orchestra, Red Cross of Tampa and Culver Academies.

A Morehead Scholar and 1981 graduate of the University of North Carolina with a Bachelor of Science degree in business administration, Ms. Steinbrenner continues her commitment to the university, serving on the UNC Board of Visitors and the Parents Council. Her daughter, Haley, received her undergraduate degree from UNC in 2008, and her son, Stephen, is currently a junior there.

Ms. Steinbrenner was born in Cleveland, Ohio, and makes her home in Tampa, Fla.

Jessica Steinbrenner

General Partner / Vice Chairperson

Jessica Steinbrenner begins her second full season as General Partner / Vice Chairperson for the New York Yankees. The younger daughter of Principal Owner George M. Steinbrenner previously served in the role of Senior Vice President for the team in 2008.

In addition, Mrs. Steinbrenner serves as the Chief Executive Officer of Bay Farms Corporation and serves on the board of the Florida Thoroughbred Breeders' and Owners' Association. She has also authored two childrens books: *My Sleepy Room* and *My Messy Room*.

She attended Culver Girls Academy and graduated from Sweet Briar College in Virginia. Mrs. Steinbrenner currently resides in Tampa, Fla., with her husband, Felix, and her four children.

Joan Z. Steinbrenner

Vice Chairperson

Joan Steinbrenner holds the position of Vice Chairperson of the New York Yankees.

Mrs. Steinbrenner has participated in many community projects and supported numerous philanthropic organizations. Among her many dignified community roles, she was named State Chairperson for the Florida Special Olympics in 1981 and 1982, and for two years was on the Board of Directors of the National Society to Prevent Blindness. She was also a charter member of Town and Gown, established in 1977 in an effort to form a bond between community supporters in the downtown Tampa area and the University of South Florida.

In addition, Mrs. Steinbrenner was a longtime board member for Children's Home, Inc., and was one of the original members of the H.B. Plant Museum Society. From 1991 to 2000 she served on the Development Council of St. Joseph's Hospital Foundation Board. She currently is a member of the Junior League of Tampa, the Chiselers, and sits on the Board of Directors for the Florida Orchestra.

A graduate of Upper Arlington High School in Columbus, Ohio, and Ohio State University, Mrs. Steinbrenner earned a degree in dental hygiene. She currently resides in Tampa, Fla., with her husband, George, their four children and 13 grandchildren.

Randy Levine

President

Randy Levine begins his 11th season as President of the New York Yankees in 2010. He was named to his position in January 2000, becoming the first person to hold the post with the club since 1986.

Under his supervision and guidance, the franchise constructed the state-of-the-art Yankee Stadium, completing the facility on time for the beginning of the 2009 season which culminated in the franchise's 27th World Championship. Mr. Levine was a principal founder of the YES Network, which was recently named the most-watched regional sports network in the United States for the seventh consecutive year (2003-09). In 2008, Mr. Levine was instrumental in creating Legends Hospitality, LLC, a new concession and merchandising company with the Dallas Cowboys which currently operates at the Yankees' and Cowboys' new stadiums. In 2004, he helped organize Yankees-Steiner, a leading sports memorabilia company.

Mr. Levine has also played a prominent role in the Yankees' international brand expansion, including the 2007 establishment of a first-of-its-kind working relationship with the Chinese Baseball Association. More recently, he led a February 2010 Yankees delegation that visited Tokyo, Beijing and Hong Kong with the 2009 World Series Trophy, marking the first-ever time that the Yankees have brought one of their World Series trophies to Asia. In addition, Mr. Levine helped develop the joint venture agreement in Japan between the Yankees and Yomiuri Shimbun, which is the parent company of the Tokyo Giants.

In 2007, the Yankees became the first Major League organization to sign players from the Israel Baseball League and also embarked on their first-ever large-scale outreach into Taiwan by holding a clinic for high school players and coaches in Taipei, Taiwan. Mr. Levine is also the Yankees' principal liason to Major League Baseball and contributes to player negotiations and contract issues.

Mr. Levine's baseball and business vision has also led to record numbers at Yankee Stadium turnstiles. The club's inaugural 2009 season in Yankee Stadium marked the franchise's seventh consecutive year topping the American League in attendance. In 2008, his direction helped the club establish the all-time AL single-season attendance record of 4,298,543 to become the only Major League franchise to exceed the 4 million mark at home in four consecutive seasons (2005-08).

Before joining the Yankees, Mr. Levine served as New York City's Deputy Mayor for Economic Development, Planning and Administration. He also served as New York City's Labor Commissioner.

From 1995 through 1997, Mr. Levine was Chief Negotiator for Major League Baseball. In 1996, he negotiated the labor agreement that for the first time included revenue sharing, luxury taxes and Interleague play. Prior to that, Mr. Levine served as Principal Associate Deputy Attorney General and Principal Deputy Attorney General at the United States Department of Justice. He has also served as a special delegate to the United States Department of Labor and was a board member for Hudson River Park. Mr. Levine presently serves on the boards of George Washington University, the ASCPA and the Yogi Berra Museum.

Mr. Levine has served on the Board of Directors of the New Jersey Nets and New Jersey Devils and is a member of the Board of Directors of the YES Network and Legends Hospitality, LLC. He is also an officer of Yankee Global Enterprises, LLC. Mr. Levine serves on the International and Diversity Committee of Major League Baseball.

Mr. Levine has been a partner in the New York law firm of Proskauer Rose Goetz & Mendelson and is presently Senior Counsel at the law firm of Akin Gump Strauss Hauer & Feld.

Born on February 22, 1955, in Brooklyn, N.Y., Mr. Levine received a Bachelor of Arts degree from George Washington University in 1977 and his J.D. from Hofstra University School of Law in 1980. Mr. Levine and his wife, Mindy, reside in Manhattan.

New York Yankees Presidents
(Chief Executive Officers)

Joseph W. Gordon	1903-06
Frank J. Farrell	1907-14
Jacob Ruppert	1915-39
Edward G. Barrow	1939-45
Leland S. Macphail	1945-47
Daniel R. Topping	1947-53
Daniel R. Topping & Del E. Webb	1954-64
Daniel R. Topping	1964-66
Michael Burke	1966-73
Gabriel Paul	1973-77
Albert Rosen	1978-79
George M. Steinbrenner	1979-80
Lou Saban	1981-82
Eugene J. McHale	1983-86
RANDY LEVINE	**2000-present**

New York Yankees president Frank Farrell presents a trophy to Yankees manager Harry Wolverton as Red Sox and Yankees players look on at Hilltop Park on April 11, 1912.

Felix M. Lopez, Jr.

Chief International Officer/Executive Vice President

Felix M. Lopez, Jr. begins his first season as Chief International Officer / Executive Vice President in 2010. From 2005-09, he served as Yankees Senior Vice President. His current responsibilities include overseeing the daily operations of George M. Steinbrenner Field, the Himes Player Development Complex and the Single-A Tampa Yankees. He is also involved with the Yankees' Latin Baseball Academy in Boca Chica, Dominican Republic, as well as player development in Latin America.

In January 2010, Mr. Lopez headed a Yankees delegation that took the club's 2009 World Series trophy to the Dominican Republic. The visit included stops at the Presidential Palace, U.S. Embassy, National Police Headquarters and Santo Domingo's Quisqueya Stadium for a Dominican Winter League playoff game.

Under Mr. Lopez' supervision, the Yankees spring training home in Tampa, Fla., has undergone several structural enhancements and renovations in recent years, including the expansion of field box seating and the redesign of the Yankees' clubhouse facilities.

Fan-friendly amenities have been at the forefront of Mr. Lopez' operational strategy, including the design of the Brighthouse Networks Dugout Club, located underneath the field box seats behind home plate. In addition, Mr. Lopez was instrumental in developing the new *Tampa Tribune* Deck, which was unveiled in 2008. Located beyond the right field wall, the unique and intimate structure features picnic-style seating for 500 people, private concessions and a full bar.

Mr. Lopez also serves on the boards of Yankee Global Enterprises, LLC, and Legends Hospitality, LLC.

Before joining the Yankees, Mr. Lopez was the president and owner of Architecture Design Construction, Inc., a company specializing in commercial construction in the southeastern United States.

Born on April 1, 1954, in Havana, Cuba, Mr. Lopez moved to Tampa, Fla., in 1969 and later graduated from Cam Tech School of Construction. He is a member of the Grand Lodge of Free and Accepted Masons of Florida and Nobles of the Mystic Shrine of North America. He also serves on the board of the Gold Shield Foundation and contributes to the efforts of the Police Athletic League (PAL).

Mr. Lopez and his wife, Jessica, reside in Tampa, Fla.

Lonn A. Trost

Chief Operating Officer

Lonn A. Trost begins his 11th season as Chief Operating Officer of the New York Yankees in 2010. He was named to the position on January 10, 2000, after serving as the club's Executive Vice President and General Counsel from 1997-99.

Mr. Trost is responsible for the overall day-to-day functioning of the Yankees' operations. Under his direction, the 2009 World Champion Yankees have seen tremendous growth in brand recognition and sponsorship opportunities, while also establishing single-season home attendance records nine times (1998-99; 2002-08). In 2009, the Yankees led the American League in home attendance for the seventh consecutive year (2003-09), drawing in excess of 16,000 more fans per game than the combined average of the other 29 Major League teams.

Additionally, Mr. Trost, along with Hal Steinbrenner and Randy Levine, spearheaded the most complex undertaking in New York Yankees history—construction and development of Yankee Stadium, which is the largest privately funded building project in the history of the Bronx. While remaining true to the architectural grandeur of the 1923 original, the current facility is the most technologically advanced stadium in baseball.

Before joining the Yankees, Mr. Trost was a partner and member of the Executive Committee of the law firm of Shea and Gould from 1972 to 1994. He was also a partner at the New York law firm of Herrick, Feinstein from 1994 through 1997. While with these firms, he served as outside general counsel for numerous sports franchises, institutions and agents. Among his clients were the New York Yankees and Mets, the New Jersey Nets and Devils, the National Baseball Hall of Fame, Little League Baseball and TCI Cable.

Mr. Trost is a member of the Board of Directors of the YES Network and an officer of Yankee Global Enterprises, LLC, New York Yankees Partnership, Legends Hospitality, LLC, and other New York Yankees affiliates. Mr. Trost is also active with the Tourette Syndrome Association, with whom he is a member of the Corporate and Professional Council.

Born on May 8, 1945, Mr. Trost began his legal career in 1971 with the United States Justice Department, Office of Chief Counsel (Treasury Department). A 1968 graduate of Hunter College in the Bronx, Mr. Trost received his J.D. from Brooklyn Law School in 1971. It's interesting to note that Mr. Trost's initial employment with the Yankees was as a grandstand vendor in the mid-1960s in the original Yankee Stadium. He resides in Monroe Township, N.J., with his wife, Carol. They have two children, Evan and Audra, and one grandchild, Ariella.

Brian Cashman

Senior Vice President, General Manager

Brian McGuire Cashman has literally grown up in the Yankees family. He joined the organization in 1986 as a 19-year-old intern in the Minor League and Scouting Department and now commands one of the most demanding jobs in sports as Yankees Senior Vice President and General Manager.

Over the course of his 23 seasons with the team, he has earned five World Series rings, including four as General Manager, becoming the first GM to win four World Series titles since the Dodgers' Buzzie Bavasi in the 1950s and '60s. Notably, he has won his titles with two different managers — Joe Torre in 1998, 1999 and 2000, and Joe Girardi in 2009.

Mr. Cashman assumed his current post on February 3, 1998. At age 31, he became the second-youngest General Manager in baseball history. In his first season, he became the youngest-ever GM to win a World Series, and with championships in 1999 and 2000, he became the only GM in baseball history to win world titles in each of his first three seasons. A pennant in 2001 gave him four straight League Championships, placing him alongside Hall-of-Fame Yankees General Managers Ed Barrow (1936-39, four) and George Weiss (1949-53, five) as the only GMs in Baseball history to win four-or-more straight league titles at any point in their careers.

Among his peers, Mr. Cashman has achieved unparalleled success while carrying on the winning tradition of the Yankees. His lifetime winning percentage of .607 (1,177-763-2) is the highest of any General Manager with five seasons of experience since 1950 and marks the best team winning percentage in the Major Leagues during that same stretch. Now in his 13th season, Mr. Cashman has the third-longest tenure among all general managers in baseball and is the longest-serving Yankees GM since George M. Steinbrenner became Principal Owner in 1973.

In all, his clubs have claimed 10 Division titles and six American League championships to go along with four World Series titles. His feat of reaching the playoffs in each of his first 10 seasons (1998-2007) remains unmatched in Baseball history.

In his present role, Mr. Cashman has been involved in dozens of high-profile Major League free-agent signings, including those of A.J. Burnett, Johnny Damon, Orlando Hernandez, Hideki Matsui, Mike Mussina, CC Sabathia, Alfonso Soriano and Mark Teixeira. Mr. Cashman has also executed more than 70 trades involving approximately 200 players, bringing the talents of Bobby Abreu, Aaron Boone, Curtis Granderson, David Justice, Alex Rodriguez, Nick Swisher and Javier Vazquez to the Bronx.

Recently, Mr. Cashman has focused on rebuilding the Yankees farm system, while still maintaining World Championship talent at the Major League level. The emphasis he and his baseball operations staff have placed on the First-Year Player Draft and international scouting is demonstrated by the organization's homegrown talent, including Alfredo Aceves, Robinson Cano, Joba Chamberlain, Brett Gardner, Phil Hughes, Zach McAllister, Mark Melancon, Jesus Montero, David Robertson and Austin Romine.

There have been three women in Major League history to hold the position of Assistant General Manager, and Mr. Cashman has hired two of them: Jean Afterman, the Yankees' current Vice President and Assistant General Manager; and Kim Ng, who is currently Vice President and Assistant General Manager of the Los Angeles Dodgers.

Various groups have honored the achievements of the Yankees and Mr. Cashman. With the club's recent World Series title, the Yankees were named "2009 Male Team of the Year" by the United States Sports Academy and were nominated as "Team of the Year" in the Laureus World Sports Awards competition. In both 1998 and 2000, the Yankees earned ESPY Awards — presented by ESPN — as "Outstanding Team of the Year," and were named "Organization of the Year" by *Baseball America* in 1998 and by *USA Today* in 1999.

Mr. Cashman has been honored as "Executive of the Year" four times: by the Boston Chapter of the BBWAA in 2000 and 2009; and in 1999 and 2003 by the New Jersey Sportswriters' Association. In 2001, he received his third consecutive "40 Under 40" Award presented by Street & Smith's *Sports Business Journal* to recognize the top 40 people under the age of 40 who have made the greatest impact in the sports business industry. He has since been inducted into the publication's "40 Under 40" Hall of Fame. In 2003, Mr. Cashman was honored by the Latino Sports Writers and Broadcasters Association with their annual "Latino Achievement Award" for his contributions to the Latino media. He was also honored with the 2005 "Ossie Davis Award for Inspirational Leadership," given each year to a key leader in an organization that works to promote opportunity in diversity.

On February 11, 2004, Mr. Cashman was given the honor of ringing the opening bell at the New York Stock Exchange. The market closed at 10,737.70 that day, its highest close since June 13, 2001.

Mr. Cashman remains committed to growing the Yankees brand and increasing the number of people who play baseball worldwide. In February 2010, he was part of the Yankees delegation that brought the 2009 World Series trophy to Tokyo, Beijing and Hong Kong. While on the Chinese mainland, the group met with the Chinese Baseball Association to discuss ways the game can be promoted in China. He was also heavily involved in bringing the Yankees to Tokyo for "Opening Series 2004" to honor the 70th anniversary of Major League Baseball's historic tour of Japan, which included Babe Ruth and Lou Gehrig.

His career as a full-time Yankees employee began following his graduation from Catholic University in 1989, when Mr. Cashman became a full-time Assistant in Baseball Operations. He was later promoted and transferred to Tampa, Fla., where he served as Assistant Farm Director from 1990 to 1992. He returned to New York and became Assistant General Manager, Baseball Administration in November 1992 .

Born on July 3, 1967, in Rockville Center, N.Y., Mr. Cashman grew up in Lexington, Ky. He attended Georgetown Prep in Rockville, Md., before attending Catholic University in Washington, D.C., where he majored in history and played intercollegiate baseball. His love for baseball developed when former Brooklyn Dodger Ralph Branca and his wife, Ann, arranged for him to serve as a bat boy for the Los Angeles Dodgers in spring training in 1982.

Mr. Cashman and his wife, Mary, have a daughter, Grace Eva, and a son, Theodore John.

Mark Newman

Senior Vice President, Baseball Operations

Mark Newman begins his 11th season as the Yankees' Senior Vice President of Baseball Operations and his 22nd season with the Yankees in 2010. Prior to being named to his current position in 2000, Mr. Newman served as the club's Vice President of Player Development and Scouting from 1997 through 1999.

During his tenure, the Yankees player development system has been recognized for producing homegrown talent including All-Stars Robinson Cano, Derek Jeter, Jorge Posada and Mariano Rivera. Under Mr. Newman's supervision over the last decade, the Yankees have drafted and stockpiled talented prospects to evolve into what has been lauded as one of the best player development systems in baseball. Entering 2010, 22 members of the club's 40-man Major League roster were either drafted by the Yankees or signed by the club as a non-drafted free agent.

In the team's 2009 championship run, 20 of the Yankees' 46 players used during the season - and 12 of 26 players appearing on the World Series roster - were products of the organization's player development system.

Over the last four seasons (2006-09), the Yankees' minor league affiliates (from the Dominican Summer League through Triple-A) have produced the most wins and the best winning percentage among all Major League franchises with a combined record of 1,896-1,426 (.571). Over the same stretch, Yankees farm teams captured eight league championships and in 2008 became the first organization since Houston in 1993 to have its Triple-A and Double-A clubs both win titles in the same season.

In addition to stringing together 14 seasons of Major League postseason play over the last 15 years (1995-2007, '09) and winning five World Championships over the stretch, the Yankees are one of only two teams, along with the Cleveland Indians, whose minor league affiliates have combined to post winning records in each of the last 20 seasons since 1990. The Yankees were selected as the "Organization of the Year" by *Baseball America* in 1998 and earned the same honor from *USA Today* in 1999.

Mr. Newman began his career in the Yankees organization in 1989 as Coordinator of Instruction and served in that position until his promotion to Director of Player Development and Scouting in 1996. He was named Vice President of Player Development and Scouting in 1997. In his first role with the club, he oversaw all managers and coaches in the farm system and planned both Major and Minor League spring training.

In 1972, Mr. Newman began his baseball coaching career at 22 years old as the pitching coach for Southern Illinois University. After spending nine successful seasons there—during which he earned his law degree with honors—he was named Head Baseball Coach at Old Dominion University in 1981. Mr. Newman's impressive 321-167-3 record in nine seasons was recognized with his induction into the ODU Hall of Fame in 1997. He was inducted into the SIU Hall of Fame in 2000.

Jean Afterman

Vice President, Assistant General Manager

Jean Afterman enters her ninth season as the Yankees' Assistant General Manager in 2010 (eighth as Vice President). She is only the third female to hold such a position in Major League Baseball history.

Ms. Afterman has been an integral part of the Yankees' efforts to spearhead operations in Asia. In her first year with the Yankees, she was instrumental in developing the club's relationship with the Yomiuri Giants of the Japan Central League and the signing of three-time Central League Most Valuable Player Hideki Matsui. She continues to cultivate relationships within the international baseball community, and in 2007 joined team President Randy Levine and General Manager Brian Cashman on a week-long trip to Asia that concluded with a working agreement with the Chinese Baseball Association. In 2010, she once again joined Randy Levine and Brian Cashman, when the Yankees brought the 2009 World Series trophy to Tokyo, Beijing and Hong Kong. While in Hong Kong, Ms. Afterman was given the honor of throwing out one of the ceremonial first pitches at the 2010 Phoenix Cup Tournament, an annual international women's baseball tournament.

In 2004, Ms. Afterman was named one of the "Power 100" by the *Sporting News* and was selected as one of the "50 Most Powerful Women in New York" by the *New York Post* in 2003 and 2007. Also in 2007, Ms. Afterman was profiled as one of *Crain's New York Business*' "100 Most Influential Women in New York Business" and in 2008, she was profiled by *Forbes Magazine* as one of the top female executives in baseball. In 2009, she was honored by the Exploring program with its "Exploring Leadership Award" for her work in providing career-orientation opportunities to local high school students. She was also named "2009 Alumni of the Year" by the Katherine Delmar Burke School in San Francisco.

Ms. Afterman joined the Yankees with a diverse business and legal background, with experience in corporate, labor and immigration law as well as international sports and licensing with an emphasis on US-Japan matters. In 1996, Ms. Afterman was appointed by the U.S. Secretary of Agriculture to a federal advisory committee, the National Organic Standards Board. Prior to joining the Yankees, Ms. Afterman managed her own practice, providing athletic representation and management with a specialization in arbitration proceedings.

From 1994 to 1999, she was General Counsel at KDN Sports, Inc. and handled business and legal affairs for international baseball clients, including Hideo Nomo, Hideki Irabu, Masato Yoshii, Alfonso Soriano and more than 30 other Major and Minor League players.

Ms. Afterman graduated from the University of California at Berkeley in 1979 and was the recipient of the Rosalynn Schneider Eisner Prize and the Mark Goodson Scholarship Grant. She received her J.D. from the University of San Francisco School of Law in 1991. In 2008, Ms. Afterman started working with an elementary school in the Bronx as part of her involvement with PENCIL, a non-profit organization that partners members of the New York business community with public schools. Projects at the school include a Mentoring Program, matching Yankees employees with 4th and 5th grade children, and an annual Read-a-Thon to encourage all students to fall in love with reading.

Commitment to Community

The New York Yankees organization takes as much pride in the championship baseball played on the field as it does in its charitable endeavors throughout the community. The Yankees' community efforts reach far beyond the Bronx and the tri-state area, encompassing programs and donations throughout the United States and even spanning into Latin America and Asia.

The Yankees strive to provide charitable partnerships with programs that support children's initiatives, education enhancement and health awareness. The club's donations, grants, tickets, promotional items and countless other contributions to such programs exceeded $3 million in 2009. Throughout the season, Yankees players and front office personnel make countless visits to various local hospitals, schools and youth groups, and the club makes every effort to recognize community excellence during pregame cermonies.

YANKEES OFFER DISASTER RELIEF

The New York Yankees continued their rich tradition of lending a helping hand to those in need when the organization contributed $500,000 to the rescue and relief efforts in Haiti in January 2010, following the country's most catastrophic earthquake in over 200 years.

In the summer of 2008, following the devastating destruction caused to the Gulf Coast by Hurricanes Gustav and Ike, the Yankees donated $1 million to assist in the area's recovery. The funds were split between the American Red Cross and Salvation Army and went directly to supporting and assisting community-based organizations along the Gulf Coast, specifically in Louisiana and Texas.

In November 2007, the Yankees donated a total of $60,000 in cash, food and supplies to the Dominican Republic and Nicaragua to aid in both countries' relief efforts after being struck by Tropical Storm Noel. Yankees players Robinson Cano, Melky Cabrera and Edwar Ramirez, along with coaches Rob Thomson and Tony Pena, presented a Yankees donation of $25,000 in Santo Domingo, D.R. Following the donation, Yankees minor league manager Jody Reed, several Yankees minor leaguers and Yankees Latin America scouts held a baseball clinic for 240 local orphans. Edwar Ramirez, along with Yankees Latin prospects and staff, helped distribute an additional $10,000 donation in food and supplies on November 18, to help rebuild a local school ravaged by the storm in Ramirez's hometown of San Juan de la Maguana in the Dominican Republic. A $25,000 donation was also made by the Yankees to the Asociacion San Francisco de Asis in Nicaragua to assist victims of Hurricane Felix, a Category 5 storm that devastated the country in early September 2007.

The Yankees made a $1 million donation to the recovery efforts following the catastrophic destruction of Hurricane Katrina in Louisiana and the Gulf Coast in September 2006. In April 2005, the Yankees donated $1 million in proceeds from their April 3 season opener against the Red Sox to victims of the tsunamis that ravaged Southeast Asia.

SHARPENING THEIR PENCILS

Beginning in 2009, Yankees front office staff members began a mentoring program with students at P.S. 35 in the Bronx. Under the leadership of Yankees Assistant GM Jean Afterman, and with the help of PENCIL, an organization that builds and supports relationships between business leaders and New York City public schools, mentors from various Yankees front office departments have worked in small groups with students on career awareness and job-readiness projects, such as designing mock advertisements, proposing new product ideas, and evaluating players' statistics. On September 28, 2009, Afterman was joined by Yankees Manager Joe Girardi in addressing the entire student body and kicking off a "Read-A-Thon" aimed at engaging students in reading and improving their language arts skills. Through the program, all of the school's 30 classes, comprising more than 700 elementary school students, are participating in a monthly reading competition for Yankees prizes.

CC Sabathia gave free haircuts for neighborhood kids at Jordan's Barber Shop in the Bronx on June 3, 2009.

CC MAKES SURPRISE VISIT

On June 12, 2009, CC Sabathia helped eighth-graders at the Bronx's Elizabeth Barrett Browning Middle School get the party started. The students were recognized with a celebration for improving their New York State exam scores as the eighth-graders raised their English language arts scores by 20 percent and their math scores by 15 percent. With chants of "Let's Go, Yankees" and "We Love CC," the eighth-graders enthusiastically welcomed the Yankees pitcher, who answered questions from the school's student council and passed out baseball caps to the honorees.

FIELD OF DREAMS

In 2009, the Yankees recognized three special teams from the area with their "Field of Dreams" program, allowing the youngsters to join the Yankees on the field during the National Anthem. Little League World Series participants from Staten Island Little League, the Fordham Prep baseball CHSAA Class A City Champions, and the Westhill High School Softball team, whose season ended on a controversial appeal, were welcomed by the Yankees to take part in the special program.

BACK TO SCHOOL

Second baseman Robinson Cano served as "Principal for a Day" at P.S. 55 in the Bronx while pitcher Alfredo Aceves assisted as "Dean of Discipline." The pair met with a group of the school's highest performing students on June 16.

YANKEES HONOR LOCAL EXCELLENCE

There's more to the South Bronx than Yankee Stadium, and the Yankees want fans to know about the vibrant community they call home. Each September, the Yankees honor organizations and businesses that are helping to make the Bronx a great place to live and work with the presentation of Hispanic Heritage Month Community Achievement Awards which recognizes local organizations and businesses in four categories — arts, athletics, business and education. The 2009 awards went to WXTV Univision 41, the Kips Bay Boys & Girls Club, Amanda Floor Covering and the New York City Department of Juvenile Justice during an on-field ceremony on Yankee Stadium.

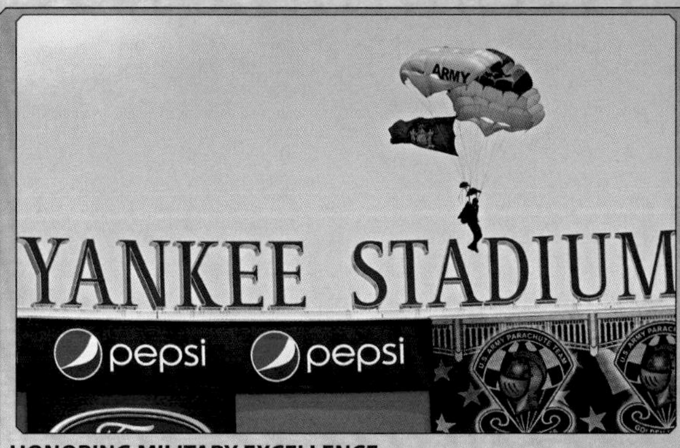

HONORING MILITARY EXCELLENCE

In their annual nod to the nation's armed services, the Yankees held their annual "Military Appreciation Day" on June 14, 2009 vs. the Mets. With a clear blue sky, the U.S. Army Golden Knights parachuted into Yankee Stadium, landing in the outfield as the Yankees showed a special Warrior Foundation video. Former U.S. Army Elite Task Force Ranger Keni Thomas, a member of the Army unit that fought in Somalia in 1993 at the Battle of Mogadishu (later depicted in the film *Black Hawk Down*), sang the national anthem. Following the anthem, the U.S. Army Materiel Command's Commanding General Ann E. Dunwoody threw out the game's ceremonial first pitch.

ANNUAL FOOD DRIVE

The Yankees held their 16th Annual Food Drive at Yankee Stadium on December 17, 2009, to benefit Bronx-area residents in need during the holiday season. Fans donating 30 pounds of nonperishable goods received a voucher valid for two tickets to one of 20 designated Yankees games in 2010 (restrictions apply). With Yankees Manager Joe Girardi, 3B Alex Rodriguez, LHP CC Sabathia and newly-acquired OF Curtis Granderson there to greet donors, a record-breaking 71,233 lbs. of food and $2,307 was collected. The Yankees reinvested the money to purchase additional canned goods from Ace Endico in Brewster, N.Y., with the company making an added food contribution. All donations were distributed throughout the Bronx to those in need.

On November 23, the Yankees and White Rose held their annual Thanksgiving Turkey Giveaway, distributing 500 vouchers to Bronx residents for redemption at a local Met Food market or Pioneer Supermarket.

In his first official day as a Yankee, Curtis Granderson [R] joins CC Sabathia [L] by accepting a food donation during the club's annual Holiday Food Drive.

NEW STADIUM OFFERS BRONX INCENTIVES

Yankee Stadium is one of the premier building projects to take place in the Bronx in the last 50 years. The hard work and dedication of engineers, architects and construction professionals in building and designing the Stadium makes the facility one of the most impressive and fan-friendly venues in Major League Baseball. Equally important was the project's dedication to support local community groups, institutions and residents as the Yankees remain devoted to the long-term development of the Bronx.

Building a new state-of-the-art facility requires an army of talented and experienced professionals. As part of the Yankees' commitment to ensure that the Stadium project creates economic opportunities in the Bronx, the Yankees made a concerted effort to recruit a wide range of vendors and employees from the local community. Of the 190 contracts awarded, 63 were allotted to Bronx-based businesses (accounting for over 33 percent of the contracts and resulting in $133 million in contracts to Bronx-based businesses). The Yankees also stayed committed to hiring at least 25 percent of the total workforce from Bronx residents, again providing incentive to the surrounding community.

In conjunction with the construction of the Stadium, the Yankees also established a $1 million training program to teach local Bronx residents professional skills and knowledge to improve their job prospects and performance. Among

YANKEES COMMUNITY PARTNERS

44th Clergy Coalition
161st St. Merchants Association
167th St. Merchants Association
ALS - Lou Gehrig Disease
American Latin Association of N.Y., Inc.
Bedford Stuyvesant Restoration Corporation
Big Brothers/Big Sisters
Bronx Arts Cultural Center
Bronx Central Council
Bronx Chamber of Commerce
Bronx Children's Psychiatric Center
Bronx Colts Youth Foundation
Bronx Community College
Bronx Dance Theatre
Bronx Kids
Bronx Lebanon Hospital Center
Bronx Little League
Bronx Museum
Bronx Neighborhood Cluster
Bronx Puerto Rican Day Parade
Bronx School for Law, Government and Justice
Bronx Tourism Council
Bronx Walk for Juvenile Diabetes
Bronx YMCA
Cardinal Hayes High School
The Claremont Center
Dreamyard Project
The Explorer Program
The First Tee
Fordham University Baseball
Grand Concourse Academy
Grand Concourse Branch Library
Greater Ridgewood Youth Council
Haven Arts
Harlem RBI
Highbridge Voices
High School for Careers in Sports
Hostos Community College
The Jackie Robinson Foundation
Junior Achievement
Kips Bay Boys & Girls Club
Knowledge is Power Program
Lincoln Medical and Mental Health Center
MAC Creations Pop Arts
Manhattan Youth-After School Program
Met Council on Jewish Poverty
Mid-Bronx Senior Citizens Council
Montefiore Medical Center
New York City Department of Education
New York City Outward Bound
New York City Parks and Recreation
New York City Sports Commission
New York City Urban League
Nos Quidamos
N.Y. Wildcards Sports Program
Out 2 Play
Ozone Howard Little League
Police Athletic League
Pregones Theater
PSAL and CHSAA Wooden Bat Grant
Renaissance EMS
Ridgewood Glendale Middle Village Maspeth Little League
SCAN New York
SCO Family Services
SCOPE
South Bronx Concerned Citizens
The Sports Foundation
Sports Professions Program
St. Angela Merici School
Steps to Albany
Thurgood Marshall Mock Trial Program
United Negro College Fund
William Hodson Senior Center
Women's Housing and Economic Development Corporation (WHEDCo)
World Vision

initiatives supported by the Yankees' grant was Project H.I.R.E. (Help In Re-entering Employment), a proven job-training program at Bronx Community College that taught Bronx residents functional construction skills for practical use in local building projects.

YANKEES LEAVE A LASTING LEGACY

As a guest of the American Red Cross in Greater New York, second baseman Robinson Cano participated in CPR training on June 5 at Chelsea Piers as part of National Cardiopulmonary Resuscitation and Automated External Defibrillator Awareness Week.

In conjunction with the 79th All-Star Game at Yankee Stadium in 2008, the Yankees were awarded a $1.5 million Legacy Grant from Major League Baseball earmarked for community distribution. The Yankees allocated the generous donation to various New York City community organizations with a focus on programs involving education, recreation and social outlets for area youth. The charitable funds went to supplies, equipment and the development of new playgrounds and facilities for numerous community groups.

Additionally, the Yankees made an $800,000 monitary donation to the Bronx Fund Advisory Panel as well as an additional $100,000 donation of sports equipment and $100,000 worth of tickets, which was distributed by the Panel to Bronx-based community organizations.

Derek Jeter and his Jeter's Leaders pack up holiday gift bags at his annual Turn 2 Holiday Express.

JETER HONORED FOR COMMUNITY WORK

Yankees All-Star shortstop Derek Jeter was selected as the 2009 recipient of the Roberto Clemente Award, recognizing the Yankees captain as the Major League Baseball player who best combines a dedication to giving back to the community with outstanding skills on the baseball field. Jeter was selected from a list of 30 nominees, one from each Major League club, by a panel of dignitaries that included Commissioner Bud Selig and Vera Clemente, wife of the late Hall of Famer. Additionally, fans were able to vote on the award via mlb.com.

In 2009, the Yankees captain continued his tireless charity work with his Turn 2 Foundation. Launched in 1996, Jeter's Foundation is aimed at creating and supporting signature programs and activities that motivate young people to turn away from drugs and alcohol and "Turn 2" healthy lifestyles. Through these ventures, the Foundation strives to create outlets that promote and reward academic excellence, leadership development and positive behavior. Turn 2's goal is to see the children of these programs grow safely and successfully into adulthood and become the leaders of tomorrow. From an annual leadership conference to baseball clinics in Michigan, New York City and Tampa, the Turn 2 Foundation is able to reward the positive behavior of children, especially those demonstrating academic achievement and leadership. Over the years, the foundation has awarded more than $10 million in grants to create and support signature programs and activities.

In March 2009, Jeter donated $500,000 to launch the "Derek Jeter Academy at Phoenix House" in Tampa, an outpatient counseling center for troubled teens combining individual and family substance abuse treatment.

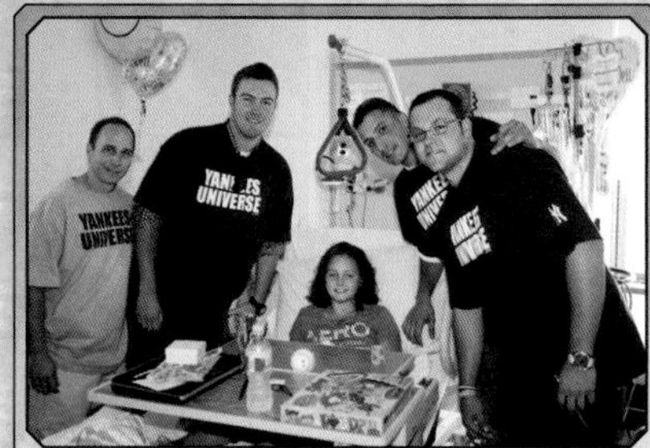

[L to R] Brian Cashman joins Yankees pitchers Phil Hughes, Andy Pettitte and Joba Chamberlain for a visit to Memorial Sloan Kettering Cancer Center in September 2009.

GOOD SPORTS

On November 21, the New York Yankees were recognized as 2009 honorees at the 11th Annual National Sportsmanship Awards for their work with Camp Sundown during the organization's inaugural HOPE Week. Pitcher A.J. Burnett and Yankees Media Relations Director Jason Zillo were on hand in St. Louis to accept the award, given by the Citizenship Through Sports Alliance and the St. Louis Sports Commission. The National Sportsmanship Awards is the signature event of the Sports Commission's Sportsmanship initiative and aims to recognize athletes and personalities from across the nation for their integrity, class, selflessness, perseverance, kindness, community service and overall commitment to sportsmanship.

Alex Rodriguez signs a ball for a young Yankees fan in Monument Park prior to a Yankees game vs. Tampa Bay. Throughout the 2009 season, Yankees players, as well as Manager Joe Girardi and General Manager Brian Cashman greeted fans entering Yankee Stadium.

Yankees HOPE Week

The Yankees celebrated their first HOPE Week from July 20-24, 2009. The creation of HOPE Week (Helping Others Persevere & Excel) was rooted in the fundamental belief that acts of goodwill provide hope and encouragement to more than just the recipient of the gesture. Over the course of HOPE Week, the Yankees brought to light five remarkable stories intended to inspire others into action in their own communities.

For the Yankees, this event was unique in that every player on the roster, along with Manager Joe Girardi and the Yankees coaching staff, participated.

Each day from Monday, July 20, through Friday, July 24, the Yankees reached out to an individual, family or organization worthy of recognition and support. Though each day's celebration culminated at Yankee Stadium, outreach often took place away from the field. Whenever possible, the Yankees' goal was to personally connect with individuals in the settings of their greatest personal successes.

Equally significant during HOPE Week was the attention media gave to the highlighted causes and organizations. The greatest challenge facing many not-for-profits is generating interest, awareness and funding for their missions.

On Monday, July 20, the Yankees reached out to Marco and Jennifer Chiappetta (pronounced Key-ah-pettah) and their Patchwork of Young Leaders Society. The Chiappettas have opened their hearts and home to become mentors to at-risk young people in their Washington Heights (N.Y.) neighborhood. Yankees players **Mariano Rivera, Robinson Cano** and **Melky Cabrera,** along with **Manager Joe Girardi** visited the Chiappettas' apartment to spend time with Marco, Jennifer and the teenagers they work with, distributing athletic equipment courtesy of Modell's and food vouchers courtesy of White Rose.

The Chiappettas, the teenagers and some of the teenagers' parents also attended the Yankees-Orioles game at Yankee Stadium that night as special guests of the team and took part in pregame ceremonies.

Andy Pettitte [L], Joba Chamberlain [C] and Alex Rodriguez escort Little Leaguer Tom Ellenson to the baseball field.

On Tuesday, July 21, the Yankees reached out to Tom Ellenson, an inspirational Little Leaguer with cerebral palsy and his father, Richard, who created a device that allows non-verbal individuals like his son to more easily communicate. Yankees players **Alex Rodriguez, Joba Chamberlain** and **Andy Pettitte,** along with **Hitting Coach Kevin Long** met Tom and his best friends for lunch at Out of the Kitchen, a Greenwich Village restaurant, then went across the street to J.J. Walker Little League Field for a celebratory rally in Tom's honor and a baseball clinic for Tom and his teammates.

Tom and his teammates attended the Yankees-Orioles game that night and were part of on-field pre-game ceremonies. Tom and his teammates took part in the ceremonial first pitch, lining up and passing the baseball from the pitcher's mound to home plate, where Tom handed the ball to Rodriguez, Chamberlain and Pettitte.

On Wednesday, July 22, the Yankees reached out to husband and wife George and Kim Murray, inviting them and their 4-year-old son, Trason, to Yankee Stadium for a surprise anniversary party with 40 of their closest family and friends. Yankees players **Derek Jeter**, **Mark Teixeira**, **Phil Hughes**, **Phil Coke**, **Hideki Matsui**, **Brian Bruney** and **Cody Ransom** joined the group in surprising George and Kim in a party suite prior to the game. The Murrays were on-field guests of the Yankees during batting practice and took part in a pre-game ceremony. Following the game, the Murrays and their immediate family received a private tour of Yankee Stadium hosted by Jeter, Teixeira, Coke and Ransom. On the tour, the group visited Monument Park, the Yankees Museum and the Yankees clubhouse.

On Tuesday, August 4, less than two weeks after his visit to Yankee Stadium, George Murray succumbed to ALS, passing away at his home in South New Berlin, N.Y., at age 38.

On Thursday, July 23, the Yankees reached out to Camp Sundown and the XP Society, which supports children who have Xeroderma Pigmentosum, a rare (approx. 250 in the U.S. and 3,000 worldwide) genetic disorder that prevents individuals from going outdoors in daylight. Camp Sundown, located in the Hudson Valley area of New York State, is a yearly retreat for the children who cannot be exposed to any UV light, including florescent lighting, which causes severe burns and eventually skin and eye cancer. More often than not, those with the disease do not live past the age of 20.

Jorge Posada [L] and Katie Mahar enjoy a postgame on-field carnival at Yankee Stadium.

XP children and their families traveled to Yankee Stadium from Camp Sundown on the evening of July 23, arriving after sunset. Thanks to a 2 hour, 43 minute rain delay prior to the start of the game, Camp Sundown was able to watch the entire game from a party suite. Immediately after the last pitch, the children and their families gathered on the field as they watched the Yankee Stadium outfield transform into a massive open-air carnival, with music, food, entertainers and a bouncy castle. XP campers and their families, along with Yankees players **Alfredo Aceves, A.J. Burnett, Brett Gardner, Jorge Posada, Cody Ransom, David Robertson, Assistant Trainer Steve Donohue**, **Bullpen Coach Mike Harkey**, and **General Manager Brian Cashman** joined in the fun, which lasted until 3:30 a.m., when the XP families had to reboard their buses in order to make it back to camp before daybreak.

In September, Yankees players autographed a replica WWE title belt that sold for $9,450 in a silent auction at yankees.com.

On Friday, July 24, the Yankees reached out to Ranjit Seal and Melvin Williams, two young men who both have developmental disabilities and work in the mailroom at the law firm of Ahmuty, Demers and McManus in Manhattan. After training from YAI/ National Institute for People with Disabilities, the two young men have integrated into the workforce and greater society. Yankees players **CC Sabathia**, **Johnny Damon** and **Nick Swisher** surprised Ranjit and Melvin (as well as the entire law firm) and took part in their day, helping them to deliver mail around the office.

A lunchtime party with catering from the Hard Rock Cafe celebrated Ranjit, Melvin and the law firm. Afterwards, Ranjit and Melvin rode back to the Bronx with the players to meet Yankee Stadium's mailroom staff. The pair then put their skills on display by helping to deliver mail to players in the Yankees clubhouse.

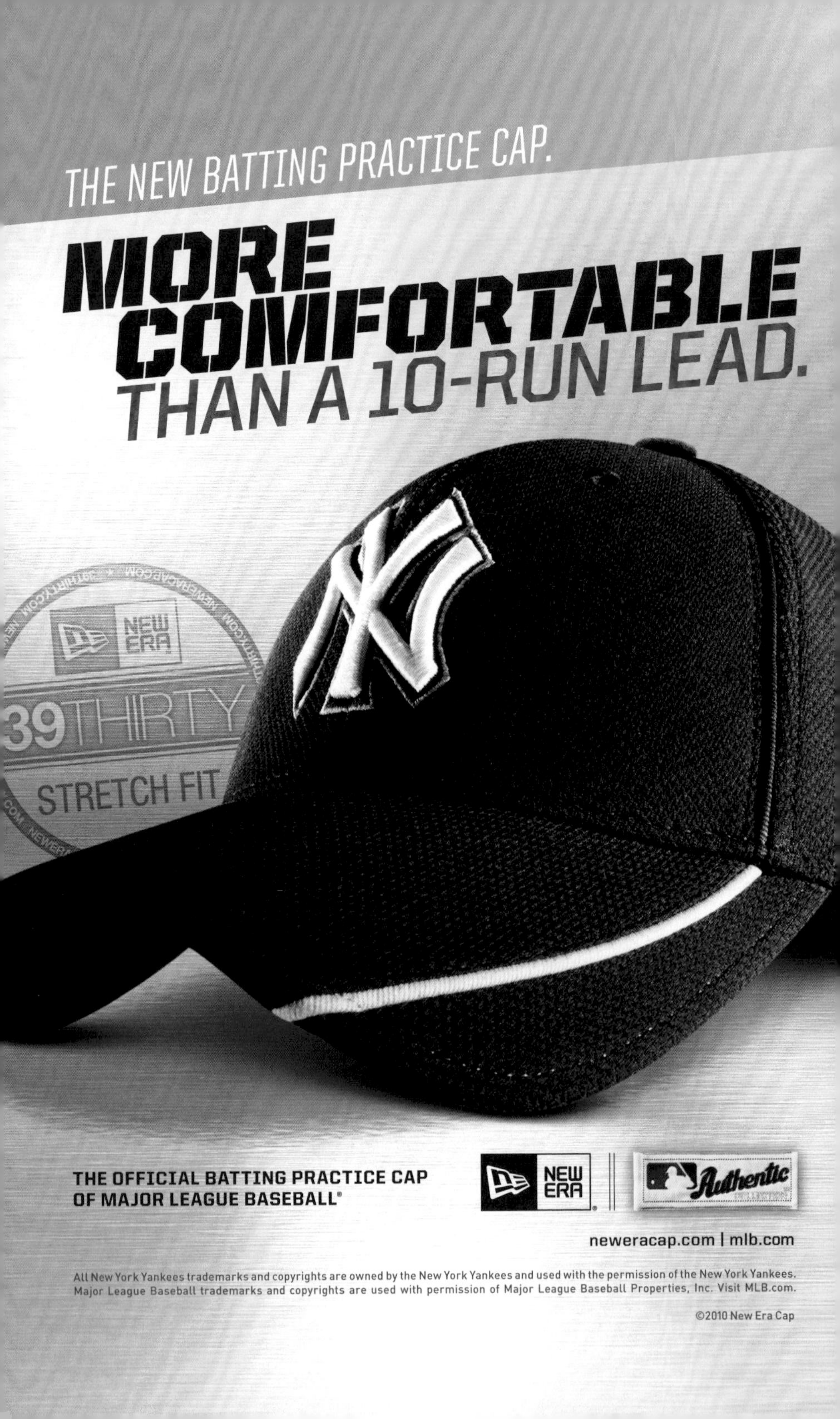

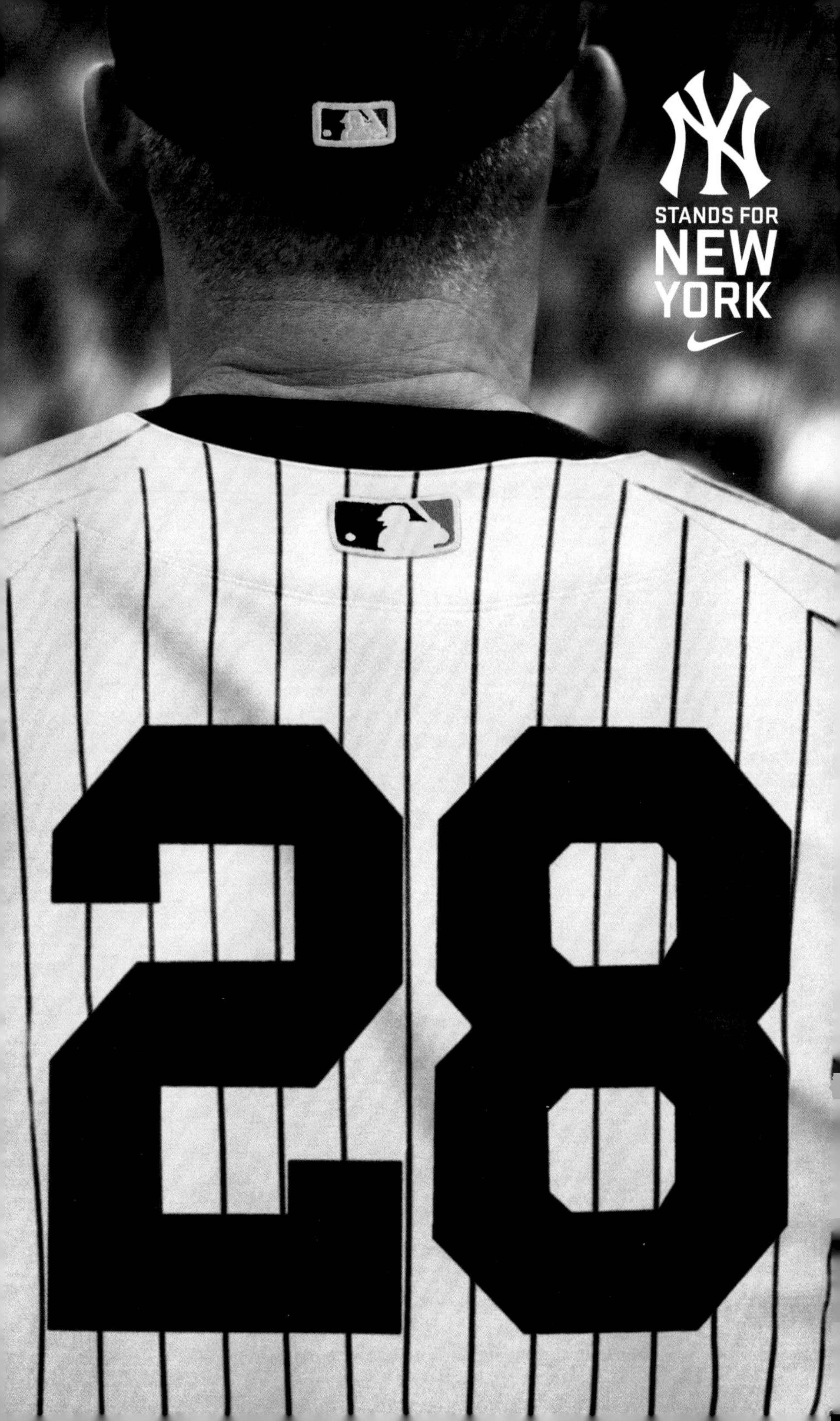
28
STANDS FOR
NEW
YORK

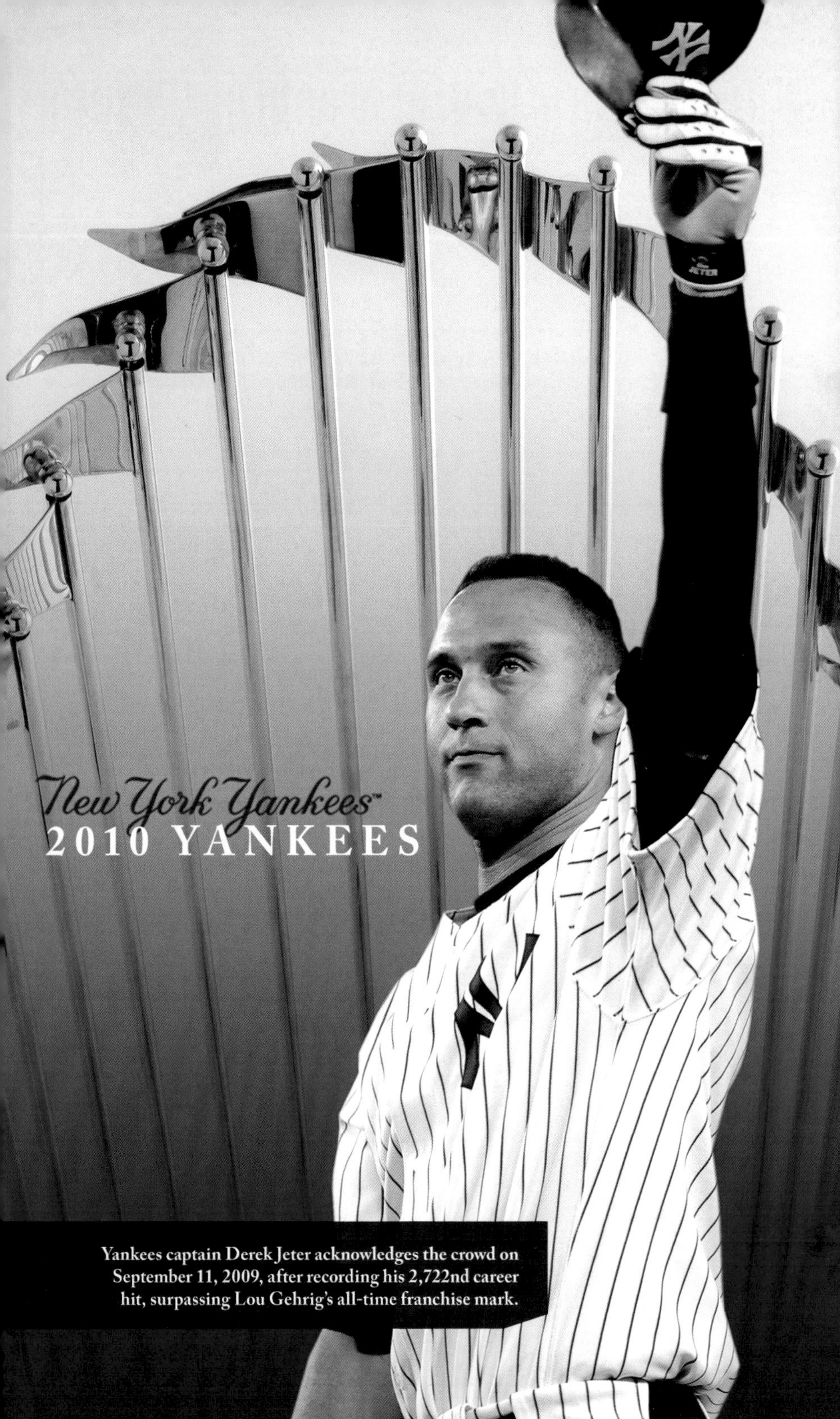

Yankees captain Derek Jeter acknowledges the crowd on September 11, 2009, after recording his 2,722nd career hit, surpassing Lou Gehrig's all-time franchise mark.

Joe Girardi

28 **Manager**

Opening Day Age: 45

Full Name
Joseph Elliott Girardi

Birthdate
October 14, 1964

Birthplace
Peoria, Ill.

Resides
Purchase, N.Y.

College
Northwestern University

Career Highlights

BBWAA

N.L. Manager of the Year
- 2006

Sporting News

N.L. Manager of the Year
- 2006

N.L. All-Star Team
- 2000

At the Helm in 2009

- Led the Yankees to their 27th World Championship in his second season as Manager, becoming the ninth Yankees manager to win a World Series...in his postseason managerial debut, joined Ralph Houk and Billy Martin as the only three Yankees to play for and manage a World Championship team...also joined Houk, Bob Lemon and Casey Stengel as the only four Yankees managers to win a World Series in their first postseason as a manager.
- Led the club to a 103-59 regular season record, marking the Majors' best record in 2009 and the Yankees' most wins since 2002 (103-58)...became the eighth Yankees manager to collect at least 100 wins in a full season, joining Miller Huggins, Joe McCarthy, Casey Stengel, Ralph Houk, Billy Martin, Dick Howser and Joe Torre...joined McCarthy, Houk, Martin and Howser as the only five Yankees skippers to accomplish the feat within their first two full seasons with the team...finished third in AL Manager of the Year voting with 34 total points, including four first-place votes.
- The Yankees' 114 total wins in 2009 tied their second-most ever in a single year behind the 125 victories by the 1998 squad (also 114W in 1927)...a member of the 1998 Yankees (114-48), became the only current Major League manager to both play for and manage teams that won at least 100 games in a season and won a World Series, according to the *Elias Sports Bureau*...became the only Major League manager in the 2000s to lead a team to 100-or-more regular season wins and a World Series title.
- The Yankees had sole possession or a share of first place in the AL East for 90 combined days in 2009, including each of the final 77...marked the first time in Girardi's managerial career his team was in first place at any point in a season.
- The Yankees led the Majors with 915R and a franchise-record 244HR...Yankees pitchers recorded a 4.26 ERA, posting their lowest mark since 2003 (4.02)...also led the AL with 1,260K, their second-highest total in franchise history according to the *Elias Sports Bureau* (1,266K in 2001).
- Guided his team to a Major League-high 51 come-from-behind wins, including a franchise-record 36 comeback victories at home...his club also produced a Major League-best 28 wins in their last at-bat, had nine wins after trailing at the end of the seventh inning and five wins when trailing at the end of the eighth...their 15 "walk-off" wins led the Majors and were the second-most in club history (17 in 1943).

Wise Beyond his Years

Joe Girardi became the youngest manager in Yankees history to win a World Series and the fourth-youngest in the Majors over the last 30 years (1980-2009) behind Minnesota's Tom Kelly (1987 and '91), the White Sox's Ozzie Guillen (2005) and the Mets' Davey Johnson (1986).

- Compiled six winning streaks of at least seven games, marking the most winning streaks of seven-or-more games for any Major League team in a single season since the 1998 Yankees...had two winning streaks of at least eight games, a first for the Yankees since 2003, and a season-high nine-game winning streak from 5/13-21.
- The Yankees committed 86 errors, marking their second-fewest miscues in a non-abbreviated season behind 2008 (83E)...the Yankees' .986 fielding percentage since Girardi took the helm in '08 ranks fifth in the Majors.
- Began the season 13-15 through 5/7, then posted a Major League-best 90-44 mark over the remaining games after 3B Alex Rodriguez was activated from the disabled list on 5/8.
- Earned his 200th career managerial win on 6/7 vs. Tampa Bay...earned his 100th win as Yankees manager on 4/29 at Detroit.
- Was ejected four times in 2009 (5/4 loss vs. Boston, 6/24 win at Atlanta, 7/6 loss vs. Toronto and 9/13 win vs. Baltimore)...has been ejected 11 times in his career, eight as a Manager (six as Yankees Manager) and seven as a Yankee (also 8/6/99 as a player).
- At 45 years old, is the third-youngest manager in the Major Leagues, behind Arizona's A.J. Hinch (35) and Cleveland's Manny Acta (41).

Managing/Coaching Career

- Was named the 32nd manager in club history on 10/30/07, becoming the 17th Yankees manager to have played for the club and fourth former Yankees catcher to skipper the team (also Bill Dickey, Ralph Houk and Yogi Berra).
- Completed his first season as Manager of the New York Yankees in 2008, guiding the club to an 89-73 record and a third-place finish in the AL East...was one of only two managers (also the Angels' Mike Scioscia) whose team did not lose more than four consecutive games during the 2008 season...won his Yankees managerial debut on 4/1/08 vs. Toronto (lost his only previous Opening Day as Manager in 2006 with Florida).
- Earned his 100th career managerial win on 5/22/08 vs. Baltimore...was ejected by HP umpire Chris Guccione in the bottom of the ninth inning in the game.
- Was named the 2006 National League "Manager of the Year" by the Baseball Writers Association of America and the *Sporting News*...guided the Florida Marlins to a 78-84 record in his first season as a Major League manager...with the award, joined the Houston Astros' Hal Lanier (1986) and the San Francisco Giants' Dusty Baker (1993) as the only managers to win the honor in their managerial debuts...at the age of 41, became the youngest manager in Marlins history (previously 47-year-old John Boles in 1996)...was named Marlins manager just two seasons after retiring as a player prior to the 2004 campaign, marking the shortest time between being an active player (2003) and making a managerial debut (2006) since 1987, when both John Wathan (Kansas City) and Larry Bowa (San Diego) became managers after last playing during the 1985 season.
- Became the first manager to improve his club's record above .500 after falling at least 20 games below the .500 mark during the same season...the Marlins were a season-low 20 games under .500 on 5/21 (11-31), but then went 62-41 through 9/12 to improve to 73-72...the only other Major League team to return to the .500 mark after falling 20 or more games below was the 1899 Louisville Colonels, who were 22 games under at 16-38 and improved to 72-72-3 before finishing with a record of 75-77-3.
- Managed Anibal Sanchez's no-hit performance on 9/6/06 vs. Arizona...was the fourth no-hitter in Marlins history and the fourth no-hitter that Girardi has been a part of, having caught two (Dwight Gooden's on 5/14/96 and David Cone's perfect game on 7/18/99) and being a teammate in one (David Wells' perfect game on 5/17/98)...according to the *Elias Sports Bureau*, Girardi became the first person since Jeff Torborg to both catch and manage a no-hitter...Torborg managed Wilson Alvarez's no-hitter on 9/11/91 with the White Sox after catching no-hitters by Sandy Koufax (perfect game, 9/9/65), Bill Singer (7/20/70) and Nolan Ryan (5/15/73).
- The 2006 Marlins club featured 22 rookies, 21 of whom appeared before 9/1, with 11 making their Major League debuts...Florida hit a then-club-record 182 home runs, featuring four players with 20 or more homers and 10 players with double-digit home run totals...became the first National League team that season to have five different pitchers record 10 or more wins, accomplishing the feat for the first time in franchise history...rookie pitchers accounted for 50 of the Marlins' 78 wins, the most rookie victories for a Major League team since the 1952 Dodgers (51).
- Made his coaching debut in 2005, serving as bench coach and catching instructor on Joe Torre's New York Yankees staff...assisted in guiding the Yankees to a 95-67 (.586) record and the American League East title.
- Appeared in 39 career postseason games as a player, most among all current American League managers...among Major League managers, only Chicago's Lou Piniella (44) and Cincinnati's Dusty Baker (40) appeared in more postseason games as a player.

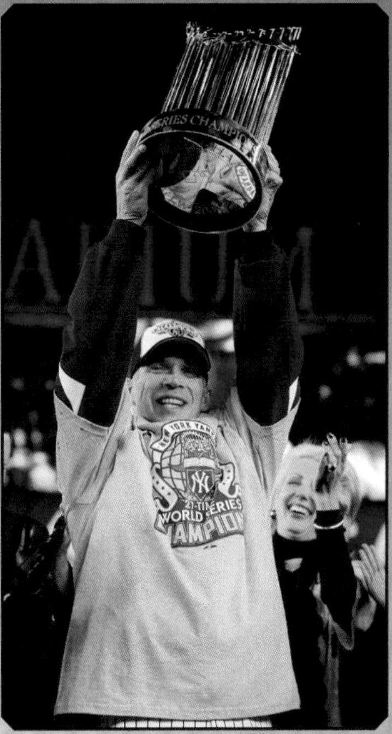

ACTIVE MANAGERS TO WIN WORLD SERIES IN THEIR FIRST POSTSEASON

JOE GIRARDI	**NYY, 2009**
Ozzie Guillen	CWS, 2005
Terry Francona	BOS, 2004
Mike Scioscia	ANA, 2002
Lou Piniella	CIN, 1990

DID YOU KNOW? Joe Girardi and Yogi Berra are the only Yankees catchers to be behind the plate for two regular season no-hitters. Girardi was the catcher for Dwight Gooden's no-hitter on 5/14/96 vs. Seattle and David Cone's perfect game on 7/18/99 vs. Montreal. Berra caught both of Allie Reynolds' no-hitters in 1951.

Playing Career

- Played parts of 15 seasons as a catcher in the Major Leagues with the Chicago Cubs (1989-92 and 2000-02), Colorado Rockies (1993-95), New York Yankees (1996-99) and St. Louis Cardinals (2003)...was a member of three World Series Championship teams in New York (1996, 1998-99) and played in a total of six postseasons with the Cubs (1989), Rockies (1995) and Yankees (1996-99).
- In 1,277 career Major League games, batted .267 (1,100-for-4,127) with 454 runs, 186 doubles, 36HR and 422RBI, finishing with a .991 career fielding percentage while throwing out 27.6% of potential base stealers...batted .184 (21-for-114) with 2 triples and 1RBI in 39 career postseason games.

GIRARDI'S CAREER MANAGERIAL RECORD

Year	Club	Position	W	L	Pct.
2006	Marlins	Fourth	78	84	.481
2008	Yankees	Third	89	73	.549
2009	Yankees	First	103	59	.636
Totals			**270**	**216**	**.556**

- Saw his first Major League action in 1989 as the Cubs' Opening Day catcher...was the first rookie catcher to start a season opener for the Cubs since Randy Hundley in 1966...was selected to *Baseball Digest's* All-Rookie Team...played in four games of the 1989 NL Championship Series against San Francisco, recording one hit.
- Played his first full big league season in 1990...stole eight bases, the most by a Cubs catcher since Gabby Hartnett's 10 in 1924...ranked second among NL catchers in assists (61) and threw out 33.3% of baserunners attempting to steal (38-of-114).
- On 8/7/91, in his first game back after missing nearly four months with a strained lower back, suffered a broken nose in a home plate collision with the Phillies' John Kruk.
- Was selected by the Rockies with the 19th pick in the Expansion Draft from the Cubs...established career highs with 8HR, 55RBI and 63R in 1995 with the Colorado Rockies.
- Acquired by the Yankees on 11/3/95 from the Rockies in exchange for LHP Mike DeJean...hit a career-high .294 with 2HR and 45RBI for the World Series Champions...stole 13 bases, marking the highest total among big league catchers and a record for a Yankees catcher...stole home on the front end of a double steal on 4/11 vs. Kansas City, becoming the first Yankees catcher to steal home since Jake Gibbs on 7/13/1968...had two triples during the 1996 postseason, including a run-scoring three-base hit off Greg Maddux in Game 6 of the World Series at Yankee Stadium.
- Was the catcher for Dwight Gooden's no-hitter on 5/14/96 vs. Seattle...in his final season as a player with the Yankees, caught David Cone's perfect game on 7/18/99 vs. Montreal...had a career-high 7RBI on 8/23/99 in a 21-3 victory at Texas, going 4-for-6 with 2 doubles and 1 triple.
- Rejoined the Cubs organization in 2000 and earned his first and only trip to an All-Star Game that season in Atlanta as a replacement for the injured Mike Piazza (did not play)...when he homered on 5/2/00 vs. Houston off Jose Lima, it was his first Cubs home run since 5/8/92...only one player, Billy Jurges (nine years, 1938-47), had a longer span between homers with the Cubs.
- Recorded his 1,000th Major League hit on 5/27/01 vs. Milwaukee off Jimmy Haynes – a seventh-inning, game-winning, two-run double.
- Was one of the Cubs' co-captains in 2001 and 2002.
- Played his final career regular season game on 9/28/03 at Arizona with the St. Louis Cardinals...his single in the ninth inning off the Diamondbacks' Edgar Gonzalez gave him 1,100 career hits.

Personal/Miscellaneous

- Graduated high school in 1982 from the Spalding Institute (Ill.), where he was an All-State selection in baseball.
- Graduated from Northwestern University in 1986 with a bachelor's degree in industrial engineering...was a three-time Academic All-American and two-time All-Big 10 selection at catcher...was elected to the College Sports Information Directors Hall of Fame on 7/1/07, becoming the first former Major Leaguer to be enshrined...also received the 2007 Distinguished Alumni Award from the Northwestern University Department of Industrial Engineering and Management Sciences.
- Established his own charity, Catch 25, which is dedicated to providing support to families and individuals across the country who have been challenged with ALS, Alzheimer's, cancer and fertility issues...Catch 25 provides assistance through scholarships, financial aid and charitable donations and is devoted to serving children and adults that may not otherwise have the financial and emotional support they may need...his father, Jerry, suffers from Alzheimer's...see www.joegirardi.com for more information...hosts the annual "Remember When, Remember Now" benefit along with Michael Kay at the Grand Central Oyster Bar in New York City, helping raise funds for his charity and Alzheimer's research.
- Received the Community Leadership Award from the New York City Chapter of the Alzheimer's Association at it's annual "Forget-Me-Not" gala on 6/1/09.
- Received the Sweetwater Clifton "City Spirit" Award from the New York Knicks on 11/22/09 for serving as a good Samaritan by stopping to aid a stranded motorist on his way home following the final game of the World Series...was the recipient of the Ben Epstein "Good Guy Award" in 1997, presented annually by the New York chapter of the BBWAA...was honored at the 2007 Lou Gehrig Sports Award Benefit Dinner.

JOE GIRARDI

- Joined New York City Mayor Michael Bloomberg and Roberto Clemente, Jr. in placing the first "pitch" on 7/29/08 at the 3rd Annual Gracie Mansion Tee Ball Game...hosted by the Mayor's Office, Little League Baseball and the Roberto Clemente Foundation, the game featured five teams, one from each New York City borough and promoted youth exercise as well as team-building sports.
- Following his retirement as a player in 2004, Girardi joined the YES Network as an analyst and won an Emmy Award for hosting YES' *Kids on Deck* series...in 2007, he rejoined YES, working as an analyst on Yankees broadcasts...also worked with FOX during the regular season and postseason...gained broadcast experience as a member of ESPN Radio's team for the 2003 National League Division Series.
- He and his wife, Kim, have three children, Serena (10), Dante (8) and Lena (3)...Kim has hosted several charitable events at Yankee Stadium, including fundraisers for stomach cancer research in which fans could purchase blue hair extensions and blue mohawks.

Girardi's Major League Playing Career

Year	Club	AVG	G	AB	R	H	2B	3B	HR	RBI	SH	SF	HP	BB	SO	SB	CS	E	OBP	SLG
1989	CHICAGO-NL	.248	59	157	15	39	10	0	1	14	1	1	2	11	26	2	1	7	.304	.331
1990	CHICAGO-NL	.270	133	419	36	113	24	2	1	38	4	4	3	17	50	8	3	11	.300	.344
1991	CHICAGO-NL	.191	21	47	3	9	2	0	0	6	1	0	0	6	6	0	0	3	.283	.234
1992	CHICAGO-NL	.270	91	270	19	73	3	1	1	12	0	1	1	19	38	0	2	4	.320	.300
1993	COLORADO-a	.290	86	310	35	90	14	5	3	31	12	1	3	24	41	6	6	6	.346	.397
1994	COLORADO	.276	93	330	47	91	9	4	4	34	6	2	2	21	48	3	3	5	.321	.364
1995	COLORADO	.262	125	462	63	121	17	2	8	55	12	1	2	29	76	3	3	10	.308	.359
1996	YANKEES-b	.294	124	422	55	124	22	3	2	45	11	3	5	30	55	13	4	3	.346	.374
1997	YANKEES-c	.264	112	398	38	105	23	1	1	50	5	2	2	26	53	2	3	5	.311	.334
1998	YANKEES	.276	78	254	31	70	11	4	3	31	8	1	2	14	38	2	4	3	.317	.386
1999	YANKEES	.239	65	209	23	50	16	1	2	27	8	2	0	10	26	3	1	8	.271	.354
2000	CHICAGO-NL-d	.278	106	363	47	101	15	1	6	40	6	3	3	32	61	1	0	5	.339	.375
2001	CHICAGO-NL	.253	78	229	22	58	10	1	3	25	2	1	0	21	50	0	1	0	.315	.345
2002	CHICAGO-NL	.226	90	234	19	53	10	1	1	13	5	1	0	16	35	1	0	6	.275	.291
2003	ST. LOUIS-e	.130	16	23	1	3	0	0	0	1	0	0	0	3	4	0	0	1	.231	.130
Minor League Totals		**.284**	**323**	**1128**	**152**	**320**	**42**	**13**	**21**	**136**	**7**	**6**	**7**	**88**	**181**	**28**	**10**	**34**	**.339**	**.393**
Major League Totals		**.267**	**1277**	**4127**	**454**	**1100**	**186**	**26**	**36**	**422**	**81**	**23**	**25**	**279**	**607**	**44**	**31**	**77**	**.315**	**.350**
NYY Totals		**.272**	**379**	**1283**	**147**	**349**	**72**	**9**	**8**	**153**	**32**	**8**	**9**	**80**	**172**	**20**	**12**	**19**	**.317**	**.361**

Drafted by the Chicago Cubs in the fifth round of the 1986 First-Year Player Draft.

a- Drafted by the Colorado Rockies from the Cubs as the 19th pick in the 1992 Expansion Draft on November 17, 1992.
b- Traded to New York-AL on November 20, 1995 in exchange for LHP Mike DeJean.
c- Signed by New York-AL as a free agent on December 3, 1996.
d- Signed by Chicago-NL as a free agent on December 15, 1999.
e- Signed by St. Louis as a free agent on December 18, 2002.
f- Signed by New York-AL as a free agent on February 4, 2004.

Girardi's Division Series Record

Year	Club/Opponent	AVG	G	AB	R	H	2B	3B	HR	RBI	BB	SO	SB
1995	COL vs. ATL	.125	4	16	0	2	0	0	0	0	0	2	0
1996	NYY vs. TEX	.222	4	9	1	2	0	0	0	0	4	1	0
1997	NYY vs. CLE	.133	5	15	2	2	0	0	0	0	1	3	0
1998	NYY vs. TEX	.429	2	7	0	3	0	0	0	0	0	1	0
1999	NYY vs. TEX	.000	2	6	0	0	0	0	0	0	0	1	0
Division Series Totals		**.170**	**17**	**53**	**3**	**9**	**0**	**0**	**0**	**0**	**5**	**8**	**0**

Girardi's League Championship Series Record

Year	Club/Opponent	AVG	G	AB	R	H	2B	3B	HR	RBI	BB	SO	SB
1989	CHC vs. SF	.100	4	10	1	1	0	0	0	0	1	2	0
1996	NYY vs. BAL	.250	4	12	1	3	0	1	0	0	1	3	0
1998	NYY vs. CLE	.250	3	8	2	2	0	0	0	0	1	0	0
1999	NYY vs. BOS	.250	3	8	0	2	0	0	0	0	0	2	0
LCS Totals		**.211**	**14**	**38**	**4**	**8**	**0**	**1**	**0**	**0**	**3**	**7**	**0**

Girardi's World Series Record

Year	Club/Opponent	AVG	G	AB	R	H	2B	3B	HR	RBI	BB	SO	SB
1996	NYY vs. ATL	.200	4	10	1	2	0	1	0	1	1	2	0
1998	NYY vs. SD	.000	2	6	0	0	0	0	0	0	0	2	0
1999	NYY vs. ATL	.286	2	7	1	2	0	0	0	0	0	1	0
World Series Totals		**.174**	**8**	**23**	**2**	**4**	**0**	**1**	**0**	**1**	**1**	**5**	**0**
POSTSEASON TOTALS		**.184**	**39**	**114**	**9**	**21**	**0**	**2**	**0**	**1**	**9**	**20**	**0**

Girardi's All-Star Game Record

Year	Club, Site	AVG	G	AB	R	H	2B	3B	HR	RBI	BB	SO	SB
2000	CHC, Atlanta				Did Not Play								

Dave Eiland

58 Pitching Coach

Opening Day Age: 43

Full Name
David William Eiland

Birthdate
July 5, 1966

Birthplace
Dade City, Fla.

Resides
Wesley Chapel, Fla.

Coaching Career

- Enters his third season as Yankees pitching coach in 2010, marking his eighth season in the Yankees organization.
- Yankees pitchers ranked fourth in the American League with a 4.26 ERA in 2009, posting their lowest mark since 2003 (4.02)...combined to strike out 1,260 batters, the second-highest total in franchise history behind the 2001 total of 1,226K (credit: *Elias*)...their .251 opponents batting average was the second-lowest in the AL behind only Seattle (.247)...led the AL with a 3.94 ERA after the All-Star break after posting a 4.54 mark in the first half (23rd in the Majors).
- Yankees starters (Burnett, Pettitte and Sabathia) worked to a 3.43 ERA in the 2009 postseason, holding the opposition to 3ER or less in 12 of their 15 playoff games...tossed at least 6.0IP with no more than 3ER allowed in each of their first seven starts of the 2009 playoffs, marking the best such stretch to start a postseason in franchise history.
- Spent 2007 as the pitching coach at Triple-A Scranton/Wilkes-Barre, where his staff ranked second in the International League with 1,101 strikeouts, tied for second with 13 shutouts and had the third-lowest ERA (3.64)...joined the Major League staff upon completion of Scranton's season.
- Previously served as the pitching coach for Double-A Trenton in 2005 and 2006...in 2006, Thunder pitchers recorded 80 wins and led the Eastern League with a 3.19 ERA and 1,107K...began his coaching career as the pitching coach for short-season Single-A Staten Island in 2003 and 2004.

Playing Career

- Appeared in 92 career Major League games (70 starts) over 10 seasons with the Yankees (1988-91, '95), San Diego Padres (1992-93) and Tampa Bay Devil Rays (1998-2000), going 12-27 with a 5.74 ERA (373.0IP, 238ER)...allowed a home run to his first-ever batter faced in the Majors on 8/3/88 at Milwaukee (Paul Molitor)...also homered in his first Major League at-bat on 4/10/92 off the Dodgers' Bob Ojeda.
- Underwent two Tommy John surgeries, forcing his retirement in 2002.
- Was originally selected by the Yankees in the seventh round of the 1987 First-Year Player Draft...earned Yankees "Minor League Pitcher of the Year" honors in 1990 as well as International League "Pitcher of the Year"...was selected to the Topps and *Baseball America* Triple-A All-Star teams.

Personal

- Married (Sandra) and has two daughters, Nicole (16) and Natalie (13)...played baseball and football at the University of Florida in 1985...transferred to the University of South Florida in 1986 to play baseball, earning All-Sun Belt Conference honors and preseason All-American honors...lettered three seasons in baseball, football and basketball at Zephyrhills (Fla.) High School and had his number retired in 2008...is active in charity work with the Pediatric Cancer Foundation.
- Served as Kevin Costner's body double in *For Love of the Game*.

Eiland's Career Major League Pitching Record

Year	Club	W-L	ERA	G	GS	CG	SHO	SV	IP	H	R	ER	BB	SO
1988	YANKEES	0-0	6.39	3	3	0	0	0	12.2	15	9	9	4	7
1989	YANKEES	1-3	5.77	6	6	0	0	0	34.1	44	25	22	13	11
1990	YANKEES	2-1	3.56	5	5	0	0	0	30.1	31	14	12	5	16
1991	YANKEES	2-5	5.33	18	13	0	0	0	72.2	87	51	43	23	18
1992	SAN DIEGO	0-2	5.67	7	7	0	0	0	27.0	33	21	17	5	10
1993	SAN DIEGO	0-3	5.21	10	9	0	0	0	48.1	58	33	28	17	14
1995	YANKEES	1-1	6.30	4	1	0	0	0	10.0	16	10	7	3	6
1998	TAMPA BAY	0-1	20.25	1	1	0	0	0	2.2	6	6	6	3	1
1999	TAMPA BAY	4-8	5.60	21	15	0	0	0	80.1	98	59	50	27	53
2000	TAMPA BAY	2-3	7.24	17	10	0	0	0	54.2	77	46	44	18	17
Minor League Totals		**109-58**	**3.42**	**248**	**241**	**33**	**8**	**0**	**1421.2**	**1404**	**627**	**540**	**261**	**815**
AL Totals		**12-22**	**5.84**	**75**	**54**	**0**	**0**	**0**	**297.2**	**374**	**220**	**193**	**96**	**129**
NL Totals		**0-5**	**5.52**	**17**	**16**	**0**	**0**	**0**	**75.1**	**91**	**54**	**45**	**22**	**24**
Major League Totals		**12-27**	**5.74**	**92**	**70**	**0**	**0**	**0**	**373.0**	**465**	**274**	**238**	**118**	**153**
NYY Totals		**6-10**	**5.23**	**36**	**28**	**0**	**0**	**0**	**160.0**	**193**	**109**	**93**	**48**	**58**

Mike Harkey

57 Bullpen Coach

Opening Day Age: 43

Full Name
Michael Anthony Harkey

Birthdate
October 25, 1966

Birthplace
San Diego, Calif.

Resides
Chino Hills, Calif.

Career Highlights

***Sporting News* Rookie of the Year**
- 1990

***USA Today* Minor League Player of the Year**
- 1988

Coaching Career

- Enters his third season as Yankees bullpen coach in 2010... Yankees relievers led the Majors in 2009 with 40 wins and tied for first with 51 saves, ranking second in opponent's batting average (.231) and fifth in strikeouts (483)...allowed 11.64 baserunners/9.0IP, marking the second-lowest ratio in the Majors behind Oakland (11.54)...the Yankees were 71-2 when leading after the end of the sixth inning.
- In 2008, the Yankees' bullpen collected a Major League-high 523K and recorded their lowest ERA (3.78) since 2002 (3.64).
- Is his second Major League coaching position, having served as bullpen coach for Joe Girardi with the Florida Marlins in 2006.
- Was the pitching coach for the Triple-A Iowa Cubs of the Pacific Coast League in 2007.
- Spent six seasons (2000-2005) as a pitching coach in the San Diego Padres organization, making stops at Single-A Rancho Cucamonga (2000), Single-A Fort Wayne (2001, '03), Single-A Lake Elsinore (2002, '04) and Double-A Mobile (2005).

Playing Career

- Appeared in 131 career Major League games (104 starts) over eight seasons with the Cubs (1988-93), Colorado Rockies (1994), Oakland Athletics (1995), California Angels (1995) and Los Angeles Dodgers (1997), going 36-36 with a 4.49 ERA (656.0IP, 327ER).
- Was named *Sporting News* 1990 "NL Rookie of the Year" after posting a 12-6 record with a 3.26 ERA in 27 starts for the Cubs...selected as *USA Today* "Minor League Player of the Year" in 1988...made his Major League debut at age 21 on 9/5/88 at Wrigley Field recording a no-decision in Game 2 of a doubleheader vs. the Phillies.
- Was a first-round pick by the Cubs in the 1987 First-Year Player Draft (fourth overall)...was originally selected by the San Diego Padres in the 18th round of the 1984 First-Year Player Draft, but chose to attend college.

Personal

- Married (Nikki) and has two sons, Tony and Cory, and a daughter, Miani...Tony is a junior infielder for Cal State Fullerton and Cory recently completed his sophomore season as a tight end with UCLA...played baseball at Cal State Fullerton, earning all-American honors as a junior...graduated from Ganesha High School in Pomona, Calif.

Harkey's Career Pitching Record

Year	Club	W-L	ERA	G	GS	CG	SHO	SV	IP	H	R	ER	BB	SO
1987	Peoria	2-3	3.55	12	12	3	0	0	76.0	81	45	30	28	48
	Pittsfield	0-0	0.00	1	0	0	0	0	2.0	1	0	0	0	2
1988	Pittsfield	9-2	1.37	13	13	3	1	0	85.2	66	29	13	35	73
	Iowa	7-2	3.55	12	12	3	1	0	78.2	55	36	31	33	62
	CHICAGO-NL	0-3	2.60	5	5	0	0	0	34.2	33	14	10	15	18
1989	Iowa	2-7	4.43	12	12	0	0	0	63.0	67	37	31	25	37
1990	CHICAGO-NL	12-6	3.26	27	27	2	1	0	173.2	153	71	63	59	94
1991	CHICAGO-NL	0-2	5.30	4	4	0	0	0	18.2	21	11	11	6	15
1992	Peoria	1-0	3.00	2	2	0	0	0	12.0	15	6	4	3	17
	Iowa	0-1	5.56	4	4	0	0	0	22.2	21	15	14	13	6
	Charlotte	0-1	5.63	1	1	1	0	0	8.0	9	5	5	0	5
	CHICAGO-NL	4-0	1.89	7	7	0	0	0	38.0	34	13	8	15	21
1993	CHICAGO-NL	10-10	5.26	28	28	1	0	0	157.1	187	100	92	43	67
	Orlando	0-0	1.69	1	1	0	0	0	5.1	4	1	1	0	5
1994	COLORADO	1-6	5.79	24	13	0	0	0	91.2	125	61	59	35	39
	Colorado Springs	1-1	12.60	2	2	0	0	0	10.0	19	14	14	3	4
1995	OAKLAND	4-6	6.27	14	12	0	0	0	66.0	75	46	46	31	28
	CALIFORNIA	4-3	4.55	12	8	1	0	0	61.1	80	32	31	16	28
1996	Albuquerque	7-11	5.38	49	13	0	0	13	118.2	146	79	71	39	90
1997	LOS ANGELES-NL	1-0	4.30	10	0	0	0	0	14.2	12	8	7	5	6
Minor League Totals		**29-28**	**3.70**	**109**	**72**	**10**	**2**	**13**	**482.0**	**482**	**267**	**214**	**179**	**349**
AL Totals		**8-9**	**5.44**	**26**	**20**	**1**	**0**	**0**	**127.1**	**155**	**78**	**77**	**47**	**56**
NL Totals		**28-27**	**4.26**	**105**	**84**	**3**	**1**	**0**	**528.2**	**565**	**278**	**250**	**178**	**260**
Major League Totals		**36-36**	**4.49**	**131**	**104**	**4**	**1**	**0**	**656.0**	**720**	**356**	**327**	**225**	**316**

Mick Kelleher

50 First Base Coach

Opening Day Age: 62

Full Name
Michael Dennis Kelleher

Birthdate
July 25, 1947

Birthplace
Seattle, Wash.

Resides
Solvang, Calif.

Coaching Career

- Begins his second season as Yankees first base coach...also serves as infield instructor...the club set an all-time Major League record with 18 consecutive errorless games in 2009 and featured two AL Gold Glove winners (SS Derek Jeter and 1B Mark Teixeira).
- Is his third tenure on a Major League coaching staff, having served three years as Detroit's first base coach from 2003-05 and as Jim Leyland's first base coach and infield instructor with Pittsburgh in 1986.
- Spent the previous three years as the Yankees' roving infield instructor (2006-08)...is in his second stint with the Yankees organization, having spent seven seasons (1996-2002) as the Yankees' roving defensive coordinator and one season (1998) as a Major League scout for the club.
- Began his coaching career with the San Diego Padres as a roving minor league instructor from 1984-85...joined the Chicago Cubs as a roving minor league infield instructor from 1987-92, taking over as manager of the organization's Triple-A Iowa club in May 1991 for the remainder of the season...also spent two seasons (1994-95) as the roving minor league infield instructor with the Milwaukee Brewers.

Playing Career

- Played 15 seasons of professional baseball, including 11 at the Major League level with the St. Louis Cardinals (1972-73, '75), Houston Astros (1974), Chicago Cubs (1976-80), Detroit Tigers (1981-82) and California Angels (1982)...finished his career with a .974 Major League fielding percentage, appearing in games at second base, third base and shortstop...since retiring in 1982, no position player has accrued as many career plate appearances without a homer.
- Was selected by St. Louis in the third round of the 1969 First-Year Player Draft.
- Paced league shortstops in fielding during four of his minor league seasons and won two Rawlings Silver Glove Awards (1972, '75) as the minors' best fielding shortstop...established an American Association record for shortstops with a .979 fielding percentage in 1972.
- Received his bachelor of science degree in political science from the University of Puget Sound in Tacoma, Wash...was an NCAA Division II All-American in 1969 and named to the NCAA Division II All-Tournament Team the same season...was also Division II All-Coast in 1968 and '69.

Personal

- He and his wife, Renee, have one daughter, Brittney, and two grandchildren...Renee is an accomplished painter and is represented at galleries throughout California...is an aficionado of the wine industry and grows his own grapes and olives...in offseason, works as a ranch hand tending to llamas and cows...also plays in senior tennis league.

Kelleher's Career Playing Record

Year	Club	AVG.	G	AB	R	H	2B	3B	HR	RBI	BB	SO	SB
1972	ST. LOUIS	.159	23	63	5	10	2	1	0	1	6	15	0
1973	ST. LOUIS	.184	43	38	4	7	2	0	0	2	4	11	0
1974	HOUSTON	.158	19	57	4	9	0	0	0	2	5	10	1
1975	ST. LOUIS	.000	7	4	0	0	0	0	0	0	0	1	0
1976	CHICAGO-NL	.228	124	337	28	77	12	1	0	22	15	32	0
1977	CHICAGO-NL	.230	63	122	14	28	5	2	0	11	9	12	0
1978	CHICAGO-NL	.253	68	95	8	24	1	0	0	6	7	11	4
1979	CHICAGO-NL	.254	73	142	14	36	4	1	0	10	7	9	2
1980	CHICAGO-NL	.146	105	96	12	14	1	1	0	4	9	17	1
1981	DETROIT	.221	61	77	10	17	4	0	0	6	7	10	0
1982	DETROIT	.000	2	1	0	0	0	0	0	0	0	0	0
	CALIFORNIA	.163	34	49	9	8	1	0	0	1	5	5	1
Major League Totals		**.213**	**622**	**1081**	**108**	**230**	**32**	**6**	**0**	**65**	**74**	**133**	**9**

Kevin Long
54
Hitting Coach
Opening Day Age: 43

Full Name
Kevin Richard Long

Birthdate
December 30, 1966

Birthplace
Van Nuys, Calif.

Resides
Scottsdale, Ariz.

Coaching Career

- Begins his fourth season as Yankees hitting coach…Yankees batters led the Majors in 2009 with 915R, 244HR, a .478 slugging percentage, a .362 on-base percentage and 663BB, and ranked second with a .283 batting average…set a franchise record in homers, surpassing the previous mark of 242 (2004)…guided an offense that featured a franchise-record five players with at least 25HR and a franchise-record nine players with at least 65RBI…coached middle infielders Derek Jeter and Robinson Cano, who became the first shortstop/second baseman combination in Baseball history to each record 200H at their respective positions in a single season…Long's offense also boasted two Silver Slugger Award winners (1B Mark Teixeria and Jeter).
- The 2008 Yankees ranked third in the AL in OBP (.342), fourth in average (.271) and tied for fourth in HR (180)…guided a Yankees offense in 2007 that led the Majors in runs (968), hits (1,656), HR (201), RBI (929), team batting average (.290), slugging percentage (.463), OBP (.366) and total bases (2,649)…the 968R were the most for the franchise since 1937 (979)…his offense also featured the AL MVP (Rodriguez), three Silver Sluggers (Jeter, Posada and Rodriguez) and four of the American League's top-15 batting averages.
- Joined the Yankees at the Major League level after serving three years as the hitting coach with the Yankees' Triple-A affiliate in Columbus (2004-06)…before joining the Yankees organization, served as the hitting coach with the Triple-A Omaha Royals (2002-03) and with the Double-A Wichita Wranglers (2000-01)…was named the Northwest League's "co-Manager of the Year" after leading the Spokane Indians to the league title in 1999…made his professional coaching debut at Single-A Wilmington in 1997.

Playing Career

- Was originally selected by the Kansas City Royals in the 31st round of the 1989 First-Year Player Draft and played in their system for eight years from 1989-96 as an outfielder.
- Led Class-A Eugene in 1989 in almost all offensive categories, including games played, at-bats, runs scored, hits, doubles and RBI…ranked eighth among all Northwest League hitters with a .312 batting average in his rookie season.
- Missed most of the 1994 season after undergoing surgery on his left wrist.

Personal

- Named a second-team All-American and first-team PAC-10 in 1989 at the University of Arizona…a three-year letter-winner, Long graduated with the Arizona record for most extra-base hits in a game (five) and ranked in the top 10 in several single-season statistical categories: third in extra-base hits (41), tied for seventh in doubles (23), eighth in multi-hit games (30), ninth in total bases (162) and tied for ninth in runs (80).
- Resides in Scottsdale, Ariz., with his wife, Marcey, daughter, Britney, and sons, Tracy and Jaron.

Long's Career Playing Record

Year	Club	AVG	G	AB	R	H	2B	3B	HR	RBI	BB	SO	SB
1989	Eugene	.312	69	260	54	81	19	1	3	45	36	40	15
1990	Baseball City	.282	85	308	53	87	17	5	5	33	32	28	22
1991	Memphis	.275	106	407	60	112	18	2	3	35	45	63	27
1992	Omaha	.228	88	312	28	71	16	3	1	29	29	41	9
1993	Memphis	.272	79	301	47	82	14	6	1	20	37	56	7
	Omaha	.255	17	51	7	13	2	0	0	4	2	13	3
1994	Memphis	.208	10	24	5	5	3	0	0	1	5	2	2
1995	Omaha	.250	22	64	7	16	3	0	0	1	5	8	1
	Wichita	.292	67	250	38	73	14	1	1	26	41	29	9
1996	Wichita	.273	128	436	62	119	31	3	3	48	56	36	9
Minor League Totals		**.273**	**671**	**2413**	**361**	**659**	**137**	**21**	**17**	**242**	**288**	**316**	**104**

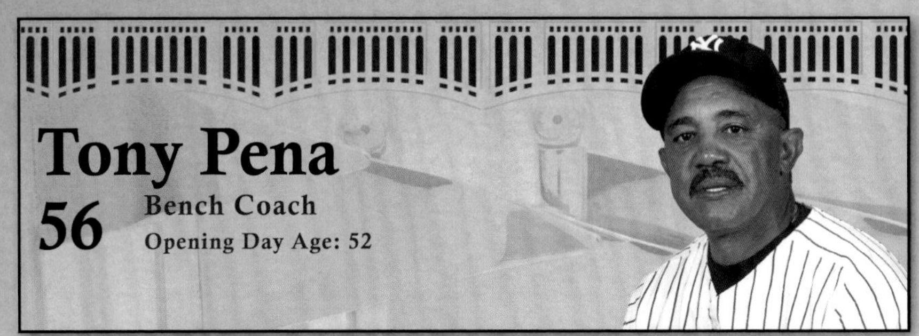

Tony Pena

56 **Bench Coach**

Opening Day Age: 52

Full Name
Antonio Francisco Pena

Birthdate
June 4, 1957

Birthplace
Monte Cristi, D.R.

Resides
Santiago, D.R.

Career Highlights

BBWAA
A.L. Manager of the Year
- 2003

N.L. All-Star Team
- 1982, 1984, 1985, 1986, 1989

N.L. Gold Glove Award
- 1983, 1984, 1985

A.L. Gold Glove Award
- 1991

Managerial/Coaching Career

- Enters his second season as Yankees bench coach...is his fifth season on the Yankees' Major League coaching staff, serving as first base coach from 2006-08 and catching instructor over the entire span...since joining the staff, Yankees catchers have caught a Major League-best 167 potential base stealers, ranking fourth in the AL with a 26.4% caught stealing rate.
- Previously spent parts of four seasons as manager of the Kansas City Royals from 2002-05.
- In his first full season as manager in 2003, led the Royals to an 83-79 record, the sixth-best turnaround in Major League history following a 100-loss season...the 2003 season marked Kansas City's first winning season since 1993, when they went 84-78.
- Was selected as the 2003 American League "Manager of the Year" by the Baseball Writers' Association of America, becoming the fourth manager since 1983 to win the award in his first full season as a Major League skipper (also Houston's Hal Lanier, 1986; San Francisco's Dusty Baker, 1993; and San Diego's Bruce Bochy, 1996)... also named the 2003 AL "Manager of the Year" by both *Sporting News* and *Sports Illustrated*.
- Became only the third Dominican-born manager in Major League history, joining Felipe Alou and Luis Pujols.
- Began his Major League coaching career in 2002 as the bench coach for the Houston Astros...was named Royals manager on 5/15/02.
- Also served as manager of Triple-A New Orleans from 1999-2001...began his coaching career as White Sox' Coordinator of Dominican Operations in 1998 and led the Aguilas Dominican team to the Caribbean Series title.

Playing Career

- A five-time National League All-Star catcher, Pena posted a .260 career batting average over an 18-year Major League career, appearing in 1,988 games for the Pittsburgh Pirates (1980-86), St. Louis Cardinals (1987-88), Boston Red Sox (1990-93), Cleveland Indians (1994-96), Chicago White Sox (1997) and Houston Astros (1997).
- Ranks fifth all-time among Major League catchers with 1,950 games behind the plate, trailing only Ivan Rodriguez (2,288), Carlton Fisk (2,226), Bob Boone (2,225) and Gary Carter (2,056).
- Won four Gold Glove Awards (1983-85, 1991) and recorded a .338 career postseason batting average...was named Topps' Rookie All-Star catcher in 1981 and was selected to the UPI Rookie All-Star Team...originally signed as a non-drafted free agent by the Pittsburgh Pirates on 7/22/75 and made his Major League debut on 9/1/80.

Personal

- Married (Amaris) with two sons: Tony, Jr. (a pitcher in the San Francisco system) and Francisco Antonio (a catcher in the New York Mets system)...also has a daughter, Jennifer Amaris, who won the Miss Dominican Republic-U.S.A. beauty pageant in 2007...his brother, Ramon, pitched with the Detroit Tigers organization.
- Tony did not play high school baseball...credits his mother, who was an outstanding softball player, with teaching him how to play the game.
- Took part in the Yankees' hurricane relief donation of $35,000 in cash and food to the Dominican Republic in October 2007.
- Joined the Yankees delegation and the World Series trophy on 1/7/10 to meet Dominican Repulilic President Dr. Leonel Fernandez at the National Palace in Santo Domingo.

TONY PENA

Pena's Career Playing Record

Year	Club	AVG	G	AB	R	H	2B	3B	HR	RBI	BB	SO	SB
1976	Bradenton	.209	33	110	10	23	2	2	1	11	4	17	5
	Charleston	.224	14	49	4	11	2	0	1	8	4	7	0
1977	Charleston	.238	29	101	10	24	4	0	3	16	7	21	2
	Salem	.276	84	319	36	88	15	3	7	46	14	60	3
1978	Shreveport	.230	104	348	34	80	14	0	8	42	15	96	3
1979	Buffalo	.313	134	515	89	161	16	4	34	97	39	83	5
1980	Portland	.329	124	450	57	148	23	13	9	77	29	75	5
1980	PITTSBURGH	.429	8	21	1	9	1	1	0	1	0	4	0
1981	PITTSBURGH	.300	66	210	16	63	9	1	2	17	8	23	1
1982	PITTSBURGH	.296	138	497	53	147	28	4	11	63	17	57	2
1983	PITTSBURGH	.301	151	542	51	163	22	3	15	70	31	73	6
1984	PITTSBURGH	.286	147	546	77	156	27	2	15	78	36	79	12
1985	PITTSBURGH	.249	147	546	53	136	27	2	10	59	29	67	12
1986	PITTSBURGH	.288	144	510	56	147	26	2	10	52	53	69	9
1987	ST. LOUIS	.214	116	384	40	82	13	4	5	44	36	54	6
1988	ST. LOUIS	.263	149	505	55	133	23	1	10	51	33	60	6
1989	ST. LOUIS	.259	141	424	36	110	17	2	4	37	35	33	5
1990	BOSTON	.263	143	491	62	129	19	1	7	56	43	71	8
1991	BOSTON	.231	141	464	45	107	23	2	5	48	37	53	8
1992	BOSTON	.241	133	410	39	99	21	1	1	38	24	61	3
1993	BOSTON	.181	126	304	20	55	11	0	4	19	25	46	1
1994	CLEVELAND	.295	40	112	18	33	8	1	2	10	9	11	0
1995	CLEVELAND	.262	91	263	25	69	15	0	5	28	14	44	1
1996	CLEVELAND	.195	67	174	14	34	4	0	1	27	15	25	0
1997	CHICAGO-AL	.164	31	67	4	11	1	0	0	8	8	13	0
	HOUSTON	.211	9	19	2	4	3	0	0	2	2	3	0
Minor League Totals		**.283**	**522**	**1892**	**240**	**535**	**76**	**22**	**63**	**297**	**112**	**359**	**23**
Major League Totals		**.260**	**1988**	**6489**	**667**	**1687**	**298**	**27**	**107**	**708**	**455**	**846**	**80**

Pena's Division Series Record

Year	Club/Opponent	AVG	G	AB	R	H	2B	3B	HR	RBI	BB	SO	SB
1995	CLE vs. BOS	.500	2	2	1	1	0	0	1	1	0	0	0
1996	CLE vs. BAL	.000	1	0	0	0	0	0	0	0	0	0	0
1997	HOU vs. ATL	.000	2	0	0	0	0	0	0	0	0	0	0
Division Series Totals		**.200**	**5**	**2**	**1**	**1**	**0**	**0**	**1**	**1**	**0**	**0**	**0**

Pena's League Championship Series Record

Year	Club/Opponent	AVG	G	AB	R	H	2B	3B	HR	RBI	BB	SO	SB
1987	STL vs. SF	.381	7	21	5	8	0	1	0	0	3	4	1
1990	BOS vs. OAK	.214	4	14	0	3	0	0	0	0	0	0	0
1995	CLE vs. SEA	.333	4	6	1	2	1	0	0	0	1	0	0
LCS TOTALS		**.317**	**15**	**41**	**6**	**13**	**1**	**1**	**0**	**0**	**4**	**4**	**1**

Pena's World Series Record

Year	Club/Opponent	AVG	G	AB	R	H	2B	3B	HR	RBI	BB	SO	SB
1987	STL vs. MIN	.409	7	22	2	9	1	0	0	4	3	2	1
1995	CLE vs. ATL	.167	2	6	0	1	0	0	0	0	0	0	0
World Series Totals		**.357**	**9**	**28**	**2**	**10**	**1**	**0**	**0**	**4**	**3**	**2**	**1**
POSTSEASON TOTALS		**.338**	**29**	**71**	**9**	**24**	**2**	**1**	**1**	**5**	**7**	**6**	**2**

Pena's All-Star Game Record

Year	Club, Site	AVG	G	AB	R	H	2B	3B	HR	RBI	BB	SO	SB
1982	PIT, Montreal	.000	1	1	0	0	0	0	0	0	0	0	1
1984	PIT, San Francisco	.000	1	0	0	0	0	0	0	0	0	0	0
1985	PIT, Minnesota	.000	1	1	0	0	0	0	0	0	0	1	0
1986	PIT, Houston	.000	1	0	0	0	0	0	0	0	0	0	0
1989	STL, Anaheim	.000	1	2	0	0	0	0	0	0	0	0	0
All-Star Game Totals		**.000**	**5**	**4**	**0**	**0**	**0**	**0**	**0**	**0**	**0**	**1**	**1**

Rob Thomson

59 Third Base Coach

Opening Day Age: 46

Full Name
Robert Thomson

Birthdate
August 16, 1963

Birthplace
Ontario, Canada

Resides
Odessa, Fla.

Coaching Career

- Begins his 21st season as a member of the Yankees organization, second as the Yankees' third base coach...served as the club's bench coach for the 2008 season.
- Managed the Yankees for three games in 2008, going 1-2, becoming the first Canadian to manage a Major League game since George (Mooney) Gibson, a Londoner, with the Pittsburgh Pirates in 1934...was 0-2 from 4/4-5 vs. Tampa Bay when Joe Girardi missed two games with an upper respiratory infection...won on 5/23 vs. Baltimore while Girardi served a one-game suspension...also guided the Yankees to a "walk-off" victory on 5/22 vs. Baltimore when Joe Girardi was ejected in the sixth inning...went in the books as Girardi's 100th career managerial victory...again took over following a Girardi ejection on 7/5 vs. Boston, also recording a "walk-off" win.
- Served as the Yankees' Major League field coordinator in 2007 after spending the previous three seasons as a special assignment instructor...was named to the Yankees' Major League coaching staff on 11/4/03.
- Joined the Yankees organization in 1990 as a third-base coach for Single-A Fort Lauderdale.
- Coached in the Yankees system for five years before taking over as manager of Single-A Oneonta of the NY-Penn League in 1995.
- Served as the third base coach at Triple-A Columbus in 1996 and 1997 before moving to the Yankees front office as a field coordinator in 1998.
- Was promoted to director of player development in 2000 and named vice president of minor league development prior to the 2003 season.

Playing Career

- Attended the University of Kansas and was selected in the 32nd round of the 1985 draft by the Detroit Tigers.
- Was a catcher and a third baseman in the Tigers system from 1985-88 before joining the Tigers' minor league coaching staff in 1988.

Personal

- Resides in Odessa, Fla., with his wife, Michele and their daughters, Jacqueline and Christina.

Thomson's Career Playing Record

Year	Club	AVG	G	AB	R	H	2B	3B	HR	RBI	BB	SO	SB
1985	Bristol	.000	2	5	0	0	0	0	0	0	1	3	0
	Gastonia	.187	39	123	7	23	6	0	0	10	5	17	0
1986	Gastonia	.252	94	298	42	75	11	1	4	38	48	44	1
	Lakeland	.182	8	22	2	4	1	0	1	4	0	2	0
1987	Lakeland	.228	71	206	21	47	12	0	1	22	25	30	2
1988	Lakeland	.000	2	7	0	0	0	0	0	0	0	2	0
Minor League Totals		**.225**	**216**	**661**	**72**	**149**	**30**	**1**	**6**	**74**	**79**	**98**	**3**

Scoring Machine

The Yankees hold the Major League record for consecutive games without being shut out, scoring at least one run in 308 straight contests from 8/3/31-8/2/33...the streak was broken by a 7-0 shutout by Philadelphia's Lefty Grove.

2010 Yankees Field Staff

Gene Monahan

Head Athletic Trainer

The 2010 season will mark his 48th consecutive season with the New York Yankees organization, the last 38 as the Head Athletic Trainer on the Major League level…is the longest-tenured active head trainer in the Major Leagues…in 2009 received the National Athletic Trainers Association "Distinguished Athletic Trainer" Award…was honored with induction into the New York State Athletic Trainers' Association Hall of Fame in 2007…began his athletic-training career with the Yankees' Class-D Ft. Lauderdale affiliate in 1963…had served as a bat boy and clubhouse attendant for the club in 1962 during his senior year at St. Thomas Aquinas High School in Ft. Lauderdale…was promoted to Double-A in 1965 and was head trainer for Columbus (Ga.) and Binghamton (N.Y.) until 1969 when he made the jump to Triple-A Syracuse (1969-72)…served as head trainer for the American League All-Star team for the fourth time in his career in 2008 at Yankee Stadium (also 1977, '86 and '92)…a 1969 graduate of Indiana University, he received a B.S. in physical education (with emphasis on professional athletic training)…was presented with the distinguished service award by the American College of Sports Medicine in 1994…is Chairman of the Professional Baseball Athletic Trainers Society's scholarship committee and a member of the National Athletic Trainers Association's Public Relations Committee…he and Yankees Assistant Trainer Steve Donohue—whom he has been paired with since 1986—were honored with the Major League Baseball "Athletic Training Staff of the Year" award in 1990…has two daughters, Kelley and Amanda.

Steve Donohue

Assistant Athletic Trainer

Begins his 32nd consecutive season in the New York Yankees organization, the last 25 as Assistant Athletic Trainer under Gene Monahan at the Major League level…served as an athletic trainer for the American League squad at the 2006 All-Star Game at Pittsburgh's PNC Park and the 1999 All-Star Game at Fenway Park…began his athletic training career in 1979 at the Yankees' Double-A West Haven affiliate before being promoted to Double-A Nashville (1980-81) and Triple-A Columbus (1982-85)…was promoted to the New York Yankees in 1986…he and Monahan—whom he has been paired with since 1986—were honored with the Major League Baseball "Athletic Training Staff of the Year" award in 1990…is a 1974 graduate of Cardinal Spellman High School in the Bronx and a 1979 graduate of the University of Louisville…was the trainer for the NCAA Champion University of Louisville basketball team in 1980…is a member of the National Athletic Trainers Association and the Eastern Athletic Trainers Association…also pens the annual Professional Baseball Athletic Trainers Society's *Confidential Directory*…lives with wife, Paula, and two daughters, Shannon and Margaret, in Bronxville, N.Y.

Dana Cavalea

Strength and Conditioning Coordinator

Enters his fourth season as the Yankees' strength and conditioning coordinator after taking over the post in May 2007…was appointed as the Yankees' strength and conditioning assistant prior to the start of the 2007 season after serving as a strength and conditioning coach during spring training from 2003-06…also served in the same capacity with the Toronto Blue Jays (2001) and Pittsburgh Pirates (2002)…founded Major League Strength, a sports performance consulting firm that teaches nutrition, injury prevention and performance maximization to coaches around the country…was born on 10/15/82 in New York, N.Y., and attended the University of South Florida in Tampa, where he earned his degree in exercise science in 2004…holds a CSCS certification from the NSCA and PES certification from the NASM…is single and resides in Long Island.

2010 Yankees Field Staff

#87 Charlie Wonsowicz

Advance Scout/Head Video Coordinator

Enters his 18th season in the Yankees organization, second in his current position…is a 1986 graduate of Tottenville High School in Staten Island (N.Y.) where he was a second-team All-American in baseball…from 1987-90, pitched at St. John's University (N.Y.) on a four-year baseball scholarship…coached the Tottenville High varsity baseball team from 1991-92 and coached in the Atlantic Coast Summer Baseball League from 1992-93…was born on 9/5/68 in Staten Island, N.Y…resides in Waldwick, N.J., with his wife, Leslie, and their three children, Paige Olivia, C.J. and Jake.

#88 Roman Rodriguez

Bullpen Catcher

Begins his ninth year with the Yankees organization as a bullpen catcher…also assists by charting pitches during games…was signed as a non-drafted free agent in 1988 by the Pittsburgh Pirates…spent eight years in the Pirates minor league system…following his playing career, was hired by the Kansas City Royals from 1997-2000 as their bullpen catcher…spent the following season (2001) as the Boston Red Sox bullpen catcher…married his wife, Carminia, on Valentine's Day in 2004 and now resides in Bradenton, Fla…was born on 3/30/69 in San Mateo, Venezuela.

Rob Cucuzza

Equipment Manager

Begins his 13th season as home clubhouse manager…has been a member of the Yankees organization since 1984, working as a bat boy (1984-86), assistant visiting clubhouse manager (1987-89) and assistant equipment manager (1990-97)…was born on 1/4/68 in the Bronx, N.Y., and is a 1985 graduate of Mount St. Michael Academy…is single and resides in White Plains, N.Y.

Lou Cucuzza, Jr.

Clubhouse Manager

Is in his 31st year in the New York Yankees organization, starting as a batboy in 1979…was honored as the 2009 MLB "Visiting Clubhouse Manager of the Year," earning the honor—as voted by his peers—for the second time (also 2006)…earned a B.A. in public accounting from Iona College…worked five years as an auditor for the accounting firm of KPMG Peat Marwick (1987-91) and five years as budgeting manager for Melville Corporation (1992-96)…was born on 8/5/64 in the Bronx, N.Y…resides in Yonkers, N.Y., with his wife Joanna and their children, Anthony and Kathryn.

Lou Cucuzza, Sr.

Clubhouse Assistant

Returns for his 34th season in the visiting clubhouse…the patriarch of the Cucuzza baseball family, has 45 years of service in professional baseball…was born on 11/19/38 in New York, N.Y., and resides in the Bronx with his wife, Joan.

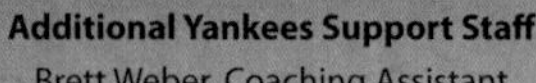

Additional Yankees Support Staff

Brett Weber, Coaching Assistant

Anthony Flynn, Assistant Video Coordinator

Lou Potter, Massage Therapist

Clubhouse Assistants:

Cesar Caceres

Chris Cruz

Joe Lee

Chris Manzione

Craig Postolowski

Jake Ryan

2010 Yankees Field Staff

Dr. Christopher Ahmad, M.D.

Team Physician

Dr. Christopher S. Ahmad begins his second season as Yankees Team Physician in 2010...has been an Assistant Attending Orthopaedic Surgeon in the Sports Medicine and Shoulder Service at New York Orthopaedic Hospital since 2001...has also served as an Associate Professor of Orthopedic Surgery at Columbia University since 2007 after having been an Assistant Professor beginning in 2001...trained in sports medicine at the Kerlan-Jobe Orthopaedic Clinic from 2000-01, which included team physician coverage for the Dodgers (MLB), Lakers (NBA), Kings (NHL), Galaxy (MLS) and Fullerton College football...was Administrative Chief Resident of Orthopaedic Surgery from 1999-2000 at Columbia University, where he served his orthopaedic surgery residency from 1996-99...completed the Frank E. Stinchfield Orthopaedic Research Fellowship at Columbia from 1994-95...received his M.D. from the NYU School of Medicine in 1994 and a B.S. in Mechanical Engineering from Columbia University in 1990...is the author of more than 50 peer-reviewed research articles as well as a textbook on minimally invasive shoulder and elbow surgery...has been elected into the American Orthopaedic Society for Sports Medicine and the American Shoulder and Elbow Surgeons Society...his practice specializes in advanced arthroscopic surgical techniques for sports-related injuries of the knee, shoulder and elbow.

Dr. Stuart J. Hershon, M.D., P.C.

Senior Advisor, Orthopedics

Born December 18, 1937, in Brooklyn, N.Y., Hershon enters his 23rd season as part of the Yankees' medical staff...is an orthopedic surgeon affiliated with Columbia Presbyterian Medical Center, Roosevelt Hospital and North Shore University Hospital, Manhasset, where he is Chief of Sports Medicine...is a graduate of Harvard University (1959) and New York Medical College (1963)...was a starting tight end for Harvard and their leading receiver in 1958...was also a standout football player at Long Beach (N.Y.) High School and was a *Newsday* "All-Scholastic" end in 1954...has also served as team physician for the New York Arrows of the Major Indoor Soccer League and Nassau Community College...Dr. Hershon and his wife, Judy, reside in Cove Neck, N.Y., and have two children, Joanna and Jordan.

Dr. Andrew G. Boyer, M.D.

Team Physician, Tampa

Enters his 16th season as a Yankees team physician...has been in private practice - Internal Medicine - since 1972...earned his undergraduate degree from Kent State University (Ohio), where he was a team captain for the track team...earned his medical degree from the University of Iowa, Iowa City, and served his internal medicine residency at the Mayo Clinic (Minn.)...was on the faculty of the University of South Florida Medical School, served as the team doctor for the Tampa Bay Rowdies professional soccer team and is presently associated with St. Joseph's Hospital, where he served as Chief of Staff...he is a member of the American Medical Association (AMA), Florida Medical Association (FMA) and the Hillsborough County Medical Association (HCMA)...is married to Ildiko and has two children, Cynthia and Andrew...Cynthia is a radiation oncologist and Andrew is an orthopedic surgeon.

First Home Runs in Franchise History

Courtesy of the *Elias Sports Bureau*

The first home run in franchise history was hit by John Ganzel on May 11, 1903. It was a fifth-inning, inside-the-park, solo homer at the Detroit Tigers' Bennett Park off George Mullin in an 8-2 Highlanders victory.

The first home run hit at home in franchise history was by Ernie Courtney on June 1, 1903. The two-run shot in the bottom of the ninth with one out at Hilltop Park came off Boston's Tom Hughes and accounted for both runs in the 8-2 Highlanders loss.

2010 Yankees Field Staff

Dr. Allen D. Miller, M.D.

Team Orthopedic Surgeon, Tampa

Begins his 14th season with the New York Yankees...is an orthopedic surgeon affiliated with Orthopedic Associates of Tampa (Fla.), where he has been in practice since 1979...is a graduate of McGill University (1975) in Montreal...also earned an MBA from the University of South Florida in 1995...is a member of both the American Academy of Orthopedic Surgeons and the Florida Orthopedic Society.

Dr. Scott L. Hegseth, D.C.

Team Chiropractor, Tampa

Begins his 24th season as the Yankees' team chiropractor...has been in private practice since 1980...earned his undergraduate degree from Mankato State University (Minn.)–which is now Minnesota State University, Mankato–and graduated from Northwestern College of Chiropractic (Minn.)...is a member of the American Chiropractic Association (ACA), Florida Chiropractic Association (FCA), Hillsborough County Chiropractic Society (HCCS) and is a Diplomat of the National Board of Chiropractic Examiners...is married to Virginia and has three children: Kelsey, Allison and Patrick.

Medical Consultants

Adam Cohen, M.D. - Assistant Team Physician
Louis Bigliani, M.D. – Consultant, Orthopedics
Conrad Blum, M.D. – Internist
Lewis Schneider, M.D. – Consultant, Gastroenterology
George Todd, M.D. – Consultant, Vascular Surgery
Darrell Rigel, M.D. – Dermatologist
Scott Levy, DDS – Dentist

Baseball Glossary

HOW TO FIGURE...

Batting Average: (H/AB) Hits divided by at-bats.

ERA: (ERx9/IP) Multiply earned runs by nine and divide the total by innings pitched.

Slugging Percentage: (TB/AB) Total bases (1B=1, 2B=2, 3B=3, HR=4) divided by at-bats.

On-Base Percentage: (H+BB+HBP)/(H+BB+HBP+SF) Add hits, walks, hit by pitch and divide by the total of hits plus walks plus hit-by-pitch plus sacrifice flies.

Fielding Percentage: (PO+A)/(PO+A+E) Total putouts plus assists divided by total chances.

Winning Percentage: The number of games won divided by the total games played.

Magic Number: Determine the number of games yet to be played, add one, then subtract the number of games ahead in the loss column of the standings from the closest opponent.

QUALIFYING RULES

Batting Championship: To qualify for a batting title, a player must make 502 or more plate appearances or 3.1 plate appearances per team game.

Pitching Championship: To qualify for the lowest ERA, a pitcher must throw at least 162.0 innings.

Fielding Championship: To qualify as the top fielder:
(a) a catcher must have played in at least 81 games.
(b) an infielder or outfielder must have played in at least 108 games.
(c) a pitcher must have 162.0 innings pitched.

Rookie: A player shall be considered a rookie unless, during a previous season or seasons, he has (a) exceeded 130 at-bats or 50 innings pitched in the major leagues; or (b) accumulated more than 45 days on the active roster of a major league club or clubs during the period of the 25-player limit.

Save: Credit a pitcher with a save when:
(1) He is the finishing pitcher in a game won by his club;
(2) He is not the winning pitcher, and
(3) He qualifies under one of the following conditions:
  a. He enters the game with a lead of no more than three runs and pitches for at least one inning, or
  b. He enters the game with the potential tying run either on base, at bat or on deck, or
  c. He pitches effectively for at least three innings
No more than one save may be credited each game.

2010 New York Yankees 40-Man Roster

MANAGER: Joe Girardi (28)
COACHES: Dave Eiland (58, Pitching), Mike Harkey (57, Bullpen), Mick Kelleher (50, First Base), Kevin Long (54, Hitting), Tony Pena (56, Bench), Rob Thomson (59, Third Base)
HEAD TRAINER: Gene Monahan **ASSISTANT TRAINER:** Steve Donohue **TEAM PHYSICIAN:** Dr. Christopher Ahmad **SPRING TRAINING PHYSICIAN:** Dr. Andrew Boyer
EQUIPMENT MANAGER: Rob Cucuzza **CLUBHOUSE MANAGER:** Lou Cucuzza, Jr. **TRAVELING SECRETARY:** Ben Tuliebitz **DIRECTOR OF MEDIA RELATIONS:** Jason Zillo

(roster as of 2/15/10)

#	PITCHERS (22)	B-T	HT.	WT.	BORN	BIRTHPLACE	2009 CLUB	W-L	ERA	G	GS	CG	SV	IP	H	R	ER	BB	SO	SVC
91	Aceves, Alfredo	R-R	6-3	220	12/8/82	San Luis Rio Colorado, Mex.	Scranton/WB	2-0	3.80	4	4	0	0	23.2	18	11	10	5	18	1.014
							YANKEES	10-1	3.54	43	1	0	1	84.0	69	36	33	16	69	
63	Albaladejo, Jonathan	R-R	6-5	260	10/30/82	San Juan, P.R.	Scranton/WB	3-0	1.75	27	0	0	11	36.0	25	8	7	3	26	1.119
							YANKEES	5-1	5.24	32	0	0	0	34.1	41	23	20	16	21	
64	Brackman, Andrew	R-R	6-10	240	12/4/85	Cincinnati, OH	Charleston	2-12	5.91	29	19	0	0	106.2	106	79	70	76	103	1.016
34	Burnett, A.J.	R-R	6-4	230	1/3/77	North Little Rock, AR	YANKEES	13-9	4.04	33	33	1	0	207.0	193	99	93	97	195	10.038
62	Chamberlain, Joba	R-R	6-2	230	9/23/85	Lincoln, NE	YANKEES	9-6	4.75	32	31	0	0	157.1	167	94	83	76	133	2.055
68	De La Rosa, Wilkin	L-L	6-0	185	2/21/85	El Seibo, D.R.	Tampa	1-0	1.29	3	3	0	0	14.0	9	2	2	4	17	0.000
							Trenton	4-5	3.48	16	16	0	0	82.2	67	37	32	41	77	
71	Garcia, Christian	R-R	6-4	215	8/24/85	Miami, FL	Trenton	2-0	0.71	5	5	0	0	25.1	15	3	2	17	24	0.000
41	Gaudin, Chad	R-R	5-10	190	3/24/83	New Orleans, LA	Portland	0-0	0.00	2	2	0	0	8.2	4	0	0	2	10	4.163
							SAN DIEGO	4-10	5.13	20	19	0	0	105.1	105	69	60	56	105	
							YANKEES	2-0	3.43	11	6	0	0	42.0	41	16	16	20	34	
65	Hughes, Phil	R-R	6-5	240	6/24/86	Mission Viejo, CA	Scranton/WB	3-0	1.86	3	3	0	0	19.1	17	4	4	3	19	2.113
							YANKEES	8-3	3.03	51	7	0	3	86.0	68	31	29	28	96	
48	Logan, Boone	R-L	6-5	215	8/13/84	San Antonio, TX	Gwinnett	4-2	3.28	29	0	0	2	35.2	26	15	13	17	39	3.002
							ATLANTA	1-1	5.19	20	0	0	0	17.1	21	12	10	9	10	
43	Marte, Damaso	L-L	6-2	213	2/14/75	Santo Domingo, D.R.	YANKEES	1-3	9.45	21	0	0	0	13.1	15	14	14	6	13	8.122
							GCL Yankees	0-0	4.50	2	2	0	0	2.0	2	1	1	0	2	
							Scranton/WB	0-1	2.45	11	0	0	0	11.0	10	3	3	4	9	
39	Melancon, Mark	R-R	6-2	215	3/28/85	Wheat Ridge, CO	Scranton/WB	4-0	2.89	32	0	0	3	53.0	37	22	17	11	54	0.077
							YANKEES	0-1	3.86	13	0	0	0	16.1	13	8	7	10	10	
45	Mitre, Sergio	R-R	6-3	225	2/16/81	Los Angeles, CA	Tampa	1-0	1.93	2	2	0	0	9.1	10	6	2	2	8	4.132
							Scranton/WB	3-1	2.40	7	7	0	0	45.0	40	13	12	5	35	
							YANKEES	3-3	6.79	12	9	0	0	51.2	71	45	39	13	32	
74	Noesi, Hector	R-R	6-2	174	1/26/87	Esperanza, D.R.	Charleston	3-4	2.38	17	11	0	0	75.2	62	24	20	11	78	0.000
							Tampa	3-0	3.92	9	9	0	0	41.1	34	18	18	4	40	
75	Nova, Ivan	R-R	6-4	210	1/12/87	San Cristobal, D.R	Trenton	5-4	2.36	12	12	0	0	72.1	65	27	19	31	47	0.000
							Scranton/WB	1-4	5.10	12	12	1	0	67.0	72	39	38	28	43	
46	Pettitte, Andy	L-L	6-5	225	6/15/72	Baton Rouge, LA	YANKEES	14-8	4.16	32	32	0	0	194.2	193	101	90	76	148	15.000
36	Ramirez, Edwar	R-R	6-3	165	3/28/81	El Cercado, D.R.	Scranton/WB	1-5	3.18	29	0	0	4	51.0	39	19	18	16	62	1.130
							YANKEES	0-0	5.73	20	0	0	0	22.0	25	15	14	18	22	
42	Rivera, Mariano	R-R	6-2	185	11/29/69	Panamá City, Panamá	YANKEES	3-3	1.76	66	0	0	44	66.1	48	14	13	12	72	14.105
30	Robertson, David	R-R	5-11	190	4/9/85	Birmingham, AL	Scranton/WB	0-3	1.84	8	0	0	2	14.2	10	7	3	6	25	1.070
							YANKEES	2-1	3.30	45	0	0	1	43.2	36	19	16	23	63	
52	Sabathia, CC	L-L	6-7	290	7/21/80	Vallejo, CA	YANKEES	19-8	3.37	34	34	2	0	230.0	197	96	86	67	197	9.000
67	Sanchez, Romulo	R-R	6-6	260	4/28/84	Carora, Venezuela	Indianapolis	1-0	4.38	10	0	0	0	12.1	11	6	6	5	15	0.097
							Scranton/WB	5-5	4.04	19	13	0	0	64.2	66	31	29	34	64	
31	Vazquez, Javier	R-R	6-2	210	7/25/76	Ponce, P.R.	ATLANTA	15-10	2.87	32	32	3	0	219.1	181	75	70	44	238	11.141

#	CATCHERS (2)	B-T	HT.	WT.	BORN	BIRTHPLACE	2009 CLUB	AVG	G	AB	R	H	2B	3B	HR	RBI	BB	SO	SB	SVC
29	Cervelli, Francisco	R-R	6-1	210	3/6/86	Valencia, Venezuela	Trenton	.190	16	58	8	11	1	0	2	7	6	13	0	0.113
							YANKEES	.298	42	94	13	28	4	0	1	11	2	11	0	
							Scranton/WB	.275	21	69	7	19	5	0	1	7	3	13	0	
							GCL Yankees	.167	2	6	1	1	0	0	0	0	1	0	0	
20	Posada, Jorge	S-R	6-2	215	8/17/71	Santurce, P.R.	YANKEES	.285	111	383	55	109	25	0	22	81	48	101	1	13.085

#	INFIELDERS (10)	B-T	HT.	WT.	BORN	BIRTHPLACE	2009 CLUB	AVG	G	AB	R	H	2B	3B	HR	RBI	BB	SO	SB	SVC
24	Cano, Robinson	L-R	6-0	205	10/22/82	San Pedro, D.R.	YANKEES	.320	161	637	103	204	48	2	25	85	30	63	5	4.153
76	Corona, Reegie	S-R	5-11	160	11/7/86	Caracas, Venezuela	Trenton	.287	85	307	56	88	21	2	3	26	56	50	12	0.000
							Scranton/WB	.200	44	160	13	32	7	0	3	14	9	20	4	
2	Jeter, Derek	R-R	6-3	195	6/26/74	Pequannock, NJ	YANKEES	.334	153	634	107	212	27	1	18	66	72	90	30	14.043
26	Johnson, Nick	L-L	6-3	235	9/19/78	Sacramento, CA	WASHINGTON	.295	98	353	47	104	16	2	6	44	63	66	2	9.041
							FLORIDA	.279	35	104	24	29	8	0	2	18	36	18	0	
							Jupiter	.333	2	3	0	1	1	0	0	0	0	2	0	
53	Miranda, Juan	L-L	6-0	220	4/25/83	Consulacion del Sur, Cuba	Scranton/WB	.290	122	438	74	127	30	2	19	82	55	101	1	0.031
							YANKEES	.333	8	9	2	3	0	0	1	3	0	4	0	
94	Nunez, Eduardo	R-R	6-0	155	6/15/87	Santo Domingo, D.R.	Trenton	.322	123	497	70	160	26	1	9	55	22	63	19	0.000
19	Pena, Ramiro	S-R	5-11	165	7/18/85	Monterrey, Mexico	YANKEES	.287	69	115	17	33	6	1	1	10	5	20	4	0.137
							Scranton/WB	.231	43	156	18	36	9	0	2	9	18	28	5	
13	Rodriguez, Alex	R-R	6-3	228	7/27/75	New York, NY	YANKEES	.286	124	444	78	127	17	1	30	100	80	97	14	15.011
77	Russo, Kevin	R-R	5-11	190	7/8/84	West Babylon, NY	Scranton/WB	.326	90	353	51	115	18	2	5	31	42	55	13	0.000
25	Teixeira, Mark	S-R	6-3	220	4/11/80	Annapolis, MD	YANKEES	.292	156	609	103	178	43	3	39	122	81	114	2	7.000

#	OUTFIELDERS (6)	B-T	HT.	WT.	BORN	BIRTHPLACE	2009 CLUB	AVG	G	AB	R	H	2B	3B	HR	RBI	BB	SO	SB	SVC
11	Gardner, Brett	L-L	5-10	183	8/24/83	Holly Hill, SC	YANKEES	.270	108	248	48	67	6	6	3	23	26	40	26	1.072
							Scranton/WB	.091	4	11	3	1	0	0	0	0	5	1	3	
27	Golson, Greg	R-R	6-0	190	9/17/85	Austin, TX	TEXAS	.000	1	1	0	0	0	0	0	0	0	1	0	0.034
							Oklahoma City	.258	123	457	46	118	17	8	2	40	29	114	20	
14	Granderson, Curtis	L-R	6-1	185	3/16/81	Blue Island, IL	DETROIT	.249	160	631	91	157	23	8	30	71	72	141	20	4.077
73	Hoffmann, Jamie	R-R	6-3	235	8/20/84	New Ulm, MN	Albuquerque	.284	68	257	44	73	14	3	8	48	32	37	10	0.025
							LOS ANGELES-NL	.182	14	22	2	4	2	0	1	7	0	5	0	
33	Swisher, Nick	S-L	5-11	210	11/25/80	Columbus, OH	YANKEES	.249	150	498	84	124	35	1	29	82	97	126	0	5.031
22	Winn, Randy	S-R	6-2	190	6/9/74	Los Angeles, CA	SAN FRANCISCO	.262	149	538	65	141	33	5	2	51	47	93	16	11.000

2010 Yankees Spring Training Invitees

#	PITCHERS (13)	B-T	HT.	WT.	BORN	BIRTHPLACE	2009 CLUB	W-L	ERA	G	GS	CG	SV	IP	H	R	ER	BB	SO	SV
90	Arias, Wilkins	L-L	6-1	150	11/4/80	San Cristobal, DR	Trenton	5-4	3.65	48	2	0	0	61.2	53	26	25	22	66	0.00
86	Bleich, Jeremy	L-L	6-2	185	6/18/87	Metairie, LA	Tampa	6-4	3.40	14	14	0	0	79.1	79	34	30	0	56	0.00
							Trenton	3-6	6.65	13	13	0	0	65.0	84	54	48	34	60	
82	Duff, Grant	R-R	6-6	210	12/19/82	Mammoth, CA	Tampa	0-1	3.82	24	1	0	1	35.1	35	17	15	11	26	0.00
							Trenton	4-2	3.22	21	0	0	1	36.1	30	15	13	16	37	
60	Hirsh, Jason	R-R	6-8	250	2/20/82	Santa Monica, CA	Colorado Springs	6-7	6.66	20	16	0	0	101.1	130	78	75	35	59	1.15
							Scranton/WB	4-0	1.35	6	6	0	0	26.2	24	4	4	6	21	
17	Igawa, Kei	L-L	6-2	212	7/13/79	Ibaraki, Japan	Scranton/WB	10-8	4.15	26	26	1	0	145.1	165	75	67	40	105	0.10
80	McAllister, Zach	R-R	6-5	230	12/8/87	Chillicothe, IL	Trenton	7-5	2.23	22	22	0	0	121.0	98	39	30	33	96	0.00
72	Mitchell, D.J.	R-R	6-2	165	5/13/87	Rural Hall, NC	Charleston	4-1	1.95	6	6	0	0	37.0	31	16	8	6	42	0.00
							Tampa	8-6	2.87	19	18	1	0	103.1	93	41	33	38	83	
40	Moseley, Dustin	R-R	6-4	190	12/26/81	Texarkana, TX	LOS ANGELES-AL	1-0	4.30	3	3	0	0	14.2	20	8	7	3	8	2.10
96	Pope, Ryan	R-R	6-3	190	5/21/86	Savannah, GA	Trenton	5-12	4.78	26	25	0	0	141.1	155	91	75	34	106	0.00
47	Ring, Royce	L-L	6-0	229	12/21/80	La Mesa, CA.	Memphis	5-2	3.04	51	0	0	4	47.1	44	18	16	15	38	1.13
93	Sanit, Amaury	R-R	5-8	204	7/4/79	Havana, Cuba	Tampa	0-0	0.00	4	0	0	0	6.0	5	0	0	0	5	0.00
							Trenton	1-2	2.95	21	0	0	10	21.1	13	7	7	8	18	
							Scranton/WB	0-3	4.13	19	0	0	0	24.0	27	12	11	7	13	
70	Segovia, Zack	R-R	6-4	215	4/11/83	Dallas, TX	Harrisburg	1-3	3.68	24	3	0	1	44.0	57	19	18	19	39	0.03
							Syracuse	2-2	2.54	27	0	0	5	28.1	18	8	8	8	27	
							WASHINGTON	1-0	7.84	8	0	0	0	10.1	11	10	9	6	4	
81	Whelan, Kevin	R-R	6-0	200	1/8/84	Kerrville, TX	Trenton	4-0	2.63	30	0	0	2	54.2	38	17	16	28	63	0.00
							Scranton/WB	0-0	2.84	14	0	0	1	12.2	7	4	4	13	22	

#	CATCHERS (6)	B-T	HT.	WT.	BORN	BIRTHPLACE	2009 CLUB	AVG	G	AB	R	H	2B	3B	HR	RBI	BB	SO	SB	SV
99	Gil, Jose	S-R	6-0	170	9/4/86	Barcelona, Venezuela	Trenton	.194	12	36	2	7	2	0	2	4	0	7	0	0.00
							Tampa	.208	29	96	10	20	4	0	0	8	5	24	0	
92	Higashioka, Kyle	R-R	6-1	190	4/20/90	Huntington Beach, CA	Staten Island	.253	60	217	24	55	11	0	2	32	26	31	0	0.00
83	Montero, Jesus	R-R	6-4	225	1/28/89	Guacara, Venezuela	Tampa	.356	48	180	26	64	15	1	8	37	14	26	0	0.00
							Trenton	.317	44	167	19	53	10	0	9	33	14	21	0	
85	Pilittere, P.J.	R-R	6-0	215	11/23/81	San Dimas, CA	Scranton/WB	.244	28	86	8	21	6	0	1	9	3	9	0	0.00
							Trenton	.198	27	96	5	19	3	0	0	8	7	8	0	
12	Rivera, Mike	R-R	6-2	219	9/8/76	Rio Piedras, PR	Nashville	.231	3	13	1	3	1	0	0	3	0	5	0	3.08
							MILWAUKEE	.228	41	114	10	26	7	0	2	14	15	32	1	
84	Romine, Austin	R-R	6-1	195	11/22/88	Lake Forest, CA	Tampa	.276	118	442	61	122	28	3	13	72	29	78	11	0.00

#	INFIELDERS (2)	B-T	HT.	WT.	BORN	BIRTHPLACE	2009 CLUB	AVG	G	AB	R	H	2B	3B	HR	RBI	BB	SO	SB	SV
97	Laird, Brandon	R-R	6-1	215	9/11/87	Cypress, CA	Tampa	.266	124	451	53	120	20	4	13	75	39	75	1	0.00
95	Vazquez, Jorge	R-R	6-0	225	3/15/82	Culiacan, Mexico	Trenton	.329	57	225	30	74	15	1	13	56	8	45	0	0.00

#	OUTFIELDERS (5)	B-T	HT.	WT.	BORN	BIRTHPLACE	2009 CLUB	AVG	G	AB	R	H	2B	3B	HR	RBI	BB	SO	SB	SV
98	Curtis, Colin	L-L	6-1	200	2/1/85	Issaquah, WA	Trenton	.268	56	213	28	57	14	4	1	19	20	37	7	0.00
							Scranton/WB	.235	70	251	29	59	10	0	6	29	24	46	1	
66	Gorecki, Reid	R-R	6-1	176	12/22/80	Queens, NY	Gwinnett	.286	106	371	57	106	27	6	9	49	34	73	14	0.04
							ATLANTA	.200	31	25	6	5	0	0	0	3	1	12	1	
38	Thames, Marcus	R-R	6-2	205	3/6/77	Louisville, MS	Toledo	.245	12	49	6	12	0	0	2	6	5	14	0	5.10
							DETROIT	.252	87	258	33	65	11	1	13	36	29	72	0	
79	Weber, Jon	L-L	5-11	185	1/20/78	Lakewood, CA	Durham	.302	117	451	63	136	46	0	14	69	56	98	3	0.00
78	Winfree, David	R-R	6-3	228	8/5/85	Virginia Beach, VA	Rochester	.273	116	422	48	115	31	3	14	61	28	88	0	0.00

New York Yankees Numerical Roster & Pronunciation Guide

Numerical Roster

2 Derek Jeter .... INF
11 Brett Gardner .... OF
12 Mike Rivera* C
13 Alex Rodriguez .... INF
14 Curtis Granderson .... OF
17 Kei Igawa* .... LHP
19 Ramiro Pena .... INF
20 Jorge Posada C
22 Randy Winn .... OF
24 Robinson Cano .... INF
25 Mark Teixeira .... INF
26 Nick Johnson DH/1B
27 Greg Golson .... OF
28 Joe Girardi .... MGR
29 Francisco Cervelli C
30 David Robertson .... RHP
31 Javier Vazquez .... RHP
33 Nick Swisher OF/1B
34 A.J. Burnett .... RHP
36 Edwar Ramirez .... RHP
38 Marcus Thames* .... OF
39 Mark Melancon .... RHP
40 Dustin Moseley* .... RHP
41 Chad Gaudin .... RHP
42 Mariano Rivera .... RHP
43 Damaso Marte .... LHP
45 Sergio Mitre .... RHP
46 Andy Pettitte .... LHP
47 Royce Ring* .... LHP
48 Boone Logan .... LHP
50 Mick Kelleher .... 1B COACH
52 CC Sabathia .... LHP
53 Juan Miranda 1B/DH
54 Kevin Long .... HITTING COACH
56 Tony Pena .... BENCH COACH
57 Mike Harkey .... BULLPEN COACH
58 Dave Eiland .... PITCHING COACH
59 Rob Thomson .... 3B COACH
60 Jason Hirsh* .... RHP
62 Joba Chamberlain .... RHP
63 Jonathan Albaladejo .... RHP
64 Andrew Brackman .... RHP
65 Phil Hughes .... RHP
66 Reid Gorecki* .... OF
67 Romulo Sanchez .... RHP
68 Wilkin De La Rosa .... LHP
70 Zack Segovia* .... RHP
71 Christian Garcia .... RHP
72 D.J. Mitchell* .... RHP
73 Jamie Hoffmann .... OF
74 Hector Noesi .... RHP
75 Ivan Nova .... RHP
76 Reegie Corona .... INF
77 Kevin Russo .... INF
78 David Winfree* .... OF
79 Jon Weber* .... OF
80 Zach McAllister* .... RHP
81 Kevin Whelan* .... RHP
82 Grant Duff* .... RHP
83 Jesus Montero* C
84 Austin Romine* C
85 P.J. Pilittere* C
86 Jeremy Bleich* .... LHP
90 Wilkins Arias* .... LHP
91 Alfredo Aceves .... RHP
92 Kyle Higashioka* C
93 Amaury Sanit* .... RHP
94 Eduardo Nunez .... INF
95 Jorge Vazquez* .... INF
96 Ryan Pope* .... RHP
97 Brandon Laird* .... INF
98 Colin Curtis* .... OF
99 Jose Gil* C

*Denotes non-roster invitee

Pronunciation Guide

Alfredo Aceves .... ah-SEV-us
Jonathan Albaladejo .... alba-la-DAY-ho
Robinson Cano .... KUH-no
Francisco Cervelli .... sir-VEL-lee
Reegie Corona .... REE-gee
Dave Eiland .... Island
Chad Gaudin .... Go-DAN
Derek Jeter .... JEE-ter
Damaso Marte .... Duh-MAH-so / MAR-tay
Mark Melancon .... Muh-LAN-son
Juan Miranda .... mur-AN-duh
Sergio Mitre .... MEE-tray
Hector Noesi .... NO-ess-e
Andy Pettitte .... pet-it
Jorge Posada .... hor-hay / po-SAH-dah
Alex Rodriguez .... rod-REE-gez
CC Sabathia .... sa-BATH-ee-a
Mark Teixeira .... Tuh-SHARE-uh
Randy Winn .... Win

How the Yankees Were Built

FIRST-YEAR PLAYER DRAFT: (10)

Andrew Brackman .... June 2007, 1st Round (30th overall)
Joba Chamberlain... June 2006, Compensation Round A (41st overall)
Christian Garcia .... June 2004, 3rd round
Brett Gardner .... June 2005, 3rd round
Phil Hughes.............. June 2004, 1st Round (23rd overall)
Derek Jeter .... June 1992, 1st Round (6th overall)
Mark Melancon .... June 2006, 9th round
Jorge Posada .... June 1990, 24th round
David Robertson...................... June 2006, 17th round
Kevin Russo........................... June 2006, 20th round

SIGNED AS A NON-DRAFTED FREE AGENT: (10)

Robinson Cano .... January 5, 2001
Francisco Cervelli .... March 1, 2003
Reegie Corona.................................. July 2, 2003
Wilkin De La Rosa .... November 15, 2001
Juan Miranda .... December 22, 2006
Hector Noesi.............................. December 3, 2004
Ivan Nova...................................... July 15, 2004
Eduardo Nunez .... February 25, 2004
Ramiro Pena .... February 18, 2005
Mariano Rivera............................ February 17, 1990

SIGNED AS A FREE AGENT: (10)

Alfredo Aceves................................ March 10, 2008
A.J. Burnett .... December 18, 2008
Nick Johnson .... December 23, 2009
Sergio Mitre .... January 14, 2009
Andy Pettitte .... December 9, 2009
Edwar Ramirez.................................... July 9, 2006
Alex Rodriguez.......................... December 13, 2007
CC Sabathia.............................. December 18, 2008
Mark Teixeira................................. January 6, 2009
Randy Winn................................. February 8, 2010

*** as of February 8, 2010**

ACQUIRED BY TRADE: (10)

PLAYER	FROM	DATE	FOR
Jonathan Albaladejo	Washington	December 5, 2007	RHP Tyler Clippard
Chad Gaudin	San Diego	August 6, 2009	Player to be named later or cash
Greg Golson	Texas	January 26, 2010	INF Mitch Hilligoss
Curtis Granderson-a	Detroit	December 9, 2009	Three team, seven player deal
Jamie Hoffmann-b	Washington	December 10, 2009	RHP Brian Bruney
Boone Logan-c	Atlanta	December 22, 2009	OF Melky Cabrera LHP Mike Dunn RHP Arodys Vizcaino
Damaso Marte-d	Pittsburgh	July 26, 2008	RHP Jeff Karstens RHP Dan McCutchen RHP Ross Ohlendorf OF Jose Tabata
Romulo Sanchez	Pittsburgh	May 16, 2009	RHP Eric Hacker
Nick Swisher-e	Chicago-AL	November 13, 2008	INF Wilson Betemit RHP Jeff Marquez OF Jhonny Nunez
Javier Vazquez-f	Atlanta	December 22, 2009	OF Melky Cabrera LHP Mike Dunn RHP Arodys Vizcaino

a – Acquired from Detroit in a three-team, seven-player deal in which the Yankees sent LHP Phil Coke and OF Austin Jackson to Detroit and RHP Ian Kennedy to Arizona.
b – Acquired from Washington as the player to be named for RHP Brian Bruney...was the first pick in the 2009 Rule 5 Draft.
c – Acquired from Atlanta along with RHP Javier Vazquez in exchange for OF Melky Cabrera, LHP Mike Dunn and RHP Arodys Vizcaino.
d – Acquired from Pittsburgh along with Xavier Nady.
e – Acquired from Chicago-AL along with RHP Kanekoa Texeira.
f – Acquired from Atlanta along with LHP Boone Logan in exchange for OF Melky Cabrera, LHP Mike Dunn and RHP Arodys Vizcaino.

2010 Yankees Birthdays

January
A.J. Burnett 1/3/1977
Ivan Nova.................. 1/12/1987
Hector Noesi.............. 1/26/1987

February
Damaso Marte............ 2/14/1975
Sergio Mitre 2/16/1981
Wilkin De La Rosa 2/21/1985

March
Francisco Cervelli 3/6/1986
Curtis Granderson.......... 3/16/1981
Chad Gaudin............... 3/24/1983
Mark Melancon 3/28/1985
Edwar Ramirez............. 3/28/1981

April
David Robertson............ 4/9/1985
Mark Teixeira.............. 4/11/1980
Juan Miranda 4/25/1983
Romulo Sanchez........... 4/28/1984

May
None

June
Tony Pena 6/4/1957
Randy Winn.................. 6/9/1974
Eduardo Nunez 6/15/1987
Andy Pettitte 6/15/1972
Phil Hughes............... 6/24/1986
Derek Jeter 6/26/1974

July
Dave Eiland................. 7/5/1966
Kevin Russo................. 7/8/1984
Ramiro Pena 7/18/1985
CC Sabathia............... 7/21/1980
Mick Kelleher 7/25/1947
Javier Vazquez 7/25/1976
Alex Rodriguez............ 7/27/1975

August
Boone Logan 8/13/1984
Rob Thomson............. 8/16/1963
Jorge Posada 8/17/1971
Jamie Hoffmann 8/20/1984
Christian Garcia........... 8/24/1985
Brett Gardner 8/24/1983

September
Greg Golson 9/17/1985
Nick Johnson 9/19/1978
Joba Chamberlain.......... 9/23/1985

October
Joe Girardi............... 10/14/1964
Robinson Cano 10/22/1982
Mike Harkey 10/25/1966
Jonathan Albaladejo 10/30/1982

November
Reegie Corona 11/7/1986
Nick Swisher............. 11/25/1980
Mariano Rivera............ 11/29/1969

December
Andrew Brackman 12/4/1985
Alfredo Aceves............. 12/8/1982
Kevin Long 12/30/1966

Alfredo Aceves

91 **Right-handed Pitcher**
6-3 • 218 • B/T: Right/Right
Opening Day Age: 28

Birthdate
December 8, 1981

Birthplace
San Luis Rio Colorado, Sonora Mexico

Resides
Sonora, Mexico

M.L. Service
1 year, 14 days

Status

- Signed by the Yankees as a minor league free agent on March 10, 2008...signed through the 2010 season.

Career Notes

- According to the *Elias Sports Bureau*, is one of five Mexican-born players to pitch for the Yankees, joining Juan Acevedo, Esteban Loaiza, Antonio Osuna and Alfonso Pulido...was the third to start (also Loaiza and Pulido).

2009

- Was 10-1 with one save and a 3.54 ERA in 43 appearances (one start) with the Yankees...opponents batted .220 (69-for-313, 10HR); LH .212 (32-for-151, 3HR), RH .228 (37-for-162, 7HR)...retired 37-of-43 first batters faced as a reliever (86.0%)...prevented 22-of-30 inherited runners from scoring (73.3%)...appeared in consecutive games seven times, once following the All-Star break (7/20-21 vs. Baltimore).
- Tossed at least 2.0IP in 24 of his 42 relief outings (57.1%)...made eight relief appearances of at least 3.0IP, holding opponents scoreless in seven of those outings...tossed at least 4.0 innings three times (5/4 vs. Boston, 7/5 vs. Toronto and 8/10 vs. Toronto).
- Led the Major Leagues with 10 wins as a reliever...according to the *Elias Sports Bureau*, was just the third Yankees rookie to reach double-digit wins in relief in one season, joining Ron Davis (14 wins in 1979) and Wilcy Moore (13 wins in 1927)...since 1990, only one Yankees pitcher recorded as many wins in relief – Lee Guetterman (11, 1990).
- Joined Ron Davis as the only Yankees rookies to win at least eight of their first nine decisions in one season over the last 50 years (Davis started 8-1 en route to a 14-2 record in 1979)—credit: *Elias Sports Bureau*.
- Was recalled from Triple-A Scranton/Wilkes-Barre on 5/4 and made his 2009 debut that night in a 6-4 Yankees loss vs. Boston, allowing 4H and 2ER while striking out a career-high seven batters in a season-high 4.1IP (2BB/1IBB, 1HR, 1HBP)...were the most strikeouts by a Yankees reliever since Brian Boehringer fanned seven batters in 3.1IP of relief on 5/4/97 at Seattle.
- Tossed a perfect 11th inning to earn his first win of the season in the Yankees' 6-4 "walk-off" victory on 5/16 vs. Minnesota (1.0IP)...also earned the win the following day on 5/17 vs. Minnesota, tossing a perfect 10th inning (1.0IP, 1K) prior to Johnny Damon's "walk-off" home run...entered 5/21 win vs. Baltimore with two outs and two runners on in the first inning after Joba Chamberlain was removed from the game with a bruised right knee...tossed 3.1 scoreless innings (3H, 1BB, 1K) to earn his third win over a span of six team victories from 5/16-21.

Single-Game Highs and Streaks

Low hit CG
N/A
IP (start)
3.1 - at MIN, 7/9/09
IP (relief)
4.1 - vs. BOS, 5/4/09
Hits
4 - 6 times
Last: at LAA, 9/22/09
Runs 4 - 3 times
Last: at SEA, 8/16/09
BB
2 - 4 times
Last: vs. LAA, 9/14/09
SO
7 - vs. BOS, 5/4/09
HR
1 - 10 times
Last: at BOS, 8/22/09
Winning Streak
7g - 6/7/09-9/3/09
Losing Streak
1g - 5/26/09

ALFREDO ACEVES

- Over 17 appearances (1GS) from 5/29-7/21, went 3-0 with one save and a 2.12 ERA (29.2IP, 20H, 7ER, 6BB, 23K)...earned his first Major League save in 7/5 win vs. Toronto, tossing 4.0 scoreless IP (1H, 5K)...became the first Yankee to record a 4.0-inning save since Orlando Hernandez on 6/28/02 vs. the Mets (4.0IP).
- Made his only start of the season in 7/9 win at Minnesota, recording a no-decision (3.1IP, 4H, 4R, 3ER, 1BB, 1HP, 2K, 1HR).
- Held opponents scoreless over his final four outings beginning on 9/25 vs. Boston (7.1IP, 3H, 0BB, 7K).
- Appeared in four postseason games, going 0-1 with a 4.15 ERA...tossed a scoreless 10th inning inning in the Yankees' 11-inning Game 2 win in the ALDS vs. Minnesota...suffered the loss in Game 3 of the ALCS at Los Angeles-AL, allowing Jeff Mathis' "walk-off" RBI double.
- Began the season with Scranton/WB and was 2-0 with a 3.80 ERA in four starts at the time of his recall, allowing 18H and 10ER in 23.2IP (11R, 5BB, 1HBP, 18K)...opponents were batting .202 (18-for-89, 3HR); LH .147 (5-for-34, 1HR), RH .236 (13-for-55, 2HR).
- Tossed 8.0 shutout innings to earn the win in a 7-0 Scranton/WB victory on 4/29 vs. Lehigh Valley in his final minor league appearance (3H, 1BB, 1HBP, 6K).

2008

- Was 1-0 with a 2.40 ERA in six games (four starts) with the Yankees...opponents batted .227 (25-for-110, 4HR); LH .238 (15-for-63, 3HR), RH .213 (10-for-47, 1HR).
- Was signed to a Major League contract and selected to the 25-man active roster from Triple-A Scranton/Wilkes-Barre prior to 8/28 win vs. Boston...made his Major League debut in 8/31 loss vs. Toronto, retiring all six of his batters faced (2.0IP, 3K).
- Threw 5.0 innings of relief in 9/4 loss at Tampa Bay (5H, 1ER, 2BB, 4K, 1HR)...was the longest relief outing by a Yankee in 2008.
- Made his first Major League start on 9/9 at Los Angeles-AL, recording the win in a 7-1 Yankees victory...allowed just 1ER on 6H in 7.0IP (0BB, 2K)...became the first Yankee to earn the win in his first Major League start since Ian Kennedy on 9/1/07 vs. Tampa Bay...was the first Yankee to do so on the road since Tyler Clippard on 5/20/07 at the Mets...joined Loaiza as the only Mexican-born pitchers to earn a win in their first start with the Yankees...held right-handed batters hitless in their first 15 Major League AB against him until Robb Quinlan's fifth-inning single.
- Started and threw 6.0 scoreless innings in 9/20 win vs. Baltimore but did not record a decision in the second-to-last-game at Yankee Stadium...recorded an unassisted double play in the first inning, catching a pop-up on Adam Jones' bunt attempt then doubling Brian Roberts off second base by himself...according to the *Elias Sports Bureau*, it was the first unassisted double play by a Major League pitcher since Dave Bush accomplished the feat on 6/23/07 vs. Kansas City w/ Milwaukee...also recorded the third out in the first inning to become the first pitcher to collect three putouts in one inning since 9/1/07 (Dan Haren w/ Oakland vs. Detroit).
- Was 8-6 with a 2.62 ERA in 25 games (23 starts) combined at Single-A Tampa, Double-A Trenton and Scranton/WB (140.2IP, 111H, 47R, 41ER, 27BB, 114K)...opponents combined to bat .217 (111-for-512, 10HR); LH .200 (42-for-210, 8HR), RH .227 (69-for-302, 2HR).
- Following the season, was ranked by *Baseball America* as the organization's seventh-best prospect and tabbed as having the "best changeup" among Yankees prospects.

2001-07

- Originally signed with the Toronto organization in 2001, playing with their DSL entry before being traded to the Mexican League the following season...went 2-1 with a 3.10 ERA in 10 games (seven starts) with the DSL Blue Jays.

ALFREDO ACEVES

- Pitched in the Mexican League from 2002-07, compiling a 34-23 record and a 4.06 ERA in 126 games (75 starts)...ranked fourth in the league in 2007 with Monterrey with a .242 opponents average, allowing 11.51 baserunners per 9.0IP (fifth-lowest average in the league)...with Yucatan in 2005, tossed a league-leading three complete games and ranked third in the league with 145.2IP and 101K.

Personal

- Married Arley following the 2008 season...his father, Alfredo Sr., was a power-hitting first baseman in the Mexican League...brother, Jonathan, played in the White Sox minor league system for 10 years (1997-2006)...became just the second Yankee to wear a uniform number in the 90's, joining Charlie Keller, who wore No. 99 in 1952.

Aceves' Career Pitching Record

Year	Club	W	L	ERA	G	GS	CG	SHO	SV	IP	H	R	ER	HR	HB	BB	SO	WP	BK
2001	DSL Blue Jays	2	1	3.10	10	1	0	0	1	29.0	29	13	10	1	1	3	24	3	0
2002	Yucatan - a	1	2	3.00	23	4	0	0	0	45.0	42	22	15	0	4	20	25	2	0
2003	Yucatan	1	1	3.35	27	2	0	0	1	43.0	49	17	16	3	4	18	29	3	0
2004	Yucatan	4	2	4.55	17	11	0	0	0	65.1	64	33	33	4	6	37	37	7	0
2005	Yucatan	9	8	4.32	22	21	3	0	0	145.2	155	77	70	12	10	44	101	7	0
2006	Monterrey	8	5	4.50	19	19	3	1	0	124.0	126	65	62	15	6	26	95	4	1
2007	Monterrey	11	5	3.64	18	18	1	0	0	106.1	96	46	43	6	7	33	70	3	2
2008	Tampa - b	4	1	2.11	8	8	0	0	0	47.0	32	16	11	1	1	8	37	2	0
	Trenton	2	2	1.80	7	7	1	1	0	50.0	37	10	10	3	0	6	35	1	0
	Scranton/WB	2	3	4.12	10	8	0	0	0	43.2	42	21	20	6	1	13	42	0	0
	YANKEES	1	0	2.40	6	4	0	0	0	30.0	25	8	8	4	0	10	16	1	0
2009	Scranton/WB	2	0	3.80	4	4	0	0	0	23.2	18	11	10	3	1	5	18	0	1
	YANKEES	10	1	3.54	43	1	0	0	1	84.0	69	36	33	10	5	16	69	0	0
Minor League Totals		**46**	**30**	**3.74**	**165**	**103**	**8**	**2**	**2**	**722.2**	**690**	**331**	**300**	**54**	**41**	**213**	**513**	**32**	**4**
Major League Totals		**11**	**1**	**3.24**	**49**	**5**	**0**	**0**	**1**	**114.0**	**94**	**44**	**41**	**14**	**5**	**26**	**85**	**1**	**0**

Signed by Toronto as a non-drafted minor league free agent on January 24, 2001.

a – Traded to Yucatan in the Mexican League along with LHP Manuel Camacho, RHP Juan Delgadillo and 3B Miguel Inzunza on April 24, 2002.

b – Signed by the Yankees as a minor league free agent on March 10, 2008.

Aceves' Division Series Record

Year	Club vs. Opp.	W	L	ERA	G	GS	CG	SHO	SV	IP	H	R	ER	HR	HP	BB	SO	WP	BK
2009	NYY vs. MIN	0	0	0.00	1	0	0	0	0	1.0	1	0	0	0	0	1	1	0	0
Division Series Totals		**0**	**0**	**0.00**	**1**	**0**	**0**	**0**	**0**	**1.0**	**1**	**0**	**0**	**0**	**0**	**1**	**1**	**0**	**0**

Aceves' League Championship Series Record

Year	Club vs. Opp.	W	L	ERA	G	GS	CG	SHO	SV	IP	H	R	ER	HR	HP	BB	SO	WP	BK
2009	NYY vs. LAA	0	1	13.50	2	0	0	0	0	1.1	3	2	2	0	0	2	0	0	0
LCS Totals		**0**	**1**	**13.50**	**2**	**0**	**0**	**0**	**0**	**1.1**	**3**	**2**	**2**	**0**	**0**	**2**	**0**	**0**	**0**

Aceves' World Series Record

Year	Club vs. Opp.	W	L	ERA	G	GS	CG	SHO	SV	IP	H	R	ER	HR	HP	BB	SO	WP	BK
2009	NYY vs. PHI	0	0	0.00	1	0	0	0	0	2.0	1	0	0	0	0	0	1	1	0
World Series Totals		**0**	**0**	**0.00**	**1**	**0**	**0**	**0**	**0**	**2.0**	**1**	**0**	**0**	**0**	**0**	**0**	**1**	**1**	**0**
POSTSEASON TOTALS		**0**	**1**	**4.15**	**4**	**0**	**0**	**0**	**0**	**4.1**	**5**	**2**	**2**	**0**	**0**	**3**	**2**	**1**	**0**

Aceves' Career Fielding Record

Position	PCT	G	PO	A	E	TC	DP
Pitcher	.889	49	5	11	2	18	3

Aceves' Regular Season Batting Record

Year	Team	AVG	G	AB	R	H	2B	3B	HR	RBI	SH	SF	HP	BB	SO	SB	CS
2009	NYY	.000	43	2	0	0	0	0	0	0	0	0	0	0	1	0	0
Major League Totals		**.000**	**49**	**2**	**0**	**0**	**0**	**0**	**0**	**0**	**0**	**0**	**0**	**0**	**1**	**0**	**0**

Triple Play

Did you know? The Yankees have now gone 6,618 regular season games over 42 seasons since turning a triple play...the last triple play turned by the Yankees was on June 3, 1968 vs. the Minnesota Twins at Yankee Stadium when Johnny Roseboro hit into a 1-5-3 triple-killing...the Yankees themselves have hit in to nine triple plays since turning their last.

Jonathan Albaladejo

63 **Right-handed Pitcher**

6-5 • 260 • B/T: Right/Right

Opening Day Age: 27

Birthdate
October 30, 1982

Birthplace
San Juan, P.R.

Resides
Vega Alta, P.R.

M.L. Service
1 year, 119 days

College
Miami-Dade Community College

Status

- Acquired from the Washington Nationals in exchange for RHP Tyler Clippard on December 5, 2007...signed through the 2010 season.

Career Notes

- In 193 games over nine minor league seasons (2001-09), has averaged just 1.70BB/9.0IP (583.1IP, 110BB).

2009

- Was 5-1 with a 5.24 ERA in 32 relief appearances over four stints with the Yankees (4/6-5/22, 7/5-10, 7/26-31 and 9/3-10/4)...opponents batted .306 (41-for-134, 6HR); LH .258 (17-for-66, 3HR), RH .353 (24-for-68, 3HR)...23 of his 32 appearances were scoreless...stranded 17-of-22 inherited runners (77.3%)...retired 21-of-32 first batters faced (65.6%)...appeared in consecutive games seven times and three straight games once (4/22-25).
- Appeared on his second career Opening Day roster (also 2008 w/ the Yankees)...made his season debut in 4/6 Opening Day loss at Baltimore, tossing 1.1 scoreless innings (2H)...tossed a career-high-tying 3.0IP in 4/13 loss at Tampa Bay, allowing 5H and 3ER (1BB, 2K, 2HR).
- Earned his first win of the season on 4/19 vs. Cleveland, retiring both batters faced and stranding three runners in the seventh inning (0.2IP).
- Was optioned to Triple-A Scranton/Wilkes-Barre on 5/22 when Chien-Ming Wang was reinstated from the 15-day disabled list...recalled from SWB on 7/5 when Wang returned to the D.L...made three scoreless relief appearances, going 2-0 (4.0IP, 3H, 1BB, 4K) before being optioned back to Scranton/WB on 7/10...recalled for a third time on 7/26 when OF Brett Gardner went on the disabled list...made one appearance in 7/27 win at Tampa Bay (0.2IP, 2H, 2ER, 1BB, 1K, 1HP) before being optioned back to Scranton/WB.
- Joined the Yankees a fourth time as a September callup in 9/3, appearing in 10 games with a 1-0 record and a 4.15 ERA (8.2IP, 4ER).
- In 27 appearances with Scranton/WB, was 3-0 with 11 saves and a 1.75 ERA...struck out 26 batters over 36.0IP with only 3BB...held opponents scoreless in 20 of his 27 appearances...converted 11-of-14 save opportunities.

Single-Game Highs and Streaks

IP (relief)
3.0 - 2 times
Last: at TB, 4/13/09

Hits
6 - vs. DET, 5/1/08

Runs
4 - 3 times
Last: vs. BAL, 5/21/09

BB
2 - 3 times
Last: vs. MIN, 5/17/09

SO
4 - vs. TB, 4/4/08

HR
1 - 6 times
Last: at TB 10/2/09

Winning Streak
1g - 9/17/07

Losing Streak
4g - 5/1/09-current

2008

- Was 0-1 with a 3.95 ERA in seven relief appearances over three stints with the Yankees (3/31-4/5; 4/14-18 and 4/25-5/10)...opponents batted .294 (15-for-51, 1HR); LH .304 (7-for-23, 0HR), RH .286 (8-for-28, 1HR)...retired 4-of-7 first batters faced...allowed just one of his five inherited runners to score.
- Made his first career Opening Day roster...Yankees debut came in 4/4 loss vs. Tampa Bay, tossing 2.2 scoreless innings (1H, 4K)...was optioned to Triple-A Scranton/Wilkes-Barre the next day when Andy Pettitte was reinstated from the D.L.

JONATHAN ALBALADEJO

- Returned to the Yankees from 4/14-18 when Joba Chamberlain was placed on the bereavement list...tossed a career-high 3.0 innings in 4/17 loss vs. Boston, allowing 4H and 2ER (1BB, 3K).
- Was recalled again on 4/25 when Brian Bruney was placed on the disabled list...made his seventh—and final—appearance of the season in 5/9 loss at Detroit, tossing 2.1 scoreless innings (2H, 1BB, 2K) before being removed from the game with a sore right elbow...was placed on the 15-day disabled list on 5/10 with a sprained right elbow, which was later diagnosed as a right elbow stress fracture...was transferred to the 60-day D.L. on 6/18...missed 125 team games.
- Began a rehab assignment on 9/2...in four combined games with short-season Single-A Staten Island and Scranton/WB (including playoff action), recorded a 3.12 ERA with no decisions (8.2IP)...threw 2.2IP in SWB's International League title-clinching game on 9/12 at Durham, allowing 3H and 1ER in the 20-2 victory.
- Pitched for Mayaguez in the Puerto Rican Winter League, allowing just 1ER in 22.0IP over 20 appearances...converted 14-of-15 save opportunities and struck out 18 batters while walking only two.

2007

- Was 1-1 with a 1.88 ERA in 14 relief appearances with the Washington Nationals (2BB, 12K)...opponents batted .149 (7-for-47, 1HR); LH .182 (4-for-22, 1HR), RH .120 (3-for-25, 0HR)...at three different levels, combined to strike out 68 batters while walking just 24.
- Was recalled from Triple-A Columbus on 9/4 and made his Major League debut vs. Florida the following day, tossing 1.2 perfect innings of relief (3K) and striking out the side in his first complete inning (David Ross, Miguel Olivo and Alejandro DeAza)...his 14 appearances in September tied him for third among all Major League rookies and tied Jesus Colome, Jon Rauch and Saul Rivera for the team lead.
- Earned his first Major League win on 9/17 vs. the Mets, allowing 1H and 1BB in 1.1IP (1K).
- Combined to go 7-3 with a 2.97 ERA in 36 relief appearances with Columbus and Double-A Harrisburg (60.2IP).
- Began the season in the Pittsburgh organization on the disabled list with lower back tightness...was reinstated from the D.L. on 4/24 and released by the Pirates that same day...signed a minor league contract with the Nationals on 5/3 and pitched in 21 games with Harrisburg, going 4-3 with two saves and a 4.17 ERA over 36.2IP (15BB, 35K).
- Was promoted to Columbus on 7/24...with the Clippers, was 3-0 with a 1.13 ERA in 15 relief appearances (7BB, 21K)...was named Columbus "Pitcher of the Month" in August...pitched in 27 games for the Tiburones de La Guaira of the Venezuelan Winter League, going 2-2 with four saves and a 2.42 ERA (26.0IP, 23H, 10R, 7ER, 8BB, 20K, 1HR)...was acquired by the Yankees from the Washington Nationals in exchange for RHP Tyler Clippard on 12/5/07.

2006

- Limited to 18 games (one start) with Double-A Altoona due to injury, going 1-2 with one save and a 4.00 ERA (5BB, 27K)...ranked second in the Eastern League in fewest walks issued per 9.0 innings pitched (1.1)...struck out 19 batters and walked just two over 21.2IP from 5/6-6/6, a span of 10 games...was placed on the disabled list on 6/7 with a right ribcage strain...started rehab assignment with the GCL Pirates on 7/22 and went 1-0 with a 2.92 ERA in three games (two starts) while walking three and striking out 16.

2005

- In his second season with Single-A Lynchburg, went 4-3 with two saves and a 3.91 ERA in 28 games (six starts)...walked just 2.4 batters per 9.0IP, striking out 76 batters while walking only 21...began the season with six consecutive starts (0-2, 6.39 ERA) before moving to the bullpen...struck out a season-high eight batters on 5/2 vs. Kinston (5.0IP)...made first relief appearance on 5/12, tossing 5.0 scoreless innings at Wilmington (2H, 5K)...was placed on the disabled list on 7/27 with right elbow tendinitis and was reinstated on 8/24...in four relief appearances after returning from the D.L., tossed 5.2IP, allowing 5H, 2R (1ER) and 3BB while striking out four.

2004

- Spent the season with Single-A Lynchburg, going 8-8 with a 4.33 ERA in 24 starts...ranked second in the Carolina League, issuing just 1.7 walks per 9.0IP...tossed his only complete game of the season in 8/15 win vs. Kinston, throwing 7.0 shutout innings (5H, 4K)...was placed on the disabled list on 8/21 with right shoulder tendonitis, ending his season.

JONATHAN ALBALADEJO

2003

- Went 12-5 with one save and a 3.11 ERA in 29 games (20 starts) for Single-A Hickory (19BB, 110K)...ranked first among all Pirates farmhands in complete games (5), tied for fourth in winning percentage (.706), tied for sixth in wins, placed seventh in ERA, ninth in innings pitched (139.0) and strikeouts, and 10th in starts...did not walk a batter over a four-start stretch from 6/13-7/4 (27.1IP, 16K)...tossed five complete games in his final 13 starts of the season, going 4-1 with a 1.58 ERA in those five games...won each of his final four starts, collecting a 2.57 ERA over the stretch (28.0IP, 16H, 8ER, 5BB, 29K).

2002

- Posted a 2.40 ERA in his second season with the GCL Pirates, going 3-2 in 12 games (10 starts)...did not allow a run or walk through his first four games (three starts), a span of 17.0IP (19H, 11K)...following the season, led the Puerto Rican Winter League with a 0.68 ERA (3ER, 40.0IP)...was rated by *Baseball America* as the No. 9 prospect in the PRWL.

2001

- In his first professional season, went 0-3 with one save and a 4.74 ERA in 10 games (two starts) with the Gulf Coast League Pirates...struck out 24 batters while walking only two and averaged 11.4 strikeouts per 9.0IP...did not allow a walk through his first seven appearances (8.2IP, 12K).

Personal

- Full name is Jonathan Albaladejo (pronounced Al-ba-la-DAY-ho) Santana...was originally selected by the Pirates in the 19th round of the 2001 First-Year Player Draft...signed by Delvy Santiago.

Albaladejo's Career Pitching Record

Year	Club	W	L	ERA	G	GS	CG	SHO	SV	IP	H	R	ER	HR	HP	BB	SO	WP	BK
2001	GCL Pirates	0	3	4.74	10	2	0	0	1	19.0	22	13	10	1	1	2	24	2	0
2002	GCL Pirates	3	2	2.40	12	10	0	0	0	60.0	71	20	16	2	3	6	37	1	0
2003	Hickory	12	5	3.11	29	20	5	0	2	139.0	114	53	48	14	4	19	110	5	1
2004	Lynchburg	8	8	4.33	24	24	1	1	0	131.0	150	72	63	10	5	25	92	6	0
2005	Lynchburg	4	3	3.91	28	6	0	0	2	78.1	74	40	34	9	2	21	76	2	1
2006	Altoona	1	2	4.00	19	1	0	0	1	36.0	41	18	16	4	3	5	27	1	0
	GCL Pirates	1	0	2.92	3	2	0	0	0	12.1	12	4	4	1	0	3	16	0	0
2007	Harrisburg	4	3	4.17	21	0	0	0	2	36.2	30	20	17	3	1	15	35	4	0
	Columbus - a	3	0	1.13	15	0	0	0	0	24.0	14	3	3	2	3	7	21	2	1
	WASHINGTON - b	1	1	1.88	14	0	0	0	0	14.1	7	3	3	1	1	2	12	0	0
2008	YANKEES - c	0	1	3.95	7	0	0	0	0	13.2	15	6	6	1	0	6	13	0	0
	Scranton/WB	0	0	1.29	4	0	0	0	0	7.0	5	2	1	1	0	4	5	0	0
	Staten Island	0	0	0.00	2	2	0	0	0	4.0	3	0	0	0	0	0	4	0	0
2009	YANKEES	5	1	5.24	32	0	0	0	0	34.1	41	23	20	6	3	16	21	0	0
	Scranton/WB	3	0	1.75	27	0	0	0	11	36	25	8	7	4	0	3	26	1	0
Minor League Totals		**39**	**26**	**3.38**	**193**	**67**	**6**	**1**	**18**	**583.1**	**561**	**253**	**219**	**51**	**22**	**110**	**473**	**24**	**3**
Major League Totals		**6**	**3**	**4.19**	**53**	**0**	**0**	**0**	**0**	**62.1**	**63**	**32**	**29**	**8**	**4**	**24**	**46**	**0**	**0**

Selected by the Pirates in the 19th round of the 2001 First-Year Player Draft.

a - Signed by Washington as a free agent on May 3, 2007.

b - Traded to New York (AL) in exchange for RHP Tyler Clippard on December 5, 2007.

c - Placed on the 15-day disabled list from May 10, 2008 through the end of the season with a right elbow stress fracture...transferred to the 60-day disabled list on June 18, 2008.

Albaladejo's Regular Season Batting Record

Year	Team	AVG	G	AB	R	H	2B	3B	HR	RBI	SH	SF	HP	BB	SO	SB	CS
2009	NYY	Did Not Bat															
Major League Totals		-	**53**	-	-	-	-	-	-	-	-	-	-	-	-	-	-

Albaladejo's Career Fielding Record

Position	PCT	G	PO	A	E	TC	DP
Pitcher	1.000	39	1	7	0	8	0

Andrew Brackman

64

Right-handed Pitcher

6-10 • 232 • B/T: Right/Right

Opening Day Age: 24

Birthdate
December 4, 1985

Birthplace
Cincinnati, Ohio

Resides
Raleigh, N.C.

M.L. Service
1 year, 16 days
(Rookie)

College
North Carolina
State University

Status

- Selected by the Yankees in the first round (30th pick overall) of the 2007 First-Year Player Draft...signed a four-year Major League contract on August 16, 2007, with three additional club-option years...contract extends through the 2013 season.

2009

- Made his regular season professional debut with Single-A Charleston, going 2-12 with a 5.91 ERA in 29 games (19 starts)...struck out 103 batters in 106.2IP...tied for first on the team in starts, ranked second in strikeouts and third in innings pitched...led the South Atlantic League in walks (76) and wild pitches (26).
- Opened the season in the rotation, then transitioned to the bullpen on 7/31 for the remainder of the season...went 1-11 with a 6.72 ERA (85.2IP, 64ER) and a .277 opponents batting average as a starter...owned a 1-1 record with a 2.57 ERA (21.0IP, 6ER) and a .218 opponents average in 10 relief appearances.
- Lost his first four decisions, remaining winless over his first eight starts of the season...held opponents to 2ER or less in six of the eight outings.
- Earned his first professional win on 5/21 vs. Lexington, limiting his opponent to 1ER on 5H in a season-high-tying 8.0IP (1BB, 6K)...walked a season-high 10 batters in his next start on 5/26 vs. Bowling Green...recorded the loss in each of his final seven starts with a 14.27 ERA (23.1IP, 37ER) over the span from 6/17-7/23.
- Held his opposition scoreless over his final four outings of the season, tossing 10.0 innings over the stretch with no walks and 9K (6H).
- Following the season, was named the organization's 10th-best prospect by *Baseball America*...also noted as having the "Best Fastball" in the organization by the publication.
- Made three appearances out of the bullpen during 2009 spring training with the Yankees, allowing 2ER in 3.0IP (3H, 1HR, 1HP).

2008

- Missed the regular season, recovering from "Tommy John" surgery performed in August 2007...following the season, was named the third-best prospect in the organization by *Baseball America*...was also tabbed by the publication as having the organization's "best fastball."
- Saw his first professional action, playing with the Waikiki BeachBoys of the Hawaiian Winter Baseball League...made eight starts, going 3-4 with a 5.56 ERA...tied for third in the league with 36K (in 34.0IP)...allowed 3ER or less in six of his starts.

2007

- Missed the professional baseball season after undergoing "Tommy John" surgery on 8/24...surgery was performed by Dr. James Andrews in Birmingham, Ala...ranked by *Baseball America* as the seventh-best overall prospect entering the draft and the third-best junior in the nation...the publication also tabbed him as having the best fastball among college pitchers entering the draft...following the season was named by *Baseball America* as the 10th-best prospect in the Yankees organization.

2006

- Played for the Orleans Cardinals of the Cape Cod League...was 1-0 with a 1.06 ERA in six games (two starts)...was named the No. 2 prospect in the league in a *Baseball America* poll of scouts, managers and coaches...left the Cape Cod League in August to join Team USA...made two appearances (one start) and did not allow an earned run in 4.0IP, pitching in the FISU World Championships in Havana, Cuba...recorded a no-decision in his lone start on 8/10 vs. Mexico (3.0IP, 1H, 1R, 0ER, 2BB, 3K).

ANDREW BRACKMAN

College Career

- Was 11-7 with a 3.80 ERA in 30 career college games (27 starts) at North Carolina State University, recording 149 strikeouts in 149.1IP...made 13 starts as a junior in 2007, going 6-4 with a 3.81 ERA and a .264 opponents batting average...named to the *Baseball America* Preseason All-America team...had his sophomore season cut short due to a stress fracture in his left hip...made just seven appearances (all starts) prior to the injury, posting a 1-3 record and a 6.35 ERA.
- As a freshman in 2005, was 4-0 with a 2.09 ERA, holding opponents to a .216 batting average...allowed just 32H in 43.0IP over 10 games (seven starts) as N.C. State won every game in which he appeared...struck out a career-high 12 batters in 7.0IP on 4/29 vs. seventh-ranked North Carolina...was the most strikeouts by an N.C. State freshman since Preston Woods struck out 13 batters on 4/26/87 vs. Georgia Tech.
- Was a communications major at N.C. State...was a college teammate of Oakland reliever and 2005 first-round pick Joey Devine...also played two seasons (2005-06) on the Wolfpack basketball team, averaging 7.6 points and 3.5 rebounds per game...appeared in all 35 games as a freshman (14 starts), averaging 19 minutes per game.

Personal

- Full name is Andrew Warren Brackman...attended Moeller High School in Cincinnati, Ohio, where he was a two-sport standout in baseball and basketball...his 1.04 career high school ERA was the seventh-best in Ohio's history when he graduated...helped his team win the state championship as a senior, going 7-0 with a 0.60 ERA and 83 strikeouts in 47.1IP... ranked as the 18th-best senior in America by *Team One Baseball* and listed as the No. 4 prospect in the state of Ohio for the 2004 Draft by *Baseball America*...was runner-up Mr. Basketball in Ohio in 2005, as awarded by the Associated Press...shared Ohio's Division 1 "Player of the Year" honors and was named first-team all-state in 2005...averaged 20.2 points and 6.5 rebounds as a senior, leading the conference in scoring and field-goal percentage (.654)...rated as the 42nd-best basketball prospect in the nation by Insiders.com and the 43rd-best basketball prospect by PrepStars following his senior year...enjoys fishing in his free time.

Brackman's Career Pitching Record

Year	Club	W	L	ERA	G	GS	CG	SHO	SV	IP	H	R	ER	HR	HP	BB	SO	WP	BK
2009	Charleston	2	12	5.91	29	19	0	0	0	106.2	106	79	70	8	10	76	103	26	0
Minor League Totals		**2**	**12**	**5.91**	**29**	**19**	**0**	**0**	**0**	**106.2**	**106**	**79**	**70**	**8**	**10**	**76**	**103**	**26**	**0**

Home Sweet Home

The Yankees were a Major League-best 57-24 (.704) at Yankee Stadium in 2009, marking their 18th consecutive winning season at home (since 1992)...according to the *Elias Sports Bureau*, it is the longest current streak of any team in the Majors and the longest such streak by any team since a 21-year streak for the Yankees from 1969–89, which included two seasons (1974-75) at Shea Stadium.

According to the *Elias Sports Bureau*, in 2009 the Yankees tied the all-time record for most wins at a ballpark in its first Major League season, matching the Red Sox who went 57-20 in their first season at Fenway Park in 1912.

The Yankees own the top two highest single-season home winning percentages: .805 (62-15) in 1932 and .802 (65-16) in 1961.

Original Yankee Stadium

A.J. Burnett

34

Right-handed Pitcher

6-4 • 230 • B/T: Right/Right

Opening Day Age: 33

Birthdate
January 3, 1977

Birthplace
North Little Rock, Ark.

Resides
Monkton, Md.

M.L. Service
10 years, 38 days

Career Highlights
No-hitter
- 5/12/01 at San Diego

Status

- Signed as a free agent by the Yankees to a five-year contract on December 18, 2008...contract extends through the 2013 season.

Career Notes

- Has recorded five consecutive seasons (2005-09) of 10-or-more wins and seven such seasons in his career (also 2001-02)...has a 51-35 record since his first season with Toronto in 2006, tying for seventh in the AL in wins over the stretch.
- Among the 381 all-time Major League pitchers with 30-or-more career decisions against AL East competition, Burnett ranks first with a .733 (33-12) career winning percentage...has held AL East batters to a .220 average in his career, eighth-lowest among the group and fourth-lowest among pitchers primarily used as starters (Nolan Ryan-.202; Andy Messersmith-.206, Pedro Martinez-.213).
- Over the previous decade (2000-09), tied for seventh in the Majors in shutouts (nine) and ranked ninth in lowest opponent's average (.236).
- Among qualifying pitchers, his 3.02 ERA in Interleague play is fifth best all time among pitchers with 30 such starts, while his .682 (15-7) career winning percentage is tied for sixth highest.

Single-Game Highs and Streaks

Low hit CG
0 - at SD, 5/12/01
IP (start)
9.0 - 16 times
Last: vs. BAL, 5/16/07
IP (relief)
2.0 - at PHI, 10/3/04
Hits
12 - 4 times
Last: at LAA, 7/4/08
Runs
9 - at BOS, 8/22/09
BB
9 - at SD, 5/12/01
SO
14 - 2 times
Last: vs. MIL, 7/6/05
HR
3 - 6 times
Last: at BOS, 8/22/09
Winning Streak
7g - 7/19-8/19/05
Losing Streak
7g - 8/24/05-4/15/06

2009

- Was 13-9 with a 4.04 ERA in 33 starts with the Yankees...his 13 wins and 33 starts were both the second-highest totals of his career (went 18-10 in 34 starts in 2008)...ranked eighth in the American League with 195K...was second in the Majors with 97BB (Arizona's Doug Davis-103BB)...opponents batted .247 (193-for-781, 25HR); LH .217 (91-for-419, 11HR); RH .282 (102- for-362, 14HR)...marked the third-lowest average against left-handed hitters among AL righties and fifth-best in the Majors (min: 200BF)...the Yankees were 21-12 in his starts.
- Tied Felix Hernandez for the Major League lead with 17 wild pitches...marked a personal single-season career high and was the second-highest total in franchise history behind Tim Leary's 23WP in 1990...matched his single-game career-high with 3WP in four games in 2009 (4/19 vs. Cleveland, 5/17 vs. Minnesota, 7/8 at Minnesota and 8/12 vs. Toronto).
- Over his final 24 starts (5/27-10/4), was 11-7 with a 3.56 ERA (149.0IP, 59ER) and a .242 batting average against (137-for-567), limiting his opponents to 3ER or less in all but four outings...was 5-2 with a 2.96 ERA (73.0IP, 24ER) in his last 11 starts at Yankee Stadium from 6/2-9/29...prior to the stretch, was 0-1 with a 4.78 ERA (32.0IP, 17ER) in five home starts to begin the season.
- Made his Yankees debut on 4/9 at Baltimore, recording the win in an 11-2 Yankees victory (5.1IP, 7H, 2ER, 1BB, 6K, 1HR)...was the Yankees' first win of the season.
- In his second start on 4/14 at Tampa Bay, retired 18 of his first 19 batters faced, surrendering a second-inning walk to DH Pat Burrell and carrying a no-hitter

Burnett's 2009 Pitching Lines

Date/Opp	Score	W/L	IP	H	R	ER	HR	BB	K	NP/K	ERA	Left game...
4/9 at BAL*	11-2	W	5.1	7	2	2	1	1	6	98/59	3.38	Leading 7-2
4/14 at TB*	7-2	W	**8.0**	3	2	2	0	1	9	103/67	2.70	Leading 3-2
4/19 vs. CLE*	7-3	ND	6.1	3	3	3	2	**7**	2	111/60	3.20	Trailing 3-1
4/25 at BOS*	11-16	ND	5.0	8	8	8	2	3	3	91/55	5.47	Tied 8-8
4/30 vs. LAA	7-4	ND	7.0	8	4	4	1	1	5	108/66	5.40	Tied 4-4
5/6 vs. TB*	3-4 (10)	ND	6.0	6	3	3	0	2	8	114/69	5.26	Trailing 3-0
5/12 at TOR	1-5	L	7.2	7	5	5	1	4	3	110/66	5.36	Trailing 5-1
5/17 vs. MIN	3-2 (10)	ND	6.2	6	2	2	0	6	7	**123**/74	5.02	Trailing 2-0
5/22 vs. PHI	3-7	L	6.0	8	5	5	**3**	2	7	95/59	5.28	Trailing 5-1
5/27 at TEX*	9-2	W	6.0	3	0	0	0	4	7	118/70	4.78	Leading 8-0
6/2 vs. TEX	12-3	W	7.0	8	3	3	1	1	8	111/71	4.69	Leading 12-3
6/9 at BOS	0-7	L	2.2	5	5	3	1	5	1	84/40	4.89	Trailing 5-0
6/14 vs. NYM*	15-0	W	7.0	4	0	0	0	4	8	111/66	4.46	Leading 15-0
6/20 at FLA	1-2	L	6.1	5	2	1	1	3	8	98/59	4.24	Trailing 2-1
6/27 at NYM	5-0	W	7.0	1	0	0	0	3	10	108/64	3.93	Leading 5-1
7/3 vs. TOR*	4-2	W	7.0	6	2	2	1	2	7	112/68	3.83	Leading 3-2
7/8 at MIN	4-3	W	6.1	7	2	2	0	4	2	100/59	3.77	Leading 4-2
7/17 vs. DET*	5-3	ND	6.0	6	3	3	1	5	1	104/57	3.81	Trailing 3-2
7/22 vs. BAL	6-4	W	7.0	6	2	2	0	3	6	104/68	3.74	Leading 5-2
7/27 at TB	11-4	W	7.0	2	1	0	0	2	5	114/69	3.53	Leading 5-1
8/1 at CWS*	4-14	L	4.2	10	7	7	0	2	4	106/62	3.89	Trailing 7-2
8/7 vs. BOS	2-0 (15)	ND	7.2	1	0	0	0	6	6	118/65	3.67	Tied 0-0
8/12 vs. TOR	4-3 (11)	ND	6.0	10	3	3	1	2	7	107/68	3.71	Tied 3-3
8/17 at OAK*	0-3 (CG)	L	**8.0**	6	3	3	0	2	5	99/66	3.69	Trailing 3-0
8/22 at BOS	1-14	L	5.0	9	**9**	**9**	**3**	2	6	97/59	4.08	Trailing 9-0
8/27 vs. TEX	2-7	L	6.0	2	3	3	1	3	**12**	105/63	4.10	Trailing 3-2
9/1 at BAL	9-6	ND	5.1	**11**	6	6	2	2	2	109/70	4.29	Tied 6-6
9/7 G2 vs. TB	11-1	W	6.0	4	1	1	0	3	8	99/64	4.19	Leading 11-1
9/12 vs. BAL*	3-7	L	7.0	7	6	6	2	2	4	108/72	4.33	Trailing 6-1
9/18 at SEA	2-3	ND	7.0	7	1	1	0	3	6	104/66	4.22	Leading 2-1
9/23 at LAA	3-2	W	5.2	7	2	2	0	3	11	101/65	4.19	Leading 3-2
9/29 vs. KC	4-3	ND	6.1	3	2	1	0	3	8	108/69	4.10	Tied 1-1
10/4 at TB*	10-2	W	5.0	7	2	1	1	1	3	84/55	4.04	Leading 10-2
Totals		**13-9**	**207.0**	**193**	**99**	**93**	**25**	**97**	**195**		**4.04**	

(*) Denotes start following a team loss **Bold = season highs**

through 6.0IP...no-hit bid was broken up by Carl Crawford's single to left field to start the seventh.

- Went winless over seven starts from 4/19-5/22, going 0-2 with a 6.04 ERA (44.2IP, 30ER) over the span...was his longest stretch without a victory in a single season since his last seven starts of the 2005 season w/ Florida (0-6, 5.87 ERA, 38.1IP, 25ER)...made four consecutive starts without drawing a decision from 4/19-5/6, marking his longest such stretch since 5/21-6/10/05 (w/ Florida).
- On 4/25 at Boston, was staked to a 6-0 lead before allowing 8ER over 2.0IP (fourth and fifth innings)...according to the *Elias Sports Bureau*, it marked just the second time in 34 career starts he did not earn a win when given a lead of five-or-more runs...the 16-11 Yankees loss marked just the third time in franchise history that the Yankees lost a game by at least five runs in a game in which they had once led by at least six runs...had last happened on 6/5/56 vs. Cleveland (led 6-0, lost 15-8)...marked the largest lead blown against Boston since 5/16/68 at Fenway Park (led 9-3 in the fourth, lost 11-10).
- Surrendered a leadoff home run to Philadelphia's Jimmy Rollins on the first pitch of the game on 5/22 at Yankee Stadium, snapping a stretch of 42 consecutive starts without allowing a first-inning home run that dated back through his first start of the 2008 season.
- Over an 11-start stretch from 5/27-7/27, was 8-2 with a 2.08 ERA (69.1IP, 16ER) and a .209 opponents average (53-for-253), limiting his opponents to 3ER or less in each outing...held his opponents scoreless three times and had one additional start in which he did not allow an earned run (7/27 at Tampa Bay: 1R/0ER)...allowed just one first-inning run over a 15-start stretch from 5/27-8/17.
- Was suspended six games by Major League Baseball on 6/4 for allegedly "intentionally throwing a pitch in the head area of Nelson Cruz of the Rangers" during the top of the fifth inning on 6/2...appealed the suspension and settled his appeal on 6/21 at a reduced penalty of five games...served the suspension from 6/21-26.
- Compiled a 0.99 ERA (27.1IP, 3ER) and went 3-1 over his four starts from 6/14-7/3, facing the team that drafted him (Mets-2GS), and the other two teams that he has pitched for in the Majors (Florida and Toronto)...allowed two-or-fewer runs with at least 7K in each of those four starts...according to the *Elias Sports Bureau*, became just the fourth Yankee to compile such a stretch in a single season in the last 40 years since Divisional play began in 1969 – also Ron Guidry (1978, '81), David Cone (1997) and Mike Mussina (2003).
- Started and won the Yankees' 15-0 victory on 6/14 vs. the Mets (7.0IP, 4H, 4BB, 8K)...marked the Yankees' largest shutout since a 15-0 win in Game 1 of a doubleheader on 9/25/77 at Toronto and their largest in a home game since a 15-0 win on 8/4/53 vs. Detroit.

- Struck out the side in the third inning in 6/20 loss at Florida on nine pitches (Johnson, Coughlan and Bonifacio – all swinging)...according to *Elias*, became the 40th pitcher all-time to accomplish the feat and just the third Yankee, joining Al Downing (1967) and Ron Guidry (1984).
- Completed the 2009 first half with an 8-4 record (.667), marking his best-ever winning percentage at the All-Star break...was just his third winning record prior to the break (also 10-8 in 2008 and 8-6 in 2002).
- Tossed 7.2 scoreless IP (1H, 6BB, 6K) on 8/7 vs. Boston while recording a no-decision in a 15-inning, 2-0 Yankees victory...allowed a single to Jacoby Ellsbury to lead off the game, then did not allow a hit to his final 27 batters faced (6BB, and a catcher's interference)...became the first Yankee to toss at least 7.2 scoreless IP and allow 1H or 0H since Mike Mussina threw a CG one-hitter on 9/2/01 at Fenway Park.
- Allowed a career-high 9R (all earned) in a 14-1 loss on 8/22 at Boston (5.0IP, 9H, 2BB, 6K, 3HR).
- Picked off Ichiro Suzuki twice in 9/18 loss at Seattle...became the first Yankees RHP to record two pickoffs in the same game since Wade Taylor on 8/17/91 vs. the White Sox.
- Won his 100th career game in his final start of the season on 10/4 at Tampa Bay, allowing 2R/1ER in 5.0IP (7H, 1BB, 3K).
- Made his postseason debut, going 1-1 with a 5.27 ERA in five starts...did not draw a decision in first career postseason start on 10/9 in Game 2 of the ALDS vs. Minnesota (6.0IP, 3H, 1ER, 5BB, 6K, 2HP)...marked the fewest hits allowed by a Yankee making his first career postseason start since Orlando Hernandez (7.0IP, 3H) in ALCS Game 4 at Cleveland on 10/10/98...earned the win in his first World Series start on 10/29 in Game 2, limiting the Phillies to 1ER on 4H in 7.0IP (2BB, 9K)...according to the *Elias Sports Bureau*, entered the 2009 playoffs tied with Brian Moehler for the fourth-most regular season starts among active pitchers without appearing in the postseason, behind only Roy Halladay (287), Randy Wolf (275) and Jamey Wright (246).

SINCE 2006
WHEN BURNETT JOINED THE AL

MOST STRIKEOUTS IN AL

1.	Justin Verlander	739
2.	Felix Hernandez	733
3.	Josh Beckett	723
4.	**A.J. BURNETT**	**720**
5.	CC SABATHIA	701

HIGHEST K/9.0IP IN AL

1.	Scott Kazmir	9.47
2.	Erik Bedard	9.19
3.	**A.J. BURNETT**	**8.88**
4.	Zack Greinke	8.61
5.	JAVIER VAZQUEZ	8.56

LOWEST OPP. AVG. IN AL

1.	Erik Bedard	.232
2.	Scott Kazmir	.243
3.	**A.J. BURNETT**	**.243**
4.	Josh Beckett	.247
5.	CC SABATHIA	.247

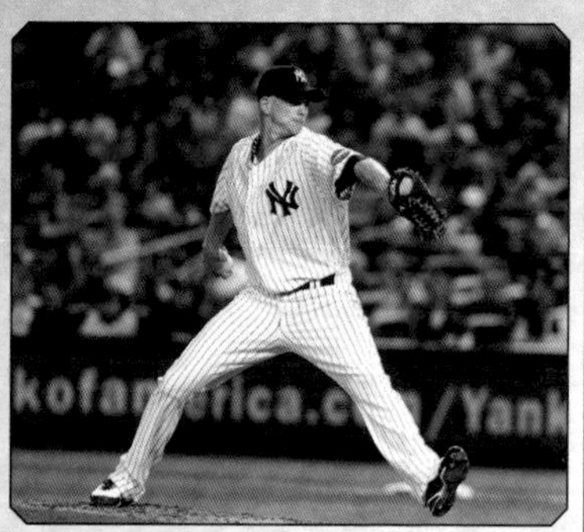

2008

- Was 18-10 with a 4.07 ERA in 35 games (34 starts) with 231 strikeouts in 221.1IP for Toronto, recording career highs in wins, innings pitched and strikeouts...opponents batted .249 (211-for-849, 19HR); LH .262 (126-for-481, 11HR), RH .231 (85-for-368, 8HR)...held the opposition to a .203 average (57-for-281) their first time through the order, and then allowed a .271 average (154-for-568) thereafter.
- Led the AL in strikeouts and strikeouts per 9.0IP (9.39), tied for tops in the AL in starts, ranked third in innings pitched and tied for fourth in wins...recorded a career-high six games with 10-or-more strikeouts...became only the third Blue Jays hurler to record at least 200 strikeouts in a season, joining Roy Halladay (2003, '06) and Roger Clemens (1997-98)...also became only the second Blue Jay to lead the league in strikeouts, joining Clemens (1997-98).
- Combined with Roy Halladay for a total of 38 victories, representing the most by any duo in Blue Jays history, surpassing the 37 by Jack Morris (21) and Juan Guzman (16) in 1992.
- Combined to go 5-3 with a 3.09 ERA (75.2IP, 31R, 26ER) in 11 starts against 2008 AL playoff teams...also won his only start against the World Series-champion Phillies on 5/17 at Citizens Bank Park, limiting Philadelphia to 2ER in 6.1IP.
- Opened the season 6-7 with a 5.42 ERA in his first 16 games (15 starts) through 6/19, as the Blue Jays went 7-9...over his final 19 starts, went 12-3 with a 3.12 ERA and 141 strikeouts as the Blue Jays went 13-6...won eight of his last nine decisions.
- Made his lone relief appearance of the season–and fourth of his career–on 4/16 vs. Texas, allowing 2ER in 1.0IP and recording the loss in the 14-inning contest.
- Did not allow an earned run over 17.0 consecutive innings from 9/9-19 facing Chicago-AL and Boston (twice)...was charged with just 4ER total over his final four starts, going 2-0 with a 1.29 ERA.

A.J. BURNETT

2007

- Went 10-8 with a 3.75 ERA in 25 starts with the Blue Jays, striking out a team-high 176 batters in 165.2 IP...ranked fourth in the AL with 9.56 K/9.0IP...opponents batted .214 (131-for-611, 23HR); LH .200 (66-for-330, 12HR), RH .231 (65-for-281, 11HR)...only Baltimore's Erik Bedard (.212) had a lower opponents average among AL starters...was the lowest batting average allowed by a right-handed pitcher against lefthanders.
- Allowed 11ER in 14.0IP over his first three starts of the season, posting a 7.07 ERA...worked to a 3.44 ERA over the remainder of the year, allowing more than 3ER just five times over his final 22 starts from 4/20 through the end of the season.
- Landed on the 15-day disabled list on 6/13 with a right shoulder strain...reinstated on 6/27 and made one start on 6/28 at Minnesota, allowing 5ER in 4.0IP in a no-decision before returning to the D.L. the next day with the same injury...made one rehab start with Triple-A Syracuse (5.0IP, 3H, 1ER, 1BB, 7K) before being returned from rehab and reinstated from the D.L. on 8/12.
- After returning from the disabled list, posted a 5-2 record with a 3.01 ERA over his final 10 starts...limited opponents to a .202 average over that span (52-for-208)...held opponents to 2ER or less in six of his first seven starts upon returning.

2006

- In his first season with Toronto, went 10-8 with a 3.98 ERA in 21 starts...was limited by two separate stints on the disabled list with scar tissue break-up caused from previous elbow surgery.
- Began the season on the D.L...made two rehab starts with Single-A Dunedin (8.0IP, 3ER) and was reinstated on 4/15...made two starts (0-1, 6.30 ERA) before returning to the D.L. on 4/22...made one rehab start each with Double-A New Hampshire (1-0, 1.50 ERA, 6.0IP, 2ER) and Triple-A Syracuse (1-0, 5.0IP, 0ER) before being returned from rehab and reinstated again on 6/22 for the remainder of the season.
- Earned his first victory as a Blue Jay on 6/27 vs. Washington, throwing his ninth career complete-game shutout (9.0IP, 6H, 7K)...became just the third Toronto pitcher to record a shutout for their first Blue Jays victory, joining Paul Mirabella (4/17/80) and Tom Underwood (5/9/78).
- Went 1-3 with a 4.33 ERA over his first six starts through 7/7...following the All-Star break, posted a 9-5 record with a 3.86 ERA in 15 starts, leading the Toronto staff in second-half wins, starts, innings pitched (100.1) and strikeouts (84).

2005

- Posted a 12-12 record with a 3.44 ERA in 32 starts with Florida...established Marlins career marks for wins (49), losses (50), shutouts (eight), complete games (14), strikeouts (753), games started (131) and innings pitched (847.2)...tied for third in the NL with four complete games.
- Tossed back-to-back complete-game victories on 4/12 vs. Philadelphia and 4/17 at New York-NL, earning NL "Pitcher of the Week" honors...limited Tampa Bay to two hits in a 9.0-inning shutout on 6/26 at Tropicana Field (2BB, 7K)...matched his franchise record with 14 strikeouts on 7/6 vs. Milwaukee.
- Won a career-high seven consecutive starts from 7/19-8/19, recording a 1.71 ERA over the stretch (52.1IP, 7ER)...following the streak, went 0-6 with 5.87 ERA in his final seven starts, marking his longest career losing streak.
- Recorded triples with his first two hits of season, becoming the first pitcher to hit two triples in a season since Mike Hampton hit three with Houston in 1999...of his 10H, five went for extra-base hits...hit third career HR on 7/24 at San Francisco, a solo shot off Kevin Correia.

2004

- Began the season on the disabled list, recovering from "Tommy John" surgery (performed 4/29/03)....returned from rehab and reinstated on 6/2 and posted a 7-6 record with a 3.68 ERA in 20 games (19 starts)...went 6-0 with a 2.80 ERA and a .188 opponents average in his 11 home games and was 1-6 with a 5.09 ERA and a .291 opponents average in his nine road games (eight starts).
- Established a Marlins club record with 14K over 8.0 innings in 8/29 win vs. Colorado...won each of his final four starts from 8/24-9/12, pitching to a 1.84 ERA over the stretch.
- First pitched on 5/18 in an extended spring training game against the Cardinals then began an official rehab assignment on 5/23...made one start each with Single-A Jupiter (ND, 4.0IP, 2H, 1R, 0ER, 2BB, 4K) and Triple-A Albuquerque (ND, 3.1IP, 7H, 4ER, 2BB, 6K, 1HR, 1HP).

A.J. BURNETT

2003

- Made four starts for the eventual World Series-champion Marlins before undergoing season-ending "Tommy John" surgery on 4/29.
- Began the season on the disabled list (retroactive to 3/21) with synovitis in his right elbow...was reinstated from the D.L. on 4/9 and made the start that night vs. the Mets, recording a no-decision in the Marlins victory (7.0IP, 5H, 2ER, 2BB, 4K).
- Went 0-2 with a 4.70 ERA before landing on the disabled list again on 4/26...had surgery to repair the torn elbow ligament performed by Dr. James Andrews in Birmingham, Ala.

2002

- Was named the "Most Improved Marlin" by the South Florida chapter of the Baseball Writers Association of America (BBWAA), going 12-9 with a 3.30 ERA in 31 games (29 starts)...posted the third-highest season strikeout total (203) and the fourth 200-plus strikeout season in franchise history...ranked sixth in the National League and seventh in the Majors in strikeouts...struck out eight or more batters in 15 of his 29 starts (51.7%)...was the third-lowest ERA in club history.
- Opponents batted .209 (153-for-732, 12HR); LH .242 (87-for-359, 5HR), RH .177 (66-for-373, 7HR)...ranked second in the NL and fourth in the Majors in lowest opponents batting average...ranked third in the Majors with a .190 opponents average at home (68-for-358)...led the Majors with five shutouts–all coming at home...tied for third in the Majors with seven complete games, one behind co-leaders Bartolo Colon and Randy Johnson.
- Made his first active Opening Day roster...tossed a four-hit shutout in his third start of the season on 4/14 vs. Atlanta...recorded a three-hit shutout on 6/15 vs. Tampa Bay.
- Was placed on the disabled list from 8/19-9/14 with a right acute bone bruise...made four appearances following his return, including his first two Major League relief appearances.

2001

- Posted an 11-12 record and a 4.05 ERA in 27 starts with the Marlins...opponents batted .231 (145-for-629, 20HR); LH .247 (80-for-320, 5HR), RH .213 (65-for-305, 15HR)...was the fifth-lowest overall opponents average in the NL.
- Began the season on the 15-day disabled list with a stress fracture to the fifth metatarsal in his right foot...made two rehab starts with Single-A Brevard County, allowing 2ER in 9.1IP (1.93 ERA)...was returned from rehab and reinstated on 5/1 and made his season debut on 5/7 at Los Angeles-NL, recording the loss despite allowing only 1ER in 6.0IP.
- Tossed the third no-hitter in Marlins history on 5/12 at San Diego in his second start of the season, striking out seven and walking nine in a 3-0 win (1HP, 1WP)...was the 203rd no-hitter since 1900, the 98th in NL history and the second in the Majors in 2001...joined Al Leiter (5/11/96 vs. Colorado) and Kevin Brown (6/10/97 at San Francisco) as the only Marlins to accomplish the feat...tied the club record for walks in a game and became the first pitcher in the modern era to issue nine walks in a complete game, nine-inning no-hitter...his 10 baserunners allowed were second only Cincinnati's Jim Maloney who surrendered 12 baserunners in a 10-inning no-hitter at Chicago-NL on 8/9/65...earned NL "Player of the Week" honors.

DID YOU KNOW?: A.J. Burnett's cap and a baseball from his 5/12/01 no-hitter at San Diego are on display at the National Baseball Hall of Fame in Cooperstown, N.Y.

2000

- Was 3-7 with a 4.79 ERA in 13 starts with the Marlins...made his season debut in the second game of a doubleheader vs. Atlanta on 7/20 after being reinstated from the D.L. earlier that day...recorded his first double-digit strikeout game on 8/28 vs. St. Louis...also hit his first career homer in the same game off Rick Ankiel.
- Opened the season on the disabled list after suffering a complete rupture of his ulnar collateral ligament in his right thumb during pitcher's fielding practice on 3/14 at spring training in Viera, Fla...underwent surgery on 3/21 at Holy Cross Hospital in Fort Lauderdale, performed by Dr. Brian Fingado.
- Made three total rehab appearances with Single-A Brevard County and Triple-A Portland, allowing 3ER in 12.1IP (2.19 ERA) with no decisions.

A.J. BURNETT

1999

- Went 4-2 with a 3.48 ERA in seven starts for the Marlins in his first Major League action...made his big league debut on 8/17 at Los Angeles-NL after being recalled to make a spot start for Alex Fernandez, allowing 1ER in 5.2IP with 2BB and 4K...became the first starting pitcher in Marlins history to earn a win in his debut...collected his first hit off Mike Judd in his second AB...was optioned back to Double-A Portland after the game.
- Recalled a second time on 8/28, making six more starts.
- Opened the season at Portland, going 6-12 with a 5.52 ERA in 26 games (23 starts)...won his first game out of the bullpen on 8/13 vs. Erie, tossing 3.0 scoreless innings.
- Selected to pitch for the U.S. team in the inaugural Futures Game...tossed 1.0 scoreless inning in the contest on 7/11 at Fenway Park.

1998

- In his first season in the Florida organization, was selected as the Marlins' "Pitcher of the Year" after posting a 10-4 record and a 1.97 ERA at Single-A Kane County.
- Led the organization in strikeouts (186) and ranked second among all hurlers in the Majors or minors...also paced the Florida organization in ERA, ranking second in the Midwest League and third among all minor leaguers...led all minor league starters with 14.07 K/9.0IP and a .179 opponents batting average (74-for-413).
- Missed the first six weeks of the season (4/9-5/16) after undergoing surgery to repair a broken right hand...named the Marlins' organizational "Player of the Month" for June...earned the Midwest League "Pitcher of the Week" for 6/22-28, going 1-0 in two starts...earned the MWL "Pitcher of the Week" for the second time for the period from 8/30-9/7.
- Was tabbed by *Baseball America* as the top prospect in the Marlins' organization and the No. 4 prospect in the Midwest League.
- Was acquired by the Marlins along with LHP Jesus Sanchez, RHP Brandon Villafuerte and a player to be named later (OF Cesar Crespo on 9/14/98) in exchange for LHP Al Leiter and INF Ralph Milliard on 2/6/98.

1997

- Went 3-2 with a 4.39 ERA in 12 combined appearances (11 starts) with the GCL Mets and short-season Single-A Pittsfield...both teams won their respective league championships...went on the D.L. from 6/17-7/1 with a broken left foot...struck out 63 combined batters in 55.1IP.

1996

- Was undefeated in 12 starts with rookie-level Kingsport, going 4-0 with a 3.88 ERA...held opponents to a .171 batting average (31-for-181) and struck out 10.55 batters per 9.0IP (68K, 58.0IP), ranking second in the Appalachian League in both categories.

1995

- Made his professional debut with the GCL Mets, going 2-3 with a 4.28 ERA in nine games (eight starts).

Personal

- Full name is Allan James Burnett...is married to Karen with two children, Allan Jr. (9) and Ashton (6)...signed by Larry Chase (Mets)...had his Central Arkansas High School jersey retired on 12/6/02...led Yankees in signing and auctioning replica WWE Championship belt to raise over $9,000 for Camp Sundown, a retreat in upstate New York for children suffering from rare genetic disorder called Xeroderma Pigmentosum, and a 2009 HOPE Week participant...accepted award on behalf of the Yankees at National Sportsmanship Awards in November, 2009 in St Louis...joined forces with the Adam Walsh Children's Fund and the National Center for Missing and Exploited Children to "Play it Safe," hosting awareness days in 2001 and 2002...also served as the national spokesman for the National Center for Missing and Exploited Children...was an active member of the Marlins' "Adopt-A-Classroom" program, serving as spokesman for Marlins @ School...enjoys fishing and playing instruments.

Burnett's Career Pitching Record

Year	Club	W	L	ERA	G	GS	CG	SHO	SV	IP	H	R	ER	HR	HP	BB	SO	WP	BK
1995	GCL Mets	2	3	4.28	9	8	1	0	0	33.2	27	16	16	2	2	23	26	7	4
1996	Kingsport	4	0	3.88	12	12	0	0	0	58.0	31	26	25	0	7	54	68	16	3
1997	GCL Mets	0	1	3.18	3	2	0	0	0	11.1	8	8	4	0	2	8	15	3	0
	Pittsfield	3	1	4.70	9	9	0	0	0	44.0	28	26	23	3	6	35	48	9	0
1998	Kane County – a	10	4	1.97	20	20	0	0	0	119.0	74	27	26	3	8	45	186	6	2
1999	Portland	6	12	5.52	26	23	0	0	0	120.2	132	91	74	15	5	71	121	16	2
	FLORIDA	4	2	3.48	7	7	0	0	0	41.1	37	23	16	3	0	25	33	0	0
2000	Brevard County	0	0	3.68	2	2	0	0	0	7.1	4	3	3	0	0	6	6	0	2
	Calgary	0	0	0.00	1	1	0	0	0	5.0	0	0	0	0	0	3	6	2	0
	FLORIDA – b	3	7	4.79	13	13	0	0	0	82.2	80	46	44	8	2	44	57	2	0
2001	FLORIDA – c	11	12	4.05	27	27	2	1	0	173.1	145	82	78	20	7	83	128	7	1
	Brevard County	0	0	1.93	2	2	0	0	0	9.1	4	2	2	0	0	4	10	0	0
2002	FLORIDA – d	12	9	3.30	31	29	7	5	0	204.1	153	84	75	12	9	90	203	14	0
2003	FLORIDA – e, f	0	2	4.70	4	4	0	0	0	23.0	18	13	12	2	2	18	21	2	0
2004	Jupiter	0	0	0.00	1	1	0	0	0	4.0	2	1	0	0	0	2	4	2	0
	Albuquerque	0	0	10.80	1	1	0	0	0	3.1	7	4	4	1	1	2	6	1	0
	FLORIDA – g	7	6	3.68	20	19	1	0	0	120.0	102	50	49	9	4	38	113	7	0
2005	FLORIDA – h	12	12	3.44	32	32	4	2	0	209.0	184	97	80	12	7	79	198	12	0
2006	Dunedin	0	0	3.38	2	2	0	0	0	8.0	9	3	3	0	1	2	6	0	0
	New Hampshire	1	0	1.50	1	1	0	0	0	6.0	2	2	1	1	0	3	9	0	0
	Syracuse	1	0	0.00	1	1	0	0	0	5.0	0	0	0	0	1	1	7	1	0
	TORONTO – i, j	10	8	3.98	21	21	2	1	0	135.2	138	67	60	14	8	39	118	6	1
2007	Syracuse	0	0	1.80	1	1	0	0	0	5.0	3	1	1	0	0	1	7	0	0
	TORONTO – k, l	10	8	3.75	25	25	2	0	0	165.2	131	74	69	23	12	66	176	5	0
2008	TORONTO – m	18	10	4.07	35	34	1	0	0	221.1	211	109	100	19	9	86	231	11	2
2009	YANKEES	13	9	4.04	33	33	1	0	0	207.0	193	99	93	25	10	97	195	17	1
Minor League Totals		**27**	**21**	**3.73**	**91**	**86**	**1**	**0**	**0**	**439.2**	**331**	**210**	**182**	**25**	**33**	**260**	**525**	**63**	**13**
AL Totals		**51**	**35**	**3.97**	**114**	**113**	**6**	**1**	**0**	**729.2**	**673**	**349**	**322**	**81**	**39**	**288**	**720**	**39**	**4**
NL Totals		**49**	**50**	**3.73**	**134**	**131**	**14**	**8**	**0**	**853.2**	**719**	**395**	**354**	**66**	**31**	**377**	**753**	**44**	**1**
Major League Totals		**100**	**85**	**3.84**	**248**	**244**	**20**	**9**	**0**	**1583.1**	**1392**	**744**	**676**	**147**	**70**	**665**	**1473**	**83**	**5**

Selected by the Mets in the eighth round of the 1995 First-Year Player Draft.

a – Acquired by the Florida Marlins along with LHP Jesus Sanchez, RHP Brandon Villafuerte and a player to be named later (OF Cesar Crespo) in exchange for LHP Al Leiter and INF Ralph Milliard on February 6, 1998.
b – Placed on the 15-day disabled list from March 17 – July 20, 2000 with a ruptured ulnar collateral ligament in his right thumb.
c – Placed on the 15-day disabled list from March 23 – May 7, 2001 with a stress fracture to the fifth metatarsal in his right foot.
d – Placed on the 15-day disabled list from August 19 – September 14, 2002 with a right acute bone bruise.
e – Placed on the 15-day disabled list from March 21 –April 9, 2003 with a sore right elbow.
f – Placed on the 15-day disabled list on April 26, 2003 with a sore right elbow…was transferred to the 60-day disabled list on May 6, 2003 and reinstated on November 19, 2003.
g – Placed on the 15-day disabled list on April 3, 2004 with a sore right elbow…was transferred to the 60-day disabled list on June 2, 2004 and reinstated on June 3, 2004.
h – Signed by Toronto as a free agent on December 6, 2005.
i – Placed on the 15-day disabled list from April 1-14, 2006 with a sore right elbow.
j – Placed on the 15-day disabled list on April 22, 2006 with a sore right elbow…was transferred to the 60-day disabled list on May 29, 2006 and reinstated on June 21, 2006.
k – Placed on the 15-day disabled list from June 13-27, 2007 with a right shoulder strain.
l – Placed on the 15-day disabled list from June 29 – August 28, 2007 with a right shoulder strain.
m – Signed by the Yankees as a free agent on December 18, 2008.

Burnett's Division Series Record

Year	Club vs. Opp.	W	L	ERA	G	GS	CG	SHO	SV	IP	H	R	ER	HR	HP	BB	SO	WP	BK
2009	NYY vs. MIN	0	0	1.50	1	1	0	0	0	6.0	3	1	1	0	2	5	6	0	0
Division Series Totals		**0**	**0**	**1.50**	**1**	**1**	**0**	**0**	**0**	**6.0**	**3**	**1**	**1**	**0**	**2**	**5**	**6**	**0**	**0**

Burnett's League Championship Series Record

Year	Club vs. Opp.	W	L	ERA	G	GS	CG	SHO	SV	IP	H	R	ER	HR	HP	BB	SO	WP	BK
2009	NYY vs. LAA	0	0	5.84	2	2	0	0	0	12.1	11	8	8	0	2	5	7	2	0
LCS Totals		**0**	**0**	**5.84**	**2**	**2**	**0**	**0**	**0**	**12.1**	**11**	**8**	**8**	**0**	**2**	**5**	**7**	**2**	**0**

Burnett's World Series Record

Year	Club vs. Opp.	W	L	ERA	G	GS	CG	SHO	SV	IP	H	R	ER	HR	HP	BB	SO	WP	BK
2009	NYY vs. PHI	1	1	7.00	2	2	0	0	0	9.0	8	7	7	1	1	6	11	0	0
World Series Totals		**1**	**1**	**7.00**	**2**	**2**	**0**	**0**	**0**	**9.0**	**8**	**7**	**7**	**1**	**1**	**6**	**11**	**0**	**0**
POSTSEASON TOTALS		**1**	**1**	**5.27**	**5**	**5**	**0**	**0**	**0**	**27.1**	**22**	**16**	**16**	**1**	**5**	**16**	**24**	**2**	**0**

Burnett's Regular Season Batting Record

Year	Team	AVG	G	AB	R	H	2B	3B	HR	RBI	SH	SF	HP	BB	SO	SB	CS
2009	NYY	.200	33	5	0	1	0	0	0	0	0	0	0	0	0	0	0
Major League Totals		**.132**	**248**	**266**	**12**	**35**	**6**	**3**	**3**	**9**	**34**	**0**	**2**	**12**	**126**	**0**	**0**

Burnett's Career Fielding Record

Position	PCT	G	PO	A	E	TC	DP
Pitcher	.923	248	97	179	23	299	10

Robinson Cano
24
Second Baseman
6-0 • 205 • B/T: Left/Right
Opening Day Age: 27

Birthdate
October 22, 1982

Birthplace
San Pedro de Macoris, D.R.

Resides
San Pedro de Macoris, D.R.

M.L. Service
4 years, 153 days

Career Highlights

A.L. All-Star Team
- 2006

A.L. Silver Slugger
- 2006

MLB All-Star Futures Game
- 2003, 2004

Status

- Signed as a non-drafted free agent on January 5, 2001...signed a four-year contract with two one-year club options on February 7, 2008...the contract extends through 2011 with options for 2012 and 2013.

Career Notes

- Has 861 hits as a second baseman since his debut on 5/3/05, most among all Major League second baseman over that span (Philadelphia's Chase Utley ranks second with 845)—credit: *Elias Sports Bureau.*
- In his career, is a .287 (437-for-1,524) batter prior to the All-Star break with 206R, 100 doubles, 9 triples, 35HR and 180RBI in 392 games...in the second half, owns a .329 (438-for-1331) career average with 200R, 99 doubles, 8 triples, 52HR and 214RBI in 342 games...over the last 50 years (since 1960), leads the Majors with a .346 (186-for-537) career BA in September and October (reg. season only/min. 300PA).
- Has played in 597 games at second base over the last four seasons (2006-09), second most in the AL over the span behind Baltimore's Brian Roberts (603)...has played more games at second base for the Yankees (728) than any other left-handed batter in franchise history...his 480 games played since the start of the 2007 season are the second-highest total in the Majors over the span (Adrian Gonzalez-483).
- Over the last four seasons (2006-09), has posted a .984 fielding percentage in each campaign...has combined to handle an American League-high 2,946 chances at second base over the four-year span.
- Collected his 500th career hit in 9/25/07 loss at Tampa Bay (came in his 1,600th AB)...according to the *Elias Sports Bureau*, since Joe DiMaggio reached that milestone in 1938 (1,503AB), the only "homegrown" Yankee to collect 500 hits in fewer at-bats than Cano was Don Mattingly in 1986 (1,549AB).

Single-Game Bests and Streaks

Hits
4 - 3 times
Last: at BOS, 8/21/09

Runs
3 - 6 times
Last: at CWS, 8/2/09

2B
2 - 8 times
Last: vs. NYM, 6/14/09

3B
1 - 12 times
Last: at CWS, 8/2/09

HR
2 - vs. OAK, 4/22/09

RBI
5 - 2 times
Last: vs. TOR, 9/22/07

BB
3 - at HOU, 6/14/08

SO
5 - at LAA, 7/7/07

SB
2 - 2 times
Last: vs. SD, 6/19/08

Hit Streak
18g - 7/25-8/13/07

2009

- Hit .320 (204-for-637) with a team-high 48 doubles, 2 triples, 25HR, 85RBI, 30BB and 5SB in 161 games at 2B with the Yankees...established career highs in runs, hits, doubles, and homers...ranked third in the AL in hits, tied for third in doubles and placed fourth in total bases (331)...had 67 multi-hit games, second-most in the Majors behind Ichiro Suzuki's 73...struck out 63 times, tied for the fifth-fewest K's among American Leaguers with at least 600 plate appearances in 2009.
- Batted .309 (68-for-220) vs. left-handed pitchers and .326 (136-for-417) vs. righties...was the sixth-highest average by a left-handed batter vs. LHP in the AL...his 10HR vs. left-handed pitchers were tied for third-most in the AL among left-handed batters.
- Collected 203H and 25HR as a second baseman, joining Bret Boone (2001) and Alfonso Soriano (2002) as the third second baseman since Rogers Hornsby retired in 1937 to have at least 200H and 25HR in a season as a 2B...over the last 70 years (since 1940), only three other Yankees players have reached those plateaus – Don Mattingly in 1985 and '86, Bernie Williams in 1999 and Soriano in 2002—credit: *Elias Sports Bureau.*

ROBINSON CANO

- Became just the third Yankees second baseman to collect 100R and 200H in the same season, joining Alfonso Soriano in 2002 and Snuffy Stirnweiss in 1944.
- Along with Derek Jeter, became the fifth pair of Yankees teammates (sixth time) each to collect at least 200 hits in the same season, joining Lou Gehrig and Earle Combs (1927), Gehrig and Joe DiMaggio (1936, '37), Bernie Williams and Jeter (1999) and Alfonso Soriano and Williams (2002)...according to *Elias*, became the first set of teammates to reach 200 hits in a season at the shortstop and second base position.
- His 48 doubles tied for fourth on the Yankees all-time single-season list and were the second-most all-time among Yankees 2B (Alfonso Soriano, 51 in 2002).
- Received three seventh-place votes for AL MVP and came in second place in AL Gold Glove balloting...had a season-high 39-game errorless stretch from 6/13-7/29.
- Hit the first unofficial HR in Yankee Stadium history with a second-inning two-run homer in the Yankees' exhibition win on 4/3 vs. the Cubs...played with the Dominican Republic in the 2009 World Baseball Classic prior to the season, going 3-for-13 (.231) with 2R and 1BB in three games.
- Made his fourth career Opening Day roster...batted .366 (34-for-93) with 18R, 5 doubles, 5HR, 16RBI, 6BB and 1SB in April after hitting .151 (16-for-106) with 6R, 3 doubles, 2HR, 7RBI and 7BB in 29 games in April 2008...marked the largest April batting average increase (.215) in the Majors (credit: *Elias Sports Bureau*).
- Established a career high with four runs scored in 4/9 win at Baltimore, going 3-for-4 with 1HR, 2RBI and 1BB...marked the most runs scored in a game by a Yankees second baseman since Jose Vizcaino on 7/25/00 at Baltimore.
- Hit safely in 33-of-34 games from 9/17/08-5/1/09...according to SABR's Trent McCotter, was one of two Yankees over the last 50 years to record a hit in 33-of-34 games with an official AB, joining Derek Jeter (39-of-40 twice, 4/8-5/25/07 and 8/20/06-4/6/07)...hit .400 (56-for-140) with 30R, 11 doubles, 6HR and 28RBI over the span.
- Compiled a career-high-tying and single-season-best 18-game hitting streak from 4/12-5/1...was the longest hitting streak by a Yankee in 2009...batted .363 (29-for-80) with 14R, 5 doubles, 4HR and 14RBI during the stretch...according to *Elias*, was the longest single-season hitting streak by a Yankees second baseman since Bobby Richardson hit safely in 19 straight in 1959.
- Recorded his fourth career multi-HR game – and first since 8/30/07 vs. Boston – in 4/25 loss at Boston, going 3-for-6 with 2R, 1 double and a career-high-tying 5RBI.
- Went a career-high 54 plate appearances without a strikeout from 5/15-28...scored 21 runs and collected 23RBI over a 26-game span from 5/20-6/17.
- Hit .330 (34-for-103) in July after posting a .327 average in July 2008 and a .385 mark in July 2007...according to the *Elias Sports Bureau*, his 109 hits during July over the last three seasons rank second in the Majors over the span behind Shane Victorino (110).
- Snapped an 0-for-22 stretch with runners in scoring position with a two-run, bases-loaded single in the sixth inning of 7/7 win at Minnesota...according to *Elias*, had been the longest hitless stretch with RISP of Cano's career and the longest by a Yankee since Rondell White in 2002 (0-for-28 stretch with RISP).
- Set a career high with his 20th home run of the season in 8/25 loss vs. Texas...hit his first career "walk-off" HR in the 10th inning and was 1-for-5 in 8/28 win vs. Chicago-AL...collected his 42nd double of the season in 9/16 win at Toronto, establishing a career high...hit his second career grand slam and was 2-for-4 with 2R and 1 double in 9/28 win vs. Kansas City.
- Batted .193 (11-for-57) with 5R, 1 double, 2 triples and 6RBI in 15 postseason games, reaching base safely in 11 of the contests.

AL SECOND BASEMEN (2006-09)*

HITS

1.	**ROBINSON CANO**	**707**
2.	Brian Roberts	.698
3.	Placido Polanco	.685
4.	Jose Lopez	.617
5.	Dustin Pedroia	.571

RUNS

1.	Brian Roberts	.403
2.	Ian Kinsler	.364
3.	Placido Polanco	.334
4.	**ROBINSON CANO**	**323**
5.	Dustin Pedroia	.322

DOUBLES

1.	Brian Roberts	.182
2.	**ROBINSON CANO**	**164**
3.	Dustin Pedroia	.141
4.	Ian Kinsler	.122
T5.	Jose Lopez	.118
	Placido Polanco	.118

HOME RUNS

1.	Ian Kinsler	.83
2.	**ROBINSON CANO**	**.70**
3.	Aaron Hill	.58
4.	Jose Lopez	.57
5.	Mark Ellis	.52

RBI

1.	**ROBINSON CANO**	**326**
2.	Jose Lopez	.309
3.	Ian Kinsler	.273
4.	Brian Roberts	.248
5.	Placido Polanco	.246

BATTING AVERAGE (min. 1,000PA)

1.	Placido Polanco	.307 (685-for-2,231)
2.	**ROBINSON CANO**	**.307 (707-for-2,306)**
3.	Dustin Pedroia	.306 (571-for-1,864)
4.	Howie Kendrick	.305 (341-for-1,117)
5.	Mark Grudzielanek	.302 (398-for-1,319)

**as a second baseman*

2008

- Hit .271 (162-for-597) with 35 doubles, 3 triples, 14HR and 72RBI in 159 games with the Yankees (154 starts at 2B)...batted .292 (50-for-171, 5HR) vs. left-handed pitchers and .263 (112-for-426, 9HR) vs. righties...was the seventh-highest average by a left-handed batter vs. left-handed pitching in the AL.
- Ranked fifth among AL second basemen with 13HR while playing the position...all but two of his 14 overall homers were solo.
- Struck out 65 times, tied with Ichiro Suzuki for the fourth-fewest K's among American Leaguers with at least 600 plate appearances.
- Hit .246 (85-for-346) with 6HR and 38RBI in 93 games prior to the All-Star break...in 66 games following the break, batted .307 (77-for-251) with 8HR and 34RBI.
- Batted .347 (114-for-329) with 56R, 27 doubles, 2 triples, 11HR and 54RBI in the 87 Yankees wins he played in...hit just .179 (48-for-268) with 14R, 8 doubles, 1 triple, 3HR and 18RBI in the 72 losses he played in...the Yankees were 34-11 when he recorded a multi-hit game.
- Recorded 800 total chances, most among AL second basemen, working to a .984 fielding percentage (13E).
- Made his third career Opening Day roster and was 1-for-3 in 4/1 Opening Day win vs. Toronto.

TOP ROAD BATTING AVERAGES, AL, 2005-09 (min. 750PA)

1.	Joe Mauer	.328 (417-for-1,270)
2.	Vladimir Guerrero	.316 (404-for-1,278)
3.	Ichiro Suzuki	.314 (540-for-1,718)
4.	DEREK JETER	.308 (486-for-1,579)
5.	**ROBINSON CANO**	**.307 (453-for-1,475)**

MOST HITS BY YANKEES 2B, SINGLE SEASON

1.	Alfonso Soriano, 2002	209
	Bobby Richardson, 1962	209
3.	Steve Sax, 1989	205
	Snuffy Stirnweiss, 1944	205
5.	**ROBINSON CANO, 2009**	**204**

- Hit .151 (16-for-106) in April after batting .306 overall in 2007 and .342 overall in 2006...according to the *Elias Sports Bureau*, was the lowest batting average during the month of April by a player coming off two straight .300 seasons (min. 50AB) since Lyman Bostock hit .148 in April 1978 with California (after .336 in 1977 and .323 in 1976 with Minnesota)...was the lowest April average among all AL qualifiers (min. 50PA)...hit at a .297 clip (146-for-491) over the remainder of the season.
- Hit game-winning, pinch-hit HR in the eighth off Al Reyes in 4/14 win at Tampa Bay...was his second career PH home run (also 6/8/05 at Milwaukee)...according to the *Elias Sports Bureau*, became the first Yankee to hit a go-ahead, pinch-hit homer since Tino Martinez on 6/25/01 vs. Cleveland.
- Batted .373 (28-for-75) with 17RBI and 11 multi-hit contests over a 20-game stretch from 6/15-7/8 as the Yankees went 12-8...led the team in hits, average and RBI over the span, raising his season average 35 points from .220 to .255.
- Drove in at least one run in six consecutive games from 6/22-28 (8 total RBI), matching his career-high RBI streak (fifth time)...was part of a stretch in which he recorded at least 1RBI in nine of 11 games from 6/20-7/2 (11RBI total).
- Hit safely in eight straight games following the All-Star Break from 7/18-26, going 18-for-35 (.514) with 3 doubles, 3HR and 10RBI and six consecutive games immediately following the break...according to the *Elias Sports Bureau*, became just the fourth player to collect at least 18H and 10RBI in his team's first eight games after the break, joining Cleveland's Earl Averill in 1936 (18H, 12RBI), Detroit's Walt Dropo in 1952 (19, 11) and San Diego's Tony Gwynn in 1988 (18, 10)...also according to *Elias*, became just the second Major Leaguer to produce multi-hit games in each of his team's first six games after the All-Star break and see his team *win* all six games (also Cincinnati's Wally Berger in 1938).
- Went a career-high 96 consecutive plate appearances without drawing a walk from 8/20-9/18...according to the *Elias Sports Bureau*, was the longest such streak by a Yankee since Alfonso Soriano in 2002 (132PA)...averaged 24.38 PA/BB in 2008, seventh-highest in the AL.
- Tied a career-high with 5RBI (sixth time) in 9/26 win at Boston, going 3-for-5 with 1R, 2 doubles and 1SF...was his most RBI in a game in exactly one year (5RBI, 9/26/07 at Tampa Bay).
- Hit safely in a season-high 11 straight games to close out the season from 9/17-9/28...batted .452 (19-for-42) over the stretch with 5 doubles, 1HR and 11RBI as the Yankees went 9-2...finished the season with 8H in his final 14AB.
- Hit .446 (29-for-65) with 2HR and 19RBI in 20 spring training games, leading the Yankees in batting average, hits and RBI.
- Appeared in 19 games with Estrellas in the Dominican Winter League, batting .267 with 8 doubles, 1HR and 15RBI.

2007

- Hit .306 (189-for-617) with 93R, 41 doubles, 7 triples, 97RBI and 39BB in 160 games with the Yankees...made 157 starts at 2B.
- Was tied (with teammate Derek Jeter) for fourth place in the American League with 61 multi-hit games, tied for sixth with 160 games played, ranked seventh with a .329 batting average at night and 10th with 189 hits, 301 total bases and 617 at-bats...drew more walks in 2007 (39 in 160 games) than he did in his previous two seasons combined (34 walks in 254 games).

- Led all AL second basemen with 97RBI...was the second-highest total by a Yankees second baseman over the last 50 years (Alfonso Soriano drove in 101 runs in 2002).
- Batted .328 (63-for-192) against lefties...was the second-highest average in the Major Leagues for a left-handed batter against left-handed pitching, trailing only Seattle's Ichiro Suzuki (.331).
- Hit .274 (90-for-328) with 40R, 24 doubles, 4 triples, 6HR, 40RBI and 15BB in 85 games prior to the All-Star break...in the second half, hit .343 (99-for-289) with 53R, 17 doubles, 3 triples, 13HR, 57RBI and 24BB in 75 games...his 99 second-half hits were tied for fifth-most in the Majors...after hitting 3HR and driving in 33 runs in his first 79G/305AB of the season (from 4/2-7/2), had 16HR and 64RBI in his last 81G/312AB of the season (from 7/3-9/30).
- Recorded 830 total chances, most among Major League second basemen...was involved in 136 double plays, the most in the Majors by a second baseman since Cleveland's Carlos Baerga in 1992 (138)...recorded 11 assists in 9/12 win at Toronto, the most in one game by a Yankees second baseman since Alfonso Soriano had 11 on 7/9/03 at Cleveland, according to the *Elias Sports Bureau.*
- Made his second straight Opening Day start at second base, going 1-for-4 with 1R in 4/2 win vs. Tampa Bay...batted in the leadoff position for the first time in his career in 4/5 loss vs. Tampa Bay, going 3-for-5 with 1R and 1RBI...including the final 13 games of 2006 and the first five games of 2007, hit safely in a career-high 18 consecutive games.
- Committed a career-high three errors in a game in 5/19 loss at the Mets...following 5/19 game, went a career-best 56 consecutive games from 5/20-7/21 without an error...according to the *Elias Sports Bureau*, it was the longest errorless streak by a Yankees second baseman since Steve Sax in 1991 (71 games from 5/11-8/7/91).
- Collected a single-game career-high three doubles and tied a career high with four hits in 5/30 win at Toronto, going 4-for-4 with 1R and 1RBI...each of his first six career four-hit games came on the road.
- Recorded his first career "walk-off" hit with a 10th-inning single on 7/17 vs. Toronto...had five extra-inning hits in 2007, third-most in the American League.
- Led the Majors with a .385 batting average in July...his 42H were tied for most in the Majors for the month and were the most in any calendar month of his Major League career...was named American League "co-Player of the Week" for the period ending 7/22 (.500, 17-for-34, 8R, 2HR, 9RBI)...was also named AL "co-Player of the Week" for the period ending 8/5 (.478, 11-for-23, 9R, 3HR, 9RBI).
- Led the Yankees with a .333 average (5-for-15) in five games during the Division Series vs. Cleveland...also hit a pair of home runs and drove in three runs.

2006

- In his sophomore season, batted .342 (165-for-482) with 41 doubles, 15HR and 78RBI in 122 games with the Yankees (115 starts at 2B, four at DH).
- Earned his first Silver Slugger Award and was selected to his first American League All-Star Team (was replaced on roster due to injury)...led the AL with a .364 road batting average and a .363 average versus right-handed pitchers, ranked third in overall batting average (.342) and tied for ninth with 41 doubles...led all Major Leaguers with a .339 average as a second baseman.
- His .342 batting average was the third-highest for a Yankee in his second season in the Majors (minimum: 400AB)...according to the *Elias Sports Bureau*, only Joe DiMaggio (.346 in 1937) and Don Mattingly (.343 in 1984) posted higher marks in the season following their rookie year.
- Went a career-long 160AB without a home run from 4/21-6/8 (a 39-game stretch).
- Was placed on the 15-day disabled list from 6/27-8/8 with a strained left hamstring (missed 35 games)...suffered the injury while running out a double in the sixth inning of 6/25 loss vs. Florida (second game of a day-night doubleheader)...made four rehab-assignment starts (three at 2B, one at DH) for Double-A Trenton (8/3-6) and was 7-for-15 with 1R, 2 doubles, 2RBI and 3BB.
- Drove in at least one run in six straight games from 8/15-20 (13RBI total) and had 16RBI over a nine-game span from 8/12-20...hit third in the lineup for the first time in his career in 9/14 win vs. Tampa Bay, going 2-for-4 with 1R, 2 doubles and 3RBI.
- Hit .373 (41-for-110) in the month of September after posting a .381 average in September 2005 (40-for-105), becoming the first player to post averages of .370-or-higher in consecutive Septembers of at least 100AB since Wade Boggs batted over .400 in three straight Septembers from 1984-86...concluded the season with a 13-game hitting streak...according to the *Elias Sports Bureau*, it was the longest hitting streak by a Yankee to conclude a season since Reggie Jackson also hit safely in 13 straight games to end the 1980 season.
- In his final 53 games of the season after being reinstated from the disabled list on 8/8, hit .365 (77-for-211) with 24 doubles, 11HR and 51RBI...the 24 doubles and 51RBI were the most in the Majors over that span...was named American League "Player of the Month" for September, batting .373 (41-for-110) with 15R, 11 doubles, 7HR, 28RBI and reached base safely in 25 of 28 games...hit .133 (2-for-15) in four Division Series games vs. the Detroit Tigers.

ROBINSON CANO

2005

- Finished second behind Oakland's Huston Street in American League "Rookie of the Year" voting...hit .297 (155-for-522) with 14HR and 62RBI in 132 games with the Yankees (130 starts at 2B) after his May recall.
- Led the AL with a .335 road batting average...led AL rookies in batting average, runs (78), hits, doubles (34), multi-hit games (47) and total bases (239)...ranked second with 52 extra-base hits and a .534 slugging percentage, fourth in RBI and fifth in HR...his 34 doubles ranked second on the team behind Hideki Matsui's 45.

- Began the season with Triple-A Columbus and batted .333 (36-for-108) with 8 doubles, 3 triples, 4HR and a club-high 24RBI in 24 games...hit safely in 21 of his contests with the Clippers...was recalled from Triple-A Columbus on 5/3 and made his Major League debut that night at Tampa Bay, starting at 2B and going 0-for-3.
- Became the 19th second baseman to start alongside Derek Jeter with the Yankees...was 2-for-4 in 5/4 loss at Tampa Bay, recording his first Major League hit with a third-inning single...doubled in five straight games from 5/10-16, the longest such streak by a Yankee since Raul Mondesi did it in five straight games from 4/1-6/03...went 15-for-27 (.556) in eight games after snapping an 0-for-18 stretch with a third-inning single in 5/10 win vs. Seattle.
- Established a single-game career high with four hits in 5/15 win at Oakland, going 4-for-5 with 1 double and 1RBI...hit his first career home run—a solo-homer in the eighth—in 5/24 win vs. Detroit...hit two-run, pinch-hit HR in seventh inning of 6/8 win at Milwaukee, the first pinch-hit HR of his career.

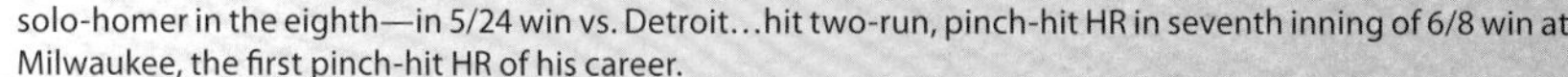

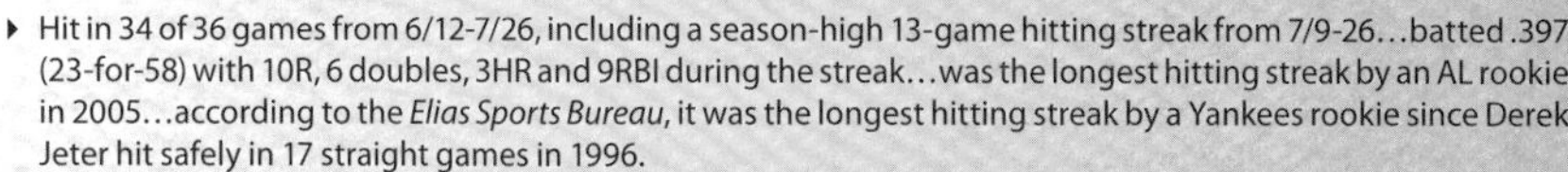

- Hit in 34 of 36 games from 6/12-7/26, including a season-high 13-game hitting streak from 7/9-26...batted .397 (23-for-58) with 10R, 6 doubles, 3HR and 9RBI during the streak...was the longest hitting streak by an AL rookie in 2005...according to the *Elias Sports Bureau*, it was the longest hitting streak by a Yankees rookie since Derek Jeter hit safely in 17 straight games in 1996.
- Had 20-game road hitting streak from 6/27-8/5, the longest such streak in the Majors in 2005 and the longest in the Majors since teammate Derek Jeter hit in 26 straight road games in 2003...was also the longest road hitting streak by a rookie since Ichiro Suzuki hit safely in 25 straight road games in 2001 (credit: *Elias Sports Bureau*).
- Established single-game career high with 5RBI in 9/15 win at Tampa Bay, going 3-for-5 with 3R, 1 double, 1 triple and game-tying, sixth-inning grand slam—the first of his Major League career (off Seth McClung)...drove in 12 runs in a three-game span from 9/14-16, going 7-for-15 with 7R, 2 doubles, 1 triple, and 3HR...recorded his first career multi-homer game in 9/16 win at Toronto with three-run HR and two-run HR and equaled single-game career highs with 3R and 5RBI (for second straight game)...homered in consecutive games (9/15-16) for the first time in his career and—according to the *Elias Sports Bureau*—became only the second rookie in the last 40 years to collect at least 5RBI in each of two consecutive games (also Brian Daubach with Boston in 1999).
- Was named the AL's "co-Player of the Week" for the period ending 9/18 after batting .429 (12-for-28) with a league-leading 13RBI and 9R...also had eight extra-base hits, including 3HR, 4 doubles and 1 triple while leading the Majors with 27TB...was the first rookie to win the honor since Hideki Matsui (6/29/03).
- Was named AL "Rookie of the Month" for September, batting .381 (40-for-105) with 22R, 9 doubles, 2 triples, 5HR and 16RBI...hit safely in 23 of 27 games played in the month.
- Hit .263 (5-for-19) in five Division Series games vs. the Angels with a team-leading 5RBI...delivered three-run double in his first postseason at-bat in Game 1.

2004

- Split the season between Double-A Trenton and Triple-A Columbus, batting a combined .283 (144-for-508) with 29 doubles, 10 triples, 13HR and 74RBI in 135 games...began the season with Trenton, batting .301 (88-for-292) with 7HR and 44RBI in 74 games...played all but four games at second base for the Thunder...hit "walk-off" homer in 6-4 win over Erie on 4/10...at time of promotion to Columbus, was tied for Eastern League lead in triples (8), ranked third in hits (88), tied for sixth in doubles (20) and was tied for 10th in RBI (44).

- Reached base in 22 consecutive games from 4/16-5/9...hit safely in 23 of last 31 games with Trenton...was promoted to Columbus on 6/28 and went 4-for-4 with 1 double and 3RBI in his Clippers debut...in 61 games with the Clippers, hit .259 (56-for-216) with 6HR and 30RBI...went 13-for-32 (.406) with 1HR and 6RBI in first 10 games with Columbus...also went 6-for-11 (.545) with 2RBI in three playoff games...appeared in the 2004 All-Star Futures Game in Houston, going 0-for-2...was ranked the No. 2 prospect in the Yankees organization by *Baseball America.*

2003

- Began the season at Single-A Tampa, batting .276 (101-for-366) with 5HR and 50RBI in 90 games...on Opening Day with Tampa, went 5-for-5 with 3R and 3RBI at Lakeland...opened the season with an 11-game hitting streak from 4/3-13...was promoted to Double-A Trenton on 7/19 and hit .280 (46-for-164) with 1HR and 13RBI in 46 games...delivered game-winning RBI single in the 10th inning on 7/21 vs. Reading...was ranked the No. 6 prospect in the Yankees organization by *Baseball America.*

2002

- Hit .276 (131-for-474) with 20 doubles, 9 triples, 14HR and 66RBI in 113 games with Single-A Greensboro...led the Bats in hits, RBI and total bases (211)...was named the starting shortstop on the South Atlantic League All-Star team and was tied for second in the league in triples...played in 22 games for short -season Single-A Staten Island, hitting .276 (24-for-87) with 1HR and 15RBI.

2001

- Spent the majority of his first professional season with the Gulf Coast League Yankees, hitting .230 (46-for-200) with 3HR and 34RBI in 57 games...also played in two games for Staten Island, going 2-for-8.

Personal

- Full name is Robinson Jose Cano...was signed by Carlos Rios...played basketball and baseball at San Pedro Apostol High School in San Pedro de Macoris...father, Jose, was originally signed by the Yankees in 1980 and made his Major League debut with Houston in 1989, pitching in six games.
- Was among 30 finalists for the 2006 Roberto Clemente Award, given annually to the Major League Baseball player who combines outstanding skills on the baseball field with devoted work in the community...on October 23, 2007, received a proclamation from New York City honoring him for his help in the fight against cancer...participated in the Yankees donation of $35,000 in cash, food and supplies to aid in hurricane relief in the Dominican Republic in November 2007...met up with the Yankees delegation and the World Series trophy on 1/7/10 to meet Dominican Republic President Dr. Leonel Fernandez at the National Palace in Santo Domingo.
- Purchased and donated an ambulance for his hometown of San Pedro de Macoris in November 2007...was inspired after a friend perished when he did not receive immediate medical attention from a local ambulance following a motorcycle accident and had to be driven nearly one hour away to Santo Domingo...joined the American Red Cross' National Celebrity Cabinet in 2008...visited with young cancer patients at Hackensack University Medical Center in May 2008...participated in the November 2008 announcement of the alliance formed between MLB, the United States Agency for International Development, the Peace Corps and six Dominican Republic non-profit agencies to use baseball as a catalyst to benefit poorer communities in the D.R.
- Participated in CPR training on 6/5/09 at Chealsea Piers as part of National Cardiopulmonary Resuscitation and Automated External Defibrillator Awareness Week...served a "Principal for a Day" at P.S. 55 in the Bronx on 6/16/09...also held a baseball clinic on Randalls Island in June 2009.
- Wears No. 24 to recognize Jackie Robinson (No. 42) whom he was named after.

ROBINSON CANO

Cano's Career Playing Record

Year	Club	AVG	G	AB	R	H	2B	3B	HR	RBI	SH	SF	HP	BB	SO	SB	CS	E	OBP	SLG
2001	GCL Yankees	.230	57	200	37	46	14	2	3	34	0	2	3	28	27	11	2	11	.330	.365
	Staten Island	.250	2	8	0	2	0	0	0	2	0	0	0	0	2	0	0	1	.250	.250
2002	Greensboro	.276	113	474	67	131	20	9	14	66	0	1	3	29	78	2	1	37	.321	.445
	Staten Island	.276	22	87	11	24	5	1	1	15	1	0	0	4	8	6	1	3	.308	.391
2003	Tampa	.276	90	366	50	101	16	3	5	50	0	3	4	17	49	1	1	13	.313	.377
	Trenton	.280	46	164	21	46	9	1	1	13	2	0	6	9	16	0	0	5	.341	.366
2004	Trenton	.301	74	292	43	88	20	8	7	44	0	4	3	24	40	2	4	12	.356	.497
	Columbus	.259	61	216	22	56	9	2	6	30	3	2	1	18	27	0	1	4	.316	.403
2005	Columbus	.333	24	108	19	36	8	3	4	24	0	0	0	6	13	0	0	4	.368	.574
	YANKEES	.297	132	522	78	155	34	4	14	62	7	3	3	16	68	1	3	17	.320	.458
2006	YANKEES - a	.342	122	482	62	165	41	1	15	78	1	5	2	18	54	5	2	9	.365	.525
	GCL Yankees	.400	1	5	0	2	0	0	0	1	0	0	0	0	0	0	0	0	.400	.400
	Trenton	.500	3	10	1	5	2	0	0	2	0	0	0	3	1	0	0	0	.615	.700
2007	YANKEES	.306	160	617	93	189	41	7	19	97	1	4	8	39	85	4	5	13	.353	.488
2008	YANKEES	.271	159	597	70	162	35	3	14	72	1	5	5	26	65	2	4	13	.305	.410
2009	YANKEES	.320	161	637	103	204	48	2	25	85	0	4	3	30	63	5	7	12	.352	.520
Minor League Totals		**.278**	**493**	**1930**	**271**	**537**	**103**	**29**	**41**	**281**	**6**	**12**	**20**	**138**	**261**	**22**	**10**	**90**	**.331**	**.425**
Major League Totals		**.306**	**734**	**2855**	**406**	**875**	**199**	**17**	**87**	**394**	**10**	**21**	**21**	**129**	**335**	**17**	**21**	**64**	**.339**	**.480**

Signed by the Yankees as a non-drafted free agent on January 5, 2001.

a – Placed on the 15-day disabled list from June 27 – August 8, 2006 with a strained left hamstring.

Cano's Division Series Record

Year	Club vs. Opp.	AVG	G	AB	R	H	2B	3B	HR	RBI	SH	SF	HP	BB	SO	SB	CS	E	OBP	SLG
2005	NYY vs. LAA	.263	5	19	3	5	3	0	0	5	0	0	0	2	4	0	1	2	.333	.421
2006	NYY vs. DET	.133	4	15	0	2	0	0	0	0	0	0	0	0	1	0	0	0	.133	.133
2007	NYY vs. CLE	.333	4	15	3	5	1	0	2	3	0	0	0	1	1	0	1	1	.375	.800
2009	NYY vs. MIN	.167	3	12	1	2	0	0	0	1	0	0	0	0	1	0	0	0	.167	.167
Division Series Totals		**.230**	**16**	**61**	**7**	**14**	**4**	**0**	**2**	**9**	**0**	**0**	**0**	**3**	**7**	**0**	**2**	**3**	**.266**	**.393**

Cano's Championship Series Record

Year	Club vs. Opp.	AVG	G	AB	R	H	2B	3B	HR	RBI	SH	SF	HP	BB	SO	SB	CS	E	OBP	SLG
2009	NYY vs. LAA	.261	6	23	4	6	1	2	0	4	0	0	2	4	3	0	0	2	.414	.478
LCS Totals		**.261**	**6**	**23**	**4**	**6**	**1**	**2**	**0**	**4**	**0**	**0**	**2**	**4**	**3**	**0**	**0**	**2**	**.414**	**.478**

Cano's World Series Record

Year	Club vs. Opp.	AVG	G	AB	R	H	2B	3B	HR	RBI	SH	SF	HP	BB	SO	SB	CS	E	OBP	SLG
2009	NYY vs. PHI	.136	6	22	0	3	0	0	0	1	0	1	0	0	5	0	0	0	.130	.136
World Series Totals		**.136**	**6**	**22**	**0**	**3**	**0**	**0**	**0**	**1**	**0**	**1**	**0**	**0**	**5**	**0**	**0**	**0**	**.130**	**.136**
POSTSEASON TOTALS		**.217**	**28**	**106**	**11**	**23**	**5**	**2**	**2**	**14**	**0**	**1**	**2**	**7**	**15**	**0**	**2**	**5**	**.276**	**.358**

Cano's All-Star Game Record

Year	Club, Site	AVG	G	AB	R	H	2B	3B	HR	RBI	SH	SF	HP	BB	SO	SB	CS	E	OBP	SLG
2006	NYY, Pittsburgh	Did Not Play - Injured																		

Cano's Career Fielding Record

Position	PCT	G	PO	A	E	TC	DP
Second Base	.982	567	1113	1703	52	2868	389

Cano's Career Home Run Chart

MULTI-HOMER GAMES: 4. **TWO-HOMER GAMES:** 4, last on 4/25/09 at Boston. **GRAND SLAMS:** 2, last on 9/28/09 vs. Kansas City (Luke Hochevar). **PINCH-HIT HR:** 2, last on 4/14/08 at Tampa Bay (Al Reyes). **INSIDE-THE-PARK HR:** None. **WALK-OFF HR:** 1, on 8/28/09 vs. Chicago-AL (Randy Williams). **LEADOFF HR:** None.

Francisco Cervelli

29 Catcher
6-1 • 210 • B/T: Right/Right
Opening Day Age: 24

Birthdate
March 6, 1986

Birthplace
Valencia, Venezuela

Resides
Valencia, Venezuela

M.L. Service
113 days

Status

- Signed by the Yankees as a non-drafted free agent on March 1, 2003...signed through the 2010 season.

Career Notes

- Has been named the organization's "Best Defensive Catcher" by *Baseball America* in each of the last four seasons (2006-09).

2009

- Hit .298 (28-for-94) with 13R, 4 doubles, 1HR and 11RBI in 42 games (25 starts at C) over two stints with the Yankees (5/5-7/8, 9/1-10/4)...threw out 13-of-21 potential base stealers (61.9%)...at the time of his first start at catcher on 5/8, was the third-youngest catcher to start a game in the Majors in 2009 (23 years old)...Pablo Sandoval (Giants, 22) and Lou Marson (Phillies, 22) had each made starts behind the plate as of 5/8/09 (credit: *Elias Sports Bureau*)...the Yankees were 17-8 when he started behind the plate.
- Was recalled from Double-A Trenton on 5/5 when Jorge Posada was placed on the disabled list...made his first appearance of the season in 5/7 loss at Tampa Bay, entering game at catcher in the fifth inning and going 0-for-2.
- Made first start of the season and collected his first Major League hit—a fourth-inning single off Jeremy Guthrie—while calling CC Sabathia's CG shutout in 5/8 win at Baltimore, going 1-for-2 with 1R, 1BB and 1SH...according to the *Elias Sports Bureau*, became the second Yankees catcher to call a complete-game shutout within his first two Major League starts, joining Thurman Munson who did so in his debut on 8/8/69, catching Al Downing's four-hit shutout vs. the Athletics.
- Made his second start in as many days on 5/9 vs. Baltimore, catching Phil Hughes...according the *Elias Sports Bureau*, the Hughes-Cervelli combination was the first for the Yankees prior to September callups with each player under the age of 24 since Steve Kline and Thurman Munson on 6/1/71.
- Hit first Major League home run in 6/24 win at Atlanta, a solo home run off RHP Kris Medlen.
- Was optioned to Triple-A Scranton/Wilkes-Barre on 7/7 when Jose Molina returned from the disabled list...returned to the Yankees on 9/1...in 17 September games (two starts at C), was 7-for-16 (.438) with 3R, 1 double and 2RBI...hit game-winning "walk-off" RBI single with one out in the ninth inning of 9/16 win vs. Toronto...was his only plate appearance after entering the game defensively in the eighth at C...was his first career "walk-off" hit, becoming the eighth different Yankee to collect a "walk-off" hit in 2009.

Single-Game Highs and Streaks

Hits
3 - vs. NYM, 6/14/09
Runs
2 - vs. NYM, 6/14/09
2B
1 - 4 times
Last: vs. KC, 9/28/09
3B
None
HR
1 - at ATL, 6/24/09
RBI
2 - at MIN, 7/7/09
BB
1 - 2 times
Last: at ATL, 6/24/09
SO
2 - 3 times
Last: at NYM, 6/26/09
SB
None
Hit Streak
5g - 9/16-30/09

FRANCISCO CERVELLI

- Began the season with Double-A Trenton, hitting .190 (11-for-58) with 8R, 1 double, 2HR, 7RBI and 6BB in 16 games at C...in 21 games with Scranton/WB, batted .275 (19-for-69) with 7R, 5 doubles, 1HR, 7RBI and 3BB...was placed on the disabled list from 8/4-25 with a left wrist contusion...made two rehab appearances with the GCL Yankees.
- Named to Yankees playoff roster in ALDS and ALCS, appearing in two games and striking out in his only at-bat.
- Played with the Lara Cardinals in the Venezuelan Winter League following the season, batting .214 (3-for-14) with 3R and 1 double in six games...participated in the WBC prior to the season, appearing in three games with Team Italy and going 1-for-7 (.143).

2008

- Appeared in three games (one start at C) with the Yankees, going hitless in five at-bats as a September call-up in his first Major League action...was recalled from Double-A Trenton prior to 9/15 win vs. Chicago-AL...made his Major League debut in 9/18 win vs. Chicago-AL, entering the game as a defensive replacement in the eighth at C (did not bat).
- Was one of three Yankees to make their Major League debut in the 9/18 game (also Juan Miranda and Humberto Sanchez)...according to the *Elias Sports Bureau*, was the first time three different Yankees made their ML debut in the same game since 3/31/03 when Hideki Matsui, Jose Contreras and Jason Anderson each debuted in the Yankees' 8-4 win at Toronto.
- Made his first Major League start (at catcher) in 9/25 loss at Toronto, going 0-for-3 against 20-game winner Roy Halladay...appeared as a defensive replacement in the season's final game on 9/28 at Boston (Game 2), going 0-for-2 in the 11-inning loss.
- Began the season on the minor league disabled list after suffering a broken right wrist in a home plate collision with Tampa Bay's Elliot Johnson on 3/8 at George M. Steinbrenner Field (then Legends Field)...was taken to St. Joseph's Hospital in Tampa for X-rays and had his wrist casted that night.
- Was reinstated from the minor league D.L. on 6/16 and assigned to Single-A Tampa...appeared in three games with Tampa, batting .300 (3-for-10) before suffering a left knee sprain and returning to the D.L.
- Returned to action on 7/30 with the GCL Yankees, appearing in three games (2-for-8, 1 double)...was transferred to Trenton on 8/4 where he batted .315 (23-for-73) with 5 doubles and 8RBI over his final 18 regular season games...also appeared in six postseason games for the Eastern League-champion Thunder, batting .200 (4-for-20) with 1 double and 2RBI...in 27 total minor league games combined at GCL, Tampa and Trenton, batted .308 (28-for-91) with 6 doubles and 9RBI...caught 7-of-14 (50.0%) potential base stealers.
- Played winter ball with the Cardenales de Lara of the Venezuelan Baseball League, batting .267 (16-for-60) with 2 doubles, 1HR and 5RBI in 26 games...caught 7-of-19 (36.8%) potential basestealers.

2007

- Hit .279 (81-for-290) with 34R, 24 doubles, 2 triples, 2HR, 32RBI and 36BB in 89 games with Single-A Tampa...led all Florida State League catchers with a 41.0% caught stealing rate (41-for-100) and a .997 fielding percentage (2E, 743TC)...ranked second with 667 putouts and 74 assists and tied for fourth with 89 games played...tied for first in doubles, ranked third in runs, hits and walks and placed fourth in RBI among all FSL catchers (min. 40G at C).
- Participated in the FSL All-Star Game, entering the game defensively in the seventh at C (was 0-for-1)...was also named to the FSL postseason All-Star team.
- Caught the entire game in a 20-inning loss vs. the Clearwater Threshers on 4/17, recording 24 putouts...fashioned a career-high 10-game hitting streak from 4/27-5/10, batting .500 (16-for-32) with 4 doubles and 4RBI during the span...hit his first career grand slam and recorded a career-high 5RBI in 5/15 win at Dunedin...was placed on the disabled list from 8/10-9/5 with a left knee sprain.
- Played for the Cardenales de Lara of the Venezuelan Baseball League, batting .212 (7-for-33) with 2R, 2 doubles, 10BB and 1SH in 16 games.

2006

- Batted .309 (42-for-306) in 42 games with short season Single-A Staten Island...led the team with a .397OBP and a .426 slugging percentage and ranked second in batting average...posted a .340 batting average at home (18-for-53) and hit .323 vs. right-handed pitchers (30-for-93)...was named to the American League team for the NY-Penn League All-Star Game...helped lead the team to their second consecutive NYPL Championship.

2005

- Played in 24 games for the GCL Yankees, batting .190 (11-for-58) with 1HR and 9RBI...reached base safely (via hit or walk) in 14 of 21 games with an official plate appearance.

FRANCISCO CERVELLI

2004

- In his second season, batted .216 (19-for-88) in 40 games with the DSL Yankees.

2003

- Made his professional debut with the Yankees' Dominican Summer League team, batting .239 (37-for-155) in 52 games.

Cervelli's Career Playing Record

Year	Club	AVG	G	AB	R	H	2B	3B	HR	RBI	SH	SF	HB	BB	SO	SB	CS	E	SLUG	OBP
2003	DSL Yankees 1	.239	52	155	14	37	4	1	0	14	2	0	11	24	25	0	0	-	.379	.277
2004	DSL Yankees 1	.216	40	88	14	19	2	0	1	14	4	4	9	19	18	1	2	-	.392	.273
2005	GCL Yankees	.190	24	58	10	11	2	0	1	9	0	2	2	8	13	1	0	2	.300	.276
2006	Staten Island	.309	42	136	21	42	10	0	2	16	1	0	7	13	30	0	0	7	.397	.426
2007	Tampa	.279	89	290	34	81	24	2	2	32	4	2	16	36	59	4	3	2	.387	.397
2008	Tampa	.300	3	10	2	3	0	0	0	1	0	0	1	0	3	0	0	0	.364	.664
	GCL Yankees	.250	3	8	0	2	1	0	0	0	0	0	0	0	1	0	0	0	.250	.375
	Trenton	.315	21	73	8	23	5	0	0	8	0	0	4	11	14	0	0	1	.432	.384
	YANKEES	.000	3	5	0	0	0	0	0	0	0	0	0	0	3	0	0	0	.000	.000
2009	Trenton	.190	16	58	8	11	1	0	2	7	0	0	0	6	13	0	0	5	.266	.310
	YANKEES	.298	42	94	13	28	4	0	1	11	4	1	0	2	11	0	3	1	.309	.372
	Scranton/WB	.275	21	69	7	19	5	0	1	7	1	1	1	3	13	0	2	3	.311	.391
	GCL Yankees	.167	2	6	1	1	0	0	0	0	0	0	0	1	0	0	0	1	.286	.167
Minor League Totals		**.262**	**313**	**951**	**119**	**249**	**54**	**3**	**9**	**108**	**12**	**9**	**51**	**121**	**189**	**6**	**7**	**21**	**.372**	**.353**
Major League Totals		**.283**	**45**	**99**	**13**	**28**	**4**	**0**	**1**	**11**	**4**	**1**	**0**	**2**	**14**	**0**	**3**	**1**	**.294**	**.354**

Signed by the Yankees as a non-drafted free agent on March 1, 2003.

Cervelli's Division Series Record

Year	Club vs. Opp.	AVG	G	AB	R	H	2B	3B	HR	RBI	SH	SF	HP	BB	SO	SB	CS	E	OBP	SLG
2009	NYY vs. MIN	On Roster - Did Not Appear																		

Cervelli's League Championship Series Record

Year	Club vs. Opp.	AVG	G	AB	R	H	2B	3B	HR	RBI	SH	SF	HP	BB	SO	SB	CS	E	OBP	SLG
2009	NYY vs. LAA	.000	1	1	0	0	0	0	0	0	0	0	0	0	1	0	0	0	.000	.000
LCS Totals		**.000**	**1**	**1**	**0**	**0**	**0**	**0**	**0**	**0**	**0**	**0**	**0**	**0**	**1**	**0**	**0**	**0**	**.000**	**.000**
POSTSEASON TOTALS		**.000**	**1**	**1**	**0**	**0**	**0**	**0**	**0**	**0**	**0**	**0**	**0**	**0**	**1**	**0**	**0**	**0**	**.000**	**.000**

Cervelli's Career Fielding Record

Position	PCT	G	PO	A	E	TC	DP	PB
Catcher	.996	45	218	14	1	233	1	1

Cervelli's Career Home Run Record

MULTI-HOMER GAMES: 0. **GRAND SLAMS:**None. **PINCH-HIT HR:** None. **INSIDE-THE-PARK HR:** None. **WALK-OFF HR:** None. **LEADOFF HR:** None.

Milestone Wins in Franchise History

1 – 4/23/1903 at Washington, 7-2
100 – 6/19/1904 at St. Louis (G1), 4-3
500 – 8/31/1909 at Cleveland (G1), 4-1
1,000 – 9/9/1916 at Philadelphia (G1), 4-1
2,000 – 6/2/1928 at Detroit, 5-2 (10 innings)
3,000 – 8/27/1938 vs. Cleveland (G1), 8-7
4,000 – 6/30/1949 at Boston, 6-3
5,000 – 9/11/1959 vs. Detroit, 9-3
6,000 – 5/8/1971 at Chicago (AL), 2-1 (11 innings)
7,000 – 8/4/1982 vs. Chicago (AL), 6-2
8,000 – 7/21/1994 at California, 11-7
9,000 – 5/17/2005 at Seattle, 6-0
*The Yankees currently have 9,457 all-time wins.

Joba Chamberlain

62

Right-handed Pitcher

6-2 • 230 • B/T: Right/Right

Opening Day Age: 24

Birthdate
September 23, 1985

Birthplace
Lincoln, Neb.

Resides
Lincoln, Neb.

M.L. Service
2 years, 55 days

College
University of Nebraska

Career Highlights
MLB All-Star Futures Game
- 2007

Status

- Selected by the Yankees in Compensation Round A (41st overall) of the 2006 First-Year Player Draft...signed through the 2010 season.

Career Notes

- Over the last two seasons (2008-09), is fourth in the AL, averaging 8.77 K/9.0IP (257.2IP, 251K) among pitchers with at least 250.0IP...has held opponents to 3ER or less in 34 of his 43 career starts including 22 of his 26 career starts of at least 5.0IP.
- Owns an 8-3 record with a 3.09 ERA (119.1IP, 41ER) and a .236 (107-for-453) opponent's BA in 45 career appearances (17 starts) against the AL East...is 7-6 with a 3.99 ERA (162.1IP, 72ER) and a .259 (159-for-613) opponents batting average against the rest of Baseball in his career.

2009

- Was 9-6 with a 4.75 ERA in 32 appearances (31 starts) with the Yankees...the Yankees were 20-11 in his starts, including 15 come-from-behind victories...were 15-4 in his 19 starts at home...opponents batted .274 (167-for-610, 21HR); LH .266 (85-for-319, 11HR), RH .282 (82-for-291, 10HR)...hit an American League-high 12 batters, matching the most HBP by a Yankees pitcher in the 2000s (Randy Johnson, 2005).
- Allowed a total of 21R (19ER) in the first inning of games (30.2IP, 5.58 first-inning ERA)...combined to allow 73R (64ER) over his other 126.2IP (for a 4.55 ERA in the second inning of the game and beyond).
- Was 5-3 with a 4.03 ERA in 13 games (12 starts) on the road...went undefeated in his first nine road starts of 2009, going 5-0 with a 2.78 ERA (55.0IP, 17ER)...went 4-3 with a 5.28 ERA (90.1IP, 53ER) in 19 starts at Yankee Stadium...was the second-highest home ERA in the AL behind Scott Kazmir (5.95).
- Did not record a decision in his first three starts of the year and 11 of his first 17 starts of 2009...according to the *Elias Sports Bureau*, Chamberlain's 10 decisions (7-3) through his first 29 career starts were the fewest in Major League history.
- Struck out a career-high 12 batters in 5/5 loss vs. Boston, including nine on called third strikes...were the most strikeouts in a game by a Yankees pitcher since Mike Mussina on 5/7/03 at Seattle (12K)...marked the most by a Yankee in a home game since Mussina on 9/24/02 vs. Tampa Bay (12K)...became the youngest Yankee to strike out 12-or-more batters since Al Downing on 6/21/64 (Game 2) at Chicago-AL (13K)...allowed the first four batters of the game to score and first five to reach, after which he permitted just one infield single, 2BB and 1HP with all 12K...according to the *Elias Sports Bureau*, only two other pitchers since 1900 struck out 12-or-more batters in a game in which they allowed four-or-more first inning runs (Herb Score in 1959 and Nolan Ryan in 1973).

Single-Game Highs and Streaks

Low hit CG
N/A
IP (start)
8.0 - 2 times
Last: at TB, 7/29/09
IP (relief)
2.0 - 9 times
Last: at LAA, 9/10/08
Hits
9 - 6 times
Last: vs. TEX, 8/25/09
Runs
8 - vs. TOR, 7/5/09
BB
7 - vs. BOS, 8/6/09
SO
12 - vs. BOS, 5/5/09
HR
2 - 4 times
Last: vs. BOS, 9/25/09
Winning Streak
5g - 6/24-8/6/09
Losing Streak
4g - 8/16-9/20/09

- *Elias* also noted that Chamberlain became one of five pitchers to strike out 12-or-more batters while pitching less than 6.0 innings in a game (also Cole Hamels in 2006, Curt Schilling in 1997, Kevin Appier in 1994 and J.R. Richard in 1978).
- Hit a batter in four consecutive starts from 4/24-5/10, matching the longest such streak for a Yankees pitcher in the last 50 years...also Rick Rhoden (1988), David Cone (1998), Orlando Hernandez (2002) and Randy Johnson (2005)-credit: *Elias*.
- Was hit in the right knee with a line drive off the bat of Adam Jones, the second batter of the game, on 5/21 vs. Baltimore (0.2IP, 2H, 1K)...exited the game with a bruised right knee after facing four batters...X-rays taken on-site at Yankee Stadium were negative...did not miss a start.

Chamberlain's 2009 Pitching Lines

Date/Opp	Score	W/L	IP	H	R	ER	HR	BB	K	NP/K	ERA	Left game...
4/12 at KC	4-6	ND	6.0	4	3	1	1	1	5	88/56	1.50	Leading 4-3
4/17 vs. CLE*	6-5	ND	4.2	6	5	5	1	5	4	93/46	5.06	Trailing 5-3
4/24 at BOS	4-5(11)	ND	5.1	**9**	2	1	0	4	2	91/49	3.94	Tied 2-2
4/29 at DET	8-6	W	7.0	3	1	1	0	3	6	88/50	3.13	Leading 8-1
5/5 vs. BOS*	3-7	L	5.2	6	4	4	1	2	**12**	**108**/65	3.77	Trailing 4-3
5/10 at BAL*	5-3	W	6.0	**9**	3	3	1	2	5	104/64	3.89	Leading 5-3
5/16 vs. MIN	6-4(11)	ND	6.0	3	2	2	1	4	6	**108**/66	3.76	Leading 3-2
5/21 vs. BAL	7-4	ND	0.2	2	0	0	0	0	1	14/8	3.70	Tied 0-0
5/26 at TEX	3-7	ND	4.0	4	3	3	1	4	5	84/46	3.97	Trailing 3-1
6/1 at CLE*	5-2	W	**8.0**	4	2	2	1	2	5	106/66	3.71	Leading 5-2
6/7 vs. TB*	4-3	ND	6.0	5	3	3	0	1	4	100/56	3.79	Trailing 3-1
6/12 vs. NYM*	9-8	ND	4.0	1	2	2	0	5	3	100/52	3.84	Leading 3-2
6/18 vs. WAS*	0-3	L	6.0	7	3	3	0	4	6	100/60	3.89	Trailing 3-0
6/24 at ATL*	8-4	W	6.1	7	3	2	1	0	5	99/68	3.81	Leading 4-2
6/30 vs. SEA	8-5	ND	5.1	**9**	3	3	1	3	4	96/55	3.89	Tied 3-3
7/5 vs. TOR	10-8	ND	3.2	**9**	**8**	3	**2**	1	1	86/53	4.04	Trailing 8-4
7/10 at LAA	6-10	ND	4.1	**9**	5	4	1	1	4	94/58	4.25	Tied 5-5
7/19 vs. DET	2-1	W	6.2	3	1	1	1	3	8	107/68	4.05	Leading 2-1
7/24 vs. OAK	8-3	W	7.0	2	1	1	0	3	6	100/56	3.86	Leading 4-1
7/29 at TB*	6-2	W	**8.0**	3	0	0	0	2	5	101/65	3.58	Leading 6-0
8/6 vs. BOS	13-6	W	5.0	6	4	4	**2**	**7**	5	**108**/62	3.73	Leading 11-4
8/11 vs. TOR*	7-5	ND	6.0	5	4	4	1	2	5	103/64	3.85	Trailing 4-3
8/16 at SEA	3-10	L	5.0	7	4	4	0	3	2	90/52	3.98	Trailing 4-3
8/25 vs. TEX	9-10	L	4.0	**9**	7	**7**	0	3	5	96/55	4.34	Trailing 7-5
8/30 vs. CWS	8-3	ND	3.0	4	2	2	0	1	1	35/23	4.38	Leading 3-2
9/4 at TOR	0-6	L	3.0	6	3	2	0	2	2	59/36	4.41	Trailing 3-0
9/9 vs. TB	4-2	ND	3.0	3	2	2	1	1	3	55/36	4.45	Trailing 2-0
9/14 vs. LAA	5-3	ND	4.0	4	1	1	1	0	2	67/41	4.39	Tied 1-1
9/20 at SEA	1-7	L	3.0	6	7	**7**	1	3	2	69/37	4.73	Trailing 7-0
9/25 vs. BOS	9-5	W	6.0	5	3	3	**2**	1	5	86/52	4.72	Leading 8-3
9/30 vs. KC	3-4	ND	3.2	7	3	3	0	4	3	91/52	4.78	Trailing 3-1
*10/4 at TB**	*10-2*	-	*1.0*	*0*	*0*	*0*	*0*	*0*	*1*	*9/7*	*4.75*	----
Totals	**9-6 (16ND)**		**157.1**	**167**	**94**	**83**	**21**	**76**	**133**		**4.75**	

(*) Denotes start following a team loss – **Bold = season highs** – *Italics = relief appearance*

- Tossed a career-high 8.0 innings on 6/1 at Cleveland, recording the win in a 5-2 Yankees victory (4H, 2ER, 2BB, 5K, 1HR).
- Was undefeated in seven consecutive starts from 5/10-6/12, going 2-0 with a 3.89 ERA (34.2IP, 15ER, 18BB, 29K).
- Following his loss on 6/18 vs. Washington, compiled a career-high nine-start undefeated streak from 6/24-8/11, going 5-0 with a 3.78 ERA (52.1IP, 22ER) over the stretch...was one of just three Major Leaguers to win at least five games and go undefeated over the nearly two-month stretch (also Houston's Wandy Rodriguez and the Angels' Jered Weaver).
- Allowed a career-high 8R (3ER) in 3.2IP on 7/5 vs. Toronto (9H, 1BB, 1K, 2HR)...was just the second time in his career he allowed multiple home runs.
- Won his first four starts immediately following the All-Star break, posting a 2.03 ERA (26.2IP, 6ER) and a .156 (14-for-90) opponent's batting average from 7/19-8/6...marked the first time in his career he recorded a win in four straight starts...was 3-0 with a 0.83 ERA over three starts from 7/19-29, allowing just 8H and 2ER in 21.2IP (8BB, 2HP, 1WP, 1BK, 1HR)...became the first Yankees pitcher to limit his opposition to 3H or fewer in three straight starts since Randy Johnson in April 2005.
- Recorded his first win at Yankee Stadium on 7/19 vs. Detroit, striking out eight batters in 6.2IP (3H, 1ER, 3BB, 1HR)...snapped a nine-start winless stretch at Yankee Stadium to begin the season (0-2, 5.36 ERA)...according to the *Elias Sports Bureau*, it marked the most winless starts at home to begin a season for a Yankees pitcher since 1990 when Andy Hawkins was 0-7 in his first 10 home starts and Tim Leary was 0-6 in his first nine home starts at the original Yankee Stadium.
- Matched his career high with 8.0IP and recorded the win on 7/29 at Tampa Bay in a 6-2 Yankees victory (3H, 0R, 2BB, 5K).

JOBA CHAMBERLAIN

- Recorded the win on 8/6 vs. Boston despite issuing a career-high 7BB...was the most walks allowed by a Yankees pitcher who also recorded a victory since David Cone walked seven in a 12-3 Yankees win on 4/9/99 vs. Detroit, according to the *Elias Sports Bureau*...allowed 4ER in 5.0IP (6H, 5K, 2HR).
- Went eight consecutive starts without a win from 8/11-9/20, going 0-4 with a 8.42 ERA (31.0IP, 44H, 29ER, 14BB, 22K, 4HR) over the stretch...allowed a season-high 7ER twice over the span (8/25 vs. Texas and 9/20 at Seattle)...lost consecutive starts for the first time in his career on 8/16 at Seattle and 8/25 vs. Texas.
- Lost his first road start of the season on 8/16 at Seattle and had his career-high nine-start undefeated streak snapped, recording the loss (5.0IP, 7H, 4ER, 3BB, 2K)...marked his first career post-All-Star Break defeat...prior to the loss, had been 8-0 and tied with Pat Darcy (1974-76) as having the most career post-All Star break wins without a defeat since the Midsummer Classic was first played in 1933.
- Set a franchise record by pitching 4.0 innings or less in six consecutive starts from 8/25-9/20, according to the *Elias Sports Bureau*...made his lone relief appearance of the season in the final team game of 2009 on 10/4 at Tampa Bay, tossing 1.0 perfect inning (1K).
- Made 10 relief appearances in the 2009 postseason, going 1-0 with a 2.84 ERA (6.1IP, 9H, 2ER, 1BB, 7K)...earned the win in Game 4 of the World Series, allowing the game-tying run on a solo homer and striking out the side in 1.0IP of relief.

MOST STRIKEOUTS/9.0IP IN THE AL, LAST TWO SEASONS (2008-09)

1. A.J. BURNETT 8.95 (428.1IP, 426K)
2. Zack Greinke 8.86 (431.2IP, 425K)
3. Justin Verlander 8.82 (441.0IP, 432K)
4. **JOBA CHAMBERLAIN .... 8.77 (257.2IP, 251K)**
5. Josh Beckett 8.64 (386.2IP, 371K)

MOST SINGLE-SEASON STRIKEOUTS BY A YANKEES ROOKIE (LAST 50 YEARS)

1. Ron Guidry 176 (1977)
2. Al Downing 171 (1963)
3. Stan Bahnsen 162 (1968)
4. Doc Medich 145 (1973)
5. Orlando Hernandez 131 (1998)
6. **JOBA CHAMBERLAIN .... 118 (2008)**
7. ANDY PETTITTE 114 (1995)
8. Dennis Rasmussen 110 (1984)

2008

- Was 4-3 with a 2.60 ERA in 42 appearances (12 starts) with the Yankees...according to the *Elias Sports Bureau*, became the first Yankee since Roy Sherid in 1929 to start his rookie season with at least 10 relief appearances before a mid-season switch resulting in at least 10 starts.
- Opponents batted .233 (87-for-373, 5HR); LH .247 (46-for-186, 2HR), RH .219 (41-for-187, 3HR)...was 3-1 with a 2.76 ERA as a starter...the Yankees were 8-4 in his starts...in 30 relief appearances, was 1-2 with a 2.31 ERA...as a reliever, retired 25-of-30 first batters faced (83.3%) and prevented 8-of-10 (80%) inherited runners from scoring.
- Began the season in the Yankees bullpen before making the transition to starting pitcher in late May.
- Among AL rookies, ranked first in ERA (2.60), second in strikeouts (118), fourth in opponents batting average (.233) and seventh in innings pitched (100.1)...allowed just 5HR, an average of 0.45HR/9.0IP, the second-lowest among all rookie Major Leaguers with at least 75.0IP (behind the Marlins' Chris Volstad, 0.32HR/9.0IP).
- His strikeout total marked the most by a Yankees rookie in a single season since Orlando Hernandez recorded 131K in 1998...were the third-most in a season by a Yankees pitcher under the age of 23, behind Al Downing's 171 in 1963 and Lefty Gomez's 150 in 1931.
- Made his first appearance of the season in 4/1 Opening Day win vs. Toronto, tossing a scoreless eighth inning (1.0IP, 1BB, 2K)...made his first Opening Day roster...was placed on the bereavement list from 4/14-19 to be with his hospitalized father, Harlan, in Nebraska (missed five team games).
- Allowed a "walk-off" single to Joe Crede to suffer his first Major League loss on 4/23 at Chicago-AL...was his fourth appearance in five games.
- Began the transition from relief pitcher to starter on 5/21 vs. Baltimore, tossing 2.0 scoreless innings (1H, 2BB, 3K)...Manager Joe Girardi announced the move following the game...tossed a relief-appearance career-high 40 pitches on 5/24 vs. Seattle (2.0IP, 1H, 1BB, 2K)...in three "transition" relief appearances, did not allow a run over 5.1IP, holding opponents to 3H and 4BB while striking out eight batters...Girardi announced on 5/30 that Chamberlain would make his first start on 6/3 vs. the Toronto Blue Jays.

- Allowed 1ER in 2.1IP (1H, 2R, 4BB, 3K, 1BK) without recording a decision in his first Major League start on 6/3 vs. Toronto...threw 62 pitches overall, facing 12 total batters and marking the first time he faced more than nine batters in a single game...opposed Roy Halladay and, according to *Elias*, joined Greg Cadaret as the only Yankee to make his first Major League start against a former Cy Young Award winner...Cadaret recorded the loss against Roger Clemens on 7/7/89 at Fenway Park after making over 100 relief appearances for the A's and Yankees.
- At 22 years old, joined Yankees pitchers Phil Hughes (21) and Ian Kennedy (23), as the first trio all age 23 or younger, to start a game in the same season for the Yankees prior to September callups since 1993 (Sterling Hitchcock, Mark Hutton and Sam Militello)...the last Yankees trio to do it as early in the season (prior to 6/4) was Gil Blanco, Al Downing and Mel Stottlemyre in 1965.
- Held opponents to 3ER or less in each of his first 11 Major League starts from 6/3-7/30, becoming the first pitcher to do so since the Marlins' Josh Johnson in 13 straight starts from 2005-06 (credit: *Elias Sports Bureau*)...was the only Yankees pitcher in 2008 to have at least 11 straight starts and allow no more than 3ER in any of them...was the first Yankee to accomplish the feat since Mike Mussina from 4/4-5/31/06 (12 straight starts)...his 2.23 ERA was the lowest for any Yankees pitcher over his first 11 Major League starts since Mel Stottlemyre in 1964 (1.97 ERA).
- Earned his first career win as a starter on 6/25 at Pittsburgh, tossing 6.2 scoreless innings...was his first time holding opponents scoreless in a Major League start...tossed a career-high 114 pitches.
- Had 124K at the time he reached 100.0 career IP on 7/25 at Boston, the most for any Yankees pitcher all time through his first 100.0 innings in the Majors...allowed just 24R in his first 100.0IP, the fewest by a Yankee since Dave Righetti allowed 23 in 1981 (credit: *Elias Sports Bureau*).
- Was removed from 8/4 loss at Texas in the fifth inning with right shoulder stiffness after allowing 8H, 5ER and 2HR in 4.2IP...had an MRI performed on 8/5 and was seen by Dr. James Andrews on 8/6...was diagnosed with rotator cuff tendinitis and placed on the 15-day disabled list on 8/6 (missed 24 team games).
- Was reinstated from the 15-day D.L. on 9/2 and returned to the bullpen...made his 21st relief appearance of the season that night at Tampa Bay, allowing 1H and 1BB in 1.1IP.
- Had a 2.38 ERA in 10 relief appearances after returning from the D.L. on 9/2, allowing 11H and 3ER in 11.1IP (14K) without recording a decision.
- Entered the 2008 season ranked by *Baseball America* as the Yankees' top prospect and the top pitching prospect in all of Baseball (third-best overall)...was also rated as having the "Best Fastball," "Best Curveball" and "Best Slider" among all pitchers in the Yankees system.

2007

- Was 2-0 with one save and a 0.38 ERA in 19 relief appearances with the Yankees, allowing only 2R (1ER) in 24.0IP...the Yankees were 17-2 in games he appeared in...opponents batted .145 (12-for-83, 1HR); LH .132 (5-for-38, 0HR), RH .156 (7-for-45, 1HR)...retired 16-of-19 first batters faced (84.2%) holding them to a .111 batting average (2-for-18, 1BB).
- Struck out 34 batters in 24.0IP, averaging 12.75 strikeouts per 9.0IP while issuing just 6BB...was the fourth-highest K/9.0IP ratio among Major League relievers with at least 20.0IP...struck out 24 of the 47 batters he recorded a first-pitch strike against (51.1%).
- Pitched more than 1.0 inning in eight of his 19 appearances...appeared in consecutive games four times...appeared in games on consecutive days just once, on 9/26 and 9/27 at Tampa Bay, tossing 1.0 scoreless inning in each appearance.
- Did not allow a run in his first 15.1 Major League innings...according to the *Elias Sports Bureau*, it was the second longest scoreless-inning streak for any pitcher in Yankees franchise history beginning his Major League career behind Slow Joe Doyle, who went 18.0 innings before allowing his first career run in 1906.
- Made his Major League debut in 8/7 win at Toronto, closing out the game with 2.0 scoreless innings (1H, 2BB, 2K)...was signed to a Major League contract and added to the roster from Triple-A Scranton/Wilkes-Barre prior to the game.
- In 8/30 win vs. Boston, allowed 1H and 1BB in 1.1IP before being ejected in the ninth inning by HP Umpire Angel Hernandez...was suspended for two games (8/31-9/1) by Major League Baseball.
- Earned his first Major League win on 9/5 vs. Seattle, tossing a perfect seventh inning (1.0IP)...became the ninth Yankees pitcher to record his first Major League win in 2007, further extending the club record (previous six, done in 1946).
- Allowed one unearned run in 1.2IP on 9/12 at Toronto, snapping his streak of 15.1 scoreless innings to begin his Major League career...allowed solo-HR to Mike Lowell in the eighth on 9/16 at Boston, snapping his streak of 17.0IP without allowing an earned run to begin his Major League career, but still came away with the win.
- Recorded his first career save on 9/23 vs. Toronto, retiring the final four batters (3K) on his 22nd birthday...according to the *Elias Sports Bureau*, he became the third pitcher to earn his first Major League save on his birthday (also Kansas City's D.J. Carrasco and the Mets' Grant Roberts, both in 2003).

- Made two appearances in the Division Series vs. Cleveland, posting a 4.91 ERA with no decisions...made his postseason debut in the seventh inning of Game 2 loss at Cleveland, recording the final two outs of the inning, inheriting two runners (none scored)...while taking the mound for the eighth, small flies known as "midges" descended on the field, congregating most densely above the pitcher's mound...did not allow a hit while completing the inning, but surrendered the tying run on 2BB, 2WP and 1HP...in Game 3 win vs. Cleveland, allowed 1ER in 2.0IP...joined Ross Ohlendorf as the first pair of teammates in Baseball history to pitch in the postseason less than two months after each made their Major League debuts (credit: *Elias Sports Bureau*).
- Combined to make 18 appearances (15 starts) with Single-A Tampa, Double-A Trenton and Scranton/WB, going 9-2 with a 2.45 ERA while registering 135K in 88.1IP...in 15 minor league starts, went 9-2 with a 2.56 ERA...in three relief appearances, tossed 4.0 scoreless innings (1H, 0BB, 10K).
- Was named to the U.S. team for the 2007 Futures Game, played on 7/8 in San Francisco...in the game, allowed 1ER on 1H and 1BB in 1.0IP (1K) in relief.
- Did not allow a run in three appearances (1GS) with Scranton/Wilkes-Barre, going 1-0 with 1BB and 18K in 8.0IP...struck out 10 batters in 5.0 shutout innings in his first and only start for Scranton/WB on 7/25 vs. Louisville.
- Entered the 2007 season ranked by *Baseball America* as the fourth-best prospect in the Yankees organization...also rated as having the "Best Fastball" among all pitchers in the Yankees system.

2006

- Selected by the Yankees in Compensation Round A (41st overall) of the 2006 First-Year Player Draft, becoming the second-highest drafted Native American in baseball history.
- Made professional debut with the West Oahu CaneFires in the Hawaiian Winter League...in nine games (six starts) with West Oahu, was 2-2 with a 2.63 ERA (37.2IP, 28H, 11ER, 3BB, 46K)...ranked second in the league in strikeouts while his ERA was tied for fifth-best in the league.

Personal

- Name is pronounced "Jah-bah"...full name is Justin Louis Chamberlain...the name "Joba" came from a young relative who could not pronounce Justin...signed by Steve Lemke and Tim Kelly...is a decendant of the Winnebago Indian Tribe...has a son, Karter (4).
- Attended Division II Nebraska-Kearney his freshman year (2004), then transferred to the University of Nebraska the next year...was 10-2 with a 2.81 ERA in 2005, establishing team highs in innings pitched (118.2) and strikeouts (130) over 18 starts and helping lead the Cornhuskers to the College World Series...led the Huskers with 102 strikeouts in 2006 and posted a 6-5 record with a 3.93 ERA in 14 starts, allowing 84 hits in 89.1IP...was named a 2006 First-Team Preseason All-American by *Collegiate Baseball* and Second-Team Preseason All-American by the National College Baseball Writers Association...won the 2005 Big 12 "Newcomer Pitcher of the Year" while being named Third-Team All-American by *Collegiate Baseball* and First-team All-Big 12.
- Wears No. 62 because the numbers add up to eight as a tribute to Nate Ruan, a childhood friend who died of brain cancer when Joba was 12 and wore No. 8.
- Spent time with area youth at the Kips Bay Boys & Girls Club in the Bronx in August 2007...handed out Christmas gifts to area youngsters from New York City's Police Athletic League in December 2007...also visited the Department of Pediatrics at Memorial Sloan-Kettering Cancer Center in Manhattan on 12/20/07 as part of their "Yankees Universe" initiative...served as spokesman for MSKCC Yankees Universe campaign in 2008.
- Honored by the New York Chapter of the BBWAA with the Joe DiMaggio "Toast of the Town" Award on 1/27/08...received a 2010 Thurman Munson Award.
- Treated Kristan Martin and his family to a trip to Disney World in February 2008...repeated the charitable endeavour in March 2009 with 11-year-old Jazmin Meyer-King, a student at Clinton Elementary School in Lincoln, Neb...participated in Health Awareness Day at Kips Bay Boys and Girls Club in New York City in April 2008 where he led the kids—along with Yankees Strength and Conditioning Coordinator Dana Cavelea—in a variety of excercises...honored as the Police Athletic League's 2008 "Athlete of the Year"...visited with children at Memorial Sloan-Kettering Cancer Clinic in September 2009...wrapped gifts on 11/17/09 at the New Yorkers for Children benefit for foster children at Madison Square Garden...passed out gifts to disadvantaged children in Winnebago, Neb., in December 2009.
- Donated himself to the Third Annual "ALS in the Heartland" Bachelor/Bachelorette Charity Auction in Omaha, Neb., on 1/23/09.

JOBA CHAMBERLAIN

Chamberlain's Career Pitching Record

Year	Club	W	L	ERA	G	GS	CG	SHO	SV	IP	H	R	ER	HR	HP	BB	SO	WP	BK
2007	Tampa	4	0	2.03	7	7	0	0	0	40.0	25	10	9	0	1	11	51	2	0
	Trenton	4	2	3.35	8	7	0	0	0	40.1	32	15	15	4	2	15	66	3	0
	Scranton/WB	1	0	0.00	3	1	0	0	0	8.0	5	0	0	0	0	1	18	1	0
	YANKEES	2	0	0.38	19	0	0	0	1	24.0	12	2	1	1	1	6	34	1	0
2008	YANKEES - a	4	3	2.60	42	12	0	0	0	100.1	87	32	29	5	2	39	118	4	2
2009	YANKEES	9	6	4.75	32	31	0	0	0	157.1	167	94	83	21	12	76	133	5	2
Minor League Totals		**9**	**2**	**2.45**	**18**	**15**	**0**	**0**	**0**	**88.1**	**62**	**25**	**24**	**4**	**3**	**27**	**135**	**6**	**0**
Major League Totals		**15**	**9**	**3.61**	**93**	**43**	**0**	**0**	**1**	**281.2**	**266**	**128**	**113**	**27**	**15**	**121**	**285**	**10**	**4**

Selected by the Yankees in Compensation Round A (41st overall) of the 2006 First-Year Player Draft

a – Placed on the 15-day disabled list from August 6 – September 2, 2008 with right shoulder tendinitis.

Chamberlain's Division Series Pitching Record

Year	Club vs. Opp.	W	L	ERA	G	GS	CG	SHO	SV	IP	H	R	ER	HR	HP	BB	SO	WP	BK
2007	NYY vs. CLE	0	0	4.91	2	0	0	0	0	3.2	3	2	2	0	1	3	4	2	0
2009	NYY vs. MIN	0	0	0.00	3	0	0	0	0	1.2	2	0	0	0	0	0	1	0	0
Division Series Totals		**0**	**0**	**3.37**	**5**	**0**	**0**	**0**	**0**	**5.1**	**5**	**2**	**2**	**0**	**1**	**3**	**5**	**2**	**0**

Chamberlain's League Championship Series Record

Year	Club vs. Opp.	W	L	ERA	G	GS	CG	SHO	SV	IP	H	R	ER	HR	HP	BB	SO	WP	BK
2009	NYY vs. LAA	0	0	5.40	4	0	0	0	0	1.2	5	1	1	0	0	0	2	0	0
LCS Totals		**0**	**0**	**5.40**	**4**	**0**	**0**	**0**	**0**	**1.2**	**5**	**1**	**1**	**0**	**0**	**0**	**2**	**0**	**0**

Chamberlain's World Series Record

Year	Club vs. Opp.	W	L	ERA	G	GS	CG	SHO	SV	IP	H	R	ER	HR	HP	BB	SO	WP	BK
2009	NYY vs. PHI	1	0	3.00	3	0	0	0	0	3.0	2	1	1	1	0	1	4	0	0
World Series Totals		**1**	**0**	**3.00**	**3**	**0**	**0**	**0**	**0**	**3.0**	**2**	**1**	**1**	**1**	**0**	**1**	**4**	**0**	**0**
POSTSEASON TOTALS		**1**	**0**	**3.60**	**12**	**0**	**0**	**0**	**0**	**10.0**	**12**	**4**	**4**	**1**	**1**	**4**	**11**	**2**	**0**

Chamberlain's Regular Season Batting Record

Year	Team	AVG	G	AB	R	H	2B	3B	HR	RBI	SH	SF	HP	BB	SO	SB	CS
2009	NYY	.000	31	2	0	0	0	0	0	0	1	0	0	0	0	0	0
Major League Totals		**.000**	**92**	**5**	**0**	**0**	**0**	**0**	**0**	**0**	**2**	**0**	**0**	**1**	**1**	**0**	**0**

Chamberlain's Career Fielding Record

Position	PCT	G	PO	A	E	TC	DP
Pitcher	.964	93	11	42	2	55	5

Futures Game History – All-Time Yankees Roster

"Major League Baseball, in conjunction with the 30 Major League Clubs, MLB.com and Baseball America, select the 25-man rosters for each club, the U.S. Team and the World Team. Each Major League organization is represented and the World Team features players from 11 different countries and territories. Players from all full-season Minor Leagues were eligible to participate. "

Five players currently on the Yankees' 40-man roster have appeared in at least one Future's Game while in the Yankees' minor league system.

2009 .... LHP Manny Banuelos (World)
C Jesus Montero (World)
2008..................... RAMIRO PENA, INF (WORLD)
2007......................JOBA CHAMBERLAIN, P (US)
2006............................ PHIL HUGHES, P (US)
Jose Tabata, CF (World)
2005........................... Melky Cabrera, OF (World)
2004.................. ROBINSON CANO, INF (WORLD)
Dioner Navarro, C (World)
2003................. ROBINSON CANO, INF (WORLD)
Chien-Ming Wang, P (World)
2002................................ Drew Henson, 3B (US)
2001......................... NICK JOHNSON, INF (US)
Juan Rivera, OF (World)
2000 .... Drew Henson, 3B (US)
Jackson Melian, OF (World)
1999......................... NICK JOHNSON, INF (US)
*Alfonso Soriano, INF (World)

*Most Valuable Player

Reegie Corona

76

Infielder

5-11 • 160 • B/T: Switch/Right

Opening Day Age: 23

Birthdate
November 7, 1986

Birthplace
Caracas, Venezuela

Resides
Miranda, Venezuela

M.L. Service
None
(Rookie)

Status

- Signed by the Yankees as a non-drafted free agent on July 2, 2003...signed through the 2010 season.

2009

- Combined to bat .257 (120-for-467) with 69R, 28 doubles, 6HR, 40RBI and 16SB in 129 games with Double-A Trenton and Triple-A Scranton/Wilkes-Barre...named to the Eastern League midseason All-Star team...appeared in 88 games at SS and 41 games at 2B.
- Was promoted to Scranton/WB on 5/14, hitting .147 (10-for-68) with 2 doubles and 1HR before being transferred back to Trenton on 6/4.
- Returned to Triple-A on 8/7 and batted .239 (22-for-92) with 5 doubles and 2HR over the final month of the season...had multiple hits in four of his last eight games of the regular season.
- Appeared in all seven postseason games for the International League runner-ups, batting .292 (7-for-24) with 3R, 3 doubles and 6BB...started six games at 2B and two games at SS.
- Tabbed by *Baseball America* as having the "Best Strikezone Discipline."
- Played with Magallanes in the Venzuelan Winter League, batting .317 (44-for-139) with 36R, 17 doubles, 2HR, 18RBI, 28BB and 19K in 44 games, playing primarily 2B...led the league in doubles.

2008

- Spent the entire season with Trenton, batting .274 (125-for-457) with 72R, 27 doubles, 3 triples, 3HR, 39RBI and 24SB in 129 games...made 99 starts at 2B and 30 at SS...tied for fourth in the Eastern League and ranked third in the Yankees organization in stolen bases...led all EL second basemen with a .994 fielding percentage (3E, 477TC).
- Hit .317 (44-for-139) with 15 extra base hits as a right-handed batter, compared to .255 (81-for-318) from the left side of the plate.
- Hit safely in 17 of his final 20 games from 8/12 through the end of the season, batting .387 (29-for-75) to raise his season batting average from .251 to .274...scored 5R in seven playoff games for the Eastern League champions, batting .148 (4-for-27) with 4RBI in the postseason.

2007

- Combined to hit .258 with 75R, 23 doubles, 3 triples, 3HR, 43RBI and 29SB in 135 games with Single-A Tampa and Trenton.
- Led Tampa in stolen bases (22), getting caught just once in his first 19 attempts...led the FSL in walks (51) and was the top-fielding shortstop in the Florida State League (.942, 27E, 466TC)...was the starting shortstop in the midseason FSL All-Star Game on 6/16 in Daytona.
- Was transferred from Tampa to Trenton on 7/30...hit safely in his first nine games at the Double-A level, compiling an 11-game hitting streak from 7/26-8/8 in games with both clubs...batted .290 (9-for-31) with a team-high 6R, 2 doubles, 2RBI and 2SB in eight postseason games for the Eastern League champions as the team's starting shortstop.
- Played for the Peoria Javelinas of the Arizona Fall League, batting .188 with 7R, 3 doubles, 1HR and 8RBI in 14 games.

REEGIE CORONA

2006

- Played in 105 games with Single-A Charleston and Tampa, batting a combined .293 for the fourth-highest average among all Yankees minor leaguers...spent majority of the season with Charleston, batting .292 with 13 doubles, 2 triples, 3HR and 26SB in 96 games (51 at 2B, 25 at SS, 10 at 3B, six in the OF and one at 1B)...ranked third among all South Atlantic League hitters with a strikeout ratio of just one per 8.93 plate appearances (45K)...batted everywhere in the lineup except cleanup.
- Homered twice and drove in all three RiverDogs runs in a 3-1 win vs. Savannah on 4/27...marked his first professional home runs...recorded six hits in an 18-inning game vs. Rome on 5/20...was on the disabled list from 5/24-6/14 with a left shoulder strain...returned from the D.L. and posted a .385 (20-for-52) batting average in 14 games during the month of June...was selected to the South Atlantic League midseason All-Star team, but did not play.
- Closed out the season with Tampa, hitting safely in eight of his nine games.

2005

- Spent majority of the season with short-season Single-A Staten Island, batting .227 with 20RBI in 72 games for the NY-Penn League champions...recorded the game-winning single in the final game of the League Championship Series...posted a 15-game hitting streak from 7/17-31, the longest streak by an SI Yankee in 2005.
- Led all NY-Penn League second basemen with a .981 fielding percentage (7E, 369TC)...also paced league second basemen in games (67), total chances, putouts (157), assists (205) and double plays (49).
- Appeared in three games for Single-A Tampa before joining Staten Island, going hitless in 12AB.

2004

- Spent his first professional season with the Gulf Coast Yankees, batting .261 in 36 games...was 4-for-4 with 3 doubles in his 13th career game on 7/9 vs. the GCL Tigers.

Corona's Career Batting Record

YEAR	CLUB	AVG	G	AB	R	H	2B	3B	HR	RBI	SH	SF	HP	BB	SO	SB	CS	E	OBP	SLG
2004	GCL Yankees	.261	36	92	12	24	5	0	0	4	2	0	0	5	13	8	2	6	.299	.315
2005	Tampa	.000	3	12	1	0	0	0	0	0	0	0	0	2	3	0	0	0	.143	.000
	Staten Island	.227	72	255	32	58	11	0	0	20	4	2	1	27	32	9	3	8	.302	.271
2006	Charleston	.292	96	359	52	105	13	2	3	40	3	5	5	30	45	26	7	20	.351	.365
	Tampa	.297	9	37	5	11	1	0	1	7	0	1	0	1	5	2	0	3	.308	.405
2007	Tampa	.271	100	395	56	107	17	3	3	37	5	5	4	51	65	22	6	27	.356	.352
	Trenton	.221	35	140	19	31	6	0	0	6	1	2	2	18	30	7	2	10	.315	.264
2008	Trenton	.274	129	457	72	125	27	3	3	39	7	4	1	51	78	24	4	12	.345	.365
2009	Trenton-a,b	.287	85	307	56	88	21	2	3	26	3	1	1	56	50	12	4	8	.397	.397
	Scranton/WB	.200	44	160	13	32	7	0	3	14	3	4	1	9	20	4	0	8	.241	.300
Minor League Totals		**.262**	**609**	**2214**	**318**	**581**	**108**	**10**	**16**	**193**	**28**	**24**	**15**	**250**	**341**	**114**	**28**	**102**	**.338**	**.342**

Signed by the Yankees as a non-drafted free agent on July 2, 2003.

a – Selected by the Mariners in the first round (2nd overall pick) of the 2008 Rule 5 Draft.
b – Returned to the Yankees on April 3, 2009.

Consecutive World Championships

New York Yankees (5)..................1949-1953
New York Yankees (4)..................1936-1939
Oakland A's (3)........................1972-1974
New York Yankees (3)..................1998-2000
Chicago Cubs (2).......................1907-1908
Philadelphia A's (2)....................1910-1911
Boston Red Sox (2)....................1915-1916
New York Giants (2) 1921-1922
New York Yankees (2)..................1927-1928
Philadelphia A's (2)....................1929-1930
New York Yankees (2)..................1961-1962
Cincinnati Reds (2) 1975-1976
New York Yankees (2)..................1977-1978
Toronto Blue Jays (2) 1992-1993

Wilkin De La Rosa

68 **Left-handed Pitcher**

6-0 • 185 • B/T: Left/Left

Opening Day Age: 25

Birthdate
February 21, 1985

Birthplace
El Seibo, D.R.

Resides
Higuey, D.R.

M.L. Service
None
(Rookie)

Status

- Was signed by the Yankees as a non-drafted free agent on November 15, 2001...signed through the 2010 season.

2009

- Was limited to 19 combined starts with Single-A Tampa and Double-A Trenton, going 5-5 with a 3.17 ERA in between three stints on the disabled list...held left-handed hitters to a .161 batting average (20-for-124, 3HR), while righties hit .246 (56-for-228, 8HR).
- Opened the season on the D.L. with left triceps tendinitis...joined Tampa on 4/23 and made three starts, going 1-0 with a 1.29 ERA...did not allow a run in his first 13.0IP of the season.
- Was promoted to Trenton on 5/8, where he went 4-5 with a 3.48 ERA in 16 starts...tossed 6.0 scoreless innings and struck out a career-high-tying nine batters to earn the win in his Double-A debut that night vs. Binghamton (5H, 1BB, 1WP)...returned to the disabled list from 6/17-7/3 with left shoulder inflammation.
- Held opponents scoreless in four of his final eight starts following his return on 7/3 before landing on the D.L. a third time on 8/10 for the remainder of the season with left triceps tendinitis.
- Did not allow a run over his final two starts of the season, combining to toss 13.0 scoreless innings and allow only 4H with 12K.

2008

- Was 9-4 with a 2.11 ERA in 32 combined appearances (11 starts) with Single-A Charleston and Single-A Tampa, ranking fifth in the organization in strikeouts (125)...opponents batted .190 (72-for-378, 2HR); LH .185 (20-for-108, 0HR), RH .193 (52-for-270, 2HR)...started the season in the bullpen and was 3-1 with a 2.74 ERA (49.1IP, 15ER) in 21 relief appearances with Charleston...tossed at least 2.0 innings in 18 of his 21 appearances out of the bullpen...in his 11 starts, went 6-3 with a 1.82 ERA (59.1IP, 12ER), limiting opponents to 2ER or less in each of those games.
- Began the season with Charleston, going 7-3 with a 2.29 ERA and 110K in 29 appearances (eight starts)...tossed a relief-appearance career-high 4.0 innings on 6/5 vs. Rome, allowing 1H and 1BB while striking out five batters...transitioned to the starting rotation on 6/21 and tossed 1.1 scoreless innings vs. Columbus (1H, 1HP, 1K)...established a career-high with 9K in 6.0IP in 7/7 win vs. Lexington...recorded the win in his final appearance with Charleston, tossing a career-high 7.0 scoreless innings on 8/4 at Greenville and allowing just 1H and 1BB (5K).
- Was promoted to Tampa on 8/8 where he made three starts, going 2-1 with a 1.10 ERA...made his first start with Tampa on 8/10 at Clearwater, recording the loss despite allowing just 1ER in 5.1IP...recorded the win on 8/22 vs. Dunedin but was removed from the game after just 5.0IP with a strained right hamstring (4H, 1R, 2BB, 3K)...was subsequently placed on the D.L. from 8/24 through the end of the season.

2007

- Was converted to a pitcher prior to the season...in his first season on the mound, was 1-0 with a 2.63 ERA in 12 relief appearances with the GCL Yankees...struck out 32 batters in 24.0IP...tossed 2.0 innings in each outing...earned his first professional win on 7/21 at the GCL Indians, allowing 1H in 2.0 scoreless IP (4K).

WILKIN DE LA ROSA

2002-2006

- Played in 94 combined games as an outfielder with Single-A Charleston and Staten Island in 2006...began the season with Charleston and batted .220 (13-for-59) in 28 games before being transferred to Staten Island...in 66 games with Staten Island, batted .201 with a team-high 35 walks...also ranked fourth among all NY-Penn League batters in walks.
- Hit .270 (50-for-185) in his first season with the GCL Yankees in 2005, ranking first in the Gulf Coast League in games played (49) and third in at-bats (185).
- Batted .223 with two home runs and 10RBI in 65 games for the Dominican Summer League in 2004...hit .250 in 15 games for the DSL Yankees in 2003...in 2002, his first professional season, batted .202 and recorded a team-high 59 walks in 64 games.

De La Rosa's Career Pitching Record

Year	Club	W	L	ERA	G	GS	CG	SHO	SV	IP	H	R	ER	HR	HP	BB	SO	WP	BK
2007	GCL Yankees	1	0	2.63	12	0	0	0	0	24.0	20	8	7	0	0	11	32	2	0
2008	Charleston	7	3	2.29	29	8	0	0	0	90.1	60	31	23	2	1	39	110	9	2
	Tampa	2	1	1.10	3	3	0	0	0	16.1	12	4	2	0	1	5	15	1	0
2009	Tampa	1	0	1.29	3	3	0	0	0	14.0	9	2	2	0	0	4	17	1	0
	Trenton	4	5	3.48	16	16	0	0	0	82.2	67	37	32	11	2	41	77	4	1
Minor League Totals		**15**	**9**	**2.61**	**63**	**30**	**0**	**0**	**0**	**227.1**	**168**	**82**	**66**	**13**	**4**	**100**	**251**	**17**	**3**

De La Rosa's Career Batting Record

Year	Club	AVG	G	AB	R	H	2B	3B	HR	RBI	SH	SF	HP	BB	SO	SB	CS	E	SLUG	OBP
2002	DSL Yankees	.202	64	218	30	44	12	3	0	19	1	0	8	59	45	4	13	--	.284	.389
2003	DSL Yankees 1	.250	15	52	5	13	1	0	1	9	2	0	1	5	13	1	0	--	.327	.328
2004	DSL Yankees 1	.223	65	202	31	45	7	0	2	10	1	1	8	29	50	5	1	--	.287	.342
2005	GCL Yankees	.270	49	185	32	50	12	2	0	30	0	2	3	21	25	7	2	4	.357	.351
2006	Charleston	.220	28	59	13	13	1	0	0	5	2	1	2	10	24	2	1	1	.237	.347
	Staten Island	.201	66	204	34	41	4	0	0	15	4	0	5	35	62	11	7	3	.221	.332
Minor League Totals		**.224**	**287**	**920**	**145**	**206**	**37**	**5**	**3**	**88**	**10**	**4**	**27**	**159**	**219**	**30**	**24**	**8**	**.285**	**.353**

Signed by the Yankees as a non-drafted free agent on November 15, 2001.

Two Great Sports Brands Unite

LEGENDS

On October 20, 2008, the New York Yankees and Dallas Cowboys, along with Goldman Sachs and Cic Partners, announced the founding of Legends Hospitality Management, LLC. Offering a broad range of sports business services, Legends has the exclusive right to operate concessions, catering and merchandising services at the state-of-the-art Yankees and Cowboys stadiums. Legends places a focus on operating catering, concessions, retail merchandising and other facility management enterprises for major sports and entertainment facilities with the intent to expand beyond the two anchor teams to provide its services to professional and college sports teams and other event facilities worldwide.

Led by Michael Rawlings, former President of Pizza Hut, Inc., Legends is headquartered in Newark, New Jersey, and offers differentiated solutions to create innovative, high-quality stadium experiences for fans. For more information, please visit Legends' website at www.legendshm.com.

Christian Garcia

71 **Right-handed Pitcher**

6-5 • 215 • B/T: Right/Right

Opening Day Age: 24

Birthdate
August 24, 1985

Birthplace
Miami, Fla.

Resides
Miami, Fla.

M.L. Service
None
(Rookie)

Status

- Selected by the Yankees in the third round of the 2004 First-Year Player Draft...signed through the 2010 season.

2009

- Was limited to just five starts with Double-A Trenton, going 2-0 with a 0.71 ERA...allowed only 2ER in 25.1IP with 24K...did not allow a run in his first two starts, combining to toss 9.1 shutout innings.
- Opened the season on the disabled list with right elbow tendinitis...was reinstated on 5/20 and joined Trenton...returned to the D.L. on 6/11 for the remainder of the season with a right elbow strain.

2008

- Combined to go 4-4 with a 4.33 ERA in 14 appearances (13 starts) with Single-A Tampa, the GCL Yankees and Double-A Trenton, striking out 74 batters in just 62.1IP...opponents batted .278 (68-for-245, 5HR); LH .214 (21-for-98, 1HR), RH .320 (47-147, 4HR).
- Began the season on the disabled list with right shoulder inflammation...was reinstated from the D.L. on 5/17 and made the start that day for Tampa at Fort Myers, allowing 6H and 1ER in 4.2IP (2R, 1BB, 1HP, 6K)...in 10 overall starts with Tampa, was 4-2 with a 2.90 ERA, allowing 45H and 16ER in 49.2IP (17BB, 60K).
- Held opponents to 3ER or less in nine of his 10 starts and 2ER or less eight times with Tampa...struck out a season-high 10 batters on 5/22 at Daytona.
- Was placed on the disabled list for the second time in 2008 from 6/9-8/4 with right elbow inflammation...began a rehab assignment with the GCL Yankees on 7/21, making three starts and going 0-2 with a 14.73 ERA (7.1IP, 19H, 12ER, 3HR, 2BB, 4HP, 9K)...was returned from rehab on 7/31 and assigned to Tampa...struck out a season-high-tying 10 batters on 8/26 at Dunedin while tossing a season-high 7.0 innings.
- Was transferred from Tampa to Trenton on 9/1...made one relief appearance with the Thunder, holding Connecticut to 4H and 2ER in 5.1IP (6BB, 5K)...also made one postseason start with the Eastern League champions, allowing 6H and 4ER in 4.0IP on 9/10 at Akron.
- Tabbed as having the "Best Curveball" among Yankees prospects by *Baseball America* following the season.

2007

- Missed the entire 2007 season recovering from right elbow surgery performed on 11/21/06...during rehab, underwent surgery on his right knee on 8/10/07...entered the season ranked as the Yankees' sixth-best prospect by *Baseball America*.

2006

- Split time between the Yankees' Gulf Coast squad and Single-A Charleston, posting a 2-4 combined record with a 4.75 ERA in 12 games (10 starts)...missed the first four months of the season while on the disabled list with a strained oblique muscle...made five starts for West Oahu in the Hawaiian Winter League, posting a 2-0 record with a 3.05 ERA and 23K in 20.0IP...entered the season ranked by *Baseball America* as the Yankees' eighth-best prospect.

CHRISTIAN GARCIA

2005

- Posted a 5-6 record with a 3.91 ERA in 21 games (20 starts) with Single-A Charleston...ranked second on the club with 103K.

2004

- In his first professional season, went 3-4 with a 2.84 ERA in 13 games (six starts) for the Yankees' Gulf Coast squad.

Personal

- Full name is Christian J. Garcia...graduated from Gulliver Preparatory High School in Miami, Fla.

Garcia's Career Pitching Record

Year	Club	W	L	ERA	G	GS	CG	SHO	SV	IP	H	R	ER	HR	HB	BB	SO	WP	BK
2004	GCL Yankees	3	4	2.84	13	6	0	0	0	38.0	26	13	12	1	2	17	47	3	0
2005	Charleston	5	6	3.91	21	20	0	0	0	106.0	102	57	46	3	10	53	103	8	3
2006	GCL Yankees	0	1	9.53	5	3	0	0	0	11.1	15	13	12	1	4	4	15	5	3
	Charleston	2	3	3.46	7	7	0	0	0	41.2	37	19	16	2	1	12	45	3	0
2007	Did Not Pitch – a																		
2008	Tampa	4	2	2.90	10	10	0	0	0	49.2	45	20	16	2	4	17	60	8	0
	GCL Yankees	0	2	14.73	3	3	0	0	0	7.1	19	12	12	3	4	2	9	0	0
	Trenton	0	0	3.38	1	0	0	0	0	5.1	4	2	2	0	0	6	5	0	0
2009	Trenton	2	0	0.71	5	5	0	0	0	25.1	15	3	2	1	1	17	24	1	2
Minor League Totals		**16**	**18**	**3.75**	**67**	**55**	**0**	**0**	**0**	**290.2**	**267**	**143**	**121**	**13**	**26**	**133**	**315**	**28**	**8**

Selected by the Yankees in the third round of the 2004 First-Year Player Draft.

a – Missed the 2007 season recovering from right elbow surgery.

Steinbrenner Field Plays Host to Additional Sporting Events

For the first time in history, four Florida universities will meet at George M. Steinbrenner Field in Tampa, Fla. to compete in "The Florida Four" on March 2, 2010. For this inaugural event, the University of South Florida (USF) and University of Miami (UM) will go head-to-head, while the University of Florida (UF) and Florida State University (FSU) will take on each other. Also in 2010, GMS Field will play host to the Tampa Bay Rowdies in the inaugural season of the United Soccer Federation Second Division.

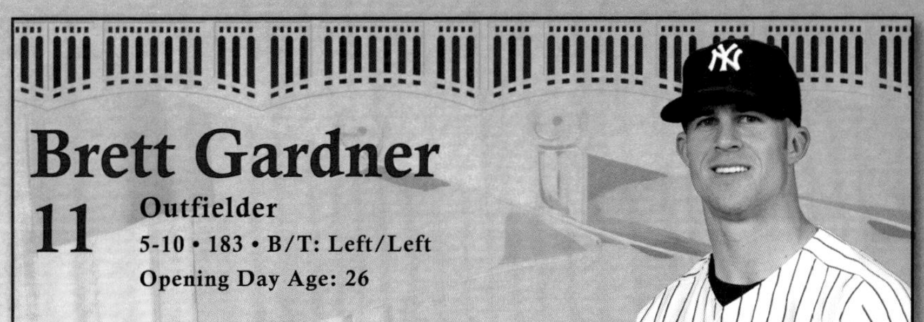

Brett Gardner

11 **Outfielder**

5-10 • 183 • B/T: Left/Left

Opening Day Age: 26

Birthdate
August 24, 1983

Birthplace
Holly Hill, S.C.

Resides
Holly Hill, S.C.

M.L. Service
1 year, 72 days

College
College of Charleston

Status

- Selected by the Yankees in the third round of the 2005 First-Year Player Draft...signed through the 2010 season.

Career Notes

- According to the *Elias Sports Bureau*, became the first player in franchise history to steal as many as 27 bases in his first 30 attempts in the Majors...*Elias* also notes his 30SB within one year of his Major League debut (6/30/08-6/29/09), marked the most for any Yankee since 1920)...has stolen 39 bases in 45 career attempts (86.7%).

2009

- Hit .270 (67-for-248) with 48R, 3HR, 23RBI and 26SB in 108 games (63 starts in CF) with the Yankees...went 26-for-31 in stolen base attempts (83.9%), ranking third among all Major League rookies...became the third Yankees rookie over the last 50 years (since 1960) to steal at least 26 bases in a season, joining Alfonso Soriano (43SB in 2001) and Willie Randolph (37SB in 1976).
- Collected a triple and home run in the same game three times in 2009 (5/13 at Toronto, 5/15 vs. Minnesota and 6/26 at the Mets), becoming the first Yankee to accomplish the feat at least three times in a single season since Hank Bauer in 1957 (also three times)—credit: *Elias Sports Bureau.*
- Made his first career Opening Day roster...started in CF in 4/6 Opening Day loss at Baltimore, going 1-for-3 with 1R and 1SH...went hitless (0-for-4) in his second game of the season on 4/8 at Baltimore, snapping his career-high 11-game hitting streak that dated back to 9/15/08.
- Hit his first Major League home run—a two-run HR in the second inning—and was 2-for-3 with 2R, 1 triple, 3RBI and 1BB in 5/13 win at Toronto...along with Ramiro Pena, became the first pair of Yankees rookies to both hit triples in the same game since 8/31/70, when Thurman Munson and Johnny Ellis did so off Mike Cuellar (credit: *Elias*).
- Hit an inside-the-park solo-HR and was 3-for-3 with 2R and 1 triple on 5/15 vs. Minnesota after entering the game defensively in the fourth in CF when Johnny Damon was ejected...was the first inside-the-park HR by a Yankee since Ricky Ledee on 8/29/99 vs. Seattle...according to *Elias*, became the fifth Yankees rookie since Divisional play began in 1969 to hit an inside-the-park HR (Johnny Ellis-1969, Deion Sanders-1990, Derek Jeter-1996 and Ricky Ledee-1999)...joined Carl Crawford (2005), Brian Giles (2002) and Fred McGriff (1993) as the only players since 1989 to hit an inside-the-park HR and triple in the same contest (credit: *Elias*)...*Elias* also notes that he became just the third Yankee since 1998 to get 3H after entering as a sub (also Lance Johnson, 2000 and Cody Ransom, 2008)
- Missed three games from 5/18-20 with a bruised right shoulder...suffered injury in 5/17 win vs. Minnesota when he was tagged out at the plate by Joe Mauer...saw team physician Dr. Christopher Ahmad and underwent an MRI at NewYork-Presbyterian Hospital on 5/18, revealing a bruised right shoulder.
- Upon his return, reached base safely (via hit, walk or HBP) in 22 straight games with an official plate appearance (including 18 starts) from 5/21-6/26, batting .371 (26-for-70) with 14R, 1 double, 2 triples, 1HR, 5RBI and 9BB.

Single-Game Bests and Streaks

Hits
5 - at NYM, 6/26/09
Runs
3 - 2 times
Last: at NYM, 6/26/09
2B
2 - at TB, 4/14/09
3B
1 - 8 times
Last: vs. OAK, 7/25/09
HR
1 - 3 times
Last: at NYM, 6/26/09
RBI
4 - at BOS, 9/26/08
BB
2 - 5 times
Last: at SEA, 9/20/09
SO
3 - 3 times
Last: vs. KC, 9/29/09
SB
3 - at TEX, 5/26/09
Single-Season Hit Streak
10g - 9/15-28/08
Hit Streak
11g - 9/15/08-4/6/09

BRETT GARDNER

- Stole a career-high three bases in 5/26 loss at Texas, going 3-for-5 with 1R...entered the game in the top of the first in CF, replacing an injured Melky Cabrera...collected three hits in a game that he did not start for the second time in 2009 (also 3-for-3 on 5/15), becoming the first player with two three-hit games off the bench in one season since John Shelby for the 1983 Orioles (credit: *Elias*).
- Hit a solo-HR and was 5-for-6 with 3R, 1 triple, 1HR, 2RBI and 1SB in 6/26 win at the Mets, establishing a career high in hits and tying his career high in runs scored...according to *Elias*, became the first player from either the Yankees or Mets with at least 5H in a Yankees/Mets game during the regular or postseason...*Elias* also notes Gardner became just the third Yankees rookie in franchise history to record at least 5H and 1HR in the same game, joining Joe DiMaggio in 1936 (5H, 1HR) and Shane Spencer in 1998 (5H, 2HR).
- Was placed on the 15-day D.L. on 7/26 with a fractured left thumb...injury occurred while sliding into second base in the first inning in 7/25 loss vs. Oakland...remained in the game and went 1-for-3 with 1 triple...was returned from rehab and reinstated on 9/7 (missed 40 team games).

HIGHEST SB PERCENTAGE IN AL, 2008-09

	Player	Pct.
1.	Ian Kinsler	89.1 (57-for-64)
2.	**BRETT GARDNER**	**86.7 (39-for-45)**
3.	Ichiro Suzuki	84.1 (69-for-82)
4.	Jacoby Ellsbury	83.9 (120-for-143)
5.	Johnny Damon	83.7 (41-for-49)

- In 56 games prior to being placed on the disabled list (5/13-7/25), batted .308 (40-for-130) with 25R, 1 double, 6 triples, 3HR, 16RBI, 17BB and 14SB...hit .214 (15-for-70) with 11R, 0HR and 4RBI in 29 games to start the season (4/6-5/12)...in 23 games after being reinstated from the 15-day D.L., batted .250 (12-for-48) with 12R, 2 doubles, 3RBI and 6SB.
- Appeared in 14 of the Yankees' postseason games, going 2-for-13 with 3R and 1SB...started the final two games (WS Game 5 and 6) in CF when Melky Cabrera was removed from the roster with a hamstring strain.
- Hit .379 (25-for-66) with 12R, 3HR and 7RBI in 27 spring training games, tying for the team lead in stolen bases (5) and ranking second in hits...won the 2009 James P. Dawson Award, given to the most outstanding rookie in Yankees spring training by the New York chapter of the BBWAA.

2008

- Hit .228 (29-for-117) with 5 doubles, 2 triples, 16RBI and 13SB in 42 games (17 starts in CF, 15 starts in LF) over two stints with the Yankees (6/30-7/25; 8/15-9/28)...the Yankees were 15-3 when he batted ninth.
- Was signed to a Major League contract and selected to the 25-man active roster from Triple-A Scranton/Wilkes-Barre on 6/30, making his Major League debut that night in a loss vs. Texas and going 0-for-3 with 1SB as the leadoff hitter...according to the *Elias Sports Bureau*, was the first Yankee to make his Major League debut in the leadoff spot since Roberto Kelly on 7/29/87 vs. Kansas City.
- Stole five bases within his first nine games...according to *Elias*, became just the third Yankee since 1938 to accomplish the feat, joining Mickey Rivers (1976) and Bobby Abreu (2006)...was 8-for-8 before being caught for the first time in 9/15 win vs. Chicago-AL...according to *Elias*, was the first Yankee to begin his Major League career with eight straight successful stolen base attempts since Andy Fox went 8-for-8 in 1996.
- Recorded his first Major League hit—a seventh-inning single off Warner Madrigal—and was 1-for-4 with 2R, 1RBI, 1BB and 1SB in 7/2 win vs. Texas, also recording his first run and RBI.
- Notched his first career multi-hit game and "walk-off" hit in 7/6 win vs. Boston, going 2-for-5 with 1R, 1RBI and 1SB...singled home Robinson Cano from second base for the winning run in the 10th inning (off Jonathan Papelbon)...according to the *Elias Sports Bureau*, became the first Yankee to record a "walk-off" hit in his sixth career game or earlier since Alfonso Soriano (also in his sixth Major League game) in 1999...*Elias* also noted he was the first Yankees rookie to provide a "walk-off" hit vs. Boston since Derek Jeter hit a 10th-inning single off Joe Hudson in a 12-11 Yankees victory on 9/21/96.
- Batted .153 (9-for-59) with 8R, 1 double, 7RBI, 1SF, 2SH and 5SB in 17 games (15 starts in LF, one start in CF) in his first stint with the Yankees before being optioned to Scranton/WB on 7/26...recalled on 8/15 and batted .294 (20-for-68) with 4 doubles, 2 triples, 9RBI and 8SB in 25 starts (16 starts in CF) in his second stint.
- Recorded his first career three-hit game and his second career "walk-off" hit on 8/16 vs. Kansas City, driving in Robinson Cano from second base with two outs in the 13th inning and going 3-for-5 with 1 double, 1RBI and 1BB...became the first Yankees rookie with two "walk-off" hits in one season since Hideki Matsui in 2003 (credit: *Elias*)...*Elias* also noted that he became the first Major Leaguer to record two game-ending RBI within his first 20 career games since Ted Simmons had two in his first seven ML games spanning from 1968-69.
- In 94 overall games with Scranton/Wilkes-Barre, batted .296 (101-for-341) with 68R, 12 doubles, 11 triples, 3HR, 32RBI, 70BB, 11SH and 37SB, while recording 27 multi-hit games...led all Yankees farmhands in stolen bases and tied for fourth in batting average...at the time of his first promotion, led all Triple-A players in triples, stolen bases and sacrifice hits and ranked first in the International League in walks, was second in OBP (.412) and fourth in runs scored.
- Hit the first "walk-off" HR in Scranton/WB Yankees history on 4/23 vs. Buffalo, a solo HR in the bottom of the ninth.
- Was tabbed as having the IL's "Best Strike Zone Judgment" and being the IL's "Best Baserunner" by *Baseball America* following the season...was also named to the publication's Triple-A All-Star team...entered the season ranked by *Baseball America* as the eighth-best prospect in the organization and as the "Fastest Baserunner."

2007

- Hit .281 (108-for-384) with 18 doubles, 8 triples, 1HR, 35RBI and 39SB in 99 combined games with Double-A Trenton and Triple-A Scranton/Wilkes-Barre...led all Yankees minor leaguers in stolen bases and tied for the Thunder team-lead with five triples.
- Began the year at Trenton, batting .300 (61-for-203) with 18SB in 54 games...missed a month of action on the disabled list from 5/5-6/8 with a fractured right hand after being hit by an errant pitch on 5/4 at New Britain.
- Was promoted to Scranton/WB on 7/13 where he hit .260 (47-for-181) and successfully stole a base in 21-of-24 attempts...hit his first professional home run on 8/21 vs. Rochester, leading off the game in a 3-1 loss.

- Following the season, played with the Peoria Javelinas, hitting safely in 24-of-26 contests and leading the Arizona Fall League in stolen bases (16) and runs scored (27) while ranking second in hits (37), tying for third in walks (17), and placing fourth in on-base percentage (.433) and fifth in batting average (.343)...was named to the 2007 Arizona Fall League Top Prospects Team.
- Entered the season ranked as the Yankees' 10th-best prospect by *Baseball America*.

2006

- Hit .298 (134-for-449) with 16 doubles, 8 triples, 35RBI and 58SB in 118 combined games with Single-A Tampa and Double-A Trenton...batted .336 (38-for-113) off left-handed pitchers.
- Ranked second among all Yankees prospects in stolen bases and was tied for second in batting average...was selected to the West Division All-Star Team for the Florida State League.
- With Tampa, reached base safely in 23 straight games from 4/17-5/11, batting .410 with 19R during the streak...also recorded 22 multi-hit games, including three four-hit games...in 55 games with Trenton, batted .272 (59-for-217) and reached base safely in 20 straight games from 6/28-7/22...missed a week of action from 8/3-10 while on the D.L. with a left knee contusion...recorded 18 bunt hits with the Thunder.
- Played in 27 games with Peoria in the Arizona Fall League, batting .250 (27-for-108) with 6SB.

2005

- Batted .284 (80-for-282) with 5HR, 32RBI and 19SB in 73 games with short-season Single-A Staten Island...reached base safely in a team-best 24 straight games from 7/17-8/10...ranked second in the league in at-bats (282), second in runs scored (52), fourth in games (73) and fifth in stolen bases (19)...hit .235 (4-for-17) with 1 double and 2RBI in four postseason games for the New York-Penn League Champions.

Personal

- He and his wife, Jessica, have one son, Hunter Thomas (1)...graduated from the College of Charleston and was the highest-drafted player in the school's history after walking on the baseball team...in his senior year at Charleston, led the Cougars with a .447 batting average (122-for-273)...helped guide the Cougars to a 48-15 regular season record and a berth in the NCAA tournament...played high school football and baseball...gave free haircuts to underprivileged kids at Jordan's Barber Shop in the Bronx on 7/8/08...makes regular visits to ailing children at NewYork-Presbyterian Morgan Stanley Children's Hospital.

Gardner's Career Playing Record

Year	Club	AVG	G	AB	R	H	2B	3B	HR	RBI	SH	SF	HP	BB	SO	SB	CS	E	OBP	SLG
2005	Staten Island	.284	73	282	62	80	9	1	5	32	3	5	6	39	49	19	3	0	.376	.377
2006	Tampa	.323	63	232	46	75	12	5	0	22	1	0	2	43	51	30	7	0	.418	.433
	Trenton	.272	55	217	41	59	4	3	0	13	1	4	2	27	39	28	5	0	.318	.352
2007	Trenton	.300	54	203	43	61	14	5	0	17	1	4	0	33	32	18	4	1	.419	.392
	Scranton/WB	.260	45	181	37	47	4	3	1	9	3	0	2	21	43	21	3	2	.331	.343
2008	Scranton/WB	.296	94	341	68	101	12	11	3	32	11	3	1	70	76	37	9	0	.414	.422
	YANKEES	.228	42	127	18	29	5	2	0	16	3	1	2	8	30	13	1	0	.283	.299
2009	YANKEES - a	.270	108	248	48	67	6	6	3	23	6	1	3	26	40	26	5	2	.345	.379
	Scranton/WB	.091	4	11	3	1	0	0	0	0	0	0	0	5	1	3	0	0	.375	.091
Minor League Totals		**.289**	**386**	**1467**	**300**	**424**	**55**	**28**	**9**	**125**	**20**	**16**	**13**	**238**	**291**	**156**	**31**	**3**	**.389**	**.383**
Major League Totals		**.256**	**150**	**375**	**66**	**96**	**11**	**8**	**3**	**39**	**9**	**2**	**5**	**34**	**70**	**39**	**6**	**2**	**.325**	**.352**

Selected by the Yankees in the third round of the 2005 First-Year Player Draft.
a – Placed on the 15-day disabled list from July 26– September 7, 2009 with a left thumb fracture.

Gardner's Division Series Record

Year	Club vs. Opp.	AVG	G	AB	R	H	2B	3B	HR	RBI	SH	SF	HP	BB	SO	SB	CS	E	OBP	SLG
2009	NYY vs. MIN	---	3	0	0	0	0	0	0	0	0	0	0	0	0	1	0	0	---	---
Division Series Totals		**---**	**3**	**0**	**0**	**0**	**0**	**0**	**0**	**0**	**0**	**0**	**0**	**0**	**0**	**1**	**0**	**0**	**---**	**---**

Gardner's Championship Series Record

Year	Club vs. Opp.	AVG	G	AB	R	H	2B	3B	HR	RBI	SH	SF	HP	BB	SO	SB	CS	E	OBP	SLG
2009	NYY vs. LAA	.667	6	3	2	2	0	0	0	0	1	0	0	0	0	0	2	0	.667	.667
LCS Totals		**.667**	**6**	**3**	**2**	**2**	**0**	**0**	**0**	**0**	**1**	**0**	**0**	**0**	**0**	**0**	**2**	**0**	**.667**	**.667**

Gardner's World Series Record

Year	Club vs. Opp.	AVG	G	AB	R	H	2B	3B	HR	RBI	SH	SF	HP	BB	SO	SB	CS	E	OBP	SLG
2009	NYY vs. PHI	.000	5	10	1	0	0	0	0	0	0	0	0	0	4	0	0	0	.000	.000
World Series Totals		**.000**	**5**	**10**	**1**	**0**	**0**	**0**	**0**	**0**	**0**	**0**	**0**	**0**	**4**	**0**	**0**	**0**	**.000**	**.000**
POSTSEASON TOTALS		**.154**	**14**	**13**	**3**	**2**	**0**	**0**	**0**	**0**	**0**	**0**	**0**	**0**	**4**	**1**	**2**	**0**	**.154**	**.154**

Gardner's Career Fielding Record

Position	PCT	G	PO	A	E	TC	DP
Outfield	.993	137	264	8	2	274	2

Gardner's Career Home Run Chart

MULTI-HOMER GAMES: None. **TWO-HOMER GAMES:** None. **GRAND SLAMS:** None. **PINCH-HIT HR:** None. **INSIDE-THE-PARK HR:** 1, on 5/15/09 vs. Minnesota (Jesse Crain). **WALK-OFF HR:** None. **LEADOFF HR:** None.

Chad Gaudin

41 Right-handed Pitcher

5-10 • 190 • B/T: Right/Right

Opening Day Age: 27

Birthdate
March 24, 1983

Birthplace
River Ridge, La.

Resides
Harahan, La.

M.L. Service
4 years, 163 days

Status

- Acquired by the Yankees from the San Diego Padres in exchange for cash considerations on August 6, 2009...signed through the 2010 season.

Career Notes

- Is 21-28 with a 4.72 ERA (409.2IP, 215ER) in 75 career starts and 13-7 with a 4.00 ERA (186.2IP, 83ER) in 141 relief appearances.

2009

- Combined to go 6-10 with a 4.64 ERA in 31 appearances (25 starts) with the Yankees and Padres in 2009...opponents batted .258 (146-for-565, 14HR); LH .296 (80-for-270, 4HR), RH .224 (66-for-295, 10HR).
- Went 5-10 with a 4.76 ERA (134.1IP, 71ER) as a starter in 2009...made six relief appearances, going 1-0 with a 3.46 ERA and 14K in 13.0IP...allowed three-of-four inherited runners to score...retired four-of-six first batters faced (66.7%)...each relief appearance lasted more than 1.0 inning.
- Allowed just 4HR in 270AB to left-handed hitters...went 77.1IP without surrendering a homer to a left-handed batter between 6/12 and 9/22.
- Averaged 8.49K/9.0IP (147.1IP, 139K), ranking him 15th among Major League pitchers with 100.0-or-more IP...received just 3.60 runs per 9.0IP of support, ranking him 170th of 183 Major League pitchers with 10-or-more starts.
- Did not record a win in a career-long 12 straight starts from 7/3-9/22, going 0-4 with a 4.58 ERA (59.0IP, 30ER)...did not record a decision in his first five starts with the Yankees, allowing just 9ER in 24.1IP (3.33 ERA)...snapped the stretch with his win on 9/28 vs. Kansas City (6.2IP, 2ER)...according to the *Elias Sports Bureau*, became the first pitcher in franchise history to record a no-decision in each of his first five starts with the club winning each game.
- Was acquired by the Yankees from the San Diego Padres on 8/6 in exchange for a player to be named later or cash considerations...was added to the Yankees' 25-man roster prior to 8/9 win vs. Boston.
- Was 2-0 with a 3.43 ERA in 11 appearances (six starts) with the Yankees, who were 8-3 in his appearances (6-0 in his starts)...opponents batted .252 (41-for-163, 7HR); LH .301 (22-for-73, 2HR), RH .211 (19-for-90, 5HR)...held his opponent to 3ER or less in each of his six starts with the Yankees, allowing just 11ER in 31.0IP (3.19 ERA)...earned the win in his Yankees debut on 8/12 vs. Toronto, tossing 2.0 scoreless IP of relief (1H, 1BB, 3K).
- Appeared on the Yankees' postseason roster in all three rounds of the 2009 playoffs...made one appearance in Game 4 of the ALCS at Los Angeles-AL, tossing 1.0 scoreless inning in the Yankees victory.
- Began the season with the Padres, going 4-10 with a 5.13 ERA in 20 games (19 starts), allowing 105H and 60ER in 105.1IP (69R, 56BB, 5HBP, 105K, 7HR)...allowed a career-high-tying 8R – and career-high 8ER – in 6/12 loss at Los Angeles-AL (3.0IP, 10H, 1K, 2HR)...earned NL "co-Player of the Week" honors (with Florida's Hanley Ramirez) for the period ending 6/28, going 2-0 with a 1.20 ERA (15.0IP, 2ER, 20K)...matched his career high with 11K in 6/23 win at Seattle (7.0IP, 4H, 2ER, 1BB, 1HR)...tossed 8.0 shutout innings in 6/28 win at Texas, limiting the Rangers to 1H and 2BB with 9K.

Single-Game Bests and Streaks

Low hit CG
4 - at SEA, 7/28/07

IP (start)
8.0 - 4 times
Last: at TEX, 6/28/09

IP (relief)
5.0 - at BOS, 9/18/03

Hits
10 - 5 times
Last: at LAA, 6/12/09

Runs
8 - 2 times
Last: at LAA, 6/12/09

BB
7 - 2 times
Last: at CHC, 5/14/09

SO
11 - 2 times
Last at SEA, 6/23/09

HR
3 - vs. STL, 6/14/05

Winning Streak
5g - 2 times
Last: 5/8-6/3/07

Losing Streak
5g - 2 times
Last: 7/12-8/7/07

CHAD GAUDIN

- Signed a minor league contract with the Chicago Cubs on 12/12/08 and attended spring training...was released on 4/8...signed with San Diego on 4/12 and made two starts with Triple-A Portland (0-0, 8.2IP, 4H, 0R, 2BB, 10K).

2008

- Combined to go 9-5 with a 4.40 ERA in 50 games (six starts) between Oakland and Chicago-NL.
- Began the season on the disabled list, recovering from offseason hip surgery...joined the A's on 4/8 and made six starts (3-2, 3.75 ERA) before transferring to the bullpen...held opponents scoreless in 14 of his 20 relief appearances...went 5-3 with a 3.59 ERA (62.2IP, 25ER) with the A's before being acquired by the Cubs on 7/8 along with RHP Rich Harden in a six-player deal.
- Went 4-2 with a 6.26 ERA in 24 games with the Cubs, striking out 27 batters in 27.1IP...posted a 2-1 record and a 1.93 ERA (14.0IP, 3ER) in 13 July outings between the A's and Cubs...allowed a career-high (as a reliever) 6ER in 2.0IP on 8/22 vs. Washington.

2007

- In his first full Major League season, went 11-13 with a 4.42 ERA in 34 starts with the A's...tossed at least 6.0 innings in 20 of his 34 starts and allowed two or fewer runs 16 times...Oakland was 18-16 in his starts.
- Prior to the All-Star break, went 8-3 with a 2.88 ERA (109.1IP, 35ER) in 18 starts, ranking fourth in the AL in ERA...in the second half, posted a 3-10 record and a 6.30 ERA (90.0IP, 63ER) over his final 16 starts.
- Went 4-0 with a 2.15 ERA (37.2IP, 9ER) in six May starts, winning a career-high-tying five straight starts from 5/8-6/3...tossed his first career complete-game on 7/28 at Seattle, limiting the Mariners to 4H in a 4-3 win (1BB, 7K)...struck out a career-high and A's season-high 11 batters in 9/30 win vs. Los Angeles-AL.
- Underwent surgery to repair a torn labrum in his left hip and a sesamoidectomy on his right foot on 12/18.

2006

- In his first season with the Athletics, went 4-2 with two saves and a 3.09 ERA in 55 relief appearances, holding opponents to a .222 batting average...stranded 28 of 35 inherited runners...posted a 3.97 ERA (34.0IP, 15ER) with 3HR prior to the All-Star break and a 2.10 ERA (30.0IP, 7ER) with 0HR following the break...had a 1.23 ERA (14.2IP, 2ER) in 16 outings on no rest.
- Was called up for the first time on 4/25 and allowed at least one run in three of four outings before being optioned back to Triple-A Sacramento on 5/4...converted his first Major League save on 5/4 at Cleveland, closing out the final 4.0 innings of a 12-4 A's victory.
- Returned to the Major League club on 5/13 for the remainder of the season...compiled a 20.1-inning scoreless streak over 20 games from 7/13-9/6, marking the longest suck streak in A's franchise history since Rick Honeycutt had a 24.1-inning scoreless stretch in 1995.
- Made three scoreless relief appearances vs. Detroit in the ALCS (3.1IP).

2005

- In his lone season in the Blue Jays organization, went 1-3 with a 13.15 ERA (13.0IP, 19ER) in five appearances (three starts) over two stints (5/29-6/16; 7/15-26).
- Won his Toronto debut on 5/31 at Seattle (5.0IP, 7H, 2ER, 2BB, 6K), becoming the youngest Blue Jay to start and win a game since Brandon Lyon in 2001.
- With Triple-A Syracuse, was 9-8 with a 3.35 ERA, ranking fourth in the International League in ERA...was the Blue Jays' Minor League "Star of the Month" in April and May and earned IL "Pitcher of the Week" for 5/16-22.
- Acquired by the Oakland Athletics on 12/5 in exchange for OF Dustin Majewski.

2004

- Made 26 appearances (four starts) with Tampa Bay, going 1-2 with a 4.85 ERA over three stints...made his first Opening Day roster.
- Went 0-1 with a 4.28 ERA (27.1IP, 13ER) in 22 relief appearances, stranding 19-of-26 inherited runners...went 1-1 with a 5.87 ERA (15.1IP, 10ER) as a starter.
- Earned his first career win as a starter on 6/17 at San Diego (5.0IP, 7H, 1ER, 1BB, 4K).
- Went 1-3 with two saves and a 4.72 ERA in 17 games (seven starts) with Triple-A Durham.
- Following the season, was acquired by Toronto on 12/12 in exchange for C Kevin Cash.

2003

- Rose from Single-A Bakersfield to Tampa Bay, going 2-0 with a 3.60 ERA in 15 games (three starts) in his first Major League action...at 20 years, 4 months, became youngest player in Tampa Bay history and fourth youngest in the Majors that season.
- Made his Major League debut on 8/1 at Kansas City, tossing 2.1 innings of relief (4H, 1ER, 1BB, 3K)...earned his first win on 8/7 vs. Kansas City with 2.0 scoreless innings of relief...made his first big league start on 8/16 at Cleveland (ND, 3.2IP, 6H, 3ER, 3BB, 0K, 1HR).
- Went 7-3 with a 1.81 ERA in 17 combined starts between Single-A Bakersfield and Double-A Orlando to open the season...named Bakersfield's "Pitcher of the Year" and was selected to play in the California League All-Star Game, but did not play due to promotion.
- Made three starts with the Orlando Rays, including the first perfect game in the franchise's history on 7/15 in game one of a doubleheader vs. Jacksonville in his first Double-A start (7.0IP, 0BB, 9K).
- Pitched 2.0 scoreless innings in the Hall of Fame Game on 6/16 at Cooperstown against the Phillies.

CHAD GAUDIN

2002

- In his first professional season, went 4-6 with a 2.26 ERA in 26 games (17 starts) with Single-A Charleston...his ERA led the Tampa Bay organization, ranked second in the South Atlantic League and 10th overall among all minor leaguers...struck out a career-high 12 batters in a 1-0 win on 7/18 at Asheville.

2001

- Selected by Tampa Bay in the 34th round of the First-Year Player Draft, but did not sign until 8/23...pitched for the Rays' instructional league team in September, holding opponents scoreless in 38.0 innings.

Personal

- Last name is pronounced GO-dan...was a *Baseball America* Third Team All-American at Crescent City High School in Metairie, La...earned all-state honors as a junior and senior and was also named MVP of his district both years.

Gaudin's Career Pitching Record

Year	Club	W	L	ERA	G	GS	CG	SHO	SV	IP	H	R	ER	HR	HB	BB	SO	WP	BK
2002	Charleston	4	6	2.26	26	17	0	0	1	119.1	106	43	30	5	11	37	106	4	3
2003	Bakersfield	5	3	2.13	14	14	1	0	0	80.1	62	23	19	2	1	23	70	0	2
	Orlando	2	0	0.47	3	3	1	1	0	19.0	8	1	1	0	0	3	23	0	0
	TAMPA BAY	2	0	3.60	15	3	0	0	0	40.0	37	18	16	4	1	16	23	1	0
2004	Durham	1	3	4.72	17	7	0	0	2	47.2	48	26	25	8	2	176	52	0	1
	TAMPA BAY	1	2	4.85	26	4	0	0	0	42.2	59	27	23	4	4	16	30	0	0
2005	Syracuse-a	9	8	3.35	23	23	2	2	0	150.1	140	61	56	12	8	35	113	5	2
	TORONTO	1	3	13.15	5	3	0	0	0	13.0	31	19	19	6	1	6	12	0	0
2006	Sacramento-b	3	0	0.37	4	4	0	0	0	24.1	14	6	1	0	0	8	26	0	0
	OAKLAND	4	2	3.09	55	0	0	0	2	64.0	51	24	22	3	1	42	36	2	2
2007	OAKLAND	11	13	4.42	34	34	1	0	0	199.1	205	108	98	21	8	100	154	3	1
2008	OAKLAND	5	3	3.59	26	6	0	0	0	62.2	63	29	25	6	3	17	44	2	1
	CHICAGO-NL-c	4	2	6.26	24	0	0	0	0	27.1	29	21	19	5	0	10	27	0	1
2009	Portland-d	0	0	0.00	2	2	0	0	0	8.2	4	0	0	0	0	2	10	1	0
	SAN DIEGO	4	10	5.13	20	19	0	0	0	105.1	105	69	60	7	5	56	105	4	1
	YANKEES-e	2	0	3.43	11	6	0	0	0	42.0	41	16	16	7	3	20	34	3	0
Minor League Totals		**24**	**20**	**2.64**	**89**	**70**	**4**	**3**	**3**	**449.2**	**383**	**160**	**132**	**27**	**22**	**125**	**400**	**10**	**8**
AL Totals		**26**	**23**	**4.33**	**172**	**56**	**1**	**0**	**2**	**463.2**	**487**	**241**	**219**	**51**	**21**	**217**	**333**	**11**	**4**
NL Totals		**8**	**12**	**5.36**	**44**	**19**	**0**	**0**	**0**	**132.2**	**134**	**90**	**79**	**12**	**5**	**66**	**132**	**4**	**2**
Major League Totals		**34**	**35**	**4.50**	**216**	**75**	**1**	**0**	**2**	**596.1**	**621**	**331**	**298**	**63**	**26**	**283**	**465**	**15**	**6**

Selected by Tampa Bay in the 34th round of the 2001 First-Year Player Draft.

a – Acquired by Toronto in exchange for C Kevin Cash on December 12, 2004.
b – Acquired by Oakland in exchange for a player to be named later (OF Dustin Majewski) on December 2, 2005.
c – Acquired by Chicago-NL along with RHP Rich Harden in exchange for LHP Sean Gallagher, C Josh Donaldson, OF Matt Murton and INF Eric Patterson on July 8, 2008.
d – Signed by San Diego as a minor league free agent on April 16, 2009.
e – Acquired by the Yankees in exchange for a player to be named later or cash on August 6, 2009.

Gaudin's Division Series Record

Year	Club vs. Opp.	W	L	ERA	G	GS	CG	SHO	SV	IP	H	R	ER	HR	HP	BB	SO	WP	BK
2006	OAK vs. MIN	On Roster - Did Not Pitch																	
2009	NYY vs. MIN	On Roster - Did Not Pitch																	
Division Series Totals		**Has Not Pitched**																	

Gaudin's League Championship Series Record

Year	Club vs. Opp.	W	L	ERA	G	GS	CG	SHO	SV	IP	H	R	ER	HR	HP	BB	SO	WP	BK
2006	OAK vs. DET	0	0	0.00	3	0	0	0	0	3.1	2	0	0	0	0	3	1	0	0
2009	NYY vs. LAA	0	0	0.00	1	0	0	0	0	1.0	0	0	0	0	0	0	0	0	0
LCS Totals		**0**	**0**	**0.00**	**4**	**0**	**0**	**0**	**0**	**4.1**	**2**	**0**	**0**	**0**	**0**	**3**	**1**	**0**	**0**

Gaudin's World Series Record

Year	Club vs. Opp.	W	L	ERA	G	GS	CG	SHO	SV	IP	H	R	ER	HR	HP	BB	SO	WP	BK
2009	NYY vs. PHI	On Roster - Did Not Pitch																	
World Series Totals		**Has Not Pitched**																	
POSTSEASON TOTALS		**0**	**0**	**0.00**	**4**	**0**	**0**	**0**	**0**	**4.1**	**2**	**0**	**0**	**0**	**0**	**3**	**1**	**0**	**0**

Gaudin's Regular Season Batting Record

Year	Team	AVG	G	AB	R	H	2B	3B	HR	RBI	SH	SF	HP	BB	SO	SB	CS
2009	SD	.036	20	28	0	1	0	0	0	0	1	0	0	1	14	0	0
	NYY	Did Not Bat															
Major League Totals		**.031**	**216**	**32**	**1**	**1**	**0**	**0**	**0**	**0**	**3**	**0**	**0**	**2**	**16**	**0**	**0**

Gaudin's Career Fielding Record

Position	PCT	G	PO	A	E	TC	DP
Pitcher	.920	216	50	65	10	125	4

Greg Golson

27 **Outfielder**

6-0 • 190 • B/T: Right/Right

Opening Day Age: 24

Birthdate
September 17, 1985

Birthplace
Austin, Texas

Resides
Austin, Texas

M.L. Service
34 days
(Rookie)

Status

- Acquired by the Yankees from the Texas Rangers in exchange for minor league infielder Mitch Hilligoss on January 26, 2010...is signed through the 2010 season.

2009

- In his first season with the Texas organization, spent the bulk of his time with Triple-A Oklahoma City, batting .258 with 46R, 17 doubles, 8 triples, 2HR, and 40RBI in 123 games...was 20-for-24 in stolen base attempts...led the team in triples and ranked second in games played.
- Appeared in one game during his one stint with Texas from 5/4-9...lone appearance came in 5/7 loss at Oakland, replacing Marlon Byrd defensively in CF in the bottom of the eighth, then striking out looking in his only Rangers at-bat to lead off the ninth inning...was optioned back to Oklahoma City on 5/9 when Joaquin Arias was added to the roster.
- Was labeled by *Baseball America* as the organization's "Best Athlete," "Fastest Baserunner" and "Best Outfield Arm" entering the season.

2008

- Saw his first Major League action as a September call up with the World Champion Phillies, going hitless in 6AB with 2R and 1SB...was selected from Double-A Reading and signed to a Major League contract on 9/1...made his Major League debut as a pinch-runner for Pat Burrell on 9/3 at Washington, stealing one base...struck out in his first big league at-bat on 9/7 at New York-NL...scored his first run on 9/22 vs. Atlanta...made first and only ML start (CF) in the Phillies' regular season finale on 9/28 vs. Washington, going 0-for-4 with 1R.
- Began the season with Double-A Reading, batting .282 with 64R, 18 doubles, 13HR, and 60RBI in 106 games...went 23-for-28 in steal attempts...set career-highs in walks (34), on-base percentage (.333), and slugging percentage (.434) and tied for sixth in the league in stolen bases...named to the Eastern League's midseason All-Star team.
- Was on the disabled list from 6/18-7/10 with a sprained left wrist, suffered while swinging on 6/13...had a .329 (70-for-213) average through the end of May...in his final 44 games after the wrist injury, batted .257 (45-for-175).
- Was a finalist for the U.S. Olympic team that played in Beijing...played for the U.S. squad in the 2008 MLB Futures Game on 7/13 at the original Yankee Stadium, going 0-for-2 after pinch-hitting and remaining in the game in LF.
- Was acquired by the Rangers on 11/20/08 in exchange for 2005 first-round pick OF John Mayberry, Jr.

2007

- Appeared in 136 combined games with Single-A Clearwater and Double-A Reading, batting .273 (156-for-571) with 86R, 32 doubles, a career-high 15HR and 68RBI...also stole 30 bases in 38 attempts.
- Began the year at Clearwater, where he led the club in doubles (27) and stolen bases (25), finishing eighth in the Florida State League in steals...was promoted to Reading on 7/26 where he finished out the season.
- Played for the Peoria Saguaros in Arizona Fall League following the season.

2006

- Combined to hit .233 (127-for-546) with 87R, 26 doubles, 13HR, 48RBI and 30SB in 133 games with Single-A Lakewood and Single-A Clearwater.
- Named the organization's June "Player of the Month" before being promoted to Clearwater on 7/20...hit for the cycle on 8/28 vs. Ft. Myers.
- Following the season, tabbed by *Baseball America* as the Phillies' 10th-best prospect.

2005

- Batted .264 with 51R, 19 doubles, 8 triples, 4HR and 27RBI in 89 games with Single-A Lakewood...also stole a team-high 25 bases (in 34 attempts)...tied for fourth in the South Atlantic League in triples.

2004

- Made his professional debut with the Gulf Coast Phillies, batting .295 with 34R, 8 doubles, 5 triples, 1HR and 22RBI in 47 games...tied for second in the league in triples and tied for sixth in batting average, leading the team in average, at-bats (183), runs, hits (54), triples, and stolen bases (12)...ranked as the Phillies' fourth-best prospect by *Baseball America*.

Personal

- Full name is Gregory Joseph Golson...graduated in 2004 from John B. Connally High School in Austin, Tex...named to the *USA Today* All-USA High School Baseball Team in 2004.

Golson's Career Batting Record

Year	Club	AVG	G	AB	R	H	2B	3B	HR	RBI	SH	SF	HP	BB	SO	SB	CS	E	OBP	SLG
2004	GCL Phillies	.295	47	183	34	54	8	5	1	22	1	2	5	10	54	12	2	1	.345	.410
2005	Lakewood	.264	89	375	51	99	19	8	4	27	2	0	6	26	106	25	9	2	.322	.389
2006	Lakewood	.220	93	387	56	85	15	4	7	31	8	3	2	19	107	23	7	3	.258	.333
	Clearwater	.264	40	159	31	42	11	2	6	17	1	0	3	11	53	7	3	1	.324	.472
2007	Clearwater	.285	99	418	66	119	27	3	12	52	2	4	4	21	124	25	8	7	.322	.450
	Reading	.242	37	153	20	37	5	2	3	16	1	1	1	2	49	5	0	0	.255	.359
2008	Reading	.282	106	426	64	120	18	4	13	60	4	5	1	34	130	23	5	8	.333	.434
	PHILADELPHIA	.000	6	6	2	0	0	0	0	0	0	0	0	0	4	1	0	1	.000	.000
2009	Oklahoma City – a	.258	123	457	46	118	17	8	2	40	8	6	0	29	114	20	4	4	.299	.344
	TEXAS – b	.000	1	1	0	0	0	0	0	0	0	0	0	0	1	0	0	0	.000	.000
Minor League Totals		**.263**	**634**	**2558**	**368**	**674**	**120**	**36**	**48**	**265**	**27**	**21**	**22**	**152**	**737**	**140**	**38**	**26**	**.308**	**.395**
Major League Totals		**.000**	**7**	**7**	**2**	**0**	**0**	**0**	**0**	**0**	**0**	**0**	**0**	**0**	**5**	**1**	**0**	**1**	**.000**	**.000**

Selected by Philadelphia in the first round (21st overall) of the 2004 First-Year Player Draft.

a – Acquired by Texas in exchange for OF John Mayberry Jr. on November 20, 2008.
b – Acquired by the Yankees in exchange for INF Mitch Hilligoss on January 26, 2010.

Golson's Career Fielding Record

Position	PCT	G	PO	A	E	TC
Outfield	.750	4	3	0	1	4

Jumpin' July

The Yankees finished July 18-9 (.667) in 2009...marked the Yankees' 17th consecutive season with a winning July record (since 1993), extending the longest all-time July winning stretch for any Major League club...according to the *Elias Sports Bureau*, Pittsburgh held the previous record with 15 straight winning Julys from 1899-1913.

Curtis Granderson

14 Outfielder
6-1 • 185 • B/T: Left/Right
Opening Day Age: 29

Birthdate
March 16, 1981

Birthplace
Blue Island, Ill.

Resides
Chicago, Ill.

M.L. Service
4 years, 77 days

College
University of Illinois

Career Highlights
A.L. All-Star Team
- 2009

Status

- Acquired by the Yankees from the Detroit Tigers in a three-team, seven-player deal in which the Yankees sent LHP Phil Coke and OF Austin Jackson to Detroit and RHP Ian Kennedy to Arizona on December 9, 2009...enters the third year of a five-year contract that extends through 2012 with a club option for 2013.

Career Highlights

- Owns 24 career lead-off home runs, marking the most in Detroit franchise history, and tying Hanley Ramirez for the sixth-most among all active players behind Alfonso Soriano (54), Jimmy Rollins (33), Ichiro Suzuki (30), Johnny Damon (26) and Rafael Furcal (25).
- Over the last five seasons (since 2005), ranks third in the Majors with 56 triples...since 2007, is tied with Boston's David Ortiz for the most extra-base hits (206) among American Leaguers.
- Among AL outfielders since 2005, ranks third with 1,745 total chances and seventh in fielding percentage (.993), committing only 13 errors over the span.
- Was the only Major Leaguer to score 100-or-more runs, collect 20-or-more doubles, 10-or-more triples, 20-or-more home runs and 10-or-more stolen bases in both 2007 and 2008.

Single-Game Bests and Streaks

Hits
5 - 2 times
Last: at CLE, 7/30/08

Runs
4 - at KC, 7/21/08

2B
2 - 6 times
Last: at BOS, 5/17/07

3B
2 - 4 times
Last: at TEX, 8/18/08

HR
2 - 4 times
Last: at TEX, 7/29/09

RBI
5 - 2 times
Last: vs. TOR, 4/4/07

BB
3 - 3 times
Last: vs. OAK, 5/17/09

SO
4 - 3 times
Last: vs. BOS, 5/8/08

SB
3 - at CWS, 9/30/07

Hit Streak
15g - 6/10-27/08

2009

- Batted .249 (157-for-631) with 91R, 23 doubles, 8 triples, 30HR, 71RBI and 20SB in 160 games for the Tigers...set a career high in home runs...was tied for fifth in the American League in triples and ranked ninth with 141K...led the Majors by grounding into a double play in just 0.9 percent of GDP situations in 2009 (1 GDP in 106 GDP).
- Was one of three American Leaguers to record 30HR and 20SB, joining Texas' Ian Kinsler and Nelson Cruz...marked his second straight season with at least 20HR and 20SB, becoming one of just three Tigers players to reach the totals in multiple seasons, joining Kirk Gibson (four times) and Alan Trammell (three times).
- Hit .275 (124-for-451) with 28HR vs. right-handed pitchers and .183 (33-for-180) with 2HR against left-handed pitchers...batted .267 (86-for-322) in 81 games on the road, tying for fourth in the AL with 20 road homers...hit .230 (71-for-309) with 10HR in 79 games at home.
- Connected for seven leadoff homers, matching his own 2007 Tigers club record.
- Was selected to the American League All-Star team for the first time in his career...tripled in his only AB (off Heath Bell) and scored the game-winning run in the eighth inning of the 4-3 AL win at St. Louis.
- Made 155 starts in CF, committing just 3E in 407 total chances (.993 fielding percentage)...ranked fifth in fielding percentage among AL outfielders with at least 125 games...did not commit an error in his first 96 games of the season from 4/6-7/26, a total of 221 errorless chances.

- Connected for three two-homer games in 2009 (4/21 at Los Angeles-AL, 6/17 at St. Louis and 7/29 at Texas).
- Hit his 100th career home run on 9/27 at Chicago's U.S. Cellular Field, a solo homer off Daniel Hudson in the first inning.
- Following the season was tabbed the third-best defensive outfielder in the American League by *Baseball America*.

2008

- Hit .280 (155-for-553) with 112R, 26 doubles, 13 triples, 22HR, 66RBI and 12SB...led the American League in triples, becoming the first Tigers player to lead the league in triples in consecutive seasons since Ty Cobb in 1917 (24) and 1918 (14)...became the fourth player in Detroit history to post double-digit totals in a single-season in doubles, triples, homers and RBI, joining Bobby Veach (1920-21), Ty Cobb (1921, 1925) and Charlie Gehringer (1929-30).
- Ranked second in the AL in runs scored, becoming the first Tigers player to score 100-or-more runs in back-to-back seasons since Tony Phillips in 1992-93...was the ninth-hardest player to double up, grounding into a double play once every 79.0AB.
- Led off a game with a home run four times (4/24 vs. Texas, 5/4 at Minnesota, 6/20 at San Diego and 8/27 vs. Cleveland).
- Began the season on the 15-day disabled list with a non-displaced fracture of the third metacarpal in his right hand...reinstated from the D.L. on 4/23, and hit safely in six of his first seven games back.
- Established a career high with a 15-game hitting streak from 6/10-27, batting .443 (27-for-61) with 4 doubles, 3 triples, 1HR and 7RBI...scored a career-high 4R in 7/21 win at Kansas City.
- Equaled a career high five hits on 7/30 at Cleveland, going 5-for-7 with 3R and 2RBI in the Tigers' 13-inning win.
- Prior to the season, agreed to terms on a five-year contract with a club option for 2013 on 2/4.

2007

- Hit .302 (185-for-612) with 122R, 38 doubles, 23 triples, 23HR, 74RBI and 26SB in 158 games for the Tigers, recording career-highs in runs, hits, doubles, triples, RBI and stolen bases...led the AL in triples, ranked third in runs scored and extra-base hits (84), fourth in total bases (338), sixth in slugging percentage (.552), seventh in strikeouts (141) and tied for ninth in multi-hit games (57).
- Became the third player in Major League history to collect at least 30 doubles, 20 triples, 20HR and 20SB in a single season, joining the Cubs' Wildfire Schulte (1911) and Philadelphia's Jimmy Rollins (also in 2007)...became the 13th player in Tigers history to post double-digits in doubles, triples, home runs and stolen bases...joined teammate Gary Sheffield as one of seven Tigers all-time to collect at least 20HR and 20SB in a single season.
- His 23 triples were the most by a Tiger since Ty Cobb finished with 24 triples in 1917, while his 122 runs were the most by a Tigers player since Ron LeFlore scored 126 runs in 1978.
- Was successful in 96.3 percent of his stolen base attempts (26-for-27), marking the best single-season stolen base percentage by a Tigers player since it became an official statistic in 1920.
- Hit .337 (166-for-493) with 20HR against right-handed pitchers, ranking fourth in the AL with a .621 slugging percentage and sixth in batting average against righties...batted .160 (19-for-119) with 3HR vs. lefthanders, recording the lowest batting average in the league against left-handed pitchers among qualifiers.
- Led all Major League outfielders with 428 putouts, tying for eighth in the AL with 10 assists...tied for the third-most putouts by a Tigers outfielder in franchise history with Barney McCosky (1939).
- Set a Detroit franchise record with seven leadoff homers (4/24 at Los Angeles-AL, 5/9 vs. Seattle, 7/14 at Seattle, 7/23 at Chicago-AL, 8/26 vs. New York-AL, 9/16 at Minnesota and 9/22 vs. Kansas City).
- Hit his first career grand slam in 4/4 win vs. Toronto, connecting in the third inning off Shaun Marcum...matched his career high with 5RBI (second time).

TWENTY GRAND

Curtis Granderson became one of four players in Major League history to collect at least 20 doubles, 20 triples, 20HR and 20SB in the same season in 2007:

Player	Year	2B	3B	HR	SB
Wildfire Schulte, CHC	1911	30	21	21	23
Willie Mays, NYG	1957	26	20	35	38
CURTIS GRANDERSON, DET	**2007**	**38**	**23**	**23**	**26**
Jimmy Rollins, PHI	2007	38	20	30	41

CURTIS GRANDERSON

- Named the AL "Player of the Week" for 7/9-15 after hitting .500 (8-for-16) with 7R in four games.
- Batted .283 (96-for-339) with 62R, 24 doubles, 15 triples, 12HR and 43RBI in 85 games prior to the All-Star break, tying for the AL lead with 51 extra-base hits...became the ninth Major League player since 1957 to post double-digit totals in doubles, triples and home runs prior to the All-Star break...hit .326 (89-for-273) with 60R, 14 doubles, 8 triples, 11HR and 31RBI in 73 games following the break.
- Collected his second career inside-the-park home run off Phil Hughes in 8/26 win vs. the Yankees...stole a career-high three bases in 9/30 win at Chicago-AL in the final game of the season.

2006

- In his first full season at the Major League level, batted .260 (155-for-596) with 31 doubles, 9 triples, 19HR, 68RBI and 8SB in 159 games (153 starts in CF)...led all AL outfielders with a .997 fielding percentage, ranking second with 389 total chances and 385 putouts...was the best fielding percentage by a Tigers centerfielder since Mickey Stanley posted a 1.000 fielding percentage in 1970.
- Led the American League with 174K, marking the third-highest single-season strikeout total in Detroit club history.
- Batted .274 (123-for-449, 15HR) against right-handed pitchers and .218 (32-for-147, 4HR) vs. lefties...hit .278 (92-for-331) with 11HR in 87 games prior to the All-Star break...in 72 games following the All-Star break, batted .238 (63-for-265) with 8HR.
- Established a career high with 5RBI and was 2-for-5 with 1 triple in 5/26 win vs. Cleveland.
- Collected his first career lead off home run in 6/18 win Chicago-AL (off Mark Prior), going 2-for-5 with 2R and 1RBI...hit six lead-off homers during the season (also 6/23 vs. St. Louis, 8/27 at Cleveland, 9/7 at Minnesota, 9/23 at Kansas City and 9/29 vs. Kansas City).
- Committed the first error of his Major League career on 7/25 at Cleveland, snapping a 150-game errorless streak...marked the longest errorless streak to begin a Major League career by a non-pitcher since Dave Roberts went his first 205 career games without an error from 8/7/99-4/20/03, and the longest such streak ever by a Tigers outfielder.
- Homered and tripled in the first inning in 9/23 win at Kansas City, going 2-for-6 with 2R and 4RBI...became just the fifth Major Leaguer since 1987 to accomplish the feat in the same inning, joining Detroit's Tony Phillips (1991), Arizona's Steve Finley (1999), Detroit's Brandon Inge (2004) and Tampa Bay's Carl Crawford (2005).
- Recorded his first career multi-homer game in 9/29 loss vs. Kansas City.
- Saw his first postseason action for the American League champions, batting .226 (12-for-53) with 3 doubles, 1 triple, 3HR, 7RBI and 2SB...went 3-for-5 with 1HR and 1RBI in his first career playoff game in Game 1 of the ALDS on 10/3 at the original Yankee Stadium.

2005

- Batted .272 (44-for-162) with 6 doubles, 3 triples, 8HR and 20RBI in 47 games over two stints with the Tigers (7/22-27; 8/15-10/2)...named the Tigers "Rookie of the Year" by the Detroit Sports Broadcasters' Association.
- Hit .318 (7-for-22) over his first five-day stay with the club, collecting 2 triples, 2HR and 4RBI in six games...hit his first Major League homer on 7/23 vs. Minnesota, a solo shot off Carlos Silva...became the first player to hit two triples and 2HR in his first four games of a season since Milwaukee's Pedro Garcia in 1974.
- Re-joined the Tigers on 8/15 for the remainder of the season...recorded his first career inside-the-park home run on 9/15 at Los Angeles-AL...went 5-for-5 with 1 double in 9/18 loss at Los Angeles-AL...hit his first career "walk-off" home run on 9/26 vs. Chicago-AL in the ninth inning off Cliff Politte.
- Opened the season with Triple-A Toledo and batted .290 (129-for-445) with 29 doubles, 13 triples, 15HR, 65RBI and 22SB, ranking second in the International League in triples...led all league outfielders with 15 assists.
- Named to the International League's postseason all-star squad...tabbed as the 19th-best prospect in the International League following the season by *Baseball America*.
- Played in 21 games with Licey in the Dominican Winter League, hitting .194 (14-for-72) with 9R, 1 double, 1HR and 8RBI.

2004

- Saw his first Major League action, appearing in nine games as a September callup with the Tigers, batting .240 (6-for-25) with 1 double and 1 triple.
- Was signed to a Major League contract and added to Detroit's active roster on 9/12...made his Major League debut the next night vs. Minnesota, starting in center field and going hitless in four at-bats in the Tigers loss...threw out Jacques Jones at third base in the fifth inning for his first career assist...collected his first hit on 9/19 at Chicago-AL, singling as a pinch-hitter in the eighth inning off Freddy Garcia.

- Began the season at Double-A Erie, batting .301 (139-for-462) with 19 doubles, 8 triples, 21HR, 94RBI and 14SB, earning the Tigers' Minor League "Player of the Year" award...ranked second in the Eastern League with a .405 on-base percentage, tied for third with 89R and 8 triples, tied for fourth in RBI, ninth with 139H and tied for ninth in batting average...selected to the Eastern League's post-season All-Star team and *Baseball America*'s Double-A All-Star team.
- Reached base safely in 33 straight games from 5/28-7/16...named Tigers Minor League "Player of the Month" for July...homered in five consecutive games from 7/30-8/3 (6HR total).
- Appeared in three games during the EL playoffs, batting .182 (2-for-11) with 1 double and 1RBI.
- Following the season, *Baseball America* named him the top prospect in the Tigers organization, the seventh-best prospect in the Eastern League, the 16th-best outfield prospect in baseball, the "Best Hitter for Average" and the "Best Strike-Zone Discipline" in the Tigers organization.
- Hit .321 (27-for-84) with 16 runs scored, 4 doubles, 1HR and 15RBI in 23 games for Grand Canyon in the Arizona Fall League following the season...named one of six nominees for the MLB.com Arizona Fall League Dernell Stenson Sportsmanship Award.

2003

- In 127 games with Single-A Lakeland, batted .286 (136-for-476) with 29 doubles, 10 triples, 11HR, 51RBI and 10SB, leading the Florida State League in triples, tying for second with 218 total bases, ranking fourth with 71R, 136H and a .458 slugging percentage, fifth with 50 extra-base hits and eighth in batting average...also tied for the lead among league outfielders with 15 assists.
- Selected to the FSL mid-season All-Star team...named the eighth-best prospect in the Tigers organization by *Baseball America* following the season.

2002

- Named the New York-Penn League's "Most Valuable Player," batting .344 (73-for-212) with 15 doubles, 4 triples, 3HR, 34RBI and 9SB in 52 games with Single-A Oneonta...was selected to the league's postseason All-Star squad and *Baseball America*'s short-season All-Star team...received the NYPL Stedler Award, given to the league player deemed likely to go the farthest in professional baseball.
- Named to *Baseball America*'s College Draft All-Star squad and rated by the publication as the fifth-best pure hitter and having the fifth-best debut among college players in the draft...named the 10th-best prospect in the New York-Penn League and 18th-best prospect in the Tigers organization following the season by *Baseball America*.
- Reached base safely via a hit or walk in 21 straight games from 7/10-8/1, batting .400 (38-for-95) with 20R, 8 doubles, 3 triples, 2HR and 6BB.

Personal

- Graduated from Thornton Fractional South High School in Illinois...was selected SICA Central All-Conference, as well as receiving *Illinois Times*, *Daily Southtown* and *Star Newspaper* All-Area recognition.
- Graduated from the University of Illinois-Chicago with a business degree, completing his final two years of school while playing in the Tigers organization...as a junior, was named Horizon League "Player of the Year" and earned All-Horizon League honors...also selected as a Second-Team All-American by *Baseball America* and *USA Today's Baseball Weekly* and a Third-Team Louisville Slugger NCAA Division I All-American...ranked second among all NCAA Division I players with a .483 batting average as a junior and established single-season records at UIC in batting average, runs (76) and hits (100)...concluded his college career as the school's all-time leader with 178R, placing second on the all-time list with 41 doubles and 24HR, third with 9 triples, fourth with 220H and 624AB, tied for fourth with 125RBI, fifth with 107BB and tied for fifth with a .350 average...inducted into the University of Illinois-Chicago Athletics Hall of Fame on 1/18/08.
- Represented Major League Baseball as an ambassador on a trip to Europe following the 2006 season, South Africa following the 2007 season and China following the 2008 season...was a studio analyst for TBS during Major League Baseball playoff broadcasts in both 2007 and 2008 and served the same role with ESPN in 2007.
- Received the Pop Lloyd Award from the Negro Leagues Baseball Museum on 1/10/09 for his baseball and community leadership.
- In 2008, established the Grand Kids Foundation to focus on improving opportunities for inner-city youth in the areas of education and youth baseball...released a children's book, *All You Can Be*, which encourages children to chase their dreams and included illustrations from fourth graders all across the state of Michigan...donated a copy of the book to each public elementary school library in Michigan.
- Received the 2009 Marvin Miller Award (as voted by MLB players) for his work on and off the field that inspires others to higher levels of achievement, and for displaying as much passion to give back to others as he shows between the lines on the baseball diamond...was also the Tigers' 2007 and 2009 Roberto Clemente Award nominee...received a 2009 Jefferson Award for Public Service from All Stars Helping Kids as a top athlete who has given back to the community.

CURTIS GRANDERSON

- Took part in announcement for the White House's anti-obesity campaign, joining First Lady Michelle Obama as MLB's representative on 2/8/10 at the White House.
- While with the Tigers, was an active participant in Play Baseball Detroit, Tigers Dreams Come True and the Detroit Tigers Autographed Memorabilia Donation Program...served as a spokesman for Gloves for Kids, reading to students in association with the Detroit Newspapers in Education, sponsored youth baseball teams during the annual Negro Leagues Weekend...judged entries in the annual Detroit Tigers Jackie Robinson Essay, Art and Poetry Contest, and attended the Rockin' Rooftop fundraising event to benefit the Coalition on Temporary Shelter (COTS).
- Took part in the Detroit Action Team, a national youth volunteer initiative administered by the Major League Baseball Players Trust and Volunteers of America that is actively recruiting the next generation of volunteers.

Granderson's Career Batting Record

Year	Club	AVG	G	AB	R	H	2B	3B	HR	RBI	SH	SF	HP	BB	SO	SB	CS	E	OBP	SLG
2002	Oneonta	.344	52	212	45	73	15	4	3	34	0	1	7	20	35	9	2	1	.417	.495
2003	Lakeland	.286	127	476	71	136	29	10	11	51	5	3	12	49	91	10	7	5	.365	.458
2004	Erie	.303	123	462	89	140	19	8	21	93	3	4	4	80	95	14	8	3	.407	.515
	DETROIT – a	.240	9	25	2	6	1	1	0	0	0	0	0	3	8	0	0	0	.321	.360
2005	Toledo	.290	111	445	79	129	29	13	15	65	2	5	3	48	129	22	6	4	.359	.515
	DETROIT	.272	47	162	18	44	6	3	8	20	2	0	0	10	43	1	1	0	.314	.494
2006	DETROIT	.260	159	596	90	155	31	9	19	68	7	6	4	66	174	8	5	1	.335	.438
2007	DETROIT	.302	158	612	122	185	38	23	23	74	5	2	5	52	141	26	1	5	.361	.552
2008	Toledo	.333	2	9	1	3	1	0	0	0	0	0	0	0	1	0	0	0	.333	.444
	West Michigan	.364	3	11	1	4	0	2	0	1	0	0	0	1	2	0	0	0	.417	.727
	DETROIT – b	.280	141	553	112	155	26	13	22	66	1	1	3	71	111	12	4	4	.365	.494
2009	DETROIT – c	.249	160	631	91	157	23	8	30	71	3	2	2	72	141	20	6	3	.327	.453
Minor League Totals		**.300**	**418**	**1615**	**286**	**485**	**93**	**37**	**50**	**244**	**10**	**13**	**26**	**198**	**353**	**55**	**23**	**13**	**.383**	**.497**
Major League Totals		**.272**	**674**	**2579**	**435**	**702**	**125**	**57**	**102**	**299**	**18**	**11**	**14**	**274**	**618**	**67**	**17**	**13**	**.344**	**.484**

Selected by the Detroit Tigers in the third round of the 2002 First-Year Player Draft.

a – Placed on the disabled list from June 21-July 3, 2004 with a left ankle sprain.
b – Placed on the disabled list from March 23-April 23, 2008 with a non-displaced fracture of the third metacarpal in his right hand.
c – Traded to the Yankees from the Detroit Tigers in a three-team, seven-player deal in which the Yankees sent LHP Phil Coke and OF Austin Jackson to Detroit and RHP Ian Kennedy to the Arizona Diamondbacks.

Granderson's Division Series Record

Year	Club vs. Opp.	AVG	G	AB	R	H	2B	3B	HR	RBI	SH	SF	HP	BB	SO	SB	CS	E	OBP	SLG
2006	DET vs. NYY	.294	4	17	3	5	0	1	2	5	0	1	0	0	1	1	0	0	.278	.765
Division Series Totals		**.294**	**4**	**17**	**3**	**5**	**0**	**1**	**2**	**5**	**0**	**1**	**0**	**0**	**1**	**1**	**0**	**0**	**.278**	**.765**

Granderson's Championship Series Record

Year	Club vs. Opp.	AVG	G	AB	R	H	2B	3B	HR	RBI	SH	SF	HP	BB	SO	SB	CS	E	OBP	SLG
2006	DET vs. OAK	.333	4	15	4	5	2	0	1	2	0	0	0	4	2	1	0	0	.474	.667
LCS Totals		**.333**	**4**	**15**	**4**	**5**	**2**	**0**	**1**	**2**	**0**	**0**	**0**	**4**	**2**	**1**	**0**	**0**	**.474**	**.667**

Granderson's World Series Record

Year	Club vs. Opp.	AVG	G	AB	R	H	2B	3B	HR	RBI	SH	SF	HP	BB	SO	SB	CS	E	OBP	SLG
2006	DET vs. STL	.095	5	21	1	2	1	0	0	0	0	0	0	1	7	0	0	0	.136	.143
World Series Totals		**.095**	**5**	**21**	**1**	**2**	**1**	**0**	**0**	**0**	**0**	**0**	**0**	**1**	**7**	**0**	**0**	**0**	**.136**	**.143**
POSTSEASON TOTALS		**.226**	**13**	**53**	**8**	**12**	**3**	**1**	**3**	**7**	**0**	**1**	**0**	**5**	**10**	**2**	**0**	**0**	**.288**	**.491**

Granderson's All-Star Game Record

Year	Club, Site	AVG	G	AB	R	H	2B	3B	HR	RBI	SH	SF	HP	BB	SO	SB	CS	E	OBP	SLG
2009	DET, St. Louis	1.000	1	1	1	1	0	1	0	0	0	0	0	0	0	0	0	0	1.000	3.000
All-Star Game Totals		**1.000**	**1**	**1**	**1**	**1**	**0**	**1**	**0**	**0**	**0**	**0**	**0**	**0**	**0**	**0**	**0**	**0**	**1.000**	**3.000**

Granderson's World Baseball Classic Record

Year	Country, Site	AVG	G	AB	R	H	2B	3B	HR	RBI	SH	SF	HP	BB	SO	SB	CS	E	OBP	SLG
2009	USA, USA	.235	7	17	1	4	0	0	0	2	0	0	0	2	5	0	0	0	.316	.235
WBC Totals		**.235**	**7**	**17**	**1**	**4**	**0**	**0**	**0**	**2**	**0**	**0**	**0**	**2**	**5**	**0**	**0**	**0**	**.316**	**.235**

Granderson's Career Fielding Record

Position	PCT	G	PO	A	E	TC
Outfield	.993	667	1724	25	13	1762

Granderson's Career Home Run Chart

MULTI-HOMER GAMES: 4. **TWO-HOMER GAMES:** 4, last on 7/29/09 at Texas. **GRAND SLAMS:** 1, on 4/4/07 vs. Toronto (Shaun Marcum). **PINCH-HIT HR:** None. **INSIDE-THE-PARK HR:** 2, last on 8/26/07 vs. New York-AL (Phil Hughes). **WALK-OFF HR:** 1, on 9/26/05 vs. Chicago-AL (Cliff Politte). **LEADOFF HR:** 15, last on 9/27/09 at Chicago-AL (Daniel Hudson).

Jamie Hoffmann

73 **Outfielder**

6-3 • 235 • B/T: Right/Right

Opening Day Age: 25

Birthdate
August 20, 1984

Birthplace
New Ulm, Minn.

Resides
New Ulm, Minn.

M.L. Service
25 days
(Rookie)

Status

- Acquired by the Yankees from the Washington Nationals on December 10, 2009 as the player to be named later to complete the trade of RHP Brian Bruney...was selected by the Nationals with the first overall pick in the 2009 Rule 5 Draft...is under contract through 2010.

Career Notes

- Was rated by *Baseball America* as the best defensive outfielder in the Dodgers' minor league system for four straight seasons (2005-08)...the publication tabbed him as having the organization's "Best Strikezone Judgment" following the 2009 season.
- He is the first Rule 5 player in Yankees spring camp since Josh Phelps in 2007 and just the second in the last 15 years (since 1996).

2009

- Saw his first Major League action, batting .182 with 2 doubles, 1HR and 7RBI in 14 games...was recalled by the Dodgers from Triple-A Albuquerque on 5/22 and made his Major League debut that night vs. Los Angeles-AL, flying out as a pinch hitter in the sixth inning.
- Hit a three-run homer for his first big league hit on 5/24 vs. Los Angeles-AL (off Matt Palmer), going 2-for-4 with 1 double, 1HR and 4RBI.
- Played in 14 games with the Dodgers, including eight pinch-hit appearances, before being optioned to Albuquerque on 6/15...was designated for assignment on 8/31 and re-signed to a minor league contract on 9/9.
- Combined to hit .291 with 69R, 23 doubles, 10HR, 64RBI and 15SB in 97 games for Double-A Chattanooga and Albuquerque...opened the year with Chattanooga and hit a grand slam and drove in five runs on 4/22 at Mississippi...went 5-for-5 on 4/28 vs. Huntsville...scored 25R in 29 games before being promoted to Albuquerque on 5/12.
- Earned the "Dodger Pride Award" in April, given on a monthly basis to the players at each level of the club's minor league system who play the game with a hustling, smart and aggressive style.
- Following the season, appeared in 21 games with Escogido of the Dominican Winter League, batting .235 (16-for-68) with 5 doubles, 5RBI, 7BB and 3SB.

Single-Game Highs and Streaks

Hits
2 - vs. LAA, 5/24/09

Runs
1 - 2 times
Last: at COL, 5/25/09

2B
1 - 2 times
Last: at COL, 5/25/09

3B
None

HR
1 - vs. LAA, 5/24/09

RBI
4 - vs. LAA, 5/24/09

BB
None

SO
2 - at CHC, 5/31/09

SB
None

Hit Streak
2g - 5/24-25/09

2008

- Batted .278 with 64R, 20 doubles, 3 triples, 10HR, 71RBI and a career-high 28 stolen bases in 37 attempts (75.7%) in 133 games, making the majority of his starts in RF...was a midseason Southern League All-Star.
- All 10 of his homers came off right-handed pitchers...hit a "walk-off" solo homer with two outs in the ninth on 8/1 vs. Mobile.
- Hit in a career-high 15 straight games from 5/9-24, batting .373 (22-for-59) over the stretch...also hit safely in 24 straight starts from 5/9-6/3.
- Played for Surprise of the Arizona Fall League following the season, batting .314 (11-for-35) with 6RBI, 8BB and 3SB in 10 games.

JAMIE HOFFMANN

2007

- Played the entire season with Single-A Inland Empire, batting .309 with 67R, a career-high 22 doubles, 7 triples, 9HR and 81RBI in 116 games...also stole 19 bases in 26 attempts...ranked 10th in the California League in batting average, leading the team in average and hits (134)...played all three outfield positions.
- Participated in the Hawaiian Winter League following the season, batting .278 and going 8-for-8 in stolen base attempts with West Oahu.

2006

- Played majority of the season with Single-A Vero Beach, batting .252 with 50R, 16 doubles, 5HR, 29RBI and 15SB in 121 games...was promoted to Triple-A Las Vegas for the final four games of the season and went 3-for-10 (.300) with 1BB, 3K and 1SB.

2005

- Began the year with Single-A Columbus and was promoted to Single-A Vero Beach on 7/5, combining to hit .285 with 79R, 19 doubles, 11 triples, 2HR, 34RBI and 13SB in 125 games.

2004

- Batted .310 with 40R, 8 doubles, 7 triples, 4HR, 36RBI and 14SB in 60 games with the GCL Dodgers, playing exclusively at 3B...led the league in hits (71), triples, RBI and runs, and ranked fourth in batting average...began his pro career with multi-hit efforts in each of his first seven games, batting .500 (16-for-32).
- Was rated by *Baseball America* as the 13th-best prospect in the GCL.

Personal

- Was an eighth-round pick of the National Hockey League's Carolina Hurricanes in the 2003 draft...played for Des Moines of the United States Hockey League during the 2002-03 season, scoring 14 goals and assisting on 25 others for a total of 39 points in 60 games...was planning to attend Colorado College to play hockey, but instead chose to sign with the Dodgers.
- Graduated from New Ulm (MN) High School...helped lead the school to Minnesota's 3A baseball state championship in 2002, setting the school's single-season hits record (53)...logged 25 goals and 32 assists during his senior year at New Ulm High.

Hoffmann's Career Batting Record

Year	Team	AVG	G	AB	R	H	2B	3B	HR	RBI	SAC	SF	HBP	BB	SO	SB	CS	E	OBP	SLG
2004	GCL Dodgers	.310	60	229	40	71	8	7	4	36	0	1	0	24	38	14	5	11	.374	.459
2005	Columbus	.308	79	321	53	99	13	9	1	24	5	2	1	39	73	10	4	5	.383	.414
	Vero Beach	.241	46	166	26	40	6	2	1	10	0	1	1	10	45	3	1	0	.287	.319
2006	Vero Beach	.252	121	433	50	109	16	0	5	29	7	2	2	35	94	15	11	6	.309	.323
	Las Vegas	.300	4	10	0	3	0	0	0	0	1	0	1	1	3	1	0	0	.417	.300
2007	Inland Empire	.309	116	433	67	134	22	7	9	81	5	6	4	47	70	19	7	3	.378	.455
2008	Jacksonville	.278	133	478	64	133	20	3	10	71	4	6	2	54	73	28	9	7	.350	.395
2009	Chattanooga	.307	29	101	25	31	9	2	2	16	0	0	6	22	18	5	3	0	.457	.495
	Albuquerque	.284	68	257	44	73	14	3	8	48	1	3	0	32	37	10	8	6	.360	.455
	LOS ANGELES-NL-a	.182	14	22	2	4	2	0	1	7	0	2	0	0	5	0	0	0	.167	.409
Minor League Totals		**.285**	**656**	**2428**	**369**	**693**	**108**	**33**	**40**	**315**	**23**	**21**	**17**	**264**	**451**	**105**	**48**	**38**	**.357**	**.407**
Major League Totals		**.182**	**14**	**22**	**2**	**4**	**2**	**0**	**1**	**7**	**0**	**2**	**0**	**0**	**5**	**0**	**0**	**0**	**.167**	**.409**

Signed by the Los Angeles Dodgers as a non-drafted free agent on August 20, 2003.

a – Selected by the Washington Nationals with the first overall pick in the 2009 Rule 5 Draft and acquired by the Yankees as the player to be named later for RHP Brian Bruney on December 10, 2009.

Hoffmann's Career Fielding Record

Position	PCT	G	PO	A	E	TC
Outfield	1.000	5	10	1	0	11

Hoffmann's Career Home Run Chart

MULTI-HOMER GAMES: 0. **GRAND SLAMS:**None. **PINCH-HIT HR:** None. **INSIDE-THE-PARK HR:** None. **WALK-OFF HR:** None. **LEADOFF HR:** None.

Phil Hughes

65 Right-handed Pitcher

6-5 • 240 • B/T: Right/Right

Opening Day Age: 23

Birthdate
June 24, 1986

Birthplace
Mission Viejo, Calif.

Resides
Tampa, Fla.

M.L. Service
2 years, 113 days

Career Highlights

Kevin Lawn Award Yankees "Minor League Pitcher of the Year"
- 2006

All-Star Futures Game
- 2006

Status

- Selected by the Yankees in the first round (23rd overall) of the 2004 First-Year Player Draft...signed through the 2010 season.

Career Notes

- According to the *Elias Sports Bureau*, Hughes' 13 career wins are the most victories by a player the Yankees selected in the first round of the First-Year Player Draft, surpassing the six career wins of Bill Burbach (Yankees 1965 first-round pick).

2009

- Was 8-3 with three saves and a 3.03 ERA in 51 appearances (seven starts) with the Yankees...opponents batted .217 (68-for-314, 8HR); LH .257 (36-for-140, 3HR), RH .184 (32-for-174, 5HR).
- In 44 relief appearances, was 5-1 with three saves and a 1.40 ERA, leading all qualifying Major League relievers in ERA...struck out 33.7% of his batters faced as a reliever (65K, 193BF), the second-highest mark in the Majors...opponents batted .172 (31-for-180, 2HR)...37 of his 44 appearances were scoreless...held opponents hitless in 24 outings...stranded 15-of-16 inherited runners (93.8%)...retired 35-of-44 first batters faced (79.5%)...appeared in consecutive games 11 times and three straight games once (8/2-5).
- The Yankees were 35-9 in his relief appearances, including a 27-4 mark following the All-Star break...the Yankees won 18 consecutive games Hughes appeared in from 8/2-9/16...allowed just 3H in 33AB with runners in scoring position as a reliever (credit: *Elias Sports Bureau*)...held opponents hitless in 26 consecutive AB with RISP from 6/14-9/22.
- Recorded the American League's lowest post-All-Star break ERA (1.64)...averaged 12.55 K/9.0IP after the All-Star break, ranking fourth in the Majors over the span.
- After stepping into the primary setup role on 7/3, the Yankees went 58-26, including a 31-5 mark in games Hughes appeared in...following his first relief appearance on 6/8, the Yankees bullpen went 27-7 with a 3.37 ERA and 37 saves in 105 games, allowing 277H and 127ER in 339.2IP (138R, 120BB, 326K, 37HR) while holding opponents to a .219 batting average...in 54 games prior to Hughes joining the bullpen, Yankees relievers were 13-10 with a 4.88 ERA, 14 saves and a .251 opponents batting average (175.1IP, 168H, 103R, 95ER, 78BB, 157K, 35HR).
- In seven starts, went 3-2 with a 5.45 ERA, allowing 37H and 21ER in 34.2IP (15BB, 31K, 6HR)...held his opponents to 3ER or less in five of his seven starts.
- Was recalled from Triple-A Scranton/Wilkes-Barre on 4/28 and made the start that night at Detroit, recording the win in an 11-0 Yankees victory...threw 6.0 scoreless innings and struck out six batters (2H, 2BB), snapping a personal four-game losing streak.
- Allowed a career-high 8ER on 8H in 1.2IP on 5/9 at Baltimore, recording the loss in a 12-5 Orioles victory...marked his shortest career start (2BB, 0K, 1HR)...tossed a scoreless first inning then allowed nine of his next 11 batters faced to reach.

Single-Game Highs and Streaks

Low hit CG
N/A

IP (start)
8.0 - 2 times
Last: at TEX, 5/25/09

IP (relief)
3.2 - at BOS, 6/10/09

Hits
9 - at BAL, 4/18/08

Runs
8 - at BAL, 5/9/09

BB
5 - at LAA, 8/20/07

SO
9 - vs. BAL, 5/20/09

HR
3 - at DET, 8/26/07

Winning Streak
4g - 8/14-9/22/09

Losing Streak
4g - 4/8-29/08

PHIL HUGHES

Hughes' 2009 Starting Pitching Lines

Date/Opp	Score	W/L	IP	H	R	ER	HR	BB	K	NP/K	ERA	Left game
4/28 at DET*	11-0	W	6.0	2	0	0	0	2	6	99/58	0.00	Leading 10-0
5/4 vs. BOS*	4-6	L	4.0	7	4	3	1	**4**	2	94/57	2.70	Trailing 4-0
5/9 at BAL	5-12	L	1.2	**8**	**8**	**8**	1	2	0	53/33	8.49	Trailing 7-0
5/15 vs. MIN	5-4	ND	5.0	6	3	3	**2**	**4**	2	93/50	7.56	Trailing 3-1
5/20 vs. BAL	11-4	W	5.0	6	3	3	**2**	1	**9**	89/57	7.06	Leading 5-3
5/25 at TEX	11-1	W	**8.0**	3	0	0	0	1	6	**101**/65	5.16	Leading 11-0
5/31 at CLE	4-5	ND	5.0	5	4	4	0	1	6	95/66	5.45	Trailing 4-2
Totals	**3-2**		**34.2**	**37**	**22**	**21**	**6**	**15**	**31**		**5.45**	

(*) Denotes start following a team loss **Bold = season highs**

- Struck out a career-high nine batters in 5/20 win vs. Baltimore, including eight on swinging third strikes...his final strikeout of the game (Nick Markakis in the fifth) was his 100th career K.
- Went undefeated over his final four starts from 5/15-31 (2-0, 3.91 ERA, 23.0IP, 10ER)...tossed 8.0 shutout innings (3H, 1BB, 6K) and recorded the win in an 11-1 Yankees victory on 5/25 at Texas...matched his career high in innings pitched (also 9/24/08 at Toronto).
- Made his first career regular season relief appearance in 6/8 win vs. Tampa Bay, tossing a perfect seventh inning (1.0IP, 1K).
- Did not allow a run over 16 consecutive outings from 6/14-7/26, tossing 21.0 shutout innings over the stretch (11H, 4BB/1IBB, 25K)...compiled a 23.1-inning scoreless stretch dating back to 6/10 at Boston, marking the longest single-season scoreless stretch for a Yankees reliever since Mariano Rivera's 30.2-inning scoreless stretch to finish the 1999 regular season (credit: *Elias*)...was also the fifth-longest by a Yankees pitcher, starter or reliever, in the last 25 seasons (1985-2009), behind Rivera, Lee Gutterman (30.2 in 1989), Steve Farr (27.0 in 1991) and Rivera (26.0 in 1996)...had his scoreless streak broken on 7/30 at Chicago-AL, when he was charged with 1ER in 2.0IP (2H, 1K)...exited with the score tied 2-2 and two runners on base before Phil Coke allowed the "walk-off" RBI single.
- Earned his first regular-season win as a reliever on 7/17 vs. Detroit, tossing 2.0 scoreless IP while striking out six-of-nine batters faced (3H, 1BK)...according to the *Elias Sports Bureau*, became just the third pitcher in Yankees history to record at least 6K in a game with all his outs being recorded via strikeout (also Joe Page, 6K vs. Detroit on 9/13/47 and Goose Gossage, 6K vs. Kansas City on 9/1/79).
- Earned his first career save in 7/23 win vs. Oakland, tossing 2.0 perfect innings...according to *Elias*, became the youngest Yankees pitcher to earn a save of at least six outs since 18-year-old Jose Rijo notched a 3.0-inning save on 4/18/84 at Cleveland.
- Opened the year with Scranton/WB, going 3-0 with a 1.86 ERA in three starts...allowed only 3BB while striking out 19 batters 19.1IP...opponents were batting .233 (17-for-73) at the time of his recall.
- Made nine postseason appearances in 2009, going 0-1 with an 8.53 ERA (6.1IP, 11H, 6ER, 4BB, 7K, 1HR)...pitched in all three Division Series wins vs. Minnesota.

2008

- Was 0-4 with a 6.62 ERA in eight starts over two stints with the Yankees (3/31-7/30; 9/13-28)...the Yankees were 3-5 in his starts...opponents batted .314 (43-for-137, 3HR); LH .333 (20-for-60, 1HR), RH .299 (23-for-77, 2HR)...his eight starts were the third-most all time by a Yankees pitcher in a winless season behind Steve Trout (9, 1987) and Ian Kennedy (9, 2008).
- Leadoff batters hit at a .412 clip (14-for-34)...according to the *Elias Sports Bureau*, opponents scored in 12 of the 17 innings the leadoff batter reached, but only two of 20 innings in which he retired the first batter.
- Opened the season as the youngest pitcher in the Majors and the second youngest player in the Majors behind Arizona's Justin Upton (20 years old, born 8/25/87)...according to the *Elias Sports Bureau*, was the youngest pitcher to begin a season in the Yankees rotation since Bill Burbach in 1969 (Opening Day age of 21 years, 232 days).
- Turned 22 on 6/24...made 19 starts with a 5-7 record and 71 career strikeouts before the age of 22...were the most starts, wins and strikeouts by a Yankees starting pitcher prior to his 22nd birthday since Bill Burbach went 6-8 with 76K in 24 starts prior to turning 22 years old on 8/22/69.
- At 21 years old, joined Yankees pitchers Joba Chamberlain (22) and Ian Kennedy (23) as the first trio—each under age 24—to start a game in the same season for the Yankees prior to September callups since 1993 (Sterling Hitchcock, Mark Hutton and Sam Militello)...the last Yankees trio to do it prior to 6/4 included Gil Blanco, Al Downing and Mel Stottlemyre in 1965.
- With his first start of the season on 4/3 vs. Toronto in the Yankees' third game, became the youngest Yankees pitcher to start one of the team's first three games since Waite Hoyt (21 years, 217 days) took the mound for the club's second game in 1921.
- Was 21 years old at the start of the season, and—with Ian Kennedy (age 23)—became the fourth pair of pitchers, each under the age of 24, to start for the Yankees within the team's first four games of a season and the first pair since Dave Righetti (23) and Mike Morgan (22) in 1982 (also Hippo Vaughn-23, Ray Fisher-23 and Ray Caldwell-22 in 1911 and Mel Stottlemyre-23 and Al Downing-23 in 1965). Credit: *Elias Sports Bureau.*

PHIL HUGHES

- Underwent an MRI on 5/1 that revealed a stress fracture in his ninth right rib and was placed on the 15-day disabled list that day...was transferred to the 60-day disabled list on 7/18 when the Yankees signed 1B Richie Sexson...was returned from rehab, reinstated from the 60-day D.L. and optioned to Charleston on 7/30...did not allow a run in two relief appearances with Charleston, going 2-0 (6.2IP, 3H, 2BB, 6K)...was promoted to Triple-A Scranton/Wilkes-Barre on 8/6 where he went 1-0 with a 5.90 ERA in six starts...in two postseason starts with Scranton/WB, was 1-0 with a 0.69 ERA, allowing 1ER in 13.0IP and striking out 23 batters (8H, 4BB)...recorded the series-clinching win in Game 4 of the Governor's Cup Series on 9/12 at Durham, allowing just 1ER in 5.0IP and striking out 12 (4H, 4BB) to establish a SWB single-game playoff strikeout record...his 23K also set a franchise-postseason record.
- Was recalled from Scranton/WB prior to 9/13 doubleheader vs. Tampa Bay and joined the Yankees the following day...made start on 9/17 vs. Chicago (AL), allowing 1ER in 4.0IP (4H, 2BB, 4K)...allowed three combined earned runs over his final two starts of the season (12.0IP), walking two and striking out 10.
- Established a career-high with 8.0IP in his final start of the season on 9/24 at Toronto...limited the Blue Jays to 2ER with 0BB and 6K...did not record a decision after the Yankees won in 10th on Bobby Abreu's grand slam.
- Pitched for the Peoria Javelinas of the Arizona Fall League following the season, making seven starts and going 2-0 with a 3.00 ERA (30.0IP, 10ER).

2007

- Was 5-3 with a 4.46 ERA in 13 starts for the Yankees in his first Major League action...at 21 years old, was the youngest member of the Yankees rotation in 2007...the Yankees were 8-5 in games he started...opponents batted .235 (64-for-272, 8HR); LH .264 (34-for-129, 6HR), RH .210 (30-for-143, 2HR)...held opponents to 3ER or less in eight of his 13 Major League starts...opponents batted just .194 (19-for-98) the first time through the order and hit .259 after that (45-for-174).
- Had contract purchased from Triple-A Scranton/Wilkes-Barre on 4/25 and made his Major League debut the next night vs. Toronto, recording the loss in a 6-0 Blue Jays victory...was the youngest Yankees pitcher (20 years, 306 days old) to debut since Jose Rijo on 4/5/84 (18 years, 328 days)...since Rijo's first appearance, the only other Yankees to make their Major League debuts under the age of 21 were Derek Jeter (20 years, 337 days), Dioner Navarro (20 years, 211 days) and Melky Cabrera (20 years, 330 days).

YOUNGEST YANKEES
LAST 25 YEARS (1985-2009)
(age at time of debut)

1.	Dioner Navarro, 2004	20 years, 211 days
2.	**PHIL HUGHES, 2007**	**20 years, 306 days**
3.	Melky Cabrera, 2005	20 years, 330 days
4.	DEREK JETER, 1995	20 years, 337 days

- According to the *Elias Sports Bureau*, was the youngest Yankees draftee to debut with the Bombers since the amateur draft began in 1965...was the youngest Yankee to debut as a starter since Gene Nelson on 5/4/81 (20 years, 152 days)...became the Yankees' first top draft choice to pitch for the club since Bill Burbach, who was chosen in 1965 (the inaugural year of the First-Year Player Draft).
- Became the fifth rookie to start for the Yankees in the team's first 21 games (also Kei Igawa, Darrell Rasner, Chase Wright and Jeff Karstens)...according to the *Elias Sports Bureau*, the only other team in the post-WWII era (since 1946) to start five rookies that early into a season was the 1998 Florida Marlins, who started Andy Larkin, Eric Ludwick, Brian Meadows, Rafael Medina and Jesus Sanchez in their first 20 games.
- Earned his first Major League win in his second start on 5/1 at Texas...tossed 6.1 hitless innings (3BB, 6K) in the Yankees' 10-1 victory before being removed in the seventh inning with a strained left hamstring...according to the *Elias Sports Bureau*, it was the furthest into a game that a Yankees starter had been removed with a no-hitter still intact since David Cone on 9/2/96, when he threw 7.0 no-hit innings in his first start after returning from aneurysm surgery (5-0 win at Oakland).
- Was placed on the 15-day disabled list with a strained left hamstring from 5/3-8/4 (retroactive to 5/2), missing 85 team games...was transferred to the 60-day D.L. on 6/9...endured a setback on 5/25 when he suffered a sprained left ankle while participating in agility drills in Tampa...made five rehab starts from 7/9-29 with Single-A Tampa, Double-A Trenton and Triple-A Scranton/WB, going 2-0 with a 0.42 ERA.
- Participated in the Triple-A All-Star Game on 7/11 at Isotopes Park in Albuquerque, pitching in relief and allowing

2H and 3ER in 0.2IP (1BB, 1K, 1HR) in a 7-5 International League win...was named International League "Pitcher of the Week" for the period from 7/23-29 (2-0. 0.00 ERA, 12.2IP, 5H, 4BB, 11K, .122 opp. avg.).

- Was returned from rehab and reinstated from the 60-day D.L. on 8/4 and started that day vs. Kansas City, recording a no-decision (4.2IP, 6ER)...surrendered his first Major League home run to David DeJesus in the fifth inning...was the first home run he allowed in either the Majors or minors in 2007, snapping a streak of 52.2 homerless innings (15.0IP Major Leagues, 37.2IP minor leagues).
- Recorded the win on 8/10 at Cleveland, allowing 4H and 1ER in 6.0IP...at 21 years, 48 days old, combined with RHP Joba Chamberlain (21 years, 322 days old) to become the youngest pair of Yankees pitchers to appear in the same game since 19-year-old Mike Jurewicz and 19-year-old Gil Blanco pitched in relief on 9/7/65 vs. Baltimore (game 2).
- Was 3-0 in September and led Yankees starters with a 2.73 ERA (29.2IP, 9ER) for the month (ninth-best in the AL)...the Yankees won each of his final five regular season starts (9/5-27) as he held opponents to 3ER or less in each of those outings.
- Appeared in two Division Series games vs. Cleveland, allowing only 1ER in 5.2IP of relief (1.59 ERA, 3H, 0BB, 6K)...tossed 2.0 innings in Game 1 loss at Jacobs Field, allowing a Ryan Garko solo-HR...at 21 years, 102 days old, became the youngest Yankees pitcher to appear in a postseason game since Bill Stafford (21 years, 58 days) in Game 5 of the 1960 World Series vs. Pittsburgh.
- Tossed 3.2 scoreless innings to earn the win in ALDS Game 3...at 21 years, 105 days old, surpassed Whitey Ford (21 years, 351 days old in 1950 World Series Game 4) as the youngest pitcher in franchise history to earn a postseason victory.
- Entered the 2007 season ranked as the top right-handed pitching prospect throughout all of Baseball by *Baseball America*...also ranked as the Yankees' No. 1 prospect for the second straight year and was rated as having the "Best Curveball" and "Best Control" among all Yankees farmhands.

2006

- Earned the 2006 "Kevin Lawn Minor League Pitcher of the Year" Award, given annually to the top pitching prospect in the Yankees organization, after posting a combined record of 12-6 with a 2.16 ERA in 26 starts with Class-A Tampa and Double-A Trenton...led all Eastern League pitchers with a 2.25 ERA and ranked fourth in the league with 138 strikeouts.
- Began the season in Tampa and went 2-3 with a 1.80 ERA, holding opponents to a .178 batting average and recording 30 strikeouts in 30.0IP...was promoted to Trenton on 4/30...in 21 starts with Trenton, went 10-3 with a Thunder franchise-record 2.25 ERA and 138 strikeouts in 116.0 innings...limited opposing batters to a .179 batting average and held left-handed hitters to just .161 (27-for-168)...was selected to participate in the Eastern League All-Star Game and was named to the U.S. team for the All-Star Futures Game at PNC Park in Pittsburgh.
- Did not allow a run in four consecutive starts from 6/23-7/17 (22.2IP, 7H, 6BB, 31K)...was named the Eastern League "Pitcher of the Week" from 8/7-13 after going 2-0 with a 0.90 ERA and 15K in 10.0IP...set a record for most strikeouts by a Thunder pitcher in a postseason game when he recorded 13K in 6.0IP on 9/6 vs. Portland in Game 1 of the Division Series.
- Following the season was named by *Baseball America* to the 2006 Minor League All-Star team as well as the Double-A All-Star squad.

2005

- In his sophomore campaign, fought through two stints on the disabled list with right shoulder inflammation to go 9-1 with a 2.19 ERA and 93 strikeouts in 17 combined appearances (16 starts) with Single-A Charleston and Single-A Tampa.
- Went 7-1 with a 1.97 ERA in 12 starts for Charleston, striking out 72 batters in 68.2IP with only 16 walks...opponents batted just .192 and right-handed hitters were held to a .172 average...struck out eight batters and allowed only two hits in 5.0 shutout innings on 4/26 at Augusta...was credited with his first career complete game in a 6/1 win vs. Greensboro (game 1), limiting the Grasshoppers to 1ER on 2H in 7.0IP for the win...was scheduled to start the South Atlantic League All-Star Game on 6/28 but was scratched after being placed on the D.L. with mild inflammation in his shoulder...went 2-0 with a 3.06 ERA in five games (four starts) for the Tampa Yankees.

2004

- Made only three starts for the Yankees' Gulf Coast League squad in his first professional season, holding opponents scoreless over 5.1IP without recording a decision (4H, 0BB, 8K)...missed most of the season with a fractured toe on his left foot.

Personal

- Graduated from Foothill High School in Santa Ana, Calif., where he owns the school record for most career wins (23) and ranks third in school history with 182 strikeouts...also spent time playing third base and first base...was named the 2004 Most Valuable Player with a 9-1 record and a 0.69 ERA...was honored as a pre-season All-American prior to his junior year and set school single-season records with 12 wins and a 0.64 ERA that season...tossed a perfect game on 4/8/04 in a 9-0 win over Laguna Hills...named to the *Los Angeles Times'* 2004 All-Star team...prior to being drafted, was named by *Baseball America* as the top right-handed pitcher in the Orange County region...was primarily a third baseman until his sophomore year of high school...was signed by Jeff Patterson.
- Visited children at Memorial Sloan-Kettering Cancer Center in New York in September 2009.

Hughes' Career Pitching Record

YEAR	CLUB	W	L	ERA	G	GS	CG	SHO	SV	IP	H	R	ER	HR	HB	BB	SO	WP	BK
2004	Yankees	0	0	0.00	3	3	0	0	0	5.0	4	0	0	0	0	0	8	0	0
2005	Charleston	7	1	1.97	12	12	1	0	0	68.2	46	19	15	1	3	16	72	3	0
	Tampa	2	0	3.06	5	4	0	0	0	17.2	8	6	6	0	3	4	21	0	0
2006	Tampa	2	3	1.80	5	5	0	0	0	30.0	19	7	6	0	1	2	30	0	0
	Trenton	10	3	2.25	21	21	0	0	0	116.0	73	30	29	5	2	32	128	5	0
2007	Tampa	0	0	0.00	1	1	0	0	0	2.0	0	1	0	0	0	2	3	0	0
	Trenton	0	0	1.29	2	2	0	0	0	7.0	5	1	1	0	0	2	11	0	0
	Scranton/WB	4	1	2.20	5	5	0	0	0	28.2	16	7	7	0	1	8	28	2	0
	YANKEES - a	5	3	4.46	13	13	0	0	0	72.2	64	39	36	8	2	29	58	4	0
2008	YANKEES - b	0	4	6.62	8	8	0	0	0	34.0	43	26	25	3	1	15	23	2	0
	Charleston	2	0	0.00	2	0	0	0	0	6.2	3	0	0	0	0	2	6	2	0
	Scranton/WB	1	0	5.90	6	6	0	0	0	29.0	34	19	19	2	2	9	31	0	0
2009	Scranton/WB	3	0	1.86	3	3	0	0	0	19.1	17	4	4	2	0	3	19	0	0
	YANKEES	8	3	3.03	51	7	0	0	3	86.0	68	31	29	8	5	28	96	4	2
Minor League Totals		**31**	**8**	**2.37**	**65**	**62**	**1**	**0**	**0**	**330.0**	**225**	**94**	**87**	**10**	**12**	**80**	**368**	**12**	**0**
Major League Totals		**13**	**10**	**4.20**	**72**	**28**	**0**	**0**	**3**	**192.2**	**175**	**96**	**90**	**19**	**8**	**72**	**177**	**10**	**2**

Selected by the Yankees in the first round (23rd overall) of the 2004 First-Year Player Draft.

a – Placed on the 15-day disabled list from May 3-August 4, 2007 with a strained left hamstring (transferred to 60-day D.L. on June 9).

b – Placed on the 15-day disabled list from May 1 – July 30, 2008 with a stress fracture in his ninth right rib (transferred to 60-day D.L. on July 18).

Hughes' Division Series Record

Year	Club vs. Opp.	W	L	ERA	G	GS	CG	SHO	SV	IP	H	R	ER	HR	HP	BB	SO	WP	BK
2007	NYY vs. CLE	1	0	1.59	2	0	0	0	0	5.2	3	1	1	1	0	0	6	1	0
2009	NYY vs. MIN	0	0	9.00	3	0	0	0	0	2.0	5	2	2	0	0	1	3	0	0
Division Series Totals		**1**	**0**	**3.52**	**5**	**0**	**0**	**0**	**0**	**7.2**	**8**	**3**	**3**	**1**	**0**	**1**	**9**	**1**	**0**

Hughes' League Championship Series Record

Year	Club vs. Opp.	W	L	ERA	G	GS	CG	SHO	SV	IP	H	R	ER	HR	HP	BB	SO	WP	BK
2009	NYY vs. LAA	0	1	3.38	3	0	0	0	0	2.2	4	1	1	0	0	1	3	0	0
LCS Totals		**0**	**1**	**3.38**	**3**	**0**	**0**	**0**	**0**	**2.2**	**4**	**1**	**1**	**0**	**0**	**1**	**3**	**0**	**0**

Hughes' World Series Record

Year	Club vs. Opp.	W	L	ERA	G	GS	CG	SHO	SV	IP	H	R	ER	HR	HP	BB	SO	WP	BK
2009	NYY vs. PHI	0	0	16.20	3	0	0	0	0	1.2	2	3	3	1	0	2	1	0	0
World Series Totals		**0**	**0**	**16.20**	**3**	**0**	**0**	**0**	**0**	**1.2**	**2**	**3**	**3**	**1**	**0**	**2**	**1**	**0**	**0**
POSTSEASON TOTALS		**1**	**1**	**5.25**	**11**	**0**	**0**	**0**	**0**	**12.0**	**14**	**7**	**7**	**2**	**0**	**4**	**13**	**1**	**0**

Hughes' Career Fielding Record

Position	PCT	G	PO	A	E	TC	DP
Pitcher	.964	72	10	17	1	28	1

Hughes' Regular Season Batting Record

Year	Team	AVG	G	AB	R	H	2B	3B	HR	RBI	SH	SF	HP	BB	SO	SB	CS
2009	NYY	Did Not Bat															
Major League Totals		-	**72**	-	-	-	-	-	-	-	-	-	-	-	-	-	-

Derek Jeter

2 **Shortstop**

6-3• 195 • B/T: Right/Right

Opening Day Age: 35

Birthdate
June 26, 1974

Birthplace
Pequannock, N.J.

Resides
Tampa, Fla.

M.L. Service
14 years, 43 days

Career Highlights

World Series MVP
- 2000

All-Star Game MVP
- 2000

A.L. All-Star Team
- 1998, 1999, 2000, 2001, 2002, 2004, 2006, 2007, 2008, 2009

A.L. Gold Glove
- 2004, 2005, 2006, 2009

A.L. Silver Slugger
- 2006, 2007, 2008, 2009

A.L. Rookie of the Year
- 1996

***Sports Illustrated* Sportsman of the Year**
- 2009

Roberto Clemente Award
- 2009

Hank Aaron Award
- 2006, 2009

Status

- Selected in the first round (sixth pick overall) of the 1992 First-Year Player Draft...signed a 10-year contract on February 9, 2001...contract extends through the 2010 season.

Career Notes

- Is one of just eight players in Baseball history with at least 1,500R, 2,500H, 200HR and 300SB (also Roberto Alomar, Craig Biggio, Barry Bonds, Rickey Henderson, Willie Mays, Paul Molitor and Joe Morgan)...is one of 15 players all time to collect 200HR, 300SB and 2,000H, joining Bobby Abreu and Johnny Damon as the only active players to reach the totals...is one of four players since 1920 with at least 2,600H, 200HR and 1,000RBI in his first 15 seasons (Hank Aaron, Stan Musial and Al Simmons)-credit: *Elias*.
- Over the last 10 seasons (2000-09), ranks second in the Majors in hits (1,940) and at-bats (6,122), third in runs scored (1,088), sixth in games played (1,500) and seventh in batting average (.317)...over the last five years (2005-09), ranks second in hits (1,013), fourth in at-bats (3,146), fifth in batting average (.322) and tied for fifth in runs scored (537)...ranks second among active players with 2,747 career hits trailing only Ken Griffey, Jr. (2,763H).
- Has reached the 200-hit plateau seven times in his career, one shy of Lou Gehrig's club record, marking the most 200H seasons by a shortstop...also owns 10 seasons with at least 190 hits, tying Stan Musial for third-most 190H seasons behind Pete Rose (13) and Ty Cobb (12)—credit: *Elias Sports Bureau*.
- His 14 consecutive seasons with at least 150 hits (since 1996), is the longest such streak among active players and the longest in franchise history (credit: *Elias*)
- Has recorded 11 seasons with at least a .300 average, surpassing Bill Dickey and Joe DiMaggio (10) for the third-most .300 seasons in club history behind Lou Gehrig (12 seasons) and Babe Ruth (13 seasons), according to the *Elias Sports Bureau*.
- Has reached the 100R plateau 12 times in his career, second-most 100R seasons in franchise history, trailing only Lou Gehrig (13)...among active players, only teammate Alex Rodriguez (13) has more 100-run seasons, according to *Elias*.
- Has reached double digits in home runs in 14 consecutive seasons (since 1996)...is one of only seven active players to record double-digit home run totals over 14 consecutive seasons at some point in their career (credit: *Elias Sports Bureau*).
- Owns the most hits in Major League history from the shortstop position, surpassing Luis Aparicio (2,673) on 8/16/09 at Seattle...according to *Elias*, only two others have played more games at shortstop while never playing any other fielding position—Aparicio (2,583) and Ozzie Smith (2,511)...according to the *Elias Sports Bureau*, is one of four players all time to record 1,500R and 1,500 games played at shortstop (also Bill Dahlen, Honus Wagner and Cal Ripken, Jr.).
- Has played 2,123 games at shortstop for the Yankees...according to the *Elias Sports Bureau*, is fifth on Baseball's all-time list in games at shortstop for one club (trails Cal Ripken-Orioles; Luke Appling-White Sox; Dave Concepcion-Reds and Alan Trammell-Tigers).

Single-Game Bests and Streaks

Hits
5 - 2 times
Last: vs. TB, 6/21/05

Runs
5 - vs. TB, 6/21/05

2B
3 - at TOR, 5/28/99

3B
2 - at DET, 9/10/96

HR
2 - 8 times
Last: at LAA, 8/27/06

RBI
5 - 3 times
Last: vs. CHC, 6/18/05

BB
3 - 20 times
Last: vs. TOR, 7/6/09

SO
4 - 2 times
Last: at PHI, 9/1/97

SB
3 - 2 times
Last: vs. BOS, 5/11/06

Hit Streak
25g - 8/20-9/16/06

DEREK JETER

- Leads all active players with 242 career games of three-or-more hits (credit: *Elias Sports Bureau*)...has posted at least a dozen games with three-or-more hits in each of the last 14 seasons (1996-2009), matching Tony Gwynn (1984-97) for the second-longest streak of its kind for any player during the expansion era (since 1961) behind Pete Rose's 19 consecutive seasons from 1963-81 (credit: *Elias Sports Bureau*)...since the start of the 1996 season, has a Major League-best 807 multi-hit games.

> **DID YOU KNOW?** Of the 2,138 career regular season games Derek Jeter has played in, there has been just one in which the Yankees had already been mathematically eliminated from postseason play (9/26/08).

- According to the *Elias Sports Bureau*, has 11 single-season hitting streaks of at least 15 games during his career, trailing Ichiro Suzuki (14) for the most among active Major League players...has hitting streaks of more than 15 games in seven different seasons (1996, '99, 2002, '04, '06, '07 and '09), most among active players...has six career single-season hitting streaks of at least 17 games (17, 19 and 20 games in 2007, 25 in 2006 and 17-game streaks in 1996 and 2004)...according to the *Elias Sports Bureau*, is tied with Nomar Garciaparra and Suzuki for the most single-season hitting streaks of at least 17 games among active players.
- Among the Yankees' all-time leaders, ranks first in hits (2,747) and at-bats (8,659), second in stolen bases (305), third in games played (2,138), fourth in runs (1,574) and doubles (438), fifth in batting average (.317), seventh in walks (885) and extra-base hits (720), and 10th in home runs (224) and RBI (1,068)...is the franchise leader in singles (2,027) and hit by pitches (143)...since Frank Crosetti (114HP) retired in 1948, no Major League shortstop has been hit by a pitch as many times as Jeter...is one of three players who hold their current franchise's all-time hits record (also Colorado's Todd Helton and Tampa Bay's Carl Crawford).
- According to the *Elias Sports Bureau*, at 1,287-849-2, has the highest personal winning percentage (.603) among active players (min. 1,000G)...*Elias* also notes that only five players who made their Major League debuts since 1929 played in more winning games than Jeter (1,197) before reaching the 2000-game mark: Yogi Berra (1,221), Pee Wee Reese (1,221), Paul Blair (1,207), Mickey Mantle (1,206) and Gil Hodges (1,200).
- Along with Jorge Posada and Mariano Rivera, is part of the first trio of teammates ever to play for the Yankees in each of 15 straight seasons (1995-2009)...Bill Dickey, Lefty Gomez and Red Ruffing (1930-42) and Whitey Ford, Elston Howard and Mickey Mantle (1955-67) played together with the Yankees for 13 straight seasons...Jeter, Posada and Rivera are the first trio of players in the Majors to play for the same team in 15 straight seasons since Jim Gantner, Paul Molitor and Robin Yount (15 years, 1978-92 with Milwaukee)—credit: *Elias*.
- His 10 All-Star Game selections are tied with Whitey Ford, Casey Stengel and Mariano Rivera for the sixth-most in club history...joins teammate Mariano Rivera as the only players to be named to the All-Star team with their current team at least 10 times, according to *Elias*.
- Has 303 hits in Interleague Play, most all time...is also Baseball's all-time Interleague leader with 895AB and 171R...is fifth all-time with a .339 career Interleague batting average (min. 300PA)...reached base safely (via hit, walk or HBP) in 51 consecutive Interleague games from 6/25/06 – 6/16/09, marking the longest such stretch since Interleague play began in 1997 (credit: *Elias Sports Bureau*).
- Owns 23 career leadoff homers, second-most in franchise history behind Rickey Henderson (24)...16 of his 23 leadoff HR have come at home and 11 have come in the month of August.
- Finished with 1,274 career hits at the original Yankee Stadium...surpassed Lou Gehrig (1,269) for the most hits all-time at the Stadium in 9/16/08 loss vs. Chicago-AL...according to the *Elias Sports Bureau*, recorded 120 career games of three-or-more hits at Yankee Stadium, most all-time ahead of second-place Gehrig (109)...his 18 career four-hit games at Yankee Stadium rank second all-time to Gehrig's 19.
- Is one of five players to play in at least 1,000 games at the original Yankee Stadium (also Mantle, Gehrig, Berra and B. Williams)...according to the *Elias Sports Bureau*, only the Angels' Garrett Anderson (1,021 at Angel Stadium) appeared in more games in any one stadium among active players.
- Ranks first on Major League Baseball's all-time postseason list with 175 career hits, 99 runs and 138 games played...also ranks second with 50 extra-base hits, and third in home runs (20), with 12 of the homers tying the game or giving the Yankees the lead...is the only player to have hit a leadoff homer in each of the three postseason rounds...is the all-time Division Series leader in hits (74), runs (37), singles (52) and games played (53)...has scored 32 runs in the World Series, fourth-most all time, while ranking fifth with 50 World Series hits...has carried at least a .300 average in five World Series (1998-2000, '03 and '09), matching Babe Ruth and Yogi Berra for the most such Series all-time.

2009

- Hit .334 (212-for-634) with 107R, 27 doubles, 1 triple, 18HR, 66RBI and 30SB in 153 games with the Yankees (147 starts at SS, five starts at DH)...was named the "Sportsman of the Year" by *Sports Illustrated*, becoming the first Yankee to win the honor in its 56-year history...also earned his fourth Silver Slugger Award, fourth Gold Glove Award and second Hank Aaron Award (as the AL's top offensive player voted on by fans)...named to the *Sporting News* AL All-Star team and finished third in AL MVP voting (193 points)...played in a total of 193 games in 2009, including spring training, World Baseball Classic, regular season, All-Star Game and postseason.
- Ranked second in the Majors in hits and fourth in batting average...ranked third in the AL in on-base percentage (.406) and tied with teammate Johnny Damon for fourth in the AL in runs scored...ranked third in the Majors with 66 multi-hit games. and third in the AL in road average (.337)...his 107R were the most among regular

shortstop in the Majors...ranked third in the Majors with a .395 (70-for-177) average vs. left-handed pitchers in 2009...led the Majors with a .409 OBP as the No. 1 batter in the lineup, while his .336 average (205-for-611) ranked third among Major League leadoff men...recorded 21 three-hit games, the highest such total of his career and third-most in the Majors behind Florida's Hanley Ramirez (24) and Minnesota's Joe Mauer (23)...were the most home runs by an AL shortstop.

- According to *Elias*, became the oldest player to post a 200-hit season for the Yankees and became the oldest regular shortstop to ever record 200H in a season (previous was Honus Wagner-201H at age 34 in 1908)...became the seventh player in Major League history to collect 200 hits in a season both before age 25 and after turning 34, joining Nap Lajoie, Ty Cobb, Tris Speaker, Paul Waner, Pete Rose and Tony Gwynn...marked the second-highest batting average by a shortstop at age 35 or older in the last 100 years behind Honus Wagner who hit .339 at age 35.
- Became the oldest player in the last 84 years and one of three players in the modern era (since 1900) to bat .334 and steal 30 bases at age 35-or-older, joining Hall-of-Famers Max Carey (1925), Eddie Collins (1923-24) and Honus Wagner (1909).
- Surpassed Lou Gehrig (2,721) for most hits in franchise history with his third-inning single to right-field off Orioles starter Chris Tillman in 9/11 loss vs. Baltimore...according to *Elias*, became the sixth different player to hold the Yankees hit record at the conclusion of a season, joining Willie Keeler (1903-11), Hal Chase (1911-22), Wally Pipp (1922-29), Babe Ruth (1929-37) and Gehrig (1937-2009)...was voted as the MLB.com "Moment of the Year"...tied Gehrig with a seventh-inning single to right field off Rays starter Jeff Niemann in 9/9 win vs. Tampa Bay, going 3-for-4 with 1 double, 1BB and 1SB.
- Along with Robinson Cano (204H), became just the fifth pair of Yankees teammates (sixth time) to each collect at least 200 hits in the same season...also Lou Gehrig and Earle Combs (1927), Gehrig and Joe DiMaggio (1936, '37), Bernie Williams and Jeter (1999) and Alfonso Soriano and Williams (2002)...also joined Cano as the first pair of teammates in Baseball history to reach 200 hits in a season at the shortstop and second base position (credit: *Elias Sports Bureau*).
- Led off the Yankees half of the first inning with a hit a Major League-best 53 times...hit four leadoff homers (8/10 vs. Toronto, 8/23 at Boston, 8/28 vs. Chicago-AL and 9/30 vs. Kansas City).
- Stole 30 bases in 35 attempts (85.7%), more SB than his totals from '07 and '08 combined (26)...marked his third season with at least 200H and 30SB, the most such seasons for any shortstop.
- Committed just eight errors in 2009, marking his fewest miscues in any full season of play...his .986 fielding percentage matched his highest career mark set in 1998 and was the highest among all AL shortstops.
- Was the AL's top overall All-Star vote-getter for the first time in his career, garnering 4,851,889 fan votes to earn his 10th career All-Star selection and sixth as the AL's starting shortstop...went 0-for-2 with 2R and 1HBP in the 4-3 American League win in St. Louis on 7/14, playing five innings as the AL's starting SS.
- Recorded the first unofficial hit by a Yankee at Yankee Stadium with a first-inning double on 4/3 vs. the Cubs in an exhibition game...played for Team USA in the World Baseball Classic, batting .276 (8-for-29) with 2 doubles in eight games (four starts at SS, three at DH).
- Made his 13th Opening Day start at SS for the Yankees, going 3-for-5 in 4/6 Opening Day loss at Baltimore...were his most hits on Opening Day since 1999 (3-for-3)...are the most Opening Day starts by a Yankees shortstop in franchise history.

MOST HITS IN FRANCHISE HISTORY

1.	**DEREK JETER**	**2,747**
2.	Lou Gehrig	2,721
3.	Babe Ruth	2,518
4.	Mickey Mantle	2,415
5.	Bernie Williams	2,336

TOP ALL-TIME NYY CAREER BATTING AVG. (min. 500G)

1.	Babe Ruth	.349
2.	Lou Gehrig	.340
3.	Joe DiMaggio	.325
4.	Earle Combs	.324
5.	**DEREK JETER**	**.317**

MOST 200-HIT SEASONS, ALL-TIME

1.	Pete Rose	10
2.	Ichiro Suzuki	9
	Ty Cobb	9
4.	Paul Waner	8
	Lou Gehrig	8
6.	**DEREK JETER**	**7**
	Wade Boggs	7
	Charlie Gehringer	7
	Rogers Hornsby	7
10.	Six others tied	6

AMONG ACTIVE MAJOR LEAGUE PLAYERS

MOST RUNS SCORED

1.	ALEX RODRIGUEZ	1,683
2.	Ken Griffey, Jr.	1,656
3.	Gary Sheffield	1,636
4.	**DEREK JETER**	**1,574**
5.	Manny Ramirez	1,506

MOST HITS

1.	Ken Griffey, Jr.	2,763
2.	**DEREK JETER**	**2,747**
3.	Ivan Rodriguez	2,711
4.	Omar Vizquel	2,704
5.	Gary Sheffield	2,689

- Hit two-run HR—his first of the season—and was 2-for-4 with 1BB and 1SB in 4/8 loss at Baltimore...did not hit his first homer in 2008 until his 32nd game (129th at-bat, on 5/10 at Detroit)...did not steal his first base in 2008 until 5/18 vs. the Mets (38th game).
- Recorded the first at-bat by a Yankee in Yankee Stadium in 4/16 loss vs. Cleveland...prior to his first-inning plate appearance, the bat used by Babe Ruth to hit the first home run in the first game at the original Yankee Stadium on 4/18/1923 was placed across the plate in a symbolic nod to the original Stadium.
- Played in his 2,000th career game and hit a solo-HR, in 4/22 win vs. Oakland...struck out in his 8,103rd career at-bat in 4/27 loss at Detroit, surpassing Mickey Mantle for sole possession of first place on the Yankees' all-time at-bats list.
- Committed his first error of the year in 5/2 loss vs. Los Angeles-AL (sixth-inning throwing error)...according to the *Elias Sports Bureau*, his 23-game errorless stretch was his longest to start a season of his career...missed two games (5/12-14) with a strained right oblique.
- Hit safely in a season-high 16 straight games from 5/17-6/2...also tied a career-high with seven consecutive multi-hit games from 5/26-6/2 (also from 6/7-14/99).
- According to the *Elias Sports Bureau*, had 2,592 hits and 1,497 runs from his first game with the Yankees on 5/29/95 through 5/28/09...were the most hits for any player within 14 years of his Major League debut since Pete Rose (2,762)...only one other player who made his Major League debut in the live ball era matched or exceeded his totals for both hits and runs within 14 years of his debut (Hank Aaron, 2,621 hits/1,520 runs).

MOST CAREER POSTSEASON HITS, ALL-TIME

1.	**DEREK JETER**	**175**
2.	Bernie Williams	128
3.	Manny Ramirez	117
4.	Kenny Lofton	97
5.	Chipper Jones	96

MOST CAREER POSTSEASON RUNS, ALL-TIME

1.	**DEREK JETER**	**99**
2.	Bernie Williams	83
3.	Manny Ramirez	67
4.	Kenny Lofton	65
5.	Chipper Jones	58

HIGHEST CAREER AVERAGES, WORLD SERIES HISTORY (min. 100 AB)

	Player	AVG.
1.	Lou Gehrig	.361 (43-for-119)
2.	Eddie Collins	.328 (42-for-128)
3.	Babe Ruth	.326 (42-for-129)
4.	**DEREK JETER**	**.321 (50-for-156)**
5.	Steve Garvey	.319 (36-for-113)

- Scored the 1,500th run of his career in the fourth inning of 6/2 win vs. Texas...became the fourth Yankee (also Babe Ruth, Lou Gehrig and Mickey Mantle) to reach the 1,500R plateau...joins Ken Griffey Jr., Alex Rodriguez, Manny Ramirez and Gary Sheffield as the only active players to score 1,500 runs...reached the milestone in his 2,035th career game...according to the *Elias Sports Bureau*, only Rickey Henderson (1,891), Alex Rodriguez (1,903), Mickey Mantle (1,949) and Willie Mays (2,009) did so in fewer games than Jeter in the expansion era (since 1961).
- Stole a base in four straight games from 6/21-25...according to *Elias*, it marked the longest such streak of his career and the longest by an individual Yankee since Alfonso Soriano had a steal in four straight from 6/28-7/1/03.
- Was 4-for-5 with 4R, 1BB and 1SB in 6/25 win at Atlanta, marking his second career game with at least 4R and 4H (also 6/21/05 vs. Tampa Bay, 5R and 5H).
- According to the *Elias Sports Bureau*, owned 2,623 career hits prior to turning 35 on 6/26, 65 more than all-time hits leader Pete Rose had on the morning of his 35th birthday...did not play on his birthday or 6/27 due to a respiratory illness.

> *"[You are] Major League Baseball's foremost champion and ambassador. You embody all the best of Major League Baseball...you have represented the sport magnificently throughout your Hall of Fame career. On and off the field, you are a man of great integrity, and you have my admiration."*
>
> **-Commissioner Bud Selig, in a letter to Derek Jeter on March 3, 2009**

- Batted at a .358 (122-for-341) clip from 7/1 through the end of the season, leading the Majors in hits and batting average over the stretch.
- Hit .357 (40-for-112) in July, marking his highest average in a single month since he batted .368 in September 2006...followed July with 46 hits in August, leading the AL and marking his first consecutive 40H months since July-August 2001...his 13 career 40-hit months are the most in club history since Joe DiMaggio (17) and the only active player with more 40-hit months is Ichiro Suzuki (21)...his August total marked his second-most hits in a single calendar month in his career, behind August 1998 (50).
- Played in the 2,085th game of his career on 8/4 at Toronto, surpassing Babe Ruth for sole possession of fourth place on the Yankees all-time list.
- Went 21-for-43 (.488) on the Yankees' 10-game road trip from 8/13-23, marking the most hits for any Major Leaguer on a trip in 2009 and the highest average on a trip by any player since Ichiro Suzuki hit .507 (34-for-67) on a 14-game trip in 2004...according to *Elias*, became the first Yankee to record at least 21H with as high an average on a road trip since Moose Skowron (.528, 28-for-53) and Mickey Mantle (.500, 21-for-42) did it on the same trip in June 1957.

DEREK JETER

- Had six straight multi-hit games from 8/15-21, going 16-for-27 and marking his most hits over a six-game span—with as few as 27AB—since 9/22-27/00 (16-for-25)...collected at least three hits in three consecutive games (8/16-18) for the fourth time in his career (also 2000, '04 and '08).
- His third-inning RBI double on 8/16 at Seattle was his 2,674th career hit as a shortstop (also has 13 hits as a DH), surpassing Luis Aparicio (2,673) for the most hits in Major League history from the shortstop position (credit: *Elias*).
- Was 2-for-3 with 1 double and 2BB in 8/25 loss vs. Texas...his first-inning walk snapped a career-long 113 plate appearance stretch (7/28-8/23) without a base-on-balls (previous long was 68 PA in 2000).
- Hit his third leadoff HR of the season in 8/28 win vs. Chicago-AL...was his 223rd career HR, surpassing Don Mattingly (222) for sole possession of 10th place on the Yankees' all-time HR list...played in his 2,117th career contest in 9/7 Game 2 win vs. Tampa Bay, surpassing Yogi Berra (2,116) for sole possession of third place on the Yankees' all-time games played list.
- Did not record a hit in either game on 9/7 vs. Tampa Bay, marking the first time in his career (32 such instances) he went hitless in both games of a doubleheader (credit: *Elias*)...went hitless for the third straight game in 9/8 win vs. Tampa Bay, his first/only time without a hit in three consecutive games this season...also struck out three times in the game for just the second time over the last two seasons (also 7/30/08 vs. Baltimore)...all three strikeouts came against David Price, marking the first time a pitcher struck out Jeter three times in a single game since Boston's Curt Schilling on 4/17/04 at Fenway Park.
- Stole his 300th career base in the first inning on 9/9, making him one of two players to steal 300 bases with the Yankees (also Rickey Henderson–326).
- Batted .344 (22-for-64) with 14R, 5 doubles, 3HR and 6RBI in 15 postseason games, leading the team in hits (22)... reached base safely in all 15 contests, trailing only Barry Bonds (17 straight in 2002) and Gary Sheffield (16 straight in 1997) for the longest streak of reaching base in a single postseason...reached base four times in ALDS Game 1 win (single, HR, 2BB)...according to the *Elias Sports Bureau*, became the third Yankee to have at least 4PA in a postseason game and reach base safely in each, score at least 3R with at least 2RBI and hit a HR (also Babe Ruth in 1926 World Series Game 4 and Reggie Jackson in Game 6 of the 1977 World Series)...collected his third career postseason leadoff HR in the ALCS Game 3 loss at Los Angeles-AL, the first leadoff HR by a Yankee in ALCS history...batted .407 (11-for-27) in the World Series, hitting safely in all six games and marking his most hits in any postseason series...became the oldest starting shortstop on a World Series-winning team since Pee Wee Reese in 1955...donated his bat from Game 6 of the World Series to the Baseball Hall of Fame.

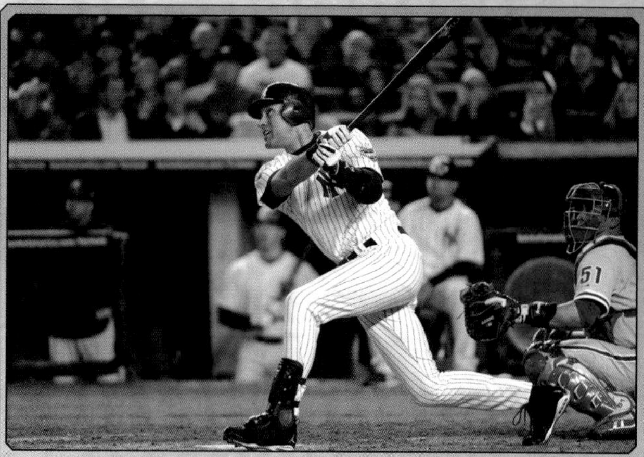

According to the *Elias Sports Bureau*, prior to Jeter setting the all-time franchise hits record on 9/11/09, Lou Gehrig had held the mark since 9/6/37, when he surpassed Babe Ruth (2,518H)...Willie Keeler led the Highlanders in hits in 1903, their first season in New York, and he remained the all-time leader for New York until Hal Chase passed him in August 1911...Chase led the franchise until September 1922, when he was followed by Wally Pipp (1922–1929), Ruth (1929–1937), then Gehrig (1937-2009). Jeter now holds the distinction.

DID YOU KNOW??? Derek Jeter hit safely in 92 of 100 games from 7/21/06-5/16/07 (G1), becoming the first player in modern Major League history (since 1900) to accomplish the feat...according to the Society for American Baseball Research, the player prior to Jeter who accomplished the feat was Wee Willie Keeler, who hit in 93 of 100 games in 1898 and 1899.

2008

- Hit .300 (179-for-596) with 88R, 25 doubles, 3 triples, 11HR and 69RBI in 150 games with the Yankees (147 starts at SS, two starts at DH).
- Struck out 85 times, the fewest for any full season in his Major League career (previous low was 88K in 2003).
- Committed 12 errors, marking his fewest miscues since 1998 (nine) while his .979 fielding percentage was his highest since 2005 (also .979)...was the second-fewest errors among AL shortstops with at least 100 games played at the position, trailing only Texas' Michael Young (10)...went 31 consecutive games without an error from 7/8-8/15.
- Was selected to his ninth All-Star Game...finished second in the AL with 3,737,437 votes (behind teammate Alex Rodriguez)...was 1-for-3 (first-inning infield single) with 1SB in the All-Star Game on 7/15 at Yankee Stadium...following the season, was named to the 2008 *Sporting News* AL All-Star team, which was selected by a panel of 41 general managers and assistant general managers from both leagues...also earned his third consectuive Silver Slugger Award.
- Was 1-for-4 in 4/1 Opening Day win vs. Toronto...was his 12th Opening Day start at SS for the Yankees, surpassing Phil Rizzuto (11) for the most Opening Day starts by a Yankees shortstop in franchise history...started his fifth straight Opening Day at shortstop with Alex Rodriguez at third base, becoming the first pair of Yankees to start on the left side of the infield in five consecutive years since Graig Nettles and Bucky Dent started six consecutive season openers from 1977-82.
- Missed six games from 4/8-13 with a strained left quadriceps...was the longest stretch of consecutive DNPs in his career, not counting times he's been on the D.L. (credit: *Elias Sports Bureau*)...upon returning, hit in seven straight games from 4/14-20, going 12-for-31 (.387) with 4R, 2 doubles, 1 triple, 10RBI and 2BB...did not score a run in nine straight games from 4/18-27, the longest such stretch of his career (credit: *Elias*).
- Hit his first home run of the season and was 2-for-5 with 2R in 5/10 win at Detroit, snapping a 128AB homerless stretch, the longest streak to begin a season of his career (credit: *Elias*).
- Recorded his first stolen base of the season in his 38th game played (5/18 loss vs. the Mets)...his 37-game streak without a steal was his longest in a single season since going 49 straight games without a steal from 6/4-7/26/96 (credit: *Elias*)...was just his second stolen base attempt of 2008 (also 4/1 vs. Toronto)...the streak of 36 games without a steal attempt was the longest of his career (previous high was 30 games in 1996).
- Went hitless in five straight games (0-for-18), his longest such streak since going hitless in seven straight from 4/21-28/04...was picked off second base in the top of the sixth inning by Dennis Sarfate in 5/27 loss at Baltimore...according to the *Elias Sports Bureau*, it was the first time he had been picked off any base since 9/2/98.

FAREWELL SPEECH: "For all of us up here, it's a huge honor to put this uniform on every day and come out here and play. Every member of this organization, past and present, has been calling this place home for 85 years. There's a lot of tradition, a lot of history, and a lot of memories. Now, the great thing about memories, is you're able to pass [them] along from generation to generation. And although things are going to change next year – we're going to move across the street – there are a few things with the New York Yankees that never change. That's pride, it's tradition, and most of all, we have the greatest fans in the world.

"We're relying on you to take the memories from this Stadium, add them to the new memories that come at the new Yankee Stadium and continue to pass them on from generation to generation. So, on behalf of the entire organization, we just want to take this moment to salute you, the greatest fans in the world."

DEREK JETER

- Turned 34 years old on 6/26...his 2,438 career hits were the most by a Yankee before turning 34 years old (17 more than Lou Gehrig when he turned 34)...was the most among all active players prior to their 34th birthday...in AL history, only Ty Cobb and Robin Yount accumulated more hits than Jeter before turning 34.
- In 7/12 win at Toronto, hit his 19th career leadoff homer and first since 9/27/05 at Baltimore...was also his 200th home run as a Yankee...the *Elias Sports Bureau* notes that with Jason Giambi (8/9) and Alex Rodriguez (8/12) also hitting their 200th Yankees homers in 2008, they became the first teammates on any club to reach the 200HR plateau together in the same season.
- Became the 88th player all time—and the sixth active Major Leaguer—to reach the 2,500-hit plateau with his first-inning single in 8/22 win vs. Baltimore...also became the third player in Yankees franchise history to tally 2,500 hits with the club, joining Lou Gehrig (2,721) and Babe Ruth (2,518)...according to the *Elias Sports Bureau*, only two players in the last 65 years were younger than Jeter (34 years, 57 days) at the time of their 2,500th hit (Hank Aaron in 1967 and Robin Yount in 1989).
- In 9/7 loss at Seattle, hit solo-HR to mark his 1,000th career RBI...had a third-inning single to tie Babe Ruth (2,518) for second place on the all-time Yankees hit list...collected his 2,519th career hit with a first-inning single off the Angels' Ervin Santana on 9/9 at Los Angeles, surpassing Ruth (2,518) for sole possession of second place on the Yankees' all-time list...marked the first time since 6/22/33 that someone other than Ruth or Gehrig occupied first or second place on the Yankees' all-time hits list (credit: *Elias Sports Bureau*).
- Was 3-for-4 in 9/13 (Game 1) loss vs. Tampa Bay and 3-for-3 with 1R, 1BB and 1SH in the Game 2 win vs. Tampa Bay, going 6-for-7 during the doubleheader...according to the *Elias Sports Bureau*, he became the first Yankee to record 3H in each game of a doubleheader in remodeled Yankee Stadium (since 1976) and only the sixth Yankee over the last 40 years to accomplish the feat at any park (Johnny Damon in 2006, Willie Randolph in 1987, Dave Winfield in 1983, Matty Alou in 1973 and Roy White in 1972)...also recorded 3H in the series finale on 9/14, finishing the series 9-for-11 and reaching base in 11 of his 13 plate appearances (1BB, 1HBP)...according to the *Elias Sports Bureau*, became the fifth player (and second Yankee) to record at least three hits in every game of a series of three games or more at Yankee Stadium joining Boston's Edgar Renteria (2005), the Yankees' Ken Griffey Sr. (1982), Oakland's Reggie Jackson (1973), and Boston's Dom DiMaggio (1949).
- Tied Lou Gehrig's all-time record of 1,269 career hits at the original Yankee Stadium in 9/14 win vs. Tampa Bay with a fifth-inning solo-HR off David Price, going 3-for-4...in 9/15 win vs. Chicago-AL, tied Gehrig (8,001) for second place on the Yankees' all-time at-bats list (according to the *Elias Sports Bureau*, Gehrig had held sole possession of first place on the franchise's all-time list since 9/6/37).
- With a first-inning single off Gavin Floyd in 9/16 loss vs. Chicago-AL, passed Lou Gehrig (1,269) in all-time hits at the original Yankee Stadium...in the same at-bat, gained sole possession of second place on the Yankees' all-time at-bats list, passing Gehrig (8,001AB)...following the game, his spikes were sent to the National Baseball Hall of Fame.
- Was 0-for-5 in the final game at the original Yankee Stadium on 9/21 vs. Baltimore, making the last Yankees out on a groundout (third base to first base)...gave a speech to the Stadium crowd following the game...the bat he used during the final homestand was sent to the National Baseball Hall of Fame...his final game speech was voted by fans as the MLB.com "Moment of the Year."
- Was scratched from the lineup prior to 9/23 win at Toronto (sore left hand)...entered the game at SS in the ninth...originally suffered the injury on 9/20 vs. Baltimore when he was hit by a Jim Miller pitch in his final at-bat of the game...left 9/26 win at Boston in the third inning with a sore wrist...missed final two games of the season.

PLAYERS TO MATCH JETER'S 2009 TOTALS (.334, 107R, 212H, 18HR, 30SB)

1. George Sisler-STL, 1920 .407, 137R, 257H, 19HR, 42SB
2. Kiki Cuyler-PIT, 1925 .357, 144R, 220H, 18HR, 41SB

according to *Baseball-Reference.com*

JETER'S CAREER BATTING AVERAGE BY POSITION

No. 1	.315	(595G, 794-for-2478, 73HR, 277RBI)
No. 2	.316	(1252G, 1616-for-5118, 133HR, 649RBI)
No. 3	.339	(128G, 171-for-505, 9HR, 66RBI)
No. 4	.000	(1G, 0-for-4)
No. 5	---	(1G, 0-for-0)
No. 6	.000	(1G, 0-for-1)
No. 7	.253	(44G, 43-for-170, 2HR, 20RBI)
No. 8	.301	(25G, 22-for-73, 1HR, 12RBI)
No. 9	.326	(91G, 101-for-310, 6HR, 44RBI)

MOST HITS BEFORE THE AGE OF 36, DURING EXPANSION ERA (Since 1961)

1. Hank Aaron	2,956
2. Robin Yount	2,868
3. Pete Rose	2,769
4. DEREK JETER	**2,747***

*turns 36 on June 26, 2010

2007

- Hit .322 (206-for-639) with 102R, 39 doubles, 12HR, 73RBI and 15SB in 156 games (153 starts at SS)...ranked third in the American League with 206 hits, tied for fourth with 61 multi-hit games and 639 at-bats, ranked seventh with 14HBP, eighth with a .334 home average, tied for eighth with a .354 average with RISP and ninth with a .322 batting average...batted .418 (28-for-67) with runners in scoring position and two outs, the third-highest average in the Majors...was elected to the AL All-Star team, the eighth All-Star selection of his career (1998-2002; 2004, 2006-07)...started at shortstop and was 1-for-3 in the AL's 5-4 win on 7/10 at AT&T Park in San Francisco...also earned a Silver Slugger Award, his second straight.
- Recorded his sixth 200-hit season...also recorded his 11th career season with 100-or-more runs scored (1996-2002; 2004-07), tying Babe Ruth for second-most such seaosns behind only Lou Gehrig (13) in franchise history.
- Fashioned 17-game, 19-game and 20-game hit streaks in the first 72 games of the season...according to the *Elias Sports Bureau*, became the first player since 1950 to record three separate hitting streaks of at least 17 games in the same season and the only player to record three hitting streaks of at least 15 games in his team's first 70 games of a season...collected four separate hitting streaks of at least 15 games in 2007, becoming the first Major Leaguer since 1941 to accomplish the feat (credit: *Elias Sports Bureau*).
- Was 1-for-4 with 2RBI and 1HP in 4/2 Opening Day win vs. Tampa Bay...was his 11th Opening Day start at SS for the Yankees, tying Phil Rizzuto's franchise record for most starts by a Yankee at SS on Opening Day.
- Hit safely in 20 straight games from 4/8-5/3 and 23 of his 24 games played with an official at-bat to begin the season...during the 20-game streak, hit .364 (32-for-88) with 17R...including the final 37 games of 2006, hit safely in 59 of 61 regular season games (since 8/20/06)...also reached base safely in each of his 25 games played to begin 2007 and 66-of-67 games dating back to the previous season (since 8/17/06)...became only the third player in Yankees history to have at least two separate single-season hitting streaks of 20 or more games (also 25 games, 8/20-9/16/06)...Joe DiMaggio had four of them (streaks of 21 and 22 in 1937, 23 in 1940 and 56 in 1941); Don Mattingly had a pair (20 games in 1985 and 24 in 1986).
- Hit safely in 25 consecutive Interleague games from 6/25/06-6/23/07, batting .396 (40-for-101) with 18R, 11 doubles, 2HR, 11RBI, 13BB and 4SB...according to the *Elias Sports Bureau,* was the second-longest hit streak in the history of Interleague play (Matt Lawton hit in 37 straight Interleague games from 6/5/99-7/12/01).
- Reached his 33rd birthday on 6/26 with 2,250 career hits, the most since Robin Yount had 2,391 at that juncture of his career (credit: *Elias Sports Bureau*)...was 83 more hits than Pete Rose (2,167)—Baseball's all-time hits leader—had at the time of his 33rd birthday.
- Hit safely in the final 15 games of the regular season, batting .386 (27-for-70), 13R, 7 doubles, 1 triple, 3HR and 11RBI during the streak...according to the *Elias Sports Bureau*, it was the longest hitting streak by a Yankee to close out a season since Bobby Murcer in 1971 (also 15 games).
- Batted .176 (3-for-17) with 1RBI in four Division Series games vs. Cleveland.

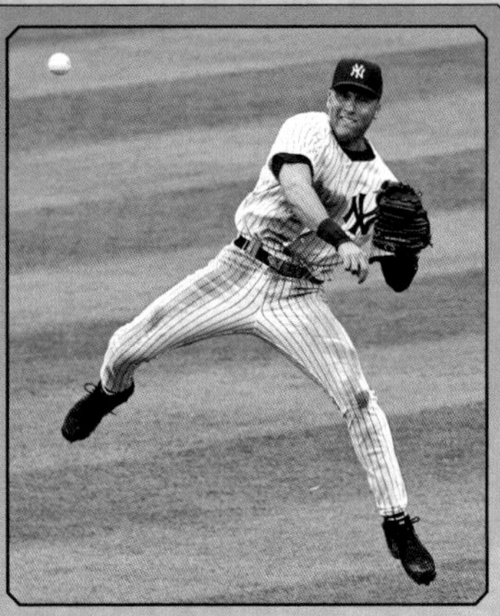

CAREER GAMES AT THE ORIGINAL YANKEE STADIUM

	Player	Games
1.	Mickey Mantle	1,213
2.	Lou Gehrig	1,080
3.	Yogi Berra	1,068
4.	Bernie Williams	1,039
5.	**DEREK JETER**	**1,004**

(Credit: *Elias Sports Bureau*)

FOUR-TIME GOLD GLOVE WINNERS AT SS

Player	Awards
Ozzie Smith	13
Omar Vizquel	11
Luis Aparicio	9
Mark Belanger	8
Dave Concepcion	5
DEREK JETER	**4**
Tony Fernandez	4
Alan Trammell	4

2006

- Finished second in American League Most Valuable Player voting while earning his first Silver Slugger Award and third consecutive Gold Glove Award...hit .343 (214-for-623) with 118R, 39 doubles, 14HR, 97RBI and a career-high 34SB in 154 games (149 starts at SS, five starts at DH)...became just the third player to reach those totals in average, runs, home runs, RBI and stolen bases in a single season, joining Kiki Cuyler with Pittsburgh in 1925 and George Sisler with St. Louis in 1920......the Hank Aaron Award, recognizing the most outstanding offensive performer.
- Ranked second in the AL in batting average, runs, average with runners in scoring position (.381) and average vs. left-handed pitchers (.390), ranked third with a .354 home batting average, tied for third with 214H, fourth with a .417 on-base percentage, tied for fifth with 12HBP, seventh with 34SB and ninth with 623AB.

DEREK JETER

- According to the *Elias Sports Bureau,* became only the fifth player since 1932 to hit .340-or-higher, drive in at least 90 runs and steal 30-or-more bases in the same season, joining Larry Walker (1997), Ellis Burks (1996), Willie Mays (1958) and Jackie Robinson (1949)...was elected to the 2006 AL All-Star team, the seventh All-Star selection of his career...started at SS and was 0-for-3 in the AL's 3-2 win on 7/11 at Pittsburgh's PNC Park.
- In 4/3 win at Oakland, made his 10th Opening Day start at SS for the Yankees...batted a career-best .398 (35-for-88) in April, hitting safely in 20 of the 23 games played.
- Became the eighth Yankee to reach the 2,000-hit plateau with a fourth-inning infield single in 5/26 loss vs. Kansas City, joining Lou Gehrig (2,721), Babe Ruth (2,518), Mickey Mantle (2,415), Bernie Williams (2,336), Joe DiMaggio (2,214), Don Mattingly (2,153) and Yogi Berra (2,148)...according to the *Elias Sports Bureau*, only one of the seven other Yankees with 2,000 hits reached the milestone in fewer games than Jeter's 1,571 (DiMaggio in 1,537 games)...in the expansion era (since 1961), only four players reached the 2,000-hit mark in fewer games than Jeter (also according to the *Elias Sports Bureau*): Wade Boggs (in 1,515 games), Kirby Puckett (1,542), Tony Gwynn (1,560) and Rod Carew (1,562).
- Missed three games (5/30-6/1) with a sprained right hand...was removed from 5/29 win at Detroit in the fifth inning after suffering the injury in a slide at second base in the third inning...on 6/2 at Baltimore, batted third for first time since 9/28/03 (vs. Baltimore)...left 6/4 loss at Baltimore with a bruised right thumb after being hit by a Rodrigo Lopez pitch in the top of the sixth inning and missed next three games (6/5-7 vs. Boston)...started following three games at DH (6/9-11).

MILESTONE HITS

Hit No.	Date/Opp.
1	5/30/95 at SEA (Tim Belcher)
100	7/17/96 at BOS (Joe Hudson)
1,000	9/25/00 vs. DET (Steve Sparks)
2,000	5/26/06 vs. KC (Scott Elarton)
2,416*	6/4/08 vs. TOR (Jesse Litsch)
2,519**	9/9/08 at LAA (Ervin Santana)
2,722***	9/11/09 vs. BAL (Chris Tillman)

* Surpassed Mickey Mantle for sole possession of third place on the Yankees' all-time list

** Surpassed Babe Ruth for sole possession of second place on the Yankees' all-time list

*** Surpassed Lou Gehrig for sole possession of first place on the Yankees' all-time list

- Hit .412 (42-for-102) in the month of July, the third time in his career that he has batted .400 or better for a calendar month.
- Was successful in 14 consecutive stolen-base attempts from 6/13-8/4, including nine straight successful steals of third base...played in the 1,648th game of his career at shortstop on 9/4 at Kansas City, surpassing Phil Rizzuto (1,647) for the most games played at shortstop in franchise history.
- Hit in a career-high 25 straight games from 8/20-9/16, batting .377 (40-for-106) with 21R, 3HR and 21RBI during the streak...was the longest hitting streak by a Yankee since Joe Gordon hit in 29 straight games in 1942...also reached base safely in 30 consecutive games, the longest such streak by a Yankee in 2006...was 3-for-3 with 3R, 1BB and 1SB in 9/30 loss vs. Toronto...recorded his 2,149th career hit, surpassing Yogi Berra (2,148) for seventh place on the club's all-time list.
- Hit safely in 36 of the last 37 games to end the season, batting .368 (57-for-155) with 33R, 4HR and 22RBI during the stretch...reached base safely in 41 of his final 42 games.
- Batted .500 (8-for-16) in four Division Series games vs. Detroit, leading the team with 4R and 4 doubles...tied the Major League record for hits in a single postseason game with five in Game 1 of the ALDS (sixth time, including Hideki Matsui in Game 3 of the 2004 ALCS at Boston), but became only the second player to go 5-for-5 (Atlanta's Marquis Grissom went 5-for-5 in Game 4 of the 1995 NLDS vs. Colorado).

2005

- Hit .309 (202-for-654) with 122R, 19HR, 70RBI and 14SB in 159 games (158 starts at SS), while earning his second consecutive Gold Glove Award...led the American League with a .354 home batting average, ranked second with 122 runs and 62 multi-hit games, third with 202H, tied for third with 654AB, sixth with a .309 batting average and a .389 on-base percentage, and ninth with 77BB...made his ninth Opening Day start at SS on 4/3 vs. Boston.

- Played in the 1,400th game of his career on 5/10 vs. Seattle and had 1,775 career hits, the most by any player through 1,400 games since Kirby Puckett had 1,830...had a leadoff single in five straight games from 5/11-16, the longest such streak of his career...hit 13th career leadoff home run–and first since 4/29/04 vs. Oakland–in 5/29 loss vs. Boston...did not play on 6/3 or 6/4 at Minnesota (chest cold), missing his first two games of the season.
- Hit grand slam and solo-HR and was 2-for-5 in 6/18 win vs. Chicago-NL...was his first career grand slam in his 136th career at-bat with the bases loaded...had 156 career home runs before the grand slam, the most home runs by any active player without a grand slam as well as the most by any player in Yankee history...was his first multi-home run game of the season and the seventh of his career (last hit 2HR in a game on 6/27/04 vs. Mets)...the 5RBI tied his career-high (third time)...was 5-for-6 with 5R, 1 double and a solo-HR in 6/21 win vs. Tampa Bay...established a career high with his five runs and tied a career high with 5H (second time, also on 5/23/01 vs. Boston).
- Hit game-winning solo home runs in consecutive games on 8/11 and 8/12 vs. Texas...made second career start at DH in 8/15 win at Tampa Bay (also 7/7/02 vs. Detroit) and was 1-for-5 with 1R...did not play in 8/22 win vs. Toronto (jammed right thumb)...in the month of August, was tied for the AL lead with 40 hits.
- Played in the 1,500th game of his career on 9/6 vs. Tampa Bay...over that span, amassed 1,906H and 1,140R...marked the most hits and runs by a Major Leaguer in his first 1,500 games since Joe DiMaggio (1,965H and 1,211R).
- Drove in at least one run in six straight games from 9/23-28, the longest streak in the Majors in 2005 from the leadoff position in the batting order...according to the *Elias Sports Bureau,* no player had a longer streak from that spot in the order since Matt Lawton had an eight-game RBI streak for Cleveland in 2002...hit leadoff HR in 9/27 loss at Baltimore, his fifth leadoff HR of the season (also 9/23 vs. Toronto, 9/4 at Oakland, 6/24 vs. NY Mets and 5/29 vs. Boston) and 17th of his career.
- Batted .333 (7-for-21) with 2HR and 5RBI in four Division Series games vs. the Angels...reached base safely in a Division Series-record 21 straight games (dating back to Game 4 of the 2000 ALDS vs. Oakland) before going 0-for-5 in Game 2.

2004

- Emerged from an early-season slump to hit .292 (188-for-643) with a career-high 44 doubles, 23HR, 78RBI and 23SB in 154 games (154 starts at SS)...committed only 13 errors and earned his first career Gold Glove...ranked second in the American League with 16 sacrifice hits, tied for fourth with 44 doubles and 14HBP, was sixth with 111R and 23SB, seventh with 188H and tied for eighth with 68 extra-base hits...was elected to the 2004 American League All-Star team, the sixth All-Star selection of his career...was the first Yankees' shortstop to be elected to start the All-Star Game since Bucky Dent in 1981...started at SS in the 7/13 AL win, going 3-for-3 with 1R.
- Was batting .189 on 5/25, going 36-for-190 in his first 43 games of the season with 17R, 8 doubles, 3HR and 17RBI...in his final 111 games, beginning on 5/26, hit .336 (152-for-453) with 94R, 36 doubles, 20HR and 61RBI.
- Made his eighth Opening Day start at SS on 3/30 at Tampa Bay in Tokyo, Japan...hit 12th lead-off home run of his career in 4/29 win vs. Oakland—and first since 8/5/03 vs. Texas—to snap an 0-for-32 stretch (longest such stretch of his career)...recorded three straight three-hit games from 5/26-28, marking the second time in his career (also in June 2000)...drove in at least one run in nine straight games from 5/23-6/2...was the longest RBI streak by a Yankee since Don Mattingly drove in at least one run in nine straight games in 1987...missed three games (6/5-8) with tightness in the left groin.
- Had his 21-game hitting streak at Camden Yards snapped on 6/23, going 0-for-4 (batted .351, 34-for-97, during that span which began on 4/4/02)...hit .396 in 23 games in June (36-for-91) with 24R, 9HR and 17RBI...set a calendar-month career high with 9HR and his .396 average was his highest monthly average since he hit .425 in July 2003.
- Was 1-for-4 with 1HBP in 7/1 win vs. Boston before being removed from the game in the bottom of the 12th inning after suffering a laceration of the chin, a bruised right cheek and a bruised right shoulder...suffered the injuries after catching a fly ball by Trot Nixon and diving into the stands to end the top of the 12th...was taken to Columbia Presbyterian where precautionary X-rays of his right cheek were negative...started at SS the following night...did not play in two straight games from 7/21-22 because of a small, non-displaced fracture of the fifth metacarpal of his right hand...sustained injury after being hit by a pitch in the sixth inning of 7/20 win at Tampa Bay.
- Before fifth-inning throwing error in 8/8 win vs. Toronto, had gone a career-high 46 consecutive games without committing an error.
- Had 17-game hitting streak from 7/30-8/17, batting .338 (25-for-74) with 12R, 1HR and 5RBI over the span...was also the longest hitting streak by a Yankee since Bernie Williams hit safely in 19 straight games from 8/7-28/02...reached the 1,000-run plateau with a solo-HR on 8/24 at Cleveland in his 1,331st game, becoming only the fifth player in the expansion era (since 1961) to accomplish the feat in fewer than 1,400 games...according to the *Elias Sports Bureau,* he joined Rickey Henderson (1,252 games), Alex Rodriguez (1,261), Kenny Lofton (1,305) and Chuck Knoblauch (1,379).
- Scored at least one run in 11 straight games from 9/5-15, the longest such streak of his career...it is the longest such streak by a Yankee since Bernie Williams scored in a career-high 13 straight games in 2000...was named the AL's "Player of the Week" for the week of 9/6-12...was the second weekly award of his career (also 8/5/01)...batted in the leadoff position in the batting order in his final 25 games of the season, hitting .388 (40-for-103) with 28R, 11 doubles, 5HR and 18RBI.

- In 11 postseason games, batted .245 (12-for-49) with 1HR and 9RBI...hit solo-HR to lead off the bottom of the first inning of ALDS Game 2 vs. Minnesota and became the 19th player to homer into the black batters-eye section of the remodeled Yankee Stadium, the third in postseason play (also Reggie Jackson in Game 6 of the 1977 World Series and Seattle's Jay Buhner in Game 3 of the 2001 ALCS)...was his second career leadoff home run in postseason play (also 10/25/00 in Game 4 of the World Series at the New York Mets).

2003

- Rebounded from an early-season injury to hit .324 (156-for-482) with 10HR, 52RBI and 11SB in 119 games (118 starts at SS)...ranked third in the AL in average and 10th in the league with a .393 on-base percentage...was placed on the 15-day disabled list on 4/1 after suffering a dislocated left shoulder in third inning of 3/31 Opening Day win at Toronto...was reinstated from the 15-day D.L. on 5/13 after missing 36 games...hit leadoff-HR in 5/27 win vs. Boston, the 10th leadoff HR of his career and first since 6/1/01 vs. Seattle...was named the 11th team captain in Yankees history by Principal Owner George Steinbrenner on 6/3.
- Was 37-for-87 (.425) in the month of July (with 17R, 8 doubles, 1HR, 12RBI, and 12BB), the second-highest batting average in the Majors during the month behind only the White Sox' Magglio Ordonez...left 7/7 win vs. Boston in third inning after being hit by pitch on right hand in the first inning...did not start the next day at Cleveland after suffering a bone bruise on his right hand...recorded a season-high four hits in 7/9 win at Cleveland, going 4-for-5 with 1R and a two-run double.
- Hit leadoff HR and two-run HR and was 2-for-4 on 8/5 vs. Texas...was his second leadoff-HR of the season and 11th of his career...was his first multi-HR game of the season and fourth of his career (last on 9/19/01 at Chicago-AL)...recorded his 1,500th career hit with a third-inning single and was 1-for-6 in 8/16 win at Baltimore...missed five games (9/1-6) after suffering strained rib-cage muscle in 8/31 win at Boston.
- Hit .314 (22-for-70) with 10R, 2HR and 5RBI in 17 postseason games.

2002

- Batted .297 (191-for-644) with 18HR, 75RBI and 32SB in 157 games (156 starts at SS, one at DH)...ranked third in the American League with 124R and 32SB, fifth in multi-hit games (58), and seventh in hits (191)...became only the fourth player since 1900 to score at least 100 runs in each of seven straight seasons starting with his rookie year...Earle Combs (1925-32) and Ted Williams (1939-49) both did it in each of their first eight seasons; Johnny Pesky did it in each of his first six (1942-50)...with Bernie Williams, were only the second set of teammates to score at least 100 runs in seven consecutive seasons (1996-2002), joining the Yankees' Earle Combs, Babe Ruth and Lou Gehrig (1926-32)...was selected by Manager Joe Torre to participate in his fifth consecutive All-Star Game on 7/9 at Miller Park in Milwaukee, Wisc...pinch-hit and was 0-for-1.
- In Opening Day loss at Baltimore, registered his 1,200th career hit and 100th career home run with two-run shot in the eighth inning...collected his 500th career RBI with a first-inning double in 4/19 win vs. Toronto...had season-high 16-game hitting streak from 5/9-25...batted .348 (24-for-69) with 3HR and 6RBI during the stretch...was longest streak by a Yankee in 2002.
- Hit leadoff home run in the first inning and was 1-for-2 with 2R, 2RBI, 1BB, 1SF and 1HBP in 6/1 win vs. Boston...was his ninth career leadoff home run...played in his 1,000th career game and hit a solo-HR in 6/10 win vs. Arizona...was 2-for-4 with 1R, 1RBI, 1BB and a career-high 3SB in 6/28 win at New York-NL...left 7/4 game vs. Cleveland in the top of the third inning after being slid into at second base by John McDonald...missed the following two games with a sprained knee and bruised lower leg...made his first career start at DH in 7/7 win vs. Toronto and hit two-run HR while going 1-for-4 with 2R and 1BB.
- Recorded season-high four hits in 8/14 win at Kansas City, going 4-for-7...hit in the final five games of the season, going 9-for-21 to raise his average from .292 to .297.
- Hit .500 (8-for-16) with 6R, 2HR and 3RBI in four Division Series games versus the Angels...collected his 100th career postseason hit in Game 4 at Anaheim on 10/5 (first-inning single off Jarrod Washburn).

2001

- Batted .311 (191-for-614) with 110R, 21HR and 74RBI in 150 games (150 starts at SS)...hit .324 (34-for-105) with 17R, 5HR and 11RBI in 26 games as a leadoff hitter and had nine first-inning hits (seven for extra bases) in 24AB...appeared in only five spring training games, going 3-for-15 with 1RBI...missed first nine games of spring training with inflammation in his right shoulder and final 14 games with a strained right quadriceps...was placed on the 15-day D.L. (retroactive to 3/23) with strained right quad to begin the season...snapped a stretch of five straight Opening Day starts at SS.
- Was activated from the 15-day D.L. prior to 4/7 game and made first appearance of the season that day vs. Toronto, going 1-for-5...his steal of home in the third inning on 5/5 win at Baltimore was the first by a Yankee since he did it on 6/18/99 at the Angels...established a career high with 5H, hit a solo-HR and was 5-for-5 with 3R and 1 double in 5/23 win vs. Boston...became first Yankee SS to have a five-hit game since Tony Kubek in 1962.
- Was selected to his fourth consecutive All-Star Game, hitting his first All-Star home run (solo shot in the sixth) in the AL's 4-1 win on 7/10 in Seattle...was the first homer by a Yankee in an All-Star Game since Yogi Berra in 1959...led the AL with 40 hits in July...was named AL "Player of the Week" for 7/30-8/5, batting .524

(11-for-21) in six games with 2HR and 5RBI (his first such award)...hit leadoff HR and was 4-for-5 with 2R and 1RBI in 8/11 loss at Oakland...was his fifth career leadoff HR and first since 8/20/97 at Anaheim...in his next start as leadoff hitter in 8/18 loss vs. Seattle, hit his second straight leadoff home run and fourth in a six-start stretch from the leadoff spot.

- His seventh-inning throwing error on 8/22 at Texas snapped his 36-game errorless streak...collected 43 hits in August (third-most in AL), marking the eighth time in his career he reached the 40-hit plateau in one month...among active players, only Tony Gwynn had more 40-hit months (19) at that time...missed four games (9/5-9) with a strained left hamstring sustained while running to first base in the second inning on 9/4 at Toronto...in 9/19 win at Chicago-AL, recorded the third multi-HR game of his career and first since 9/9/98 at Boston...in his last 82 games of the season (since 6/24), batted .334 (111-for-332) with 68R, 16HR and 39RBI.
- Batted .226 (14-for-62) in 17 postseason games...in five Division Series games vs. Oakland, batted .444 (8-for-18)...made famous "flip play" on 10/13/01 in Game 3 at Oakland, relaying Shane Spencer's errant throw to Jorge Posada in time to nail Jeremy Giambi at the plate in the seventh inning...was 2-for-3 in Game 5 of the ALDS and established a Major League record for most career postseason hits with 87 (in 66 games), surpassing Pete Rose's 86 hits (in 67 games)...had his 12-game postseason hitting streak snapped in Game 3 of the ALDS...had his 14-game World Series hitting streak snapped in Game 1 of the World Series...his streak tied Roberto Clemente for the third-longest streak of all time (behind only Hank Bauer, Yankees, 17 straight games, 1956-58; and Marquis Grissom, Atlanta-Cleveland, 15, 1995-97).

2000

- Was a member of his fourth World Series championship team, becoming the first player in Major League history to be named MVP of the Fall Classic and All-Star Game in the same season...the only other player to win both awards in his career is Frank Robinson, World Series MVP in 1966 and All-Star MVP in 1971...at 26 years old, only Joe DiMaggio and Mickey Mantle (at 24) and Billy Martin (25) earned four World Championships at a younger age...hit .339 with 15HR and 73RBI in 148 games (148 starts at SS).
- Recorded his third straight 200-hit season, becoming only the third Yankee to compile three consecutive 200-hit seasons (joining Lou Gehrig, 1927-29 and Don Mattingly, 1984-86)...joined Bernie Williams in reaching the 100-run plateau for the fifth straight season...was only the third time since 1900 that teammates have each scored 100 or more runs in at least five consecutive seasons...the Yankees' Babe Ruth, Lou Gehrig and Earle Combs accomplished the feat in seven consecutive seasons (1926-32) and Cincinnati's Joe Morgan and Pete Rose broke the 100-run plateau in five straight seasons (1972-76).
- Reached his 26th birthday on 6/26 with 887 career hits...only two Yankees had more hits at age 26 (Mickey Mantle, 1,080 and Joe DiMaggio, 970)...only three active players at the time had more hits before turning 26 (Roberto Alomar, 1054; Ken Griffey, Jr., 1039 and Ivan Rodriguez, 948)...was selected to his third All-Star Game by Manager Joe Torre...went 3-for-3 with 1R and 2RBI in his first start and was named Most Valuable Player of the 71st All-Star Game in Atlanta, Ga...became the first player in Yankees history to be named MVP of the All-Star Game and the fourth shortstop to take home the honor.
- Made fifth straight Opening Day start at SS...reached base safely in 26 of the first 28 games of the season (4/3-5/6)–including 23 straight from 4/7-5/3...scored his 500th career run on 4/23 at Toronto, becoming only the fourth Yankee to reach the 500-run plateau before his 26th birthday (joining Gehrig, DiMaggio and Mantle)...was hitless in four straight games (5/7-9, 5/11) for the first time since 4/26-29/97...left game in third inning on 5/11 vs. Tampa Bay and missed five games (5/12-17) with an abdominal strain...was placed on the 15-day disabled list from 5/19-27.
- Compiled a streak of 10 consecutive games with at least one walk from 8/14-23, (14BB total)...was the longest such streak by a Yankee since Jesse Barfield also walked in 10 straight games from 8/9-19/90...reached the 1,000-hit plateau with a fifth-inning single and was 3-for-4 on 9/25 vs. Detroit...at 26, became the second-youngest Yankee to reach 1,000 hits (behind only Mickey Mantle, who was 25 when he collected his 1,000th hit in 1957).
- Hit .317 (20-for-63) and led the Yankees with 13R and 4HR in the postseason...had his 17-game postseason hitting streak snapped in Game 1 of the Division Series at Oakland, going 0-for-3...was the World Series MVP, hitting .409 (9-for-22) with two doubles, one triple, 2HR and 2RBI in five games...set a five-game World Series record with 19 total bases and tied five-game records with 9H and 6R...also became the eighth player to lead off a World Series game with a home run in Game 4.
- Became the third shortstop to ever win the World Series MVP Award, joining the Yankees' Bucky Dent in 1978 and Detroit's Alan Trammell in 1984...hit safely in all five World Series games, extending his hitting streak in the Series to 14 games.

1999

- Culminated his season with a third World Championship in his first four full seasons...only two other Yankee players (Mickey Mantle, 21 years old and Joe DiMaggio, 23 years old) have won three championships at a younger age than Jeter (25)...hit .349 with 37 doubles, 24HR and 102RBI in 158 games (all at SS)...set career highs in nearly every offensive category, including batting average, runs (134), hits (219), triples (9), home runs, RBI, and walks (91)...was named to his second All-Star team by Yankees manager Joe Torre (was 0-for-1).

- Was among the AL leaders in multi-hit games (first-67), hits (first), batting average (second), runs (second), triples (tied for second), on-base percentage (third-.438) and total bases (tied for fourth-346)...his 102RBI were the second-most ever by a Yankees shortstop in a single season behind only Lyn Lary's 107 in 1931...led the Yankees in hits for the fourth straight season and became the first player since Ernie Banks to lead his team in hits in each of his first four full seasons...his 219 hits were the fourth-highest single-season total by a Yankee and most since 1986 (Don Mattingly, 238)...joined centerfielder Bernie Williams as the first pair of Yankee teammates to record 200 or more hits in the same season since DiMaggio and Lou Gehrig accomplished the feat in 1939...became the first player to score at least 100 runs in four straight seasons starting with his rookie year since Jim Gilliam did it for the Brooklyn Dodgers from 1953-56.
- Reached base safely in each of the first 53 games of the season, the longest streak in the Majors in 1999 and the longest by a Yankee in the post-expansion era (since 1961)...the streak ended in a 7-2 loss on 6/6 vs. New York-NL...had six hitting streaks of at least 10 games, including a season-high 16-game streak from 5/4-22.
- Tied his career high with 5RBI in a 10-1 win on 5/7 vs. Seattle...posted seven consecutive multi-hit games from 6/7-14, the most by a Yankee since Dave Winfield in 1988...batted third for the first time in his career on 6/18 vs. Anaheim and went 2-for-3 with 2R, 1RBI and 1HBP...also stole home on the front end of a double steal with Chili Davis...hit in the third position from 6/18-7/1, batting .395 (17-for-43) and hitting safely in each of the 11 games...batted fourth for the first time ever on 7/10 at New York-NL...was 0-for-4 with 1IBB.
- Snapped an 0-for-17 skid with the game-winning two-run home run off David Wells in the eighth inning of a 3-1 victory on 8/2 vs. Toronto...the home run was his 20th of the season, making him the first Yankees shortstop ever to hit 20HR in a season.
- Hit .375 (18-for-48) and led the Yankees with 10R in the postseason...hit safely in all 12 games and 17 consecutive postseason games dating back to 1998, tying Hank Bauer for the all-time record.

1998

- Batted .324 with 19HR and 84RBI in 149 games (148 starts at SS)...finished third in the American League MVP voting behind Juan Gonzalez and Nomar Garciaparra...was among the American League leaders in runs (first-127), multi-hit games (tied for second), hits (third-203), triples (tied for fourth-8), batting average (fifth) and at-bats (sixth-626)...broke the single-season home run record for Yankees shortstops (previously held by Roy Smalley in 1982 with 16)...with 203 hits, joined Phil Rizzuto as the second Yankees shortstop to collect 200 or more hits in a season (Rizzuto had 200 in 1950).
- Set a Major League record for most runs scored by a shortstop in his first three full seasons with 352, surpassing the previous mark of 343 held by Detroit's Donie Bush from 1908-11...joined Frank Crosetti as the only Yankees shortstops to score 100 or more runs in three or more consecutive seasons (Crosetti did it in four straight seasons from 1936-39)...combined with 2B Chuck Knoblauch to become the first pair of Yankees middle infielders to each hit 15 or more home runs in the same season (Knoblauch had 17)...they also became the third pair of middle-infield teammates in AL history to record at least 30 stolen bases each in a single season (also SS Jack Barry and 2B Eddie Collins of the 1911 Philadelphia Athletics and SS Bert Campaneris and 2B Phil Garner of the 1976 Oakland Athletics)...was named to his first All-Star team by Cleveland manager Mike Hargrove and went 0-for-1 in the game.
- Drove in a career-high five runs on 5/6 at Texas...had a season-high 15-game hitting streak from 5/2-20, batting .456 (31-for-68) with 4HR and 19RBI during the streak...was placed on the disabled list for the first time in his career on 6/4 with a strained abdominal muscle sustained on a check swing on 6/3 vs. Tampa Bay (missed 12 team games)...was named the American League's "Player of the Month" for August, batting .382 (50-for-131) with 30R, 9 doubles, 4HR and 22RBI in 32 games.
- With 50 hits in August, he became the first Yankee to collect 50 hits in a month since Joe DiMaggio had 53 in July 1941...joined Alex Rodriguez (54 hits in August 1996) as the only players to reach 50 hits in a month in the 1990s.
- Started every game of the postseason, batting .235 (12-for-51) with 7R and 3RBI...hit .353 (6-for-17) vs. San Diego in the World Series.

1997

- In his sophomore campaign, batted .291 with 10HR and 70RBI in 159 games (all starts at SS)...led the American League with 748 plate appearances and tied for first with 142 singles...ranked third in at-bats (654) and hits (190) and tied for fourth in games played (159)...also ranked fourth in runs scored (116), tied for fifth in triples (7) and ninth in stolen bases (23).
- Had a team-leading 57 multi-hit games, tying him for third in the American League...scored at least 100 runs in each of his first two seasons, making him only the second Yankee to accomplish the feat (Joe DiMaggio 1936-37)...became only the fifth Yankee to play 140 or more games in each of their first two seasons seasons (also Earle Combs, Tony Lazzeri, Tom Tresh and Alvaro Espinoza)...in 102 games in the leadoff spot, hit .321 (137-for-427) with 6HR and 45RBI.
- Had a season-high 11-game hitting streak from 5/4-15...snapped a career-high 75-game homerless drought with a leadoff homer on 8/7 at Texas...had his first career multi-homer game with 2HR and 4RBI on 8/20 at Anaheim (G2).

- Started all five games of the Division Series vs. Cleveland at SS, hitting .333 (7-for-21) with 2HR and 2RBI…hit the second of three consecutive home runs in the sixth inning of Game 1 (between Tim Raines and Paul O'Neill), marking the first time three consecutive home runs have ever been hit in postseason play.

1996

- Hit .314 with 10HR and 78RBI, winning the American League "Rookie of the Year" Award…was the fifth time a Yankee had won the award and the first since Thurman Munson in 1970…became the club's first Opening Day rookie shortstop since Tom Tresh in 1962…hit his first Major League home run on Opening Day on 4/2 at Cleveland, a solo shot off Dennis Martinez…led the Yankees with 183H and 156 games started (all at SS) and tied with Tino Martinez for the team lead in multi-hit games with 49.
- Played the most games of any AL rookie (157) and had a stretch of 105 consecutive starts before sitting out the second game of a doubleheader on 9/25 vs. Milwaukee…had a season-high 17-game hitting streak from 9/7-25, the longest by a Yankees rookie since Joe DiMaggio's streak of 18 games in 1936…his 77RBI were the most by a rookie shortstop since Julio Franco drove in 80 in 1980…hit an inside-the-park home run on 8/2 at Kansas City, the first by a Yankee since Alvaro Espinoza on 7/21/90 at Minnesota.
- Hit .361 with 12R, 1HR and 3RBI in the postseason…scored the game-winning run in the bottom of the 12th inning in Game 2 of the Division Series vs. Texas after 3B Dean Palmer overthrew first base on a Charlie Hayes bunt…hit controversial game-tying home run off Armando Benitez in the eighth inning of Game 1 of the ALCS when a young fan reached over the wall and deflected the ball (Yankees would win 5-4 in 11 innings).

1995

- Saw his first Major League action, batting .250 (12-for-48) with 4 doubles and 7RBI in 15 games across two stints with the Yankees…contract was purchased on 5/29 after Tony Fernandez was placed on the disabled list with a strained rib cage muscle…made 13 starts and batted .234 with 0HR and 6RBI before he was optioned back to Columbus on 6/11…was recalled on 9/3, appearing in two games and raising his average to .250…was named to the International League All-Star team…his .317 batting average led all Yankees minor leaguers and ranked third among Triple-A shortstops…ranked third among Triple-A players with 96R, tied for fifth with 9 triples and was seventh with 154 hits.

1994

- Was named Minor League "Player of the Year" by *Baseball America*, *Sporting News*, *USA Today Baseball Weekly* and Topps/NAPBL after hitting .344 with 5HR, 68RBI and 50SB combined at Triple-A Columbus, Double-A Albany and Single-A Tampa…became the first Yankees prospect to win the *Baseball America* and *USA Today* awards…was also named MVP of the Florida State League…his .344 average led all minor league shortstops and ranked 10th in the minors overall…also ranked among all minor leaguers with 186 hits (second), 103R (10th) and 50SB (tied for 14th)…was named the Yankees "Minor League Player of the Year" after leading the organization in batting average, stolen bases, runs, hits and triples…was named the organization's "Player of the Month" for May after hitting .391 and leading the organization with 31R…earned a June promotion to Albany after hitting .367 in his last 49 games at Tampa.
- Was the Florida State League's "Player of the Month" for June…had a five-hit game on 6/10 at Sarasota…hit .420 in July at Albany and was named Topps' Eastern League "Player of the Month."…was promoted to Columbus on 8/1…hit safely in 28-of-35 games with the Clippers and did not go hitless in consecutive games…finished the season with a five-game hitting streak, batting .579 (11-for-19), including a 4-for-4 performance on 8/31 vs. Toledo…Yankees affiliates combined for a .621 winning percentage (87-53) with Jeter on the roster and a .502 winning percentage without him (138-137)…committed 25 errors in 616 chances at shortstop…played for Chandler in the Arizona Fall League and hit .278 with 9RBI, 2SB and 11 errors in 16 games before he was sidelined with mild inflammation in his right shoulder.

1993

- Was voted the "Most Outstanding Major League Prospect" by South Atlantic League managers after hitting .295 with 5HR, 71RBI and 18SB at Class-A Greensboro…was named to the All-Star team after finishing second in the league in triples (11), third in hits (152) and 11th in batting average…ranked fifth in the organization in batting average…committed 56 errors in 126 games at shortstop, ranking second in the league in errors by a shortstop…was voted by *Baseball America* as the South Atlantic League's "Best Defensive Shortstop," "Most Exciting Player" and "Best Infield Arm."

1992

- Was the Yankees' first-round selection and the sixth pick overall in the June 1992 First-Year Player Draft…was the first high school player chosen in the draft…became the third shortstop in Yankees history selected with a first-round pick, joining Rex Hudler (1978) and Dennis Sherrill (1974)…combined to hit .210 with 4HR and 29RBI in 58 games at Single-A Tampa and Single-A Greensboro…had 12 errors in 211 chances at Tampa and nine errors in 48 chances at Greensboro.

DEREK JETER

Personal

- Full name is Derek Sanderson Jeter...was signed by Dick Groch...graduated in 1992 from Kalamazoo Central High School (Mich.), where he hit .508 (30-for-59) with 4HR, 23RBI, 21BB and 1K in 23 games as a senior...was 12-for-12 in stolen base attempts, had an .831 slugging percentage and a .637 on-base percentage...hit .557 with 7HR as a junior...was named 1992 High School "Player of the Year" by the American Baseball Coaches Association...was elected into the Kalamazoo High School Hall of Fame in December 2007.
- Was the recipient of the Joan Payson Award for community service in 1997, presented annually by the New York chapter of the BBWAA...received the New York Press Photographers' annual "Good Guy" Award for 1998...also received the Babe Ruth Award from the New York Chapter of the BBWAA in 2000, awarded annually to the Postseason MVP...was one of three finalists for the 2008 "Marvin Miller Man of the Year" Award given annually by the MLB Players' Association to the player in either league whose on-field performance and contributions to his community inspire others to higher levels of achievement...was the recipient of the Joe DiMaggio "Toast of the Town" Award New York Chapter of the BBWAA for the third time in 2009 (also 1999 and 2000)...also honored along with teammates Andy Pettitte, Jorge Posada and Mariano Rivera with the "Willie, Mickey and the Duke" Award from the New York BBWAA in 2009.
- Selected as the 2009 "Roberto Clemente Award" winner, given annually to the Major League Baseball player who combines a dedication to giving back to the community with outstanding skills on the baseball field...hosted Saturday Night Live on 12/1/01...was honored with the *Sporting News* "Good Guy in Sports" Award in 2002 and also received an ESPY for the Best Play Award that same year for his "flip play" in Game 3 of the 2001 ALDS at Oakland.
- Named the No. 1 sports celebrity in WFAN's (660AM) Top 20 New York Athletes of the Last 20 Years in December 2007...selected as a member of *Time Out New York's* "Top 40 under 40" in 2008.
- Since 1996, Derek's Turn 2 Foundation has enjoyed 14 years of supporting various programs and activities designed to motivate youth to "Turn 2" a healthy lifestyle, academic achievement and leadership development and "turn away" from drugs and alcohol...the Foundation has awarded more than $10 million to support signature programs in Tampa, where Derek resides, New York, where he works, and West Michigan, where he grew up...along with his "Jeter's Leaders," hosted a leadership conference at the University of Texas at Arlington in August 2008, that brought together high school student leaders from New York, West Michigan, Louisville and Chicago...held his annual Holiday Express on 12/3/09 at Yankee Stadium, assembling approximately 1,000 gift bags with the New York Jeter's Leaders and the Yankees to be distributed to deserving youngsters...following the assembly, held a private holiday party at the Stadium...also joined Santa at the Air Zoo in Portage, Mich., on 12/8/09 to celebrate the holidays with the Kalamazoo Jeter's Leaders...hosted the Seventh Annual Derek Jeter Celebrity Golf Classic in Tampa, Fla., in January 2010...the sold-out event brought together celebrities from MLB, the NBA and the NFL as well as musicians and actors, raising nearly $1 million...hosts annual baseball clinics in Michigan, New York City and Tampa.
- Donated $500,000 to launch the "Derek Jeter Center at Phoenix House" in Tampa, an outpatient counseling center for troubled teens combining individual and family substance abuse treatment...attended ribbon-cutting on 10/2/09.

Jeter's Career Batting Record

Year	Club	AVG	G	AB	R	H	2B	3B	HR	RBI	SH	SF	HP	BB	SO	SB	CS	E	OBP	SLG
1992	GCL Yankees	.202	47	173	19	35	10	0	3	25	0	2	5	19	36	2	2	12	.296	.312
	Greensboro	.243	11	37	4	9	0	0	1	4	0	0	1	7	16	0	1	9	.378	.324
1993	Greensboro	.295	128	515	85	152	14	11	5	71	2	4	11	58	95	18	9	56	.376	.394
1994	Tampa	.329	69	292	61	96	13	8	0	39	3	3	3	23	30	28	2	12	.380	.428
	Albany	.377	34	122	17	46	7	2	2	13	3	1	1	15	16	12	2	6	.446	.516
	Columbus	.349	35	126	25	44	7	1	3	16	3	1	1	20	15	10	4	7	.439	.492
1995	Columbus	.317	123	486	96	154	27	9	2	45	2	5	4	61	56	20	12	29	.394	.422
	YANKEES	.250	15	48	5	12	4	1	0	7	0	0	0	3	11	0	0	2	.294	.375
1996	YANKEES	.314	157	582	104	183	25	6	10	78	6	9	9	48	102	14	7	22	.370	.430
1997	YANKEES	.291	159	654	116	190	31	7	10	70	8	2	10	74	125	23	12	18	.370	.405
1998	YANKEES - a	.324	149	626	*127	203	25	8	19	84	3	3	5	57	119	30	6	9	.384	.481
	Columbus	.400	1	5	2	2	2	0	0	0	0	0	0	0	2	0	0	1	.400	.800
1999	YANKEES	.349	158	627	134	*219	37	9	24	102	3	6	12	91	116	19	8	14	.438	.552
2000	YANKEES - b	.339	148	593	119	201	31	4	15	73	3	3	12	68	99	22	4	24	.416	.481
	Tampa	.667	1	3	2	2	1	0	0	0	0	0	0	0	0	0	0	0	.667	1.000
2001	YANKEES - c	.311	150	614	110	191	35	3	21	74	5	1	10	56	99	27	3	15	.377	.480
2002	YANKEES	.297	157	644	124	191	26	0	18	75	3	3	7	73	114	32	3	14	.373	.421
2003	YANKEES - d	.324	119	482	87	156	25	3	10	52	3	1	13	43	88	11	5	14	.393	.450
	Trenton	.444	5	18	2	8	1	1	0	5	0	0	1	3	0	0	0	1	.545	.611
2004	YANKEES	.292	154	643	111	188	44	1	23	78	16	2	14	46	99	23	4	13	.352	.471
2005	YANKEES	.309	159	654	122	202	25	5	19	70	7	3	11	77	117	14	5	15	.389	.450
2006	YANKEES	.343	154	623	118	214	39	3	14	97	7	4	12	69	102	34	5	15	.417	.483
2007	YANKEES	.322	156	639	102	206	39	4	12	73	3	2	14	56	100	15	8	18	.388	.452
2008	YANKEES	.300	150	596	88	179	25	3	11	69	7	4	9	52	85	11	5	12	.363	.408
2009	YANKEES	.334	153	634	107	212	27	1	18	66	4	1	5	72	90	30	5	8	.406	.465
Minor League Totals		**.308**	**454**	**1777**	**313**	**548**	**82**	**32**	**16**	**218**	**13**	**16**	**27**	**206**	**266**	**90**	**32**	**133**	**.385**	**.418**
Major League Totals		**.317**	**2138**	**8659**	**1574**	**2747**	**438**	**58**	**10**	**68**	**78**	**44**	**143**	**885**	**1466**	**305**	**80**	**213**	**.388**	**.459**

* denotes league leader

Selected by New York (AL) in the first round (sixth pick overall) of the 1992 First-Year Player Draft.

a - Placed on the 15-day disabled list on June 6, 1998 with a strained abdominal muscle.
b - Placed on the 15-day disabled list from May 19-27, 2000 (retroactive to May 12) with a strained abdominal muscle.
c - Placed on the 15-day disabled list from March 31 - April 7, 2001 (retroactive to March 23) with a strained right quad.
d - Placed on the 15-day disabled list from April 1 - May 13, 2003 with a dislocated left shoulder.

DEREK JETER

Jeter's Division Series Record

Year	Club vs. Opp.	AVG	G	AB	R	H	2B	3B	HR	RBI	SH	SF	HP	BB	SO	SB	CS	E	OBP	SLG
1996	NYY vs. TEX	.412	4	17	2	7	1	0	0	1	0	0	0	0	2	0	0	2	.412	.471
1997	NYY vs. CLE	.333	5	21	6	7	1	0	2	2	0	0	0	3	5	1	0	0	.417	.667
1998	NYY vs. TEX	.111	3	9	0	1	0	0	0	0	1	0	0	2	2	0	0	0	.273	.111
1999	NYY vs. TEX	.455	3	11	3	5	1	1	0	0	0	0	0	2	3	0	0	0	.538	.727
2000	NYY vs. OAK	.211	5	19	1	4	0	0	0	2	0	0	1	2	3	0	1	0	.318	.211
2001	NYY vs. OAK	.444	5	18	2	8	1	0	0	1	0	1	1	1	0	0	1	0	.476	.500
2002	NYY vs. ANA	.500	4	16	6	8	0	0	2	3	0	1	0	2	3	0	0	1	.526	.875
2003	NYY vs. MIN	.429	4	14	2	6	0	0	1	1	0	0	0	4	2	1	0	1	.556	.643
2004	NYY vs. MIN	.316	4	19	3	6	1	0	1	4	1	0	0	1	4	1	0	1	.350	.526
2005	NYY vs. LAA	.333	5	21	4	7	0	0	2	5	0	1	0	1	5	1	0	0	.348	.619
2006	NYY vs. DET	.500	4	16	4	8	4	0	1	1	0	0	0	1	2	0	1	1	.529	.938
2007	NYY vs. CLE	.176	4	17	0	3	0	0	0	1	0	0	0	0	4	0	0	0	.176	.176
2009	NYY vs. MIN	.400	3	10	4	4	2	0	1	2	0	0	0	3	0	0	0	0	.538	.900
Division Series Totals		**.356**	**53**	**208**	**37**	**74**	**11**	**1**	**10**	**23**	**2**	**3**	**2**	**22**	**35**	**4**	**3**	**6**	**.417**	**.563**

Jeter's League Championship Series Record

Year	Club vs. Opp.	AVG	G	AB	R	H	2B	3B	HR	RBI	SH	SF	HP	BB	SO	SB	CS	E	OBP	SLG
1996	NYY vs. BAL	.417	5	24	5	10	2	0	1	1	0	0	0	0	5	2	0	0	.417	.625
1998	NYY vs. CLE	.200	6	25	3	5	1	1	0	2	2	0	0	2	5	3	0	0	.259	.320
1999	NYY vs. BOS	.350	5	20	3	7	1	0	1	3	0	0	0	2	3	0	0	2	.409	.550
2000	NYY vs. SEA	.318	6	22	6	7	0	0	2	5	0	0	0	6	7	1	0	0	.464	.591
2001	NYY vs. SEA	.118	5	17	0	2	0	0	0	2	1	1	0	2	2	0	0	0	.200	.118
2003	NYY vs. BOS	.233	7	30	3	7	2	0	1	2	0	0	0	2	4	1	0	0	.281	.400
2004	NYY vs. BOS	.200	7	30	5	6	1	0	0	5	2	0	0	6	2	1	0	2	.333	.233
2009	NYY vs. LAA	.259	6	27	5	7	0	0	2	3	0	0	0	6	5	0	1	1	.394	.481
LCS Totals		**.262**	**47**	**195**	**30**	**51**	**7**	**1**	**7**	**23**	**5**	**1**	**0**	**26**	**33**	**8**	**1**	**5**	**.347**	**.415**

Jeter's World Series Record

Year	Club vs. Opp.	AVG	G	AB	R	H	2B	3B	HR	RBI	SH	SF	HP	BB	SO	SB	CS	E	OBP	SLG
1996	NYY vs. ATL	.250	6	20	5	5	0	0	0	1	1	0	1	4	6	1	0	2	.400	.250
1998	NYY vs. SD	.353	4	17	4	6	0	0	0	1	0	0	0	3	3	0	0	0	.450	.353
1999	NYY vs. ATL	.353	4	17	4	6	1	0	0	1	0	0	0	1	3	3	1	0	.389	.412
2000	NYY vs. NYM	.409	5	22	6	9	2	1	2	2	0	0	0	3	8	0	0	0	.480	.864
2001	NYY vs. ARI	.148	7	27	3	4	0	0	1	1	0	0	1	0	6	0	0	0	.179	.259
2003	NYY vs. FLA	.346	6	26	5	9	3	0	0	2	0	0	1	1	7	0	0	1	.393	.462
2009	NYY VS. PHI	.407	6	27	5	11	3	0	0	1	0	0	0	1	6	0	0	0	.429	.519
World Series Totals		**.321**	**38**	**156**	**32**	**50**	**9**	**1**	**3**	**9**	**1**	**0**	**3**	**13**	**39**	**4**	**1**	**3**	**.384**	**.449**
POSTSEASON TOTALS		**.313**	**138**	**559**	**99**	**175**	**27**	**3**	**20**	**55**	**8**	**4**	**5**	**61**	**107**	**16**	**5**	**14**	**.383**	**.479**

Jeter's All-Star Game Record

Year	Club, Site	AVG	G	AB	R	H	2B	3B	HR	RBI	SH	SF	HP	BB	SO	SB	CS	E	OBP	SLG
1998	NYY, Colorado	.000	1	1	0	0	0	0	0	0	0	0	0	0	1	0	0	0	.000	.000
1999	NYY, Boston	.000	1	1	0	0	0	0	0	0	0	0	0	0	1	0	0	0	.000	.000
2000	NYY, Atlanta	1.000	1	3	1	3	1	0	0	2	0	0	0	0	0	0	0	0	1.000	1.333
2001	NYY, Seattle	1.000	1	1	1	1	0	0	1	1	0	0	0	0	0	0	0	0	1.000	4.000
2002	NYY, Milwaukee	.000	1	1	0	0	0	0	0	0	0	0	0	0	1	0	0	0	.000	.000
2004	NYY, Houston	1.000	1	3	1	3	0	0	0	0	0	0	0	0	0	0	0	0	1.000	1.000
2006	NYY, Pittsburgh	.000	1	3	0	0	0	0	0	0	0	0	0	0	2	0	0	0	.000	.000
2007	NYY, San Francisco	.333	1	3	0	1	0	0	0	0	0	0	0	0	0	0	0	0	.333	.333
2008	NYY, New York (AL)	.333	1	3	0	1	0	0	0	0	0	0	0	0	0	1	0	0	.333	.333
2009	NYY, St. Louis	.000	1	2	2	0	0	0	0	0	0	0	1	0	0	0	0	0	.333	.000
All-Star Game Totals		**.429**	**10**	**21**	**5**	**9**	**1**	**0**	**1**	**3**	**0**	**0**	**1**	**0**	**5**	**1**	**0**	**0**	**.455**	**.619**

Jeter's World Baseball Classic Record

Year	Country, Site	AVG	G	AB	R	H	2B	3B	HR	RBI	SH	SF	HP	BB	SO	SB	CS	E	OBP	SLG
2006	USA, USA	.450	6	20	5	9	0	1	0	1	1	0	1	2	1	0	0	2	.522	.550
2009	USA, USA	.276	8	29	2	8	2	0	0	0	0	0	1	4	1	0	1	1	.382	.345
WBC Totals		**.347**	**14**	**49**	**7**	**17**	**2**	**1**	**0**	**1**	**1**	**0**	**2**	**6**	**2**	**0**	**1**	**3**	**.439**	**.429**

Jeter's Career Fielding Record

Position	PCT	G	PO	A	E	TC	DP
Shortstop	.976	2123	3159	5353	213	8725	1133

Jeter's Career Home Run Chart

MULTI-HOMER GAMES: 8. **TWO HOMER GAMES:** 8, last on 8/27/06 at Los Angeles-AL (Joe Saunders). **GRAND SLAMS:** 1, 6/18/06 vs. Chicago-NL (Joe Borowski). **PINCH-HIT HR:** None. **INSIDE-THE-PARK HR:** 1, on 8/2/96 at Kansas City (Jeff Montgomery). **WALK-OFF HR:** 1, on 4/5/05 vs. Boston (Keith Foulke). **LEADOFF HR:** 23, last on 9/30/09 vs. Kansas City (Robinson Tejeda).

Nick Johnson

26 Designated Hitter/First Baseman

6-3 • 235 • B/T: Left/Left

Opening Day Age: 31

Birthdate
September 19, 1978

Birthplace
Sacramento, Calif.

Resides
Fair Oaks, Calif.

M.L. Service
9 years, 41 days

Career Highlights
All-Star Futures Game
- 1999, 2001

Status
- Signed by the Yankees as a free agent on December 23, 2009...contract extends through the 2010 season.

2009
- Split the season between the Nationals and Marlins organization after being acquired by Florida at the 7/31 trading deadline in exchange for LHP Aaron Thompson...combined to bat a career-high .291 (133-for-457) with 71R, 24 doubles, 8HR, 62RBI and 99BB in 133 games...ranked second in the National League with a .426 on-base percentage and sixth in walks.
- Posted the third-highest on-base percentage in the Majors, trailing only AL MVP Joe Mauer (.444) and NL MVP Albert Pujols (.443)...also ranked third in the Majors with 4.36 pitches per plate appearances.
- Opened the season with the Nationals and hit .295 with 16 doubles, 6HR and 44RBI in 98 games...tied his career high with 5RBI (second time) in 5/12 loss at San Francisco then matched his career high with 4H (fifth time) in the next day's win at the Giants.
- With the Marlins, hit .279 with 8 doubles, 2HR and 18RBI in 35 games...went 2-for-3 with 2BB and 1HBP in his Marlins debut on 8/1 vs. Chicago-NL, becoming the first player in franchise history to reach base five times in his Marlins debut.
- Suffered a strained right hamstring in 8/16 win vs. Colorado...went on the 15-day disabled list on 8/26 (retroactive to 8/17)...played in two rehab games with Single-A Jupiter before he was returned from rehab and reinstated from the D.L. on 9/3 (missed 15 team games)...was batting .302 on 9/16, but closed out the season with 2H over his final 23AB.

Single-Game Highs and Streaks

Hits
4 - 5 times
Last: at SF, 5/13/09

Runs
4 -vs. DET, 9/10/03

2B
2 - 13 times
Last: vs. NYM, 6/6/09

3B
1 - 5 times
Last: at NYY, 6/17/09

HR
2 - 4 times
Last: vs. LAD, 5/28/06

RBI
5 - 2 times
Last: at SF, 5/12/09

BB
3 - 20 times
Last: at PHI, 10/4/09

SO
4 - 2 times
Last: at PHI, 8/20/06

SB
1 - 27 times
Last: vs. CHC, 7/18/09

Hit Streak
16g - 4/10-26/05

2008
- Returned to action after missing the entire 2007 season, but appeared in just 38 games before landing on the disabled list for the final four-and-a-half months of the season.
- Hit .220 with 8 doubles, 5HR and 20RBI before sustaining a right wrist tendon sheath injury on a swing on 5/13 at the Mets...the injury came at Shea Stadium, the same ballpark as his 2006 fractured right femur...had season-ending surgery to repair the tendon sheath in the right wrist performed by Dr. Richard Berger on 6/24 in Washington, D.C.

2007
- Missed the entire season, rehabbing from his fractured right femur injury...underwent two subsequent surgeries in 2007 to remove hardware...on 1/16, had a distal screw removed in a procedure performed by Dr. Richard Marder...on 8/21, had final hardware removal performed by Dr. David Lewellen at the Mayo Clinic in Rochester, Minn...began taking batting practice on 7/31.

2006
- Batted .290 with 100R, 46 doubles, 23HR, 77RBI and 10SB in 147 games, setting career highs in games, runs scored, doubles, home runs, RBI, on-base percentage (.428) and

slugging (.520)...also walked a career-high 110 times with only 99K...among National Leaguers, tied for third in walks, ranked fourth in OBP, tied for seventh in doubles and intentional walks (15), and tied for 10th in HBP (13)...took 64.9% of pitches he faced, ranking third in the Majors, while his total of 1,746 pitches seen were fourth-most in the Majors...led the NL with a walk once every 5.71PA and ranked second with 4.28 pitches/PA.

- Joined San Francisco's Barry Bonds, San Diego's Brian Giles and Houston's Morgan Ensberg as the only four players to walk at least 100 times, yet not record 100 strikeouts in 2006.
- Came in fourth place in NL Gold Glove balloting for 1B, working to a .988 fielding percentage (15E, 1,273TC).
- Collected his first "walk-off" home run on 7/1 vs. Tampa Bay, hitting a two-out solo homer off Brian Meadows in the 10th inning.
- Celebrated his birthday on 9/19 vs. Atlanta, going 2-for-4 with a solo home run and becoming the first Washington National to hit a homer on his birthday.
- Season ended prematurely on 9/23 at the Mets when he collided with RF Austin Kearns attempting to catch a David Wright popup in the eighth inning...suffered a fractured right femur and underwent surgery that night at Queens Hospital New York performed by Dr. Peter Dzenis and Nationals orthopedist Dr. Ben Shaffer.
- Signed a three-year contract extension (through 2009) with the Nationals during 2006 spring training.

CAREER AVERAGE BY BATTING POSITION

No. 1	NA
No. 2	.284 (204G, 211-for-743, 39 doubles, 20HR, 100RBI, 148BB, .413OBP)
No. 3	.276 (91G, 83-for-301, 26 doubles, 13HR, 48RBI, 60BB, .406OBP)
No. 4	.269 (224G, 194-for-721, 60 doubles, 28HR, 121RBI, 161BB, .414OBP)
No. 5	.293 (54G, 58-for-198, 12 doubles, 5HR, 22RBI, 32BB, .397OBP)
No. 6	.284 (31G, 27-for-95, 7 doubles, 2HR, 10RBI, 15BB, .387OBP)
No. 7	.230 (48G, 34-for-148, 6 doubles, 7HR, 26RBI, 24BB, .349OBP)
No. 8	.258 (57G, 42-for-163, 10 doubles, 6HR, 27RBI, 29BB, .386OBP)
No. 9	.259 (61G, 44-for-170, 5 doubles, 8HR, 25RBI, 18BB, .360OBP)

2005

- Batted .289 with 66R, 35 doubles, 15HR, 74RBI and 80BB in 131 games with the Nationals in the franchise's first season in Washington...posted a .408 on-base percentage, ranking sixth in the NL and eighth all-time on the franchise's single-season list...ranked 10th in the NL having seen 4.10 pitches per plate appearance...tied for third in the NL with a .996 fielding percentage...his 11 game-winning RBI and 21 go-ahead RBI were each second-most on the team...walked once every 6.84 AB, ranking eighth in the NL...hit in six different spots in the lineup (second-seventh).
- Compiled a career-high 16-game hitting streak from 4/10-26, batting .310 (18-for-58) with 4 doubles, 1 triple, 1HR, 4RBI and 8BB over the stretch...named NL "co-Player of the Week" for the period ending 6/5 (shared with Albert Pujols).
- Left 4/26 game vs. Philadelphia with a contusion on the back of his left leg (missed one game)...sustained a right heel contusion on 6/26 vs. Toronto while scoring from first base on a double...in trying to avoid catcher Gregg Zaun, landed awkwardly on home plate...was placed on the 15-day disabled list from 7/3 (retroactive to 6/27) to 7/26 (missed 24 games)...played in three rehab games with Triple-A New Orleans.

2004

- In his first season with the Expos/Nationals organization, was limited to 73 games due to two stints on the disabled list...batted .251 with 16 doubles, 7HR and 33RBI.
- Injured his lower back at the end of spring training and missed the first 46 games of the season...was reinstated from the 15-day disabled list on 5/28...went 8-for-18 with 2 doubles, 2HR (including his second career grand slam on 8/14 vs. Houston) and 10RBI from 8/10-15, to earn his first NL "Player of the Week" award.
- Returned to the disabled list on 8/21 for the remainder of the season after fracturing his right cheekbone on a batted ball that took a bad hop.

2003

- Appeared in 96 games with the Yankees, batting .284 with 60R, 19 doubles, 14HR and 47RBI...ranked fifth in the Majors (second in the AL), seeing 4.28 pitches per plate appearance...posted more walks than strikeouts (70BB, 57K)...drew at least one walk in 17 consecutive games from 4/16-5/3.
- Collected his first multi-homer game on 4/21 at Minnesota in a 15-1 Yankees win...established a career-high with 4H, including his first career grand slam, in 8/8 win vs. Seattle.
- Was placed on the 15-day disabled on 5/16 with a stress fracture of the third metacarpal bone of the right hand...missed 61 games before being reinstated on 7/25.
- Acquired by the Expos along with LHP Randy Choate and OF Juan Rivera in exchange for RHP Javier Vazquez on 12/16.

2002

- In his first full season in the Majors, batted .243 with 56R, 15 doubles, 15HR and 58RBI in 129 games (59 starts at 1B, 49 at DH and two in LF)...named to the Topps Rookie All-Star Team.
- Left 5/4 game vs. Seattle after experiencing pain in his right knee (MRI exam was negative with a bone bruise)

and missed one game...on 8/7 vs. Kansas City, left game after injuring his left wrist while catching a Raul Ibanez line drive...MRI and CAT scan examinations on 8/8 at Beth Israel North Hospital revealed a bone bruise of the left wrist...placed on 15-day disabled list on 8/10 (retroactive to 8/8) -9/3 with a left-wrist strain, missing 24 games.

- Was recipient of the "James P. Dawson" Award as the Yankees' outstanding rookie in spring training (voted by NYBBWA).

2001

- Saw his first Major League action, appearing in 23 games and batting .194 with 2 doubles, 2HR and 8RBI...recalled on 8/21 and went 2-for-4 with 1RBI in his Major League debut that night at Texas, recording his first Major League hit with an RBI single in the second inning off Doug Davis...became the first Yankee to collect two hits in his big league debut since 1984 when Mike Pagliarulo (3H on 7/7) and Victor Mata (2H on 7/22) accomplished the feat...hit his first homer—a two-run HR off Hideo Nomo—in a 9/9 win vs. Boston...did not appear on any of the Yankees' three postseason rosters.
- Began the season with Triple-A Columbus and hit .256 with 68R, 20 doubles, 18HR and 49RBI in 110 games...led the IL with a .407 on-base percentage and led the team in games, runs, total bases (166), extra-base hits (38), doubles, HR, HBP (14), BB (81) and K (105)...spent time on the D.L. from 5/18-6/2 with a strained left thumb.
- Named "Best Defensive 1B" in the IL and ranked as the Yankees' No. 2 prospect by *Baseball America*...was selected to play in the 2001 MLB Futures Game at SAFECO Field on 7/8, going 1-for-1 with 1R...selected as the starting 1B in the Triple-A All-Star Game on 7/11 at Indianapolis.

MAJOR LEAGUE LEADERS, SINCE 2001

HIGHEST OBP

1.	Barry Bonds	.531
2.	Todd Helton	.433
3.	Albert Pujols	.427
4.	Lance Berkman	.415
5.	Manny Ramirez	.415
6.	Chipper Jones	.415
7.	Jason Giambi	.410
8.	Joe Mauer	.408
9.	**NICK JOHNSON**	**.402**
10.	Bobby Abreu	.400

FEWEST PA/BB

1.	Barry Bonds	3.43
2.	Jim Thome	5.84
3.	Jason Giambi	5.87
4.	Adam Dunn	5.93
5.	Todd Helton	6.36
6.	Lance Berkman	6.39
7.	**NICK JOHNSON**	**6.40**
8.	Chipper Jones	6.59
9.	Bobby Abreu	6.67
10.	Brian Giles	6.70

MOST PITCHES/PA

1.	Kevin Youkilis	4.32
2.	Bobby Abreu	4.32
3.	Brad Wilkerson	4.27
4.	Adam Dunn	4.26
5.	NICK SWISHER	4.25
6.	**NICK JOHNSON**	**4.24**
7.	Jason Giambi	4.22
8.	Frank Thomas	4.22
9.	Pat Burrell	4.18
10.	Casey Blake	4.17

2000

- Missed entire season with a strained muscle in his right hand...injury occurred on a check swing during a 3/10 split-squad spring training game at Cincinnati (in Sarasota, Fla.)...was placed on the 15-day disabled list with a strained muscle in his right hand on 3/25...transferred to the 60-day D.L. on 4/30.
- Was ranked as the Yankees' No. 1 prospect by *Baseball America*.

1999

- Made his Double-A debut with Norwich, batting .345 with 33 doubles, 14HR and 87RBI in 132 games...was the Yankees' "co-Minor League Player of the Year" (with D'Angelo Jimenez)...led all minor leaguers with 123BB and a .525 on-base percentage, becoming the only minor leaguer in the '90s to post an on-base percentage of .500 or better in a single season...also led the Eastern League in batting average and runs (114)...set EL record for HBP (37).
- Was named to the Eastern League midseason and post-season All-Star teams...was also the Topps Double-A All-Star 1B...played for USA in Futures Game on 7/11 at Fenway Park...was named EL's "Best Defensive 1B" and ranked as the Yankees' No. 1 prospect by *Baseball America*.
- Reached base safely via hit, walk or HBP in 63 consecutive games from 5/16-7/27...after the streak ended, reached base in 25 of next 35 plate appearances.

1998

- Named the Yankees' Minor League "Player of the Year" after batting .317 with 69R, 14 doubles, 17HR, 58RBI and 68BB in 92 games with Single-A Tampa...ranked second among all minor leaguers with a .466 on-base percentage...named the third-best prospect in the FSL by *Baseball America*.

1997

- With Single-A Greensboro, hit .273 with 77R, 23 doubles, 16HR, 75RBI and 16SB in 127 games...led the team in home runs, RBI, walks (76) and on-base percentage (.398).

1996

- Hit .287 with 33RBI in 47 games for the GCL Yankees in first professional season...led the Gulf Coast League with a .422 OBP.

Personal

- Full name is Nicholas Robert Johnson...married to Liz, with two children: Brianna (4) and Nicholas Robert Jr. (1)...graduated from C.K. McClatchy High School (Calif.)...is the nephew of Larry Bowa.

NICK JOHNSON

Johnson's Career Batting Record

Year	Team	AVG	G	AB	R	H	2B	3B	HR	RBI	SAC	SF	HBP	BB	SO	SB	CS	E	OBP	SLG
1996	GCL Yankees	.287	47	157	31	45	11	1	2	33	0	3	9	30	35	0	0	3	.422	.408
1997	Greensboro	.273	127	433	77	118	23	1	16	75	0	6	18	76	99	16	3	16	.398	.441
1998	Tampa	.317	92	303	69	96	14	1	17	58	0	3	19	68	76	1	4	12	.466	.538
1999	Norwich	.345	132	420	114	145	33	5	14	87	0	1	37	123	88	8	6	20	.525	.548
2000		Did Not Play - Injured-a																		
2001	Columbus	.256	110	359	68	92	20	0	18	49	0	5	14	81	105	9	2	10	.407	.462
	YANKEES	.194	23	67	6	13	2	0	2	8	0	0	4	7	15	0	0	0	.308	.313
2002	YANKEES-b	.243	129	378	56	92	15	0	15	58	3	0	12	48	98	1	3	7	.347	.402
	Columbus	.091	3	11	1	1	0	0	0	0	0	0	0	1	4	0	0	0	.167	.091
2003	YANKEES-c	.284	96	324	60	92	19	0	14	47	3	1	8	70	57	5	2	5	.422	.472
	Columbus	.500	3	10	1	5	2	0	1	3	0	0	0	2	2	0	0	1	.583	1.000
	Trenton	.417	4	12	3	5	1	0	0	1	0	0	1	5	0	0	0	0	.611	.500
2004	Brevard County-d, e	.190	6	21	3	4	0	0	1	5	0	0	0	4	6	0	0	0	.320	.333
	Edmonton	.222	3	9	2	2	1	0	0	0	0	0	0	4	3	0	0	0	.462	.333
	MONTREAL-f	.251	73	251	35	63	16	0	7	33	0	1	3	40	58	6	3	4	.359	.398
2005	WASHINGTON-g	.289	131	453	66	131	35	3	15	74	0	2	12	80	87	3	8	5	.408	.479
	New Orleans	.000	3	6	0	0	0	0	0	0	0	0	0	1	2	0	0	0	.143	.000
2006	WASHINGTON	.290	147	500	100	145	46	0	23	77	2	3	13	110	99	10	3	15	.428	.520
2007		Did Not Play - Injured-h																		
2008	WASHINGTON-i	.220	38	109	15	24	8	0	5	20	0	1	4	33	25	0	0	0	.415	.431
2009	WASHINGTON	.295	98	353	47	104	16	2	6	44	0	2	6	63	66	2	2	7	.408	.402
	FLORIDA-j, k, l	.279	35	104	24	29	8	0	2	18	1	3	6	36	18	0	2	5	.477	.413
	Jupiter	.333	2	3	0	1	1	0	0	0	0	0	0	0	2	0	0	0	.333	.667
Minor League Totals		**.295**	**532**	**1744**	**369**	**514**	**106**	**8**	**69**	**311**	**0**	**18**	**98**	**395**	**422**	**34**	**15**	**62**	**.447**	**.483**
AL Totals		**.256**	**248**	**769**	**122**	**197**	**26**	**0**	**31**	**113**	**6**	**1**	**24**	**125**	**170**	**6**	**5**	**12**	**.376**	**.424**
NL Totals		**.280**	**522**	**1770**	**287**	**496**	**129**	**5**	**58**	**266**	**3**	**12**	**44**	**362**	**353**	**21**	**18**	**36**	**.412**	**.457**
Major League Totals		**.273**	**770**	**2539**	**409**	**693**	**165**	**5**	**89**	**379**	**9**	**13**	**68**	**487**	**523**	**27**	**23**	**48**	**.402**	**.447**

Selected by the Yankees in the third round of the 1996 First-Year Player Draft.

a – Placed on the 15-day disabled list with a sprained right wrist on March 25, 2000 through the end of the season...transferred to 60-day D.L. on April 30, 2000.
b – Placed on the 15-day disabled list with a strained left wrist from August 9-September 3, 2002.
c - Placed on the 15-day disabled list with a stress fracture in his third metacarpal bone of his right hand from May 16-July 25, 2003.
d - Acquired by Montreal from the Yankees along with LHP Randy Choate and OF Juan Rivera in exchange for RHP Javier Vazquez on December 16, 2003.
e - Placed on the 15-day disabled list with a back strain from March 31-May 28, 2004.
f - Placed on the 15-day disabled list with a right-cheekbone fracture from August 21, 2004 through the end of the season. Transferred to the 60-day D.L. on September 14, 2004.
g - Placed on the 15-day disabled list with a right heel contusion from June 27-July 26, 2005.
h – Placed on 15-day disabled list recovering from surgery on a broken right femur from March 28, 2007 through the end of the season...transferred to the 60-day D.L. on May 16, 2007.
i - Placed on the 15-day disabled list with an injury to his right wrist tendon sheath on May 15, 2008 through the end of the season...transferred to the 60-day D.L. on June 26, 2008.
j - Acquired by Florida from Washington in exchange for LHP Aaron Thompson on July 31, 2009.
k - Placed on the 15-day disabled list with a right hamstring strain from August 17-September 3, 2009.
l – Signed by the Yankees as a free agent to a one-year contract on December 23, 2009.

Johnson's Division Series Record

Year	Club vs. Opp.	AVG	G	AB	R	H	2B	3B	HR	RBI	SH	SF	HP	BB	SO	SB	CS	E	OBP	SLG
2002	NYY vs. ANA	.182	3	11	1	2	0	0	0	1	0	0	0	1	5	0	0	0	.250	.182
2003	NYY vs. MIN	.077	4	13	2	1	1	0	0	2	0	0	1	3	2	0	0	0	.294	.154
Division Series Total		**.125**	**7**	**24**	**3**	**3**	**1**	**0**	**0**	**3**	**0**	**0**	**1**	**4**	**7**	**0**	**0**	**0**	**.276**	**.167**

Johnson's Championship Series Record

Year	Club vs. Opp.	AVG	G	AB	R	H	2B	3B	HR	RBI	SH	SF	HP	BB	SO	SB	CS	E	OBP	SLG
2003	NYY vs. BOS	.231	7	26	4	6	1	0	1	3	0	0	0	2	4	0	0	0	.286	.385
LCS Totals		**.231**	**7**	**26**	**4**	**6**	**1**	**0**	**1**	**3**	**0**	**0**	**0**	**2**	**4**	**0**	**0**	**0**	**.286**	**.385**

Johnson's World Series Record

Year	Club vs. Opp.	AVG	G	AB	R	H	2B	3B	HR	RBI	SH	SF	HP	BB	SO	SB	CS	E	OBP	SLG
2003	NYY vs. FLA	.294	6	17	3	5	1	0	0	0	0	0	0	2	3	0	0	0	.368	.353
World Series Totals		**.294**	**6**	**17**	**3**	**5**	**1**	**0**	**0**	**0**	**0**	**0**	**0**	**2**	**3**	**0**	**0**	**0**	**.368**	**.353**
POSTSEASON TOTALS		**.209**	**20**	**67**	**10**	**14**	**3**	**0**	**1**	**6**	**0**	**0**	**1**	**8**	**14**	**0**	**0**	**0**	**.303**	**.299**

Johnson's Career Fielding Record

Position	PCT	G	PO	A	E	TC
First Base	.992	666	5249	420	48	5717
Outfield	1.000	2	2	0	0	2

Johnson's Career Home Run Chart

MULTI-HOMER GAMES: 4. **TWO-HOMER GAMES:** 4, last on 5/28/06 vs. Los Angeles-NL. **GRAND SLAMS:** 2, 8/14/04 vs. Houston (off Chad Qualls); 8/18/03 vs. Seattle (off Ryan Franklin). **PINCH-HIT HR:** None. **INSIDE-THE-PARK HR:** None. **WALK-OFF HR:** 1, on 7/1/06 vs. Tampa Bay (Brian Meadows). **LEADOFF HR:** None

Boone Logan

48 Left-handed Pitcher

6-5 • 215 • B/T: Right/Left

Opening Day Age: 25

Birthdate
August 13, 1984

Birthplace
San Antonio, Texas

Resides
Helotes, Texas

M.L. Service
3 years, 2 days

College
Temple College (Tex.)

Status

- Acquired by the Yankees along with RHP Javier Vazquez in exchange for OF Melky Cabrera, LHP Mike Dunn and RHP Arodys Vizcaino on December 22, 2009...signed through the 2010 season.

2009

- In his first season with the Atlanta organization, split the year between the Braves and Triple-A Gwinnett...went 1-1 with a 5.19 ERA in 20 relief appearances with the Braves...opponents batted .292 (21-for-72, 1HR); LH .231 (9-for-39, 0HR), RH .364 (12-for-33, 1HR)...retired 16-of-20 first batters faced (80.0%)...stranded 11-of-13 inherited runners (84.6%)...eight of his appearances were less than 1.0IP...appeared in consecutive games once and three straight once (8/17-19).
- Was recalled from Gwinnett on 6/25 and made his Braves debut that night vs. the Yankees, allowing 2ER on 1H and 2BB in 1.1IP...did not allow an earned run over his next nine appearances from 6/30-7/29 (7.2IP).
- Went 22 days between outings from 8/27-9/17.
- Began the season with Gwinnett, going 4-2 with two saves and a 3.28 ERA in 29 relief appearances...held opponents scoreless in 19 of his outings and did not allow an earned run 21 times.

Single-Game Highs and Streaks

IP (relief)
3.0 - 2 times
Last: vs. DET, 4/25/07

Hits
6 - at TB, 5/16/06

Runs
5 - 2 times
Last: vs. MIN, 7/6/07

BB
2 - 11 times
Last: at COL, 7/12/09

SO
5 - at CLE, 5/2/06

HR
2 - 2 times
Last: at MIN 9/23/08

Winning Streak
2g - 4/24-8/2/07

Losing Streak
2g - 7/13-8/9/08

2008

- Made his second Opening Day roster and spent the majority of the season with the White Sox, going 2-3 with a 5.95 ERA in 55 relief appearances...established a career high with 42K and averaged 8.9K/9.0IP...30 of his outings were less than 1.0IP.
- Opponents batted. 317 (57-for-180, 7HR); LH .291 (30-for-103, 5HR), RH .351 (27-for-77, 2HR)...marked the third-highest opponents batting average among AL relievers...retired 41-of-55 first batters faced (74.5%)...stranded 32-of-44 inherited runners (72.7%)...appeared in consecutive games nine times, three straight games twice and four straight once (4/20-24).
- Went 2-1 with a 1.95 ERA (32.1IP, 7ER) through his first 36 appearances of the season (through 7/9) with opponents batting .223 (27-for-121, 2HR)...posted an 0-2 record and an 18.90 ERA (10.0IP, 21ER) over his remaining 19 appearances from 7/10 until the end of the season as opponents batted .508 (30-for-59, 5HR).
- Made 17 straight scoreless outings from 4/29-6/14 (14.2 P) and held the opposition hitless in six consecutive games from 5/24-6/4 (20AB)...did not allow a run in 10 relief appearances in May (7.2IP).
- Was optioned to Triple-A Charlotte on 8/10 and recalled on 8/31...went 0-1 with a 6.00 ERA in five games with the Knights...worked to an 18.00 ERA (2.0IP, 4ER) in seven games following his return to the Sox.

2007

- Went 2-1 with a 4.97 ERA in 68 relief appearances in his first full season with the White Sox...tied for sixth in appearances among AL lefthanders and tied for 10th-most games on the club's all-time list by a lefthander...opponents batted .298 (59-for-198, 7HR); LH .221 (19-for-86, 1HR), RH .357 (40-for-112, 6HR)...tied Milwaukee's Brian Shouse for the Major League lead with 78 inherited runners...stranded 56-of-78 inherited runners (71.8%)...retired 46-of-68 first batters faced (67.6%)...appeared in consecutive games 10 times, three consecutive games seven times and four straight games once (8/5-9).

BOONE LOGAN

- Of his 68 appearances, 48 were scoreless…40 of his outings were less than 1.0IP…posted a 2.88 ERA (25.0IP, 8ER) on the road, compared to a 7.01 mark (25.2IP, 20ER) at home.
- Matched his career high (second time) with 3.0IP in 4/25 loss vs. Detroit, allowing 2ER in 3.0 innings of relief (4H).
- Began the season with Triple-A Charlotte, going 0-1 with a 2.16 ERA and one save in four games with the Knights...was recalled from Charlotte on 4/17…earned his first Major League win on 4/24 at Kansas City (0.2IP, 1BB, 2K)…made eight straight scoreless appearances from 7/31-8/14 (8.0IP).

2006

- Saw his first Major League action, making the White Sox' Opening Day roster after not having appeared above Single-A in his professional career…became the first Sox player to jump from Single-A to the Majors in consecutive seasons since Mike Caruso in 1997 and 1998.
- Posted an 8.31 ERA with one save and no decisions in 21 relief appearances with the White Sox…opponents hit .288 (21-for-73, 2HR), including a .357 (10-for-28, 1HR) mark by lefthanders…first-batters faced were just 1-for-14 (.071)…appeared inconsecutive games four times and three straight once (9/8-10).
- Made his Major League debut in 4/4 loss vs. Cleveland, tossing 2.0 scoreless innings…recorded his first career save on 4/25 at Seattle, allowing 1ER over a career-high 3.0IP…was optioned to Triple-A Charlotte on 5/16, going 3-1 with a 3.38 ERA and 11 saves in 38 relief appearances before being recalled on 9/1…compiled a 15.43 ERA (4.2IP, 8ER) in his second stint with the White Sox.
- Pitched in five games for LaGuaira in the Venezuelan Winter League, recording a 2.08 ERA (4.1IP, 1ER).

2005

- Combined to go 1-1 with a 3.54 ERA and two saves in 25 relief appearances between rookie-level Great Falls and Single-A Winston-Salem, working exclusively out of the bullpen the entire season…lowered the arm angle in his delivery prior to the season.

2004

- Spent his second full season at Great Falls…went 2-5 with a 6.26 ERA (41.2IP, 29 ER) in nine starts and 1-2 with a 4.37 ERA (22.2IP, 11ER) and one save in nine relief appearances…earned his first professional save on 8/18 vs. Provo (3.0IP).

2003

- Made his professional debut at Great Falls, going 3-3 with a 6.58 ERA in 16 games (14 starts).

Personal

- Was selected to the San Antonio All-Star Team at O'Connor High School…lost a pregame, on-field cow-milking contest to the Angels' Brandon Wood on 5/4/07 at Angels Stadium.

Logan's Career Pitching Record

Year	Team	W	L	ERA	G	GS	CG	SHO	SV	IP	H	R	ER	HR	HB	BB	SO	WP	BK
2003	Great Falls	3	3	6.58	16	14	0	0	0	67.0	76	60	49	4	11	31	48	8	1
2004	Great Falls	3	7	5.60	18	9	0	0	1	64.1	74	48	40	7	4	31	48	8	2
2005	Great Falls	1	1	3.31	21	0	0	0	2	35.1	34	15	13	1	3	4	29	4	0
	Winston-Salem	0	0	5.06	4	0	0	0	0	5.1	7	3	3	2	0	4	5	0	0
2006	Charlotte	3	1	3.38	38	0	0	0	11	42.2	35	18	16	1	9	12	57	3	0
	CHICAGO-AL	0	0	8.31	21	0	0	0	1	17.1	21	18	16	2	3	15	15	1	0
2007	Charlotte	0	1	2.16	4	0	0	0	1	8.1	8	2	2	1	0	4	11	0	0
	CHICAGO-AL	2	1	4.97	68	0	0	0	0	50.2	59	30	28	7	0	20	35	2	0
2008	CHICAGO-AL	2	3	5.95	55	0	0	0	0	42.1	57	31	28	7	1	14	42	1	0
	Charlotte	0	1	6.00	5	0	0	0	0	9.0	10	8	6	2	3	6	7	1	0
2009	Gwinnett-a	4	2	3.28	29	0	0	0	2	35.2	26	15	13	2	6	17	39	4	0
	ATLANTA-b	1	1	5.19	20	0	0	0	0	17.1	21	12	10	1	1	9	10	0	0
Minor League Totals		**14**	**16**	**4.77**	**135**	**23**	**0**	**0**	**17**	**267.2**	**270**	**169**	**142**	**20**	**36**	**109**	**244**	**28**	**3**
Major League Totals		**5**	**5**	**5.78**	**164**	**0**	**0**	**0**	**1**	**127.2**	**158**	**91**	**82**	**17**	**5**	**58**	**102**	**4**	**0**

Selected by the Chicago White Sox in the 20th round of the 2002 First-Year Player Draft.

a – Acquired by the Atlanta Braves along with RHP Javier Vazquez in exchange for INFs Jon Gilmore and Brent Lillibridge, C Tyler Flowers and LHP Santos Rodriguez on December 4, 2008.

b – Acquired by the Yankees along with RHP Javier Vazquez in exchange for OF Melky Cabrera, LHP Mike Dunn and RHP Arodys Vizcaino on December 22, 2009.

Logan's Regular Season Batting Record

Year	Team	AVG	G	AB	R	H	2B	3B	HR	RBI	SH	SF	HP	BB	SO	SB	CS
2009	Atlanta	Did Not Bat															
Major League Totals		-	**164**	-	-	-	-	-	-	-	-	-	-	-	-	-	-

Logan's Career Fielding Record

Position	PCT	G	PO	A	E	TC	DP
Pitcher	.885	164	9	14	3	26	1

Damaso Marte

43 Left-handed Pitcher
6-2 • 213 • B/T: Left/Left
Opening Day Age: 35

Birthdate
February 14, 1975

Birthplace
Santo Domingo, D.R.

Resides
Santo Domingo, D.R.

M.L. Service
8 years, 122 days

Status

- Acquired by the Yankees along with OF Xavier Nady from the Pittsburgh Pirates in exchange for OF Jose Tabata and RHPs Ross Ohlendorf, Jeff Karstens and Daniel McCutchen...signed to a three-year contract with a one-year option on November 12, 2008...contract extends through 2011 with a team option for 2012.

Career Notes

- Among left-handed relievers in the Majors since 2004, ranks seventh in strikeouts (320) and appearances (373), and 10th in opponents batting average (.228).
- Owns a career record of 3-4 with a 2.37ERA (83.2 IP, 22ER) in 93 appearances vs. the AL East.
- Reached the 50-appearance plateau in seven consecutive seasons from 2002-08, one of only seven pitchers to accomplish the feat over the span.

2009

- Was 1-3 with a 9.45 ERA in 21 relief appearances with the Yankees...opponents batted .278 (15-for-54, 3HR); LH .120 (3-for-25, 1HR), RH .414 (12-for-29, 2HR)...15 of his 21 appearances were scoreless...stranded 17-of-21 inherited runners (81.0%)...retired 16-of-21 first batters faced (76.2%)...appeared in consecutive games once and three straight games twice (4/22-25 and 9/22-25).
- Made his eighth career Opening Day roster...allowed 1H in 0.1IP in the Yankees' Opening Day loss at Baltimore on 4/6...surrendered a career-high-tying 6R/6ER (second time, also 1999) in 4/16 loss vs. Cleveland, throwing 1.0 inning of relief in the first regular season game at Yankee Stadium (3H, 1BB, 1HP, 2HR)...on 4/24 at Boston, allowed "walk-off" solo-HR to Kevin Youkilis in the bottom of the 11th to suffer his first loss (1.1IP, 1H, 1ER, 3K).
- Was placed on the 15-day disabled list on 5/3 (retroactive to 4/26) with left shoulder inflammation...began throwing program in Tampa on 5/23...was examined by Dr. James Andrews in Birmingham, Ala., on 6/15, who seconded the Yankees' diagnosis of left shoulder inflammation...was transferred to the 60-day D.L. on 8/8...made 12 rehab appearances, combining to go 0-1 with a 3.00 ERA (12.0IP, 10H, 4ER, 4BB, 10K, 2HR) with Scranton/WB and the GCL Yankees.
- Was returned from rehab on 8/14 and excused for personal reasons...was reinstated from the disabled list on 8/21, prior to the Yankees' 20-11 win at Fenway Park...retired both of his batters faced (0.2IP, 1K) that night in the Yankees victory, entering with the bases loaded in the seventh inning in first appearance since 4/25.
- Held opponents scoreless in 12 of his 14 outings after returning from the disabled list...four of his five runs allowed over the span came in 9/11 loss vs. Baltimore, in which he was tagged with the loss...snapped a 14-game winning streak by the Yankees bullpen, dating back to 8/5.
- Did not allow a run in eight postseason appearances, holding opponents to 2H with 0BB and 5K in 4.0IP...after allowing singles to his first two hitters faced in the ALDS, retired his final 12 batters of the postseason...tied eight other pitchers for the fifth-most appearances in a single postseason without allowing any runs.

Single-Game Highs and Streaks

Low hit CG
N/A
IP (start)
N/A
IP (relief)
4.0 - vs. ARI, 7/20/99
Hits
10 - vs. ARI, 7/20/99
Runs
6 - 2 times
Last: vs. CLE, 4/16/09
BB
4 - 2 times
Last: vs. MIL, 8/16/06
SO
5 - 3 times
Last: at FLA, 6/17/04
HR
2 - 5 times
Last: vs. CLE, 4/16/09
Single-Season Winning Streak
4g - 4/23-5/25/08
Winning Streak
7g - 8/22/06-5/25/08
Single-Season Losing Streak
7g - 4/5-8/16/06
Losing Streak
8g - 9/9/05-8/16/06

- Faced eight batters in four World Series appearances vs. Philadelphia, recording 5K (Utley twice, Howard twice and Werth)...faced Ryan Howard in all four outings, retiring him each time.
- Made two scoreless relief appearances with the Dominican Republic in the World Baseball Classic prior to the season (2.0IP, 1H, 2K)...missed a little over a week upon return from the WBC with left shoulder inflammation.

2008

- Was 5-3 with a 4.02 ERA in 72 combined relief appearances between the Yankees and Pirates...was acquired by the Yankees along with OF Xavier Nady on 7/26 in exchange for OF Jose Tabata and RHPs Ross Ohlendorf, Jeff Karstens and Daniel McCutchen.
- Opponents batted .214 (52-for-243, 5HR); LH .247 (21-for-85, 1HR), RH .196 (31-for-158, 4HR)...appeared in consecutive games 16 times, three straight once (5/24-27) and four straight once (8/27-30)...stranded 37-of-46 inherited runners (80.4%)...retired 55-of-72 first-batters faced (76.4%)...tossed more than 1.0 inning 13 times, including a season-high 2.0 innings four times...was called upon to face one batter seven times, including five times with the Yankees.
- In 25 games with the Yankees, went 1-3 with a 5.40 ERA...while with the Yankees, retired 15-of-25 first batters faced (60.0%)...stranded 11-of-15 inherited runners (73.3%)...opponents batted .206 (14-for-68, 1HR); LH .233 (7-for-30, 0HR); RH .184 (7-for-38, 1HR).
- Made his Yankees debut in 7/26 win at Boston, striking out only batter faced (Ortiz) with two on and one out in the seventh (0.1IP, 1K)...arrived at Fenway Park less than two hours before first pitch following the trade.
- Suffered first loss of the season on 8/4 at Texas, allowing "walk-off" grand slam in the bottom of the ninth to Marlon Byrd...according to the *Elias Sports Bureau*, became the fourth Yankee since 1960 to allow a game-ending grand slam, joining Lindy McDaniel (7/7/70 at Baltimore, Brooks Robinson), Cecilio Guante (6/21/88 at Detroit, Alan Trammell) and Mariano Rivera (7/14/02 at Cleveland, Bill Selby).
- Recorded his first win as a Yankee in 9/13 Game 2 victory vs. Tampa Bay, tossing a perfect seventh (2K) after the Yankees rallied from 4-1 deficit.
- Was 4-0 with five saves and a 3.47 ERA in 47 relief appearances with the Pirates, striking out 47 batters in 46.2 innings pitched (16BB) before being acquired by the Yankees...at the time of the trade, opponents were batting .217 (38-for-175, 4HR); LH .255 (14-for-55, 1HR), RH .200 (24-for-120, 3HR)...was a member of Pittsburgh's Opening Day roster for the third straight year.
- Walked two of three batters faced and allowed two runs in 0.1IP on 3/31 Opening Day in Atlanta...was charged with 4ER in his next outing on 4/2 at Atlanta, combining for an 81.00 ERA over his first two appearances of the season (0.2IP, 4H, 6ER, 2BB, 1K, 1HR)...over his next 45 outings from 4/5-7/23, posted a 2.35 ERA (46.0IP, 12ER) before being acquired by the Yankees.
- Picked up his first career NL save on 6/12 vs. Washington and his first save since 8/27/05 (w/ Chicago-AL)...became the Pirates' full-time closer on 7/2 when Matt Capps was placed on the disabled list...converted each of his five save opportunities from 7/2-23.

2007

- Spent second straight full season with Pittsburgh, going 2-0 with a 2.38 ERA in 65 appearances...opponents batted .200 (32-for-160, 2HR); LH .094 (6-for-64, 0HR), RH .271 (26-for-96, 2HR)...prevented 45-of-56 inherited runners from scoring (80.4%)...retired 45-of-65 first batters faced (69.0%)...both of his home runs allowed were to switch hitters who were batting right-handed – Tony Clark at Arizona on 8/9 and Lance Berkman at Houston on 9/14...pitched 1.0 inning or less in 58 of his 65 appearances.
- Held opponents without an earned run in his first 21G at PNC Park from 4/9-8/14 (17.2IP, 6H, 1R, 5BB, 23K).
- Did not allow an earned run in his first eight outings (6.1IP, 1R)...allowed his first earned run in 4/21 loss at Los Angeles (NL)...following that outing, made 13 consecutive scoreless appearances from 4/22-5/26 (10.2IP)...was scored upon once in 12 outings during May and held opponents to a .118 average (4-for-34) for the month.
- Held left-handed batters hitless in 32 consecutive at-bats from 5/18-8/9, marking the longest such streak in the Majors in 2007...streak was snapped on 8/11 at San Francisco when Ryan Klesko's fly ball to left was lost in the sun by Jason Bay and ruled a double...held left-handed hitters to just two hits in their final 44AB (.045) from 5/18 through the remainder of the season.
- Had 13 consecutive scoreless appearances from 6/27-8/2 (11.2IP), throwing 10.1 shutout innings in July (10 appearances).

2006

- Was 1-7 with a 3.70 ERA in a career-high 75 appearances with Pittsburgh...was three games shy of the club record for a left-handed pitcher (Scott Sauerbeck with 78 in 2002)...worked 1.0 inning or less in 66 of his 75 outings...averaged 9.7 K/9.0IP (58.1IP, 63K)...opponents batted .244 (51-for-209, 5HR); LH .225 (20-for-89, 2HR), RH .258 (31-for-120, 3HR)...retired 48-of-75 first batters faced (64.0%)...prevented 29-of-40 inherited runners from scoring (72.5%).
- Lost his first seven decisions from 4/5-8/16, marking a career high losing streak.

DAMASO MARTE

- Suffered a blown save on Opening Day loss at Milwaukee...was scored upon just three times in his first 19 games through 5/17 (12.0IP, 3ER, 2.25 ERA)...retired only batter faced on 8/22 at Atlanta to pick up lone victory of the season...was scored upon just once in final 10 appearances (10.0IP, 2ER).
- Made two appearances in Dominican Winter League (3.2IP, 0R).
- Went 0-1 with a 20.25 ERA (1.1IP, 3ER) in three relief appearances for the Dominican Republic in the inaugural World Baseball Classic...returned to Bradenton, Fla., prior to the end of the WBC with left shoulder irritation...was limited to one game in spring training while battling left shoulder irritation and a stiff neck.

2005

- Was 3-4 with four saves and a 3.77 ERA in 66 games for the World Series-champion Chicago White Sox...averaged 10.7K/9.0IP (45.1IP, 54K), his best mark since 2002 (also 10.7).
- Opponents batted .256 (45-for-176, 5HR); LH .267 (24-for-90, 1HR), RH .244 (21-for-86, 4HR)...converted 4-of-8 save chances...was scored upon in just 16-of-66 appearances...stranded 28-of-37 inherited runners (75.7%)...retired 31-of-52 first batters faced (59.6%), holding them to a .173 (9-for-52) average, the seventh-lowest mark in the AL...threw a season-high 2.0 innings twice (both scoreless)...57 of his outings were 1.0 inning or less.
- Had 14 consecutive scoreless outings on the road from 5/6-7/30 (10.2IP, 8H, 6BB, 10K).
- Did not pitch from 6/8-13 due to a sore left bicep...was placed on the 15-day disabled list from 6/27-7/14 with an inflamed left trapezius...made one rehab appearance with Triple-A Charlotte on 7/10 at Louisville (1.2IP, 4H, 1ER, 1BB, 2K)...was returned from rehab and reinstated from the D.L. on 7/14, throwing 1.0 scoreless inning in that night's win at Cleveland.
- Made one appearance in the AL Division Series against Boston, walking two batters and allowing one hit in Game 3 win on 10/7 at Boston...was not on the ALCS roster vs. the Angels...was the winning pitcher in Game 3 of the World Series, tossing 1.2 scoreless innings in Chicago's 7-5, 14-inning victory at Houston.

2004

- Was 6-5 with six saves and a 3.42 ERA in 74 appearances with the White Sox...ranked seventh in the American League in appearances, recording the eighth-highest total in White Sox history and fifth-highest among club lefthanders at the time...also established a career high in wins.
- Opponents batted .217 (56-for-258, 10HR); LH .143 (14-for-98, 2HR), RH .263 (42-for-160, 8HR)...prevented 30-of-40 inherited runners from scoring (75.0%)...retired 55-of-75 first batters faced (73.3%)...converted 6-of-12 save opportunities.
- Posted a 2.45 ERA (40.1IP, 11ER) prior to the All-Star break and a 4.59 ERA (33.1IP, 17ER) in the second half.
- Suffered a blown save and recorded the loss on Opening Day at Kansas City, surrendering a game-tying, three-run homer to Mendy Lopez and a game-winning, two-run shot to Carlos Beltran without recording an out...compiled a 1.69 ERA (42.2IP, 8ER) over his next 38 games from 4/11-7/24...matched his career high with 5K in 6/17 loss at Florida (2.0IP).

2003

- Was 4-2 with 11 saves and a 1.58 ERA in 71 appearances with the White Sox...established career highs in saves, innings pitched (79.2) and strikeouts (87)...ranked fourth among AL relievers in ERA, recording the second-lowest mark by a Sox reliever since Ed Farmer in 1979 (1.07)...also ranked among AL relief leaders in strikeouts (fifth).
- Converted 11-of-18 save opportunities, including each of his final seven chances...was scored upon in just 11 of his 71 total appearances.
- Opponents batted .185 (50-for-271, 3HR); LH .168 (21-for-125, 1HR), RH .199 (29-for-146, 2HR)...was the third-lowest average against left-handers among AL relievers...prevented 37-of-53 inherited runners from scoring (69.8%)...retired 49-of-71 first batters faced (69.0%).
- Made 18 straight scoreless outings from 4/20-6/10, allowing just 8H and 5BB, while striking out 20 batters over the stretch...the streak came to an end on 6/12 vs. San Francisco when he gave up game-winning grand slam to Rich Aurilia after inheriting bases-loaded jam...matched his career high with 5K in 8/20 win vs. Anaheim...compiled a 1.09 ERA (49.2IP, 6ER) over his final 39 outings and a 0.84 ERA (21.1IP, 2ER) over his final 16.
- Pitched in five games for Estrellas in the Dominican Winter League, going 1-0 with a 0.00 ERA (6.1IP).

2002

- Spent first full season in the Majors with Chicago-AL after being acquired from Pittsburgh in exchange for RHP Matt Guerrier on 3/27.
- Was 1-1 with a 2.83 ERA in 68 appearances with the White Sox, striking out 72 batters in 60.1IP...led the staff in appearances and the bullpen in ERA and strikeouts...his average of 10.74K/9.0IP ranked second among relievers in Sox history behind Roberto Hernandez (12.67 in 1995).

- Opponents batted .204 (44-for-216, 5HR); LH .149 (15-for-101, 2HR), RH .252 (29-for-115, 3HR)...was the lowest mark in the AL and lowest figure by a Sox pitcher since Kevin Hickey in 1981 (.146)...prevented 36-of-50 inherited runners from scoring (72.0%)...retired 45-of-68 first batters faced (66.1%).
- Earned his first Major League win on 4/16 vs. Cleveland (1.2IP, 1H, 1ER, 1BB, 4K).
- Compiled a 1.92 ERA (51.2IP, 11ER) in 57 appearances from 5/1 through the end of the season...earned first Major League save on 7/6 vs. Cleveland, recording 1.2 scoreless innings (1BB)...converted all 10 saves chances over the remainder of the season.
- Pitched for Estrellas in the Dominican Winter League, going 0-1 with a 3.97 ERA (11.1IP, 5ER) and 14K in 12 appearances...went 3-0 with a 1.69 ERA (10.2IP, 2ER) and 17K in the playoffs.

2001

- Was 0-1 with a 4.71 ERA in 23 games with Pittsburgh...was acquired by the Pirates from the Yankees in exchange for INF Enrique Wilson on 6/13 and was assigned to Triple-A Nashville.
- Had his contract purchased by Pittsburgh on 6/23 and made his National League debut the next day, tossing 3.0 scoreless innings in 6/24 loss vs. Montreal (1H, 1BB, 1K)...made four straight scoreless outings (6.0IP) before giving up three runs in 0.2IP in 7/5 loss at Cincinnati...surrendered just 1ER over eight outings from 7/24-8/22 (14.0IP), lowering his ERA from 6.75 to 2.61...established a career high with five strikeouts in 8/31 loss at Cincinnati.
- Began season with the Yankees' Double-A affiliate Norwich, going 3-1 with a 3.50 ERA in 23 games...held lefthanders to a .194 average (6-for-31)...went 2-0 with a 1.20 ERA (15.0IP, 3R, 2ER) in nine games during the month of April...notched first professional save on 5/6 at New Haven (3.0IP, 5H, 1ER, 1K).
- Appeared in four games with Nashville before joining Major League club, posting a 3.38 ERA with no decisions.

2000

- Opened season on the disabled list from 4/7-8/22 with a left elbow strain...made two rehab starts for the Peoria Mariners of the Arizona Rookie League, surrendering just 1H with 6K in 5.0IP...was transferred to Double-A New Haven on 8/22...did not record a decision in his four Double-A outings.

1999

- Was 0-1 with a 9.35 ERA in five appearances with Seattle in his first Major League action...was recalled from Triple-A Tacoma on 6/30 and made his Major League debut that night at Oakland (1.0IP, 2H, 3ER, 1BB)...threw a career-high 4.0 innings in 7/20 loss vs. Arizona in his final outing before being optioned back to Tacoma on 7/22.
- Posted a 3-3 record with a 5.13 ERA in 31 games (11 starts) at Triple-A Tacoma...went 1-2 with a 5.94 ERA as a starter (47.0, 31ER) with opponents batting .287 (54-for-188)...in 20 relief appearances, was 2-1 with a 3.71 ERA (26.2IP, 11ER) and a .243 opponents average (25-for-103).

1998

- In his first action at the Double-A level, was 7-6 with a 5.27 ERA with Orlando...ranked second on the staff in strikeouts (99) and third in innings pitched (121.1)...began season on D.L. with a left elbow strain...was reinstated on 5/2 and tossed 5.0 innings that night in a 9-1 win vs. Knoxville...tossed 6.2 scoreless innings in a 13-0 win vs. West Tenn on 8/15...returned to D.L. from 9/2-22 with a left forearm strain...made two appearances with Escogido in the Dominican Winter League.

1997

- Was 8-8 with a 4.13 ERA in 25 starts with Single-A Lancaster...was on the D.L. with tendinitis in his left elbow from 4/3-17...set minor league career high in strikeouts (127)...won eight of his 10 decisions from 6/19-8/26, including four straight wins from 6/29-7/30...named California League "Pitcher of the Week" on 8/16 after going 2-0 with a 0.56 ERA (16.0IP, 1ER) in two starts...tossed four-hit shutout at Stockton on 8/15 (11K)...pitched with Escogido in the Dominican Winter League following the season.

DAMASO MARTE

1996

- Was 8-6 with a 4.49 ERA in 26 starts with Single-A Wisconsin...led club in strikeouts (115) and ranked second in starts and innings pitched (142.1)...established a minor league career high in innings pitched...pitched four-hit shutout vs. South Bend on 7/6.

1995

- Was 2-2 with a 2.21 ERA in 11 games (five starts) with Single-A Everett...held opposing batters to a .195 average (25-for-128).

1993-94

- Went 7-0 with a 3.86 ERA (65.1IP, 28ER) in 17 games (13 starts) for Santo Domingo in the Dominican Summer League in 1994.
- Made professional debut with Santo Domingo in the Dominican Summer League in 1993, going 2-5 with a 6.55 ERA in 17 games (15 starts).

Personal

- Damaso Savinon Marte ("DAH-mah-so" "MAR-tay")...signed his first professional contract at the age of 16.
- Visited with kids at P.S. 55 in the Bronx for National Literacy Day in September 2008.

Marte's Career Pitching Record

Year	Club	W	L	ERA	G	GS	CG	SHO	SV	IP	H	R	ER	HR	HB	BB	SO	WP	BK
1993	DSL Mariners	2	5	6.55	17	15	2	0	0	56.1	62	48	41	5	7	50	29	4	4
1994	DSL Mariners	7	0	3.86	17	13	0	0	0	65.1	53	41	28	5	0	48	80	12	1
1995	Everett	2	2	2.21	11	5	0	0	0	36.2	25	11	9	2	1	10	39	3	0
1996	Wisconsin	8	6	4.49	26	26	2	1	0	142.1	134	82	71	8	6	75	115	4	3
1997	Lancaster	8	8	4.13	25	25	2	1	0	139.1	144	75	64	15	8	62	127	8	4
1998	Orlando	7	6	5.27	22	20	0	0	0	121.1	136	82	71	14	2	47	99	6	2
1999	Tacoma	3	3	5.13	31	11	0	0	0	73.2	79	43	42	13	2	40	59	1	2
	SEATTLE	0	1	9.35	5	0	0	0	0	8.2	16	9	9	3	0	6	3	0	0
2000	Peoria	0	0	0.00	2	2	0	0	0	5.0	1	0	0	0	1	0	6	0	0
	New Haven - a	0	0	1.59	4	0	0	0	0	5.2	6	1	1	1	0	2	4	0	1
2001	Norwich - b	3	1	3.50	23	0	0	0	0	36.1	34	21	19	5	3	12	39	1	0
	Nashville	0	0	3.58	4	0	0	0	0	5.1	3	2	2	2	0	0	4	0	0
	PITTSBURGH	0	1	4.71	23	0	0	0	0	36.1	34	21	19	5	3	12	39	1	0
2002	CHICAGO-AL - c	1	1	2.83	68	0	0	0	10	60.1	44	19	19	5	4	18	72	3	1
2003	CHICAGO-AL	4	2	1.58	71	0	0	0	11	79.2	50	16	14	3	3	34	87	1	0
2004	CHICAGO-AL	6	5	3.42	74	0	0	0	6	73.2	56	28	28	10	3	34	68	3	0
2005	Charlotte-d	0	0	5.40	1	0	0	0	0	1.2	4	1	1	0	0	1	2	1	0
	CHICAGO-AL - e	3	4	3.77	66	0	0	0	4	45.1	45	21	19	5	3	33	54	1	1
2006	PITTSBURGH	1	7	3.70	75	0	0	0	0	58.1	51	30	24	5	4	31	63	3	1
2007	PITTSBURGH	2	0	2.38	65	0	0	0	0	45.1	32	14	12	2	2	18	51	0	1
2008	PITTSBURGH - f	4	0	3.47	47	0	0	0	5	46.2	38	18	18	4	1	16	47	1	0
	YANKEES	1	3	5.40	25	0	0	0	0	18.1	14	11	11	1	1	10	24	0	0
2009	YANKEES - g	1	3	9.45	21	0	0	0	0	13.1	15	14	14	3	1	6	13	0	0
	GCL Yankees	0	0	4.50	2	2	0	0	0	2.0	2	1	1	0	0	0	2	0	0
	Scranton/WB	0	1	2.45	11	0	0	0	0	11.0	10	3	3	2	0	4	9	0	1
Minor League Totals		**40**	**32**	**4.46**	**196**	**119**	**6**	**2**	**1**	**701.2**	**688**	**406**	**348**	**70**	**29**	**346**	**611**	**39**	**19**
AL Totals		**16**	**19**	**3.43**	**330**	**0**	**0**	**0**	**31**	**299.1**	**240**	**118**	**114**	**30**	**15**	**141**	**321**	**8**	**23**
NL Totals		**7**	**8**	**3.52**	**210**	**0**	**0**	**0**	**5**	**186.2**	**155**	**83**	**73**	**16**	**10**	**77**	**200**	**5**	**2**
Major League Totals		**23**	**27**	**3.46**	**540**	**0**	**0**	**0**	**36**	**486.0**	**395**	**201**	**187**	**46**	**25**	**218**	**521**	**13**	**25**
NYY Totals		**2**	**6**	**7.11**	**46**	**0**	**0**	**0**	**0**	**31.2**	**29**	**25**	**25**	**4**	**2**	**16**	**37**	**0**	**0**

Signed by Seattle as a non-drafted free agent on November 6, 1992.

a – Signed by the Yankees as a minor league free agent on November 16, 2000
b – Acquired by Pittsburgh for the Yankees in exchange for INF Enrique Wilson on June 13, 2001.
c – Acquired by Chicago-AL from Pittsburgh in exchange for RHP Matt Guerrier on March 27, 2002.
d – Placed on the 15-day disabled list from June 27 – July 14, 2005 with an inflamed left trapezius.
e – Acquired by Pittsburgh from Chicago-AL in exchange for INF/OF Rob Mackowiak on December 13, 2005.
f – Acquired by the Yankees from Pittsburgh with OF Xavier Nady in exchange for RHPs Jeff Karstens, Dan McCutchen and Ross Ohlendorf and OF Jose Tabata on July 26, 2008.
g – Placed on the 15-day disabled list from May 3 (retroactive to April 26) – August 19, 2009 with left shoulder inflammation (transferred to 60-day disabled list on August 8).

DAMASO MARTE

Marte's Division Series Record

Year	Club vs. Opp.	W	L	ERA	G	GS	CG	SHO	SV	IP	H	R	ER	HR	HP	BB	SO	WP	BK
2005	CWS vs. BOS	0	0	---	1	0	0	0	0	0.0	1	0	0	0	0	2	0	0	0
2009	NYY vs. MIN	0	0	---	1	0	0	0	0	0.0	2	0	0	0	0	0	0	0	0
Division Series Totals		**0**	**0**	**---**	**2**	**0**	**0**	**0**	**0**	**0.0**	**3**	**0**	**0**	**0**	**0**	**2**	**0**	**0**	**0**

Marte's League Championship Series Record

Year	Club vs. Opp.	W	L	ERA	G	GS	CG	SHO	SV	IP	H	R	ER	HR	HP	BB	SO	WP	BK
2005	CWS vs. LAA	Did Not Pitch - Not on Roster																	
2009	NYY vs. LAA	0	0	0.00	3	0	0	0	0	1.1	0	0	0	0	0	0	0	0	0
LCS Totals		**0**	**0**	**0.00**	**3**	**0**	**0**	**0**	**0**	**1.1**	**0**	**0**	**0**	**0**	**0**	**0**	**0**	**0**	**0**

Marte's World Series Record

Year	Club vs. Opp.	W	L	ERA	G	GS	CG	SHO	SV	IP	H	R	ER	HR	HP	BB	SO	WP	BK
2005	CWS vs. HOU	1	0	0.00	1	0	0	0	0	1.2	0	0	0	0	0	2	3	0	0
2009	NYY vs. PHI	0	0	0.00	4	0	0	0	0	2.2	0	0	0	0	0	0	5	0	0
World Series Totals		**1**	**0**	**0.00**	**5**	**0**	**0**	**0**	**0**	**4.1**	**0**	**0**	**0**	**0**	**0**	**2**	**8**	**0**	**0**
POSTSEASON TOTALS		**1**	**0**	**0.00**	**10**	**0**	**0**	**0**	**0**	**5.2**	**3**	**0**	**0**	**0**	**0**	**4**	**8**	**0**	**0**

Marte's World Baseball Classic Record

Year	Country, Site	W	L	ERA	G	GS	CG	SHO	SV	IP	H	R	ER	HR	HP	BB	SO	WP	BK
2006	D.R., USA	0	1	20.25	3	0	0	0	1	1.1	4	4	3	0	0	1	2	0	0
2009	D.R., Puerto Rico	0	0	0.00	2	0	0	0	0	2.0	1	0	0	0	0	0	2	0	0
WBC Totals		**0**	**1**	**8.10**	**5**	**0**	**0**	**0**	**1**	**3.1**	**5**	**4**	**3**	**0**	**0**	**1**	**4**	**0**	**0**

Marte's Regular Season Batting Record

Year	Team	AVG	G	AB	R	H	2B	3B	HR	RBI	SH	SF	HP	BB	SO	SB	CS
2009	NYY	Did Not Bat															
Major League Totals		**.000**	**540**	**9**	**0**	**0**	**0**	**0**	**0**	**0**	**0**	**0**	**0**	**0**	**3**	**0**	**0**

Marte's Career Fielding Record

Position	PCT	G	PO	A	E	TC	DP
Pitcher	.986	540	14	58	1	73	3

Yankees in Interleague Play

The Yankees lead the Majors in all-time Interleague wins and winning percentage (.583, 133-95)...the Yankees went 10-8 vs. the NL in 2009, matching their record from each of the previous three years and collecting their 12th straight non-losing season of Interleague play...SS Derek Jeter has recorded 303 hits and scored 171 runs in Interleague Play, ranking first all time in both categories...RHP Mariano Rivera ranks first with 59 Interleague saves while LHP Andy Pettitte is tied for second in starts (45)...Yankees pitchers have batted a combined .103 (27-for-263) all-time in Interleague play with 8 doubles...no Yankees pitcher has ever homered in Interleague play.

YEAR-BY-YEAR INTERLEAGUE RESULTS

Year	Opponents	Record
1997	(NYM, ATL, MON, FLA, PHI)	5-10
1998	(NYM, ATL, MON, FLA, PHI)	13-3
1999	(NYM, ATL, MON, FLA, PHI)	9-9
2000	(NYM, ATL, MON, FLA, PHI)	11-6
2001	(NYM, ATL, MON, FLA, PHI)	10-8
2002	(NYM, SF, ARI, CL, SD)	11-7
2003	(NYM, CIN, CHC, HOU, StL)	13-5
2004	(NYM, COL, SD, ARI, LAD)	10-8
2005	(NYM, MIL, StL, PIT, CHC)	11-7
2006	(NYM, WAS, PHI, FLA, ATL)	10-8
2007	(NYM, PIT, ARI, COL, SF)	10-8
2008	(NYM, HOU, SD, CIN, PIT)	10-8
2009	(NYM, PHI, WAS, FLA, ATL)	10-8

TOP INTERLEAGUE WINNING PCTS., ALL-TIME

Rk.	Opponents	Record (Pct.)
1.	YANKEES	133-95 (.583)
2.	Minnesota	132-96 (.580)
3.	Chicago-AL	128-101 (.559)
4.	Los Angeles-AL	128-102 (.557)
	Oakland	128-102 (.557)

Mark Melancon

39 Right-handed Pitcher
6-2 • 215 • B/T: Right/Right
Opening Day Age: 25

Birthdate
March 28, 1985

Birthplace
Wheat Ridge, Colo.

Resides
Marble Falls, Tex.

M.L. Service
77 days

College
University of Arizona

Status

- Selected by the Yankees in the ninth round of the 2006 First-Year Player Draft...signed through 2010.

2009

- Was 0-1 with a 3.86 ERA in 13 relief appearances over three stints with the Yankees (4/25-5/8; 7/10-8/8 and 9/1-10/4)...opponents batted .217 (13-for-60, 0HR); LH .276 (8-for-29), RH .161 (5-for-31)...stranded 7-of-15 inherited runners (46.7%)...retired 7-of-13 first batters faced (53.8%)...appeared in consecutive games once (7/31-8/1).
- Was signed to a Major League contract and selected to the Yankees' 25-man roster on 4/25 from Triple-A Scranton/Wilkes-Barre...made his Major League debut the next night in 4/26 loss at Boston, tossing 2.0 scoreless IP (1H, 1BB, 1HBP, 1K).
- Suffered his first blown save in 5/1 win vs. Los Angeles-AL, allowing 1H and 1ER in 0.1IP (1BB, 1WP)...was the first run allowed in his Major League career...entered the game with two outs and the bases loaded in the sixth inning and allowed all three inherited runners to score on a Gary Matthews Jr. triple...was optioned to Scranton/WB on 5/8.
- Recalled on 7/10 and allowed 3R (2ER) on 3H in 2.1IP of relief that night at Los Angeles-AL...did not pitch again for 18 days (14 games) until 7/28 at Tampa Bay, tossing a career-high-tying 2.1 scoreless innings (1H, 2K).
- Was optioned back to Scranton/WB on 8/8 when RHP Josh Towers joined the Major League staff.
- Was recalled for a third time prior to 9/1 win at Baltimore...allowed a run in three of his final four outings during September.
- In 32 relief appearances with Scranton/WB, was 4-0 with three saves and a 2.89 ERA (53.0IP, 37H, 22R, 17ER, 11BB, 54K, 3HR)...recorded 10.1 scoreless IP in relief and struck out 17 batters over six appearances with Scranton/WB prior to his first recall.
- Appeared in six spring training games as a non-roster invitee, recording a 7.94 ERA without a decision (5.2IP, 9H, 6R, 5ER, 3BB, 5K, 2HR).

Single-Game Highs and Streaks

IP (relief)
2.1 - 2 times
Last: at TB, 7/28/09

Hits
3 - at LAA, 7/10/09

Runs
3 - at LAA, 7/10/09

BB
3 - vs. BOS, 5/5/09

SO
2 - 3 times
Last: vs. TOR, 9/15/09

HR
None

Winning Streak
None

Losing Streak
1g - 7/10/09

2008

- Combined at three stops (Single-A Tampa, Double-A Trenton and Triple-A Scranton/Wilkes-Barre) to go 8-1 with a 2.27 ERA in 41 relief appearances, holding opponents to a .202 batting average (69-for-341, 6HR)...lefthanders batted just .163 (21-for-129, 2HR)...threw more than 1.0 inning in 40 of his 44 outings.
- Opened the year at Tampa, allowing 6ER in his first three outings (4.2IP, 11.57 ERA)...surrendered just 2ER over his next 20.2IP (0.90 ERA) before being promoted to Trenton on 5/13...tossed at least 2.0 innings in all 19 appearances with the Thunder and converted both his save opportunities.
- Promoted to SWB on 7/29, where he struck out 22 batters in 20.0IP...appeared in two postseason games with the International League champions, going 1-0 with 3.0 scoreless IP...following the season, was selected as the organization's ninth-best prospect by *Baseball America*.

2007

- Missed the season after having "Tommy John" surgery on 10/31/06...entered the 2007 season ranked as the ninth-best prospect in the Yankees organization by *Baseball America*.

2006

- Made professional debut with short-season Single-A Staten Island, making seven relief appearances and going 0-1 with a 3.52 ERA and two saves...helped lead the Yankees to their second consecutive NY-Penn League Championship, tossing 3.1 perfect innings in three postseason appearances with 6K.

Personal

- Full name is Mark David Melancon...last name is pronounced "Muh-LAN-son"...married to Mary Catherine...drafted out of the University of Arizona, where he holds the school's single-season and career saves records...also set a freshman team record with 29 appearances in 2004...previously drafted by the Los Angeles Dodgers in 2003 (30th round)...was a three-sport athlete at Golden (Colo.) High School.

Melancon's Career Pitching Record

Year	Team	W	L	ERA	G	GS	CG	SHO	SV	IP	H	R	ER	HR	HP	BB	SO	WP	BK
2006	Staten Island	0	1	3.52	7	0	0	0	2	7.2	9	7	3	0	0	2	8	1	0
2007		Did Not Pitch - Injured																	
2008	Tampa	1	0	2.84	13	0	0	0	0	25.1	26	9	8	2	1	6	20	0	0
	Trenton	6	0	1.81	19	0	0	0	2	49.2	32	14	10	3	0	12	47	1	0
	Scranton/WB	1	1	2.70	12	0	0	0	1	20.0	11	7	6	1	1	4	22	1	0
2009	Scranton/WB	4	0	2.89	32	0	0	0	3	53.0	37	22	17	3	6	11	54	5	0
	YANKEES	0	1	3.86	13	0	0	0	0	16.1	13	8	7	0	4	10	10	3	0
Minor League Totals		**12**	**2**	**2.54**	**83**	**0**	**0**	**0**	**8**	**155.2**	**115**	**59**	**44**	**9**	**8**	**35**	**151**	**8**	**0**
Major League Totals		**0**	**1**	**3.86**	**13**	**0**	**0**	**0**	**0**	**16.1**	**13**	**8**	**7**	**0**	**4**	**10**	**10**	**3**	**0**

Selected by the Yankees in the ninth round of the 2006 First-Year Player Draft.

Melancon's Career Fielding Record

Position	PCT	G	PO	A	E	TC	DP
Pitcher	1.000	13	1	4	0	5	0

Deck the Hall

Following the inaugural game at Yankee Stadium on 4/16/09, the National Baseball Hall of Fame and Museum in Cooperstown, N.Y. received the spikes worn by Yankee starter **LHP CC Sabathia**, who threw the Stadium's first pitch; the bat used by Cleveland's Grady Sizemore to hit the Stadium's first grand slam; and a game-used baseball autographed by Indians starter and winning pitcher Cliff Lee.

Following the Yankees' 2009 Game 6 World Series-clinching victory vs. Philadelphia, the Baseball Hall of Fame secured eight Yankees items to remain on display in the Autumn Glory exhibit in Cooperstown through the 2010 postseason: **RHP Mariano Rivera** postseason hat; **DH Hideki Matsui** Game 6 bat; **SS Derek Jeter Game** 6 bat; **LHP Andy Pettitte** cap from the World Series; **LF Johnny Damon** spikes from Game 4 when he stole two bases on one pitch; **C Jorge Posada** mask from the postseason; **C Jose Molina** mask from the postseason; radio broadcaster **Suzyn Waldman** Game 6 scorecard.

Juan Miranda

53 First Baseman
6-0 • 220 • B/T: Left/Left
Opening Day Age: 26

Birthdate
April 25, 1983

Birthplace
Consulacion del Sur, Cuba

Resides
Santiago, D.R.

M.L. Service
31 days
(Rookie)

Status

- Signed as a non-drafted free agent to a four-year Major League contract on December 22, 2006...contract extends through the 2010 season.

2009

- Batted .333 (3-for-9) with 2R, 1HR and 3RBI in eight games (one start at 1B) over two stints with the Yankees (4/17-18, 9/18-10/4)...was recalled from Triple-A Scranton/Wilkes-Barre on 4/17, and was optioned back on 4/18 when RHP Anthony Claggett was recalled...recalled again from Scranton/WB prior to 9/18 loss at Seattle...made his season debut in 9/19 win at Seattle, singling in the ninth inning as a pinch-hitter for Hideki Matsui.
- Hit "walk-off" infield single in 9/29 win vs. Kansas City after entering the game defensively in the top of the ninth at 1B...was his first career "walk-off" hit...became the ninth different Yankee to collect a "walk-off" hit in 2009 and the second rookie to do so (also Francisco Cervelli on 9/16 vs. Toronto).
- Hit first Major League home run in 10/2 loss at Tampa Bay, a two-run HR off Dale Thayer in the eighth inning.
- Batted .290 (127-for-438) with 74R, 30 doubles, 19HR and 82RBI in 122 games for Scranton/WB...ranked third in the International League in RBI...named International League "Player of the Week" for the period 4/9-12...appeared in seven postseason games for the IL North Division champs, batting .231 (6-for-26) with 1 double 1 triple, 1HR, 6RBI and 4BB.
- Played winter ball with Licey in the Dominican Winter League, batting .409 (18-for-44) with 5 doubles, 2HR and 11RBI in 13 games.

Single-Game Highs and Streaks

Hits
2 - at TOR, 9/24/08
Runs
1 - 4 times
Last: at TB, 10/4/09
2B
1 - at TOR, 9/24/08
3B
None
HR
1 - at TB, 10/2/09
RBI
2 - at TB, 10/2/09
BB
2 - vs. CWS, 9/18/08
SO
2 - at KC 9/28/09
SB
None
Hit Streak
2g - 2 times
Last: 9/28/08-9/19/09

2008

- Batted .400 (4-for-10) with 1 double and 1RBI in five games (three starts at 1B) with the Yankees as a September callup in his first Major League action...reached base safely in four of his five games...doubled in his only at-bat vs. a left-handed pitcher on 9/24 at Toronto (Jesse Carlson).
- Was recalled from Triple-A Scranton/Wilkes-Barre on 9/17...made his Major League debut in 9/18 win vs. Chicago (AL), starting at 1B and going 0-for-2 with 1R and 2BB...became the 15th Cuban-born player to appear in a game with the Yankees.
- Was one of three Yankees to make their Major League debut in the 9/18 game (also Cervelli and Sanchez)...according to the *Elias Sports Bureau*, was the first time three different Yankees made their debut in the same game since 3/31/03 when Hideki Matsui, Jose Contreras and Jason Anderson each debuted in the Yankees' 8-4 win at Toronto.
- Made his second Major League start in 9/24 win at Toronto, going 2-for-4 with 1 double...collected his first hit with a fourth-inning single off A.J. Burnett...recorded his first RBI in 9/28 Game 2 loss at Boston with a ninth-inning sacrifice fly.
- Batted .287 (102-for-356) in 99 games with Triple-A Scranton/Wilkes-Barre, with 22 doubles, 12HR, 52RBI and 55BB...ranked fifth in the International League with a .384 on-base percentage...ranked second on the team with 102H...committed just 5E in 670 total chances at 1B (.993 fielding percentage) with Scranton/WB...hit .332 (79-for-228) with 10HR vs. right-handed pitchers.

- Was placed on the disabled list twice with a right shoulder strain (4/30-5/12 and 5/19-6/16).
- Batted .265 (9-for-34) with a league-high 11RBI in eight postseason games for the International League-champion SWB Yankees...homered and drove in a single-game postseason franchise-record six runs in SWB's 20-2 win on 9/12 vs. Durham to clinch the IL title.
- Batted .301 (22-for-73) with 14R, 7 doubles, 2 triples, 5HR and 20RBI in 19 games with the Peoria Javelinas of the Arizona Fall League...did not commit an error in nine starts at 1B (81 TC).

2007

- Combined to hit .265 (118-for-446) with 64R, 34 doubles, 16HR and 96RBI in 122 games with Single-A Tampa and Double-A Trenton...ranked first among all Yankees farmhands in RBI and fourth in HR...collected 10 sacrifice flies, tying for fourth-most among all minor leaguers...batted .317 with runners in scoring position (44-for-139, 7HR, 78RBI).
- Began the season with Tampa, batting .264 (66-for-250) with 35R, 9HR and 50RBI in 67 games...hit .284 (52-for-183) off right-handers...was tied for third among Florida State League first basemen (min: 500TC) with a .991 fielding percentage (5E, 566TC).
- Recorded his first career multi-home run game on 5/24 at Vero Beach with a pair of two-run homers...beginning with that game, fashioned a 15-game hitting streak from 5/24-6/10, batting .426 (23-for-54) with 12R, 9 doubles, 1 triple, 4HR, 22RBI, 8BB and six multi-hit games during the stretch...drove in at least one run in 13 of those games, including nine straight from 5/31-6/10...the team went 12-3 during his hitting streak.
- Was promoted to Double-A Trenton on 6/22 and hit .265 (52-for-196) with 29R, 7HR and 46RBI in 55 games...drove in an organization-high 27R in 25 July games...helped lead Trenton to its ninth straight win on 7/8 at Harrisburg, hitting his first career grand slam off Jerome Williams and establishing a career-high 5RBI...also recorded with 5RBI on 8/9 at Binghamton...appeared in two postseason games with Trenton, batting .250 (2-for-8) with 1R, 1 double, 1RBI and 1HBP.
- Played for the Peoria Javelinas of the Arizona Fall League, hitting .295 (23-for-78) with 16R, 5 doubles and 5HR in 22 games...led the league, averaging one home run every 15.6AB, tied for fourth with 5HR, placed fifth in on-base percentage (.423), tied for fifth in RBI (17), ranked sixth in slugging percentage (.551) and tied for seventh with 16BB...was named to the 2007 AFL Top Prospects Team.

Career

- Began his professional career in Cuba, playing first base and left field for Pinar Del Rio in Cuba's Serie Nacional from 2001-04...in his Cuban career, batted .303 with 27HR and 73BB while striking out just 87 times...while playing in Cuba, was a teammate of former Yankee Jose Contreras...also played against other current Major Leaguers, including Kansas City's Yuniesky Betancourt and the Angels' Kendry Morales.

Personal

- Full name is Juan Miguel Miranda...signed by Ramon Valdivio...has one son, Edgar Miguel (2)...defected to the Dominican Republic in 2004, established residency in 2005 and was granted citizenship in 2006.

Miranda's Career Playing Record

Year	Club	AVG	G	AB	R	H	2B	3B	HR	RBI	SH	SF	HB	BB	SO	SB	CS	E	OBP	SLG
2007	Tampa	.264	67	250	35	66	17	3	9	50	0	7	7	29	60	1	0	5	.348	.464
	Trenton	.265	55	196	29	52	17	2	7	46	0	3	5	23	46	0	1	4	.352	.480
2008	Scranton/WB	.287	99	356	40	102	22	0	12	52	0	3	3	55	79	2	1	5	.384	.449
	YANKEES	.400	5	10	2	4	1	0	0	1	0	1	1	2	4	0	0	0	.500	.500
2009	Scranton/WB	.290	122	438	74	127	30	2	19	82	55	6	3	55	101	1	0	10	.369	.498
	YANKEES	.333	8	9	2	3	0	0	1	3	0	0	0	0	4	0	0	0	.333	.667
Minor League Totals		**.280**	**343**	**1240**	**178**	**347**	**86**	**7**	**47**	**230**	**162**	**19**	**18**	**162**	**286**	**4**	**2**	**24**	**.366**	**.474**
Major League Totals		**.368**	**13**	**19**	**4**	**7**	**1**	**0**	**1**	**4**	**2**	**1**	**1**	**2**	**8**	**0**	**0**	**0**	**.435**	**.579**

Selected by the Yankees in the third round of the 2005 First-Year Player Draft

Miranda's Career Fielding Record

Position	PCT	G	PO	A	E	TC
First Base	1.000	13	49	3	0	52

Cuban Born Yankees

In 2008, Juan Miranda became the 15th Cuban-born player to appear in a game for the Yankees. The complete list of Cuban-born Yankees: OF Angel Aragon, OF Armando Marsans, INF Willie Miranda, RHP Pedros Ramos, RHP Luis Tiant, C Bobby Ramos, INF Bert Campaneris, 1B Orestes Destrade, RHP Orlando Hernandez, LHP Tony Fossas, OF Jose Canseco, RHP Adrian Hernandez, C Michel Hernandez, RHP Jose Contreras and 1B Juan Miranda.

Sergio Mitre

45 **Right-handed Pitcher**

6-3 • 225 • B/T: Right/Right

Opening Day Age: 29

Birthdate
February 16, 1981

Birthplace
Los Angeles, Calif.

Resides
Chula Vista, Calif.

M.L. Service
4 years, 132 days

College
San Diego City College

Status

- Signed as a free agent on January 14, 2009...signed through the 2010 season.

2009

- Was 3-3 with a 6.79 ERA in 12 appearances (nine starts) with the Yankees...did not record a decision in his three relief outings, posting a 4.70 ERA...went 3-3 with a 7.16 ERA as a starter, allowing 65H in 44.0IP...opponents batted .321 (71-for-221, 10HR); LH .421 (40-for-95, 6HR); RH .246 (31-for-126, 4HR).
- Allowed at least one run in the first inning of six of his nine starts, compiling an 8.00 first-inning ERA (9.0IP, 8ER)...had a 6.94 ERA (35.0IP, 27ER) from the second inning onward.
- Was signed to a Major League contract and selected to the Yankees' 25-man roster from Triple-A Scranton/Wilkes-Barre on 7/21...started and recorded the win that night vs. Baltimore at Yankee Stadium, allowing 3ER and 8H in 5.2IP (4R, 1BB, 4K)...was his first Major League start since 9/15/07 w/ Florida at Colorado and his first Major League win since 7/29/07 w/ Florida at San Francisco.
- Went winless over his next four starts from 7/26-8/10, going 0-1 with a 7.79 ERA (17.1IP, 15ER).
- Moved to the bullpen for the final two weeks of the season and made two relief appearances...tossed 5.0 scoreless innings in 9/20 loss at Seattle (1H, 1BB, 5K)...was the longest relief outing of his career (previous was 3.0IP) and longest by a Yankees reliever in 2009.
- Opened the year on the disabled list, recovering from "Tommy John" surgery...also served a 50-game suspension at the start of the season for violating Major League Baseball's Drug Prevention and Treatment Program.
- Made nine combined starts with Single-A Tampa and Triple-A Scranton/Wilkes-Barre, going 4-1 with a 2.32 ERA...held opponents to 3ER or less in each start and 2ER or less in seven of those starts.
- Saw his first action with Tampa, making his season debut on 5/30 vs. Charlotte County...was his first appearance since 9/15/07 w/ Florida...named the International League "Pitcher of the Week" with Scranted/Wilkes-Barre for the period from 7/6-12.

Single-Game Highs and Streaks

Low hit CG
5 - vs. FLA, 6/14/05

IP (start)
9.0 - vs. FLA, 6/14/05

IP (relief)
5.0 - at SEA, 9/20/09

Hits
12 - at KC, 6/15/07

Runs
11 - at TOR, 9/6/09

BB
4 - 5 times
Last: at COL, 9/15/07

SO
8 - vs. NYM, 5/25/07

HR
4 - vs. TOR, 9/15/09

Winning Streak
2g - 4 times Last: 8/15-29/09

Losing Streak
7g - 4/11/06-4/11/07

2008

- Underwent "Tommy John" surgery on 7/15 and did not pitch the entire season...opened the year on the disabled list with a right elbow strain.

2007

- Went 5-8 with a 4.65 ERA in 27 starts with the Marlins, setting career highs in wins, games, starts, IP (149.0) and strikeouts (80)...began the season with a 1.59 ERA (56.2IP, 10ER) through his first 10 starts.
- Left his third start on 4/17 at Houston with a blister on his right middle finger and was placed on the 15-day disabled list from 4/18-5/5...did not allow an earned run in 24.2 consecutive innings over five starts from 5/20-6/15...was winless over his final eight starts from 8/4-9/15 (0-3, 7.96 ERA).

2006

- Went 1-5 with 5.71 ERA in 15 games (seven starts) in his first season with the Florida Marlins...was 1-4 with a 4.89 ERA in seven starts, and 0-1 with a 10.50 ERA in eight relief outings...was placed on the 15-day disabled list with right shoulder inflammation on 5/15 and transferred to the 60-day D.L. on 5/26...was reinstated on 8/8 and pitched out of the bullpen for the remainder of the season...was shut down in September.

2005

- Appeared in 21 games over three stints (5/10-12; 5/24-8/5; 9/4-9/30) with Chicago-NL, making seven starts and going 2-5 with a 5.37 ERA.

- Recorded his first Major League shutout and first complete game with 14-0 win vs. Florida on 6/14, allowing just 5H and striking out three in 9.0IP...was the second of back-to-back starts without allowing a run (also 6/8 vs. Toronto – 7.0IP, 2H).
- Pitched for Hermosillo in the Mexican Winter League, going 0-1 with 4.15 ERA in three starts...was acquired by the Marlins following the season in a trade for OF Juan Pierre.

2004

- Made his first career Opening Day roster and went 2-4 with a 6.62 ERA in 12 appearances (nine starts) over two stints with the Cubs...earned his first Major League win in his start on 4/21 at Pittsburgh, allowing only 4H over 6.0 scoreless innings in a 12-1 victory.
- While with Triple-A Iowa, went 6-3 with a 2.98 ERA in 18 games (15 starts)...collected his first professional save on 7/6 vs. Albuquerque, tossing the final 4.0 innings of the game (1H, 1ER, 1BB, 5K, 1HR)...tossed a 9.0-inning one-hit shutout on 8/13 vs. Albuquerque with 1BB and 9K.

2003

- Saw his first Major League action, going 0-1 with an 8.31 ERA in three games (two starts) over three stints...was signed to a Major League contract and added to the Cubs' 40-man roster on 7/21 in place of the injured Mark Prior...made his debut on 7/22 at Atlanta in an emergency start, recording the loss in an 8-4 Braves victory (3.2IP, 10H, 8ER, 3BB, 0K, 1HR).
- Made 25 appearances (24 starts) with Double-A West Tenn, going 7-9 with a 3.34 ERA...held his opponents to 1ER or less in 13 starts, including eight of his final 10 outings.

2002

- Spent the season at Single-A Lansing, where he went 8-10 with a 2.83 ERA in 27 starts...ranked fourth in the Midwest League in innings pitched (168.2) and sixth in ERA...walked just 27 batters.

2001

- Made his professional debut with short-season Single-A Boise, going 8-4 with a 3.07 ERA...ranked second in the Northwest League in wins, innings pitched (91.0) and starts (15) and 10th in ERA...threw the first shutout of his pro career on 7/24 at Tri-City, allowing just 3H in a 9-0 victory.

Personal

- Full name is Sergio Armando Mitre (MEE-tray)...originally selected by Chicago-NL in the seventh round of the 2001 First-Year Player Draft...graduated from Montgomery High School (Calif.) in 1999...attended San Diego City College...he and his wife, Tonya, have one son, Sam (3).

Mitre's Career Pitching Record

Year	Club	W	L	ERA	G	GS	CG	SHO	SV	IP	H	R	ER	HR	HP	BB	SO	WP	BK
2001	Boise	8	4	3.07	15	15	1	1	0	91.0	85	37	31	2	3	18	71	3	3
2002	Lansing	8	10	2.83	27	27	2	0	0	168.2	166	72	53	7	10	27	96	10	0
2003	West Tenn	7	9	3.34	25	24	0	0	0	145.2	162	75	54	6	12	41	128	6	0
	CHICAGO	0	1	8.31	3	2	0	0	0	8.2	15	8	8	1	0	4	3	0	0
2004	Iowa	6	3	2.98	18	15	1	1	1	102.2	97	38	34	9	6	39	95	7	1
	CHICAGO	2	4	6.62	12	9	0	0	0	51.2	71	38	38	6	4	20	37	5	1
2005	Iowa	5	6	4.33	13	13	1	0	0	70.2	72	34	34	5	1	22	55	4	2
	CHICAGO - a	2	5	5.37	21	7	1	1	0	60.1	62	37	36	11	3	23	37	5	0
2006	FLORIDA - b	1	5	5.71	15	7	0	0	0	41.0	44	28	26	7	6	20	31	1	0
	GCL Marlins	0	0	0.00	1	1	0	0	0	1.0	0	0	0	0	0	1	0	0	0
2007	FLORIDA - c	5	8	4.65	27	27	0	0	0	149.0	180	88	77	9	10	41	80	6	0
	Jupiter	2	0	1.00	2	1	0	0	0	9.0	5	1	1	0	0	0	4	0	0
2008		Injured - Did Not Pitch - d																	
2009	Tampa - e, f	1	0	1.93	2	2	0	0	0	9.1	10	6	2	0	1	2	8	1	0
	Scranton/WB	3	1	2.40	7	7	0	0	0	45.0	40	13	12	3	3	5	35	1	0
	YANKEES	3	3	6.79	12	9	0	0	0	51.2	71	45	39	10	3	13	32	3	0
Minor League Totals		**40**	**33**	**3.09**	**110**	**105**	**5**	**2**	**1**	**643.0**	**637**	**276**	**221**	**32**	**36**	**155**	**492**	**32**	**6**
NL Totals		**10**	**23**	**5.36**	**78**	**52**	**1**	**1**	**0**	**310.2**	**372**	**199**	**185**	**34**	**23**	**108**	**188**	**17**	**1**
Major League Totals		**13**	**26**	**5.56**	**90**	**61**	**1**	**1**	**0**	**362.1**	**443**	**244**	**224**	**44**	**26**	**121**	**220**	**20**	**1**

Selected by Chicago-NL in the seventh round of the 2001 First-Year Player Draft.

a - Traded to Florida from Chicago-NL with RHP Carlos Nolasco and LHP Renyel Pinto in exchange for OF Juan Pierre on December 7, 2005.
b - Placed on the 15-day disabled list from May 13 - August 9, 2006 with right shoulder tendinitis(transferred to 60-day disabled list on May 26).
c - Placed on the 15-day disabled list from April 18 - May 5, 2007 with a blister on his right middle finger.
d - Placed on the 15-day disabled list on March 21, 2008 with a right elbow strain (transferred to the 60-day disabled list on April 18)...was released on September 29, 2008.
e - Signed by New York-AL as a free agent on November 16, 2008.
f - Served a 50-game suspension from April 9 - June 1, 2009 for violating Major League Baseball's Drug Prevention and Treatment Program.

Mitre's Regular Season Batting Record

Year	Team	AVG	G	AB	R	H	2B	3B	HR	RBI	SH	SF	HP	BB	SO	SB	CS
2009	Yankees	Did Not Bat															
Major League Totals		**.141**	**90**	**78**	**5**	**11**	**4**	**0**	**0**	**2**	**13**	**0**	**0**	**3**	**33**	**0**	**0**

Mitre's Career Fielding Record

Position	PCT	G	PO	A	E	TC	DP
Pitcher	.949	90	38	73	6	117	3

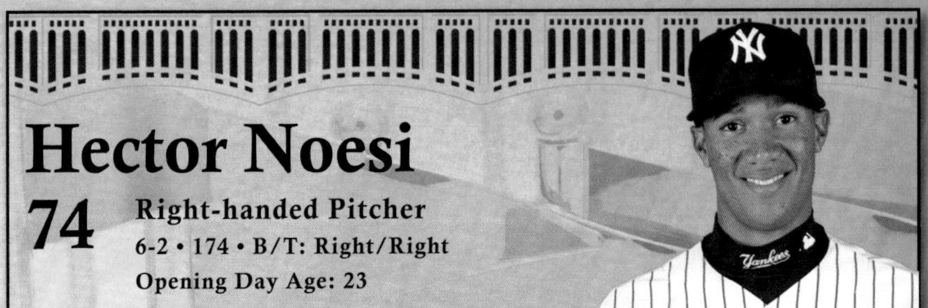

Hector Noesi

74 Right-handed Pitcher

6-2 • 174 • B/T: Right/Right

Opening Day Age: 23

Birthdate
January 26, 1987

Birthplace
Esperanza, D.R.

Resides
Mao, D.R.

M.L. Service
None
(Rookie)

Status

- Signed by the Yankees as a non-drafted free agent on December 3, 2004.

Minor League Career

- Has averaged 8.54K and just 1.55BB per 9.0 innings pitched in his career.

2009

- Appeared in 26 combined games (20 starts) with Single-A Charleston and Single-A Tampa, going 6-4 with a 2.92 ERA and 118 strikeouts in 117.0 IP...combined to hold opponents to a .220 batting average (96-for-436) with only 15 walks...struck out at least seven batters in nine of his starts.
- Began the season with 27.1 consecutive scoreless innings over his first nine appearances (three starts), striking out 35 batters with only three walks over the stretch...was named a midseason All-Star with Charleston.
- Went on the disabled list from 7/19-8/2 with right shoulder tendinitis.
- Made two postseason relief appearances for the FSL Champion Tampa squad, allowing 4ER in 7.0IP...earned the win in Game 1 of the Championship Series at Port Charlotte.

2008

- Combined to go 3-2 with a 3.33 ERA in 14 appearances (seven starts) with the GCL Yankees and short-season Single-A Staten Island...began the season with the GCL Yankees, going 2-1 with a 3.65 ERA in nine appearances (two starts)...was promoted to Staten Island on 8/10 and went 1-1 with a 3.00 ERA in five starts.

2007

- Suffered a season-ending right elbow strain on 6/23 that limited him to only five starts with Single-A Charleston, going 1-1 with a 4.50 ERA...began the season serving a 50-day suspension for violating the Minor League Drug Prevention and Treatment Program.

2006

- Was limited to just five relief appearances with the Yankees' Gulf Coast League team, beginning the season on the disabled list with a strained right shoulder (6/18-7/31)...walked only one batter while recording 11 strikeouts in 7.0IP.

2005

- Made his professional debut with the Yankees' Dominican Summer League team, going 5-3 with a 1.60 ERA in 13 games (10 starts).

Noesi's Career Pitching Record

YEAR	CLUB	W	L	ERA	G	GS	CG	SHO	SV	IP	H	R	ER	HR	HB	BB	SO	WP	BK
2005	DSL Yankees 1	5	3	1.60	13	10	0	0	0	50.2	34	19	9	2	5	8	36	2	1
2006	GCL Yankees	0	0	1.29	5	0	0	0	1	7.0	5	1	1	0	0	1	11	0	0
2007	Charleston	1	1	4.50	5	5	0	0	0	20.0	25	10	10	2	0	8	11	2	0
2008	GCL Yankees	2	1	3.65	9	2	0	0	0	24.2	23	11	10	2	1	3	24	1	0
	Staten Island	1	1	3.00	5	5	0	0	0	24.0	20	12	8	5	1	7	31	3	1
2009	Charleston	3	4	2.38	17	11	0	0	0	75.2	62	24	20	3	0	11	78	0	1
	Tampa	3	0	3.92	9	9	0	0	0	41.1	34	18	18	3	1	4	40	2	0
Minor League Totals		**15**	**10**	**2.81**	**63**	**42**	**0**	**0**	**1**	**243.1**	**203**	**95**	**76**	**17**	**8**	**42**	**231**	**10**	**3**

Signed by the Yankees as a non-drafted free agent on December 3, 2004.

Ivan Nova

75

Right-handed Pitcher

6-4 • 210 • B/T: Right/Right

Opening Day Age: 23

Birthdate
January 12, 1987

Birthplace
San Cristobal, D.R.

Resides
San Cristobal, D.R.

M.L. Service
None

Status

- Signed by the Yankees as a non-drafted free agent on July 15, 2004...signed through the 2010 season.

2009

- Made 24 combined starts with Double-A Trenton and Triple-A Scranton/Wilkes-Barre, going 6-8 with a 3.68 ERA (139.1IP, 57ER).
- Held opponents to 2ER or less in 10 of his 12 starts with Trenton, including each of his final seven outings...left-handers batted just .188 (25-for-133, 1HR) against him at the Double-A level.
- Tossed 5.2 scoreless innings and allowed just 1H in his Triple-A debut on 6/29 vs. Rochester, earning the win in a 5-0 SWB victory (3BB, 5K)...was credited with his first career complete game on 7/30 vs. Durham, throwing all 7.0 innings and recording the loss in Game 1 of a doubleheader (6H, 6R, 5ER, 3BB, 2K, 1HR).
- Made two postseason starts for Scranton/WB, going 1-0 with a 1.93 ERA, allowing just three earned runs in 14.0IP and striking out 10 batters.
- Following the season, appeared in five games (four starts) with Esogido in the Dominican Winter League, going 1-0 with a 1.05 ERA (25.2IP, 17H, 3ER, 4BB, 17K).
- Was selected by the San Diego Padres in the second round of the 2008 Rule 5 Draft...attended Major League Spring Training with the Padres, allowing 11R (8ER) on 13H in 8.2IP over eight relief appearances...was returned to the Yankees on 3/29/09.

2008

- Made a career-high 26 appearances (24 starts) with Single-A Tampa, going 8-13 with a 4.36 ERA and striking out a career-high 109 batters...ranked second among Florida State League pitchers with 148.2IP...led the team in starts, tied for most wins and ranked second in strikeouts.

2007

- Was 6-8 with a 4.98 ERA in 21 starts with Single-A Charleston...was placed on the disabled list from 7/7-14 with a left hip strain.
- Made one relief appearance for Leones del Escogido of the Dominican Winter League, throwing 1.2 scoreless innings and earning the win (1BB, 1K).

2006

- Posted a 3-0 record with a 2.72 ERA in 10 games (five starts) with the Gulf Coast League Yankees...ranked second in the league with 5HR allowed.

2005

- Made professional debut with the Yankees' Dominican Summer League squad, going 0-1 with a 2.29 ERA in 11 games (seven starts).

Nova's Career Pitching Record

YEAR	CLUB	W	L	ERA	G	GS	CG	SHO	SV	IP	H	R	ER	HR	HB	BB	SO	WP	BK
2005	DSL Yankees 1	0	1	2.29	11	7	0	0	0	39.1	29	11	10	2	3	11	38	5	0
2006	GCL Yankees	3	0	2.72	10	5	0	0	1	43.0	36	13	13	5	3	7	36	3	0
2007	Charleston	6	8	4.98	21	21	0	0	0	99.1	121	64	55	8	6	31	54	4	0
2008	Tampa-a	8	13	4.36	26	24	0	0	0	148.2	168	81	72	6	9	46	109	12	1
2009	Trenton-b	5	4	2.36	12	12	0	0	0	72.1	65	27	19	3	2	31	47	5	3
	Scranton/WB	1	4	5.10	12	12	1	0	0	67.0	72	39	38	4	3	28	43	4	0
Minor League Totals		**23**	**30**	**3.97**	**92**	**81**	**1**	**0**	**1**	**469.2**	**491**	**235**	**207**	**28**	**26**	**154**	**327**	**33**	**4**

Signed by the Yankees as a non-drafted free agent on July 15, 2004.

a – Selected by the San Diego Padres in the Rule 5 Draft on December 11, 2008.
b – Returned to the Yankees on March 29, 2009.

Eduardo Nunez

94 **Infielder**

6-0 • 155 • B/T: Right/Right

Opening Day Age: 22

Birthdate
June 15, 1987

Birthplace
Santo Domingo, D.R.

Resides
Azua, D.R.

M.L. Service
None
(Rookie)

Status

- Signed by the Yankees as a non-drafted free agent on February 25, 2004...signed through the 2010 season.

2009

- Batted .322 (160-for-497) with 9HR, 55RBI and 19SB in 123 games with Double-A Trenton in 2009, making 120 starts at shortstop...set career highs in hits, doubles and home runs in his first season at the Double-A level...ranked second in the Eastern League in hits and third in batting average...committed 33 errors, most among Eastern League players.
- Was named the top shortstop in the EL, earning a spot on the postseason All-Star team...was also the starting shortstop for the North Division in the Eastern League midseason All-Star Game, the lone Thunder player to earn both midseason and postseason All-Star honors in 2009.
- Compiled five hitting streaks of eight-or-more games, including a career-high-tying 11-game hitting streak from 4/30-5/11, in which he batted .378 (17-for-45) over the stretch with just 5K.
- Appeared in four games with Toros del Este in the Dominican Winter League, going 2-for-10 (.200)

2008

- Spent the entire season with Single-A Tampa, batting .271 with 18 doubles, 6HR and 42RBI in 94 games...appeared in 92 games at shortstop...batted .269 (28-for-104, 1HR) against left-handed pitchers and .271 (73-for-269, 5HR) off righties.
- Opened the season on the disabled list with a sprained right thumb and was activated on 4/20...returned to the D.L. from 5/12-6/3 with a sprained left thumb.
- Recorded a career-high five consecutive multi-hit games from 6/8-12 (all two hits).

2007

- Combined to hit .251 with 15 doubles, 2HR and 41RBI in 121 games with Single-A Charleston and Tampa...went more than two straight games without a hit just twice.
- Began the season with the RiverDogs and was named the starting shortstop for the North Division in the South Atlantic League All-Star Game.
- Promoted to Tampa on 7/30...recorded multiple hits in 13 of his 30 games with Tampa.

2006

- Combined to hit .214 in 127 games with Tampa and Charleston, seeing time at 2B, 3B and SS...began the season with Tampa and batted .184 in 37 games before being transferred to Charleston on 5/18...in 90 games with the RiverDogs, hit .227 with 16SB.

EDUARDO NUNEZ

2005

- Batted .313 with 11 doubles, 3HR and 46RBI in 73 games with short-season Single-A Staten Island...was selected to participate in the NY-Penn League All-Star Game and was 1-for-3 with 1R and 1RBI in the contest...ranked third in the NYPL in hits (88), tied for third in triples (6), fourth in games played (73), fourth in at-bats (281) and ninth in average (.313)...following the season, was named the sixth-best prospect in the Yankees organization by *Baseball America*.

2004

- Played in 63 games with the DSL Yankees 1, batting .249 with 7 doubles and 33RBI.

Nunez' Career Batting Record

YEAR	CLUB	AVG	G	AB	R	H	2B	3B	HR	RBI	SH	SF	HP	BB	SO	SB	CS	E	OBP	SLG
2004	DSL Yankees 1	.249	63	229	27	57	7	1	0	33	1	2	5	13	23	5	4	--	.301	.288
2005	Staten Island	.313	73	281	37	88	11	6	3	46	6	0	3	20	43	6	3	28	.365	.427
2006	Tampa	.184	37	147	17	27	5	3	4	26	4	2	0	8	28	16	5	14	.223	.340
	Charleston	.227	90	344	36	78	11	3	2	40	0	2	2	23	48	16	5	26	.278	.294
2007	Charleston	.238	91	328	36	78	10	2	1	28	2	3	2	25	42	20	8	27	.293	.290
	Tampa	.285	30	123	16	35	5	0	1	13	0	1	3	7	18	9	0	6	.336	.350
2008	Tampa	.271	94	373	45	101	18	3	6	42	5	4	1	19	48	14	10	19	.305	.383
2009	Trenton	.322	123	497	70	160	26	1	9	55	4	4	1	22	63	19	7	33	.349	.433
Minor League Totals		**.266**	**595**	**2284**	**286**	**608**	**95**	**23**	**29**	**270**	**23**	**16**	**16**	**151**	**331**	**106**	**40**	**153**	**.314**	**.366**

Signed by the Yankees as a non-drafted free agent on February 25, 2004.

College Football Returns to Yankee Stadium

Beginning in 2010, college football will return to Yankee Stadium as Notre Dame and Army renew their rivalry in the Bronx on November 20...the two historic programs met 22 times at the original Yankee Stadium, with the Irish holding a 14-5-3 record in games played from 1925-29, 1931-46, and 1969 (the 100th anniversary of college football)...in addition, Army is scheduled to play home games at Yankee Stadium in 2011 vs. Rutgers, 2012 vs. Air Force and 2014 vs. Boston College...the original Yankee Stadium played host to more than 100 college football games over its 86-year history.

The Army-Air Force football game returns to Yankee Stadium in 2012.

Ramiro Pena

19

Infielder

5-11 • 165 • B/T: Switch/Right

Opening Day Age: 24

Birthdate
July 18, 1985

Birthplace
Monterrey, Mexico

Resides
San Nicolas de los Garza, Mexico

M.L. Service
137 days

Status

- Signed as a non-drafted free agent on February 18, 2005...signed through the 2010 season.

2009

- Batted .287 (33-for-115) with 17R, 6 doubles, 1HR and 10RBI in 69 games (14 starts at 3B, 11 at SS, three at 2B) over three stints with the Yankees (4/4-7/1; 8/7-21 and 9/1-10/4) in his first Major League action.
- Made his first career Opening Day roster...was signed to a Major League contract and selected to the Yankees' 25-man roster on 4/4...became the first Yankee without experience above the Double-A level to make the club's Opening Day active Major League roster since RHP Jose Contreras in 2003 and the first such position player since 3B Scott Seabol in 2001.
- Made his Major League debut in 4/6 Opening Day loss at Baltimore, entering the game as a pinch-runner in the eighth inning and remaining in the game at 3B...batted .267 (23-for-86) with 5 doubles, 1 triple and 7RBI in 46 games during his first stint with the Yankees...played in 24G/14GS at 3B, the majority of which came while Alex Rodriguez was on the D.L...also appeared at SS (18G/8GS) and 2B (2G/1GS).
- Collected his first career Major League hit—in his first plate appearance—and scored his first run in 4/9 win at Baltimore, singling to center off Chris Ray in the ninth and scoring...became the first Yankee to record a hit in his first Major League plate appearance since Andy Cannizaro on 9/8/06...according to *Elias*, was only the second Yankee in the last 43 years to do so during the first week of a season (also Hideki Matsui in 2003).
- Made his first Major League start (at 3B) in 4/14 win at Tampa Bay, going 0-for-3 with 1BB.
- Established a career high with 3H in 5/1 win vs. Los Angeles-AL, going 3-for-4 with 2RBI and 1SB...recorded a two-run, bases-loaded hit in the eighth inning for the second straight game...stole his first career base in the second inning.
- Made his first career start at SS in 5/12 loss at Toronto, going 1-for-3 with 1 double.
- Both he and Brett Gardner tripled on 5/13 at Toronto, becoming the first pair of Yankees rookies to hit triples in the same game since 8/31/70, when Thurman Munson and Johnny Ellis did so off Mike Cuellar (credit: *Elias Sports Bureau*).
- Was optioned to Triple-A Scranton/Wilkes-Barre on 7/1 when INF/OF Eric Hinske was added to the 25-man roster...was recalled by the Yankees on 8/7 and optioned back to Scranton/WB on 8/21 when LHP Damaso Marte was activated from the disabled list...was recalled for a third time on 9/1 for the remainder of the season.
- Recorded the Yankees' only hit of the game off Roy Halladay in 9/4 loss at Toronto, going 1-for-3 with 1 double...hit solo-HR—the first of his career and sixth of his professional career—and was 2-for-4 with 2R, 2RBI and 1SB in 9/28 win vs. Kansas City.
- Was added to the Yankees' World Series roster prior to Game 5 when Melky Cabrera sustained an injury (did not appear).

Single-Game Highs and Streaks

Hits
3 - 2 times
Last: at NYM, 6/26/09

Runs
2 - 2 times
Last: vs. KC, 9/28/09

2B
2 - at NYM, 6/26/09

3B
1 - at TOR, 5/13/09

HR
1 - vs. KC, 9/28/09

RBI
2 - 3 times
Last: vs. KC, 9/28/09

BB
1 - 5 times
Last: vs. TEX, 6/4/09

SO
2 - 3 times
Last: at NYM, 6/27/09

SB
1 - 4 times
Last: vs. KC, 9/28/09

Hit Streak
4g - 5/6-13/09

- In 43 games with Scranton/WB, batted .231 (36-for-156) with 9 doubles, 2HR, 9RBI and 5SB, appearing in games at SS (22 games), 2B (11), CF (seven) and 3B (three)...marked his first career action in the outfield.
- Following the season, appeared in 26 games with Culiacan in the Mexican Winter League, batting .247 (21-for-85) with 10R, 3 doubles, 4RBI and 11BB.
- Attended spring training with the Yankees as a non-roster invitee, batting .277 (18-for-65) with 12R, 2 doubles, 1 triple and 7RBI in 30 games.

2008

- Played the entire season at Double-A Trenton, batting .266 with 20 doubles, 7 triples, 2HR and 45RBI in 111 games (all at shortstop)...set career highs in nearly every offensive category.
- Appeared on the World Team at the 2008 Futures Game during All-Star weekend at the original Yankee Stadium, going 0-for-1 with 1BB.
- Batted .345 (10-for-29) with 6R and 2SB in seven postseason games for the Eastern League champions...following the season, was tabbed as the "Best Defensive Infielder" in the Yankees organization and Eastern League by *Baseball America*...played winter ball with Culiacan in the Mexican Winter League.

2007

- Was limited to 52 games with Double-A Trenton due to injuries, batting .252 with 7 doubles, 1 triple and 10RBI.
- Went on the disabled list from 5/24-6/1 with a groin strain...returned on 6/2 and played in 11 more games before his season was cut short on 6/14 with a dislocated right shoulder...suffered the injury on 6/13 vs. Connecticut, sliding into second base in the seventh inning.

2006

- Endured three stints on the disabled list and batted .257 in 80 combined games with Double-A Trenton and Single-A Tampa.
- Began the season with Trenton and batted .198 in 26 games...was placed on the disabled list on 5/11 after suffering a right knee contusion on 5/10 at Portland...was reinstated from the D.L. on 5/24 and transferred to Tampa...played in 51 games before suffering a sprained right ankle on 7/20 vs. Palm Beach...was placed on the D.L. the next day and missed a week of action...was reinstated on 7/28 and played in three games before being placed on the disabled list for a third time for the remainder of the season, this time with a left thumb injury.
- Played in 33 games with Culiacan of the Mexican Winter League, batting .221 (15-for-68).

2005

- In his first professional season, played in 91 combined games with Single-A Tampa and Double-A Trenton...began the season with Tampa, batting .247 in 23 games before being promoted to Trenton on 6/14...in 68 games with the Thunder, batted .250 with 5 doubles and 12RBI.

Pena's Career Batting Record

YEAR	CLUB	AVG	G	AB	R	H	2B	3B	HR	RBI	SH	SF	HP	BB	SO	SB	CS	E	OBP	SLG
2005	Tampa	.247	23	73	11	18	4	1	1	6	2	2	0	9	12	1	0	4	.321	.370
	Trenton	.250	68	236	28	59	5	2	0	12	8	1	0	10	48	4	1	15	.279	.288
2006	Trenton	.198	26	86	6	17	2	0	0	6	5	1	1	5	19	0	1	2	.247	.221
	Tampa	.280	54	218	31	661	4	2	0	23	4	4	4	16	26	8	4	12	.335	.317
2007	Trenton	.252	52	202	23	51	7	1	0	10	7	0	2	22	33	7	3	4	.332	.297
2008	Trenton	.266	111	443	57	118	20	7	2	45	12	6	4	41	86	8	6	21	.330	.357
2009	YANKEES	.287	69	115	17	33	6	1	1	10	1	0	0	5	20	4	1	5	.317	.383
	Scranton/WB	.231	43	156	18	36	9	0	2	9	6	0	0	18	28	5	1	2	.310	.327
Minor League Totals		**.255**	**377**	**1414**	**174**	**360**	**51**	**13**	**5**	**111**	**44**	**14**	**11**	**121**	**252**	**33**	**16**	**60**	**.315**	**.320**
Major League Totals		**.287**	**69**	**115**	**17**	**33**	**6**	**1**	**1**	**10**	**1**	**0**	**0**	**5**	**20**	**4**	**1**	**5**	**.317**	**.383**

Signed by the Yankees as a non-drafted free agent on February 18, 2005.

Pena's World Series Record

Year	Club vs. Opp.	AVG	G	AB	R	H	2B	3B	HR	RBI	SH	SF	HP	BB	SO	SB	CS	E	OBP	SLG
2009	NYY vs. PHI	Added to Roster - Did Not Play																		

Pena's Career Fielding Record

Position	PCT	G	PO	A	E	TC	DP
Shortstop	.953	34	21	40	3	64	9
Third Base	.952	27	10	30	2	42	5
Second Base	1.000	8	7	10	0	17	2

Andy Pettitte

46 Left-handed Pitcher
6-5 • 225 • B/T: Left/Left
Opening Day Age: 37

Birthdate
June 15, 1972

Birthplace
Baton Rouge, La.

Resides
Deer Park, Tex.

M.L. Service
15 years

College
San Jacinto JC (Tex.)

Career Highlights
ALCS MVP
- 2001

A.L. All-Star Team
- 1996, 2001

***Sporting News* A.L. All-Star Team**
- 1996, 2003

Status

- Signed as a free agent on December 9, 2009 to a one-year contract...contract extends through the 2010 season.

Career Notes

- Among active Major League pitchers, ranks second in career wins (229), third in starts (458), fourth in innings pitched (2,926.1), fifth in strikeouts (2,150) and seventh in winning percentage (.629, min. 140 decisions)...is second among active left-handed pitchers in wins, starts, innings pitched and strikeouts – trailing only Jamie Moyer in each category.
- Over the last 10 years (2000-09), led the Majors in wins (148), ranked ninth in games started (300) and 10th in strikeouts (1,441).
- Has won 49.8% of his 458 career starts (is 228-134 in his starts), marking the third-best percentage among active pitchers with at least 250 career GS.
- Reached 30 games started for the 12th time in his career, and 10th time as a Yankee in 2009 – most in franchise history...is tied for the third-most seasons with at least 30GS among active pitchers.
- Has a .686 (118-54) career winning percentage and a 3.62 ERA after the All-Star break compared to a .578 (111-81) career mark and 4.17 ERA before the break.
- Has recorded 192 wins as a Yankee, marking the most for any pitcher with his current club (credit: *Elias Sports Bureau*)...ranks third in franchise history in wins, strikeouts (1,722), and games started (375), sixth in IP (2,406.2), and eighth in appearances (384)...is the first Yankees draft pick to win 200 games in the Majors.
- As a Yankee, is 81-44 (.648) in regular season starts immediately following a Yankees loss (credit: *Elias*).
- Owns the highest all-time career winning pct. vs. the AL East (82-35, .701) among the 202 pitchers with at least 50 AL East decisions.
- With 229 career wins, trails only Ted Lyons (260) all time among Louisiana-born pitchers...former Yankees LHP Ron "Louisiana Lightning" Guidry finished with 170 wins.
- Has recorded the most pickoffs (97) since they became an official stat in 1974.
- Finished with 95 regular season wins at the remodeled original Yankee Stadium (1976-2008), trailing only Ron Guidry (99) for most all-time...his 167 starts at remodeled original Yankee Stadium were the most all-time while his 1,120.0IP ranked second only to Guidry's 1,256.2IP.
- According to the *Elias Sports Bureau*, at 26-15, has the most April wins in franchise history (Mel Stottlemyre-23, Whitey Ford-22, Red Ruffing-21).
- Has made an all-time franchise high 108 consecutive starts as a Yankee without throwing a complete game, surpassing Roger Clemens (104GS from 6/3/00-7/24/03) for the all-time franchise mark, according to the *Elias Sports Bureau*...last completed a game as a Yankee on 8/9/03 vs. Seattle in a 2-1 Mariners victory...also has made 107 consecutive career starts without a complete game, marking the longest such career stretch (last CG on 8/16/06 w/ Houston vs. Chicago-NL in a 1-0 Cubs victory).

Single-Game Highs and Streaks

Low hit CG
2 - vs. OAK, 5/29/00
IP (start)
9.0 - 21 times
Last: vs. CHC, 8/16/06
IP (relief)
3.1 - at BOS, 5/13/95
Hits
14 - at BOS, 4/15/01
Runs
10 - 3 times
Last: vs. KC, 6/7/08
BB
7 - 2 times
Last: at TOR, 7/19/98
SO
12 - 2 times
Last: at TB, 7/28/02
HR
4 - vs. TB, 5/7/09
Winning Streak
8g - 2 times
Last: 6/14-7/29/03
Losing Streak
5g - 8/26-9/16/08

- Is 18-9 with a 3.90 ERA in 40 career postseason starts, ranking first all time in wins, starts and innings pitched (249.0), and third in strikeouts (164)...24 of his starts have been "quality" (6.0 or more IP, 3ER or less)...has appeared in eight World Series, second only to Whitey Ford who pitched in 11...is 6-2 with a 3.95 ERA (70.2IP, 31ER) in 12 starts in possible series clinchers, recording the most series-clinching wins all time.
- Is undefeated in last eight postseason starts, marking the longest current undefeated streak of postseason starts among active Major League pitchers.
- As a Yankee, is 17-8 with a 3.86 ERA in 36 career postseason starts (223.2IP, 96ER)...is the Yankees' all-time postseason leader in wins, starts, innings pitched and strikeouts (148).

2009

- Was 14-8 with a 4.16 ERA in 32 starts with the Yankees...marked his fewest losses in a non-injury shortened season since going 21-8 with the Yankees in 2003...lasted at least 5.0IP in 29 of his 32 starts and exited 24 of his 32 starts in the lead or with the game tied...the Yankees were 21-11 in his starts.
- Ranked fourth among AL starters (min: 5GS) with a .326 slugging percentage against and ranked fifth with a .226 batting average against in 14 starts after the All-Star break, going 6-3 with a 3.31 ERA in 87.0IP...surrendered just 6HR in 94.2IP on the road in 2009 (0.57HR/9.0IP), marking the third-lowest rate among AL pitchers.
- Allowed just three stolen bases in his last 21 starts from 6/8 to the end of the season...picked off Torii Hunter in the first inning of his start on 5/1 vs. Los Angeles-AL, marking his 95th career pickoff to surpass Kenny Rogers for the most pickoffs since they became an official stat in 1974.
- Opponents batted .259 (193-for-746, 20HR); LH .282 (62-for-220, 6HR); RH .249 (131-for-526, 14HR)...limited opponents to a .236 (38-for-161) batting average with runners in scoring position in 2009, the second-lowest single-season mark of his career (.203 with RISP w/ Houston in 2005)...allowed a .195 (17-for-87, 1HR) batting average to opposing hitters in the No. 1 slot in the order, seventh-lowest in the Majors (min: 50BF)...over the last three seasons since 2007, has allowed a .197 (59-for-300, 1HR) BA to No. 1 hitters.
- Earned the win in his season debut on 4/10 at Kansas City in the Royals' home opener (7.0IP, 3H, 1ER, 1BB, 6K)...improved his career record vs. the Royals to 13-3, including a current eight-game winning streak...only Johan Santana (nine straight) has a longer current winning streak vs. Kansas City.
- Recorded the victory in his Yankee Stadium debut on 4/21 vs. Oakland in a 5-3 Yankees victory, (7.0IP, 9H, 2ER, 0BB, 0K)...marked the fourth start in his career that he did not walk a batter or record a strikeout...became the first Yankees starter to throw at least 7.0IP without a walk or a strikeout since current Yankees pitching coach Dave Eiland did so on 10/6/91 vs. Cleveland.

Pettitte's 2009 Pitching Lines

Date/Opp	Score	W/L	IP	H	R	ER	HR	BB	K	NP/K	ERA	Left game...
4/10 at KC	4-1	W	7.0	3	1	1	0	1	6	99/64	1.29	Leading 4-1
4/15 at TB	4-3	ND	7.1	6	3	3	1	1	4	96/38	2.51	Tied 3-3
4/21 vs. OAK	5-3	W	7.0	9	2	2	0	0	0	105/67	2.53	Leading 5-2
4/26 at BOS*	1-4	L	6.0	6	4	3	0	4	6	**116**/65	2.96	Trailing 1-4
5/1 vs. LAA	10-9	ND	5.2	9	5	5	0	4	2	108/61	3.82	Leading 4-2
5/7 vs. TB*	6-8	ND	6.0	9	5	5	**4**	1	5	115/72	4.38	Trailing 5-4
5/13 at TOR*	8-2	W	6.0	5	2	1	0	4	2	106/64	4.00	Leading 8-2
5/18 vs. MIN	7-6	W	6.2	**12**	4	4	1	1	3	105/71	4.18	Leading 6-4
5/23 vs. PHI*	5-4	ND	7.0	5	4	4	2	2	5	114/67	4.30	Trailing 4-2
5/29 at CLE	3-1	W	5.0	6	1	1	0	5	1	84/45	4.10	Leading 3-0
6/3 vs. TEX	2-4	L	5.0	7	4	4	0	**6**	6	104/59	4.33	Trailing 4-1
6/8 vs. TB*	5-3	W	6.0	5	3	2	1	3	7	104/64	4.22	Leading 4-3
6/13 vs. NYM	2-6	L	5.0	11	5	5	1	1	3	104/66	4.52	Trailing 6-1
6/19 at FLA*	5-1	W	7.0	3	1	1	1	0	7	108/66	4.26	Leading 5-1
6/25 at ATL	11-7	ND	3.2	7	6	3	0	3	4	95/59	4.38	Leading 8-6
7/1 vs. SEA	4-2	W	7.0	6	2	2	1	1	5	98/63	4.25	Leading 4-2
7/6 vs. TOR	6-7	L	6.0	5	6	**6**	2	5	3	109/58	4.53	Trailing 4-1
7/11 at LAA*	8-14	L	4.1	7	6	**6**	1	2	1	83/47	4.85	Tied 4-4
7/20 vs. BAL	2-1	ND	7.1	6	1	1	1	2	8	109/76	4.62	Tied 1-1
7/25 vs. OAK	4-6	L	6.1	5	4	4	0	1	7	99/66	4.67	Tied 1-1
7/30 at CWS	2-3	ND	6.1	5	2	1	0	0	8	101/71	4.51	Tied 1-1
8/4 at TOR	5-3	W	6.2	4	1	1	0	4	6	103/57	4.35	Leading 2-1
8/9 vs. BOS	5-2	ND	7.0	5	0	0	0	2	4	112/68	4.14	Leading 1-0
8/14 at SEA	4-2	ND	6.0	6	2	2	0	1	**10**	111/67	4.09	Tied 2-2
8/21 at BOS	20-11	W	5.0	7	**7**	5	0	2	4	105/64	4.25	Leading 15-5
8/26 vs. TEX*	9-2	W	7.0	5	2	2	1	3	7	103/61	4.18	Leading 9-2
8/31 at BAL	5-1	W	**8.0**	2	1	1	1	0	8	104/73	4.03	Leading 5-1
9/5 at TOR*	6-4	W	6.0	4	4	4	1	5	3	101/60	4.10	Leading 5-4
9/11 vs. BAL	4-10	ND	5.0	5	3	3	0	3	5	103/59	4.14	Leading 4-3
9/21 at LAA*	2-5	L	6.0	5	3	3	0	2	3	91/57	4.15	Trailing 3-1
9/27 vs. BOS	4-2	W	6.0	7	2	2	0	3	4	97/63	4.11	Leading 3-2
10/3 at TB*	3-5	L	4.1	6	5	3	1	4	1	95/54	4.16	Trailing 3-2
Totals	**14-8**		**194.2**	**193**	**101**	**90**	**20**	**76**	**148**	--	**4.16**	

(*) Denotes start following a Yankees loss – **Bold = season highs**

ANDY PETTITTE

- Took the loss on 4/26 at Boston in a 4-1 Red Sox victory (6.0IP, 6H, 4R, 3ER, 4BB, 6K) as the Yankees were swept in a three-game series at Fenway Park...was just the second loss for Pettitte in 24 career starts for the Yankees when the team was facing a sweep (fell to 17-2).
- Surrendered a career-high 4HR on 5/7 vs. Tampa Bay, recording a no-decision in the 8-6 Rays victory...allowed two first-inning homers (Bartlett and Pena) for the first time since 4/4/06 w/ Houston vs. Florida (Miguel Cabrera and Josh Willingham) and the first time ever as a Yankee.
- Recorded the win on 5/18 vs. Minnesota, allowing 4ER on 12H in 6.2IP (1BB, 3K, 1HR)...were his most hits allowed since 5/20/06 vs. Texas (also 12H) and most as a Yankee since 8/19/01 vs. Seattle (13H)...was the first time he has won a game when allowing at least 12H since 4/9/01 at Kansas City (12H in 8.1IP)...included was 4H allowed to Justin Morneau, marking the first time in his career he surrendered 4H in the same game to a left-handed batter.
- His win on 5/29 at Cleveland was saved by Mariano Rivera, marking the 58th time the Yankees closer had recorded a save in a game in which Pettitte was the winning pitcher...according to the *Elias Sports Bureau*, surpassed Oakland's Dennis Eckersley and Bob Welch (57) for the most win-save combinations for any pair of pitchers since the save became an official statistic in 1969.
- Made his 357th start as a Yankee on 6/19 at Florida, surpassing Mel Stottlemyre (356) for sole possession of third place on the franchise's all-time list...limited the Marlins to 1ER on 3H with 0BB and 7K in 7.0IP...according to the *Elias Sports Bureau*, was the first time in Pettitte's regular season career that he allowed three-or-fewer hits, 0BB and recorded at least 7K.

ANDY, CY & TOM

Andy Pettitte has posted a record of .500 or better and made at least 15 starts in each of his 15 seasons since the start of his Major League career in 1995...according to the *Elias Sports Bureau*, that ties Cy Young (15 seasons, 1890-1904) and Tom Seaver (15, 1967-81) for the longest such streak in Major League history.

Posted a winning record in each of his first 13 seasons to begin his Major League career (1995-2007)...marked the third-longest streak of consecutive winning seasons to start a Major League career behind Grover Alexander (19) and Cy Young (15).

- Went undefeated over a nine-start stretch from 7/30-9/11, going 5-0 with a 3.00 ERA (57.0IP, 19ER)...among AL pitchers over the stretch, ranked third in opponents batting average against (.210), tied for third in wins and eighth in ERA.
- Limited opponents to 2ER or less in four straight starts from 7/30-8/14, going 1-0 with a 1.38 ERA (26.0IP, 4ER)...struck out a season-high 10 batters on 8/14 at Seattle, marking his most strikeouts since 8/21/06 w/ Houston at Cincinnati (10K)...marked his most K's as a Yankee since 7/6/03 vs. Boston (10K).
- Was 4-0 with a 2.50 ERA (39.2IP, 11ER) in six starts in August, tying for second in the AL in wins and ranking third in ERA for the month...according to the *Elias Sports Bureau*, owns a .725 (50-19 in 87GS) career winning percentage during the month of August, trailing only Lefty Gomez (.736, 39-14) and Roger Clemens (.726, 69-26) among pitchers since 1900 (min. 60 August starts).
- Tossed 7.0 shutout innings on 8/9 vs. Boston, recording a no-decision in a 5-2 Yankees victory (5H, 2BB, 4K) to complete a four-game sweep of the Red Sox...was the third straight game a Yankees starter tossed at least 7.0 innings without allowing a run (also Burnett and Sabathia vs. Boston), marking the first time the Yankees recorded three consecutive starts of at least 7.0 innings each not allowing a run since 9/27-29/73 (Pat Dobson, Mel Stottlemyre and Doc Medich), according to the *Elias Sports Bureau*.
- Allowed 2ER in 7.0IP and recorded the victory in a 9-2 Yankees win on 8/26 vs. Texas, (5H, 3BB, 7K, 1HR)...allowed a seventh-inning homer to David Murphy, snapping a 49.2-inning homerless streak (since 7/20)...the six-start streak without allowing a home run was his longest since a 10-start stretch in 2002.
- Limited the O's to 2H and 1ER in a season-high 8.0IP (0BB, 8K, 1HR) on 8/31 at Baltimore...retired his first 20 batters faced, carrying a perfect game through 6.2IP and marking the farthest into a game that Pettitte has ever remained perfect...also marked his furthest into a game with a no-hit bid intact...was his 190th win as a Yankee, surpassing Lefty Gomez for sole possession of third place on the franchise's all-time wins list.
- Missed his regularly schedule start on 9/16, suffering from shoulder fatigue...returned on 9/21 at Los Angeles-AL and recorded the loss in a 5-2 Angels victory (6.0IP, 5H, 3ER, 2BB, 3K)...left the start with the team trailing 3-1, snapping a 12-start streak from 7/11-9/11 in which he was not removed from a game with his team behind.

- Made his 384th career appearance as a Yankee and took the loss on 10/3 at Tampa Bay (4.1IP, 5R, 3ER) in his regular season finale, surpassing Johnny Murphy (383) for sole possession of eighth place on the Yankees' all-time games pitched list.
- Was a member of his fifth World Championship team, going 4-0 with a 3.52 ERA (30.2IP, 12ER) in five postseason starts...became the second Yankees pitcher (also David Wells, 4-0 in 1998) and the 14th pitcher in Major League history to win four-or-more games in a single postseason...became the first pitcher ever to start and win all three clinching games in a single postseason (ALDS, ALCS, WS)...following the playoffs, donated his postseason hat to the Baseball Hall of Fame.
- Went 2-0 with a 5.40 ERA in two World Series starts in Games 3 and 6...won the Game 6 clincher on 11/4/09 vs. Philadelphia (5.2IP, 4H, 3ER, 5BB, 3K, 1HR), marking his second career World Series-clinching victory and making him one of 10 pitchers all time to own two such wins...start came on three days' rest, marking his first start on short rest since September 2006 and his third career World Series start on short rest (also 1996 and 2003)...became the oldest pitcher to start and win on three-days' rest in the World Series since Early Wynn in 1956 w/ Cleveland...improved to 3-0 with a 1.19 ERA (22.2IP, 3ER) in World Series starts on short rest...the three wins match the total of all the other World Series starters combined since 1993...became the first Yankees pitcher to start and win two games in a single World Series since Mike Torrez in 1977.

2008

- Was 14-14 with a 4.54 ERA in 33 starts...the Yankees were 15-18 in games he started...led the team with 204.0IP, surpassing 200.0IP for the fourth straight season and 10th time in his career...was his highest ERA since 1999 (4.70)...opponents batted .290 (233-for-804, 19HR); LH .203 (47-for-231, 3HR), RH .325 (186-for-573, 16HR).
- Picked off 10 runners in 2008, second-most in the Majors behind Oakland's Greg Smith (15)...were his most since a career-high 14 in 1997.
- Began the season on the 15-day disabled list with lower back spasms (missed four team games)...was reinstated from the D.L. prior to his first start on 4/5 vs. Tampa Bay, recording the loss in the 6-3 Rays victory...according to the *Elias Sports Bureau*, was the first time since 1999 that Pettitte did not start one of his team's first four games.
- Carried a perfect game into the fifth inning in 4/20 win at Baltimore before Jay Payton's two-out infield single broke it up...his 3-1 record through his first four starts of the season marked his best start since 2003, when he also began the year 3-1.
- Became the 115th pitcher and 35th lefthander in Major League history to reach the 400-start plateau on 5/6 vs. Cleveland, recording a no-decision in a 5-3 Indians victory...at 204-116, Pettitte's .638 winning percentage was the highest for a pitcher at the time of his 400th start since rotation-mate Mike Mussina was 206-114 (.644), heading into his 400th start on 6/11/04 vs. San Diego...according to the *Elias Sports Bureau*, since 1946, only eight pitchers had a higher winning percentage than Pettitte at the time of their 400th start: Whitey Ford, Juan Marichal, Tom Seaver, Jim Palmer, Roger Clemens, Dwight Gooden, Randy Johnson and Mussina.
- Was undefeated in eight consecutive starts from 5/23-6/28, going 6-0 with a 3.54 ERA (53.1 IP, 21ER).
- Recorded his first home win of the season on 5/23 vs. Seattle, snapping his four-game losing streak at the Stadium that dated back to 2007...had been the first time in his career that Pettitte had lost more than two consecutive decisions at Yankee Stadium and the first time he had failed to record a win in any of his first four starts at Yankee Stadium in any season.
- Blew three leads in the same game for the first time in his career, recording a no-decision in 6/2 loss at Minnesota...gave up leads of 2-0, 4-2 and 5-4, becoming the first Yankee since Matt Keough on 8/12/83 at Detroit to blow three leads in the same game (credit: *Elias Sports Bureau*).
- On 6/7 vs. Kansas City, recorded a no-decision in the Yankees' 12-11, ninth-inning, "walk-off" win...tied career highs, allowing 10R (third time) and 10ER (second time).
- Held opponents scoreless for 20.0 consecutive innings from 6/12-28, the second-longest stretch of his career (went 23.0 straight scoreless innings from 6/25-7/16/97)...held opponents to five hits or less in each of his four starts during the span for the first time since 8/31-9/15/05 (w/ Houston)...included in the scoreless stretch were back-to-back scoreless starts on 6/17 vs. San Diego (7.0IP) and 6/22 vs. Cincinnati (6.0IP), accomplishing the feat for the first time since 8/31-9/5/05 (w/ Houston).
- Reached the All-Star Break with a 10-7 record, recording his most wins prior to the break since 2003 (11-6)...collected his final win before the break on 7/8 vs. Tampa Bay, throwing 8.0 scoreless innings...his seventh-inning strikeout of Carlos Pena was his 1,500th as a Yankee...was his longest scoreless start since a three-hit shutout on 5/14/06 (w/ Houston) vs. Colorado.
- Went winless over a four-start stretch from 7/31-8/15 (0-2, 2ND), marking his longest post-All-Star break winless streak since 8/19-9/4/01...recorded the loss on 8/5 at Texas, snapping an eight-game winning streak in August that dated back to 8/26/06 (w/ Houston)...was his second straight loss, marking the first time he lost back-to-back post-All-Star outings since 8/19-24/01.

- Lost a career-high five straight starts from 8/26-9/16, pitching to a 6.91 ERA over the stretch...was the longest losing streak by a Yankees starter in 2008.
- Started and earned the win the final game at Yankee Stadium on 9/21 vs. Baltimore, allowing 2ER in 5.0IP (7H, 3R, 1BB, 3K).

2007

- Was 15-9 with a 4.05 ERA in 34 starts (career-high-tying 36 appearances)...the Yankees were 21-13 in games he started...opponents batted .286 (238-for-832, 16HR); LH .298 (59-for-198, 7HR), RH .282 (179-for-634, 9HR)...tied for first in the American League in games started (with seven other pitchers) and ranked ninth in the AL with 215.1IP...were his most innings pitched with the Yankees since 1998 (216.1) and his 34 starts were his second-most as a Yankee (35 in 1997)...also recorded five pickoffs, tying with Chicago's Mark Buehrle and Seattle's Ryan Feierabend for the AL lead.
- Earned his 200th career win on 9/19 vs. Baltimore, becoming the 107th pitcher all time to reach the plateau and the 27th left-hander...according to the *Elias Sports Bureau*, he became the seventh pitcher in the expansion era to record his 200th career win as a Yankee, joining Whitey Ford (1964), Catfish Hunter (1976), Tommy John (1980), David Wells (2003), Mike Mussina (2004) and Kevin Brown (2004)...also became the first pitcher drafted by the Yankees to win 200 games in the Major Leagues.
- Was 11-3 with a 3.84 ERA (103.0IP, 44ER) in 16 starts following the All-Star break, leading the Major Leagues in wins in the second half...allowed three or fewer earned runs in 25 of 34 starts (14-5, six no-decisions)...according to the *Elias Sports Bureau*, his 1.32 first-inning ERA was tops in the Major Leagues (5ER, 34GS).
- Made his season debut on 4/5 vs. Tampa Bay, his first appearance in pinstripes since 9/26/03 vs. Baltimore...made his first of two relief appearances in 2007 on 4/8 vs. Baltimore, tossing 1.0 scoreless inning with 1BB and 1K...was his first relief appearance since 7/28/06 (w/ Houston) vs. Arizona, and his first relief appearance as a Yankee since 9/25/98 vs. Tampa Bay...also made a relief appearance on 4/22 at Boston (1.0IP, 1BB).
- Earned his first win of the season on 4/10 at Minnesota, becoming the ninth pitcher in franchise history to reach the 150-win plateau.

MOST WINS IN THE 2000s

1.	**ANDY PETTITTE**	**148**
2.	Randy Johnson	143
3.	Jamie Moyer	140
4.	Roy Halladay	139
T5.	Tim Hudson	137
	Roy Oswalt	137

BEST WINNING PERCENTAGE, POST ALL-STAR BREAK, ACTIVE PITCHERS (min. 50 post-All-Star starts)

1.	Johan Santana	.763 (61-19)
2.	Roy Oswalt	.761 (70-22)
3.	Rich Harden	.718 (28-11)
4.	Tim Hudson	.701 (75-32)
5.	**ANDY PETTITTE**	**.686 (118-54)**

MOST WINS, ACTIVE LEFT-HANDERS

1.	Jamie Moyer	258
2.	**ANDY PETTITTE**	**229**
3.	Mike Hampton	148
4.	CC SABATHIA	136
5.	Mark Buehrle	135

- Went 6-0 in August with a 2.36 ERA, leading the Majors in wins and earning the AL "Pitcher of the Month" Award...was his fifth career monthly award and third with the Yankees...was also selected by the fans as the "Major League Baseball Clutch Performer of the Month Presented by Pepsi" for August...according to the *Elias Sports Bureau*, became the fourth Yankees pitcher in the last 30 seasons to win at least six games in a calendar month (also Roger Clemens, 6-0, June 2001; Ed Figueroa, 7-0, September 1978; and Catfish Hunter, 6-0, August 1978).
- Recorded the loss in an 8-2 Devil Rays victory on 9/2 at Yankee Stadium, allowing a season-high 11 hits (two home runs)...the loss snapped his six-game winning streak and was his first loss to the Devil Rays since 9/16/98 at Tampa Bay, snapping a 17-start undefeated streak in which he went 12-0, the longest winning streak he has ever posted against one team (credit: *Elias Sports Bureau*).

- Made one start in the Division Series vs. Cleveland in Game 2 at Jacobs Field, recording a no-decision in the 2-1, 11-inning Indians victory...held the Indians scoreless for 6.1 innings (7H, 2BB, 5K), exiting the game with a 1-0 lead...was his 35th career postseason start, tying him with Tom Glavine for the most all time...the start also gave him 218.1 career innings pitched in the postseason, also tied with Glavine for the most all-time.

2006

- Went 14-13 with a 4.20 ERA in 36 appearances (35 starts) for the Houston Astros...tied a career high with 35 starts (also 1997)...his 178 strikeouts were tied for 10th in the NL and were two shy of his career-high of 180 set in 2003.
- Struck out a season-high 10 batters three times: 7/15 at Florida, 8/11 vs. San Diego and 8/21 at Cincinnati...tossed two complete games, his highest total since he logged three in 2002...allowed 238H, fifth-most in the NL...his 14 wins ranked second among NL lefties...was 7-4 with a 2.80 ERA (93.1IP, 29ER) in 16 second-half outings (15 starts).
- Carried a no-hitter into the seventh inning on 4/24 vs. Los Angeles-NL that was broken up by a J.D. Drew home run and eventually won by the Dodgers, 6-2...marked the second time in his career that he pitched at least 7.0 innings and allowed only one hit with his team losing both games...also 8/3/03 at Oakland while with the Yankees (8.0IP, 1H, 1R, 1ER, 2BB, 6K).
- Tossed his fourth career complete-game shutout on 5/14 vs. Colorado, allowing three hits in a 3-0 win...made his eighth career relief appearance on 7/28 vs. Arizona (first since 9/25/98 vs. Tampa Bay), allowing 1ER in the 11th inning to record the loss (1.0IP).
- Hit his first career home run (off Chan Ho Park) and recorded the win on 8/11 vs. San Diego while tying a season-high with 10K.
- Was 4-2 with a 2.27 ERA in August, leading Major League pitchers with 49 strikeouts, the most strikeouts by a Houston pitcher in August since Randy Johnson struck out 61 in 1998...his 2.27 ERA was his lowest of any month in 2006...was 1-0 in five September starts with a 2.60 ERA...left the game on 9/12 at St. Louis after just 2.2 innings with a strained flexor muscle in his left elbow and missed one start.

2005

- Named 2005 Astros "Pitcher of the Year" by the Houston chapter of the BBWAA after finishing 17-9 with a career-low 2.39 ERA in 33 starts...allowed three or fewer earned runs in 31 of his 33 starts...led the Majors with a 2.12 ERA at home, was tied with Chris Carpenter for the MLB lead in "quality starts" with 27 and ranked second in overall ERA...also ranked third all-time in single-season ERA by a lefty starter in club history...Houston was 21-12 in his 33 starts...did not allow more than one home run in any of his starts and allowed none 16 times.
- Ranked third in the NL in road ERA at 2.69, tied for fifth in wins, ranked sixth with a .230 opponent's batting average and eighth with a .654 winning percentage...was named NL "Pitcher of the Month" in both July and September, the first Astro to capture the award twice in one season...was one of six National League finalists for the MLB "Comeback Player of the Year Award" (Cliff Floyd, Brian Fuentes, Troy Glaus, Ken Griffey, Jr., and Todd Jones).
- Went 14-2 with a 1.56 ERA (24ER/138.2IP) in his last 20 starts of the season from 6/20-10/1, leading the Majors in ERA and wins during that time span...pitched 7.0 or more innings in 12 of his 16 starts after the All-Star Break...led the Majors with a 1.69 ERA and a .201 opponent batting average in the second half...tied Jose Contreras for the most wins after the All-Star break with 11.
- Went 5-0 with an 0.90 ERA (4ER/40.0IP) in six July starts, the second-lowest ERA among NL starters and the lowest for one month in his career...also marked the third-lowest ERA for an Astros pitcher in a single month since 1969 (Nolan Ryan, 0.20, May 1984 and J.R. Richard, 0.67, Aug. 1979)...tossed 8.0 scoreless innings on 7/30 vs. NY Mets, marking his eighth straight start pitching at least 5.0 innings and not allowing more than one run (6/20-7/30)...it was the longest streak by a NL pitcher since Bill Gullickson in 1986, and only four other NL pitchers had done the same since 1960: Sandy Koufax (1962), Don Drysdale (1968), Bob Gibson (1968), and J.R. Richard (1979).
- Won seven consecutive starts from 8/21-9/20, compiling a 1.70 ERA over the stretch with 8BB and 37K...tossed 5.2 scoreless innings on 9/5 at Philadelphia, but had his start cut short after being hit in the left foot with a line drive in the third inning.
- Was 1-1 in four postseason starts with a 4.26 ERA...earned the win in NLDS Game 1 at Atlanta, allowing 4H and 3ER in 7.0IP (6K)...suffered the loss in NLCS Game 1 at St. Louis...left two games in 2005 playoffs with a 4-2 lead, only to receive no-decisions...allowed two runs in 6.1 innings of NLCS Game 5 and two runs in 6.0 innings in World Series Game 2.

ANDY PETTITTE

2004

- Made 15 starts in his first season with Houston, finishing 6-4 with a 3.90 ERA...was placed on the disabled list three times: 4/7-29 (left elbow strain); 5/27-6/28 (left forearm strain); 8/13-10/3 (left elbow surgery)...suffered the loss in his first start with Houston on 4/6 vs. San Francisco, allowing 6ER on 11H over 5.1IP....was placed on the 15-day D.L. on 4/10 (retroactive to 4/7) with a strained left elbow...suffered the injury during a checked swing in his first start on 4/6 vs. San Francisco and missed 19 games.
- Earned the 150th win of his career on 4/29 at Pittsburgh, his first win of the season...left his start on 5/26 vs. Chicago-NL after 4.0 innings with a left forearm strain...was placed on the 15-day D.L. on 5/27 and missed 28 games...made two rehab starts at Double-A Round Rock on 6/18 and 6/23.
- Was reinstated from the D.L. on 6/28 and received a no-decision in his start that night at Chicago-NL, allowing 3ER over 5.0IP...made his longest start of the year, tossing 8.0 innings for the win in a 5-2 victory on 7/21 at Arizona...took the loss on 7/26 vs. Arizona, allowing 2ER before leaving the game after the fifth inning with a sore left elbow.
- Returned to New York to face the Mets on 8/12 and did not record a decision, allowing 1ER over 5.2IP in the Astros' 2-1 loss...was placed on the D.L. the following day and underwent season-ending surgery on 8/24 to repair a torn flexor tendon in his left elbow...the surgery was performed by Dr. James Andrews and Dr. David Lintner.

2003

- Finished the season 21-8 with a 4.02 ERA in 33 starts...the Yankees were 23-10 in games he started...tied for second in the American League in wins, was fifth with a .724 winning percentage, and ranked sixth with 180 strikeouts and 7.8 strikeouts per nine innings...with 21 victories, equaled his single-season career high (also 1996)...his 33 starts were the most since starting 35 games in 1997...opponents batted .272 (227-for-835, 21HR); LH .321 (72-for-224, 5HR), RH .254 (155-for-611, 16HR).
- Became the first pitcher in the post-expansion era (since 1961) to win at least 12 games in each of his first nine seasons, according to the *Elias Sports Bureau*...became the first pitcher since Hall of Famer Stan Coveleski (from 1916-1926) to accomplish the feat.
- Lost four straight starts/decisions from 5/6-22 for the first time in his career (a span of 206 games)...in Major League history, only four pitchers had more decisions to start their careers before a four-game losing streak: Whitey Ford (306 decisions), Juan Marichal (267), Ed Reulbach (227), and Mike Mussina (208).
- Won a career-high eight consecutive decisions from 6/14-7/29 with a 3.36 ERA over the nine-game stretch...on 8/9 vs. Seattle, recorded the loss in a 2-1 Mariners victory despite throwing his first complete game of the season (9.0IP, 5H, 2ER, 1BB, 5K).
- Went 3-1 with a 2.10 ERA in five postseason starts...collected the win in Game 2 of the Division Series vs. Minnesota...fanned 10 batters and allowed one earned run in 7.0 innings...started Game 2 and Game 6 of the ALCS vs. Boston...was 1-1 with an 0.57 ERA (1ER/15.2IP) in two World Series starts...notched his 13th career playoff win in the Yankees' 6-1 victory vs. Florida in Game 2 of the World Series, pitching on three-days' rest (1ER, 8.2IP)...was the losing pitcher in the Marlins' series-clinching Game 6 victory despite allowing 2R (1ER) in 7.0IP.

2002

- Was 13-5 with a 3.27 ERA and a team-high three complete games in 22GS...the Yankees were 16-6 in games he started...won 11 of his final 13 decisions of the season, 10 of his last 11 and five straight to conclude the season...opponents batted .272 (144-for-529, 6HR); LH .255 (26-for-102, 2HR), RH .276 (118-for- 427, 4HR)...became the first pitcher in the post-expansion era (since 1961) to win at least 12 games in each of his first eight seasons (credit: *Elias Sports Bureau*).
- Allowed homers in only five of his 22 starts (6HR total)...recorded the victory in his first start of the season on 4/5 vs. Tampa Bay in the home opener at Yankee Stadium, tossing 6.0 scoreless innings in the Yankees 4-0 win (2H, 0BB, 6K)...with his first-inning strikeout of Steve Cox, became the eighth pitcher in Yankees history to reach the 1,000K plateau.
- Was placed on the 15-day disabled list on 4/21 (retroactive to 4/16) with tendinitis of the left elbow...made four rehab assignment starts, tossing 15.1 innings (8H, 2ER, 1BB, 13K) before being reinstated from the D.L. on 6/14...on 6/30 vs. New York-NL, recorded his third career shutout (first since 6/29/00 vs. Detroit), in an 8-0 Yankees win (9.0IP, 3H, 2BB, 8K)...tied a career high with 12K in 7/28 win at Tampa Bay...was scratched from his scheduled start on 8/31 with a stiff lower back.
- Started Game 2 of the Division Series vs. Anaheim, allowing 4ER and 8H in 3.0IP but did not receive the decision in an 8-6 Angels win.

2001

- Was 15-10 with a 3.99 ERA in 31 starts...the Yankees were 18-13 in games he started...opponents batted .281 (224-for-796, 14HR); LH .251 (42-for-167, 3HR), RH .289 (182-for-629, 11HR)...collected 103 wins over a six-season span (1996-2001), the most by any pitcher in the American League and second-most in the Majors during that span behind Greg Maddux (107)...became one of only five pitchers in the last 40 years to win at least 12 games in each of his first seven seasons in the Major Leagues, joining Dean Chance (1962-68), Tom Seaver (1967-73), Dennis Leonard (1975-81) and Fernando Valenzuela (1981-87)...became the first Yankees pitcher to make at least 25 starts for seven consecutive seasons (1995-2001) since Mel Stottlemyre did it in nine straight from 1965-73 and Fritz Peterson recorded eight straight from 1966-73.
- Averaged a career-low 1.8 walks per 9.0IP...allowed only 19BB in 17 GS/101.0IP after being reinstated from D.L. on 7/1 and allowed only one walk to a left-handed batter in his final 14 starts of the season...concluded the season with a 5-7 road record, his first losing record on the road since going 4-7 in his rookie campaign in 1995.
- In his 5/23 start vs. Boston, became the fourth youngest pitcher to start 200 games for the Yankees...only Waite Hoyt (27), Mel Stottlemyre (28) and Lefty Gomez (28) accomplished the feat at a younger age...on 6/15 at New York-NL, left the game after 3.1IP with a strained left groin and was placed on the 15-day disabled list on 6/16...was reinstated on 7/1.
- On 9/26 vs. Tampa Bay, left the game after two batters when he was hit on the left elbow by a Ben Grieve line drive, suffering a contusion (0.0IP, 2H)...did not pitch again until 10/6 at Tampa Bay, tossing 5.0 shutout innings (5H, 2BB, 2K) in his final outing of the regular season.
- Was 2-3 with a 4.55 ERA in five postseason starts...started and lost Game 2 of the Division Series at Oakland, snapping a streak of nine consecutive postseason wins for the Yankees in which Pettitte made the start (last lost on 10/9/98 in Game 3 of the ALCS at Cleveland).
- Was named Most Valuable Player of the American League Championship Series, going 2-0 with a 2.51 ERA in two starts...earned the win in Game 1 and the Game 5 clincher.

MOST WINS-SAVE COMBINATIONS
Since saves became an official statistic in 1969
Courtesy of the *Elias Sports Bureau*

1.	**ANDY PETTITTE/MARIANO RIVERA (NYY)**	**63**
2.	Bob Welch/Dennis Eckersley (OAK)	57
3.	Mike Mussina/MARIANO RIVERA (NYY)	49
4.	Dave Stewart/Dennis Eckersley (OAK)	43
T5.	Jimmy Key/ Tom Henke (TOR)	37
	Kevin Tapani/Rick Aguilera (MIN)	37

YANKEES ALL-TIME WINS

1.	Whitey Ford (LHP)	236
2.	Red Ruffing (RHP)	231
3.	**ANDY PETTITTE (LHP)**	**192**
4.	Lefty Gomez (LHP)	189
5.	Ron Guidry (LHP)	170

10-WIN SEASONS AS A YANKEE

1.	Whitey Ford (LHP)	13
T2.	**ANDY PETTITTE (LHP)**	**12**
	Red Ruffing (RHP)	12

MOST POSTSEASON WINS ALL-TIME

1.	**ANDY PETTITTE**	**18**
2.	John Smoltz	15
3.	Tom Glavine	14
4.	Roger Clemens	12
5.	Greg Maddux	11
	Curt Schilling	11

MOST POSTSEASON STARTS ALL-TIME

1.	**ANDY PETTITTE**	**40**
2.	Tom Glavine	35
3.	Roger Clemens	34
4.	Greg Maddux	30
5.	John Smoltz	27

ANDY PETTITTE

2000

- Went 19-9 with a 4.35 ERA in 32 starts...his 88 wins over five seasons (1996-2000) were the third most in the Majors during that span behind only Pedro Martinez (90) and Greg Maddux (90)...earned his 100th career win on 9/24 vs. Detroit, becoming the 15th Yankee to record 100 career wins and the first since Ron Guidry in 1982...at 100-54, only four then-active pitchers had fewer losses at the time of their 100th win (Dwight Gooden, 100-37; Mike Mussina, 100-43; Roger Clemens, 100-47 and Pedro Martinez, 100-49).
- Allowed only 1HR to left-handed batters in 2000 (Robin Ventura, NY Mets on 6/10 at Yankee Stadium)...was placed on the 15-day disabled list on 4/13 (retroactive to 4/8) with a strained muscle on the left side of his back...was reinstated on 4/26 and pitched 5.0 shutout innings vs. Minnesota (3H, 1BB, 4K), but did not record a decision in a 2-0 Yankees win...on 5/29 vs. Oakland, allowed a career-low two hits while registering his 15th career complete game (first since 8/19/98 at Minnesota) in a Yankees' 4-1 win...lone run came on ninth inning Randy Velarde homer.
- Was 2-0 with a 2.84 ERA in five postseason starts...started the Yankees' World-Series clinching Game 5 on 10/25 at Shea Stadium...did not receive a decision, allowing two unearned runs in 7.0IP and leaving with the score tied at 2-2...was his third straight World Series road start in which he did not allow an earned run (22.2IP).

1999

- Was 14-11 with a 4.70 ERA in 31 games (all starts)...his 69 wins over four seasons (1996-99) trailed only Pedro Martinez (72) and Greg Maddux (71) for the most wins in the Majors...compiled 81 wins in the 1990s, the most by any Yankee during the decade (David Cone was second with 60)...after going 5-7 with a 5.59 ERA (93.1IP, 58ER) in his first 16 starts, finished the season with a 9-4 record and a 3.84 ERA (98.1IP, 42ER) over his last 15 starts.
- Left his first–and only–spring training start on 3/7 vs. Minnesota after seven pitches with a strained left elbow...was placed on the 15-day disabled list on 4/4 with a strained elbow (retroactive to 3/26)...on 4/6 suffered a sprained right ankle during agility drills...was reinstated from the 15-day D.L. on 4/17...started that night vs. Detroit and pitched six shutout innings but did not record a decision in a 3-1 Yankees loss...earned his first win of the season on 5/5 at Minnesota...the win snapped Pettitte's three-game losing streak dating back to 1998...after 102 decisions, the three-game skid marked the first streak of at least three losses in his career...since 1900, only two pitchers have had more decisions at the start of their careers before compiling a three-game losing streak: Dwight Gooden (139) and Mike Mussina (119).
- Was 2-0 with a 3.93 ERA in three postseason starts...won Game 2 of the Division Series vs. Texas on 10/7, allowing only 1ER in 7.1IP...earned the win in Game 4 of the ALCS at Boston on 10/17, limiting the Red Sox to 2ER in 7.1IP...saw his streak of 15.2 scoreless innings in World Series play come to an end in the Yankees' come-from-behind win in Game 3 on 10/26 at Atlanta, allowing 10H and 5ER in 3.2IP...did not draw a decision in the game.

1998

- Went 16-11 with a 4.24 ERA in 33 games (32 starts)...tied for fifth in the American League in wins...led the AL with 55 wins combined from 1996-98, trailing only Atlanta's John Smoltz (56)...tossed a career-high five complete games...became the first Yankees pitcher to throw over 200.0 innings in three straight seasons since Ron Guidry did it in four straight from 1977-80.
- Made the first Opening Day start of his career in a 4-1 loss on 4/1 at Anaheim, allowing 4ER in 6.0IP (9H, 3BB, 3K)...began the season 0-2 with a 5.54 ERA in his first two starts, then won five straight starts from 4/11-5/2 (33.1IP, 7ER, 1.89 ERA)...tossed his first complete game of the season in a 9-1 win over Roger Clemens and the Blue Jays on 4/22 at Toronto in his 100th career start...with a .671 winning percentage after 100 career starts, owned the seventh-highest winning percentage of any pitcher in the post-expansion era (1961) after 100 career starts...the top six after 100 career starts: Ron Guidry, .765 (62-19); Dwight Gooden, .756 (59-19); Roger Clemens, .718 (56-22); Juan Guzman, .708 (46- 19); Mike Mussina, .696 (55-24); and Jim Palmer, .671 (51-25).
- Threw a career-high 143 pitches in a complete-game 3-2 victory on 7/3 vs. Baltimore...missed 8/4 start at Oakland with a strain in his left trapezius...made his only relief appearance of the season on 9/25 vs. Tampa Bay, tossing three shutout innings in relief of Orlando Hernandez in a 6-1 Yankees win.
- Was 2-1 with a 3.32 ERA in three postseason starts, making one start in each round of the playoffs...won Game 2 of the Division Series on 9/30 vs. Texas, limiting the Rangers to 1ER on 3H in 7.0IP in a 3-1 Yankees victory...lost Game 3 of the ALCS on 10/9 at Cleveland in a 6-1 Indians win (4.2IP, 8H, 6ER)...won Game 4 of the World Series on 10/21 at San Diego, throwing 7.1 scoreless innings (5H) in the Yankees' 3-0 victory to clinch the Series.

ANDY PETTITTE

1997

- Was 18-7 with a 2.88 ERA in 35 starts...set career bests for starts and innings pitched (240.1)...compiled an American League-high 39 wins over 1996 and '97, tying him with Atlanta's John Smoltz for the Major League lead...the Yankees were 24-11 in his starts, scoring 217 runs (6.2 runs/start - third-best in the AL)...opponents batted .256 (233-for-910, 7HR); LH hit .321 (62-for-193, 1HR), RH hit .238 (171-for-717, 6HR)...led American League pitchers with 35 starts, 14 pickoffs and 36 ground-ball double plays induced...allowed an AL-low 0.26HR/9.0IP (7HR, 240.1IP)...ranked fourth in the AL in ERA, wins and winning percentage (.720)...ranked third in innings pitched, tied for sixth in complete games (4) and was eighth in strikeouts (166).
- Earned his third win of the season in Game 1 of a 4/13 doubleheader vs. Oakland in the Yankees' 10th game of the season, the second straight season he won three of the Yankees' first 10 games...joined Waite Hoyt (1922 and '29) as the only Yankees pitchers to accomplish the feat twice...finished April with a 5-0 record and a 2.32 ERA, joining Mel Stottlemyre (1969 and '74) as the only Yankees pitchers to win five games in April...became the first Yankee to start the season 5-0 since Bob Wickman opened 8-0 in 1993.
- Recorded consecutive losses for first time in 54 starts on 5/26 vs. Baltimore (last recorded two straight losses on 8/21 and 8/25/95)...tossed his first career shutout on 7/5 at Toronto (6H) in an 8-0 Yankees victory...had a season-high 23.0-inning scoreless streak snapped in an 11-5 win on 7/16 at Chicago-AL...was the longest by a Yankees starter since Jimmy Key also tossed 23.0 scoreless innings from 4/5-21/93...lasted just one inning on 9/5 vs. Baltimore after being hit in the face by a Cal Ripken line drive (suffered contusions of the left thumb, lip and nose as well as a small laceration of the nose)...struck out a career-high 12 batters on 9/16 vs. Boston (G1), tossing eight shutout innings in a 2-0 victory (did not walk a batter).
- Was 0-2 with an 8.49 ERA in two starts vs. Cleveland in the Division Series...took the loss in Game 2, allowing 7ER on nine hits in five innings on 10/2 at Yankee Stadium...was the losing pitcher in Cleveland's series-clinching Game 5, allowing 4ER in 6.2IP on 10/6 at Jacobs Field in the 4-3 Indians victory.

1996

- Went 21-8 with a 3.87 ERA in 35 games (34 starts)...finished second to Toronto's Pat Hentgen in American League Cy Young Award voting...led the AL in wins and was eighth in ERA...the Yankees were 24-10 in his starts, scoring 195R (5.7 runs/start)...led the Majors with 11 pickoffs...opponents hit .271 (229-for-844, 23HR); LH .329 (50-for-152, 1HR), RH .259 (179-for-692, 22HR)...was 13-3 after a Yankees loss and 11-1 in day games...was named to the *Sporting News* All-Star team...at 23 years, nine months and 24 days, became the youngest Yankees pitcher to start the home opener since James "Hippo" Vaughn started on 4/14/10 vs. Boston at Hilltop Park.
- Made his only relief appearance of the season on 5/1 at Baltimore, tossing 3.0 shutout innings for the win in an 11-6, 15-inning victory...was his first relief appearance since 5/13/95, snapping a streak of 32 consecutive starts...recorded his 10th win of the season on 6/11 at Toronto, becoming only the fourth Yankees pitcher in the post-expansion era to record 10 wins in the team's first 60 games (Whitey Ford 10-2 in 1961, Ron Guidry 10-0 in 1978 and Tommy John 10-1 in 1979).
- Won his 15th game of the season on 7/24 vs. Texas, making him the third fastest Yankees pitcher to win 15 games in a season...won his 20th game of the season in a 10-3 victory on 9/4 at Oakland, becoming the Yankees' first 20-game winner since Ron Guidry in 1985...picked up his league-leading 21st win in a 4-1 victory on 9/13 vs. Toronto.
- Was 2-1 with a 4.78 ERA in the postseason...received no-decisions in his first two postseason starts, both Yankees wins (5-4 in Game 2 of the Division Series vs. Texas and 5-4 in Game 1 of the ALCS vs. Baltimore)...started Game 1 of the World Series vs. Atlanta and recorded his first career postseason loss in a 12-1 Braves victory (2.1IP, 7ER)...in Game 5 at Atlanta, tossed 8.1 shutout innings, out-dueling John Smoltz in the Yankees' 1-0 victory.

1995

- Finished third in American League "Rookie of the Year" voting after going 12-9 with a 4.17 ERA in 31 games (26 starts)...his 16 points in the voting trailed Minnesota's Marty Cordova (105) and California's Garret Anderson (99)...led all American League rookies in wins...led the American League with 12 pickoffs...began the season in the bullpen, making five appearances without recording a decision (5.14 ERA)...made his Major League debut on 4/29 at Kansas City (0.2IP, 3H, 2ER, 1K).
- Was optioned to Triple-A Columbus on 5/16 to make room for Mariano Rivera on the 25-man roster...was recalled on 5/27 and made his first Major League start that day at Oakland, suffering the loss in a 3-0 Athletics win (5.1IP, 7H, 3R, 1ER, 2BB, 3K, 1HR)...stayed in the Yankees' starting rotation for the remainder of the season...threw his first career complete game in his second Major League start on 6/2 vs. California, but suffered the loss in a 3-2 Angels win.

- Earned his first Major League win on 6/7 vs. Oakland in a 6-1 Yankees victory, allowing 1ER in 7.0IP (4H, 1BB, 3K)...suffered the shortest start of his career on 8/21 at Oakland in a 13-4 Athletics win, leaving after 0.2IP (6ER, 8H)...tossed a complete-game five-hitter, tying his season high with eight strikeouts, in a 4-1 victory on 8/30 vs. the Angels (retired 20 of his first 21 batters faced).
- Did not allow a home run to a left-handed batter until he allowed a two-run shot to Rafael Palmeiro in the ninth inning of a 5-4 win on 9/14 at Baltimore...went 5-1 with a 3.38 ERA in six September starts...became only the fifth Yankees rookie starter to ever win five games after 9/1, joining Russ Ford (7-0 in 1910), Ernie Bonham (6-1 in 1940), Mel Stottlemyre (5-2 in 1964) and Bob Wickman (5-1 in 1992).
- Made his lone postseason start in Game 2 of the Division Series on 10/4 vs. Seattle and recorded a no-decision in the Yankees' 7-5, 15-inning victory (7.0IP, 9H, 4ER, 3BB, 1HR).

1994

- Was named the Yankees' Minor League "Pitcher of the Year" after going 14-4 with a 2.86 ERA in 27 combined starts at Triple-A Columbus and Double-A Albany...tied with Mark Cumberland for the organization lead in victories...also ranked among the organizational leaders in ERA (second), innings pitched (third, 169.2) and strikeouts (ninth, 111)...opponents hit .250, including .220 with 5HR at Albany and .272 with 3HR at Columbus...was added to the 40-man roster on 11/18.
- Was 7-2 with a 2.98 ERA in 16 starts at Columbus...recorded the loss in a 10-2 defeat on 6/10 vs. Ottawa in his Triple-A debut...walked an average of 1.96 batters per 9.0IP, fifth-best ratio in the International League.
- Began the season at Albany and went 7-2 with a 2.71 ERA in 11 starts before he was promoted on 6/10...was named the "Pitcher of the Month" for May after going 4-1 with a 3.66 ERA in six starts...was named the Eastern League's "Pitcher of the Week" from 5/30-6/5.

1993

- Went 12-9 with a 3.06 ERA in 26 starts at Single-A Prince William and one start at Double-A Albany...ranked among the organizational leaders with a 3.06 ERA (third), 12 wins (tied for fourth), 27 starts (tied for fifth) and 135 strikeouts (fifth)...led Prince William with 129 strikeouts...Carolina-League opponents hit .248 off him...tossed a two-hitter for Prince William in a 2-0 victory on 7/29 vs. Kinston.

1992

- Was 10-4 with a 2.20 ERA in 27 starts at Single-A Greensboro...led the Yankees organization and ranked second in the South Atlantic League in ERA...led league pitchers with 45 assists...also ranked among organizational leaders with a .714 winning percentage (second), 168.0 IP (third) and 27 starts (tied for third)...opponents hit just .232 off him...threw a three-hitter in a 4-0 victory on 5/2 vs. Gastonia...allowed one hit in an eight-inning outing on 6/13 vs. Charleston.

1991

- In his first professional season, went 6-3 with a 1.55 ERA in 12 starts with the Gulf Coast League Yankees and Short-A Oneonta...led organization short-season pitchers in ERA...was 4-1 with a 0.98 ERA in six starts at Tampa and 2-2 with a 2.18 ERA in six starts at Oneonta.

Personal

- Full name is Andrew Eugene Pettitte...he and his wife, Laura, have four children: sons Joshua Blake (15), Jared (11) and Luke Jackson (4), and daughter, Lexy Grace (9)...was selected by the Yankees in the 22nd round of the 1990 First-Year Player Draft, but chose to attend San Jacinto (Texas) Junior College...was eventually signed by Joe Robison on 5/25/91...graduated from Deer Park (Texas) High School...his father-in-law has been the pastor of the same Deer Park Baptist church for more than 40 years...Andy and Laura are members of the church, where they teach youth classes and sing in the choir.
- Participated in a game of Tee Ball on the White House South Lawn during the summer of 2005 while the Astros were in town playing the Washington Nationals...the game featured teams from Little League Baseball's Challenger Division for physically and mentally disabled children...President George W. Bush was in attendance.

- Was honored by the New York Sports Photographers with the "Good Guy" Award for 1996...also received a special recognition award for his work with the RBI program in 1996...received the 2003 Warren Spahn Award, given annually to the top left-handed pitcher in baseball, from the Oklahoma Sports Museum...tabbed by the Houston Chapter of the BBWAA as the "Greater Houston Major League Player of the Year" in 1996 and again in 2003...named the Astros' recipient of the 2005 Roberto Clemente Award and one of 30 nominees for the award...also in 2005, was Houston's nominee for the Marvin Miller "Man of the Year" Award...received the Thurman Munson Award in 2006, presented by the Association for the Help of Retarded Children...honored along with teammates Derek Jeter, Mariano Rivera and Jorge Posada with the 2009 "Willie, Mickey and the Duke" Award from the New York Baseball Writer's Association of America.
- Is an active supporter of the San Jacinto College Foundation, a non-profit corporation that helps to enhance the level of achievement at the college he attended...as the official spokesman of the fund's annual gold tournament, the foundation has raised over $550,000 since 1996...visited the St. Cabrini Nursing Home in New York in April 2008...joined Joba Chamberlain, Phil Hughes and Brian Cashman at Memorial Sloan-Kettering Cancer Center in September 2009.

Pettitte's Career Pitching Record

Year	Club	W	L	ERA	G	GS	CG	SHO	SV	IP	H	R	ER	HR	HP	BB	SO	WP	BK
1991	GCL Yankees	4	1	0.98	6	6	0	0	0	36.2	16	6	4	0	1	8	51	4	6
	Oneonta	2	2	2.18	6	6	1	0	0	33.0	33	18	8	1	0	16	32	4	0
1992	Greensboro	10	4	2.20	27	27	2	1	0	168.0	141	53	41	4	5	55	130	11	2
1993	Prince William	11	9	3.04	26	26	2	1	0	159.2	146	68	54	7	5	47	129	8	1
	Albany	1	0	3.60	1	1	0	0	0	5.0	5	4	2	0	0	2	6	0	0
1994	Albany	7	2	2.71	11	11	0	0	0	73.0	60	32	22	5	1	18	50	5	1
	Columbus	7	2	2.98	16	16	3	0	0	96.2	101	40	32	3	2	21	61	5	0
1995	YANKEES	12	9	4.17	31	26	3	0	0	175.0	183	86	81	15	1	63	114	8	1
	Columbus	0	0	0.00	2	2	0	0	0	11.2	7	0	0	0	0	0	8	1	0
1996	YANKEES	*21	8	3.87	35	34	2	0	0	221.0	229	105	95	23	3	72	162	6	1
1997	YANKEES	18	7	2.88	35	#35	4	1	0	240.1	233	86	77	7	3	65	166	7	0
1998	YANKEES	16	11	4.24	33	32	5	0	0	216.1	226	110	102	20	6	87	146	5	0
1999	Tampa	1	0	0.00	1	1	0	0	0	5.0	4	0	0	0	0	2	8	0	0
	YANKEES - a	14	11	4.70	31	31	0	0	0	191.2	216	105	100	20	3	89	121	3	1
2000	YANKEES - b	19	9	4.35	32	32	3	1	0	204.2	219	111	99	17	4	80	125	2	3
2001	YANKEES - c	15	10	3.99	31	31	2	0	0	200.2	224	103	89	14	6	41	164	2	2
2002	YANKEES - d	13	5	3.27	22	22	3	1	0	134.2	144	58	49	6	4	32	97	2	1
	Tampa	0	0	0.00	2	2	0	0	0	5.0	3	0	0	0	0	0	4	0	0
	Norwich	0	0	1.42	1	1	0	0	0	6.1	2	1	1	0	0	0	5	0	0
2003	YANKEES	21	8	4.02	33	33	1	0	0	208.1	227	109	93	21	1	50	180	5	0
2004	HOUSTON - e,f,g,h	6	4	3.90	15	15	0	0	0	83.0	71	37	36	8	0	31	79	4	0
	Round Rock	0	0	2.25	2	2	0	0	0	8.0	4	2	2	1	0	2	9	0	0
2005	HOUSTON	17	9	2.39	33	33	0	0	0	222.1	188	66	59	17	3	41	171	2	0
2006	HOUSTON	14	13	4.20	36	#35	2	1	0	214.1	238	114	100	27	2	70	178	2	1
2007	YANKEES - i	15	9	4.05	36	#34	0	0	0	215.1	238	106	97	16	1	69	141	3	0
2008	YANKEES - j	14	14	4.54	33	33	0	0	0	204.0	233	112	103	19	7	55	158	6	1
2009	YANKEES	14	8	4.16	32	32	0	0	0	194.2	193	101	90	20	4	76	148	3	0
Minor League Totals		**43**	**20**	**2.46**	**101**	**101**	**8**	**2**	**0**	**608.0**	**522**	**224**	**166**	**21**	**14**	**171**	**493**	**38**	**10**
AL Totals		**192**	**109**	**4.02**	**384**	**375**	**23**	**3**	**0**	**2406.2**	**2565**	**1192**	**1075**	**198**	**43**	**779**	**1722**	**52**	**10**
NL Totals		**37**	**26**	**3.38**	**84**	**83**	**2**	**1**	**0**	**519.2**	**497**	**217**	**195**	**52**	**5**	**142**	**428**	**8**	**1**
Major League Totals		**229**	**135**	**3.91**	**468**	**458**	**25**	**4**	**0**	**2926.1**	**3062**	**1409**	**1270**	**250**	**48**	**921**	**2150**	**60**	**11**

*Denotes league leader #Tied for league lead

Selected by the New York Yankees in the 22nd round of the June 1990 free-agent draft; signed on May 25, 1991.

a - Placed on disabled list, April 4-17, 1999 with a strained left elbow.
b - Placed on disabled list, April 13-26, 2000 with a back strain.
c - Placed on disabled list, June 16-July 1, 2001 with a strained left groin.
d - Placed on disabled list, April 21-June 14, 2002 with left elbow tendinitis.
e - Signed by Houston as a free agent on Dec. 12, 2003.
f - Placed on disabled list, April 10-29, 2004 with a strained left elbow.
g - Placed on disabled list, May 31-June 29, 2004 with a strained left forearm.
h - Placed on disabled list, August 18, 2004 through remainder of season with left elbow surgery.
i - Signed by New York (AL) as a free agent on December 21, 2006.
j - Placed on the disabled list from March 31 - April 5, 2008 with lower back spasms.

Zeroes Across

From 8/7-9/09 vs. Boston, Yankees starters **A.J. Burnett**, **CC Sabathia** and **Andy Pettitte** each tossed at least 7.0 innings without allowing a run, marking the first time the Yankees recorded three consecutive starts of at least 7.0IP each not allowing a run since 9/27-29/73 (Pat Dobson, Mel Stottlemyre and Doc Medich), according to the *Elias Sports Bureau*...Burnett (7.2IP, 1H, 0R on 8/7) and Sabathia (7.2IP, 2H, 0R on 8/8) became just the third Yankees starters in franchise history to toss at least 7.0 innings while allowing no runs and no more than two hits in back-to-back games...the feat was also accomplished on 5/23-24/47 vs. Boston (Allie Reynolds and Spud Chandler) and 4/11-12/73 vs. Cleveland (Mel Stottlemyre and Steve Kline).

ANDY PETTITTE

Pettitte's Division Series Record

Year	Club vs. Opp.	W	L	ERA	G	GS	CG	SHO	SV	IP	H	R	ER	HR	HP	BB	SO	WP	BK
1995	NYY vs. SEA	0	0	5.14	1	1	0	0	0	7.0	9	4	4	1	0	3	0	0	0
1996	NYY vs. TEX	0	0	5.68	1	1	0	0	0	6.1	4	4	4	2	0	6	3	1	0
1997	NYY vs. CLE	0	2	8.49	2	2	0	0	0	11.2	15	11	11	1	0	1	5	0	0
1998	NYY vs. TEX	1	0	1.29	1	1	0	0	0	7.0	3	1	1	0	0	0	8	0	0
1999	NYY vs. TEX	1	0	1.23	1	1	0	0	0	7.1	7	1	1	1	0	0	5	0	0
2000	NYY vs. OAK	1	0	3.97	2	2	0	0	0	11.1	15	5	5	0	0	3	7	0	0
2001	NYY vs. OAK	0	1	1.42	1	1	0	0	0	6.1	7	1	1	1	0	2	4	0	0
2002	NYY vs. ANA	0	0	12.00	1	1	0	0	0	3.0	8	4	4	2	0	0	1	0	0
2003	NYY vs. MIN	1	0	1.29	1	1	0	0	0	7.0	4	1	1	1	0	3	10	1	0
2005	HOU vs. ATL	1	0	3.86	1	1	0	0	0	7.0	4	3	3	2	0	2	6	0	0
2007	NYY vs. CLE	0	0	0.00	1	1	0	0	0	6.1	7	0	0	0	0	2	5	0	0
2009	NYY vs. MIN	1	0	1.42	1	1	0	0	0	6.1	3	1	1	0	0	1	7	0	0
Division Series Totals		**6**	**3**	**3.74**	**14**	**14**	**0**	**0**	**0**	**86.2**	**86**	**36**	**36**	**11**	**0**	**23**	**61**	**2**	**0**

Pettitte's League Championship Series Record

Year	Club vs. Opp.	W	L	ERA	G	GS	CG	SHO	SV	IP	H	R	ER	HR	HP	BB	SO	WP	BK
1996	NYY vs. BAL	1	0	3.60	2	2	0	0	0	15.0	10	6	6	4	0	5	7	0	1
1998	NYY vs. CLE	0	1	11.57	1	1	0	0	0	4.2	8	6	6	4	0	3	1	0	0
1999	NYY vs. BOS	1	0	2.45	1	1	0	0	0	7.1	8	2	2	0	0	1	5	0	0
2000	NYY vs. SEA	1	0	2.70	1	1	0	0	0	6.2	9	2	2	0	0	1	2	0	0
2001	NYY vs. SEA	2	0	2.51	2	2	0	0	0	14.1	11	4	4	0	0	2	8	0	0
2003	NYY vs. BOS	1	0	4.63	2	2	0	0	0	11.2	17	6	6	2	0	4	10	0	0
2005	HOU vs. STL	0	1	5.11	2	2	0	0	0	12.1	15	7	7	1	1	4	6	0	0
2009	NYY vs. LAA	1	0	2.84	2	2	0	0	0	12.2	14	4	4	2	0	2	8	0	0
LCS Totals		**7**	**2**	**3.93**	**13**	**13**	**0**	**0**	**0**	**84.2**	**92**	**37**	**37**	**13**	**1**	**22**	**47**	**0**	**1**

Pettitte's World Series Record

Year	Club vs. Opp.	W	L	ERA	G	GS	CG	SHO	SV	IP	H	R	ER	HR	HP	BB	SO	WP	BK
1996	NYY vs. ATL	1	1	5.91	2	2	0	0	0	10.2	11	7	7	1	0	4	5	0	0
1998	NYY vs. SD	1	0	0.00	1	1	0	0	0	7.1	5	0	0	0	0	3	4	0	0
1999	NYY vs. ATL	0	0	12.27	1	1	0	0	0	3.2	10	5	5	0	0	1	1	1	0
2000	NYY vs. NYM	0	0	1.98	2	2	0	0	0	13.2	16	5	3	0	1	4	9	0	0
2001	NYY vs. ARI	0	2	10.00	2	2	0	0	0	9.0	12	10	10	1	1	2	9	0	0
2003	NYY vs. FLA	1	1	0.57	2	2	0	0	0	15.2	12	3	1	0	0	4	14	0	0
2005	HOU vs. CWS	0	0	3.00	1	1	0	0	0	6.0	8	2	2	0	0	0	4	0	0
2009	NYY VS. PHI	2	0	5.40	2	2	0	0	0	11.2	9	7	7	3	0	8	10	1	0
World Series Totals		**5**	**4**	**4.06**	**13**	**13**	**0**	**0**	**0**	**77.2**	**83**	**39**	**35**	**5**	**2**	**26**	**56**	**2**	**0**
POSTSEASON TOTALS		**18**	**9**	**3.90**	**40**	**40**	**0**	**0**	**0**	**249.0**	**261**	**112**	**108**	**29**	**3**	**71**	**164**	**4**	**1**

Pettitte's All-Star Game Record

Year	Club, Site	W	L	ERA	G	GS	CG	SHO	SV	IP	H	R	ER	HR	HP	BB	SO	WP	BK
1996	NYY, Philadelphia	Selected - Did Not Pitch																	
2001	NYY, Seattle	0	0	0.00	1	0	0	0	0	1.0	1	0	0	0	0	0	1	0	0
All-Star Game Totals		**0**	**0**	**0.00**	**1**	**0**	**0**	**0**	**0**	**1.0**	**1**	**0**	**0**	**0**	**0**	**0**	**1**	**0**	**0**

Pettitte's Regular Season Batting Record

Year	Team	AVG	G	AB	R	H	2B	3B	HR	RBI	SH	SF	HP	BB	SO	SB	CS
2009	NYY	.200	32	5	1	1	1	0	0	1	1	0	0	0	2	0	0
Major League Totals		**.134**	**369**	**186**	**6**	**25**	**6**	**0**	**1**	**13**	**32**	**1**	**0**	**6**	**6**	**0**	**0**

Pettitte's Career Fielding Record

Position	PCT	G	PO	A	E	TC	DP
Pitcher	.954	468	119	486	29	634	30

Home Runs by Yankees Pitchers

Fifty-eight Yankees pitchers have combined to hit 154 home runs in the franchise's 106-year history. The top five: Red Ruffing, 30; Tommy Byrne, 10; Spud Chandler, 9; Don Larsen, 8; Mel Stottlemyre, 7...the first home run hit by a Yankee pitcher was by Clark Griffith on July 14, 1903...the last was hit by Lindy McDaniel on September 28, 1972 off Mickey Lolich at Detroit...no Yankee pitcher has ever homered in a postseason game. Four current Yankees pitchers – A.J. Burnett (three times), Andy Pettitte (once), CC Sabathia (three times) and Javier Vazquez (once) – have homered in a Major League game.

Jorge Posada

20 Catcher

6-2 • 215 • B/T: Switch/Right

Opening Day Age: 38

Birthdate
August 17, 1971

Birthplace
Santurce, P.R.

Resides
Miami, Fla.

M.L. Service
13 years, 85 days

College
Calhoun Community College

Career Highlights

A.L. All-Star Team
- 2000, 2001, 2002, 2003, 2007

A.L. Silver Slugger Award
- 2000, 2001, 2002, 2003 2007

Status

- Selected in the 24th round of the 1990 First-Year Player Draft...signed a four-year contract on November 29, 2007...contract extends through the 2011 season.

Career Notes

- Ranks eighth on the Yankees' all-time lists with 243HR and 838BB, ninth with 342 doubles and 12th with 964RBI.
- Along with Derek Jeter and Mariano Rivera, is part of the first trio of teammates ever to play for the Yankees in each of 15 straight seasons (1995-2009)...Bill Dickey, Lefty Gomez and Red Ruffing (1930-42) and Whitey Ford, Elston Howard and Mickey Mantle (1955-67) played together with the Yankees for 13 straight seasons...Jeter, Posada and Rivera are the first trio of players in the Majors to play for the same team in 15 straight seasons since Jim Gantner, Paul Molitor and Robin Yount (15 years, 1978-92 with Milwaukee)—credit: *Elias Sports Bureau.*
- Is one of six catchers all-time to hit at least 20HR in eight seasons, joining Mike Piazza (11), Johnny Bench (11), Yogi Berra (10), Gary Carter (9) and Carlton Fisk (8)—credit: *Elias*...is one of eight catchers all-time to reach the 200HR plateau...according to the *Elias Sports Bureau*, has homered in more ballparks (28) than any player in franchise history...his 233HR as a catcher rank second on the Yankees' all-time list behind only Yogi Berra (306).
- Started 68 consecutive postseason games from 10/27/99 (World Series Game 4)-10/5/05 (Division Series Game 2)...his 43 Division Series games are the third-most on Baseball's all-time list...is tied for fourth on Baseball's all-time list with 111 career postseason games played...his 110 postseason contests at catcher are the most all-time (Yogi Berra is second with 63)...has recorded 21 postseason doubles, third-most all time.

Single-Game Bests and Streaks

Hits
4 - 16 times
Last: at TOR, 9/3/09

Runs
4 - 3 times
Last: vs. SEA, 9/4/07

2B
3 - at CWS, 4/23/08

3B
1 - 9 times
Last: at CLE, 4/26/08

HR
2 - 16 times
Last: at BAL, 9/1/09

RBI
7 - vs. DET, 9/10/03

BB
4 - 2 times
Last: at CLE, 7/9/03

SO
4 - 5 times
Last: at ATL, 6/23/09

SB
1 - 17 times
Last: at DET, 4/29/09

Hit Streak
15g - 5/3-20/07

2009

- Hit .285 (109-for-383) with 55R, 25 doubles, 22HR and 81RBI in 111 games (88 starts at C and nine at DH) with the Yankees...batted .290 (36-for-124, 5HR) vs. left-handed pitchers and .282 (73-for-259, 17HR) vs. righties.
- Played in 100 games at catcher in a season in which he turned 38 years old, the most games ever for a Yankees catcher in a season at that age and the most by any catcher since Benito Santiago in 2003 w/ San Francisco...among all-time Major League catchers, only Carlton Fisk (130G, 37HR and 107RBI in 1985 with Chicago-AL) reached Posada's totals in games, home runs and RBI in a season in which they entered at 37 years of age or older.
- Among Major League catchers, ranked fourth in HR, fifth in RBI and tied for seventh in doubles...ranked seventh in the Majors with a 4.73AB/RBI ratio (383AB, 81RBI)...had the most RBI for any player with fewer than 400 at-bats.
- Reached base safely in each of his 11 games against Boston in 2009, going 16-for-40 (.400) with 6R, 3 doubles, 2HR, 7RBI and 11BB...batted .432 (16-for-37) with 6RBI out of the cleanup spot.

JORGE POSADA

- Made his 10th straight Opening Day start at catcher (2000-09), the most consecutive starts by a Yankee at C on Opening Day since Thurman Munson made 10 straight starts there from 1970-79...only Bill Dickey (14, 1930-43) has made more consecutive starts behind the plate for the Yankees on Opening Day.
- Hit solo-HR and was 1-for-3 with 1BB in 4/6 Opening Day loss at Baltimore, marking his third career Opening Day homer.
- Hit the first home run in Yankee Stadium history in the fifth inning in the Yankees' 4/16 home opening loss vs. Cleveland.
- Hit go-ahead, two-run, pinch-hit HR in the seventh and was 1-for-2 in 4/19 win vs. Cleveland...was his third career pinch-hit home run and first since 8/29/04 at Toronto...the home run was reviewed via replay, becoming the first HR to go under umpire review in Yankee Stadium...was the first reviewed home run in the Majors in 2009.
- Caught all 14 innings in 4/22 win vs. Oakland...marked the seventh time in his career he caught at least 14.0 innings and the first since catching 17.0 innings on 6/1/03 at Detroit.
- Was 1-for-4 with 1R, 1BB and 1SB in 4/29 win at Detroit...was his first SB since 7/14/07 at Tampa Bay.
- Was placed on the 15-day disabled list from 5/5-29 with a Grade 2 right hamstring strain (missed 22 team games)...rehabbed at Yankees minor league complex in Tampa, Fla., appearing in simulated, intrasquad and extended spring training games.
- Tied a career-high with four strikeouts in 6/23 loss at Atlanta, going 0-for-4...was only the fifth 4K game of his career (last on 7/19/02 vs. Boston).
- Hit solo-HR and game-winning "walk-off" single in the 12th inning on 7/4 vs. Toronto, going 2-for-6...according to the *Elias Sports Bureau*, the 12th-inning RBI single—in his 1,533rd Major League game—was his first career "walk-off" RBI in extra innings...the last player whose first extra-inning "walk-off" RBI came as far into his career as Posada's was Tony Fernandez, who finally accomplished the feat in his 2,123rd big league game in 2001 w/ Toronto.
- Missed three games (8/27-29) with bruised left ring finger.
- Recorded his 16th career multi-HR game (all 2HR-games) with a solo-HR and two-run HR in 9/1 win at Baltimore...was his first multi-homer game since 9/4/07 vs. Seattle.
- Hit his second pinch-hit homer of the season in 9/9 win vs. Tampa Bay (also 4/19 vs. Cleveland), hitting the game-winning three-run homer in the eighth...was his fourth career pinch-hit homer.
- Was suspended for three games by Major League Baseball for his actions during eighth-inning altercation in 9/15 loss vs. Toronto...was 1-for-3 with 2R and 1BB the game before being ejected by HP umpire Jim Joyce in the bottom of the eighth inning (fighting)...was his fifth career ejection and first since 8/24/07...served his suspension from 9/16-19.
- Did not play in 9/23 win at Los Angeles-AL (bruised right toes), undergoing X-rays (negative) that day...was scratched from lineup prior to 9/26 win vs. Boston with a stiff neck (also missed 9/27 game).
- Was selected by Joe Girardi to manage the Yankees' final regular season game, guiding the team to a 10-2 win on 10/4 at Tampa Bay.
- Appeared in all 15 Yankees postseason games (10 starts), batting .260 (13-for-50) with 5R, 2 doubles, 2HR and 8RBI...reached base in 14 of the contests...hit go-ahead solo home run in the seventh inning in Game 3 clincher of ALDS at Minnesota.

MAJOR LEAGUE CATCHERS (SINCE 2000*)

MOST HITS

1.	Jason Kendall	1,517
2.	Ivan Rodriguez	1,326
3.	A.J. Pierzynski	1,223
4.	**JORGE POSADA**	**1,177**
5.	Bengie Molina	1,152

MOST HOME RUNS

1.	**JORGE POSADA**	**199**
2.	Mike Piazza	159
3.	Ivan Rodriguez	156
4.	Jason Varitek	146
5.	Ramon Hernandez	134

MOST RBI

1.	**JORGE POSADA**	**774**
2.	Bengie Molina	631
3.	Ivan Rodriguez	621
4.	Ramon Hernandez	590
5.	Jason Varitek	582

MOST GAMES STARTED

1.	Jason Kendall	1,399
2.	**JORGE POSADA**	**1,135**
3.	Ivan Rodriguez	1,114
4.	A.J. Pierzynski	1,112
5	Benjie Molina	1,099

WALKS

1.	**JORGE POSADA**	**650**
2.	Jason Varitek	508
3.	Jason Kendall	501
4.	Brad Ausmus	377
5.	Gregg Zaun	336

DOUBLES

1.	**JORGE POSADA**	**274**
2.	Ivan Rodriguez	270
3.	Jason Kendall	257
4.	A.J. Pierzynski	250
5.	Jason Varitek	232

*as a catcher

2008

- Hit .268 (45-for-168) with 13 doubles, 3HR and 22RBI in 51 games with the Yankees before being placed on the disabled list from 7/21 through the conclusion of the season with a right shoulder strain...made 28 starts at C, 15 at DH, three at 1B...marked his most starts at 1B since 2000 (8GS).
- Was placed on the 15-day D.L. on 7/21 (retroactive to 7/20)...underwent season-ending arthroscopic surgery on his right shoulder on 7/30 at the Hospital for Special Surgery in New York...the procedure was performed by Dr. David Altcheck (missed 63 team games).
- Was his second stint on the D.L. in 2008...was also on the 15-day D.L. from 4/28-6/3 with a right shoulder strain that was later diagnosed as right rotator cuff tendinitis (missed 32 team games)...had never spent time on the disabled list prior to the 2008 season...according to the *Elias Sports Bureau*, at the time of his injury, Posada was one of six current players with at least 10 years of service that had never been placed on the disabled list along with Brad Ausmus, Johnny Damon, Andruw Jones, Derek Lowe and Livan Hernandez...prior to 4/28/08, the Yankees' last game without Posada on the active roster was 9/1/96 at California (Jim Leyritz started at C).
- Had started at least 120 games behind the plate in each of his previous eight seasons (2000-07), a streak equaled only by Jason Kendall.
- Caught just three of 37 potential base stealers (8.1%).
- Made his ninth straight Opening Day start at catcher (2000-2008) in 4/1 win vs. Toronto...was 0-for-2 with 1BB in 4/1 Opening Day win vs. Toronto, allowing three stolen bases...missed the next two games from 4/2-3 with a strained right shoulder.
- Made four consecutive starts at DH for the first time in his career from 4/10-14...made his 13th career start at 1B in 4/19 loss at Baltimore, going 1-for-5.
- Established a career high with three doubles and tied a career best with four hits in 4/23 win at Chicago-AL, going 4-for-5 with 2RBI...according to the *Elias Sports Bureau*, became the first Yankees catcher to collect three doubles in a game since Buddy Rosar on 4/20/41.
- Made first appearance on the D.L. on 4/28...in seven extended spring training rehab appearances, was 10-for-27 (.370) with 2 doubles and 6BB in 7GS (6-C/1-DH)...was returned from rehab and reinstated from the disabled list on 6/4...started at C and was 1-for-3 with 1BB in 6/5 win vs. Toronto in his first game back...hit safely in eight of his first 11 games following his return from D.L.
- Made his final appearance of the season with the Yankees in 7/19 win vs. Oakland, starting at C and going 1-for-5.

DID YOU KNOW? JORGE POSADA has caught at least one game for 15 straight years. The last man to accomplish that with the same team was Johnny Bench with the Reds from 1967-83 (17 consecutive seasons). Credit: *Elias Sports Bureau*.

MOST GAMES CAUGHT IN YANKEES FRANCHISE HISTORY

	Player	Games
1.	Bill Dickey	1,708
2.	Yogi Berra	1,695
3.	**JORGE POSADA**	**1,490**
4.	Thurman Munson	1,278
5.	Elston Howard	1,030

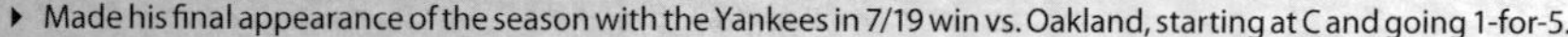

2007

- Hit a career-high .338 (171-for-506) while establishing career highs in hits, doubles (42) and slugging percentage (.543)...also hit 20HR and drove in 90 runs in 144 games with the Yankees (125 starts at C, five at DH and one at 1B).
- Ranked fourth in the American League in average, becoming the first Yankees catcher to finish a season in the top 10 in the league in batting average since Thurman Munson finished 10th in 1978 with a .297 average...also became the only player in Major League history to bat at least .330 with 40 doubles, 20HR and 90RBI in a year in which he caught in at least half of his games played (credit: *Elias Sports Bureau*)...led the AL with a .344 road average, ranked third with a .426 overall on-base percentage, eighth with a .543 slugging percentage and tied for eighth in doubles.
- Won his fifth career Silver Slugger Award and was named the starting catcher on both the *Baseball America* and the *Sporting News* Major League All-Star teams.
- His .338 batting average was 61 points higher than in 2006 (.277), the largest increase for any Major Leaguer who qualified for the batting title in 2006 and 2007...according to the *Elias Sports Bureau*, from 1939-2008, the only other Yankee to improve his batting average by 60 or more points from one season to the next was Bobby Murcer who hit .331 in 1971 after posting a .251 average in 1970 (an 80 point increase)...from 1940-2007, only four players appearing primarily at catcher recorded a higher single-season batting average: St. Louis' Joe Torre (.363 in 1971), the Dodgers' Mike Piazza (.362 in 1997 and .346 in 1995) and Minnesota's Joe Mauer (.347 in 2006).
- His average never went below .311 (on 4/29) and he never went more than three games without hitting safely...his eighth-inning single on 8/16 vs. Detroit snapped an 0-for-11 stretch, his longest hitless streak of the season.

- His 42 doubles established a franchise record for a catcher, surpassing his own record of 40 set in 2002...joined Ivan Rodriguez (47 in 1996 and 40 in 1998) as the only two catchers in Major League history to have two seasons of 40 or more doubles (credit: *Elias*)...became only the 17th player in Major League history to collect at least 300 career doubles while appearing in at least 1,000 games at catcher.
- Was selected to the 2007 American League All-Star team, his fifth career All-Star selection and first since 2003...went 1-for-3 with 1 double in 7/10 AL win, pinch-hitting for Josh Beckett in the fifth inning and remaining in game at C.
- Combined with Alex Rodriguez for a .325 batting average, 74HR and 246RBI...according to *Elias*, no Yankees teammates had combined for numbers that high in each of those categories since 1937, when Joe DiMaggio and Lou Gehrig had a .349BA, 83HR and 326RBI between them.
- Hit solo-HR—his second career Opening Day HR and the 199th of his career—and was 2-for-4 with 2R in 4/2 win vs. Tampa Bay...hit his 200th career home run in 4/17 win vs. Cleveland...did not play in 4/21 loss at Boston (bruised left thumb).
- Compiled a career-high 15-game hitting streak from 5/3-20, batting .448 (26-for-58) with 13R, 7 doubles, 3HR and 8RBI...was the longest hitting streak for a Yankees catcher since Bob Geren hit safely in 15 straight games in 1989.
- Hit solo home runs from each side of the plate and tied career highs with 4H and 4R in 9/4 win vs. Seattle, going 4-for-4 with 1BB...was the second time in 2007 (also 8/1 vs. Chicago-AL) and the eighth time in his career he hit homers from both sides of the plate in the same game, tying Bernie Williams for the second most in team history and marking the most single-game switch-hit HR by a catcher all-time.
- Recorded his 300th career double and was 2-for-3 with a solo-HR, 3R and 2BB in 9/11 win at Toronto...according to the *Elias Sports Bureau*, became only the 17th player to reach the 300-double plateau while appearing in at least 1,000 games at catcher.
- Went a career-high 37 plate appearances without a strikeout from 8/31-9/12 (previous high was 33PA in 1997).
- Hit a team-best .395 in September (30-for-76), fifth-highest in the AL for the month...according to the *Elias Sports Bureau*, only two players have had a higher September average than Posada in a year in which they caught at least 130 games: the Dodgers' Mike Piazza in 1997 (.406) and Pittsburgh's Jason Kendall in 2004 (.400)...named honorary Yankees Manager for the regular season finale on 10/1 at Baltimore.
- Batted .133 (2-for-15) in four Division Series games vs. Cleveland.

2006

- Batted .277 (129-for-465) with 23HR and 93RBI in 143 games (121 starts at C, two at DH)...was the sixth time in a seven-year span (2000-06) he hit at least 20HR and drove in at least 80 runs...ranked 10th in the American League with 1RBI every 5.0AB.
- In 4/3 win at Oakland, made his seventh straight Opening Day start at catcher (2000-06)...hit two-run "walk-off" home run and was 2-for-3 with 2R, 2RBI, 1BB and 2SF in 5/16 win vs. Texas...was his second career "walk-off" HR (also on 5/5/00 vs. Baltimore).
- Missed two games (5/20-21) with tightness in his upper back...suffered tear in his hamstring tendon behind his left knee on 5/23 at Boston and missed four games (5/24-28)...hit two-run HR and was 1-for-3 with 1BB in 6/11 loss vs. Oakland, hitting his first home run of the season as a right-handed batter and first since 9/22/05 vs. Baltimore (a span of 58AB)...was scratched from lineup on 7/19 vs. Seattle with a bruised right index finger...threw out three runners on 8/8 at Chicago for the second time in his career (also 8/6/02 vs. Kansas City).
- Snapped career-high 0-for-25 stretch with a second-inning single in 8/14 win vs. the Angels...hit two three-run HRs in back-to-back at-bats in the sixth and eighth innings and was 2-for-3 with 3R and a season-high 6RBI and 1BB in 9/6 win at Kansas City...was his second multi-home-run game of the season (also 4/9 at Los Angeles-AL) and the 13th of his career (all 2HR games).
- Hit .500 (7-for-14) with 1HR and 2RBI in four Division Series games vs. Detroit.

2005

- Hit .262 (124-for-474) with 19HR and 71RBI in 142 games (122 starts at C, three starts at DH)...threw out 39-of-129 potential base stealers (30.2%)...homered from both sides of the plate in 5/24 win vs. Detroit, hitting solo-HR in the fourth and three-run HR in the fifth.
- Did not strike out in 32 straight plate appearances before fanning in third inning of 6/3 loss at Minnesota...recorded his 1,000th career hit with a seventh-inning double in 8/20 win at Chicago-AL, going 1-for-2 with 2R and 2BB...did not play in 9/10 loss vs. Boston (jammed right shoulder)...hit solo-HR and three-run HR in 9/22 win vs. Baltimore...was his second multi-HR game of the season (also 5/24 vs. Detroit) and the 11th of his career.
- Hit .231 (3-for-13) with 1HR, 2RBI and 6BB in five games vs. the Angels in the Division Series...had his streak of 68 consecutive postseason starts snapped in Game 3 of the ALDS (had started each of the Yankees' postseason games since Game 4 of the 1999 World Series).

2004

- Batted .272 (122-for-449) with 21HR and 81RBI in 137 games (126 starts at C)...led the American League in games caught for the second time in his career, becoming the first Yankee to lead the league in games caught more than once since Thurman Munson in 1970, 1972 and 1973...was tied for third in the AL with 88BB and ranked fourth with a .400 on-base percentage.
- Homered from both sides of the plate (three-run homers in the fifth and seventh innings) and was 2-for-5 with 6RBI in 3/31 win vs. Tampa Bay at Tokyo Dome...accomplished the feat for the fifth time in his career, tying Roy White for third place on the club's all-time list.
- Missed four games after suffering a broken nose in 5/12 game vs. Anaheim (was hit in the nose by a ball thrown by Angels shortstop Alfredo Amezaga in a double-play attempt in bottom of the second inning)...was taken to Columbia Presbyterian Hospital where he was seen by ear, nose and throat specialist, Dr. Hector Rodriguez and surgery was performed to set the fracture.
- Drew at least one walk in a career-high 13 straight games from 5/9-29...hit solo-HR and was 2-for-2 with 2RBI in 7/11 win vs. Tampa Bay before being removed in the third with a sprained right ankle (precautionary X-rays were negative)...hit first-inning grand slam in 7/26 win at Toronto, the seventh of his career to tie Charlie Keller for ninth place on the club's all-time list...missed three games from 8/6-8 with a bruised right thumb...missed two games on 8/14-15, suffering from a low-grade viral infection.
- Hit pinch-hit solo-HR off Jason Frasor in the ninth inning of 8/29 loss at Toronto...was his second career pinch-hit HR (also on 6/16/01 vs. Baltimore off Mike Trombley).
- Hit .244 (11-for-45) with 2RBI in 11 postseason games...caught every inning of the postseason for the Yankees.

2003

- Ranked third in American League Most Valuable Player voting behind Texas' Alex Rodriguez and Toronto's Carlos Delgado...batted .281 (135-for-481) and established career highs with 30HR and 101RBI in 142 games (131 starts at C, two at DH)...his 30HR tied the Yankees' single-season record for home runs by a catcher (Yogi Berra hit 30 in 1952 and 1956).
- Earned his fourth consecutive Silver Slugger Award...ranked fifth in the American League with a .405 on-base percentage and sixth with 93 walks.
- Was elected to start the 2003 All-Star Game at catcher for second straight season, his fourth consecutive All-Star selection (was 0-for-2 at U.S. Cellular Field)...made fourth straight Opening Day start at catcher on 3/31 at Toronto...hit two-run HR in 4/1 win at Toronto, snapping the longest HR drought of his career (140AB/37G since previous HR on 8/17/02)...with seven home runs in April, tied his highest HR total for any single month (also hit 7HR in April 2000 and May 2002)...was ejected in the eighth inning of 5/24 loss vs. Toronto by 2B umpire Fieldin Culbreth for arguing interference call.
- Tied his career high with four walks in 7/9 win at Cleveland, going 0-for-2 with 1R (also 4BB on 5/30/00 vs. Oakland)...missed two games (8/8-9) vs. Seattle with a stiff neck...tied his career high with four hits (ninth time) in 8/12 win at Kansas City, going 4-for-5 with 2R, 1 double and 2RBI...hit two home runs and was 2-for-5 with 2R and 3RBI in 8/30 win at Boston, snapping an 0-for-17 stretch...was the eighth multi-home-run game of his career and first since 6/28/02 vs. New York-NL.
- Hit grand slam and was 3-for-4 with 2R, a career-high 7RBI and 1BB in 9/10 win vs. Detroit...the 7RBI were the most by a Yankee since Bernie Williams also collected 7RBI on 6/17/00 vs. Chicago...was his sixth career grand slam.
- Batted .222 (14-for-63) with 1HR and 7RBI in 17 postseason games.

2002

- Batted .268 (137-for-511) with 40 doubles, 20HR and 99RBI in 143 games (131 starts at C, five at DH and one at 1B)...the 40 doubles were the most by a catcher since Texas' Ivan Rodriguez had 45 in 1996...his 99RBI were the most by any catcher in the Majors in 2002 and his 266RBI from 2000-02 trailed only Mike Piazza (279) for most RBI by a catcher over that span.
- Earned his third Silver Slugger Award...was elected to his third career All-Star Game on 7/9 at Miller Park in Milwaukee...started at catcher and was 0-for-3...made third straight Opening Day start (and appearance) at catcher on 4/1 at Baltimore...tied a career high with 4R and was 3-for-6 with 1 double and 1RBI in 6/19 win at Colorado.
- Homered from both sides of the plate for fourth time in his career in 6/28 win vs. New York (NL)...hit three-run homer from the left side in the third and hit two-run shot in the fifth from the right side...hit grand slam and was 1-for-3 with 1BB in 7/2 win vs. Cleveland...was his first grand slam of the season and fourth of his career...hit two-run HR, the 100th HR of his career, and was 1-for-3 with 1BB in 7/5 win vs. Toronto...hit second grand slam of the season—and fifth of his career—and was 3-for-5 with 2R, 1 double and 6RBI in 7/13 win at Cleveland.
- Missed 7/15 game at Toronto to be with wife, Laura, for birth of their second child, Paulina, born that morning in New York...was 1-for-2 in 7/23 loss at Cleveland before being removed from game in fifth with laceration of the left ear (missed 7/24 game at Cleveland)...did not homer in the season's last 40 regular season games (134AB) after 8/17 at Seattle.
- Hit .235 (4-for-17) with 1HR and 3RBI in four Division Series games vs. the Angels.

JORGE POSADA

2001

- Batted .277 with 22HR and 95RBI in 138 games (126 starts at C, six at DH, one at 1B)...hit a three-run HR—his first on Opening Day—and was 3-for-4 with 1R, 1 double and 4RBI in 4/2 win vs. Kansas City...was his second straight Opening Day start for the Yankees at catcher...hit first career grand slam in 4/8 win vs. Toronto.
- Homered in career-high three straight games from 4/7-9...did not appear at catcher for seven games (6/4-10) because of a sprained ligament in his left thumb (3-DH; 3-DNP; 1-PH).
- Pinch-hit for Todd Greene in the eighth and hit game-winning grand slam in 6/6 win vs. Baltimore...was his second career grand slam and second of the season (also 4/8 vs. Toronto)...was his first career pinch-hit home run and the first by a Yankee in 2001...was the 21st pinch-hit grand-slam in Yankees history and first since Glenallen Hill on 7/28/00 at Minnesota.
- On 6/9 vs. Atlanta hit the 20th home run (in the regular season) into the "batter's eye" section of the center-field bleachers since the remodeled Yankee Stadium opened in 1976...tallied 18RBI on 13-game homestand from 6/1-6/14, appearing in just 10 games with eight starts.
- Was selected to his second All-Star Game, going 1-for-1 in the American League's 4-1 win on 7/10 in Seattle...missed three straight games (7/31-8/2) with a stomach illness...was ejected from 9/3 win by HP Umpire Andy Fletcher in the ninth after being called out on strikes for second time...appealed six-game suspension by MLB and had sentence reduced by one game (served five-game suspension from 9/26-10/1)...hit third grand slam of the season (and career) and tied a season high with 5RBI in 9/18 win at Chicago.
- Struck out in 12 straight games from 8/30-9/19, the longest such streak by a Yankee since Jim Leyritz also fanned in 12 straight games in 1995.
- Batted .273 (15-for-55) with 2HR and 3RBI in 17 postseason games...in Game 3 of the ALDS on 10/13 at Oakland, became only the 10th player in postseason history—and second Yankee—to hit a home run in a 1-0 game (also Tommy Henrich in Game 1 of the 1949 World Series vs. Brooklyn at Yankee Stadium).

2000

- Batted .287 with 28HR and 86RBI in 151 games (136 starts at C, eight at 1B and three at DH)...drew 107BB, including 95 while appearing in games at catcher, breaking the club record for most walks in a single season by a catcher (Wally Schang, 1921 and Bill Dickey, 1939 each drew 77BB at catcher).
- With 26HR as a catcher, fell four shy of tying Yogi Berra for the most home runs in a single season by a Yankees catcher (Berra hit 30 home runs in 1952 and '56)...threw out 34-of-104 potential base stealers (32.7%)...was selected to his first All-Star Game by Manager Joe Torre and was 0-for-2...in 13 games batting from the second spot in the order, hit .364 (20-for-55) with 12R, 3HR and 10RBI.
- Homered from both sides of the plate for the third time in his career on 4/23 at Toronto, going 3-for-5 with 2R and 3RBI...along with OF Bernie Williams, became the first pair of players in Major League history to hit switch-hit home runs in the same game.
- Hit three-run "walk-off" home run in the ninth and was 4-for-5 with 4RBI in 5/5 win vs. Baltimore...set a career high with 4BB on 5/30 vs. Oakland.
- Established a career high with 4R, in 6/19 win at Boston...was ejected on 7/1 at Tampa Bay for fighting and served a one-game suspension on 7/17 vs. Philadelphia...batted second for the first time in his career on 8/4 vs. Seattle and tied a career high with 4H (sixth time), going 4-for-5 with 2R, 2 doubles and 4RBI.
- Hit .204 (11-for-54) in 16 postseason games with four doubles and 5RBI.

1999

- Batted .245 with 12HR and 57RBI in 112 games (98 starts at C, one at DH and one at 1B)...threw out 20-of-95 potential stealers (21.1%)...team posted a 4.20 ERA in games he caught...did not play in the three-game series at Detroit (4/16-18) after being scratched from the lineup before 4/16 game with a sore right calf (suffered when he was doubled off first base in sixth inning in 4/15 loss vs. Baltimore)...on 4/28 at Texas hit upper-deck home run to snap an 0-for-25 streak from the left side of the plate to begin the season.
- Collected his first career triple on 6/23 at Tampa Bay...was 1-for-3 with an RBI double on 6/25 at Baltimore before leaving the game in the seventh inning with a mild contusion of his left thumb (missed two games, 6/26-27).
- Hit two home runs and was 2-for-5 on 7/10 at Shea Stadium–the third multi-HR game of his career...became only the second catcher in Baseball history to have switch-hit homers in two separate games (Todd Hundley also five times)...established a career-high with 4H (4-for-6) and had 3R and 3RBI on 7/24 vs. Cleveland...was a single shy of hitting for the cycle on 8/22 at Minnesota.
- Batted .182 with 1HR and 3RBI in six postseason games (five starts at C)...hit two-run home run in pennant-clinching win at Boston on 10/18 in ALCS Game 5.

1998

- In first season as the Yankees' primary catcher, batted .268 with 17HR and 63RBI in 111 games...made 91 starts (85 at C, five at DH and one at 1B)...threw out 29-of-76 potential base stealers (38.1%)...team posted a 3.83 ERA in games he caught (792.0IP, 337ER)...hit the Yankees' first home run of the season in his first start of the season on 4/5 at Oakland (was 3-for-5 with 2R and 2RBI in the 9-7 win).

- Caught David Wells' perfect game on 5/17 vs. Minnesota...made his first career start at first base on 6/26 at New York-NL...had the first multi-homer game of his career in 5-2 win on 7/31 at Seattle (two solo HRs)...became only the sixth Yankee ever to homer from both sides of the plate in recording the second multi-home run game of his career (and season) on 8/23 at Texas.
- Batted .227 with 2HR and 4RBI in nine postseason games, six starts at C...belted his first career postseason home run in the Yankees' 7-2 victory in Game 6 of the ALCS vs. Cleveland (a solo shot off Chad Ogea)...batted .333 (3-for-9) with 1HR and 2RBI in the World Series vs. San Diego...hit his first career World Series home run in the Yankees' 9-3 victory in Game 2 at Yankee Stadium (a two-run homer off ex-Yankee Brian Boehringer).

1997

- Hit .250 with 6HR and 25RBI in his first full season in the Majors...played 60 games, making 52 starts (all at C)...team posted a 4.71 ERA in games he caught (479.1IP, 251ER)...threw out 9-of-48 potential base stealers (18.8%)...was the only rookie on the Yankees' 25-man Opening Day roster...won the James P. Dawson Award, given annually to the Yankees' top rookie in spring training (.357, 2HR, 11RBI)...became the Yankees' second switch-hitting catcher to appear in at least two games in the last 50 years (also Butch Wynegar, 1982-86).
- Hit his first Major League home run on 5/4 at Kansas City, a solo HR off Jim Converse.
- Appeared in two games of the Division Series vs. Cleveland, going 0-for-2...hit .224 (17-for-76) with 2HR and 13RBI for Santurce of the Puerto Rican Winter League.

1996

- Hit .071 (1-for-14) in eight games with the Yankees over four stints in the Majors (4/3-5/11, 5/22-24, 6/29-7/6 and 9/2-9/29)...batted .271 with 11HR and 62RBI at Triple-A Columbus...caught a team-high 94 games...led the International League with 79 walks...was the International League's "Player of the Week" from 5/6-12...was named to the International League All-Star team for the second straight season.

1995

- Spent most of the season at Triple-A Columbus, batting .255 with 8HR and 51RBI in 108 games...started 93 games behind the plate...was named to the International League All-Star team...homered from each side of the plate on 5/1 at Ottawa (off Dennis Gray and Tim Crabtree)...was the International League's "Player of the Week" from 8/13-19, batting .391 with 1HR and 10RBI...was on the disabled list from 5/3-12 with a sore back...was third in the International League with 32 doubles before being promoted on 8/31...appeared in one game for the Yankees, making his Major League debut on 9/4 vs. Seattle (caught the ninth inning).
- Appeared in one game of the Division Series vs. Seattle, pinch-running for Wade Boggs in the bottom of the 12th inning of Game 2...scored the tying run, making it 5-5 (Yankees won 7-5 in 15 innings).

1994

- Hit .240 with 11HR and 48RBI in 92 games at Triple-A Columbus...caught 79 games...hit .188 with 5HR vs. LHP and .277 with 6HR vs. RHP...tied for the International League lead in errors by a catcher (11)...threw out 18-of-83 potential base stealers (21.7%)...season was cut short on 7/25 vs. Norfolk when he suffered a fractured left fibula and a dislocated left ankle after a collision at home plate with Pat Howell...hit .429 in four games prior to the injury and had 16 hits in his last 50 at-bats (.320 BA)...was added to the Yankees' 40-man roster on 11/18.

1993

- Combined to hit .260 in 118 games at Single-A Prince William and seven games at Double-A Albany...was named to the Carolina League All-Star team after hitting .259 with 17HR, 61RBI and 17SB at Prince William...ranked second on the team in HR and RBI behind Tate Seefried (21HR, 89RBI)...hit a grand slam on 7/16 off Lynchburg's Joel Bennett...committed 15 errors in 107 games at catcher and one at third base...played for Ponce of the Puerto Rican Winter League, batting .234 with 6HR and 25RBI.

1992

- Made the transition from second base to catcher and hit .277 with 12HR and 58RBI in 101 games at Single-A Greensboro...had a 15-game hitting streak from 4/25-5/25...played 41 games at catcher and five at third base.

1991

- Batted .235 with 4HR and 33RBI in 71 games, playing his first professional season at Short-A Oneonta...led New York-Penn League second basemen in double plays turned (42).

JORGE POSADA

Personal

- Full name is Jorge Rafael de Posada, Jr...first name pronounced HOR-hay...he and his wife, Laura, have a son, Jorge Jr. (10), and a daughter, Paulina (7).
- Received the Ted Williams Community Award from the Ted Williams Museum and Hitters Hall of Fame on 3/20/09...honored by the New York BBWAA along with Derek Jeter, Andy Pettitte and Mariano Rivera as the "Willie, Mickey and the Duke" Award winner at the 2010 annual dinner.
- Selected as the Yankees' recipient of the 2007 Roberto Clemente Award, which is given annually to the Major League Baseball player who combines outstanding skills on the baseball field with devoted work in the community...was his second nomination (also 2005)...also received the Kids in Distressed Situtations' 2007 Mentor Award and the Bart Giamatti Award at the 2007 Baseball Assistance Team (B.A.T.) dinner...the award is presented annually to the individual associated with the baseball community who best exemplifies the compassion demonstrated by the late Baseball Commissioner...received the 2004 "Good Guy" Award by the New York Press Photographers Association...given the 2001 Milton Richman "You Gotta' Have Heart" Award by the New York Chapter of the BBWAA...received the 2001 Thurman Munson Award for his baseball accomplishments and philanthropic work in New York.
- In the fall of 2000, initiated the Jorge Posada Foundation, part of the Giving Back Fund family of charities...proceeds support families of children who suffer from craniosynostosis and provide athletic programs for children in New York City and Puerto Rico...held the Foundation's third annual Family Day in San Juan, Puerto Rico, in July 2008...the event included games, rides, food and live entertainment...held the foundation's Annual Heroes for Hope Gala in June 2008...hosted the second annual BaseBowl charity event in Puerto Rico in January 2009, raising funds for the foundation.
- Was honored at the first annual Puerto Rican Yankees Festival in 2007 at the Puerto Rican Sports Museum in Guaynabo...the festival was established to raise money for underprivileged children in Puerto Rico...Jorge Posada, Sr. presented his son with a plaque that commemorated the thirty Puerto Ricans who have played for the Yankees during the team's history...wife, Laura, received the 2007 "Commitment to Family" Award from the Boys and Girls Town of New York, and was honored as an "Inspiring Woman" by *Siempre Mujer* in 2008.
- Teamed up with Charity Wines to make "Jorge Cabernet" in 2008 with proceeds going to the Jorge Posada Foundation...the wine, from the Clos LaChance Winery and Estate Vineyard in San Martin, Calif. (Napa Valley), is available across the Tri-State area and retails for $13.
- Was signed by Leon Wurth...uncle, Leo Posada, was an instructor for the Dodgers...father, Jorge, is a scout for the Rockies...was a baseball All-Star in 1988-89 at Colegio Alejandrino High School...also participated in basketball, volleyball and track...in 1991, he received an Associate's degree from Calhoun Community College in Decatur, Ala...at Calhoun, he was voted best hitter in 1990 and was a co-captain and all-conference selection in 1991...in 2006, was elected to the Alabama Community College Athletic Hall of Fame...inducted into the Hall of Fame at Pfitzner Stadium on 8/25/07, having played there during the 1993 season with Single-A Prince William...became the seventh member of their Hall of Fame, joining Barry Bonds (2004), Bernie Williams (2004), Andy Pettitte (2004), Art Silber (2005), Bobby Bonilla (2005) and Albert Pujols (2006).

Posada's Career Batting Record

ear	Club	AVG	G	AB	R	H	2B	3B	HR	RBI	SH	SF	HP	BB	SO	SB	CS	E	OBP	SLG
1991	Oneonta	.235	71	217	34	51	5	5	4	33	7	1	4	51	51	6	5	21	.388	.359
1992	Greensboro	.277	101	339	60	94	22	4	12	58	0	3	6	58	87	11	6	11	.389	.472
1993	Prince William	.259	118	410	71	106	27	2	17	61	1	6	6	67	90	17	5	15	.366	.459
	Albany	.280	7	25	3	7	0	0	0	0	0	0	0	2	7	0	0	2	.333	.280
1994	Columbus	.240	92	313	46	75	13	3	11	48	4	5	1	32	81	5	5	11	.308	.406
1995	Columbus	.255	108	368	60	94	32	5	8	51	6	3	1	54	101	4	4	4	.350	.435
	YANKEES	.000	1	0	0	0	0	0	0	0	0	0	0	0	0	0	0	0	.000	.000
1996	Columbus	.271	106	354	76	96	22	6	11	62	1	3	3	79	86	3	3	10	.405	.460
	YANKEES	.071	8	14	1	1	0	0	0	0	0	0	0	1	6	0	0	0	.133	.071
1997	YANKEES	.250	60	188	29	47	12	0	6	25	1	2	3	30	33	1	2	3	.359	.410
1998	YANKEES	.268	111	358	56	96	23	0	17	63	0	4	0	47	92	0	1	4	.350	.475
1999	YANKEES	.245	112	379	50	93	19	2	12	57	0	2	3	53	91	1	0	5	.341	.401
2000	YANKEES	.287	151	505	92	145	35	1	28	86	0	4	8	107	151	2	2	8	.417	.527
2001	YANKEES	.277	138	484	59	134	28	1	22	95	0	5	6	62	132	2	6	11	.363	.475
2002	YANKEES	.268	143	511	79	137	40	1	20	99	0	3	3	81	143	1	0	12	.370	.468
2003	YANKEES	.281	142	481	83	135	24	0	30	101	0	4	10	93	110	2	4	6	.405	.518
2004	YANKEES	.272	137	449	72	122	31	0	21	81	0	1	9	88	92	1	3	9	.400	.481
2005	YANKEES	.262	142	474	67	124	23	0	19	71	0	4	2	66	94	1	0	3	.352	.430
2006	YANKEES	.277	143	465	65	129	27	2	23	93	0	5	11	64	97	3	0	9	.374	.492
2007	YANKEES	.338	144	506	91	171	42	1	20	90	0	3	6	74	98	2	0	5	.426	.543
2008	YANKEES - a, b	.268	51	168	18	45	13	1	3	22	0	1	2	24	38	0	0	1	.364	.411
2009	YANKEES - c	.285	111	383	55	109	25	0	22	81	0	5	2	48	101	1	0	7	.363	.522
Minor League Totals		**.258**	**603**	**2026**	**350**	**523**	**121**	**25**	**63**	**313**	**19**	**21**	**21**	**343**	**503**	**46**	**28**	**74**	**.368**	**.436**
Major League Totals		**.277**	**1594**	**5365**	**817**	**1488**	**342**	**9**	**243**	**964**	**1**	**43**	**65**	**838**	**1278**	**17**	**18**	**83**	**.379**	**.480**

Selected by New York (AL) in the 24th round of the 1990 First-Year Player Draft.

a – Placed on the 15-day disabled list from April 28 – June 3, 2008 with a right shoulder strain.

b – Placed on the 15-day disabled list from July 21 – September 28, 2008 with a right shoulder strain.

c – Placed on the 15-day disabled list from May 5-27, 2009 with a Grade 2 right hamstring strain.

Posada's Division Series Record

Year	Club vs. Opp.	AVG	G	AB	R	H	2B	3B	HR	RBI	SH	SF	HP	BB	SO	SB	CS	E	OBP	SLG
1995	NYY vs. SEA	---	1	0	1	0	0	0	0	0	0	0	0	0	0	0	0	0	---	---
1997	NYY vs. CLE	.000	2	2	0	0	0	0	0	0	0	0	0	0	1	0	0	0	.000	.000
1998	NYY vs. TEX	.000	1	2	1	0	0	0	0	0	0	0	0	1	2	0	0	0	.333	.000
1999	NYY vs. TEX	.250	1	4	0	1	1	0	0	0	0	0	0	0	0	0	0	0	.250	.500
2000	NYY vs. OAK	.235	5	17	2	4	2	0	0	1	0	0	0	3	5	0	0	0	.350	.353
2001	NYY vs. OAK	.444	5	18	3	8	1	0	1	2	0	0	0	2	2	1	0	0	.500	.667
2002	NYY vs. ANA	.235	4	17	2	4	0	0	1	3	0	1	0	0	3	0	0	1	.222	.412
2003	NYY vs. MIN	.176	4	17	1	3	1	0	0	0	0	0	0	0	6	0	0	0	.176	.235
2004	NYY vs. MIN	.222	4	18	2	4	0	0	0	0	0	0	0	0	6	0	0	0	.222	.222
2005	NYY vs. LAA	.231	5	13	3	3	1	0	1	2	0	0	0	6	2	0	0	0	.474	.538
2006	NYY vs. DET	.500	4	14	2	7	1	0	1	2	0	0	0	2	2	0	0	0	.563	.786
2007	NYY vs. CLE	.133	4	15	1	2	1	0	0	0	0	0	0	2	3	0	0	0	.235	.200
2009	NYY vs. MIN	.364	3	11	1	4	0	0	1	2	0	0	0	0	2	0	0	0	.364	.636
Division Series Totals		**.270**	**43**	**148**	**19**	**40**	**8**	**0**	**5**	**12**	**0**	**1**	**0**	**16**	**34**	**1**	**0**	**1**	**.339**	**.426**

Posada's League Championship Series Record

Year	Club vs. Opp.	AVG	G	AB	R	H	2B	3B	HR	RBI	SH	SF	HP	BB	SO	SB	CS	E	OBP	SLG
1998	NYY vs. CLE	.182	5	11	1	2	0	0	1	2	0	0	0	4	2	0	1	0	.400	.455
1999	NYY vs. BOS	.100	3	10	1	1	0	0	1	2	0	0	0	1	2	0	0	1	.182	.400
2000	NYY vs. SEA	.158	6	19	2	3	1	0	0	3	0	0	1	5	5	0	1	0	.360	.211
2001	NYY vs. SEA	.214	5	14	4	3	1	0	0	0	0	0	0	6	7	0	0	0	.450	.286
2003	NYY vs. BOS	.296	7	27	5	8	4	0	1	6	0	0	0	3	4	0	0	0	.367	.556
2004	NYY vs. BOS	.259	7	27	4	7	1	0	0	2	0	1	1	7	1	0	0	0	.417	.296
2009	NYY vs. LAA	.200	6	20	3	4	1	0	1	1	0	0	0	5	5	1	0	0	.360	.400
LCS Totals		**.219**	**39**	**128**	**20**	**28**	**8**	**0**	**4**	**16**	**0**	**1**	**2**	**31**	**26**	**1**	**2**	**1**	**.377**	**.375**

Posada's World Series Record

Year	Club vs. Opp.	AVG	G	AB	R	H	2B	3B	HR	RBI	SH	SF	HP	BB	SO	SB	CS	E	OBP	SLG
1998	NYY vs. SD	.333	3	9	2	3	0	0	1	2	0	0	0	2	2	0	0	0	.455	.667
1999	NYY vs. ATL	.250	2	8	0	2	1	0	0	1	0	0	0	0	3	0	0	0	.250	.375
2000	NYY vs. NYM	.222	5	18	2	4	1	0	0	1	0	0	0	5	4	0	0	0	.391	.278
2001	NYY vs. AZ	.174	7	23	2	4	1	0	1	1	0	0	0	3	8	0	0	1	.269	.348
2003	NYY vs. FLA	.158	6	19	0	3	1	0	0	1	0	0	0	5	7	1	1	0	.333	.211
2009	NYY vs. PHI	.263	6	19	1	5	1	0	0	5	0	1	0	2	7	0	0	1	.318	.316
World Series Totals		**.219**	**29**	**96**	**7**	**21**	**5**	**0**	**2**	**11**	**0**	**1**	**0**	**17**	**31**	**1**	**1**	**2**	**.333**	**.333**
POSTSEASON TOTALS		**.239**	**111**	**372**	**46**	**89**	**21**	**0**	**11**	**39**	**0**	**3**	**2**	**64**	**91**	**3**	**3**	**4**	**.351**	**.384**

Posada's All-Star Game Record

Year	Club, Site	AVG	G	AB	R	H	2B	3B	HR	RBI	SH	SF	HP	BB	SO	SB	CS	E	OBP	SLG
2000	NYY, Atlanta	.000	1	2	0	0	0	0	0	0	0	0	0	0	1	0	0	0	.000	.000
2001	NYY, Seattle	1.000	1	1	0	1	1	0	0	0	0	0	0	0	0	0	0	0	1.000	2.000
2002	NYY, Milwaukee	.000	1	3	0	0	0	0	0	0	0	0	0	0	2	0	0	0	.000	.000
2003	NYY, Chicago (AL)	.000	1	2	0	0	0	0	0	0	0	0	0	0	2	0	0	0	.000	.000
2007	NYY, San Francisco	.333	1	3	0	1	1	0	0	0	0	0	0	0	0	0	0	0	.333	.333
All-Star Game Totals		**.182**	**5**	**11**	**0**	**2**	**2**	**0**	**0**	**0**	**0**	**0**	**0**	**0**	**5**	**0**	**0**	**0**	**.182**	**.364**

Posada's Career Fielding Record

Position	PCT	G	PO	A	E	TC	PB
Catcher	.992	1490	9447	672	82	10201	134
First Base	.992	27	117	12	1	130	---

Posada's Career Home Run Chart

MULTI-HOMER GAMES: 16. **TWO-HOMER GAMES:** 16, last 9/1/09 at Baltimore. **GRAND SLAMS:** 7, last on 7/26/04 at Toronto (Sean Douglass). **PINCH-HIT HR:** 4, last on 9/9/09 vs. Tampa Bay (Grant Balfour). **INSIDE-THE-PARK HR:** None. **WALK-OFF HR:** 2, last on 5/16/06 vs. Texas (Akinori Otsuka). **LEADOFF HR:** None.

Most Seasons with Same Team, Active Players

1. Chipper Jones .... Atlanta 17 (1993-2009)
2. **DEREK JETER .... YANKEES .... 15 (1995-2009)**
   JORGE POSADA .... YANKEES 15 (1995-2009)
   MARIANO RIVERA .... YANKEES 15 (1995-2009)

Edwar Ramirez

36

Right-handed Pitcher
6-3 • 167 •B/T: Right/Right
Opening Day Age: 29

Birthdate
March 28, 1981

Birthplace
El Cerdado, D.R.

Resides
El Cercado, D.R.

M.L. Service
1 year, 130 days

Status

- Signed by the Yankees as a free agent on July 9, 2006...signed through the 2010 season.

2009

- Made 20 relief appearances with the Yankees, posting a 5.73 ERA with no decisions over two stints (4/6-5/19, 9/1-10/4)...opponents batted .281 (25-for-89, 6HR); LH .302 (16-for-53, 3HR), RH .250 (9-for-36, 3HR)...13 of his 20 appearances were scoreless...stranded 14-of-21 inherited runners (66.7%)...retired 11-of-20 first batters faced (55.0%)...appeared in consecutive games once and three straight games once (5/4-6)...nine of his 15R allowed came via the home run.
- Appeared on his first career Opening Day roster...made season debut in 4/8 loss at Baltimore, tossing 1.1 scoreless IP...recorded his 100th career strikeout (Shin-Soo Choo) in fourth inning of 4/18 loss vs. Cleveland...tossed a career-high 3.1IP in 5/9 loss at Baltimore (4H, 3ER, 2K, 2HR).
- Was optioned to Triple-A Scranton/Wilkes-Barre on 5/19 when Brian Bruney was reinstated from the 15-day disabled list...recalled from Scranton/WB on 9/1 and held opponents scoreless in three of his five September outings.
- In 29 overall relief appearances with Scranton/WB, was 1-5 with four saves and a 3.18 ERA (51.0IP, 39H, 18ER, 16BB, 62K, 3HR)...pitched at least 2.0IP in 16 of his outings...following the All-Star break, went 1-1 with one save and a 1.57 ERA (23.0IP, 4ER) in 14 appearances with only 6BB and 26K.
- Made three regular season appearances with Licey in the Dominican Winter League following the season, allowing 1ER in 2.2IP with no decisions...also made three relief appearance in the playoffs allowing 3ER in 2.1IP with 4K and no walks.

Single-Game Highs and Streaks

IP (relief)
3.1 - at BAL, 5/9/09
Hits
4 - 4 times
Last: at BAL, 5/9/09
Runs
5 - at LAA, 8/9/08
BB
4 - vs. TB, 7/20/07
SO
5 - at TOR, 9/11/07
HR
2 - 4 times
Last: at BAL, 5/9/09
Winning Streak
3g - 5/25-8/3/08
Losing Streak
1g - 2 times Last: 8/9/08

2008

- Was 5-1 with one save and a 3.90 ERA in a career-high 55 relief appearances over two stints with the Yankees (4/18-19; 4/29-9/28)...opponents batted .215 (44-for-205, 7HR); LH .229 (27-for-118, 4HR), RH .195 (17-for-87, 3HR)...retired 40-of-54 first batters faced (72.2%)...stranded 26-of-40 inherited runners (65.0%)...appeared in consecutive games 12 times.
- Averaged 10.25 K/9.0IP (63K, 55.1IP), leading Yankees relievers and ranking seventh among AL relievers...posted a 1.33 ERA (27.0IP, 4ER) when working on one or no days' rest...owned a 6.35 ERA (28.1IP, 20ER) when receiving two or more days of rest.
- Made two appearances in which he allowed 4ER without retiring a batter each time (6/3 vs. Toronto and 8/9 at Los Angeles-AL)...in his 53 other appearances, combined for a 2.60 ERA (55.1IP, 16ER)...pitched to a 59.40 ERA (1.2IP, 11ER) against the Angels and a 2.18 ERA (53.2IP, 13ER) against all other Major League teams.
- Was recalled from Triple-A Scranton/Wilkes-Barre on 4/18 and made his first appearance of the season that night at Baltimore, tossing 2.1 scoreless innings in the Yankees' loss...was optioned back the next day and then recalled a second time on 4/29.

- Did not allow a run in his first 21 relief appearances of the season with the Yankees and Triple-A Scranton/Wilkes-Barre...in his first 13 appearances with the Yankees, allowed 10H and 6BB in 14.2IP (15K)...did not allow a run in eight appearances with Scranton/WB, going 1-0 and holding opponents to a .069 average (2-for-29) over 9.0IP (1BB, 1HB, 13K).
- Allowed his first run of the season (minors and Majors) in 5/31 win at Minnesota, giving up a seventh-inning solo home run to record his first blown save of the season.
- Was ejected by home plate umpire Mark Wegner from 7/30 win vs. Baltimore after entering the game and throwing one pitch to Kevin Millar...Wegner deemed him intentionally throwing at the batter...marked his first career ejection...appealed a three-game suspension given by Major League Baseball on 7/31 and served a reduced two-game suspension from 9/15-16.
- Had 12 consecutive scoreless outings from 6/29-7/30, going 1-0 and allowing just 1H (13.1IP, 3BB, 17K)...lowered his ERA from 3.60 to 2.35...did not allow a run in 10 July appearances (11.1IP)...held opponents hitless for 37 consecutive at-bats from 7/3-8/3...according to the *Elias Sports Bureau*, marked the longest such stretch by a Yankee since Randy Johnson in 2005 (39AB).
- Had hitless streak snapped on 8/3 vs. Los Angeles (AL)...struck out first two batters faced in the eighth before allowing a Chone Figgins single...two batters later (2BB), surrendered a Mark Teixeira grand slam that tied the game...still came away with the win after the Yankees scored six runs in the bottom of the frame...according to *Elias*, became first Yankee in franchise history to be credited with a win while being charged with at least four runs with no more than 1.0IP...was the first Major Leaguer to win in those circumstances since Boston's Keith Foulke in 2005.
- Recorded his only loss of the season on 8/9 at Los Angeles (AL), allowing a career-high 5R (4ER) and 4H (1HR) without retiring any of the five batters he faced in the eighth...allowed just 1ER over his next 10 outings from 8/11-30 (8.1IP).
- Began year at Scranton/Wilkes-Barre and did not allow a run in six relief appearances before being recalled the first time (7.0IP, 2H, 1HB, 1BB, 11K)...opponents were batting .087 (2-for-23)...ranked third among relief pitchers in the International League with a 14.14K/9.0IP ratio at the time of his initial call-up...did not allow a run in eight overall appearances with SWB in 2008 (9.0IP).

2007

- Was 1-1 with one save and an 8.14 ERA in 21 relief appearances over two stints with the Yankees (7/1-21; 8/15-9/30)...opponents batted .286 (24-for-84, 6HR); LH .342 (13-for-38, 3HR), RH .239 (11-for-46, 3HR)...retired 12-of-20 first batters faced (60.0%) and prevented 10-of-19 inherited runners from scoring (53.6%).
- Struck out 31 batters in 21.0IP, leading all Major League pitchers with a ratio of 13.3 strikeouts/9.0IP (min. 20 appearances).
- Had contract purchased from Triple-A Scranton/Wilkes-Barre on 7/1...made Major League debut in 7/3 win vs. Minnesota, striking out the side in a perfect ninth inning (1.0IP, 3K)...according to the *Elias Sports Bureau*, became the first Yankee to strike out each of the first three batters faced in his first Major League inning since Stan Bahnsen on 9/9/66 vs. Boston (struck out Joe Foy, Carl Yastrzemski and Tony Conigliaro).
- Earned his first Major League win on 7/6 vs. Los Angeles (AL), allowing 2H and 1ER in 1.1IP (1BB, 1K)...suffered his first career blown save in the game (allowed game-tying run to score in the sixth).
- Recorded his first Major League save in 8/19 win vs. Detroit, tossing 2.0 perfect innings (3K)...struck out a career-high five batters in 9/11 win at Toronto, tossing 2.0 scoreless innings (2H).
- Was on the Yankees' Division Series roster vs. Cleveland but did not make an appearance.
- Was 4-0 with seven saves and a 0.70 ERA in 34 combined minor league relief appearances at Double-A Trenton and Scranton/WB (26H, 5ER, 22BB)...struck out 102 batters in 56.2IP and allowed only 1HR, averaging a minor league-best 16.2K/9.0IP (min: 50.0IP)...tabbed by *Baseball America* as the top relief pitcher on their All-Minor League All-Star team.
- Began the season with Trenton and tossed 8.2 shutout innings of one-hit ball over his first five appearances of the season from 4/7-24...was 1-0 with six saves and a 0.90 ERA in 25 relief appearances over two stints for Scranton/WB, compiling a 19.1-inning scoreless stretch with 38K over 13 outings from 6/8-8/2 (7H, 1BB).
- Pitched with the Tigres del Licey in the Dominican Winter League, appearing in three games without recording a decision (6.75 ERA).
- Following the season, was tabbed by *Baseball America* as having the organization's "Best Changeup".

2006

- Began the season in the Angels organization, but was released on 3/31...made 25 appearances with Edinburg of the Independent United League, leading the league with 16 saves while posting a 1-1 record and a 1.07 ERA...recorded 46 strikeouts in 25.1IP...ranked second in the league with 24 games finished.

EDWAR RAMIREZ

- Had his contract purchased by the Yankees on 7/9 and was added to the Single-A Tampa roster…in 19 relief appearances for Tampa, went 4-1 with a 1.17 ERA and 47 strikeouts in 30.2 IP…limited opponents to a .133 (14-for-105) batting average with 0HR and held right-handers to just .118 (8-for-68)…did not allow an earned run over his final 11 appearances, striking out 29 and walking only two in 18.1IP…pitched with Tigres del Licey in the Dominican Winter League, allowing 11ER in 21.2IP (4.57 ERA) without a decision.

2005

- Posted a 2-2 record and 1.45 ERA in 43 relief appearances with Pensacola of the Independent Central League…recorded 93 strikeouts while walking only 15 batters in 62.0IP…had his contract purchased by the Angels on 9/1 and made one appearance for Triple-A Salt Lake (2.0IP, 0ER).

2004

- Did not play during the season after being released by the Angels on 3/31.

2003

- Combined to post a 1-3 record with a 5.40 ERA in 10 games (five starts) with Single-A Rancho Cucamonga and Single-A Cedar Rapids in the Angels organization…began the season with Rancho and was 0-2 with an 8.10 ERA in four starts…was transferred to Cedar Rapids and made six appearances from 8/12-9/1, going 1-1 with a 3.32 ERA.

2002

- Made professional debut with the Angels' rookie-league Arizona club, posting a 2-5 record with a 3.69 ERA in 13 games (7GS) and 45K in 46.1IP…made two appearances with Provo and allowed 10ER in 9.2IP…was originally signed by the Angels as a non-drafted free agent on 2/6/01.

Personal

- Signed by Leo Perez (Angels)...attended Prof. Luis Guarionex Landestoy High School in the Dominican Republic…participated in the Yankees' donation of $25,000 in cash, food and supplies to aid in hurricane relief in the Dominican Republic in November 2007…was joined by Yankees Latin prospects and staff to distribute an additional $10,000 donation in food and supplies to help rebuild a local school ravaged by the storm in Ramirez' hometown…is a regular participant in Yankees players visits to local Bronx hospitals and schools…joins teammates at Jordan's Barber Shop in the Bronx on 7/8/08, helping to give haircuts to underprivileged kids.

Ramirez' Career Pitching Record

YEAR	CLUB	W	L	ERA	G	GS	CG	SHO	SV	IP	H	R	ER	HR	HB	BB	SO	WP	BK
2002	Angels	2	5	3.69	13	7	0	0	0	46.1	47	22	19	1	4	13	45	1	0
	Provo	1	0	9.31	2	1	0	0	0	9.2	14	10	10	0	3	4	4	2	0
2003	Rancho Cuca	0	2	8.1	4	4	0	0	0	16.2	29	16	15	5	0	7	9	1	0
	Cedar Rapids	1	1	3.32	6	1	0	0	0	19.0	17	7	7	2	1	8	15	1	0
2004								Did Not Pitch											
2005	Pensacola (IND)	2	2	1.45	43	0	0	0	11	62.0	37	12	10	4	8	15	93	4	1
	Salt Lake - a	0	0	0.00	1	0	0	0	0	2.0	0	0	0	0	0	0	2	0	0
2006	Edinburg (IND)	1	1	1.07	25	0	0	0	16	25.1	14	6	3	2	1	10	46	4	0
	Tampa - b	4	1	1.17	19	0	0	0	3	30.2	14	4	4	0	1	6	47	2	0
2007	Trenton	3	0	0.54	9	0	0	0	1	16.2	6	1	1	1	1	8	33	1	0
	Scranton/WB	1	0	0.90	25	0	0	0	6	40.0	20	4	4	0	3	14	69	3	1
	YANKEES	1	1	8.14	21	0	0	0	1	21.0	24	19	19	6	3	14	31	4	0
2008	Scranton/WB	1	0	0.00	8	0	0	0	0	9.0	2	0	0	0	1	1	13	1	0
	YANKEES	5	1	3.90	55	0	0	0	1	55.1	44	25	24	7	3	24	63	3	0
2009	Scranton/WB	1	5	3.18	29	0	0	0	4	51.0	39	19	18	3	0	16	62	8	0
	YANKEES	0	0	5.73	20	0	0	0	0	22.0	25	15	14	6	0	18	22	1	0
Minor League Totals		**14**	**14**	**2.91**	**116**	**13**	**0**	**0**	**14**	**241.0**	**188**	**83**	**78**	**12**	**14**	**77**	**299**	**20**	**1**
Major League Totals		**6**	**2**	**5.22**	**96**	**0**	**0**	**0**	**2**	**98.1**	**93**	**59**	**57**	**19**	**6**	**56**	**116**	**8**	**0**

Signed by Los Angeles-AL as a non-drafted free agent on February 6, 2001.

Minor League totals do not include Independent League statistics

a - Signed by Los Angeles-AL as a free agent on September 1, 2005.
b - Signed by the Yankees as a free agent on July 9, 2006.

Ramirez' Regular Season Batting Record

Year	Team	AVG	G	AB	R	H	2B	3B	HR	RBI	SH	SF	HP	BB	SO	SB	CS
2009					Did Not Bat												
Major League Totals		-	**96**	-	-	-	-	-	-	-	-	-	-	-	-	-	-

Ramirez' Fielding Record

Position	PCT	G	PO	A	E	TC
Pitcher	1.000	96	7	7	0	14

Mariano Rivera

42
Right-handed Pitcher
6-2 • 185 • B/T: Right/Right
Opening Day Age: 40

Birthdate
November 29, 1969

Birthplace
Panama City, Panama

Resides
La Chorrera, Panama

M.L. Service
14 years, 105 days

Career Highlights

A.L. All-Star Team
- 1997, 1999, 2000, 2001, 2002, 2004, 2005, 2006, 2008, 2009

League Championship Series MVP
- 2003

World Series MVP
- 1999

***Sporting News* Pro Athlete of the Year**
- 2009

***Sporting News* A.L. Reliver of the Year**
- 1997, 1999, 2009

A.L. Rolaids Relief Man Award
- 1999, 2001, 2004, 2005, 2006, 2009

MLB Delivery Man of the Year
- 2005, 2006, 2009

Status

- Signed as a non-drafted free agent on February 17, 1990...signed a three-year contract on December 17, 2007 that extends through the 2010 season.

Career Notes

- Owns 526 career saves, the most in AL history and second-most all time behind Trevor Hoffman (591)...has an 89.5% career conversion rate in 588 save opportunities.
- Has reached the 40-save mark seven times in his career, second-most all time behind Trevor Hoffman (nine)...saved at least 35 games in a season 10 times in his career, ranking second all time to Hoffman's 12...has reached the 30-save plateau 12 times in his career, including each of his last seven seasons...according to the *Elias Sports Bureau*, is the fourth player in Major League history to register at least 30 saves in seven straight seasons, joining Hoffman (eight, 1995-2002), Robb Nen (1996-2002) and Troy Percival (1998-2004)...has recorded at least 25 saves in 13 consecutive seasons (since 1997) tying Lee Smith (13 straight seasons 1983-95) for the longest such streak since saves became an official statistic in 1969.
- Since earned runs became an official statistic in the National League (in 1912) and American League (in 1913), his 2.25 career ERA is the second-lowest all time among pitchers with at least 1,000.0IP behind only Eddie Cicotte (2.20), according to the *Elias Sports Bureau*...has recorded a sub-2.00 ERA nine times in his career.
- Over the last 10 years (2000-09) leads the Majors with 397 saves and ranks third with 651 appearances...over the last five years, (2005-09) has 190 saves in 204 chances, ranking first in the Majors in save percentage (93.1) and fourth in saves.
- Has made 60 appearances 12 times in his career, tied with four other pitchers for the second-most such seasons all time behind Mike Stanton (13).
- Has the most saves in Yankees franchise history...his 917 appearances are the most in club history (395 more than second-place Dave Righetti's 522) and rank 20th on Baseball's all-time list...ranks 11th in club history with 1,006K...owns eight of the 10 highest single-season save totals in franchise history (1. 53 in 2004; 2. 50 in 2001; 4. 45 in 1999; 5. 44 in 2009; T6. 43 in 1997 and 2005; 9. 40 in 2003; 10. 39 in 2008)...Dave Righetti's 46 saves in 1986 ranks third and John Wetteland's 43 saves in 1996 is tied for sixth.
- Along with Derek Jeter and Jorge Posada, are the first trio of teammates ever to play for the Yankees in each of 15 straight seasons (1995-2009)...Bill Dickey, Lefty Gomez and Red Ruffing (1930-42) and Whitey Ford, Elston Howard and Mickey Mantle (1955-67) played together with the Yankees for 13 straight seasons...Jeter, Posada and Rivera became the first trio of players in the Majors to play for the same team in 15 straight seasons since Jim Gantner, Paul Molitor and Robin Yount (15 years, 1978-92 with Milwaukee). Credit: *Elias Sports Bureau*.
- Owns 114 career saves when recording more than three outs and 11 saves when tossing at least 2.0 innings.

Single-Game Highs and Streaks

Low-hit CG
NA
IP (start)
8.0 – at CWS, 7/4/95
IP (relief)
5.1 – at SEA, 8/25/95
Hits
8 – at CAL, 5/23/95
Runs (start)
7 – vs. OAK, 6/6/95
Runs (relief)
6 – at CLE, 7/14/02
BB
4 – 2 times
Last: at SEA, 8/23/97
SO
11 – at CWS, 7/4/95
HR
2 - 4 times
Last: vs. TB, 5/7/09
Winning Streak
5g – 3 times
Last: 5/28-7/25/03
Losing Streak
3g – 2 times
Last: 6/3-7/14/02
Consecutive Saves
36 - 4/30-9/14/09

MARIANO RIVERA

- According to the *Elias Sports Bureau*, has converted 113-of-118 (95.8%) save opportunities since blowing his first two saves of the 2007 season, marking the best conversion rate in the Majors over that span (since 4/21/07)...has converted each of his last 47 save opportunities at home (last blown save at home came on 8/13/07 vs. Baltimore)...is tied with John Smoltz (6/3/02-4/8/04) for the third-longest such streak all time (Eric Gagne-51, Trevor Hoffman-49).
- Is the all-time leader in Interleague saves with 59...since blowing a save on 7/14/01 at Florida, has converted 34 of his last 35 save opportunities in Interleague play, including each of his last 15 (credit: *Elias*).
- Recorded his 1,000th strikeout on 9/18/09 at Seattle, at which time he had walked just 255 batters in his career...according to *Elias*, only three pitchers since 1900 (Shane Reynolds-233; Ben Sheets-247; and Billy Wagner-255) had as many or fewer walks at the time of their 1,000th strikeout.
- Has been selected to 10 All-Star teams, joining teammate Derek Jeter as the only players to be named to the All-Star team with their current team at least 10 times, according to *Elias Sports Bureau*...is tied for the fourth-most All-Star selections by a pitcher all time.
- According to the *Elias Sports Bureau*, his 230 saves at the original Yankee Stadium are the most by any one pitcher in any one ballpark...saved his final 23 chances at the Stadium, including all 20 in 2008 in its final season.
- Has 39 career postseason saves—including 11 in the World Series—both Major League records...his 24 World Series appearances are the most all time...owns a 0.74 ERA (133.1IP, 11ER) in 88 postseason games, the lowest ERA all-time (min. 30.0IP) and the most postseason appearances for any pitcher in Major League history...owns 14 career 2.0-inning saves in the postseason.

LOWEST ERAs ALL-TIME, MIN. 1000.0IP (Since becoming an official statistic in NL-1912 and AL-1913 / credit: *Elias*)

1.	Eddie Cicotte	2.20
2.	**MARIANO RIVERA**	**2.25**
3.	Jim Scott	2.26
4.	Babe Ruth	2.28

ALL-TIME SAVES LEADERS

1.	Trevor Hoffman	591
2.	**MARIANO RIVERA**	**526**
3.	Lee Smith	478
4.	John Franco	424
5.	Dennis Eckersley	390

MOST SAVES, LAST 10 YEARS

1.	**MARIANO RIVERA**	**397**
2.	Trevor Hoffman	363
3.	Jason Isringhausen	284
	Billy Wagner	284
5.	Francisco Cordero	250

BEST CAREER SAVE PERCENTAGE, Since 1969 (min. 200 save opps.)

1.	Eric Gagne	91.7 (187-for-204)
2.	Joe Nathan	89.5 (247-for-276)
3.	**MARIANO RIVERA**	**89.5 (526-for-588)**
4.	Trevor Hoffman	89.3 (591-for-662)
5.	Troy Percival	86.3 (358-for-415)

MOST CAREER POSTSEASON SAVES

1.	**MARIANO RIVERA**	**39**
2.	Brad Lidge	16
3.	Dennis Eckersley	15
4.	Jason Isringhausen	11
	Rob Nenn	11

MOST GAMES PITCHED, ACTIVE PLAYERS

1.	Trevor Hoffman	985
2.	David Weathers	964
3.	**MARIANO RIVERA**	**917**
4.	Eddie Guardado	908
5.	Tom Gordon	890

2009

- Was 3-3 with a 1.76 ERA and 44 saves in 66 relief appearances for the Yankees...ranked second in the Majors with a 95.7% (44-for-46) save percentage and third in saves...placed fifth in the American League with 55 games finished...tabbed as *Sporting News* "Pro Athlete of the Year," becoming the second Yankees pitcher to receive the honor (also Ron Guidry in 1978)...also earned the MLB "Delivery Man of the Year" Award, "Closer of the Year" by MLB.com and *Sporting News* "Reliever of the Year"...named co-winner of the 2009 "Rolaids Relief Man" Award, joining Dan Quisenberry (1980, '82-85) as the only five-time winners of the award...received four votes for AL MVP (17 points).
- Made appearances in consecutive games 14 times, three-straight games twice (6/28-7/1; 7/17-19) and four straight games twice (4/19-24 and 6/4-8)...recorded saves in two consecutive games 10 times, on two consecutive days 10 times, in three straight games twice and three straight "days" once (7/17-19 at Detroit)...recorded seven saves of more than 1.0IP, including a season-high 2.0IP in 5/16 win vs. Minnesota...retired 47-of-66 first batters faced (71.2%)...prevented 15-of-20 inherited runners from scoring (75.0%)...opponents batted .197 (48-for-244, 7HR); LH .182 (22-for-121, 3HR), RH .211 (26-for-123, 4HR).
- In his final 40 appearances of the season (from 6/16), went 2-1 with a 0.68 ERA and converted 30-of-31 save opportunities (39.2IP, 21H, 3ER, 9BB, 40K, 2HR)...over his first 26 appearances (from 4/9-6/12), went 1-2 with a 3.38 ERA while going 14-of-15 in save opportunities (26.2IP, 27H, 10ER, 3BB, 32K, 5HR).
- Converted a career-high 36 straight save opportunities from 4/30-9/14...went 2-2 with a 1.44 ERA over the stretch (50.0IP, 30H, 9R, 8ER, 11BB, 53K, 4HR), allowing just 2ER in save situations.
- Allowed 7HR, his most in a single season since a career-high 11 in 1995 (his rookie season)...surrendered 5HR over his first 17G (72 opp. AB) through 5/20, then allowed just 2HR over his final 49 appearances (172 opp. AB).
- Was named to his 10th All-Star team...earned the save in the American League win in St. Louis on 7/14, tossing a perfect ninth inning (1.0IP, 1K)...was his fourth career All-Star save, surpassing Dennis Eckersley for most all time.
- Made his 14th Opening Day roster...in 4/17 win vs. Cleveland, tossed a scoreless ninth inning to earn the first save in Yankee Stadium history (1.0IP, 2H, 2K).

- Allowed back-to-back solo-HR in the ninth (Carl Crawford and Evan Longoria) to suffer the loss (0.2IP, 2H, 2ER, 1K) on 5/7 vs. Tampa Bay...surrendered consecutive home runs for the first time in his career, and allowed two HR in an appearance for only the fourth time in his career (first since 7/18/98 at Toronto—Mike Stanley and Ed Sprague).
- Issued his first walk of the season in 5/14 win at Toronto in his 13th appearance of the season...was his first walk since 8/24/08 at Baltimore, a span of 23.2IP.
- In 5/29 win at Cleveland, tossed a scoreless ninth for his 10th save (1.0IP, 1H, 2K)...was his 58th save in a game in which Andy Pettitte was the winning pitcher, surpassing Bob Welch and Dennis Eckersley (57) for the highest total for any pair of pitchers since saves became an official statistic in 1969 (credit: *Elias*).

MOST WIN-SAVE COMBINATIONS, ALL-TIME

1.	ANDY PETTITTE/**MARIANO RIVERA (NYY)**	63
2.	Bob Welch/Dennis Eckersley (OAK)	57
3.	Mike Mussina/**MARIANO RIVERA (NYY)**	49
4.	Dave Stewart/Dennis Eckersley (OAK)	43
T5.	Jimmy Key/ Tom Henke (TOR)	37
	Kevin Tapani/Rick Aguilera (MIN)	37

- Did not allow a run over 21 straight appearances from 6/16-8/9, compiling a 22.1-inning scoreless stretch dating back to the ninth inning on 6/12...according to the *Elias Sports Bureau*, was the fourth-longest scoreless stretch of his career (behind 30.2IP in 1999, 26.0IP in 1996 and 23.0IP in 2005)...did not allow a run in a save situation over 25 save chances from 5/20-8/9, a 25.1-inning scoreless span.
- In 6/24 win at Atlanta, struck out all four batters faced to earn his 16th save (1.1IP)...was the first time in his career he faced at least four batters and retired each of them via strikeout...marked the fourth time since the start of the 1997 season he struck out four-or-more hitters in a game (all 4K: 7/9/08 vs. Tampa Bay; 5/20/06 at the Mets; 8/19/99 vs. Kansas City)...also made second career regular season plate appearance in the game, lining out to CF in the ninth.
- Earned his 500th career save (18th of the season) in 6/28 win at the Mets, tossing 1.1 scoreless innings (1H, 2K)...also recorded his first career RBI with a bases-loaded walk off Francisco Rodriguez in the ninth inning...according to *Elias*, was the first AL pitcher to record both a save and RBI in the same game since Detroit's Chad Durbin at Atlanta on 6/25/07.
- Was named the AL "co-Player of the Week" for the period ending 6/28...was his second career weekly award (also 6/9/08).
- On 6/30 vs. Seattle, threw out the ceremonial first pitch in recognition of earning his 500th career save and tossed a perfect ninth for his 19th save (1.0IP, 1K).

MARIANO RIVERA SAVES BREAKDOWN

Category	2009	Career
0.1IP	2	21 (last, 7/22/09 vs. Baltimore)
0.2IP	1	13 (last, 8/31/09 at Baltimore)
1.0IP	34	378 (last, 9/27/09 vs. Boston)
1.1IP	7	69 (last, 8/4/09 at Toronto)
1.2IP	0	34 (last, 8/29/08 vs. Toronto)
2.0IP	0	10 (last, 7/16/06 vs. Chicago-AL)
2.1IP	0	1 (8/23/96 vs. Oakland)
Three consecutive games		28 times (last 7/17-19/09)
Four consecutive games		2 times (6/1-4/04; 6/23-27/97)
Three consecutive days		21 times (last 7/17-19/09)
Four consecutive days		1 time (6/1-4/04)

- Was named the winner of the "Major League Baseball Delivery Man of the Month" Award for July for the second time in his career (also April 2008)...recorded a Major League-best 10 saves during the month, successfully converting each of his save opportunities without allowing a run...marked just the second time in his career he earned at least 10 saves in a single month without allowing a run (also August 1999).
- Made his 900th Major League appearance in 8/14 win at Seattle, tossing a perfect ninth (1.0IP) for his 34th save...became the 22nd Major Leaguer to reach the milestone.
- Made his 907th career appearance in 9/7 Game 1 win vs. Tampa Bay, surpassing Cy Young for sole possession of 20th place on Baseball's all-time games pitched list.
- Allowed a two-run "walk-off" home run to Ichiro Suzuki with two outs in the bottom of the ninth on 9/19 at Seattle...marked just the fifth "walk-off" homer allowed by Rivera in his career (also Cleveland's Bill Selby-7/14/02, Boston's Bill Mueller-7/24/04, Toronto's Vernon Wells-7/20/06 and Oakland's Marco Scutaro-4/15/07)...was just the second time Rivera allowed a game-ending homer to a team after they were down to their final out with no one on base (also Scutaro)...snapped a career-high streak of 36 straight converted save chances...his strikeout of Mike Carp in the ninth was the 1,000th K of his career.
- Was a part of his fifth World Championship team, making 12 postseason appearances in 2009, recording five saves (in five opportunities) and allowing just 1ER in 16.0IP (0.56 ERA)...six of the outings were more than 1.0 inning, including two 2.0-inning saves (Game 6 of ALCS and Game 2 of WS)...was on the mound for the clinching game in each of the three rounds for the fourth time in his career...made his 23rd career World Series appearance in Game 4 on 11/1 at Philadelphia, surpassing Whitey Ford (22) for most all time...with two World Series saves, became the second-oldest pitcher to earn a save in a World Series game behind Baltimore's Dick Hall (age 40 in 1971)...tossed a World Series career-high 41 pitches in Game 6 on 11/4 at Yankee Stadium...has been the Yankees final pitcher in each of their last four World Series wins (1998, '99, 2000 and '09)...donated his postseason cap to the Baseball Hall of Fame.

2008

- Was 6-5 with 39 saves (in 40 chances) and a 1.40 ERA in a team-high 64 appearances with the Yankees...were his most wins and saves and his lowest ERA since 2005 (7, 43, 1.38)...established a career high with a 97.5% save percentage, the highest mark by an AL closer since Boston's Tom Gordon in 1998 (97.9%, 46-for-47)...finished fifth in AL Cy Young Award voting.
- Opponents batted .165 (41-for-249, 4HR); LH .147 (19-for-129, 2HR), RH .183 (22-for-120, 2HR)...was the lowest opponents average among qualifying AL relievers, trailing only the Cubs' Carlos Marmol (.135) among all Major League relievers...stranded 16-of-20 inherited runners (80.0%)...retired 47-of-64 first batters faced (73.4%)...pitched consecutive games nine times, three straight three times and four straight three times...appeared in four straight games four times combined over his previous four years (2004-07)...saved consecutive games five times and earned the save in three straight games three times.
- Had the Majors' lowest ERA among all pitchers with at least 70.0IP...ranked third among AL relievers in strikeouts and was tied with Joe Nathan for fifth in the AL in saves.

- According to the *Elias Sports Bureau*, Rivera's 12.83-to-1 strikeouts-to-walks ratio (77K, 6BB) was the third highest in modern Major League history (min. 50.0IP), behind Dennis Eckersley's 1989 (18.33-to-1) and 1990 (18.25-for-1) campaigns.
- Converted his first 28 save opportunities to start the season, marking a career best (converted first 12 chances in 2004)...was not charged with a run in any of his first 22 save opportunities, becoming the first pitcher since 1975 (when the current save rules came into effect) to accomplish the feat (credit: *Elias*).

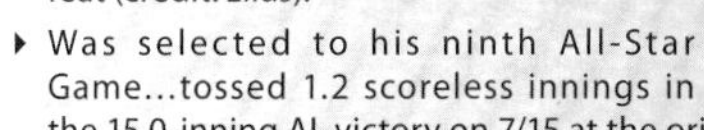

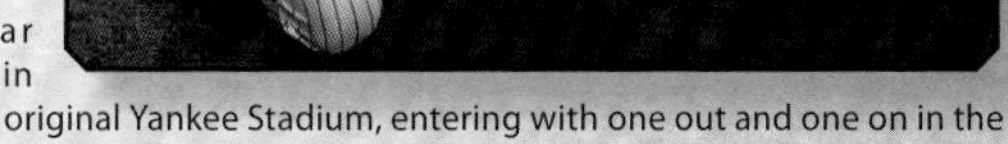

- Was selected to his ninth All-Star Game...tossed 1.2 scoreless innings in the 15.0-inning AL victory on 7/15 at the original Yankee Stadium, entering with one out and one on in the ninth...donated his jersey as well as dirt from the mound to the Baseball Hall of Fame.
- Recorded his second career Opening Day save—the most in franchise history—tossing a perfect ninth inning (1.0IP, 1K) in 4/1 win vs. Toronto...made his 13th career Opening Day roster...did not allow a run or walk in his first 14 appearances (4/1-5/10), recording 10 saves and striking out 12 batters in 15.0IP (6H)...was the longest scoreless streak to begin a season in his career...named the April winner of the "DHL Presents the Major League Baseball Delivery Man of the Month" Award.
- On 5/13 at Tampa Bay, in his 15th appearance of the year, allowed "walk-off" RBI single in the 11th to suffer the loss (1.0IP, 3H, 1ER, 1K)...was his first run allowed of the season, marking the latest into a season he had gone without allowing a run...previous best was in 1998 when he first allowed a run in his 11th appearance on 5/14/98 vs. Texas.
- Was named AL "Player of the Week" for the period ending 6/1, earning his first career weekly award...in 6/7 win vs. Kansas City, recorded his second win of the season despite allowing a home run to David DeJesus, his first batter faced, on his first pitch (1.0IP, 1H, 1ER, 1K, 1HR)...was his first HR allowed since 8/15/07 vs. Baltimore (Aubrey Huff) and marked the first time he had allowed a HR on his first pitch after entering a game since 8/23/97 at Seattle to Roberto Kelly (credit: *Elias*).
- Allowed his first run of the season in a save opportunity in 7/5 win vs. Boston...allowed 1ER and loaded the bases with no outs (2HP) before retiring the final three batters of the game to earn his 23rd save...according to the *Elias Sports Bureau*, it was the first time Rivera escaped a bases-full-none-out jam with the tying run on third in the game's final inning.
- In 7/29 loss vs. Baltimore, pitched the ninth to surpass the 1000.0IP plateau...on 8/1 at Los Angeles-AL, allowed one-out ninth-inning "walk-off" RBI-single to Chone Figgins on his first and only pitch of the game as the Angels won 1-0...was the second time he threw just one pitch (also 8/7/05 at Toronto – earned the save).
- In 8/12 win at Minnesota, allowed game-tying three-run HR to Delmon Young in the eighth for his first and only blown save of the season (1.2IP, 2H, 1ER)...in 8/15 loss vs. Kansas City, allowed the go-ahead run to score on a wild pitch...was just the second time in his career he allowed a run on a wild pitch (also 6/24/00 at Chicago-AL) and his first time allowing the go-ahead run on a WP (credit: *Elias*).
- Saved all three games of the Yankees' series at Baltimore from 8/22-24, marking the sixth time in his career he has saved all of the games in a series of three or more games (previous 6/1-3/04 vs. Baltimore)...was also the 19th time in his career he recorded a save on three or more consecutive days...the only other Yankees pitchers to earn a save in each game of a series (of at least three games) are Dave Righetti (1986), Steve Howe (1994) and John Wetteland (twice in 1996).

- Recorded his 479th career save in 9/15 win vs. Chicago-AL, surpassing Lee Smith (478) for sole possession of second place on Baseball's all-time saves list.
- Threw 1.0 scoreless inning in the final game at Yankee Stadium on 9/21 vs. Baltimore, inducing a Brian Roberts groundout to 1B Cody Ransom with the game's final pitch to secure the Yankees victory.
- Returned to New York during the season's final road trip to undergo an MRI on his shoulder that revealed calcification in the AC joint in his right shoulder.
- Collected his 39th and final save of the season in 9/28 Game 1 win at Boston...tossed 1.1 scoreless innings to save Mike Mussina's 20th win of the season...was the second time he recorded a save in a pitcher's 20th win (also Roger Clemens in 2001).
- Underwent surgery on the AC Joint in his right shoulder on 10/7...procedure was done by Dr. David Altchek at the Hospital for Special Surgery in New York.

2007

- Was 3-4 with a 3.15 ERA and 30 saves in 67 relief appearances for the Yankees...ranked fourth in the American League with 59 games finished and tied for eighth with 30 saves...opponents batted .248 (68-for-274, 4HR); LH .255 (35-for-137, 1HR), RH .241 (33-for-137, 3HR)...converted 30-of-34 save opportunities (88.2%).
- Saved consecutive games five times and earned the save in three consecutive games once, from 7/14-16...made appearances in consecutive games 11 times and three straight games once...recorded 11 saves of more than 1.0IP...tossed a season-high 2.0IP twice...retired 43-of-67 first batters faced (64.2%)...prevented 19-of-26 inherited runners from scoring (73.1%).
- In his final 59 appearances of the season (from 4/28), went 2-2 with a 2.23 ERA and converted 30-of-32 save opportunities (64.2IP, 58H, 16ER, 9BB, 66K)...in his first eight games (4/2-27), went 1-2 with a 12.15 ERA while blowing both of his save opportunities (6.2IP, 10H, 9ER, 3BB, 8K).
- Allowed three-run "walk-off" home run to Marco Scutaro with two strikes and two outs in the ninth inning on 4/15 at Oakland, suffering the loss and blown save...was the first time in his career that he blew a multiple-run lead against a team that was down to its last out with the bases empty (credit: *Elias Sports Bureau*)...according to *Elias*, it was Rivera's first home run allowed on an 0-2 pitch since Marquis Grissom hit a 10th-inning game-winner on 7/14/97 vs. Cleveland...was the fourth "walk-off" home run allowed in his career in the regular season and first since 7/20/06 at Toronto (Vernon Wells)...was also the 14th time that Rivera was on the mound for a "walk-off" loss in a regular season game.
- Blew his second save chance on 4/20 at Boston, allowing 3H and 2ER in 0.2IP (1K)...following the consecutive setbacks, converted 19 consecutive save opportunities from 4/28-8/12, allowing just 3ER in 22.2IP (1.19 ERA) with no walks and 24K.
- Recorded saves in both games of a doubleheader on 5/3 at Texas...according to the *Elias Sports Bureau*, was the fifth time in his career that he has recorded two saves on the same day (in either official doubleheaders or split day/night games), becoming one of only three pitchers in Major League history to accomplish the feat, joining Sparky Lyle and Jose Mesa.
- Notched his fourth save of the season in 5/30 win at Toronto, his first save and save opportunity since 5/3 at Texas (a span of 27 days)...was the longest gap between save opportunities since becoming the Yankees closer in 1997.
- Appeared in three games (no save opportunites) in the Division Series vs. Cleveland, throwing 4.2 scoreless innings with 1BB and 6K.

YANKEES ALL-TIME SAVES

1.	**MARIANO RIVERA**	**526**
2.	Dave Righetti	224
3.	Goose Gossage	151
4.	Sparky Lyle	141

MOST GAMES PITCHED, YANKEES, ALL-TIME

1.	**MARIANO RIVERA**	**917**
2.	Dave Righetti	522
3.	Whitey Ford	498
4.	Mike Stanton	456
5.	Red Ruffing	426

MOST SAVES, SINGLE SEASON (Last 10 seasons, 2000-09)

1.	Francisco Rodriguez-2008-LAA	62
2.	Eric Gagne, 2003-LAD	55
	John Smoltz, 2002-ATL	55
4.	**MARIANO RIVERA, 2004-NYY**	**53**
5.	Eric Gagne, 2002-LAD	52
6.	**MARIANO RIVERA, 2001-NYY**	**50**
7.	Francisco Cordero, 2004-TEX	49

LOWEST CAREER AVERAGE AGAINST LEFT-HANDERS AMONG ACTIVE MAJOR LEAGUE RIGHT-HANDED PITCHERS

1.	Troy Percival	.201 (263-for-1307)
2.	**MARIANO RIVERA**	**.205 (427-for-2086)**
3.	Joe Nathan	.214 (243-for-1134)
4.	Tim Lincecum	.215 (243-for-1132)
5.	Trevor Hoffman	.215 (390-for-1813)

2006

- Went 5-5 with a 1.80 ERA and 34 saves in 63 relief appearances for the Yankees, winning his second consecutive "DHL Delivery Man of the Year" Award and third straight "Rolaids Relief Man of the Year" Award...ranked second in the American League with 59 games finished and ninth with 34 saves.

MARIANO RIVERA

- Converted 34-of-37 save opportunities (91.9%)...saved consecutive games four times...made appearances in consecutive games nine times, three straight games three times and four consecutive games once...recorded at least six outs in eight appearances (tossed 2.0 innings seven times and 3.0 innings once)...retired 48-of-63 first batters faced (76.2%)...prevented 11-of-18 inherited runners from scoring (61.1%)...opponents batted .223 (61-for-274, 3HR); LH .194 (25-for-129, 1HR), RH .248 (36-for-145, 2HR).
- Was selected to the American League All-Star team, his eighth career selection...tossed a scoreless ninth to earn the save in the American League's 3-2 victory on 7/11 at PNC Field in Pittsburgh...was his third career All-Star save, tying Dennis Eckersley for most saves in All-Star history.
- Tossed 3.0 scoreless innings on 5/30 at Detroit to earn the win, marking his longest outing in the regular season since 9/6/96 vs. Toronto when he also went 3.0 innings...in 6/6 win vs. Boston, tossed a perfect ninth for his 12th save of the season and the 391st of his career, surpassing Dennis Eckersley for fourth place on Baseball's all-time list.
- On 7/20 at Toronto, allowed 11th-inning "walk-off" home run to Vernon Wells to record fifth loss (1.1IP, 2H, 1ER)...was the third "walk-off" home run allowed in his career in the regular season and the first since 7/24/04 at Boston (Bill Mueller)...had gone 51.0 innings without allowing a home run in 2006 and had gone 73.0 innings since he had last allowed a home run (Eduardo Perez on 8/16/05 at Tampa Bay), marking the longest such streak by a Yankees pitcher since Andy Pettitte in 2002 (also 73.0 innings)...missed 22 games from 9/1-20 with a strained right forearm.
- Made one relief appearance in the Division Series vs. Detroit, allowing 1H in 1.0IP in Game 1 win on 10/13.

2005

- Was 7-4 with a career-low 1.38 ERA and 43 saves in 71 relief appearances...won his second straight "Rolaids Relief Man of the Year" Award...also was named "DHL Delivery Man of the Year"...became only the third pitcher in Major League history to save at least 40 games with a sub-1.50 ERA while working 75.0 innings or more (also John Wetteland in 1993 and Eric Gagne in 2003)...led the American League with 67 games finished, was tied for third with 43 saves and was tied for eighth with 71 games...led all American League relievers in ERA and opponent's batting average (.177)...was tied for seventh with 78.1IP...allowed more than one earned run in an appearance only once (2ER in 2.0IP on 8/13 vs. Texas)...allowed only 1ER on the road in 34 appearances (35.0IP) the entire season (0.26 ERA).
- Converted 43-of-47 save opportunities (91.5%)...saved consecutive games five times...saved three consecutive games three times...made appearances in consecutive games 13 times and three straight games six times...retired 58-of-71 first batters faced (81.7%)...prevented 16-of-18 inherited runners from scoring (88.9%)...opponents batted .177 (50-for-283, 2HR); LH .177 (25-for-141, 1HR), RH .176 (25-for-142, 1HR).
- Was selected to the 2005 American League All-Star team, his seventh career All-Star selection...retired the final batter of the All-Star Game at Detroit to record his second career All-Star save.
- Blew his first two save chances of the season on consecutive days, 4/5 and 4/6 vs. Boston, the first time he blew consecutive save opportunities in the regular season since 7/24/04 at Boston and 7/26/04 at Toronto (he had never blown saves on consecutive days)...following the back-to-back setbacks, converted 31 straight save opportunities from 4/9-8/11, the longest such streak of his career, allowing only 1ER in 31.2IP (0.28 ERA) while limiting batters to a .140 batting average (15-for-107, 3BB, 33K)...allowed only 4ER in his 46 overall appearances during that same span (51.2IP, 0.70ERA).
- Did not allow a run in 22 appearances from 5/9-7/4 (23.0IP, 8H, 5BB, 23K)...the longest single-season scoreless innings streak by a Yankees pitcher since Mike Mussina threw 23.0 straight scoreless innings in 2001...was the longest such streak by any Yankees reliever since 1999, when Rivera finished the regular season with 30.2 shutout innings, the longest streak of his career.
- On 8/16 at Tampa Bay, allowed game-tying ninth-inning home run (Eduardo Perez) to record fourth blown save of the season and second in span of three opportunities...prior to blowing the save, had recorded 33 consecutive saves vs. the Devil Rays, the most saves—without a blown save—by a pitcher against one particular opponent in AL history.
- Recorded saves in each of his two appearances versus the Angels in the Division Series (3.0IP, 1H, 1ER, 1BB, 1K)...recorded the 15th Division Series save of his career in Game 4 vs. the Angels, tossing 2.0 perfect innings for his first two-inning postseason save since Game 5 of the 2003 ALCS at Boston...it also was his Major League-leading 34th career postseason save (in 39 opportunities).

2004

- Was 4-2 with a 1.94 ERA and a single-season franchise-record 53 saves in career-high 74 relief appearances...led the Major Leagues in saves and was tied for fourth in the American League in appearances...his 53 saves tied Randy Myers (Chicago Cubs, 1993) and Trevor Hoffman (San Diego Padres, 1998) for fourth place on Baseball's single-season all-time list...joined Eric Gagne as the only relievers in Major League history to record two 50-save seasons...earned his third "Rolaids Relief Man of the Year" Award...converted 53-of-57 save opportunities (93.0%)...saved two consecutive games seven times...saved three consecutive games four times, and saved four straight games once...made appearances in consecutive games 13 times, three straight games seven times, and four straight games once...retired 53-of-74 first batters faced (71.6%)...prevented 11-of-17 inherited runners from scoring (64.7%)...opponents batted .225 (65-for-289, 3HR); LH .234 (36-for-154, 2HR), RH .215 (29-for-135, 1HR)...was selected to the 2004 American League All-Star team, his sixth career All-Star selection...pitched a perfect ninth inning in the American League's 9-4 win on 7/13.

- In 5/11 win vs. Anaheim, allowed 2ER in 1.0IP to suffer his first blown save of the season, snapping a stretch of 28 consecutive save conversions...in 5/19 win at Anaheim, tossed perfect ninth to record league-leading 15th save in the Yankees' 39th game of the season...became the first Yankees reliever to reach 15 saves in fewer than 50 games into any season...became the 17th pitcher in Major League history—and first Yankee—to reach the 300-save plateau in 5/28 win at Tampa Bay...became the fifth-youngest pitcher to reach 300 saves—at 34 years, 181 days—behind Robb Nen (32 years, 251 days), Lee Smith (33/264), John Wetteland (33/265) and Trevor Hoffman (33/306)...with 11 saves in June, tied his career high for any calendar month.
- In 7/8 win vs. Tampa Bay, pitched a perfect 1.2 innings (1K) to earn his 30th save...tied the then-American League record for fewest team games in a season to reach the 30-save plateau, joining Bobby Thigpen of the Chicago White Sox (1990) and Boston's Lee Smith (1993), who also reached 30 saves in their team's 83rd game...record later surpassed by the Angels' Francisco Rodriguez in 2008 (76 games)...established an AL record with 32 saves before the All-Star break (fell two shy of the Major League mark of 34 set by Atlanta's John Smoltz in 2003)...surrendered "walk-off," two-run home run to Bill Mueller in the bottom of the ninth in 7/24 loss at Boston.
- Recorded save No. 40 in 8/14 win at Seattle (Game 116), becoming the quickest to the 40-save plateau and breaking Bobby Thigpen's record of 118 games set with the Chicago White Sox in 1990...record later broken by the Angels' Francisco Rodriguez in 2008 (98 games)...earned his 45th save of the season in the Yankees' 18-6 win on 8/28 at Toronto, retiring last four batters of the game (entered the game with a 9-6 lead and two runners on base)......first Yankee to earn a save in a game in which the Yankees won by at least 12 runs was Ed Figueroa, who earned a save in a 16-3 Yankees win on 5/14/80 vs. Kansas City.
- Was 1-0 with two saves and a 0.71 ERA in nine postseason appearances...earned his 10th career LCS save in Game 2 vs. Boston...recorded back-to-back blown saves for the first time in his postseason career in Games 4 and 5 of the ALCS at Boston.

2003

- Was 5-2 with a 1.66 ERA and 40 saves in 64 relief appearances with the Yankees...ranked third in the American League with 40 saves despite missing the first 25 games of the season and having only four saves through the Yankees' 59th game...had 36 saves in the final 104 games of the season...converted 40-of-46 save opportunities (87.0%)...saved two consecutive games eight times and three consecutive games twice (6/24-26 and 6/28-30)...retired 44-of-64 first batters faced (68.8%)...prevented 18-of-35 inherited runners from scoring (51.4%)...opponents batted .235 (61-for-260, 3HR); LH .197 (29-for-147, 1HR), RH .281 (32-for-113, 2HR)...made appearances in consecutive games 11 times, three straight games five times and four straight games once.
- Began the season on the 15-day D.L. (retroactive to 3/25) with a strained right groin...suffered the injury on the last pitch of 3/24 spring training outing vs. Detroit...was reinstated from the D.L. on 4/29 (missed first 25 games of the season)...made his 2003 debut in 4/30 win vs. Seattle andrecorded his first save of the season in 5/1 win vs. Seattle...in 6/13 win vs. St. Louis, pitched a perfect ninth to save Roger Clemens' 300th victory.
- Did not allow a run in his final 15 appearances of the season (16.1IP, 10H, 3BB, 16K) and saved all 16 of his opportunities from 8/19 through the conclusion of the regular season.
- Was 1-0 with a 0.56 ERA and five saves in eight postseason relief appearances...also struck out 14 batters without allowing a walk in postseason play...was named American League Championship Series Most Valuable Player, going 1-0 with a 1.13 ERA and two saves in four appearances vs. Boston...earned the win in Game 7, pitching 3.0 scoreless innings–his first three-inning stint since 9/6/96 vs. Toronto.

2002

- Battled through three stints on the disabled list to go 1-4 with a 2.74 ERA and 28 saves in 45 games...in 5/9 win at Tampa Bay, recorded the 225th save of his career to surpass Dave Righetti (224) as the club's all-time saves leader...converted 28-of-32 save opportunities (87.5%)...had to record more than three outs in four of his 28 saves...saved two consecutive games five times and three consecutive twice...retired 35-of-45 first batters faced (77.8%)...prevented 11-of-20 inherited runners from scoring (55.0%)...made appearances in consecutive games 12 times and three straight games twice...opponents batted .203 (35-for-172, 3HR); LH .181 (15-for-83, 1HR), RH .225 (20-for-89, 2HR)...was selected to his fifth All-Star Game by Manager Joe Torre and pitched a scoreless ninth inning (1H) on 7/9 at Miller Park in Milwaukee, as the game ended tied in the 13th inning.
- Was placed on the 15-day disabled list three separate times in 2002 (entering the season had been placed on the disabled list once in his eight-year Major League career)...was placed on the 15-day D.L. from 6/9-25 with a strained right groin...on 6/26 at Baltimore, struck out the side in first appearance since reinstatement, pitching in the seventh inning for first time since 10/1/00 at Baltimore...was removed from 7/20 win vs. Boston—after six pitches—with tightness in his right shoulder (1H, 1ER in 0.1IP)...was placed on the 15-day

disabled list for a second time from 7/26 (retroactive to 7/21) to 8/8 with a mild muscle strain of the right shoulder...was placed on 15-day D.L. for a third time from 8/19 (retroactive to 8/16) to 9/21 with a muscle strain of the right shoulder.

- Converted 17 consecutive save opportunities from 4/23-7/11 without allowing a run (17.0IP, 8H)...on 7/14 at Cleveland, allowed "walk-off" grand slam by Bill Selby in the ninth inning to suffer his second consecutive blown save and fourth loss on the season (0.2IP, 5H, 6ER, 1IBB, 1K)...was his second game-winning home run allowed in 2002 (also Shea Hillenbrand on 4/13 at Boston) and fourth of his career...6ER were the most allowed in a relief appearance in his career.
- Made one appearance in the Division Series vs. the Angels, saving Game 1 (1.0IP, 1H).

DID YOU KNOW? MARIANO RIVERA has saved wins for five former Cy Young Award winners (Dwight Gooden, David Cone, Roger Clemens, Randy Johnson and CC Sabathia)...only two pitchers have saved wins for six former Cy Young winners: *Goose Gossage*-Ron Guidry, LaMarr Hoyt, Catfish Hunter, Sparky Lyle, Gaylord Perry and Rick Sutcliffe and *John Franco*-John Denny, Dwight Gooden, Orel Hershiser, Bret Saberhagen, Tom Glavine and Frank Viola. Credit: *Elias Sports Bureau*

2001

- Went 4-6 with a 2.34 ERA and 50 saves in 71 games...became only the sixth player in Major League history to reach the 50-save plateau in a single season...saved at least 30 games for the fifth straight season, surpassing Dave Righetti for most 30-save seasons by a Yankee.
- Converted 50-of-57 save opportunities (87.7%)...had to record more than three outs in 13 of his 50 saves...saved two consecutive games nine times and three consecutive games three times (4/27-29; 6/14-16; 7/16-18)...retired 57-of-71 first batters faced (80.3%) and prevented 20-of-25 inherited runners from scoring (80.0%)...made appearances in consecutive games 13 times, three straight games six times and pitched in four straight games once...opponents batted .209 (61-for-292, 5HR); LH .187 (26-for-139, 0HR), RH .229 (35-for-153, 5HR)...was selected to participate in the All-Star Game, but did not attend to rest an injured right ankle.
- Saved all three games a series vs. Oakland from 4/27-29...in 8/1 win vs. Texas, recorded his 200th career save, pitching 2.0 scoreless innings (2K).

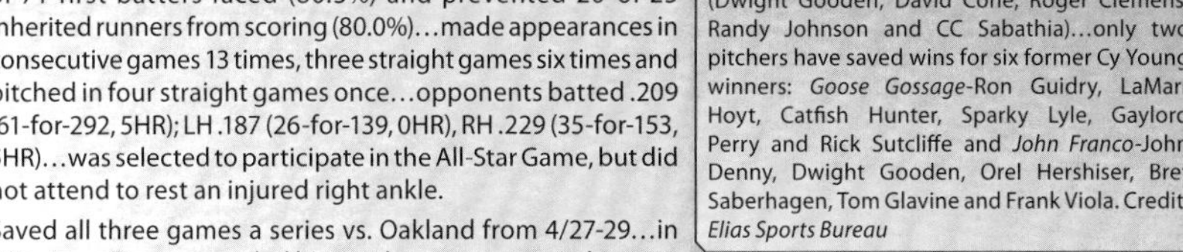

- Was 2-1 with a 1.13 ERA and five saves in 11 postseason relief appearances...allowed two runs in the bottom of the ninth in Game 7 of the World Series at Arizona and recorded the loss...was his first career blown save in World Series play (had been 8-for-8 in save opportunities)...had converted 23 consecutive saves in postseason play (last blown save was Game 4 of 1997 ALDS at Cleveland).

2000

- Was 7-4, with a 2.85 ERA and 36 saves in 66 appearances...converted 36-of-41 save opportunities (87.8%)...saved two consecutive games three times and three consecutive games twice...was asked to record more than three outs in 13 of his 36 saves...retired 51-of-66 first batters faced (77.3%)...prevented 14-of-24 inherited runners from scoring (58.3%)...opponents batted .208 (58-for-279, 4HR); LH .210 (28-for-143, 1HR), RH .206 (28-for-136, 3HR).
- Made his first Opening Day appearance on 4/3 at Anaheim and recorded the save, allowing 1ER in 1.0IP...tossed 2.2IP to record his second win of the season on 4/19 at Texas, his longest outing since tossing 3.0IP and earning the win on 9/6/96 vs. Toronto...recorded his first loss and second blown save of season on 5/7 vs. Baltimore, allowing 4H and 3ER in the ninth inning...was the first time he received the loss when leading by two or more runs in the ninth inning or later since 8/2/96 at Kansas City when he allowed 4ER in 0.2IP.
- Saved both games of 7/8 doubleheader vs. the Mets (Game 1 at Shea Stadium and Game 2 at Yankee Stadium), pitching scoreless ninth innings.
- Was 0-0 with a 1.72 ERA and six saves in a team-high 10 postseason relief appearances...with his save in Game 5 of the Division Series at Oakland on 10/8, Rivera established the Major League record for most saves in postseason play with 16 (surpassing Dennis Eckersley-15)...had his postseason record scoreless streak end at 33.1IP in Game 6 of the ALCS on 10/17 vs. Seattle, allowing 1ER in 2.0IP...streak had covered 23 appearances, dating back to Sandy Alomar's solo-HR in Game 4 of the 1997 Division Series at Cleveland...surpassed Whitey Ford's 33.0 consecutive scoreless innings from 1960-62...had his World Series scoreless streak snapped at 14.1 innings when he allowed 2ER in the ninth inning of Game 2 vs. the Mets on 10/22...saved Games 4 and 5 of the World Series to bring his career Series saves total to seven, the most all-time, surpassing Rollie Fingers' six.

1999

- Made 66 appearances out of the Yankees bullpen, going 4-3 with a 1.83 ERA and 45 saves...converted 45-of-49 save opportunities (91.8%)...led the American League in saves, save percentage and relief ERA...became the first Yankees pitcher to have two 40-save seasons (also had 43 saves in 1997)...retired 60-of-66 first batters faced (90.9%)...prevented 22-of-27 inherited runners from scoring (81.5%)...opponents batted .176 (43-for-245, 2HR); LH .143 (20-for-140, 1HR), RH .219 (23-for-105, 1HR).
- Appeared in a career-high six consecutive games from 4/20-27, recording four saves over the stretch...was selected to participate in his second All-Star Game, but did not attend because of personal matters in his native country of Panama...was named AL "Pitcher of the Month" in August...saved a league-leading 11 games in the month and did not allow a run in 13 appearances (14.2IP, 15K).
- Did not allow a run in his final 28 appearances of the season (30.2IP), converting his last 22 save opportunities.
- Tossed 12.1 scoreless innings in eight postseason appearances and was 6-for-6 in save opportunities...pitched 4.2 scoreless innings with a win and two saves in three games in the World Series vs. the Atlanta Braves and was selected as the Most Valuable Player...became only the third reliever to be named World Series MVP, joining Oakland's Rollie Fingers in 1974 and former Yankee John Wetteland in 1996...including postseason play, did not allow a run in his final 43.0IP of the season over a span of 36 appearances.

1998

- Posted 36 saves and was 3-0 with a 1.91 ERA in 54 relief appearances...converted 36-of-41 save opportunities (87.8%)...retired 41-of-54 first-batters faced (75.9%)...prevented 20-of-24 inherited runners from scoring (83.3%)...opponents batted .215 (48-for-223, 3HR); LH .235 (27-for-115, 0HR), RH .194 (21-for-108, 3HR).
- Threw 1.1IP in his season debut on 4/5 at Oakland, leaving the game with a strained right groin...was placed on the 15-day disabled list the next day (missed 13 games)...returned on 4/24 and did not allow a run in his next nine appearances (9.2IP), going 7-for-7 in save opportunites...in a 6/1 blown save vs. Chicago-AL, was asked to record as many as six outs for the save for the first time in his career...entered in the eighth with no outs and a 4-2 lead, but allowed two inherited runners to score (Yankees won 5-4 in 10 innings)...following that game, converted 22 consecutive save opportunities before blowing a save on 8/18 at Kansas City (Yankees won 3-2).
- Tossed 13.1 scoreless innings in 10 postseason appearances and was 6-for-6 in save opportunities...saved three of the Yankees' four wins vs. San Diego in the World Series...earned his first career World Series save in the Yankees' 9-6 victory in Game 1 at Yankee Stadium...completed the Yankees' sweep with a save in Game 4 at San Diego, retiring Mark Sweeney on a ground ball to third base for the final out.

1997

- Took over as the Yankees' full-time closer, going 6-4 with a 1.88 ERA and 43 saves in 66 relief appearances...ranked second among American League relievers in ERA and saves...also led the AL in save opportunities (52), ranked sixth in games finished (56) and batting average with runners in scoring position (.151, 11-for-73) and seventh in save percentage (82.7%, 43-for-52)...opponents batted .237 (65-for-274, 5HR); LH .243 (37-for-152, 1HR), RH .230 (28-for-122, 4HR).
- Recorded saves in four straight games from 6/23-27, becoming only the third Yankees pitcher to save four consecutive games during the regular season...John Wetteland accomplished the feat twice in 1996 and Sparky Lyle did it in 1973...his 27 saves at the All-Star break were the sixth-highest total since the inception of the save rule...became the first Yankee to earn a save in the All-Star Game, tossing a perfect ninth on 7/8 at Jacobs Field in his All-Star debut...became only the sixth Yankees reliever to record 30 saves in a season with his save on 7/17 at Chicago-AL...saved both games of a doubleheader on 9/16 vs. Boston.
- Was 0-0 with a 4.50 ERA and one save in two games vs. Cleveland in the Division Series...earned his first career postseason save in the Yankees' 8-6 victory in Game 1 at Yankee Stadium...suffered a blown save in the Yankees' 3-2 loss in Game 4 at Cleveland, surrendering the game-tying home run to Sandy Alomar, Jr. in the bottom of the eighth inning.

1996

- Was 8-3 with a 2.09 ERA and five saves in 61 appearances in his first season of full-time relief...led all Yankees pitchers in ERA and led all Yankees relievers in wins, tying for most relief wins in the American League...was the most wins by a Yankees reliever since Lee Guetterman recorded 11 victories in 1990...opponents batted just .189 (73-for-386, 1HR); LH .215 (46-for-214, 1HR), RH .157 (27-for-172, 0HR)...struck out the side (facing only three batters) four times...had at least one strikeout in 54 of his 61 appearances...first batters were 5-for-56 (.089) with 27K, 4BB and 1HBP...recorded 130 strikeouts in 107.2 innings, the most ever by a Yankees reliever (Gossage had 122 in 1978)...permitted only one home run (Baltimore's Rafael Palmiero on 6/28 at Yankee Stadium).

- Had a 26.0-inning scoreless streak from 4/19-5/21, the most by a Yankee since Steve Farr went 27.0 innings without allowing a run from 5/29-8/4/91...picked up wins vs. Minnesota on 4/26 and 4/28, tossing three no-hit innings in each game...had a streak of 15.0 consecutive hitless innings over six appearances snapped on 5/5 vs. Chicago-AL...recorded six strikeouts in three innings on 9/6 vs. Toronto, the most by a Yankees reliever in 1996.
- Was 1-0 with a 0.63 ERA in the postseason (14.1IP, 1ER)...picked up his second career postseason victory in the Yankees' 5-4, 11-inning victory in Game 1 of the ALCS vs. Baltimore.

1995

- Saw his first Major League action, going 5-3 with a 5.54 ERA in 19 appearances (nine starts) with the Yankees...was 3-3 with a 5.94 ERA as a starter and 2-0 with a 4.32 ERA as a reliever...opponents batted .266 (71-for-267, 11HR); LH .246 (35-for-142, 6HR), RH .288 (36-for-1125, 5HR).
- Was recalled from Columbus on 5/16 and made his Major League debut on 5/23 at California, losing a 10-0 decision (3.1IP, 8H, 5ER, 3BB, 5K)...became the first Yankees rookie to lose his starting debut since Jeff Johnson in 1991...earned his first Major League victory in a 4-1 win on 5/28 at Oakland (5.1IP, 7H, 1ER, 3BB, 1K)...allowed two home runs for the first time in his career, including a grand slam to Geronimo Berroa, in an 8-6 loss on 6/6 vs. Oakland...was optioned back to Columbus on 6/11 and made just one start with the Clippers because of a sore right shoulder...in that start (on 6/26), pitched a five-inning, rain-shortened no-hitter.
- Was recalled on 7/4 and started that night at Chicago-AL, recording 11K in 8.0 shutout innings (both career highs) as the Yankees won 4-1...his 11K were the most by a Yankees rookie since Al Leiter, who also struck out 11 on 4/14/88 at Toronto...made his first Major League relief appearance on 8/1 vs. Milwaukee, picking up the win despite blowing his first save opportunity...was optioned back to Columbus between games of an 8/10 doubleheader vs. Cleveland...started Game 1 and did not receive a decision...tossed a career-high 5.1 innings of relief on 8/25 at Seattle, allowing 1ER on 2Hin a 7-4 loss (2BB, 5K, 1HR)...allowed his second career grand slam (Bobby Bonilla) in an 8-1 loss on 9/15 at Baltimore.
- Overall with Columbus, was 2-2 with a 2.10 ERA in seven starts.
- Was 1-0 with a 0.00 ERA in three appearances vs. Seattle in the Division Series (5.1IP, 8K)...won his postseason debut, tossing 3.1 scoreless innings of relief in a 7-5, 15-inning victory in Game 2 at Yankee Stadium (2H, 5K).

1994

- Combined to go 10-2 with a 3.09 ERA in 22 starts at Triple-A Columbus, Double-A Albany and Single-A Tampa...began the season at Tampa, was promoted to Albany on 6/5 and promoted to Columbus on 7/22...ranked sixth in the organization in ERA...in 131.0IP, allowed just 126 hits and 30 walks while striking out 89...combined to go 6-0 with a 2.25 ERA in 16 starts at Albany and Tampa...was on Tampa's disabled list from 4/23-5/9 with a strained right shoulder...went 4-2 with a 5.81 ERA in six starts at Columbus...was on the Clippers' disabled list from 8/4-14 with a strained left hamstring.

1993

- Went 1-1 with a 2.08 ERA in 12 starts combined at Single-A Greensboro and Single-A Tampa...opponents batted just .208 off him...combined on a shutout with Sandi Santiago, Bruce Pool and Billy Coleman on 7/4 vs. Hickory.

1992

- Suffered through an injury-plagued season at Single-A Ft. Lauderdale...went 5-3 with a 2.28 ERA in 10 starts...allowed just 40 hits and five walks in 59.1IP...averaged less than a walk for every 9.0IP...had a strikeout/walk ratio of 8.4...season was cut short due to surgery on his right elbow...surgery was performed by Dr. Frank Jobe on 8/27...was rated the ninth-best prospect in the Yankees' system by *Baseball America*.

1991

- Went 4-9 with a 2.75 ERA in 29 games (15 starts) at Single-A Greensboro...struck out 123 batters in 114.2IP, averaging 9.7 strikeouts per nine innings...allowed 103 hits and 36 walks.

1990

- Spent his first season of professional ball with the Gulf Coast Yankees, going 5-1 with a league-leading 0.17 ERA in 22 appearances (one start)...allowed just one earned run in 52.0IP, surrendering only 17 hits and seven walks while striking out 58...was named Gulf Coast League "Star of Stars"...threw a seven-inning no-hitter in his lone start on 8/31 vs. Bradenton.

Personal

- He and his wife, Clara have three sons, Mariano Jr., Jafet, and Jaziel...was signed by Herb Raybourn...received the Buck Canel Award by the BBWAA as the top Latin American player in 1996...donated his 2001 Rolaids Relief Man Award to the FDNY...received the 2003 Thurman Munson Award for his accomplishments on the field and his philanthropic work within the community...along with Bobby Abreu, delivered Christmas gifts to the Kips Bay Boys and Girls Club in the Bronx in December 2007...sponsored a youth baseball tournament at Franz Siegel Park in the Bronx in September 2008...delivered holiday gifts to kids at Harlem's Gregorio Luperon High School in December 2008...served as a spokesman for President Obama's United We Serve campaign in 2009...was honored along with teammates Derek Jeter, Andy Pettitte and Jorge Posada with the 2009 "Willie, Mickey and the Duke" Award from the New York Baseball Writer's Association of America.
- In 2004, helped open two Intel Computer Clubhouses in Panama City as part of an after-school program that provides area youth with access to computers and adult mentors in order to develop self-confidence and learning skills...spends time in the off-season in his native Panama, where he provides Christmas gifts for many of the local children...helped finance the construction of a new elementary school and a new church building in Puerto Caimito, Panama...is the first cousin of former Yankee, Ruben Rivera...is the only active player currently wearing uniform No. 42.
- Joined with jeweler Michael C. Fina and *Hearts on Fire* to announce Yankee Stadium's "Final Engagement" via the in-stadium Diamond Vision scoreboard during the 9/18/08 game vs. Chicago-AL...registrations were $1 with all proceeds going to the Mariano Rivera Foundation.
- Is a four-time recipient of the LatinoMVP "American League Reliever of the Year" Award (2003-06)...was also honored with the Citizen Award from latinobaseball.com for his commitment to the well-being of children throughout the United States and Latin America...participates in annual baseball clinics in the Dominican Republic during the offseason...received the prestigious Manuel Amador Guerrero Order during Panama's Independence Day parade on 11/3/99 in Panama City.
- Named the No. 7 sports celebrity on WFAN's (660 AM) Top 20 New York Athletes of the Last 20 Years in December 2007.

Rivera's Career Pitching Record

Year	Club	W	L	ERA	G	GS	CG	SHO	SV	IP	H	R	ER	HR	HP	BB	SO	WP	BK
1990	GCL Yankees	5	1	0.17	22	1	1	1	1	52.0	17	3	1	0	2	7	58	2	0
1991	Greensboro	4	9	2.75	29	15	1	0	0	114.2	103	48	35	2	3	36	123	3	0
1992	Ft. Lauderdale	5	3	2.28	10	10	3	1	0	59.1	40	17	15	5	0	5	42	0	0
1993	GCL Yankees	0	1	2.25	2	2	0	0	0	4.0	2	1	1	0	0	1	6	1	0
	Greensboro	1	0	2.06	10	10	0	0	0	39.1	31	12	9	0	0	15	32	2	0
1994	Tampa	3	0	2.21	7	7	0	0	0	36.2	34	12	9	2	2	12	27	0	0
	Albany	3	0	2.27	9	9	0	0	0	63.1	58	20	16	5	0	8	39	1	1
	Columbus	4	2	5.81	6	6	1	0	0	31.0	34	22	20	5	0	10	23	0	1
1995	Columbus	2	2	2.10	7	7	1	1	0	30.0	25	10	7	2	0	3	30	0	0
	YANKEES	5	3	5.51	19	10	0	0	0	67.0	71	43	41	11	2	30	51	0	1
1996	YANKEES	8	3	2.09	61	0	0	0	5	107.2	73	25	25	1	2	34	130	1	0
1997	YANKEES	6	4	1.88	66	0	0	0	43	71.2	65	17	15	5	0	20	68	2	0
1998	YANKEES - a	3	0	1.91	54	0	0	0	36	61.1	48	13	13	3	1	17	36	0	0
1999	YANKEES	4	3	1.83	66	0	0	0	*45	69.0	43	15	14	2	3	18	52	2	1
2000	YANKEES	7	4	2.85	66	0	0	0	36	75.2	58	26	24	4	0	25	58	2	0
2001	YANKEES	4	6	2.34	71	0	0	0	*50	80.2	61	24	21	5	1	12	83	1	0
2002	YANKEES - b, c, d	1	4	2.74	45	0	0	0	28	46.0	35	16	14	3	2	11	41	1	1
	GCL Yankees	0	0	0.00	1	1	0	0	0	2.0	2	0	0	0	0	1	2	0	0
2003	YANKEES - e	5	2	1.66	64	0	0	0	40	70.2	61	15	13	3	4	10	63	0	0
2004	YANKEES	4	2	1.94	74	0	0	0	*53	78.2	65	17	17	3	5	20	66	0	0
2005	YANKEES	7	4	1.38	71	0	0	0	43	78.1	50	18	12	2	4	18	80	0	0
2006	YANKEES	5	5	1.80	63	0	0	0	34	75.0	61	16	15	3	5	11	55	0	0
2007	YANKEES	3	4	3.15	67	0	0	0	30	71.1	68	25	25	4	6	12	74	1	0
2008	YANKEES	6	5	1.40	64	0	0	0	39	70.2	41	11	11	4	2	6	77	1	0
2009	YANKEES	3	3	1.76	66	0	0	0	44	66.1	48	14	13	7	1	12	72	1	0
Minor League Totals		**27**	**18**	**2.35**	**103**	**68**	**7**	**3**	**1**	**432.1**	**346**	**145**	**113**	**21**	**7**	**98**	**382**	**9**	**2**
Major League Totals		**71**	**52**	**2.25**	**917**	**10**	**0**	**0**	**526**	**1090.0**	**848**	**295**	**273**	**60**	**38**	**256**	**1006**	**12**	**3**

*Denotes league leader

Signed by New York (AL) as a non-drafted free agent on February 17, 1990.

a - Was placed on the 15-day disabled list with a strained right groin on April 6 - 24, 1998.
b - Was placed on the 15-day disabled list with a strained groin from June 9 - 25, 2002.
c - Was placed on the 15-day disabled list with a right shoulder muscle strain from July 21 - August 8, 2002
d - Was placed on the 15-day disabled list with a right shoulder muscle strain from August 19 - September 21, 2002.
e - Was placed on the 15-day disabled list from March 30 - April 29, 2003 with a strained right groin.

Rivera's Division Series Record

Year	Club vs. Opp.	W	L	ERA	G	GS	CG	SHO	SV	IP	H	R	ER	HR	HP	BB	SO	WP	BK
1995	NYY vs. SEA	1	0	0.00	3	0	0	0	0	5.1	3	0	0	0	0	1	8	0	0
1996	NYY vs. TEX	0	0	0.00	2	0	0	0	0	4.2	0	0	0	0	0	1	1	0	0
1997	NYY vs. CLE	0	0	4.50	2	0	0	0	1	2.0	2	1	1	1	0	0	1	0	0
1998	NYY vs. TEX	0	0	0.00	3	0	0	0	2	3.1	1	0	0	0	0	1	2	0	0
1999	NYY vs. TEX	0	0	0.00	2	0	0	0	2	3.0	1	0	0	0	0	0	3	1	0
2000	NYY vs. OAK	0	0	0.00	3	0	0	0	3	5.0	2	0	0	0	0	0	2	0	0
2001	NYY vs. OAK	0	0	0.00	3	0	0	0	2	5.0	4	1	0	0	0	0	4	0	0
2002	NYY vs. ANA	0	0	0.00	1	0	0	0	1	1.0	1	0	0	0	0	0	0	0	0
2003	NYY vs. MIN	0	0	0.00	2	0	0	0	2	4.0	0	0	0	0	0	0	4	0	0
2004	NYY vs. MIN	1	0	0.00	4	0	0	0	0	5.2	2	0	0	0	0	0	2	0	0
2005	NYY vs. LAA	0	0	3.00	2	0	0	0	2	3.0	1	1	1	0	0	1	2	0	0
2006	NYY vs. DET	0	0	0.00	1	0	0	0	0	1.0	1	0	0	0	0	0	0	0	0
2007	NYY vs. CLE	0	0	0.00	3	0	0	0	0	4.2	2	0	0	0	1	1	6	0	0
2009	NYY vs. MIN	0	0	0.00	3	0	0	0	1	3.2	4	0	0	0	0	1	7	0	0
Division Series Totals		**2**	**0**	**0.35**	**34**	**0**	**0**	**0**	**16**	**51.1**	**24**	**3**	**2**	**1**	**1**	**6**	**42**	**1**	**0**

Rivera's League Championship Series Record

Year	Club vs. Opp.	W	L	ERA	G	GS	CG	SHO	SV	IP	H	R	ER	HR	HP	BB	SO	WP	BK
1996	NYY vs. BAL	1	0	0.00	2	0	0	0	0	4.0	6	0	0	0	0	1	5	0	0
1998	NYY vs. CLE	0	0	0.00	4	0	0	0	1	5.2	0	0	0	0	0	1	5	0	0
1999	NYY vs. BOS	1	0	0.00	3	0	0	0	2	4.2	5	0	0	0	0	0	3	0	0
2000	NYY vs. SEA	0	0	1.93	3	0	0	0	1	4.2	4	1	1	0	0	0	1	0	0
2001	NYY vs. SEA	1	0	1.93	4	0	0	0	2	4.2	2	1	1	0	0	1	3	2	0
2003	NYY vs. BOS	1	0	1.13	4	0	0	0	2	8.0	5	1	1	0	0	0	6	0	0
2004	NYY vs. BOS	0	0	1.29	5	0	0	0	2	7.0	6	1	1	0	0	2	6	0	0
2009	NYY vs. LAA	0	0	1.29	5	0	0	0	2	7.0	3	1	1	0	0	2	4	0	0
LCS Totals		**4**	**0**	**0.99**	**30**	**0**	**0**	**0**	**12**	**45.2**	**31**	**5**	**5**	**0**	**0**	**7**	**33**	**2**	**0**

Rivera's World Series Record

Year	Club vs. Opp.	W	L	ERA	G	GS	CG	SHO	SV	IP	H	R	ER	HR	HP	BB	SO	WP	BK
1996	NYY vs. ATL	0	0	1.59	4	0	0	0	0	5.2	4	1	1	0	0	3	4	0	0
1998	NYY vs. SD	0	0	0.00	3	0	0	0	3	4.1	5	0	0	0	0	0	4	0	0
1999	NYY vs. ATL	1	0	0.00	3	0	0	0	2	4.2	3	0	0	0	0	1	3	0	0
2000	NYY vs. NYM	0	0	3.00	4	0	0	0	2	6.0	4	2	2	1	1	1	7	0	0
2001	NYY vs. ARI	1	1	1.42	4	0	0	0	1	6.1	6	2	1	0	1	1	7	0	0
2003	NYY vs. FLA	0	0	0.00	2	0	0	0	1	4.0	2	0	0	0	0	0	4	0	0
2009	NYY vs. PHI	0	0	0.00	4	0	0	0	2	5.1	3	0	0	0	0	2	3	0	0
World Series Totals		**2**	**1**	**0.99**	**24**	**0**	**0**	**0**	**11**	**36.1**	**27**	**5**	**4**	**1**	**2**	**8**	**32**	**0**	**0**
POSTSEASON TOTALS		**8**	**1**	**0.74**	**88**	**0**	**0**	**0**	**39**	**133.1**	**82**	**13**	**11**	**2**	**3**	**21**	**107**	**3**	**0**

Rivera's All-Star Game Record

Year	Club, Site	W	L	ERA	G	GS	CG	SHO	SV	IP	H	R	ER	HR	HP	BB	SO	WP	BK
1997	NYY, Cleveland	0	0	0.00	1	0	0	0	1	1.0	0	0	0	0	0	0	1	0	0
1999	NYY, Boston	Selected - Did Not Pitch																	
2000	NYY, Atlanta	0	0	0.00	1	0	0	0	0	1.0	2	1	0	0	0	0	0	0	0
2001	NYY, Seattle	Selected - Did Not Pitch																	
2002	NYY, Milwaukee	0	0	0.00	1	0	0	0	0	1.0	1	0	0	0	0	0	0	0	0
2004	NYY, Houston	0	0	0.00	1	0	0	0	0	1.0	0	0	0	0	0	0	0	0	0
2005	NYY, Detroit	0	0	0.00	1	0	0	0	1	0.1	0	0	0	0	0	0	1	0	0
2006	NYY, Pittsburgh	0	0	0.00	1	0	0	0	1	1.0	0	0	0	0	0	0	0	0	0
2008	NYY, New York (AL)	0	0	0.00	1	0	0	0	0	1.2	2	0	0	0	0	0	2	0	0
2009	NYY, St. Louis	0	0	0.00	1	0	0	0	1	1.0	0	0	0	0	0	0	1	0	0
All-Star Game Totals		**0**	**0**	**0.00**	**8**	**0**	**0**	**0**	**4**	**8.0**	**5**	**1**	**0**	**0**	**0**	**0**	**5**	**0**	**0**

Rivera's Regular Season Batting Record

Year	Team	AVG	G	AB	R	H	2B	3B	HR	RBI	SH	SF	HP	BB	SO	SB	CS
2009	NYY	.000	66	1	0	0	0	0	0	1	0	0	0	1	0	0	0
Major League Totals		**.000**	**917**	**2**	**0**	**0**	**0**	**0**	**0**	**1**	**0**	**0**	**0**	**1**	**1**	**0**	**0**

Rivera's Career Fielding Record

Position	PCT	G	PO	A	E	TC	DP
Pitcher	.981	917	101	216	6	323	11

Century City

The Yankees reached 100 wins in a season for the 19th time in franchise history in 2009, hitting triple digits in victories for the first time since 2004 (101-61)...no other franchise has more than 10 such seasons (OAK/PHI Athletics franchise-10)...the 2009 World Series championship marked the 12th time in which they won the title after posting a 100-win season.

From 2002–04, the Yankees compiled three consecutive 100-win seasons for the first time in franchise history...they joined the 1929-31 Philadelphia Athletics, 1942-44 St. Louis Cardinals, 1969-71 Baltimore Orioles and 1997-99 Atlanta Braves as the only teams in Major League history to record three straight 100-win seasons.

David Robertson

30 **Right-handed Pitcher**

5-11 • 190 • B/T: Right/Right

Opening Day Age: 24

Birthdate
April 9, 1985

Birthplace
Birmingham, Ala.

Resides
Tampa, Fla.

M.L. Service
1 year, 70 days

College
University of Alabama

Status

- Selected in the 17th round of the 2006 First-Year Player Draft...signed through the 2010 season.

2009

- Was 2-1 with one save and a 3.30 ERA (43.2IP, 16ER) in 45 relief appearances over three stints with the Yankees (4/16; 4/24-5/9; 5/26-10/4)...opponents batted .216 (36-for-167, 4HR); LH .189 (14-for-74, 2HR), RH .237 (22-for-93, 2HR)...stranded 16-of-25 inherited runners (64.0%)...retired 34-of-45 first batters faced (75.6%)...appeared in consecutive games eight times...threw less than 1.0 inning 12 times.
- Had a 12.98K/9.0IP ratio (43.2IP, 63K)...among pitchers with at least 40.0IP, marked the second-best K/9.0IP ratio in the Majors behind the Dodgers' Jonathan Broxton (13.50).
- Was recalled from Triple-A Scranton/Wilkes-Barre prior to the Yankees' first-ever regular season game at Yankee Stadium on 4/16...made his first appearance of the season in the loss that day vs. Cleveland, striking out three batters in 2.0 scoreless innings (2H)...was optioned back to Scranton/WB the next day...recalled a second time on 4/24 when RHP Chien-Ming Wang was placed on the D.L...appeared in four games (2.2IP, 2H, 3R, 2ER, 4BB, 4K) before being optioned back to Scranton/WB.
- Was recalled a third time on 5/26 and pitched out of the Yankees bullpen for the remainder of the season...did not allow a run in any of his first seven appearances following his third recall (5.0IP, 2H, 2BB, 6K).
- Threw one pitch (Elvis Andrus flyout to LF) to earn his first win of the season on 6/4 vs. Texas...was his second career one-pitch win (also 7/22/08 vs. Minnesota).
- Held opposing left-handed batters hitless in 18 consecutive at-bats from 4/25-6/18...streak was snapped in 6/23 loss at Atlanta, when he allowed a solo-HR to Brian McCann in 1.0IP (1K)...was his first HR surrendered since 8/27/08 vs. Boston (Dustin Pedroia grand slam), snapping a 20.0-inning homerless span over 21 relief appearances...earned his first career save on 7/27 at Tampa Bay, closing out the final 1.1 innings (2H, 1ER, 1K, 1HR)...suffered his first Major League loss in his next outing on 7/31 at Chicago-AL, allowing 2H and 1ER in 2.0IP (1BB, 2K).
- Struck out three batters in 0.2IP in 8/6 win vs. Boston, becoming the first Yankee to record at least three strikeouts without completing a full inning of work since Ron Davis on 9/17/80 vs. Toronto (0.2IP, 3K).
- Was shut down for three weeks from 9/6-28 with elbow stiffness...had an MRI on 9/7 and was seen by Dr. James Andrews in Pensacola, Fla., on 9/10...Dr. Andrews recommended 10-14 days of rest before beginning a throwing program...returned to the mound in 9/29 win vs. Kansas City, allowing 1BB in 0.2IP (1K).

Single-Game Highs and Streaks

Low hit CG
N/A

IP (start)
N/A

IP (relief)
2.0 - 8 times
Last: at CWS, 7/31/09

Hits
4 - 3 times
Last: at LAA, 8/9/08

Runs
5 - vs. BAL, 7/28/08

BB
3 - 2 times
Last: at MIN, 7/9/09

SO
4 - 2 times
Last: at FLA, 6/21/09

HR
1 - 7 times
Last: vs. TEX, 8/27/09

Winning Streak
5g - 7/19/08-6/4/09

Losing Streak
1g - at CWS, 7/31/09

DAVID ROBERTSON

- Did not allow a run in five appearances during the 2009 playoffs, tossing 5.1 scoreless innings (4H, 3BB, 3K)...earned the win in each of his first two postseason appearances (Game 2 of ALDS vs. Minnesota and Game 2 of ALCS vs. Los Angeles-AL), as the Yankees recorded "walk-off" wins in each contest.
- In eight relief appearances with Scranton/WB, went 0-3 with two saves and a 1.84 ERA (14.2IP, 10H, 7R, 3ER, 6BB, 25K)...held left-handed batters to a .100 batting average (2-for-20) with 11K.

2008

- Was 4-0 with a 5.34 ERA in 25 relief appearances over two stints with the Yankees (6/28-8/28; 9/13-28)...opponents batted .257 (29-for-113, 3HR); LH .259 (14-for-54, 0HR), RH .254 (15-for-59, 3HR)...retired 16-of-25 first batters faced (64.0%)...prevented 6-of-14 inherited runners from scoring (42.9%)...pitched in three consecutive games twice (7/13-18 and 8/24-27)...tossed a season-high 2.0 innings on six occasions.
- Was signed to a Major League contract and selected to the Yankees' 25-man roster on 6/28...made his Major League debut in 6/29 loss at the Mets, allowing 1ER in 2.0IP (4H, 1K)...struck out his first batter faced (Oliver Perez).
- Allowed just 3H and 1ER in his next 10.1IP over 10 games from 7/1-26 (0.87 ERA).
- Held left-handed batters hitless over 16AB from 6/29-7/21 (9G) before Luke Scott's leadoff single in the sixth on 7/28 vs. Baltimore.
- Pitched a scoreless 12th inning and recorded his first Major League victory on 7/19 vs. Oakland (1.0IP, 1H, 1BB, 1K) after Jose Molina was hit by a pitch with the bases loaded, bringing in the game-winning run.
- Recorded his second Major League victory (within a four-game span) on 7/22 vs. Minnesota, stranding two inherited runners and getting the final out in the sixth on one pitch...became the seventh Major League pitcher in 2008 to throw one pitch and record a win (third in the AL).
- In 7/28 loss vs. Baltimore, allowed a grand slam to Adam Jones and set a career high with 5ER...was his first HR allowed as a professional after 148.1 career IP (minors-136.0IP from 2007-08 and Majors-12.1IP).
- Allowed 16ER over 10 outings (13.1IP) from 7/28-8/27 and was optioned to Scranton/WB on 8/28.
- Was recalled from Scranton/WB on 9/13...did not allow a run over four appearances in his second stint (4.2IP, 2H, 3BB, 7K).
- In 53.2 combined minor league innings with Scranton/WB and Double-A Trenton, went 4-0 with three saves and a 1.67 ERA over 30 relief appearances (28H, 13R, 10ER, 23BB, 77K)...opponents batted .158 (28-for-176, 1HR); LH .182 (15-for-82, 1HR), RH .125 (13-for-104, 0HR)...has averaged 12.39 K/9.0IP in his minor league career (138.0IP, 190K).
- Made three postseason relief appearances with IL-champion SWB, allowing 3ER in 4.1IP (6.23 ERA, 2H, 1HP, 4BB, 6K).
- Named the International League's "Best Reliever" in *Baseball America*'s 2008 Best Tools survey.

2007

- In his first professional season, pitched at Single-A Charleston, Single-A Tampa and Double-A Trenton, combining to go 8-3 with four saves and a 0.96 ERA in 44 relief appearances (32BB, 113K).
- Ranked third among minor league relievers, with a .154 opponents batting average...was named to the South Atlantic League's midseason All-Star team (w/ Charleston)...39 of his 44 outings were 2.0 innings and all but two were more than 1.0 inning...held opponents scoreless in 35 of his appearances and did not allow a hit in 16 of his games...converted on four of five save opportunities.
- Was 5-2 with three saves and a 0.77 ERA (47.0IP, 4ER) in 24 appearances with Charleston...began his career with 10 consecutive scoreless outings from 4/3-5/3, allowing just 7H in 18.1IP (6BB, 27K).
- Went 3-1 with one save and a 1.08 ERA with Tampa...did not allow an earned run in nine appearances at home (17.1IP, 8H, 2R, 9BB, 12K).
- Made two regular season appearances with Trenton, allowing 1ER in 4.0IP (2.25 ERA)...appeared in two postseason games for the Eastern League champion Thunder, surrendering 2ER in 5.0 IP (3.60 ERA) and striking out five batters.

DAVID ROBERTSON

Personal

- Full name is David Alan Roberston...married Erin in January 2009...older brother, Connor, was drafted by Oakland in 2004.
- Was drafted by the Yankees out of the University of Alabama...ranked among all-time school career leaders in strikeouts, appearances and saves...was named to the 2005 Louisville Slugger Freshmen All-America team as well as the 2005 Freshman All-SEC team as selected by the league's head coaches...named a freshman All-America by *Baseball America* and *Collegiate Baseball Magazine*...was also a Freshman All-SEC selection by SEBaseball.com and a Third-Team All-SEC pick by SEBaseball.com after leading the team in games (32) wins (seven), ERA (2.92) and saves (eight) and setting the single-season rookie record for most strikeouts (105) and overall highest average of strikeouts per nine innings pitched (12.8)...also led the SEC in lowest opponents average (.105)...became the fifth former Alabama player to wear pinstripes, joining Joe Sewell, Ken Sears, Butch Hobson and Andy Phillips.
- Is a 2004 graduate of Paul W. Bryant High School, where he played baseball and led the Stampede to the Class 6A state playoffs in the school's first year of existence.

Robertson's Career Pitching Record

YEAR	Club	W	L	ERA	G	GS	CG	SHO	SV	IP	H	R	ER	HR	HB	BB	SO	WP	BK
2007	Charleston	5	2	0.77	24	0	0	0	3	47.0	25	5	4	0	0	15	67	5	0
	Tampa	3	1	1.08	18	0	0	0	1	33.1	18	6	4	0	0	15	37	2	0
	Trenton	0	0	2.25	2	0	0	0	0	4.0	2	1	1	0	0	2	9	1	0
2008	Trenton	0	0	0.96	9	0	0	0	2	18.2	8	2	2	0	1	6	26	1	0
	Scranton/WB	4	0	2.06	21	0	0	0	1	35.0	20	11	8	1	1	17	51	1	0
	YANKEES	4	0	5.34	25	0	0	0	0	30.1	29	18	18	3	0	15	36	6	0
2009	Scranton/WB	0	3	1.84	8	0	0	0	2	14.2	10	7	3	0	0	6	25	0	0
	YANKEES	2	1	3.30	45	0	0	0	1	43.2	36	19	16	4	1	23	63	6	0
Minor League Totals		**12**	**6**	**1.24**	**82**	**0**	**0**	**0**	**9**	**152.2**	**83**	**32**	**22**	**1**	**2**	**61**	**215**	**10**	**0**
Major League Totals		**6**	**1**	**4.14**	**70**	**0**	**0**	**0**	**1**	**74.0**	**65**	**37**	**34**	**7**	**1**	**38**	**99**	**12**	**0**

Selected by the Yankees in the 17th round of the 2006 First-Year Player Draft.

Robertson's Division Series Record

Year	Club vs. Opp.	W	L	ERA	G	GS	CG	SHO	SV	IP	H	R	ER	HR	HP	BB	SO	WP	BK
2009	NYY vs. MIN	1	0	0.00	1	0	0	0	0	1.0	1	0	0	0	0	0	0	0	0
Division Series Totals		**1**	**0**	**0.00**	**1**	**0**	**0**	**0**	**0**	**1.0**	**1**	**0**	**0**	**0**	**0**	**0**	**0**	**0**	**0**

Robertson's League Championship Series Record

Year	Club vs. Opp.	W	L	ERA	G	GS	CG	SHO	SV	IP	H	R	ER	HR	HP	BB	SO	WP	BK
2009	NYY vs. LAA	1	0	0.00	2	0	0	0	0	2.0	1	0	0	0	0	2	1	0	0
LCS Totals		**1**	**0**	**0.00**	**2**	**0**	**0**	**0**	**0**	**2.0**	**1**	**0**	**0**	**0**	**0**	**2**	**1**	**0**	**0**

Robertson's World Series Record

Year	Club vs. Opp.	W	L	ERA	G	GS	CG	SHO	SV	IP	H	R	ER	HR	HP	BB	SO	WP	BK
2009	NYY vs. PHI	0	0	0.00	2	0	0	0	0	2.1	2	0	0	0	0	1	2	0	0
World Series Totals		**0**	**0**	**0.00**	**2**	**0**	**0**	**0**	**0**	**2.1**	**2**	**0**	**0**	**0**	**0**	**1**	**2**	**0**	**0**
POSTSEASON TOTALS		**2**	**0**	**0.00**	**5**	**0**	**0**	**0**	**0**	**5.1**	**4**	**0**	**0**	**0**	**0**	**3**	**3**	**0**	**0**

Robertson's Regular Season Batting Record

Year	Team	AVG	G	AB	R	H	2B	3B	HR	RBI	SH	SF	HP	BB	SO	SB	CS
2009	NYY	Did Not Bat															
Major League Totals		-	**70**	-	-	-	-	-	-	-	-	-	-	-	-	-	-

Robertson's Career Fielding Record

Position	PCT	G	PO	A	E	TC	DP
Pitcher	1.000	70	1	6	0	7	0

Highest Single-Season Road Attendance

ATTENDANCE	CLUB	YEAR
3,308,666	**New York Yankees**	**2004**
3,130,043	Boston Red Sox	2007
3,107,743	Boston Red Sox	2008
3,080,268	**New York Yankees**	**2006**
3,056,535	Boston Red Sox	2005
3,016,074	Cincinnati Reds	2000
2,997,599	**New York Yankees**	**2005**
2,978,206	**New York Yankees**	**2007**
2,953,637	Chicago Cubs	2005
2,940,048	**New York Yankees**	**2002**

Alex Rodriguez

13

Third Baseman

6-3 • 228 • B/T: Right/Right

Opening Day Age: 34

Birthdate
July 27, 1975

Birthplace
New York, N.Y.

Resides
Miami, Fla.

M.L. Service
15 years, 11 days

Career Highlights

A.L. Most Valuable Player
- 2003, 2005, 2007

A.L. All-Star Team
- 1996, 1997, 1998, 2000, 2001, 2002, 2003, 2004, 2005, 2006, 2007, 2008

A.L. Silver Slugger Award
- 1996, 1998, 1999, 2000, 2001, 2002, 2003, 2005, 2007, 2008

Gold Glove Award
- 2002, 2003

***Baseball America* Player of the Year**
- 2000, 2002, 2007

***Sporting News* Player of the Year**
- 1996, 2002, 2007

Status

- Acquired from the Texas Rangers with cash in exchange for 2B Alfonso Soriano and a player to be named later (INF Joaquin Arias) on February 16, 2004...signed a seven-year contract with player options for three additional years on December 11, 2000...opted out of the contract on October 28, 2007...re-signed by the Yankees to a 10-year contract on December 17, 2007...contract extends through the 2017 season.

Career Notes

- Is tied with Mark McGwire for eighth place on Baseball's all-time list with 583 career homers...in 2009, passed Hall of Famers Reggie Jackson (563) and Harmon Killebrew (573) as well as Rafael Palmiero (569)...ranks ninth on the Yankees' all-time list with 238 career homers.
- Is the only player in Baseball history to collect at least 30HR and 100RBI at least 13 times in his career.
- Has reached 30HR in 12 consecutive seasons and 13 times in his career...only two players have hit at least 30HR in as many consecutive seasons: Barry Bonds (13) and Jimmie Foxx (12)...is tied with Babe Ruth and Mike Schmidt for the fifth-most 30-homer seasons all-time behind Hank Aaron (15) and Bonds (14)...his 12 consecutive seasons with at least 25HR is tied for fourth-longest in Major League history behind Babe Ruth (15 straight), Barry Bonds (15) and Willie Mays (13)...his 13 overall seasons of at least 25HR is tied with Manny Ramirez and Jim Thome for most among active players...his 14 consecutive seasons of at least 20HR are tied with five other players (Chipper Jones, Eddie Mathews, Rafael Palmeiro, Mike Schmidt and Manny Ramirez) for the fourth-longest in Major League history behind Hank Aaron (20), Babe Ruth (16) and Barry Bonds (15)—credit: *Elias Sports Bureau*.
- Owns eight seasons of at least 40HR, tying Barry Bonds, Hank Aaron and Harmon Killebrew for second-most all-time behind Babe Ruth (11)...compiled six straight seasons with 40-or-more home runs from 1998-2003, matching Sammy Sosa (1998-2003) for the second longest streak of 40-homer seasons in Major League history behind Babe Ruth (7, 1926-32).
- Has hit at least 50HR in three separate seasons (54-2007; 57-2002; 52-2001), becoming the fourth player in Major League history to have more than two seasons with at least 50HR: Babe Ruth, Mark McGwire and Sammy Sosa each did it four times (credit: *Elias Sports Bureau*)...is one of only three players to hit 50-or-more home runs in a season with more than one club, joining Jimmie Foxx (58HR w/ Philadelphia in 1932; 50 w/ Boston in 1938) and Mark McGwire (52 w/ Oakland in 1996; 70 w/ St. Louis in 1998 and 65 w/ St. Louis in 1999), according to SABR'S David Vincent.
- According to the *Elias Sports Bureau*, his 572HR were the most for any player prior to turning 34 years old (7/27/09) while his 1,661 career RBI were third-most for any player before turning 34, behind Jimmie Foxx (1,851) and Lou Gehrig (1,763)...his 2,462 career hits were the most for any player at his age since Robin Yount (2,585).

Single-Game Bests and Streaks

Hits
5 - 5 times
Last: at TEX, 5/25/09

Runs
5 - 2 times
Last: vs. TB,4/18/05

2B
3 - vs. SEA, 4/7/01

3B
1 - 27 times
Last: at BOS, 8/21/09

HR
3 - 3 times
Last: vs. LAA, 4/26/05

RBI
10 - vs. LAA, 4/26/05

BB
5 - vs. KC, 4/23/00

SO
4 - 4 times
Last: at KC,4/8/08

SB
3 - 2 times
Last: vs. BOS, 9/25/09

Single-Season Hit Streak
20g - 8/16-9/4/96

Hit Streak
23g - 9/25/06-4/23/07

- Is one of only three players in Major League history to have three career "walk-off" grand slams, joining Vern Stephens (1946 with St. Louis-AL, '49 and '50 with Boston-AL) and the Philadelphia Phillies' Cy Williams (one in 1924 and two in 1926)...owns six "walk-off" homers as a Yankee, the most since Graig Nettles had six from 1973-81...19 of his career home runs have come in the ninth inning or later and either tied the game or given his team the lead...has nine game-ending home runs in his career, tied with Vladimir Guerrero for third-most among active players behind Jim Thome (11) and David Ortiz (10)...his 18 career grand slams are tied for fourth-most all-time, second-most among active players (Manny Ramirez-20).
- Has collected 100RBI in 12 consecutive seasons and 13 times in his career...marks the longest current streak of its kind in the Majors and his 13 overall 100RBI seasons match Jimmie Foxx, Lou Gehrig and Babe Ruth for the most all time.
- Had his streak of consecutive 100R seasons snapped at 13 in 2009, remaining tied with Hank Aaron (13, 1955-67) and Gehrig (13, 1926-38) as the only players in Baseball history to accomplish the feat...reached the 100RBI and 100R plateaus in 11 consecutive seasons from 1998-2008, trailing only Lou Gehrig all time (13 straight seasons from 1926-38).
- Is one of 15 players all time to collect 500HR and 2,500H and one of three active players to accomplish the feat (also Gary Sheffield and Ken Griffey, Jr.).
- Is one of four players all time with 400 doubles, 500HR and 250SB, joining Barry Bonds (601/762/514), Willie Mays (523/660/338) and Gary Sheffield (467/509/253).
- Over the last 10 seasons (2000-09), led the Major Leagues with 1,190R, 435HR and 1,243RBI and ranked fourth with 1,524 games played...over the last five seasons (2005-09), ranked second in the Majors in runs (562) and RBI (610) and third in home runs (202).
- Owns 238HR with the Yankees after hitting 189HR with Seattle and 156HR with Texas...according to the *Elias Sports Bureau*, joins Gary Sheffield, Paul Konerko and Jermaine Dye as the only active players with at least 300HR for teams other than the one for which they made their Major League debut.
- Has complied over 3,000AB with the Yankees and Seattle, joining Manny Ramirez (Indians and Red Sox) and Ken Griffey, Jr. (Seattle and Cincinnati) as the only current Major Leaguers with at least 3,000AB for each of two different teams...joins Dave Winfield (3,997AB with San Diego) as the only players to accumulate 3,000 at-bats with the Yankees and at least that many at-bats for another team (credit: *Elias Sports Bureau*).
- Is the all-time leader with 163 Interleague RBI and ranks second in Interleague hits (253) and third in runs (153).
- Played in 431 career games at the original Yankee Stadium, marking the fifth-highest total among New York City-born players, behind Lou Gehrig (1,080), Phil Rizzuto (825), Joe Pepitone (525) and Snuffy Stirnweiss (442), according to the *Elias Sports Bureau*.
- Compiled 344HR as a shortstop, one shy of the all-time record held by Cal Ripken Jr., who played in 2,303 games with 8,934 at-bats at shortstop...his eight consecutive 20-homer seasons as a shortstop (1996-2003) is the second-longest such streak, two behind Cal Ripken Jr. (1982-91).

MOST GRAND SLAMS, ALL TIME

	Player	
1.	Lou Gehrig	23
2.	Manny Ramirez	21
3.	Eddie Murray	19
4.	Willie McCovey	18
	Robin Ventura	18
	ALEX RODRIGUEZ	**18**

MOST "WALK-OFF" HOME RUNS AMONG ACTIVE PLAYERS

	Player	
1.	Jim Thome	11
2.	David Ortiz	10
3.	**ALEX RODRIGUEZ**	**9**
	Vladimir Guerrero	9

credit: *Elias Sports Bureau*

MOST HOME RUNS, ALL-TIME

	Player	
1.	Barry Bonds	762
2.	Hank Aaron	755
3.	Babe Ruth	714
4.	Willie Mays	660
5.	Ken Griffey, Jr.	630
6.	Sammy Sosa	609
7.	Frank Robinson	586
8.	**ALEX RODRIGUEZ**	**583**
	Mark McGwire	583
10.	Harmon Killebrew	573

2009

- Hit .286 (127-for-444) with 17 doubles, 1 triple, 30HR, 100RBI and 14SB in 124 games (113 starts at 3B, nine at DH) with the Yankees...missed 28 team games at the beginning of the season due to injury...became the 12th player all time to reach 30HR and 100RBI in a season in which he played fewer than 125G, first since Manny Ramirez in 2002.

ALEX RODRIGUEZ

- The Yankees went 90-44 (.672) following his return from the disabled list on 5/8, marking the best winning percentage in the Majors over the stretch...ranked second in the American League in RBI and tied for second in the AL in home runs after coming off the D.L., trailing only teammate Mark Teixeira...the Yankees record since 2004 with Alex Rodriguez in the lineup: 538-353 (.604); without Rodriguez, 41-40 (.506).
- Was involved in scoring or driving in the game-winning or tying run in six of the Yankees' 15 "walk-off" innings in 2009 (two game-ending home runs, one game-tying home run, two game-winning runs scored and hit a pop-up resulting in a two-run "walk-off" error vs. the Mets)...batted .310 (18-for-58) with 8HR and 21RBI in "close and late" situations, tying for second-most HR in the Majors in such situations.
- According to *Elias*, 15 of his 30HR either tied the game or put the team ahead...had 12HR in the seventh inning or later, seven of which tied the game or put the Yankees ahead...51 of his 100RBI tied the game or put the team ahead, tying for second in the AL with 29 go-ahead RBI...had 33RBI in the seventh inning or later, 15 of which tied the game or put the team ahead.
- Became the third Yankee to reach the 100RBI plateau in fewer than 125 games in a season (also Joe DiMaggio in 1939 and Bill Dickey in 1936).
- Was placed on the 15-day D.L. from 4/4–5/8 (retroactive to 3/27)...missed 28 team games...underwent arthroscopic surgery on 3/9 to repair his right hip labrum, remove an impingement in the joint and drain a cyst in the hip...the procedure was performed by Dr. Marc Philippon at the Vail Valley Surgery Center in Vail, Colo...the cyst and tear were discovered during an MRI taken on 2/28...cyst was originally drained on 3/5.
- In 44 overall plate appearances during rehab assignment from 4/30-5/7, was 7-for-36 (.194) with 3HR, 8BB and 8K...reported to Tampa on 4/13 to continue his rehab program...in four spring training games prior to the surgery, hit .429 (3-for-7) with 2 doubles, 1HR and 5RBI...was selected to participate in the World Baseball Classic with Team Dominican Republic, but was unable to play (hip surgery).
- Missed the Opening Day active roster for the first time since 1995, snapping a stretch of 13 straight Opening Day starts.
- Hit three-run HR on his first pitch seen of the season and was 1-for-4 in 5/8 win at Baltimore...became the first Yankee to homer on the first pitch of his first plate appearance of a season since Andy Phillips on 9/26/04 at Boston, in the first PA of his Major League career...was the second time that Rodriguez hit a HR in his first AB of a season (also 2006).

MOST RBI, SINGLE POSTSEASON, ALL TIME

1.	Sandy Alomar, Jr.	19 (1997, CLE)
	David Ortiz	19 (2004, BOS)
	Scott Spiezio	19 (2002, ANA)
4.	**ALEX RODRIGUEZ**	**18 (2009, NYY)**

FEWEST AT-BATS PER HOME RUN, ALL-TIME (min. 3,000AB)

	Player	AB/HR	AB	HR
1.	Mark McGwire	10.61	6,187	583
2.	Babe Ruth	11.76	8,399	714
3.	Barry Bonds	12.92	9,847	762
4.	Jim Thome	13.66	7,706	564
5.	Adam Dunn	13.98	4,417	316
6.	Albert Pujols	14.06	5,146	366
7.	Ralph Kiner	14.11	5,205	369
8.	Harmon Killebrew	14.22	8,147	573
9.	**ALEX RODRIGUEZ**	**14.24**	**8,304**	**583**
10.	Sammy Sosa	14.47	8,813	609

- Seven of his first 10 hits after returning from the disabled list on 5/8 were home runs...according to the *Elias Sports Bureau*, was the first Yankee in franchise history to collect 7HR within his first 10H of the season.
- Homered on four straight days from 5/16-19, marking the eighth time in his career he homered in at least four consecutive games, most among active players...according to *Elias*, his five streaks of four straight games with a HR as a Yankee tie him with Babe Ruth, Lou Gehrig and Yogi Berra for the most in franchise history.
- Both Rodriguez and Teixeira each hit 4HR over a four-game span from 5/16-19, becoming the first pair of Yankees teammates since 1977 (Reggie Jackson and Bucky Dent) to each hit at least 4HR over the same four-game span—credit: *Elias Sports Bureau*.
- Hit 6HR on the Yankees' 10-game homestand from 5/15-24, matching his most HR hit during any homestand in his Major League career (third time).
- Was 1-for-5 with 1 double in 6/12 win vs. the Mets...was the final batter of the game, coming to bat with two runners on and two outs and reaching base on Luis Castillo's fielding error (missed Rodriguez pop-up to 2B)...both Yankees runners on base scored for the seventh "walk-off" win of the season...marked the Yankees first "walk-off" win on an error since 7/7/03 vs. Boston, when Hideki Matsui scored on Todd Walker's throwing error.

- Reached the 14-year anniversary of his first HR (Tom Gordon on 6/12/95 w/ Seattle vs. Kansas City) with 561 homers...according to the *Elias Sports Bureau*, his career total of within 14 years of hitting his first were most all time...the next-highest home run totals as of the 14th anniversary of their first were Mark McGwire (552) and Sammy Sosa (539).
- Hit two-run HR—the 564th of his career to surpass Reggie Jackson for 11th place on Baseball's all-time list—in 6/26 win at the Mets.
- Hit two-run "walk-off" HR in the 15th inning of 8/7 win vs. Boston, becoming the fifth player in Baseball history to hit a "walk-off" HR in the 15th inning or later to break a scoreless tie, joining Old Hoss Radbourn in 1882 w/ Providence (18th inning), Earl Averill in 1935 w/ Cleveland (15th inning), Willie Mays in 1963 w/ San Francisco (16th inning) and Adrian Garrett in 1975 w/ Chicago-NL (16th inning)—credit: *Elias Sports Bureau*...was his ninth career extra-inning HR.
- The homer snapped a single-season career-high 72AB homerless stretch dating back to 7/19 (third-longest of his career).
- Two games later, hit the go-ahead solo-HR in the seventh in 8/9 win vs. Boston...according to the *Elias Sports Bureau*, became the first player in Major League history to snap scoreless ties by hitting home runs in the seventh inning or later twice in one series.
- Recorded his 2,500th hit with a fifth-inning single in 9/2 win at Baltimore, becoming the 78th player all time to reach the hit total...according to the *Elias Sports Bureau* - at the age of 34 years, 37 days old – became the third-youngest player to reach the 2,500H plateau in the Expansion era, behind Hank Aaron (33 years, 127 days) and Robin Yount (33 years, 289 days)...among active players, only teammate Derek Jeter (1,999G) collected his 2,500th hit in fewer games than him (2,141G).
- Was ejected for the fifth time in his career – and first since 7/24/04 at Boston – in the middle of the fifth by Marty Foster for arguing balls and strikes in 9/13 win vs. Baltimore.
- Tied his career high with 3SB in 9/26 win vs. Boston, going 3-for-3 with 3R, 1 double and 1HR (also 6/24/98 w/ Seattle at San Diego)...became just the fifth player in the last 50 years to collect at least 1HR, 4RBI and 3SB in 9/26 win vs. Boston, joining Edgar Rentaria (6/28/03), Mike Cameron (5/16/02), Davey Lopes (4/7/78) and Bert Campaneris (6/12/65).
- Homered twice in the sixth inning of the Yankees regular season finale win at Tampa Bay on 10/4, with a three-run home run and a grand slam...the 7RBI marked the most in a single inning by an American Leaguer...became the second player in the modern era (since 1900) to drive in seven-or-more runs in an inning (also Fernando Tatis—8RBI on 4/23/99 vs. Los Angeles-NL)...became just the third player in the last 55 years (since 1955) to collect at least 7RBI in a season finale, joining Philadelphia's Dick Allen (7RBI in 1968) and Minnesota's Kirby Puckett (7RBI in 1994 on the day before the strike took effect)...became the 10th player since 1900 to hit two home runs in one inning, one of which was a grand slam...was the second time in his career he has homered twice in the same inning (also 9/5/07 vs. Seattle), marking the sixth time a Yankee has homered twice in the same frame and becoming the first Yankee to accomplish the feat twice in pinstripes.
- Became the first player to homer on his first pitch and last pitch of a season since Detroit's Craig Paquette in 2000 (credit: *Elias*).
- Hit .365 (19-for-52) with 15R, 5 doubles, 6HR and 18RBI in the postseason, leading the team in average, runs, home runs, RBI and tying for tops in doubles...hit three game-tying HR in the seventh inning or later in the 2009 postseason, the most such HR ever for a player in their postseason career (credit: *Elias*)...hit ninth-inning, two-run home run (off Joe Nathan) to tie game in Game 2 win of ALDS vs. Minnesota and solo

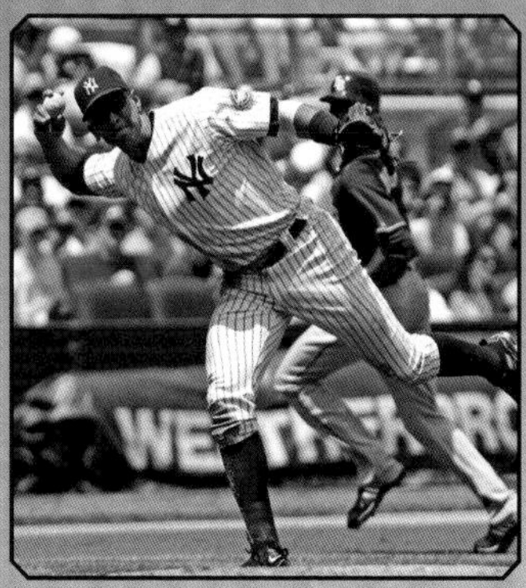

AMONG ACTIVE PLAYERS

GAMES PLAYED

1.	Omar Vizquel	2,742
2.	Ken Griffey, Jr.	2,638
3.	Gary Sheffield	2,576
4.	Ivan Rodriguez	2,338
5.	Jim Thome	2,284
6.	Manny Ramirez	2,207
7.	**ALEX RODRIGUEZ**	**2,166**
	Chipper Jones	2,166
9.	Garrett Anderson	2,148
10.	DEREK JETER	2,138

RUNS SCORED

1.	**ALEX RODRIGUEZ**	**1,683**
2.	Ken Griffey, Jr.	1,656
3.	Gary Sheffield	1,636
4.	DEREK JETER	1,574
5.	Manny Ramirez	1,506

HITS

1.	Ken Griffey, Jr.	2,763
2.	DEREK JETER	2,747
3.	Ivan Rodriguez	2,711
4.	Omar Vizquel	2,704
5.	Gary Sheffield	2,689
6.	**ALEX RODRIGUEZ**	**2,531**
7.	Garrett Anderson	2,501
8.	Manny Ramirez	2,494
9.	Johnny Damon	2,425
10.	Chipper Jones	2,406

RBI

1.	Ken Griffey, Jr.	1,829
2.	Manny Ramirez	1,788
3.	**ALEX RODRIGUEZ**	**1,706**
4.	Gary Sheffield	1,676
5.	Jim Thome	1,565

HR (off Carl Pavano) to tie game in seventh inning of Game 3 ALDS clincher at Minnesota...tied the game with a solo HR (off Brian Fuentes) in the 11th inning of ALCS Game 2 win vs. Los Angeles-AL...matched Bernie Williams (6HR in 1996) for the most HR in a single postseason in franchise history, and was 1HR shy of tying the AL record (7-ANA Troy Glaus-2002 and TB B.J. Upton-2008)...his solo HR on 10/31/09 in Game 4 of World Series at Philadelphia became the first playoff homer to be reviewed by video replay.

- Drove in a run in 11 games and set a franchise record with 18RBI, falling one RBI shy of the all-time postseason record shared by Sandy Alomar, Jr. (1997, CLE), Scott Spiezio (2002, ANA) and David Ortiz (2004, BOS)...eight of his RBI tied the game or put the Yankees ahead...drove in at least one run in eight straight playoff games from 10/8/07 (ALDS Game 4)-10/20/09 (ALCS Game 4), matching the all-time record, (also Lou Gehrig and Ryan Howard)...joined Boston's David Ortiz (2004) as the only two players to record three game-tying or go-ahead RBI hits in the ninth inning or later in a single postseason.
- Collected 11 extra-base hits in the 2009 playoffs, tying six others – including teammate Hideki Matsui (2004) – for most in a single postseason (credit: *Elias*)...was hit by a pitch three times in the World Series, tying Pittsburgh's Max Carey (1925) and teammate Mark Teixeira (2009) for the all-time record.
- Won the Babe Ruth Award from the New York Chapter of the Baseball Writers Association of America as the postseason MVP.

LAST 10 SEASONS, MAJORS (2000-2009)

MOST HOME RUNS

1.	**ALEX RODRIGUEZ**	**435**
2.	Jim Thome	368
3.	Albert Pujols	366
4.	Manny Ramirez	348
5.	Carlos Delgado	324

MOST RUNS SCORED

1.	**ALEX RODRIGUEZ**	**1,190**
2.	Johnny Damon	1,115
3.	DEREK JETER	1,088
4.	Albert Pujols	1,071
5.	Bobby Abreu	1,061

MOST RBI

1.	**ALEX RODRIGUEZ**	**1,243**
2.	Albert Pujols	1,112
3.	Manny Ramirez	1,106
4.	Miguel Tejada	1,046
5.	Carlos Delgado	1,045

2008

- Hit .302 (154-for-510) with 104R, 33 doubles, 35HR, 103RBI and 18SB in 138 games with the Yankees (131 starts at 3B, seven at DH).
- Led the American League with a .573 slugging percentage, ranked third with 35HR and a 14.6 AB/HR ratio, fourth with 14HBP, tied for fifth with 104R, fifth with a .392 on-base percentage, seventh with a .316 average vs. right-handed pitchers and a .339 day batting average, tied for eighth with 103RBI, ninth with a 5.0 AB/RBI ratio and 10th with a .324 home batting average...finished eighth in AL MVP voting.
- According to the *Elias Sports Bureau*, recorded his fourth consecutive season (2005-08) of hitting 20-or-more home runs at the original Yankee Stadium...only Babe Ruth (six straight seasons) had a longer such stretch in original Yankee Stadium history (1926-31)...batted .324 (60-for-185) with 17HR and 47RBI in his last 50 games at the original Yankee Stadium beginning 6/7.
- Was named to his 12th All-Star team, marking his 11th selection via the fan vote and fifth overall selection as a third baseman...tallied the most votes in the Majors (3,934,518) for the second straight season, becoming the first back-to-back leader since Ichiro Suzuki (three seasons, 2001-03)...was 0-for-2 in the 15-inning AL victory on 7/15 at Yankee Stadium, starting at 3B.
- Following the season, was named to the 2008 *Sporting News* AL All-Star team, which was selected by a panel of 41 general managers and assistant general managers from both leagues...also earned his 10th career Silver Slugger Award.
- Made his fifth straight Opening Day start at 3B for the Yankees—the 13th OD start of his career—and was 2-for-3 with 1R, 1 double, 1RBI and 1BB in 4/1 win vs. Toronto...started his fifth straight Opening Day at third base with Derek Jeter at shortstop, becoming the first pair of Yankees to start on the left side of the infield in five consecutive years since Graig Nettles and Bucky Dent started six consecutive from 1977-82.
- Was 0-for-4 in 4/8 loss at Kansas City, striking out a career-high-tying four times for the fourth time in his career (third as a Yankee, first since 8/25/06 at Los Angeles-AL).
- Was placed on the 15-day D.L. from 4/30-5/20 with a strained right quadriceps (missed 16 team games, Yankees were 6-10)...was his first stint on the disabled list since 7/8-24/00 (w/ Seattle) when he missed 15 games with a right knee strain...originally injured his quad running out a ground ball on 4/20 at Baltimore...missed three games from 4/22-24 (spent three days from 4/21-23 in Miami, Fla., welcoming the birth of his second daughter, Ella Alexander, on 4/21)...returned to the lineup on 4/25 and played in four games before being removed for PH (Damon) in the eighth inning of 4/28 win at Cleveland (left game with discomfort in his right quad).

- In his final 114 games of the season after returning from the D.L. on 5/20, hit .305 (128-for-419) with 90R, 26 doubles, 31HR, 92RBI, 59BB and 17SB...the Yankees were 68-46 (.596) over the stretch as he led the AL in home runs and ranked third in runs and RBI...was the third-highest winning percentage in the AL following his return.
- Hit two-run HR on 5/20 vs. Baltimore and solo-HR on 5/21 vs. Baltimore, becoming the first player to homer in each of his first two games after spending at least three weeks on the D.L. since Chris Richard from 7/31-8/1/02 with Baltimore (credit: *Elias Sports Bureau*).
- Hit game-winning solo-HR in the 12th—his 200th homer as a Yankee—and was 1-for-6 on 8/12 at Minnesota...became the 15th player in franchise history to reach 200 home runs with the Yankees, including two others who did it within the previous month: Derek Jeter (7/12) and Jason Giambi (8/9)...according to the *Elias Sports Bureau*, it marked the first time that any set of teammates on one club accomplished the feat in the same season...*Elias* also notes that Rodriguez became the second-fastest Yankee to reach 200HR, doing so in 729 games with the club (Babe Ruth reached 200HR with the Yankees in 586 games).
- Grounded into 11 double plays in the month of August, the most in a single month in franchise history since GDPs were first recorded in the American League in 1939 (credit: *Elias Sports Bureau*).
- His solo-HR on 9/2 at Tampa Bay was the 1,000th extra-base hit of his career, coming at the age of 33 years, 37 days...according to the *Elias Sports Bureau*, only Jimmie Foxx (32 years, 294 days on 8/13/40) reached the milestone at a younger age.
- Was scratched from the lineup before 9/13 Game 1 loss vs. Tampa Bay (stiff neck).
- Hit grand-slam-HR in the first inning and was 2-for-4 with 2R and 1 double in 9/14 win vs. Tampa Bay...according to *Elias*, became the first Yankees cleanup hitter to hit a grand slam after the first three batters of the game reached base since Mel Hall on 6/24/89 at Kansas City and the first such Yankee at Yankee Stadium since Dave Winfield on 7/16/84 vs. Texas.

2007

- Won his third career American League MVP Award and his second in four seasons with the Yankees, hitting .314 (183-for-583) with 143R, 54HR, 156RBI and 24SB in 158 games (154 starts at 3B, four starts at DH)...established career highs in runs and RBI...received 26-of-28 first-place votes in BBWAA MVP voting (382 total points)...became the ninth player in Major League history to win at least three MVP Awards and fifth AL player...became the sixth player to win multiple MVP's with the Yankees, joining Lou Gehrig (two), Joe DiMaggio (three), Mickey Mantle (three), Yogi Berra (three) and Roger Maris (two)...became just the fourth player to win the MVP Award three times within a five-year span, joining Roy Campanella, Berra and Barry Bonds.
- Was elected to the 2007 AL All-Star team, the 11th All-Star selection of his career (1996-98; 2000-07)...was the first time he led the Majors in All-Star balloting (3,890,515 votes)...started at 3B and went 1-for-3 in the 7/10 American League win...also named "Major League Player of the Year" by *Baseball America* and the *Sporting News* and was named starting 3B on each publication's All-Star team...became just the third player in the 72-year history of the *Sporting News* Award to win at least three times, joining Ted Williams (five) and Barry Bonds (three)...received his ninth career Silver Slugger Award, fourth career Hank Aaron Award, the Oscar Charleston Legacy Award and Josh Gibson Award presented by the Negro Leagues Baseball Museum, and was named the MLB.com "Clutch Performer of the Year," This Week in Baseball's "Hitter of the Year" and the Latinosports.com "2007 LatinoMVP Player of the Year"...was also named the Sid Mercer "Player of the Year" by the New York chapter of the BBWAA and was selected by his peers as the Players Choice 2007 "Player of the Year" and the American League's "Outstanding Player"...was named American League "Player of the Week" three times in 2007 (4/2-9, 6/4-10 and 9/3-9).
- Led the Majors in runs, home runs and RBI...since RBI became an official statistic in 1920, became only the fourth player (and the first in the past 50 years) to finish a season with the outright Major League lead in each of those categories, according to the *Elias Sports Bureau*: Babe Ruth (three times: 1920-21, 1926), Ted Williams (1942-also won Triple Crown) and Mickey Mantle (1956-also won Triple Crown)...also led the Major Leagues with a .645 slugging percentage and an average of 1RBI every 3.7 at-bats...tied for the lead with three grand slams.

Most MVPs by Franchise

YANKEES	**22**
Cardinals	16
Giants	12
Reds	11
Athletics	10

Yankees MVPs

Berra	3
DiMaggio	3
Mantle	3
Gehrig	2
Maris	2
RODRIGUEZ	**2**
Chandler	1
Gordon	1
Howard	1
Mattingly	1
Munson	1
Rizzuto	1
Ruth	1

- Led the American League with 376 total bases, ranked second with 85 extra-base hits, 21HBP and 1HR/10.8AB, fourth with a .422 on-base percentage, tied for fourth with nine sacrifice flies, seventh with a .326 road batting average and a .340 day average, tied for seventh with 95BB and eighth with a .327 average vs. right-handed pitching.
- Hit .463 (19-for-41) with 8HR, 21RBI, 9BB and 7K in the ninth inning of games, leading the Majors in ninth-inning homers...tied Philadelphia's Ryan Howard and Houston's Lance Berkman for the Major League lead with 22HR that tied the game or put his team ahead (credit: *Elias Sports Bureau*).
- Became the fifth player in Major League history to have 140R, 50HR and 150RBI in a season, joining Sammy Sosa (2001), Jimmie Foxx (1932), Hack Wilson (1930) and Babe Ruth (1921, '27) and the first to also record 20SB...according to the

ALEX RODRIGUEZ

Elias Sports Bureau, is only the fourth player to post two seasons of at least 50HR, 130R and 130RBI (2001, '07)...Babe Ruth accomplished the feat four times; Jimmie Foxx and Sammy Sosa both did it twice.

- With 54HR, established the Yankees franchise record for most home runs in a single season by a right-handed batter...were the most by any Yankees player since Roger Maris (61HR in 1961) and were tied for the fourth-highest single-season total in franchise history...the Yankees were 35-11 in games in which he homered.
- Established the Major League record for most home runs in a single season by a third baseman with 52 homers (hit two as DH), surpassing Mike Schmidt (48 with Philadelphia in 1980) and Adrian Beltre (48 with Los Angeles-NL in 2004).
- Finished with 26HR at home, tying his own record (established in 2005) for the most home runs in a single season at Yankee Stadium by a right-handed batter...Yankees were 21-2 in games in which he homered at Yankee Stadium...hit 28HR on the road...only four Yankees have hit more road homers in a single-season: Babe Ruth in 1927 (32), Roger Maris in 1961 (31), Mickey Mantle in 1961 (30) and Jason Giambi in 2003 (29).
- His 156RBI were the most by a Yankee in a single season since 1937 when Joe DiMaggio had 167 and Lou Gehrig had 159...was the second-highest single-season total by a right-handed hitter in franchise history behind only DiMaggio's 167 in 1937...the total also ranks 10th on the Yankees' all-time single-season list and were the most in the American League since Manny Ramirez in 1999 with Cleveland (165RBI)...drove in 111 runs in his final 105 games of the season...became the first Yankee to record multiple seasons of at least 130RBI (2005, '07) since Joe DiMaggio accomplished the feat in 1937, '38, '40 and '48 (credit: *Elias Sports Bureau*).
- His 143 runs scored were the highest single-season total in the American League since the Yankees' Rickey Henderson scored 146 runs in 1985 and was the second-highest single-season total by a Yankee in the last 70 years (since 1938).

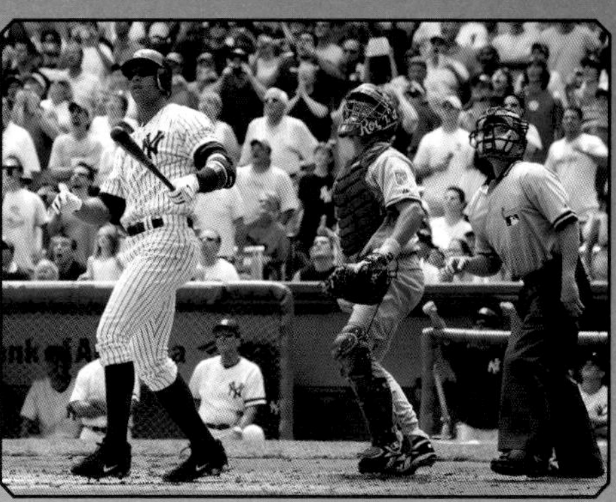

YOUNGEST PLAYERS TO HIT 500 CAREER HOME RUNS

Player	Age (Yrs-Days) when hit 500th	Career Total
ALEX RODRIGUEZ	**32-008**	**553**
Jimmie Foxx	32-338	534
Willie Mays	34-131	660
Sammy Sosa	34-133	609
Hank Aaron	34-160	755

** Courtesy* *Elias Sports Bureau*

MOST HOME RUNS BY A YANKEE IN A SINGLE SEASON

No.	Player	Year
61	Roger Maris	1961
60	Babe Ruth	1927
59	Babe Ruth	1921
54	**ALEX RODRIGUEZ**	**2007**
54	Mickey Mantle	1961
54	Babe Ruth	1928
54	Babe Ruth	1920

50 OR MORE HOME RUNS, THREE DIFFERENT SEASONS

No.	Player	Years
4	Babe Ruth	1920-21, '27-28
	Mark McGwire	1996-99
	Sammy Sosa	1998-2001
3	**ALEX RODRIGUEZ**	**2001-02, '07**

SEASONS WITH 35-OR-MORE HOME RUNS (ALL-TIME)

	Player	
1.	Babe Ruth	12
	ALEX RODRIGUEZ	**12**
3.	Hank Aaron	11
	Mike Schmidt	11

140 Runs, 50 Home Runs, 150 RBI In One Season

Year	Player	Team	(R-HR-RBI)
1921	Babe Ruth	New York-AL	177-59-171
1927	Babe Ruth	New York-AL	158-60-164
1930	Hack Wilson	Chicago-NL	146-56-191
1932	Jimmie Foxx	Philadelphia-AL	151-58-169
2001	Sammy Sosa	Chicago-NL	146-64-160
2007	**ALEX RODRIGUEZ**	**New York-AL**	**143-54-156**

- Drove in 100 runs through the club's first 99 games of the season...according to the *Elias Sports Bureau*, became the first Yankee to reach the 100-RBI mark in fewer than 100 "team games" into a season since 1937, when both Joe DiMaggio (91 games) and Lou Gehrig (96 games) did so.
- His 24 stolen bases were the most for any player from the cleanup spot in the batting order since Preston Wilson stole 36 bases from that spot for the 2000 Marlins...became just the fourth player all-time to record at least 50HR and at least 20SB in a single season, joining Willie Mays (1955, New York Giants), Brady Anderson (1996, Baltimore) and Ken Griffey, Jr. (1998, Seattle).
- Hit two-run HR—his third career Opening Day home run and second as a Yankee—and was 2-for-5 with 2R and 1SB in 4/2 win vs. Tampa Bay...was his fourth straight Opening Day start at 3B for the Yankees and 12th Opening Day start of his career.

- Hit two-run HR and "walk-off" grand slam in the ninth inning in 4/7 win vs. Baltimore, and was 3-for-4 with 4R, 1 double and 1BB...according to the *Elias Sports Bureau*, became the third player in franchise history to hit a game-ending grand slam with the Yankees trailing when they came to the plate: also Jason Giambi on 5/27/02 vs. Minnesota and Babe Ruth in 1925...marked only the eighth time in franchise history that the Yankees won a game with a "walk-off" grand slam and the first since Giambi in 2002...was his third career "walk-off" grand slam (also on 7/27/02 w/ Texas vs. Oakland and 7/31/03 w/ Texas vs. Boston).
- According to the *Elias Sports Bureau*, became only the second player in AL history to hit six home runs through his team's first seven games, joining Ken Griffey, Jr. (1997)...became the first player in Yankees franchise history to hit 7HR in the team's first 10 games of the season and 8HR in the first 12 games...hit 12HR in the first 15 games of the season, joining Mike Schmidt (12HR in the first 15 games of 1976) as the fastest players in Major League history to reach 12 home runs...drove in 31 runs in the first 16 games of the season, the most of any Major Leaguer over any 16-game span since Sammy Sosa had 32 in May/June 1998.

MOST HOME RUNS IN A SINGLE SEASON BY A RIGHT HANDED BATTER IN YANKEES HISTORY

1.	**ALEX RODRIGUEZ, 2007**	**54**
2.	**ALEX RODRIGUEZ, 2005**	**48**
3.	Joe DiMaggio, 1937	46
4.	Joe DiMaggio, 1948	39
	Alfonso Soriano, 2002	39

- Drove in 16 runs in his first eight games of the season (4/2-11), the most RBI for any AL player through his club's first eight games of a season since Minnesota's Brant Alyea in 1970 (credit: *Elias Sports Bureau*).
- According to the *Elias Sports Bureau*, became the first player in Yankees history (and the only Major Leaguer since 1958) to collect an extra-base hit in each of his team's first eight games of a season...his streak of 11 straight regular season games with an extra base hit (dating back to 2006) was the longest for any player in franchise history, breaking the mark of 10 straight shared by Don Mattingly (1987) and Paul O'Neill (2001).
- Hit three-run "walk-off" HR in the ninth inning—his third home run in a three-game span—and was 1-for-5 in 4/19 win vs. Cleveland...was his second "walk-off" home run of the season (also 4/7 vs. Baltimore) and seventh of his career (fourth as a Yankee)...according to *Elias*, became the fourth player in Major League history to hit two "walk-off" home runs so early in the season (through his team's first 14 games), joining Pat Burrell (nine games in 2002), Robin Yount (12 games in 1991) and Tommy Henrich (12 games in 1949)...is only the third player in Yankees history to hit a pair of "walk-off" homers within a span of five home games at any point in a season, joining Babe Ruth (August 1922) and Claudell Washington (September 1988) who each hit two "walk-off" home runs in three-game spans.
- In his 18th game, on 4/23 at Tampa Bay, became the fastest player in Major League history to reach 14HR to begin a season (previous record was held by Albert Pujols, who hit 14HR in the first 24 games of 2006)...according to the *Elias Sports Bureau*, only two players hit more than 14HR over an 18-game span for their team at any point during a season: Sammy Sosa in 1998 (16) and Barry Bonds in 2001 (15)...three others also hit 14 over a period of 18 games (Rudy York, 1937 Tigers; Albert Belle, 1995 Indians; and Mark McGwire, 1998 Cardinals).
- Began the season with an 18-game hitting streak, the longest hitting streak by an American Leaguer to start a season since George Brett hit safely in his first 19 games of the 1983 season...dating back to 2006, hit safely in a career-high 23 straight games.
- Was named the AL "Player of the Month" for April, hitting .355 (33-for-93) and leading the Majors with 14HR, 34RBI and 27R in 23 games...tied the mark for most home runs hit in April (also Albert Pujols in 2006) and finished 1RBI shy of Juan Gonzalez's Major League record for April (35) set in 1998 with Texas...with 14HR, fell 1HR shy of tying a career high for any calendar month (15HR with Texas in August 2003)...established a single-month career high with 34RBI (previous high was 31RBI with Texas in August 2003)...according to the *Elias Sports Bureau*, became the first player in Major League history to record at least 14HR and 34RBI by the end of April.
- Became the first Yankee with at least 14HR and 34RBI in any calendar month since Roger Maris in June 1961 (15HR, 35RBI)...according to the *Elias Sports Bureau*, the only other Yankees with more home runs in a calendar month were Babe Ruth, who did it four times (17 in September 1927; 15 in May 1928, August 1929 and June 1930), Joe DiMaggio (15 in July 1937) and Mickey Mantle (16 in May 1956)...only Harmon Killebrew (15 with the Washington Senators in May 1959) has hit more home runs in any calendar month all time among Major League third basemen.
- Went 47 consecutive games without committing an error from 5/30-7/23, the longest errorless streak by a Yankees third baseman since he went 61 straight games without an error from 6/23-9/1/05.
- Hit game-winning solo-HR in the ninth and was 2-for-5 with 2RBI in 6/3 win at Boston...was his second ninth-inning, game-winning home run at Fenway Park since joining the Yankees (also 7/14/05 off Curt Schilling)...over the last 20 years, only two other Yankees have hit a game-winning homer in the ninth inning at Fenway: Bernie Williams and Alfonso Soriano (one each in 2001)...hit grand slam in the ninth—his third ninth-inning homer of the road trip—and was 2-for-4 with 1IBB in 6/7 win at Chicago-AL...according to the *Elias Sports Bureau*, became the second player in Yankees history to hit two grand slams in the ninth inning or later in the same season, joining Darryl Strawberry who hit two pinch-hit grand slams in 1998.

- Was named the AL "Player of the Month" for June, his second "Player of the Month" Award in 2007, fifth as a Yankee and ninth of his career—the most among American Leaguers...led the AL with 28R, 9HR, 34RBI, a .773 slugging percentage and a .496 on-base percentage, while ranking fourth with a .402 batting average...his 34RBI tied his personal best for any calendar month of his career, which he set in in April, and were the most by any Yankee in June since Roger Maris (35RBI) in 1961...no Yankee had posted as high of calendar-month numbers in average, home runs and RBI in over 50 years since Mickey Mantle batted .414 with 16HR and 35RBI in May 1956.
- Missed his first game of the season in 7/5 win vs. Minnesota (strained left hamstring)...was the only Yankee to start each of the first 81 games of 2007.
- Set personal highs for home runs (30) and RBI (86) before the All-Star break...according to the *Elias Sports Bureau*, Lou Gehrig (90 in 1934) is the only player in franchise history to have as many RBI at the break...was the first Yankee to lead the Majors in home runs at the All-Star break since Roger Maris in 1961 (33HR)...led the Major Leagues in runs (79), HR (30) and RBI (86) at the All-Star break, becoming the first player in the Majors to accomplish the feat since the Yankees' Mickey Mantle in 1956 (credit: *Elias Sports Bureau*)...also reached the All-Star break with 20HR for the Major League-record seventh consecutive season.
- Hit three-run HR in the first inning—the 500th of his career—and was 3-for-4 with 3R, 1BB and 1SB in 8/4 win vs. Kansas City...became the 22nd player in Major League history to reach the 500-HR plateau...according to the *Elias Sports Bureau*, became the youngest player to hit 500 career home runs (32 years, 8 days), surpassing Jimmie Foxx (32 years, 338 days)...became the third player to hit his 500th home run as a Yankee (also Babe Ruth and Mickey Mantle) and only the second to hit his 500th at Yankee Stadium (Mantle on 5/14/67 off Baltimore's Stu Miller)...according to the *Elias Sports Bureau*, is one of only two players with at least 500 career HR to have hit 100 or more with three different teams (Seattle-189; Yankees-208: Texas-156), joining Reggie Jackson (Oakland-269; Yankees-144; California-123)...went 28AB between home runs #499 and #500...according to the *Elias Sports Bureau*, that tied Mickey Mantle for the third-longest homerless streak between #499 and #500 (Jimmie Foxx-61AB, Harmon Killebrew-43AB).
- His 44HR were the most for a Yankee through the end of August since 1961, when Roger Maris and Mickey Mantle began September with 51 and 48 home runs, respectively (credit: *Elias Sports Bureau*)...hit solo-HR and two-run HR in the seventh inning and was 2-for-3 with 1BB in 9/5 win vs. Seattle...hit two home runs in the same inning for the first time in his career becoming the fourth Yankee to accomplish the feat (first since Cliff Johnson in the eighth inning on 6/30/77 at Toronto).
- Hit two-run HR and was 2-for-5 with 2R in 9/9 win at Kansas City, homering in his fifth consecutive game (7HR overall) from 9/4-9/9, tying a career high (also 8/11-16/99 and 8/17-21/03)...was the first Yankee to homer in five straight games since Tino Martinez did so from 5/7-11/05...joined Albert Pujols as the only Major Leaguers to homer in at least five straight games in 2007.
- On 9/28 at Baltimore, became the second player in Major League history (since RBI became an official statistic in 1920) to reach 1,500 career runs and 1,500 career RBI in the same game...according to the *Elias Sports Bureau*, Houston's Jeff Bagwell reached both milestones on 9/18/04 vs. Milwaukee...became the third-youngest player to reach 1,500 career RBI, behind Jimmie Foxx and Lou Gehrig (credit: *Elias Sports Bureau*)...hit his 54th and final home run of the season in the game, going 3-for-5...came in his 1,903rd career game, marking the fourth-fewest games needed to reach the plateaus since 1920 (when RBIs became an official statistic) behind Lou Gehrig (1,715 games), Ted Williams (1,761) and Jimmie Foxx (1,850).
- Batted .267 (4-for-15) in four Division Series games vs. Cleveland with 1HR and 1RBI.

2006

- In his third season with the Yankees, hit .290 (166-for-572) with 113R, 35HR, 121RBI and 15SB in 154 games (148 starts at 3B, three at DH)...ranked fourth in the American League in RBI, fifth in runs scored and a .340 average vs. lefthanders, seventh with 139 strikeouts, eighth with 90BB, tied for eighth in home runs and ninth with 1RBI every 4.7 at bats...was elected to the 2006 American League All-Star team, the 10th All-Star selection of his career (1996-98; 2000-06)...started at 3B and was 0-for-2 in the American League's 3-2 victory on 7/11.
- In 4/3 Opening Day win at Oakland, hit the 12th grand slam of his career...was the fourth grand slam by a Yankee on Opening Day (also Russ Derry on 4/17/45 vs. Boston; Bobby Murcer on 4/9/81 vs. Texas; and Alfonso Soriano on 3/31/03 at Toronto)...became the 56th Yankee to hit a home run on Opening Day...made his third straight Opening Day start at 3B for the Yankees and the 11th of his career...hit two-run HR and solo-HR and scored a season-high four runs in 5/27 win vs. Kansas City.
- Was named AL "Player of the Month" for May...reached base safely in 25 of 28 games during the month, batting .330 (36-for-109) with 8HR while tying Boston's David Ortiz and Cleveland's Travis Hafner for the AL lead with 28RBI...finished the month with a nine-game hitting streak...was his seventh career "Player of the Month" Award, third as a Yankee, and marked the second consecutive year he won the award for the month of May.
- Missed two games (6/2-3) at Baltimore with a stomach virus...hit two-run "walk-off" home run (#16) in the 12th inning and was 2-for-5 with 3RBI and 1BB in 6/28 win vs. Atlanta...was the fifth "walk-off" home run of his career and first since 8/4/04 vs. Oakland...was also the first by a Yankee to end an extra-inning game when trailing since 5/17/02 when Jason Giambi hit a 14th-inning grand slam to give the Yankees a 13-12 win

vs. Minnesota...the home run was the 100th of his career as a Yankee, making him the third player in Major League history to record at least 100 home runs with three different teams (also 189HR with Seattle, 156 with Texas)...according to the *Elias Sports Bureau*, Reggie Jackson (269 with KC/Oakland A's, 144 with the Yankees and 123 with California) and Darrell Evans (131 with Atlanta, 142 with San Francisco and 141 with Detroit) also accomplished the feat.

- In 7/17 win vs. Seattle, committed three errors in a single game for the first time in his career...hit a three-run home run in 7/21 loss at Toronto, six days shy of his 31st birthday, becoming only the eighth player in Major League history to accumulate 2,000 hits before age 31, according to the *Elias Sports Bureau*...joined Ty Cobb (29), Rogers Hornsby (29), Met Ott (30), Hank Aaron (30), Joe Medwick (30), Jimmie Foxx (30) and Robin Yount (30)...was also his 450th career home run and at 30 years, 359 days old, became the youngest player in Major League history to reach the 450 mark, surpassing Ken Griffey Jr. who was 31 years, 261 days old when he hit his 450th career home run on 8/9/01.
- Was named the AL "Player of the Week" for the week of 8/28-9/3...hit solo-HR and three-run HR and was 3-for-5 with 5RBI in 9/3 win vs. Minnesota...was his fourth multi-home run game of the season and second in a three-game span (also 9/1 vs. Minnesota)...missed two games (9/9-10 at Baltimore) with a stomach virus...made only two errors in his final 34 games at third base (8/19-9/30)... hit .071 (1-for-14) in four Division Series games vs. Detroit.

2005

- Captured his second career American League Most Valuable Player Award, hitting .321 (194-for-605) and leading the American League with 124R and 48HR while driving in 130 runs in 162 games with the Yankees (161 starts at 3B, one start at DH)...became the first Yankee to win the AL home run title since Reggie Jackson (41) in 1980.
- Led the AL with a .610 slugging percentage, tied for the lead with 162 games played, ranked second with a .321 batting average, .351 home batting average, .421 on-base percentage and 369 total bases, third with 91 walks, 139 strikeouts and a .327 average vs. right-handed pitching, fourth with 130RBI and 78 extra-base hits, tied for fifth with 16HBP, tied for sixth with 194H, and tied for eighth with 53 multi-hit games...joined Willie Mays (New York Giants, 1955), Barry Bonds (San Francisco Giants, 1993) and Larry Walker (Colorado Rockies, 1997) as the only players to bat .300, hit 45 or more home runs and steal 20 or more bases in a single season.
- Was elected to the 2005 American League All-Star team, the ninth All-Star selection of his career (1996-98; 2000-05)...started at 3B and was 1-for-2 with 1R and 1BB...also earned his eighth career Louisville Slugger "Silver Slugger" Award.
- Established the franchise record for most home runs in a single season by a right-handed batter (later passed with 54HR in 2007), breaking Joe DiMaggio's mark of 46 set in 1937...his 48 home runs were the most by any Yankee since Roger Maris hit 61 and Mickey Mantle hit 54 in 1961...hit 26 home runs at Yankee Stadium in 2005, establishing the single-season club record for right-handed batters (previous record was 19HR by Joe DiMaggio in 1937 and Gary Sheffield in 2004)...with Hideki Matsui, became the first pair of Yankees to each play in every game in the same season since 1945, when Nick Etten and Snuffy Stirnweiss accomplished the feat for the second straight year (credit: *Elias Sports Bureau*)...committed 12 errors in his second season at third base and only two over his last 91 games of the season...among third basemen with 400 or more chances, only the Rangers' Hank Blalock (11) had fewer errors.
- On 4/5 vs. Boston, became only the second player to hit a home run into the black "batter's-eye" section of remodeled original Yankee Stadium both as a Yankee and as an opponent (also 8/17/96 w/ Seattle), joining Tony Clark.
- Hit a three-run HR in the first inning, a two-run HR in the third and a grand slam in the fourth and was 4-for-5 with a career-high 10RBI in 4/26 win vs. the Angels...was the 38th multi-homer game of his career and his second of the season (was his third three-home run game and first since 8/17/02 with Texas vs. Toronto)...became the 19th Yankee to hit three home runs in a single regular season game and the first since Tony Clark on 8/28/04 at Toronto (24th time overall)...his 10RBI were the most by a Yankee since Tony Lazzeri established the franchise- and American League record with 11 in a 25-2 win at Philadelphia on 5/24/36 (the Major League record for RBI in a single game is 12 by the Cardinals' Jim Bottomley on 9/16/24 and the Cardinals' Mark Whiten on 9/7/93)...became the 11th player in Major League history to drive in at least 10 runs in a game and the first since Boston's Nomar Garciaparra on 5/10/99 vs. Seattle...became the first and only player ever to accomplish the feat at the original Yankee Stadium.
- Became the first player to hit eight home runs at Yankee Stadium in April (in a single season)...the previous record was five (by Lou Gehrig in 1933 and Paul O'Neill in 2001)...was named co-winner of the AL's "Player of the Week" award (with White Sox pitcher Jon Garland) for the week ending 5/1...was his ninth career "Player of the Week" Award...was named the AL "Player of the Month" for May...reached base safely in 10 straight plate appearances from 5/26-29.
- Had his fourth multi-home-run game of the season in 6/8 win at Milwaukee, the 40th of his career (37th 2HR game)...the two home runs were the 399th and 400th home runs of his career...at 29 years, 316 days old, became the youngest player in Major League history to reach the 400 mark...became the sixth player to hit his 400th career home run as a Yankee, joining Babe Ruth (on 9/2/27 at Philadelphia), Lou Gehrig (on 7/10/36 vs.

Cleveland), Mickey Mantle (on 9/10/62 at Detroit), Reggie Jackson (on 8/11/80 vs. Chicago) and Gary Sheffield (on 7/27/04 at Toronto).

- Hit a solo-HR—his second in as many games—and was 1-for-3 with 1HP in 8/26 win vs. Kansas City...his home run was his second "batter's eye" home run of the season (also 4/5 vs. Boston) and the third of his career (also on 8/17/96 with Seattle), tying Danny Tartabull and Bernie Williams for the most by any player.
- Named AL "Player of the Month" for August...went 61 consecutive games without committing an error from 6/23-9/2...was the longest such streak by an AL third baseman since Boston's John Valentin in 1998 (65 games)...hit solo-HR and was 4-for-5 with 2R and 1 double in AL East-clinching win on 10/1 at Boston...hit six home runs against the Red Sox in 2005, the most by any Yankee since Mickey Mantle hit six in 1964...hit .133 (2-for-15) with 6BB in five Division Series games vs. Los Angeles-AL.

2004

- In his first season with the Yankees, batted .286 (172-for-601) with 112R, 36HR, 106RBI and a team-high 28SB in 155 games (155 starts at 3B)...ranked fifth in the American League in runs and stolen bases, was tied for sixth in home runs, was ninth with 80BB and ranked 10th with 308TB...was elected to the 2004 American League All-Star team, the eighth All-Star selection of his career (1996-98; 2000-04)...started at 3B and was 1-for-3 with an RBI triple in the American League's 9-4 win on 7/13 at Houston's Minute Maid Park.
- With three-run HR in 5/4 win at Oakland, became the 70th player to reach 350 career home runs and, at 28 years, 282 days old, also became the youngest player ever to reach the 350 mark (previous youngest to reach 350 home runs was Ken Griffey, Jr., who was 28 years, 308 days old)...with his 4RBI on 5/4, he reached 1,001 in his career to become the third-youngest player ever to reach the 1,000 RBI plateau (behind only Mel Ott, 27 years, 94 days; and Jimmie Foxx, 27 years, 236 days)...reached base safely in a career-high 53 consecutive games from 4/18–6/18 (longest previous such streak was 37 straight games from 4/6-6/22/99 w/ Seattle)...was the longest such streak in the Major Leagues in 2004 and the longest by a Yankee within a single season since Derek Jeter reached base safely in the first 53 games of the 1999 season.
- Hit three-run HR and two-run HR and collected a season-high 5RBI in 6/22 win at Baltimore, his second multi-home-run game of the season (also 5/15 vs. Seattle) and the 35th of his career...was successful in 17 straight stolen-base attempts from 4/20-6/29, the longest such streak of his career...hit two solo home runs in 7/15 win at Detroit, his third multi-homer game of the season and the 36th of his career...was 0-for-1 with 1R and 1HBP before being ejected (fighting) in the top of the third inning of 7/24 loss at Boston.
- Had 369 career home runs before his 29th birthday, the most of any Major League player...hit two-run "walk-off" HR (#29) in the 11th inning on 8/4 vs. Oakland...was his fourth career "walk-off" HR and first since 7/31/03 (w/ Texas) vs. Boston.
- Did not play in 8/13 win at Seattle, missing his first game of the season with a viral infection...in 9/6 win vs. Tampa Bay, batted second in the lineup for the first time since 10/2/99 (w/ Seattle vs. Oakland) and was 2-for-4 with two doubles, 3RBI and 1BB...remained second in the lineup for the remainder of the season, batting .301 (28-for-93) with 19R, 3HR and 25RBI in 24 games.
- Hit .320 (16-for-50) with 11R, 3HR and 8RBI in 11 postseason games...went 4-for-6 with 3RBI in Game 2 of the Division Series, driving in the game-tying run with a 12th-inning double...with five runs scored in Game 3 of the ALCS, matched the single-game postseason record for runs scored (also Hideki Matsui in the same game)...homered in back-to-back games in the ALCS, driving in game-tying run in Game 3 and go-ahead run in Game 4.

2003

- Earned his first American League MVP Award, batting .298 (181-for-607) with 47HR and 118RBI in 161 games with Texas (158 starts at SS, one at DH)...was tied for the Major League lead in home runs and led the AL in HR, runs (124) and slugging precentage (.600)...ranked second in the league in RBI and total bases (364), placed third in extra base hits (83) and was eighth in walks (87) and on-base percentage (.396)...became the third player in the last 71 years to win three consecutive AL home run titles and the fifth since 1954 to top the league in homers, runs and slugging percentage in the same year...was second in the AL in go-ahead RBI (30) and tied for third in game-winning RBI (16), including three consecutive games, 8/17-19.
- Won his second consecutive Rawlings Gold Glove Award, leading all Major League shortstops with a .989 fielding percentage (8E/699TC), the highest figure in Rangers history and a career best...were the fewest errors ever for a Texas shortstop (among qualifers) and the fewest of his career...led AL shortstops in double plays (111), tied for second in games (158), and placed third in putouts (227), assists (464) and total chances...longest errorless streak was 33 games from 6/1-7/9...won the AL Silver Slugger Award (SS) for the fifth consecutive year and seventh time overall...won third consecutive AL Hank Aaron Award as league's top offensive player and the latinosports.com LatinoMVP American League Award.
- Was elected as starting shortstop for seventh time on the AL All-Star team...went 1-for-3 with 1R on 7/15 at Chicago's U.S. Cellular Field...won Players' Choice Award as the American League's Outstanding Player...won the Negro Leagues Baseball Museum Oscar Charleston Legacy Award (AL MVP) and his third consecutive Josh Gibson Legacy Award (AL Home Run Leader).

- Tied Philadelphia's Jim Thome for the most home runs in the Majors, becoming the first player to lead Majors in home runs in consecutive seasons since Mark McGwire in 1998-99 and the second Ranger to accomplish the feat (Juan Gonzalez in 1992-93)...homered once every 12.9 at-bats, the AL's top ratio...had three two-homer games (4/16 vs. Anaheim, 8/28 at Kansas City and 9/20 vs. Anaheim)...connected for 10th career grand slam to win the game in the bottom of 11th inning on 7/31 vs. Boston, becoming the 11th player ever with at least two "walk-off" grand slams...tied the club record at the time with home runs in five consecutive games from 8/17-21...had 25 homers in his last 62 games beginning 7/23...led the Majors and tied the club mark for homers in a month with a career-high 15HR in August...of that total, 14 came while playing shortstop, the highest monthly total ever for a player at that position...established team mark for homers vs. an opponent with 11 against Anaheim.
- Connected for his 300th career home run off Ramon Ortiz on 4/2 at Anaheim at the age of 27 years, 249 days, becoming the youngest player in history to reach the milestone (79 days younger than Jimmie Foxx)...had 322 homers before turning 28, also the most ever by that age...homered as the DH on 8/31/03 vs. Minnesota...drove in 53 runs in last 54 games beginning 7/31...tied for the Major League lead with 31RBI in August.
- Had appeared in 546 consecutive games—the 25th longest streak in Major League history—before sitting out on 9/24 at Oakland...was first missed contest since 7/23/00 with starts in 542 of those games...had played in all 482 games since joining the Rangers, a club record for consecutive contests...became the 35th player in history to appear in 500 consecutive contests on 8/5 at New York...did not start due to bruised left knee on 6/7-8 vs. Montreal in San Juan, Puerto Rico, but pinch-hit in both games...hit safely in 25 of 26 games from 7/27-8/22 with streaks of 12 (7/27-8/8) and 13 (8/10-22) games, the latter the longest by a Ranger in 2003...selected as the AL and Texas Rangers' "Player of the Month" for August.
- Tied club record and career-high with five hits on 4/27 vs. New York-AL and followed with 4H on 4/29 in Toronto, the first Ranger ever with nine hits in consecutive games...became the second youngest player ever to score 1,000 career runs at 28 years, 47 days on 9/12 vs. Oakland, topped only by the New York Giants' Mel Ott (27 years, 104 days in 1936).

2002

- Led the Major Leagues with 57HR, 142RBI and 389TB, the first player to lead the Majors in all three categories since Boston's Tony Armas in 1984...batted .300 (187-for-624) and finished among American League leaders in games (tied for first, 162), runs (second, 125), slugging (third, .623), extra base hits (tied for third, 86), multi-hit games (tied for sixth, 57), intentional walks (seventh, 12), on-base percentage (eighth, .392), hits (ninth), walks (ninth, 87), and at-bats (10th)...started 160 games at shortstop while setting career bests for homers, RBI, and intentional walks...selected as the Major League "Player of the Year" by the *Sporting News*.
- Had the sixth-most home runs in AL history, the most since Roger Maris' AL-record 61 in 1961, and the most ever for a shortstop for the second consecutive year...his 57 homers were tied for the 12th most ever in Major League history and were the most ever in a season for a Major League infielder other than a first baseman...was one shy of the AL record for homers in a season by a right-handed batter, shared by Jimmie Foxx in 1932 and Hank Greenberg in 1938...became just the fifth player in Major League history to post consecutive 50-homer seasons, tying the AL record for consecutive 50-homer campaigns with Babe Ruth (1920-21; 1927-28) and Ken Griffey, Jr. (1997-98).
- Became the first player to lead the Majors in homers and RBI since Detroit's Cecil Fielder in 1991...was just the third time a shortstop has ever led the Majors in homers, joining the Cubs' Ernie Banks in 1958 (47) and 1960 (41)...the only other times a shortstop has led his league in homers were both in the AL: Vern Stephens of the St. Louis Browns in 1945 (24) and Rodriguez in 2001 (52)...was the first shortstop to lead the Majors in RBI since Banks in both 1958 and 1959 and the sixth all-time, also joining Pittsburgh's Honus Wagner in 1908 and Vern Stephens, then with the Boston Red Sox in 1949 and 1950 (tied both years)...Stephens (three times, also with the Browns in 1944) is the only other shortstop to top the AL in RBI...became first shortstop to lead Majors in total bases since Ripken (368) in 1991...led the AL in total bases for the second consecutive year, the first player to do so since Belle in 1994 and 1995...his 109 homers in 2001-02 are the most ever by an American League player in consecutive seasons.
- His postseason honors included his first Rawlings Gold Glove and his second consecutive Rangers "Player of the Year" Award...named Major League "Player of the Year" by players in MLBPA Players Choice Award voting and by *Baseball America*...won second consecutive AL Hank Aaron Award as league's top offensive player as well as his second consecutive Josh Gibson Legacy Award from the Negro Leagues Baseball Museum (NLBM) for winning the AL home run crown...finished second in BBWAA AL MVP voting to Oakland's Miguel Tejada (21 first place votes and 356 points) with five first place votes and 254 points.
- Selected to AL Silver Slugger team for fifth consecutive year and sixth time overall...named as shortstop on *Baseball America* Major League All-Star team and AL All-Star squad selected by the *Sporting News*.
- Hit 250th career home run on 4/30 at Toronto at 26 years, 277 days of age, the second youngest ever to reach the figure behind Foxx (26 yrs., 269 days)...had Texas-record 10 multi-homer games, one shy of the Major League mark shared by Hank Greenberg (1938) and Sammy Sosa (1998)...tied club record with three homers on 8/17 vs. Toronto, the 11th time that had been done in Rangers history...joined Ernie Banks, Nomar Garciaparra and Miguel Tejada as only shortstops with two three-homer contests.

- Was the AL "Player of the Month" for both July (.349, 12 HR, 27 RBI) and August (.339, 12 HR, 27 RBI), the first player to win that honor in consecutive months since Cleveland's Albert Belle in August and September, 1995...named the AL "Player of the Week" for 7/11-14 and 8/12-18 (shared with Bernie Williams).

2001

- In his first season with Texas, batted .318 (201-for-632) with 52HR and 135RBI in 162 games...led the American League in homers, runs (133) and total bases (393)...tied for the league lead in games and extra-base hits (87), ranked third in RBI, slugging percentage (.622), tied for third in hit by pitches (16), and was also among the AL leaders in hits (fourth), at-bats (sixth), multi-hit games (sixth, 55), sacrifice flies (tied for sixth, 9), average (seventh) and on-base percentage (eighth, .399)...established Rangers club records for homers, runs, total bases and hit by pitches, had the second most extra-base hits, and the fourth-highest RBI total...became the fourth player, first since 1932, with 50 homers and 200 hits in a season.
- Was named the Rangers' "Player of the Year" and finished sixth in BBWAA AL MVP voting...named as shortstop on *Baseball America* Major League All-Star team and AL All-Star squad as selected by the *Sporting News*...named the Rangers' "Player of the Month" for May and a was a two-time selection as AL "Player of the Week," 4/9-15 and 9/17-23...his .318 average was the second highest of his career since his .358 in 1996...led the AL with a .361 (113-for-313) home average, ranked sixth with a .323 (162-for-501) mark vs. right-handers, and was seventh with a .329 (48-146) average in day games...tied club record with three doubles on 4/7 vs. Seattle...singled for 1,000th hit on 5/5 vs. Chicago-AL.

2000

- Batted .316 (175-for-554) with a career-high 134R, 41HR and 132RBI in 148 games (148 starts at SS) in his final season with the Mariners...was second in the AL in runs scored and ranked among the league leaders in homers (tied for fourth), sacrifice flies (tied for fourth, 11), slugging percentage (fifth, .606), RBI (sixth), extra-base hits (sixth, 77), total bases (tied for sixth, 336), on-base percentage (seventh, .420), walks (10th, 100) and average (15th)...led Seattle in runs, total bases, homers, and sacrifice flies...had AL's third-highest road average at .356 (103-for-289) and .370 (34-for-92) mark vs. left-handers was fourth-best...set a career-high with 100BB...joined Edgar Martinez (three consecutive years from 1995-97) as the only Mariners to have a .300 average with 100R, 100RBI and 100BB in one season.
- Selected as the Major League "Player of the Year" by *Baseball America*, finished third in AL MVP voting and was named Seattle's MVP by local BBWAA chapter...selected as shortstop on the Major League All-Star teams by the Associated Press and *Baseball America* and on AL All-Star squad by the *Sporting News*...named the AL "Player of the Week" for the week of 4/10-16...sustained a concussion while trying to break up a double play on 7/7 vs. Los Angeles-AL...also strained his right knee in the collision and was placed on 15-day disabled list on 7/14 (retroactive to 7/8)...missed 13 games with the injury...activated on 7/24...walked a club-record five times on 4/23 vs. Kansas City and tied team mark with five runs scored on 4/16 at Texas, establishing career-highs in both categories.

1999

- Despite missing 32 games while on the disabled list with a left knee injury, batted .285 (143-for-502) with 42HR and 111RBI in 129 games at SS with Seattle...joined Ernie Banks as the only shortstops in Major League history to hit 40 or more home runs more than once...teamed with David Bell (21) to hit more home runs than any middle-infield combo in Major League history (62)...ranked second on club in runs (110), total bases (294), homers, and RBI...ranked fifth in the AL in homers and sixth in slugging percentage (.586).
- Won AL Silver Slugger Award...played in just two games before going on D.L. on 4/7...had surgery the following day to repair torn cartilage in his left knee...activated on 5/14 and homered in his first at-bat that night vs. Kansas City...missed 32 games with injury...homered in five straight games from 8/11-16 to become only the fourth Seattle player to homer in five straight games...was at .315 at end of August before hitting .173 in September...scored 15 runs in a six-game span from 5/23-29...recorded his 100th career stolen base on 6/1 vs. Baltimore.

1998

- Batted .310 with 42HR, 124RBI and 46SB in 161 games with Seattle, joining Jose Canseco (1988) and Barry Bonds (1996) as the only players in history with 40 or more homers and 40 or more steals in a single season...led the AL in at-bats (686), hits (213), and multi-hit games (64) and ranked among the league leaders in runs (third, 123), total bases (third, 384), extra-base hits (tied for fourth, 82), RBI (fifth), and homers (seventh)...became the first Mariner ever with at least 30 homers and 30 steals in a season...tied AL record with eight extra base hits over three games from 4/18-20.
- Was selected as Players Choice AL "Player of the Year" and was Seattle's co-MVP with Ken Griffey, Jr...finished ninth in AL MVP balloting...named to Associated Press Major League All-Star Team and AL All-Star Club picked by the *Sporting News*...won second Silver Slugger Award...batted leadoff for first time in career from 5/10-14...voted starting shortstop for the second straight All-Star Game (third overall selection).

ALEX RODRIGUEZ

1997

- Batted .300 with 23HR and 84RBI in 141 games (140 starts at SS) with the Mariners...tied for the team lead in doubles (40) and ranked third in hits (176) and total bases (291)...had three hitting streaks of at least 10 games, including a 16-game streak from 6/1-7/3...hit for the cycle on 6/5 at Detroit, with a homer in the first inning, single in the fourth, triple in the eighth and double in the ninth...was the second Mariner ever to accomplish the feat and at 21 years, 10 months, was fifth-youngest in Baseball history to hit for the cycle.
- Suffered a deep bruise of his chest wall in a collision with Roger Clemens on 6/11 at Toronto...was placed on the 15-day disabled list and missed 14 games...ejected for the first time in his career on 8/9 at Chicago-AL...became the first AL shortstop other than Cal Ripken to start an All-Star Game since 1983 (Milwaukee's Robin Yount).

1996

- In his first full Major League season, batted .358 (215-for-601) with 36HR and 123RBI in 146 games and was selected by both the *Sporting News* and Associated Press as the Major League "Player of the Year"...finished three points behind Juan Gonzalez in AL MVP voting, matching the second-closest AL MVP voting in history...was the AL batting champ with a .358 average, highest for an AL right-handed batter since Joe DiMaggio (.381) in 1939...at 21 years, one month, was the AL's third youngest batting leader ever behind Al Kaline (20, in 1955) and Ty Cobb (20, in 1907)...was the first Major League shortstop to win a batting title since Pittsburgh's Dick Groat in 1960 (.325) and the first in the AL since Cleveland's Lou Boudreau (.327) in 1944...was the third-highest single-season batting average ever for a shortstop.
- Was a postseason All-Star shortstop and won first AL Silver Slugger Award...led the AL in runs (141), total bases (379) and doubles (54) and ranked among the league leaders in hits (second, 215), extra-base hits (second, 91), multi-hit games (third, 65), slugging percentage (fourth, .631), RBI (eighth, 123), and on-base percentage (eighth, .414)...posted then-records for a shortstop in runs, hits, doubles, extra-base hits and slugging percentage...established Seattle club records for average, runs, hits, doubles and total bases...named the AL "Player of the Month" for August and won league "Player of the Week" awards for weeks ending 8/19 and 9/1...hit in a single-season career-high 20 consecutive games from 8/16-9/4...was on the D.L. with pulled left hamstring from 4/22-5/7.

1995

- Batted .232 (33-for-142) with 5HR and 19RBI in 48 games over four stints with Seattle (5/6-27; 6/8-23; 7/20-8/15; and 8/31-10/2), starting 38 games at SS...connected for first Major League HR off Tom Gordon on 6/12 vs. Kansas City...despite playing in just 54 games at Triple-A Tacoma, batted .360 and was named to *Baseball America*'s Triple-A All-Star team...also selected by the publication as the Pacific Coast League's "Most Exciting Player."

1994

- Advanced from Single-A Appleton to Seattle in his first pro season at age 19...hit a combined .300 (144-for-480) with 21HR and 86RBI in 131 games...joined Seattle on 7/7 and made his Major League debut as the starting shortstop on 7/8 at Boston at 18 years, 11 months and 11 days of age, just the Majors' third 18-year-old shortstop since 1900 (Kansas City's Tony LaRussa in 1963 and Milwaukee's Robin Yount in 1974)...became the Majors' first 18-year-old player since Yankees pitcher Jose Rijo in 1984...was the youngest position player in Seattle history with pitcher Edwin Nunez (18 yrs, 10 months, 11 days in 1982) the only younger player...singled off Boston's Sergio Valdez for first hit on 7/9 at Fenway Park (2-for-4, 1SB)...started 17 games at SS before being optioned to Triple-A Calgary for rest of season on 8/2.

18-YEAR-OLD SHORTSTOPS, SINCE 1900	
ALEX RODRIGUEZ, Seattle Mariners	**1994**
Robin Yount, Milwaukee Brewers	1974
Tony LaRussa, Kansas City Athletics	1963

- Started the season at Appleton, hitting .319 in 65 games...went 2-for-4 in pro debut on 4/8 at Quad City and hit first homer on 4/24 vs. Fort Wayne...selected to play in Midwest League All-Star Game on 6/20 but was promoted to Double-A Jacksonville on 6/16...named to Southern League's postseason All-Star squad...homered in first Double-A at-bat on 6/16 against Port City...played in 17 games before joining Seattle...played with Escogido in Dominican Winter League.

ALEX RODRIGUEZ

Personal

- Full name is Alexander Enmanuel Rodriguez...has two daughters, Natasha (5) and Ella (1)...signed by Fernando Arguelles...had outstanding three-year career at Westminster Christian High School in Miami, Fla. (graduated in 1993)...batted .419 with 17HR, 70RBI and 90SB in 100 games as team went 86-13-1...was first team prep All-American as a senior, hitting .505 with 9HR, 36RBI and 35SB (in 35 attempts) in 33 games...selected as the USA Baseball Junior "Player of the Year" and as Gatorade's "National Baseball Student Athlete of the Year"...was the first high school player to try out for Team USA in 1993 and also play with U.S. Junior National Squad that summer...participated in Little League and American Legion programs...also played basketball and football in high school...hobbies include basketball, golf and boating...favorite players growing up were Keith Hernandez, Dale Murphy and Cal Ripken, Jr.
- Joined the Boys & Girls Club of Miami-Dade in 1982 at the age of 7 and remained a member until the day he was drafted in 1993...since reaching the Major Leagues, has worked extensively with the Boys & Girls Club of Miami-Dade, dedicating time, effort and resources toward its continued development...created the Alex Rodriguez Evening with the All-Stars in 1998...five benefits have since been hosted, raising over $500,000 for the Club ...has also served as a national spokespersons for the Boys & Girls Clubs of America...championed Campaign 3 p.m., which is the Boys & Girls Clubs national initiative to enroll every child in America in an after-school program...hosted a two-hour clinic at the Boys & Girls Club in November 2007 for approximately 85 youngsters between the ages of 9 and 14 on a field named after him.
- In 2007, personally donated $500,000 to the Alex Rodriguez Learning Center which opened in January 2010...the 8,000 square foot educational facility for the advancement of literacy, computer study and math, includes three separate classrooms, a computer technology lab and a research technology lab with 25 computers...an additional wing houses the teen center with a study hall with computers and a teen lounge with games, a big screen television and books.
- In January of 2003, donated $3.9 million to the University of Miami...the money was directed to construction costs stemming from the remodeling of the baseball stadium, as well as scholarship money for the Boys & Girls Clubs of Miami-Dade...one student from the Club will be awarded a four-year scholarship to the University each year...the scholarship will be awarded in perpetuity, so an unlimited number of children benefit from this donation...in 2005, donated $200,000 to the Children's Aid Society, a New York City-based children's advocacy and charity group...his donation supported the placement of therapists into schools located in Washington Heights—the neighborhood in which Alex was born...the donation will fund the project for an entire school year...also in 2005, Alex donated $50,000 to the Dominican Republic branch of UNICEF...this donation fully funded five day-care centers outside of Santo Domingo...these five centers were able to purchase enough school supplies, food and personal hygiene products for one full year, with over 1,500 students benefiting from his contribution.
- Is dedicated to positively impacting families in distress by supporting programs focusing on improved quality of life, education and mental health...teamed up with hip-hop icon Jay-Z on 11/15/06 to host a celebrity poker tournament with over $500,000 in proceeds going to charitable endeavors of both men...co-hosted Family Fun Day at the Miami Seaquarium in January 2007 with the Ronald McDonald House Charities of South Florida...authored a children's picture book in February 2007, "Out of the Ballpark," published in English and Spanish...hosted a book signing at FAO Schwartz in Manhattan on 7/20/07 and read to a group of 9 year olds...participated in a Q & A session with Michael Kay for 500 kids from local community groups at Niketown in New York on 8/1/07.
- Received a 2007 Thurman Munson Award for his accomplishments on the field and his philanthropic work within the community...was also honored with the 2008 Sid Mercer Award, presented by the New York chapter of the BBWAA to their "Player of the Year"...was presented the Key to the City by New York City Mayor Michael Bloomberg on 8/16/07 during an on-field, pregame ceremony in recognition of his 500th home run.
- Was presented with a plaque by the United Youth Baseball League on 4/4/08 after donating $10,000 to the league to help pay for field fees, insurance and uniforms for the kids...spoke to 2,000 local Bronx kids about the importance of education and practice in life at Macombs Dam Park, adjacent to Yankee Stadium in July 2008...held a hitting clinic at a youth sports complex in Mexico City in November 2008.
- Donated $250,000 towards the completion of the new Pediatric Outpatient Unit at Bronx-Lebanon Hospital in New York City in 2008, aimed at providing quality medical attention for local children who are not covered by insurance...also pledged another $250,000 over the next five years to fund the Community DentCare Network from the Columbia University College of Dentistry, sponsoring mobile vans in the Bronx and Washington Heights areas that provide dental care and education to those who cannot otherwise afford it.
- Joined actor Richard Gere as coaches for an All-Star Little League game at Franz Sigel Park in the Bronx on 6/6/09...served as "Chef-for-a-Day" with Cody Ransom and GM Brian Cashman on 7/1 at El Nuevo Caridad Restaurant in Washington Heights, feeding nearly 50 neighborhood kids...played in community stickball game across from Yankee Stadium on 8/29/09.

Rodriguez' Career Playing Record

Year	Club	AVG	G	AB	R	H	2B	3B	HR	RBI	SH	SF	HP	BB	SO	SB	CS	E	OBP	SLG
1994	Appleton	.319	65	248	49	79	17	6	14	55	1	3	2	24	44	16	5	19	.379	.605
	Jacksonville	.288	17	59	7	17	4	1	1	8	0	0	0	10	13	2	1	3	.391	.441
	SEATTLE	.204	17	54	4	11	0	0	0	2	1	1	0	3	20	3	0	6	.241	.204
	Calgary	.311	32	119	22	37	7	4	6	21	0	0	1	8	25	2	4	3	.359	.588
1995	Tacoma	.360	54	214	37	77	12	3	15	45	1	2	2	18	44	2	4	10	.411	.654
	SEATTLE	.232	48	142	15	33	6	2	5	19	1	0	0	6	42	4	2	8	.264	.408
1996	SEATTLE - a	*.358	146	601	*141	215	*54	1	36	123	6	7	4	59	104	15	4	15	.414	.631
	Tacoma	.200	2	5	0	1	0	0	0	0	0	0	0	2	1	0	0	1	.429	.200
1997	SEATTLE - b	.300	141	587	100	176	40	3	23	84	4	1	5	41	99	29	6	24	.350	.496
1998	SEATTLE	.310	161	*686	123	*213	35	5	42	124	3	4	10	45	121	46	13	18	.360	.560
1999	SEATTLE - c	.285	129	502	110	143	25	0	42	111	1	8	5	56	109	21	7	14	.357	.586
2000	SEATTLE - d	.316	148	554	134	175	34	2	41	132	0	11	7	100	121	15	4	10	.420	.606
2001	TEXAS - e	.318	#162	632	*133	201	34	1	*52	135	0	9	16	75	131	18	3	18	.399	.622
2002	TEXAS	.300	#162	624	125	187	27	2	*57	*142	0	4	10	87	122	9	4	10	.392	.623
2003	TEXAS	.298	161	607	*124	181	30	6	*47	118	0	6	15	87	126	17	3	8	.396	*.600
2004	YANKEES - f	.286	155	601	112	172	24	2	36	106	0	7	10	80	131	28	4	13	.375	.512
2005	YANKEES	.321	#162	605	*124	194	29	1	*48	130	0	3	16	91	139	21	6	12	.421	*.610
2006	YANKEES	.290	154	572	113	166	26	1	35	121	0	4	8	90	139	15	4	24	.392	.523
2007	YANKEES	.314	158	583	*143	183	31	0	*54	*156	0	9	21	95	120	24	4	13	.422	*.645
2008	YANKEES - g	.302	138	510	104	154	33	0	35	103	0	5	14	65	117	18	3	10	.392	*.573
2009	YANKEES - h	.286	124	444	78	127	17	1	30	100	0	3	8	80	97	14	2	9	.402	.532
Minor League Totals		**.327**	**170**	**645**	**115**	**211**	**40**	**14**	**36**	**129**	**2**	**5**	**5**	**62**	**127**	**22**	**14**	**36**	**.388**	**.600**
Major League Totals		**.305**	**2166**	**8304**	**1683**	**2531**	**445**	**27**	**583**	**1706**	**16**	**82**	**149**	**1060**	**1738**	**297**	**69**	**212**	**.390**	**.576**
NYY Total		**.300**	**891**	**3315**	**674**	**996**	**160**	**5**	**238**	**716**	**0**	**31**	**77**	**501**	**743**	**120**	**23**	**81**	**.401**	**.567**

* League leader # Tied for league lead

Selected by Seattle in the first round (first pick overall) of the 1993 First-Year Player Draft.

a - Placed on the 15-day disabled list from April 22 - May 7, 1996 with a pulled left hamstring.
b - Placed on the 15-day disabled list from June 12-27, 1997 with a deep chest bruise.
c - Placed on the 15-day disabled list from April 7 - May 14, 1999 with torn cartilage in his left knee.
d - Placed on the 15-day disabled list from July 8-24, 2000 with a right knee strain.
e - Signed by Texas as a free agent on December 11, 2000.
f - Traded to New York (AL) on February 16, 2004 with cash in exchange for 2B Alfonso Soriano and player to be named later (INF Joaquin Arias).
g - Placed on the 15-day disabled list from April 30 - May 20, 2008 with a strained right quadriceps.
h – Placed on the 15-day disabled list on April 4 (retroactive to March 27) – May 8, 2009 with a right hip labral tear.

Steinbrenner High School

Named after the Yankees Principal Owner, George M. Steinbrenner High School opened in August 2009 on Lutz Lake Fern Road just north of Tampa.

"Over the years, Mr. Steinbrenner has been deeply involved in the community, particularly with the schools and the school system," said Steven Ayers, director of community relations for Hillsborough County public schools. "He's been very involved and very philanthropic. He's probably donated in tens of millions over the length of time. He's had a significant amount of money and significant amount of involvement in the community."

In addition to traditional classroom curriculum, the school also offers classes for students preparing for a career in sports with sports marketing, sports medicine and the business of sports (BOSS). The school's nickname is the Warriors. The school's colors are navy and gold.

Rodriguez' Division Series Record

YEAR	TEAM	AVG	G	AB	R	H	2B	3B	HR	RBI	SH	SF	HP	BB	SO	SB	CS	E	OBP	SLG
1995	SEA vs. NYY	.000	1	1	1	0	0	0	0	0	0	0	0	0	0	0	0	0	.000	.000
1997	SEA vs. BAL	.313	4	16	1	5	1	0	1	1	0	0	0	0	5	0	0	0	.313	.563
2000	SEA vs. CWS	.308	3	13	0	4	0	0	0	2	1	0	0	0	2	0	1	0	.308	.308
2004	NYY vs. MIN	.421	4	19	3	8	3	0	1	3	0	0	0	2	1	2	1	0	.476	.737
2005	NYY vs. LAA	.133	5	15	2	2	1	0	0	0	0	0	2	6	5	1	1	1	.435	.200
2006	NYY vs. DET	.071	4	14	0	1	0	0	0	0	0	0	1	0	4	0	0	1	.133	.071
2007	NYY vs. CLE	.267	4	15	2	4	0	0	1	1	0	0	0	2	6	0	0	0	.353	.467
2009	NYY vs. MIN	.455	3	11	4	5	0	0	2	6	0	0	0	1	2	0	0	0	.500	1.000
Division Series Totals		**.279**	**28**	**104**	**13**	**29**	**5**	**0**	**5**	**13**	**1**	**0**	**3**	**11**	**25**	**3**	**3**	**2**	**.364**	**.471**

Rodriguez' League Championship Series Record

Year	Club vs. Opp.	AVG	G	AB	R	H	2B	3B	HR	RBI	SH	SF	HP	BB	SO	SB	CS	E	OBP	SLG
1995	SEA vs. CLE	.000	1	1	0	0	0	0	0	0	0	0	0	0	1	0	0	0	.000	.000
2000	SEA vs. NYY	.409	6	22	4	9	2	0	2	5	0	0	0	3	8	1	0	0	.480	.773
2004	NYY vs. BOS	.258	7	31	8	8	2	0	2	5	0	0	2	4	6	0	0	0	.378	.516
2009	NYY vs. LAA	.429	6	21	6	9	2	0	3	6	0	1	0	8	3	1	0	0	.567	.952
LCS Totals		**.347**	**20**	**75**	**18**	**26**	**6**	**0**	**7**	**16**	**0**	**1**	**2**	**15**	**18**	**2**	**0**	**0**	**.462**	**.707**

Rodriguez' World Series Record

Year	Club vs. Opp.	AVG	G	AB	R	H	2B	3B	HR	RBI	SH	SF	HP	BB	SO	SB	CS	E	OBP	SLG
2009	NYY vs. PHI	.250	6	20	5	5	3	0	1	6	0	0	3	3	8	1	0	1	.423	.550
World Series Totals		**.250**	**6**	**20**	**5**	**5**	**3**	**0**	**1**	**6**	**0**	**0**	**3**	**3**	**8**	**1**	**0**	**1**	**.423**	**.550**
POSTSEASON TOTALS		**.302**	**54**	**199**	**36**	**60**	**14**	**0**	**13**	**35**	**1**	**1**	**8**	**29**	**51**	**6**	**3**	**3**	**.409**	**.568**

Rodriguez' All-Star Game Record

Year	Club, Site	AVG	G	AB	R	H	2B	3B	HR	RBI	SH	SF	HP	BB	SO	SB	CS	E	OBP	SLG
1996	SEA, Philadelphia	.000	1	1	0	0	0	0	0	0	0	0	0	0	0	0	0	0	.000	.000
1997	SEA, Cleveland	.333	1	3	0	1	0	0	0	0	0	0	0	0	2	0	0	0	.333	.333
1998	SEA, Colorado	.667	1	3	2	2	0	0	1	1	0	0	0	0	1	0	0	0	.667	1.667
2000	SEA, Atlanta	Injured - Did Not Play																		
2001	TEX, Seattle	.000	1	2	0	0	0	0	0	0	0	0	0	0	2	0	0	0	.000	.000
2002	TEX, Milwaukee	.000	1	2	0	0	0	0	0	0	0	0	0	0	2	0	0	0	.000	.000
2003	TEX, Chicago (AL)	.333	1	3	1	1	0	0	0	0	0	0	0	0	1	0	0	0	.333	.333
2004	NYY, Houston	.333	1	3	0	1	0	1	0	1	0	0	0	0	1	0	0	0	.333	1.000
2005	NYY, Detroit	.500	1	2	1	1	0	0	0	0	0	0	0	1	0	0	0	0	.667	.500
2006	NYY, Pittsburgh	.000	1	2	0	0	0	0	0	0	0	0	0	0	0	0	0	0	.000	.000
2007	NYY, San Francisco	.333	1	3	0	1	0	0	0	0	0	0	0	0	0	0	0	0	.333	.333
2008	NYY, New York (AL)	.000	1	2	0	0	0	0	0	0	0	0	0	0	1	0	0	0	.000	.000
All-Star Game Totals		**.269**	**11**	**26**	**4**	**7**	**0**	**1**	**1**	**2**	**0**	**0**	**0**	**1**	**10**	**0**	**0**	**0**	**.296**	**.462**

Rodriguez' World Baseball Classic Record

Year	Country, Site	AVG	G	AB	R	H	2B	3B	HR	RBI	SH	SF	HP	BB	SO	SB	CS	E	OBP	SLG
2006	USA, USA	.333	6	21	3	7	1	0	0	3	0	0	0	2	7	0	0	0	.391	.381

Rodriguez' Career Fielding Record

Position	PCT	G	PO	A	E	TC
Third Base	.962	752	490	1314	72	1876
Shortstop	.977	1272	2014	3605	131	5750

Rodriguez's Home Run Chart

MULTI-HOMER GAMES: 54. **TWO-HOMER GAMES:** 51, last on 10/4/09 at Tampa Bay. **THREE-HOMER GAMES:** 3, last on 4/26/05 vs. Los Angeles-AL. **GRAND SLAMS:** 18, last on 10/4/09 at Tampa Bay (Andy Sonnanstine). **PINCH-HIT HR:** None. **INSIDE-THE-PARK HR:** None. **WALK-OFF HR:** 9 (six as a Yankee), last on 8/7/09 vs. Boston (Junichi Tazawa). **LEADOFF HR:** None.

Kevin Russo

77

Infielder

5-11 • 190 • B/T: Right/Right

Opening Day Age: 25

Birthdate
July 8, 1984

Birthplace
West Babylon, N.Y.

Resides
Boulder, Colo.

M.L. Service
None
(Rookie)

College
Baylor University

Status

- Selected by the Yankees in the 20th round of the 2006 First-Year Player Draft...signed through the 2010 season.

Minor League Career

- Is a career .312 batter (264-for-845) with 10HR in his career against right-handed pitchers...owns a .265 (82-for-310) mark with 2HR vs. lefthanders.

2009

- Played the entire season with Triple-A Scranton/Wilkes-Barre, batting .326 (115-for-353) with 51R, 18 doubles, 5HR, 31RBI and 13SB in 90 games...led all Yankees minor leaguers in batting average...ranked third in the International League in batting average and fourth in the IL with a team-high .397 on-base percentage...had 34 multi-hit games.
- Was named to the International League's 2009 postseason All-Star team as the league's top second baseman and the Topps Triple-A All-Star Team as the top 2B...also appeared in games at shortstop and third base.
- Batted primarily in the leadoff position, hitting .329 (112-for-340) as the No. 1 batter...owned a .407 batting average in the first inning (33-for-81).
- Hit safely in his first six games of the season and 12 of the first 13...had two stints on the disabled list with a strained right hamstring, from 4/16-5/3 and 5/12-6/6...batted .600 (9-for-15) in four games between stints.
- Collected three doubles and was 3-for-4 with 3R in 4-0 win on 7/27 at Toledo.
- Appeared in all seven postseason games for the SWB Yankees, batting .125 (4-for-32) with 4RBI.
- Was a spring invitee with the Yankees, appearing in 11 games.

2008

- Hit .307 with 17 doubles, 3 triples, 2HR and 33RBI in 71 games with Double-A Trenton, appearing in games at 2B, 3B and the outfield.
- Missed nearly two months from 6/14-7/30 on the disabled list after fracturing his left cheekbone when he was hit by a batting practice grounder prior to 6/6 game.
- Started all seven postseason games at 3B for the Eastern League champions, batting .174 (4-for-23).
- Appeared in 30 games with the Peoria Javelinas of the Arizona Fall League following the season, batting .309 with 16R, 8 doubles, 3HR and 16RBI, leading Yankees winter leaguers with 34H.

2007

- With Single-A Tampa, hit .281 with 22 doubles, 3 triples, 2HR and 45RBI in 109 games...was successful in 19-of-25 stolen base attempts, including 10 of his first 11 tries.
- Named by *Baseball America* as the best defensive second baseman in the Florida State League...started at 2B in the FSL midseason All-Star Game...appeared in 104 games at 2B, recording a .977 fielding percentage (13E, 559TC)...was involved in 81 double plays, second-most among FSL second basemen.
- Hit safely in 19 of 20 games from 4/26-5/22, including a career-high 12 straight games from 4/26-5/12 (.426, 20-for-47)...batted .338 in July (25-for-74).

KEVIN RUSSO

2006

- Made professional debut with the Yankees' Gulf Coast League team, batting .273 in 45 games (36 at 2B, 11 at 3B)...was among the most difficult batters in the league to strike out, ranking third in K/PA ratio (1/10.06)...ranked fifth in the league with a .383 on-base percentage.
- Led all GCL second basemen with a .986 fielding percentage, committing only two errors in 142 total chances.

Personal

- Was drafted out of Baylor University, where he was named to the 2006 Preseason All-Big 12 Conference team by *Baseball America*, received a 2005 All-Big 12 Conference Honorable Mention and was a three-time member of the Big 12 Conference Commissioner's Honor Roll...was one of four players to start every game in 2005, establishing a school record...at San Jacinto JC in 2004, earned Junior College World Series all-tournament honors...graduated from Fairview High School in Boulder, Colo., where he was a first-team all-state honoree as a senior and a two-time first-team All-Centennial League and first-team all-region selection.

Russo's Career Batting Record

Year	Club	AVG	G	AB	R	H	2B	3B	HR	RBI	SH	SF	HP	BB	SO	SB	CS	E	OBP	SLG
2006	GCL Yankees	.273	45	150	23	41	10	0	3	23	1	2	8	20	18	6	2	4	.383	.400
2007	Tampa	.281	109	385	47	108	22	3	2	45	3	6	5	15	66	19	6	14	.311	.369
2008	Trenton	.307	71	267	46	82	17	3	2	33	3	3	2	23	42	8	3	9	.363	.416
2009	Scranton/WB	.326	90	353	51	115	18	2	5	31	3	5	3	42	55	13	7	12	.397	.431
Minor League Totals		**.300**	**315**	**1155**	**167**	**346**	**67**	**8**	**12**	**132**	**10**	**16**	**18**	**100**	**181**	**46**	**18**	**39**	**.360**	**.403**

Selected by the Yankees in the 20th round of the 2006 First-Year Player Draft.

Green Initiatives at Yankee Stadium

The Yankees are committed to promoting a sustainable environment and have implemented many green initiatives at Yankee Stadium, including a partnership with Hess Energy to support greener sources of power. In addition, Yankee Stadium uses environmentally friendly lighting that saves approximately 207,000 pounds of CO2 emissions during every night game. Yankee Stadium also composts grass clippings, food waste, beverage cups and food packaging and recycles cardboard, glass, plastics, paper and waste cooking oil, diverting much of Yankee Stadium trash away from landfills.

CC Sabathia

52 Left-handed Pitcher

6-7 • 290 • B/T: Left/Left

Opening Day Age: 29

Birthdate
July 21, 1980

Birthplace
Vallejo, Calif.

Resides
Alpine, N.J.

M.L. Service
9 years

Career Highlights

A.L. Cy Young Award
- 2007

A.L. All-Star Team
- 2003, 2004, 2007

ALCS MVP
- 2009

Status

- Signed as a free agent to a seven-year contract on December 18, 2008...contract extends through the 2015 season.

Career Notes

- Was 82-46 (.641) over the last five seasons (2005-09), leading the Majors in wins and IP (1,113.1)...tied for first in shutouts (nine) and ranked third in strikeouts (990) over the stretch.
- Since his debut in 2001, has a 136-81 (.627) record, marking the second-most wins in the Majors over the span (Roy Oswalt–137)...is second in shutouts (11), ranks third in complete games (28), fourth in strikeouts (1,590), fifth in IP (1889.1), and tied for sixth in games started (288, also Jeff Suppan) over the stretch.
- His .627 career winning percentage is 10th-best among lefthanders who began their careers in 1950 or later (min: 140 decisions).
- Leads all active Major League pitchers under the age of 30 in career wins (136), strikeouts (1,590) and innings pitched (1889.1)...the last Major Leaguer to compile as many wins prior to his 30th birthday was Greg Maddux who won 151 games before turning 30.
- According to the *Elias Sports Bureau*, is the first pitcher since Mike Mussina (2001-03) to win at least 17 games in three straight seasons...has accomplished the feat while pitching for three different clubs over the stretch (19-7 w/ Cleveland, 2007; 17-10 w/ Cleveland and Milwaukee, 2008; and 19-8 w/ the Yankees, 2009), joining Randy Johnson (over two overlapping spans of three seasons from 1997-99 and 1998-2000 with Seattle, Houston and Arizona) as the only pitchers to accomplish the feat in the last 100 years (Credit: *Elias*).
- Has recorded at least 11 wins in each of his first nine seasons to begin his Major League career, marking the longest current such streak among active pitchers.
- Has held lefthanders homerless in his last 33 regular season starts at home, since giving up a pair of homers to Jim Thome on Opening Day in 2008 (3/31/08 w/ Cleveland vs. Chicago-AL).
- Has participated in the postseason in each of the last three seasons with three different clubs (2009 w/ the Yankees, 2008 w/ Milwaukee and 2007 w/ Cleveland).

Single-Game Bests and Streaks

Low hit CG
1 - at PIT, 8/31/08

IP (start)
9.0 - 23 times
Last: at BAL, 5/8/09

IP (relief)
N/A

Hits
13 - at MIN, 7/15/06

Runs
9 - 5 times
Last: at TB, 10/2/09

BB
6 - 2 times
Last: at OAK, 9/11/04

SO
13 - vs. KC, 9/14/07

HR
3 - 6 times
Last: at DET, 7/5/07

Winning Streak
12g - 6/10-8/31/08

Losing Streak
5g - 7/6-30/05

2009

- Was 19-8 with a 3.37 ERA and two complete games in 34 starts with the Yankees, tying for the Major League lead in wins with Seattle's Felix Hernandez, Detroit's Justin Verlander and St. Louis' Adam Wainwright...matched his personal single-season high (was 19-7 w/ Cleveland in 2007)...was third in the American League with a .232 opponents batting average against (197-for-849, 18HR), and fourth in both IP (230.0) and ERA (3.37)...left-handed batters hit just .198 (39-for-197, 3HR) against him, while righties batted .242 (158-for-652, 15HR)...the Yankees were 22-12 in his starts.

CC SABATHIA

Date/Opp	Score	W/L	IP	H	R	ER	HR	BB	K	NP/K	ERA	Left game
4/6 at BAL	5-10	L	4.1	8	6	**6**	0	**5**	0	96/50	12.46	Trailing 5-1
4/11 at KC	6-1	W	7.2	6	0	0	0	0	6	108/73	4.50	Leading 6-0
4/16 vs. CLE	2-10	ND	5.2	5	1	1	0	**5**	4	122/70	3.57	Tied 1-1
4/22 vs. OAK	9-7 (14)	ND	6.2	6	7	**6**	1	4	2	112/66	4.81	Tied 7-7
4/27 at DET*	2-4	(CG) L	8.0	6	4	4	1	0	7	99/70	4.73	Trailing 1-4
5/2 vs. LAA	4-8	L	6.2	8	5	4	0	1	5	119/78	4.85	Trailing 4-1
5/8 at BAL*	4-0	(CG) W	**9.0**	4	0	0	0	1	8	112/79	3.94	Leading 4-0
5/14 at TOR	3-2	W	8.0	5	2	2	1	4	5	111/65	3.70	Leading 3-2
5/19 vs. BAL	9-1	W	7.0	3	1	1	0	1	7	105/69	3.43	Leading 9-1
5/24 vs. PHI	3-4 (11)	ND	8.0	9	3	3	0	0	4	110/75	3.42	Trailing 3-2
5/30 at CLE	10-5	W	7.0	5	3	3	1	3	8	113/70	3.46	Leading 8-3
6/6 vs. TB	7-9	ND	8.0	5	5	4	**2**	3	5	101/64	3.56	Tied 5-5
6/11 at BOS*	3-4	L	7.0	6	4	4	1	2	6	**123**/79	3.68	Leading 3-2
6/16 vs. WAS	5-3	W	7.2	6	3	3	1	1	2	109/75	3.67	Leading 4-3
6/21 at FLA*	5-6	ND	1.1	3	1	1	0	1	1	28/16	3.71	Trailing 1-0
6/26 at NYM	9-1	W	7.0	3	1	1	1	0	8	99/67	3.55	Leading 7-1
7/2 vs. SEA	4-8	L	5.2	**10**	6	**6**	1	3	8	107/70	3.85	Trailing 6-4
7/7 at MIN	10-2	W	7.0	3	1	1	1	1	3	100/68	3.85	Leading 10-1
7/12 at LAA	4-5	L	6.2	9	5	5	0	3	6	114/71	3.86	Trailing 5-2
7/18 vs. DET	2-1	W	7.0	5	0	0	0	3	4	114/66	3.66	Leading 2-0
7/23 vs. OAK	6-3	W	7.0	9	3	3	0	0	4	109/71	3.67	Leading 6-3
7/28 at TB	2-6	L	5.2	9	6	5	1	2	6	109/69	3.83	Trailing 1-6
8/2 at CWS*	8-5	W	7.0	**10**	5	5	**2**	0	5	100/71	3.95	Leading 7-4
8/8 vs. BOS	5-0	W	7.2	2	0	0	0	2	9	**123**/81	3.76	Leading 2-0
8/13 at SEA	11-1	W	8.0	3	1	1	1	2	**10**	105/74	3.64	Leading 11-1
8/18 at OAK*	7-2	W	8.0	5	2	2	**2**	1	7	94-66	3.58	Leading 7-2
8/23 at BOS*	8-4	W	6.2	8	4	3	0	0	8	118/80	3.59	Leading 7-4
8/28 vs CWS*	5-2	ND	7.0	8	2	2	0	1	**10**	113/78	3.56	Tied 2-2
9/2 at BAL	10-2	W	7.0	7	1	1	0	1	9	105/73	3.48	Leading 3-1
9/7 vs. TB*	4-1	ND	7.0	3	1	1	1	4	**10**	118/71	3.40	Tied 1-1
9/13 vs. BAL*	13-3	W	7.0	5	3	3	0	4	1	108/66	3.42	Leading 5-3
9/19 at SEA*	10-1	W	7.0	4	1	0	0	2	8	105/69	3.31	Leading 8-1
9/26 vs. BOS	3-0	W	7.0	1	0	0	0	2	8	96/57	3.21	Leading 1-0
10/2 at TB*	4-13	L	2.2	8	**9**	5	0	**5**	3	82/47	3.37	Trailing 9-1
Totals	**19-8**	**(7ND)**	**230.0**	**197**	**96**	**86**	**18**	**67**	**197**	--	**3.37**	

Sabathia's 2009 Pitching Lines

(*) Denotes start following a team loss – **Bold indicates season highs**

- With 19 wins, surpassed Dock Ellis (17-8 in 1976) for the most single-season victories by an African-American pitcher in Yankees franchise history...marked the most wins by a Yankee in his first season with the franchise since Tommy John in 1979 (21-9)...were the most wins by a Yankees left-hander since Andy Pettitte went 21-8 in 2003.
- Began the season 1-3 with a 4.85 ERA (39.0IP, 21ER) in his first six starts, then posted an 18-5 record with a 3.06 ERA (191.0IP, 65ER) in 28 starts from 5/8 through the end of the season.
- Led the Majors in wins after the All-Star break, compiling an 11-2 record with a 2.74 ERA in 15 starts...the Yankees went 13-2 in his post-All-Star break starts, which included an 11-start undefeated stretch from 8/2-9/26 in which he went 9-0 with a 2.04 ERA (79.1IP, 56H, 18ER, 19BB, 85K, 6HR)...his nine-game winning streak over that same period was the longest in the AL in 2009...according to the *Elias Sports Bureau*, was the longest post-All-Star break winning streak by a Yankee since Aaron Small went 10-0 (8-0 as a starter) in 2005.
- Compiled a 12-6 record with a 3.53 ERA on the road, tying Texas' Scott Feldman and St. Louis' Adam Wainwright for the most wins away from home among all Major League pitchers...marked the most road wins by a Yankee in the last 31 seasons, since Ron Guidry went 13-2 away from the original Yankee Stadium in 1978.
- Became the 10th lefthander in Yankees history to win 19-or-more games in a season, joining Whitey Ford, Lefty Gomez, Ron Guidry, Tommy John, Eddie Lopat, Herb Pennock, Fritz Peterson, Andy Pettitte and David Wells.
- Compiled an American League-best 1.59 first-inning ERA (34.0IP, 6ER - min 20GS), according to the *Elias Sports Bureau*.
- Tossed at least 7.0IP in 24 of his 34 starts, including 10 of his final 12 outings...marked the most starts of at least 7.0IP in a season by a Yankee since Melido Perez (27) in 1992 and the most such starts while also allowing 3ER or less (20) since Mike Mussina in 2001 (21)...strung together eight straight starts with at least 7.0IP from 5/8-6/16, marking the longest such single-season streak by a Yankee since David Cone (eight straight from 6/24-8/2/98)...threw at least 100 pitches in 27-of-34 starts, marking the most 100-pitch starts by a Yankee in a single season since Roger Clemens in 2001 (also 27).
- Allowed just 1HR to a left-handed batter in his final 21 starts (122AB) from 6/16 to the end of the season (Jim Thome on 8/2 at Chicago-AL)...did not allow an extra-base hit to a lefty from 8/8 to 9/26 (spanning 63AB)...held lefthanders to a .127 batting average over the stretch, allowing just eight singles and 3BB.
- For the third straight year, was selected as the recipient of the "Warren Spahn Award" as the season's top left-handed pitcher...the award is given by the Oklahoma Sports Museum and is based on a combination of wins, strikeouts and earned run average...placed fourth in AL Cy Young Award voting and received one eighth-place vote for AL MVP.

CC SABATHIA

- Made his sixth career Opening Day start on 4/6 at Baltimore, recording the loss in a 10-5 Orioles victory (4.1IP, 8H, 6ER, 5BB, 0K)...marked just the fifth time in his career that he failed to strike out a batter and first since 7/25/05 at Oakland (w/ Cleveland)...according to *Elias*, he became the first Yankees starter to not record a strikeout in an Opening Day assignment since George Mogridge in 1918.
- Became the Yankees' sixth different Opening Day starting pitcher in the last seven years and the team's first free-agent signing to make an Opening Day start immediately after signing with the club during the previous offseason since Roger Clemens in 2003...was the ninth left-hander to make an Opening Day start for the Yankees over the last 50 years (1960-2009), joining Randy Johnson (2005-06), Andy Pettitte (1998), Jimmy Key (1993-95), Dave LaPoint (1990), Dennis Rasmussen (1987), Tommy John (1981), Ron Guidry (1978-80, '82-84, '86) and Whitey Ford (1961-62, '64, '66)...was the Yankees' first African-American Opening Day starter.
- Earned his first win of the season in his second start on 4/11 at Kansas City in a 6-1 Yankees victory, tossing 7.2 scoreless innings (6H, 0BB, 6K).
- Started the first-ever regular season game in Yankee Stadium on 4/16 vs. Cleveland, leaving without a decision in a 10-2 Indians victory...limited his former club to 1ER in 5.2IP (5H, 5BB, 4K)...exited in the sixth with the game tied 1-1 before Cleveland scored 9R in the seventh...opposed 2008 Cy Young Award winner Cliff Lee, marking the first time the last two AL Cy Young Award winners faced off since 2003 when Roger Clemens and Barry Zito squared off on 5/4/03 at the original Yankee Stadium.

MAJOR LEAGUE LEADERS (since 2007)

WINS

1.	**CC SABATHIA**	**55**
2.	Roy Halladay	53
3.	Josh Beckett	49
4.	Justin Verlander	48
5.	Dan Haren	45

STRIKEOUTS

1.	Tim Lincecum	676
2.	**CC SABATHIA**	**657**
3.	JAVIER VAZQUEZ	651
4.	Dan Haren	621
5.	Justin Verlander	615

INNINGS PITCHED

1.	**CC SABATHIA**	**724.0**
2.	Roy Halladay	710.1
3.	Dan Haren	668.0
4.	James Shields	649.2
5.	JAVIER VAZQUEZ	644.1

- Recorded a complete-game loss on 4/27 at Detroit in a 4-2 Tigers victory (8.0IP, 6H, 4ER, 0BB, 7K, 1HR)...was his 27th career complete game, and the sixth complete-game loss of his career...was the first CG loss by a Yankee since Randy Johnson on 8/24/06 in a 4-2 loss at Seattle.
- Recorded a 4-0 complete-game shutout victory on 5/8 at Baltimore...marked the first CG-shutout by a Yankee since Chien Ming Wang on 7/28/06 vs. Tampa Bay (2H, 2BB, 1K), snapping a franchise-record 414-game stretch without a Yankees pitcher recording a shutout (credit: *Elias*)...became the first Yankees lefthander to throw a shutout at Baltimore since Ron Guidry in 1985 at Memorial Stadium.
- Faced his former club again on 5/30 at Cleveland, recording the win in a 10-5 Yankees victory in his first start at Progressive Field since being traded by the Indians last July (7.0IP, 5H, 3ER, 3BB, 8K, 1HR)...according to the *Elias Sports Bureau*, became the first pitcher with 100 career wins with the Indians to subsequently defeat Cleveland since Early Wynn did so with the White Sox in 1962.
- Exited his start on 6/21 at Florida after 1.1IP with a sore left biceps muscle...allowed 1ER on 3H in 1.1IP (1BB, 1K)...was his shortest start since 6/26/04 vs. Colorado, when he left that game after 1.0 inning with irritation in his left shoulder...did not miss a start.
- Was 5-0 with a 1.63 ERA (49.2IP, 9ER) in his last seven home starts from 7/18 until the end of the season, allowing just 33H and 16BB with 46K.
- Reached 1,500 career strikeouts on 7/28 at Tampa Bay, catching Carl Crawford looking in the fifth inning...recorded the loss in a 6-2 Rays victory (5.2IP, 9H, 6R, 5ER, 2BB, 6K, 1HR).

SABATHIA'S AL RANKS IN 2009

STAT	TOTAL	AL RANK
Wins	19	T-1st
ERA	3.37	4th
IP	230.0	4th
Strikeouts	197	7th
Opp. Avg.	.232	3rd
HR/9.0IP	0.70	3rd

- Allowed 4R/3ER in 6.2IP (8H, 0BB, 8K) on 8/23 at Boston while becoming the Majors' first 15-game winner, defeating Josh Beckett (8.0IP, 8ER)...according to the *Elias Sports Bureau*, became the first Yankee to be the first pitcher in the Majors to win 15 games since Roger Clemens in 2001 and just the second since David Cone in 1998...became only the second pitcher since 1946 to reach the mark first in his first season with a team, joining Roger Clemens (w/ Toronto in 1997).
- Struck out at least seven batters in a career-high seven straight starts from 8/8-9/7, matching Mike Mussina (4/2-5/7/03 – 7GS) and Ron Guidry (7/14-8/15/78 – 7GS) as the only three Yankees pitchers since 1954 to post seven such consecutive games.
- Allowed a career-high-tying 9R (5ER) in 2.2IP on 10/2 at Tampa Bay in his final regular season start...marked his shortest non-injury-shortened start since 6/21/06 w/Cleveland vs. Chicago-NL...matched his season high with 5BB (also 4/6 at Baltimore and 4/16 vs. Cleveland).

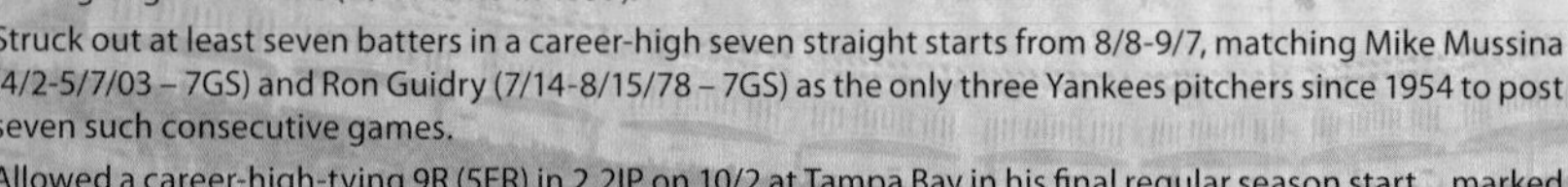

CC SABATHIA

- Made five postseason starts, going 3-1 with a 1.98 ERA (36.1IP, 28H, 9R, 8ER, 9BB, 32K, 4HR, 1HP), limiting opponents to 3ER or less in each outing...started Game 1 in all three rounds, making his two other starts on three-days' rest...earned ALCS MVP after winning both starts with a 1.13 ERA (16.0IP, 2ER)...won his Yankees postseason debut on 10/7 in Game 1 of the ALDS vs. Minnesota (6.2IP, 8H, 2R, 1ER, 0BB, 8K, 1HP), marking just the fifth time in postseason franchise history a Yankees pitcher recorded at least 8K without walking a batter...became the third African-American Yankees pitcher to start a World Series game, joining Dock Ellis and Al Downing...became the seventh Yankee to record three-or-more wins in a single postseason, joining David Wells (1998), Andy Pettitte (2003 and '09), Mike Stanton (2000), Orlando Hernandez (1999 and 2000), Dave Righetti (1981) and Sparky Lyle (1977).

2008

- Went 17-10 with a 2.70 ERA in 35 combined starts with Cleveland and Milwaukee...led the Majors in innings pitched (253.0), complete games (10) and shutouts (five), ranked second in strikeouts (251) and fourth in ERA...despite midseason trade, finished fifth in National League Cy Young Award voting and sixth in NL MVP voting.
- Opponents batted .237 (223-for-942, 19HR); LH .205 (48-for-234, 5HR), RH .247 (175-for-708, 14HR)...his five shutouts were the second-most in a single season over the last 15 years (1994-2008), behind Randy Johnson's six in 1998...only Johnson (12 CG in 1999) recorded more complete games in a single season than Sabathia's 10 over the last 10 years (1999-2008)...marked the most innings pitched by any Major League pitcher since Montreal's Livan Hernandez in 2004 (255.0).
- Lost his first three decisions (0-3, 4GS, 13.50 ERA)...over his remaining 31 starts (beginning 4/22), posted a 17-7 record and a 1.88 ERA, leading the Majors in ERA over the span.
- Opened the year at Cleveland, going 6-8 with a 3.83 ERA in 18 starts before being acquired by Milwaukee on 7/7...finished with 106 wins as an Indian, ranking second all time among club lefthanders behind Sam McDowell (122).
- Won a career-high 12 straight decisions over 16 starts from 6/10-8/31, pitching to a 1.55 ERA over the stretch and striking out 126 batters in 128.0IP with only 28 walks.
- Was acquired by Milwaukee on 7/7 in exchange for OF Matt LaPorta, LHP Zach Johnson, RHP Rob Bryson and a player to be named later (OF Michael Brantley)...became the fifth defending Cy Young Award winner to be traded before the end of the following season, joining Frank Viola, David Cone, Pedro Martinez and Roger Clemens...was leading the AL with 123K at the time of the trade.

MOST MAJOR LEAGUE WINS BY LHP (2001-09)

1.	**CC SABATHIA**	**136**
2.	Mark Buehrle	131
3.	ANDY PETTITTE	129
4.	Jamie Moyer	127
5.	Barry Zito	126

HIGHEST SINGLE-SEASON K/BB RATIO, ALL-TIME BY A LHP

1.	Randy Johnson, ARI	2004	6.59
2.	**CC SABATHIA, CLE**	**2007**	**5.65**
3.	David Wells, NYY	1998	5.62
4.	Greg Swindell, CLE	1991	5.45
5.	Sandy Koufax, LA-NL	1965	5.38

Courtesy: *BASEBALL REFERENCE*

MOST RBI, ALL-TIME IN INTERLEAGUE PLAY BY AL PITCHER (1997-2009)

1.	**CC SABATHIA**	**8**
2.	Josh Beckett	5
	Felix Hernandez	5
	Mike Mussina	5
5.	Jon Garland	4
	Jarrod Washburn	4

MOST COMPLETE GAMES SINCE 2001

1.	Roy Halladay	47
2.	Livan Hernandez	31
3.	**CC SABATHIA**	**28**
4.	Mark Mulder	25
5.	Mark Buehrle	24
	Randy Johnson	24

- Went 11-2 with a 1.65 ERA in 17 starts as a Brewer, tossing seven complete games and three shutouts...the Brewers went 14-3 in his starts...opponents batted .222 (106-for-478, 6HR)...after joining the Brewers, led the Majors in ERA, tied Cliff Lee for most wins and ranked second in strikeouts (128)...the Brewers went 41-32 (.562) from 7/8 (Sabathia's first start) through the remainder of the year, recording the fifth-best winning percentage in the NL over the span.
- Won his first nine decisions over his first 13 starts after joining Milwaukee, winning the NL "Player of the Month" Award in July (4-0, 2.27 ERA) and August (5-0, 1.12).
- Became the second pitcher in the last 90 years to win his first nine decisions following a midseason change of teams, joining Doyle Alexander who went 9-0 after going from the Braves to the Tigers in 1987.
- Collected three straight complete games from 7/13-28, allowing only 3ER in 27.0IP (1.00 ERA)...became the first Brewer to toss three consecutive CGs since Cal Eldred in 1994...streak was capped off by a three-hit shutout on 7/23 at St. Louis.
- Tossed a one-hit shutout on 8/31 at Pittsburgh in a 7-0 win for his ninth career shutout...lone hit was an Andy LaRoche check-swing dribbler back to Sabathia in the fifth inning.
- Made each of his final three starts of the season on three-days' rest, going 2-1 with a 0.83 ERA...included was a complete-game, 3-1 win on 9/28 vs. the Cubs to clinch the Brewers' Wild Card berth (9.0IP, 4H, 1R, 0ER, 1BB, 7K) on the final day of the season.
- Recorded the loss in his only postseason start on 10/2 at Philadelphia in Game 2 of the NLDS, allowing 5ER in 3.2IP.

CC SABATHIA

2007

- Won the American League Cy Young Award after compiling a 19-7 record with a 3.21 ERA and 209K...set career highs in wins, starts (34), innings pitched (241.0), ERA and strikeouts...became just the second Indian to win the award, joining Gaylord Perry (1972)...marked the most wins by a Cleveland left-hander since Sam McDowell (20) in 1970.
- Became the first Cleveland left-hander to lead the Majors in innings pitched, the first Indian since Early Wynn in 1954 to lead the AL in innings pitched and the first Indian since Bob Feller in 1947 to lead the Majors in innings pitched...were the most IP by an Indian since Charles Nagy in 1992.
- Bested Boston's Josh Beckett (119 points to 86) to become the first African-American Cy Young Award winner since Dwight Gooden in 1985 and the first in the AL since Vida Blue in 1971...also placed 14th in AL MVP voting...was named AL "Pitcher of the Year" by the MLBPA and the *Sporting News* and was named Indians "Man of the Year" by the Cleveland chapter of the BBWAA.
- Tied for first in the AL in starts, tied for second in wins, ranked second in complete games (four), third in pitches thrown (3,582), tied for third in winning percentage (.731), placed fifth in strikeouts and tied for ninth in GIDPs induced (23)...along with teammate Fausto Carmona (19 wins), became the first set of Tribe teammates since 1956 to each win at least 19 games...allowed 2ER or less in 20 of 34 starts and lasted 6.0IP in 32 starts.
- Reached double-digit wins for the seventh straight season to begin his career, becoming the second pitcher (and only LHP) in club history to accomplish the feat, joining RHP Addie Joss (1902-09)...no other Indians lefty has won 10+ games in seven straight years at any point in his career.
- Collected the most strikeouts by an Indian since Bartolo Colon (201) in 2001 and the most by an Indians lefthander since Sam McDowell in 1970 (304)...recorded the second-highest K/BB ratio (MLB-best 5.65) by a LHP in MLB history and the highest K/BB ratio ever by an AL lefty...finished second in the AL to Paul Byrd, averaging just 1.38 BB/9.0IP.
- Became the first pitcher to beat the Twins' Johan Santana three times in the same season (8/3, 8/29 and 9/3).
- Made his fourth career Opening Day start and won at Chicago-AL on 4/2 (6.0IP, 8H, 3R/ER)...began the year 5-0 for the first time in his career, winning nine of his first 10 decisions and 12 of his first 14.
- Went 16 consecutive starts without walking more than one batter from 4/20-7/5, the longest such streak in the Majors in 2007 and longest such stretch by a Cleveland pitcher since 1957.
- Notched his 1,000th career strikeout in 5/21 win vs. Seattle (Ichiro Suzuki in the fifth inning)...collected his fifth career complete-game shutout on 6/5 vs. Kansas City, then tossed 9.0 shutout innings (ND) in his next start on 6/10 at Cincinnati, a 12-inning 1-0 loss to the Reds...stretched his scoreless innings streak to 22.0 in his 6/15 start vs. Atlanta, but lost a 5-4 decision...was named AL "Player of the Week" for 6/25-7/1 (2-0 innings, 2.25ERA, 16.0IP, 15H, 4ER, 0BB, 16K).
- Did not allow a homer over a 41.0-inning stretch from 7/19-8/19...struck out a career-high 13 batters on 9/14 vs. Kansas City.
- Collected his 19th win of the season and 100th career win in his final start at Kansas City on 9/28 (7.0IP, 8H, 3ER)...became the youngest Major League pitcher (27 years, 70 days) since Greg Maddux in 1993 to win 100 games...of the 16 pitchers to win 300 games from 1900-2007, only three (Christy Mathewson, Maddux and Walter Johnson) were younger than Sabathia at the time of their 100th win...became the youngest Indians lefty ever to win 100 games and youngest overall pitcher since Bob Feller in 1941.
- Went 1-2 with an 8.80 ERA in three playoff starts (15.1IP, 21H, 15ER, 13BB, 14K).

2006

- In a career-low 28 starts, went 12-11 with a 3.22 ERA...was his sixth straight season to begin his career with double-digit wins, becoming just the second pitcher in club history to accomplish the feat, joining Hall of Famer Addie Joss (first eight seasons 1902-09)...became the only lefty in club history with six straight seasons of 10+ wins at any point in a career.
- Opponents batted .247 (182-for-738, 17HR); LH .271 (29-for-107, 3HR), RH .242 (153-for-631, 14HR).
- Led the Majors with six complete games, the most by an Indians LHP since Greg Swindell tossed seven in 1991...had the lowest road ERA (2.90) in the AL and the second-lowest day ERA (2.33) in the AL...ranked third in the AL in ERA, sixth in K/9.0IP (8.03) and opponents' average, and tied for eighth in strikeouts (172).
- Made his third career Opening Day start on 4/2 at Chicago-AL and left the game in the third inning with a strained right oblique muscle (2.1IP, 3H, 3ER, 1BB, 3K)...was placed on the 15-day disabled list the following day...made a rehab assignment on 4/27 for Triple-A Buffalo vs. Syracuse (5.0IP, 6H, 2R, 1ER, 1BB, 5K)...was his second career stint on the D.L...was activated prior to his 5/2 start vs. Chicago-AL, earning his first win of the season...recorded back-to-back complete games (5/19 and 5/24), becoming the first Indians pitcher since Bartolo Colon in May 2002 to accomplish the feat...repeated the act on 7/7 and 7/15.

- Named AL "Pitcher of the Month" for May, going 5-1 with a 1.20 ERA in six starts after coming off the D.L. on 5/2...tossed his third career shutout on 5/24 at Minnesota (9.0IP, 6H, 0R, 0BB, 8K)...tossed his seventh career complete game while allowing only 3H in 5/19 win vs. Pittsburgh (9.0IP, 1R/ER, 1BB, 9K).
- Underwent arthroscopic surgery on his right knee on 9/29 at the Cleveland Clinic to remove torn cartilage.

CAREER WINNING PERCENTAGE, ACTIVE LHP (min. 150 dec.)

	Player	Pct.
1.	Johan Santana	.670 (122-60)
2.	ANDY PETTITTE	.629 (229-135)
3.	**CC SABATHIA**	**.627 (136-81)**
4.	Mark Buehrle	.582 (135-97)
5.	Jamie Moyer	.570 (258-195)

YOUNGEST TO REACH 100 WINS SINCE

Youngest	Since Date	Years+Days
CC SABATHIA (CLE)	**9/28/07**	**27+069**
P G. Maddux (ATL)	5/31/93	27+047
AL P B. Saberhagen (KC)	5/10/91	27+029
LHP F. Valenzuela (LAD)	4/12/87	26+162
AL LHP V. Blue (OAK)	7/23/76	26+361

Courtesy: *BASEBALL REFERENCE*

YOUNGEST TO REACH 1,000 STRIKEOUTS SINCE...

Youngest	Since Date	Years+Days
CC SABATHIA (CLE)	**5/21/07**	**26+304**
P K. Wood (CHC)	8/11/03	26+056
AL P R. Clemens (BOS)	4/31/89	26+252
LHP F. Valenzuela (LAD)	8/31/85	24+303
AL LHP F. Tanana (DET)	6/20/78	24+325

Courtesy: *BASEBALL REFERENCE*

2005

- Went 15-10 with a 4.03 ERA in 31 starts...ranked sixth in the AL in K/9.0IP (7.37), seventh in strikeouts, tied for eighth in wins and placed 10th in opponents' average...opponents batted .248 (185-for-745, 19HR); LH .248 (27-for-109, 4HR), RH .248 (158-for-636, 15HR).
- Began the season on the 15-day D.L. (placed on D.L. officially on 3/25; activated on 4/16) after straining his right oblique muscle warming up prior to his first spring start on 3/6 vs. Detroit...was his first trip to the Major League disabled list in his career.
- Hit his first career homer on 5/25 in Cincinnati in the fourth inning off Elizardo Ramirez...had 4RBI on the year (most by an Indians pitcher since 1972).
- Lost a career-high five straight starts from 7/6-7/30, then won seven straight starts from 8/5-9/7, recording the longest winning streak for an Indians pitcher since Ken Schrom in June/July of 1986.
- Tossed a four-hit complete game on 9/7 at Detroit, retiring his last 21 batters faced.
- Had his 2006 club option exercised by Cleveland and was then signed to a two-year extension through 2008 on 4/27.

2004

- Posted an 11-10 record with a 4.12 ERA in 30 starts...was selected to his second consecutive All-Star team, pitching 1.0 inning in the AL win at Houston...had six potential wins blown by the Cleveland bullpen.
- Made his second consecutive Opening Day start on 4/5 at Minnesota (7.0IP, 2H, 0R, 4BB, 9K)...was scratched from his start on 4/22 vs. Kansas City due to an irritated left biceps tendon and did not start from 4/17-30.
- Made his 100th career start on 5/1 vs. Baltimore, earning the win...became only the second Indian to make 100 career starts before age 24, joining Hall of Famer Bob Feller (175GS).
- Left his start on 6/26 vs. Colorado after 1.0 inning with irritation in his left shoulder...after MRI results in Cleveland were negative, traveled for a second opinion to Birmingham, Ala., on 6/28 to visit Dr. James Andrews, who cleared him to return...was 3-0 with a 2.57 ERA in six June starts (35.0IP, 27H, 10ER, 11BB, 26K).
- Notched his 50th career win on 7/27 vs. Detroit at the age of 24 years, 6 days, becoming the youngest pitcher to reach 50 career wins since Atlanta's Steve Avery (10/1/93 at 23 years, 170 days)...according to *Elias*, was the youngest active pitcher at the time to reach 50 career wins
- Tossed the second complete-game shutout of his Major League career on 9/6 at Seattle (9.0IP, 5H, 0R, 1BB, 8K) as he allowed just two runners to second base...sat out last two weeks of season due to a strained right hamstring.

2003

- Was 13-9 with a 3.60 ERA in 30 starts, earning his first career All-Star selection...did not appear in the Midsummer Classic, and at 22 years, 352 days, became the youngest Indians All-Star since RHP Dennis Eckersley in 1977 and the first Tribe All-Star LHP since Greg Swindell in 1989.
- Ranked sixth among AL pitchers with a 3.09 home ERA, eighth with a 3.38 night ERA and 10th in overall ERA...threw at least 5.0 innings in 29 of his 30 starts as the Indians averaged just 3.8 runs per game during his starts (the fifth worst run support among AL starting pitchers).
- Made his first career Opening Day start on 3/31 at Baltimore (ND, 7.0IP, 8H, 2ER, Riske BS) and was the youngest Opening Day starting pitcher (22 years, 252 days) in the Major Leagues since Dwight Gooden (22 years, 143 days) started for the New York Mets on 4/8/86 at Pittsburgh...was also the youngest Indians pitcher to start on Opening Day since Eckersley (21 years old) on 4/10/76 vs. Detroit.

- Tossed his first career complete-game shutout on 8/15 vs. Tampa Bay in a 1-0 win (9.0IP, 4H, 0R, 3BB, 9K)...was the first complete game, 1-0 shutout by a Tribe hurler since Bud Black in 1990 and the Tribe's first 1-0 win since 1997...collected a pinch-hit single off Mike Williams in 15.0-inning game on 6/20 at Pittsburgh in the 11th inning, becoming first Cleveland pitcher with a pinch-hit base hit since Dick Donovan on 7/28/63.

2002

- Went 13-11 with a 4.37 ERA in 33 starts, leading Cleveland pitchers in wins, IP (210.0), starts and strikeouts (149)...was tied for fourth in the AL with a 2.48 day ERA, tied for sixth with 24 induced GIDP, ranked seventh with 0.73 HR allowed per 9.0IP (17HR, 210.0IP), ninth with 3,379 pitches thrown and 10th in strikeouts.
- Became the fifth pitcher since 1987 to win 30 games over his first two seasons in the Majors.
- Took a no-hitter into the eighth inning of his second start at Detroit on 4/7 before yielding a lead-off single to Randall Simon...collected his first Major League hit on 6/15 at Colorado, a single off Dennys Reyes...tossed his first career complete game in 8/18 loss at Anaheim (8.0IP, 8H, 4ER, 3BB, 4K).
- Signed a four-year contract through 2005 with a club option for 2006 on 2/23.

2001

- Saw his first Major League action as a 20-year-old, going 17-5 with a 4.39 ERA in 33 starts, leading all rookie pitchers in wins, starts (33) and strikeouts (171)...became the first Indians rookie since Gene Bearden (20-7) in 1948 to win 17-or-more games in his rookie season...finished second to Seattle's Ichiro Suzuki in the AL BBWAA "Rookie of the Year" voting with 73 points...was the youngest active player in the big leagues all season...led AL rookie pitchers in innings (180.1) and ERA.
- Overall among AL pitchers, ranked third in winning percentage (.773) tied for sixth in wins and ranked seventh in strikeouts...his .228 average against (149-for-654) was the second-lowest mark among AL starters...led the AL with 13 road wins...also paced the AL, allowing a league-low 7.44 H/9.0IP.
- Became the first player to finish a season under 22 years of age with at least 17 wins since Atlanta's Steve Avery (18-8) in 1991 and the first AL pitcher to accomplish the feat since Chicago's Britt Burns in 1980 (19-13)...was the most wins by a left-handed rookie pitcher since Seattle's Dave Fleming in 1992 (17-10).
- After the season, was named the *Sporting News'* AL "Rookie Pitcher of the Year" and was selected to the *Baseball Digest* & Topps Major League All-Rookie Teams.
- Was a member of the Opening Day roster and made his Major League debut on 4/8 vs. Baltimore, drawing a no-decision in Cleveland's 4-3 win (5.2IP, 3H, 3ER, 2BB, 3K, 1HR)...was the youngest pitcher to start and appear in a game for Cleveland since Julian Tavarez in August 1993...registered his first Major League win in his second start on 4/13 at Detroit (5.0IP, 5H, 4R/ER, 2BB, 2K) in a 9-8 Indians victory.
- Won the AL "Rookie of the Month" Award in July, going 3-0 with a 2.83 ERA as the Indians went 6-0 in his starts.
- Won his first postseason start in Game 3 of the ALDS vs. Seattle (6.0IP, 6H, 2ER, 5BB, 5K), becoming the second-youngest pitcher to win a Division Series game behind only the Dodgers' Fernando Valenzuela (defeated Houston in 1981)...also became the youngest Indians pitcher to start a Division Series game and the third-youngest pitcher in Division Series history (youngest in ALDS history) to start a game behind Valenzuela (1981, 20 years, 339 days) and St. Louis' Rick Ankiel (2000, 21 years, 77 days).

2000

- Split the season between Single-A Kinston and Double-A Akron, posting a combined 3.57 ERA (146.1IP, 58ER) in 27 starts over the two stops while striking out an organization-high 159 batters.
- Began the year at Kinston and went 3-2 with a 3.54 ERA in 10 starts, which included a 9.0-inning, two-hit, complete game shutout in his final start there on 5/23 at Myrtle Beach...was promoted to Akron on 5/27, throwing 5.0 or more innings in 23 of his 27 starts with the Aeros.
- Started the Hall of Fame Game for Cleveland against the Arizona Diamondbacks on 7/24 in Cooperstown, N.Y...did not record a decision in the outing (3.0IP, 3H, 3ER, 2BB, 4K, HR)...also pitched in the Futures Game in Atlanta, Ga. for Team USA on 7/10.
- Tabbed as the top prospect in the organization and the No. 2 prospect in the Eastern League by *Baseball America* after the season.

CC SABATHIA

1999

- Missed the first two and half months of the season with a bone bruise in his left pitching elbow...was activated off the D.L. on 6/20 and assigned to short-season Single-A Mahoning Valley...made six starts with the Scrappers, which increased by 1.0-inning increments, before being promoted to Single-A Columbus of the South Atlantic League on 7/17...was promoted to Single-A Kinston of the Carolina League on 8/2 where he spent the remainder of the season...combined on the year between his three minor league stops to go 5-3 with a 3.29 ERA in 16 starts (68.1IP, 47H, 25ER, 36BB, 76K)...overall, minor league hitters hit .198 (47-for-237) off him with 4HR.

1998

- Signed on 6/29 and was assigned to rookie-level Burlington, where he made five starts and struck out 35 batters in 18.0IP (17.50K/9.0IP)...was ranked by *Baseball America* as Cleveland's second-best prospect, the fourth-best prospect in the Appalachian League and was tabbed as having the best fastball in the organization.

Personal

- Full name is Carsten Charles Sabathia...he and his wife, Amber, have one son, Carsten Charles III (6) and two daughters, Jaden Arie (4) and Cyia Cathleen (1)...attended Vallejo Senior High School where he compiled a mark of 6-0 with a 0.77 ERA (46.2IP, 14H, 4ER, 14BB, 82K) during his senior season...was the top high school prospect coming out of Northern California according to *Baseball America*...was also an all-conference tight end in football at Vallejo...had scholarship offers to play college football and had signed a letter of intent at Hawaii...was selected to the 2000 United States Olympic Team Roster and appeared in one pre-Olympic tournament game in Sydney, Australia, but was not on the official 24-man, Gold Medal-winning roster.
- In 2008, established the CC Sabathia Family Foundation's "PitCCh In" along with his wife, Amber...the foundation is committed to the care and needs of inner-city children while helping to raise self-esteem through sports activities and education.
- Through "PitCCh In," the Sabathia's provided backpacks filled with back-to-school essentials and an autographed photo on 8/19/09 at his elementary school, Loma Vista School in Vallejo, Calif...for Thanksgiving 2009, joined Safeway to deliver 500 dinners to Vallejo families in need...played secret Santa for 22 Vallejo teenagers in foster care for Christmas 2009, taking the kids on a shopping spree...provided holiday gifts to children in need through "Toys for Tots" for the third straight year...also provided sports equipment to the Madison Square Boys & Girls Club in New York City...renovated Thurmon Field, his former Little League field, in Vallejo, Calif., and held a clinic on 1/30/10.

- Was honored at the Vallejo Mayor's Community Recognition Dinner on 11/28/09 where he received the Mayor's Achievement Awards.
- Joined Carl Crawford at Tropicana Field on 7/29/09 to speak to African-American youth and encourage them to get involved with baseball...also served as an MLB spokesman for RBI (Reviving Baseball in Inner Cities)...gave free haircuts to Bronx neighborhood kids at Jordan's Barber Shop on 6/3/09.
- Purchased 500 tickets to a Golden State Warriors basketball game in 2009 and distributed them to children from the Boys & Girls Clubs in Oakland and Vallejo...assisted in funding two programs for inner-city children at Tony La Russa's Animal Rescue Foundation in 2009...purchased lights for the 2008 Macy's Holiday Tree as part of a fundraising benefit for the University of California-San Francisco Children's Hospital.
- Was a regular participant in the Indians' Winter Press Caravan and was involved in numerous community endeavors during his tenure with Cleveland, including: OfficeMax Parent-Child Clinics, the Larry Doby RBI Program, Red Cross' "Fire Prevention Week", the Cleveland Scholarship Program, Grand Slam Summer Literacy, High Achievers and the Giant Eagle week-long baseball camps...was also a regular visitor to area hospitals as part of the "Tribe Loving Care" program...co-chaired the Swim for Diabetes and participated in the Dick's Sporting Goods "Shop with a Pro" in 2006-07...danced in the Oakland Ballet's "Nutcracker" in 2005 along with Barry Zito and Tony La Russa...organized the Sabathia Baseball Clinic in his hometown of Vallejo in 2003.
- Since 2005, has teamed with Barry Zito's foundation "Strikeouts For Troops," a national program which provides "comforts of home" to wounded troops being treated in military hospitals nationwide and assists their families...has personally contributed $100 for each strikeout since 2005...hasparticipated in adopting 25 military families and providing Thanksgiving and Christmas dinner as well as Christmas gifts for the children each of the last three years (2007-09).

CC SABATHIA

Sabathia's Career Pitching Record

Year	Club	W	L	ERA	G	GS	CG	SHO	SV	IP	H	R	ER	HR	HP	BB	SO	WP	BK
1998	Burlington	1	0	4.50	5	5	0	0	0	18.0	20	14	9	1	1	8	35	1	1
1999	Mahoning Valley	0	0	1.83	6	6	0	0	0	19.2	9	5	4	0	0	12	27	0	0
	Columbus	2	0	1.08	3	3	0	0	0	16.2	8	2	2	1	1	5	20	1	0
	Kinston	3	3	5.34	7	7	0	0	0	32.0	30	22	19	3	1	19	29	6	0
2000	Kinston	3	2	3.54	10	10	2	2	0	56.0	48	23	22	4	2	24	69	2	1
	Akron	3	7	3.59	17	17	0	0	0	90.1	75	41	36	6	7	48	90	2	1
2001	CLEVELAND	17	5	4.39	33	33	0	0	0	180.1	149	93	88	19	3	95	171	7	3
2002	CLEVELAND	13	11	4.37	33	33	2	0	0	210.0	198	109	102	17	1	88	149	6	*3
2003	CLEVELAND	13	9	3.60	30	30	2	1	0	197.2	190	85	79	19	6	66	141	4	2
2004	CLEVELAND	11	10	4.12	30	30	1	1	0	188.0	176	90	86	20	7	72	139	1	1
2005	Akron	0	1	1.00	2	2	0	0	0	9.0	4	3	1	0	1	2	9	1	0
	CLEVELAND – a	15	10	4.03	31	31	1	0	0	196.2	185	92	88	19	7	62	161	7	0
2006	CLEVELAND – b	12	11	3.22	28	28	*6	*2	0	192.2	182	83	69	17	7	44	172	3	0
	Buffalo	1	0	1.80	1	1	0	0	0	5.0	6	2	1	0	0	1	5	1	0
2007	CLEVELAND	19	7	3.21	34	*34	4	1	0	*241.0	238	94	86	20	8	37	209	1	0
2008	CLEVELAND	6	8	3.83	18	18	3	2	0	122.1	117	54	52	13	3	34	123	1	2
	MILWAUKEE – c	11	2	1.65	17	17	*7	#3	0	130.2	106	31	24	6	4	25	128	1	0
2009	YANKEES – d	#19	8	3.37	34	34	2	1	0	230.0	197	96	86	18	9	67	197	5	0
Minor League Totals		**13**	**13**	**3.43**	**51**	**51**	**2**	**2**	**0**	**246.2**	**200**	**112**	**94**	**15**	**13**	**119**	**284**	**14**	**3**
AL Totals		**125**	**79**	**3.77**	**271**	**271**	**21**	**8**	**0**	**1758.2**	**1632**	**796**	**736**	**162**	**55**	**565**	**1462**	**35**	**11**
NL Totals		**11**	**2**	**1.65**	**17**	**17**	**7**	**3**	**0**	**130.2**	**106**	**31**	**24**	**6**	**4**	**25**	**128**	**1**	**0**
Major League Totals		**136**	**81**	**3.62**	**288**	**288**	**28**	**11**	**0**	**1889.1**	**1738**	**827**	**760**	**168**	**59**	**590**	**1590**	**36**	**11**

* League leader # Tied for league lead

Selected by Cleveland in the first round (20th overall) of the 1998 First-Year Player Draft.

a – Placed on the 15-day disabled list from March 25 – April 15, 2005 with a right oblique strain.
b – Placed on the 15-day disabled list from April 3 – May 2, 2006 with a right oblique strain.
c – Acquired by Milwaukee from Cleveland on July 7, 2008 in exchange for OF Matt LaPorta, LHP Zach Jackson, RHP Rob Bryson and a player to be named later.
d – Signed by New York (AL) as a free agent on December 18, 2008.

Sabathia's Division Series Record

Year	Club vs. Opp.	W	L	ERA	G	GS	CG	SHO	SV	IP	H	R	ER	HR	HP	BB	SO	WP	BK
2001	CLE vs. SEA	1	0	3.00	1	1	0	0	0	6.0	6	2	2	0	0	5	5	0	0
2007	CLE vs. NYY	1	0	5.40	1	1	0	0	0	5.0	4	3	3	2	0	6	5	0	0
2008	MIL vs. PHI	0	1	12.27	1	1	0	0	0	3.2	6	5	5	1	0	4	5	0	0
2009	NYY vs. MIN	1	0	1.35	1	1	0	0	0	6.2	8	2	1	0	1	0	8	1	0
Division Series Totals		**3**	**1**	**4.64**	**4**	**4**	**0**	**0**	**0**	**21.1**	**24**	**12**	**11**	**3**	**1**	**15**	**23**	**1**	**0**

Sabathia's League Championship Series Record

Year	Club vs. Opp.	W	L	ERA	G	GS	CG	SHO	SV	IP	H	R	ER	HR	HP	BB	SO	WP	BK
2007	CLE vs. BOS	0	2	10.45	2	2	0	0	0	10.1	17	12	12	1	3	7	9	1	0
2009	NYY vs. LAA	2	0	1.13	2	2	0	0	0	16.0	9	2	2	1	0	3	12	0	0
LCS Totals		**2**	**2**	**4.78**	**4**	**4**	**0**	**0**	**0**	**26.1**	**26**	**14**	**14**	**2**	**3**	**10**	**21**	**1**	**0**

Sabathia's World Series Record

Year	Club vs. Opp.	W	L	ERA	G	GS	CG	SHO	SV	IP	H	R	ER	HR	HP	BB	SO	WP	BK
2009	NYY vs. PHI	0	1	3.29	2	2	0	0	0	13.2	11	5	5	3	0	6	12	0	0
World Series Totals		**0**	**1**	**3.29**	**2**	**2**	**0**	**0**	**0**	**13.2**	**11**	**5**	**5**	**3**	**0**	**6**	**12**	**0**	**0**
POSTSEASON TOTALS		**5**	**4**	**4.40**	**10**	**10**	**0**	**0**	**0**	**61.1**	**61**	**31**	**30**	**8**	**4**	**31**	**56**	**2**	**0**

Sabathia's All-Star Game Record

Year	Club, Site	W	L	ERA	G	GS	CG	SHO	SV	IP	H	R	ER	HR	HP	BB	SO	WP	BK
2003	CLE, Chicago (AL)						Selected - Did Not Pitch												
2004	CLE, Houston	0	0	27.00	1	0	0.0	0	0	1.0	4	3	3	0	0	0	0	0	0
2007	CLE, San Francisco	0	0	0.00	1	0	0	0	0	1.0	1	0	0	0	0	0	0	0	0
All-Star Game Totals		**0**	**0**	**13.50**	**2**	**0**	**0**	**0**	**0**	**2.0**	**5**	**3**	**3**	**0**	**0**	**0**	**0**	**0**	**0**

Sabathia's Regular Season Batting Record

Year	Team	AVG	G	AB	R	H	2B	3B	HR	RBI	SH	SF	HP	BB	SO	SB	CS
2009	NYY	.250	34	4	1	1	0	0	0	1	0	0	0	0	1	0	0
Major League Totals		**.261**	***289**	**92**	**7**	**24**	**3**	**0**	**3**	**14**	**3**	**0**	**0**	**1**	**23**	**0**	**0**

*one game as pinch-hitter

Sabathia's Career Fielding Record

Position	PCT	G	PO	A	E	TC	DP
Pitcher	.952	288	31	188	11	230	14

Romulo Sanchez
67
Right-handed Pitcher
6-5 • 260 • B/T: Right/Right
Opening Day Age: 25

Birthdate
April 28, 1984

Birthplace
Carora, Venezuela

Resides
Carora, Venezuela

M.L. Service
97 days
(Rookie)

Status

- Acquired by the Yankees from the Pittsburgh Pirates in exchange for minor league RHP Eric Hacker on May 16, 2009...signed through the 2010 season.

2009

- Spent the year at the Triple-A level, combining to go 6-5 with a 4.09 ERA and 79 strikeouts in 29 games (13 starts) with Indianapolis (PIT) and Scranton/Wilkes-Barre (NYY)...was acquired by the Yankees on 5/16 in exchange for minor league RHP Eric Hacker.
- Went 5-5 with a 4.04 ERA in 19 games (13 starts) with Scranton/WB...struck out 55 batters in 55.1IP as a starter, posting a 4-5 record and a 3.90 ERA...went 1-0 with a 4.82 ERA as a reliever...became a permanent fixture in the rotation on 7/20, making his final nine appearances as a starter...tossed 7.0 scoreless innings and earned the win on 8/27 vs. Syracuse, limiting the Chiefs to 2H with 9K (2BB, 2HP).
- Made two postseason starts for the International League North Division champs, going 1-1 with a 2.70 ERA and 17 strikeouts in 10.0IP...earned the win in his postseason debut, tossing 5.0 scoreless innings at Gwinnett on 9/9 (5H, 3BB, 9K).
- Made 10 relief appearances with Indianapolis prior to being traded, going 1-0 with a 4.38 ERA...held opponents scoreless in seven outings...struck out four of his eight batters faced on 4/22 at Toledo (2.0IP, 1H, 2BB).
- Pitched with both Lara and Caracas in the Venezuelan Winter League, going 6-4 with one save and a 3.82 ERA in 26 relief appearances...struck out 47 batters in 33.0IP.

Single-Game Bests and Streaks

Low hit CG
N/A
IP (start)
N/A
IP (relief)
3.0 - at MIL, 9/1/07
Hits
4 - vs. ARI, 9/27/07
Runs
3 - 2 times
Last: vs. ARI, 9/27/07
BB
3 - vs. NYM, 8/16/08
SO
3 - at CHC, 9/23/07
HR
1 - 2 times
Last: at CHC, 9/23/07
Winning Streak
1g - 9/14/07
Losing Streak
N/A

2008

- Made 10 relief appearances, posting a 4.05 ERA with no decisions over three stints with the Pirates (6/29-7/13; 8/5-23 and 9/2-28)...earned his first Major League save in his first outing of the season on 7/1 at Cincinnati (1.0IP, 2H, 1ER, 1BB)...tossed 2.1 scoreless innings (1H, 1HP) on 8/20 at St. Louis, prior to being optioned back to the minors a second time...collected three straight scoreless appearances from 9/7-14 (2.2IP) when recalled a third time.
- Spent majority of the season with Triple-A Indianapolis, going 5-1 with a 3.46 ERA in 33 total relief appearances...allowed runs in just two of his eight April outings, going 2-0 with one save...tossed five straight scoreless outings from 7/18-8/1 in between recalls (10.1IP, 5H, 2BB, 5K).
- Pitched with Caracas in the Venezuelan Winter League, going 2-2 with an 11.70 ERA in 12 relief appearances.

ROMULO SANCHEZ

2007

- Went 1-0 with a 5.00 ERA (18.0IP, 10ER) in 16 relief appearances with the Pirates in his first Major League action...was recalled by Pittsburgh on 8/25 and made his Major League debut the following night at Houston, tossing 0.2 scoreless innings of relief...struck out in his first career plate appearance on 9/1 at Milwaukee.
- Led Pirates pitchers with 14 relief appearances in September...held opponents scoreless in nine of his first 11 outings...pitched a career-high 3.0IP in his third career outing on 9/1 at Milwaukee (3H, 1ER, 1BB, 1K) earned his first win on 9/14 at Houston, striking out his only batter faced...allowed a run in three of his final five outings (5.1IP, 8ER).
- Opened the year with Double-A Altoona, going 6-3 with a 2.81 ERA in 40 relief appearances...struck out 52 batters with just 17 walks and held opponents to a .204 batting average (43-for-211)...right-handers hit just .155 (18-for-116, 4HR)...did not allow an earned run over 12 consecutive outings from 4/24-5/21 (11.1IP, 2H, 1R, 4BB, 10K)...earned his lone save on 5/27 at Bowie (1.0P, 1H, 1BB).
- Pitched with Caracas in the Venezuelan Winter League, going 1-2 with a 4.30 ERA in 14 relief appearances.

2006

- Appeared in 37 combined games (three starts) with Single-A Hickory, Single-A Lynchburg and Double-A Altoona, going 0-3 with a 5.86 ERA.
- Opened the year in Hickory...converted back-to-back save chances on 7/1 and 7/3 at Lakewood...was promoted to Lynchburg on 7/13, holding opponents scoreless in seven of his eight outings there and allowing only 12 baserunners (7H, 4BB, 1HP)...closed the season with Altoona after a promotion on 8/6...made 10 relief appearances with Caracas in the Venezuelan Winter League, posting a 4.66 ERA with no decisions.

2005

- Played at three levels, combining to go 5-3 with a 4.15 ERA with the GCL Pirates, Double-A Altoona and Single-A Hickory...won his Double-A debut on 7/5 vs. Erie, allowing just 1ER in 5.0IP (6H)...pitched for Caracas of the Venezuelan Winter League, advancing to the Caribbean World Series.

2004

- Signed with the Pirates organization on 5/7 after being released by the Dodgers on 3/12...spent the entire season pitching for Pittsburgh's Venezuelan Summer League entry...led the team in appearances (21) and saves (6)...tossed a 9.0-inning no-hitter on 8/3 vs. Ciudad Alienza, striking out 12 batters, in his final start of the season.

2002-03

- Opened his career in the Dodgers organization, playing his first two seasons with the Dominican League Dodgers.

Sanchez' Career Pitching Record

YEAR	CLUB	W	L	ERA	G	GS	CG	SHO	SV	IP	H	R	ER	HR	HB	BB	SO	WP	BK
2002	DSL Dodgers	1	4	4.44	15	0	0	0	1	24.1	24	16	12	4	6	10	22	4	0
2003	DSL Dodgers	2	3	4.46	9	9	0	0	0	38.1	40	25	19	1	4	10	21	7	0
2004	VSL Pirates-a	4	2	1.03	21	2	1	1	6	43.2	33	9	5	0	7	7	49	3	0
2005	GCL Pirates	1	0	1.80	2	1	0	0	0	10.0	7	2	2	1	0	4	7	0	0
	Altoona	1	0	3.60	2	2	0	0	0	10.0	11	4	4	2	0	4	5	1	0
	Hickory	3	3	4.70	10	10	0	0	0	53.2	59	34	28	5	10	19	24	4	1
2006	Hickory	0	3	7.08	21	3	0	0	4	40.2	51	36	32	4	6	18	28	6	1
	Lynchburg	0	0	1.04	8	0	0	0	1	8.2	7	1	1	0	1	4	6	0	0
	Altoona	0	0	5.00	8	0	0	0	0	9.0	8	5	5	1	0	8	5	0	0
2007	Altoona	6	3	2.81	40	0	0	0	1	57.2	43	24	18	8	3	17	52	5	1
	PITTSBURGH	1	0	5.00	16	0	0	0	0	18.0	16	10	10	2	1	8	11	1	0
2008	Indianapolis	5	1	3.46	33	0	0	0	4	54.2	50	27	21	5	3	19	32	2	0
	PITTSBURGH	0	0	4.05	10	0	0	0	1	13.1	14	6	6	0	1	6	3	4	0
2009	Indianapolis	1	0	4.38	10	0	0	0	0	12.1	11	6	6	1	1	5	15	0	0
	Scranton/WB-b	5	5	4.04	19	13	0	0	0	64.2	66	31	29	3	5	34	64	8	2
Minor League Totals		**29**	**24**	**3.83**	**198**	**40**	**1**	**1**	**17**	**427.2**	**410**	**220**	**182**	**35**	**46**	**159**	**330**	**40**	**5**
Major League Totals		**1**	**0**	**4.60**	**26**	**0**	**0**	**0**	**1**	**31.1**	**30**	**16**	**16**	**2**	**2**	**14**	**14**	**5**	**0**

Signed by the Los Angeles Dodgers as a non-drafted free agent on March 8, 2002.

a – Signed by the Pittsburgh Pirates as a minor league free agent on May 7, 2004.
b – Acquired by the Yankees from the Pirates in exchange for minor league RHP Eric Hacker on May 16, 2009.

Sanchez' Career Fielding Record

Position	PCT	G	PO	A	E	TC
Pitcher	1.000	26	4	4	0	8

Nick Swisher

33 Outfielder/Infielder

5-11 • 210 • B/T: Switch/Left

Opening Day Age: 29

Birthdate
November 25, 1980

Birthplace
Columbus, Ohio

Resides
Parkersburg, W. Va.

M.L. Service
5 years, 31 days

College
Ohio State University

Status

- Acquired by the Yankees along with RHP Kanekoa Texeira from the Chicago White Sox on November 13, 2008, in exchange for INF Wilson Betemit and RHPs Jeff Marquez and Jhonny Nunez...signed a five-year contract on May 11, 2007 (w/ Oakland)...contract extends through the 2011 season.

Career Notes

- Is the only player to have hit 15 or more home runs with three different franchises since 2007 (22 w/ Oakland in 2007, 24 w/ Chicago-AL in 2008 and 29 w/ the Yankees in 2009)...according to *Elias*, the only other player to cap such a three-year streak with the Yankees was Reggie Jackson (36HR for the 1975 Athletics, 27HR for the 1976 Orioles and 32 for the 1977 Yankees)...has hit at least 20HR in five straight seasons (2005-09).
- His 131HR since 2005 are the third-most among Major League switch-hitters over the last five seasons.

2009

- Hit .249 (124-for-498) with 84R, 35 doubles, 29HR and 82RBI in 150 games (126 starts in RF, 10 at 1B, four in LF, one at DH) in his first season with the Yankees...batted .250 (84-for-336, 20HR) as a left-handed batter and .247 (40-for-162, 9HR) as a right-handed batter.
- Ranked third among Major League switch-hitters in home runs, tied for third with 97BB and ranked sixth in RBI...ranked second overall in the AL in walks, marking the most free passes by a Yankees switch-hitter since Jorge Posada in 2000 (107)...ranked second in the American League and seventh in the Majors with 4.26 pitches seen per plate appearance...led the AL with a .585 slugging percentage on the road.
- Homered from both sides of the plate three times in 2009 (4/29 at Detroit, 7/27 at Tampa Bay and 9/8 vs. Tampa Bay)...according to SABR's David Vincent, his 10 career switch-hit homers are the most among active players and tied with Ken Caminiti, Tony Clark and Mickey Mantle for the third-most all-time behind Chili Davis and Eddie Murray (11 each).
- According to the *Elias Sports Bureau*, his three sets of switch-hit homers in 2009 tied his high for any season (also 2007) and tied the AL single-season mark, also shared by Tony Clark (1998 with Detroit) and teammate Mark Teixeira, who joined Swisher in accomplishing the feat in 2009.
- Homered from seven different spots in the batting order in 2009 (two through eight)...over the last 35 years, the only other player to homer from seven different batting order positions in one season for the Yankees was Dan Pasqua in 1987—credit: *Elias*...became the first player in franchise history to hit 21 of his first 24HR of the season on the road.
- He and teammate Mark Teixeira became the third set of Yankees teammates over the last 50 years to each hit at least 25HR in their first full season in pinstripes (also Alex Rodriguez/Gary Sheffield in 2004 and Jason Giambi/Robin Ventura in 2002).
- Made his Yankees debut in Opening Day loss at Baltimore on 4/6, going 1-for-1 with a pinch-hit double...was his fifth career Opening Day roster.

Single-Game Bests and Streaks

Hits
4 - at TB, 9/8/06

Runs
3 - 17 times
Last: at DET, 4/28/09

2B
2 - 10 times
Last: vs. TOR, 9/15/09

3B
1 - 6 times
Last: at KC, 4/11/09

HR
2 - 14 times
Last: vs. TB, 9/8/09

RBI
5 - 3 times
Last: at BAL, 4/9/09

BB
3 - 17 times
Last: vs. OAK, 4/22/09

SO
5 - at SD, 6/29/06

SB
1 - 7 times
Last: at MIN, 7/31/08

Hit Streak
11g - 4/30-5/11/06

NICK SWISHER

- Started his first game of the season on 4/9 at Baltimore in the Yankees first win of the season, going 3-for-5 with 2R, 1 double, 1HR and a career-high-tying 5RBI…according to the *Elias Sports Bureau*, became the first player to drive in four-or-more runs in his first career start with the Yankees since Roger Maris on 4/19/60 at Boston, when he went 4-for-5 with 2HR and 4RBI…*Elias* also noted that Swisher became just the second Yankee in franchise history (since RBI became an official statistic in 1920) to record five-or-more RBI in a single game within his first three contests with the club (also Bob Tillman on 8/13/67 at Cleveland, third game w/ NYY, 2-for-5, 1HR, 6RBI).
- Recorded a hit in each of his first nine games with an official at-bat, the longest hitting streak to begin a season of his career…batted .406 (13-for-32) with 5 doubles, 1 triple, 4HR and 11RBI over the stretch…according to the *Elias Sports Bureau*, set a franchise record with nine extra-base hits (4 doubles, 1 triple, 4HR) in his first eight games with the Yankees, surpassing Roger Maris, who had seven in 1960…*Elias* also notes his 11RBI tied the franchise record for most RBI in a player's first eight games with the club, matching Maris in 1960 and Robin Ventura in 2002.
- Reached base safely in each of his first 17 games, becoming the first Yankee to accomplish the feat since Matty Alou reached in his first 19 games in 1973 (credit: *Elias*).
- Hit solo-HR and was 1-for-3 with 2R and 1BB in 4/13 loss at Tampa Bay…also pitched a scoreless eighth inning (1.0IP, 1H, 1BB, 1K), becoming the Yankees' first position player to pitch in a game since Wade Boggs on 8/19/97 at Anaheim…also became the first Yankee to homer and record a strikeout while pitching in the same game since Lindy McDaniel on 9/28/72 at Detroit…according to the *Elias Sports Bureau*, since Divisional play began in 1969, only two other position players have homered and pitched in the same game (Pittsburgh's Keith Osik on 5/20/00 and Texas' Jeff Kunkel on 5/20/89).
- Led the team with 7HR and 19RBI in April, becoming the first offseason acquisition to lead the Yankees in March/April RBI in his first year with the club since Dave Winfield tied Bucky Dent for the team lead with nine April RBI in 1981…also became the first to hold the outright lead in both categories since Bobby Bonds in 1975 (4HR and 15RBI).
- Was 0-for-3 in 5/6 loss vs. Tampa Bay before being ejected in the seventh inning following a called third strike…was his second career ejection (also 9/16/07 w/ Oakland vs. Texas).

MOST WALKS IN THE AL, 2005-09

1. David Ortiz 476
2. **NICK SWISHER 431**
3. ALEX RODRIGUEZ 421
4. Grady Sizemore 389
5. Jason Giambi 384

MOST HOME RUNS BY MAJOR LEAGUE SWITCH-HITTERS, 2005-09

1. MARK TEIXEIRA 178
2. Lance Berkman 157
3. **NICK SWISHER 131**
4. Carlos Beltran 127
5. Chipper Jones 116

MOST GAMES WITH HOMERS FROM BOTH SIDES OF THE PLATE

1. Chili Davis 11
   Eddie Murray 11
3. Ken Caminiti 10
   Tony Clark 10
   Mickey Mantle 10
   NICK SWISHER 10

- Hit solo-HR—the first of back-to-back-to-back HR with Robinson Cano and Melky Cabrera—and was 1-for-2 with 2R and 2BB in 5/20 win vs. Baltimore…was his first homer at Yankee Stadium after hitting his first 8HR of the season on the road…according to *Elias*, became the first Yankee to hit each of his first 8HR of a season on the road since Bernie Williams in 2003 (first 9HR on the road)…was the first player to hit his first 8HR *as a Yankee* on the road since Chuck Knoblauch in 1998 (8HR).
- Reached base safely in 30 consecutive games from 7/17-8/22, the longest such streak by a Yankee in 2009 and the second-longest streak of his career (36 games in 2006 w/ Oakland).
- Hit solo-HR in the second and "walk-off" solo-HR in the ninth and was 2-for-3 with 1BB in 9/8 win vs. Tampa Bay…was his second career "walk-off" hit and home run (also 8/5/08 w/ Chicago-AL vs. Detroit)…was his third multi-HR game in 2009 and 14th of his career…became just the fourth Yankee to homer from both sides of the plate in the same game with one of those home runs being a "walk-off" (also Mickey Mantle in 1956, Roy White in 1976 and Melky Cabrera on 4/22/09)…marked the eighth time it happened in Baseball history (also Donnie Scott in 1985, Kevin Bass in 1987 and 1989 and Carlos Guillen in 2006)—credit: *Elias Sports Bureau*.
- Appeared in 14 of the Yankees' 15 postseason games in 2009, batting .128 (6-for-47) with 5R, 2 doubles, 1HR, 2RBI and 7BB…hit his first career postseason homer in Game 3 of the World Series at Philadelphia.

2008

- Hit .219 (109-for-497) with 21 doubles, 24HR and 69RBI in 153 games in his only season with the White Sox (69 starts in CF, 47 at 1B, 16 in LF and 11 in RF)…was his fourth consecutive season with 20-or-more home runs.
- Led all AL switch-hitters in home runs and finished second in RBI to Texas' Milton Bradley…batted .227 (83-for-365) with 18HR as a left-handed batter and .197 (26-for-132) with 6HR from the right side…hit in eight different spots in the lineup.
- Led the AL with 4.51 pitches seen per plate appearance and tied for eighth with 82BB…owned the third-lowest batting average among AL qualifiers, ahead of only Oakland's Daric Barton (.214) and Jack Hannahan (.216)…hit .247 (64-for-259) with 19HR at U.S. Cellular Field, while batting .189 (45-for-238) with 5HR on the road…batted .385 (5-for-13) with 2HR and 19RBI with the bases loaded.
- Made just two errors in 481 chances at 1B (.996 fielding percentage), while making 5E in 202TC as an outfielder (.975).
- Made his fourth career Opening Day roster and start in 3/31 loss at Cleveland, going 2-for-4 with 2R.
- Walked in six consecutive plate appearances from 4/4-5 at Detroit, becoming the first player to walk six straight times since Ivan Rodriguez in 2003 and the first White Sox player to do so since Chet Lemon in 1980.

NICK SWISHER

- Hit his first career leadoff home run off Justin Verlander on 4/6 at Detroit...hit his first career "walk-off" home run on 8/5 vs. Detroit, a 14th-inning, three-run shot off Joel Zumaya...homered in a career-high four straight games from 8/18-21...included was his 100th career home run on 8/20 vs. Seattle.
- Snapped a career-high 0-for-19 stretch with an eighth-inning double on 9/2 at Cleveland.
- Went 1-for-4 (.250) with 1R and 2BB in three ALDS games vs. Tampa Bay.
- Was traded to Chicago-AL from Oakland on 1/3/08 in exchange for RHP Fautino De Los Santos, LHP Giovany Gonzalez and OF Ryan Sweeney.

2007

- Hit .262 (141-for-539) with 36 doubles, 22HR, 78RBI and 100BB in 150 games with Oakland (57 starts in CF, 46 in RF, 39 at 1B, and five at DH)...set career highs in average, doubles, walks and on-base percentage (.381).
- Ranked sixth in the American League in walks, seventh in pitches per plate appearance (4.25) and 10th in strikeouts (131)...also ranked among the AL leaders in sacrifice flies (tied for fourth, nine), intentional walks (tied for fifth, 12) and percent of pitches taken (seventh, 62.8).
- His 22HR ranked second among AL switch-hitters behind Cleveland's Victor Martinez (25) and tied for the third-highest total in Athletics history for a switch-hitter...of his 22 homers, 15 were solo shots and 10 either tied the game or gave the A's the lead...had three multi-HR games, homering from both sides of the plate each time (4/23 at Baltimore, 7/26 at Seattle and 9/9 at Texas).
- Became the third player in Oakland history to start at least 30 games at three different positions, joining Jay Payton (2006) and Jason Giambi (1996)...had a .993 fielding percentage at 1B (3E), .986 in CF (2E) and 1.000 in RF (0E).
- Hit .291 (44-for-151) with 6HR, 22RBI and a .458 on-base percentage vs. left-handed pitchers and .250 (97-for-388) with 16HR, 56RBI and a .348OBP vs. righties.
- Established a career high with 5RBI on 5/21 at Chicago-AL, becoming the eighth player in Oakland history to drive in five runs without a home run.
- Committed his first error of the season on 8/2 vs. Los Angeles-AL in his 98th game...also snapped a career-high 103-game errorless stretch dating back to 9/24/06.
- Scored a run in 10 consecutive games from 9/5-15 (15R overall).
- Served a three-game suspension from 9/18-21 after being ejected on 9/16 vs. Texas for charging the mound when he was hit by a Vicente Padilla pitch in his first at-bat...marked his third straight game of being hit by a pitch (also 9/14 and 9/15 vs. Texas)...also homered in each of those games.

2006

- Batted .254 (141-for-556) with 106R, 35HR, 95RBI and 97BB in 157 games with Oakland (80 starts at 1B, 71 in LF)...led the team in games played, runs scored, walks, extra-base hits (61), total bases (254), intentional walks (seven) and strikeouts...led all AL switch-hitters and ranked eighth in the AL in home runs...became just the 23rd switch-hitter in Major League history to homer at least 30 times in a season...ranked sixth in the AL in walks and eighth in runs scored...tied for fourth in the AL with 152K, the highest total by an A's player since Jose Canseco also had 152 in 1991.
- Hit .291 (41-for-141) with 8HR vs. left-handed pitchers and .241 (100-for-415) with 27HR vs. right-handers...hit .412 (7-for-17) with 2HR and 20RBI with the bases loaded.
- Became the first player in Oakland history to start at least 70 games at two different positions and was the first to do so in the Majors since Cleveland's Carlos Baerga in 1991...started 63-of-88 games in LF before the All-Star break and 59-of-74 at 1B after the break.
- Reached base safely in 36 consecutive games from 4/7-5/19, going 41-for-131 (.313) with 12HR, 33RBI and 35R...hit his first career grand slam on 4/22 vs. Los Angeles-AL off Jeff Weaver.
- Compiled a career-high 11-game hitting streak from 4/30-5/11, batting .341 (14-for-41) with 12R, 6 doubles, 3HR, 10RBI and 8BB during the stretch.
- Started all seven postseason games at 1B for the Athletics (three vs. Minnesota-ALDS and four vs. Detroit-ALCS), batting .200 (4-for-20) with 1RBI and 7BB.

2005

- Hit .236 (109-for-462) with 32 doubles, 21HR and 74RBI in 131 games with Oakland (115 starts in RF, 13 at 1B)...ranked fourth among AL switch hitters in RBI and tied for fourth in home runs...ranked eighth in the AL with an average of 4.13 pitches per plate appearance.
- Finished sixth in the AL "Rookie of the Year" balloting after leading all Major League rookies in walks (55) and extra-base hits (62)...among American League rookies, led in RBI, tied for the lead in home runs, ranked third in doubles and total bases (206), fourth in runs (66) and slugging percentage (.446), fifth in multi-hit games (26) and sixth in hits.
- Batted .203 (25-for-123) with 3HR vs. left-handed pitchers and .248 (84-for-339) with 18HR vs. right-handers.
- Was placed on the 15-day disabled list on 5/2 with a right AC joint sprain after running into the wall on a Jeremy Reed fly ball on 5/1 vs. Seattle...was reinstated from the D.L. on 5/25...missed 19 team games.

NICK SWISHER

- Had a 34-game, 119AB homerless stretch from 4/13-6/16, the longest such streaks of his career.
- Homered from both sides of the plate for the first time in his career on 6/26 vs. San Francisco, becoming the second player in Oakland history—and third in Athletics history—to accomplish the feat.
- Drew a bases-loaded, "walk-off" walk on 9/7 vs. Seattle—the fifth run scored in the inning by the A's—capping the largest ninth-inning comeback in Oakland history.

2004

- Hit .250 (15-for-60) with 11R, 4 doubles, 2HR and 8RBI in 20 games with Oakland (11 starts in LF, three in RF, two at 1B and two at DH).
- Was recalled by the Athletics from Triple-A Sacramento on 9/3, making his Major League debut that day at Toronto and going 1-for-3 with 2R, 1 double and 2BB...walked in his first plate appearance and doubled off Ted Lilly in the fourth inning for his first Major League hit...hit his first career home run on 9/5 at Toronto off Sean Douglass...started 13 of the A's first 14 games after his recall, replacing an injured Jermaine Dye.
- Began the season with Sacramento, batting .269 (119-for-443) with 109R, 29HR, 92RBI and 103BB in 125 games...led all minor leaguers in walks and tied for fourth in runs scored...topped the Pacific Coast League in walks and runs and ranked eighth in on-base percentage (.406)...tied Dan Johnson for the most homers among A's farmhands...reached base safely in 26 straight games from 6/11-7/7...recorded 2HR and 6RBI on 7/24 at Las Vegas...hit 20HR in his last 69 games after homering just nine times in his first 56 contests.

2003

- Split the season between Single-A Modesto and Double-A Midland, combining to hit .256 (122-for-476) with 15HR and 86RBI in 127 games...his 11SF tied for fifth in the minors.
- Began the season at Modesto, batting .296 (56-for-189) with 10HR and 43RBI in 51 games...was named California League "Player of the Week" for the period from 4/28-5/4...reached base safely in 31 consecutive games from 4/17-5/24 and 47 of his 51 games overall...was promoted to Midland on 6/8 where he hit .230 (66-for-287) with 36R, 24 doubles and 43RBI in 76 games.

2002

- Combined to hit .242 (55-for-227) with 6HR and 35RBI in 62 games with Single-A Vancouver and Single-A Visalia...began his career at Vancouver, but was promoted to Visalia after just 13 games.

Personal

- Full name is Nicholas Thomas Swisher...was signed by Rich Sparks (Athletics)...was selected by the Athletics with Boston's first-round pick in 2002 as compensation for the loss of free agent Johnny Damon.
- Established the Nick Swisher Foundation "Swish's Wishes" in 2007 to assist children with life-threatening illnesses and to help lift the spirits of kids going through difficult times...in 2009, provided Christmas dinner for the families of children battling cancer at the Ronald McDonald House in New York and was the co-Ambassador to the Entertainment Industry Foundation's Lee Denim Day to help raise money for breast cancer research...continued his practice of hosting "Swish's Wishes Days" at Yankee Stadium, inviting children to his home ballpark throughout the year as he did in Oakland and Chicago...made a $10,000 donation to the United Way Alliance of the Mid-Ohio Valley in November 2009...also purchased uniforms for the football team at his junior high school.
- Is a regular visitor at children's hospitals...supports Lynn Sage Cancer Center in Chicago...in the past, has dyed his goatee pink on Mother's Day to raise awareness for breast cancer and blue on Father's Day to raise awareness for prostate cancer...provides holiday gifts and a party for mentally challenged children at Janet Pomeroy School in San Francisco...supports UCSF Medical Center in San Francisco, where he served as the honorary chairman for the 2007 Macy's Tree Lighting Ceremony...has also funded programs at the Children's Hospital & Research Center in Oakland and frequently reads books to children in the hospital...teamed with Columbia Pictures in 2007 to host a private screening of the movie "Water Horse: Legend of the Deep" for 400 sick and low-income Bay Area children.
- Participates in Strikeouts For Troops, a non-profit organization that provides assistance to wounded war veterans and their children by providing "comforts of home" while they recover in military hospitals nationwide...toured U.S. bases in Spain, Greece and Italy on a goodwill mission to visit American soldiers and their families stationed abroad in January 2007...helped fund two programs for low-income children in need at Tony La Russa's Animal Rescue Foundation...participated in adopting 25 military families in need and provided Thanksgiving and Christmas dinner as well as Christmas gifts for the children in 2007, 2008 and 2009.
- Threw out the first pitch to eight-year-old Adam Bender on 7/1/08 vs. Cleveland...Bender lost his leg to cancer at the age of 1 and was flown from Kentucky to Chicago with his parents, older brother and younger sister by Swisher's foundation to celebrate the one-year anniversary of "Swish's Wishes"...Bender played catcher for his Little League team in Lexington, Ky...Swisher provided Bender with a personalized White Sox jersey and a bat autographed by the team.

NICK SWISHER

- In honor of his grandmother, Betty, who lost her battle with cancer in 2005, Nick joined as an ambassador to the EIF Foundation and the Women's Cancer Research Fund...went without a haircut for nearly one year in 2007 as part of the non-profit Pantene Beautiful Lengths program that encourages people to grow, cut and donate their hair to create live hair wigs for women who have lost their hair due to cancer treatments...his father, Steve, made the "kindest cut of all" on the field in Oakland on 5/19/07, cutting Nick's hair to be donated to the program...also supports childhood diabetes, prostate and breast cancer, and the Special Olympics...was the Athletics' 2007 Roberto Clemente Award nominee.
- Appeared as himself in an episode of the television show *How I Met Your Mother* in February 2010...also appeared as himself in the television show *The Game* in 2007 and 2008.
- Attended Ohio State University where he was named Big Ten "Freshman of the Year" in 2000 after hitting .299 with 10HR and 48RBI...was All-Big Ten at first base as a sophomore in 2001 after hitting .322 with a league-best 15HR and 56RBI...also earned All-Conference honors as an outfielder in 2002 when he batted .348 with 10HR and 52RBI...graduated from Parkersburg (W. Va.) High School.
- Is the son of Steve Swisher, who batted .216 (305-for-1,414) in 509 Major League games with Chicago-NL (1974-77), St. Louis (1978-80) and San Diego (1981-82)...Steve was selected by the White Sox in the first round (21st overall) of the 1973 draft.

Swisher's Career Playing Record

Year	Club	AVG	G	AB	R	H	2B	3B	HR	RBI	SH	SF	HP	BB	SO	SB	CS	E	OBP	SLG
2002	Vancouver	.250	13	44	10	11	3	0	2	12	0	1	2	13	11	3	0	0	.433	.455
	Visalia	.240	49	183	22	44	13	2	4	23	2	1	2	26	48	3	1	4	.340	.399
2003	Modesto	.296	51	189	38	56	14	2	10	43	0	5	2	41	49	0	2	4	.418	.550
	Midland	.230	76	287	36	66	24	2	5	43	0	6	6	37	76	0	1	5	.324	.380
2004	Sacramento	.269	125	443	109	119	28	2	29	92	0	5	3	103	109	3	3	7	.406	.537
	OAKLAND	.250	20	60	11	15	4	0	2	8	0	1	2	8	11	0	0	3	.352	.417
2005	OAKLAND - a	.236	131	462	66	109	32	1	21	74	0	1	4	55	110	0	1	2	.322	.446
	Sacramento	.391	6	23	4	9	3	0	0	1	0	0	1	2	7	0	1	0	.462	.522
2006	OAKLAND	.254	157	556	106	141	24	2	35	95	2	6	11	97	152	1	2	8	.372	.492
2007	OAKLAND	.262	150	539	84	141	36	1	22	78	1	9	10	100	131	3	2	5	.381	.455
2008	CHICAGO (AL) – b	.219	153	497	86	109	21	1	24	69	1	4	4	82	135	3	3	7	.332	.410
2009	YANKEES - c	.249	150	498	84	124	35	1	29	82	3	6	3	97	126	0	0	6	.371	.498
Minor League Totals		**.261**	**320**	**1169**	**219**	**305**	**85**	**8**	**50**	**214**	**2**	**18**	**16**	**222**	**300**	**9**	**8**	**20**	**.381**	**.476**
Major League Totals		**.245**	**761**	**2612**	**437**	**639**	**152**	**6**	**133**	**406**	**7**	**27**	**34**	**439**	**665**	**7**	**8**	**31**	**.357**	**.460**

Selected by Oakland in the first round (16th overall) of the 2002 First-Year Player Draft.

a – Placed on the 15-day disabled list from May 2-25,2005 with a right shoulder sprain.

b – Acquired by Chicago-AL on January 3, 2008 in exchange for RHP Fautino De Los Santos, LHP Giovany Gonzalez and OF Ryan Sweeney.

c – Acquired by the Yankees along with RHP Kanekoa Texeira on November 13, 2008 in exchange for INF Wilson Betemit and RHPs Jeff Marquez and Jhonny Nunez.

Swisher's Division Series Record

Year	Club vs. Opp.	AVG	G	AB	R	H	2B	3B	HR	RBI	SH	SF	HP	BB	SO	SB	CS	E	OBP	SLG
2006	OAK vs. MIN	.300	3	10	3	3	2	0	0	1	0	0	0	2	2	0	0	0	.417	.500
2008	CWS vs. TB	.250	3	4	1	1	0	0	0	0	0	0	0	2	1	0	0	0	.500	.250
2009	NYY vs. MIN	.083	3	12	0	1	1	0	0	1	0	0	0	0	4	0	0	0	.083	.167
Division Series Totals		**.192**	**9**	**26**	**4**	**5**	**3**	**0**	**0**	**2**	**0**	**0**	**0**	**4**	**7**	**0**	**0**	**0**	**.300**	**.308**

Swisher's Championship Series Record

Year	Club vs. Opp.	AVG	G	AB	R	H	2B	3B	HR	RBI	SH	SF	HP	BB	SO	SB	CS	E	OBP	SLG
2006	OAK vs. DET	.100	4	10	0	1	0	0	0	0	0	0	0	5	5	0	0	0	.400	.100
2009	NYY vs. LAA	.150	6	20	2	3	0	0	0	0	1	0	1	3	7	0	0	0	.292	.150
LCS Totals		**.133**	**10**	**30**	**2**	**4**	**0**	**0**	**0**	**0**	**1**	**0**	**1**	**8**	**12**	**0**	**0**	**0**	**.333**	**.133**

Swisher's World Series Record

Year	Club vs. Opp.	AVG	G	AB	R	H	2B	3B	HR	RBI	SH	SF	HP	BB	SO	SB	CS	E	OBP	SLG
2009	NYY vs. PHI	.133	5	15	3	2	1	0	1	1	0	0	0	4	4	0	0	0	.316	.400
World Series Totals		**.133**	**5**	**15**	**3**	**2**	**1**	**0**	**1**	**1**	**0**	**0**	**0**	**4**	**4**	**0**	**0**	**0**	**.316**	**.400**
POSTSEASON TOTALS		**.155**	**24**	**71**	**9**	**11**	**4**	**0**	**1**	**3**	**1**	**0**	**1**	**16**	**23**	**0**	**0**	**0**	**.318**	**.254**

Swisher's Career Fielding Record

Position	PCT	G	PO	A	E	TC
Outfield	.982	553	1083	19	20	1122
First Base	.994	249	1721	114	11	1846

Swisher's Career Home Run Chart

MULTI-HOMER GAMES: 14. **TWO-HOMER GAMES:** 14, last on 9/8/09 vs. Tampa Bay. **GRAND SLAMS:** 4, last on 6/30/08 vs. Cleveland (Jeremy Sowers). **PINCH-HIT HR:** None. **INSIDE-THE-PARK HR:** 1, on 6/11/06 at New York-AL (Shawn Chacon). **WALK-OFF HR:** 2, last on 9/8/09 vs. Tampa Bay (Dan Wheeler). **LEADOFF HR:** 1, on 4/6/08 at Detroit (Justin Verlander).

Mark Teixeira

25

First Baseman

6-3 • 220 • B/T: Switch/Right

Opening Day Age: 29

Birthdate
April 11, 1980

Birthplace
Annapolis, Md.

Resides
Greenwich, Conn.

M.L. Service
7 years

College
Georgia Tech

Career Highlights

A.L. All-Star Team
- 2005, 2009

A.L. Gold Glove
- 2005, 2006, 2009

A.L. Silver Slugger
- 2004, 2005, 2009

Status

- Signed as a free agent to an eight-year contract on January 6, 2009…contract extends through the 2016 season.

Career Notes

- Is one of only three Major Leaguers to reach 30HR and 100RBI in each of the last six seasons (2004-09), joining Albert Pujols and teammate Alex Rodriguez…according to *Elias*, is one of three 1B all time to surpass 30HR and 100RBI in six straight years by age 29 (also Jimmie Foxx and Pujols).
- Has reached the 25HR plateau in each of his first seven Major League seasons…according to *Elias*, is just the fifth player in Baseball history to accomplish the feat, joining Eddie Mathews (11 seasons), Albert Pujols (nine), Darryl Strawberry (nine) and Frank Robinson (seven).
- Has hit 242 career home runs, marking the most ever by a switch-hitter in his first seven seasons…among active players, only Albert Pujols (282) hit more home runs in his first seven Major League seasons.
- Since returning to the AL on 7/29/08, leads the league in RBI (165) and ranks third in home runs (52).
- Ranks second among all active first basemen with a .99625 career fielding percentage at 1B, fractionally behind Doug Mientkiewicz (.99626).
- Played in his 1,000th career Major League game in 7/28/09 loss at Tampa Bay, going 1-for-4 with 1R and 1 double…the double was the 250th of his career—and with 228HR—became only the second active player to accumulate at least 250 doubles and 225HR through his first 1,000 games (also Albert Pujols – 273 doubles, 266 HR)—credit: *Elias Sports Bureau.*

Single-Game Bests and Streaks

Hits
4 - 17 times
Last: at SEA, 9/19/09

Runs
4 - 2 times
Last: at CIN, 8/20/07

2B
3 - at NYY, 5/10/07

3B
1 - 16 times
Last at SEA, 9/19/09

HR
3 - 2 times
Last: vs. SEA, 6/22/08

RBI
7 - 2 times
Last: at BAL, 7/13/06

BB
5 - 2 times
Last: at BOS, 4/25/09

SO
5 - at DET, 8/18/03

SB
1 - 15 times
Last: at CWS, 8/2/09

Hit Streak
14g - 5/18-6/1/09

2009

- Batted .292 (178-for-609) with 103R, 43 doubles, 39HR and 122RBI in 156 games (150 starts at 1B, five at DH) in his first season with the Yankees…hit .282 (122-for- 432) with 30HR as a left-handed batter and .316 (56-for-177) with 9HR as a right-handed batter…earned his third Gold Glove Award and third Silver Slugger Award.
- From 5/8 (when Alex Rodriguez returned to the lineup) through the end of the season, batted .310 (159-for-513) with 89R, 39 doubles, 34HR, 107RBI and 62BB in 131G (the Yankees were 88-43 in those games)…led the AL in home runs and RBI over the span…prior to Rodriguez's return, Teixeira hit .198 (19-for-96) with 14R, 4 doubles, 5HR, 15RBI and 19BB in 25G.
- Led the American League in RBI and tied Tampa Bay's Carlos Pena for the lead in home runs…led the Majors in home runs (24) and RBI (71) at home…led the AL in go-ahead RBI (31) and ranked second in go-ahead home runs (13).
- With 103R, 43 doubles and 39HR, was one of only two players in the Majors to collect at least 100R, 40 doubles and 35HR, joining St. Louis' Albert Pujols (124R, 45 doubles, 47HR).
- Became just the second player ever to lead or tie for the AL lead in home runs in his first season with the Yankees, joining Babe Ruth in 1920 (54HR)-credit: *Elias Sports Bureau*…*Elias* also noted Teixeira was one of three Yankees to lead the AL in RBI in

their first season with the club, joining Ruth (136RBI) and Roger Maris (112 in 1960)...became one of just three players to reach 39HR and 122RBI in their first season with the Yankees, joining Babe Ruth in 1920 (54HR, 136RBI) and Jason Giambi in 2002 (41HR, 122RBI)—credit: *Elias*.

- According to the *Elias Sports Bureau*, became the eighth player to hit at least 30HR in his first season with the Yankees (did so in his 112th game of the season), joining Babe Ruth (1920), Roger Maris (1960), Bobby Bonds (1975), Reggie Jackson (1977), Jason Giambi (2002), Alex Rodriguez (2004) and Gary Sheffield (2004)...only two of those players hit their 30th homer fewer games into the season than Teixeira (Maris in 82 games and Ruth in 88 games).
- Became the fifth Yankee to reach 100R, 40 doubles, 35HR and 100RBI in a season (also Babe Ruth-1921 and '23; Lou Gehrig-1927, '30 and '34; Don Mattingly-1985 and Alfonso Soriano-2002)...is the only player to do so in his first season with the club.
- With teammate Nick Swisher, became the third set of Yankees teammates over the last 50 years to each hit at least 25HR in their first full season in pinstripes (also Alex Rodriguez/Gary Sheffield in 2004 and Jason Giambi/Robin Ventura in 2002)—credit: *Elias*.
- Homered from both sides of the plate three times in 2009 (5/4 vs. Boston, 5/18 vs. Minnesota and 9/19 at Seattle)...became the 11th Yankee all time to accomplish the feat and one of three in 2009 (also Melky Cabrera and Nick Swisher)...is one of five Yankees to homer from both sides of the plate in multiple games during a single season, joining Mickey Mantle (1955 and '56), Bernie Williams (2000), Jorge Posada (2007) and Swisher (2009)...along with Swisher (2007 and 2009), tied Tony Clark (1998 w/ Detroit) for the most switch-hit homers in a single season.
- His 43 doubles were the most by a Yankees first baseman in a season since Don Mattingly had 53 in 1986...85 of his 178 hits (47.8%) went for extra bases (43 doubles, 3 triples and 39HR)...batted .355 (22-for-62) with 31RBI with RISP and two outs.

MOST GO-AHEAD RBI IN AL IN 2009

1.	**MARK TEIXEIRA, NYY**	**31**
2.	ALEX RODRIGUEZ, NYY	29
	Jose Lopez, SEA	29
4.	Adam Lind, TOR	27
5.	Nick Markakis, BAL	26

MOST HR, FIRST YEAR W/ NYY

	Player	HR
1.	Babe Ruth	54 (1920)
2.	Jason Giambi	41 (2002)
3.	Roger Maris	39 (1960)
	MARK TEIXEIRA	**39 (2009)**

MOST GAMES WITH A SWITCH-HIT HR, ACTIVE PLAYERS

1.	NICK SWISHER	10
2.	JORGE POSADA	8
	MARK TEIXEIRA	**8**
4.	Carlos Beltran	6
	Chipper Jones	6

Credit: SABR's David Vincent

- Was voted as the AL's starting first baseman in the 2009 All-Star Game...went 0-for-3 in the AL's 4-3 win in St. Louis on 7/14, playing five innings at 1B...was named the starting AL All-Star at 1B for the second time in his career (also 2005)...was the first Yankee 1B to start an All-Star Game since Jason Giambi in 2004...became the sixth Yankee to start an All-Star game in his first year with the club after signing as a free agent and first since Hideki Matsui in 2003 (credit: *Elias*).
- Batted .200 (14-for-70) with 3HR and 10RBI in April...hit at a .304 (164-for-539) clip over the remainder of the season...was 0-for-4 with 1BB in 4/6 Opening Day loss at Baltimore, making his seventh career Opening Day roster and sixth Opening Day start at 1B...missed three games (4/11-13) with left wrist tendinitis.
- Collected the 1,000th hit of his career with a third-inning infield single in 4/24 loss at Boston.
- Tied a career high with 5BB in 4/25 loss at Boston...also walked five times on 9/23/04 w/ Texas vs. Oakland...is the only current Major Leaguer to walk five times in two games (credit: *Elias*)...*Elias* also noted he became the first player to draw 5BB in two nine-inning contests since Mel Ott who had three (1929, 1943 and 1944)...were the most walks drawn by a Yankee since Roger Maris drew 5BB in a 12-inning game against the Angels on 5/22/62...were the most walks by a Yankee in a nine-inning game since Russ Derry drew 5BB in Game 1 of a doubleheader on 9/6/45 vs. Detroit...according to Yankees records, the 5BB tied a club mark for a nine-inning game, now done eight times.
- Hit 13HR in May, tying a career-high for his most HRs in any calendar month (also July 2004))...were the most by a Yankee since Alex Rodriguez hit 14HR in April 2007...led the Majors in HR and RBI (34) during May and, according to *Elias*, matched the most RBI for a Yankees player in a calendar month over the past 20 years: Tino Martinez (April 1997), Bernie Williams (August 1999) and Alex Rodriguez (April 2007 and June 2007).
- Both he and Alex Rodriguez each hit 4HR over a four-game span from 5/16-19, becoming the first pair of Yankees teammates since 1977 (Reggie Jackson and Bucky Dent) to accomplish the feat (credit: *Elias*).
- Hit safely in a career-high 14 straight games from 5/18-6/1...during the stretch, hit .397 (23-for-58) with 14R, 5 doubles, 8HR and 20RBI...was scratched from the lineup with a bruised right ankle prior to 6/3 loss vs. Texas.
- Had 47RBI through his first 50 games with the Yankees, matching Harry Rice, Joe Gordon and Roger Maris for the third-most for any player in franchise history over his first 50 games with the team since 1920 when RBI became an official statistic...only Babe Ruth (57) and Joe DiMaggio (56) had more through their first 50 games (credit: *Elias*).
- Made ninth-inning throwing error in 7/2 loss vs. Seattle, snapping a 72-game stretch at 1B to start the season without committing an error...had been the longest errorless streak in one season for a Yankees first baseman since Tino Martinez went 82 straight games without an error in 1996 (credit: *Elias*)...also snapped a 106-game errorless stretch at 1B overall, dating back to 8/20/08.

- Snapped a career-long 95AB homerless stretch with solo-HR in 7/9 win at Minnesota.
- Hit game-winning solo-HR in the eighth—the second of back-to-back homers with Johnny Damon—and was 2-for-4 on 8/9 vs. Boston...was the sixth time he and Damon hit back-to-back HR, setting a franchise record for consecutive homers by Yankees teammates and breaking a tie with Gary Sheffield/Alex Rodriguez (5, 2005), Lou Gehrig/Joe DiMaggio (5, 1936) and Gehrig/Babe Ruth (5, 1927)—credit: *Elias*.
- Drove in his 100th run of the season with a three-run home run in 8/30 win vs. Chicago-AL in his 126th game of the season...according to *Elias*, only four players reached the 100RBI milestone fewer games into their Yankees career than Teixeira: Babe Ruth in 1920 (97 games), Joe DiMaggio in 1936 (102), Roger Maris in 1960 (118) and Tony Lazzeri in 1926 (125).
- Hit three-run HR and solo-HR and tied a career-high with four hits in 9/19 win at Seattle, finishing a double shy of the cycle...was 4-for-5 with 1 triple and a season-high 5RBI before being removed defensively in the ninth...according to *Baseball Reference*, became the first Yankee to record 2HR and 1 triple in a game since Elston Howard in 1962...was his fourth multi-HR game of the season (also 5/4 vs. Boston, 5/18 vs. Minnesota and 9/7 vs. Tampa Bay-Game 2) and the 25th of his career (23rd two-HR game).
- Collected three triples over a 15AB span from 9/14-19, after having no triples in his previous 1,289 regular season at-bats and just three triples over his previous three seasons (2006-08).
- Batted .180 (11-for-61) with 2 doubles, 2HR and 8RBI in the 2009 postseason...hit "walk-off" solo home run off Jose Mijares in 11th inning in Game 2 of ALDS vs. Minnesota, marking his first career postseason home run and first career "walk-off" HR (regular and postseason)...was the Yankees' second "walk-off" homer in ALDS play (also Jim Leyritz in 1995 vs. Seattle)...scored a run in five of the six World Series games...was hit by a pitch three times in the WS, joining Alex Rodriguez (also 2009) and Pittsburgh's Max Carey (1925) as the only players to get plunked three times in a single Series.

TOP OFFENSIVE MONTHS BY A YANKEE SINCE 1954 (min. .330 Avg. / 13HR / 34RBI)

Player	Month	Avg. / HR / RBI
Mickey Mantle	May 1956	.414 / 16 / 35
Roger Maris	June 1960	.331 / 14 / 34
ALEX RODRIGUEZ	April 2007	.355 / 14 / 34
MARK TEIXEIRA	**May 2009**	**.330 / 13 / 34**

MOST BACK-TO-BACK HOME RUNS IN A SINGLE SEASON BY THE SAME YANKEES TANDEM (Credit: *Elias*)

	Tandem	Total (Year)
1.	**Johnny Damon/MARK TEIXEIRA**	**6 (2009)**
2.	Gary Sheffield/ALEX RODRIGUEZ	5 (2005)
	Lou Gehrig/Joe DiMaggio	5 (1936)
	Lou Gehrig/Babe Ruth	5 (1927)

2008

- In 157 combined games with Atlanta and Los Angeles-AL, batted .308 (177-for-574) with 41 doubles, 33HR and 121RBI...ranked sixth in the Majors in RBI.
- Hit 20 home runs for the Braves and 13 with the Angels in 2008, a year after hitting 13 homers for the Rangers and 17 for the Braves...according to *Elias*, he became the first player in history to hit at least 30 home runs in each of back-to-back seasons while playing for more than one team in both years.
- Batted .366 (83-for-227) with 18 doubles, 16HR and 52RBI in 64 games after the All-Star break, ranking third in the Majors in batting average behind Manny Ramirez (.388) and Albert Pujols (.368)...hit .271 (94-for-347) with 23 doubles, 17HR and 69RBI in 93 games prior to the break.
- Opened the season with Atlanta, hitting .283 (108-for-381) with 27 doubles, 20HR and 78RBI in 103 games prior to being dealt...at the time of the trade, ranked fifth in the NL in walks (65) and tied for 10th in doubles (27).
- Compiled 134RBI in 157 games with the Braves over 2007-08...according to the *Elias Sports Bureau*, only one Major League player had as many RBI in so few career games for one team – Juan Gonzalez, who had 140RBI for the Indians in 141 games (140 games in 2001 and one game in 2005).
- Recorded his second career three-homer game in 6/22 win vs. Seattle, homering from each side of the plate for the fifth time in his career...became the first Brave with a three-homer game at Turner Field.
- Was acquired by the Angels on 7/29 in exchange for 1B Casey Kotchman and RHP Steve Marek...hit .358 (122-for-393) with 14 doubles, 13HR and 43RBI in 54 games with Los Angeles-AL, reaching base safely in 49 of those contests...recorded the highest average, on-base percentage (.449) and slugging percentage (.632) in the AL following the trade, the sixth-most RBI, tied for the sixth-most home runs and tied for the ninth-most hits and extra-base hits.
- Collected 66H in his first 50 games with Angels, tallying the fourth-most base hits by an Angel in their first 50 contests with the club behind Johnny Ray (79), Alex Johnson (71) and Vladimir Guerrero (70).
- Hit .386 (39-for-101) in August, ranking fifth in the AL and marking his highest average for any month in his career...hit his first homer as an Angel in 8/3 loss at Yankee Stadium, an eighth-inning grand slam...was just the third player in club history whose first homer as an Angel was a slam.
- Connected for his 200th career home run on 9/14 vs. Seattle off Felix Hernandez.
- Saw his first career postseason action, batting .467 (7-for-15) with 4R, 1RBI and 4BB in four Division Series games against Boston.

MARK TEIXEIRA

2007

- Combined with Texas and Atlanta to hit .306 (151-for-494) with 86R, 33 doubles, 30HR and 105RBI in 132 games...was acquired by the Braves at the 7/31 trade deadline in a seven-player deal.
- Was one of just eight players to record a .300 average with 30HR and 100RBI in 2007, doing so in the fewest at-bats (494) and games (132)...Boston's David Ortiz needed the second-fewest at-bats (549) and games (149) to reach the plateaus.
- Batted .357 (55-for-154) with 6HR off left-handed pitching, and .282 (96-for-340) with 24HR against right-handers...his .405 (53-for-131) average with runners in scoring position ranked third in the Majors (min. 100AB)...was a .382 (50-for-131) hitter during the day and .278 (101-for-363) hitter at night.
- Opened the year with Texas and batted .297 with 24 doubles, 13HR and 49RBI in 78 games with the Rangers prior to the trade.
- Tied for second in the AL in May with 27RBI and 19 extra-base hits while hitting .348 with 7HR for the month...his 38 hits were a career high for any month.
- Was on the 15-day disabled list from 6/9-7/13 with a strained left quadriceps (missed 27 games)...snapped his consecutive games played streak at 507 games.
- Batted .317 with 17HR and 56RBI in 54 games with Atlanta, hitting safely in 33 of his last 38 games and in 43 of 54 games overall with the Braves...also drove in a run in 32 of his 54 Braves games...had 21 multi-hit games and 14 multi-RBI games, including three contests with four-or-more RBI.
- Homered in each of his first three games with Atlanta from 8/1-4, becoming the first Brave to accomplish the feat since Gary Sheffield from 4/1-4/02...went 1-for-4 with a three-run homer and 4RBI in his Atlanta debut on 8/1 vs. Houston...walked with the bases loaded in the first inning for his 500th career RBI.
- Earned the NL "Player of the Month" award in August, hitting .315 (35-for-111) with 32RBI and 10HR...marked the most RBI in the Majors in August and tied for the most homers...named NL "co-Player of the Week" (with Jason Isringhausen) for 8/20-26, hitting .414 (12-for-29) with 8R, 3HR and 11RBI over the stretch.
- Homered twice in back-to-back games on 8/19 (vs. Arizona) and 8/20 (at Cincinnati) to become the fourth player in Atlanta history with consecutive multi-homer games and first since Chipper Jones in July 2003.
- Drove in the "walk-off" run in the 11th inning on 9/22 vs. Milwaukee with an RBI single...homered in three straight games from 9/25-27.

MOST HOME RUNS AMONG ACTIVE PLAYERS IN FIRST SEVEN MLB SEASONS

1.	Albert Pujols	282 (2001-07)
2.	**MARK TEIXEIRA**	**242 (2003-09)**
3.	Adam Dunn	238 (2001-07)
4.	Ryan Howard	222 (2004-09)
5.	Todd Helton	219 (1997-2003)

LAST FIVE YEARS (2005-09)

MOST HOME RUNS

1.	Ryan Howard	220
2.	Albert Pujols	206
3.	ALEX RODRIGUEZ	202
4.	Adam Dunn	198
5.	David Ortiz	187
6.	**MARK TEIXEIRA**	**178**

MOST RBI

1.	Ryan Howard	635
2.	ALEX RODRIGUEZ	610
3.	Albert Pujols	608
4.	**MARK TEIXEIRA**	**602**
5.	David Ortiz	590

MOST EXTRA-BASE HITS

1.	Albert Pujols	409
2.	**MARK TEIXEIRA**	**390**
3.	David Ortiz	379
4.	Miguel Cabrera	373
5.	Chase Utley	365

2006

- Played in all 162 games for Texas, batting .282 (177-for-628) with 45 doubles, 33HR and 110RBI...won his second straight AL Gold Glove at first base, becoming the first Rangers first baseman to win the award twice.
- Became the first Ranger since Pete Incaviglia (1986-90) to record 20-or-more homers in each of his first four Major League seasons and the fourth player in club history to record three consecutive seasons of at least 30 home runs.
- Led the AL in game-winning RBI (19), ranked third in extra-base hits (79), fifth in doubles, sixth in at-bats (628), seventh in total bases (323), eighth in intentional walks (12) and ninth in walks (89).
- Collected his third consecutive 100-RBI season, becoming the fourth player in Texas history to accomplish the feat...also became the fourth Ranger to notch 30HR and 100RBI in consecutive seasons...was second on the club with 26 go-ahead RBI as well as 40 two-out RBI.
- Ranked by *Baseball America* as the best defensive first baseman in a survey of AL managers...posted a .997 fielding percentage (4E, 1572 TC), ranking second among all Major League first baseman behind Tampa Bay's Travis Lee (.998) for the second consecutive season.
- Hit .302 (51-for-169) off lefties and .275 (126-for-459) against right-handed pitching...totaled 21HR from the left side of the plate and 12HR from the right.
- Batted .275 (97-for-353) with 9HR and 49RBI prior to the All-Star break...following the break, hit .291 (80-for-275) with 24HR and 61RBI in the second half, ranking first in the Majors in homers, tied for second in RBI, placed fourth in walks (42) and slugging percentage (.604) and eighth in runs scored (51).
- Named Rangers' July "Player of the Month," batting .316 (15-for-37) with seven home runs and 18RBI.

- Tied a club record with a career-high 3HR on 7/13 at Baltimore in the first game after the All-Star break, and also tied career high with 7RBI...was the third time he homered from both sides in the same game...according to the *Elias Sports Bureau*, he became the first player to hit three-or-more home runs in his team's first game after the All-Star break.
- Reached base safely in 36 consecutive games from 7/3-8/13 (.352, 44-for-125, 27R, 10HR, 26RBI, 22BB), matching the second-longest streak in the Majors in 2006 behind Orlando Cabrera's 63-game run.
- Participated in the inaugural World Baseball Classic for the United States, going hitless in four games.

2005

- Hit .301 with 41 doubles, 43HR and 144RBI in 162 games with Texas...set club records for home runs and RBI as a first baseman...established a Major League record for RBI by a switch hitter in a single season, surpassing the previous mark of 136 by the New York Giants' George Davis in 1896...finished seventh in AL Most Valuable Player voting.
- Led the AL in total bases (370), ranked second in extra-base hits (87), tied for second in RBI (144), placed fourth in home runs (43) and multi-hit games (59), fifth in slugging percentage (.575), tied for sixth in hits (194) and at-bats (644), ranked seventh in doubles (41), tied for seventh in runs (112) and finished 10th in on-base percentage (.379)...batted .366 (59-for-161) with runners in scoring position, placing second in the AL...hit .334 (104-for-311) with 30HR and 88RBI in 81 games at home, recording the fourth-best home average in the AL.
- Batted .292 (50-171) with 6HR and 29 RBI against left-handers and .304 (144-for-473) with 37HR and 115RBI against right-handers...hit his first 27 home runs from the left side of the plate, the most ever by a switch-hitter from one side of the plate to begin a season.
- Of his 43HR, 40 came as a first baseman...was the fourth-highest HR total in Major League history by a switch-hitter...became the fourth player in Texas history to record a 40-homer season, joining Juan Gonzalez, Rafael Palmeiro and Alex Rodriguez...became the 30th player all time with 20-or-more home runs in each of his first full Major League campaigns...averaged one home run every 15.0 at-bats, the eighth-best ratio in the AL.
- Registered 133RBI as a first baseman, leading all Major Leaguers and breaking his own club record of 112RBI as a first baseman, set in 2004...became just the fifth player in Texas history to record consecutive 100-RBI seasons...had the AL's third-best RBI ratio, averaging one every 4.5 at-bats.
- Earned his first career All-Star nod, receiving 2,187,115 fan votes and becoming the first Texas first baseman elected to start an All-Star game...started at 1B in the AL win on 7/12 at Detroit, going 1-for-3 with a sixth inning HR off Florida's Dontrelle Willis...the homer came from the right side, his first right-handed homer in any game (including spring training) in 2005...participated in the Home Run Derby on 7/11 and homered twice.

CAREER AVERAGE BY SPOTS 3-5 IN THE ORDER

No. 3 ... .305 (604-for-1980), 508G, 148 doubles, 121HR, 414RBI
No. 4 ..... .279 (351-for-1260), 340G, 69 doubles, 77HR, 248RBI
No. 5 .... .263 (121-for-460), 121G, 29 doubles, 26HR, 81RBI

SWITCH-HITTING RECORD

Year		AVG	AB	H	HR	RBI
2003	Left	.244	353	86	15	52
	Right	.290	176	51	11	32
2004	Left	.266	376	100	27	77
	Right	.314	169	53	11	35
2005	Left	.304	470	143	37	115
	Right	.293	174	51	6	29
2006	Left	.276	457	126	21	78
	Right	.298	171	51	12	32
2007	Left	.284	335	95	24	69
	Right	.352	159	56	6	36
2008	Left	.311	379	118	26	80
	Right	.303	195	59	7	41
2009	Left	.282	432	122	30	91
	Right	.316	177	56	9	31
Totals	**Left**	**.282**	**2802**	**790**	**180**	**562**
	Right	**.309**	**1221**	**377**	**62**	**236**

- Received his first career Rawlings Gold Glove Award, joining Rafael Palmeiro (1999) as the only Texas first basemen to claim the honor...made 154 starts at first base and led all qualifying AL first basemen with a .998 fielding percentage (3E, 1483TC), trailing only Cincinnati's Sean Casey among all Major League first basemen...was the eighth-best fielding percentage by a first baseman since 1986...led AL first basemen in total chances (1,483), putouts (1,378) and innings played at the position (1,358.0), and ranked second in assists (102).
- Earned an AL Silver Slugger Award for the second consecutive year.
- Named AL "Player of the Week" for the periods of 5/16-22 and 8/29-9/4.
- Hit his 100th career home run on 9/6 at Minnesota, joining Ralph Kiner, Albert Pujols, Eddie Mathews and Joe DiMaggio as the fifth player in Major League history to reach 100HR in their first three seasons...hit his 100th homer in his 430th career game, becoming one of four then-active Major Leaguers to reach 100 career home runs in 430-or-fewer games (also Albert Pujols-415 games, Mike Piazza-422 and Juan Gonzalez-423).
- Batted .356 (37-for-104) with 9HR and a Major League-best 35RBI in 27 games in September...marked the highest September RBI total for a Major Leaguer since Don Mattingly had 37RBI in September 1985...matched Carlton Fisk (1977) for the second-highest September RBI total since Divisional play began in 1969.

MARK TEIXEIRA

2004

- In his sophomore campaign, batted .281 (153-for-545) with 101R, 34 doubles, 38HR and 112RBI in 145 games with the Rangers...ranked fifth in the American League in home runs and extra base hits (74), tied for fifth in intentional walks (12), placed sixth in slugging percentage (.560), seventh in RBI and was the eighth hardest to double up, averaging 90.8 at-bats per GIDP...led the team in each of those categories as well as on-base percentage (.370)...received his first AL Silver Slugger Award.
- Had a .313 (51-for-163) batting average with 11HR from the right side and hit .267 (102-for-382) with 27HR from the left side...hit .314 (43-for-137) with runners in scoring position.
- Recorded the highest home run total in Major League history by a switch-hitter 24 years old or younger, surpassing Mickey Mantle's 37HR in 1955 at age 23...led the AL with 33HR after 6/1...became the 12th player in club history to record a 30-homer season, joining Ruben Sierra (1987) and Mickey Tettleton (1995) as the only switch-hitters to do so...averaged a home run every 14.3 at-bats, the fifth-best ratio in the AL.
- All 112 of his RBI came as a first baseman, surpassing the club record set by Rafael Palmeiro (105) in 1993.
- Made 138 starts at 1B, four in RF and two as DH...led AL first basemen in assists (98) and ranked second in total chances...had just one error in his final 35 games (311 chances) in the field.
- Was placed on the 15-day disabled list from 4/13-28 with a strained left oblique muscle...played one rehab game with Frisco on 4/27 at El Paso, going 0-for-3.
- Named AL "Player of the Month" and Rangers "Player of the Month" for July, batting .300 (30-for-100) with 27R, 13HR and 30RBI and becoming the first Texas player other than Alex Rodriguez to win the monthly award since 1999...tied for the Major League lead in homers, RBI and runs scored for the month...was the fourth-highest home run total in club history for a single month...homered 12 times in a span of 18 games from 6/28-7/19, including home runs in five consecutive games from 7/11-19 (5HR) to match a club record...also matched the second-longest home run streak ever by a switch-hitter.
- Homered from both sides of the plate for the first time in his career in 7/4 win at Houston, including a grand slam...named AL "Player of the Week" for the period ending 7/4...also connected for a grand slam in 7/18 win at Toronto.
- Recorded his first career four-hit game in 8/17 win vs. Cleveland, hitting for the cycle (third-inning double, fourth-inning homer, fifth-inning triple, seventh-inning single)...became the second player in Rangers history to hit for the cycle in a game, joining Oddibe McDowell who accomplished the feat on 7/23/85 vs. Cleveland...recorded 7RBI in the game, the most in a cycle game since Boston's Rich Gedman on 9/18/85...at the time, became the 14th switch-hitter to hit for the cycle, and first since Jose Valentin on 4/27/00...was the sixth switch-hitter with a cycle in AL history...recorded two hits from each side of the plate in the cycle, becoming just the third known switch-hitter to accomplish the feat (also Mickey Mantle and Wes Parker).

HITTING FOR THE CYCLE

On August 17, 2004 vs. Cleveland, Teixeira became the second Rangers player in franchise history to hit for the cycle, joining Oddibe McDowell (July 23, 1985 vs. Cleveland). Was the 245th cycle in Baseball history, 223rd since 1900 and 110th in the American League. Teixeira became the 14th switch-hitter to hit for the cycle and just the sixth American League switch-hitter to accomplish the feat. Was the fifth player to hit for the cycle in 2004 and the first switch-hitter, since 1970, to complete the cycle with a single. Became the first player to hit for the cycle in Rangers Ballpark (formerly Ameriquest Field) and the third player to do it in the city of Arlington, joining McDowell and Baltimore's Cal Ripken, Jr. (May 6, 1984) who both accomplished the feat at Arlington Stadium.

First AB: .... Strikeout vs. Cliff Lee (first inning)
Second AB: .... Double off Lee (third inning)
Third AB: .... Home run off Rick White (fourth inning)
Fourth AB: .... Triple off White (fifth inning)
Fifth AB: .... Single off Cliff Bartosh (seventh inning)

2003

- In his first Major League season, hit .259 (137-for-529) with 29 doubles, 5 triples, 26HR and 84RBI in 146 games with Texas...led all rookies in homers and extra base hits (60), ranked second in RBI and walks (44), third in slugging percentage (.480), fourth in hits, total bases (254) and triples, and fifth in runs (66) and doubles...were the second-most homers ever for a Texas first-year player behind Pete Incaviglia (30) in 1986...the total also tied for the third-most ever by a rookie switch-hitter.
- Selected as the first baseman on the *Baseball Digest* and Topps Major League All-Star Rookie teams...named Rangers "Rookie of the Year" by local BBWAA chapter.
- Started 104 games at 1B and was also in the starting lineup at 3B (11), LF (10), RF (8) and DH (5)...had never played 1B prior to the 2003 season...ranked fifth among AL first basemen with a .996 fielding percentage (4E, 1006TC)...did not commit an error in his final 36 games at 1B beginning 8/20.
- Made his first Opening Day roster having played in just 86 professional games, the fewest for a Ranger since Incaviglia went directly from college to the Majors in 1986.
- Started at DH in his Major League debut on 4/1 at Anaheim, going 1-for-3 with 1BB...went hitless in his first 16AB before doubling off Mark Mulder on 4/9 vs. Oakland...connected for his first homer off Ted Lilly the next day vs. Oakland...hit his first grand slam off Baltimore's Rick Helling on 5/25, marking the first slam for a Texas rookie since Mike Stanley on 7/3/87 at the Yankees.
- Set a club record for spring training homers (8).

MARK TEIXEIRA

2002

- Combined to bat .318 (102-for-321) with 19HR and 69RBI in 86 games at Single-A Charlotte and Double-A Tulsa in his first professional season...despite missing the first two months of the season, was selected as the third baseman on the *Baseball America* overall Minor League All-Star team as well as the Rangers' "Minor League Player of the Year."
- Opened season on the D.L. after rupturing a tendon in his left elbow and forearm while attempting to catch a foul pop in March...activated on 6/1 and hit safely in his first 12 games at a .354 (17-for-48) clip...named the Topps Florida State League "Player of the Month" for June.
- Promoted to Tulsa on 7/12 and hit .316 with 10HR and 28RBI in 47 starts at third base and one as the DH...had a .243 (9-for-37) average with 1HR and 4RBI in 10 Texas League playoff games.
- Selected as the top prospect in the both the Texas League and Florida State League by *Baseball America*...played for Peoria in Arizona Fall League, batting .333 (33-for-99) with 7HR and 23RBI in 27 games...ranked among the league leaders in slugging (second, .616), homers (tied for third), RBI (tied for fourth) and average (fifth) despite missing the last two weeks of the season with a strained abdominal muscle.

2001

- Was the fifth overall pick by the Rangers in the 2001 First-Year Player Draft, Texas' highest selection since 1989...signed a four-year contract through 2006 on 8/22 and participated in the Rangers' Florida Instructional League program, batting .246 with a team-high 13RBI in 20 games.

Personal

- Full name is Mark Charles Teixeira...he and his wife, Leigh, have a son, Jack Gordan (3) and daughter Addison Leigh (2)...met his wife, an industrial-design Major, as a freshman at Georgia Tech...signed by Zackary Hoyrst (Rangers)...hobbies include hunting and golf...his favorite team growing up was the Baltimore Orioles and his favorite player was Don Mattingly...is a natural right-handed hitter...decided to become a dedicated switch hitter at the age of 13...is of Portugese decent...his father, John, is a former Navy pilot who played high school baseball with Bucky Dent...his uncle, Pete, played in the Braves minor league system.
- In 2006, Mark and his wife established the Mark Teixeira Charitable Fund that supported six $5,000 scholarships at three high schools in the Dallas/Ft. Worth area...in 2007, he increased the number of scholarships to 12...following the 2007 season, he held the first Tex's Holiday Hold 'Em poker tournament that raised over $55,000 for his foundation...other community groups that have been helped by the Teixeiras include Cook Children's Medical Center, the Arlington Boys & Girls Club and the Arlington Police Department, where they worked to start a local Police Athletic League (PAL) for the youth of Arlington...won the 2006 "Harold McKinney Good Guy Award" as voted on by the Dallas/Ft. Worth chapter of the BBWAA.
- Teamed up with Coppertone's "Help Strike Out Sun Damage" program in 2009 as a spokesman for the National Foundation for Cancer Research.
- Batted .409 (216-528) with 36HR and 165RBI in 140 games in three seasons at Georgia Tech...became just the second player in Atlantic Coast Conference history to have a career .400 average, joining Wake Forest's Bill Merrifield (.400 from 1981-83)...batted .419 (26-for-62) with 5HR and 20RBI in 16 games for the Yellow Jackets as a senior in 2001...fractured right ankle in season's seventh game on 2/23 vs. Elon...won the Dick Howser Trophy as the "National Collegiate Player of the Year" in 2000, hitting .427 (103-for-241) with 18HR and 80RBI in 66 games...selected as "National Player of the Year" by *Baseball America* and the Sporting News, was the ACC "Player of the Year" and was a consensus first-team All-American...led the ACC in batting average, runs (school-record 104), homers, walks (67), slugging percentage (.772) and on-base percentage (.547)...was a three-time ACC "Player of the Week"...named to all-tournament team in NCAA regional in Atlanta with 2HR and 7RBI...hit .387 (87-for-225) with 13HR and 65RBI in 58 games in 1999...named ACC Rookie of the Year and was first-team all-conference selection...picked as "National Freshman of the Year" by *Collegiate Baseball*...set Georgia Tech freshman records for hits and RBI and tied the doubles mark (18)...led Tech in batting, becoming the first freshman to do so since 1978...spent summer of 2000 with USA Baseball National Team, leading the club in batting (.385), runs (26), hits (46), RBI (23) and total bases (70)...hit .289 with 7HR and 26RBI for Orleans in the Cape Cod League in the summer of 1999...earned team MVP in league All-Star Game and received Robert A. McNeese Award as Cape League's most outstanding pro prospect.
- Makes an annual donation to the Georgia Tech baseball scholarship, including a $500,000 pledge in February 2009.
- Played baseball, basketball and soccer at Mt. St. Joseph's High School in Baltimore (graduated 1998)...set Maryland state records for career homers (29), RBI (105) and runs (128)...in 1998, earned first-team High School All-American honors from *Baseball America, USA Today/Sports Weekly, Collegiate Baseball*, and the American Baseball Coaches Association, hitting .548 with 12 homers and 36 RBI...was named Maryland "Player of the Year" in 1997 and 1998...also played in the Babe Ruth League and American Legion programs...endowed a scholarship at Mt. St. Joseph in the name of his friend Nick Libertore who was killed in a car accident while to two were in school.

MARK TEIXEIRA

Teixeira's Career Playing Record

Year	Club	AVG	G	AB	R	H	2B	3B	HR	RBI	SH	SF	HP	BB	SO	SB	CS	E	OBP	SLG
2002	Charlotte	.320	38	150	32	48	10	2	9	41	0	1	3	21	24	2	0	9	.411	.593
	Tulsa	.316	48	171	31	54	11	3	10	28	0	0	4	25	36	3	2	12	.415	.591
2003	TEXAS	.259	146	529	66	137	29	5	26	84	0	2	14	44	120	1	2	4	.331	.480
2004	TEXAS – a	.281	145	545	101	153	34	2	38	112	0	2	10	68	117	4	1	10	.370	.560
	Frisco	.000	1	3	0	0	0	0	0	0	0	0	1	0	1	0	0	0	.250	.000
2005	TEXAS	.301	#162	644	112	194	41	3	43	144	0	3	11	72	124	4	0	3	.379	.575
2006	TEXAS	.282	#162	628	99	177	45	1	33	110	0	6	4	89	128	2	0	4	.371	.514
2007	TEXAS – b	.297	78	286	48	85	24	1	13	49	9	1	3	45	66	0	0	1	.397	.524
	Frisco	.000	1	2	0	0	0	0	0	0	0	0	0	2	0	0	0	0	.500	.000
	ATLANTA – c	.317	54	208	38	66	9	1	17	56	0	1	4	27	46	0	0	4	.404	.615
2008	ATLANTA	.283	103	381	63	108	27	0	20	78	0	2	3	65	70	0	0	2	.390	.512
	LOS ANGELES-AL – d	.358	54	193	39	69	14	0	13	43	0	5	4	32	23	2	0	3	.449	.632
2009	YANKEES – e	.292	156	609	103	178	43	3	#39	*122	0	5	12	81	114	2	0	4	.383	.565
Minor League Totals		**.313**	**88**	**326**	**63**	**102**	**21**	**5**	**19**	**69**	**0**	**1**	**8**	**48**	**61**	**5**	**2**	**21**	**.413**	**.583**
AL Totals		**.289**	**903**	**3434**	**568**	**993**	**230**	**15**	**205**	**664**	**0**	**24**	**58**	**431**	**692**	**15**	**3**	**37**	**.375**	**.544**
NL Totals		**.295**	**157**	**589**	**101**	**174**	**36**	**1**	**37**	**134**	**0**	**3**	**7**	**92**	**116**	**0**	**0**	**6**	**.395**	**.548**
Major League Totals		**.290**	**1060**	**4023**	**669**	**1167**	**266**	**16**	**242**	**798**	**0**	**27**	**65**	**523**	**808**	**15**	**3**	**43**	**.378**	**.545**

#Tied for league lead

Selected by Boston in the ninth round of the 1998 First-Year Player Draft but did not sign.
Selected by Texas in the first round (fifth pick overall) of the 2001 First-Year Player Draft.

a – Placed on the 15-day disabled list from April 13-29, 2004 with a strained left oblique.
b – Placed on the 15-day disabled list from June 9 – July 13, 2007 with a strained left quadriceps.
c – Traded to the Atlanta Braves along with LHP Ron Mahay from the Texas Rangers in exchange for C Jarrod Saltalamacchia, INF Elvis Andrus, RHP Neftali Perez and LHPs Matt Harrison and Beau Jones on July 31, 2007.
d – Traded to the Los Angeles Angels from the Atlanta Braves in exchange for INF Casey Kotchman and RHP Steve Marek on July 29, 2008.
e – Signed as a free agent by the Yankees to an eight-year contract on January 6, 2009.

Teixeira's Division Series Record

Year	Club vs. Opp.	AVG	G	AB	R	H	2B	3B	HR	RBI	SH	SF	HP	BB	SO	SB	CS	E	OBP	SLG
2008	LAA vs. BOS	.467	4	15	4	7	0	0	0	1	0	1	0	4	3	0	0	0	.550	.467
2009	NYY vs. MIN	.167	3	12	3	2	0	0	1	1	0	0	0	1	1	0	0	0	.231	.417
Division Series Totals		**.333**	**7**	**27**	**7**	**9**	**0**	**0**	**1**	**2**	**0**	**1**	**0**	**5**	**4**	**0**	**0**	**0**	**.424**	**.444**

Teixeira's League Championship Series Record

Year	Club vs. Opp.	AVG	G	AB	R	H	2B	3B	HR	RBI	SH	SF	HP	BB	SO	SB	CS	E	OBP	SLG
2009	NYY vs. LAA	.222	6	27	2	6	1	0	0	4	0	1	0	3	8	0	0	0	.290	.259
LCS Totals		**.222**	**6**	**27**	**2**	**6**	**1**	**0**	**0**	**4**	**0**	**1**	**0**	**3**	**8**	**0**	**0**	**0**	**.290**	**.259**

Teixeira's World Series Record

Year	Club vs. Opp.	AVG	G	AB	R	H	2B	3B	HR	RBI	SH	SF	HP	BB	SO	SB	CS	E	OBP	SLG
2009	NYY vs. PHI	.136	6	22	5	3	1	0	1	3	0	0	3	2	8	0	0	0	.296	.318
World Series Totals		**.136**	**6**	**22**	**5**	**3**	**1**	**0**	**1**	**3**	**0**	**0**	**3**	**2**	**8**	**0**	**0**	**0**	**.296**	**.318**
POSTSEASON TOTALS		**.237**	**19**	**76**	**14**	**18**	**2**	**0**	**2**	**9**	**0**	**2**	**3**	**10**	**20**	**0**	**0**	**0**	**.341**	**.342**

Teixeira's All-Star Game Record

Year	Club, Site	AVG	G	AB	R	H	2B	3B	HR	RBI	SH	SF	HP	BB	SO	SB	CS	E	OBP	SLG
2005	TEX, Detroit	.333	1	3	1	1	0	0	1	2	0	0	0	0	0	0	0	0	.333	1.333
2009	NYY, St. Louis	.000	1	3	0	0	0	0	0	0	0	0	0	0	0	0	0	0	.000	.000
All-Star Game Totals		**.167**	**2**	**6**	**1**	**1**	**0**	**0**	**1**	**2**	**0**	**0**	**0**	**0**	**0**	**0**	**0**	**0**	**.167**	**.667**

Teixeira's World Baseball Classic Record

Year	Country, Site	AVG	G	AB	R	H	2B	3B	HR	RBI	SH	SF	HP	BB	SO	SB	CS	E	OBP	SLG
2006	USA, USA	0	4	15	0	0	0	0	0	0	0	0	0	0	4	1	0	0	.000	.000

Teixeira's Career Fielding Record

Position	PCT	G	PO	A	E	TC	DP
First Base	.996	1005	8723	584	35	9342	854
Outfield	.974	32	37	0	1	38	0
Third Base	.811	15	10	20	7	37	0

Teixeira's Career Home Run Chart

MULTI-HOMER GAMES: 25. **TWO-HOMER GAMES:** 23, last on 9/19/09 at Seattle. **THREE-HOMER GAMES:** 2, last on 6/22/08 vs. Seattle. **GRAND SLAMS:** 4, last on 8/3/08 at New York-AL (Edwar Ramirez). **PINCH-HIT HR:** None. **INSIDE-THE-PARK HR:** None. **WALK-OFF HR:** None. **LEADOFF HR:** None.

Javier Vazquez

31 Right-handed Pitcher

6-2 • 210 •B/T: Right/Right

Opening Day Age: 33

Birthdate
July 25, 1976

Birthplace
Ponce, P.R.

Resides
Ponce, P.R.

M.L. Service
11 years, 141 days

Career Highlights
A.L. All-Star Team
- 2004

Status

- Acquired by the Yankees along with LHP Boone Logan in exchange for OF Melky Cabrera, RHP Arodys Vizcaino and LHP Mike Dunn on December 22, 2009...is in the fifth year of a five-year contract through 2010.

Career Notes

- Has never been on the disabled list in his career (see chart on pg. 221).
- Is the only active pitcher to record at least 10 wins, 30 starts and 150K in each of the last nine seasons.
- Has recorded at least 10 wins and 150K in each of the last 10 seasons (since 2000)...according to the *Elias Sports Bureau*, he became only the 10th pitcher in Major League history to accomplish the feat (eight of which are Hall of Famers)...joins Steve Carlton (1970s) as the only two pitchers to collect such a span over a "conventional decade."
- Owns nine seasons of at least 200.0IP...is one of only four pitchers to reach 200.0IP in each of the last five seasons (2005-09), joining Dan Haren, Mark Buehrle and Bronson Arroyo...missed 200.0IP just once over the last 10 years (2000-09), falling just shy of the mark in 2004 with the Yankees with 198.0IP.
- Has struck out at least one batter in 320 consecutive starts...marks the eighth-longest such streak since 1954, behind Tom Seaver (411), Nolan Ryan (382), Curt Schilling (378), David Cone (347), Dwight Gooden (347), Randy Johnson (342) and Pedro Martinez (327)...trails only Martinez among active pitchers.
- Has struck out 10 or more batters in a game 40 times in his career, fifth-most among active pitchers behind Pedro Martinez (108), Johan Santana (47), John Smoltz (44) and Kerry Wood (41).
- Among Major Leaguers since debuting in 1998, ranks second in starts (385), innings pitched (2,490.0) and strikeouts (2,253), seventh in "quality starts" (210) and eighth in K/9.0IP (8.14)
- Has received Gold Glove votes in eight of the last nine seasons (2001-03, '05-09), finishing as high as third place in 2001 balloting.

Single-Game Highs and Streaks

Low hit CG
1 - at LAD, 9/14/99

IP (start)
9.0 - 23 times
Last: at WAS, 9/25/09

IP (relief)
2.0 - at PHI, 10/3/04

Hits
12 - 3 times
Last: at PIT, 9/6/05

Runs
9 - 2 times
Last: vs. HOU, 6/25/06

BB
6 - 2 times
Last: vs. NYY, 8/10/06

SO
14 - at CHC, 4/9/03

HR
3 - 14 times
Last: vs. NYM, 5/4/09

Winning Streak
6g - 8/12-9/7/01

Losing Streak
7g - 8/4-9/5/02

2009

- In his lone season with Atlanta, went 15-10 with a career-low 2.87 ERA and 238K in 32 starts...came in fourth place in the NL Cy Young voting, receiving one second-place vote.
- Ranked third in the Majors (second in the NL) in K/BB ratio (5.41), fourth (second in the NL) in strikeouts, fifth (third in the NL) with 9.77 K/9.0IP and ninth (sixth in the NL) in ERA...tied for fourth in the NL in wins.
- Made 22 "quality starts" and held opponents to 3ER or less in all but eight starts...tossed at least 6.0 innings 28 times and at least 7.0 innings in 18 starts with the Braves going 13-5 in those games.

JAVIER VAZQUEZ

- Over his final 22 starts, beginning 5/30, made 16 "quality starts," pitched to a 2.49 ERA (155.1IP, 43ER), limited opponents to a .217 average and collected 160K with just 29BB.
- Named the NL "Player of the Week" for the period ending 9/13, going 2-0 with a 1.13 ERA and 17K in wins at Houston and St. Louis.
- Hit safely in nine of his last 18 games, going 10-for-34 (.294) over the span...led the Majors with 20 sacrifice hits on the year.
- Pitched for Puerto Rico in the World Baseball Classic prior to the season, winning both of his starts and allowing just 1ER in 9.1IP (0.96 ERA).

Vazquez' 2009 Pitching Lines

Date/Opp	Score	W/L	IP	H	R	ER	HR	BB	K	NP/K	ERA	Left game
4/8 at PHI	11-12	ND	6.0	5	3	3	1	**4**	5	102/61	4.50	Leading 9-3
4/14 vs. FLA	1-5	L	6.0	5	3	3	0	1	**12**	106/73	4.50	Trailing 3-1
4/19 at PIT*	11-1	W	6.0	5	0	0	0	1	8	98/71	3.00	Leading 6-0
4/24 at CIN	4-3	W	6.0	7	2	1	0	1	9	102/67	2.63	Leading 4-2
4/29 vs. STL	3-5	L	8.0	9	5	5	0	1	8	99/71	3.38	Trailing 5-3
5/4 vs. NYM*	4-6	L	6.2	7	**6**	**6**	**3**	3	8	110/73	4.19	Trailing 6-3
5/9 at PHI*	6-2	W	7.2	4	2	2	2	0	7	115/74	3.88	Leading 6-2
5/15 vs. ARI	4-3	ND	7.0	5	2	2	0	2	10	107/68	3.71	Trailing 3-2
5/20 vs. COL	12-4	W	5.0	3	1	0	0	1	6	71/49	3.39	Leading 10-1
5/25 at SF	2-8	L	5.2	8	5	5	0	1	5	107/66	3.80	Trailing 5-2
5/30 at ARI	2-3 (11)	ND	6.1	7	2	1	0	1	8	99/64	3.58	Tied 2-2
6/6 vs. MIL*	0-3	L	6.0	4	2	2	1	0	7	80/56	3.54	Trailing 2-0
6/11 vs. PIT*	1-3	ND	8.0	2	1	1	1	0	**12**	113/**79**	3.31	Tied 1-1
6/17 at CIN*	3-4	L	8.0	4	4	4	2	2	7	99/69	3.41	Trailing 3-4
6/22 vs. CHI*	2-0	W	6.2	9	0	0	0	2	5	116/74	3.18	Leading 1-0
6/27 vs. BOS*	0-1	L	7.2	6	1	1	0	3	8	121/83	3.04	Trailing 1-0
7/2 vs. PHI	5-2	ND	5.1	7	2	2	0	0	5	109/72	3.05	Tied 2-2
7/7 at CHI*	2-1	W	7.0	5	1	1	0	0	6	108/78	2.95	Leading 2-1
7/19 vs. NYM*	7-1	W	7.0	6	1	1	0	1	5	101/63	2.86	Leading 7-1
7/24 at MIL*	9-4	W	7.0	7	4	4	1	3	9	110/74	2.98	Leading 8-4
7/30 at FLA*	6-3	ND	7.1	5	3	3	1	1	8	110/71	3.01	Leading 3-2
8/4 at SD*	9-2	W	7.0	4	2	2	1	2	6	98/68	2.99	Leading 9-2
8/9 at LAD	8-2	W	8.0	5	1	1	0	2	7	113/73	2.90	Leading 5-1
8/16 vs. PHI	1-4	L	7.0	6	4	4	2	2	7	107/69	2.99	Trailing 4-1
8/21 vs. FLA	3-5	L	6.2	**10**	5	5	2	1	8	105/69	3.14	Trailing 5-0
8/27 vs. SD*	9-1	W	7.0	5	0	0	0	0	6	88/63	3.02	Leading 9-0
9/2 at FLA	7-8	ND	5.1	7	5	5	1	1	7	**120**/75	3.18	Leading 3-2
9/8 at HOU*	2-1	W	7.0	3	0	0	0	**4**	9	110/69	3.06	Leading 2-0
9/13 at STL	9-2	W	**9.0**	7	2	2	0	0	8	94/70	3.01	Leading 9-2
9/19 vs. PHI*	6-4	W	7.0	3	0	0	0	3	6	102/58	2.91	Leading 6-0
9/25 at WSH	4-1	W	**9.0**	3	1	1	1	1	7	103/72	2.83	Leading 4-1
9/30 vs. FLA*	4-5	L	6.0	8	5	3	1	0	9	91/65	2.87	Trailing 5-0
Totals		**15-10**	**219.1**	**181**	**75**	**70**	**20**	**44**	**238**	**--**	**2.87**	

(*) Denotes start following a team loss **Bold=indicates season highs**

2008

- Made 33 starts in his final season with the White Sox, going 12-16 with a 4.67 ERA and 200K...became just the third pitcher (fifth time) in White Sox history to record back-to-back seasons with 200K, joining Ed Walsh (1907-08 and '10-12) and Tom Bradley (1971-72)...the total tied for the 13th-highest single-season mark in Sox history.
- Ranked fourth among American League pitchers in strikeouts and K/9.0IP (8.64), tied for fifth in starts and placed ninth in innings pitched (208.1)...was one of 10 AL pitchers to not commit an error (46TC).
- Went 3-0 with a 2.21 ERA (20.1IP, 5ER) from 4/2-18 without allowing a home run in his first five outings.
- Named "co-AL Player of the Week" for the period ending on 8/17 (also Melvin Mora), going 2-0 with a 0.56 ERA (16.0IP, 1ER) and 18K, marking his first career weekly award.
- Collected his 2,000th career strikeout in 9/14 (Game 1) win vs. Detroit, fanning Edgar Renteria in the fifth inning...became the 62nd pitcher in Baseball history to reach the plateau.
- Acquired by the Atlanta Braves on 12/4/08 along with LHP Boone Logan in exchange for INFs Jon Gilmore and Brent Lillibridge, C Tyler Flowers and LHP Santos Rodriguez.

2007

- Was 15-8 with a 3.74 ERA and 213K in 32 starts with the White Sox...the strikeout total was the sixth-highest single-season mark in White Sox history...he became the first pitcher to lead the club in strikeouts in consecutive seasons since Mike Sirotka (1998-2000), the first right-hander since Alex Fernandez (1995-96).
- Lowered his ERA from 4.84 in 2006 to 3.74 in 2007, the fourth-best ERA improvement in the AL...ranked fourth in the American League in strikeouts, fifth in K/BB ratio (4.3), K/9.0IP (8.9) and baserunners/9.0IP (10.6), sixth in opponents average (.242), and seventh in IP (216.2)...tossed 6.0 innings or more 30 times and at least 7.0IP in 15 starts.
- Led all pitchers with 56K in September...marked the second-highest monthly total in White Sox history behind Wilbur Wood (58 in September 1971)...reached 2,000 career IP in his start on 8/10 vs. Seattle...agreed to terms on a three-year contract extension on 3/6.

JAVIER VAZQUEZ

2006

- Went 11-12 with a 4.84 ERA and 184K in 33 games (32 starts) in his first season with the White Sox...led the staff in strikeouts, ranking fourth in the AL...compiled five games with at least 10K, marking the most by a White Sox pitcher since Britt Burns in 1985...posted a 9-4 record before the All-Star Break and went 2-8 in the second half...his 98K after the All-Star break ranked second in the AL behind Minnesota's Johan Santana (107)...ranked second in the AL with 15 hit batsmen.
- Recorded his 1,500th strikeout on 7/1 at Chicago-NL (Greg Maddux)...made his second career relief outing on 7/9 vs. Boston in a 19-inning victory, tossing 1.2 scoreless innings...registered his 100th career win on 8/10 vs. the Yankees...struck out 50 batters in September, leading the AL and tying Jack McDowell (July 1994) for the third-highest monthly total in franchise history...went 0-3 with a 3.82 ERA for the month, becoming one of four pitchers to strike out at least 50 in a month without recording a win, joining Pedro Martinez (0-1, 55 K in 5/06), Kerry Wood (0-3, 55 K in 8/02) and Randy Johnson (0-2, 59 SO in 9/92).
- Competed for Puerto Rico in the inaugural World Baseball Classic, going 1-0 with a 2.25 ERA (8.0IP, 2ER) in two starts.

DURING THE 2000s (2000-09)

MOST IP

1.	Livan Hernandez	2201.1
2.	**JAVIER VAZQUEZ**	**2163.0**
3.	Mark Buehrle	2061.0
4.	Barry Zito	1999.0
5.	Jamie Moyer	1980.1

MOST STRIKEOUTS

1.	Randy Johnson	2,182
2.	**JAVIER VAZQUEZ**	**2,001**
3.	Johan Santana	1,733
4.	Pedro Martinez	1,620
5.	CC SABATHIA	1,590

MOST STARTS

1.	Livan Hernandez	332
2.	**JAVIER VAZQUEZ**	**327**
3.	Jeff Suppan	321
4.	Barry Zito	320
5.	Jamie Moyer	315

Best K/BB AMONG ACTIVE PLAYERS

1.	Pedro Martinez	4.15
2.	Johan Santana	3.66
3.	Roy Oswalt	3.58
4.	**JAVIER VAZQUEZ**	**3.48**
5.	Roy Halladay	3.29

2005

- Acquired by Arizona prior to the season...went 11-15 with a 4.42 ERA in 33 starts in his only season with the Diamondbacks...recorded his fifth season with at least 200.0IP but set career highs in losses and home runs allowed (35)...ranked eighth in the NL in strikeouts (192)...received one run of support or less in 14 of his 15 losses.
- Was the Diamondbacks' Opening Day starter on 4/4 vs. Chicago-NL, recording the loss...did not issue a walk in a club-record 54.1 consecutive IP (220 batters faced) from 4/25-6/9...issued a free pass to Minnesota's Michael Cuddyer in the fifth inning on 6/9 to end the streak...hit his first career home run on 5/28 vs. Los Angeles-NL (off Duaner Sanchez).
- Acquired by the White Sox along with cash considerations in exchange for RHP Orlando Hernandez, RHP Luiz Vizcaino and OF Chris Young on 12/20/05.

2004

- In his first and only season with the Yankees, went 14-10 with a 4.91 ERA in 32 starts...recorded his fifth consecutive campaign with at least 32 starts...named to his first All-Star team in his initial season in the American League.
- Allowed 33HR, marking the fifth-most in the AL and the third-most HR surrendered in a single season by a Yankee behind Ralph Terry (40 in 1962) and Orlando Hernandez (34 in 2000)...was also charged with 12WP, third-most in the AL.
- Won his AL debut on 4/8 vs. Chicago-AL, allowing just 1ER in 8.0IP...was scratched from his start on 8/11 at Texas due to conjunctivitis...allowed his first stolen base on 8/17, ending his string of 36 starts without allowing a steal.
- Made his first postseason start on 10/9 in Game 4 of the ALDS at Minnesota, drawing a no-decision in the Yankees' 6-5 extra-inning victory (5.0IP, 7H, 5ER, 2BB, 6K, 1HR, 2HP)...made two relief appearances in the ALCS vs. Boston, allowing 7ER in 6.1IP...earned his first career playoff win on 10/16 in Game 3 at Fenway Park, despite allowing 4ER in 4.1IP.

2003

- In his final season with Montreal, posted a 13-12 record with a 3.24 ERA in 34 starts, setting career bests in innings pitched (230.2) and strikeouts (241) and matching his most career starts...marked the third-highest strikeout total in Expos history behind Pedro Martinez (305 in 1997) and Bill Stoneman (251 in 1971).
- Ranked second among National League pitchers in IP, third in strikeouts, tied for third in starts, fourth in K/9.0IP (9.4), tied for fifth in complete games (4), seventh in opponents average (.229) and 10th in ERA...threw 3,741 pitches, second only to Oakland's Barry Zito (3,747)...notched nine games with at least 10K, tied for second-most in the Majors.

JAVIER VAZQUEZ

- Suffered a strained right calf prior to Opening Day, preventing him from making his third consecutive start to begin the season...recorded his 1,000th strikeout on 8/2 vs. Milwaukee (Eric Young)...tossed 29.0 consecutive scoreless IP from 8/18-9/2, the longest stretch of the season in the Majors.

MOST SERVICE DAYS AMONG ACTIVE PITCHERS WHO HAVE NEVER BEEN ON A MAJOR LEAGUE DISABLED LIST

PLAYER	YEARS, DAYS
1. Derek Lowe	12 yrs, 100 days
2. Livan Hernandez	12 yrs, 96 days
3. JAVIER VAZQUEZ	**11 yrs, 141 days**

2002

- Posted his third consecutive 10-win/200.0IP season, going 10-13 with a 3.91 ERA in 34 starts with Montreal...led the National League in hits allowed (243), ranked fourth in IP (230.1), tied for fifth in starts and placed ninth in strikeouts (179)...made his second straight Opening Day start (4/2 vs. Florida).

2001

- Set a career high in wins, going 16-11 with a 3.42 ERA, five complete games and three shutouts in 32 starts with the Expos...tied with Greg Maddux for the most shutouts in the National League...tied for second in the NL in complete games, ranked fourth in road ERA (2.86), fifth in strikeouts (208), eighth in innings pitched (223.2) and ninth in opponents batting average (.235).
- Made Opening Day start on 4/2 at Wrigley Field...was 7-9 with a 4.93 ERA prior to the All-Star break and 9-2 with a 1.60 ERA in the second half...named the NL "Pitcher of the Month" for August going 5-1 with a 0.55 ERA (49.0IP, 3ER).
- Was hit by a Ryan Dempster pitch on 9/17 vs. Florida...X-rays taken at St. Mary's Hospital revealed a fractured right eye socket, cutting his season short.

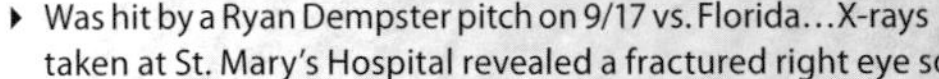

2000

- Was 11-9 with a 4.05 ERA and two complete games in 33 starts with Montreal...ranked fourth in the National League leaders in strikeout-to-walk ratio (4.73), sixth in strikeouts (196), tied for ninth in starts and tied for 10th in innings pitched (217.2).
- Recorded his first career shutout on 9/10 at Atlanta (4-0), striking out 11 while allowing only 6H.

1999

- Went 9-8 with a 5.00 ERA in 26 starts with the Expos, leading the team in wins and ranking second in innings pitched (154.2)...tied for ninth in the NL with three complete games.
- Went 2-4 with a 6.63 ERA in his first 11 starts before being optioned to Triple-A Ottawa on 6/6...recalled on 7/18 and suffered the loss that night at Yankee Stadium (7.0IP, 6ER) as David Cone tossed a perfect game.
- Tossed back-to-back complete games on 7/23 vs. Pittsburgh and 7/28 vs. Chicago-NL...hurled a one-hitter with a season-high 10K on 9/14 at Los Angeles-NL.

1998

- In his first Major League action, went 5-15 with a 6.06 ERA in 33 games (32 starts) with the Expos...led all National League rookies in starts, ranked second in strikeouts (139) and third in innings pitched (172.1).
- Made Montreal's Opening Day roster and made his Major League debut on 4/3 at Chicago-NL, recording the loss in the 6-2 Cubs victory (5.0IP, 3ER)...recorded his first hit on 4/19 at Houston (double)...earned his first win on 5/1 vs. Arizona in his sixth big league start...was ejected on 7/17 vs. Pittsburgh after hitting Aramis Ramirez with a pitch...served a suspension from 7/23-26...pitched with Ponce in the Puerto Rican Winter League following the season.

JAVIER VAZQUEZ

1997

- Was named the Montreal Player Development "Pitcher of the Year" for the second consecutive season after combining to go 10-3 with a 1.86 ERA in 25 starts between Single-A West Palm Beach and Double-A Harrisburg...marked the lowest ERA among all minor-league pitchers, while his .200 opponents average against ranked as the fifth-lowest...was named to the Florida State League All-Star Team and was tabbed by *Baseball America* as the No. 3 Prospect in the Expos farm system following the season.

1996

- Earned Montreal Player Development "Pitcher of the Year" honors, going 14-3 with a 2.68 ERA in 27 starts with Single-A Delmarva...led all minor leaguers with an .824 winning percentage, and ranked second in the South Atlantic League in wins, third in strikeouts (173) and ninth in ERA.

1995

- Went 6-6 with a 5.08 ERA in 21 starts with Single-A Albany.

1994

- Made his pro debut, going 5-2 with a 2.53 ERA in 15 games (11 starts) with the GCL Expos.

Personal

- Full name is Javier Carios Vazquez...he and wife Kamille have three children: daughters Kamila and Kariana and son Javier Josue...attended Colegio Ponceno where he played baseball and basketball...was a member of the 2000 MLB All-Star Team that toured Japan...in 2007, he participated in a clinic with the Professional Baseball Athletic Trainer Society (PBATS) and partnered with the American Diabetes Association (ADA) to provide P.L.A.Y. Day for local children.
- Created his "K's for Kids" Foundation along with his wife Kamille to provide assistance to children and families who are trying to cope with Juvenile Diabetes Type 1...their daughter Kamila was diagnosed with the chronic disease at 2 years old...hold an annual K's for Kids Gala to raise funds for diabetes prevention, treatment and research programs...previous charitable endeavors involved raising funds for an elementary school for deaf children in his hometown of Ponce, P.R.

Vazquez' Career Pitching Record

Year	Team	W	L	ERA	G	GS	CG	SHO	SV	IP	H	R	ER	HR	HB	BB	SO	WP	BK
1994	GCL Expos	5	2	2.53	15	11	1	1	0	67.2	37	25	19	0	3	15	56	9	2
1995	Albany	6	6	5.08	21	21	1	0	0	102.2	109	67	58	8	9	47	87	2	2
1996	Delmarva	14	3	2.68	27	27	1	0	0	164.1	138	64	49	12	7	57	173	12	2
1997	West Palm Beach	6	3	2.16	19	19	1	0	0	112.2	98	40	27	8	6	28	100	2	2
	Harrisburg	4	0	1.07	6	6	1	0	0	42.0	15	5	5	2	2	12	47	2	0
1998	MONTREAL	5	15	6.06	33	32	0	0	0	172.1	196	121	116	31	11	68	139	2	0
1999	MONTREAL	9	8	5.00	26	26	3	1	0	154.2	154	98	86	20	4	52	113	2	0
	Ottawa	4	2	4.85	7	7	0	0	0	42.2	45	24	23	7	2	16	46	0	0
2000	MONTREAL	11	9	4.05	33	33	2	1	0	217.2	247	104	98	24	5	61	196	3	0
2001	MONTREAL	16	11	3.42	32	32	5	3	0	223.2	197	92	85	24	3	44	208	3	1
2002	MONTREAL	10	13	3.91	34	34	2	0	0	230.1	243	111	100	28	4	49	179	3	0
2003	MONTREAL	13	12	3.24	34	34	4	1	0	230.2	198	93	83	28	4	57	241	11	1
2004	YANKEES-a	14	10	4.91	32	32	0	0	0	198.0	195	114	108	33	11	60	150	12	2
2005	ARIZONA-b	11	15	4.42	33	33	3	1	0	215.2	223	112	106	35	5	46	192	7	0
2006	CHICAGO-AL-c	11	12	4.84	33	32	1	0	0	202.2	206	116	109	23	15	56	184	7	0
2007	CHICAGO-AL	15	8	3.74	32	32	2	0	0	216.2	197	95	90	29	7	50	213	5	0
2008	CHICAGO-AL	12	16	4.67	33	33	1	0	0	208.1	214	113	108	25	6	61	200	2	0
2009	ATLANTA-d, e	15	10	2.87	32	32	3	0	0	219.1	181	75	70	20	4	44	238	6	0
Minor League Totals		**39**	**16**	**3.06**	**95**	**91**	**5**	**1**	**0**	**532.0**	**442**	**225**	**181**	**37**	**29**	**175**	**509**	**27**	**8**
AL Totals		**52**	**46**	**4.52**	**130**	**129**	**4**	**0**	**0**	**825.2**	**812**	**438**	**415**	**110**	**39**	**227**	**747**	**26**	**2**
NL Totals		**90**	**93**	**4.02**	**257**	**256**	**22**	**7**	**0**	**1664.1**	**1639**	**806**	**744**	**210**	**40**	**421**	**1506**	**37**	**2**
Major League Totals		**142**	**139**	**4.19**	**387**	**385**	**26**	**7**	**0**	**2490.0**	**2451**	**1244**	**1159**	**320**	**79**	**648**	**2253**	**63**	**4**

Selected by the Montreal Expos in the fifth round of the 1994 First-Year Player Draft.

a – Acquired by the Yankees from Montreal in exchange for LHP Randy Choate, INF Nick Johnson and OF Juan Rivera on December 16, 2003.

b – Acquired by Arizona from the Yankees along with LHP Brad Halsey, C Dioner Navarro and cash considerations in exchange for LHP Randy Johnson on January 11, 2005.

c – Acquired by Chicago-AL from Arizona along with cash considerations in exchange for RHPs Orlando Hernandez and Luis Vizcaino and OF Chris Young on December 20, 2005.

d – Acquired by Atlanta from Chicago-AL along with LHP Boone Logan in exchange for INFs Jonny Gilmore and Brent Lillibridge, C Tyler Flowers and LHP Santos Rodriguez on December 4, 2008.

e – Acquired by the Yankees from Atlanta along with LHP Boone Logan in exchange for OF Melky Cabrera, RHP Arodys Vizcaino and LHP Mike Dunn on December 22, 2009.

JAVIER VAZQUEZ

Vazquez' Division Series Record

Year	Club vs. Opp.	W	L	ERA	G	GS	CG	SHO	SV	IP	H	R	ER	HR	HP	BB	SO	WP	BK
2004	NYY vs. MIN	0	0	9.00	1	1	0	0	0	5.0	7	5	5	1	2	2	6	0	0
2008	CWS vs. TB	0	1	12.46	1	1	0	0	0	4.1	8	6	6	2	0	1	6	0	0
Division Series Totals		**0**	**1**	**10.61**	**2**	**2**	**0**	**0**	**0**	**9.1**	**15**	**11**	**11**	**3**	**2**	**3**	**12**	**0**	**0**

Vazquez' Championship Series Record

Year	Club vs. Opp.	W	L	ERA	G	GS	CG	SHO	SV	IP	H	R	ER	HR	HP	BB	SO	WP	BK
2004	NYY vs. BOS	1	0	9.95	2	0	0	0	0	6.1	9	7	7	3	0	7	6	0	0
LCS Totals		**1**	**0**	**9.95**	**2**	**0**	**0**	**0**	**0**	**6.1**	**9**	**7**	**7**	**3**	**0**	**7**	**6**	**0**	**0**
POSTSEASON TOTALS		**1**	**1**	**10.34**	**4**	**2**	**0**	**0**	**0**	**15.2**	**24**	**18**	**18**	**6**	**2**	**10**	**18**	**0**	**0**

Vazquez' All-Star Game Record

Year	Club, Site	W	L	ERA	G	GS	CG	SHO	SV	IP	H	R	ER	HR	HP	BB	SO	WP	BK
2004	NYY, Houston	0	0	0.00	1	0	0	0	0	1.0	0	0	0	0	0	0	2	0	0

Vazquez' World Baseball Classic Record

Year	Country, Site	W	L	ERA	G	GS	CG	SHO	SV	IP	H	R	ER	HR	HP	BB	SO	WP	BK
2006	Puerto Rico	1	0	2.25	2	2	0	0	0	8.0	6	2	2	1	1	2	7	0	0
2006	Puerto Rico	2	0	0.96	2	2	0	0	0	9.1	8	1	1	0	0	1	5	0	0
WBC Totals		**3**	**0**	**1.56**	**4**	**4**	**0**	**0**	**0**	**17.1**	**14**	**3**	**3**	**1**	**1**	**3**	**12**	**0**	**0**

Vazquez' Regular Season Batting Record

Year	Team	AVG	G	AB	R	H	2B	3B	HR	RBI	SH	SF	HP	BB	SO	SB	CS
2009	Atlanta	.176	37	68	6	12	3	0	0	3	20	0	0	3	14	0	0
Major League Totals		**.207**	**387**	**503**	**38**	**104**	**13**	**2**	**1**	**27.0**	**94**	**2**	**1**	**20**	**85**	**0**	**1**

Vazquez' Career Fielding Record

Position	PCT	G	PO	A	E	TC	DP
Pitcher	.977	387	141	375	12	528	40

James P. Dawson Award

The James P. Dawson Award is presented annually to the top rookie in the Yankees' spring training camp. The award is named in honor of Dawson (1896-1953), who began a 45-year career with the New York Times as a copy boy in 1908 before becoming editor of boxing eight years later and covering boxing and baseball until his death during spring training in 1953. All-time list of James P. Dawson Award Winners:

2009 – Brett Gardner, OF
2008 – Shelley Duncan, INF/OF
2007 – Kei Igawa, LHP
2006 – Eric Duncan, INF
2005 – Andy Phillips, INF
2004 – Bubba Crosby, OF
2003 – Hideki Matsui, OF
2002 – Nick Johnson, 1B
2001 – Alfonso Soriano, 2B
2000 – None selected
1999 – None selected
1998 – Homer Bush, INF
1997 – Jorge Posada, C
1996 – Mark Hutton, RHP
1995 – None selected
1994 – Sterling Hitchcock, LHP
1993 – Mike Humphreys, OF
1992 – Gerald Williams, OF
1991 – Hensley Meullens, OF
1990 – Alan Mills, RHP
1989 – None selected
1988 – Al Leiter, LHP
1987 – Kevin Hughes, OF
1986 – Bob Tewskberry, RHP
1985 – Scott Bradey, C
1984 – Jose Rijo, RHP
1983 – Don Mattingly, 1B
1982 – Andre Robertson, SS
1981 – Gene Nelson, RHP
1980 – Mike Griffin, RHP
1979 – Paul Mirabella, LHP
1978 – Jim Beattie, RHP
1977 – George Zeber, INF
1976 – Willie Randolph, 2B
1975 – Tippy Martinez, LHP
1974 – Tom Buskey, RHP
1973 – Otto Velez, OF
1972 – Rusty Torres, OF
1971 – None selected
1970 – John Ellis, 1B/C
1969 – Jerry Kenney, OF and Bill Burbach, RHP
1968 – Mike Ferraro, 3B
1967 – Bill Robinson, OF
1966 – Roy White, OF
1965 – Arturo Lopez, OF
1964 – Pete Mikkelsen, RHP
1963 – Pedro Gonzalez, 2B
1962 – Tom Tresh, SS
1961 – Rollie Sheldon, RHP
1960 – Johnny James, RHP
1959 – Gordon Windhorn, OF
1958 – Johnny Blanchard, C
1957 – Tony Kubek, SS
1956 – Norm Siebern, OF

Randy Winn

22 Outfielder

6-2 • 193• B/T: Switch/Right

Opening Day Age: 35

Birthdate
June 9, 1974

Birthplace
Los Angeles, Calif.

Resides
Burlingame, Calif.

M.L. Service
11 years

College
Santa Clara University

Career Highlights
A.L. All-Star Team
- 2002

Status

- Signed by the Yankees as a free agent on February 8, 2010...signed through the 2010 season.

Career Notes

- Has never gone on the disabled list in his Major League career...only sidelined once, coming in his first season as a professional with Single-A Elmira (8/22-9/11/95).
- Enters the 2010 season having not made an error in his last 209 games (443 TC) dating back to 2008, marking his career-long errorless game streak.
- Over the last eight years (2002-09), is tied for seventh place among all Major Leaguers in games (1,234) and doubles (304) and has compiled the eighth-most hits (1,378).
- In his career, owns a .289 (1,250-for-4,330) batting average with 73HR batting left-handed and a .279 (460-for-1,651) mark with 33HR from the right side...among all active switch-hitters, ranks fourth in hits (1,710).
- With 1,601 career games, has appeared in the most Major League games without playing in a postseason game, among active players (Credit: *Elias*).

Single-Game Bests and Streaks

Hits
5 - 2 times
Last: at DET, 8/21/04
Runs
4 - at LAD, 5/10/09
2B
3 - 2 times
Last: at MIL, 9/23/06
3B
2 - at KC, 8/14/98
HR
2 - 5 times
Last: at CIN, 8/30/08
RBI
6 - vs. DET, 7/30/03
BB
3 - 8 times
Last: vs. ARI, 8/22/06
SO
4 – at BAL, 8/19/98
SB
2 – 16 times
Last: vs. COL, 9/14/09
Hitting Streak
20g - 4/29-5/21/07

2009

- Batted .262 (141-for-538) with 33 doubles, 2HR and 51RBI in 149 games with San Francisco (90 starts in RF, 34 in LF, 11 in CF, one as DH)...also went 16-for-18 in stolen base attempts (88.9%), leading the team in steals.
- Led the team with a .319 average (37-for-116) with runners in scoring position and hit .370 (20-for-54) with RISP and two outs, fourth-highest in the National League...hit .292 (122-for-418) batting left-handed and .158 (19-for-120) as a right-hander...combined to bat .354 (45-for-127) in the fifth and sixth holes in lineup, but .234 (96-for-411) elsewhere.
- His two home runs on the year were tied for third-fewest among all Major League players with at least 500PA...only the Mets' Luis Castillo (1HR) and the Marlins' Emilio Bonifacio (1HR) had fewer homers than Winn...ended the season with a 477 consecutive at-bat homerless drought, marking the longest homerless streak of his career.
- Was the only NL outfielder to not commit an error in 2009 (min. 800 innings)...was only one of five outfielders in the Majors to not have a miscue, joining Boston's Jason Bay, Cleveland's Grady Sizemore and Kansas City's David DeJesus and Mitch Maier.
- Made his 10th career Opening Day roster and was an Opening Day starter for the ninth straight season...hit his second career Opening Day home run on 4/7 vs. Milwaukee with an eighth-inning HR off Jorge Julio (also 2001 vs. Toronto).
- Hit his second—and final—homer of the year in 4/25 win at Arizona (off Max Scherzer)...scored a career-high four runs in 5/10 win at Los Angeles-NL, going 4-for-6 with 1 double and 2RBI and driving in game winning runs with a bases-loaded two-run single in the 13th inning ...also played all three outfield positions in that game for the first time his career (7.0 innings in RF, 2.0 innings in LF and 4.0 innings in CF).
- Collected "walk-off" RBI single in the 10th inning on 7/29 vs. Pittsburgh, giving the Giants a 1-0 victory.

RANDY WINN

2008

- Batted career-high-tying .306 with 84R, 38 doubles, 2 triples, 10HR and 64RBI in team-high 155 games (127 starts in RF, 13 in LF, seven in CF and two as DH)...also went 25-for-27 in stolen base attempts, collecting his most steals since 2002 (27)...his 183 hits marked the second-most in his career and were tied for fourth-most in the National League...also tied for fifth in the NL in sacrifice flies (9), ranked seventh in average, ninth in average vs. right handers (.313) and tied for 10th in stolen bases.
- Homered from both sides of the plate twice (5/29 at Arizona and 8/30 at Cincinnati), marking the first time in his career he accomplished the feat twice in a single season.
- Made his eighth straight Opening Day start (ninth Opening Day roster of his career)...missed 4/20 game in St. Louis with a bruise on his right foot (suffered by fouling pitch off foot previous day)...also missed 4/24-25 games with a stiff neck.
- Batted .400 (46-for-115) in August, leading the NL in hits and ranking third in average for the month.
- Hit his 100th career home run in 8/15 win at Atlanta, a solo HR off Will Ohman in the eighth inning.

MOST HITS BY OUTFIELDERS SINCE 2002*

	Player	Hits
1.	Ichiro Suzuki	1,753
2.	Juan Pierre	1,371
3.	**RANDY WINN**	**1,356**
4.	Bobby Abreu	1,338
5.	Carlos Lee	1,309

*as an outfielder

HIGHEST AVERAGES, SEVENTH INNING AND LATER, NL IN 2009

	Player	AVG
1.	Matt Kemp, LAD	.346 (74-for-214)
2.	Justin Upton, ARI	.339 (56-for-165)
3.	Juan Pierre, LAD	.336 (51-for-152)
4.	NICK JOHNSON, WSH-FLA	.326 (45-for-138)
5.	Gerardo Parra, ARI	.323 (50-for-155)
6.	Derrek Lee, CHC	.322 (49-for-152)
7.	Albert Pujols, STL	.317 (53-for-167)
8.	**RANDY WINN, SF**	**.316 (54-for-171)**

MOST SERVICE DAYS AMONG ACTIVE PLAYERS WHO HAVE NEVER BEEN ON A MAJOR LEAGUE DISABLED LIST

	PLAYER	YEARS, DAYS
1.	Brad Ausmus	16 yrs, 70 days
2.	Derek Lowe	12 yrs, 100 days
3.	Livan Hernandez	12 yrs, 96 days
4.	JAVIER VAZQUEZ	11 yrs, 141 days
5.	**RANDY WINN**	**11 yrs**

2007

- Played in a team-high 155 games with the Giants, batting .300 with 73R, 42 doubles, 1 triple, 14HR, 65RBI and 15SB...also led the club in average, hits (178), doubles, extra-base hits (57), multi-hit games (47) and three-hit games (16)...started 143 games (98 in RF, 31 in CF, 14 in LF), hitting safely in a team-high 112 contests.
- Became just the sixth player in Giants franchise history to post at least 40 doubles in a season, tying for the sixth-highest single-season total in club history.
- Compiled a career-high 20-game hitting streak from 4/29-5/21, batting .388 (33-for-85) over the stretch...was the longest hitting streak by switch-hitter in San Francisco history and was the longest by a Giant since Robby Thompson had 21-game run in 1993.
- Made his first career appearance at third base for the final out of the 10th inning on 6/8 vs. Oakland, ending the frame by catching a foul pop.

2006

- Appeared in 149 games with the Giants, batting .262 with 82R, 34 doubles, 5 triples, 11HR and 56RBI...made 136 starts (69 in RF, 57 in CF and 10 in LF)...ranked second on the team in doubles and third with 35 multi-hit contests.
- Tied for sixth among NL outfielders with 359 total chances and tied for 10th with a team-high eight outfield assists.
- Exited 5/8 win vs. Houston in the sixth inning after fouling a ball off his right knee...suffered a severe contusion but did not miss a game.

2005

- Combined with Seattle and San Francisco to bat .306 (189-for-617) with 85R, 47 doubles, 6 triples, 20HR, 63RBI and 19SB in 160 games...set career highs in average, games, hits, doubles and homers.
- Began the season in Seattle, hitting .275 (106-for-386) with 25 doubles in 102 games.
- Was acquired by San Francisco on 7/30 in exchange for C Yorvit Torrealba and RHP Jesse Foppert...hit .359 (83-for-231) with 39R, 22 doubles, 5 triples, 14HR in 58 games with the Giants...led the Majors in hits and doubles from 8/1 through the end of the season, while ranking third in average...the 14HR marked the second-most HR in franchise history by player acquired in the middle of a season behind Kevin Mitchell (15HR in 1987).

FLIP THE SWITCH: In 2005, Randy Winn became just the third switch-hitter ever to bat over .300 with at least 185H, 45 doubles and 20HR in a single season:

Player	Year	AVG/Hits/Doubles/HR
Jose Vidro, MON	2000	.330/200/51/24
Lance Berkman, HOU	2001	.331/191/55/34
RANDY WINN, SEA-SF	**2005**	**.306/189/47/20**

RANDY WINN

- Earned NL "Player of the Month" award for September, becoming first Giant other than Barry Bonds to win a monthly honor since Jeff Kent in June 2000...led Majors with 51 hits for the month, most by any Giants player in any single month in at least 35 years...also paced the Majors with a .447 average (51-for-114), 100 total bases and an .877 slugging percentage, while his 11HR tied for the Major League high.
- Hit for the cycle in 8/15 win at Cincinnati, collecting a first-inning single, third-inning solo home run, fourth-inning double and sixth-inning triple...became the 21st player in franchise history (eighth in SF annals) to accomplish the feat.

2004

- Hit .286 with 84R, 34 doubles, 6 triples, 14HR, 81RBI and 21SB in 157 games, setting a career high in RBI...was Seattle's Opening Day center fielder, making 119 starts in CF and 32 in LF.
- Hit his second career "walk-off" homer in the 12th inning on 8/28 vs. Kansas City in Game 2 of a doubleheader.

2003

- In his first season with Seattle, batted .295 with 103R, 37 doubles, 4 triples, 11HR, 75RBI and 23SB in 157 games...made 139 appearances in LF, 20 in CF and four in RF...started in LF on Opening Day and doubled in his first Mariners at-bat at Oakland...led the team in doubles...ranked fourth in the AL with a .349 batting average with runners in scoring position and tied for eighth in the AL in stolen bases.
- Hit .268 (91-for-339) with 2HR and 32RBI prior to the All-Star break, and batted .330 (86-for-261) with 9HR and 43RBI in the second half.
- Collected a career-high 6RBI in 7/30 win vs. Detroit, going 2-for-6 with 3R and 2HR.

2002

- Was named team MVP by the Tampa Bay Baseball Writers Association, after batting .298 with 87R, 39 doubles, 9 triples, 14HR, 75RBI and 27SB in 152 games...joined Toronto's Shannon Stewart as the only two players to finish in the AL top 10 in 2002 in singles (10th-119), doubles (tied-eighth) and triples (second)...ranked second in the AL in stolen bases and fourth with 13 outfield assists.
- Established a Tampa Bay franchise record with 181 hits...also set a club record for most hits in any month with 42 hits in June (both have since been broken).
- Selected to the AL All-Star team, and went 1-for-2 with 1R, 1 double, 1BB and 1SB in the tie game on 7/10 at Milwaukee's Miller Park.
- Hit a pinch-hit grand slam in 4/4 win vs. Detroit (off Matt Miller)...tied an AL record with eight extra-base hits over three games from 6/9-11, going 10-for-14 with 6 doubles, 2HR and 6RBI.
- Following the season, was acquired by Seattle in exchange for infielder Antonio Perez...deal was contingent upon Tampa Bay reaching and agreement with Lou Piniella for their managerial position.

2001

- Played his first full season in the Majors, appearing in 128 games with Tampa Bay and batting .273 with 54R, 25 doubles, 6 triples, 6HR and 50RBI in 128 games...led the team and ranked sixth in the AL with 12 outfield assists.
- Homered in his first at-bat of the season vs. Toronto's Kelvim Escobar...broke up Tim Wakefield's no-hit bid with nobody out in the ninth inning on 6/19 vs. Boston, delivering an RBI-single.
- Played for Santurce in the Puerto Rican Winter League following the season, batting .316 with 6HR and 16RBI in 37 games.

2000

- Batted .252 with 28R, 5 doubles, 1HR and 16RBI in 51 games over three stints with Tampa Bay.
- Appeared in 79 games with Triple-A Durham, leading all Tampa Bay farmhands with a .330 average.

1999

- Made his first career Opening Day roster, and batted .267 with 44R, 16 doubles, 4 triples, 2HR, 24RBI and 9SB in 79 games over three stints with Tampa Bay.
- Hit his first career grand slam in the season finale on 10/3 vs. the Yankees, connecting for inside-the-park homer off Jeff Juden...marked 171st inside-the-park grand slam in Major League history, and first by AL player since Seattle's Dan Wilson 5/3/98 vs. Detroit.

RANDY WINN

1998

- Selected by Tampa Bay in the third round of the 1998 Expansion Draft...batted .278 with 51R, 9 doubles, 9 triples, 1HR and 17RBI in 109 games during the franchise's inaugural season...also stole 26 bases in 38 attempts...led all Major League rookies and became one of eight AL rookies during the 90s to steal at least 25 bases...also led AL rookies in triples...led Tampa Bay with 28 infield hits.
- Made his Major League debut on 5/11 vs. Cleveland, pinch running in the eighth and getting caught stealing...recorded his first hit on 5/14 vs. Kansas City, an infield single off the Royals' Scott Service...was Roger Clemens' 3,000th strikeout victim on 7/5 at Toronto...hit his first big league home run in 7/29 win at Chicago-AL (off Jim Parque).

1997

- Combined at Single-A Brevard County and Double-A Portland to bat .298 (157-for-527) with 23 doubles, 8 triples, 8HR, 51RBI and 51SB in 132 games...ranked eighth among all Double-A players with 35SB in Portland...collected 8HR with Portland after going homerless over the first two-and-a-half seasons of his career (870AB).

1996

- Spent the season with Single-A Kane County, batting .270 with 16 doubles, 3 triples, 35RBI and 30SB (in 48 attempts) in 130 games.

1995

- Made his professional debut with short-season Single-A Elmira, batting .315 with 38R and 19SB in 51 games...tied for ninth in the New York-Penn League in batting average...appeared on the disabled list from 8/22-9/11 with a strained left quad.

Personal

- Full name is Dwight Randolph Winn...graduated from San Ramon Valley (Danville, Calif.) HS, where he excelled in both baseball and basketball...was named *Oakland Tribune*'s "Scholar Athlete of Year" following his senior year...attended Santa Clara (Calif.) University, advancing to the NCAA Tournament in both baseball and basketball...earned All-West Coast Conference honors in 1995 in baseball...shared Broncos' point guard duties with Steve Nash, two-time NBA MVP with the Phoenix Suns...lettered in basketball in 1993 and 1994, while playing on Santa Clara squad that knocked off No. 2 seed Arizona in 1993 NCAA Tournament...won a 2002 Mitsubishi Lancer when he netted half-court shot before fourth quarter of Cleveland Cavaliers-Los Angeles Clippers game 1/18/02 at Staples Center and gave the car to his mom...married to Blessings...has two children, Sadia and Sayscar.
- Is the only active player who appears on the board of directors for the Baseball Assistance Team (B.A.T.), which assists former players and members of the Baseball family...was active in San Francisco community during time with Giants, participating in variety of programs...participated in MLB's Buses for Baseball program by hosting group of kids at the ballpark for meet and greet before games...attended 2007 Strikeouts For Troops Giants Jam...was the Giants' recipient of 2008 MLBPAA Heart and Hustle Award.
- Lent his voice, image and time to WritersCorps, a San Francisco program that encourages young people to express themselves through writing and spoken word...appeared in an anti-drug poster used by Contra Costa Sheriff's Department...taped a PSA for Edgewood Center and met with families...he and his wife are supporters of Camp Erin (created by Jamie Moyer's Foundation)...donated a television to University Preparatory High School, charter school in Oakland, California.

Most Games Played by Yankees in the 2000s by Position
Credit: Stats, LLC

Pitcher – Mariano Rivera (651), Mike Stanton (252), Mike Mussina (249)
Catcher – Jorge Posada (1,217), Jose Molina (175), John Flaherty (131)
First Base – Jason Giambi (501), Tino Martinez (425), Andy Phillips (170)
Second Base – Robinson Cano (728), Alfonso Soriano (467), Miguel Cairo (161)
Third Base – Alex Rodriguez (868), Scott Brosius (254), Robin Ventura (217)
Shortstop – Derek Jeter (1,486), Enrique Wilson (83), Erick Almonte (35)
Outfielder – Bernie Williams (841), Hideki Matsui (632), Melky Cabrera (559)
Designated Hitter – Jason Giambi (373), Hideki Matsui (252), Bernie Williams (120)

RANDY WINN

Winn's Career Batting Record

Year	Team	AVG	G	AB	R	H	2B	3B	HR	RBI	SAC	SF	HBP	BB	SO	SB	CS	E	OBP	SLG
1995	Elimira	.315	51	213	38	67	7	4	0	22	0	2	3	15	31	19	7	5	.365	.385
1996	Kane County	.270	130	514	90	139	16	3	0	35	11	1	8	47	115	30	18	8	.340	.313
1997	Brevard County	.315	36	143	26	45	8	2	0	15	2	1	5	16	28	16	8	0	.400	.399
	Portland	.292	96	384	66	112	15	6	8	36	6	1	7	42	92	35	20	4	.371	.424
1998	Durham-a	.285	29	123	25	35	5	2	1	16	4	0	0	15	24	10	4	2	.362	.382
	TAMPA BAY	.278	109	338	51	94	9	9	1	17	11	0	1	29	69	26	12	4	.337	.367
1999	TAMPA BAY	.267	79	303	44	81	16	4	2	24	1	2	1	17	63	9	9	1	.307	.366
	Durham	.353	46	207	38	73	20	3	3	30	2	0	1	16	27	9	6	4	.402	.522
2000	Durham	.330	79	303	67	100	24	5	7	40	3	1	3	48	53	18	5	7	.425	.512
	TAMPA BAY	.252	51	159	28	40	5	0	1	16	2	1	2	26	25	6	7	1	.362	.302
2001	TAMPA BAY	.273	128	429	54	117	25	6	6	50	5	2	6	38	81	12	10	5	.339	.401
2002	TAMPA BAY	.298	152	607	87	181	39	9	14	75	1	5	6	55	109	27	8	3	.360	.461
2003	SEATTLE-b	.295	157	600	103	177	37	4	11	75	6	5	8	41	108	23	5	3	.346	.425
2004	SEATTLE	.286	157	626	84	179	34	6	14	81	9	7	8	53	98	21	7	4	.346	.427
2005	SEATTLE	.275	102	386	46	106	25	1	6	37	6	3	4	37	53	12	6	0	.342	.391
	SAN FRANCISCO-c	.359	58	231	39	83	22	5	14	26	4	0	1	11	38	7	5	1	.391	.680
2006	SAN FRANCISCO	.262	149	573	82	150	34	5	11	56	3	4	7	48	63	10	8	3	.324	.396
2007	SAN FRANCISCO	.300	155	593	73	178	42	1	14	65	4	5	7	44	85	15	3	2	.353	.445
2008	SAN FRANCISCO	.306	155	598	84	183	38	2	10	64	1	9	0	59	88	25	2	3	.363	.426
2009	SAN FRANCISCO-d	.262	149	538	65	141	33	5	2	51	3	8	1	47	93	16	2	0	.318	.353
Minor League Totals		**.303**	**467**	**1887**	**350**	**571**	**95**	**25**	**19**	**194**	**28**	**6**	**27**	**199**	**370**	**137**	**68**	**30**	**.376**	**.410**
AL Totals		**.283**	**935**	**3448**	**497**	**975**	**190**	**39**	**55**	**375**	**41**	**25**	**36**	**296**	**606**	**136**	**64**	**22**	**.343**	**.408**
NL Totals		**.290**	**666**	**2533**	**343**	**735**	**169**	**18**	**51**	**262**	**15**	**26**	**16**	**209**	**367**	**73**	**20**	**8**	**.345**	**.432**
Major League Totals		**.286**	**1601**	**5981**	**840**	**1710**	**359**	**57**	**106**	**637**	**56**	**51**	**52**	**505**	**973**	**209**	**84**	**30**	**.344**	**.418**

Selected by Florida in third round of 1995 First-Year Player Draft.

a - Selected by Tampa Bay in third round of 1998 Expansion Draft.
b - Acquired by Seattle in exchange for IF Antonio Perez on October 28, 2002. Deal contingent on Lou Piniella signing as manager with Tampa Bay.
c - Acquired by San Francisco in exchange for C Yorvit Torrealba and RHP Jesse Foppert on July 30, 2005.
d - Signed by the Yankees as a free agent on February 8, 2010.

Winn's All-Star Record

Year	Club, Site	AVG	G	AB	R	H	2B	3B	HR	RBI	SH	SF	HP	BB	SO	SB	CS	E	OBP	SLG
2002	TB, Milwaukee	.500	1	2	1	1	1	0	0	0	0	0	0	1	1	1	0	0	.667	1.000
All-Star Game Totals		**.500**	**1**	**2**	**1**	**1**	**1**	**0**	**0**	**0**	**0**	**0**	**0**	**1**	**1**	**1**	**0**	**0**	**.667**	**1.000**

Winn's World Baseball Classic Record

Year	Country, Site	AVG	G	AB	R	H	2B	3B	HR	RBI	SH	SF	HP	BB	SO	SB	CS	E	OBP	SLG
2006	USA, USA	.273	4	11	3	3	0	0	0	0	1	0	1	0	1	0	0	0	.273	.273

Winn's Career Fielding Record

Position	PCT	G	PO	A	E	TC
Outfield	.992	1532	3597	77	30	3704
Third base	1.000	1	1	0	0	1

Winn's Career Home Run Chart

MULTI-HOMER GAMES: 5. **TWO-HOMER GAMES:** 5, last on 8/30/08 at Cincinnati. **GRAND SLAMS:** 6, last on 7/14/07 vs. Los Angeles-NL (off Chin-hui Tsao). **PINCH-HIT HR:** 3, 4/14/01 at Baltimore (off Ryan Kohlmeier); 4/4/02 vs. Detroit (off Matt Miller); 9/14/04 vs. Anaheim (off Brendan Donnelly). **INSIDE-THE-PARK HR:** 3, last on 9/22/03 at Anaheim. **WALK-OFF HR:** 2, 5/11/02 vs. Baltimore (off Jorge Julio); 8/28/04 (Game 2) vs. Kansas City (off Matt Kinney). **LEADOFF HR:** 16, last on 8/30/08 at Cincinnati (off Ramon Ramirez).

Most Seasons with the Yankees
(as a player only)

Player	Seasons
Yogi Berra	18 (1946-63)
Mickey Mantle	18 (1951-68)
Frank Crosetti	17 (1932-48)
Bill Dickey	17 (1928-43, '46)
Lou Gehrig	17 (1923-39)
Whitey Ford	16 (1950, '53-67)
Bernie Williams	16 (1991-2006)
DEREK JETER	**15 (1995-2009)**
JORGE POSADA	**15 (1995-2009)**
MARIANO RIVERA	**15 (1995-2009)**
Babe Ruth	15 (1920-34)

New York Yankees
2009 REVIEW

With his teammates by his side, Yankees closer Mariano Rivera hoists the Commissioner's Trophy in celebration of the Yankees' all-time record 27th World Championship and first since 2000.

2009 Postseason Summary

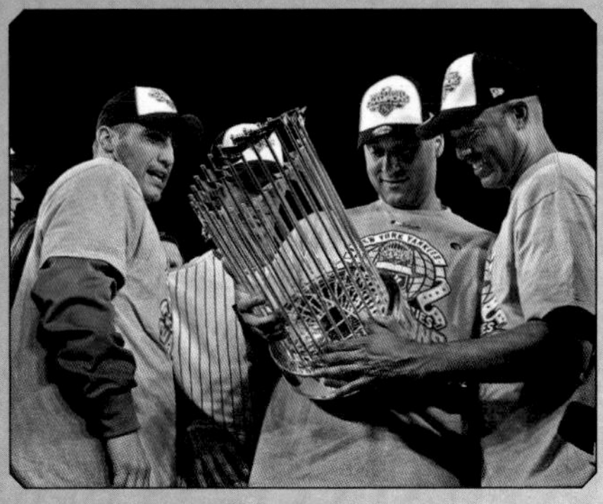

The Yankees won their unprecedented 27th World Championship in 2009, advancing to the postseason for the 14th time in the last 15 seasons. The club returned to the playoffs after missing out in 2008, defeating the Minnesota Twins in the Division Series, the Los Angeles Angels in the Championship Series and the Philadelphia Phillies in the World Series. **Manager Joe Girardi** made his postseason managerial debut and joined Billy Martin and Ralph Houk as the third Yankees skipper to both play for and manage a World Championship Yankees team.

The Yankees employed three starters throughout the 2009 postseason (**LHP CC Sabathia, RHP A.J. Burnett** and **LHP Andy Pettitte**), becoming the first team to win the World Series using only three postseason starters since the 1991 Twins (Morris, Tapani, Erickson). The threesome combined to go 8-2 with a 3.43 ERA (94.1IP, 36ER) in the 2009 playoffs, allowing 3ER or less in 12 of the 15 playoff contests, including 1ER or less in seven starts. Opponents batted just .221 (76-for-344) off the trio, with 81K and 36BB.

The Yankees offense accounted for 20HR in the 2009 playoffs, setting a franchise high (prev. was 16–1996, 2001, '03) and tying for the third-highest postseason total ever by an AL team. **3B Alex Rodriguez** batted .365 (19-for-52) with 15R, 6HR, 18RBI and 12BB in the 2009 postseason, and was selected as the Postseason MVP by the New York chapter of the BBWAA. He set a franchise record for most RBI in a single postseason and tied Bernie Williams (6HR in 1996) for the most HR by a Yankee in a single postseason. Eight of his RBI tied the game or put the Yankees ahead while his three game-tying homers in the seventh inning or later in 2009 accounted for the most such HR ever for a player in their postseason career (credit: *Elias*).

2009 ALDS RECAP

New York Yankees	3
Minnesota Twins	0

The Yankees swept the Minnesota Twins (three-games-to-none) in the 2009 ALDS, marking their third ALDS sweep all time (1998 and '99 vs. Texas) and fourth "best-of-five" series sweep all time (also 1981 ALCS vs. Oakland)...came back to win in all three contests, and out-homered the Twins, 6-0...Yankees starters combined to allow just 3ER in 19.0IP (1.42 ERA), with 21K and only three extra-base hits...Yankees pitchers struck out 34 batters in 29.0 overall innings pitched, marking the first time they had more K's than innings pitched in a postseason series since the 2001 World Series.

GAME 1 – October 7 at Yankee Stadium

	1 2 3	4 5 6	7 8 9	-	R	H	E
MIN	0 0 2	0 0 0	0 0 0	-	2	10	1
NYY	0 0 2	1 3 0	1 0 x	-	7	9	0

WP: CC Sabathia **LP:** Brian Deunsing **SV:** ---

HR: NYY, D. Jeter (inning: 3, 1 out, 1 on) off B. Duensing, H. Matsui (inning: 5, 2 out, 1 on) off F. Liriano

In the first-ever postseason contest in Yankee Stadium, the Yankees defeated Minnesota in Game 1 of the 2009 ALDS, 7-2...scored five of their seven runs with two outs...LHP CC Sabathia (6.2IP, 8H, 2R, 1ER, 8K, 1WP, 1HP) snapped his personal three-game postseason losing streak...SS Derek Jeter (2-for-2) hit a game-tying two-run homer in the third and reached base in all four plate appearances (also 2BB)...tied his postseason career high with 3R (fourth time)...3B Alex Rodriguez (2-for-4) had two two-out RBI singles after entering the game hitless in 40 consecutive postseason at-bats with runners in scoring position...DH Hideki Matsui (1-for-3) hit his seventh career postseason home run...RF Nick Swisher (1-for-4) drove in the go-ahead run with a fourth-inning double.

GAME 2 – October 9 at Yankee Stadium

	1 2 3	4 5 6	7 8 9	10 11	-	R	H	E
MIN	0 0 0	0 0 1	0 2 0	0 0	-	3	12	1
NYY	0 0 0	0 0 1	0 0 2	0 1	-	4	7	0

WP: David Robertson **LP:** Jose Mijares **SV:** ---

HR: NYY, M. Teixeira (inning: 11, 0 out, 0 on) off J. Mijares, A. Rodriguez (inning: 9, 0 out, 1 on) off J. Nathan.

The Yankees "walked off" with a 4-3 win in 11 innings at Yankee Stadium...1B Mark Teixeira (2-for-5) hit his first career "walk-off" HR, including the regular season, with a solo HR down the left-field line in the bottom of the 11th...3B Alex Rodriguez (2-for-4) tied the game in the bottom of the ninth with a two-run HR off Joe Nathan...RHP A.J. Burnett made his first career postseason start, holding the Twins to 1ER on 3H in 6.0IP in the no-decision (5BB, 6K, 1HBP)...RHP David Robertson (1.0IP, 1H) earned the win in his first career postseason appearance, escaping a bases-loaded, no-out jam in the 11th without allowing a run.

GAME 3 – October 11 at the Metrodome

	1 2 3	4 5 6	7 8 9	-	R	H	E
NYY	0 0 0	0 0 0	2 0 2	-	4	7	0
MIN	0 0 0	0 0 1	0 0 0	-	1	7	0

WP: Andy Pettitte **LP:** Carl Pavano **SV:** Mariano Rivera

HR: NYY, A. Rodriguez (inning: 7, 1 out, 0 on) off C. Pavano, J. Posada (inning: 7, 2 out, 0 on) off C. Pavano.

The Yankees completed the series sweep with a 4-1 win in the final game ever at the Metrodome...LHP Andy Pettitte limited the Twins to 3H and 1ER in 6.1IP (1BB, 7K) to earn the win...was his 15th career postseason win (tying Tom Glavine for most all time) and his fourth career postseason series-clinching win, tying for most all time...RHP Mariano Rivera (1.1IP, 1H, 2K) earned his first save of the 2009 postseason and the 35th of his career...3B Alex Rodriguez (1-for-3) hit a two-run, opposite-field solo homer in the seventh inning to put the Yankees on the board...two batters later C Jorge Posada (2-for-4) put the Yankees ahead with a solo HR.

2009 ALCS RECAP

New York Yankees 4
Los Angeles Angels 2

The Yankees defeated the Angels 4-games-to-2 for their 11th ALCS victory and 40th American League title...hit 8HR and drew 38BB over the six games, while holding the Majors' second-highest scoring team to an average of 3.2R/G...LHP CC Sabathia earned ALCS MVP honors after going 2-0 with a 1.13 ERA (16.0IP, 2ER) in two starts...3B Alex Rodriguez batted a team-high .429 (9-for-21) with 6R, 3HR, 6RBI and 8BB...RHP Mariano Rivera collected two saves, including a 2.0-inning save in the series clincher.

GAME 1 – October 16 at Yankee Stadium

	123	456	789	- R	H	E
LAA	000	100	000	- 1	4	3
NYY	200	011	00x	- 4	10	0

WP: CC Sabathia **LP:** John Lackey **SV:** Mariano Rivera
HR: None

The Yankees won Game 1 of the ALCS vs. the Angels, 4-1...three Angels errors led to three Yankees runs...LHP CC Sabathia improved to 2-0 in the 2009 postseason, holding Los Angeles to 1ER on 4H in 8.0IP (1BB, 7K)...marked his first career LCS victory and longest career postseason outing...LF Johnny Damon (2-for-5) doubled and scored twice...SS Derek Jeter (2-for-5) led off the first inning with a hit and scored the game's first run...recorded his 45th career multi-hit postseason game, extending his all-time record...RHP Mariano Rivera (1.0IP, 1BB) recorded his 39th postseason save.

GAME 2 – October 17 at Yankee Stadium

	123	456	789	10	11	12	13	- R	H	E
LAA	000	020	000	0	1	0	0	- 3	8	2
NYY	011	000	000	0	1	0	1	- 4	13	3

WP: David Robertson **LP:** Ervin Santana **SV:** ---
HR: NYY, D. Jeter (inning: 3, 1 out, 0 on) off J. Saunders, A. Rodriguez (inning: 11, 0 out, 0 on) off B. Fuentes.

The Yankees "walked off" with a 4-3 win in the 13th inning in Game 2 at Yankee Stadium...marked the Yankees' longest postseason game (in innings) since Game 5 of the 2004 ALCS (14 inn.)...set an ALCS record with 21 players used...PH Jerry Hairston, Jr. (1-for-1) led off the 13th inning with a single and scored the game-winning run on Maicer Izturis' throwing error two batters later...3B Alex Rodriguez (1-for-6) homered to tie the game in the 11th...SS Derek Jeter (1-for-5) hit his 19th career postseason HR, moving him into sole possession of third place on Baseball's all-time list...Manager Joe Girardi became just the second manager to win his first five career postseason games, joining Colorado's Clint Hurdle in 2007 (credit: *Elias*).

GAME 3 – October 19 at Angel Stadium

	123	456	789	10	11	- R	H	E
NYY	100	110	010	0	0	- 4	8	0
LAA	000	012	100	0	1	- 5	13	0

WP: Ervin Santana **LP:** Alfredo Aceves **SV:** ---
HR: NYY, D. Jeter (inning: 1, 0 out, 0 on) off J. Weaver, J. Damon (inning: 5, 1 out, 0 on) off J. Weaver, A. Rodriguez (inning: 4, 0 out, 0 on) off J. Weaver, J. Posada (inning: 8, 1 out, 0 on) off K. Jepsen; LAA, V. Guerrero (inning: 6, 2 out, 1 on) off A. Pettitte, LAA, H. Kendrick (inning: 5, 1 out, 0 on) off A. Pettitte.

The Yankees fell in 11 innings at Angel Stadium, 5-4, for their first playoff loss in 2009...all 4R came via four solo home runs (Jeter, Rodriguez, Damon, Posada)...marked the Yankees' first ALCS loss when holding a three-run lead (had been 30-0)...LHP Andy Pettitte did not draw a decision, allowing 3ER on 7H in 6.1IP (1BB, 2K, 2HR)...RHP Alfredo Aceves recorded the loss, allowing the game-winning hit to Jeff Mathis...SS Derek Jeter (1-for-6) hit his third career postseason leadoff HR, homering in consecutive postseason games for the first time since the 2000 World Series...C Jorge Posada (2-for-4) hit a solo HR in the eighth to tie the game.

CC Sabathia became the eighth Yankee to earn the ALCS MVP award.

GAME 4 – October 20 at Angel Stadium

	123	456	789	- R	H	E
NYY	000	320	023	- 10	13	0
LAA	000	010	000	- 1	5	1

WP: CC Sabathia **LP:** Scott Kazmir **SV:** ---
HR: NYY, J. Damon (inning: 8, 2 out, 1 on) off M. Palmer, A. Rodriguez (inning: 5, 0 out, 1 on) off J. Bulger; LAA, K. Morales (inning: 5, 1 out, 0 on) off C. Sabathia.

The Yankees took a 3-games-to-1 series lead with a 10-1 win at Angel Stadium...marked the Yankees' most runs and largest margin of victory in a postseason contest since a 19-8 win in Game 3 of the 2004 ALCS at Boston...LHP CC Sabathia improved to 3-0 and became the seventh Yankee to record three wins in a single postseason, holding the Angels to 1ER on 5H in 8.0IP (2BB, 5K, 1HR) on three-days' rest...CF Melky Cabrera (3-for-4) drove in a playoff career-high four runs...3B Alex Rodriguez (3-for-4) hit his fifth homer of the 2009 playoffs and scored three runs.

GAME 5 – October 22 at Angel Stadium

	123	456	789	- R	H	E
NYY	000	000	600	- 6	9	0
LAA	400	000	30x	- 7	12	0

WP: Kevin Jepsen **LP:** Phil Hughes **SV:** Brian Fuentes
HR: None

The Yankees fell, 7-6, at Angel Stadium...trailed 4-0 after the first inning...scored all 6R in the seventh (all with two outs) to take the lead, before allowing 3R in the bottom of the frame...marked their most runs scored in an inning in the postseason since Game 4 of the 2003 ALDS at Minnesota (6R in fourth)...1B Mark Teixeira (2-for-5) had a bases-clearing double...3B Alex Rodriguez (1-for-3) extended his postseason hitting streak to 10G...SS Derek Jeter (1-for-4) extended his postseason hitting streak to nine games, leading off a game with a hit for the fifth time in eight playoff games in 2009.

GAME 6 – October 25 at Yankee Stadium

	123	456	789	- R	H	E
LAA	001	000	010	- 2	9	2
NYY	000	300	02x	- 5	9	0

WP: Andy Pettitte **LP:** Joe Saunders **SV:** Mariano Rivera
HR: None

The Yankees wrapped up the series victory with a 5-2 win at Yankee Stadium and clinched their 40th American League pennant...the game was postponed one day due to inclement weather...the Yankees drew 9BB, marking their most since Game 4 of the 2001 ALCS vs. Seattle...LHP Andy Pettitte recorded his record-setting 16th postseason win, limiting the Angels to 1ER on 7H in 6.1IP (1BB, 6K)...also notched his record fifth postseason series-clinching win...RHP Mariano Rivera collected his 13th career 2.0-inning save in postseason play...allowed his first postseason run at home since Game 2 of the 2000 World Series...3B Alex Rodriguez (2-for-2) extended his postseason hitting streak to 11G...also walked three times.

2009 WORLD SERIES RECAP

New York Yankees 4
Philadelphia Phillies 2

The Yankees won their 27th World Championship, defeating the Phillies 4-games-to-2, for their second title of the decade (also 2000 vs. the Mets)...improved to 6-2 all time in the World Series against the defending champion...DH Hideki Matsui was named World Series MVP, marking the first time a Japanese-born player earned the honor...was the unanimous winner after batting .615 (8-for-13) with 1 double, 3HR and 8RBI.

GAME 1 – October 28 at Yankee Stadium

The Yankees fell in Game 1 of the World Series, 6-1, vs. the Phillies...marked their first home loss, first loss to a LH starter, largest margin of defeat and fewest runs scored in the 2009 postseason...LHP CC Sabathia suffered his first postseason loss of 2009, allowing 2ER on 4H in 7.0IP (3BB, 6K)...both runs came via Chase Utley solo HRs...was opposed by former Indians teammate LHP Cliff Lee who hurled a complete game...marked just the second time that two former Cy Young Award winners faced off in the first game of the World Series (also 1995 - Greg Maddux vs. Orel Hershiser)...also marked the first time former teammates opposed each other in Game 1 of the WS since 2005 when two former Yankees squared off (Houston's Roger Clemens vs. the White Sox's Jose Contreras)...SS Derek Jeter (3-for-4) recorded at least 3H in a World Series game for the fourth time in his career, breaking a tie with several others for most such games all time...also scored the Yankees' only run of the night in the ninth.

	123	456	789	-	R	H	E
PHI	0 0 1	0 0 1	0 2 2	-	6	9	1
NYY	0 0 0	0 0 0	0 0 1	-	1	6	0

Philadelphia	AB	R	H	RBI	BB	SO
Rollins, SS	4	2	1	0	1	0
Victorino, CF	4	1	1	1	1	0
Utley, 2B	4	2	2	2	1	1
Howard, 1B	5	0	2	1	0	2
Werth, RF	2	0	1	0	2	1
Ibanez, DH	4	0	1	2	0	2
Francisco, B, LF	3	0	0	0	1	0
Feliz, 3B	4	0	0	0	0	1
Ruiz, C	4	1	1	0	0	0
Totals	**34**	**6**	**9**	**6**	**6**	**7**

BATTING: 2B: Howard 2, Ruiz; HR: Utley 2 (2, 3rd inning off Sabathia, 0 on, 2 out; 6th inning off Sabathia, 0 on, 1 out); GIDP: Feliz.
BASERUNNING: SB: Rollins (1).
FIELDING: E: Rollins (1, throw); DP: (Rollins-Howard).

NY Yankees	AB	R	H	RBI	BB	SO
Jeter, SS	4	1	3	0	0	1
Damon, LF	4	0	1	0	0	0
Teixeira, 1B	4	0	0	0	0	2
Rodriguez, A, 3B	4	0	0	0	0	3
Posada, C	4	0	1	0	0	2
Matsui, H, DH	3	0	1	0	0	1
Cano, 2B	3	0	0	0	0	0
Swisher, RF	3	0	0	0	0	1
Cabrera, Me, CF	3	0	0	0	0	0
Sabathia, P	0	0	0	0	0	0
Totals	**32**	**1**	**6**	**0**	**0**	**10**

BATTING: 2B: Jeter.
FIELDING: Outfield assists: Swisher (Victorino at home); DP: (Rodriguez, A-Cano-Teixeira).

Philadelphia	IP	H	R	ER	BB	SO	HR	ERA
Lee, Cl (W, 1-0)	9.0	6	1	0	0	10	0	0.00
Totals	**9.0**	**6**	**1**	**0**	**0**	**10**	**0**	**0.00**

NY Yankees	IP	H	R	ER	BB	SO	HR	ERA
Sabathia (L, 0-1)	7.0	4	2	2	3	6	2	2.57
Hughes, P	0.0	0	2	2	2	0	0	--
Marte, D	0.2	0	0	0	0	1	0	0.00
Robertson, D	0.1	1	0	0	1	0	0	0.00
Bruney	0.1	3	2	2	0	0	0	54.00
Coke	0.2	1	0	0	0	0	0	0.00
Totals	**9.0**	**9**	**6**	**6**	**6**	**7**	**2**	**6.00**

Hughes, P pitched to 2 batters in the 8th.

GAME 2 – October 29 at Yankee Stadium

The Yankees recorded their first 2009 World Series win with a 3-1 victory vs. Philadelphia...snapped a four-game World Series losing streak...earned their sixth comeback win of the 2009 playoffs...RHP A.J. Burnett earned the win in his first career World Series start, limiting the Phillies to 1ER on 4H in 7.0IP with 2BB and 9K...RHP Mariano Rivera tossed 2.0 scoreless innings for his 10th World Series save (2H, 1BB, 2K)...1B Mark Teixeira (1-for-3) hit his first career World Series homer, tying the game, 1-1, in the fourth...DH Hideki Matsui (2-for-3) provided the go-ahead run in the sixth with his second career World Series home run...C Jose Molina (0-for-1) made his first career World Series start and picked off Jayson Werth in the fourth, marking the first pickoff by a Yankees catcher in the postseason since Yogi Berra in 1950 vs. the Phillies (credit: researcher Bill Chuck).

	1 2 3	4 5 6	7 8 9	-	R	H	E
PHI	0 1 0	0 0 0	0 0 0	-	1	6	0
NYY	0 0 0	1 0 1	1 0 x	-	3	8	0

Philadelphia	AB	R	H	RBI	BB	SO
Rollins, SS	2	0	0	0	2	1
Victorino, CF	4	0	1	0	0	1
Utley, 2B	3	0	0	0	1	0
Howard, 1B	4	0	0	0	0	4
Werth, RF	4	0	1	0	0	0
Ibanez, LF	4	1	2	0	0	2
Stairs, DH	4	0	1	1	0	2
Feliz, 3B	3	0	0	0	0	1
Ruiz, C	3	0	1	0	0	0
Totals	**31**	**1**	**6**	**1**	**3**	**11**

BATTING: 2B: Ibanez 2, Ruiz; GIDP: Utley.
BASERUNNING: PO: Werth (1st base by Molina, J).
FIELDING: DP: (Howard-Rollins).

NY Yankees	AB	R	H	RBI	BB	SO
Jeter, SS	4	0	1	0	0	3
Damon, LF	4	0	0	0	0	1
Teixeira, 1B	3	1	1	1	0	1
Rodriguez, A, 3B	4	0	0	0	0	3
Matsui, H, DH	3	1	2	1	1	1
Cano, 2B	4	0	1	0	0	0
Hairston, J, RF	3	0	1	0	0	1
1-Gardner, PR-CF	1	1	0	0	0	1
Cabrera, Me, CF-RF	3	0	1	0	0	1
Molina, J, C	1	0	0	0	1	0
a-Posada, PH-C	1	0	1	1	0	0
Totals	**31**	**3**	**8**	**3**	**2**	**12**

a-Singled for Molina, J in the 7th.
1-Ran for Hairston, J in the 7th.

BATTING: 2B: Jeter; HR: Teixeira (1, 4th inning off Martinez, P, 0 on, 0 out), Matsui, H (1, 6th inning off Martinez, P, 0 on, 2 out).
FIELDING: DP: (Cano-Jeter-Teixeira); Pickoffs: Molina, J (Werth at 1st base).

Philadelphia	IP	H	R	ER	BB	SO	HR	ERA
Martinez, P (L, 0-1)	6.0	6	3	3	2	8	2	4.50
Park	0.1	1	0	0	0	1	0	0.00
Eyre, S	0.2	0	0	0	0	0	0	0.00
Madson	1.0	1	0	0	0	3	0	0.00
Totals	**8.0**	**8**	**3**	**3**	**2**	**12**	**2**	**1.59**

NY Yankees	IP	H	R	ER	BB	SO	HR	ERA
Burnett, A (W, 1-0)	7.0	4	1	1	2	9	0	1.29
Rivera, Ma (S, 1)	2.0	2	0	0	1	2	0	0.00
Totals	**9.0**	**6**	**1**	**1**	**3**	**11**	**0**	**3.50**

Martinez, P pitched to 2 batters in the 7th.

GAME 3 – October 31 at Citizens Bank Park

The Yankees took the series lead with an 8-5 win at Citizens Bank Park...came back from a three-run deficit, marking their largest WS comeback since Game 3 of the 1999 Series vs. Atlanta (4R deficit overcome in 6-5 win)...scored their most runs in a WS game since a 9-3 win vs. San Diego in Game 2 of the 1998 Series...starter LHP Andy Pettitte tossed 6.0 innings (5H, 4ER, 3BB, 7K, 2HR) and earned the win...also drove in a run with a single, marking the first World Series RBI by a Yankees pitcher since Jim Bouton on 10/14/64 in a Game 6 win at St. Louis...was his 11th World Series start (second-most all time behind Whitey Ford-22)...3B Alex Rodriguez (1-for-2) hit his sixth HR of the 2009 postseason, which was the first playoff HR reviewed by video replay...PH Hideki Matsui (1-for-1) became the eighth Yankee to hit a pinch-hit HR in a World Series game and first since Jason Giambi in 2003.

	1 2 3	4 5 6	7 8 9	-	R	H	E
NYY	0 0 0	2 3 1	1 1 0	-	8	8	1
PHI	0 3 0	0 0 1	0 0 1	-	5	6	0

NY Yankees	AB	R	H	RBI	BB	SO
Jeter, SS	5	1	1	0	0	1
Damon, LF	4	1	1	2	1	0
Teixeira, 1B	3	1	0	0	2	2
Rodriguez, A, 3B	2	1	1	2	1	0
Posada, C	5	0	1	1	0	0
Cano, 2B	4	0	0	0	0	2
Swisher, RF	4	2	2	1	0	0
Gardner, CF	0	0	0	0	0	0
Cabrera, Me, CF-RF	4	0	0	0	0	2
Pettitte, P	3	1	1	1	0	1
Chamberlain, P	0	0	0	0	0	0
a-Matsui, H, PH	1	1	1	1	0	0
Marte, D, P	0	0	0	0	0	0
Hughes, P, P	0	0	0	0	0	0
Rivera, Ma, P	0	0	0	0	0	0
Totals	**35**	**8**	**8**	**8**	**4**	**8**

a-Homered for Chamberlain in the 8th.

BATTING: 2B: Swisher, Damon; HR: Rodriguez, A (1, 4th inning off Hamels, 1 on, 1 out), Swisher (1, 6th inning off Happ, 0 on, 1 out), Matsui, H (2, 8th inning off Myers, 0 on, 2 out).
BASERUNNING: SB: Damon (1).
FIELDING: E: Rodriguez, A (1, throw).

Philadelphia	AB	R	H	RBI	BB	SO
Rollins, SS	4	0	1	1	1	0
Victorino, CF	3	0	0	1	0	0
Utley, 2B	4	0	0	0	0	2
Howard, 1B	4	0	0	0	0	3
Werth, RF	4	2	2	2	0	1
Ibanez, LF	4	0	0	0	0	2
Feliz, 3B	4	1	1	0	0	1
Ruiz, C	2	2	1	1	2	0
Hamels, P	1	0	1	0	0	0
Happ, P	0	0	0	0	0	0
a-Bruntlett, PH	1	0	0	0	0	0
Durbin, C, P	0	0	0	0	0	0
Myers, P	0	0	0	0	0	0
Madson, P	0	0	0	0	0	0
b-Stairs, PH	1	0	0	0	0	0
Totals	**32**	**5**	**6**	**5**	**3**	**9**

a-Flied out for Happ in the 6th. b-Grounded out for Madson in the 9th.

BATTING: 2B: Feliz; HR: Werth 2 (2, 2nd inning off Pettitte, 0 on, 0 out; 6th inning off Pettitte, 0 on, 0 out), Ruiz (1, 9th inning off Hughes, P, 0 on, 1 out); S: Hamels; SF: Victorino.
BASERUNNING: SB: Rollins (2).

NY Yankees	IP	H	R	ER	BB	SO	HR	ERA
Pettitte (W, 1-0)	6.0	5	4	4	3	7	2	6.00
Chamberlain (H, 1)	1.0	0	0	0	0	0	0	0.00
Marte, D	1.0	0	0	0	0	2	0	0.00
Hughes, P	0.1	1	1	1	0	0	1	81.00
Rivera, Ma	0.2	0	0	0	0	0	0	0.00
Totals	**9.0**	**6**	**5**	**5**	**3**	**9**	**3**	**4.00**

Philadelphia	IP	H	R	ER	BB	SO	HR	ERA
Hamels (L, 0-1)	4.1	5	5	5	2	3	1	10.38
Happ	1.2	1	1	1	0	1	1	5.40
Durbin, C	1.0	1	1	1	1	2	0	9.00
Myers	1.0	1	1	1	0	2	1	9.00
Madson	1.0	0	0	0	1	0	0	0.00
Totals	**9.0**	**8**	**8**	**8**	**4**	**8**	**3**	**3.81**

GAME 4 – November 1 at Citizens Bank Park

The Yankees won their third straight game, defeating the Phillies, 7-4...posted three runs in the ninth with two outs...LF Johnny Damon (3-for-5) scored 2R, including the game-winner...stole two bases on the same pitch in the ninth, taking second base then advancing to third on the throw when no one covered the base due to an infield shift...3B Alex Rodriguez (1-for-4) doubled home Damon for the go-ahead run...C Jorge Posada (1-for-3) drove in a postseason career-high three runs...LHP CC Sabathia limited the Phillies to 3ER on 7H in 6.2IP (3BB, 6K, 1HR), working on three-days' rest in the no-decision...RHP Mariano Rivera tossed a scoreless ninth in his 23rd career World Series appearance, surpassing Whitey Ford for the most all time.

	1 2 3	4 5 6	7 8 9	-	R	H	E
NYY	2 0 0	0 2 0	0 0 3	-	7	9	1
PHI	1 0 0	1 0 0	1 1 0	-	4	8	1

NY Yankees	AB	R	H	RBI	BB	SO
Jeter, SS	4	1	2	1	1	1
Damon, LF	5	2	3	1	0	1
Teixeira, 1B	4	1	0	1	0	1
Rodriguez, A, 3B	4	1	1	1	0	1
Posada, C	3	0	1	3	1	2
Cano, 2B	4	0	1	0	0	1
Swisher, RF	2	1	0	0	2	2
Cabrera, Me, CF	3	1	1	0	0	0
Gardner, CF	1	0	0	0	0	0
Sabathia, P	3	0	0	0	0	2
Marte, D, P	0	0	0	0	0	0
Chamberlain, P	0	0	0	0	0	0
a-Matsui, H, PH	1	0	0	0	0	0
Rivera, Ma, P	0	0	0	0	0	0
Totals	**34**	**7**	**9**	**7**	**4**	**11**

a-Popped out for Chamberlain in the 9th.

BATTING: 2B: Damon, Rodriguez, A; SF: Posada.
BASERUNNING: SB: Damon 2 (3).
FIELDING: E: Posada (1, missed catch).

Philadelphia	AB	R	H	RBI	BB	SO
Rollins, SS	5	0	1	0	0	0
Victorino, CF	4	1	1	0	1	0
Utley, 2B	4	1	2	2	0	0
Howard, 1B	4	1	1	0	0	1
Werth, RF	3	0	0	0	1	2
Ibanez, LF	4	0	0	0	0	3
Feliz, 3B	4	1	3	2	0	0
Ruiz, C	3	0	0	0	1	1
Blanton, P	2	0	0	0	0	2
a-Francisco, B, PH	1	0	0	0	0	0
Park, P	0	0	0	0	0	0
Madson, P	0	0	0	0	0	0
Lidge, P	0	0	0	0	0	0
b-Stairs, PH	1	0	0	0	0	0
Totals	**35**	**4**	**8**	**4**	**3**	**9**

a-Flied out for Blanton in the 6th. b-Grounded out for Lidge in the 9th.

BATTING: 2B: Victorino, Utley; HR: Utley (3, 7th inning off Sabathia, 0 on, 2 out), Feliz (1, 8th inning off Chamberlain, 0 on, 2 out).
BASERUNNING: SB: Howard (1).
FIELDING: E: Ibanez (1, throw); Outfield assists: Ibanez.

NY Yankees	IP	H	R	ER	BB	SO	HR	ERA
Sabathia	6.2	7	3	3	3	6	1	3.29
Marte, D (H, 1)	0.1	0	0	0	0	0	0	0.00
Chamberlain (BS, 1) (W, 1-0)	1.0	1	1	1	0	3	1	4.50
Rivera, Ma (S, 2)	1.0	0	0	0	0	0	0	0.00
Totals	**9.0**	**8**	**4**	**4**	**3**	**9**	**2**	**4.00**

Philadelphia	IP	H	R	ER	BB	SO	HR	ERA
Blanton	6.0	5	4	4	2	7	0	6.00
Park	1.0	0	0	0	1	1	0	0.00
Madson	1.0	1	0	0	1	2	0	0.00
Lidge (L, 0-1)	1.0	3	3	3	0	1	0	27.00
Totals	**9.0**	**9**	**7**	**7**	**4**	**11**	**0**	**4.63**

GAME 5 – November 2 at Citizens Bank Park
The Yankees' comeback bid fell short in an 8-6 loss at Citizens Bank Park…trailed 6-1 after three innings and 8-2 after the seventh…RHP A.J. Burnett exited after 2.0IP, allowing 6ER on 4H with 4BB, 2K and 1HBP…marked the shortest non-injury start and most runs allowed by a Yankees pitcher in the Series since LHP Andy Pettitte in Game 6 in 2001 vs. Arizona (2.0IP, 6ER)…3B Alex Rodriguez (2-for-4) doubled twice and drove in three runs, matching his single-game career postseason high (fourth time)…LF Johnny Damon (3-for-4) recorded his second straight 3H game.

	1 2 3	4 5 6	7 8 9	-	R	H	E
NYY	1 0 0	0 1 0	0 3 1	-	6	10	0
PHI	3 0 3	0 0 0	2 0 x	-	8	9	0

NY Yankees	AB	R	H	RBI	BB	SO
Jeter, SS	5	0	1	0	0	0
Damon, LF	4	2	3	1	1	0
Teixeira, 1B	5	1	1	0	0	1
Rodriguez, A, 3B	4	1	2	3	0	0
Swisher, RF	3	0	0	0	1	0
Cano, 2B	3	0	1	1	0	0
Gardner, CF	4	0	0	0	0	1
Molina, J, C	1	0	0	0	0	0
a-Posada, PH-C	3	1	1	0	0	1
Burnett, A, P	1	0	0	0	0	1
Robertson, D, P	0	0	0	0	0	0
b-Hinske, PH	0	1	0	0	1	0
Aceves, A, P	0	0	0	0	0	0
c-Hairston, J, PH	1	0	0	0	0	0
Coke, P	0	0	0	0	0	0
Hughes, P, P	0	0	0	0	0	0
d-Matsui, H, PH	1	0	1	0	0	0
Totals	**35**	**6**	**10**	**5**	**3**	**4**

a-Grounded out for Molina, J in the 5th. b-Walked for Robertson, D in the 5th. c-Flied out for Aceves, A in the 7th. d-Singled for Hughes, P in the 9th.

BATTING: 2B: Rodriguez, A 2, Teixeira, Posada; SF: Cano; GIDP: Jeter.
FIELDING: DP: (Cano-Jeter-Teixeira).

Philadelphia	AB	R	H	RBI	BB	SO
Rollins, SS	4	1	2	0	1	1
Victorino, CF	3	1	0	0	0	0
Francisco, B, CF	0	0	0	0	0	0
Utley, 2B	3	3	2	4	1	0
Howard, 1B	2	1	0	0	2	2
Werth, RF	4	1	1	1	0	1
Ibanez, LF	4	1	2	2	0	0
Feliz, 3B	4	0	0	0	0	1
Ruiz, C	4	0	1	1	0	1
Lee, Cl, P	3	0	1	0	0	1
Park, P	0	0	0	0	0	0
a-Stairs, PH	1	0	0	0	0	0
Madson, P	0	0	0	0	0	0
Totals	**32**	**8**	**9**	**8**	**4**	**7**

a-Grounded into a double play for Park in the 8th.

BATTING: HR: Utley 2 (5, 1st inning off Burnett, A, 2 on, 0 out; 7th inning off Coke, 0 on, 0 out), Ibanez (1, 7th inning off Coke, 0 on, 2 out).
BASERUNNING: SB: Utley (1).
FIELDING: DP: (Rollins-Utley-Howard).

NY Yankees	IP	H	R	ER	BB	SO	HR	ERA
Burnett, A (L, 1-1)	2.0	4	6	6	4	2	1	7.00
Robertson, D	2.0	1	0	0	0	2	0	0.00
Aceves, A	2.0	1	0	0	0	1	0	0.00
Coke	0.2	2	2	2	0	1	2	13.50
Hughes, P	1.1	1	0	0	0	1	0	16.20
Totals	**8.0**	**9**	**8**	**8**	**4**	**7**	**3**	**4.91**

Philadelphia	IP	H	R	ER	BB	SO	HR	ERA
Lee, Cl (W, 2-0)	7.0	7	5	5	3	3	0	2.81
Park	1.0	0	0	0	0	0	0	0.00
Madson (S, 1)	1.0	3	1	1	0	1	0	2.25
Totals	**9.0**	**10**	**6**	**6**	**3**	**4**	**0**	**4.91**

Burnett, A pitched to 4 batters in the 3rd.
Lee, Cl pitched to 3 batters in the 8th.

GAME 6 –November 4 at Yankee Stadium
The Yankees clinched their 27th World Championship with a 7-3 win…DH Hideki Matsui (3-for-4) doubled, homered and drove in six of the Yankees' seven runs…tied the Yankees' Bobby Richardson (Game 2, 1960 vs. Pittsburgh) for the most RBI in a World Series game all time…Matsui's two-run homer in the second marked the first runs of the game and was his team-leading third HR of the World Series…LHP Andy Pettitte earned the Series-clinching win, limiting the Phillies to 3ER on 4H in 5.2IP (5BB, 3K, 1HR)…SS Derek Jeter (3-for-5) collected his all-time best fifth World Series game of three-or-more hits…RHP Mariano Rivera closed out the game with 1.2 scoreless innings (1H, 1BB, 1K), throwing 41 pitches – his most ever in a WS game.

	1 2 3	4 5 6	7 8 9	-	R	H	E
PHI	0 0 1	0 0 2	0 0 0	-	3	6	0
NYY	0 2 2	0 3 0	0 0 x	-	7	8	0

Philadelphia	AB	R	H	RBI	BB	SO
Rollins, SS	4	0	0	1	0	0
Victorino, CF	4	0	1	0	1	0
Utley, 2B	3	1	0	0	1	2
Howard, 1B	4	1	1	2	0	1
Werth, RF	2	0	0	0	2	2
Ibanez, DH	3	0	2	0	1	0
Feliz, 3B	4	0	0	0	0	0
Francisco, B, LF	3	0	0	0	0	2
a-Stairs, PH	1	0	0	0	0	0
Ruiz, C	2	1	2	0	2	0
Totals	**30**	**3**	**6**	**3**	**7**	**7**

a-Lined out for Francisco, B in the 9th.

BATTING: 2B: Ibanez 2; 3B: Ruiz; HR: Howard (1, 6th inning off Pettitte, 1 on, 1 out); SF: Rollins; GIDP: Utley; Rollins.
BASERUNNING: SB: Rollins (3).

NY Yankees	AB	R	H	RBI	BB	SO
Jeter, SS	5	2	3	0	0	0
Damon, LF	1	1	0	0	1	1
Hairston, J, LF	2	0	0	0	0	0
Teixeira, 1B	3	1	1	1	0	1
Rodriguez, A, 3B	2	2	1	0	2	1
Matsui, H, DH	4	1	3	6	0	1
Posada, C	3	0	0	0	1	2
Cano, 2B	4	0	0	0	0	2
Swisher, RF	3	0	0	0	1	1
Gardner, CF	4	0	0	0	0	2
Totals	**31**	**7**	**8**	**7**	**5**	**11**

BATTING: 2B: Jeter, Matsui, H; HR: Matsui, H (3, 2nd inning off Martinez, P, 1 on, 0 out); S: Hairston, J.
BASERUNNING: SB: Rodriguez, A (1).
FIELDING: PB: Posada (1); DP: 2 (Cano-Jeter-Teixeira, Rodriguez, A-Cano-Teixeira).

Philadelphia	IP	H	R	ER	BB	SO	HR	ERA
Martinez, P (L, 0-2)	4.0	3	4	4	2	5	1	6.30
Durbin, C	0.1	2	3	3	1	0	0	27.00
Happ	1.0	1	0	0	1	3	0	3.38
Park	1.0	1	0	0	0	1	0	0.00
Eyre, S	1.1	0	0	0	1	2	0	0.00
Madson	0.1	1	0	0	0	0	0	2.08
Totals	**8.0**	**8**	**7**	**7**	**5**	**11**	**1**	**5.37**

NY Yankees	IP	H	R	ER	BB	SO	HR	ERA
Pettitte (W, 2-0)	5.2	4	3	3	5	3	1	5.40
Chamberlain	1.0	1	0	0	1	1	0	3.00
Marte, D (H, 2)	0.2	0	0	0	0	2	0	0.00
Rivera, Ma	1.2	1	0	0	1	1	0	0.00
Totals	**9.0**	**6**	**3**	**3**	**7**	**7**	**1**	**4.58**

In a Clinch

LHP Andy Pettitte, in 2009, became the first pitcher ever to start and earn the win in the series-clinching game in all three rounds of a single postseason (ALDS, ALCS, WS)…his six career postseason series-clinching wins are more than any player all time.

2009 Cumulative Postseason Stats

PLAYER	AVG	G	AB	R	H	TB	2B	3B	HR	RBI	SH	SF	HP	BB	IBB	SO	SB	CS	DP	E	SLG	OBP
Cabrera	.271	13	48	5	13	15	2	0	0	4	2	0	0	3	0	14	0	0	0	0	.313	.314
RIGHT	.300		20		6	6	0	0	0	2	2	0	0	0	0	5			0		.300	.300
LEFT	.250		28		7	9	2	0	0	2	0	0	0	3	0	9			0		.321	.323
Cano	.193	15	57	5	11	16	1	2	0	6	0	1	2	4	1	9	0	0	2	2	.281	.266
Cervelli	.000	2	1	0	0	0	0	0	0	0	0	0	0	0	0	1	0	0	0	0	.000	.000
Damon	.281	15	64	10	18	27	3	0	2	9	0	0	0	5	0	9	3	0	0	0	.422	.333
Gardner	.154	14	13	3	2	2	0	0	0	0	1	0	0	0	0	4	1	2	0	0	.154	.154
Guzman	.000	2	1	0	0	0	0	0	0	0	0	0	0	0	0	1	0	0	0	0	.000	.000
RIGHT	.000		1		0	0	0	0	0	0	0	0	0	0	0	1			0		.000	.000
LEFT	.000		0		0	0	0	0	0	0	0	0	0	0	0	0			0		.000	.000
Hairston	.250	6	8	1	2	2	0	0	0	0	1	0	0	0	0	2	0	0	0	0	.250	.250
Hinske	.000	1	0	1	0	0	0	0	0	0	0	0	0	1	0	0	0	0	0	0	.000	1.000
Jeter	.344	15	64	14	22	36	5	0	3	6	0	0	0	10	2	11	0	1	2	1	.563	.432
Matsui	.349	15	43	5	15	29	2	0	4	13	0	0	0	9	0	10	0	0	1	0	.674	.462
Molina	.167	5	6	0	1	1	0	0	0	0	0	0	0	1	0	1	0	0	0	0	.167	.286
Posada	.260	15	50	5	13	21	2	0	2	8	0	1	0	7	1	14	1	0	2	1	.420	.345
RIGHT	.158		19		3	4	1	0	0	0	0	0	0	2	1	6			1		.211	.238
LEFT	.323		31		10	17	1	0	2	8	0	1	0	5	0	8			1		.548	.405
Rodriguez	.365	15	52	15	19	42	5	0	6	18	0	1	3	12	3	13	2	0	0	1	.808	.500
Swisher	.128	14	47	5	6	11	2	0	1	2	1	0	1	7	0	15	0	0	0	0	.234	.255
RIGHT	.227		22		5	10	2	0	1	2	1	0	0	4	0	3			0		.455	.346
LEFT	.040		25		1	1	0	0	0	0	0	0	1	3	0	12			0		.040	.172
Teixeira	.180	15	61	10	11	19	2	0	2	8	0	1	3	6	0	17	0	0	2	0	.311	.282
RIGHT	.214		28		6	11	2	0	1	5	0	1	0	4	0	7			2		.393	.303
LEFT	.152		33		5	8	0	0	1	3	0	0	3	2	0	10			0		.242	.263
Burnett	.000	5	1	0	0	0	0	0	0	0	0	0	0	0	0	1	0	0	0	0	.000	.000
Pettitte	.333	5	3	1	1	1	0	0	0	1	0	0	0	0	0	1	0	0	0	0	.333	.333
Sabathia	.000	5	3	0	0	0	0	0	0	0	0	0	0	0	0	2	0	0	0	0	.000	.000
YANKEES	**.257**	**15**	**522**	**80**	**134**	**222**	**24**	**2**	**20**	**75**	**5**	**4**	**9**	**65**	**7**	**125**	**7**	**3**	**9**	**5**	**.425**	**.347**
OPPONENTS	**.237**	**15**	**523**	**52**	**124**	**201**	**29**	**3**	**14**	**50**	**5**	**3**	**6**	**53**	**7**	**122**	**12**	**1**	**13**	**12**	**.384**	**.313**

PITCHER	W	L	ERA	G	GS	CG	GF	SHO	SV	IP	H	R	ER	HR	HB	BB	IBB	SO	WP	BK	AVG
Aceves	0	1	4.15	4	0	0	1	0	0	4.1	5	2	2	0	0	3	1	2	1	0	.313
Bruney	0	0	54.00	1	0	0	0	0	0	0.1	3	2	2	0	0	0	0	0	0	0	.750
Burnett	1	1	5.27	5	5	0	0	0	0	27.1	22	16	16	1	5	16	1	24	2	0	.218
Chamberlain	1	0	2.84	10	0	0	0	0	0	6.1	9	2	2	1	0	1	0	7	0	0	.333
Coke	0	0	6.75	6	0	0	1	0	0	2.2	4	2	2	2	0	1	0	3	0	0	.400
Gaudin	0	0	0.00	1	0	0	1	0	0	1.0	0	0	0	0	0	0	0	0	0	0	.000
Hughes	0	1	8.53	9	0	0	1	0	0	6.1	11	6	6	1	0	4	0	7	0	0	.379
Marte	0	0	0.00	8	0	0	0	0	0	4.0	2	0	0	0	0	0	0	5	0	0	.154
Pettitte	4	0	3.52	5	5	0	0	0	0	30.2	26	12	12	5	0	11	0	25	1	0	.239
Rivera	0	0	0.56	12	0	0	9	0	5	16.0	10	1	1	0	0	5	1	14	0	0	.175
Robertson	2	0	0.00	5	0	0	2	0	0	5.1	4	0	0	0	0	3	2	3	0	0	.200
Sabathia	3	1	1.98	5	5	0	0	0	0	36.1	28	9	8	4	1	9	2	32	1	0	.209
YANKEES	**11**	**4**	**3.26**	**15**	**15**	**0**	**15**	**0**	**5**	**140.2**	**124**	**52**	**51**	**14**	**6**	**53**	**7**	**122**	**5**	**0**	**.237**
OPPONENTS	**4**	**11**	**4.82**	**15**	**15**	**1**	**14**	**0**	**2**	**136.1**	**134**	**80**	**73**	**20**	**9**	**65**	**7**	**125**	**3**	**0**	**.257**

Postseason Doodles

A NEW HOUSE: The Yankees became the third team to win the World Series in their first season in their current stadium (also the 2006 St. Louis Cardinals and 1912 Boston Red Sox)—credit: *Elias*...the Yankees also advanced to the World Series in their first season at the original Yankee Stadium in 1923 (defeating the New York Giants), as well in the first season of the remodeled Stadium in 1976 (swept by Cincinnati).

THREE AMIGOS: LHP Andy Pettitte, SS Derek Jeter and RHP Mariano Rivera all appeared in the Yankees' World Series Game 3 win at Philadelphia, 13 years after playing together for the first time in a World Series in 1996...according to the *Elias Sports Bureau*, it is the longest such span for any trio of teammates in Series history...prior to 2009, the trios with the longest spans between World Series as teammates bookended their appearances with different teams: Nippy Jones, Del Rice and Red Schoendienst (1946 Cardinals and 1957 Braves); Joe Morgan, Tony Perez and Pete Rose (1972 Reds and 1983 Phillies).

MO' OF THE SAME: RHP Mariano Rivera has converted 11-of-12 career World Series save opportunities...with his two saves in the 2009 World Series, became the second-oldest pitcher ever to record a WS save behind Baltimore's Dick Hall (1970 at age 40 and 1971 at age 41), according to Retrosheet's Dave Smith...his 12 appearances in the 2009 playoffs were his most in any postseason (prev. 11G in 2001)...the 2009 playoffs marked the fourth time he was the final pitcher in the clinching game for all three rounds of a postseason.

ON BASE SAFELY: SS Derek Jeter reached base in all 15 games of the 2009 postseason, hitting safely in 14 of the contests and scoring at least 1R in 11 games...was the third-longest single-postseason streak of reaching base safely, trailing only Barry Bonds (17 straight in 2002) and Gary Sheffield (16 straight in 1997)...batted .407 (11-for-27) in the World Series, joining Babe Ruth and Yogi Berra as the only three players to hit at least .300 in at least five World Series.

2009 Transactions

January 6	Signed **1B Mark Teixeira** to an eight-year contract; designated **INF/OF Shelley Duncan** for assignment.
January 14	Invited 20 non-roster players to spring training: **C Kyle Anson, INF Doug Bernier, INF Angel Berroa, C Kevin Cash, OF Colin Curtis, INF/OF Shelley Duncan, LHP Kei Igawa, OF Austin Jackson, RHP Jason Johnson, INF Justin Leone, OF Todd Linden, RHP Mark Melancon, RHP Sergio Mitre, C Jesus Montero, INF Eduardo Nunez, INF Ramiro Pena, C P.J. Pilittere, OF John Rodriguez, C Austin Romine, INF Kevin Russo; INF/OF Shelley Duncan** cleared waivers and was outrighted to Triple-A Scranton/Wilkes-Barre.
January 20	Signed **OFs Melky Cabrera** and **Xavier Nady** to one-year contracts, avoiding arbitration.
January 26	Signed **LHP Andy Pettitte** to a one-year contract; designated **LHP Chase Wright** for assignment.
January 30	Signed **RHP Brian Bruney** to a one-year contract, avoiding arbitration.
February 4	Acquired **OF/C Eric Fryer** from Milwaukee in exchange for **LHP Chase Wright**.
February 11	Invited **RHPs J.B. Cox, George Kontos** and **Kanekoa Texeira** to spring training.
February 13	Signed **RHP Brett Tomko** to a minor league contract with a spring training invite.
March 9	Optioned **RHP Andrew Brackman** to Single-A Charleston; reassigned **RHPs J.B. Cox, George Kontos** and **Kanekoa Texeira** to minor league camp; assigned **LHP Wilkin De La Rosa** and **RHP Eric Hacker** to minor league camp.
March 14	Reassigned **OF Colin Curtis** and **C Austin Romine** to minor league camp; assigned **LHP Michael Dunn** to minor league camp.
March 15	Assigned **RHP Ian Kennedy** to minor league camp and **RHP Christian Garcia** to Double-A Trenton; reassigned **C Kyle Anson, RHP Mark Melancon, C Jesus Montero** and **INF Kevin Russo** to minor league camp.
March 16	Optioned **LHP Wilkin De La Rosa** to Single-A Tampa; optioned **LHP Michael Dunn** and **RHPs Christian Garcia** and **Eric Hacker** to Double-A Trenton; optioned **RHP Ian Kennedy** to Triple-A Scranton/Wilkes-Barre; **LHP Zach Kroenke** was returned to the Yankees from the Marlins after Florida selected him in the 2008 Rule 5 draft.
March 20	Optioned **RHPs Anthony Claggett** and **Steven Jackson** to Triple-A Scranton/Wilkes-Barre.
March 21	Optioned **RHP Phil Hughes** to Triple-A Scranton/Wilkes-Barre; optioned **RHP Humberto Sanchez** and **C Francisco Cervelli** to Double-A Trenton; reassigned **RHP Jason Johnson** and **RHP Sergio Mitre** to minor league camp.
March 23	Reassigned **LHP Kei Igawa** to minor league camp.
March 24	Optioned **INF Juan Miranda** to Triple-A Scranton/Wilkes-Barre; reassigned **INF Eduardo Nunez** and **OF Austin Jackson** to minor league camp.
March 28	Optioned **RHP David Robertson** to Triple-A Scranton/Wilkes-Barre; reassigned **INF Justin Leone, INF Doug Bernier, INF/OF Shelley Duncan, OF Todd Linden, OF John Rodriguez, C P.J. Pilittere** and **C Chris Stewart** to minor league camp.
March 29	**RHP Ivan Nova** was returned to the Yankees from the Padres after San Diego selected him in the 2008 Rule 5 draft.
March 31	Optioned **RHPs Alfredo Aceves** and **Dan Giese** to Triple-A Scranton/Wilkes-Barre…reassigned **RHP Brett Tomko** and **C Kevin Cash** to minor league camp.
April 3	**INF Reegie Corona** was returned to the Yankees from the Mariners after Seattle selected him in the 2008 Rule 5 draft.
April 4	Placed **3B Alex Rodriguez** on the 15-day disabled list retroactive to 3/27 with a right hip labral tear; signed to a Major League contract and selected **INF Ramiro Pena** to the 40-man roster; designated **RHP Dan Giese** for assignment; reassigned **INF Angel Berroa** to minor league camp.
April 8	**RHP Dan Giese** was claimed off waivers by the Oakland Athletics.
April 16	Placed **OF Xavier Nady** on the 15-day disabled list with an ulnar collateral ligament injury of the right elbow; recalled **RHP David Robertson** from Triple-A Scranton/Wilkes-Barre.
April 17	Optioned **RHP David Robertson** to Triple-A Scranton/Wilkes-Barre; recalled **1B Juan Miranda** from Scranton/WB.
April 18	Optioned **1B Juan Miranda** to Triple-A Scranton/Wilkes-Barre; recalled **RHP Anthony Claggett** from Scranton/WB.
April 19	Optioned **RHP Anthony Claggett** to Triple-A Scranton/Wilkes-Barre; recalled **RHP Stephen Jackson** from Scranton/WB.
April 24	Placed **RHP Chien-Ming Wang** on the 15-day disabled list with weakness in his hip abductor; recalled **RHP David Robertson** from Triple-A Scranton/Wilkes-Barre.
April 25	Placed **RHP Brian Bruney** on the 15-day disabled list with a flexor muscle strain in his right elbow; placed **INF Cody Ransom** on the 60-day disabled list with a strained right quadriceps muscle; signed **INF Angel Berroa** and **RHP Mark Melancon** to Major League contracts and selected them to the 25-man roster from Triple-A Scranton/Wilkes-Barre; released **RHP Humberto Sanchez**.
April 28	Recalled **RHP Phil Hughes**; optioned **RHP Steven Jackson** to Triple-A Scranton/Wilkes-Barre.
May 3	Placed **LHP Damaso Marte** on the 15-day disabled list with inflammation in his left shoulder; recalled **RHP Anthony Claggett** from Triple-A Scranton/Wilkes-Barre.
May 4	Recalled **RHP Alfredo Aceves** from Triple-A Scranton/Wilkes-Barre; optioned **RHP Anthony Claggett** to Scranton/WB.
May 5	Placed **C Jorge Posada** on the 15-day disabled list with a Grade 2 right hamstring strain; recalled **C Francisco Cervelli** from Double-A Trenton.
May 8	Returned from rehab and reinstated **3B Alex Rodriguez** from the 15-day disabled list; optioned **RHP Mark Melancon** to Triple-A Scranton/Wilkes-Barre; placed **C Jose Molina** on the 15-day disabled list with a strained left quadriceps; signed **C Kevin Cash** to a Major League contract and selected him to the 25-man roster from Triple-A Scranton/Wilkes-Barre; designated **RHP Steven Jackson** for assignment.
May 9	Signed **RHP Brett Tomko** to a Major League contract and selected him to the 25-man roster from Triple-A Scranton/Wilkes-Barre; optioned **RHP David Robertson** to Scranton/WB; designated **RHP Eric Hacker** for assignment.
May 16	Acquired **RHP Romulo Sanchez** from the Pittsburgh Pirates in exchange for **RHP Eric Hacker.**
May 18	**RHP Steven Jackson** was claimed off waivers by the Pittsburgh Pirates.
May 19	Returned from rehab and reinstated **RHP Brian Bruney** from the 15-day disabled list; optioned **RHP Edwar Ramirez** to Triple-A Scranton/Wilkes-Barre.
May 22	Returned from rehab and reinstated **RHP Chien-Ming Wang** from the 15-day disabled list; optioned **RHP Jonathan Albaladejo** to Triple-A Scranton/Wilkes-Barre.
May 26	Placed **RHP Brian Bruney** on the 15-day disabled list with a right elbow strain (retroactive to 5/20); recalled **RHP David Robertson** from Triple-A Scranton/Wilkes-Barre.

May 29	Reinstated **C Jorge Posada** from the 15-day disabled list; optioned **C Kevin Cash** to Triple-A Scranton/Wilkes-Barre.
June 16	Reinstated **RHP Brian Bruney** from the 15-day disabled list; designated **RHP Jose Veras** for assignment.
June 24	Traded **RHP Jose Veras** to the Cleveland Indians in exchange for cash considerations; returned from rehab and reinstated **INF Cody Ransom** from the 60-day disabled list; designated **INF Angel Berroa** for assignment.
June 30	Acquired **INF/OF Eric Hinske** and cash considerations from the Pittsburgh Pirates in exchange for minor league **OF Eric Fryer** and minor league **RHP Casey Erickson.**
July 1	Optioned **INF Ramiro Pena** to Triple-A Scranton/Wilkes-Barre.
July 5	Placed **RHP Chien-Ming Wang** on the 15-day disabled list with a right shoulder strain; recalled **RHP Jonathan Albaladejo** from Triple-A Scranton/Wilkes-Barre.
July 6	Released **INF Angel Berroa.**
July 7	Returned from rehab and reinstated **C Jose Molina** from the 15-day disabled list; optioned **C Francisco Cervelli** to Triple-A Scranton/Wilkes-Barre.
July 10	Recalled **RHP Mark Melancon** from Triple-A Scranton/Wilkes-Barre; optioned **RHP Jonathan Albaladejo** to Scranton/WB.
July 21	Signed **RHP Sergio Mitre** to a Major League contract and selected him to the 25-man roster from Triple-A Scranton/Wilkes-Barre; designated **RHP Brett Tomko** for assignment.
July 26	Placed **OF Brett Gardner** on the 15-day disabled list with a fractured left thumb; recalled **RHP Jonathan Albaladejo** from Triple-A Scranton/Wilkes-Barre.
July 29	Acquired **RHP Jason Hirsh** from the Colorado Rockies for a player to be named later and assigned him to Triple-A Scranton/Wilkes-Barre; released **RHP Brett Tomko.**
July 31	Acquired **INF/OF Jerry Hairston, Jr.** from the Cincinnati Reds in exchange for minor league **C Chase Weems**; signed **INF/OF Shelley Duncan** to a Major League contract and selected him to the 25-man roster from Triple-A Scranton/Wilkes-Barre; optioned **RHP Jonathan Albaladejo** to Scranton/WB; transferred **RHP Chien-Ming Wang** and **OF Xavier Nady** to the 60-day disabled list.
Aug. 1	Added **INF/OF Jerry Hairston, Jr.** to the 25-man roster; optioned **INF/OF Shelley Duncan** to Triple-A Scranton/Wilkes-Barre.
Aug. 5	Recalled **RHP Anthony Claggett** from Triple-A Scranton/Wilkes-Barre; designated **INF Cody Ransom** for assignment.
Aug. 6	Acquired **RHP Chad Gaudin** from the San Diego Padres in exchange for a player to be named later or cash considerations.
Aug. 7	Recalled **INF Ramiro Pena** from Triple-A Scranton/Wilkes-Barre; optioned **RHP Anthony Claggett** to Scranton/WB.
Aug. 8	Signed **RHP Josh Towers** to a Major League contract and selected him to the 25-man roster from Triple-A Scranton/Wilkes-Barre; optioned **RHP Mark Melancon** to Scranton/WB.
Aug. 9	Added **RHP Chad Gaudin** to the 25-man roster; designated **RHP Josh Towers** for assignment.
Aug. 14	Returned **LHP Damaso Marte** from rehab.
Aug. 21	Reinstated **LHP Damaso Marte** from the 60-day disabled list; optioned **INF Ramiro Pena** to Triple-A Scranton/Wilkes-Barre.
Sept. 1	Recalled **LHP Michael Dunn**, **RHP Mark Melancon**, **RHP Edwar Ramirez**, **C Francisco Cervelli** and **INF Ramiro Pena** from Triple-A Scranton/Wilkes-Barre.
Sept. 3	Recalled **RHP Jonathan Albaladejo** from Triple-A Scranton/Wilkes-Barre.
Sept. 5	Signed **RHP Josh Towers** to a Major League contract, selected him to the active roster from Triple-A Scranton/Wilkes-Barre; released **C Kevin Cash.**
Sept. 7	Returned from rehab and reinstated **CF Brett Gardner** from the disabled list; recalled **INF/OF Shelley Duncan** from Triple-A Scranton/Wilkes-Barre.
Sept. 14	Signed **OF Freddy Guzman** to a Major League contract and selected him to the active roster from Triple-A Scranton/Wilkes-Barre; designated **RHP Anthony Claggett** for assignment.
Sept. 15	Recalled **1B Juan Miranda** from Triple-A Scranton/Wilkes-Barre.
Sept. 16	Recalled **RHP Ian Kennedy** from Triple-A Scranton/Wilkes-Barre.
Sept. 24	**RHP Anthony Claggett** claimed off waivers by Pittsburgh.
Nov. 11	Outrighted **RHP Josh Towers**; elected free agency.
Nov. 13	Outrighted **OF Freddy Guzman**; elected free agency.
Nov. 17	Declined option on **RHP Sergio Mitre.**
Nov. 20	Added **RHPs Hector Noesi**, **Ivan Nova** and **Romulo Sanchez**; **INFs Reegie Corona**, **Eduardo Nunez** and **Kevin Russo**; and **OF Austin Jackson** to 40-man roster.
Nov. 25	Outrighted **INF/OF Shelley Duncan**, elected free agency.
Dec. 7	Traded **RHP Brian Bruney** to the Washington Nationals in exchange for a player to be named later.
Dec. 9	Yankees signed **LHP Andy Pettitte** to a one-year contract; acquired **OF Curtis Granderson** from the Detroit Tigers in a three-team trade that sent **LHP Phil Coke** and **OF Austin Jackson** to the Tigers and **RHP Ian Kennedy** to the Arizona Diamondbacks.
Dec. 10	Acquired **OF Jamie Hoffmann** (No. 1 pick in Rule 5 Draft) from the Washington Nationals as the player to be named later for **RHP Brian Bruney.**
Dec. 12	Declined to offer a 2010 Major League contract to **RHP Chien-Ming Wang.**
Dec. 21	Acquired **RHP Javier Vazquez** and **LHP Boone Logan** from the Atlanta Braves in exchange for **OF Melky Cabrera**, **LHP Mike Dunn** and **RHP Arodys Vizcaino.**
Dec. 23	Signed **DH Nick Johnson** to a one-year contract.

2010

Jan. 7	Signed **RHP Sergio Mitre** to a one-year contract, avoiding arbitration.
Jan. 18	Signed **RHP Chad Gaudin** and **LHP Boone Logan** to one-year contracts, avoiding arbitration.
Jan. 26	Acquired **OF Greg Golson** from the Texas Rangers in exchange for minor league **INF Mitch Hilligoss.**
Feb. 8	Signed **OF Randy Winn** to a one-year contract.
	Invited 20 non-roster players to spring training: **LHP Wilkins Arias, LHP Jeremy Bleich, OF Colin Curtis, RHP Grant Duff, OF Reid Gorecki, C Kyle Higashioka, RHP Jason Hirsh, LHP Kei Igawa, RHP Zach McAllister, C Jesus Montero, C P.J. Pilittere, LHP Royce Ring, C Mike Rivera, C Austin Romine, RHP Amaury Sanit, RHP Zack Segovia, OF Marcus Thames, RHP Kevin Whelan** and **OF David Winfree.**
Feb. 16	Invited **RHP's D.J. Mitchell, Dustin Moseley** and **Justin Pope** and **INF's Brandon Laird** and **Jorge Vazquez** to spring training

2009 Day-by-Day

Gm	Date	Opponent	W/L	Score	Winning Pitcher	Losing Pitcher	Save	Rec.	Pos.	GA/GB	Att.
1	4/6	at Baltimore	L	5-10	Guthrie (1-0)	Sabathia (0-1)	-	0-1	5th	-1.0	*48,607
	4/7		OFF DAY						T4th	-1.5	
2	4/8	at Baltimore	L	5-7	Uehara (1-0)	Wang (0-1)	Sherrill (1)	0-2	5th	-2.0	22,856
3	4/9	at Baltimore	W	11-2	Burnett (1-0)	Simon (0-1)	-	1-2	T4th	-1.5	28,534
4	4/10	at Kansas City	W	4-1	Pettitte (1-0)	Ponson (0-1)	Rivera (1)	2-2	T3rd	-1.5	*38,078
5	4/11	at Kansas City	W	6-1	Sabathia (1-1)	Ramirez (0-1)	-	3-2	3rd	-1.5	31,072
6	4/12	at Kansas City	L	4-6	Cruz (1-0)	Coke (0-1)	Soria (3)	3-3	T3rd	-1.5	17,473
7	4/13	at Tampa Bay	L	5-15	Kazmir (2-0)	Wang (0-2)	-	3-4	4th	-2.5	*36,973
8	4/14	at Tampa Bay	W	7-2	Burnett (2-0)	Howell (0-1)	-	4-4	T3rd	-2.0	*36,973
9	4/15	at Tampa Bay	W	4-3	Bruney (1-0)	Percival (0-1)	Rivera (2)	5-4	3rd	-1.5	25,171
10	4/16	Cleveland	L	2-10	Lee (1-2)	Veras (0-1)	-	5-5	3rd	-2.5	*48,271 (1)
11	4/17	Cleveland	W	6-5	Bruney (2-0)	Lewis (1-1)	Rivera (3)	6-5	3rd	-1.5	45,101
12	4/18	Cleveland	L	4-22	Carmona (1-2)	Wang (0-3)	-	6-6	3rd	-2.5	45,167
13	4/19	Cleveland	W	7-3	Albaladejo (1-0)	Lewis (1-2)	-	7-6	2nd	-2.5	43,068
	4/20	Oakland			Ppd., Rain (make-up game scheduled for 7/23 at 7:05 p.m.)				T2nd	-2.5	
14	4/21	Oakland	W	5-3	Pettitte (2-0)	Eveland (0-1)	Rivera (4)	8-6	2nd	-1.5	42,065
15	4/22	Oakland	W	9-7 (14)	Veras (1-1)	Giese (0-2)	-	9-6	T2nd	-1.5	43,342
	4/23		OFF DAY						T2nd	-2.0	
16	4/24	at Boston	L	4-5 (11)	Ramirez (2-0)	Marte (0-1)	-	9-7	3rd	-3.0	*38,163
17	4/25	at Boston	L	11-16	Okajima (1-0)	Albaladejo (1-1)	-	9-8	3rd	-3.0	*37,699
18	4/26	at Boston	L	1-4	Masterson (2-0)	Pettitte (2-1)	Saito (2)	9-9	3rd	-4.0	*38,154
19	4/27	at Detroit	L	2-4	Verlander (1-2)	**Sabathia (1-2)**	-	9-10	3rd	-4.0	28,784
20	4/28	at Detroit	W	11-0	Hughes (1-0)	Perry (0-1)	-	10-10	3rd	-4.0	25,519
21	4/29	at Detroit	W	8-6	Chamberlain (1-0)	Porcello (1-3)	-	11-10	3rd	-3.0	28,348
22	4/30	Los Angeles-AL	W	7-4	Coke (1-1)	Speier (0-1)	Rivera (5)	12-10	3rd	-2.0	43,388
23	5/1	Los Angeles-AL	W	10-9	Albaladejo (2-1)	Fuentes (0-2)	-	13-10	3rd	-2.0	44,058
24	5/2	Los Angeles-AL	L	4-8	Palmer (2-0)	Sabathia (1-3)	-	13-11	3rd	-3.0	44,970
	5/3	Los Angeles-AL			Ppd. Rain (make-up game scheduled for 9/14 at 7:05 p.m.)				3rd	-3.5	
25	5/4	Boston	L	4-6	Lester (2-2)	Hughes (1-1)	Papelbon (7)	13-12	3rd	-3.5	46,426
26	5/5	Boston	L	3-7	Beckett (3-2)	Chamberlain (1-1)	-	13-13	3rd	-4.5	46,810
27	5/6	Tampa Bay	L	3-4 (10)	Balfour (1-0)	Coke (1-2)	Percival (5)	13-14	3rd	-5.5	42,585
28	5/7	Tampa Bay	L	6-8	Shouse (1-0)	Rivera (0-1)	-	13-15	3rd	-5.5	43,769
29	5/8	at Baltimore	W	4-0	**Sabathia (2-3)**	Guthrie (2-3)	-	14-15	3rd	-4.5	36,926
30	5/9	at Baltimore	L	5-12	Eaton (2-3)	Hughes (1-2)	-	14-16	4th	-5.5	41,825
31	5/10	at Baltimore	W	5-3	Chamberlain (2-1)	Johnson (2-1)	Rivera (6)	15-16	3rd	-5.5	33,290
	5/11		OFF DAY						3rd	-5.5	
32	5/12	at Toronto	L	1-5	**Halladay (7-1)**	Burnett (2-1)	-	15-17	3rd	-6.5	43,737
33	5/13	at Toronto	W	8-2	Pettitte (3-1)	Richmond (4-2)	-	16-17	3rd	-5.5	20,164
34	5/14	at Toronto	W	3-2	Sabathia (3-3)	Carlson (0-2)	Rivera (7)	17-17	3rd	-4.5	22,667
35	5/15	Minnesota	W	5-4	Veras (2-1)	Nathan (1-1)	-	18-17	3rd	-4.5	43,856
36	5/16	Minnesota	W	6-4 (11)	Aceves (1-0)	Breslow (1-2)	-	19-17	3rd	-4.5	45,455
37	5/17	Minnesota	W	3-2 (10)	Aceves (2-0)	Crain (2-2)	-	20-17	3rd	-4.5	44,804
38	5/18	Minnesota	W	7-6	Pettitte (4-1)	Perkins (1-3)	Coke (1)	21-17	3rd	-4.5	43,244
39	5/19	Baltimore	W	9-1	Sabathia (4-3)	Bergensen (1-2)	-	22-17	3rd	-3.5	42,838
40	5/20	Baltimore	W	11-4	Hughes (2-2)	Guthrie (3-4)	Rivera (8)	23-17	3rd	-2.5	43,903
41	5/21	Baltimore	W	7-4	Aceves (3-0)	Eaton (2-5)	Rivera (9)	24-17	3rd	-1.5	43,342
42	5/22	Philadelphia	L	3-7	Myers (4-2)	Burnett (2-2)	-	24-18	3rd	-1.5	46,288
43	5/23	Philadelphia	W	5-4	Veras (3-1)	Lidge (0-2)	-	25-18	T2nd	-0.5	46,887
44	5/24	Philadelphia	L	3-4 (11)	Condrey (4-0)	Tomko (0-1)	-	25-19	3rd	-1.0	46,988
45	5/25	at Texas	W	11-1	Hughes (3-2)	Harrison (4-4)	-	26-19	2nd	-1.0	*48,914
46	5/26	at Texas	L	3-7	Jennings (2-1)	Aceves (3-1)	-	26-20	2nd	-1.0	33,397
47	5/27	at Texas	W	9-2	Burnett (3-2)	Holland (1-2)	-	27-20	T1st	---	38,409
	5/28		OFF DAY						2nd	-0.5	
48	5/29	at Cleveland	W	3-1	Pettitte (5-1)	Lee (2-6)	Rivera (10)	28-20	1st	+0.5	32,802
49	5/30	at Cleveland	W	10-5	Sabathia (5-3)	Carmona (2-5)	-	29-20	1st	+1.5	34,396
50	5/31	at Cleveland	L	4-5	Wood (2-2)	Coke (1-3)	-	29-21	1st	+0.5	29,405
51	6/1	at Cleveland	W	5-2	Chamberlain (3-1)	Aquino (1-1)	Rivera (11)	30-21	1st	+1.0	23,651
52	6/2	Texas	W	12-3	Burnett (4-2)	Padilla (3-3)	-	31-21	1st	+1.0	43,948
53	6/3	Texas	L	2-4	Feldman (5-0)	Pettitte (5-2)	Francisco (12)	31-22	T1st	---	44,452
54	6/4	Texas	W	8-6	Robertson (1-0)	Wilson (3-3)	Rivera (12)	32-22	T1st	---	45,713

2009 Day-by-Day

Gm	Date	Opponent	W/L	Score	Winning Pitcher	Losing Pitcher	Save	Rec.	Pos.	GA/GB	Att.
	6/5	Tampa Bay			Ppd. Rain (make-up game scheduled for 9/7 at 7:05 p.m.)				1st	+0.5	
55	6/6	Tampa Bay	L	7-9	Howell (1-2)	Rivera (0-2)	Choate (3)	32-23	2nd	-0.5	46,205
56	6/7	Tampa Bay	W	4-3	Aceves (4-1)	Balfour (2-1)	Rivera (13)	33-23	1st	+0.5	46,465
57	6/8	Tampa Bay	W	5-3	Pettitte (6-2)	Sonnanstine (4-6)	Rivera (14)	34-23	1st	+1.0	44,706
58	6/9	at Boston	L	0-7	Beckett (7-2)	Burnett (4-3)	-	34-24	T1st	---	*37,883
59	6/10	at Boston	L	5-6	Wakefield (8-3)	Wang (0-4)	Papelbon (15)	34-25	2nd	-1.0	*38,121
60	6/11	at Boston	L	3-4	Saito (1-0)	Sabathia (5-4)	Papelbon (16)	34-26	2nd	-2.0	*38,153
61	6/12	New York-NL	W	9-8	Rivera (1-2)	Rodriguez (1-1)	-	35-26	2nd	-2.0	47,967
62	6/13	New York-NL	L	2-6	Nieve (1-0)	Pettitte (6-3)	-	35-27	2nd	-3.0	48,056
63	6/14	New York-NL	W	15-0	Burnett (5-3)	Santana (8-4)	-	36-27	2nd	-2.0	47,943
	6/15		OFF DAY						2nd	-2.0	
64	6/16	Washington	W	5-3	Sabathia (6-4)	Villone (3-4)	Rivera (15)	37-27	2nd	-2.0	44,873
65	6/17	Washington	L	2-3	Lannan (4-5)	Wang (0-5)	MacDougal (1)	37-28	2nd	-3.0	46,052
66	6/18	Washington	L	0-3	Stammen (1-2)	Chamberlain (3-2)	MacGougal (2)	37-29	2nd	-3.0	45,143
67	6/19	at Florida	W	5-1	Pettitte (7-3)	West (2-2)	-	38-29	2nd	-2.0	35,027
68	6/20	at Florida	L	1-2	Johnson (7-1)	Burnett (5-4)	Lindstrom (13)	38-30	2nd	-3.0	46,427
69	6/21	at Florida	L	5-6	Volstad (5-7)	Tomko (0-2)	Lindstrom (14)	38-31	2nd	-4.0	35,827
	6/22		OFF DAY						2nd	-4.0	
70	6/23	at Atlanta	L	0-4	Hanson (3-0)	Wang (0-6)	-	38-32	T2nd	-5.0	40,828
71	6/24	at Atlanta	W	8-4	Chamberlain (4-2)	Medlen (2-3)	Rivera (16)	39-32	T2nd	-5.0	42,315
72	6/25	at Atlanta	W	11-7	Aceves (5-1)	Lowe (7-6)	Rivera (17)	40-32	2nd	-4.0	*47,508
73	6/26	at New York-NL	W	9-1	Sabathia (7-4)	Pelfrey (5-3)	-	41-32	2nd	-4.0	*41,278
74	6/27	at New York-NL	W	5-0	Burnett (6-4)	Redding (1-3)	-	42-32	2nd	-4.0	*41,302
75	6/28	at New York-NL	W	4-2	Wang (1-6)	Hernandez (5-3)	Rivera (18)	43-32	2nd	-3.0	*41,315
	6/29		OFF DAY						2nd	-3.5	
76	6/30	Seattle	W	8-5	Bruney (3-0)	White (2-1)	Rivera (19)	44-32	2nd	-2.5	46,181
77	7/1	Seattle	W	4-2	Pettitte (8-3)	Washburn (4-6)	Rivera (20)	45-32	2nd	-2.5	45,285
78	7/2	Seattle	L	4-8	Batista (5-2)	Sabathia (7-5)	-	45-33	2nd	-3.0	46,142
79	7/3	Toronto	W	4-2	Burnett (7-4)	Tallet (5-6)	Rivera (21)	46-33	2nd	-2.0	46,308
80	7/4	Toronto	W	6-5 (12)	Tomko (1-2)	Camp (0-4)	-	47-33	2nd	-1.0	46,620
81	7/5	Toronto	W	10-8	Albaladejo (3-1)	Ryan (1-1)	Aceves (1)	48-33	2nd	-1.0	46,320
82	7/6	Toronto	L	6-7	Romero (7-3)	Pettitte (8-4)	Frasor (3)	48-34	2nd	-1.0	46,450
83	7/7	at Minnesota	W	10-2	Sabathia (8-5)	Baker (6-7)	-	49-34	2nd	-1.0	29,540
84	7/8	at Minnesota	W	4-3	Burnett (8-4)	Swarzak (2-3)	Rivera (22)	50-34	2nd	-1.0	38,115
85	7/9	at Minnesota	W	6-4	Albaladejo (4-1)	Liriano (4-9)	Rivera (23)	51-34	T1st	---	40,142
86	7/10	at Los Angeles-AL	L	6-10	Bulger (4-1)	Melancon (0-1)	Fuentes (25)	51-35	2nd	-1.0	*44,076
87	7/11	at Los Angeles-AL	L	8-14	Weaver (10-3)	Pettitte (8-5)	-	51-36	2nd	-2.0	42,602
88	7/12	at Los Angeles-AL	L	4-5	Lackey (4-4)	Sabathia (8-6)	Fuentes (26)	51-37	2nd	-3.0	41,532
	7/13-16				(80th All-Star Game on 7/14 at Busch Stadium, 4-3 American League win)						
89	7/17	Detroit	W	5-3	Hughes (4-2)	Zumaya (3-3)	Rivera (24)	52-37	2nd	-3.0	46,197
90	7/18	Detroit	W	2-1	Sabathia (9-6)	Verlander (10-5)	Rivera (25)	53-37	2nd	-2.0	46,423
91	7/19	Detroit	W	2-1	Chamberlain (5-2)	Jackson (7-5)	Rivera (26)	54-37	2nd	-1.0	46,937
92	7/20	Baltimore	W	2-1	Aceves (6-1)	Johnson (3-4)	-	55-37	T1st	---	46,342
93	7/21	Baltimore	W	6-4	Mitre (1-0)	Hill (3-3)	Rivera (27)	56-37	1st	+1.0	45,589
94	7/22	Baltimore	W	6-4	Burnett (9-4)	Berken (1-8)	Rivera (28)	57-37	1st	+2.0	47,134
95	7/23	Oakland	W	6-3	Sabathia (10-6)	Mazzaro (2-7)	Hughes (1)	58-37	1st	+2.5	44,206
96	7/24	Oakland	W	8-3	Chamberlain (6-2)	Anderson (5-8)	-	59-37	1st	+2.5	46,068
97	7/25	Oakland	L	4-6	Gonzalez (2-2)	Pettitte (8-6)	Bailey (11)	59-38	1st	+1.5	46,412
98	7/26	Oakland	W	7-5	Coke (2-3)	Braden (7-9)	Rivera (29)	60-38	1st	+2.5	46,163
99	7/27	at Tampa Bay	W	11-4	Burnett (10-4)	Shields (6-7)	Robertson (1)	61-38	1st	+2.5	33,442
100	7/28	at Tampa Bay	L	1-6	Kazmir (5-6)	Sabathia (10-7)	-	61-39	1st	+2.5	32,304
101	7/29	at Tampa Bay	W	6-2	Chamberlain (7-2)	Garza (7-8)	-	62-39	1st	+3.5	32,398
102	7/30	at Chicago-AL	L	2-3	Thornton (5-2)	Hughes (4-3)	-	62-40	1st	+2.5	31,305
103	7/31	at Chicago-AL	L	5-10	Pena (1-0)	Robetrson (1-1)	-	62-41	1st	+1.5	*38,228
104	8/1	at Chicago-AL	L	4-14	Danks (9-7)	Burnett (10-5)	-	62-42	1st	+0.5	*38,763
105	8/2	at Chicago-AL	W	8-5	Sabathia (11-7)	Buehrle (11-5)	Rivera (30)	63-42	1st	+0.5	36,325
	8/3		OFF DAY						1st	+0.5	
106	8/4	at Toronto	W	5-3	Pettitte (9-6)	**Halladay (11-5)**	Rivera (31)	64-42	1st	+1.5	33,669
107	8/5	at Toronto	W	8-4	Aceves (7-1)	Rzepczynski (1-3)	-	65-42	1st	+2.5	31,402
108	8/6	Boston	W	13-6	Chamberlain (8-2)	Smoltz (2-5)	-	66-42	1st	+3.5	*49,005 (2)
109	8/7	Boston	W	2-0 (15)	Coke (3-3)	Tazawa (0-1)	-	67-42	1st	+4.5	*48,262 (3)
110	8/8	Boston	W	5-0	Sabathia (12-7)	Buchholz (1-2)	-	68-42	1st	+5.5	*48,796 (4)

2009 Day-by-Day

Gm	Date	Opponent	W/L	Score	Winning Pitcher	Losing Pitcher	Save	Rec.	Pos.	GA/GB	Att.
111	8/9	Boston	W	5-2	Coke (4-3)	Bard (0-1)	Rivera (32)	69-42	1st	+6.5	*48,190 (5)
112	8/10	Toronto	L	4-5	Camp (1-5)	Mitre (1-1)	Frasor (5)	69-43	1st	+5.5	46,376
113	8/11	Toronto	W	7-5	Robertson (2-1)	Carlson (1-5)	Rivera (33)	70-43	1st	+5.5	46,523
114	8/12	Toronto	W	4-3 (11)	Gaudin (1-0)	Camp (1-6)	-	71-43	1st	+5.5	47,113
115	8/13	at Seattle	W	11-1	Sabathia (13-7)	Snell (0-1)	-	72-43	1st	+6.5	33,585
116	8/14	at Seattle	W	4-2	Hughes (5-3)	Lowe (1-5)	Rivera (34)	73-43	1st	+6.5	36,769
117	8/15	at Seattle	W	5-2	Mitre (2-1)	French (2-3)	Rivera (35)	74-43	1st	+7.5	44,272
118	8/16	at Seattle	L	3-10	Fister (1-0)	Chamberlain (8-3)	-	74-44	1st	+7.5	*45,210
119	8/17	at Oakland	L	0-3	Tomko (2-2)	**Burnett (10-6)**	Bailey (18)	74-45	1st	+7.0	24,409
120	8/18	at Oakland	W	7-2	Sabathia (14-7)	Marshall (0-1)	-	75-45	1st	+7.0	25,383
121	8/19	at Oakland	W	3-2	Aceves (8-1)	Anderson (7-9)	Rivera (36)	76-45	1st	+7.0	35,067
	8/20		OFF DAY						1st	+6.5	
122	8/21	at Boston	W	20-11	Pettitte (10-6)	Penny (7-8)	-	77-45	1st	+7.5	*37,869
123	8/22	at Boston	L	1-14	Tazawa (2-2)	Burnett (10-7)	-	77-46	1st	+6.5	*37,277
124	8/23	at Boston	W	8-4	Sabathia (15-7)	Beckett (14-5)	-	78-46	1st	+7.5	*38,008
	8/24		OFF DAY						1st	+7.0	
125	8/25	Texas	L	9-10	Millwood (10-8)	Chamberlain (8-4)	-	78-47	1st	+6.0	46,511
126	8/26	Texas	W	9-2	Pettitte (11-6)	Holland (7-8)	-	79-47	1st	+6.0	46,461
127	8/27	Texas	L	2-7	Grilli (2-2)	Burnett (10-8)	-	79-48	1st	+6.0	47,209
128	8/28	Chicago-AL	W	5-2 (10)	Bruney (4-0)	Williams (0-1)	-	80-48	1st	+6.0	46,318
129	8/29	Chicago-AL	W	10-0	Mitre (3-1)	Contreras (5-13)	-	81-48	1st	+6.0	46,193
130	8/30	Chicago-AL	W	8-3	Aceves (9-1)	Garcia (0-2)	-	82-48	1st	+6.0	46,664
131	8/31	at Baltimore	W	5-1	Pettitte (12-6)	Guthrie (9-13)	Rivera (37)	83-48	1st	+6.5	25,063
132	9/1	at Baltimore	W	9-6	Marte (1-1)	Ray (0-3)	Rivera (38)	84-48	1st	+6.5	25,782
133	9/2	at Baltimore	W	10-2	Sabathia (16-7)	Mickolio (0-2)	Hughes (2)	85-48	1st	+7.5	21,126
134	9/3	at Toronto	W	10-5	Aceves (10-1)	Romero (11-7)	-	86-48	1st	+7.5	22,773
135	9/4	at Toronto	L	0-6	**Halladay (14-8)**	Chamberlain (8-5)	-	86-49	1st	+7.5	22,179
136	9/5	at Toronto	W	6-4	Pettitte (13-6)	Cecil (6-4)	Hughes (3)	87-49	1st	+8.5	31,295
137	9/6	at Toronto	L	8-14	Tallet (6-9)	Mitre (3-2)	-	87-50	1st	+7.5	30,873
138	9/7	Tampa Bay	W	4-1	Hughes (6-3)	Cormier (2-2)	Rivera (39)	88-50	1st	+8.5	47,436
139	9/7	Tampa Bay	W	11-1	Burnett (11-8)	Sonnanstine (6-9)	-	89-50	1st	+9.0	45,953
140	9/8	Tampa Bay	W	3-2	Rivera (2-2)	Wheeler (4-4)	-	90-50	1st	+9.0	45,350
141	9/9	Tampa Bay	W	4-2	Albaladejo (5-1)	Cormier (2-3)	Coke (2)	91-50	1st	+9.0	45,848
	9/10		OFF DAY						1st	+9.0	
142	9/11	Baltimore	L	4-10	Tillman (2-3)	Marte (1-2)	Hendrickson (1)	91-51	1st	+8.5	46,771
143	9/12	Baltimore	L	3-7	Matusz (5-2)	Burnett (11-9)	-	91-52	1st	+7.5	46,497
144	9/13	Baltimore	W	13-3	Sabathia (17-7)	Guthrie (10-14)	-	92-52	1st	+7.0	46,413
145	9/14	Los Angeles-AL	W	5-3	Hughes (7-3)	Weaver (15-6)	Rivera (40)	93-52	1st	+7.5	44,701
146	9/15	Toronto	L	4-10	Halladay (15-9)	Mitre (3-3)	-	93-53	1st	+6.5	45,847
147	9/16	Toronto	W	5-4	Rivera (3-2)	Frasor (6-3)	-	94-53	1st	+6.5	46,046
	9/17		OFF DAY						1st	+7.0	
148	9/18	at Seattle	L	2-3	**Hernandez (16-5)**	Rivera (3-3)	-	94-54	1st	+6.0	28,395
149	9/19	at Seattle	W	10-1	Sabathia (18-7)	Fister (2-3)	-	95-54	1st	+6.0	43,173
150	9/20	at Seattle	L	1-7	Snell (5-2)	Chamberlain (8-6)	-	95-55	1st	+5.0	35,885
151	9/21	at Los Angeles-AL	L	2-5	Sanders (14-7)	Pettitte (13-7)	Fuentes (44)	95-56	1st	+5.0	*38,667
152	9/22	at Los Angeles-AL	W	6-5	Hughes (8-3)	Palmer (10-2)	Rivera (41)	96-56	1st	+6.0	*40,374
153	9/23	at Los Angeles-AL	W	3-2	Burnett (12-9)	Kazmir (9-9)	Rivera (42)	97-56	1st	+6.0	35,760
	9/24		OFF DAY						1st	+5.5	
154	9/25	Boston	W	9-5	Chamberlain (9-6)	Lester (14-8)	-	98-56	1st	+6.5	*48,449 (6)
155	9/26	Boston	W	3-0	Sabathia (19-7)	Matsuzaka (3-6)	Rivera (43)	99-56	1st	+7.5	*48,809 (7)
156	9/27	Boston	W	4-2	Pettitte (14-7)	Byrd (1-3)	Rivera (44)	100-56	1st	+8.5	47,576
157	9/28	Kansas City	W	8-2	Gaudin (2-0)	Hochevar (7-12)	-	101-56	1st	+9.5	45,348
158	9/29	Kansas City	W	4-3	Bruney (5-0)	Farnsworth (1-5)	-	102-56	1st	+10.5	44,794
159	9/30	Kansas City	L	3-4	Wright (3-5)	Marte (1-3)	Soria (30)	102-57	1st	+10.5	46,956
	10/1		OFF DAY						1st	+10.0	
160	10/2	at Tampa Bay	L	4-13	Price (10-7)	Sabathia (19-8)	-	102-58	1st	+9.0	22,704
161	10/3	at Tampa Bay	L	3-5	Niemann (13-6)	Pettitte (14-8)	Balfour (4)	102-59	1st	+8.0	30,084
162	10/4	at Tampa Bay	W	10-4	Burnett (13-9)	Davis (2-2)	-	103-59	1st	+8.0	28,699

BOLD (Complete Game)

*Denotes Sellout (#Home Sellouts)

2009 Major League Standings

AMERICAN LEAGUE

***NEW YORK**	**103**	**59**	**.636**	**–**
#BOSTON	95	67	.586	8.0
TAMPA BAY	84	78	.519	19.0
TORONTO	75	87	.463	28.0
BALTIMORE	64	98	.395	39.0

AL CENTRAL	WON	LOST	PCT.	GB
*MINNESOTA	87	76	.534	-
DETROIT	86	77	.528	0.5
CHICAGO	79	83	.488	7.0
CLEVELAND	65	97	.401	21.0
KANSAS CITY	65	97	.401	21.0

AL WEST	WON	LOST	PCT.	GB
*LOS ANGELES	97	65	.599	-
TEXAS	87	75	.537	10.0
SEATTLE	85	77	.525	12.0
OAKLAND	75	87	.463	22.0

* - DIVISION WINNER
\# - WILD CARD WINNER

NATIONAL LEAGUE

NL EAST	WON	LOST	PCT.	GB
*PHILADELPHIA	93	69	.574	-
FLORIDA	87	75	.537	6.0
ATLANTA	86	76	.531	7.0
NEW YORK	70	92	.432	23.0
WASHINGTON	59	103	.364	34.0

NL CENTRAL	WON	LOST	PCT.	GB
*ST. LOUIS	91	71	.562	-
CHICAGO	83	78	.516	7.5
MILWAUKEE	80	82	.494	11.0
CINCINNATI	78	84	.481	13.0
HOUSTON	74	88	.457	17.0
PITTSBURGH	62	99	.385	28.5

NL WEST	WON	LOST	PCT.	GB
*LOS ANGELES	95	67	.586	-
#COLORADO	92	70	.568	3.0
SAN FRANCISCO	88	74	.543	7.0
SAN DIEGO	75	87	.463	20.0
ARIZONA	70	92	.432	25.0

2009 Yankees Club Statistics

	HOME		ROAD		TOTALS	
	W	L	W	L	W	L
VS. BALTIMORE	7	2	6	3	13	5
VS. BOSTON	7	2	2	7	9	9
VS. TAMPA BAY	6	3	5	4	11	7
VS. TORONTO	6	3	6	3	12	6
VS. EAST	**26**	**10**	**19**	**17**	**45**	**27**

	HOME		ROAD		TOTALS	
	W	L	W	L	W	L
VS. CLEVELAND	2	2	3	1	5	3
VS. CHICAGO	3	0	1	3	4	3
VS. DETROIT	3	0	2	1	5	1
VS. KANSAS CITY	2	1	2	1	4	2
VS. MINNESOTA	4	0	3	0	7	0
VS. CENTRAL	**14**	**3**	**11**	**6**	**25**	**9**

	HOME		ROAD		TOTALS	
	W	L	W	L	W	L
VS. LOS ANGELES	3	1	2	4	5	5
VS. OAKLAND	5	1	2	1	7	2
VS. SEATTLE	2	1	4	3	6	4
VS. TEXAS	3	3	2	1	5	4
VS. WEST	**13**	**6**	**10**	**9**	**23**	**15**
TOTALS VS. A.L.	**53**	**19**	**40**	**32**	**93**	**51**

	HOME		ROAD		TOTALS	
	W	L	W	L	W	L
VS. ATLANTA	0	0	2	1	2	1
VS. FLORIDA	0	0	1	2	1	2
VS. WASHINGTON	1	2	0	0	1	2
VS. NEW YORK	2	1	3	0	5	1
VS. PHILADELPHIA	1	2	0	0	1	2
TOTALS VS. N.L.	**4**	**5**	**6**	**3**	**10**	**8**
TOTALS	**57**	**24**	**46**	**35**	**103**	**59**

	HOME		ROAD		TOTALS	
	W	L	W	L	W	L
SHUTOUTS	5	1	3	4	8	5
SHO - INDIVIDUAL	0	0	1	1	1	1
EXTRA INNINGS	7	2	0	1	7	3
ONE-RUN DECISIONS	16	7	6	9	22	16
TWO-RUN DECISIONS	18	5	8	4	26	9
VS. LH STARTERS	20	10	16	8	36	18
VS. RH STARTERS	37	14	30	27	67	41
GRASS FIELDS	57	24	32	28	89	52
ARTIFICIAL FIELDS	0	0	14	7	14	7
DAY GAMES	24	11	10	11	34	22
NIGHT GAMES	33	13	36	24	69	37

	NYY	OPP
DOUBLE PLAYS	131	167
TRIPLE PLAYS	0	0
LEFT ON BASE	1238	1144
GRAND SLAM HR	3	5
HOME RUNS - HOME	136	101
HOME RUNS - ROAD	108	80

DOUBLEHEADERS (HOME)	WON 1	LOST 0	SPLIT 0
DOUBLEHEADERS (ROAD)	WON 0	LOST 0	SPLIT 0

	WON	LOST
STARTERS	63	42
RELIEVERS	40	17
STREAKS	9	5

ATTENDANCE

HOME	3,719,358	(81 DATES)	45,918 AVG
ROAD	2,792,495	(81 DATES)	34,475 AVG

2009 Final Yankees Statistics

PLAYER	AVG	G	AB	R	H	TB	2B	3B	HR	RBI	SH	SF	HP	BB	IBB	SO	SB	CS	DP	E	SLG	OBP
Aceves	.000	43	2	0	0	0	0	0	0	0	0	0	0	0	0	1	0	0	0	2	.000	.000
Berroa	.136	21	22	6	3	4	1	0	0	1	1	0	1	0	0	6	0	0	1	3	.182	.174
Burnett	.200	33	5	0	1	1	0	0	0	0	0	0	0	0	0	1	0	0	0	3	.200	.200
Cabrera	.274	154	485	66	133	202	28	1	13	68	4	4	4	43	4	59	10	2	15	3	.416	.336
Cano	.320	161	637	103	204	331	48	2	25	85	0	4	3	30	2	63	5	7	22	12	.520	.352
Cash	.231	10	26	1	6	8	2	0	0	3	0	1	1	0	0	5	0	0	1	0	.308	.250
Cervelli	.298	42	94	13	28	35	4	0	1	11	4	1	0	2	0	11	0	3	1	1	.372	.309
Chamberlain	.000	32	2	0	0	0	0	0	0	0	1	0	0	0	0	0	0	0	0	2	.000	.000
Coke	.000	72	1	0	0	0	0	0	0	0	0	0	0	0	0	1	0	0	0	2	.000	.000
Damon	.282	143	550	107	155	269	36	3	24	82	2	1	2	71	1	98	12	0	9	5	.489	.365
Duncan	.200	11	15	1	3	3	0	0	0	1	0	0	0	0	0	5	0	0	1	0	.200	.200
Gardner	.270	108	248	48	67	94	6	6	3	23	6	1	3	26	0	40	26	5	3	2	.379	.345
Guzman	.167	10	6	2	1	1	0	0	0	1	0	1	0	0	0	1	4	1	0	0	.167	.143
Hairston	.237	45	76	15	18	29	5	0	2	12	2	1	3	11	0	8	0	1	1	2	.382	.352
Hinske	.226	39	84	13	19	43	3	0	7	14	0	2	2	10	1	25	1	0	2	0	.512	.316
Jeter	.334	153	634	107	212	295	27	1	18	66	4	1	5	72	4	90	30	5	18	8	.465	.406
Matsui	.274	142	456	62	125	232	21	1	28	90	0	2	4	64	1	75	0	1	4	0	.509	.367
Miranda	.333	8	9	2	3	6	0	0	1	3	0	0	0	0	0	4	0	0	0	0	.667	.333
Molina	.217	52	138	15	30	37	4	0	1	11	1	1	1	14	0	28	0	0	6	1	.268	.292
Nady	.286	7	28	4	8	12	4	0	0	2	0	0	0	1	0	6	0	0	2	0	.429	.310
Pena	.287	69	115	17	33	44	6	1	1	10	1	0	0	5	0	20	4	1	2	5	.383	.317
Pettitte	.200	32	5	1	1	2	1	0	0	1	1	0	0	0	0	2	0	0	0	2	.400	.200
Posada	.285	111	383	55	109	200	25	0	22	81	0	5	2	48	4	101	1	0	13	7	.522	.363
Ransom	.190	31	79	11	15	26	9	1	0	10	0	0	0	7	0	25	2	0	3	4	.329	.256
Rivera	.000	66	1	0	0	0	0	0	0	1	0	0	0	1	0	0	0	0	0	0	.000	.500
Rodriguez	.286	124	444	78	127	236	17	1	30	100	0	3	8	80	7	97	14	2	13	9	.532	.402
Sabathia	.250	34	4	1	1	1	0	0	0	1	0	0	0	0	0	1	0	0	0	0	.250	.250
Swisher	.249	150	498	84	124	248	35	1	29	82	3	6	3	97	2	126	0	0	13	6	.498	.371
Teixeira	.292	156	609	103	178	344	43	3	39	122	0	5	12	81	9	114	2	0	13	4	.565	.383
Tomko	.000	15	1	0	0	0	0	0	0	0	0	0	0	0	0	1	0	0	0	0	.000	.000
Wang	.000	12	3	0	0	0	0	0	0	0	1	0	0	0	0	0	0	0	1	0	.000	.000
YANKEES	**.283**	**162**	**5660**	**915**	**1604**	**2703**	**325**	**21**	**244**	**881**	**31**	**39**	**54**	**663**	**35**	**1014**	**111**	**28**	**144**	**86**	**.478**	**.362**
OPPONENTS	**.251**	**162**	**5523**	**753**	**1386**	**2251**	**274**	**24**	**181**	**711**	**28**	**49**	**71**	**574**	**28**	**1260**	**125**	**52**	**110**	**97**	**.408**	**.327**

PITCHER	W	L	ERA	G	GS	CG	GF	SHO	SV	IP	H	R	ER	HR	HB	BB	IBB	SO	WP	BK	AVG
Aceves	10	1	3.54	43	1	0	10	0	1	84.0	69	36	33	10	5	16	2	69	0	0	.220
Albaladejo	5	1	5.24	32	0	0	5	0	0	34.1	41	23	20	6	3	16	2	21	0	0	.306
Bruney	5	0	3.92	44	0	0	6	0	0	39.0	36	17	17	6	1	23	3	36	2	0	.243
Burnett	13	9	4.04	33	33	1	0	0	0	207.0	193	99	93	25	10	97	0	195	17	1	.247
Chamberlain	9	6	4.75	32	31	0	0	0	0	157.1	167	94	83	21	12	76	2	133	5	2	.274
Claggett	0	0	33.75	2	0	0	1	0	0	2.2	11	10	10	2	0	4	0	3	1	0	.579
Coke	4	3	4.50	72	0	0	13	0	2	60.0	44	34	30	10	1	20	4	49	7	0	.209
Dunn	0	0	6.75	4	0	0	3	0	0	4.0	3	3	3	1	0	5	0	5	1	0	.200
Gaudin	2	0	3.43	11	6	0	4	0	0	42.0	41	16	16	7	3	20	1	34	3	0	.252
Hughes	8	3	3.03	51	7	0	6	0	3	86.0	68	31	29	8	5	28	1	96	4	2	.217
Kennedy	0	0	0.00	1	0	0	0	0	0	1.0	0	0	0	0	1	2	0	1	0	0	.000
Marte	1	3	9.45	21	0	0	6	0	0	13.1	15	14	14	3	1	6	1	13	0	0	.278
Melancon	0	1	3.86	13	0	0	4	0	0	16.1	13	8	7	0	4	10	0	10	3	0	.217
Mitre	3	3	6.79	12	9	0	2	0	0	51.2	71	45	39	10	3	13	0	32	3	0	.321
Pettitte	14	8	4.16	32	32	0	0	0	0	194.2	193	101	90	20	4	76	1	148	3	0	.259
Ramirez	0	0	5.73	20	0	0	2	0	0	22.0	25	15	14	6	0	18	0	22	1	0	.281
Rivera	3	3	1.76	66	0	0	55	0	44	66.1	48	14	13	7	1	12	1	72	1	0	.197
Robertson	2	1	3.30	45	0	0	20	0	1	43.2	36	19	16	4	1	23	1	63	6	0	.216
Sabathia	19	8	3.37	34	34	2	0	1	0	230.0	197	96	86	18	9	67	7	197	5	0	.232
Swisher	0	0	0.00	1	0	0	1	0	0	1.0	1	0	0	0	0	1	0	1	0	0	.250
Tomko	1	2	5.23	15	0	0	7	0	0	20.2	19	12	12	5	0	7	0	11	1	0	.247
Towers	0	0	3.38	2	0	0	2	0	0	5.1	6	3	2	0	1	1	1	2	0	0	.273
Veras	3	1	5.96	25	0	0	10	0	0	25.2	23	17	17	5	4	14	0	18	0	0	.235
Wang	1	6	9.64	12	9	0	2	0	0	42.0	66	46	45	7	2	19	1	29	3	0	.365
YANKEES	**103**	**59**	**4.26**	**162**	**162**	**3**	**159**	**8**	**51**	**1450.0**	**1386**	**753**	**687**	**181**	**71**	**574**	**28**	**1260**	**66**	**5**	**.251**
OPPONENTS	**59**	**103**	**5.32**	**162**	**162**	**4**	**158**	**5**	**24**	**1432.0**	**1604**	**915**	**846**	**244**	**54**	**663**	**35**	**1014**	**46**	**6**	**.283**

2009 Yankees Starting Pitchers

STARTERS	W	L	PCT	ERA	G	GS	CG	IP	H	TBF	R	ER	HR	SH	SF	HB	BB	IBB	SO	WP	BK	AVG
Aceves	0	0	.000	8.10	1	1	0	3.1	4	17	4	3	1	0	0	1	1	0	2	0	0	.267
Burnett	13	9	.591	4.04	33	33	1	207.0	193	896	99	93	25	2	5	10	97	0	195	17	1	.247
Chamberlain	9	6	.600	4.78	31	31	0	156.1	167	706	94	83	21	6	5	12	76	2	132	5	2	.275
Gaudin	1	0	1.000	3.19	6	6	0	31.0	28	137	11	11	4	0	2	3	15	1	23	3	0	.239
Hughes	3	2	.600	5.45	7	7	0	34.2	37	158	22	21	6	0	4	5	15	0	31	1	0	.276
Mitre	3	3	.500	7.16	9	9	0	44.0	65	211	41	35	8	0	4	2	12	0	27	2	0	.337
Pettitte	14	8	.636	4.16	32	32	0	194.2	193	834	101	90	20	4	4	4	76	1	148	3	0	.259
Sabathia	19	8	.704	3.37	34	34	2	230.0	197	938	96	86	18	4	9	9	67	7	197	5	0	.232
Wang	1	6	.143	11.38	9	9	0	34.0	57	173	44	43	6	2	1	2	17	1	22	3	0	.377
TOTALS	**63**	**42**	**.600**	**4.48**	**162**	**162**	**3**	**935.0**	**941**	**4070**	**512**	**465**	**109**	**18**	**34**	**48**	**376**	**12**	**777**	**39**	**3**	**.262**

2009 Yankees Relievers

RELIEVERS	W	L	PCT	ERA	APP	GF	SV	IP	H	TBF	R	ER	HR	SH	SF	HB	BB	IBB	SO	WP	BK	AVG
Aceves	10	1	.909	3.35	42	10	1	80.2	65	320	32	30	9	1	2	4	15	2	67	0	0	.218
Albaladejo	5	1	.833	5.24	32	5	0	34.1	41	158	23	20	6	1	4	3	16	2	21	0	0	.306
Bruney	5	0	1.000	3.92	44	6	0	39.0	36	175	17	17	6	2	1	1	23	3	36	2	0	.243
Chamberlain	0	0	.000	0.00	1	0	0	1.0	0	3	0	0	0	0	0	0	0	0	1	0	0	.000
Claggett	0	0	.000	33.75	2	1	0	2.2	11	23	10	10	2	0	0	0	4	0	3	1	0	.579
Coke	4	3	.571	4.50	72	13	2	60.0	44	238	34	30	10	1	5	1	20	4	49	7	0	.209
Dunn	0	0	.000	6.75	4	3	0	4.0	3	20	3	3	1	0	0	0	5	0	5	1	0	.200
Gaudin	1	0	1.000	4.09	5	4	0	11.0	13	51	5	5	3	0	0	0	5	0	11	0	0	.283
Hughes	5	1	.833	1.40	44	6	3	51.1	31	193	9	8	2	0	0	0	13	1	65	3	2	.172
Kennedy	0	0	.000	0.00	1	0	0	1.0	0	6	0	0	0	0	0	1	2	0	1	0	0	.000
Marte	1	3	.250	9.45	21	6	0	13.1	15	62	14	14	3	1	0	1	6	1	13	0	0	.278
Melancon	0	1	.000	3.86	13	4	0	16.1	13	74	8	7	0	0	0	4	10	0	10	3	0	.217
Mitre	0	0	.000	4.70	3	2	0	7.2	6	30	4	4	2	0	0	1	1	0	5	1	0	.214
Ramirez	0	0	.000	5.73	20	2	0	22.0	25	110	15	14	6	0	2	0	18	0	22	1	0	.281
Rivera	3	3	.500	1.76	66	55	44	66.1	48	257	14	13	7	0	0	1	12	1	72	1	0	.197
Robertson	2	1	.667	3.30	45	20	1	43.2	36	191	19	16	4	0	0	1	23	1	63	6	0	.216
Swisher	0	0	.000	0.00	1	1	0	1.0	1	5	0	0	0	0	0	0	1	0	1	0	0	.250
Tomko	1	2	.333	5.23	15	7	0	20.2	19	85	12	12	5	1	0	0	7	0	11	1	0	.247
Towers	0	0	.000	3.38	2	2	0	5.1	6	25	3	2	0	0	1	1	1	1	2	0	0	.273
Veras	3	1	.750	5.96	25	10	0	25.2	23	118	17	17	5	2	0	4	14	0	18	0	0	.235
Wang	0	0	.000	2.25	3	2	0	8.0	9	33	2	2	1	1	0	0	2	0	7	0	0	.300
TOTALS	**40**	**17**	**.702**	**3.91**	**461**	**159**	**51**	**515.0**	**445**	**2177**	**241**	**224**	**72**	**10**	**15**	**23**	**198**	**16**	**483**	**27**	**2**	**.231**

2009 Yankees Pinch-Hitters

BATTER	AVG	APP	AB	R	H	TB	2B	3B	HR	RBI	SH	SF	HP	BB	IBB	SO	SB	CS	GDP	SLG	OBP
Berroa	.000	1	1	0	0	0	0	0	0	0	0	0	0	0	0	0	0	0	0	.000	.000
Cabrera	.000	7	6	1	0	0	0	0	0	0	0	0	0	1	0	2	0	0	0	.000	.143
Cano	.500	2	2	0	1	1	0	0	0	0	0	0	0	0	0	0	0	0	0	.500	.500
Cervelli	.000	1	1	0	0	0	0	0	0	0	0	0	0	0	0	0	0	0	0	.000	.000
Damon	.000	8	4	0	0	0	0	0	0	0	0	0	1	3	0	2	0	0	0	.000	.500
Duncan	.000	3	3	0	0	0	0	0	0	0	0	0	0	0	0	1	0	0	0	.000	.000
Gardner	.333	6	6	1	2	3	1	0	0	0	0	0	0	0	0	1	1	0	0	.500	.333
Guzman	.000	1	0	0	0	0	0	0	0	1	0	1	0	0	0	0	0	0	0	.000	.000
Hairston	.000	4	2	1	0	0	0	0	0	1	0	1	0	1	0	1	0	0	0	.000	.250
Hinske	.167	9	6	1	1	1	0	0	0	1	0	1	0	2	0	2	1	0	0	.167	.333
Jeter	.000	1	1	0	0	0	0	0	0	0	0	0	0	0	0	0	0	0	0	.000	.000
Matsui	.381	26	21	2	8	13	2	0	1	4	0	0	0	5	1	5	0	0	0	.619	.500
Miranda	1.000	1	1	0	1	1	0	0	0	0	0	0	0	0	0	0	0	0	0	1.000	1.000
Molina	.000	1	1	0	0	0	0	0	0	0	0	0	0	0	0	1	0	0	0	.000	.000
Pena	.000	3	3	0	0	0	0	0	0	0	0	0	0	0	0	1	0	0	0	.000	.000
Posada	.364	14	11	3	4	10	0	0	2	7	0	1	0	2	0	6	0	0	1	.909	.429
Rodriguez	.000	2	1	0	0	0	0	0	0	0	0	0	0	1	0	0	0	0	0	.000	.500
Swisher	.200	6	5	0	1	2	1	0	0	0	0	0	0	1	0	1	0	0	0	.400	.333
Teixeira	.000	1	1	0	0	0	0	0	0	0	0	0	0	0	0	0	0	0	0	.000	.000
TOTALS	**.237**	**97**	**76**	**9**	**18**	**31**	**4**	**0**	**3**	**14**	**0**	**4**	**1**	**16**	**1**	**23**	**2**	**0**	**1**	**.408**	**.361**

2009 Yankees Fielding Statistics

PITCHERS

PLAYER	PCT	G	GS	PO	A	E	TC	DP	TP
Aceves	.846	43	1	2	9	2	13	1	0
Albaladejo	1.000	32	0	1	7	0	8	0	0
Bruney	1.000	44	0	0	3	0	3	0	0
Burnett	.893	33	33	5	20	3	28	0	0
Chamberlain	.947	32	31	8	28	2	38	4	0
Claggett	.000	2	0	0	0	0	0	0	0
Coke	.857	72	0	3	9	2	14	0	0
Dunn	.000	4	0	0	0	0	0	0	0
Gaudin	1.000	11	6	3	8	0	11	1	0
Hughes	1.000	51	7	4	5	0	9	0	0
Kennedy	.000	1	0	0	0	0	0	0	0
Marte	1.000	21	0	0	1	0	1	0	0
Melancon	1.000	13	0	1	4	0	5	0	0
Mitre	.833	12	9	3	12	3	18	1	0
Pettitte	.938	32	32	3	27	2	32	1	0
Ramirez	1.000	20	0	1	2	0	3	0	0
Rivera	1.000	66	0	2	16	0	18	1	0
Robertson	1.000	45	0	0	3	0	3	0	0
Sabathia	1.000	34	34	3	28	0	31	0	0
Swisher	.000	1	0	0	0	0	0	0	0
Towers	.000	2	0	0	0	0	0	0	0
Wang	1.000	12	9	3	7	0	10	1	0
Tomko	1.000	15	0	2	1	0	3	0	0
Veras	1.000	25	0	3	1	0	4	0	0

FIRST BASE

PLAYER	PCT	G	GS	PO	A	E	TC	DP	TP
Miranda	1.000	8	1	19	1	0	20	2	0
Molina	1.000	3	0	4	2	0	6	1	0
Posada	1.000	2	0	3	2	0	5	0	0
Ransom	1.000	1	1	5	2	0	7	1	0
Swisher	.989	20	10	89	5	1	95	7	0
Teixeira	.997	152	150	1222	49	4	1275	110	0

SECOND BASE

PLAYER	PCT	G	GS	PO	A	E	TC	DP	TP
Cano	.984	161	158	308	424	12	744	96	0
Hairston	1.000	3	0	3	2	0	5	0	0
Pena	1.000	8	3	7	10	0	17	2	0
Ransom	1.000	1	1	4	2	0	6	1	0

THIRD BASE

PLAYER	PCT	G	GS	PO	A	E	TC	DP	TP
Berroa	.880	16	6	6	16	3	25	3	0
Hairston	.920	16	9	3	20	2	25	2	0
Hinske	1.000	10	2	3	3	0	6	0	0
Molina	.000	1	0	0	0	0	0	0	0
Pena	.952	27	14	10	30	2	42	5	0
Ransom	.911	23	18	10	31	4	45	2	0
Rodriguez	.967	116	113	66	200	9	275	17	0

SHORTSTOP

PLAYER	PCT	G	GS	PO	A	E	TC	DP	TP
Hairston	1.000	11	2	6	10	0	16	2	0
Jeter	.986	150	147	206	340	8	554	75	0
Pena	.954	34	11	21	41	3	65	9	0
Ransom	1.000	3	2	2	5	0	7	0	0

OUTFIELDERS

PLAYER	PCT	G	GS	PO	A	E	TC	DP	TP
Cabrera	.990	151	130	300	3	3	306	1	0
Damon	.978	132	128	220	6	5	231	2	0
Duncan	1.000	8	2	5	0	0	5	0	0
Gardner	.990	99	63	186	3	2	191	2	0
Guzman	1.000	7	0	4	0	0	4	0	0
Hairston	1.000	19	10	22	1	0	23	0	0
Hinske	1.000	24	17	32	0	0	32	0	0
Nady	1.000	6	6	10	0	0	10	0	0
Swisher	.980	134	130	249	2	5	256	1	0

CATCHERS

PLAYER	PCT	G	GS	PO	A	E	TC	DP	TP	PB
Cash	1.000	10	7	57	10	0	67	1	0	0
Cervelli	.995	40	25	207	14	1	222	1	0	0
Molina	.997	49	42	366	21	1	388	1	0	3
Posada	.990	100	88	648	48	7	703	6	0	8

2009 Yankees Highs & Lows

Individual Batting

Longest Hitting Streak	18	Cano (4/12-5/1)
Most Runs, Game, Yankees	4	3x, Last by Matsui (8/13 at SEA)
Most Runs, Game, Opponents	4	2x, Last by Pedroia (8/22 at BOS)
Most Hits Game, Yankees	5	2x, Last by Gardner (6/26 at NYM)
Most Hits Game, Opponents	5	Upton (10/2 at TB)
Most Total Bases, Game	12	Teixeira (9/19 at SEA)
Most Total Bases, Game, Opponents	11	Upton (10/2 at TB)
Most Doubles, Game	3	Cano (9/19 at SEA)
Most Triples, Game	1	21x, last by Teixeira (9/19 at SEA)
Most Home Runs, Game	2	16x, Last by Rodriguez (10/4 at TB)
Most Home Runs, Game, Opponents	2	6x, Last by Snider (9/15 vs. TOR)
Most Extra-base Hits, Game	3	8x, Last by Cano and Teixeira (9/19 at SEA)
Most Extra-base Hits, Game, Opponents	3	3x, Last by Upton (10/2 at TB)
Most RBI, Game, Yankees	7	2x, Last by Rodriguez (10/4 at TB)
Most RBI, Game, Opponents	6	5x, last by Upton (10/2 at TB)
Most SB, Game	3	2x, Last by Rodriguez (9/25 vs. BOS)
Most SB, Game, Opponents	3	Suzuki (6/30 vs. SEA)
Pinch-Hit HR, Yankees	1	3x, Posada (4/19 vs. CLE; 9/9 vs. TB) and Matsui (9/21 at LAA)
Pinch-Hit HR, Opponents	1	Morales (9/21 vs. LAA)

Individual Pitching

Most Strikeouts, Game, Starter	12	2x, Last by Burnett (8/27 vs. TEX)
Most Strikeouts, Game, Reliever	7	Aceves (5/4 vs. BOS)
Most Strikeouts, Game, Opponent	10	2x, Last by Floyd (7/30 at CWS)
Most Walks, Game, Yankees	7	2x, Last by Chamberlain (8/6 vs. BOS)
Most Walks, Game, Opponent	7	Nipppert (6/10 at OAK)
Low-hit, Complete Game	4	Sabathia (5/8 at BAL)
Most Innings, Game, Starter	9.0	Sabathia (5/8 at BAL)
Most Innings, Game, Reliever	5.0	Mitre (9/20 at SEA)
Most Innings, Game, Opponents	9.0	4x, Last by Hernandez (9/18 at SEA)
Most HR Allowed, Game	4	2x, Last by Mitre (9/15 vs. TOR)
Most HR Allowed, Game, Opponents	5	Beckett (8/23 at BOS)
Longest Winning Streak	9	Sabathia (8/2-9/26)
Longest Losing Streak	4	Burnett (8/1-27)
Most Consecutive Scoreless Innings	21.1	Rivera (6/16-8/9)

Team Batting

Most Runs Game, Yankees	20	8/21 at BOS
Most Runs Game, Both Clubs	31	8/21 at BOS
Most Runs Inning, Yankees	10	2x, Last on 10/4 at TB (6th Inning)
Most Hits Game, Yankees	23	8/21 at BOS
Most Hits, Both Clubs	35	8/21 at BOS
Most Hits Inning, Yankees	8	5x, Last on 9/14 vs. LAA
Most Total Bases, Game	39	8/21 at BOS
Most Doubles, Game	8	8/21 at BOS
Most Triples, Game	3	5/13 at TOR
Most Home Runs, Game	5	4x, Last on 9/1 at BAL
Most Home Runs, Both Clubs	8	2x, Last on 5/7 vs. TB
Most Extra-base Hits, Game	11	8/21 at BOS
Most Walks, Game	11	2x, Last on 6/28 at NYM
Most Walks, Both Clubs	18	8/6 at BOS
Most Strikeouts, Game	14	2x, Last on 8/7 vs. BOS (15 innings)
Most Strikeouts, Both Clubs	28	8/7 vs. BOS (15 innings)
Most Stolen Bases, Game	7	9/25 vs. BOS
Most Stolen Bases, Opponent	4	3x, Last on 7/11 at LAA
Most GIDP, Game	3	10x, last on 9/7 vs. TB
Most LOB, Game	15	2x, Last on 4/24 at BOS (11 Innings)
Most LOB, Both Clubs	28	4/24 at BOS (11 Innings)

Team Pitching

Most Runs Allowed, Game	22	4/18 vs. CLE
Most Runs Allowed, Inning	14	4/18 vs. CLE
Most Hits Allowed, Game	25	4/18 vs. CLE
Most Hits Allowed, Inning	13	4/18 vs. CLE
Most Total Bases Allowed, Game	50	4/18 vs. CLE
Most Home Runs Allowed, Game	6	2x, Last on 5/7 vs. TB
Most Extra-base Hits Allowed, Game	13	4/18 vs. CLE
Most Strikeouts Game	15	2x, Last on 9/23 vs. LAA
Most Walks, Game	12	8/6 at BOS

Team Fielding

Most Errors, Game	4	9/6 at TOR
Most Errors, Both Clubs	6	6/6 vs. TB
Most DPs Turned Game, Yankees	4	2x, Last on 8/26 vs. TEX
Most DPs Turned, Both Clubs	7	4/24 at BOS (11 innings)

2009 Yankees Highs & Lows

Miscellaneous

Longest Winning Streak	9	5/13-21
Longest Losing Streak	5	5/2-7
Longest Winning Streak, Home	8	7/17-24
Longest Losing Streak, Home	5	5/2-7
Longest Winning Streak, Road	8	6/24-7/9
Longest Losing Streak, Road	4	4/24-27
Longest Game, Innings	15	8/7 vs. BOS
Longest Game, Time	5:33	8/7 vs. BOS (15 innings)
Longest Game, Time (9 inn.)	4:21	2x, Last on 4/25 at BOS
Shortest Game, Time	2:15	8/17 at OAK
Highest Attendance, Home	49,005	8/6 vs. BOS
Highest Attendance, Road	48,914	5/25 at TEX
Largest Margin of Victory	15	6/14 vs. NYM
Largest Margin of Defeat	18	4/18 at CLE
Largest Shutout Victory	15-0	6/14 vs. NYM
Largest Shutout Defeat	7-0	6/9 at BOS
Left on base average, Yankees	7.6	
Solo Home runs	148	
Two-Run Home Runs	64	
Three-Run Home Runs	29	
Grand Slams, Yankees	3	
Grand Slams, Opponents	5	
"Walk-off" Wins	15	
"Walk-off" Losses	4	
Come-From-Behind Wins	51	
10-Plus Runs Games	23	
10-Plus Hits Games	82	
Five Hits or Fewer Games	14	
Players Used	45	
Starting Pitchers Used	9	
Ejections	8	

YANKEES RECORDS, 2009

Pre-All-Star Break	51-37
Post-All-Star Break	52-22
vs. LH starters	36-18
vs. RH starters	67-41
Yankees Score First	66-20
Opponents Score First	36-39
Yankees Score 4 Runs or More	92-29
Yankees Score 3 Runs or Fewer	99-39
Yankees Outhit Opp.:	86-14
Opp. Outhits Yankees:	17-40
One-Run Games:	22-16
Leading After 6:	71-2
Trailing After 6:	16-52
Tied After 6:	16-5
Leading After 7:	79-4
Trailing After 7:	9-55
Tied After 7:	15-0
Leading After 8:	85-2
Trailing After 8:	5-53
Tied After 8:	14-4
Extra-Inning Games:	7-3
On Grass	89-52
On Turf	14-7
Day	34-22
Night	69-37
April	12-10
May	17-11
June	15-11
July	18-9
August	21-7
Sept./Oct.	20-11
Series Record:	36-14-3
Series Record, home:	19-6-2
Series Record, road:	17-8-1
Series Openers:	31-22
vs. AL East	45-27
vs. AL Central	25-9
vs. AL West	23-15
vs. NL	10-8

YANKEES LINEUPS

2009 STARTS BY POSITION

PLAYER	C	1B	2B	3B	SS	LF	CF	RF	DH
Berroa	--	--	--	6	--	--	--	--	--
Cabrera	--	--	--	--	--	20	97	13	--
Cano	--	--	158	--	--	--	--	--	--
Cash	7	--	--	--	--	--	--	--	--
Cervelli	25	--	--	--	--	--	--	--	--
Damon	--	--	--	--	--	129	--	--	4
Duncan	--	--	--	--	--	--	--	2	1
Gardner	--	--	--	--	--	--	63	--	--
Hairston	--	--	--	9	2	8	2	--	--
Hinske	--	--	--	2	--	1	--	15	1
Jeter	--	--	--	--	147	--	--	--	5
Matsui	--	--	--	--	--	--	--	--	116
Miranda	--	1	--	--	--	--	--	--	--
Molina	42	--	--	--	--	--	--	--	1
Nady	--	--	--	--	--	--	--	6	1
Pena	--	--	3	14	11	--	--	--	--
Posada	88	--	--	--	--	--	--	--	9
Ransom	--	1	1	18	2	--	--	--	--
Rodriguez	--	--	--	113	--	--	--	--	9
Swisher	--	10	--	--	--	4	--	126	1
Teixeira	--	150	--	--	--	--	--	--	5

2009 STARTS BY BATTING ORDER

PLAYER	1	2	3	4	5	6	7	8	9
Berroa	--	--	--	--	--	--	--	4	2
Cabrera	--	1	--	--	--	7	34	56	32
Cano	--	1	1	--	50	45	61	--	--
Cash	--	--	--	--	--	--	--	1	6
Cervelli	--	--	--	--	--	--	1	8	16
Damon	4	127	2	--	--	--	--	--	--
Duncan	--	--	--	--	1	1	1	--	--
Gardner	11	3	--	--	--	--	5	12	32
Hairston	--	4	--	--	--	--	4	10	3
Hinske	--	1	--	--	1	--	4	10	3
Jeter	147	5	--	--	--	--	--	--	--
Matsui	--	--	1	21	63	4	27	--	--
Miranda	--	--	--	--	--	--	1	--	--
Molina	--	--	--	--	--	--	2	6	36
Nady	--	--	--	1	2	--	4	--	--
Pena	--	--	--	--	--	--	--	12	16
Posada	--	--	--	9	29	59	--	--	--
Ransom	--	--	--	--	--	--	1	14	7
Rodriguez	--	--	--	122	--	--	--	--	--
Swisher	--	20	4	8	16	46	18	30	--
Teixeira	--	--	154	1	--	--	--	--	--

New York Yankees™ OPPONENTS

The Braves' Warren Spahn [L] and the Yankees' Whitey Ford [R] started against each other four times in World Series play, including three times in the 1958 Fall Classic which the Yankees won in seven games.

Baltimore Orioles

Series Results, Last 10 Years

Year	Hm	Rd	Tot
2009	7-2	6-3	13-5
2008	6-3	5-4	11-7
2007	5-4	4-5	9-9
2006	5-4	7-3	12-7
2005	7-2	4-5	11-7
2004	7-3	7-2	14-5
2003	6-4	7-2	13-6
2002	7-3	6-3	13-6
2001	5-3	8-2	13-5
2000	4-2	3-3	7-5

Oriole Park at Camden Yards, 333 W. Camden St. • Baltimore, MD 21201
(410) 685-9800 • (410) 547-6272 - Fax
Capacity: 48,190 **Dimensions:** 330 LF, 400 CF, 318 RF

President, Baseball Operations: Andy MacPhail
Manager: Dave Trembley
Director, Public Relations: Monica Barlow

2009 Record, Finish .... 64-98, 5th in AL East (-39.0 games)

Yankees vs. Baltimore

vs. BAL, 2009 13-5
at BAL, 2009 6-3
at New York, 2009 7-2
at Camden Yards 88-49-1

vs. BAL, All-Time 497-414-3
at BAL, All-Time.............. 240-213-2
at New York, All-Time 257-201-1
at original Yankee Stadium 241-190-1

Series Sweeps at New York	by NYY	by BAL
3-game	7/20-22/09	6/6-8/86
4-game	9/19-22/05	9/21-23/76

Series Sweeps at Baltimore	by NYY	by BAL
3-game	8/31-9/2/09	4/15-17/05
4-game	8/14-17/03	9/5-7/66

Longest Winning Streaks

by NYY .... 10 games (5/10-9/2/2009; 4/21-6/29/1955)
by BAL.................................... 9 games (8/15/67-5/22/1968)

2010 Schedule

at New York............................ May 3-5, June 1-3, September 6-8
at Baltimore .... April 27-29, June 8-10, September 17-19

Boston Red Sox

Series Results, Last 10 Years

Year	Hm	Rd	Tot
2009	7-2	2-7	9-9
2008	4-5	5-4	9-9
2007	6-3	4-5	10-8
2006	4-6	7-2	11-8
2005	5-4	5-5	10-9
2004	5-4	3-7	8-11
2003	5-5	5-4	10-9
2002	5-4	5-5	10-9
2001	8-1	5-4	13-5
2000	2-4	5-2	7-6

Fenway Park, 4 Yawkey Way, Boston, MA 02215
(617) 267-9440 • (617) 375-0944 - Fax
Capacity: 37,402 (night); 36,974 (day) **Dimensions:** 310 LF, 420 CF, 380 RF

Executive Vice President/General Manager: Theo Epstein
Manager: Terry Francona
Director, Media Relations: Pam Ganley

2009 Record, Finish .... 95-67, 2nd in AL East (-8.0 games) AL Wild Card

Yankees vs. Boston

vs. BOS, 2009 9-9
at BOS, 2009 2-7
at New York, 2009 7-2
at Fenway Park....... 458-442-4

vs. BOS, All-Time.......... 1104-907-14
at BOS, All-Time 507-503-7
at New York, All-Time 597-404-7
at original Yankee Stadium....... 484-285-4

Series Sweeps at New York	by NYY	by BOS
3-game	9/25-27/09	4/23-25/04
4-game	8/6-9/09	none
5-game	*9/28-30/51	*7/9-13/39

Series Sweeps at Boston	by NYY	by BOS
3-game	8/31-9/2/01	6/09-11/09
4-game	10/2-5/86	6/4-7/90
5-game	**8/18-21/06	none

* includes two doubleheaders ** includes one doubleheader

Longest Winning Streaks

by NYY .... 12 games (8/16/1952-4/23/1953; 5/27-8/23/1936)
by BOS .... 17 games (10/3/1911-7/1/1912)

2010 Schedule

at New York........................ May 17-18, August 6-9, September 24-26
at Boston .... April 4-7, May 7-9, October 1-3

Chicago White Sox

Series Results, Last 10 Years

Year	Hm	Rd	Tot
2009	3-0	1-3	4-3
2008	3-1	2-1	5-2
2007	2-1	4-3	6-4
2006	3-0	1-2	4-2
2005	1-2	2-1	3-3
2004	2-2	2-1	4-3
2003	1-2	1-2	2-4
2002	1-2	3-0	4-2
2001	3-0	2-1	5-1
2000	1-5	3-3	4-8

US Cellular Field, 333 West 35th St., Chicago, IL 60616
(312) 674-5300 • (312) 674-5116 - Fax
Capacity: 40,615 **Dimensions:** 330 LF, 400 CF, 335 RF

Senior Vice President/General Manager: Ken Williams
Manager: Ozzie Guillen
Director, Media Relations: Bob Beghtol

2009 Record, Finish . . . . 79-83, 3rd in AL Central (-7.5 games)

Yankees vs. Chicago

vs. CWS, 2009	4-3	vs. CWS, All-Time	1031-798-14
at CWS, 2009	1-3	at CWS, All-Time	481-436-9
at New York, 2009	3-0	at New York, All-Time	550-362-5
at U.S. Cellular Field:	45-41	at original Yankee Stadium:	428-255-3

Series Sweeps at New York	**by NYY**	**by CWS**
3-game	8/28-30/09	9/14-16/92
4-game	6/6-8/69	6/15-18/00

Series Sweeps at Chicago	**by NYY**	**by CWS**
3-game	5/27-29/02	8/6-8/91
4-game	6/17-20/76	8/17-20/64

Longest Winning Streaks
by NYY . . . . .10 games (4/22-6/22/1964; 8/14/1944-5/26/1945)
by CWS . . . . .8 games (9/3/1972-7/10/1973; 6/10-8/22/1967; 7/16-8/22/1906)

2010 Schedule
at New York . . . . April 30-May 2
at Chicago . . . . August 27-29

Cleveland Indians

Series Results, Last 10 Years

Year	Hm	Rd	Tot
2009	2-2	3-1	5-3
2008	1-2	2-2	3-4
2007	3-0	3-0	6-0
2006	2-1	2-2	4-3
2005	3-1	1-2	4-3
2004	2-1	2-1	4-2
2003	4-0	1-2	5-2
2002	3-0	3-3	6-3
2001	3-3	2-1	5-4
2000	1-3	4-2	5-5

Progressive Field, 2401 Ontario St., Cleveland, OH 44115
(216) 420-4200 • Fax: (216) 420-4396
Capacity: 43,421 **Dimensions:** 325 LF, 405 CF, 325 RF

Executive Vice President, General Manager: Mark Shapiro
Manager: Manny Acta
Director, Media Relations: Bart Swain

2009 Record, Finish . . . . .65-97, T4th in AL Central (-21.5 games)

Yankees vs. Indians

vs. CLE, 2009	5-3	vs. CLE, All-Time	1065-844-12
at CLE, 2009	3-1	at CLE, All-Time	487-466-7
at New York, 2009	2-2	at New York, All-Time	578-378-5
at Progressive Field:	44-25	at original Yankee Stadium:	456-262-1

Series Sweeps at New York	**by NYY**	**by CLE**
3-game	4/17-19/07	4/7-9/89
4-game	7/17-20/03	none

Series Sweeps at Cleveland	**by NYY**	**by CLE**
3-game	8/10-12/07	9/11-13/70
4-game	6/21-23/96	*6/15-17/62

* includes one doubleheader

Longest Winning Streaks
by NYY . . . . 13 games (7/2/1976-7/7/1977)
by CLE . . . . 13 games (7/13-9/23/1908)

2010 Schedule
at New York . . . . May 28-31
at Cleveland . . . . July 26-29

Detroit Tigers

Series Results, Last 10 Years

Year	Hm	Rd	Tot
2009	3-0	2-1	5-1
2008	0-3	2-1	2-4
2007	3-1	1-3	4-4
2006	2-1	3-1	5-2
2005	3-0	2-1	5-1
2004	1-2	2-2	3-4
2003	3-0	2-1	5-1
2002	501	3-0	8-1
2001	3-0	2-4	5-4
2000	3-3	1-5	4-8

Comerica Park, 2100 Woodward Avenue, Detroit, MI 48201
(313) 471-2000 • (313) 471-2138 - Fax
Capacity: 41,255 **Dimensions:** 345 LF, 420 CF, 330 RF

President/CEO/General Manager: Dave Dombrowski
Manager: Jim Leyland
Director, Baseball Media Relations: Brian Britten

2009 Record, Finish .... 86-77, 2nd in AL Central (-1.0 game)

Yankees vs. Detroit

vs. DET, 2009	5-1	vs. DET, All-Time	1016-899-10
at DET, 2009	2-1	at DET, All-Time	462-495-6
at New York, 2009	3-0	at New York, All-Time	554-404-4
at Comerica Park	20-19	at original Yankee Stadium	433-288-2

Series Sweeps at New York	**by NYY**	**by DET**
3-game	7/17-19/09	4/29-5/1/08
4-game	9/8-11/88	6/13-15/58

Series Sweeps at Detroit	**by NYY**	**by DET**
3-game	9/20-22/02	5/12-14/00
4-game	6/8-11/26	*8/12-13/45

* includes two doubleheaders

Longest Winning Streaks
by NYY .... 11 games (7/12-9/17/1942)
by DET .... 12 games (6/10-8/18/1908)

2010 Schedule
at New York .... August 16-19
at Detroit .... May 10-13

Kansas City Royals

Series Results, Last 10 Years

Year	Hm	Rd	Tot
2009	2-1	2-1	4-2
2008	4-3	1-2	5-5
2007	3-0	6-1	9-1
2006	5-1	2-1	7-2
2005	3-0	0-3	3-3
2004	3-0	2-1	5-1
2003	3-0	1-2	4-2
2002	2-1	3-0	5-1
2001	3-0	3-0	6-0
2000	5-1	3-1	8-2

Kauffman Stadium, One Royal Way, Kansas City, MO 64129
(816) 921-8000 • (816) 921-5775 - Fax
Capacity: 37,840 **Dimensions:** 330 LF, 400 CF, 330 RF

Senior VP & General Manager – Baseball Operations: Dayton Moore
Manager: Trey Hillman
VP – Communications & Broadcasting: Mike Swanson

2009 Record, Finish .... 65-97, T4th in AL Central (-21.5 games)

Yankees vs. Kansas City

vs. KC, 2009	4-2	vs. KC, All-Time	256-174-1
at KC, 2009	2-1	at KC, All-Time	113-101-1
at New York, 2009	2-1	at New York, All-Time	143-73
All-Time at Kauffman Stadium:	100-90	at original Yankee Stadium:	134-67

Series Sweeps at New York	**by NYY**	**by KC**
3-game	8/3-5/07	6/3-5/94
4-game	*8/7-9/98	none
5-game	7/12-15/84	none

Series Sweeps at Kansas City	**by NYY**	**by KC**
3-game	9/7-9/07	5/31-6/2/05
4-game	none	none

* includes one doubleheader

Longest Winning Streaks
by NYY .... 12 games (8/13/1997-8/18/1998)
by KC .... 5 games (5/26-7/4/1990; 5/14-7/24/1978)

2010 Schedule
at New York .... July 22-25
at Kansas City .... August 12-15

Los Angeles Angels

Series Results, Last 10 Years

Year	Hm	Rd	Tot
2009	3-1	2-4	5-5
2008	2-2	1-5	3-7
2007	2-4	1-2	3-6
2006	2-2	2-4	4-6
2005	3-3	1-3	4-6
2004	2-4	2-1	4-5
2003	1-2	5-1	6-3
2002	2-1	2-2	4-3
2001	2-2	1-2	3-4
2000	2-2	3-3	5-5

Angel Stadium of Anaheim, 2000 Gene Autry Way, Anaheim, CA 92806
(714) 940-2000 • (714) 940-2205 - Fax
Capacity: 45,285 **Dimensions:** 365 LF, 400 CF, 365 RF

Vice President & General Manager: Tony Reagins
Manager: Mike Scioscia
Vice President, Communications: Tim Mead

2009 Record, Finish .... 97-65, 1st in AL West (+10.0 games)

Yankees vs. Los Angeles

vs. LAA, 2009	5-5	vs. LAA, All-Time	322-271
at LAA, 2009	2-4	at LAA, All-Time	144-157
at New York, 2009	3-1	at New York, All-Time	178-114
All-Time at Angel Stadium:	120-136	at original Yankee Stadium:	166-109

Series Sweeps at New York	**by NYY**	**by LAA**
3-game	8/29-31/95	5/25-27/07
4-game	7/22-25/93	none

Series Sweeps at Los Angeles	**by NYY**	**by LAA**
3-game	7/29-31/03	7/10-12/09
4-game	7/21-24/94	none

Longest Winning Streaks
by NYY .... 7 games (8/23/1980-5/4/1981)
by LAA................................. 5 games (4x, last 4/27-7/23/2005)

2010 Schedule
at New York.. April 13-15, July 20-21
at Los Angeles .... April 23-25

Minnesota Twins

Series Results, Last 10 Years

Year	Hm	Rd	Tot
2009	4-0	3-0	7-0
2008	3-0	3-4	6-4
2007	3-1	2-1	5-2
2006	2-1	1-2	3-3
2005	2-1	1-2	3-3
2004	3-0	1-2	4-2
2003	3-0	4-0	7-0
2002	3-0	3-0	6-0
2001	1-2	1-2	2-4
2000	3-3	2-2	5-5

Target Field, 1 Twins Way, Minneapolis, MN 55403
(612) 659-3400 • (612) 659-4029 - Fax
Capacity: 39,800 **Dimensions:** 339 LF, 404 CF, 328 RF

Senior Vice President, General Manager: Bill Smith
Manager: Ron Gardenhire
Director, Baseball Communications: Mike Herman

2009 Record, Finish .... 87-76, 1st in AL Central (+1.0 game)

Yankees vs. Minnesota

vs. MIN, 2009	7-0	vs. MIN, All-Time	324-240-1
at MIN, 2009	3-0	at MIN, All-Time	154-133
at New York, 2009	4-0	at New York, All-Time	170-107-1
All-Time at Metrodome:	77-64	at original Yankee Stadium:	159-103-1

Series Sweeps at New York	**by NYY**	**by MIN**
3-game	7/21-23/08	8/9-11/68
4-game	5/15-18/09	none

Series Sweeps at Minnesota	**by NYY**	**by MIN**
3-game	7/7-9/09	9/6-8/91
4-game	4/18-21/03	7/3-5/67

Longest Winning Streaks
by NYY .... 13 games (5/10/2002-4/21/2003)
by MIN.................................. 6 games (3x, last 5/24-6/4/1969)

2010 Schedule
at New York... May 14-16
at Minnesota.. May 25-27

Oakland Athletics

Series Results, Last 10 Years

Year	Hm	Rd	Tot
2009	5-1	2-1	7-2
2008	3-0	2-1	5-1
2007	1-2	1-2	2-4
2006	2-4	1-2	3-6
2005	2-1	5-1	7-2
2004	5-1	2-1	7-2
2003	1-2	2-4	3-6
2002	3-3	2-1	5-4
2001	3-0	0-6	3-6
2000	4-2	2-1	6-3

Oakland Alameda-County Coliseum, 7000 Coliseum Way • Oakland, CA 94621
(510) 638-4900 • (510) 562-1633 - Fax
Capacity: 34,077 **Dimensions:** 330 LF, 400 CF, 330 RF

Vice President and General Manager: Billy Beane
Manager: Bob Geren
Director of Public Relations: Bob Rose

2009 Record, Finish .... 75-87, 4th in AL West (-22.0 games)

Yankees vs. Oakland

vs. OAK, 2009	7-2	vs. OAK, All-Time	246-217
at OAK, 2009	2-1	at OAK, All-Time	110-119
at New York, 2009	5-1	at New York, All-Time	136-98
All-Time at County Coliseum:	110-119	at original Yankee Stadium:	124-92

Series Sweeps at New York	**by NYY**	**by OAK**
3-game	7/18-20/08	6/9-11/06
4-game	9/5-8/85	7/14-16/72

Series Sweeps at Oakland	**by NYY**	**by OAK**
3-game	5/13-15/05	8/10-12/01
4-game	7/6-8/79	none

Longest Winning Streaks
by NYY .... 8 games (3x, last 6/12/2008-7/24/2009)
by OAK .... 16 games (9/9/1989-5/1/1991)

2010 Schedule
at New York .... July 5-7
at Oakland .... April 20-22

Seattle Mariners

Series Results, Last 10 Years

Year	Hm	Rd	Tot
2009	2-1	4-3	6-4
2008	6-0	1-2	7-2
2007	4-3	1-2	5-5
2006	2-1	1-2	3-3
2005	3-0	4-3	7-3
2004	2-1	4-2	6-3
2003	3-3	2-1	5-4
2002	0-3	4-2	4-5
2001	1-5	2-1	3-6
2000	1-3	3-3	4-6

Safeco Field, 1250 First Ave. South, Seattle, WA 98134
(206) 346-4000 • (206) 346-4400 - Fax
Capacity: 47,447 **Dimensions:** 331 LF, 405 CF, 326 RF

Executive Vice President & General Manager: Jack Zduriencik
Manager: Don Wakamatsu
Director, Baseball Information: Tim Hevly

2009 Record, Finish .... 85-77, 3rd in AL West (-12.0 games)

Yankees vs. Seattle

vs. SEA, 2009	6-4	vs. SEA, All-Time	197-157
at SEA, 2009	4-3	at SEA, All-Time	97-83
at New York, 2009	2-1	at New York, All-Time	100-74
All-Time at Safeco Field:	30-21	at original Yankee Stadium:	98-73

Series Sweeps at New York	**by NYY**	**by SEA**
3-game	5/23-25/08	5/3-5/02
4-game	none	none

Series Sweeps at Seattle	**by NYY**	**by SEA**
3-game	5/9-11/05	8/26-28/96
4-game	8/5-8/99	none

Longest Winning Streaks
by NYY .... 8 games (9/4/2007-5/25/2008; 5/9-8/29/1999)
by SEA .... 5 games (3x, last 5/29-6/10/1995)

2010 Schedule
at New York .... June 29-July 1, August 20-22
at Seattle .... July 8-11

Tampa Bay Rays

Series Results, Last 10 Years

Year	Hm	Rd	Tot
2009	6-3	5-4	11-7
2008	6-3	5-4	11-7
2007	5-4	5-4	10-8
2006	7-2	6-3	13-5
2005	3-6	5-5	8-11
2004	10-0	5-4	15-4
2003	6-3	8-2	14-5
2002	7-2	6-3	13-5
2001	8-1	5-5	13-6
2000	4-2	2-4	6-6

Tropicana Field, One Tropicana Drive, St. Petersburg, FL 33705
(727) 825-3137 • (727) 825-3111 - Fax
Capacity: 36,973 **Dimensions:** 315 LF, 404 CF, 320 RF

Executive Vice President, Baseball Operations: Andrew Friedman
Manager: Joe Maddon
Vice President, Communications: Rick Vaughn

2009 Record, Finish .... 84-78, 3rd in AL East (-19.0 games)

Yankees vs. Tampa Bay

vs. TB, 2009 .... 11-7 | vs. TB, All-Time................ *133-69
at TB, 2009.................. 5-4 | at TB, All-Time 61-39
at New York, 2009........... 6-3 | at New York, All-Time 71-29
at Tropicana Field .... 61-39 | at original Yankee Stadium....... 65-26

* includes 2 games at Tokyo from 3/30-31/04

Series Sweeps at New York	**by NYY**	**by TB**
3-game	9/12-14/06	none
4-game	*9/7-9/09	none

* includes one doubleheader

Series Sweeps at Tampa Bay	**by NYY**	**by TB**
3-game	9/13-15/05	9/26-28/00
4-game	7/9-12/98	none

Longest Winning Streaks

by NYY .... 11 games (9/17/1998-9/24/1999)
by TB .... 4 games (5/3-6/20/2005)

2010 Schedule

at New York........................ May 19-20, July 16-18, September 20-23
at Tampa Bay .... April 9-11, July 30-August 1, September 13-15

Texas Rangers

Series Results, Last 10 Years

Year	Hm	Rd	Tot
2009	3-3	2-1	5-4
2008	1-2	2-2	3-4
2007	2-1	3-0	5-1
2006	2-2	6-0	8-2
2005	5-2	2-1	7-3
2004	2-1	3-3	5-4
2003	2-4	2-1	4-5
2002	2-2	2-1	4-3
2001	1-2	2-2	3-4
2000	5-1	5-1	10-2

Ballpark in Arlington, 1000 Ballpark Way, Suite #400, Arlington, TX 76011
(817) 273-5222 • (817) 273-5110 - Fax
Capacity: 48,911 **Dimensions:** 332 LF, 400 CF, 325 RF

General Manager: Jon Daniels
Manager: Ron Washington
Senior Director, Baseball Media Relations: Rich Rice

2009 Record, Finish .... 87-75, 2nd in AL West (-10.0 games)

Yankees vs. Texas

vs. TEX, 2009 .... 5-4 | vs. TEX, All-Time 232-170
at TEX, 2009................. 2-1 | at TEX, All-Time................ 101-97
at New York, 2009........... 3-3 | at New York, All-Time 131-73
At Rangers Ballpark:....... 43-28 | at original Yankee Stadium: 120-66

Series Sweeps at New York	**by NYY**	**by TEX**
3-game	6/7-9/91	5/16-18/03
4-game	8/11-14/05	none

Series Sweeps at Texas	**by NYY**	**by TEX**
3-game	5/1-3/07*	4/6-7/96
4-game	none	7/20-23/89

* includes one doubleheader

Longest Winning Streaks

by NYY .... 8 games (7/24/2006-5/9/2007; 7/20/2005-5/7/2006)
by TEX...7 games (4/20-9/10/1990)

2010 Schedule

at New York.. April 16-18
at Texas.............................. August 10-11, September 10-12

Toronto Blue Jays

Series Results, Last 10 Years

Year	Hm	Rd	Tot
2009	6-3	6-3	12-6
2008	5-4	4-5	9-9
2007	5-4	5-4	10-8
2006	6-3	4-5	10-8
2005	6-4	6-2	12-6
2004	6-3	6-4	12-7
2003	4-6	6-3	10-9
2002	6-3	4-6	10-9
2001	5-5	6-3	11-8
2000	4-2	1-5	5-7

Rogers Centre, 1 Blue Jays Way, Suite 3200 • Toronto, Ontario M5V 1J1
(416) 341-1000 • (416) 341-1250 - Fax
Capacity: 49,160 .... **Dimensions:** 328 LF, 400 CF, 328 RF

Senior VP, Baseball Operations and GM: Alex Anthopoulos
Manager: Cito Gaston
Vice President, Communications: Jay Stenhouse

2009 Record, Finish .... 75-87, 4th in AL East (-28.0 games)

Yankees vs. Toronto

vs. TOR, 2009	12-6	vs. TOR, All-Time	259-205
at TOR, 2009	6-3	at TOR, All-Time	129-102
at New York, 2009	6-3	at New York, All-Time	130-103
All-Time at Rogers Centre:	81-71	at original Yankee Stadium:	124-100

Series Sweeps at New York	by NYY	by TOR
3-game	8/1-3/06	7/31-8/2/92
4-game	9/18-21/95	5/22-25/03

Series Sweeps at Toronto	by NYY	by TOR
3-game	3/31-4/2/03	9/19-21/00
4-game	none	none

Longest Winning Streaks
by NYY .... 13 games (5/10/1995-6/4/1996)
by TOR .... 10 games (4/14-9/25/1992)

2010 Schedule
at New York .... July 2-4, August 2-4, September 3-5
at Toronto .... June 4-6, August 23-25, September 27-29

Arizona Diamondbacks

Series Results, Last 10 Years

Year	Hm	Rd	Tot
2007	3-0	-	3-0
2004	-	2-1	2-1
2002	2-1	-	2-1

Chase Field, 401 E. Jefferson Street, Phoenix, AZ 85004
(602) 462-6500 • (602) 462-6117 - Fax
Capacity: 48,652 **Dimensions:** 330 LF, 407 CF, 334 RF

Executive Vice President & General Manager: Josh Byrnes
Manager: A.J. Hinch
Vice President, Communications: Shaun Rachau

2009 Record, Finish .... 70-92, 5th in NL West (-25.0 games)

Yankees vs. Arizona

vs. ARI, 2009	NA	vs. ARI, All-Time	7-2
at ARI, 2009	NA	at ARI, All-Time	2-1
at New York, 2009	NA	at New York, All-Time	5-1
at Chase Field	2-1	at original Yankee Stadium	5-1

Series Sweeps at New York	by NYY	by ARI
3-game	6/12-14/07	none
4-game	none	none

Series Sweeps at Arizona	by NYY	by ARI
3-game	none	none
4-game	none	none

2010 Schedule
at Arizona .... June 21-23

Houston Astros

Series Results, Last 10 Years

Year	Hm	Rd	Tot
2008	-	3-0	3-0
2003	2-1	-	2-1

Minute Maid Park, 501 Crawford, Suite 400, Houston, TX 77002
(713) 259-8000 • (713) 259-8025 - Fax
Capacity: 40,976 **Dimensions:** 315 LF, 435 CF, 326 RF

General Manager: Ed Wade
Manager: Brad Mills
Director, Media Relations: Gene Dias

2009 Record, Finish................ 74-88, 5th in NL Central (-17.0 games)

Yankees vs. Houston

vs. HOU, 2009	NA	vs. HOU, All-Time	5-1
at HOU, 2009	NA	at HOU, All-Time	3-0
at New York, 2009	NA	at New York, All-Time	2-1
at Minute Maid Park	3-0	at original Yankee Stadium	2-1

Series Sweeps at New York	by NYY	by HOU
3-game	none	none
4-game	none	none

Series Sweeps at Houston	by NYY	by HOU
3-game	6/13-15/08	none
4-game	none	none

2010 Schedule
at New York...June 11-13

Los Angeles Dodgers

Series Results, Last 10 Years

Year	Hm	Rd	Tot
2004	-	1-2	1-2

Dodger Stadium, 1000 Elysian Park Avenue, Los Angeles, CA 90090
(323) 224-1301 • (323) 224-1459 - Fax
Capacity: 56,000 **Dimensions:** 330 LF, 395 CF, 330 RF

General Manager: Ned Colletti
Manager: Joe Torre
Vice President, Communications: Josh Rawitch

2009 Record, Finish.................. 95-67, 1st in NL West (+3.0 games)

Yankees vs. Los Angeles

vs. LAD, 2009	NA	vs. LAD, All-Time	1-2
at LAD, 2009	NA	at LAD, All-Time	1-2
at New York, 2009	NA	at New York, All-Time	NA
at Dodger Stadium	1-2	at original Yankee Stadium	NA

Series Sweeps at New York	by NYY	by LAD
3-game	none	none
4-game	none	none

Series Sweeps at Los Angeles-NL	by NYY	by LAD
3-game	none	none
4-game	none	none

2010 Schedule
at Los Angeles...June 25-27

New York Mets

Series Results, Last 10 Years

Year	Hm	Rd	Tot
2009	2-1	3-0	5-1
2008	0-3	2-1	2-4
2007	2-1	1-2	3-3
2006	2-1	1-2	3-3
2005	1-2	2-1	3-3
2004	2-1	0-3	2-4
2003	3-0	3-0	6-0
2002	2-1	1-2	3-3
2001	2-1	2-1	4-2
2000	2-1	2-1	4-2

Citi Field, 126th Street, Flushing, NY 11368
(718) 507-6387 • (718) 639-3619 - Fax
Capacity: 41,800 **Dimensions:** 335 LF, 408 CF, 330 RF

Executive VP/General Manager: Omar Minaya
Manager: Jerry Manuel
Vice President, Media Relations: Jay Horwitz

2009 Record, Finish .... 70-92, 4th in NL East (-23.0 games)

Yankees vs. Mets

vs. NYM, 2009 5-1
at NYM, 2009 3-0
at New York-AL, 2009........ 2-1
at Shea Stadium 17-16
vs. NYM, All-Time 42-30
at NYM, All-Time.................20-16
at New York-AL, All-Time 22-14
at original Yankee Stadium.......20-13

Series Sweeps at Yankees	by NYY	by NYM
3-game	6/27-29/03	none
4-game	none	none

Series Sweeps at Mets	by NYY	by NYM
3-game	6/26-28/09	7/2-4/04
4-game	none	none

Longest Winning Streaks

by NYY .... 7 games (6/30/2002-6/29/2003)
by NYM.................................3 games (3x, last 5/17-6/27/2008)

2010 Schedule

at New York Yankees ....June 18-20
at New York Mets .... May 21-23

Philadelphia Phillies

Series Results, Last 10 Years

Year	Hm	Rd	Tot
2009	1-2	-	1-2
2006	-	2-1	2-1
2001	-	2-1	2-1
2000	2-1	-	2-1

Citizens Bank Park, One Citizens Bank Way, Philadelphia, PA 19148
(215) 463-1000 • (215) 389-3050 - Fax
Capacity: 43,647 **Dimensions:** 329 LF, 401 CF, 330 RF

Senior Vice President & General Manager: Ruben Amaro, Jr.
Manager: Charlie Manuel
Vice President, Communications: Bonnie Clark

2009 Record, Finish .... 93-69, 1st in NL East (+6.0 games)

Yankees vs. Philadelphia

vs. PHI, 2009 1-2
at PHI, 2009................ NA
at New York, 2009........... 1-2
at Citizens Bank Park 2-1
vs. PHI, All-Time..................11-10
at PHI, All-Time 5-7
at New York, All-Time 6-3
at original Yankee Stadium..........5-1

Series Sweeps at New York	by NYY	by PHI
3-game	6/30-7/2/98	none
4-game	none	none

Series Sweeps at Philadelphia	by NYY	by PHI
3-game	none	9/1-3/97
4-game	none	none

2010 Schedule

at New York...June 15-17

All-Time Series Results by Year

YEAR	BAL	BOS	CWS	CLE	DET	KC	LAA	MIL	MIN	OAK	SEA	TB	TEX	TOR
2009	13-5	9-9	4-3	5-3	5-1	4-2	5-5	–	7-0	7-2	6-4	11-7	5-4	12-6
2008	11-7	9-9	5-2	3-4	2-4	5-5	3-7	–	6-4	5-1	7-2	11-7	3-4	9-9
2007	9-9	10-8	6-4	6-0	4-4	9-1	3-6	–	5-2	2-4	5-5	10-8	5-1	10-8
2006	12-7	11-8	4-2	4-3	5-2	7-2	4-6	–	3-3	3-6	3-3	13-5	8-2	10-8
2005	11-7	10-9	3-3	4-3	5-1	3-3	4-6	1-2	3-3	7-2	7-3	8-11	7-3	12-6
2004	14-5	8-11	4-3	4-2	3-4	5-1	4-5	–	4-2	7-2	6-3	15-4	5-4	12-7
2003	13-6	10-9	2-4	5-2	5-1	4-2	6-3	–	7-0	3-6	5-4	14-5	4-5	10-9
2002	13-6	10-9	4-2	6-3	8-1	5-1	4-3	–	6-0	5-4	4-5	13-5	4-3	10-9
2001	13-5	13-5	5-1	5-4	5-4	6-0	3-4	–	2-4	3-6	3-6	13-6	3-4	11-8
2000	7-5	7-6	4-8	5-5	4-8	8-2	5-5	–	5-5	6-3	4-6	6-6	10-2	5-7
1999	9-4	4-8	7-5	7-3	7-5	4-5	4-6	–	6-4	6-4	9-1	8-4	8-4	10-2
1998	9-3	7-5	7-4	7-4	8-3	10-0	5-6	–	7-4	8-3	8-3	11-1	8-3	6-6
1997	4-8	8-4	9-2	6-5	10-2	8-3	7-4	7-4	8-3	6-5	4-7	–	7-4	7-5
1996	10-3	6-7	7-6	9-3	8-5	8-4	6-7	6-6	7-5	9-3	3-9	–	5-7	8-5
1995	7-6	8-5	2-3	6-6	8-5	7-3	5-7	6-5	4-3	4-9	4-9	–	6-3	12-1
1994	6-4	7-3	2-4	9-0	3-3	2-4	8-4	7-2	5-4	7-5	8-4	–	3-2	3-4
1993	7-6	7-6	8-4	7-6	9-4	6-6	6-6	9-4	8-4	6-6	7-5	–	3-9	5-8
1992	8-5	6-7	4-8	6-7	8-5	7-5	5-7	7-6	5-7	6-6	6-6	–	6-6	2-11
1991	8-5	7-6	4-8	7-6	5-8	5-7	6-6	7-6	2-10	6-6	3-9	–	5-7	6-7
1990	7-6	4-9	2-10	8-5	6-7	4-8	6-6	7-6	6-6	0-12	9-3	–	3-9	5-8
1989	5-8	6-7	6-5	4-9	7-6	6-6	6-6	5-8	6-6	3-9	8-4	–	5-7	7-6
1988	10-3	4-9	9-3	7-6	5-8	6-6	6-6	7-6	9-3	6-6	5-7	–	5-6	6-7
1987	10-3	6-7	7-5	7-6	8-5	7-5	9-3	6-7	6-6	5-7	7-5	–	5-7	6-7
1986	8-5	8-5	6-6	8-5	7-6	8-4	5-7	5-8	8-4	5-7	8-4	–	7-5	7-6
1985	12-1	8-5	6-6	7-6	3-9	7-5	9-3	6-7	9-3	7-5	9-3	–	8-4	6-7
1984	8-5	6-7	5-7	11-2	6-7	7-5	4-8	7-6	4-8	8-4	7-5	–	6-6	8-5
1983	7-6	6-7	4-8	7-6	8-5	6-6	7-5	9-4	8-4	8-4	7-5	–	7-5	7-6
1982	2-11	6-7	4-8	9-4	5-8	7-5	5-7	5-8	10-2	7-5	6-6	–	7-5	6-7
1981	6-7	3-3	7-5	5-7	7-3	10-2	2-2	3-3	3-3	4-3	2-3	–	5-4	2-3
1980	6-7	10-3	7-5	8-5	8-5	4-8	10-2	8-5	8-4	8-4	9-3	–	7-5	10-3
1979	6-5	8-5	8-4	8-5	6-7	7-5	5-7	4-9	5-7	9-3	6-6	–	8-4	9-4
1978	9-6	9-7	9-1	9-6	11-4	5-6	5-5	5-10	7-3	8-2	6-5	–	6-4	11-4
1977	7-8	7-8	7-3	12-3	9-6	5-5	7-4	7-8	8-2	9-2	6-4	–	7-3	9-6
1976	5-13	11-7	11-1	12-4	8-9	5-7	7-5	13-5	10-2	6-6	–	–	9-3	–
1975	10-8	5-11	6-6	9-9	12-6	5-7	5-7	9-9	8-4	6-6	–	–	8-4	–
1974	7-11	7-11	8-4	11-7	7-11	8-4	9-3	9-9	8-4	7-5	–	–	8-4	–
1973	9-9	4-14	4-8	11-7	11-7	6-6	6-6	8-10	9-3	4-8	–	–	8-4	–
1972	6-7	9-9	5-7	11-7	9-7	5-7	8-4	9-9	6-6	3-9	–	–	8-4	–
1971	7-11	11-7	7-5	10-8	8-10	7-5	6-6	10-2	4-8	5-7	–	–	7-11	–
1970	7-11	8-10	7-5	10-8	11-7	11-1	7-5	9-3	7-5	6-6	–	–	10-8	–
1969	7-11	7-11	9-3	8-9	8-10	7-5	9-3	7-5	2-10	6-6	–	–	10-8	–
1968	5-13	8-10	12-6	8-10	8-10	–	12-6	–	6-12	10-8	–	–	14-4	–
1967	5-13	6-12	6-12	9-9	8-10	–	9-9	–	6-12	11-7	–	–	12-6	–
1966	3-15	10-8	9-9	6-12	7-11	–	7-11	–	10-8	13-5	–	–	5-10	–
1965	5-13	9-9	10-8	6-12	8-10	–	12-6	–	5-13	11-7	–	–	11-7	–
1964	8-10	9-9	12-6	15-3	10-8	–	11-7	–	10-8	12-6	–	–	12-6	–
1963	11-7	12-6	10-8	11-7	10-8	–	13-5	–	11-6	12-6	–	–	14-4	–
1962	7-11	12-6	10-8	7-11	11-7	–	10-8	–	11-7	13-5	–	–	15-3	–
1961	9-9	13-5	12-6	14-4	10-8	–	12-6	–	14-4	14-4	–	–	11-7	–
1960	13-9	15-7	12-10	16-6	14-8	–	–	–	12-10	15-7	–	–	–	–
1959	10-12	9-13	9-13	11-11	8-14	–	–	–	15-7	17-5	–	–	–	–
1958	14-8	13-9	15-7	15-7	10-12	–	–	–	12-10	13-9	–	–	–	–
1957	13-9	14-8	14-8	13-9	12-10	–	–	–	13-9	19-3	–	–	–	–
1956	13-9	14-8	13-9	12-10	10-12	–	–	–	17-5	18-4	–	–	–	–
1955	19-3	14-8	11-11	9-13	12-10	–	–	–	16-6	15-7	–	–	–	–
1954	17-5	13-9	15-7	11-11	16-6	–	–	–	13-9	18-4	–	–	–	–
1953	17-5	11-10	13-9	11-11	16-6	–	–	–	14-6	17-5	–	–	–	–
1952	14-8	14-8	14-8	12-10	13-9	–	–	–	15-7	13-9	–	–	–	–
1951	17-5	11-11	14-8	15-7	12-10	–	–	–	16-6	13-9	–	–	–	–
1950	17-5	13-9	14-8	14-8	11-11	–	–	–	14-8	15-7	–	–	–	–
1949	17-5	13-9	15-7	12-10	11-11	–	–	–	15-7	14-8	–	–	–	–
1948	16-6	8-14	16-6	12-10	13-9	–	–	–	17-5	12-10	–	–	–	–
1947	15-7	13-9	12-10	15-7	14-8	–	–	–	15-7	13-9	–	–	–	–
1946	14-8	8-14	14-8	12-10	9-13	–	–	–	14-8	16-6	–	–	–	–
1945	7-15	16-6	12-9	9-12	7-15	–	–	–	14-8	16-6	–	–	–	–
1944	10-12	11-11	12-10	14-8	8-14	–	–	–	15-7	13-9	–	–	–	–
1943	17-5	17-5	12-10	13-9	12-10	–	–	–	11-11	16-6	–	–	–	–
1942	15-7	10-12	15-7	15-7	15-7	–	–	–	17-5	16-6	–	–	–	–
1941	18-4	13-9	14-8	15-7	11-11	–	–	–	16-6	14-8	–	–	–	–
1940	14-8	13-9	11-11	12-10	8-14	–	–	–	17-5	13-9	–	–	–	–
1939	19-3	8-11	18-4	15-7	13-9	–	–	–	15-7	18-4	–	–	–	–
1938	15-7	11-11	14-8	13-8	14-8	–	–	–	16-6	16-5	–	–	–	–
1937	16-6	15-7	13-9	15-7	13-9	–	–	–	16-6	14-8	–	–	–	–
1936	14-8	15-7	14-7	16-6	14-8	–	–	–	13-9	16-6	–	–	–	–
1935	12-10	12-9	11-9	14-8	11-11	–	–	–	15-7	14-6	–	–	–	–
1934	17-5	12-10	17-5	11-11	10-12	–	–	–	12-10	15-7	–	–	–	–
1933	14-7	14-8	15-7	13-7	15-7	–	–	–	8-14	12-9	–	–	–	–
1932	16-6	17-5	17-5	15-7	17-5	–	–	–	11-11	14-8	–	–	–	–
1931	16-6	16-6	15-6	9-13	14-8	–	–	–	13-9	11-11	–	–	–	–
1930	16-6	16-6	14-8	12-10	13-9	–	–	–	5-17	10-12	–	–	–	–

All-Time Series Results by Year

YEAR	BAL	BOS	CWS	CLE	DET	KC	LAA	MIL	MIN	OAK	SEA	TB	TEX	TOR
1929	14-8	17-5	16-6	8-14	13-9	–	–	–	12-10	8-14	–	–	–	–
1928	12-10	16-6	13-9	16-6	15-7	–	–	–	13-9	16-6	–	–	–	–
1927	21-1	18-4	17-5	12-10	14-8	–	–	–	14-8	14-8	–	–	–	–
1926	16-6	17-5	14-8	11-11	12-10	–	–	–	12-10	9-13	–	–	–	–
1925	11-11	13-9	9-13	12-10	8-14	–	–	–	7-15	9-13	–	–	–	–
1924	12-10	17-5	16-6	14-8	9-13	–	–	–	9-13	12-8	–	–	–	–
1923	15-5	14-8	15-7	10-12	12-10	–	–	–	16-6	16-6	–	–	–	–
1922	14-8	9-13	13-9	15-7	11-11	–	–	–	15-7	17-5	–	–	–	–
1921	13-9	15-7	9-13	14-8	17-5	–	–	–	13-8	17-5	–	–	–	–
1920	12-10	13-9	12-10	13-9	15-7	–	–	–	11-11	19-3	–	–	–	–
1919	12-8	9-10	8-12	7-13	12-8	–	–	–	14-6	18-2	–	–	–	–
1918	10-10	11-6	6-12	7-11	10-9	–	–	–	8-11	8-4	–	–	–	–
1917	13-9	9-13	10-12	7-15	9-13	–	–	–	8-13	15-7	–	–	–	–
1916	9-13	11-11	12-10	10-12	8-14	–	–	–	15-7	15-7	–	–	–	–
1915	12-10	12-10	7-15	13-9	5-17	–	–	–	9-13	11-9	–	–	–	–
1914	11-11	11-11	10-12	14-8	9-13	–	–	–	7-15	8-14	–	–	–	–
1913	11-11	6-14	10-11	8-14	11-11	–	–	–	6-16	5-17	–	–	–	–
1912	13-9	2-19	9-13	8-13	6-16	–	–	–	7-15	5-17	–	–	–	–
1911	16-5	10-12	9-13	8-14	15-7	–	–	–	12-10	6-15	–	–	–	–
1910	16-6	13-9	13-8	13-8	9-13	–	–	–	15-7	9-12	–	–	–	–
1909	13-8	9-13	8-14	14-8	8-14	–	–	–	14-6	8-14	–	–	–	–
1908	5-17	10-12	6-16	6-16	7-15	–	–	–	9-13	8-14	–	–	–	–
1907	8-14	12-8	10-12	7-15	8-13	–	–	–	15-7	10-9	–	–	–	–
1906	13-8	17-5	10-12	11-10	11-11	–	–	–	15-7	13-8	–	–	–	–
1905	15-7	8-13	7-15	10-12	8-13	–	–	–	15-7	8-11	–	–	–	–
1904	16-6	10-12	10-12	11-9	15-7	–	–	–	18-4	12-9	–	–	–	–
1903	15-5	7-13	11-7	6-14	9-10	–	–	–	14-5	10-8	–	–	–	–
Totals	**1208-813**	**1104-908**	**1031-798**	**1065-844**	**1016-899**	**256-174**	**322-271**	**208-182**	**1079-747**	**1094-787**	**197-157**	**133-69**	**353-244**	**259-205**

Orioles include St. Louis Browns, 1903-1953 (711-399). Brewers include Seattle Pilots, 1969 (7-5). Twins include original Washington Senators, 1903-1960 (755-507). A's include Philadelphia A's, 1903-1954 (665-445) and Kansas City A's, 1955-1967 (183-75). Rangers include Washington Senators, 1961-1971 (121-74).

Most Recent Trades with Each Team

AMERICAN LEAGUE EAST

Baltimore (Nov. 12, 2006): Yankees acquire RHP Chris Britton for RHP Jaret Wright.

Boston (Aug. 13, 1997): Yankees acquire 1B/DH Mike Stanley and minor league INF Randy Brown for RHP Tony Armas and a player to be named later.

Tampa Bay (May 25, 2006): Yankees acquire INF Nick Green for cash considerations.

Toronto (July 1, 2002): Yankees acquire OF Raul Mondesi for RHP Scott Wiggins.

AMERICAN LEAGUE CENTRAL

Chicago (Nov. 13, 2008): Yankees acquire INF/OF Nick Swisher and RHP Kanekoa Texeira for INF Wilson Betemit and RHPs Jeff Marquez and Jhonny Nunez.

Cleveland (June 24, 2009): Yankees trade RHP Jose Veras for cash considerations.

Detroit (Dec. 9, 2009): Yankees acquire OF Curtis Granderson for LHP Phil Coke and OF Austin Jackson in a three-team, seven-player trade (also sent RHP Ian Kennedy to Arizona).

Kansas City (Aug. 11, 2000): Yankees acquire INF Nick Ortiz for INF Wilson Delgado.

Minnesota (Sept. 3, 2003): Yankees acquire RHP Juan Padilla as player to be named following 8/31/03 trade for LHP Jesse Orosco.

AMERICAN LEAGUE WEST

Los Angeles (July 21, 2007) Yankees acquire C Jose Molina for RHP Jeff Kennard.

Oakland (July 5, 2002): Yankees acquire RHP Jeff Weaver for LHP Ted Lilly, RHP Jason Arnold and OF John-Ford Griffin.

Seattle (Aug. 6, 2003): Yankees acquire RHP Jeff Nelson for RHP Armando Benitez and cash considerations.

Texas (January 26, 2010): Yankees acquire OF Greg Golson for INF Mitch Hilligoss.

NATIONAL LEAGUE EAST

Atlanta (Dec. 22, 2009): Yankees acquire RHP Javier Vazquez and LHP Boone Logan for OF Melky Cabrera, RHP Arodys Vizcaino and LHP Mike Dunn.

Florida (Dec. 16, 2005): Yankees acquire LHP Ron Villone for LHP Ben Julianel.

Washington (Dec. 7, 2009): Yankees acquire a player to be named later (OF Jamie Hoffmann) for RHP Brian Bruney.

New York (December 3, 2004): Yankees acquire LHP Mike Stanton for LHP Felix Heredia.

Philadelphia (July 30, 2006): Yankees acquire OF Bobby Abreu and RHP Cory Lidle for INF C.J. Henry, C Jesus Sanchez, RHP Carlos Monasterios and LHP Matt Smith.

NATIONAL LEAGUE CENTRAL

Chicago (Aug. 27, 2005): Yankees acquire OF Matt Lawton for RHP Justin Berg.

Cincinnati (July 31, 2009): Yankees acquire INF/OF Jerry Hairston, Jr. for C Chase Weems.

Houston (July 30, 2008): Yankees acquire 2B Matt Cusick for RHP LaTroy Hawkins and cash considerations.

Milwaukee (Feb. 4, 2009): Yankees acquire OF/C Eric Fryer for LHP Chase Wright.

Pittsburgh (June 30, 2009): Yankees acquire INF/OF Eric Hinske and cash considerations for OF Eric Fryer and RHP Casey Erickson.

St. Louis (Aug. 22, 2003): Yankees acquire RHP Justin Pope and LHP Ben Julianel for LHP Sterling Hitchcock.

NATIONAL LEAGUE WEST

Arizona (Jan. 9, 2007): Yankees send RHP Ian Kennedy to Arizona in a three-team, seven-player trade (also sent LHP Phil Coke and OF Austin Jackson to Detroit in exchange for OF Curtis Granderson).

Colorado (July 29, 2009): Yankees acquire RHP Jason Hirsh for cash considerations.

Los Angeles (July 31, 2007): Yankees acquire INF Wilson Betemit for RHP Scott Proctor.

San Diego (Aug. 6, 2009): Yankees acquire RHP Chad Gaudin for cash considerations.

San Francisco (Dec. 13, 2001): Yankees acquire OF John Vander Wal for RHP Jay Witasick.

Home Record vs. AL Opponents, 1976-2009

YEAR	BAL	BOS	CWS	CLE	DET	KC	LAA	MIL	MIN	OAK	SEA	TB	TEX	TOR	TOTAL
2009	7-2	7-2	3-0	2-2	3-0	2-1	3-1	---	4-0	5-1	2-1	6-3	3-3	6-3	53-19
2008	6-3	4-5	3-1	1-2	0-3	4-3	2-2	---	3-0	3-0	6-0	6-3	1-2	5-4	48-33
2007	5-4	6-3	2-1	3-0	3-1	3-0	2-4	---	3-1	1-2	4-3	5-4	2-1	5-4	44-28
2006	5-4	4-6	3-0	2-1	2-1	5-1	2-2	---	2-1	2-4	2-1	7-2	2-2	6-3	44-28
2005	7-2	5-4	1-2	3-1	3-0	3-0	3-3	---	2-1	2-1	3-0	3-6	5-2	6-4	46-26
2004	7-3	5-4	2-2	2-1	1-2	3-0	2-4	---	3-0	5-1	2-1	10-0	2-1	6-3	50-22
2003	6-4	5-5	1-2	4-0	3-0	3-0	1-2	---	3-0	1-2	3-3	6-3	2-4	4-6	42-31
2002	7-3	5-4	1-2	3-0	5-1	2-1	2-1	---	3-0	3-3	0-3	7-2	2-2	6-3	52-28
2001	5-3	8-1	3-0	3-3	3-0	3-0	2-2	---	1-2	3-0	1-5	8-1	1-2	5-5	46-24
2000	4-2	2-4	1-5	1-3	3-3	5-1	2-2	---	3-3	4-2	1-3	4-2	5-1	4-2	39-33
1999	4-3	2-4	4-2	4-2	5-1	1-2	2-4	---	2-2	2-2	5-1	3-3	4-2	5-1	43-29
1998	6-0	3-3	4-1	4-1	5-1	5-0	3-3	---	5-1	4-1	4-1	6-0	4-2	2-4	55-18
1997	1-5	4-2	4-1	3-2	4-2	4-2	2-2	5-0	3-2	4-2	2-4	---	4-1	3-3	43-28
1996	4-3	4-2	5-2	3-3	4-3	5-1	3-3	5-1	3-2	4-2	2-4	---	4-2	3-3	49-31
1995	4-2	6-1	0-2	2-4	4-2	3-1	4-2	3-3	2-2	3-4	3-3	---	5-0	7-0	46-26
1994	3-3	4-2	1-2	7-0	1-2	0-3	3-3	1-2	3-0	3-3	3-3	---	2-0	2-1	33-24
1993	4-3	4-3	4-2	4-2	5-1	4-2	4-2	4-2	4-2	4-2	4-2	---	2-4	3-4	50-31
1992	3-3	4-2	1-5	3-4	4-3	4-2	4-2	5-2	2-4	4-2	3-3	---	3-3	1-5	41-40
1991	5-2	3-4	3-3	4-2	3-3	2-4	2-4	3-3	2-4	3-3	2-4	---	4-2	3-4	39-42
1990	3-3	4-2	1-5	4-3	3-4	3-3	3-3	3-4	3-3	0-6	4-2	---	3-3	3-3	37-44
1989	2-5	4-3	4-2	1-5	5-1	3-3	5-1	3-3	3-3	1-5	3-3	---	4-2	3-4	41-40
1988	5-1	2-4	5-1	4-3	5-2	2-4	3-3	6-1	4-2	4-2	2-4	---	3-2	1-5	46-34
1987	6-1	4-3	4-2	4-2	5-1	6-0	4-2	3-3	4-2	3-3	3-3	---	3-3	2-5	51-30
1986	2-4	2-4	2-4	5-2	4-3	4-2	3-3	4-3	3-3	3-3	3-2	---	4-2	2-4	41-39
1985	7-0	5-2	4-2	3-3	2-3	5-1	5-1	3-3	6-0	5-1	5-1	---	6-0	2-5	58-22
1984	4-2	2-4	3-3	7-0	3-3	6-0	2-4	5-2	3-3	5-1	2-4	---	3-3	5-1	50-30
1983	4-3	4-3	2-4	5-2	3-3	3-3	5-1	6-0	5-1	4-2	3-3	---	3-3	5-2	52-30
1982	2-4	3-3	1-5	3-4	3-4	3-3	3-3	4-3	5-1	4-2	3-3	---	4-2	4-2	42-39
1981	5-2	2-1	4-2	2-4	3-0	5-1	0-0	2-1	1-2	2-1	1-1	---	4-2	1-2	32-19
1980	3-3	3-3	3-3	5-2	5-2	2-4	6-0	3-4	4-2	5-1	5-1	---	4-2	5-1	53-28
1979	4-3	3-3	6-0	3-3	3-3	4-2	4-3	2-4	3-3	4-2	5-1	---	5-1	5-2	51-30
1978	3-4	4-1	6-2	6-2	3-3	3-2	3-4	5-3	3-2	5-0	4-1	---	4-1	6-1	55-26
1977	6-2	4-1	6-1	3-4	4-1	4-1	4-4	3-4	4-1	5-1	5-0	---	3-2	4-4	55-26
1976	9-2	5-1	5-3	4-5	2-4	2-4	1-8	8-1	5-1	2-4	---	---	4-2	---	47-35

Road Record vs. AL Opponents, 1976-2009

YEAR	BAL	BOS	CWS	CLE	DET	KC	LAA	MIL	MIN	OAK	SEA	TB	TEX	TOR	TOTAL
2009	6-3	2-7	1-3	3-1	2-1	2-1	2-4	---	3-0	2-1	4-3	5-4	2-1	6-3	40-32
2008	5-4	5-4	2-1	2-2	2-1	1-2	1-5	---	3-4	2-1	1-2	5-4	2-2	4-5	41-40
2007	4-5	4-5	4-3	3-0	1-3	6-1	1-2	---	2-1	1-2	1-2	5-4	3-0	5-4	40-32
2006	7-3	7-2	1-2	2-2	3-1	2-1	2-4	---	1-2	1-2	1-2	6-3	6-0	4-5	43-29
2005	4-5	5-5	2-1	1-2	2-1	0-3	1-3	---	1-2	5-1	4-3	5-5	2-1	6-2	38-34
2004	7-2	3-7	2-1	2-1	2-2	2-1	2-1	---	1-2	2-1	4-2	5-4	3-3	6-4	41-31
2003	7-2	5-4	1-2	1-2	2-1	1-2	5-1	---	4-0	2-4	2-1	8-2	2-1	6-3	46-25
2002	6-3	5-5	3-0	3-3	3-0	3-0	2-2	---	3-0	2-1	4-2	6-3	2-1	4-6	51-30
2001	8-2	5-4	2-1	2-1	2-4	3-0	1-2	---	1-2	0-6	2-1	5-5	2-2	6-3	39-33
2000	3-3	5-2	3-3	4-2	1-5	3-1	3-3	---	2-2	2-1	3-3	2-4	5-1	1-5	37-35
1999	5-1	2-4	3-3	3-1	2-4	3-3	2-2	---	4-2	4-2	4-0	5-1	4-2	5-1	46-26
1998	3-3	4-2	3-3	3-3	3-2	5-0	2-3	---	2-3	4-2	4-2	5-1	4-1	4-2	46-27
1997	3-3	4-2	5-1	3-3	6-0	4-1	5-2	2-4	5-1	2-3	2-3	---	3-3	4-2	48-28
1996	6-0	2-5	2-4	6-0	4-2	3-3	3-4	1-5	4-3	5-1	1-5	---	1-5	5-2	43-39
1995	3-4	2-4	2-1	4-2	4-3	4-2	1-5	3-2	2-1	1-5	1-6	---	1-3	5-1	33-39
1994	3-1	3-1	1-2	2-0	2-1	2-1	5-1	6-0	2-4	4-2	5-1	---	1-2	1-3	37-19
1993	3-3	3-3	4-2	3-4	4-3	2-4	2-4	5-2	4-2	2-4	3-3	---	1-5	2-4	38-43
1992	5-2	2-5	3-3	3-3	4-2	3-3	1-5	2-4	3-3	2-4	3-3	---	3-3	1-6	35-46
1991	3-3	4-2	1-5	3-4	2-5	3-3	4-2	4-3	0-6	3-3	1-5	---	1-5	3-3	32-49
1990	4-3	0-7	1-5	4-2	3-3	1-5	3-3	4-2	3-3	0-6	5-1	---	0-6	2-5	30-51
1989	3-3	2-4	2-3	3-4	2-5	3-3	1-5	2-5	3-3	2-4	5-1	---	1-5	4-2	33-47
1988	5-2	2-5	4-2	3-3	0-6	4-2	3-3	1-5	5-1	2-4	3-3	---	2-4	5-2	39-42
1987	4-2	2-4	3-3	3-4	3-4	1-5	5-1	3-4	2-4	2-4	4-2	---	2-4	4-2	38-43
1986	6-1	6-1	4-2	3-3	3-3	4-2	2-4	1-5	5-1	2-4	5-2	---	3-3	5-2	49-33
1985	5-1	3-3	2-4	4-3	1-6	2-4	4-2	3-4	3-3	2-4	4-2	---	2-4	4-2	39-42
1984	4-3	4-3	2-4	4-2	3-4	1-5	2-4	2-4	1-5	3-3	5-1	---	3-3	3-4	37-45
1983	3-3	2-4	2-4	2-4	5-2	3-3	2-4	3-4	3-3	4-2	4-2	---	4-2	2-4	39-41
1982	0-7	3-4	3-3	6-0	2-4	4-2	2-4	1-5	5-1	3-3	3-3	---	3-3	2-5	37-44
1981	1-5	1-2	3-3	3-3	4-3	5-1	2-2	1-2	2-1	2-2	1-2	---	1-2	1-1	27-29
1980	3-4	7-0	4-2	3-3	3-3	2-4	4-2	5-1	4-2	3-3	4-2	---	3-3	5-2	50-31
1979	4-2	5-1	2-5	3-4	4-2	1-5	2-2	2-5	2-4	5-1	1-5	---	3-3	4-2	38-41
1978	6-3	5-0	3-4	5-2	2-3	2-3	6-2	0-7	4-1	3-2	2-4	---	2-3	5-3	45-37
1977	1-6	3-2	6-2	6-2	1-4	3-3	3-4	4-4	4-1	4-1	1-4	---	4-1	5-2	45-36
1976	4-5	6-0	7-1	4-4	3-3	5-1	4-5	5-4	5-1	4-2	---	---	5-1	---	52-27

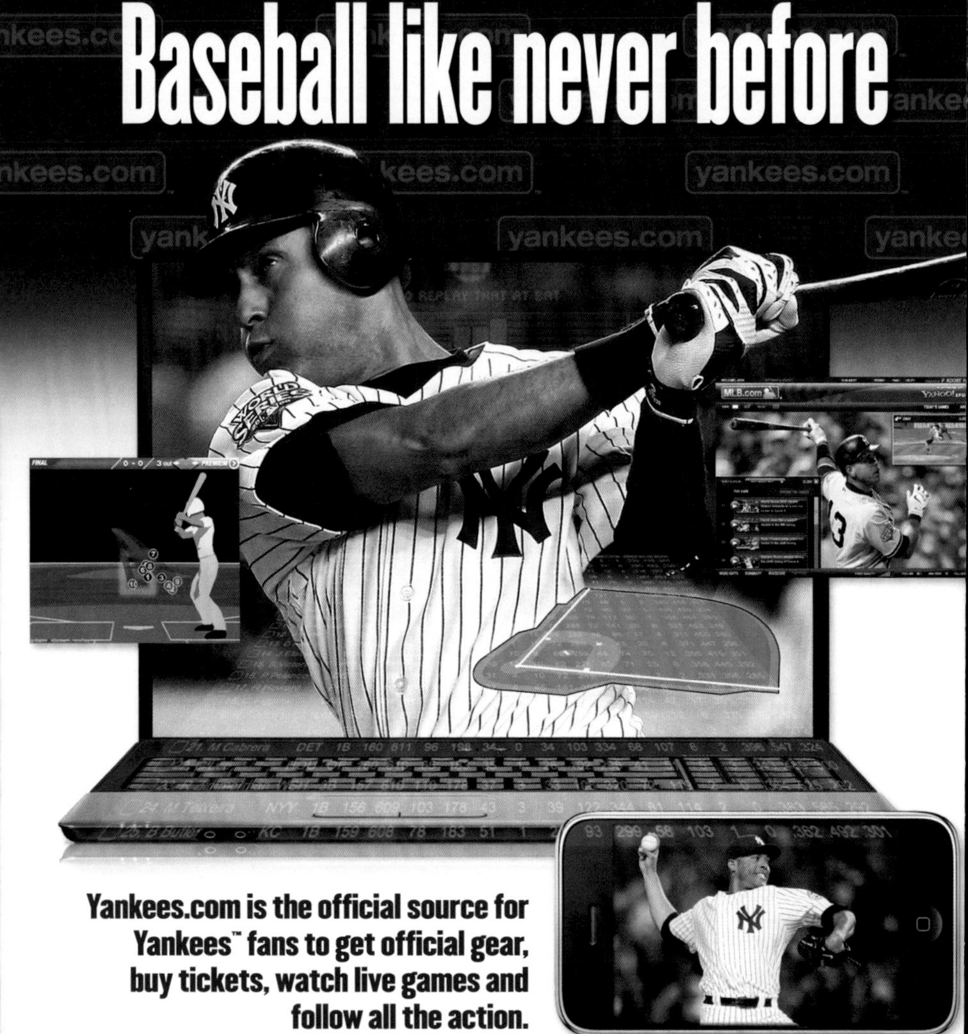

New York Yankees™

HISTORY & RECORDS

Manager Miller Huggins [at L] and Yankees owner Jacob Ruppert [at R] led the Yankees to their first World Series appearance in 1921 and first World Series title in 1923.

History of the New York Yankees

The Yankees are Baseball's most storied franchise. With 27 World Championships and 40 American League pennants to its name, the franchise stands alone in both categories.

The team's glorious history has surprisingly humble origins at the start of the previous century, when the upstart American League declared itself a Major League following the 1900 season. At that time, the league sought to place a team in New York for the 1901 campaign. But due to the political strength of the National League's New York Giants, the American League instead put a team in Baltimore, calling it the Orioles, with the intent to move it to New York as soon as possible.

Managed by John McGraw, the 1901 Orioles finished 68-65 and failed to draw substantial crowds. The following season, McGraw, fearing the team would relocate to New York without him in 1903, precipitated a midseason release from his contract. He immediately teamed with Giants owner Andrew Freedman and Cincinnati Reds owner John T. Brush, helping them acquire a majority interest in the Orioles. With control of Baltimore's players, the pair of owners decimated the squad, divvying up the players between them. On July 17, 1902, the Baltimore Orioles were left with five players on their roster and were forced to forfeit their game against the St. Louis Browns. The American League quickly stepped in and lent Baltimore players from other teams so they could finish the season.

Prior to the 1903 campaign, the two leagues reached a truce, part of which involved the National League agreeing to allow an American League team in New York City. Racehorse owner Frank Farrell and ex-New York chief of police Bill Devery purchased the remnants of the Baltimore franchise for $18,000 and reestablished it in upper Manhattan.

The New York Americans, as they were formally named, were New York City's third Major League team, joining the Giants and Brooklyn Dodgers of the National League. They played home games at American League Park, a hastily constructed all-wooden structure at 168th Street and Broadway. Because the site was one of the highest spots in Manhattan, the team was commonly called the "Hilltoppers" or "Highlanders" and their home field "Hilltop Park." The club played its inaugural game on April 22, 1903, at Washington, losing 3-1 to the Senators. The next day, they defeated the Senators, 7-2, recording the very first win in franchise history.

Led by future Hall of Famers Jack Chesboro, Clark Griffith and Wee Willie Keeler, the Highlanders finished with a 72-62 record, 17.0 games out of first place. They nearly captured the American League pennant in 1904—finishing 1.5 games behind the Boston Pilgrims—as Chesboro went 41-12 with a 1.82 ERA in 454.2 innings pitched, setting a modern-era (since 1900) record with his win total. That season marked the first of three second-place finishes for the club between 1904 and 1910.

After a spectacular fire severely damaged the Polo Grounds in 1911, the Highlanders' owners invited the Giants to share Hilltop Park until their home could be rebuilt. Two years later, the Giants returned the favor and allowed the Highlanders to become tenants in their rebuilt and vastly superior facility. With

The 1927 Yankees were known as "Murderers' Row."

the move in 1913, the Highlanders officially changed their name to "Yankees," by which they had actually been known for most of their history.

From 1911 to 1919, the Yankees won as many as 80 games in a season only twice. But three key moves—the January 11, 1915, purchase of the ballclub by Colonel Jacob Ruppert and Colonel Tillinghast L'Hommedieu Huston, the 1918 hiring of Manager Miller Huggins by Ruppert (without Huston's blessing) and the 1919 midseason trade for right-handed pitcher Carl Mays (26 wins in 1920 and 27 wins in 1921)—set the stage for the most course-altering transaction in baseball history.

On January 3, 1920, the Yankees purchased the contract of George Herman "Babe" Ruth from the Boston Red Sox for $125,000 and a $350,000 loan against the mortgage on Fenway Park.

Ruth's impact was immediate. The Yankees won 95 games in 1920, their highest victory total up to that point, then captured their first American League pennant a year later. With the Babe hitting 54 home runs in 1920—more than any other *team* in the American League—Yankees attendance at the Polo Grounds doubled to 1,289,422. In 1921, the Giants, being outdrawn in their own park, asked the Yankees to vacate the Polo Grounds as soon as possible. Now bitter rivals, the two teams squared off in the World Series in 1921 and 1922 with the Giants winning both times.

Though he came up on the wrong end in both Series, Yankees pitcher—and 1969 Hall of Fame inductee—Waite Hoyt allowed just one earned run over 35.0 combined innings over the two Fall Classics. Remarkably, he went 2-2 in his five appearances (four starts), including a 1-0, Series-clinching loss (on an unearned run) in Game 8 of the 1921 best-of-nine championship.

With their departure from the Polo Grounds inevitable, the Yankees' owners set out to build a ballpark of their own. Designed to be baseball's first triple-decked structure with an advertised capacity of 70,000, it would also be the first baseball facility to be labeled a "stadium."

Construction began on May 5, 1922, and in only 284 working days, Yankee Stadium was ready for its inaugural game on April 18, 1923 vs. the Boston Red Sox. An announced crowd of 74,200 fans packed Yankee Stadium for a glimpse of Baseball's grandest facility while thousands milled around outside after the fire department finally ordered the gates closed. Appropriately, Ruth christened his new home with a three-run homer to cap a four-run third inning as the Yankees won, 4-1.

Playing in their new stadium, the Yankees won the American League by 16.0 games in 1923, using just eight pitchers all season. Each of their five starters—Bob Shawkey, Joe Bush, Waite Hoyt, Sam Jones and Herb Pennock—won at least 16 games. Yet it was Ruth's tremendous power that people were coming to see, and Yankee Stadium quickly became known as "The House That Ruth Built." Later that season, the Stadium hosted the first of 37 World Series at the structure, and the Yankees won their first World Championship over their former landlord, the Giants.

On June 1, 1925, in a 5-3 loss vs. Washington, Huggins inserted a 21-year-old rookie first baseman as a pinch-hitter for light-hitting shortstop Paul "Pee Wee" Wanninger. No one could have imagined at the time that this appearance would be the first of 2,130 consecutive games played by Lou Gehrig, who, with Ruth and later Joe DiMaggio, anchored some of the greatest ballclubs of all time.

After a tough loss to the St. Louis Cardinals in the 1926 World Series, the Yankees rolled to World Championships in both 1927 and 1928, sweeping Pittsburgh and St. Louis, respectively. The 1927 club, the second Yankees team to be labeled "Murderers' Row" (the first was the 1919 squad), is often the yardstick by which team greatness is measured. During that season, Ruth broke his own single-season home run record (previously 59 in 1921) with his 60th on September 30, 1927, off Washington's Tom Zachary. Gehrig also added 47 homers and 175 RBI.

In his 15 seasons in pinstripes, Ruth helped build a winning tradition with seven American League pennants and four World Championships (also 1932). He finished his unparaleled career with 714 home runs (including 49 with the Red Sox from 1914-19 and six with the Boston Braves in 1935), 12 American League home run titles and six RBI crowns, including five seasons with more than 150 RBI. A charter member of Baseball's Hall of Fame, he remains widely regarded as the greatest player of all time.

Throughout Ruth's time in pinstripes, he often overshadowed the soft-spoken, Manhattan-born Gehrig. Yet the "Iron Horse" posted incredible numbers in his own right. From 1926 through 1938, Gehrig drove in at least 112 runs each season. A member of six World Championship clubs (1927-28, 1932, 1936-38), he finished with a .340 lifetime batting average and 493 career home runs in just 8,001 at-bats. He was the AL's starting first baseman in each of the first five Major League Baseball All-Star Games, and in 1934, he became the first of two Yankees in franchise history (also Mickey Mantle in 1956) to win the Triple Crown, hitting .363

Lou Gehrig

with a career-best 49 homers and 165 RBI. He also still holds the American League record for RBI in a single season with 184 in 1931.

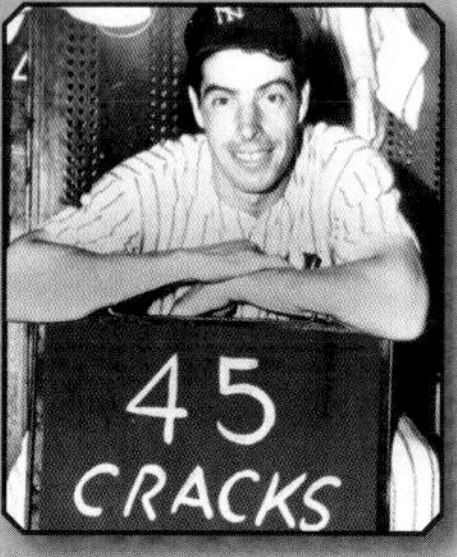

Joe DiMaggio

After the 1934 season, Ruth's last in New York, the Yankees purchased the contract of a budding star named Joe DiMaggio from the San Francisco Seals of the Pacific Coast League. Two years later, DiMaggio made his debut in pinstripes and helped the Yankees to an incredible string of four consecutive World Championships under Manager Joe McCarthy from 1936 through 1939. The 1930s also produced one of the game's greatest lefty-righty pitching combinations in future Hall of Famers Lefty Gomez and Red Ruffing. A four-time 20-game winner—including 24-7 in 1932 and 26-5 in 1934—Gomez posted a 6-0 record over five World Series. Ruffing, who was acquired in May 1930 from the Boston Red Sox for outfielder Cedric Durst and $50,000, had been 39-96 with the Red Sox since his 1924 rookie season. After coming to the Yankees, however, he forged a legacy worthy of Cooperstown, going 231-124 in pinstripes while posting 20, 20, 21 and 21 wins on the four World Championship clubs from 1936 through 1939. He was also an exceptionally good hitter for a pitcher, totaling 36 career home runs and a .269 lifetime batting average.

From 1931 through part of the 1946 season, the Yankees were led by McCarthy, who compiled a Yankees-record 1,460 wins in his time at the helm. Having also spent time leading the Chicago Cubs (1926-1930) and the Boston Red Sox (1948-50), he stands at eighth place on the all-time managerial wins list with 2,125 victories heading into the 2010 season. With the Yankees, he reached eight World Series (1932, 1936-39, 1941-43), winning a World Championship in all but one—the 1942 Fall Classic against St. Louis.

Sadly, in 1939, Gehrig was diagnosed with a crippling disease, eventually determined to be amyotrophic lateral sclerosis (ALS), and his streak of playing in 2,130 consecutive games came to an end on May 2, when he took himself out of the lineup prior to the Yankees' 22-2 win at Detroit. He never played in a Major League game again.

On July 4 of the same season, the Yankees honored their captain with an emotional Lou Gehrig Appreciation Day at Yankee Stadium, and his uniform No. 4 became the first in Baseball to be retired. He died on June 2, 1941.

With Gehrig's retirement, DiMaggio became the pillar of the next generation of Yankees champions. In his 13 seasons in pinstripes (1936-42 and '46-51), DiMaggio made the AL All-Star team every year, and his club played in the World Series in all but three years (1940, '46, '48), winning nine World Series titles. Along the way, he tallied three AL MVP Awards (1939, '41, '47) and batted .324 over his career, marking the third-highest average in franchise history. The legendary "Yankee Clipper" compiled one of the game's most remarkable—and perhaps unbreakable—records in 1941, when he hit safely in an all-time-best 56 consecutive games.

DiMaggio's retirement after the 1951 season at the age of 37 was made easier by the emergence of Mickey Mantle, who played side-by-side with DiMaggio in the outfield in the Yankee Clipper's final campaign. With contributions from future Hall of Famers Yogi Berra, Whitey Ford and Phil Rizzuto, the Yankees were nearly unstoppable from the late 1940s through the early 1960s. Manager Casey Stengel sublimely handled the Yankees juggernaut following his surprising appointment prior to the 1949 season as the club marched to an all-time record five consecutive World Series titles from 1949 through 1953.

His emphasis on platooning players (often to their chagrin) allowed him to exploit matchups in a way not emphasized in his era. Nicknamed "The Old Perfessor," with a vernacular called "Stengelese," he remains one of the most colorful personalities in the game's history. In 12 seasons as manager of the Yankees, he brought his club to the World Series 10 times, winning on seven occasions (also 1956 and 1958).

Mantle would achieve greatness despite suffering from osteomyelitis (a painful inflammatory bone disease) and numerous other injuries. The powerful switch-hitter belted 536 home runs, collected 2,415 hits and batted .300 or higher 10 times in an 18-year career. In his first 14 seasons in pinstripes (1951-64), the Yankees missed the World Series only twice (1954 and 1959) and won the Fall Classic seven times. With his .353 batting average, 52 homers and 130 RBI in 1956, he remains the last Yankees player to win the Triple Crown.

Ford, who played his whole career in pinstripes, is the Yankees' all-time

Lefty Gomez

Mickey Mantle and Roger Maris

wins leader. His lifetime record of 236-106 gives him the second-best career winning percentage (.690) of any modern-era (since 1900) pitcher with 100 or more decisions, trailing only career-Yankee Spud Chandler (.717, 109-43). Ford paced the American League in victories three times and in ERA and shutouts twice. He still holds many World Series records, including those for wins (10), consecutive scoreless innings (33.0) and strikeouts (94).

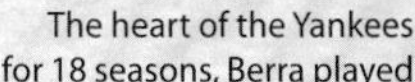

The heart of the Yankees for 18 seasons, Berra played on an incredible 14 pennant winners and 10 World Championship teams—a record number for any individual player in Baseball history. He is one of only 10 players in Major League history to win three MVP Awards, and he was selected to the All-Star team in every season from 1948 through 1962.

Rizzuto played on 10 pennant winners and eight World Series championship teams from 1941 through 1956, capturing the league's MVP award in 1950, batting .324 with 200 hits and 125 runs scored. Eventually elected to the Baseball Hall of Fame in 1994, he gave one of the most memorable induction speeches in the history of the ceremony.

Not every notable Yankee was a future Hall of Famer. In Game 5 of the 1956 World Series vs. the Brooklyn Dodgers at Yankee Stadium, right-hander Don Larsen authored one of the game's greatest pitching performances when he retired all 27 Dodger batters for the only perfect game in World Series history.

The Yankees opened the 1960s winning pennants in the first five seasons (1960-64) and World Series titles in 1961 and 1962. Incredibly, in the 29 seasons from 1936 to 1964, the Yankees won 22 pennants and 16 World Championships. The 1961 club is still regarded as one of the best teams in Baseball history. With Mantle and Roger Maris embroiled in a season-long race to break Ruth's single-season home run record, the Yankees rolled to 109 wins en route to a World Championship. Maris broke Ruth's record when he belted his 61st home run on October 1 off Boston's Tracy Stallard at Yankee Stadium in the last game of the season.

Age finally caught up with the ballclub after a seven-game Series loss to the St. Louis Cardinals in 1964. The Yankees would finish above fourth place just once in the next nine seasons and actually fell to last place in 1966 for the first time in 53 years.

The team's fall from grace ended on January 2, 1973, when it was sold by CBS to a group headed by George M. Steinbrenner III. With the addition of Catfish Hunter, Baseball's first marquee free agent, shrewd trades that brought Ed Figueroa, Mickey Rivers, Chris Chambliss and Willie Randolph to the club, and a strong nucleus that included Thurman Munson, Graig Nettles, Roy White and Sparky Lyle, the Yankees returned to the postseason in 1976, ending an 11-year drought (1965-1975) by winning their first American League East title. Then on October 14, 1976, in the deciding Game 5 of the AL Championship Series vs. Kansas City, Chambliss launched a ninth-inning, pennant-winning home run to put the Yankees back in the World Series.

This newfound success took place in a remodeled Yankee Stadium. The 1974 and '75 Yankees played in Shea Stadium for two years while vast improvements were made to the original Yankee Stadium (for more details, see "History of Original Yankee Stadium").

After a disheartening four-game sweep by the Cincinnati Reds in the 1976 World Series, the Yankees introduced Reggie Jackson—the most prolific slugger of his era—as the club's newest free-agent acquisition. Jackson capped an exciting 1977 season with one of baseball's greatest individual performances. In the Game 6 World Series-clinching win vs. Los Angeles at Yankee Stadium, "Mr. October" belted three home runs on three swings of the bat to join Babe Ruth as the only players to hit three home runs in a single World Series game.

In 1978, the Yankees overcame a 14.0-game deficit in the American League East to force a one-game

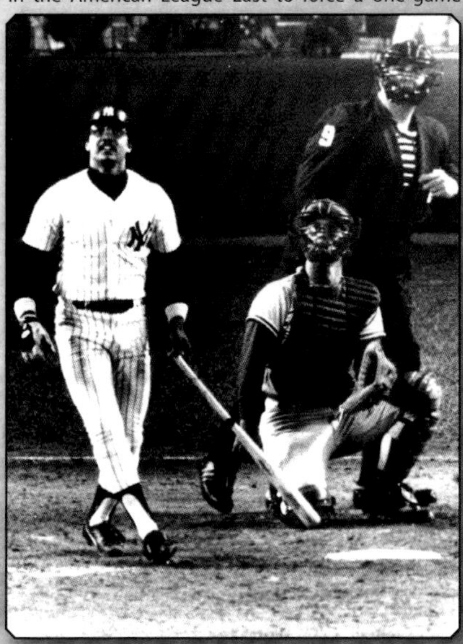
Reggie Jackson hit three home runs in Game 6 of the 1977 World Series.

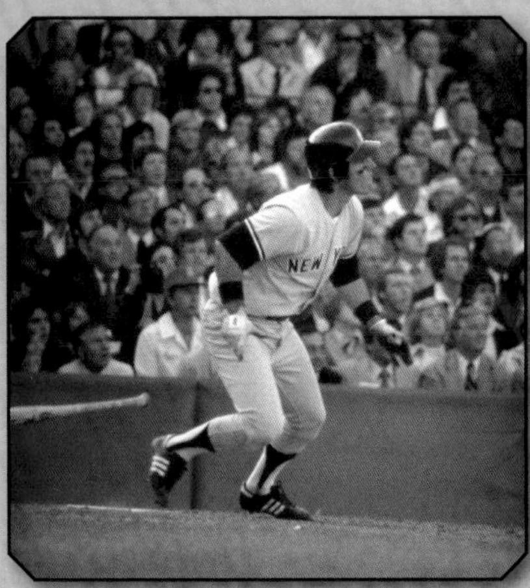

Bucky Dent hits his famous three-run home run in the one-game AL East playoff contest on Oct. 2, 1978 at Fenway Park.

playoff with the Boston Red Sox at Fenway Park to decide the American League pennant. Shortstop Bucky Dent erased a 2-0, seventh-inning Red Sox lead with a dramatic three-run homer, and the Yankees went on to a 5-4 win en route to a second straight World Championship over the Dodgers.

The 1978 season also saw the emergence of Ron Guidry as one the franchise's greatest pitchers. A four-time American League All-Star, Guidry compiled one of the most dominating seasons in baseball history while becoming known as "Louisiana Lightning." He went 25-3 with a 1.74 ERA in leading the Yankees to their dramatic comeback, compiling a club-record 248 strikeouts and nine shutouts en route to a unanimous selection as the AL Cy Young Award recipient. On June 17, 1978 vs. the California Angels at Yankee Stadium, Guidry set a club record by striking out 18 batters. A five-time Gold Glove Award winner, Guidry also racked up 20-win seasons in 1983 (21-9) and 1985 (22-6).

The 1970s ended with tragedy. Thurman Munson, the Yankees' first captain since Gehrig, was killed when his private jet crashed on August 2, 1979. Only 32 years old at the time of his death, Munson was the undisputed leader of the clubs that won three consecutive pennants and two World Championships. After the captain's death, the Yankees would make only one more World Series appearance (1981) in the next 17 years despite compiling the best record in the Major Leagues during the 1980s.

Thurman Munson, Goose Gossage

During this period, Don Mattingly became one of the most popular players in franchise history, batting .307 in a 14-year career (1982-95) played entirely in pinstripes. He compiled an incredible six-year stretch from 1984 through 1989, in which he batted .327 and topped 100 RBI five times, including a career-high 145 in 1985, when he captured the AL MVP Award. A year earlier, he outdueled teammate Dave Winfield for the 1984 AL batting crown (.343 to .340), going 4-for-5 on the final day of the season. His performance and loyalty were recognized when he was named the 10th captain in Yankees history from 1991-95.

Winfield, who came to the Yankees as the game's most sought-after free agent in 1981, compiled Hall of Fame credentials in his eight-plus seasons in pinstripes (1981-90). With the Yankees, he belted 205 home runs with 818 RBI and won five Gold Glove Awards.

After a 13-year absence (1982-94), the Yankees returned to postseason play in 1995 as the American League's first-ever "Wild Card" entry. A heart-wrenching five-game loss to the Seattle Mariners in the Division Series marked the start of a 13-year run of consecutive postseason appearances (1995-2007), a record topped only by the Atlanta Braves' 14-season streak (1991-93, 1995-2005).

In 1996 under new skipper Joe Torre, the Yankees returned to the World Series against Atlanta, coming back from an 0-2 deficit to win four straight games, including Games 3, 4 and 5 in Atlanta. Following a Division Series exit in 1997, the Yankees won three straight World titles from 1998 through 2000, giving them four championships in five years. Their 114 victories in 1998 shattered the 44-year-old American League mark of 111 wins set by the 1954 Cleveland Indians (since broken by Seattle in 2001) and their 125 total victories, including 11 postseason wins, remains the highest single-season total in baseball history.

Rudy Giuliani, George Steinbrenner and Joe Torre

The Yankees' most recent era of accomplishment has featured a lineup of homegrown talent to rival any period in franchise history. Since the signing of nondrafted free agent Bernie Williams in 1991, the Yankees farm system has produced All-Stars Robinson Cano, Derek Jeter, Andy Pettitte, Jorge Posada and Mariano Rivera. In addition, trades and free-agent acquisitions have brought such All-Stars as Wade Boggs, Scott Brosius, David Cone, Jimmy Key, Tino Martinez, Hideki Matsui and Mike Mussina to the Bronx. Another of those players, Paul O'Neill, acquired in a November 3, 1992, trade with Cincinnati, became adored by Yankees fans for his intense and gritty approach. A winner of the 1994 batting title (.359) and often described as a "warrior," he is typically thought of as the heart and soul of the club's turn-of-the-century success.

In 2001, the Yankees fell just shy of becoming the second team in history to win four consecutive World Series titles, but they nevertheless captured

Scott Brosius hits a two-run, ninth-inning, game-tying homer in Game 5 of the 2001 World Series vs. Arizona.

the hearts of the nation in the aftermath of the terrorist attacks of September 11. The Yankees dropped the first two games of the Series at the Arizona Diamondbacks' Bank One Ballpark but rallied to win the next three at Yankee Stadium behind dramatic ninth-inning comebacks in both Games 4 and 5. On consecutive nights, Martinez and Brosius erased two-run, ninth-inning Diamondbacks leads with home runs, and the Yankees won both games in extra innings. It was in Game 4 that Jeter earned his "Mr. November" nickname with a 10th-inning "walk-off" home run. The victories marked the first time in World Series history that a team won two games in the same Series when trailing by at least two runs in the ninth inning.

No one personifies the Yankees' success since 1996 more than Jeter, who was a rookie on that squad. Over the last 10 seasons (2000-09), his 1,940-hit total is second in the Majors, and his personal career winning percentage of .603 (1,287-849-2) is the best among active Major League players who have played in a minimum of 1,000 games. In 2009, he further cemented his legacy by becoming the Yankees' all-time hits leader (2,747), passing Lou Gehrig (2,721), who had held the mark since 1937. Jeter also recorded his seventh 200-hit season and is one of two players in franchise history along with Gehrig (eight) with as many as four. In fact, according to the *Elias Sports Bureau*, no other player has had as many as four 200-hit seasons while playing at least 100 games at shortstop per year.

Posada and Rivera have crafted special places for themselves in the annals of the franchise. Posada, a 24th-round selection in the 1990 First-Year Player Draft, is one of six catchers in Major League history to hit at least 20 home runs in eight seasons while playing a minimum of 50 percent of his games behind the plate. Known for his toughness and durability, the Puerto Rico-born backstop started at least 120 games in eight consecutive seasons from 2000-07. Rivera, with 526 career saves going into 2010, ranks second on Baseball's all-time list behind only Trevor Hoffman (591). His reputation has been cemented by postseason excellence, which includes an 8-1 record and 0.74 ERA in 88 career postseason games (133.1 innings pitched). His Major League-leading 39 career postseason saves is almost as many as the totals of the second, third and fourth place pitchers on the list combined (42). His 2.25 career ERA is the second-lowest all time among pitchers with at least 1.000.0IP since ERA was made an official statistic in 1912 in NL and 1913 in AL (Eddie Cicotte 2.20).

In 2004, the organization acquired Alex Rodriguez in a trade from the Texas Rangers. Since his arrival in the Bronx, the now 12-time All-Star transitioned to a new position at third base and was voted the AL MVP in 2005 and 2007, while becoming the 22nd—and youngest—player in baseball history reach the 500-home run plateau in 2007.

Former Yankees catcher Joe Girardi was named the 32nd manager in franchise history on October 30, 2007, giving him the reins heading into the final season of the original Yankee Stadium. The 2008 season was full of nostalgia, and notable events included the third Papal Mass in Stadium history on April 20 and a 15-inning, 4-3 American League victory in the All-Star Game on July 15. Though the Yankees played their last-ever home game in the original Stadium on September 21, defeating the Baltimore Orioles, 7-3, the drama of the season didn't end until its final day as Mike Mussina earned a win in the first game of a doubleheader over Boston at Fenway Park to become the oldest first-time 20-game winner in baseball history.

The past season proved nothing short of storybook material as the club finished the inaugural season in the newly-constructed Yankee Stadium with the best regular season record in the Majors (103-59) and a six-game World Series win over the Phillies. The 2009 season featured 15 "walk-off" wins along with an all-time Major League-record 18-consecutive errorless games from May 14 through June 1. Free-agent acquisitions CC Sabathia (19 wins), A.J. Burnett (13 wins) and Mark Teixeira (second in AL MVP voting, 39 homers, 122 RBI) each played major roles in the club's success.

Looking forward, the Yankees will continue to concentrate on procuring and nurturing young talent. Pitchers Joba Chamberlain and Phil Hughes, and second baseman Robinson Cano are illustrative of the team's commitment to youth and international scouting. With the 2010 season at hand, the Yankees will strive toward the singular goal of bringing a 28th championship back to the Bronx.

Derek Jeter

History of the Yankees Uniform

When the Yankees (then "Highlanders") first took the field for their inaugural season in 1903, their uniforms did not much resemble the iconic style for which they are known today. A large ornate "N" decorated one breast and a large ornate "Y" the other. Two years later for the 1905 season, the "N" and "Y" were merged side by side into a monogram on the left breast, creating a forerunner of the now legendary emblem.

It wasn't until 1909 that the most recognizable insignia in sports—the interlocking "NY"—made its first appearance on the caps and left sleeves of Highlanders uniforms. The design was created in 1877 by Louis C. Tiffany for a medal to be given by the New York City Police Department to Officer John McDowell, the first NYC policeman shot in the line of duty. Perhaps because one of the club's owners, Bill Devery, was a former NYC police chief, the design was adopted by the organization. The familiar "NY" eventually migrated from the left sleeve to the left breast of home uniforms from 1912-16, albeit in a larger version than is currently worn today.

In 1912, their final season at Hilltop Park, the Yankees (as they were commonly known by then) made a fashionable debut at their April 11 home opener by wearing pinstripes for the first time in their history. The club was not the first team to wear pinstripes (eight of Baseball's other 15 teams had already worn them at some point), and they would actually abandon the look in the following two seasons (1913-14). By 1915, though, home pinstripes were back for good.

Jack Chesbro models the franchise's earliest "NY" design in 1903.

In 1917, the Yankees removed the "NY" monogram from the jersey and went with a plain, pinstripes-only look. The "NY" remained off the uniform—except for the cap—for the next 20 years until it was reinstated in 1936. Babe Ruth, whose Yankees career spanned 1920-1934, played his entire Yankees career without ever wearing the club's now-legendary insignia on his jersey.

The Yankees utilized numerous cap designs from 1903 until 1921—including pinstripes in 1915, '16, '19 and '21—until they finally settled on a solid navy cap with the interlocking "NY" insignia in 1922.

Babe Ruth sports the pinstriped-cap look of 1921.

The club's road uniforms have remained relatively unchanged since 1918—solid grey with "NEW YORK" in block letters across the chest. The notable exception was from 1927-30, when "NEW YORK" was replaced by "YANKEES." In 1973, with the introduction of more breathable double-knit uniforms, Yankees road jerseys added navy-and-white banded trim to the cuffs of the sleeves as well as white shadowing behind the jersey lettering.

Lou Gehrig and Tony Lazzeri display the pre-1936 home uniform without insignia.

The home uniform remains the Yankees' signature look. With the exception of minor alterations—including bolder pinstripes in the 1940s—it has remained mostly unchanged for more than 70 years.

For the 2008 season, the Yankees wore an All-Star Game patch on their left sleeve and a Yankee Stadium Final Season tribute patch on their right sleeve. In 2009, the club wore a patch on their left sleeve, as well as a specially-designed patch on the back of their cap, each to commemorate the inaugural season of Yankee Stadium.

Origin of Numbered Uniforms

Numbers first appeared on Major League uniforms on June 26, 1916, when the Cleveland Indians wore large numerals on their left sleeves in an experiment that lasted just a few weeks. Another brief trial by Cleveland the next season and a similar sleeve trial by the St. Louis Cardinals in 1923 both proved temporary. It wasn't until the 1929 season that another attempt was made, as both Cleveland and the New York Yankees began their seasons with numbers as a permanent part of their respective uniforms. Though the Yankees are typically credited as being the team with the longest-standing such policy, it should be noted that the Indians began their season two days earlier than the Bombers, as the Yankees' April 16 Opening Day contest was rained out.

The initial distribution of numbers to the Yankees roster was made according to the player's position in the batting order. Therefore, in 1929, leadoff hitter Earle Combs wore No. 1, Mark Koenig No. 2, Babe Ruth No. 3, Lou Gehrig No. 4, Bob Meusel No. 5, Tony Lazzeri No. 6, Leo Durocher No. 7, Johnny Grabowski No. 8, Benny Bengough No. 9 and Bill Dickey No. 10 (Grabowski, Bengough and Dickey shared the catching duties). By the mid-1930s, other teams adopted the idea, and uniform numbers became the standard for all teams.

Important Dates in Yankees History

*** Event occurred at the original Yankee Stadium**

Hilltop Park, first home of the Yankees

Jan. 9, 1903 - Frank Farrell and Bill Devery purchase the defunct Baltimore franchise of the American League for $18,000, then move the team to Manhattan.

March 12, 1903 - The New York franchise is approved as a member of the American League. The team will play in a hastily constructed, all-wood park at 168th Street and Broadway. Because the site is one of the highest spots in Manhattan, their home field is referred to as "Hilltop Park."

April 22, 1903 - The Highlanders (as the Yankees were commonly known then) play their first game, a 3-1 loss at Washington.

April 23, 1903 - The Highlanders record the first win in franchise history, a 7-2 victory at Washington. Harry Howell records the win.

April 30, 1903 - The Highlanders notch a 6-2 win vs. Washington in their inaugural home opener at Hilltop Park.

April 11, 1912 - Pinstripes first appear on Highlanders uniforms, creating a look that would become the most famous uniform design in sports.

April 1913 - The Highlanders are officially renamed "Yankees" after moving to the Polo Grounds, home of the National League's New York Giants.

Jan. 11, 1915 - Col. Jacob Ruppert and Col. Tillinghast L'Hommedieu Huston purchase the Yankees for $465,000.

April 24, 1917 - George Mogridge becomes the first Yankee to throw a no-hitter in a 2-1 win at Fenway Park.

Jan. 3, 1920 - The Yankees purchase the contract of Babe Ruth from the Boston Red Sox for $125,000 and a $350,000 loan against the mortgage on Fenway Park.

Oct. 5, 1921 - The Yankees play their first postseason game in franchise history, as Carl Mays tosses a complete game shutout to defeat the New York Giants at the Polo Grounds in Game 1 of the World Series.

***May 5, 1922** - Construction begins on Yankee Stadium.

May 21, 1922 - Col. Ruppert buys out Col. Huston for $1.5 million.

***April 18, 1923** - Yankee Stadium opens with a 4-1 win over the Boston Red Sox before an announced crowd of 74,200. Babe Ruth hits the Stadium's first home run.

Oct. 15, 1923 - The Yankees defeat the New York Giants, 6-4, at the Polo Grounds in Game 6 of the World Series, clinching the first World Championship in franchise history.

***June 1, 1925** - Lou Gehrig begins his record streak of 2,130 consecutive games played, pinch-hitting for "Pee Wee" Wanniger in a 5-3 loss to Washington at Yankee Stadium.

Oct. 6, 1926 - Babe Ruth becomes the first player to hit three home runs in a single World Series game in Game 4 at St. Louis.

***Sept. 30, 1927** - Babe Ruth breaks his own single-season Major League record by hitting his 60th home run (off Tom Zachary) in a 4-2 win over Washington at Yankee Stadium.

***April 20, 1928** - Yankee Stadium's left field stands are enlarged to three decks.

Oct. 9, 1928 - In Game 4 of the World Series vs. the Cardinals at St. Louis' Sportsman's Park, Babe Ruth hits three home runs, marking his second three-homer World Series game.

***April 18, 1929** - The Yankees wear numbered uniforms for the first time in their history, two days after the Cleveland Indians permanently adopt them as well (Numbers would become standard for all teams by 1932).

Sept. 24, 1929 - The Yankees celebrate Babe Ruth Day at Fenway Park by winning, 5-3, over Boston. Ruth goes 2-for-3 with a double and Tom Zachary (pitching for the Yankees) records his final decision of the season, improving to 12-0, still a Major League record for most wins in a season without a loss.

Sept. 25, 1929 - Manager Miller Huggins, who guided the Yankees to their first six AL pennants and three World Championships, dies of blood poisoning.

Origin of the Names "Highlanders" and "Yankees"

When the American League moved the Baltimore Orioles to New York for the 1903 season, the club made its home at 168th Street and Broadway, one of the highest spots in Manhattan. As a result, the team became known as the "Hilltoppers" and their field "Hilltop Park," even though their formal team name was "New York Americans" and formal ballpark name "American League Park."

The name "Highlanders," as the team of that era is most-popularly remembered today, also started in the club's formative years. It originated not only as a nod to their elevated Manhattan perch, but also as a reference to club president Joseph W. Gordon, whose last name conjured up thoughts of the famous British army unit, the Gordon Highlanders.

Other nicknames for the team were "Porch Climbers," "Burglars," and "Invaders"—all three usually reserved for writers sympathetic to the New York Giants, who held lingering animosity at having American League competition in such close proximity.

As early as 1904, however, the name "Yankees" became common in the press. The earliest known use was in an April 7, 1904, article in the *New York Evening Journal* that bore the headline "YANKEES WILL START HOME FROM SOUTH TODAY," which was published following a successful spring training spent in the Southern U.S. A week later, the same newspaper's coverage of Opening Day was headlined "YANKEES BEAT BOSTON," and the term also appeared in the article's lead sentence.

"Yankees" was a natural fit given the club's formal name, but likely owes its success to newspaper typesetters and editors grateful for a team name with fewer letters than "Highlanders" or "Hilltoppers." When the franchise moved from Hilltop Park to the Polo Grounds in 1913, it officially changed its name to "New York Yankees."

June 3, 1932 - Lou Gehrig becomes the first player to hit four home runs in a single game in the Yankees' 20-13 win at Philadelphia. The news is overshadowed by the retirement announcement of New York Giants Manager John McGraw. Gehrig remains the only Yankee to hit four home runs in one game.

Aug. 13, 1932 - Red Ruffing throws a complete game shutout and hits a 10th-inning solo home run off Washington Senators pitcher Al Thomas, giving the Yankees a 1-0 victory at Griffith Stadium. Though not the first to do so, no Major League pitcher has since thrown a complete game shutout and hit a home run in a 1-0 game.

Oct. 1, 1932 - In the fifth inning of the Yankees' 7-5 victory over the Chicago Cubs at Wrigley Field in Game 3 of the World Series, Babe Ruth gestures toward the bleachers before hitting his second home run of the game. Though Lou Gehrig also hits two homers that day, the game will be remembered for Ruth's much-debated "called shot."

June 6, 1934 - Myril Hoag goes 6-for-6 in a 15-3, nine-inning win in Game 1 of a doubleheader at Boston, becoming the first of only two Yankees to go 6-for-6 in a single game (see June 7, 2008 - Johnny Damon).

Nov. 21, 1934 - The Yankees purchase Joe DiMaggio from the San Francisco Seals of the Pacific Coast League for $50,000.

Joe DiMaggio

May 24, 1936 - Tony Lazzeri hits three home runs (including two grand slams) and a triple, setting a still-standing AL record with 11RBI in a single game in a 25-2 win at Philadelphia.

***April 20, 1937** - The Yankees' 15th season at Yankee Stadium opens with the right-field stands enlarged to three decks. Wooden bleachers are replaced by a concrete structure, and the distance to center field drops from 490 feet to 461 feet.

***May 30, 1938** - A franchise-record crowd of 81,841 attends a doubleheader sweep of the Boston Red Sox at Yankee Stadium.

***Aug. 27, 1938** - Monte Pearson authors the first Yankee Stadium no-hitter by a Yankee, defeating Cleveland, 13-0, in Game 2 of a doubleheader.

May 2, 1939 - Lou Gehrig's playing streak of 2,130 consecutive games ends when he does not make an appearance in a 22-2 Yankees win at Detroit. Babe Dahlgren plays first base for the Yankees and contributes a double and a home run.

***July 4, 1939** - "Lou Gehrig Appreciation Day" is held at Yankee Stadium in between games of a doubleheader vs. Washington. His uniform No. 4 is the first to be retired in Major League Baseball. Gehrig makes his famous "luckiest man on the face of the earth" speech.

***May 15, 1941** - Joe DiMaggio's 56-game hitting streak begins with a single off Edgar Smith in a 13-1 loss vs. Chicago at Yankee Stadium.

June 2, 1941 - Lou Gehrig dies of Amyotrophic Lateral Sclerosis at the age of 37 in the Riverdale section of the Bronx.

July 17, 1941 - Joe DiMaggio's consecutive-game hitting streak ends at 56 when he goes 0-for-3 in a 4-3 Yankees win at Cleveland. Indians third baseman Ken Keltner twice robs DiMaggio of hits with great fielding plays. DiMaggio hits safely in his next 16 games, giving him hits in 72 of 73 games.

Jan. 25, 1945 - Dan Topping, Del Webb and Larry MacPhail purchase the Yankees for $2.8 million from the estate of the late Col. Jacob Ruppert. MacPhail replaces Ed Barrow as President and General Manager.

***May 28, 1946** - The first night game is played at Yankee Stadium, a 2-1 loss vs. Washington before 49,917 fans.

***April 27, 1947** - "Babe Ruth Day" is celebrated at Yankee Stadium and throughout Major League Baseball.

***June 13, 1948** - Babe Ruth's uniform No. 3 is retired at Yankee Stadium's 25th Anniversary celebration. The visit marks the Babe's final Stadium appearance.

Aug. 16, 1948 - Babe Ruth dies of throat cancer in New York at age 53.

Oct. 12, 1948 - The Yankees announce that Casey Stengel will replace Bucky Harris as manager.

***Oct. 1-2, 1949** - The Yankees come back from a one-game deficit with two games to play, defeating the Boston Red Sox in the final two games of the season at Yankee Stadium, 5-4 and 5-3, respectively, marking the first of five consecutive American League pennants.

***Oct. 5, 1949** - In Game 1 of the World Series vs. Brooklyn at Yankee Stadium, Tommy Henrich breaks up a scoreless pitchers' duel between the Yankees' Allie Reynolds and the Dodgers' Don Newcombe, hitting a game-winning solo home run in the bottom of the ninth.

***April 17, 1951** - Mickey Mantle makes his Major League debut, going 1-for-4 in a 4-0 win vs. Boston at Yankee Stadium. The game also marks Bob Sheppard's first as Yankees public-address announcer. Boston's Dom DiMaggio is the first hitter announced.

***Sept. 28, 1951** - In an 8-0 Game 1 win in a doubleheader vs. Boston at Yankee Stadium, Allie Reynolds becomes the second of four players in Baseball history to toss two no-hitters in the same season (also Johnny Vander Meer in 1938, Virgil Trucks in 1952 and Nolan Ryan in 1973). Reynolds had previously no-hit the Indians at Cleveland's Municipal Stadium on July 12 in a 1-0 win.

Dec. 12, 1951 - Joe DiMaggio officially announces his retirement.

April 17, 1953 - Exactly two years after his Yankees debut, Mickey Mantle hits what is recognized as the game's first "tape-measure" home run, a 565-foot shot off the Senators' Chuck Stobbs at Washington's Griffith Stadium.

***Oct. 5, 1953** - Billy Martin singles home the winning run in the ninth inning of a 4-3, Game 6 victory over the Brooklyn Dodgers at Yankee Stadium. The win clinches the Yankees' fifth-consecutive World Championship.

***Oct. 4, 1955** - Brooklyn's Johnny Podres outduels Yankees starter Tommy Byrne and two relievers, 2-0, clinching the Dodgers' first World Series Championship. The World Series loss snaps the Yankees' string of seven consecutive team appearances in the Fall Classic without losing a Series (1943, '47, '49-53). It also marks the Yankees' first World Series loss to Brooklyn after wins in 1941, '47, '49, '52 and '53.

***May 30, 1956** - Batting against Pedro Ramos in Game 1 of a doubleheader vs. Washington, Mickey Mantle nearly hits a home run out of Yankee Stadium, with the ball striking the upper deck frieze in right field.

***Oct. 8, 1956** - Don Larsen hurls the only perfect game in World Series history, a 2-0 win over Brooklyn in Game 5 at Yankee Stadium.

Oct. 10, 1956 - Johnny Kucks pitches a complete game shutout, defeating the Brooklyn Dodgers at Ebbets Field, 9-0, to win Game 7 of the World Series.

April 22, 1959 - Whitey Ford pitches a 1-0, 14-inning complete game shutout at Washington, allowing just seven hits and striking out 15.

***October 8, 1960** - Second baseman Bobby Richardson sets an all-time World Series record (since tied by Hideki Matsui on 11/4/09 in Game 6 vs. Philadelphia) with 6RBI in Game 3 of the World Series vs. Pittsburgh, hitting a grand slam in the first inning and two-run single in the fourth inning of a 10-0 Yankees win.

***Oct. 1, 1961 -** Roger Maris hits his 61st home run in the season's final game, establishing a then-Major League record and still-standing AL record.

June 24, 1962 - Jack Reed's two-run, 22nd-inning home run ends the longest game in Yankees history, a 9-7 win at Detroit.

Oct. 16, 1962 - In Game 7 of the World Series, superb fielding from outfielder Roger Maris holds Matty Alou at third base after a two-out, ninth-inning Willie Mays double. Bobby Richardson then snares a screaming line drive off the bat of Willie McCovey for the game's final out, securing a 1-0, Series-clinching victory over the San Francisco Giants at Candlestick Park. New York scores the game's only run when Tony Kubek grounds into a fifth-inning double play. It would be the last championship for the Yankees for 15 seasons.

***May 22, 1963 -** In an 8-7, 11-inning win vs. the Kansas City A's, Mickey Mantle hits the upper deck frieze in right field for the second time in his career, this time off righthander Bill Fischer.

Nov. 2, 1964 - CBS purchases 80 percent of the Yankees for $11.2 million. The network later buys the remaining 20 percent.

***May 14, 1967 –** Mickey Mantle becomes only the sixth player—and second Yankee—to reach the 500 home run plateau, when he connects off Baltimore's Stu Miller at Yankee Stadium.

***June 8, 1969** - "Mickey Mantle Day" is celebrated at Yankee Stadium and his uniform No. 7 is retired.

***June 24, 1970 -** Bobby Murcer hits home runs in four consecutive at-bats over two games of a doubleheader vs. Cleveland at Yankee Stadium.

Aug. 8, 1972 - The Yankees sign a 30-year lease to play in a remodeled Yankee Stadium. Completion is scheduled for 1976.

Jan. 3, 1973 - A limited partnership, headed by George M. Steinbrenner III as its managing general partner, purchases the Yankees for a net price of $8.7 million from CBS.

April 6, 1974 - The Yankees begin the first of two seasons at Shea Stadium as Yankee Stadium is remodeled. The Yankees will go 90-69 at Shea over the two seasons (1974-75).

Dec. 31, 1974 - Free agent Catfish Hunter signs a then-record five-year contract.

Aug. 1, 1975 - Billy Martin replaces Bill Virdon for his first of five stints as manager.

Jim "Catfish" Hunter

***April 15, 1976 -** Remodeled Yankee Stadium opens with an 11-4 win over the Minnesota Twins. The Twins' Dan Ford hits the first home run.

***April 17, 1976 -** Thurman Munson hits the first homer by a Yankee in remodeled Yankee Stadium in a 10-0 win vs. the Minnesota Twins (off Jim Hughes).

***Oct. 14, 1976** - Chris Chambliss' ninth-inning home run off Mark Littell in Game 5 of the ALCS vs. Kansas City at Yankee Stadium gives the Yankees their 30th AL pennant and first trip to the World Series since 1964.

Nov. 29, 1976 - Free agent Reggie Jackson signs a five-year contract.

Oct. 9, 1977 – The Yankees rally for one run in the eighth inning and three runs in the ninth for a 5-3, series-clinching win in the decisive Game 5 of the 1977 ALCS at Kansas City. Sparky Lyle earns the win for the second consecutive night, finishing the game with 1.1 scoreless innings on no rest following his scoreless 5.1-inning relief appearance at Kauffman Stadium in Game 4.

Sparky Lyle

***Oct. 18, 1977 -** Reggie Jackson hits three home runs (on three consecutive pitches) in Game 6 of the World Series vs. the Los Angeles Dodgers at Yankee Stadium. He joins Babe Ruth as the only players to hit three home runs in a single World Series game.

***June 17, 1978** - Ron Guidry establishes a franchise record by striking out 18 batters in the Yankees' 4-0 win vs. California.

July 24, 1978 - Billy Martin resigns as manager.

July 25, 1978 - Bob Lemon is named manager, replacing Billy Martin.

***July 29, 1978 -** On Old-Timers' Day, the Yankees announce that Billy Martin will return as Yankees manager in 1980 and Bob Lemon will become General Manager.

Oct. 2, 1978 - The Yankees, 14.0 games behind Boston as late as July 19, defeat the Red Sox, 5-4, at Fenway Park in only the second one-game playoff in AL history. Bucky Dent's three-run, seventh-inning home run becomes one of the most memorable in Baseball history.

June 18, 1979 - Billy Martin returns as Yankees manager, replacing Bob Lemon.

Aug. 2, 1979 - Yankees Captain Thurman Munson dies in a plane crash in Canton, Ohio, at age 32. His No. 15 is immediately retired.

***Aug. 6, 1979 -** After delivering a eulogy at Thurman Munson's funeral earlier that morning in Canton, Ohio, Bobby Murcer hits a three-run seventh inning homer and a two-run ninth-inning single, accounting for all five of the Yankees' runs in an emotional 5-4 comeback win vs. Baltimore at Yankee Stadium.

Dec. 15, 1980 - Free agent Dave Winfield signs a then-record 10-year contract.

Sept. 6, 1981 - Bob Lemon is named manager for a second time, replacing Gene Michael.

April 26, 1982 - Gene Michael becomes manager for a second time, replacing Bob Lemon.

Aug. 3, 1982 - Clyde King is named Yankees manager, replacing Gene Michael.

July 4, 1983 - Dave Righetti pitches the sixth regular season no-hitter in franchise history and the first since 1951 in a 4-0 win vs. Boston at Yankee Stadium. Righetti strikes out Wade Boggs for the final out.

***July 24, 1983 -** The Yankees and Kansas City play the infamous "Pine Tar" game at Yankee Stadium. George Brett hits a two-out, ninth-inning home run off Goose Gossage to give the Royals an apparent 5-4 lead. Manager Billy Martin points out that the pine tar on Brett's bat is above the allowable 18 inches and Brett is subsequently called out for using an illegal bat. The Yankees (temporarily) win 4-3 (see Aug. 18, 1983).

"The Pine Tar Game"

***Aug. 18, 1983** - Kansas City's protest is upheld and play is resumed at Yankee Stadium from the point immediately after Brett's home run. Yankees pitcher Ron Guidry plays center field while lefthanded first baseman Don Mattingly plays second base. Royals' reliever Dan Quisenberry retires the Yankees in order in the bottom of the ninth for a 5-4 Royals win.

April 28, 1985 - Billy Martin is named manager for the fourth time, replacing Yogi Berra.

***August 4, 1985** - The Yankees celebrate "Phil Rizzuto Day" at Yankee Stadium, dedicating a plaque in his honor and retiring his No. 10. The Yankees lose their scheduled game to the Chicago White Sox, 4-1, as Tom Seaver wins his 300th career game.

Oct. 6, 1985 - Phil Niekro tosses a four-hit complete game shutout in an 8-0 victory at Toronto's Exhibition Stadium for his 300th career win.

Oct. 17, 1985 - Lou Piniella is named manager, replacing Billy Martin.

July 18, 1987 - Don Mattingly homers off Texas' Jose Guzman to tie Dale Long's Major League record of hitting a home run in eight consecutive games (Mattingly hits 10 HR during the streak).

***Sept. 29, 1987** - Don Mattingly hits a grand slam off Boston's Bruce Hurst, setting a Major League record (tied by Travis Hafner in 2008) with six grand slams in a season.

June 23, 1988 - Billy Martin is replaced as manager of the Yankees for the fifth and final time. Lou Piniella is named manager for the second time.

Dec. 9, 1988 - The Yankees sign a 12-year television contract with the Madison Square Garden Network.

Dec. 25, 1989 - Billy Martin dies in an automobile accident at age 61.

***Sept. 4, 1993** - Jim Abbott tosses a 4-0, no-hit win vs. Cleveland at Yankee Stadium.

Aug. 13, 1995 - Mickey Mantle dies of cancer at age 63 in Dallas, Tex.

Sept. 6, 1995 - Lou Gehrig's Major League record of 2,130 consecutive games played is broken when Baltimore's Cal Ripken, Jr. plays in his 2,131st.

***Oct. 4, 1995** - The Yankees play the longest postseason game in their history, a 15-inning, 7-5 win over Seattle at Yankee Stadium, giving them a 2-0 series lead. The contest was the final Yankee Stadium game for Don Mattingly.

Nov. 2, 1995 - Joe Torre is named the Yankees' 31st manager.

Mar. 1, 1996 - The Yankees defeat the Cleveland Indians, 5-2, in the first ever game at Legends Field (renamed George M. Steinbrenner Field in 2008), the club's new spring training home.

***May 14, 1996** - Dwight Gooden hurls the eighth regular season no-hitter in Yankees history, a 2-0 blanking of the Seattle Mariners at Yankee Stadium.

June 16, 1996 - Mel Allen, the legendary "Voice of the Yankees" from 1939-64, dies at age 83 in Greenwich, Connecticut.

***Aug. 25, 1996** - A monument in honor of Mickey Mantle is unveiled in Yankee Stadium's Monument Park.

Oct. 23, 1996 - In Game 4 of the World Series at Atlanta's Fulton County Stadium, Jim Leyritz hits a three-run eighth inning homer off the Braves' Mark Wohlers, knotting the game at 6-6. The Yankees went on to win, 8-6, in 10 innings.

Oct 24, 1996 - The Yankees' Andy Pettitte (8.1IP) outduels Atlanta's John Smoltz (8.0IP), 1-0, in Game 5 in Atlanta, giving the Yankees a 3 games to 2 World Series lead.

***Oct. 26, 1996** - In Game 6 of the World Series at Yankee Stadium, John Wetteland closes out a 3-2 win vs. Atlanta, giving the Yankees their first World Championship in 18 years.

***May 17, 1998** - David Wells tosses the first regular-season perfect game by a Yankee, the 14th in Baseball history.

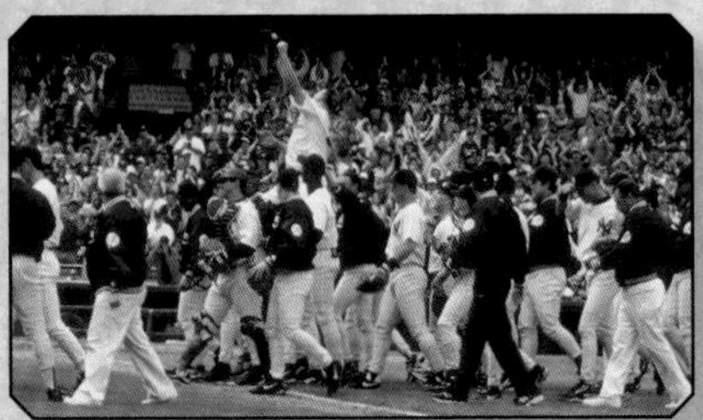

David Wells' perfect game

***Sept. 25, 1998** - The Yankees establish an American League record with their 112th win of the season (a 6-1 win vs. Tampa Bay at Yankee Stadium), breaking the mark of 111 by the 1954 Cleveland Indians (they complete the season with a then AL-record 114th victory on September 27 vs. Tampa Bay).

Oct. 21, 1998 - The Yankees complete an incredible season with a four-game World Series sweep of the San Diego Padres to capture the franchise's 24th World Championship. The 3-0 win gives the club a 125-50 record over the entire season (114-48 in the regular season, 11-2 in postseason).

March 8, 1999 - Joe DiMaggio dies at age 84 in Hollywood, Fla.

***April 25, 1999** - A monument in honor of Joe DiMaggio is unveiled in Yankee Stadium's Monument Park in front of a sold out Stadium and many of DiMaggio's former teammates. Paul Simon sings "Mrs. Robinson" while standing in center field.

***July 18, 1999** - On "Yogi Berra Day," David Cone tosses the 15th regular season perfect game in Baseball history, one season after David Wells accomplishes the feat. Amazingly, Don Larsen—who tossed a perfect game in the 1956 World Series—throws out the ceremonial first pitch.

***Oct. 27, 1999** - The Yankees play Baseball's last game of the century and complete a four-game sweep of the Atlanta Braves, capturing their 25th World Championship.

***July 8, 2000** - The Yankees and Mets play their first-ever dual stadium day/night doubleheader: Game 1 is a 4-2 Yankees win at Shea Stadium and Game 2 is another 4-2 Yankees win at Yankee Stadium.

***Oct. 21, 2000** - The Yankees' World Series Game 1 win vs. the Mets at Yankee Stadium marks their 13th consecutive victory in World Series play, breaking the 12-game record of the 1927, 1928 and 1932 Yankees.

Oct. 26, 2000 - The Yankees win World Series Game 5 over the Mets at Shea Stadium, clinching their third consecutive World Championship in the first "Subway Series" since 1956. It marks the first time a club has won three consecutive World Series titles since the 1972-74 Oakland Athletics.

Oct. 13, 2001 - With a 1-0 lead and two-out in the bottom of the seventh of Game 3 of the ALDS in Oakland, Derek Jeter picks up Shane Spencer's errant throw from the outfield and "flips" the ball in a backhand motion to Jorge Posada, who tags Jeremy Giambi for the final out of the inning. The Yankees go on to win the game, 1-0, and the series 3 games to 2. The play will be known as the "Flip Play."

***Oct. 30, 2001** - President George W. Bush throws out the first pitch prior to the Yankees' 2-1 World Series Game 3 win vs. Arizona at Yankee Stadium.

***Oct. 31, 2001** - In Game 4 of the World Series vs. Arizona at Yankee Stadium, Tino Martinez's two-out, bottom-of-the ninth, two-run home run off Byung-Hyun Kim sends the game into extra innings. Shortly after the stroke of midnight, Derek Jeter wins the game with a "walk-off" solo home run in the 10th, earning him the nickname "Mr. November."

***Nov. 1, 2001** - In the late innings of Game 5 of the World Series vs. Arizona at Yankee Stadium, fans serenade Paul O'Neill, who is playing in his last game at Yankee Stadium. Scott Brosius' two-out, bottom-of-the ninth, two-run home run off Byung-Hyun Kim sends the game into extra innings, and Alfonso Soriano singles in the winning run in the 12th.

***May 17, 2002** - Jason Giambi becomes only the 21st player—and second Yankee—to hit a "walk-off" grand slam with his team trailing by three runs (Babe Ruth did it on 9/24/25). His 14th-inning slam off Minnesota's Mike Trombley erases a 12-9 Twins lead, giving the Yankees a 13-12 win.

***June 13, 2003** - In a 5-2 win vs. the St. Louis Cardinals at Yankee Stadium, Roger Clemens records both his 300th career win and 4,000 career strikeout (Edgar Renteria).

***Oct. 16, 2003** – In Game 7 of the ALCS vs. Boston at Yankee Stadium, Aaron Boone becomes only the fifth player—and second Yankee—to end a postseason series with a "walk-off" home run (also Chris Chambliss, 1976 ALCS vs. Kansas City), when his 11th-inning leadoff solo shot off Tim Wakefield clinches the Yankees' 39th pennant.

***July 1, 2004** - Derek Jeter makes his most famous catch, diving into Yankee Stadium's third base stands to nab a 12th-inning popup off the bat of Boston's Trot Nixon. John Flaherty wins the game with a 13th-inning RBI single.

***April 26, 2005** - Alex Rodriguez hits three home runs (all off Bartolo Colon) and becomes just the second Yankee in franchise history to record at least 10 RBI in a game (also Tony Lazzeri, 11 on 5/24/36) in a 12-4 win vs. the Angels at Yankee Stadium.

June 15, 2005 – The Yankees announce plans for a new Yankee Stadium to be constructed in Macombs Dam and John Mullaly Parks, which are located on the north side of 161st Street (adjacent to the original Stadium's longtime site).

***Sept. 25, 2005** – The Yankees conclude their 81-game home schedule at Yankee Stadium with a season attendance of 4,090,696, establishing a single-season American League record. They become only the third franchise in sports history to reach the 4 million mark, joining the Toronto Blue Jays (1991-93) and Colorado Rockies (1993). The Yankees will subsequently break their home attendance mark in each of the next three seasons (2006-08).

***May 16, 2006** - The Yankees tie a franchise record by overcoming a nine-run deficit vs. Texas to win, 14-13, in nine innings. Jorge Posada hits a two-run "walk-off" home run off Akinori Otsuka.

***Aug. 16, 2006** – The Yankees break ground for a new Yankee Stadium, scheduled to be ready for Opening Day 2009.

Groundbreaking ceremony for the new Yankee Stadium

***Aug. 4, 2007** - Alex Rodriguez becomes the 22nd and youngest (32 years, 8 days) player in Baseball history to reach the 500-home run mark in a 16-8 win vs. Kansas City at Yankee Stadium. He is the third player to hit his 500th career homer as a Yankee, joining Babe Ruth and Mickey Mantle.

Oct. 30, 2007 - Joe Girardi is named the 32nd manager in Yankees franchise history.

March 27, 2008 - Prior to the Yankees' final home exhibition game of spring training, Legends Field is renamed George M. Steinbrenner Field.

***June 7, 2008** - Johnny Damon goes 6-for-6 in the Yankees' 12-11 win vs. Kansas City, matching the franchise record for hits in a nine-inning game (see June 6, 1934 - Myril Hoag) and becoming the only Yankee in original Yankee Stadium history to record six hits in a game of any length. His final hit is a "walk-off" single.

***September 16, 2008** - Derek Jeter singles off Chicago's Gavin Floyd in the first inning for his 1,270th career hit at Yankee Stadium, surpassing Lou Gehrig for the most all-time hits at the ballpark. Jeter finishes the game 2-for-3 in the 6-2 loss.

***September 21, 2008** - The Yankees play their last ever game in the original Yankee Stadium. Julia Ruth Stevens, daughter of Babe Ruth, throws out the ceremonial first pitch, and Jose Molina hits the park's final home run in the fourth inning. Following the Yankees' 7-3 win over Baltimore, Derek Jeter thanks the fans over the Stadium public address system.

September 28, 2008 - On the final day of the season in the first game of a doubleheader at Boston's Fenway Park, Mike Mussina records his 20th win of the year, becoming the oldest pitcher in Major League history to win 20 games for the first time.

***November 8, 2008** - Local Bronx high school youth groups are joined by Scott Brosius, David Cone, Jeff Nelson and Paul O'Neill of the Yankees' 1998 World Championship team and Yankees General Partner and Vice Chairperson Jennifer Steinbrenner Swindal in removing home plate, the pitcher's rubber and pails of dirt from the original Yankee Stadium, then installing them in the current Yankee Stadium.

April 3-4, 2009 – The Yankees play their first exhibition games in Yankee Stadium, defeating the Chicago Cubs, 7-4 and 10-1, respectively. Chien-Ming Wang tosses the first pitch in the April 3 contest.

April 16, 2009 – The Yankees play the first regular season game in Yankee Stadium history, falling to Cleveland, 10-2. CC Sabathia tosses the Stadium's first official pitch, Johnny Damon records the first hit (first-inning single off Cliff Lee) and Jorge Posada hits the first home run (fifth-inning off Lee).

May 14 – June 1, 2009 – The Yankees set an all-time Major League mark with 18 consecutive errorless games, safely handling 660 chances over the stretch.

September 11, 2009 – Derek Jeter breaks Lou Gehrig's all-time franchise mark of 2,721 hits with a single off Baltimore's Chris Tillman at Yankee Stadium. Gehrig had held the mark since 9/6/37.

October 4, 2009 – Alex Rodriguez hits a three-run home run and a grand slam in the sixth-inning of the season finale at Tampa Bay in a 10-2 Yankees victory, setting an all-time AL mark with 7RBI in an inning.

November 4, 2009 – The Yankees win their 27th World Championship, defeating Philadelphia in Game 6 of the World Series, 7-3. Hideki Matsui ties Bobby Richardson's all-time World Series mark (1960 Game 3 vs. Pittsburgh) with 6RBI. Andy Pettitte records the win, becoming the first pitcher to start and record the win in the clinching game in all three rounds of a single postseason. Manager Joe Girardi joins Billy Martin and Ralph Houk as the only individuals in franchise history to win a World Series with the Yankees as a player and as a manger.

Lou Gehrig Appreciation Day - July 4, 1939

Prior to the Yankees' May 2, 1939, game at Detroit's Briggs Stadium, captain Lou Gehrig gave the umpires his team's lineup card—which did not have his name on it. He watched the entire game from the bench, marking the end of his 2,130-consecutive-games-played streak. "The Iron Horse" was suffering the effects of amyotrophic lateral sclerosis (ALS), a disease since known as Lou Gehrig's Disease. He would never play again.

Just over two months later, on July 4, 1939, Lou Gehrig Appreciation Day was held in front of approximately 62,000 fans in Yankee Stadium. Ceremonies were held between games of a doubleheader against the Washington Senators. Gehrig and his teammates were joined by members of the 1927 Yankees. After speeches by Mayor Fiorello La Guardia and Postmaster James A. Farley, Manager Joe McCarthy said his public goodbye to Gehrig: "Lou, what can I say except that it was a sad day in the life of everybody who knew you when you came to my hotel room that day in Detroit and told me you were quitting as a ballplayer because you felt yourself a hindrance to the team.

"My God, man, you were never that."

Various gifts were presented to Gehrig from club employees and the rival New York Giants. His teammates gave him a trophy, which was inscribed with a poem by *New York Times* writer John Kiernan. As the crowd chanted, "We want Lou; We want Lou…," Gehrig stepped to the microphone to deliver one of the most touching and oft-quoted speeches in American history.

"Fans, for the past two weeks you have been reading about the bad break I got. Yet today I consider myself the luckiest man on the face of the Earth. I have been in ballparks for 17 years and have never received anything but kindness and encouragement from you fans.

"Look at these grand men. Which of you wouldn't consider it the highlight of his career just to associate with them for even one day? Sure, I'm lucky. Who wouldn't consider it an honor to have known Jacob Ruppert? Also, the builder of baseball's greatest empire, Ed Barrow? To have spent six years with that wonderful little fellow, Miller Huggins? Then to have spent the next nine years with that outstanding leader, that smart student of psychology, the best manager in baseball today, Joe McCarthy? Sure, I'm lucky.

"When the New York Giants, a team you would give your right arm to beat, and vice versa, sends you a gift—that's something. When everybody down to the groundskeepers and those boys in white coats remember you with trophies—that's something. When you have a wonderful mother-in-law who takes sides with you in squabbles with her own daughter—that's something. When you have a father and a mother who work all their lives so you can have an education and build your body—it's a blessing. When you have a wife who has been a tower of strength and shown more courage than you dreamed existed—that's the finest I know.

"So I close in saying that I might have been given a bad break, but I've got an awful lot to live for."

During the ceremony, Gehrig had his No. 4 retired by the Yankees, becoming the first person in sports to be given such an honor. To this day he remains the only Yankee ever to wear the number.

Gehrig died on June 2, 1941, at his home in the Riverdale section of the Bronx. He was 37.

Babe Ruth Day - April 27, 1947

On April 27, 1947, Babe Ruth Day was celebrated throughout Major League Baseball, as the Babe said goodbye in an on-field ceremony at Yankee Stadium. Dressed in a topcoat and hat, Ruth, weakened by throat cancer, made the following remarks:

"Thank you very much, ladies and gentlemen. You know how bad my voice sounds—well it feels just as bad.

"You know this baseball game of ours comes up from the youth. That means the boys. And after you're a boy and grow up to know how to play ball, then you come to the boys you see representing themselves today in your national pastime. The only real game—I think—in the world is baseball.

"As a rule, some people think if you give them a football, or a baseball, or something like that—naturally they're athletes right away. But you can't do that in baseball. You've gotta start from way down [at] the bottom, when you're 6 or 7 years of age. You can't wait until you're 15 or 16. You gotta let it grow up with you. And if you're successful, and you try hard enough, you're bound to come out on top—just like these boys have come to the top now.

"There has been so many lovely things said about me, and I'm glad that I've had the opportunity to thank everybody. Thank you."

Ruth returned to Yankee Stadium once more, on June 13, 1948, to celebrate the 25th anniversary of Yankee Stadium and have his uniform No. 3 retired.

He died on Aug. 16, 1948, at Memorial Hospital in New York at age 53. His body lay in state at the entrance of Yankee Stadium on Aug. 17 and 18, before his funeral on Aug. 19 at New York's St. Patrick's Cathedral.

Bob Sheppard "The Voice of Yankee Stadium"

Known to generations of fans as the "Voice of Yankee Stadium," Bob Sheppard began his tenure as Yankees public address announcer on April 17, 1951—Opening Day of Joe DiMaggio's final season. By virtue of his dedicated service and sheer excellence, the sound of his voice remains a common link among Yankees fans of the last 60 years. Yankee Stadium's media dining room was named "Sheppard's Place" prior to the 2009 season to commemorate his legacy.

Born in Ridgewood, Queens, and later moving within the borough to Richmond Hills, Sheppard went to St. John's College, which eventually became St. John's University. Always a talented athlete, he received a full athletic scholarship to the school, playing quarterback on the football team all four years. He later enrolled at Columbia University, where he received his master's degree in speech and worked his way up from teacher-in-training to substitute teacher to permanent teacher to department chairman. In order to supplement his teaching salary, Sheppard played semiprofessional football on Sundays in Long Island with the Valley Stream Red Riders and the Hempstead Monitors, earning $25 a game.

By the time World War II broke out, Sheppard was married with three small children, and he sought out a position as a naval officer to best provide for his family. He finished a two-year tour of duty and was released from his military commitment with honor. He returned to teaching as chairman of the speech department at John Adams High School in Ozone Park, Queens, where he stayed for 25 years.

Sheppard's incredible career behind the microphone started when he volunteered his services for a charity football game in Freeport, Long Island, in the late 1940s. An executive from the Brooklyn Dodgers football team of the All-America Conference was at the game. He liked Sheppard's style ("clear, concise and correct") and hired him. The football Dodgers folded after only one season at Ebbets Field (1948), but one of their opponents—the New York football Yankees—heard Sheppard's booming voice and offered him their PA job at Yankee Stadium. Baseball's Yankees then heard him and offered him the same role for them for the 1950 season. But Sheppard's teaching schedule could not accommodate the 77-game home schedule for baseball (plus World Series games), and he turned down the offer.

"You must remember that in those days there were a lot of afternoon games," Sheppard said. "It was just not possible to do both things."

But the Yankees were persistent and again offered the PA job to Sheppard for the 1951 season with one attractive addition. The Yankees would allow Sheppard to hire a replacement for any games he would have to miss. The rest, as they say, is history.

"A temporary job," Sheppard said, "that lasted a half century."

Among the approximately 4,500 baseball games he worked were an incredible 121 consecutive postseason contests (1951-2006), including 62 games in 22 World Series. Additionally, Sheppard was the public address voice for the football Giants for 50 seasons—from their move to Yankee Stadium in 1956 until his retirement after the 2005 season. Some of the events he lists as the most memorable of his incredible career are: Don Larsen's perfect game in Game 5 of the 1956 World Series on October 8, 1956; Roger Maris' 61st home run on October 1, 1961; Reggie Jackson's three home runs in Game 6 of the World Series on October 18, 1977; and the Giants-Colts overtime NFL Championship Game on December 28, 1958.

Sheppard also served the New York Titans of the American Football League at the Polo Grounds, the New York Stars of the World Football League at Downing Stadium, the New York Cosmos (soccer) and St. John's University basketball and football. Sheppard also handled PA duties for five Army-Navy football games in Philadelphia.

Over the years, the eloquent linguist has also written and delivered hundreds of moving tributes and eulogies including those for Mickey Mantle (1995), Joe DiMaggio (1999), Ray Charles (2004), President Ronald Reagan (2004), and those lost in the attacks of September 11, 2001.

In 1998, Sheppard was presented with the prestigious William J. Slocum "Long and Meritorious Service" Award by the New York chapter of the BBWAA as well as the "Pride of the Yankees" award by the ballclub. He was even honored with a ceremonial first pitch before Game 2 of the 1998 World Series at Yankee Stadium (he recorded his own introduction). And, during his 50th season as the Yankees' PA announcer in 2000, he presented his most-recent Yankee Stadium microphone to the Baseball Hall of Fame during induction ceremonies in Cooperstown, N.Y.

BOB SHEPPARD
THE VOICE OF
YANKEE STADIUM

In one of the game's truly memorable moments, Sheppard introduced President George W. Bush before Game 3 of the 2001 World Series (on October 30) as Mr. Bush became the first sitting President to throw out a ceremonial first pitch at Yankee Stadium.

On September 21, 2008, he provided a valedictory in the bottom of the seventh inning of the final game at Yankee Stadium. Unable to say goodbye in person as he continued to recover from illness that had kept him away from the Stadium since the final weeks of the 2007 season, Sheppard gave his tribute through a taped segment played on the video board. He recited, "Farewell, old Yankee Stadium, farewell / What a wonderful story you can tell / DiMaggio, Mantle, Gehrig and Ruth / A baseball cathedral in truth."

The native New Yorker has been elected to the St. John's University Sports Hall of Fame, the Long Island Sports Hall of Fame and the New York Sports Hall of Fame. He has been awarded honorary doctorates from St. John's University (Pedagogy) and Fordham University (Rhetoric), and in 2007, received St. John's' Medal of Honor, the highest award that the university can confer on a graduate.

Sheppard has also made cameo appearances in numerous motion pictures and television shows, including *61**, *It's My Turn*, *It Could Happen to You*, *Anger Management*, *Seinfeld* and *Mad About You*.

"Most men go to work, but I go to a game," Sheppard said. "How many men would love to do that?"

He resides on Long Island with his wife, Mary. They have four children, four grandchildren and nine great grandchildren.

BOB SHEPPARD'S FIRST LINEUP CARD

April 17, 1951

Boston Red Sox	New York Yankees
Dom DiMaggio, CF	Jackie Jensen, LF
Billy Goodman, RF	Phil Rizzuto, SS
Ted Williams, LF	Mickey Mantle, RF
Vern Stephens, 3B	Joe DiMaggio, CF
Walt Dropo, 1B	Yogi Berra, C
Bobby Doerr, 2B	Johnny Mize, 1B
Lou Boudreau, SS	Billy Johnson, 3B
Buddy Rosar, C	Jerry Coleman, 2B
Billy Wright, P	Vic Raschi, P

Voices Before Sheppard

Hard to believe, but Bob Sheppard was not the only Public Address Announcer in the original Yankee Stadium's fabled history. But no one—not even Sheppard himself—could remember who immediately preceded the current Stadium P.A. announcer behind the microphone. After all, the last game by this mystery man would likely have been the fourth and final game of the 1950 World Series between the Yankees and Philadelphia's "Whiz Kids" Phillies.

But, after years of search and research, the answer may have turned up in the transcript of an interview conducted in 1991 by writer Paul Doherty with Don Carney, the producer-director of Yankees telecasts for more than three decades.

Extolling Sheppard's longevity, Carney told Doherty that "Bob's been around forever. He followed Red Patterson, who was the club's Public Relations Director and also did the P.A."

Red Patterson: The man who preceded Sheppard

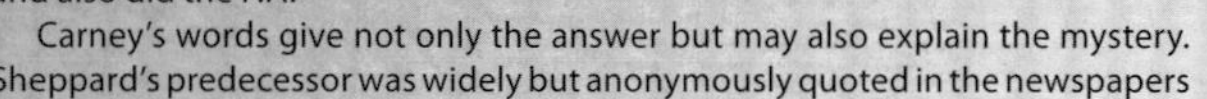

Carney's words give not only the answer but may also explain the mystery. Sheppard's predecessor was widely but anonymously quoted in the newspapers for an infamous gaffe he made during a Yankees-Philadelphia Athletics game on May 31, 1946. "Will the spectators in the front row please remove their clothing…" he began, with the rest of his announcement: "from the front railing," drowned out by the crowd's laughter.

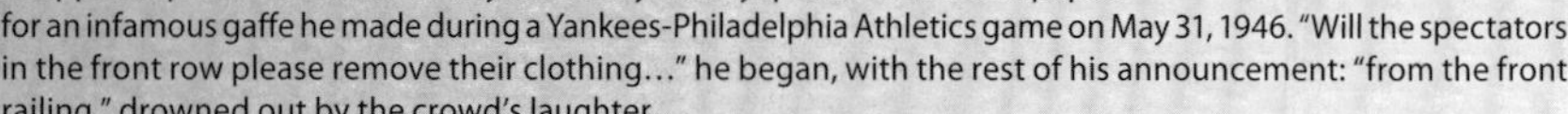

The story got into the papers, but the identity of the speaker did not. Of course, it didn't. The writers didn't want to embarrass their main conduit for information about the club!

Additional research shows that Yankee Stadium was the last ballpark in the Majors to install a public-address system. It debuted in Game 3 of the 1936 World Series and was manned by Jack Lenz and George Levy, two veterans of the time when information was still relayed to the crowd by megaphone.

The careers of Lenz and Levy began in 1915 when the Yankees and Giants shared the Polo Grounds. When the Yankees hopped across the Harlem River in 1923, Levy stayed with the Giants while Lenz took the Yankee post. "I grabbed the offer," Lenz said. "Who wouldn't, with the old Bambino holding forth at the Stadium?"

To do his job, Lenz sat in a box alongside the Yankees dugout (then on the third-base side of Yankee Stadium) and shouted the batting orders and batteries (each team's pitcher and catcher) as well as the changes throughout the game. Unlike today, players were not announced each time they came to bat and Lenz was called upon only when a change was made.

Jack Lenz: "The little man with the big voice."

According to a feature article which appeared in the *New York Evening News* in the early 1930s to celebrate a career of more than 2,000 consecutive games, Lenz—the "mild-mannered megaphone man"—would receive the lineups and batting orders from both managers approximately 15 minutes before the start of the game (3:15 p.m. in those days). After telephoning the press box with the "necessary dope," Lenz would pick up his megaphone and shout the batting orders and batteries. He directed his voice first toward the bleachers, then to the upper tiers of the grandstand and again to the lower stands.

Due to the vast size of their new ballpark, the Yankees actually began the 1927 season with two public address announcers to service Yankee Stadium. After the idea proved successful before a crowd of more than 65,000 on Opening Day, the "two-ply announcer system" of Lenz and Levy was used again for the second game when the crowd was only about 7,000. The experiment was likely short lived.

Research for "The Voices Before Sheppard" by Keith Olbermann.

Yankees in Cooperstown

There are 48 members of the Baseball Hall of Fame that have played, managed or been an executive for the New York Yankees at one time or another. The Yankees' first inductee was Babe Ruth, who entered the Hall in its inaugural 1936 class along with Ty Cobb, Walter Johnson, Christy Mathewson and Honus Wagner. The Yankees' most recent inductees are Joe Gordon and Rickey Henderson, who were formally enshrined in Cooperstown on July 26, 2009.

Currently, the choice of which insignia appears on the cap of each Hall of Famer's plaque belongs to the Hall of Fame itself. The decision is based on the "historical accomplishments" of the player and "where that player makes his most indelible mark" (though the wishes of the inductee are always considered). It is important to remember that caps have not always had insignias and some players' images are cast as profiles without visible insignias.

*** Information listed below each photo includes name of Hall of Famer, primary career position, year inducted, years with Yankees, number of games played with Yankees and insignia on Hall of Fame cap.**

Frank "Home Run" Baker
3B (1955)
1916-22, 676 games
Cap: No insignia (A's style)

Ed Barrow
Executive (1953)
1920-45
No Cap

Yogi Berra
C (1972)
1946-63 (player), 2,116 games
1964, 1984-85 (Mgr), 340 games
Cap turned, insignia unseen

Wade Boggs
3B (2005)
1993-97, 602 games
Cap: Boston Red Sox

Frank Chance
1B/Manager (1946)
1913-14 (1B), 12 games
1913-14 (Mgr), 285 games
Cap: Chicago Cubs

Jack Chesbro
RHP (1946)
1903-09, 269 games
Cap: Head turned, insignia unseen

Earle Combs
CF (1970)
1924-35, 1,454 games
Cap: New York Yankees

Stan Coveleski
RHP (1969)
1928, 12 games
Cap: Cleveland Indians

Bill Dickey
C (1954)
1928-46 (Player), 1,789 games
1946 (Mgr), 105 games
Cap: New York Yankees

Joe DiMaggio
CF (1955)
1936-51, 1,736 games
Cap: New York Yankees

Leo Durocher
Manager (1994)
1925, 28-29 (INF), 210 games
Cap: Brooklyn Dodgers

Whitey Ford
LHP (1974)
1950-67, 498 games
Cap: New York Yankees

Lou Gehrig
1B (1939)
1923-39, 2,164 games
Cap: New York Yankees

Lefty Gomez
LHP (1972)
1930-42, 367 games
Cap: New York Yankees

Joe Gordon
2B (2009)
1938-43, '46, 1000 games
Cap: New York Yankees

Rich "Goose" Gossage
RHP (2008)
1978-83, 89, 319 games
Cap: New York Yankees

Clark Griffith
Player, Manager, Executive (1946)
1903-07 (RHP), 87 games
1903-08 (Mgr), 789 games
Cap: No insignia

Burleigh Grimes
RHP (1964)
1934, 10 games
Cap: Brooklyn Dodgers

Bucky Harris
Mgr (1975)
1947-48, 308 games
Cap: Washington Senators

Rickey Henderson
CF/LF (2009)
1985-89, 596 games
Cap: Oakland A's

Waite Hoyt
RHP (1969)
1921-30, 365 games
Cap: New York Yankees

Miller Huggins
Mgr (1964)
1918-29, 1,786 games
Cap: New York Yankees

Jim "Catfish" Hunter
RHP (1987)
1975-79, 137 games
Cap: No insignia

Reggie Jackson
RF (1993)
1977-81, 653 games
Cap: New York Yankees

Willie Keeler
RF (1939)
1903-09, 873 games
Cap: Brooklyn Dodgers

Tony Lazzeri
2B (1991)
1926-37, 1,658 games
Cap: New York Yankees

Bob Lemon
RHP (1976)
1978-79, 81-82 (Mgr), 172 games
Cap: Cleveland Indians

Larry MacPhail
Executive (1978)
1945-47
No Cap

Lee MacPhail
Executive (1998)
1949-58, 1966-73
No Cap

Mickey Mantle
CF (1974)
1951-68, 2,401 games
Cap: New York Yankees

Joe McCarthy
Mgr (1957)
1931-46, 2,327 games
Cap: New York Yankees

Bill McKechnie
Mgr (1962)
1913 (INF), 44 games
Cap: Cincinnati Reds

Johnny Mize
1B (1981)
1949-53, 375 games
Cap: No insignia

Phil Niekro
RHP (1997)
1984-85, 65 games
Cap: Atlanta Braves

Herb Pennock
LHP (1948)
1923-33, 346 games
Cap: No insignia

Gaylord Perry
RHP (1991)
1980, 10 games
Cap: San Francisco Giants

Branch Rickey
Executive (1967)
1907 (OF, C, 1B), 52 games
No Cap

Phil Rizzuto
SS (1994)
1941-42, 46-56, 1,661 games
Cap: New York Yankees

Red Ruffing
RHP (1967)
1930-42, 45-46, 426 games
Cap: New York Yankees

Babe Ruth
OF (1936)
1920-34, 2,084 games
Cap: New York Yankees

Joe Sewell
SS (1977)
1931-33, 389 games
Cap: Cleveland Indians

Enos Slaughter
OF (1985)
1954-55, 56-59, 350 games
Cap: St. Louis Cardinals

Casey Stengel
Mgr (1966)
1949-60, 1,845 games
Cap: New York Yankees

Dazzy Vance
RHP (1955)
1915, 1918, 10 games
Cap: Brooklyn Dodgers

Phil Rizzuto gives his Hall of Fame Induction speech in 1994.

Paul Waner
RF (1952)
1944-45, 10 games
Cap: Pittsburgh Pirates

George Weiss
Executive (1971)
1932-60
No Cap

Dick Williams
Executive (2008)
1995-2001
Cap: Oakland A's

Dave Winfield
RF (2001)
1981-90, 1,172 games
Cap: San Diego Padres

Goose Gossage and Dick Williams at the 2008 Baseball Hall of Fame induction ceremony.

NATIONAL BASEBALL HALL OF FAME AND MUSEUM

25 Main Street, Cooperstown, New York 13326
Phone: (607) 547-7200 **Fax:** (607) 547-2044
Public Relations: (607) 547-0215
e-mail address: info@baseballhalloffame.org
Web site: baseballhall.org
Summer Hours: Memorial Day Weekend - Labor Day Weekend: 9 a.m. to 9 p.m.
Regular Hours: 9 a.m. to 5 p.m.
Holiday Closings: Thanksgiving Day, Christmas Day, and New Year's Day.

DIRECTORY: Jane Forbes Clark (Chairman), Joe Morgan (Vice Chairman), Jeff Idelson (President), Bill Haase (Senior Vice President), Sean Gahagan (Vice President, Retail Marketing & Licensing), Erik Strohl (Senior Director of Exhibits and Collections), Ken Meifert (Senior Director, Development), Brad Horn (Senior Director, Communications & Education), Jim Gates (Librarian), Tim Wiles (Research Director)
COMMUNICATIONS CONTACTS: Craig Muder (Comm. Director), Jackie Brown (Comm. Associate)

HALL OF FAME WEEKEND 2010: July 23-26

Induction Ceremony:
Sunday, July 25, 1:30 p.m. EDT, Clark Sports Center

HALL OF FAME CLASSIC

Sunday, June 20, 2 p.m., Doubleday Field;
For more information, visit **baseballhall.org**

YANKEES IN THE HALL OF FAME

A total of 48 former players, managers and executives in the Hall of Fame spent some of their professional careers with the New York Yankees, including 2009 Inductees Rickey Henderson (1985-1989) and Joe Gordon (1938-1943, 1946). Twenty-five of these 48 spent the majority of their careers in a Yankees uniform, including: Yogi Berra, Bill Dickey, Joe DiMaggio, Whitey Ford, Lou Gehrig, Mickey Mantle, Joe McCarthy, Phil Rizzuto, Babe Ruth and Casey Stengel. For a complete list of New York Yankees in the Hall of Fame, visit the "Hall of Famers" team pages at **www.baseballhall.org**.

HALL OF FAME ARTIFACTS FROM 2009 WORLD CHAMPIONSHIP

- Bat used by World Series MVP Hideki Matsui during Game 6.
- Bat used by Derek Jeter and spikes worn by Alex Rodriguez during Game 6.
- Scorecard from Game 6 used by Suzyn Waldman, the first female World Series broadcaster.
- Spikes worn by Johnny Damon during Game 4, when he stole two bases.
- First ball taken out of play during the first WS game at Yankee Stadium.
- Caps worn by Andy Pettitte and Mariano Rivera during the World Series.

2009 World Series artifacts

OTHER NOTABLE YANKEES ARTIFACTS IN COOPERSTOWN

- Derek Jeter's batting gloves from Sept. 11, 2009, when he passed Lou Gehrig on the Yankees all-time list with his 2,722nd hit.
- Helmet worn by Melky Cabrera during his cycle on Aug. 2, one of the record-tying eight in MLB during 2009.
- Ball and Andy Pettitte cap from May 30, 2009, when Pettitte and Mariano Rivera set record for combined win-saves (58).
- Spikes worn by starting pitcher CC Sabathia on April 16, 2009, and a ticket from the home opener at new Yankee Stadium.
- Ticket to last game and spikes worn by Jose Molina to record final home run in old Yankee Stadium on Sept. 21, 2008.
- Helmet worn by Alex Rodriguez to hit his 500th home run on Aug. 4, 2007, the youngest player to reach the mark.
- Bat used by Aaron Boone to end Game Seven of the 2003 ALCS against the Boston Red Sox.
- Batting helmet worn by World Series MVP Derek Jeter in the 2000 World Series.
- Cap, ball, ticket and beanie baby giveaway from David Wells' perfect game on May 17, 1998.
- Bat used by Mickey Mantle to hit his 500th career home run on May 14, 1967.
- Ticket to Lou Gehrig Day on July 4, 1939, when he made the "Luckiest Man" speech.
- Bats used by Hall of Famer Babe Ruth to hit his 57th, 58th, and 60th home runs in 1927.
- Ball thrown by New York Governor Alfred Smith at Yankee Stadium dedication ceremony, April 18, 1923.

A LOOK AHEAD TO 2011

Ballots for the 2011 Hall of Fame/BBWAA election will be distributed in early December with results from the voting scheduled to be announced in January 2011. A partial list of first-year candidates for election include: Carlos Baerga, Jeff Bagwell, Bret Boone, Kevin Brown, John Franco, Juan Gonzalez, Marquis Grissom, Charles Johnson, Al Leiter, Tino Martinez, Raul Mondesi, John Olerud, Rafael Palmeiro, B.J. Surhoff and Larry Walker. Historical voting data from all past BBWAA elections can be accessed at **www.baseballhall.org** or by contacting the Hall of Fame Public Relations department.

CONNECT TO COOPERSTOWN

- For up-to-the-minute news from Cooperstown, visit at **www.baseballhall.org**. Stay up-to-date on all the activity at the Hall of Fame's official Web site and through social networking at Facebook, LinkedIn and Twitter.
- If you would like to receive interesting stories and timely news items direct from the Hall of Fame and get the inside track on the latest happenings in Cooperstown, sign up for ***Inside Pitch***. There's no cost to receive our weekly electronic newsletter in your e-mail box at home or work and it's easy to enroll: Just log on to **www.baseballhall.org**.
- If you have an interest in receiving ***Around The Horn***, the Hall's monthly media newsletter, please send an e-mail to **info@baseballhalloffame.org**. Be sure to include your name, name of organization and e-mail address.

RESEARCH ASSISTANCE

The Hall of Fame is pleased to provide assistance in baseball research and members of the media are encouraged to utilize this valuable baseball resource whenever necessary by calling the Public Relations department at (607) 547-0215, or the Library Reference desk at (607) 547-0330.

Yankees Retired Uniform Numbers

Beginning with Lou Gehrig's No. 4 in 1939, the Yankees have retired 15 uniform numbers to honor 16 players and managers.

1 Billy Martin (Number retired in 1986)

Born: May 16, 1928 in Berkeley, Calif. • **Died:** Dec. 25, 1989 in Binghamton, N.Y.
Height: 5-11 • **Weight:** 165 • **B/T:** R/R

Had as much "Yankee Pride" as any player or manager to wear pinstripes, and he implanted his own fierce desire to win in his teams. Played an integral part in four World Series in the 1950s as a player, and added another ring managing the Yankees in 1977. His .333 lifetime series batting average is sixth with at least 75 AB on the all-time series list. Combative and daring, Martin was a brilliant baseball strategist and a legend in Yankees history.

3 Babe Ruth (Number retired in 1948)

Born: Feb. 6, 1895 in Baltimore, Md. • **Died:** Aug. 16, 1948 in New York, N.Y.
Height: 6-2 • **Weight:** 215 • **B/T:** L/L

Baseball's greatest slugger and the most colorful figure in the game's history. Debuted as a pitcher for the Boston Red Sox, winning 89 games over six seasons before being converted to the outfield because of his tremendous power. Was sold to the Yankees in 1920 and his 54 home runs that year were more than any other American League team. En route to 714 career home runs, won 12 home run titles, hitting 60 in 1927. Added 15 home runs in World Series competition as he led the Yankees to seven Series appearances and four World Championships. A member of the inaugural class of Hall of Fame inductees in 1936.

4 Lou Gehrig (Number retired in 1939)

Born: June 19, 1903 in New York, N.Y. • **Died:** June 2, 1941 in Riverdale, N.Y.
Height: 6-1 • **Weight:** 212 • **B/T:** L/L

Durable, powerhitting first baseman who played in an amazing 2,130 consecutive games between 1925 and 1939. Drove in at least 100 runs for 13 straight seasons (1926-38) and established an American League record with 184 RBI in 1931. Compiled a .340 lifetime batting average and belted 493 home runs in a career shortened by terminal illness. Was honored at Yankee Stadium on July 4, 1939, and made memorable, "Today, I consider myself the luckiest man on the face of the earth" speech. Life was immortalized in classic 1942 motion picture, *The Pride of the Yankees*, starring Gary Cooper. Elected to the Hall of Fame in 1939.

5 Joe DiMaggio (Number retired in 1952)

Born: Nov. 25, 1914 in Martinez, Calif. • **Died:** March 8, 1999 in Hollywood, Fla.
Height: 6-2 • **Weight:** 193 • **B/T:** R/R

The "Yankee Clipper" is considered by many experts as the best all-around baseball player in history. Was a sensational hitter for average and power, and a splendid, graceful, ball-hawking center fielder. Owned a powerful and accurate arm, and was a daring and alert baserunner. Compiled a .325 lifetime batting average from 1936 to 1951. A two-time batting champion and three-time MVP, he powered the Yankees to the first of four consecutive World Championships in his 1936 rookie season. Many rate his 56-consecutive-game batting streak in 1941 as the top baseball feat of all time. Elected to the Hall of Fame in 1955.

7 Mickey Mantle (Number retired in 1969)

Born: Oct. 20, 1931 in Spavinaw, Okla. • **Died:** Aug. 14, 1995 in Dallas, Tex.
Height: 6-0 • **Weight:** 201 • **B/T:** S/R

"The Mick" was the most feared hitter on some of the most successful teams in history. Could run like the wind and hit tape measure homers, like his famous 565-footer in Washington in 1953. In the 14 seasons between 1951 and 1964, he led the Yanks to 12 Fall Classics and seven World Championships. He still owns records for most homers, RBI, runs and walks in World Series play. In 1956, Mantle had one of the greatest seasons ever at the plate, hitting 52 homers with 130 RBI and a .353 average to win the Triple Crown. Elected to the Hall of Fame in 1974.

8 Yogi Berra (Number retired in 1972)

Born: May 12, 1925 in St. Louis, Mo.
Height: 5-8 • **Weight:** 191 • **B/T:** L/R

A mainstay behind the plate for some of the most dominating teams in history from the end of World War II until the early 1960s. Although he never led the league in a single major offensive category, he was just the third man to win three Most Valuable Player Awards. Was selected to play in the All-Star Game in 15 successive seasons (1948-62). Played on 14 pennant winners and 10 World Champions, more than anyone in history. Led the Yankees to the 1964 pennant as manager. Elected to the Hall of Fame in 1972.

Yankees Retired Uniform Numbers

8 Bill Dickey (Number retired in 1972)

Born: June 6, 1907 in Bastrop, La. • **Died:** Nov. 12, 1993 in Little Rock, Ark.
Height: 6-1 • **Weight:** 185 • **B/T:** L/R

Regarded as one of the greatest catchers of all-time. A durable and tireless worker, he caught more than 100 games in 13 consecutive seasons (1929-41), an American League record. In 1931, he did not allow a single passed ball in 125 games behind the plate, another AL record. Dickey also excelled at the plate, batting over .300 in 10 of his first 11 full seasons, while hitting 202 homers during his career. He handled Yankees pitching staffs on eight World Series teams, winning seven championships.

9 Roger Maris (Number retired in 1984)

Born: Sept. 10, 1934 in Hibbing, Minn. • **Died:** Dec. 14, 1985 in Houston, Tex.
Height: 6-0 • **Weight:** 197 • **B/T:** L/R

In one of the most dramatic assaults on a baseball record, Maris caught, then surpassed Babe Ruth's famous home run record of 60. Maris hit 61 home runs in 1961, a Major League record which stood until 1998 and is still the American League mark. The two-time American League MVP (1960-61) is also considered as one of the best-fielding right fielders in Yankees history.

10 Phil Rizzuto (Number retired in 1985)

Born: Sept. 25, 1917 in New York, N.Y. • **Died:** Aug. 13, 2007 in West Orange, N.J.
Height: 5-6 • **Weight:** 150 • **B/T:** R/R

Playing 13 years for the Yankees, "Scooter" went to nine World Series. That stat may best explain why the diminutive shortstop is regarded as a true Yankees legend. He was durable, a skilled bunter and an enthusiastic baserunner with a solid .273 career batting average. In 1950, Rizzuto earned the AL MVP Award, batting .324 with 200 hits, 92 walks and 125 runs scored. He batted .320 in the 1951 World Series and was named Series MVP. He also spent 40 years as a Yankees broadcaster (1957-96) and was elected to the Hall of Fame in 1994.

15 Thurman Munson (Number retired in 1979)

Born: June 7, 1947 in Akron, Ohio • **Died:** Aug. 2, 1979 in Canton, Ohio
Height: 5-11 • **Weight:** 190 • **B/T:** R/R

Was the undisputed leader and most respected man on Yankees teams that won three consecutive AL pennants (1976-78) and two World Championships. Munson was a tremendous defensive catcher, winning the Gold Glove Award in three consecutive seasons (1973-75). From 1975-77, Thurman drove in more than 100 runs and hit better than .300 in each season. He hit the first Yankees home run in remodeled Yankee Stadium. There is no more tragic date in Yankees history than August 2, 1979, when Munson passed away in a plane crash.

16 Whitey Ford (Number retired in 1974)

Born: Oct. 21, 1928 in New York, N.Y.
Height: 5-10 • **Weight:** 181 • **B/T:** L/L

"The Chairman of the Board" was the ace pitcher on great Yankees teams of the 1950s and early '60s. The wily southpaw's lifetime record of 236-106 gives him the best winning percentage (.690) of any left-handed pitcher in the 20th century with 100 or more wins. He paced the American League in victories three times, and in ERA and shutouts twice. The 1961 Cy Young Award winner still holds many World Series records, including 10 wins, 33 consecutive scoreless innings and 94 strikeouts. Elected to the Hall of Fame in 1974.

23 Don Mattingly (Number retired in 1997)

Born: April 20, 1961 in Evansville, Ill.
Height: 6-0 • **Weight:** 185 • **B/T:** L/L

"Donnie Baseball" was only the 10th captain to be named by the Yankees in their storied history. The premier first baseman of his era, Mattingly was a nine-time Gold Glove winner. The 1985 American League MVP set records for most grand slams in a season (6) and most home runs in seven consecutive games (9) and eight consecutive games (10). A humble man of grace and dignity, Mattingly carried on the legacy of the pinstripe tradition and dedicated his career to the pursuit of excellence.

Yankees Retired Uniform Numbers

32 Elston Howard (Number retired in 1984)

Born: Feb. 23, 1929 in St. Louis, Mo. • **Died:** Dec. 14, 1980 in New York, N.Y.
Height: 6-2 • **Weight:** 196 • **B/T:** R/R

Became the first black player in Yankees history when he made the club in the spring of 1955. The versatile two-time Gold Glove catcher was an important member of AL pennant-winning Yankees teams in nine of his first 10 seasons with the club. The 1963 American League MVP, Howard was a clubhouse leader who was respected as both a player and a man. Howard's dignified manner off the field and competitive spirit on the field set a powerful example for his teammates.

37 Casey Stengel (Number retired in 1970)

Born: July 30, 1889 in Kansas City, Mo. • **Died:** Sept. 29, 1975 in Glendale, Calif.
Height: 5-11 • **Weight:** 175 • **B/T:** L/L

In a distinguished 54-year professional career, "The Old Perfessor" emerged as one of the game's greatest managers. His feat of guiding the Yankees to 10 pennants and seven world tities in a 12-year span ranks as one of the top managerial accomplishments of all time. Simply put, Casey Stengel was one of the best things to ever happen to the game of Baseball. He was an authentic baseball ambassador, making the game fun for millions of Americans. Elected to the Hall of Fame in 1966.

44 Reggie Jackson (Number retired in 1993)

Born: May 18, 1946 in Wyncote, Pa.
Height: 5-10 • **Weight:** 181 • **B/T:** L/L

One of the game's premier power hitters, "Mr. October" blasted 563 career home runs, good for 11th place on Baseball's all-time list. In Game 6 of the 1977 World Series, Jackson hit three home runs, all on the first pitch, as the Yankees beat the Dodgers to wrap up the club's first World Championship since 1962. Jackson was an exciting clutch player and an intimidating clean-up hitter with a .490 career slugging percentage. The 1973 American League MVP once said, "Some people call October a time of pressure. I call it a time of character." He was elected to the Hall of Fame in 1993.

49 Ron Guidry (Number retired in 2003)

Born: Aug. 28, 1950 in Lafayette, La.
Height: 5-11 • **Weight:** 165 • **B/T:** L/L

Known as "Louisiana Lightning," Ron Guidry was a four-time American League All-Star and three-time 20-game winner. He compiled one of the most dominating seasons in Baseball history in 1978, going 25-3 with a 1.74 ERA. He led the Yankees to a dramatic comeback from 14.0 games behind the Boston Red Sox to capture their second straight World Championship. That season, he also compiled a club-record 248 strikeouts and nine shutouts en route to a unanimous selection as the American League's Cy Young Award winner. On June 17, 1978 vs. California at Yankee Stadium, Guidry struck out 18 Angels, breaking the club's single-game record. With Willie Randolph, he served as the Yankees' co-captain from 1986 through his retirement in 1989. He remains in the Top 10 on the Yankees' all-time list in games pitched (368), innings pitched (2392.0), wins (170), winning percentage (.651), strikeouts (1778) and shutouts (26).

Yankees retired numbers are immortalized in Yankee Stadium's Monument Park.

All-Time Roster

In the Yankees' 107 seasons in the American League, 1,459 players have appeared in at least one game.

*Deceased

A (41)

Jim Abbott............. 1993-94
Harry Ables*.................1911
Bobby Abreu............. 2006-08
Juan Acevedo...............2003
Alfredo Aceves........... 2008-09
Spencer Adams*............1926
Doc Adkins*.................1903
Steve Adkins................1990
Luis Aguayo.................1988
Jack Aker................ 1969-72
Jonathan Albaladejo..... 2008-09
Mike Aldrete.................1996
Doyle Alexander... 1976, 1982-83
Walt Alexander*......... 1915-17
Bernie Allen............. 1972-73
Johnny Allen*............ 1932-35
Neil Allen.......... 1985, 1987-88
Carlos Almanzar............2001
Erick Almonte..........2001, 2003
Sandy Alomar............ 1974-76
Felipe Alou.............. 1971-73
Matty Alou...................1973
Dell Alston............... 1977-78
Ruben Amaro............ 1966-68
Jason Anderson........2003, 2005
John Anderson*.......... 1904-05
Rick Anderson*..............1979
Ivy Andrews*... 1931-32, 1937-38
Pete Appleton*..............1933
Angel Aragon*..... 1914, 1916-17
Alex Arias...................2002
Rugger Ardizoia.............1947
Mike Armstrong.......... 1984-86
Brad Arnsberg........... 1986-87
Luis Arroyo............. 1960-63
Tucker Ashford..............1981
Paul Assenmacher...........1993
Joe Ausanio............. 1994-95
Jimmy Austin*........... 1909-10
Chick Autry*.................1924
Oscar Azocar.................1990

Yogi Berra

B (136)

Loren Babe*............. 1952-53
Stan Bahnsen...... 1966, 1968-71
Bill Bailey*...................1911
Frank Baker*.... 1916-19, 1921-22
Frank Baker............. 1970-71
Steve Balboni... 1981-83, 1989-90
Neal Ball*................ 1907-09
Scott Bankhead.............1995
Willie Banks............. 1997-98
Steve Barber*............ 1967-68
Jesse Barfield............ 1989-92
Cy Barger*.............. 1906-07
Ray Barker.............. 1965-67
Frank Barnes*...............1930
Honey Barnes*...............1926
Ed Barney*...................1915
Chris Basak..................2007
George Batten*..............1912
Hank Bauer*............. 1948-59
Paddy Baumann*........ 1915-17
Don Baylor............... 1983-85
Walter Beall*............ 1924-27
T.J. Beam....................2006
Colter Bean.............. 2005-07
Jim Beattie............... 1978-79
Rich Beck....................1965
Zinn Beck*...................1918
Fred Beene.............. 1972-74
Joe Beggs*...................1938
John Bell*....................1907
Zeke Bella...................1957
Mark Bellhorn...............2005
Clay Bellinger.......... 1999-2001
Benny Bengough*....... 1923-30
Juan Beniquez...............1979
Armando Benitez............2003
Lou Berberet*........... 1954-55
Dave Bergman.........1975, 1977
Juan Bernhardt..............1976
Walter Bernhardt*...........1918
Dale Berra.............. 1985-86
Yogi Berra............... 1946-63
Angel Berroa................2009
Wilson Betemit.......... 2007-08
Bill Bevens*............. 1944-47
Monte Beville*.......... 1903-04
Harry Billiard*...............1908
Doug Bird............... 1980-81
Ewell Blackwell*......... 1952-53
Rick Bladt....................1975
Paul Blair............... 1977-80
Walter Blair*............ 1907-11
Johnny Blanchard*. 1955, 1959-65
Gil Blanco....................1965
Wade Blasingame............1972
Steve Blateric...............1972
Gary Blaylock................1959
Curt Blefary*............ 1970-71
Elmer Bliss*..................1903
Ron Blomberg..... 1969, 1971-76
Mike Blowers............ 1989-91
Eddie Bockman..............1946
Ping Bodie*............. 1918-21
Len Boehmer..........1969, 1971
Brian Boehringer... 1995-97, 2001
Wade Boggs............. 1993-97
Don Bollweg*................1953
Bobby Bonds*...............1975
Ricky Bones..................1996
Ernie Bonham*.......... 1940-46
Juan Bonilla...........1985, 1987
Aaron Boone.................2003
Luke Boone*............ 1913-16
Frenchy Bordagaray*.........1941
Rich Bordi.............1985, 1987
Joe Borowski............ 1997-98
Hank Borowy*........... 1942-45
Babe Borton*................1913
Daryl Boston.................1994
Jim Bouton.............. 1962-68
Clete Boyer*............ 1959-66
Ryan Bradley.................1998
Scott Bradley............ 1984-85
Neal Brady*...........1915, 1917
Darren Bragg................2001
Ralph Branca.................1954
Norm Branch*........... 1941-42
Marshall Brant...............1980
Garland Braxton*........ 1925-26
Don Brennan*................1933
Jim Brenneman*.............1965
Ken Brett*....................1976
Marv Breuer*............ 1939-43
Billy Brewer..................1996
Fritzie Brickell*.......... 1958-59
Jim Brideweser*.......... 1951-53
Marshall Bridges*........ 1962-63
Harry Bright*............ 1963-64
Ed Brinkman*................1975
Chris Britton............. 2007-08
Johnny Broaca*.......... 1934-37
Lew Brockett*....1907, 1909, 1911
Jim Bronstad.................1959
Tom Brookens................1989
Scott Brosius...........1998-2001
Bob Brower...................1989
Jim Brower...................2007
Boardwalk Brown*....... 1914-15

Wade Boggs

Dr. Bobby Brown... 1946-52, 1954
Bobby Brown............ 1979-81
Curt Brown...................1984
Hal Brown....................1962
Jumbo Brown*.. 1932-33, 1935-36
Kevin Brown............. 2004-05
Brian Bruney............ 2006-09
Jim Bruske...................1998
Billy Bryan.............. 1966-67
Jess Buckles*................1916
Mike Buddie............. 1998-99
Jay Buhner.............. 1987-88
Bill Burbach............. 1969-71
Lew Burdette*...............1950
Tim Burke....................1992
A.J. Burnett..................2009
George Burns*........... 1928-29
Alex Burr*...................1914
Ray Burris....................1979
Homer Bush....... 1997-98, 2004
Joe Bush*............... 1922-24
Tom Buskey*............ 1973-74
Ralph Buxton*...............1949
Joe Buzas*...................1945
Harry Byrd*..................1954
Sammy Byrd*............ 1929-34
Tommy Byrne*..... 1943, 1946-51, 1954-57
Marty Bystrom.......... 1984-85

C (118)

Melky Cabrera........... 2005-09
Greg Cadaret............ 1989-92
Miguel Cairo....... 2004, 2006-07
Charlie Caldwell*............1925
Ray Caldwell*........... 1910-18
Johnny Callison*........ 1972-73
Howie Camp*................1917
Bert Campaneris.............1983
Archie Campbell*............1928
John Candelaria.......... 1988-89
Andy Cannizaro..............2006
Robinson Cano.......... 2005-09
Jose Canseco................2000
Mike Cantwell*...............1916
Andy Carey............. 1952-60
Roy Carlyle*..................1926
Duke Carmel.................1965
Dick Carroll*.................1909
Ownie Carroll*...............1930
Tommy Carroll........... 1955-56
Chuck Cary............. 1989-91
Hugh Casey*..................1949
Kevin Cash...................2009
Alberto Castillo..............2002
Roy Castleton*...............1907
Bill Castro....................1981
Danny Cater............. 1970-71
Rick Cerone...1980-84, 1987, 1990
Bob Cerv......... 1951-56, 1960-62
Francisco Cervelli........ 2008-09
Shawn Chacon........... 2005-06
Joba Chamberlain........ 2007-09
Chris Chambliss.... 1974-79, 1988
Frank Chance*........... 1913-14
Spud Chandler*.......... 1937-47
Les Channell*..........1910, 1914
Darrin Chapin................1991
Ben Chapman*........... 1930-36
Mike Chartak*.........1940, 1942
Hal Chase*.............. 1905-13
Jack Chesbro*........... 1903-09
Randy Choate............ 2000-03
Justin Christian..............2008
Clay Christiansen............1984
Al Cicotte*...................1957
Anthony Claggett............2009
Allie Clark....................1947
George Clark*................1913
Jack Clark....................1988
Tony Clark...................2004
Horace Clarke............ 1965-74
Walter Clarkson*......... 1904-07
Brandon Claussen...........2003
Ken Clay................ 1977-79
Roger Clemens... 1999-2003, 2007
Pat Clements............ 1987-88
Tex Clevenger........... 1961-62
Lu Clinton*.............. 1966-67
Tyler Clippard................2007
Al Closter............... 1971-72
Andy Coakley*...............1911
Jim Coates......... 1956, 1959-62

Chris Chambliss

Jim Cockman*................1905
Rich Coggins............. 1975-76
Phil Coke................ 2008-09
Rocky Colavito...............1968
King Cole*.............. 1914-15
Curt Coleman*...............1912
Jerry Coleman........... 1949-57
Michael Coleman............2001
Rip Coleman*............ 1955-56
Bob Collins*..................1944
Dave Collins..................1982
Joe Collins*............. 1948-57
Orth Collins*.................1904
Pat Collins*............. 1926-28
Rip Collins*............. 1920-21
Frank Colman*.......... 1946-47
Loyd Colson..................1970
Earle Combs*............ 1924-35
David Cone............1995-2000
Tom Connelly*........... 1920-21
Joe Connor*..................1905
Wid Conroy*............. 1903-08
Jose Contreras........... 2003-04
Andy Cook....................1993
Doc Cook*.............. 1913-16
Dusty Cooke*............ 1930-32
Ron Coomer..................2002
Johnny Cooney*.............1944
Phil Cooney*.................1905
Don Cooper..................1985
Guy Cooper*.................1914
Dan Costello*................1913
Henry Cotto............. 1985-87
Ensign Cottrell*..............1915
Clint Courtney*..............1951
Ernie Courtney*..............1903
Stan Coveleski*...............1928

Billy Cowan 1969
Joe Cowley 1984-85
Bobby Cox.............. 1968-69
Casey Cox............... 1972-73
Birdie Cree*............. 1908-15
Lou Criger*..................1910
Herb Crompton*............1945
Bubba Crosby............ 2004-06
Frank Crosetti*.......... 1932-48
Ivan Cruz 1997
Jose Cruz 1988
Jack Cullen......... 1962, 1965-66
Roy Cullenbine*..............1942
Nick A. Cullop*.......... 1916-17
Nick Cullop *.................1926
John Cumberland........ 1968-70
Jim Curry* 1911
Chad Curtis.............. 1997-99
Fred Curtis*...................1905

D (66)

Babe Dahlgren*.......... 1937-40
Bud Daley 1961-64
Tom Daley*.............. 1914-15
Johnny Damon 2006-09
Bert Daniels*............ 1910-13
Bobby Davidson 1989
Chili Davis 1998-99
George Davis* 1912
Kiddo Davis*..................1926
Lefty Davis*...................1903
Ron Davis............... 1978-81
Russ Davis 1994-95
Brian Dayett 1983-84
John Deering* 1903
Jim Deidel 1974
Ivan DeJesus..................1986
Frank Delahanty* .. 1905-06, 1908
Wilson Delgado...............2000
Bobby Del Greco......... 1957-58
David Dellucci 2003
Jim Delsing* 1949-50
Joe DeMaestri 1960-61
Ray Demmitt*................1909
Rick Dempsey............ 1973-76
Bucky Dent 1977-82
Jorge DePaula 2003-05
Claud Derrick* 1913
Russ Derry*.............. 1944-45
Matt DeSalvo 2007
Jim Deshaies..................1984
Jimmie Deshong*........ 1934-35
Orestes Destrade.............1987
Charlie Devens*.......... 1932-34
Al DeVormer*............ 1921-22
Bill Dickey* 1928-43, 1946
Murry Dickson* 1958
Joe DiMaggio* .. 1936-42, 1946-51
Kerry Dineen............. 1975-76
Craig Dingman................2000
Art Ditmar 1957-61
Sonny Dixon 1956
Pat Dobson*............. 1973-75
Cozy Dolan* 1911-12
Atley Donald*............ 1938-45
Mike Donovan*...............1908
Wild Bill Donovan*....... 1915-16
Brian Dorsett............. 1989-90
Octavio Dotel..................2006
Richard Dotson 1988-89
Patsy Dougherty*........ 1904-06
John Dowd* 1912
Al Downing.............. 1961-69
Brian Doyle 1978-80
Jack Doyle* 1905
Slow Joe Doyle*.......... 1906-10
Doug Drabek 1986
Bill Drescher* 1944-46
Karl Drews*.............. 1946-48
Monk Dubiel*............ 1944-45
Joe Dugan*.............. 1922-28
Mariano Duncan 1996-97
Shelley Duncan 2007-09
Michael Dunn..................2009
Ryne Duren 1958-61
Leo Durocher* 1925, 1928-29
Cedric Durst* 1927-30

E (26)

Mike Easler 1986-87
Rawly Eastwick................1978
Doc Edwards..................1965
Foster Edwards* 1930
Robert Eenhoorn......... 1994-96
Dave Eiland........ 1988-91, 1995
Darrell Einertson 2000
Kid Elberfeld*............ 1903-09
Gene Elliott* 1911
Dock Ellis*............... 1976-77
John Ellis 1969-72
Kevin Elster 1994-95
Alan Embree..................2005
Red Embree*..................1948
Clyde Engle*............. 1909-10
Jack Enright*..................1917
Morgan Ensberg 2008
Todd Erdos 1998-2000
Roger Erickson........... 1982-83
Scott Erickson.................2006
Juan Espino..... 1982-83, 1985-86
Felix Escalona............ 2004-05
Alvaro Espinoza.......... 1988-91
Bobby Estalella................2001
Nick Etten* 1943-46
Barry Evans 1982

F (44)

Charles Fallon*...............1905
Kyle Farnsworth.......... 2006-08
Steve Farr................ 1991-93
Doc Farrell*.............. 1932-33
Sal Fasano 2006
Alex Ferguson* ... 1918, 1921, 1925
Frank Fernandez 1967-69
Tony Fernandez..............1995
Mike Ferraro 1966, 1968
Wes Ferrell*.............. 1938-39
Tom Ferrick*............. 1950-51
Chick Fewster*........... 1917-22
Cecil Fielder.............. 1996-97
Mike Figga............... 1997-99
Ed Figueroa.............. 1976-80
Pete Filson 1987
Happy Finneran*.............1918
Mike Fischlin..................1986
Brian Fisher 1985-86
Gus Fisher* 1912
Ray Fisher*.............. 1910-17
Mike Fitzgerald* 1911
John Flaherty 2003-05
Tim Foli.........................1984
Ray Fontenot 1983-84
Barry Foote 1981-82
Ben Ford.......................2000
Russ Ford* 1909-13

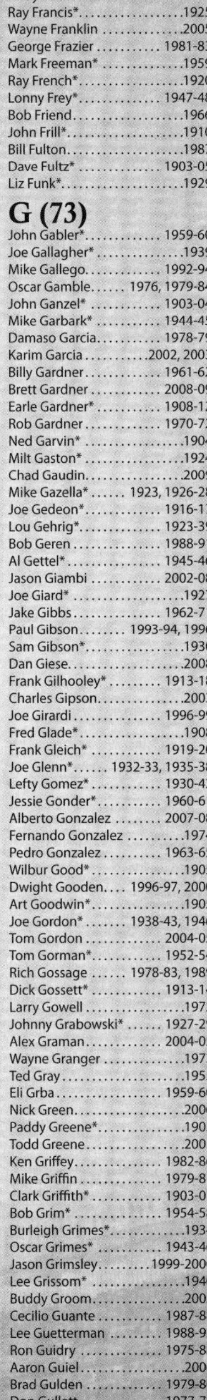

Whitey Ford........ 1950, 1953-67
Tony Fossas....................1999
Eddie Foster* 1910
Jack Fournier* 1918
Andy Fox 1996-97
Ray Francis*...................1925
Wayne Franklin 2005
George Frazier 1981-83
Mark Freeman* 1959
Ray French*...................1920
Lonny Frey*............. 1947-48
Bob Friend.....................1966
John Frill*......................1910
Bill Fulton......................1987
Dave Fultz* 1903-05
Liz Funk*......................1929

G (73)

John Gabler*............. 1959-60
Joe Gallagher* 1939
Mike Gallego............. 1992-94
Oscar Gamble...... 1976, 1979-84
John Ganzel* 1903-04
Mike Garbark* 1944-45
Damaso Garcia........... 1978-79
Karim Garcia 2002, 2003
Billy Gardner............. 1961-62
Brett Gardner 2008-09
Earle Gardner* 1908-12
Rob Gardner 1970-72
Ned Garvin* 1904
Milt Gaston* 1924
Chad Gaudin..................2009
Mike Gazella* 1923, 1926-28
Joe Gedeon*............. 1916-17
Lou Gehrig*.............. 1923-39
Bob Geren 1988-91
Al Gettel*................ 1945-46
Jason Giambi 2002-08
Joe Giard* 1927
Jake Gibbs............... 1962-71
Paul Gibson........ 1993-94, 1996
Sam Gibson*..................1930
Dan Giese......................2008
Frank Gilhooley* 1913-18
Charles Gipson...............2003
Joe Girardi 1996-99
Fred Glade*...................1908
Frank Gleich* 1919-20
Joe Glenn*...... 1932-33, 1935-38
Lefty Gomez* 1930-42
Jessie Gonder*........... 1960-61
Alberto Gonzalez 2007-08
Fernando Gonzalez 1974
Pedro Gonzalez 1963-65
Wilbur Good*.................1905
Dwight Gooden.... 1996-97, 2000
Art Goodwin*.................1905
Joe Gordon* 1938-43, 1946
Tom Gordon 2004-05
Tom Gorman*............ 1952-54
Rich Gossage 1978-83, 1989
Dick Gossett* 1913-14
Larry Gowell 1972
Johnny Grabowski* 1927-29
Alex Graman............. 2004-05
Wayne Granger 1973
Ted Gray 1955
Eli Grba.................. 1959-60
Nick Green.....................2006
Paddy Greene*...............1903
Todd Greene..................2001
Ken Griffey............... 1982-86
Mike Griffin 1979-81
Clark Griffith* 1903-07
Bob Grim* 1954-58
Burleigh Grimes*.............1934
Oscar Grimes* 1943-46
Jason Grimsley.........1999-2000
Lee Grissom* 1940
Buddy Groom..................2005
Cecilio Guante 1987-88
Lee Guetterman 1988-92
Ron Guidry 1975-88
Aaron Guiel....................2006
Brad Gulden 1979-80
Don Gullett 1977-78
Bill Gullickson.................1987
Randy Gumpert*.......... 1946-48
Larry Gura 1974-75
Freddy Guzman...............2009

H (111)

John Habyan............. 1990-93
Bump Hadley* 1936-40
Kent Hadley*..................1960
Ed Hahn* 1905-06
Noodles Hahn* 1906
Hinkey Haines* 1923
Jerry Hairston, Jr..............2009
George Halas* 1919
Bob Hale.......................1961
Jimmie Hall 1969
Mel Hall.................. 1989-92
Brad Halsey 2004

Elston Howard

Roger Hambright 1971
Steve Hamilton* 1963-70
Chris Hammond 2003
Mike Handiboe* 1911
Jim Hanley*....................1913
Truck Hannah*........... 1918-20
Ron Hansen.............. 1970-71
Harry Hanson*................1913
Jim Hardin*....................1971
Bubbles Hargrave* 1930
Harry Harper*.................1921
Toby Harrah...................1984
Greg Harris 1994
Joe Harris*.....................1914
Jim Ray Hart 1973-74
Roy Hartzell*............. 1911-16
Buddy Hassett* 1942
Ron Hassey 1985-86
Andy Hawkins 1989-91
LaTroy Hawkins 2008
Chicken Hawks*..............1921
Charlie Hayes 1992, 1996-97
Fran Healy 1976-78
Mike Heath 1978
Neal Heaton 1993
Don Heffner* 1934-37
Mike Hegan........1964, 1966-67,
.... 1973-74
Fred Heimach*........... 1928-29
Woodie Held*..........1954, 1957
Charlie Hemphill*........ 1908-11
Rollie Hemsley*.......... 1942-44
Bill Henderson* 1930
Rickey Henderson........ 1985-89
Harvey Hendrick* 1923-24
Elrod Hendricks* 1976-77
Tim Hendryx*............ 1915-17
Sean Henn............... 2005-07
Tommy Henrich* 1937-42, 1946-50
Bill Henry 1966
Drew Henson 2002-03
Felix Heredia............. 2003-04
Adrian Hernandez........ 2001-02
Leo Hernandez................1986
Michel Hernandez 2003
Orlando Hernandez ... 1998-2002,
.....................................2004
Xavier Hernandez............1994
Ed Herrmann 1975
Hugh High*.............. 1915-18
Oral Hildebrand*......... 1939-40
Glenallen Hill 2000
Jesse Hill*......................1935
Shawn Hillegas 1992

Rickey Henderson

Frank Hiller* 1946, 1948-49
Mack Hillis* 1924
Eric Hinkse 2009
Rich Hinton 1972
Sterling Hitchcock 1992-95, 2001-03
Myril Hoag* 1931-32, 1934-38
Butch Hobson 1982
Red Hoff* 1911-13
Danny Hoffman* 1906-07
Solly Hofman* 1916
Fred Hofmann* 1919-25
Bill Hogg* 1905-08
Bobby Hogue* 1951-52
Ken Holcombe 1945
Bill Holden* 1913-14
Al Holland 1986-87
Ken Holloway* 1930
Darren Holmes 1998
Fred Holmes* 1903
Roger Holt 1980
Ken Holtzman 1976-78
Rick Honeycutt 1995
Don Hood 1979
Wally Hood* 1949
Johnny Hopp* 1950-52
Shags Horan* 1924
Ralph Houk 1947-54
Elston Howard* 1955-67
Matt Howard 1996
Steve Howe* 1991-96
Harry Howell* 1903
Jay Howell 1982-84
Dick Howser* 1967-68
Waite Hoyt* 1921-30
Rex Hudler 1984-85
Charlie Hudson 1987-88
Keith Hughes 1987
Phil Hughes 2007-09
Long Tom Hughes* 1904
Tom Hughes* ... 1906-07, 1909-10
John Hummel* 1918

Waite Hoyt

Mike Humphreys 1991-93
Ken Hunt* 1959-60
Billy Hunter 1955-56
Catfish Hunter* 1975-79
Mark Hutton 1993-94, 1996
Ham Hyatt* 1918

I (3)

Pete Incaviglia 1997
Kei Igawa 2007-08
Hideki Irabu 1997-99

J (44)

Fred Jacklitsch* 1905
Grant Jackson 1976
Reggie Jackson 1977-81
Dion James 1992-93, 95-96
Johnny James 1958, 1960-61
Stan Javier 1984
Domingo Jean 1993
Stanley Jefferson 1989
Jackie Jensen* 1950-52
Mike Jerzembeck 1998
Derek Jeter 1995-2009
D'Angelo Jimenez 1999
Elvio Jimenez 1964
Brett Jodie 2001
Tommy John 1979-82, 1986-89
Alex Johnson 1974-75
Billy Johnson* 1943, 1946-51
Cliff Johnson 1977-79
Darrell Johnson* 1957-58
Deron Johnson* 1960-61
Don Johnson 1947, 1950
Ernie Johnson* 1923-25
Hank Johnson* ... 1925-26, '28-32
Jeff Johnson 1991-93
Johnny Johnson* 1944
Ken Johnson 1969
Lance Johnson 2000
Nick Johnson 2001-03
Otis Johnson* 1911
Randy Johnson 2005-06
Roy Johnson* 1936-37
Russ Johnson 2005
Jay Johnstone 1978-79
Darryl Jones 1979
Gary Jones 1970-71
Jimmy Jones 1989-90
Ruppert Jones 1980
Sad Sam Jones* 1922-26
Tim Jordan* 1903
Art Jorgens* 1929-39
Felix Jose 2000
Jeff Juden 1999
Mike Jurewicz 1965
David Justice 2000-01

K (52)

Jim Kaat 1979-80
Scott Kamieniecki 1991-96
Bob Kammeyer* 1978-79
Frank Kane* 1919
Bill Karlon* 1930
Herb Karpel* 1946
Steve Karsay 2002-05
Jeff Karstens 2006-07
Benny Kauff* 1912
Curt Kaufman 1982-83
Eddie Kearse* 1942
Ray Keating* 1912-16, 1918
Bob Keefe* 1907
Willie Keeler* 1903-09
Randy Keisler 2000-01
Mike Kekich 1969-73
Charlie Keller* ... 1939-43, '45-49, '52
Pat Kelly 1991-97
Roberto Kelly 1987-92, 2000
Steve Kemp 1983-84
Ian Kennedy 2007-09
John Kennedy 1967
Jerry Kenney 1967, 1969-72
Matt Keough 1983
Jimmy Key 1993-96
Steve Kiefer 1989
Dave Kingman 1977
Harry Kingman* 1914
Fred Kipp 1960
Frank Kitson* 1907
Ron Kittle 1986-87
Ted Kleinhans* 1936
Red Kleinow* 1904-10
Ed Klepfer* 1911, 1913
Ron Klimkowski* ... 1969-70, 1972
Steve Kline 1970-74
Mickey Klutts 1976-78
Bill Knickerbocker* 1938-40
Brandon Knight 2001-02
John Knight* 1909-11, 1913
Chuck Knoblauch 1998-2001
Mark Koenig* 1925-30
Jim Konstanty* 1954-56
Andy Kosco 1968
Steve Kraly 1953
Jack Kramer* 1951
Ernie Krueger* 1915
Dick Kryhoski* 1949
Tony Kubek 1957-65
Johnny Kucks 1955-59
Bill Kunkel* 1963
Bob Kuzava 1951-54

L (63)

Joe Lake* 1908-09
Bill Lamar* 1917-19
Hal Lanier 1972-73
Dave Lapoint 1989-90
Frank LaPorte* 1905-10
Dave LaRoche 1981-83
Don Larsen 1955-59
Lyn Lary* 1929-34
Chris Latham 2003
Marcus Lawton 1989
Matt Lawton 2005
Gene Layden* 1915
Tony Lazzeri* 1926-37
Tim Leary 1990-92
Ricky Ledee 1998-00
Travis Lee 2004
Joe Lefebvre 1980
Al Leiter 1987-89, 2005
Mark Leiter 1990
Frank Leja* 1954-55
Jack Lelivelt* 1912-13
Eddie Leon 1975
Louis LeRoy* 1905-06
Ed Levy* 1942, 1944
Duffy Lewis* 1919-20
Jim Lewis 1982
Terry Ley 1971
Jim Leyritz 1990-96, 1999-2000
Cory Lidle* 2006
Jon Lieber 2004
Ted Lilly 2000-02
Paul Lindblad* 1978
Johnny Lindell* 1941-50
Phil Linz 1962-65
Bryan Little 1986
Jack Little* 1912
Clem Llewellyn* 1922
Graeme Lloyd 1996-98
Esteban Loaiza 2004
Gene Locklear 1976-77
Kenny Lofton 2004
Sherm Lollar* 1947-48
Tim Lollar 1980
Phil Lombardi 1986-87
Dale Long* 1960, 1962-63
Herman Long* 1903
Terrence Long 2006
Ed Lopat* 1948-55
Art Lopez 1965
Hector Lopez 1959-66
Baldy Louden* 1907
Slim Love* 1916-18
Torey Lovullo 1991
Mike Lowell 1998
Johnny Lucadello* 1947
Joe Lucey* 1920
Roy Luebbe* 1925
Matt Luke 1996
Jerry Lumpe 1956-59
Scott Lusader 1991
Sparky Lyle 1972-78
Al Lyons* 1944, 1946-47
Jim Lyttle 1969-71

M (151)

Duke Maas* 1958-61
Kevin Maas 1990-93
Bob MacDonald 1995
Danny MacFayden* 1932-34
Ray Mack* 1947
Tommy Madden* 1910
Elliott Maddox 1974-76
Dave Madison* 1950
Lee Magee* 1916-17
Sal Maglie* 1957-58
Stubby Magner* 1911
Jim Magnuson* 1973
Fritz Maisel* 1913-17
Hank Majeski* 1946
Frank Makosky* 1937
Pat Malone* 1935-37
Pat Maloney* 1912
Al Mamaux* 1924
Rube Manning* 1907-10
Mickey Mantle* 1951-68
Jeff Manto 1999
Josias Manzanillo 1995
Cliff Mapes* 1948-51
Roger Maris* 1960-66
Cliff Markle* 1915-16, 1924
Jim Marquis* 1925
Armando Marsans* 1917-18
Cuddles Marshall* .. 1946, 1948-49
Sam Marsonek 2004
Damaso Marte 2008-09
Billy Martin* 1950-53, 1955-57
Hersh Martin* 1944-45
Jack Martin* 1912
Tino Martinez 1996-2001, 2005
Tippy Martinez 1974-76
Jim Mason 1974-76
Vic Mata 1984-85
Hideki Matsui 2003-09
Don Mattingly 1982-95
Carlos May 1976-77
Darrell May 2005
Rudy May 1974-76, 1980-83
John Mayberry 1982
Carl Mays* 1919-23
Lee Mazzilli 1982
Larry McCall 1977-78
Joe McCarthy* 1905
Pat McCauley* 1903
Larry McClure* 1910
George McConnell* ... 1909, '12-13
Mike McCormick 1970
Lance McCullers 1989-90
Lindy McDaniel 1968-73
Mickey McDermott* 1956
Danny McDevitt 1961
Dave McDonald 1969
Donzell McDonald 2001
Jim McDonald 1952-54
Gil McDougald 1951-60
Jack McDowell 1995
Sam McDowell 1973-74
Lou McEvoy* 1930-31
Herm McFarland* 1903
Andy McGaffigan 1981
Lynn McGlothen* 1982
Bob McGraw* 1917-20
Deacon McGuire* 1904-07
Marty McHale* 1913-15
Irish McIlveen* 1908-09
Tim McIntosh 1996
Bill McKechnie* 1913
Rich McKinney 1972
Frank McManus* 1904
Norm McMillan* 1922
Tommy McMillan* 1912
Mike McNally* 1921-24

Herb McQuaid* 1926
George McQuinn*........ 1947-48
Bobby Meacham......... 1983-88
Charlie Meara*..............1914
Jim Mecir............... 1996-97
George Medich 1972-75
Mark Melancon 2009
Bob Melvin 1994
Ramiro Mendoza. 1996-2002, 2005
Fred Merkle*............ 1925-26
Andy Messersmith 1978
Tom Metcalf 1963
Bud Metheny*........... 1943-46
Hensley Meulens......... 1989-93
Bob Meusel*............ 1920-29
Bob Meyer..................1964
Danny Miceli.................2003
Gene Michael........... 1968-74
Ezra Midkiff*............ 1912-13
Doug Mientkiewicz 2007
Pete Mikkelsen*.......... 1964-65
Larry Milbourne.......... 1981-83
Sam Militello............ 1992-93
Bill Miller* 1952-54
Elmer Miller*.... 1915-18, 1921-22
John Miller..................1966
Alan Mills............... 1990-91
Buster Mills*................1940
Mike Milosevich*......... 1944-45
Paul Mirabella................1979
Juan Miranda 2008-09
Willie Miranda* 1953-54
Bobby Mitchell...............1970
Fred Mitchell*...............1910
Johnny Mitchell*......... 1921-22
Sergio Mitre 2009
Johnny Mize*........... 1949-53
Keven Mmahat..............1989
Chad Moeller 2008
George Mogridge*....... 1915-20
Dale Mohorcic 1988-89
Fenton Mole.................1949
Jose Molina.............. 2007-09
Bill Monbouquette....... 1967-68
Raul Mondesi 2002-03
Ed Monroe*............. 1917-18
Zack Monroe............ 1958-59
John Montefusco 1983-86
Rich Monteleone......... 1990-93
Archie Moore 1964-65
Earl Moore*.................1907
Wilcy Moore* ... 1927-29, 1932-33
Ray Morehart* 1927
Omar Moreno........... 1983-85
Mike Morgan 1982
Tom Morgan*... 1951-52, 1954-56
George Moriarty* 1906-08
Jeff Moronko.................1987
Hal Morris 1988-89
Ross Moschitto.........1965, 1967
Jerry Moses..................1973
Terry Mulholland............1994
Charlie Mullen* 1914-16
Jerry Mumphrey 1981-83
Bob Muncrief* 1951
Bobby Munoz................1993
Thurman Munson*....... 1969-79
Bobby Murcer* 1965-66,
.... 1969-74, 1979-83

Johnny Murphy*...1932,'34-43,'46
Rob Murphy 1994
Dale Murray 1983-85
George Murray*.............1922
Larry Murray............ 1974-76
Mike Mussina 2001-08
Mike Myers 2006-07

N (28)

Xavier Nady............. 2008-09
Jerry Narron 1979
Dan Naulty 1999
Dioneer Navarro 2004
Denny Neagle 2000
Bots Nekola*.................1929
Gene Nelson.................1981
Jeff Nelson....... 1996-2000, 2003
Luke Nelson* 1919
Graig Nettles............ 1973-83
Tex Neuer*...................1907
Ernie Nevel* 1950-51
Floyd Newkirk* 1934
Bobo Newsom*..............1947
Doc Newton* 1905-09
Gus Niarhos*....... 1946, 1948-50
Joe Niekro* 1985-87
Phil Niekro.............. 1984-85
Jerry Nielsen.................1992
Scott Nielsen....... 1986, 1988-89
Wil Nieves 2005-07
Harry Niles*.................1908
C. J. Nitkowski...............2004
Otis Nixon 1983
Matt Nokes 1990-94
Irv Noren 1952-56
Don Nottebart*..............1969
Les Nunamaker* 1914-17

O (27)

Johnny Oates* 1980-81
Mike O'Berry................1984
Andy O'Connor* 1908
Jack O'Connor* 1903
Paddy O'Connor* 1918
Heinie Odom* 1925
Lefty O'Doul* 1919-20, 1922
Rowland Office 1983
Ross Ohlendorf 2007-08
Bob Ojeda 1994
Rube Oldring* 1905, 1916
John Olerud 2004
Bob Oliver 1975
Joe Oliver....................2001
Nate Oliver 1969
Paul O'Neill 1993-2001
Steve O'Neill* 1925
Jesse Orosco.................2003
Queenie O'Rourke* 1908
Al Orth* 1904-09
Donovan Osborne 2004
Champ Osteen*..............1904
Joe Ostrowski*........... 1950-52
Antonio Osuna...............2003
Bill Otis* 1912
Stubby Overmire*...........1951
Spike Owen..................1993

Bobby Murcer

P (63)

John Pacella 1982
Del Paddock* 1912
Juan Padilla..................2004
Dave Pagan............. 1973-76
Joe Page*............... 1944-50
Mike Pagliarulo 1984-89
Donn Pall 1994
Christian Parker..............2001
Clay Parker.............. 1989-90
Ben Paschal*............ 1924-29
Dan Pasqua.............. 1985-87
Gil Patterson.................1977
Jeff Patterson 1995
Mike Patterson........... 1981-82
Scott Patterson 2008
Carl Pavano........ 2005, 2007-08
Dave Pavlas.............. 1995-96
Monte Pearson*.......... 1936-40
Roger Peckinpaugh* 1913-21
Steve Peek*..................1941
Hipolito Pena 1988
Ramiro Pena 2009
Herb Pennock*........... 1923-33
Joe Pepitone............. 1962-69
Marty Perez..................1977
Melido Perez............ 1992-95
Pascual Perez 1990-91
Robert Perez..................2001
Cecil Perkins 1967
Cy Perkins* 1931
Gaylord Perry 1980
Fritz Peterson 1966-74
Andy Pettitte ...1995-2003, 2007-09
Josh Phelps..................2007
Ken Phelps.............. 1988-89
Andy Phillips............ 2004-07
Eddie Phillips* 1932
Jack Phillips*............ 1947-49
Cy Pieh* 1913-15
Bill Piercy* 1917, 1921
Duane Pillette........... 1949-50
Lou Piniella 1974-84
George Pipgras* 1923-24, 1927-33
Wally Pipp* 1915-25
Jim Pisoni*............... 1959-60
Eric Plunk............... 1989-91
Dale Polley...................1996
Luis Polonia....1989-90, '94-95, '00
Sidney Ponson.........2006, 2008
Bob Porterfield*.......... 1948-51
Jorge Posada 1995-2009
Scott Pose 1997
Jack Powell* 1904-05
Jake Powell* 1936-40
Mike Powers* 1905
Del Pratt*............... 1918-20
Jerry Priddy*............ 1941-42
Curtis Pride 2003
Johnny Priest* 1911-12
Bret Prinz............... 2003-04
Scott Proctor............ 2004-07
Alfonso Pulido 1986
Ambrose Puttmann* 1903-05

Q (5)

Paul Quantrill 2004-05
Mel Queen*...1942, 1944, 1946-47
Ed Ouick*....................1903
Jack Ouinn*..... 1909-12, 1919-21
Jamie Quirk..................1989

R (81)

Tim Raines.............. 1996-98
Dave Rajsich 1978
Edwar Ramirez........... 2007-09
Bobby Ramos................1982
Domingo Ramos..............1978
John Ramos 1991
Pedro Ramos............ 1964-66
Lenny Randle 1979
Willie Randolph.......... 1976-88
Cody Ransom............ 2008-09
Vic Raschi*.............. 1946-53
Dennis Rasmussen....... 1984-87
Darrell Rasner........... 2006-08
Shane Rawley............ 1982-84
Jeff Reardon 1994

Tim Redding.................2005
Jack Reed............... 1961-63
Kevin Reese............. 2005-06
Jimmie Reese*.......... 1930-31
Hal Reniff*.............. 1961-67
Bill Renna....................1953
Tony Rensa* 1933
Roger Repoz............. 1964-66
Rick Reuschel................1981
Dave Reverning.......... 1981-82
Al Reyes 2003
Allie Reynolds*.......... 1947-54
Bill Reynolds*........... 1913-14
Rick Rhoden 1987-88

Allie Reynolds

Gordon Rhodes*......... 1929-32
Harry Rice* 1930
Bobby Richardson........ 1955-66
Nolen Richardson*...........1935
Branch Rickey*...............1907
Dave Righetti 1979, 1981-90
Jose Rijo.....................1984
Danny Rios 1997
Juan Rivera 2001-03
Mariano Rivera.........1995-2009
Ruben Rivera 1995-96
Mickey Rivers 1976-79
Phil Rizzuto* 1941-42, 1946-56
Roxey Roach*............ 1910-11
Dale Roberts.................1967
Andre Robertson......... 1981-85
David Robertson......... 2008-09
Gene Robertson* 1928-29
Aaron Robinson*... 1943, 1945-47
Bill Robinson*........... 1967-69
Bruce Robinson.......... 1979-80
Eddie Robinson 1954-56
Hank Robinson* 1918
Jeff Robinson 1990
Alex Rodriguez........... 2004-09
Aurelio Rodriguez*....... 1980-81
Carlos Rodriguez.............1991
Eddie Rodriguez 1982
Ellie Rodriguez...............1968
Felix Rodriguez 2005
Henry Rodriguez.............2001
Ivan Rodriguez...............2008
Gary Roenicke 1986
Oscar Roettger*.......... 1923-24
Jay Rogers* 1914
Kenny Rogers........... 1996-97
Tom Rogers*.................1921
Jim Roland...................1972
Red Rolfe* 1931, 1934-42
Buddy Rosar*............ 1939-42
Larry Rosenthal* 1944
Steve Roser*............. 1944-46
Braggo Roth* 1921
Jerry Royster.................1987
Muddy Ruel*............ 1917-20
Dutch Ruether* 1926-27
Red Ruffing* 1930-42, 1945-46
Allen Russell* 1915-19
Marius Russo*...... 1939-43, 1946
Babe Ruth* 1920-34
Blondy Ryan* 1935
Rosy Ryan* 1928

S (142)

CC Sabathia.....2009
Johnny Sain*..... 1951-55
Lenn Sakata.....1987
Mark Salas.....1987
Jack Saltzgaver*.... 1932, 1934-37
Billy Sample.....1985
Celerino Sanchez*..... 1972-73
Humberto Sanchez.....2008
Rey Sanchez.....1997, 2005
Deion Sanders..... 1989-90
Roy Sanders*.....1918
Scott Sanderson..... 1991-92
Charlie Sands.....1967
Fred Sanford..... 1949-51
Rafael Santana.....1988
Bronson Sardinha.....2007
Don Savage*..... 1944-45
Rick Sawyer..... 1974-75
Steve Sax..... 1989-91
Ray Scarborough*..... 1952-53
Germany Schaefer*.....1916
Harry Schaeffer*.....1952
Roy Schalk*.....1932
Art Schallock..... 1951-55
Wally Schang*..... 1921-25
Bob Schmidt.....1965
Butch Schmidt*.....1909
Johnny Schmitz..... 1952-53
Pete Schneider*.....1919
Dick Schofield.....1966
Paul Schreiber*.....1945
Art Schult.....1953
Al Schulz*..... 1912-14
Don Schulze.....1989
Pius Schwert*..... 1914-15
Everett Scott*..... 1922-25
George Scott.....1979
Rodney Scott.....1982
Rod Scurry*..... 1985-86
Scott Seabol.....2001
Ken Sears*.....1943
Bob Seeds*.....1936
Kal Segrist.....1952
Fernando Seguignol.....2003
George Selkirk*..... 1934-42
Ted Sepkowski*.....1947
Hank Severeid*.....1926
Joe Sewell*..... 1931-33
Richie Sexson.....2008
Howard Shanks*.....1925
Billy Shantz*.....1960
Bobby Shantz..... 1957-60
Bob Shawkey*..... 1915-27
Spec Shea*..... 1947-49, 1951
Al Shealy*.....1928
George Shears*.....1912
Tom Sheehan*.....1921
Gary Sheffield..... 2004-06
Rollie Sheldon.....1961-62,
..... 1964-65
Skeeter Shelton*.....1915
Roy Sherid*..... 1929-31
Pat Sheridan.....1991
Dennis Sherrill.....1978, 1980
Ben Shields*..... 1924-25
Steve Shields.....1988
Bob Shirley..... 1983-87
Urban Shocker*...1916-17, 1925-28
Tom Shopay.....1967, 1969
Ernie Shore*..... 1919-20
Bill Short.....1960
Norm Siebern..... 1956, 1958-59
Ruben Sierra.... 1995-96, 2003-05
Charlie Silvera..... 1948-56
Dave Silvestri..... 1992-95
Ken Silvestri*..... 1941, 1946-47
Hack Simmons*.....1912
Dick Simpson.....1969
Harry Simpson*..... 1957-58
Duke Sims..... 1973-74
Bill Skiff*.....1926
Camp Skinner*.....1922
Joel Skinner..... 1986-88
Lou Skizas.....1956
Bill Skowron..... 1954-62
Roger Slagle.....1979
Don Slaught..... 1988-89
Enos Slaughter*. 1954-55, 1956-59

Yankees Serving Their Country

The following Yankees lost Major League service time for military service:

Phil Rizzuto is one of 40 Yankees that lost Major League service for military service.

Rich Beck.....1967
Norm Branch..... 1943-45
Bobby Brown..... 1952-54
Tommy Byrne..... 1944-45
Tommy Carroll.....1958
Jerry Coleman..... 1952-53
Bill Dickey..... 1944-45
Joe DiMaggio..... 1943-45
Frank Fernandez.....1967
Whitey Ford..... 1950-51
Joe Gordon..... 1944-45
Randy Gumpert..... 1943-45
Buddy Hassett..... 1943-45
Mike Hegan.....1967
Rollie Hemsley.....1945
Tommy Henrich..... 1943-45
Billy Johnson..... 1944-46
Jerry Kenney.....1968
Tony Kubek.....1962
Al Lyons.....1945
Hank Majeski..... 1943-45
Billy Martin..... 1954-55
Tom Morgan..... 1952-53
Ross Moschitto.....1966
Bobby Murcer..... 1967-68
Steve Peck..... 1942-45
Mel Queen..... 1945-46
Phil Rizzuto..... 1943-45
Araron Robinson.....1944
Red Ruffing..... 1943-44
Marius Russo..... 1944-45
Ken Sears..... 1944-45
George Selkirk..... 1943-45
Ken Silvestri..... 1942-45
Charley Stanceu..... 1943-44
Johnny Sturm..... 1942-45
Jake Wade.....1945
Roy Weatherly..... 1944-45
Bob Wiesler..... 1951-52
Butch Wensloff..... 1945-46

Aaron Small..... 2005-06
Roy Smalley..... 1982-84
Walt Smallwood*.....1917, 1919
Charley Smith*..... 1967-68
Elmer Smith*..... 1922-23
Joe Smith*.....1913
Keith Smith..... 1984-85
Klondike Smith*.....1912
Lee Smith.....1993
Matt Smith.....2006
Harry Smythe*.....1934
J.T. Snow.....1992
Eric Soderholm.....1980
Luis Sojo.. 1996-99, 2000-01, 2003
Tony Solaita*.....1968
Alfonso Soriano.....1999-2003
Steve Souchock*.....1946, 1948
Jim Spencer*..... 1978-81
Shane Spencer.....1998-2002
Charlie Spikes.....1972
Russ Springer.....1992
Bill Stafford*..... 1960-65
Jake Stahl*.....1908
Roy Staiger.....1979
Tuck Stainback*..... 1942-45
Gerry Staley*..... 1955-56
Charley Stanceu*.....1941, 1946
Andy Stankiewicz..... 1992-93
Fred Stanley..... 1973-80
Mike Stanley..... 1992-95, 1997
Mike Stanton....1997-2002, 2005
Dick Starr..... 1947-48
Dave Stegman.....1982
Dutch Sterrett*..... 1912-13
Bud Stewart*.....1948
Chris Stewart.....2008
Lee Stine*.....1938
Kelly Stinnett.....2006
Snuffy Stirnweiss*..... 1943-50
Tim Stoddard..... 1986-88
Mel Stottlemyre..... 1964-74
Hal Stowe.....1960

Darryl Strawberry..... 1995-99
Gabby Street*.....1912
Marlin Stuart*.....1954
Bill Stumpf*..... 1912-13
Tom Sturdivant*..... 1955-59
Johnny Sturm*.....1941
Tanyon Sturtze..... 2004-06
Bill Sudakis.....1974
Steve Sundra*..... 1936, 1938-40
Dale Sveum.....1998
Ed Sweeney*..... 1908-15
Nick Swisher.....2009
Ron Swoboda..... 1971-73

T (54)

Fred Talbot..... 1966-69
Vito Tamulis*..... 1934-35
Frank Tanana.....1993
Jesse Tannehill*.....1903
Tony Tarasco.....1999
Danny Tartabull..... 1992-95
Wade Taylor.....1991
Zack Taylor*.....1934
Mark Teixeira.....2009
Frank Tepedino.... 1967, 1969-72
Walt Terrell.....1989
Ralph Terry..... 1956-57, 1959-64
Jay Tessmer..... 1998-00, 2002
Dick Tettelbach*.....1955
Bob Tewksbury..... 1986-87
Marcus Thames.....2002
Ira Thomas*..... 1906-07
Lee Thomas.....1961
Myles Thomas*..... 1926-29
Stan Thomas.....1977
Gary Thomasson.....1978
Homer Thompson*.....1912
Kevin Thompson..... 2006-07
Ryan Thompson.....2000
Tommy Thompson*.....1912
Jack Thoney*.....1904

Hank Thormahlen*..... 1917-20
Marv Throneberry*... 1955, 1958-59
Mike Thurman.....2002
Luis Tiant..... 1979-80
Dick Tidrow..... 1974-79
Bobby Tiefenauer*.....1965
Eddie Tiemeyer*.....1909
Ray Tift*.....1907
Bob Tillman*.....1967
Thad Tilllotson..... 1967-68
Dan Tipple*.....1915
Wayne Tolleson..... 1986-90
Brett Tomko.....2009
Earl Torgeson*.....1961
Rusty Torres..... 1971-72
Mike Torrez.....1977
Cesar Tovar*.....1976
Josh Towers.....2009
Billy Traber.....2008
Bubba Trammell.....2003
Tom Tresh*..... 1961-69
Gus Triandos..... 1953-54
Steve Trout.....1987
Virgil Trucks.....1958
Frank Truesdale*.....1914
Bob Turley..... 1955-62
Chris Turner.....2000
Jim Turner*..... 1942-45

U (4)

George Uhle*..... 1933-34
Tom Underwood..... 1980-81
Bob Unglaub*.....1904
Cecil Upshaw*.....1974

V (20)

Elmer Valo*.....1960
Russ Van Atta*..... 1933-35
Dazzy Vance*.....1915, 1918
Joe Vance*..... 1937-38
John Vander Wal.....2002

Bobby Vaughn* 1909
Hippo Vaughn* 1908, 1910-12
Javier Vazquez 2004
Bobby Veach* 1925
Randy Velarde ... 1987-1995, 2001
Otto Velez 1973-76
Mike Vento 2005
Robin Ventura 2002-03
Jose Veras 2006-09
Joe Verbanic 1967-68, 1970
Frank Verdi 1953
Sammy Vick* 1917-20
Ron Villone 2006-07
Jose Vizcaino 2000
Luis Vizcaino 2007

W (94)

Jake Wade* 1946
Dick Wakefied* 1950
Jim Walewander 1990
Curt Walker* 1919
Dixie Walker* 1931, 1933-36
Mike Wallace 1974-75
Jimmy Walsh* 1914
Joe Walsh* 1910-11
Roxy Walters* 1915-18
Danny Walton 1971
Paul Waner* 1944-45
Chien-Ming Wang 2005-09
Jack Wanner* 1909
Pee Wee Wanninger* 1925
Aaron Ward* 1917-26
Gary Ward 1987-89
Joe Ward* 1909
Pete Ward 1970
Jack Warhop* 1908-15
George Washburn* 1941
Claudell Washington . 1986-88, '90
Gary Waslewski 1970-71
Allen Watson 1999-2000
Bob Watson 1980-82
Roy Weatherly* 1943, 1946
David Weathers 1996-97
Jeff Weaver 2002-03
Jim Weaver* 1931
Dave Wehrmeister 1981
Lefty Weinert* 1931
David Wells 1997-98, 2002-03
Ed Wells* 1929-32
Butch Wensloff* 1943, 1947
Julie Wera* 1927, 1929
Billy Werber* 1930, 1933
Dennis Werth 1979-81
Jake Westbrook 2000
John Wetteland 1995-96
Stefan Wever 1982
Steve Whitaker 1966-68
Gabe White 2003-04
Rondell White 2002
Roy White 1965-79
Wally Whitehurst 1996
George Whiteman* 1913
Mark Whiten 1997
Terry Whitfield 1974-76
Ed Whitson 1985-86
Kemp Wicker* 1936-38
Al Wickland* 1919
Bob Wickman 1992-96
Chris Widger 2002
Bob Wiesler 1951, 1954-55
Bill Wight* 1946-47
Ted Wilborn 1980
Ed Wilkinson* 1911
Bernie Williams 1991-2006
Bob Williams* 1911-13
Gerald Williams . 1992-96, 2001-02
Harry Williams* 1913-14
Jimmy Williams* 1903-07
Stan Williams 1963-64
Todd Williams 2001
Walt Williams 1974-75
Archie Wilson* 1951-52
Enrique Wilson 2001-04
George Wilson* 1956
Craig Wilson 2006
Kris Wilson 2006
Pete Wilson* 1908-09
Snake Wiltse* 1903
Gordie Windhorn 1959
Dave Winfield 1981-90
Jay Witasick 2001
Mickey Witek* 1949
Mike Witt 1990-91, 1993
Whitey Witt* 1922-25
Mark Wohlers 2001
Bill Wolfe* 1903-04
Harry Wolter* 1910-13
Harry Wolverton* 1912
Dooley Womack 1966-68
Tony Womack 2005
Gene Woodling* 1949-54
Ron Woods 1969-71
Dick Woodson 1974
Hank Workman 1950
Chase Wright 2007
Jaret Wright 2005-06
Ken Wright 1974
Yats Wuestling* 1930
John Wyatt* 1968
Butch Wynegar 1982-86
Jimmy Wynn 1977

X (0)

Y (5)

Ed Yarnall 1999-2000
Joe Yeager* 1905-06
Jim York 1976
Curt Young 1992
Ralph Young* 1913

Z (8)

Tom Zachary* 1928-30
Jack Zalusky* 1903
George Zeber 1977-78
Rollie Zeider* 1913
Todd Zeile 2003
Guy Zinn* 1911-12
Bill Zuber* 1943-46
Paul Zuvella 1986-87

YANKEES FAMILY WHO PASSED AWAY SINCE LAST PUBLICATION

Johnny Blanchard
Tony Fantasia
Lonny Frey
John Gabler
Woodie Held
Tommy Henrich
Ron Klimkowski
Max Margulis
Jack Phillips
Arthur Richman
Tom Sturdivant
Harvey Winston
Mark Zettelmeyer

All-Time Yankees Captains

1. Hal Chase 1912
2. Roger Peckinpaugh 1914-1921
3. Babe Ruth 5/20/22-5/25/22
4. Everett Scott 1922-1925
5. Lou Gehrig 4/21/35-6/2/41
6. Thurman Munson 4/17/76-8/2/79
7. Graig Nettles 1/29/82-3/30/84
8. Willie Randolph 3/4/86-10/2/88
9. Ron Guidry 3/4/86-7/12/89
10. Don Mattingly 2/28/91-1995
11. **DEREK JETER 6/3/03-PRESENT**

Coaches Roster

Available records show that 115 men have served as a coach for the Yankees through the 2009 season.

***Deceased**

A (2)

Neil Allen 2005
Joe Altobelli 1981-82, 1986

B (8)

Loren Babe* 1967
Vern Benson* 1965-66
Yogi Berra 1963, 1976-83
Larry Bowa 2006-07
Clete Boyer* 1988, 1992-94
Cloyd Boyer* 1975, 1977
Jimmy Burke* 1931-33
Brian Butterfield 1994-95

C (11)

Jose Cardenal 1996-99
Chris Chambliss ... 1988, 1996-2000
Tony Cloninger 1992-2001
Earle Combs* 1936-44
Mark Connor 1984-85, 1986-87, 1990-93
Billy Connors 1989-90, 1994-95, 2000
Nardi Contreras 1995
Pat Corrales 1989
John Corriden* 1947-48
Bobby Cox 1977
Frank Crosetti* 1946-68

D (6)

Tom Daly* 1914
Cot Deal* 1965
Gary Denbo 2001
Bill Dickey* 1949-57, 1960
Rick Down 1993-95, 2002-03
Chuck Dressen* 1947-48

E (4)

Dave Eiland 2008-09
Lee Elia 1989
Sammy Ellis 1982-84, 1986
Darrell Evans 1990

F (6)

Duke Farrell* .. 1909, 1911, 1915-17
Mike Ferraro 1979-82, 1987-91
Art Fletcher* 1927-45
Whitey Ford ... 1964, 1968, 1974-75
Art Fowler* 1977-79, 1983,1988
Charlie Fox* 1989

G (4)

Joe Girardi 2005
Jimmy Gleeson* 1964
Ron Guidry 2006-07
Randy Gumpert* 1957

H (10)

Mike Harkey 2008-09
Jim Hegan* 1960-73, 1979-80
Tommy Henrich 1951
Marc Hill 1991
Doug Holmquist* 1984-85
Willie Horton 1985
Ralph Houk 1953-54, 1958-60
Elston Howard* 1969-79
Frank Howard 1989, 1991-93
Dick Howser* 1969-78

K (4)

Mick Kelleher 2009
Charlie Keller* 1957, 1959
Joe Kerrigan 2006-07
Clyde King 1978, 1981-82, 1988

L (5)

Charlie Lau* 1979-81
Bob Lemon* 1976
Dale Long* 1963
Kevin Long 2007-09
Eddie Lopat* 1960

M (15)

Mickey Mantle* 1970
Harry Mathews* 1929
Don Mattingly 2004-07
Lee Mazzilli 2000-03, 2006
Jerry McNertney 1984
Bobby Meacham 2008
Fred Merkle* 1925-26
Stump Merrill 1985, 1987
Russ "Monk" Meyer* 1992
Gene Michael 1976, 1978, 1984-86, 1988-89
George Mitterwald 1988
Bill Monbouquette 1985-86
Rich Monteleone 2002-04
Tom Morgan* 1979
Wally Moses* 1961-62, 1966

N (4)

Ed Napoleon 1992-93
Graig Nettles 1991
Tom Nieto 2000-02
Johnny Neun* 1944-46

O (2)

Paddy O'Connor* 1918-19
Charlie O'Leary* 1921-30

P (4)

Tony Pena 2006-09
Joe Pepitone 1982
Cy Perkins* 1932-33
Lou Piniella 1984-85

R (3)

Willie Randolph 1994-2004
Red Rolfe* 1946
Frank Roth* 1921-22

S (13)

Johnny Sain* 1961-63
Germany Schaefer* 1916
Paul Schreiber* 1942, 1945
John Schulte* 1934-48
Joe Sewell* 1934-35
Bob Shawkey* 1929
Glenn Sherlock 1995
Buck Showalter 1990-91
Luis Sojo 2004-05
Joe Sparks 1990
John Stearns 1989
Mel Stottlemyre 1996-2005
Champ Summers 1989-90

T (5)

Rob Thomson 2008-09
Jeff Torborg 1979-88
Earl Torgeson* 1961
Gary Tuck 1997-99, 2003-04
Jim Turner* 1949-59, 1966-73

V (1)

Mickey Vernon* 1982

W (7)

Jerry Walker 1981-82
Lee Walls* 1983
Jay Ward 1987
Roy White .. 1983-84, 1986, 2004-05
Stan Williams 1980-82, 1987-88
George Wiltse* 1925
Mel Wright* 1974-75

Z (1)

Don Zimmer .... 1983, 1986, '96-03

Yankees by the Numbers

In 1929, the New York Yankees and Cleveland Indians became the first teams to make numbers a permanent part of the uniform. Other teams quickly adopted the idea and, by 1932, uniform numbers became standard for all teams. The initial distribution of numbers to the Yankees' roster was made according to the player's spot in the batting order. Therefore, in 1929, leadoff hitter Earle Combs wore No. 1, Mark Koenig No. 2, Babe Ruth No. 3, Lou Gehrig No. 4, Bob Meusel No. 5, Tony Lazzeri No. 6, Leo Durocher No. 7, Johnny Grabowski No. 8, Benny Bengough No. 9, Bill Dickey No. 10 (Grabowski, Bengough and Dickey shared the catching duties). After some exhaustive research, the Yankees' Media Relations staff compiled the following list of Yankees uniform numbers. The list represents uniform numbers worn by players, coaches (c) and managers (m) on Yankees' active regular-season rosters. Numbers that have since been retired by the Yankees are denoted by boldface text.

Yogi Berra congratulates Roger Maris on hitting his 61st home run on Oct. 1, 1961.

1

Earle Combs 1929-35
George Selkirk 1934
Roy Johnson 1936
Frank Crosetti 1937-44
Tuck Stainback 1944
Snuffy Stirnweiss 1945-50
Billy Martin 1951-57
Bobby Richardson 1958-66
Bobby Murcer 1969-74
Billy Martin (m) .... 1975-79, '83, '85, '88

2

Mark Koenig 1929-30
Yats Wuestling 1930
Lyn Lary 1931-34
Red Rolfe 1931, 1934-42
Snuffy Stirnweiss 1943-44
Frank Crosetti 1945-46
Frank Crosetti (c) 1947-68
Jerry Kenney 1969-72
Matty Alou 1973
Sandy Alomar 1974-76
Paul Blair 1977-79
Darryl Jones 1979
Bobby Murcer 1979-83
Graig Nettles 1983
Tim Foli 1984
Dale Berra 1985-86
Wayne Tolleson 1986-90
Graig Nettles 1991
Mike Gallego 1992-94
Derek Jeter 1995-2009

3

Babe Ruth 1929-34
George Selkirk 1935-42
Bud Metheny 1943-46
Eddie Bockman 1946
Hal Peck 1946
Roy Weatherly 1946
Allie Clark 1947
Frank Colman 1947
Cliff Mapes 1948

Derek Jeter wears No. 2.

4

Lou Gehrig 1929-39

5

Bob Meusel 1929
Tony Lazzeri 1930-31
Frank Crosetti 1932-36
Nolen Richardson 1935
Joe DiMaggio ... 1937-42, '46-51
Nick Etten 1943-45

6

Tony Lazzeri 1929, 1934-37
Dusty Cooke 1930-31
Ben Chapman 1932-33
Joe Gordon .... 1938-43, '46
Don Savage 1944-45
Bobby Brown 1947-52
Mickey Mantle 1951
Andy Carey 1952-60
Deron Johnson 1960-61
Clete Boyer 1961-66
Charley Smith 1967-68
Roy White 1969-79
Brad Gulden 1980
Ken Griffey 1982
Roy White (c) .... 1983-84, '86
Mike Pagliarulo 1985
Rick Cerone 1987
Jack Clark 1988
Clete Boyer (c) 1988, 1992-94
Steve Sax 1989-91
Tony Fernandez 1995
Joe Torre (m) 1996-2007

7

Leo Durocher 1929
Ben Chapman .... 1930-31, '34-36
Jack Saltzgaver 1932
Tony Lazzeri 1933
Jake Powell 1936-38
Tommy Henrich 1939-42
Roy Cullenbine 1942
Billy Johnson 1943
Oscar Grimes 1944-46
Bobby Brown 1946
Aaron Robinson 1946
Chuck Dressen (c) 1947-48
Cliff Mapes 1949-51
Bob Cerv 1951
Mickey Mantle 1951-68
Mickey Mantle (c) 1970

8

Johnny Grabowski 1929
Bill Dickey 1930-43
Johnny Lindell 1944-45
Aaron Robinson .... 1945, '47
Frank Colman 1946
Bill Dickey (m) 1946
Yogi Berra 1948-63
Yogi Berra (c) .... 1963, '76-83
Yogi Berra (m) .... 1964, '84-85

9

Benny Bengough 1929
Bubbles Hargrave 1930
Cy Perkins 1931
Art Jorgens 1932-35
Joe Glenn 1933
Joe DiMaggio 1936
Myril Hoag 1937-38
Charlie Keller .... 1939-43, '45, '49
Ed Levy 1944
Tuck Stainback 1944
Hersh Martin 1944-45
Nick Etten 1946
Aaron Robinson 1946
George McQuinn 1947-48
Dick Wakefield 1950
Hank Workman 1950
Jim Brideweser 1951
Bobby Brown 1951
Hank Bauer 1952-59
Roger Maris 1960-66
Steve Whitaker 1968
Dick Simpson 1969
Ron Woods 1969-71
Graig Nettles 1973-82

10

Bill Dickey 1929
Benny Bengough 1930
Art Jorgens 1931
Tony Rensa 1933
George Pipgras 1932-33
Don Heffner 1934-37
Bill Knickerbocker 1938-40
Phil Rizzuto .... 1941-42, '46-56
Roy Weatherly 1943
Mike Garbark 1944-45
Tony Kubek 1958-65
Dick Howser 1967-68
Frank Fernandez 1969
Danny Cater 1970-71
Celerino Sanchez 1972-73
Chris Chambliss 1974-79
Rick Cerone 1980-84

11

Herb Pennock 1929
Ownie Carroll 1930
Waite Hoyt 1930
Lefty Gomez 1932-42
Tommy Byrne 1943
Rip Collins 1944
Joe Page 1945-50
Johnny Sain 1951-55
Jerry Lumpe 1956-59
Hector Lopez 1959-66
Bill Robinson 1967-69
Danny Walton 1971
Bernie Allen 1972-73
Fred Stanley 1973-80
Sandy Alomar 1974
Gene Michael (m) 1981-82
Jeff Torborg (c) 1983
Toby Harrah 1984
Billy Sample 1985
Gary Roenicke 1986
Lenn Sakata 1987
Don Slaught 1988-89
Rick Cerone 1990

Buck Showalter (c) 1991
Buck Showalter (m) 1992-95
Dwight Gooden......... 1996-97
Chuck Knoblauch 1998-2001
Chris Widger 2002
Erick Almonte...............2003
David Dellucci 2003
Curtis Pride 2003
Gary Sheffield........... 2004-06
Doug Mientkiewicz 2007
Morgan Ensberg 2008
Brett Gardner 2008-09

12

Waite Hoyt..................1929
George Pipgras 1930-31
Herb Pennock........... 1932-33
Jack Saltzgaver.......... 1934-37
Babe Dahlgren........... 1938-40
Buddy Rosar 1941-42
Oscar Grimes 1943
Mike Milosevich.............1944
Joe Buzas....................1945
Charlie Keller 1945-49
Vic Raschi....................1946
Ralph Buxton 1949
Ed Kleiman..................1949
Billy Martin 1950
Gil McDougald........... 1951-60
Billy Gardner............ 1961-62
Mike Hegan..................1964
Phil Linz 1965
Ruben Amaro............ 1966-68
Billy Cowan 1969
Ron Blomberg 1969, 1971-77
Jim Spencer............. 1978-81
Dave Revering 1981-82
Roy Smalley............. 1983-84
Ron Hassey 1985-86
Joel Skinner............. 1986-88
Tom Brookens 1989
Alvaro Espinoza.............1990
Jim Leyritz .... 1990-92, '99
Torey Lovullo 1991
Carlos Rodriguez............1991
Wade Boggs 1993-97
Roger Clemens..............1999
Denny Neagle 2000
Clay Bellinger 2001
Alfonso Soriano 2002-03
Kenny Lofton 2004
Tony Womack...............2005
Andy Phillips............ 2006-07
Kevin Thompson............2007
Alberto Gonzalez 2008
Ivan Rodriguez..............2008
Cody Ransom...............2009
Josh Towers.................2009

13

Spud Chandler..............1937
Lee Stine.....................1938
Cliff Mapes...................1948
Curt Blefary 1970-71
Walt Williams 1974-75
Bobby Brown 1980-81
Keith Smith 1985
Mike Pagliarulo 1986-89
Mike Blowers 1989
Alvaro Espinoza.............1990
Torey Lovullo 1991
Gerald Williams 1992
Jim Leyritz 1993-96,
.......................1999-2000
Charlie Hayes 1997
Willie Banks.................1998
Mike Figga.............. 1998-99
Jeff Manto 1999
Jose Vizcaino................2000
Michael Coleman 2001
Lee Mazzilli (c) 2002
Antonio Osuna...............2003
Alex Rodriguez........... 2004-09

14

George Pipgras 1929
Hank Johnson 1930-31
Ed Wells 1932
Russ Van Atta 1933-35
Bump Hadley 1936-40
Jerry Priddy............. 1941-42
Butch Wensloff..............1943
Monk Dubiel............. 1944-45
Bill Bevens...................1946
Cuddles Marshall............1946
Rugger Ardizoia.............1947
Ted Sepkowski 1947
Lonny Frey.............. 1947-48
Jerry Coleman 1948
Gene Woodling 1949-54
Bill Skowron 1955-62
Harry Bright 1963-64
Pedro Ramos............ 1964-66
Jerry Kenney................1967
Bobby Cox............... 1968-69
Ron Swoboda............ 1971-73
Lou Piniella 1974-84
Lou Piniella (c) 1984-85
Lou Piniella (m) 1986-88
Mike Blowers 1991
Pat Kelly 1991-97
Hideki Irabu 1998-99
Wilson Delgado..............2000
Luis Sojo.....................2000
Joe Oliver....................2001
Enrique Wilson........... 2001-04
Robinson Cano 2005

Spud Chandler wore No. 13 in 1937.

Russ Johnson 2005
Andy Phillips................2005
Miguel Cairo 2006
Kevin Thompson 2007
Matt DeSalvo 2007
Wilson Betemit........... 2007-08
Angel Berroa................2009
Eric Hinske..................2009

15

Hank Johnson 1929
Art Jorgens 1929
Roy Sherid............... 1930-31
Red Ruffing .... 1932-42, '46
Hank Borowy 1943-45
Charlie Keller 1945
Tommy Henrich.......... 1946-50
Tommy Henrich (c)..........1951
Archie Wilson 1952
Joe Collins 1953-57
Jim Pisoni................ 1959-60
Jack Reed....................1961
Tom Tresh............... 1961-69
Thurman Munson...... 1969-79

16

Tom Zachary............. 1929-30
Herb Pennock............ 1930-31
Gordon Rhodes..............1932
Wilcy Moore 1932-33
Jimmy DeShong 1934-35
Monte Pearson........... 1936-40
Johnny Lindell 1941
Tuck Stainback........... 1942-43
Joe Page 1944
Mel Queen...................1944
Herb Crompton..............1945
Frank Hiller 1946
Charley Stanceu.............1946
Bill Bevens.............. 1946-47
Ernie Nevel 1950
Whitey Ford........... 1953-67
Whitey Ford (c) ..1964, '68, '74-75

17

Fred Heimach................1929
Ed Wells 1930-31
Hank Johnson 1932
Danny MacFayden 1932-34
Jumbo Brown............ 1935-36
Babe Dahlgren...............1937
Tommy Henrich.......... 1938-39
Jake Powell 1939-40
Buster Mills 1940
Charley Stanceu.............1941
Ed Levy......................1942
Bill Zuber 1943-46
Mel Queen............... 1946-47
Vic Raschi............... 1947-53

Enos Slaughter........... 1954-59
Bobby Richardson........ 1955-56
Elmer Valo 1960
Bob Cerv................. 1960-62
Lee Thomas..................1961
Bobby Murcer............ 1965-66
Tom Shopay 1967
Gene Michael............ 1968-74
Mickey Rivers 1976-79
Oscar Gamble............ 1979-84
Vic Mata 1985
Mike Easler 1986-87
Paul Zuvella..................1987
Rafael Santana...............1988
Bucky Dent (m) 1989
Claudell Washington 1990
Scott Lusader 1991
Pat Sheridan 1991
Andy Stankiewicz 1992
Spike Owen..................1993
Luis Polonia............. 1994-95
Ruben Rivera 1995
Kenny Rogers............ 1996-97
Dale Sveum..................1998
Ricky Ledee............1999-2000
Dwight Gooden..............2000
Darren Bragg 2001
Gerald Williams 2001-02
Alex Arias....................2002
John Flaherty 2003-05
Nick Green...................2006
Chris Basak 2007
Jeff Karstens 2007
Shelley Duncan 2007-08
Justin Christian 2008
Steven Jackson 2009
Kevin Cash...................2009
Jerry Hairston, Jr.............2009

18

Wilcy Moore 1929
Bill Henderson 1930
Lou McEvoy..................1930
Tom Zachary.................1930
Red Ruffing 1931
Johnny Allen............ 1932-35
Art Jorgens 1936-39
Steve Peek...................1941
Johnny Lindell 1942-43
Johnny Johnson 1944
Tuck Stainback...............1945
Karl Drews...................1946
Randy Gumpert.......... 1946-48
Bob Porterfield........... 1948-50
Fenton Mole 1949
Dave Madison 1950
Jack Kramer..................1951
Bob Muncrief 1951
Ray Scarborough.............1952

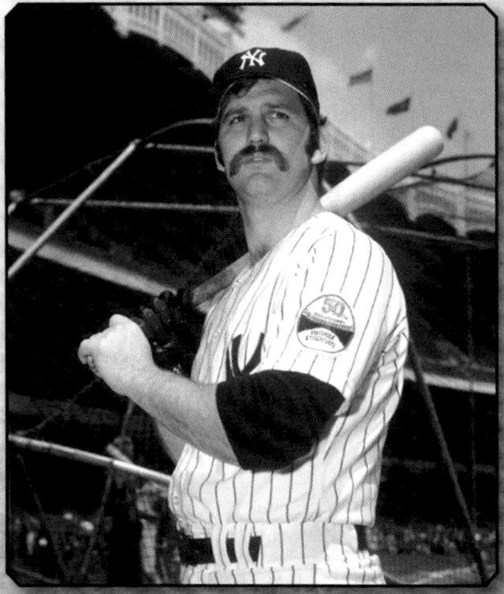

Thurman Munson's No. 15 was retired in 1979.

Jim McDonald 1952-54
Don Larsen 1955-59
Eli Grba 1960
Fred Kipp 1960
Hal Reniff 1961-67
Steve Barber 1967-68
Mike Kekich 1969-73
Dave Pagan 1973
Mike Hegan 1973-74
Larry Murray 1974
Dave Bergman 1975
Tippy Martinez 1976
Ellie Hendricks 1976-77
Dennis Sherrill 1978
Brian Doyle 1979-80
Larry Milbourne 1981-82
Mike Patterson 1982
Rodney Scott 1982
Andre Robertson 1982-85
Claudell Washington 1986-88
Jamie Quirk 1989
Deion Sanders 1989
Randy Velarde 1989-95
Mariano Duncan 1996-97
Andy Fox 1997
Mike Stanley 1997
Scott Brosius 1998-2001
Marcus Thames 2002
Jeff Weaver 2002-03
Homer Bush 2004
John Olerud 2004
Bubba Crosby 2005
Andy Phillips 2005
Johnny Damon 2006-09

19

Ed Wells 1929
Harry Rice 1930
Gordon Rhodes 1930-31
Lefty Weinert 1931
Jumbo Brown 1932-33
Johnny Murphy ...1934-41, '43, '46
Al Lyons 1944
Hersh Martin 1944
Larry Rosenthal 1944
Ken Holcombe 1945
Vic Raschi 1947
Karl Drews 1947-48
Dick Starr 1948
Cuddles Marshall 1949
Whitey Ford 1950
Bob Porterfield 1951
Spec Shea 1951
Jim McDonald 1952
Ray Scarborough 1953
Harry Byrd 1954
Art Schallock 1954
Bob Turley 1955-62
Stan Williams 1963-64
Bob Friend 1966
Fritz Peterson 1967-74
Dick Tidrow 1974-79
Rick Anderson 1979
Brad Gulden 1980
Dave Righetti 1981-90
Dion James 1992-93
Kevin Elster 1994
Bobby Ojeda 1994
Jack McDowell 1995
Luis Sojo 1996-2001
Luis Polonia 2000
Roberto Kelly 2000
Robin Ventura 2002-03
Aaron Boone 2003
Al Leiter 2005
Bubba Crosby 2004-06
Chris Basak 2007
Kevin Thompson 2007
Tyler Clippard 2007
Chad Moeller 2008
Ramiro Pena 2009

20

Myles Thomas 1929
Julie Wera 1929
Billy Werber 1930
Lefty Gomez 1931
Charlie Devens 1932
Johnny Murphy 1932
Don Brennan 1933
Burleigh Grimes 1934
Floyd Newkirk 1934
Harry Smythe 1934
Johnny Broaca 1935-37
Kemp Wicker 1937-38
Oral Hildebrand 1939-40
Tiny Bonham 1940-46
Cuddles Marshall 1946
Spec Shea 1947-49
Ernie Nevel 1950
Clint Courtney 1951
Art Schallock 1951-52
Willy Miranda 1953-54
Billy Hunter 1955-56
Marv Throneberry 1958-59
Joe DeMaestri 1960-61
Bill Kunkel 1963
Horace Clarke 1965-74
Ed Brinkman 1975
Eddie Leon 1975
Mickey Klutts 1976
Bucky Dent 1977-82
Edwin Rodriguez 1982
Rowland Office 1983
Bobby Meacham 1983-88
Keith Smith 1984
Alvaro Espinoza 1989-91
Bucky Dent (m) 1990
Mike Stanley .... 1992-95, '97
Mike Aldrete 1996
Robert Eenhoorn 1996
Jorge Posada 1997-2009

21

George Burns 1929
Gordon Rhodes ....1929, '31
Bill Henderson 1930
Red Ruffing 1930
Joe Sewell 1932-33
Johnny Broaca 1934
John Schulte (c) 1934
Pat Malone 1935-37
Spud Chandler ....1938-44, '46, '47
Johnny Cooney 1944
Bill Bevens 1944-45
Cuddles Marshall 1948
Fred Sanford 1949-50
Bob Kuzava 1951-54
Jim Konstanty 1954-56
Sonny Dixon 1956
Ralph Terry 1956-57
Sal Maglie 1957-58
Virgil Trucks 1958
Mark Freeman 1959
Tex Clevenger 1962
Johnny Keane (m) 1965-66
Roy White 1968
Jim Lyttle 1969
Nate Oliver 1969
Frank Tepedino 1970-71
Danny Walton 1971
Rusty Torres 1971-72
Bill Virdon (m) 1974-75
Cloyd Boyer (c) ....1975, '77
Bob Lemon (c) 1976
Jay Johnstone 1978
Bob Lemon (m) 1978-79,
.... 1981-82
Eric Soderholm 1980
Steve Kemp 1983-84
Dan Pasqua 1985-87
Jose Cruz 1988
Ken Phelps 1988-89
Hal Morris 1989
Mike Blowers 1990
Kevin Maas 1990
Deion Sanders 1990
Scott Sanderson 1991-92
Paul O'Neill 1993-2001
LaTroy Hawkins 2008

22

Gene Robertson 1929
Lefty Gomez 1930
Ivy Andrews 1931
Doc Farrell 1932-33
Johnny Broaca 1934
Lyn Lary 1934
Vito Tamulis 1934-35
Bob Seeds 1936
Tommy Henrich 1937
Roy Johnson 1937
Joe Beggs 1938
Mel Queen 1942
Marius Russo 1939-43
Russ Derry 1944
Bill Drescher 1944
Paul Waner 1945
Red Ruffing 1945-46
Allie Reynolds 1947-54
Rip Coleman 1955
Mickey McDermott 1956
Darrell Johnson 1958
Gary Blaylock 1959
Jim Bronstad 1959
Billy Short 1960
Bill Stafford 1960-65
Fred Talbot 1966-69
Jack Aker 1969-72
Ron Klimkowski 1972
Hal Lanier 1973
Jim Mason 1974-76
Gil Patterson 1977
Bobby Brown 1979
Ruppert Jones 1980
Jerry Mumphrey 1981-83
Omar Moreno 1983-85
Mike Fischlin 1986
Gary Ward 1987-89
Hal Morris 1989
Luis Polonia 1989-90
Mike Witt 1990
Stump Merrill (m) 1991
Scott Kamieniecki 1992
Jimmy Key 1993-96
Jorge Posada 1997
Mark Whiten 1997
Homer Bush 1998
Tony Tarasco 1999
Roger Clemens ..... 1999-2003, '07
Jon Lieber 2004
Robinson Cano 2005-06
LaTroy Hawkins 2008
Xavier Nady 2008-09

23

Tony Lazzeri 1932
Frank Makosky 1937
Steve Sundra 1940
Tiny Bonham 1946
Dick Kryhoski 1949
Fenton Mole 1949
Bob Porterfield 1951
Archie Wilson 1951
Bill Miller 1952-54
Tommy Byrne 1954-57
Murry Dickson 1958
Ralph Terry 1959-64
Rich Beck 1965
Jim Brenneman 1965
Billy Bryan 1966-67
Bob Tillman 1967
Ellie Rodriguez 1968
Don Nottebart 1969
John Ellis 1969-72
Jerry Moses 1973
Alex Johnson 1974-75
Oscar Gamble 1976
Stan Thomas 1977
Damaso Garcia 1978
Luis Tiant 1979-80
Barry Foote 1981-82
Don Zimmer (c) 1983
Don Mattingly.......... 1984-95
Don Mattingly (c) 2004-07

24

Lyn Lary 1929-30
Jim Weaver 1931
Sammy Byrd 1932
Billy Werber 1933
Charlie Devens 1934
Vito Tamulis 1934
Steve Sundra 1936
Spud Chandler 1937
Ivy Andrews 1937-38
Marv Breuer 1939-43
Al Lyons 1944
Paul Waner 1944
Steve Roser 1945
Gus Niarhos 1946
Billy Johnson 1946-51
Stubby Overmire 1951
Tom Gorman 1952-54
Ralph Branca 1954
Gerry Staley 1955-56
Al Cicotte 1957
Duke Maas 1958-60
Danny McDevitt 1961
Al Downing 1961-69
Ron Klimkowski 1970
Felipe Alou 1971-73
Otto Velez .... 1973-74, '76
Rick Bladt 1975
Mike Torrez 1977
Jimmy Wynn 1977
Mickey Klutts 1978
Gary Thomasson 1978
Dennis Werth 1979-81
Butch Hobson 1982
Lee Mazzilli 1982
John Montefusco 1983-84
Rickey Henderson 1985-89
Marcus Lawton 1989
Deion Sanders 1989
Mike Blowers 1990
Kevin Maas 1990-93
Russ Davis 1994-95
Tino Martinez ......1996-2001, '05
Ruben Sierra 2003-04
Sidney Ponson 2006
Robinson Cano 2007-09

Tino Martinez wore No. 24.

25

Ben Paschal ... 1929
Jimmie Reese ... 1930
Sammy Byrd ... 1933-34
Jesse Hill ... 1935
Ted Kleinhans ... 1936
Kemp Wicker ... 1936-37
Joe Vance ... 1937-38
Wes Ferrell ... 1938-39
Marius Russo ... 1939
Steve Sundra ... 1940
Eddie Kearse ... 1942
Aaron Robinson ... 1943
Larry Rosenthal ... 1944
Al Gettel ... 1945-46
Ray Mack ... 1947
Butch Wensloff ... 1947
Hank Bauer ... 1948-51
Jackie Jensen ... 1952
Irv Noren ... 1952-56
Zeke Bella ... 1957
Norm Siebern ... 1958-59
Kent Hadley ... 1960
Dale Long ... 1960
Jesse Gonder ... 1961
Joe Pepitone ... 1962-69
Pete Ward ... 1970
Len Boehmer ... 1971
Johnny Callison ... 1972-73
Bobby Bonds ... 1975
Grant Jackson ... 1976
Willie Randolph ... 1976
George Zeber ... 1977-78
Brian Doyle ... 1978
Tommy John ... 1979-82, '86-89
Stefan Wever ... 1982
Don Baylor ... 1983-85
Greg Cadaret ... 1989-92
Jim Abbott ... 1993-94
Scott Bankhead ... 1995
Ruben Sierra ... 1995-96
Cecil Fielder ... 1996
Ruben Sierra ... 1996
Joe Girardi ... 1996-99
Chris Turner ... 2000
Randy Velarde ... 2001
Jason Giambi ... 2002-08
Mark Teixeira ... 2009

26

Cedric Durst ... 1929
Sammy Byrd ... 1930
Jimmie Reese ... 1931
Joe Glenn ... 1932, 1935-38
George Uhle ... 1933-34
Johnny Broaca ... 1934
Buddy Rosar ... 1939-40
Ken Silvestri ... 1941
Ken Sears ... 1943
Steve Roser ... 1944, '46
Mike Milosevich ... 1945
Bill Drescher ... 1946
Karl Drews ... 1946
Marius Russo ... 1946
Don Johnson ... 1947, '50
Hugh Casey ... 1949
Tom Ferrick ... 1950-51
Ernie Nevel ... 1951
Art Schallock ... 1951
Gus Triandos ... 1953-54
Ryne Duren ... 1958-61
Tex Clevenger ... 1961-62
Dale Long ... 1962-63
Archie Moore ... 1964-65
John Kennedy ... 1967
John Miller ... 1966
Mike Ferraro ... 1968
Jimmie Hall ... 1969
Ron Klimkowski ... 1969
Frank Baker ... 1970-71
Fernando Gonzalez ... 1974
Rich Coggins ... 1975-76
Juan Bernhardt ... 1976
Cesar Tovar ... 1976
Domingo Ramos ... 1978
Juan Beniquez ... 1979
Johnny Oates ... 1980-81
Shane Rawley ... 1982-84
Neil Allen ... 1985
John Montefusco ... 1985-86

Tommy Byrne wore No. 28 from 1946-51 and again in 1954.

Joe Niekro ... 1985-86
Ivan DeJesus ... 1986
Bryan Little ... 1986
Paul Zuvella ... 1986
Rick Rhoden ... 1987-88
Stan Jefferson ... 1989
Steve Kiefer ... 1989
Jimmy Jones ... 1989-90
Steve Farr ... 1991-93
Daryl Boston ... 1994
Kevin Elster ... 1995
Darryl Strawberry ... 1995
Andy Fox ... 1996-97
Homer Bush ... 1997
Scott Pose ... 1997
Rey Sanchez ... 1997, 2005
Orlando Hernandez ... 1998-'02, '04
Mark Bellhorn ... 2005
Sal Fasano ... 2006
Koyie Hill ... 2006
Terrence Long ... 2006
Wil Nieves ... 2006-07
Jose Molina ... 2007-09

27

Sammy Byrd ... 1929
Cedric Durst ... 1930
Joe Sewell ... 1931
Myril Hoag ... 1932
Dixie Walker ... 1933-36
Zack Taylor ... 1934
Blondy Ryan ... 1935
Spud Chandler ... 1939
Joe Gallagher ... 1939
Lee Grissom ... 1940
Buster Mills ... 1940
Frenchy Bordagaray ... 1941
Mike Chartak ... 1942
Rollie Hemsley ... 1943-44
Russ Derry ... 1945
Johnny Lindell ... 1946-50
Lew Burdette ... 1950
Jackie Jensen ... 1951
Tom Morgan ... 1951
Jim Brideweser ... 1952-53
Bobby Brown ... 1954
Marlin Stuart ... 1954
Woodie Held ... 1954, '57
Bobby Del Greco ... 1957-58
Johnny James ... 1958
Jesse Gonder ... 1960
Frank Leja ... 1960
Jack Reed ... 1962-63
Duke Carmel ... 1965
Dick Schofield ... 1966
Tom Shopay ... 1967, '69
Jim Lyttle ... 1970-71
Rich McKinney ... 1972
Elliott Maddox ... 1974-76
Marty Perez ... 1977
Dell Alston ... 1977-78
Jay Johnstone ... 1978-79
Brad Gulden ... 1979
Darryl Jones ... 1979
Bobby Murcer ... 1979
Paul Blair ... 1980
Aurelio Rodriguez ... 1980-81
Butch Wynegar ... 1982-86
Keith Hughes ... 1987
Mark Salas ... 1987
Neil Allen ... 1988
Mel Hall ... 1989-92
Bob Wickman ... 1993-96
Graeme Lloyd ... 1996-98
Tony Fossas ... 1999
Allen Watson ... 1999-2000
Rondell White ... 2002
Luis Sojo ... 2003
Todd Zeile ... 2003
Kevin Brown ... 2004-05
Kevin Reese ... 2006
Kevin Thompson ... 2006
Darrell Rasner ... 2007
Joe Girardi (m) ... 2008-09

28

Liz Funk ... 1929
Art Jorgens ... 1930
Myril Hoag ... 1931, 1934-36
Ivy Andrews ... 1932
Joe Glenn ... 1933
Babe Dahlgren ... 1937
Frank Makosky ... 1937
Atley Donald ... 1938-45
Spud Chandler ... 1944-45
Hank Majeski ... 1946
Tommy Byrne ... 1946-51, '54
Bill Wight ... 1947
Tom Morgan ... 1951-52, 1954-56
Charlie Keller ... 1952
Bill Renna ... 1953
Art Ditmar ... 1957-61
Bud Daley ... 1961-64
Gil Blanco ... 1965
Steve Whitaker ... 1966-67
Andy Kosco ... 1968
Thurman Munson ... 1969
Ron Hansen ... 1970-71
Sparky Lyle ... 1972-78
Mike Griffin ... 1979
Bob Watson ... 1980-82
John Mayberry ... 1982
Steve Balboni ... 1983
Bill Monbouquette (c) ... 1985
Rod Scurry ... 1986
Henry Cotto ... 1987
Jerry Royster ... 1987
Al Leiter ... 1988-89
Jesse Barfield ... 1989
Marcus Lawton ... 1989
Hensley Meulens ... 1989
Dale Mohorcic ... 1989
Hal Morris ... 1989
Dave Eiland ... 1989, '91
Brian Dorsett ... 1990
Alan Mills ... 1990
Charlie Hayes ... 1992
Andy Stankiewicz ... 1993
Scott Kamieniecki ... 1993-96
Ruben Rivera ... 1996
Chad Curtis ... 1997-99
David Justice ... 2000-01
John Vander Wal ... 2002
Karim Garcia ... 2003
Charles Gipson ... 2003
Chris Latham ... 2003
Esteban Loaiza ... 2004
Ruben Sierra ... 2005
Melky Cabrera ... 2006-08
Anthony Claggett ... 2009
Brett Tomko ... 2009
Shelley Duncan ... 2009

29

Bob Shawkey (c) ... 1929
Lou McEvoy ... 1930
Bob Shawkey (m) ... 1930
Sammy Byrd ... 1931
Art Fletcher (c) ... 1932-39
George Washburn ... 1941
Oscar Grimes ... 1943
Bill Bevens ... 1944
Bill Drescher ... 1945-46
Johnny Murphy ... 1946
Steve Souchock ... 1946
Charley Stanceu ... 1946
Johnny Lucadello ... 1947
Sherm Lollar ... 1947-48
Charlie Silvera ... 1949-56
Bobby Richardson ... 1957
Fritz Brickell ... 1958-59
Hal Stowe ... 1960
Duke Maas ... 1961
Earl Torgeson (c) ... 1961
Hal Brown ... 1962
Tom Metcalf ... 1963
Mike Jurewicz ... 1965
Bobby Tiefenauer ... 1965
Bill Henry ... 1966
Rocky Colavito ... 1968
Mike McCormick ... 1970
Jim Hardin ... 1971
Wade Blasingame ... 1972
Casey Cox ... 1973
Sam McDowell ... 1973
Tom Buskey ... 1973-74
Dick Woodson ... 1974
Catfish Hunter ... 1975-79
Dave Collins ... 1982
Bob Shirley ... 1983-87
Al Holland ... 1987
Paul Zuvella ... 1987
Randy Velarde ... 1987-88
Luis Aguayo ... 1988
Dave LaPoint ... 1989
Jesse Barfield ... 1989-92
Mike Humphreys ... 1993
Andy Stankiewicz ... 1993
Gerald Williams ... 1994-96
Ricky Bones ... 1996
Mike Stanton ... 1997-2002, '05
Bubba Trammell ... 2003
Tony Clark ... 2004
Felix Escalona ... 2005
Tim Redding ... 2005
Octavio Dotel ... 2006
Kei Igawa ... 2007-08
Xavier Nady ... 2008
Cody Ransom ... 2008
Juan Miranda ... 2009
Francisco Cervelli ... 2009

30

Bots Nekola ... 1929
Gordon Rhodes ... 1929
Art Fletcher (c) ... 1930-31
Jimmy Burke (c) ... 1932
Cy Perkins (c) ... 1933
Joe Sewell (c) ... 1934-35
Earle Combs (c) ... 1936-39
Mike Chartak ... 1940
Norm Branch ... 1941-42
Jim Turner ... 1942-45
Bill Wight ... 1946
Dick Starr ... 1947

Eddie Lopat ... 1948-55
Rip Coleman ... 1955-56
Bobby Shantz ... 1957-60
Marshall Bridges ... 1962-63
Mel Stottlemyre ... 1964-74
Willie Randolph ... 1976-88
Bucky Dent (m) ... 1989
Willie Randolph (c) ... 1994-2004
Cory Lidle ... 2006
Matt Smith ... 2006
Scott Patterson ... 2008
David Robertson ... 2008-09

31

Roy Sherid ... 1929
Charles O'Leary (c) ... 1930
Jimmy Burke (c) ... 1931, '33
Cy Perkins (c) ... 1932
John Schulte (c) ... 1935-39
Art Fletcher (c) ... 1940-45
Red Rolfe (c) ... 1946
John Corriden (c) ... 1947-48
Jim Turner (c) ... 1949-59, '66-73
Johnny Sain (c) ... 1961-63
Jim Gleeson (c) ... 1964
Cot Deal (c) ... 1965
Mel Wright (c) ... 1974-75
Ed Figueroa ... 1976-80
Jeff Torborg (c) ... 1979
Dave Winfield ... 1981-90
Hensley Meulens ... 1990-91, '93
Mike Humphreys ... 1992
Bob Wickman ... 1992
Frank Tanana ... 1993
Xavier Hernandez ... 1994
Brian Boehringer ... 1995
Tim Raines ... 1996-98
Dan Naulty ... 1999
Brian Dorsett ... 1999
Ben Ford ... 2000
Glenallen Hill ... 2000
Lance Johnson ... 2000
Ed Yarnall ... 2000
Steve Karsay ... 2002-05
Jason Anderson ... 2005
Aaron Small ... 2005
Jose Veras ... 2006
Josh Phelps ... 2007
Edwar Ramirez ... 2007
Ian Kennedy ... 2008
Michael Dunn ... 2009

32

Art Jorgens ... 1929
Frank Barnes ... 1930
Ken Holloway ... 1930
Bill Karlon ... 1930
Dusty Cooke ... 1932
Eddie Phillips ... 1932
Tommy Henrich ... 1937
Steve Sundra ... 1938-39
Earle Combs (c) ... 1940-44
Johnny Neun (c) ... 1944-46
Johnny Neun (m) ... 1946
Ralph Houk ... 1947-52
Ralph Houk (c) ... 1953-54
Elston Howard ... 1955-67
Elston Howard (c) ... 1969-79

33

Charles O'Leary (c) ... 1929
Sam Gibson ... 1930
Jim Weaver ... 1931
Pete Appleton ... 1933
Charlie Devens ... 1933
Lee Stine ... 1938
John Schulte (c) ... 1940-48
Bill Dickey (c) ... 1949-57, '60
Randy Gumpert (c) ... 1957
Charlie Keller (c) ... 1957-59
Doc Medich ... 1974-75
Bob Lemon (c) ... 1976
Bobby Cox (c) ... 1977
Gene Michael (c) ... 1978
Mike Ferraro (c) ... 1979-82
Ken Griffey ... 1983-86
Tim Stoddard ... 1986
Claudell Washington ... 1986
Ron Kittle ... 1986-87
Jack Clark ... 1988
Steve Shields ... 1988
Bob Brower ... 1989
Scott Nielsen ... 1989
Eric Plunk ... 1989-91
Melido Perez ... 1992-95
Charlie Hayes ... 1996
David Wells ... 1997-98, 2002-03
Jose Canseco ... 2000
Ryan Thompson ... 2000
Alfonso Soriano ... 2000-01
Javier Vazquez ... 2004
Jaret Wright ... 2005
Kelly Stinnett ... 2006
Brian Bruney ... 2006-08
Nick Swisher ... 2009

34

Art Fletcher (m) ... 1929
Foster Edwards ... 1930
Lou McEvoy ... 1931
Ivy Andrews ... 1931-32
Frank Makosky ... 1937
Johnny Sturm ... 1941
Buddy Hassett ... 1942
Ed Bockman ... 1946
Ken Silvestri ... 1946-47
Bobo Newsom ... 1947
Jack Phillips ... 1948
Bob Cerv ... 1952
Harry Schaeffer ... 1952
Kal Segrist ... 1952
Tony Kubek ... 1957
Clete Boyer ... 1959-61
Bob Hale ... 1961
Phil Linz ... 1962-64
Mike Hegan ... 1966-67
Dick Howser (c) ... 1969-78
Lenny Randle ... 1979
Dick Howser (m) ... 1980
Dave LaRoche ... 1981-83
Roy Smalley ... 1982
Matt Keough ... 1983
Scott Bradley ... 1984-85
Mike Armstrong ... 1986
Doug Drabek ... 1986
Mike Ferraro (c) ... 1987-88
Bob Davidson ... 1989
Rich Dotson ... 1989
Don Schulze ... 1989
Walt Terrell ... 1989
Pascual Perez ... 1990-91
Mike Humphreys ... 1992
Jerry Nielsen ... 1992
Andy Cook ... 1993
Sterling Hitchcock ... 1993
Sam Militello ... 1993
Greg Harris ... 1994
Rob Murphy ... 1994
Bob MacDonald ... 1995
Mel Stottlemyre (c) ... 1996-2005
Jaret Wright ... 2006
Sean Henn ... 2007
Phil Hughes ... 2008
Damaso Marte ... 2008
A.J. Burnett ... 2009

35

Dixie Walker ... 1931
Spud Chandler ... 1937
Paul Schreiber (c) ... 1945
Aaron Robinson ... 1946
Yogi Berra ... 1947
Red Embree ... 1948
Mickey Witek ... 1949
Duane Pillette ... 1949-50
Joe Ostrowski ... 1950-52
Steve Kraly ... 1953
Johnny Schmitz ... 1953
Lou Berberet ... 1955
Ralph Houk (c) ... 1958-60
Ralph Houk (m) ... 1961-63, '66-73
Vern Benson (c) ... 1965-66
Don Gullett ... 1977-78
Bill Castro ... 1981
Roger Erickson ... 1982-83
Phil Niekro ... 1984-85
Bob Tewksbury ... 1986-87
Steve Trout ... 1987
Lee Guetterman ... 1988-92
Curt Young ... 1992
Andy Stankiewicz ... 1993
Paul Gibson ... 1993-1994
John Wetteland ... 1995-96
Hideki Irabu ... 1997
Clay Bellinger ... 1999-2000
Mike Mussina ... 2001-08

36

Mel Queen ... 1942
Bill Drescher ... 1945
Vic Raschi ... 1946
Jake Wade ... 1946
Al Lyons ... 1946-1947
Jack Phillips ... 1947-49
Dick Starr ... 1948
Johnny Mize ... 1949-53
Dave Madison ... 1950
Eddie Robinson ... 1954-56
Norm Siebern ... 1956
Harry Simpson ... 1957-58
Eddie Lopat (c) ... 1960
Wally Moses (c) ... 1961-62, '66
Loren Babe (c) ... 1967
Hal Lanier ... 1972
Pat Dobson ... 1973-75
Dock Ellis ... 1976-77
Stan Thomas ... 1977
Mike Torrez ... 1977
Rawley Eastwick ... 1978
Paul Lindblad ... 1978
Dave Rajsich ... 1978
Don Hood ... 1979
Paul Mirabella ... 1979
Jim Kaat ... 1979-80
Gaylord Perry ... 1980
Rick Reuschel ... 1981
Steve Balboni ... 1982
Mike Armstrong ... 1984-86
Al Holland ... 1986
Phil Lombardi ... 1986
Brad Arnsberg ... 1987
Jeff Moronko ... 1987
Rich Dotson ... 1988
Billy Connors (c) ... 1989-90, '94-95
Mike Humphreys ... 1991
Mike Witt ... 1991
Shawn Hillegas ... 1992
Dave Silvestri ... 1992
Russ Springer ... 1992
Gerald Williams ... 1993
David Cone ... 1995-2000
Bobby Estalella ... 2001
Nick Johnson ... 2002-03
Tom Gordon ... 2004-05
Mike Myers ... 2006-07
Jim Brower ... 2007
Ian Kennedy ... 2007
Edwar Ramirez ... 2008-09

37

Herb Karpel ... 1946
Gus Niarhos ... 1946
Bucky Harris (m) ... 1947-48
Casey Stengel (m) ... 1949-60

38

Marius Russo ... 1939
Hank Borowy ... 1942
Yogi Berra ... 1946
Frank Hiller ... 1946
Mel Queen ... 1946
Karl Drews ... 1947
Gus Niarhos ... 1948-50
Johnny Hopp ... 1950-52
Loren Babe ... 1952-53
Willy Miranda ... 1953
Art Schallock ... 1953-55
Johnny Blanchard ... 1955, 1959-65
Doc Edwards ... 1965
Frank Fernandez ... 1967-68
Len Boehmer ... 1969
Steve Kline ... 1970-74
Cecil Upshaw ... 1974
Ken Brett ... 1976
Carlos May ... 1976-77
Jerry Narron ... 1979
Tom Underwood ... 1980-81
Barry Evans ... 1982
Curt Kaufman ... 1982
Dave Stegman ... 1982
Dave LaRoche ... 1983
Jose Rijo ... 1984
Ed Whitson ... 1985-86
Leo Hernandez ... 1986
Pat Clements ... 1987-88
Hal Morris ... 1988
Scott Nielsen ... 1988
Clay Parker ... 1989-90
Matt Nokes ... 1990-94
Josias Manzanillo ... 1995
Jeff Patterson ... 1995
Matt Howard ... 1996
Homer Bush ... 1997
Scott Pose ... 1997
Ricky Ledee ... 1998
Jason Grimsley ... 1999-2000
Randy Choate ... 2001-03
Drew Henson ... 2003
Brett Prinz ... 2003
Travis Lee ... 2004
Buddy Groom ... 2005
Ramiro Mendoza ... 2005
T.J. Beam ... 2006
Kris Wilson ... 2006
Chase Wright ... 2007
Chris Stewart ... 2008
Dan Giese ... 2008
Brian Bruney ... 2009
Ian Kennedy ... 2009

39

Mike Chartak ... 1942
Rollie Hemsley ... 1942
Tommy Byrne ... 1946
Frank Hiller ... 1948-49
Wally Hood Jr. ... 1949
Loren Babe ... 1952
Harry Schaeffer ... 1952
Bob Wiesler ... 1954-55
Ted Gray ... 1955
George Wilson ... 1956
Darrell Johnson ... 1957
Jim Coates ... 1959-62
Steve Hamilton ... 1963-70
Gary Jones ... 1970-71
Rob Gardner ... 1971
Casey Cox ... 1972
Wayne Granger ... 1973
Jim Magnuson ... 1973
Larry Gura ... 1974-75
Gene Michael (c) ... 1976
Mickey Klutts ... 1977
Ron Davis ... 1979-81
Mike Morgan ... 1982
Ron Smalley Jr. ... 1982
Bert Campaneris ... 1983
Larry Milbourne ... 1983
Don Cooper ... 1985
Neil Allen ... 1985
Joe Niekro ... 1986-87
Pat Clements ... 1987
Roberto Kelly ... 1987-92
Mike Humphreys ... 1993
Mike Witt ... 1993
Donn Pall ... 1994
Dion James ... 1995-96
Brian Boehringer ... 1996
Paul Gibson ... 1996
Matt Luke ... 1996
Darryl Strawberry ... 1996-99
Mark Wohlers ... 2001
Ron Coomer ... 2002
Chris Hammond ... 2003
Andy Phillips ... 2004
Melky Cabrera ... 2005
Kevin Reese ... 2005
Shawn Chacon ... 2005-06
Craig Wilson ... 2006
Chris Britton ... 2007-08
Ross Ohlendorf ... 2008
Richie Sexson ... 2008
Anthony Claggett ... 2009
Mark Melancon ... 2009

40

Herb Karpel ... 1946
Roy Weatherly ... 1946
Cuddles Marshall ... 1948
Charlie Silvera ... 1948
Jackie Jensen ... 1950-51
Bob Wiesler ... 1951
Bobby Hogue ... 1951-52

Johnny Schmitz..............1952
Ewell Blackwell............ 1952-53
Tom Carroll 1955-56
John Gabler.............. 1959-60
Jack Cullen..................1962
Lou Clinton 1966-67
Bill Monbouquette....... 1967-68
Lindy McDaniel 1968-73
Rick Sawyer..................1974
Tippy Martinez............ 1974-76
Fran Healy 1976-78
Ron Davis...................1978
Bob Kammeyer 1978
Larry McCall 1978
Charlie Lau (c)........... 1979-81
Mickey Vernon (c) 1982
Don Zimmer (c) ....1983, '86
Gene Michael (c)......... 1984-86
Clyde King (c) 1988
Steve Shields 1988
Andy Hawkins 1989-91
Scott Kamieniecki............1991
Tony Cloninger (c)......1992-2001
Darren Holmes...............1998
Dan Miceli 2003
Gabe White 2003-04
C.J. Nitkowski 2004
Chien-Ming Wang........ 2005-09

41

Frank Hiller 1946
Steve Souchock..........1946, '48
Joe Collins 1949-52
Bob Cerv................. 1953-56
Marv Throneberry............1955
Zeke Bella 1957
Jake Gibbs............... 1962-71
Frank Tepedino 1972
Otto Velez 1973
Duke Sims 1974
Mike Wallace............. 1974-75
Rick Sawyer..................1975
Cliff Johnson............. 1977-79
George Scott.................1979
Jeff Torborg (c)........... 1980-83
Sammy Ellis (c)....... 1983-84, '86
Joe Cowley 1984-85
Scott Nielsen.................1986
Charlie Hudson 1987-88
Lance McCullers 1989-90
Stump Merrill (m) 1990
Darrell Evans (c)..............1990
Wade Taylor..................1991
Tim Burke....................1992
Russ Springer 1992
Jake Gibbs (c).................1993
Sterling Hitchcock... 1994-95,'01-03
Jorge Posada 1996
Brian Boehringer....1996-97,2001
Tony Cloninger (c)............1998
Denny Neagle 2000
Mike Buddie 1999
Ed Yarnall 2000
Jorge DePaula 2003
Miguel Cairo 2004
Randy Johnson 2005-06
Miguel Cairo 2007
Jose Veras 2007-09
Chad Gaudin.................2009

42

Bill Drescher 1946
Vic Raschi 1946
Butch Wensloff...............1947
Joe Collins 1948
Bud Stewart 1948
Jerry Coleman 1949-57
Jesse Gonder 1960
Pedro Gonzalez 1963-65
Ray Barker 1965-67
Charlie Spikes................1972
Doc Medich...................1973
Ken Wright...................1974
Bob Oliver 1975
Art Fowler (c) ...... 1977-79, '83, '88
Tom Morgan (c) 1979
Stan Williams (c) ..... 1980-82, '88
Clyde King (c) 1981
Clyde King (m) 1982
Jerry Walker (c)...............1982
Jerry McNertney (c) 1984
Doug Holmquist (c) 1984-85
Stump Merrill (c) 1985-87
Billy Connors (c)..............1989
Dave LaPoint............. 1989-90
John Habyan............. 1991-93
Domingo Jean 1993
Mariano Rivera.........1995-2009

43

Frank Hiller 1946
Vic Raschi....................1947
Art Schult....................1953
Deron Johnson 1960
Roger Repoz.............. 1964-66
Mike Ferraro 1966
Dale Roberts.................1967
Rob Gardner............. 1970-72
Terry Ley.....................1971
Jim Magnuson 1973
Jim Ray Hart 1973-74
Jim Deidel 1974
Rudy May................ 1974-76
Jim York 1976
Ken Clay................. 1978-79
Doug Bird................ 1980-81
George Frazier 1981-83
Jeff Torborg (c)...............1984
Rich Bordi....................1985
Tim Stoddard 1986-88
Lee Elia (c) 1989
Gene Michael (c) 1989
Jeff Robinson 1990
Torey Lovullo 1991
Jeff Johnson 1991-93
Sam Militello.................1992
Paul Assenmacher 1993
Bob Melvin 1994
Nardi Contreras (c) 1995
Dave Silvestri 1995
Jeff Nelson......... 1996-2000, '03
Todd Greene.................2001
Christian Parker..............2001
Ted Lilly......................2002
Raul Mondesi 2002-03
Jorge DePaula 2004
Scott Proctor............. 2005-07
Darrell Rasner................2008
Damaso Marte 2009

44

Bob Seeds 1936
Frank Verdi...................1953
Dick Tettelbach 1955
Gordie Windhorn 1959
Ken Hunt 1959-60
Jim Hegan (c) 1960-73
Bill Sudakis 1974
Terry Whitfield 1975-76
Reggie Jackson........ 1977-81
Jeff Torborg (c)........... 1984-88
John Stearns (c)..............1989
Mike Ferraro (c) 1990-91

45

Clint Courtney 1951
Don Bollweg..................1953
Lou Skizas 1956
Mark Freeman 1959
Roland Sheldon... 1961-62, '64-65
Roger Repoz..................1965
Jack Cullen............... 1965-66
John Miller...................1966
Steve Barber 1967
Stan Bahnsen 1968-71
Larry Gowell 1972
Rich Hinton...................1972
Ed Herrmann 1975
Jim Beattie............... 1978-79
Rudy May................ 1980-83
Dennis Rasmussen 1984-87
Bill Gullickson................1987
John Candelaria.......... 1988-89
Kevin Mmahat 1989
Steve Balboni 1990
Alan Mills 1991
Rich Monteleone.............1991
Danny Tartabull.......... 1992-95
Andy Fox 1995
Joe Girardi 1996
Cecil Fielder.............. 1996-97
Chili Davis 1998-99
Felix Jose 2000
Ryan Thompson 2000
Henry Rodriguez.............2001
Jay Witasick..................2001
Alberto Castillo 2002
Ted Lilly......................2002
Jason Anderson..............2003
Armando Benitez 2003
Felix Heredia............. 2003-04
Carl Pavano.......... 2005, '07-08
Sergio Mitre 2009

46

Frank Coleman...............1946
Charlie Silvera................1948
Dave Madison 1950
Bill Short.....................1960
Frank Tepedino 1969
Bobby Mitchell...............1970
Roger Hambright 1971
Otto Velez 1973
Rick Dempsey............ 1973-76
Gene Locklear 1976-77
Mike Heath 1978
Don Hood 1979
Joe Lefebvre 1980
Gene Nelson..................1981
Joe Pepitone (c)..............1982
Shane Rawley 1982
Don Mattingly 1982-83
Mike Pagliarulo 1984
Henry Cotto 1985-86
Juan DeJesus 1986
Rich Bordi....................1987
Roberto Kelly 1987
Jerry Royster.................1987
Hipolito Pena 1988
Randy Velarde 1988
Dallas Green (m) 1989
Stump Merrill (m) 1990
Joe Sparks (c)................1990
Frank Howard (c)......... 1991-93
Terry Mulholland.............1994
Donovan Osborne 2004
Alan Embree.................2005
Darrell May 2005
Scott Erickson................2006
Aaron Guiel..................2006
Jose Veras 2006
Andy Pettitte ...1995-2003, '07-09

47

Frank Colman................1947
Eli Grba 1959
Tom Sturdivant 1955-59
Billy Shantz 1960
Luis Arroyo 1960-63
Bob Schmidt..................1965
Stan Bahnsen 1966
Frank Tepedino 1967
Fred Beene 1972-74
Kerry Dineen.................1976
Larry Murray.................1976
Bob Lemon (m) 1978
Andy Messersmith 1978
Jim Kaat 1979
Jeff Torborg (c)...............1979
Bruce Robinson.......... 1979-80
Dennis Sherrill 1980
Curt Kaufman................1982
Ray Fontenot 1983-1984
Rod Scurry...................1985
Al Pulido.....................1986
Juan Bonilla..................1987
Pete Filson...................1987
Alvaro Espinoza..............1988
Scott Nielsen.................1988
Pat Corrales (c)...............1989
Champ Summers (c)...... 1989-90
Marc Hill (c)..................1991
Lee Smith....................1993
Dave Silvestri 1993-94
Dave Eiland 1995
Rick Honeycutt...............1995
Billy Brewer 1996
Dave Pavlas..................1996
Ruben Rivera 1996
Ivan Cruz 1997
Shane Spencer.........1998-2002
Erick Almonte................2003
Jesse Orosco.................2003
Al Reyes 2003
Brett Prinz 2004
Felix Rodriguez 2005
Ron Villone 2006-07
Colter Bean 2007
Chris Britton 2008
Sidney Ponson................2008
Freddy Guzman..............2009

48

Frank Colman................1947
John Gabler..................1959
Elvio Jimenez 1964
Pedro Ramos.................1964
Roy White............... 1965-68
Cecil Perkins 1967
Sam McDowell........... 1973-74
Dave Kingman 1977
Mike Torrez 1977
Clyde King (c) 1978
Jim Hegan (c) 1979-80
Joe Altobelli (c) ...... 1981-82, '86
Dale Murray 1983-85
Willie Horton (c)..............1985
Neil Allen 1987
Gene Michael (c) 1988
George Mitterwald (c)........1988
Frank Howard (c).............1989
Buck Showalter (c) 1990
John Ramos 1991
Russ Meyer (c) 1992
Rick Down (c) 1993-95
Don Zimmer (c).......... 1996-97
Chris Chambliss (c).....1998-2000
Randy Keisler 2001
Robert Perez 2001
Scott Seabol 2001
Brandon Knight..............2002
Jay Tessmer..................2002
Fernando Seguignol 2003
Paul Quantrill 2004-05
Wayne Franklin 2005
Kyle Farnsworth.......... 2006-08
Phil Coke 2008-09

49

Lou Berberet.................1954
Jim Bronstad.................1959
Bob Meyer...................1964
Stan Bahnsen 1966
Charlie Sands 1967
Loyd Colson 1970
Kerry Dineen.................1975
Ron Guidry.... 1975-88, (c) 2006-07
Jeff Johnson 1992

50

Ralph Houk..................1947
Bill Bryan 1967
Bill Burbach.............. 1969-71
Alan Closter.............. 1971-72
Doc Medich..................1972
Dave Pagan...................1973
Duke Sims 1973
Ken Clay 1977
Roger Slagle 1979
Clyde King (c) 1981
Lynn McGlothen 1982
John Pacella 1982
Jay Howell 1983-84
Marty Bystrom 1985
Phil Lombardi................1986
Jay Ward (c)..................1987
Chris Chambliss..............1988
Chris Chambliss (c)....... 1996-97
Steve Balboni 1989
Oscar Azocar.................1990
John Habyan..................1990
Alan Mills 1991
Ed Napoleon (c).......... 1992-93
Robert Eenhoorn......... 1994-95
Don Zimmer (c) 1998-99
Todd Erdos 2000
Rich Monteleone (c)...... 2003-04
Matt Lawton 2005
Larry Bowa (c)........... 2006-07
Bobby Meacham (c)..........2008
Mick Kelleher (c) 2009

51

George McQuinn............1947
Frank Leja................1954-55
Gordie Windhorn...........1959
Pete Mikkelsen...........1964-65
Ralph Houk (m)............1966
Tony Solaita..............1968
John Wyatt................1968
Ron Klimkowski............1969
Terry Whitfield...........1974
Larry McCall..............1977
Dom Scala (c)............1978-86
Cecilio Guante...........1987-88
Chuck Cary...............1989-91
Bernie Williams........1991-2006

52

Johnny Lucadello..........1947
Ken Silvestri.............1947
Jim Delsing...............1949
Wally Hood Jr.............1949
Tom Morgan................1951
Jim Coates................1956
Bobby Murcer..............1965
Fritz Peterson............1966
Joe Verbanic...........1967-1970
Larry Murray..............1974
Otto Velez................1975
Doyle Alexander...1976, '82-1983
Dave Rajsich..............1978
Mike Griffin...........1979-1981
Otis Nixon................1983
Mark Connor (c)....1984-87, '90-93
Juan Espino...............1985
Orestes Destrade..........1987
Dave Eiland...............1988
Bob Geren.................1988
Mike Ferraro (c)..........1989
Charlie Fox (c)...........1989
Mark Hutton............1994, '96
David Weathers...........1996-97
Joe Borowski..............1997
Pete Incaviglia...........1997
Danny Rios................1997
Mike Buddie...............1998
Ed Yarnall................1999
Don Zimmer (c)............2000
Gary Denbo (c)............2001
Jose Contreras...........2003-04
Joe Girardi...............2005
Tony Pena (c).............2006
Luis Vizcaino.............2007
Dave Eiland (c)...........2008
CC Sabathia...............2009

53

Bob Wiesler...............1951
Bill Skowron..............1954
Johnny Kucks.............1955-59
Johnny James.............1960-61
Ross Moschitto..........1965, '67
Dave Pagan...............1974-76
Ken Holtzman.............1976-78
Ron Davis.................1978
Larry McCall..............1978
Ray Burris................1979
Bob Kammeyer..............1979
Tim Lollar................1980
Jerry Walker (c)..........1981
Jay Howell...............1982-83
Lee Walls (c).............1983
Marty Bystrom.............1984
Neil Allen................1985
Orestes Destrade..........1987
Bob Geren................1989-91
Glen Sherlock (c)......1992, '94-95
Neal Heaton...............1993
Mark Hutton...............1993
Jose Cardenal (c)........1996-99
Alfonso Soriano...........2000
Mike Thurman..............2002
Don Zimmer (c)............2001
Lee Mazzilli (c)..........2003
Luis Sojo (c)............2004-05
Larry Bowa (c)............2006
Bobby Abreu..............2006-08
Melky Cabrera.............2009

54

Jim Delsing...............1950
Andy Carey................1952
Thad Tillotson...........1967-68
Ken Johnson...............1969
Gary Waslewski...........1970-71
Steve Blateric............1972
Jim Roland................1972
Jim Deidel................1974
Alex Johnson..............1974
Dave Bergman..............1977
Cecilio Guante............1987
Rich Gossage........1978-83, '89
Brian Fisher.............1985-86
Jay Buhner...............1987-98
Dale Mohorcic............1988-89
Tim Leary................1990-92
Sterling Hitchcock........1992
Bobby Munoz...............1993
Jeff Reardon..............1994
Joe Ausanio..............1994-95
Jim Mecir................1996-97
Todd Erdos...............1998-99
Lee Mazzilli (c).......2000-01, '06
Don Zimmer (c)...........2002-03
Roy White (c)............2004-05
Kevin Long (c)...........2007-09

55

Bob Grim.................1954-58
Zach Monroe..............1958-59
Spud Murray (c)..........1961-69
Dave McDonald.............1969
Paul Mirabella............1979
Roger Holt................1980
Andre Robertson...........1981
Roy Smalley...............1982
Stan Javier...............1984
Vic Mata..................1984
Juan Bonilla..............1985
Mike Fennell (c).........1987-89
Rich Monteleone......1990, '92-93
Brian Butterfield (c)....1994-95
Jorge Posada..............1996
Wally Whitehurst..........1996
Ramiro Mendoza.........1997-2002
Hideki Matsui............2003-09

56

Jim Bouton...............1962-68
John Cumberland..........1968-70
Mike McCormick............1970
Dave Righetti.............1979
Ted Wilborn...............1980
Bill Castro...............1981
Mike Patterson...........1981-82
Andre Robertson...........1982
Bert Campaneris...........1983
Curt Brown................1984
Rex Hudler...............1984-85
Al Leiter.................1987
Brian Dorsett.............1989
Mark Leiter...............1990
Dave Silvestri............1992
Andy Cook.................1993
Dave Pavlas...............1995
Dale Polley...............1996
Darrell Einertson..........2000
Ted Lilly.................2000
Juan Rivera...............2001
Todd Williams.............2001
Rick Down (c)............2002-03
Scott Proctor.............2004
Tanyon Sturtze...........2004-06
Tony Pena (c)............2007-09

57

Art Lopez.................1965
Roy Staiger...............1979
Clyde King (c)............1980
Tucker Ashford............1981
Bobby Ramos...............1982
Juan Bonilla..............1987
Bob Geren.................1988
Hensley Meulens...........1989
Steve Howe...............1991-96
Ramiro Mendoza............1996
Joe Borowski..............1998
Jeff Juden................1999
Jay Tessmer............1999-2000
Jake Westbrook............2000
Carlos Almanzar...........2001
Erick Almonte.............2001
Mark Wohlers..............2001
Karim Garcia..............2002
Drew Henson...............2002
Juan Acevedo..............2003
Michael Hernandez.........2003
Jorge DePaula.............2004
Alex Graman...............2004
Brad Halsey...............2004
Scott Proctor.............2004
Neil Allen (c)............2005
Joe Kerrigan (c).........2006-07
Mike Harkey (c)..........2008-09

58

Dooley Womack............1966-68
Bobby Brown...............1979
Bruce Robinson............1979
Andy McGaffigan...........1981
Dave Wehrmeister..........1981
Sammy Ellis (c)...........1982
Juan Espino............1982, '86
Mike O'Berry..............1984
Bob Geren.................1988
Hensley Meulens...........1989
Dave Eiland...............1990
Mike Jerzembeck...........1998
Alfonso Soriano...........1999
Randy Choate..............2000
Randy Keisler.............2001
Jorge DePaula.............2005
Alex Graman...............2005
Sean Henn.................2005
Mike Vento................2005
Colter Bean..............2005-06
T.J. Beam.................2006
Jeff Karstens............2006-07
Darrell Rasner............2006
Dave Eiland (c)...........2009

59

Damaso Garcia.............1979
Steve Adkins..............1990
Hensley Meulens...........1992
Billy Brewer..............1996
Ryan Bradley..............1998
D'Angelo Jimenez..........1999
Donzell McDonald..........2001
Juan Rivera..............2002-03
Rob Thomson (c)..........2007-09

60

Hipolito Pena.............1988
John Habyan...............1990
Darrin Chapin.............1991
J.T. Snow.................1992
Tim McIntosh..............1996
Homer Bush................1997
Mike Lowell...............1998
Craig Dingman.............2000
Brett Jodie...............2001
Nick Johnson..............2001
Brandon Knight............2002
Erick Almonte.............2003
Brandon Claussen..........2003
Felix Escalona............2004
Sam Marsonek..............2004
Wil Nieves...............2005-06
Ross Ohlendorf............2007

61

Marshall Brant............1980
Jim Lewis.................1982
Phil Lombardi.............1987
John Habyan...............1990
Jim Bruske................1998
Ted Lilly.................2001
Brad Halsey...............2004
Juan Padilla..............2004
Jorge DePaula.............2005
Darrell Rasner............2006
Matt DeSalvo..............2007
Billy Traber..............2008

62

Cloyd Boyer...............1975
Brian Dayett.............1983-84
Brad Arnsberg.............1986
Hal Morris................1988
Steve Adkins..............1990
Jorge Posada..............1995
Willie Banks..............1997
Jay Tessmer...............1998
Brandon Knight............2001
Bubba Crosby..............2004
Sean Henn.................2006
Joba Chamberlain.........2007-09

63

Mike Morgan...............1982
Jim Walewander............1990
Mike Figga................1997
Danny Rios................1997
Randy Keisler.............2000
Andy Cannizaro............2006
Alberto Gonzalez..........2007
Jonathan Albaladejo.....2008-09
Chris Britton.............2008

64

Bill Fulton...............1987
Steve Kiefer..............1989
Bronson Sardinha..........2007
Francisco Cervelli........2008

65

Clyde King (c)...........1981-82
Juan Espino...............1983
Adrian Hernandez.........2001-02
Phil Hughes..............2007-09

66

Bob Lemon (c).............1981
Steve Balboni............1981-83
Jim Deshaies..............1984
Juan Miranda..............2008

67

Clay Christiansen.........1984
Dale Mohoricic............1988

68

Dioner Navarro............2004

69

Alan Mills................1990

72

Juan Miranda..............2009

77

Humberto Sanchez..........2008

91

Alfredo Aceves...........2008-09

99

Charlie Keller............1952
Brian Bruney..............2009

Unknown:
Sam Gibson (1930), Roy Schalk (1932)

(c) denotes coach
(m) denotes manager

All-Time Opening Day Lineups

2009 at Baltimore
SS ... JETER
LF ... Damon
1B ... TEIXEIRA
DH ... Matsui
C ... POSADA
2B ... CANO
RF ... Nady
3B ... Ransom
CF ... GARDNER
P ... SABATHIA

2008 vs. Toronto
LF ... Damon
SS ... JETER
RF ... Abreu
3B ... RODRIGUEZ
1B ... Giambi
2B ... CANO
C ... POSADA
DH ... Matsui
CF ... Cabrera
P ... Wang

2007 vs. Tampa Bay
CF ... Damon
SS ... JETER
RF ... Abreu
3B ... RODRIGUEZ
DH ... Giambi
LF ... Matsui
C ... POSADA
2B ... CANO
1B ... Phelps
P ... Pavano

2006 at Oakland
CF ... Damon
SS ... JETER
RF ... Sheffield
3B ... RODRIGUEZ
1B ... Giambi
LF ... Matsui
C ... POSADA
DH ... Williams
2B ... CANO
P ... Johnson

2005 vs. Boston
SS ... JETER
3B ... RODRIGUEZ
RF ... Sheffield
DH ... Sierra
LF ... Matsui
C ... POSADA
1B ... Giambi
CF ... Williams
2B ... Womack
P ... Johnson

2004 at Tampa Bay
SS ... JETER
LF ... Matsui
3B ... RODRIGUEZ
1B ... Giambi
RF ... Sheffield
C ... POSADA
DH ... Sierra
2B ... Wilson
CF ... Lofton
P ... Mussina

2003 at Toronto
2B ... Soriano
SS ... JETER
1B ... Giambi
CF ... Williams
LF ... Matsui
C ... POSADA
3B ... Ventura
RF ... Mondesi
DH ... Johnson
P ... Clemens

2002 at Baltimore
2B ... Soriano
SS ... JETER
1B ... Giambi
CF ... Williams
3B ... Ventura
C ... POSADA
LF ... White
RF ... Spencer
DH ... JOHNSON
P ... Clemens

2001 vs. Kansas City
LF ... Knoblauch
2B ... Soriano
RF ... O'Neill
CF ... Williams
DH ... Justice
1B ... Martinez
C ... POSADA
SS ... Sojo
3B ... Brosius
P ... Clemens

2000 at Anaheim
2B ... Knoblauch
SS ... JETER
RF ... O'Neill
DH ... Williams
1B ... Martinez
CF ... Ledee
C ... POSADA
LF ... Spencer
3B ... Brosius
P ... Hernandez

1999 at Oakland
2B ... Knoblauch
SS ... JETER
RF ... O'Neill
CF ... Williams
1B ... Martinez
DH ... Davis
LF ... Ledee
3B ... Brosius
C ... Girardi
P ... Clemens

1998 at Anaheim
2B ... Knoblauch
SS ... JETER
RF ... O'Neill
CF ... Williams
1B ... Martinez
DH ... Davis
LF ... Curtis
3B ... Brosius
C ... Girardi
P ... PETTITTE

1997 at Seattle
SS ... JETER
3B ... Boggs
CF ... Williams
DH ... Fielder
1B ... Martinez
RF ... O'Neill
LF ... Strawberry
2B ... Duncan
C ... Girardi
P ... Cone

1996 at Cleveland
3B ... Boggs
2B ... Duncan
RF ... O'Neill
DH ... Sierra
1B ... Martinez
CF ... B. Williams
LF ... G. Williams
C ... Girardi
SS ... JETER
P ... Cone

1995 vs. Texas
3B ... Boggs
DH ... Leyritz
LF ... O'Neill
RF ... Tartabull
1B ... Mattingly
C ... Stanley
CF ... Williams
SS ... Fernandez
2B ... Kelly
P ... Key

1994 vs. Texas
LF ... Polonia
3B ... Boggs
1B ... Mattingly
DH ... Tartabull
RF ... O'Neill
C ... Stanley
CF ... Williams
SS ... Gallego
2B ... Kelly
P ... Key

1993 at Cleveland
CF ... Williams
3B ... Boggs
1B ... Mattingly
RF ... Tartabull
LF ... O'Neill
C ... Nokes
DH ... Maas
SS ... Owen
2B ... Kelly
P ... Key

1992 vs. Boston
SS ... Velarde
1B ... Mattingly
CF ... R. Kelly
LF ... Hall
DH ... Tartabull
C ... Nokes
RF ... Barfield
3B ... Hayes
2B ... P. Kelly
P ... Sanderson

1991 at Detroit
2B ... Sax
1B ... Mattingly
CF ... Kelly
DH ... Maas
LF ... Meulens
RF ... Barfield
C ... Leyritz
3B ... Blowers
SS ... Espinoza
P ... Leary

1990 vs. Cleveland
2B ... Sax
SS ... Espinoza
1B ... Mattingly
DH ... Winfield
LF ... Hall
RF ... Barfield
CF ... Kelly
C ... Geren
3B ... Blowers
P ... LaPoint

1989 at Minnesota
LF ... Henderson
2B ... Sax
DH ... Brookens
1B ... Balboni
RF ... Ward
3B ... Pagliarulo
C ... Slaught
SS ... Espinoza
CF ... R. Kelly
P ... John

1988 vs. Minnesota
LF ... Henderson
2B ... Randolph
1B ... Mattingly
DH ... Ward
RF ... Winfield
CF ... Kelly
3B ... Pagliarulo
C ... Skinner
SS ... Santana
P ... Rhoden

1987 at Detroit
CF ... Henderson
2B ... Randolph
1B ... Mattingly
DH ... Ward
RF ... Winfield
LF ... Pasqua
3B ... Pagliarulo
C ... Skinner
SS ... Tolleson
P ... Rasmussen

1986 vs. Kansas City
CF ... Henderson
2B ... Randolph
1B ... Mattingly
RF ... Winfield
DH ... Roenicke
LF ... Cotto
3B ... Berra
C ... Wynegar
SS ... Meacham
P ... Guidry

1985 at Boston
CF ... Moreno
2B ... Randolph
1B ... Mattingly
RF ... Winfield
DH ... Baylor
LF ... Griffey
3B ... Pagliarulo
C ... Wynegar
SS ... Meacham
P ... P. Niekro

1984 at Kansas City
CF ... Moreno
2B ... Randolph
LF ... Kemp
DH ... Baylor
RF ... Winfield
3B ... Harrah
1B ... Griffey
C ... Cerone
SS ... Foli
P ... Guidry

1983 at Seattle
2B ... Randolph
SS ... Smalley
LF ... Winfield
RF ... Kemp
DH ... Baylor
1B ... Griffey
3B ... Nettles
CF ... Mumphrey
C ... Wynegar
P ... Guidry

1982 vs. Chicago
2B ... Randolph
CF ... Mumphrey
RF ... Griffey
LF ... Winfield
1B ... Revering
DH ... Watson
3B ... Nettles
C ... Cerone
SS ... Dent
P ... Guidry

1981 vs. Texas
2B ... Randolph
CF ... Mumphrey
LF ... Winfield
1B ... Watson
RF ... Piniella
C ... Cerone
3B ... Nettles
DH ... Werth
SS ... Dent
P ... John

1980 at Texas
2B ... Randolph
CF ... Jones
1B ... Watson
RF ... Jackson
LF ... Piniella
DH ... Soderholm
3B ... Nettles
C ... Cerone
SS ... Dent
P ... Guidry

1979 vs. Milwaukee
CF ... Rivers
2B ... Randolph
C ... Munson
DH ... Johnson
1B ... Chambliss
3B ... Nettles
LF ... White
RF ... Blair
SS ... Dent
P ... Guidry

1978 at Texas
2B ... Randolph
CF ... Rivers
DH ... Munson
RF ... Jackson
LF ... Piniella
C ... Johnson
1B ... Chambliss
3B ... Nettles
SS ... Dent
P ... Guidry

1977 vs. Milwaukee
CF ... Rivers
LF ... White
C ... Munson
1B ... Chambliss
RF ... Jackson
3B ... Nettles
DH ... Wynn
2B ... Randolph
SS ... Dent
P ... Hunter

1976 at Milwaukee
CF ... Rivers
LF ... White
DH ... Munson
1B ... Chambliss
RF ... Gamble
3B ... Nettles
2B ... Randolph
C ... Dempsey
SS ... Mason
P ... Hunter

1975 at Cleveland
2B ... Alomar
LF ... Piniella
CF ... Bonds
RF ... Blomberg
3B ... Nettles
DH ... Herrmann
1B ... Chambliss
C ... Munson
SS ... Mason
P ... Medich

1974 vs. Cleveland
LF ... White
1B ... Hegan
C ... Munson
CF ... Murcer
RF ... Blomberg
3B ... Nettles
DH ... Sudakis
2B ... Michael
SS ... Mason
P ... Stottlemyre

1973 at Boston
2B ... Clarke
LF ... White
RF ... M. Alou
CF ... Murcer
3B ... Nettles
DH ... Blomberg
1B ... F. Alou
C ... Munson
SS ... Michael
P ... Stottlemyre

1972 at Baltimore
SS ... Kenney
3B ... McKinney
CF ... Murcer
LF ... White
1B ... Blomberg
RF ... Callison
C ... Munson
2B ... Allen
P ... Stottlemyre

1971 at Boston
2B ... Clarke
C ... Munson
LF ... White
CF ... Murcer
1B ... Cater
RF ... Lytle
3B ... Kenney
SS ... Michael
P ... Bahnsen

1970 vs. Boston
2B ... Clarke
C ... Munson
LF ... White
1B ... Ellis
3B ... Cater
CF ... Murcer
RF ... Blefary
SS ... Michael
P ... Stottlemyre

1969 at Washington
2B ... Clarke
CF ... Kenney
3B ... Murcer
LF ... White
1B ... Pepitone
SS ... Tresh
RF ... Robinson
C ... Gibbs
P ... Stottlemyre

1968 vs. California
2B ... Clark
3B ... Ferraro
1B ... Mantle
LF ... Tresh
RF ... Robinson
CF ... Pepitone
C ... Fernandez
SS ... Michael
P ... Stottlemyre

1967 at Washington
LF .... Tresh
RF .... Robinson
1B .... Mantle
CF .... Pepitone
C .... Howard
3B .... C. Smith
2B .... Clarke
SS .... Kennedy
P .... Stottlemyre

1966 vs. Detroit
2B .... Richardson
LF .... Tresh
RF .... Maris
CF .... Mantle
3B .... Boyer
1B .... Pepitone
C .... Howard
SS .... Amaro
P .... Ford

1965 at Minnesota
CF .... Tresh
2B .... Richardson
RF .... Maris
LF .... Mantle
C .... Howard
1B .... Pepitone
3B .... Boyer
SS .... Kubek
P .... Bouton

1964 vs. Boston
SS .... Linz
2B .... Richardson
RF .... Maris
CF .... Mantle
LF .... Tresh
1B .... Pepitone
C .... Howard
3B .... Boyer
P .... Ford

1963 at Kansas City
SS .... Kubek
2B .... Richardson
LF .... Tresh
CF .... Mantle
1B .... Pepitone
C .... Howard
RF .... Lopez
3B .... Boyer
P .... Terry

1962 vs. Baltimore
2B .... Richardson
SS .... Tresh
RF .... Maris
CF .... Mantle
C .... Howard
1B .... Skowron
LF .... Lopez
3B .... Boyer
P .... Ford

1961 vs. Minnesota
2B .... Richardson
LF .... Lopez
C .... Berra
CF .... Mantle
RF .... Maris
1B .... Skowron
SS .... Kubek
3B .... Boyer
P .... Ford

1960 at Boston
RF .... Maris
2B .... Richardson
3B .... McDougald
LF .... Lopez
CF .... Mantle
1B .... Skowron
C .... Howard
SS .... Kubek
P .... Coates

1959 vs. Boston
RF .... Bauer
LF .... Siebern
CF .... Mantle
C .... Berra
2B .... McDougald
1B .... Throneberry
3B .... Carey
SS .... Richardson
P .... Turley

1958 at Boston
RF .... Bauer
SS .... McDougald
CF .... Mantle
C .... Berra
1B .... Skowron
LF .... Howard
3B .... Carey
2B .... Richardson
P .... Larsen

1957 vs. Washington
RF .... Bauer
2B .... Martin
CF .... Mantle
C .... Berra
1B .... Skowron
SS .... McDougald
LF .... Howard
3B .... Carey
P .... Ford

1956 at Washington
RF .... Bauer
SS .... Lumpe
CF .... Mantle
C .... Berra
1B .... Skowron
2B .... Martin
LF .... Howard
3B .... Carey
P .... Larsen

1955 vs. Washington
2B .... McDougald
3B .... Carey
CF .... Mantle
C .... Berra
1B .... Skowron
RF .... Bauer
LF .... Cerv
SS .... Rizzuto
P .... Ford

1954 at Washington
RF .... Bauer
1B .... Collins
CF .... Mantle
C .... Berra
3B .... McDougald
LF .... Woodling
2B .... Coleman
SS .... Rizzuto
P .... Ford

1953 vs. Philadelphia
SS .... Rizzuto
1B .... Collins
RF .... Bauer
CF .... Mantle
C .... Berra
LF .... Woodling
3B .... McDougald
2B .... Martin
P .... Raschi

1952 at Philadelphia
SS .... Rizzuto
CF .... Jensen
RF .... Mantle
3B .... McDougald
LF .... Bauer
1B .... Mize
2B .... Coleman
C .... Silvera
P .... Raschi

Singer Paul Simon throws out the ceremonial first pitch for the 1969 home opener.

1951 vs. Boston
LF .... Jensen
SS .... Rizzuto
RF .... Mantle
CF .... DiMaggio
C .... Berra
1B .... Mize
3B .... Johnson
2B .... Coleman
P .... Raschi

1950 at Boston
SS .... Rizzuto
1B .... Henrich
RF .... Bauer
CF .... DiMaggio
C .... Berra
3B .... Johnson
LF .... Lindell
2B .... Coleman
P .... Reynolds

1949 vs. Washington
2B .... Stirnweiss
SS .... Rizzuto
CF .... Woodling
RF .... Henrich
LF .... Bauer
3B .... Brown
1B .... Kryhoski
C .... Niarhos
P .... Lopat

1948 at Washington
2B .... Stirnweiss
RF .... Henrich
LF .... Keller
CF .... DiMaggio
1B .... McQuinn
3B .... Johnson
SS .... Rizzuto
C .... Niarhos
P .... Reynolds

1947 vs. Philadelphia
SS .... Rizzuto
2B .... Stirnweiss
1B .... McQuinn
LF .... Keller
RF .... Berra
CF .... Lindell
3B .... Johnson
C .... Robinson
P .... Chandler

1946 at Philadelphia
SS .... Crosetti
3B .... Stirnweiss
RF .... Henrich
CF .... DiMaggio
1B .... Etten
LF .... Lindell
C .... Dickey
2B .... Grimes
P .... Chandler

1945 vs. Boston
2B .... Stirnweiss
LF .... Martin
RF .... Derry
CF .... Lindell
1B .... Etten
SS .... Buzas
3B .... Savage
C .... Garbark
P .... Donald

1944 at Boston
2B .... Stirnweiss
RF .... Metheny
1B .... Etten
CF .... Lindell
3B .... Savage
LF .... Levy
SS .... Grimes
C .... Garbark
P .... Borowy

1943 vs. Washington
SS .... Stirnweiss
CF .... Weatherly
LF .... Keller
2B .... Gordon
1B .... Etten
3B .... Johnson
C .... Dickey
RF .... Lindell
P .... Bonham

1942 at Washington
3B .... Priddy
SS .... Rizzuto
RF .... Henrich
CF .... DiMaggio
LF .... Keller
2B .... Gordon
C .... Dickey
1B .... Levy
P .... Ruffing

1941 at Washington
SS .... Rizzuto
3B .... Rolfe
RF .... Henrich
CF .... DiMaggio
LF .... Keller
2B .... Gordon
C .... Dickey
1B .... Sturm
P .... Russo

1940 at Philadelphia
SS .... Crosetti
3B .... Rolfe
RF .... Selkirk
LF .... Keller
C .... Dickey
2B .... Gordon
CF .... Henrich
1B .... Dahlgren
P .... Ruffing

1939 vs. Boston
SS .... Crosetti
3B .... Rolfe
LF .... Powell
CF .... DiMaggio
1B .... Gehrig
C .... Dickey
RF .... Gallagher
2B .... Gordon
P .... Ruffing

1938 at Boston
SS .... Crosetti
3B .... Rolfe
LF .... Selkirk
1B .... Gehrig
C .... Dickey
RF .... Henrich
CF .... Hoag
2B .... Gordon
P .... Ruffing

1937 vs. Washington
SS .... Crosetti
3B .... Rolfe
LF .... Johnson
1B .... Gehrig
C .... Dickey
RF .... Selkirk
2B .... Lazzeri
CF .... Hoag
P .... Gomez

1936 at Washington
3B .... Rolfe
LF .... Johnson
RF .... Selkirk
1B .... Gehrig
C .... Dickey
CF .... Chapman
2B .... Lazzeri
SS .... Crosetti
P .... Gomez

1935 vs. Boston
LF .... Combs
3B .... Rolfe
RF .... Selkirk
1B .... Gehrig
C .... Dickey
CF .... Chapman
2B .... Lazzeri
SS .... Crosetti
P .... Gomez

1934 at Philadelphia
CF .... Combs
SS .... Rolfe
LF .... Ruth
1B .... Gehrig
RF .... Chapman
3B .... Lazzeri
C .... Dickey
2B .... Heffner
P .... Gomez

1933 vs. Boston
CF .... Combs
3B .... Sewell
RF .... Ruth
1B .... Gehrig
LF .... Chapman
2B .... Lazzeri
C .... Dickey
SS .... Crosetti
P .... Gomez

1932 at Philadelphia
CF .... Byrd
2B .... Saltzgaver
LF .... Ruth
1B .... Gehrig
RF .... Chapman
3B .... Crosetti
C .... Dickey
SS .... Lary
P .... Gomez

1931 vs. Boston
CF.......... Combs
SS.............Lary
RF............ Ruth
1B.......... Gehrig
3B.......... Lazzeri
2B........ Chapman
LF............Cooke
C............ Dickey
P...........Ruffing

1930 at Philadelphia
CF.......... Combs
SS..........Koenig
LF............ Ruth
1B.......... Gehrig
2B.......... Lazzeri
RF...........Cooke
3B........ Chapman
C............ Dickey
P...........Pipgras

1929 vs. Boston
CF.......... Combs
3B..........Koenig
RF............ Ruth
1B.......... Gehrig
LF..........Meusel
2B.......... Lazzeri
SS.........Durocher
C........Grabowski
P...........Pipgras

1928 at Philadelphia
CF.......... Combs
SS..........Koenig
LF............ Ruth
1B.......... Gehrig
RF..........Meusel
3B.......... Dugan
2B.........Durocher
C.......... Collins
P..........Pennock

1927 vs. Philadelphia
CF.......... Combs
SS..........Koenig
RF............ Ruth
1B.......... Gehrig
LF..........Meusel
2B.......... Lazzeri
3B.......... Dugan
C........Grabowski
P............. Hoyt

1926 at Boston
SS..........Koenig
CF.......... Combs
1B.......... Gehrig
LF............ Ruth
RF..........Meusel
2B.......... Lazzeri
3B.......... Dugan
C........... Collins
P......... Shawkey

1925 vs. Washington
RF..........Paschal
3B.......... Dugan
CF.......... Combs
LF..........Meusel
1B.............Pipp
2B......... A. Ward
SS............Scott
C.......... O'Neill
P..........Shocker

1924 at Boston
CF.............Witt
3B.......... Dugan
LF............ Ruth
1B.............Pipp
RF..........Meusel
2B............Ward
C...........Schang
SS............Scott
P......... Shawkey

1923 vs. Boston
CF.............Witt
3B.......... Dugan
RF............ Ruth
1B.............Pipp
LF..........Meusel
C...........Schang
2B............Ward
SS............Scott
P......... Shawkey

1922 at Washington
CF............ Miller
LF.......... Fewster
3B............Baker
RF........McMillan
1B.............Pipp
2B............Ward
SS............Scott
C...........Schang
P............ Jones

1921 vs. Philadelphia
2B......... Fewster
SS.....Peckinpaugh
LF............ Ruth
1B.............Pipp
RF..........Meusel
CF........... Bodie
3B............Ward
C...........Schang
P.............Mays

1920 at Philadelphia
RF...........Gleich
SS.....Peckinpaugh
1B.............Pipp
CF............ Ruth
LF............Lewis
3B..........Meusel
2B............ Pratt
C..............Ruel
P......... Shawkey

1919 vs. Boston
RF.............Vick
SS.....Peckinpaugh
1B.............Pipp
3B............Baker
2B............ Pratt
CF........... Lewis
LF........... Bodie
C.......... Hannah
P........ Mogridge

1918 at Washington
RF........Gilhooley
CF............ Miller
2B............ Pratt
1B.............Pipp
3B............Baker
LF........... Bodie
SS.....Peckinpaugh
C.......... Hannah
P........ Mogridge

1917 vs. Boston
RF........Gilhooley
LF............ High
2B...........Maisel
1B.............Pipp
3B............Baker
CF.......... Magee
SS.....Peckinpaugh
C....... Nunamaker
P..........Caldwell

1916 vs. Washington
CF.......... Maisel
RF........Gilhooley
LF.......... Magee
3B............Baker
2B......... Gedeon
1B.............Pipp
SS.....Peckinpaugh
C....... Nunamaker
P..........Caldwell

Yankees Managers on Opening Day

MANAGER	G	W	L	PCT.
Joe McCarthy*	16	10	6	.625
Miller Huggins*	12	9	3	.750
Casey Stengel*	12	10	2	.833
Joe Torre*	12	7	5	.583
Ralph Houk	10	5	5	.500
Clark Griffith	6	5	1	.833
Billy Martin	5	2	3	.400
Buck Showalter*	4	4	0	1.000
Yogi Berra	3	0	3	.000
Bill Donovan	3	0	3	.000
Frank Chance	2	1	1	.500
JOE GIRARDI*	**2**	**1**	**1**	**.500**
Bucky Harris	2	1	1	.500
Johnny Keane	2	0	2	.000
Bob Lemon	2	0	2	.000
Lou Piniella*	2	2	0	1.000
George Stallings+	2	0	1	.000 (1 tie)
Bill Virdon*	2	1	1	.500
Hal Chase	1	1	0	1.000
Dallas Green*	1	1	0	1.000
Bucky Dent	1	1	0	1.000
Dick Howser	1	0	1	.000
Stump Merrill	1	0	1	.000
Gene Michael*	1	1	0	1.000
Bob Shawkey	1	0	1	.000
Harry Wolverton	1	0	1	.000
Total	**107**	**62**	**44**	**.585 (1 tie)**

* Won Yankees managerial debut on Opening Day.
+ 1910 opener called due to darkness tied 4-4.

1915 at Washington
3B...........Maisel
LF............ High
CF............ Cree
1B.............Pipp
RF............Cook
SS.....Peckinpaugh
2B............Boone
C.........Sweeney
P..........Warhop

1914 vs. Philadelphia
3B...........Maisel
2B.......... Hartzell
LF...........Walsh
1B.........Williams
CF.......... Holden
RF............Cook
SS.....Peckinpaugh
C.........Sweeney
P...........McHale

1913 at Washington
RF..........Daniels
CF.......... Wolter
3B......... Hartzell
LF.............Cree
2B...........Chase
1B..........Sterrett
C.........Sweeney
SS...........Young
P....... McConnell

1912 vs. Boston
RF.......... Wolter
CF......... Daniels
1B...........Chase
LF.............Cree
SS.......... Hartzell
3B...........Dolan
2B.........Gardner
C.............Street
P..........Caldwell

1911 at Philadelphia
RF.......... Wolter
CF....... Hemphill
1B...........Chase
3B......... Hartzell
2B.......... Knight
LF.............Cree
SS..........Johnson
C.............Blair
P.......... Vaughn

1910 vs. Boston
CF....... Hemphill
RF.......... Wolter
1B...........Chase
LF........... Engle
2B.........Gardner
SS...........Foster
3B...........Austin
C.........Sweeney
P.......... Vaughn

1909 at Washington
CF....... Hemphill
RF...........Keeler
3B........Elberfeld
LF........... Engle
1B............Ward
2B.............. Ball
SS.......... Knight
C..........Kleinow
P..........Newton

1908 vs. Washington
2B............Niles
RF...........Keeler
LF............Stahl
SS........Elberfeld
1B...........Chase
CF....... Hemphill
3B..........Conroy
C..........Kleinow
P............ Doyle

1907 at Washington
CF........ Hoffman
RF...........Keeler
SS........Elberfeld
2B.........Williams
3B......... LaPorte
LF..........Conroy
1B.........Moriarty
C..........Kleinow
P............. Orth

1906 vs. Boston
LF...... Dougherty
RF...........Keeler
SS........Elberfeld
3B......... LaPorte
2B.........Williams
CF.......... Conroy
1B...........Chase
C..........McGuire
P..........Chesbro

1905 at Washington
LF...... Dougherty
RF...........Keeler
SS........Elberfeld
2B.........Williams
CF....... Anderson
3B..........Conroy
1B...........Chase
C..........Kleinow
P..........Chesbro

1904 vs. Boston
3B..........Conroy
CF.............Fultz
RF...........Keeler
SS........Elberfeld
LF....... Anderson
2B.........Williams
1B..........Ganzel
C..........McGuire
P..........Chesbro

1903 at Washington
LF............Davis
RF...........Keeler
CF.............Fultz
2B.........Williams
1B..........Ganzel
3B..........Conroy
SS.............Long
C.........O'Connor
P..........Chesbro

2009 Opening Day Roster

PITCHERS (12): RHP Jonathan Albaladejo, RHP Brian Bruney, RHP A.J. Burnett, RHP Joba Chamberlain, LHP Phil Coke, LHP Damaso Marte, LHP Andy Pettitte, RHP Edwar Ramirez, RHP Mariano Rivera, LHP CC Sabathia, RHP Jose Veras, RHP Chien-Ming Wang. **CATCHERS (2):** Jose Molina, Jorge Posada. **INFIELDERS (5):** Robinson Cano, Derek Jeter, Ramiro Pena, Cody Ransom, Mark Teixeira. **OUTFIELDERS (6):** Melky Cabrera, Johnny Damon, Brett Gardner, Hideki Matsui, Xavier Nady, Nick Swisher. **DISABLED LIST (1):** Alex Rodriguez

All-Time Opening Day Results

YEAR	OPPONENT	W/L	SCORE	WP	LP
2009	at Baltimore	L	10-5	Guthrie	Sabathia
2008	vs. Toronto	W	3-2	Wang	Halladay
2007	vs. Tampa Bay	W	9-5	Vizcaino	Stokes
2006	at Oakland	W	15-2	Johnson	Zito
2005	vs. Boston	W	9-2	Johnson	Wells
2004	at Tampa Bay*	L	8-3	Zambrano	Mussina
2003	at Toronto	W	8-4	Clemens	Halladay
2002	at Baltimore	L	10-3	Erickson	Clemens
2001	vs. Kansas City	W	7-3	Clemens	Suppan
2000	at Anaheim	W	3-2	Hernandez	Hill
1999	at Oakland	L	5-3 (8)	Matthews	Stanton
1998	at Anaheim	L	4-1	Finley	Pettitte
1997	at Seattle	L	4-2	Fassero	Cone
1996	at Cleveland	W	7-3	Cone	Martinez
1995	vs. Texas	W	8-6	Key	Rogers
1994	vs. Texas	W	5-3	Key	Brown
1993	at Cleveland	W	9-1	Key	Nagy
1992	vs. Boston	W	4-3	Sanderson	Clemens
1991	at Detroit	L	6-4	Gibson	Cadaret
1990	vs. Cleveland	W	6-4	Plunk	Orosco
1989	at Minnesota	W	4-2	John	Viola
1988	vs. Minnesota	W	8-0	Rhoden	Viola
1987	at Detroit	W	2-1 (10)	Righetti	Morris
1986	vs. Kansas City	W	4-2	Guidry	Black
1985	at Boston	L	9-2	Boyd	Niekro
1984	at Kansas City	L	4-2	Black	Guidry
1983	at Seattle	L	5-4	Clark	Erickson
1982	vs. Chicago (AL)	L	7-6 (12)	Hickey	Gossage
1981	vs. Texas	W	10-3	John	Matlack
1980	at Texas	L	1-0 (12)	Lyle	Underwood
1979	vs. Milwaukee	L	5-1	Caldwell	Guidry
1978	at Texas	L	2-1	Matlack	Gossage
1977	vs. Milwaukee	W	3-0	Hunter	Travers
1976	at Milwaukee	L	5-0	Slaton	Hunter
1975	at Cleveland	L	5-3	Perry	Medich
1974	vs. Cleveland	W	6-1	Stottlemyre	Perry
1973	at Boston	L	15-5	Tiant	Stottlemyre
1972	at Baltimore	L	3-1	Dobson	Stottlemyre
1971	at Boston	L	3-1	Culp	Bahnsen
1970	vs. Boston	L	4-3	Peters	Stottlemyre
1969	at Washington	W	8-4	Stottlemyre	Pascual
1968	vs. California	W	1-0	Stottlemyre	Brunet
1967	at Washington	W	8-0	Stottlemyre	Richert
1966	vs. Detroit	L	2-1	Lolich	Ford
1965	at Minnesota	L	5-4(11)	Fosnow	Ramos
1964	vs. Boston	L	4-3(11)	Radatz	Ford
1963	at Kansas City	W	8-2	Terry	Segui
1962	vs. Baltimore	W	7-6	Terry	Brown
1961	vs. Minnesota	L	6-0	Ramos	Ford
1960	at Boston	W	8-4	Coates	Brewer
1959	vs. Boston	W	3-2	Turley	Brewer
1958	at Boston	W	3-0	Larsen	Nixon
1957	vs. Washington	W	2-1	Ford	Stobbs
1956	at Washington	W	10-4	Larsen	Pascual
1955	vs. Washington	W	19-1	Ford	McDermott
1954	at Washington	L	5-3	Dixon	Reynolds
1953	vs. Philadelphia	L	5-0	Kellner	Raschi
1952	at Philadelphia	W	8-1	Raschi	Kellner
1951	vs. Boston	W	5-0	Raschi	Wight
1950	at Boston	W	15-10	Johnson	Masterson
1949	vs. Washington	W	3-2	Lopat	Hudson
1948	at Washington	W	12-4	Reynolds	Wynn
1947	vs. Philadelphia	L	6-1	Marchildon	Chandler
1946	at Philadelphia	W	5-0	Chandler	Christopher
1945	vs. Boston	W	8-4	Donald	Cecil
1944	at Boston	W	3-0	Borowy	Terry
1943	vs. Washington	W	5-4	Murphy	Haeffner
1942	at Washington	W	7-0	Ruffing	Hudson
1941	at Washington	W	3-0	Russo	Leonard
1940	at Philadelphia	L	2-1 (10)	Dean	Ruffing
1939	vs. Boston	W	2-0	Ruffing	Grove
1938	at Boston	L	8-4	Bagby	Ruffing
1937	vs. Washington	L	3-2	Weaver	Gomez
1936	at Washington	L	1-0	Newsom	Gomez
1935	vs. Boston	L	1-0	Ferrell	Gomez
1934	at Philadelphia	L	6-5	Cascarella	Smythe
1933	vs. Boston	W	4-3	Gomez	Andrews
1932	at Philadelphia	W	12-6	Gomez	Earnshaw
1931	vs. Boston	W	6-3	Ruffing	Moore
1930	at Philadelphia	L	6-2	Grove	Pipgras
1929	vs. Boston	W	7-3	Pipgras	Ruffing
1928	at Philadelphia	W	8-3	Pennock	Grove
1927	vs. Philadelphia	W	8-3	Hoyt	Grove
1926	at Boston	W	12-11	Shawkey	Ehmke
1925	vs. Washington	W	5-1	Shocker	Mogridge
1924	at Boston	W	2-1	Shawkey	Ehmke
1923	vs. Boston	W	4-1	Shawkey	Ehmke
1922	at Washington	L	6-5	Mogridge	Jones
1921	vs. Philadelphia	W	11-1	Mays	Perry
1920	at Philadelphia	L	3-1	Perry	Shawkey
1919	vs. Boston	L	10-0	Mays	Mogridge
1918	at Washington	W	6-3	Mogridge	Johnson
1917	vs. Boston	L	10-3	Ruth	Caldwell
1916	vs. Washington	L	3-2 (11)	Johnson	Caldwell
1915	at Washington	L	7-0	Johnson	Warhop
1914	vs. Philadelphia	W	8-2	McHale	Bush
1913	at Washington	L	2-1	Johnson	McConnell
1912	vs. Boston	L	5-3	Wood	Caldwell
1911	at Philadelphia	W	2-1	Vaughn	Bender
1910	vs. Boston	T	4-4	Game called because of darkness	
1909	at Washington	L	4-1	Smith	Newton
1908	vs. Philadelphia	W	1-0 (12)	Carter	Doyle
1907	at Washington	W	3-2	Orth	Hughes
1906	vs. Boston	W	2-1	Chesbro	Young
1905	at Washington	W	4-2	Chesbro	Patten
1904	vs. Boston	W	8-2	Chesbro	Young
1903	at Washington	L	3-1	Orth	Chesbro

*at Tokyo Dome, Yankees were visiting team

OPENING DAY HOME RUNS

The Yankees have hit 94 Opening Day home runs by 57 different players. The last Yankees Opening Day home run came in 2009 when DH Hideki Matsui went deep in the seventh inning off Baltimore's Chris Ray. Joe Pepitone (pictured) was the last Yankee to homer twice on Opening Day.

MULTI-HOME RUN GAMES ON OPENING DAY (6)

Player	Date	Opponent
Babe Ruth (2)	4/12/32	at Philadelphia
Sammy Byrd (2)	4/12/32	at Philadelphia
Russ Derry (2)	4/17/45	vs. Boston
Mickey Mantle (2)	4/17/56	at Washington
Roger Maris (2)	4/19/60	at Boston
Joe Pepitone (2)	4/9/63	at Kansas City

Home Opener Ceremonial First Pitches

2009 Yogi Berra
2008 Reggie Jackson
2007 Melanie Lidle and Christopher Lidle, widow and son of Cory Lidle
2006 Yogi Berra
2005 Yogi Berra
2004 Yogi Berra, Whitey Ford, and Phil Rizzuto
2003 Yogi Berra and Whitey Ford
2002 Michael Bloomberg, New York City Mayor
2001 Mel Stottlemyre
2000 Yogi Berra
1999 Yogi Berra
1998 Joe DiMaggio
1997 Joe DiMaggio
1996 Joe DiMaggio
1995 Joe DiMaggio
1994 Joe DiMaggio
1993 Dean Smith, University of North Carolina Head Basketball Coach (representing North Carolina State University Head Basketball Coach Jim Valvano, who was too ill to attend)
1992 Joe DiMaggio
1991 General Colin Powell, Chairman, Joint Chiefs of Staff
1990 Bill Martin Jr.
1989 P.J. Carlesimo, Seton Hall University Head Basketball Coach
1988 Diane Munson, widow of Thurman Munson; and Arlene Howard, widow of Elston Howard
1987 Rachel Robinson, widow of Jackie Robinson
1986 Robert Merrill, Metropolitan Opera
1985 Mickey Mantle
1984 Scott Hamilton, U.S. Olympic Skater
1983 Joe DiMaggio
1982 Jimmy Esposito, Head Groundskeeper whose crew got the field in shape after a heavy snow storm
1981 Elston Howard Jr.
1980 Eric Heiden, Mike Eruzione, and Herb Brooks; 1980 U.S. Olympic Heroes
1979 Lucielle James, widow of World War II hero
1978 No first-pitch ceremony (Mickey Mantle and Roger Maris raised 1977 championship flag)
1977 Vince Polito, randomly selected fan
1976 Bob Shawkey, Yankees starting pitcher at opener of Yankee Stadium on 4/18/23
1975 Five children of slain "Good Samaritan" Frank J. Walker
1974 Ted Kennedy Jr., son of United States Senator Ted Kennedy
1973 Herb Bluestone, who attended opening of Yankee Stadium in 1923
1972 Jim Farley, former Postmaster General of the United States
1971 John Lindsay, New York City Mayor
1970 Whitney Young Jr., President of the National Urban League
1969 Paul Simon, singer/songwriter
1968 Marianne Moore, famed 81-year-old poet and baseball fan
1967 John Lindsay, New York City Mayor
1966 John Lindsay, New York City Mayor
1965 Rick O'Keefe, 7-year-old fan (he would later be a first-round draft pick of the Milwaukee Brewers in 1975)
1964 William Bracciodieta, Columbia University student and baseball player (second winner of Yogi Berra Scholarship Award)
1963 Joe DiMaggio
1962 Claire Ruth, widow of Babe Ruth
1961 James Lyons, Bronx Borough President (standing in for Mayor Robert Wagner, who was ill)
1960 Joe Cronin, Hall of Famer and President of the American League
1959 Will Harridge, recently-retired President of the American League
1958 James Lyons, Bronx Borough President
1957 Robert F. Wagner Jr., New York City Mayor
1956 Robert F. Wagner Jr., New York City Mayor

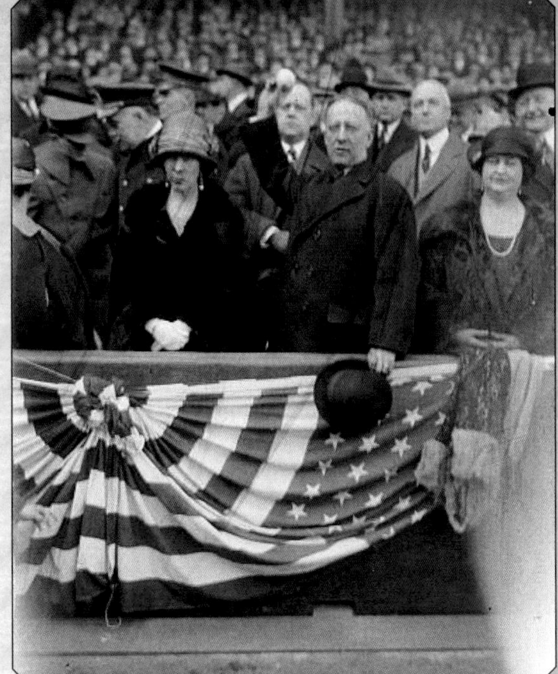

New York Governor Al Smith throws out the ceremonial first pitch at Yankee Stadium's inaugural game on April 18, 1923.

1955 Robert F. Wagner Jr., New York City Mayor
1954 James Lyons, Bronx Borough President
1953 Vincent Impellitteri, New York City Mayor
1952 Joe DiMaggio, who retired after the 1951 season
1951 Whitey Ford (in military service)
1950 Ed Barrow, former Yankees President
1949 Gary Simpson, student at St. Mary's Industrial School in Baltimore, Md. (which was attended by Babe Ruth, who passed away the previous season)...Ruth monument also unveiled.
1948 Thomas Dewey, New York Governor
1947 Sgt. Anthony Guzzetta, wounded World War II veteran
1946 Sgt. Hulon B. Whittington, Congressional Medal of Honor recipient
1945 Fiorello LaGuardia, New York City Mayor
1944 Fiorello LaGuardia, New York City Mayor
1943 Fiorello LaGuardia, New York City Mayor
1942 Fiorello LaGuardia, New York City Mayor
1941 Fiorello LaGuardia, New York City Mayor
1940 Fiorello LaGuardia, New York City Mayor
1939 Fiorello LaGuardia, New York City Mayor
1938 Newbold Morris, New York City Council President
1937 Fiorello LaGuardia, New York City Mayor
1936 Fiorello LaGuardia, New York City Mayor
1935 Fiorello LaGuardia, New York City Mayor
1934 Fiorello LaGuardia, New York City Mayor
1933 John O'Brien, New York City Mayor
1932 Jimmy Walker, New York City Mayor
1931 Jimmy Walker, New York City Mayor
1930 Jimmy Walker, New York City Mayor
1929 Joseph V. McKee, President of the New York City Board of Aldermen (substituting for Mayor Walker)
1928 Jimmy Walker, New York City Mayor
1927 Jimmy Walker, New York City Mayor
1926 Jimmy Walker, New York City Mayor
1925 Rear Admiral Charles P. Plunkett
1924 John F. Hylan, New York City Mayor
1923 Al Smith, New York Governor
1922 John F. Hylan, New York City Mayor
1921 John F. Hylan, New York City Mayor
1920 Lt. General Robert Bullard
1919 Robert Moran, President of the New York City Board of Aldermen
1918 Brigadier General William Mann
1917 Major General Leonard Wood
1916 Al Smith, Sheriff of New York
1915 John Mitchell, New York City Mayor
1914 Robert Wagner, New York Lieutenant Governor
1913 Bill Devery, co-owner
1912 Edward B. McCall, judge
1911 City Chamberlain Hyde
1910 Bill Devery, co-owner
1909 Tim Foley, Sheriff of New York
1908 George McClellan, New York City Mayor
1907 Diamond Jim Brady
1906 John M. Ward, former player
1905 Game was rained out (Congressman Tim Sullivan had thrown the first pitch)
1904 William Olcott, judge
1903 Ban Johnson, President of the American League

Yankees Championship Clubs

40 American League Pennant Winners, 27 World Championship Teams

Year	Won	Lost	Pct.	GA	Manager	World Series Opponent	Record W	L
1921	98	55	.641	4.5	Miller Huggins	Giants	3	5
1922	94	60	.610	1.0	Miller Huggins	Giants**	0	4
1923*	98	54	.645	16.0	Miller Huggins	Giants	4	2
1926	91	63	.591	3.0	Miller Huggins	Cardinals	3	4
1927*	110	44	.714	19.0	Miller Huggins	Pirates	4	0
1928*	101	53	.656	2.5	Miller Huggins	Cardinals	4	0
1932*	107	47	.695	13.0	Joe McCarthy	Cubs	4	0
1936*	102	51	.667	19.5	Joe McCarthy	Giants	4	2
1937*	102	52	.662	13.0	Joe McCarthy	Giants	4	1
1938*	99	53	.651	9.5	Joe McCarthy	Cubs	4	0
1939*	106	45	.702	17.0	Joe McCarthy	Reds	4	0
1941*	101	53	.656	17.0	Joe McCarthy	Dodgers	4	1
1942	103	51	.689	9.0	Joe McCarthy	Cardinals	1	4
1943*	98	56	.636	13.5	Joe McCarthy	Cardinals	4	1
1947*	97	57	.630	12.0	Bucky Harris	Dodgers	4	3
1949*	97	57	.630	1.0	Casey Stengel	Dodgers	4	1
1950*	98	56	.636	3.0	Casey Stengel	Phillies	4	0
1951*	98	56	.636	5.0	Casey Stengel	Giants	4	2
1952*	95	59	.617	2.0	Casey Stengel	Dodgers	4	3
1953*	99	52	.656	8.5	Casey Stengel	Dodgers	4	2
1955	96	58	.623	3.0	Casey Stengel	Dodgers	3	4
1956*	97	57	.630	9.0	Casey Stengel	Dodgers	4	3
1957	98	56	.636	8.0	Casey Stengel	Braves	3	4
1958*	92	62	.597	10.0	Casey Stengel	Braves	4	3
1960	97	57	.630	8.0	Casey Stengel	Pirates	3	4
1961*	109	53	.673	8.0	Ralph Houk	Reds	4	1
1962*	96	66	.593	5.0	Ralph Houk	Giants	4	3
1963	104	57	.646	10.5	Ralph Houk	Dodgers	0	4
1964	99	63	.611	1.0	Yogi Berra	Cardinals	3	4
1976	97	62	.610	10.5	Billy Martin	Reds	0	4
1977*	100	62	.617	2.5	Billy Martin	Dodgers	4	2
1978*	100	63	.613	1.0	Martin-Lemon	Dodgers	4	2
1981†	34	22	.607	2.0	Gene Michael			
	25	26	.490	-5.0	Michael-Lemon	Dodgers	2	4
1996*	92	70	.568	4.0	Joe Torre	Braves	4	2
1998*	114	48	.704	22.0	Joe Torre	Padres	4	0
1999*	98	64	.605	4.0	Joe Torre	Braves	4	0
2000*	87	74	.540	2.5	Joe Torre	Mets	4	1
2001	95	65	.594	13.5	Joe Torre	Diamondbacks	3	4
2003	101	61	.623	6.0	Joe Torre	Marlins	2	4
2009*	103	59	.636	8.0	Joe Girardi	Phillies	4	2
Yankees World Series Totals						**Tie game in 1922	**134**	**90**

* World Champions † 1st-Half Winner

60th Anniversary of the 1950 World Champion Yankees

The 2010 season marks the 60th anniversary of the Yankees' 1950 World Championship season. Led by Manager Casey Stengel and AL MVP Phil Rizzuto, who batted .324 with 125 runs scored, the Yankees went 98-56 in capturing the pennant by 3.0 games. In the World Series, the Yankees swept four games from the Philadelphia Phillies to win the 13th championship in team history. Yankees pitchers allowed just five runs (three earned) all Series, tallying a 0.73 combined ERA in 37.0IP. Each of the first three games were decided by one run, including a 1-0 victory behind Vic Raschi in Game 1, and a 2-1, 10-inning win behind Allie Reynolds in Game 2. Whitey Ford earned the first of his record 10 career World Series wins in the Game 4 clincher as Reynolds came out of the bullpen to strike out the final batter of the game with two runners on base. The victory marked the second of five consecutive Fall Classics won by the Yankees from 1949 through 1953.

Front Row: Whitey Ford, Phil Rizzuto, Billy Martin, Ed Lopat, Jim Turner, Frank Crosetti, Casey Stengel, Bill Dickey, Jackie Jensen, Billy Johnson, Gene Woodling, Charley Silvera, John Mize. **Second Row:** Gus Mauch, Bob Porterfield, Wally Hood, Dave Madison, Jerry Coleman, Bobby Brown, Tommy Henrich, Hank Bauer, Joe Collins, Lou Burdette, Joe Ostrowski, Ernie Nevel, Johnny Hopp. **Back Row:** Tommy Byrne, Cliff Mapes, Hank Workman, Fred Sanford, Tom Ferrick, Yogi Berra, Joe Page, Ralph Houk, Joe DiMaggio, Allie Reynolds, Vic Raschi. **Seated on Ground (Batboys):** Bert Padell, Joseph Carrieri.

Year-by-Year Results

Year	AL/WS	Position	GA/GB	Won	Lost	Pct.	Manager	Attendance	Stadium
1903		Fourth	-17.0	72	62	.537	Clark Griffith	211,808	Hilltop Park
1904		Second	-1.5	92	59	.609	Clark Griffith	438,919	Hilltop Park
1905		Sixth	-21.5	71	78	.477	Clark Griffith	309,100	Hilltop Park
1906		Second	-3.0	90	61	.596	Clark Griffith	434,700	Hilltop Park
1907		Fifth	-21.0	70	78	.473	Clark Griffith	350,020	Hilltop Park
1908		Eighth	-39.5	51	103	.331	Griffith-Kid Elberfeld	305,500	Hilltop Park
1909		Fifth	-23.5	74	77	.490	George Stallings	501,000	Hilltop Park
1910		Second	-14.5	88	63	.583	Stallings-Hal Chase	355,857	Hilltop Park
1911		Sixth	-25.5	76	76	.500	Hal Chase	302,444	Hilltop Park
1912		Eighth	-55.0	50	102	.329	Harry Wolverton	242,194	Hilltop Park
1913		Seventh	-38.0	57	94	.377	Frank Chance	357,551	Polo Grounds
1914		Sixth	-30.0	70	84	.455	Chance-Roger Peckinpaugh	359,477	Polo Grounds
1915		Fifth	-32.5	69	83	.454	Bill Donovan	256,035	Polo Grounds
1916		Fourth	-11.0	80	74	.519	Bill Donovan	469,211	Polo Grounds
1917		Sixth	-28.5	71	82	.464	Bill Donovan	330,294	Polo Grounds
1918		Fourth	-13.5	60	63	.488	Miller Huggins	282,047	Polo Grounds
1919		Third	-7.5	80	59	.576	Miller Huggins	619,164	Polo Grounds
1920		Third	-3.0	95	59	.617	Miller Huggins	1,289,422	Polo Grounds
1921	AL	First	+4.5	98	55	.641	Miller Huggins	1,230,696	Polo Grounds
1922	AL	First	+1.0	94	60	.610	Miller Huggins	1,026,134	Polo Grounds
1923	WS	First	+16.0	98	54	.645	Miller Huggins	1,007,066	Orig. Yankee Stadium
1924		Second	-2.0	89	63	.586	Miller Huggins	1,053,533	Orig. Yankee Stadium
1925		Seventh	-28.5	69	85	.448	Miller Huggins	697,267	Orig. Yankee Stadium
1926	AL	First	+3.0	91	63	.591	Miller Huggins	1,027,095	Orig. Yankee Stadium
1927	WS	First	+19.0	110	44	.714	Miller Huggins	1,164,015	Orig. Yankee Stadium
1928	WS	First	+2.5	101	53	.656	Miller Huggins	1,072,132	Orig. Yankee Stadium
1929		Second	-18.0	88	66	.571	Huggins-Art Fletcher	960,148	Orig. Yankee Stadium
1930		Third	-16.0	86	68	.558	Bob Shawkey	1,169,230	Orig. Yankee Stadium
1931		Second	-13.5	94	59	.614	Joe McCarthy	912,437	Orig. Yankee Stadium
1932	WS	First	+13.0	107	47	.695	Joe McCarthy	962,320	Orig. Yankee Stadium
1933		Second	-7.0	91	59	.607	Joe McCarthy	728,014	Orig. Yankee Stadium
1934		Second	-7.0	94	60	.610	Joe McCarthy	854,682	Orig. Yankee Stadium
1935		Second	-3.0	89	60	.597	Joe McCarthy	657,508	Orig. Yankee Stadium
1936	WS	First	+19.5	102	51	.667	Joe McCarthy	976,913	Orig. Yankee Stadium
1937	WS	First	+13.0	102	52	.662	Joe McCarthy	998,148	Orig. Yankee Stadium
1938	WS	First	+9.5	99	53	.651	Joe McCarthy	970,916	Orig. Yankee Stadium
1939	WS	First	+17.0	106	45	.702	Joe McCarthy	859,785	Orig. Yankee Stadium
1940		Third	-2.0	88	66	.571	Joe McCarthy	988,975	Orig. Yankee Stadium
1941	WS	First	+17.0	101	53	.656	Joe McCarthy	964,722	Orig. Yankee Stadium
1942	AL	First	+9.0	103	51	.669	Joe McCarthy	988,251	Orig. Yankee Stadium
1943	WS	First	+13.5	98	56	.636	Joe McCarthy	645,006	Orig. Yankee Stadium
1944		Third	-6.0	83	71	.539	Joe McCarthy	789,995	Orig. Yankee Stadium
1945		Fourth	-6.5	81	71	.533	Joe McCarthy	881,846	Orig. Yankee Stadium
1946		Third	-17.0	87	67	.565	McCarthy-Bill Dickey-Johnny Neun	2,265,512	Orig. Yankee Stadium
1947	WS	First	+12.0	97	57	.630	Bucky Harris	2,178,937	Orig. Yankee Stadium
1948		Third	-2.5	94	60	.610	Bucky Harris	2,373,901	Orig. Yankee Stadium
1949	WS	First	+1.0	97	57	.630	Casey Stengel	2,281,676	Orig. Yankee Stadium
1950	WS	First	+3.0	98	56	.636	Casey Stengel	2,081,380	Orig. Yankee Stadium
1951	WS	First	+5.0	98	56	.636	Casey Stengel	1,950,107	Orig. Yankee Stadium
1952	WS	First	+2.0	95	59	.617	Casey Stengel	1,629,665	Orig. Yankee Stadium
1953	WS	First	+8.5	99	52	.656	Casey Stengel	1,537,811	Orig. Yankee Stadium
1954		Second	-8.0	103	51	.669	Casey Stengel	1,475,171	Orig. Yankee Stadium
1955	AL	First	+3.0	96	58	.623	Casey Stengel	1,490,138	Orig. Yankee Stadium
1956	WS	First	+9.0	97	57	.680	Casey Stengel	1,491,138	Orig. Yankee Stadium
1957	AL	First	+8.0	98	56	.636	Casey Stengel	1,497,134	Orig. Yankee Stadium
1958	WS	First	+10.0	92	62	.597	Casey Stengel	1,428,438	Orig. Yankee Stadium
1959		Third	-15.0	79	75	.513	Casey Stengel	1,552,030	Orig. Yankee Stadium
1960	AL	First	+8.0	97	57	.630	Casey Stengel	1,627,349	Orig. Yankee Stadium
1961	WS	First	+8.0	109	53	.673	Ralph Houk	1,747,725	Orig. Yankee Stadium
1962	WS	First	+5.0	96	66	.593	Ralph Houk	1,493,574	Orig. Yankee Stadium
1963	AL	First	+10.5	104	57	.646	Ralph Houk	1,308,920	Orig. Yankee Stadium
1964	AL	First	+1.0	99	63	.611	Yogi Berra	1,305,638	Orig. Yankee Stadium
1965		Sixth	-25.0	77	85	.475	Johnny Keane	1,213,552	Orig. Yankee Stadium
1966		Tenth	-26.5	70	89	.440	Keane-Houk	1,124,648	Orig. Yankee Stadium
1967		Ninth	-20.0	72	90	.444	Ralph Houk	1,259,514	Orig. Yankee Stadium
1968		Fifth	-20.0	83	79	.512	Ralph Houk	1,185,666	Orig. Yankee Stadium
1969		Fifth	-28.5	80	81	.497	Ralph Houk	1,067,996	Orig. Yankee Stadium
1970		Second	-15.0	93	69	.574	Ralph Houk	1,136,879	Orig. Yankee Stadium
1971		Fourth	-21.0	82	80	.506	Ralph Houk	1,070,771	Orig. Yankee Stadium
1972		Fourth	-6.5	79	76	.510	Ralph Houk	966,328	Orig. Yankee Stadium
1973		Fourth	-17.0	80	82	.494	Ralph Houk	1,262,103	Orig. Yankee Stadium

Year-by-Year Results

Year		Position	GA/GB	Won	Lost	Pct.	Manager	Attendance	
1974		Second	-2.0	89	73	.549	Bill Virdon	1,273,075	Shea Stadium
1975		Third	-12.0	83	77	.519	Virdon-Billy Martin	1,288,048	Shea Stadium
1976	AL	First	+10.5	97	62	.610	Billy Martin	2,012,434	Orig. Yankee Stadium (R)
1977	WS	First	+2.5	100	62	.617	Billy Martin	2,103,092	Orig. Yankee Stadium (R)
1978	WS	First	+1.0	100	63	.613	Martin-Bob Lemon	2,335,871	Orig. Yankee Stadium (R)
1979		Fourth	-13.5	89	71	.556	Lemon-Martin	2,537,765	Orig. Yankee Stadium (R)
1980		First	+3.0	103	59	.636	Dick Howser	2,627,417	Orig. Yankee Stadium (R)
1981	AL	First	+2.0	34	22	.607	Gene Michael		
		Sixth	-5.0	25	26	.490	Michael-Lemon	1,614,353	Orig. Yankee Stadium (R)
1982		Fifth	-16.0	79	83	.488	Lemon-Michael-Clyde King	2,041,219	Orig. Yankee Stadium (R)
1983		Third	-7.0	91	71	.562	Billy Martin	2,257,976	Orig. Yankee Stadium (R)
1984		Third	-17.0	87	75	.537	Yogi Berra	1,821,815	Orig. Yankee Stadium (R)
1985		Second	-2.0	97	64	.602	Berra-Martin	2,214,587	Orig. Yankee Stadium (R)
1986		Second	-5.5	90	72	.556	Lou Piniella	2,268,030	Orig. Yankee Stadium (R)
1987		Fourth	-9.0	89	73	.549	Lou Piniella	2,427,672	Orig. Yankee Stadium (R)
1988		Fifth	-3.5	85	76	.528	Martin-Piniella	2,633,701	Orig. Yankee Stadium (R)
1989		Fifth	-14.5	74	87	.460	Dallas Green-Bucky Dent	2,170,485	Orig. Yankee Stadium (R)
1990		Seventh	-21.0	67	95	.414	Dent-Stump Merrill	2,006,436	Orig. Yankee Stadium (R)
1991		Fifth	-21.0	71	91	.438	Stump Merrill	1,863,733	Orig. Yankee Stadium (R)
1992		Fourth	-20.0	76	86	.469	Buck Showalter	1,748,773	Orig. Yankee Stadium (R)
1993		Second	-7.0	88	74	.543	Buck Showalter	2,416,965	Orig. Yankee Stadium (R)
1994		First	+6.5	70	43	.619	Buck Showalter	1,675,556	Orig. Yankee Stadium (R)
1995		Second	-7.0	79	65	.549	Buck Showalter	1,705,263	Orig. Yankee Stadium (R)
1996	WS	First	+4.0	92	70	.568	Joe Torre	2,250,877	Orig. Yankee Stadium (R)
1997		Second	-2.0	96	66	593	Joe Torre	2,580,445	Orig. Yankee Stadium (R)
1998	WS	First	+22.0	114	48	.704	Joe Torre	2,919,046	Orig. Yankee Stadium (R)
1999	WS	First	+4.0	98	64	.605	Joe Torre	3,292,736	Orig. Yankee Stadium (R)
2000	WS	First	+2.5	87	74	.540	Joe Torre	3,227,657	Orig. Yankee Stadium (R)
2001	AL	First	+13.5	95	65	.594	Joe Torre	3,264,777	Orig. Yankee Stadium (R)
2002		First	+10.5	103	58	.640	Joe Torre	3,461,644	Orig. Yankee Stadium (R)
2003	AL	First	+6.0	101	61	.623	Joe Torre	3,465,585	Orig. Yankee Stadium (R)
2004		First	+3.0	101	61	.623	Joe Torre	3,775,292	Orig. Yankee Stadium (R)
2005		First	0.0	95	67	.586	Joe Torre	4,090,692	Orig. Yankee Stadium (R)
2006		First	+10.0	97	65	.599	Joe Torre	4,243,780	Orig. Yankee Stadium (R)
2007		Second	-2.0	94	68	.580	Joe Torre	4,271,083	Orig. Yankee Stadium (R)
2008		Third	-8.0	89	73	.549	Joe Girardi	4,298,543	Orig. Yankee Stadium (R)
2009	WS	First	+8.0	103	59	.636	Joe Girardi	3,719,358	Yankee Stadium
Totals	**27WS/40AL**			**9,457**	**7,141**	**.570**		(R) Remodeled Orig. Yankee Stadium	

Yankees Silver Slugger Award Winners by Year

Award given since 1980

Year:	Player (Position)
1980:	Willie Randolph (2B)
1981:	Dave Winfield (OF)
1982:	Dave Winfield (OF)
1983:	Dave Winfield (OF), Don Baylor (DH)
1984:	Dave Winfield (OF)
1985:	Don Mattingly (1B), Rickey Henderson (OF), Dave Winfield (OF), Don Baylor (DH)
1986:	Don Mattingly (1B)
1987:	Don Mattingly (1B)
1988:	None
1989:	None
1990:	None
1991:	None
1992:	None
1993:	Mike Stanley (C), Wade Boggs (3B)
1994:	Wade Boggs (3B)
1995:	None
1996:	None
1997:	Tino Martinez (1B)
1998:	None
1999:	None
2000:	Jorge Posada (C)
2001:	Jorge Posada (C)
2002:	Jorge Posada (C), Jason Giambi (1B), Alfonso Soriano (2B), Bernie Williams (OF)
2003:	Jorge Posada (C)
2004:	Gary Sheffield (OF)
2005:	Alex Rodriguez (3B), Gary Sheffield (OF)
2006:	Robinson Cano (2B), Derek Jeter (SS)
2007:	Jorge Posada (C), Alex Rodriguez (3B), Derek Jeter (SS)
2008:	Alex Rodriguez (3B), Derek Jeter (SS)
2009:	Mark Teixeira (1B), Derek Jeter (SS)

Yankees Silver Slugger Award Winners by Position

Position	Winner (Years)
Catcher	Mike Stanley (1993); Jorge Posada (2000-03, '07)
First Base	Don Mattingly (1985-87); Tino Martinez (1997); Jason Giambi (2002); Mark Teixeira (2009)
Second Base	Willie Randolph (1980); Alfonso Soriano (2002), Robinson Cano (2006)
Third Base	Wade Boggs (1993-94), Alex Rodriguez (2005, '07-08)
Shortstop	Derek Jeter (2006-09)
Outfield	Dave Winfield (1981-85); Rickey Henderson (1985); Bernie Williams (2002), Gary Sheffield (2004-05)
Designated Hitter	Don Baylor (1983, '85)

Year-by-Year Team Hitting Statistics

YEAR	AVG	AB	R	H	HR	RBI	SB	BB	SO	E
1903	.249	4565	579	1136	18	474	160	332	465	264
1904	.259	5220	598	1354	27	499	163	312	548	275
1905	.248	4957	587	1228	23	480	200	360	537	293
1906	.264	5095	641	1345	17	528	192	331	--	272
1907	.249	5042	604	1257	15	497	206	304	--	334
1908	.236	5036	456	1187	13	372	230	288	--	337
1909	.248	4981	591	1234	16	473	187	407	--	330
1910	.248	5050	629	1252	20	492	289	464	--	285
1911	.272	5056	686	1375	25	577	270	493	--	328
1912	.259	5095	632	1320	18	502	247	463	--	382
1913	.237	4880	529	1157	8	430	203	534	617	293
1914	.229	4992	536	1144	12	416	251	577	711	238
1915	.233	4982	583	1162	31	459	198	570	668	217
1916	.246	5200	575	1277	35	492	179	516	632	225
1917	.239	5136	524	1226	27	445	136	496	535	219
1918	.257	4224	491	1085	20	406	88	367	370	161
1919	.267	4775	582	1275	45	499	101	386	479	193
1920	.280	5176	838	1448	115	747	64	539	626	194
1921	.300	5249	948	1576	134	861	89	588	567	222
1922	.287	5245	758	1504	95	674	62	497	532	157
1923	.291	5347	823	1554	105	770	69	521	516	144
1924	.289	5340	798	1516	98	734	69	478	420	156
1925	.275	5353	706	1471	110	638	67	470	482	160
1926	.289	5221	847	1508	121	794	79	642	580	210
1927	.307	5347	975	1644	158	908	90	635	605	195
1928	.296	5337	894	1578	133	817	51	562	544	194
1929	.295	5379	899	1587	142	828	51	554	518	178
1930	.309	5448	1062	1683	152	986	91	644	569	207
1931	.297	5608	1067	1667	155	990	139	748	554	169
1932	.286	5477	1002	1564	160	955	77	766	527	188
1933	.283	5274	927	1495	144	849	74	700	506	165
1934	.278	5368	842	1494	135	791	71	700	597	157
1935	.280	5214	818	1462	104	755	68	604	469	151
1936	.300	5591	1065	1676	182	995	76	700	594	163
1937	.283	5487	979	1554	174	922	60	709	607	170
1938	.274	5410	966	1480	174	917	91	749	616	169
1939	.287	5300	967	1521	166	903	72	701	543	126
1940	.259	5286	817	1371	155	757	59	648	606	152
1941	.269	5444	830	1464	151	774	51	616	565	165
1942	.269	5305	801	1429	108	744	69	591	556	142
1943	.256	5282	669	1350	100	635	46	624	562	160
1944	.264	5331	674	1410	96	631	91	523	627	156
1945	.259	5176	676	1343	93	639	64	618	567	175
1946	.248	5139	684	1275	136	649	48	627	706	150
1947	.271	5308	794	1439	115	746	27	610	581	109
1948	.278	5324	857	1480	139	806	24	623	478	120
1949	.269	5196	829	1396	115	759	58	731	539	138
1950	.282	5361	914	1511	159	863	41	687	463	119
1951	.269	5194	798	1395	140	741	78	605	547	144
1952	.267	5294	727	1411	129	672	52	566	652	127
1953	.273	5194	801	1420	139	762	34	656	644	126
1954	.268	5226	805	1400	133	747	34	650	632	126
1955	.260	5161	762	1342	175	722	55	609	658	128
1956	.270	5312	857	1433	190	788	51	615	755	136
1957	.268	5271	723	1412	145	682	49	562	709	123
1958	.268	5294	759	1418	164	715	48	537	822	128
1959	.260	5379	687	1397	153	651	45	457	828	131
1960	.260	5290	746	1377	193	699	37	537	818	129
1961	.263	5559	827	1461	240	781	28	543	785	124
1962	.267	5644	817	1509	199	791	42	584	842	131
1963	.252	5506	714	1387	188	666	42	434	808	110
1964	.253	5705	730	1442	162	688	54	520	976	109
1965	.235	5470	611	1286	149	576	35	489	951	137
1966	.235	5330	611	1254	162	569	49	485	817	142
1967	.225	5443	522	1225	100	473	63	532	1043	154
1968	.214	5310	536	1137	109	501	90	566	958	139
1969	.235	5308	562	1247	94	521	119	565	840	131
1970	.251	5492	680	1381	111	627	105	588	808	130
1971	.254	5413	648	1377	97	607	75	581	717	125
1972	.249	5168	557	1288	103	526	71	491	689	134
1973	.261	5492	641	1435	131	616	47	489	680	156
1974	.263	5524	671	1451	101	637	53	515	690	142

YEAR	AVG	AB	R	H	HR	RBI	SB	BB	SO	E
1975	.264	5415	681	1430	110	642	102	486	710	135
1976	.269	5555	730	1496	120	682	163	470	616	126
1977	.281	5605	831	1576	184	784	93	533	681	132
1978	.267	5583	735	1489	125	693	98	505	695	113
1979	.266	5421	734	1443	150	594	64	509	590	122
1980	.267	5553	820	1484	189	772	86	643	739	138
1981	.252	3529	421	889	100	403	46	391	434	72
1982	.256	5526	709	1417	161	666	69	590	719	128
1983	.273	5631	770	1535	153	728	84	533	686	139
1984	.276	5661	758	1560	130	725	62	534	673	142
1985	.267	5458	839	1458	176	793	155	620	771	126
1986	.271	5570	797	1512	188	745	139	645	911	127
1987	.262	5511	788	1445	196	749	105	604	949	102
1988	.263	5592	772	1469	148	713	146	588	935	134
1989	.269	5458	698	1470	130	657	137	502	831	122
1990	.241	5483	603	1322	147	561	119	427	1027	126
1991	.256	5541	674	1418	147	630	109	473	861	133
1992	.261	5593	733	1462	163	703	78	536	903	114
1993	.279	5615	821	1568	178	793	39	629	910	105
1994	.290	3986	670	1155	139	632	55	530	660	80
1995	.276	4947	749	1365	122	709	50	625	851	74
1996	.288	5628	871	1621	162	830	96	632	909	91
1997	.287	5710	891	1636	161	846	99	676	954	104
1998	.288	5643	965	1625	207	907	153	653	1025	98
1999	.282	5568	900	1568	193	855	104	718	978	111
2000	.277	5556	871	1541	205	833	99	631	1007	109
2001	.267	5577	804	1488	203	774	161	519	1035	109
2002	.275	5601	897	1540	223	857	100	640	1171	127
2003	.271	5605	877	1518	230	845	98	684	1042	114
2004	.268	5527	897	1483	242	863	84	670	982	99
2005	.276	5624	886	1552	229	847	84	637	989	95
2006	.285	5651	930	1608	210	902	139	649	1053	104
2007	.290	5717	968	1656	201	929	123	637	991	88
2008	.271	5572	789	1512	180	758	118	535	1015	83
2009	.283	5660	915	1604	244	881	111	663	1014	86

Year-by-Year Team Pitching Statistics

YEAR	W-L	ERA	CG	SHO	SV	SO	BB
1903	72-62	3.08	111	7	2	463	245
1904	92-59	2.57	123	15	1	684	311
1905	71-78	2.93	88	10	9	642	396
1906	90-61	2.78	99	18	5	605	351
1907	70-78	3.03	93	9	7	511	428
1908	51-103	3.16	91	11	6	584	457
1909	74-77	2.68	94	16	14	597	422
1910	88-63	2.59	110	14	10	654	364
1911	76-76	3.54	91	5	9	667	406
1912	50-102	4.13	109	3	3	637	436
1913	57-94	3.27	78	7	6	530	455
1914	70-84	2.81	97	5	7	563	390
1915	69-83	3.09	100	11	2	559	517
1916	80-74	2.77	83	10	18	616	476
1917	71-82	2.66	87	9	7	571	427
1918	60-63	3.03	59	9	11	369	463
1919	80-59	2.78	85	14	7	500	433
1920	95-59	3.31	88	16	11	480	420
1921	98-55	3.79	92	7	15	481	470
1922	94-60	3.39	98	7	14	458	423
1923	98-54	3.66	102	9	10	506	491
1924	89-63	3.86	76	13	13	487	522
1925	69-85	4.33	80	8	13	492	505
1926	91-63	3.86	64	4	20	486	478
1927	110-44	3.20	82	11	20	431	409
1928	101-53	3.74	82	13	21	487	452
1929	88-66	4.17	64	12	18	484	485
1930	86-68	4.88	65	7	15	572	524
1931	94-59	4.20	78	4	17	686	543
1932	107-47	3.98	95	11	15	780	561
1933	91-59	4.36	70	8	22	711	612
1934	94-60	3.76	83	13	10	656	542
1935	89-60	3.60	76	12	13	594	516
1936	102-51	4.17	77	6	21	624	663
1937	102-52	3.65	82	15	21	652	506
1938	99-53	3.91	91	11	13	567	566
1939	106-45	3.31	87	13	26	565	567

Urban Shocker

YEAR	W-L	ERA	CG	SHO	SV	SO	BB
1940	88-66	3.89	76	10	14	559	511
1941	101-53	3.53	75	13	26	589	598
1942	103-51	2.91	88	18	17	558	431
1943	98-56	2.93	83	14	13	653	489
1944	83-71	3.39	78	9	13	529	532
1945	81-71	3.45	78	9	14	474	485
1946	87-67	3.13	68	17	17	653	552
1947	97-57	3.39	73	14	21	691	628
1948	94-60	3.75	62	16	24	654	641
1949	97-57	3.69	59	12	36	671	812
1950	98-56	4.15	66	12	31	712	708
1951	98-56	3.56	66	24	22	664	562
1952	95-59	3.14	72	17	27	666	581
1953	99-52	3.20	50	16	39	604	500
1954	103-51	3.26	51	16	37	655	552
1955	96-58	3.23	52	19	33	732	688
1956	97-57	3.63	50	10	35	732	652
1957	98-56	3.00	41	13	42	810	580
1958	92-62	3.22	53	21	33	796	557
1959	79-75	3.60	38	15	28	836	594
1960	97-57	3.52	38	16	42	712	609
1961	109-53	3.46	47	14	39	866	542
1962	96-66	3.70	33	10	42	838	499
1963	104-57	3.07	59	19	31	965	476
1964	99-63	3.15	46	18	45	989	504
1965	77-85	3.28	41	11	31	1001	511
1966	70-89	3.42	29	7	32	842	443
1967	72-90	3.24	37	16	27	898	480
1968	83-79	2.79	45	14	27	831	424
1969	80-81	3.23	53	13	20	801	522
1970	93-69	3.25	36	6	49	777	451
1971	82-80	3.45	67	15	12	707	423
1972	79-76	3.05	35	19	39	625	419
1973	80-82	3.34	47	16	39	708	457
1974	89-73	3.31	53	13	24	829	528
1975	83-77	3.29	70	11	20	809	502
1976	97-62	3.19	62	15	37	448	674
1977	100-62	3.61	52	16	34	758	486
1978	100-63	3.18	39	16	36	817	478
1979	89-71	3.83	43	10	37	731	455
1980	103-59	3.58	29	15	50	845	463
1981	59-48	2.90	16	13	30	606	287
1982	79-83	3.99	24	8	39	939	491
1983	91-71	3.86	47	12	32	892	455
1984	87-75	3.78	15	12	43	992	518
1985	97-64	3.69	25	9	49	907	518
1986	90-72	4.11	13	8	58	878	492
1987	89-73	4.36	19	10	47	900	542
1988	85-76	4.25	16	4	43	861	487
1989	74-87	4.50	15	9	44	787	521
1990	67-95	4.21	15	6	41	909	618
1991	71-91	4.42	3	11	37	936	506
1992	76-86	4.21	20	9	44	851	612
1993	88-74	4.35	11	13	38	899	552
1994	70-43	4.34	8	2	31	656	398
1995	79-65	4.56	18	5	35	908	535
1996	92-70	4.65	6	9	52	1139	610
1997	96-66	3.84	11	10	51	1165	532
1998	114-48	3.82	22	16	48	1080	466
1999	98-64	4.13	6	10	50	1111	581
2000	87-74	4.76	9	6	40	1040	577
2001	95-65	4.02	7	9	57	1266	465
2002	103-58	3.87	9	11	53	1135	403
2003	101-61	4.02	8	12	49	1119	375
2004	101-61	4.69	1	5	59	1058	445
2005	95-67	4.52	8	14	46	985	463
2006	97-65	4.41	5	8	43	1019	496
2007	94-68	4.49	1	5	34	1009	578
2008	89-73	4.28	1	11	42	1141	489
2009	103-59	4.26	3	8	51	1260	574

Bob Turley

Whitey Ford

Ron Guidry

Mike Mussina

Year-by-Year Hitting Leaders

AVERAGE

Year	Leader	Avg.
1903	Keeler	.318
1904	Keeler	.343
1905	Keeler	.302
1906	Chase	.323
1907	Chase	.287
1908	Hemphill	.297
1909	LaPorte	.298
1910	Knight	.312
1911	Cree	.348
1912	Paddock	.288
1913	Cree	.272
1914	Cook	.283
1915	Maisel	.281
1916	Pipp	.262
1917	Baker	.282
1918	Baker	.306
1919	Peckinpaugh	.305
1920	Ruth	.376
1921	Ruth	.377
1922	Pipp	.329
1923	Ruth	.394
1924	Ruth*	.378
1925	Combs	.343
1926	Ruth	.372
1927	Gehrig	.373
1928	Gehrig	.374
1929	Lazzeri	.353
1930	Gehrig	.379
1931	Ruth	.373
1932	Gehrig	.349
1933	Gehrig	.334
1934	Gehrig*	.363
1935	Gehrig	.329
1936	Dickey	.362
1937	Gehrig	.351
1938	DiMaggio	.324
1939	DiMaggio*	.381
1940	DiMaggio*	.352
1941	DiMaggio	.357
1942	Gordon	.322
1943	Johnson	.280
1944	Stirnweiss	.319
1945	Stirnweiss*	.309
1946	DiMaggio	.290
1947	DiMaggio	.315
1948	DiMaggio	.320
1949	Henrich	.287
1950	Rizzuto	.324
1951	McDougald	.306
1952	Mantle	.311
1953	Bauer	.304
1954	Noren	.319
1955	Mantle	.306
1956	Mantle*	.353
1957	Mantle	.365
1958	Mantle	.304
1959	Richardson	.301
1960	Skowron	.309
1961	Howard	.348
1962	Mantle	.321
1963	Howard	.287
1964	Howard	.318
1965	Tresh	.279
1966	Mantle	.288
1967	Clarke	.272
1968	White	.267
1969	White	.290
1970	Munson	.302
1971	Murcer	.331
1972	Murcer	.292
1973	Murcer	.304
1974	Piniella	.305
1975	Munson	.318
1976	Rivers	.312
1977	Rivers	.326
1978	Piniella	.314
1979	Piniella, Jackson	.297
1980	Watson	.307
1981	Mumphrey	.307
1982	Mumphrey	.300
1983	Baylor	.303
1984	Mattingly*	.343
1985	Mattingly	.324
1986	Mattingly	.352
1987	Mattingly	.327
1988	Winfield	.322
1989	Sax	.315
1990	R. Kelly	.285
1991	Sax	.304
1992	Mattingly	.288
1993	O'Neill	.311
1994	O'Neill*	.359
1995	Boggs	.324
1996	JETER	.314
1997	O'Neill	.324
1998	B. Williams*	.339
1999	JETER	.349
2000	JETER	.339
2001	JETER	.311
2002	B. Williams	.333
2003	JETER	.324
2004	Matsui	.298
2005	RODRIGUEZ	.321
2006	JETER	.343
2007	POSADA	.338
2008	Damon	.303
2009	JETER	.334

RUNS

Year	Leader	Runs
1903	Keeler	98
1904	Dougherty*	80
1905	Keeler	81
1906	Keeler	96
1907	Hoffman	81
1908	Hemphill	62
1909	Demmitt	68
1910	Daniels	68
1911	Cree	90
1912	Daniels	72
1913	Hartzell	60
1914	Maisel	78
1915	Maisel	77
1916	Pipp	70
1917	Pipp	82
1918	Baker, Pratt	65
1919	Peckinpaugh	89
1920	Ruth*	158
1921	Ruth*	177
1922	Witt	98
1923	Ruth*	151
1924	Ruth*	143
1925	Combs	117
1926	Ruth*	139
1927	Ruth*	158
1928	Ruth*	163
1929	Gehrig	127
1930	Ruth	150
1931	Gehrig*	163
1932	Combs	142
1933	Gehrig*	138
1934	Gehrig	128
1935	Gehrig*	125
1936	Gehrig*	167
1937	DiMaggio*	151
1938	Rolfe	132
1939	Rolfe*	139
1940	Gordon	112
1941	DiMaggio	122
1942	DiMaggio	123
1943	Keller	97
1944	Stirnweiss*	125
1945	Stirnweiss*	107
1946	Keller	98
1947	Henrich	109
1948	Henrich*	138
1949	Rizzuto	110
1950	Rizzuto	125
1951	Berra	92
1952	Berra	97
1953	Mantle	105
1954	Mantle*	128
1955	Mantle	121
1956	Mantle*	132
1957	Mantle*	121
1958	Mantle*	127
1959	Mantle	104
1960	Mantle*	119
1961	Maris*	132
1962	Richardson	99
1963	Tresh	91
1964	Mantle	92
1965	Tresh	94
1966	Pepitone	85
1967	Clarke	74
1968	White	89
1969	Clarke, Murcer	82
1970	White	109
1971	Murcer	94
1972	Murcer*	102
1973	White	88
1974	Maddox	75
1975	Bonds	93
1976	White*	104
1977	Nettles	99
1978	Randolph	87
1979	Randolph	98
1980	Randolph	99
1981	Randolph	59
1982	Randolph	85
1983	Winfield	99
1984	Winfield	106
1985	Henderson*	146
1986	Henderson*	130
1987	Randolph	96
1988	Henderson	118
1989	Sax	88
1990	R. Kelly	85
1991	Sax	85
1992	Mattingly	86
1993	Tartabull	87
1994	B. Williams	80
1995	B. Williams	93
1996	B. Williams	108
1997	JETER	116
1998	JETER*	127
1999	JETER	134
2000	JETER	119
2001	JETER	110
2002	Soriano*	128
2003	Soriano	114
2004	Sheffield	117
2005	RODRIGUEZ*	124
2006	RODRIGUEZ	121
2007	RODRIGUEZ*	143
2008	RODRIGUEZ	104
2009	Damon, JETER	107

HITS

Year	Leader	Hits
1903	Keeler	164
1904	Keeler	185
1905	Keeler	169
1906	Chase	193
1907	Chase	143
1908	Hemphill	150
1909	Engle	137
1910	Chase	152
1911	Cree	181
1912	Chase	143
1913	Cree	145
1914	Cook	133
1915	Maisel	149
1916	Pipp	143
1917	Baker	156
1918	Baker	154
1919	Baker	166
1920	Pratt	180
1921	Ruth	204
1922	Pipp	190
1923	Ruth	205
1924	Ruth	200
1925	Combs	203
1926	Ruth	184
1927	Combs*	231
1928	Gehrig	210
1929	Combs	202
1930	Gehrig	220
1931	Gehrig*	211
1932	Gehrig	208
1933	Gehrig	198
1934	Gehrig	210
1935	Rolfe	192
1936	DiMaggio	206
1937	DiMaggio	215
1938	Rolfe	196
1939	Rolfe*	213
1940	DiMaggio	179
1941	DiMaggio	193
1942	DiMaggio	186
1943	Johnson	166
1944	Stirnweiss*	205
1945	Stirnweiss*	195
1946	Keller	148
1947	DiMaggio	168
1948	DiMaggio	190
1949	Rizzuto	169
1950	Rizzuto	200
1951	Berra	161
1952	Mantle	171
1953	McDougald	154
1954	Berra	179
1955	Mantle	158
1956	Mantle	188
1957	Mantle	173
1958	Mantle	158
1959	Mantle	154
1960	Skowron	166
1961	Richardson	173
1962	Richardson*	209
1963	Richardson	167
1964	Richardson	181
1965	Tresh	168
1966	Richardson	153
1967	Clarke	160
1968	White	154
1969	Clarke	183
1970	White	180
1971	Murcer	175
1972	Murcer	171
1973	Murcer	187
1974	Murcer	166
1975	Munson	190
1976	Chambliss	188
1977	Rivers	184
1978	Munson	183
1979	Randolph, Chambliss	155
1980	Jackson	154
1981	Winfield	114
1982	Randolph	155
1983	Winfield	169
1984	Mattingly*	207
1985	Mattingly	211
1986	Mattingly*	238
1987	Mattingly	186
1988	Mattingly	186
1989	Sax	205
1990	R. Kelly	183
1991	Sax	198
1992	Mattingly	184
1993	Boggs	169
1994	O'Neill	132
1995	B. Williams	173
1996	JETER	183
1997	JETER	190
1998	JETER	203
1999	JETER*	219
2000	JETER	201
2001	JETER	191
2002	Soriano*	209
2003	Soriano	198
2004	JETER	188
2005	JETER	202
2006	JETER	214
2007	JETER	206
2008	Abreu	180
2009	JETER	212

DOUBLES

Year	Leader	Doubles
1903	Williams	30
1904	Williams	31
1905	Williams	20
1906	Williams	25
1907	Chase	23
1908	Conroy	22
1909	Engle	20
1910	Knight	25
1911	Chase	32
1912	Daniels	25
1913	Cree	25
1914	Maisel	23
1915	Pipp	20
1916	Baker	23
1917	Pipp	29
1918	Baker	24
1919	Pratt, Bodie	27
1920	Meusel	40
1921	Ruth	44
1922	Pipp	32
1923	Ruth	45
1924	Meusel	40
1925	Combs	36
1926	Gehrig	47
1927	Gehrig*	52
1928	Gehrig*	47
1929	Lazzeri	37
1930	Gehrig	42
1931	Lary	35
1932	Gehrig	42
1933	Gehrig	41
1934	Gehrig	40
1935	Chapman	38
1936	DiMaggio	44
1937	Gehrig	37
1938	Rolfe	36
1939	Rolfe*	46
1940	Gordon	32
1941	DiMaggio	43
1942	Henrich	30
1943	Etten	35
1944	Stirnweiss	35
1945	Stirnweiss	32
1946	Keller	29
1947	Henrich	35
1948	Henrich	42
1949	Rizzuto	22
1950	Rizzuto	36
1951	McDougald	23
1952	Mantle	37
1953	McDougald	27
1954	Berra	28
1955	Mantle	25
1956	Berra	29
1957	Mantle	28
1958	Bauer, Skowron	22
1959	Berra, Kubek	25
1960	Skowron	34
1961	Kubek	38
1962	Richardson	38
1963	Tresh	28
1964	Howard	27
1965	Tresh	29
1966	Boyer	22
1967	Tresh	23
1968	White	20
1969	White	30
1970	White	30
1971	Murcer	25
1972	Murcer	30
1973	Murcer, Munson	29
1974	Maddox, Piniella	26
1975	Chambliss	38
1976	Chambliss	32
1977	Jackson	39
1978	Piniella	34
1979	Chambliss	27
1980	Cerone	30
1981	Winfield	25
1982	Mumphrey, Winfield	24
1983	Baylor	33
1984	Mattingly*	44
1985	Mattingly*	48
1986	Mattingly*	53
1987	Mattingly	38
1988	Winfield	37
1989	Mattingly	37
1990	R. Kelly	32
1991	Sax	38
1992	Mattingly	40
1993	O'Neill	34
1994	B. Williams	29
1995	Mattingly	32
1996	O'Neill	35
1997	O'Neill	42
1998	O'Neill	40
1999	O'Neill	39
2000	B. Williams, Martinez	37
2001	B. Williams	38
2002	Soriano	51
2003	Matsui	42
2004	JETER	44
2005	Matsui	45
2006	CANO	41
2007	POSADA	42
2008	Abreu	39
2009	CANO	48

Year-by-Year Hitting Leaders

TRIPLES

Year	Leader	Triples
1903	Williams, Conroy	12
1904	Anderson, Conroy	12
1905	Conroy	11
1906	Chase, Conroy	10
1907	Conroy, LaPorte, Williams	11
1908	Hemphill	9
1909	Demmitt	12
1910	Cree	16
1911	Cree	22
1912	Hartzell, Daniels	11
1913	Peckinpaugh	7
1914	Maisel, Hartzell	9
1915	Pipp	13
1916	Pipp	14
1917	Pipp	12
1918	Pipp	9
1919	Pipp	10
1920	Pipp	14
1921	Ruth, Meusel	16
1922	Meusel	11
1923	Ruth	13
1924	Pipp*	19
1925	Combs	13
1926	Gehrig*	20
1927	Combs*	23
1928	Combs*	21
1929	Combs	15
1930	Combs*	22
1931	Gehrig	15
1932	Lazzeri	16
1933	Combs	16
1934	Chapman*	13
1935	Selkirk	12
1936	DiMaggio*, Rolfe*	15
1937	DiMaggio	15
1938	DiMaggio	13
1939	Rolfe	10
1940	Keller	15
1941	DiMaggio	11
1942	DiMaggio	13
1943	Lindell*	12
1944	Stirnweiss*, Lindell*	16
1945	Stirnweiss*	22
1946	Keller	10
1947	Henrich*	13
1948	Henrich*	14
1949	Rizzuto, Woodling	7
1950	Bauer, DiMaggio	10
1951	Woodling	8
1952	Rizzuto	10
1953	McDougald	7
1954	Mantle	12
1955	Mantle*, Carey*	11
1956	Bauer	7
1957	Bauer*, McDougald*	9
1958	Bauer	6
1959	McDougald	8
1960	Maris	7
1961	Mantle, Kubek	6
1962	Skowron	6
1963	Howard, Richardson	6
1964	Tresh, Boyer	5
1965	Tresh, Boyer	6
1966	Boyer, Clarke, Tresh, Pepitone	4
1967	Pepitone, Smith, Tresh, Whitaker	3
1968	White, Robinson	7
1969	Clarke	7
1970	Kenney	7
1971	Clarke, White	7
1972	Murcer	7
1973	Munson	4
1974	White	8
1975	White	5
1976	Rivers	8
1977	Randolph	11
1978	Rivers	8
1979	Randolph	13
1980	Randolph	7
1981	Mumphrey	5
1982	Mumphrey	10
1983	Winfield	8
1984	Moreno	6
1985	Winfield	6
1986	Henderson, Winfield	5
1987	Henderson, Pagliarulo	3
1988	Washington	3
1989	R. Kelly, Sax, Slaught	3
1990	R. Kelly	4
1991	B.Williams, P. Kelly	4
1992	Hall	3
1993	B. Williams	4
1994	Polonia	6
1995	B. Williams	9
1996	B. Williams	7
1997	JETER	7
1998	JETER	8
1999	JETER	9
2000	B. Williams	6
2001	JETER, Soriano, Knoblauch	3
2002	Soriano, Spencer	2
2003	B. Williams, Wilson, Soriano	5
2004	Lofton	7
2005	JETER	5
2006	Damon	5
2007	CABRERA	8
2008	Damon	5
2009	GARDNER	6

HOME RUNS

Year	Leader	HR
1903	McFarland	5
1904	Ganzel	6
1905	Williams	6
1906	Conroy	4
1907	Hoffman	5
1908	Niles	4
1909	Chase, Demmitt	4
1910	Wolter, Cree	4
1911	Wolter, Cree	4
1912	Zinn	6
1913	Wolter, Sweeney	2
1914	Peckinpaugh	3
1915	Peckinpaugh	5
1916	Pipp*	12
1917	Pipp*	9
1918	Baker	6
1919	Baker	10
1920	Ruth*	54
1921	Ruth*	59
1922	Ruth	35
1923	Ruth*	41
1924	Ruth*	46
1925	Meusel*	33
1926	Ruth*	47
1927	Ruth*	60
1928	Ruth*	54
1929	Ruth*	46
1930	Ruth*	49
1931	Ruth*, Gehrig*	46
1932	Ruth	41
1933	Ruth	34
1934	Gehrig*	49
1935	Gehrig	30
1936	Gehrig*	49
1937	DiMaggio*	46
1938	DiMaggio	32
1939	DiMaggio	30
1940	DiMaggio	31
1941	Keller	33
1942	Keller	26
1943	Keller	31
1944	Etten*	22
1945	Etten	18
1946	Keller	30
1947	DiMaggio	20
1948	DiMaggio*	39
1949	Henrich	24
1950	DiMaggio	32
1951	Berra	27
1952	Berra	30
1953	Berra	27
1954	Mantle	27
1955	Mantle*	37
1956	Mantle*	52
1957	Mantle	34
1958	Mantle*	42
1959	Mantle	31
1960	Mantle*	40
1961	Maris*	61
1962	Maris	33
1963	Howard	28
1964	Mantle	35
1965	Tresh	26
1966	Pepitone	31
1967	Mantle	22
1968	Mantle	18
1969	Pepitone	27
1970	Murcer	23
1971	Murcer	25
1972	Murcer	33
1973	Murcer, Nettles	22
1974	Nettles	22
1975	Bonds	32
1976	Nettles*	32
1977	Nettles	37
1978	Jackson, Nettles	27
1979	Jackson	29
1980	Jackson*	41
1981	Jackson, Nettles	15
1982	Winfield	37
1983	Winfield	32
1984	Baylor	27
1985	Mattingly	35
1986	Mattingly	31
1987	Pagliarulo	32
1988	Clark	27
1989	Mattingly	23
1990	Barfield	25
1991	Nokes	24
1992	Tartabull	25
1993	Tartabull	31
1994	O'Neill	21
1995	O'Neill	22
1996	B. Williams	29
1997	Martinez	44
1998	Martinez	28
1999	Martinez	28
2000	B. Williams	30
2001	Martinez	34
2002	Giambi	41
2003	Giambi	41
2004	RODRIGUEZ, Sheffield	36
2005	RODRIGUEZ*	48
2006	Giambi	37
2007	RODRIGUEZ*	54
2008	RODRIGUEZ	35
2009	TEIXEIRA*	39

RBI

Year	Leader	RBI
1903	Williams	82
1904	Anderson	82
1905	Williams	60
1906	Williams	77
1907	Chase	68
1908	Hemphill	44
1909	Engle	71
1910	Chase	73
1911	Hartzell	91
1912	Chase	58
1913	Cree	63
1914	Peckinpaugh	51
1915	Pipp	58
1916	Pipp	99
1917	Pipp	72
1918	Baker	68
1919	Baker	78
1920	Ruth*	137
1921	Ruth*	171
1922	Ruth	96
1923	Ruth*	131
1924	Ruth	121
1925	Meusel*	138
1926	Ruth*	145
1927	Gehrig*	175
1928	Gehrig*, Ruth*	142
1929	Ruth	154
1930	Gehrig*	174
1931	Gehrig*	184
1932	Gehrig	151
1933	Gehrig	139
1934	Gehrig*	165
1935	Gehrig	119
1936	Gehrig	152
1937	DiMaggio	167
1938	DiMaggio	140
1939	DiMaggio	126
1940	DiMaggio	133
1941	DiMaggio*	125
1942	DiMaggio	114
1943	Etten	107
1944	Lindell	103
1945	Etten*	111
1946	Keller	101
1947	Henrich	98
1948	DiMaggio*	155
1949	Berra	91
1950	Berra	124
1951	Berra	88
1952	Berra	98
1953	Berra	108
1954	Berra	125
1955	Berra	108
1956	Mantle*	130
1957	Mantle	94
1958	Mantle	97
1959	Lopez	93
1960	Maris*	112
1961	Maris*	141
1962	Maris	100
1963	Pepitone	89
1964	Mantle	111
1965	Tresh	74
1966	Pepitone	83
1967	Pepitone	64
1968	White	62
1969	Murcer	62
1970	White	94
1971	Murcer	94
1972	Murcer	96
1973	Murcer	95
1974	Murcer	88
1975	Munson	102
1976	Munson	105
1977	Jackson	110
1978	Jackson	97
1979	Jackson	89
1980	Jackson	111
1981	Winfield	68
1982	Winfield	106
1983	Winfield	116
1984	Mattingly	110
1985	Mattingly*	145
1986	Mattingly	113
1987	Mattingly	115
1988	Winfield	107
1989	Mattingly	113
1990	Barfield	78
1991	Hall	80
1992	Mattingly	86
1993	Tartabull	102
1994	O'Neill	83
1995	O'Neill	96
1996	Martinez	117
1997	Martinez	141
1998	Martinez	123
1999	B. Williams	115
2000	B. Williams	121
2001	Martinez	113
2002	Giambi	122
2003	Giambi	107
2004	Sheffield	121
2005	RODRIGUEZ	130
2006	RODRIGUEZ	121
2007	RODRIGUEZ*	156
2008	RODRIGUEZ	103
2009	TEIXEIRA*	122

STOLEN BASES

Year	Leader	SB
1903	Conroy	33
1904	Conroy	30
1905	Fultz	44
1906	Hoffman	33
1907	Conroy	41
1908	Hemphill	42
1909	Austin	30
1910	Daniels	41
1911	Cree	48
1912	Daniels	37
1913	Daniels	27
1914	Maisel*	74
1915	Maisel	51
1916	Magee	29
1917	Maisel	29
1918	Bodie	16
1919	Pratt	22
1920	Ruth	14
1921	Meusel, Pipp, Ruth	17
1922	Meusel	13
1923	Ruth	17
1924	Meusel	26
1925	Paschal	14
1926	Meusel	16
1927	Meusel	24
1928	Lazzeri	15
1929	Combs, Lazzeri	11
1930	Combs	16
1931	Chapman*	61
1932	Chapman*	38
1933	Chapman*	27
1934	Chapman	26
1935	Chapman	17
1936	Crosetti	18
1937	Crosetti	13
1938	Crosetti*	27
1939	Selkirk	12
1940	Gordon	18
1941	Rizzuto	14
1942	Rizzuto	22
1943	Stirnweiss	11
1944	Stirnweiss*	55
1945	Stirnweiss*	33
1946	Stirnweiss	18
1947	Rizzuto	11
1948	Rizzuto	6
1949	Rizzuto	18
1950	Rizzuto	12
1951	Rizzuto	18
1952	Rizzuto	17
1953	Mantle	8
1954	Mantle, Carey	5
1955	Hunter	9
1956	Mantle	10
1957	Mantle	16
1958	Mantle	18
1959	Mantle	21
1960	Mantle	14
1961	Mantle	12
1962	Richardson	11
1963	Richardson	15
1964	Tresh	13
1965	Richardson	7
1966	White	14
1967	Clarke	21
1968	Clarke, White	20
1969	Clarke	33
1970	Clarke, White	23
1971	Clarke	17
1972	White	23
1973	White	16
1974	White	15
1975	Bonds	30
1976	Rivers	43
1977	Rivers	22
1978	Randolph	36
1979	Randolph	32
1980	Randolph	30
1981	Randolph	14
1982	Randolph	16
1983	Baylor	17
1984	Moreno	20
1985	Henderson*	80
1986	Henderson*	87
1987	Henderson	41
1988	Henderson*	93
1989	Sax	43
1990	Sax	43
1991	R. Kelly	32
1992	R. Kelly	28
1993	P. Kelly	14
1994	Polonia	20
1995	Polonia	10
1996	B. Williams	17
1997	JETER	23
1998	Knoblauch	31
1999	Knoblauch	28
2000	JETER	22
2001	Soriano	43
2002	Soriano*	41
2003	Soriano	35
2004	RODRIGUEZ	28
2005	Womack	27
2006	JETER	34
2007	Damon	27
2008	Damon	29
2009	JETER	30

*** Denotes League Leader**

Year-by-Year Pitching Leaders

STRIKEOUTS

Year	Leader	SO
1903	Chesbro	147
1904	Chesbro	239
1905	Chesbro	156
1906	Chesbro	152
1907	Doyle	94
1908	Chesbro	124
1909	Lake	117
1910	Ford	209
1911	Ford	158
1912	Ford	112
1913	Fisher	92
1914	Keating	109
1915	Caldwell	130
1916	Shawkey	122
1917	Caldwell	102
1918	Love	95
1919	Shawkey	123
1920	Shawkey	126
1921	Shawkey	126
1922	Shawkey	133
1923	Bush, Shawkey	125
1924	Shawkey	114
1925	Jones	92
1926	Pennock	78
1927	Hoyt	86
1928	Pipgras	139
1929	Pipgras	125
1930	Ruffing	117
1931	Gomez	150
1932	Ruffing*	190
1933	Gomez*	163
1934	Gomez*	158
1935	Gomez	138
1936	Pearson	118
1937	Gomez*	194
1938	Gomez	129
1939	Gomez	102
1940	Ruffing	97
1941	Russo	105
1942	Borowy	85
1943	Chandler	134
1944	Borowy	107
1945	Bevens	76
1946	Chandler	138
1947	Reynolds	129
1948	Raschi	124
1949	Byrne	129
1950	Reynolds	160
1951	Raschi*	164
1952	Reynolds*	160
1953	Ford	110
1954	Ford	125
1955	Turley	210
1956	Ford	141
1957	Turley	152
1958	Turley	168
1959	Ford	114
1960	Terry	92
1961	Ford	209
1962	Terry	176
1963	Ford	189
1964	Downing*	217
1965	Downing	179
1966	Downing	152
1967	Downing	171
1968	Bahnsen	162
1969	Peterson	150
1970	Stottlemyre	127
1971	Peterson	139
1972	Stottlemyre	110
1973	Medich	145
1974	Dobson	157
1975	Hunter	177
1976	Hunter	173
1977	Guidry	176
1978	Guidry	248
1979	Guidry	201
1980	Guidry	166
1981	Guidry	104
1982	Righetti	163
1983	Righetti	169
1984	Niekro	136
1985	Niekro	149
1986	Guidry	140
1987	Rhoden	107
1988	Candelaria	121
1989	Hawkins	98
1990	Leary	138
1991	Sanderson	130
1992	M. Perez	218
1993	Key	173
1994	M. Perez	109
1995	McDowell	157
1996	PETTITTE	162
1997	Cone	222
1998	Cone	209
1999	Cone	177
2000	Clemens	188
2001	Mussina	214
2002	Clemens	192
2003	Mussina	195
2004	VAZQUEZ	150
2005	Johnson	211
2006	Johnson, Mussina	172
2007	PETTITTE	141
2008	PETTITTE	158
2009	SABATHIA	197

INNINGS PITCHED

Year	Leader	IP
1903	Chesbro	324.2
1904	Chesbro*	454.2
1905	Orth	305.1
1906	Orth*	338.2
1907	Orth	248.2
1908	Chesbro	289.0
1909	Warhop	243.1
1910	Ford	299.2
1911	Ford	281.1
1912	Ford	291.2
1913	Fisher	246.1
1914	Warhop	216.2
1915	Caldwell	305.0
1916	Shawkey	276.2
1917	Shawkey	236.1
1918	Mogridge	230.1
1919	Quinn	264.0
1920	Mays	312.0
1921	Mays*	336.2
1922	Shawkey	299.2
1923	Bush	275.2
1924	Pennock	286.1
1925	Pennock*	277.0
1926	Pennock	266.1
1927	Hoyt	256.1
1928	Pipgras	300.2
1929	Pipgras*	225.1
1930	Pipgras	221.0
1931	Gomez	243.0
1932	Gomez	265.1
1933	Gomez, Ruffing	235.0
1934	Gomez*	281.2
1935	Gomez	246.0
1936	Ruffing	271.0
1937	Gomez	278.1
1938	Ruffing	247.1
1939	Ruffing	233.1
1940	Ruffing	226.0
1941	Russo	209.2
1942	Chandler	200.2
1943	Chandler	253.0
1944	Borowy	252.2
1945	Bevens	184.0
1946	Chandler	257.1
1947	Reynolds	241.2
1948	Reynolds	236.1
1949	Raschi	274.2
1950	Raschi	256.2
1951	Raschi	258.1
1952	Reynolds	244.1
1953	Ford	207.0
1954	Ford	210.2
1955	Ford	253.2
1956	Ford	225.2
1957	Sturdivant	201.2
1958	Turley	245.1
1959	Ford	204.0
1960	Ditmar	200.0
1961	Ford*	283.0
1962	Terry*	298.2
1963	Ford*	269.1
1964	Bouton	271.1
1965	Stottlemyre*	291.0
1966	Stottlemyre	251.0
1967	Stottlemyre	255.0
1968	Stottlemyre	278.2
1969	Stottlemyre	303.0
1970	Stottlemyre	271.0
1971	Peterson	274.0
1972	Stottlemyre	260.0
1973	Stottlemyre	273.0
1974	Dobson	281.0
1975	Hunter*	328.0
1976	Hunter	298.2
1977	Figueroa	239.0
1978	Guidry	273.2
1979	John	276.0
1980	John	265.0
1981	May	148.0
1982	Guidry	222.0
1983	Guidry	250.1
1984	Niekro	215.2
1985	Guidry	259.0
1986	Rasmussen	202.0
1987	John	187.2
1988	Rhoden	197.0
1989	Hawkins	208.1
1990	Leary	208.0
1991	Sanderson	208.0
1992	M. Perez	247.2
1993	Key	236.2
1994	Key	168.0
1995	McDowell	217.2
1996	PETTITTE	221.0
1997	PETTITTE	240.1
1998	PETTITTE	216.1
1999	O. Hernandez	214.1
2000	PETTITTE	204.2
2001	Mussina	228.2
2002	Mussina	215.2
2003	Mussina	214.2
2004	VAZQUEZ	198.0
2005	Johnson	225.2
2006	Wang	218.0
2007	PETTITTE	215.1
2008	PETTITTE	204.0
2009	SABATHIA	230.0

WINS

Year	Leader	Wins
1903	Chesbro	21-15
1904	Chesbro*	41-12
1905	Chesbro	20-15
1906	Orth*	27-17
1907	Orth	14-21
1908	Chesbro	14-20
1909	Lake	14-11
1910	Ford	26-6
1911	Ford	22-11
1912	Ford	13-21
1913	Fisher, Ford	11-17, 11-18
1914	Caldwell	17-9
1915	Caldwell	19-16
1916	Shawkey	23-14
1917	Shawkey	13-15
1918	Mogridge	16-13
1919	Shawkey	20-11
1920	Mays	26-11
1921	Mays*	27-9
1922	Bush	26-7
1923	Jones	21-8
1924	Pennock	21-9
1925	Pennock	16-17
1926	Pennock	23-11
1927	Hoyt*	22-7
1928	Pipgras*	24-13
1929	Pipgras	18-12
1930	Pipgras, Ruffing	15-15, 15-5
1931	Gomez	21-9
1932	Gomez	24-7
1933	Gomez	16-10
1934	Gomez*	26-5
1935	Ruffing	16-11
1936	Ruffing	20-12
1937	Gomez*	21-11
1938	Ruffing*	21-7
1939	Ruffing	21-7
1940	Ruffing	15-12
1941	Ruffing, Gomez	15-6, 15-5
1942	Bonham	21-5
1943	Chandler*	20-4
1944	Borowy	17-12
1945	Bevens	13-9
1946	Chandler	20-8
1947	Reynolds	19-8
1948	Raschi	19-8
1949	Raschi	21-10
1950	Raschi	21-8
1951	Raschi, Lopat	21-10, 21-9
1952	Reynolds	20-8
1953	Ford	18-6
1954	Grim	20-6
1955	Ford*	18-7
1956	Ford	19-6
1957	Sturdivant	16-6
1958	Turley*	21-7
1959	Ford	16-10
1960	Ditmar	15-9
1961	Ford*	25-4
1962	Terry*	23-12
1963	Ford*	24-7
1964	Bouton	18-13
1965	Stottlemyre	20-9
1966	Stottlemyre, Peterson	12-20, 12-11
1967	Stottlemyre	15-15
1968	Stottlemyre	21-12
1969	Stottlemyre	20-14
1970	Peterson	20-11
1971	Stottlemyre	16-12
1972	Peterson	17-15
1973	Stottlemyre	16-16
1974	Dobson, Medich	19-15, 19-15
1975	Hunter*	23-14
1976	Figueroa	19-10
1977	Guidry, Figueroa	16-7, 16-11
1978	Guidry*	25-3
1979	John	21-9
1980	John	22-9
1981	Guidry	11-5
1982	Guidry	14-8
1983	Guidry	21-9
1984	Niekro	16-8
1985	Guidry*	22-6
1986	Rasmussen	18-6
1987	Rhoden	16-10
1988	Candelaria	13-7
1989	Hawkins	15-15
1990	Guetterman	11-7
1991	Sanderson	16-10
1992	M. Perez	13-16
1993	Key	18-6
1994	Key*	17-4
1995	McDowell	15-10
1996	PETTITTE*	21-8
1997	PETTITTE	18-7
1998	Cone*	20-7
1999	O. Hernandez	17-9
2000	PETTITTE	19-9
2001	Clemens	20-3
2002	Wells	19-7
2003	PETTITTE	21-8
2004	Lieber, VAZQUEZ	14-8, 14-10
2005	Johnson	17-8
2006	Wang*	19-6
2007	Wang	19-7
2008	Mussina	20-9
2009	SABATHIA*	19-8

ERA

Year	Leader	ERA
1903	Griffith	2.70
1904	Chesbro	1.82
1905	Chesbro	2.20
1906	Clarkson	2.32
1907	Chesbro	2.53
1908	Chesbro	2.93
1909	Lake	1.88
1910	Ford	1.65
1911	Ford	2.28
1912	McConnell	2.75
1913	Caldwell	2.43
1914	Caldwell	1.94
1915	Fisher	2.10
1916	Cullop	2.05
1917	Shawkey	2.44
1918	Mogridge	2.27
1919	Mogridge	2.50
1920	Shawkey*	2.45
1921	Mays	3.04
1922	Shawkey	2.91
1923	Hoyt	3.01
1924	Pennock	2.83
1925	Pennock	2.96
1926	Shocker	3.38
1927	W. Moore*	2.28
1928	Pennock	2.56
1929	Sherid	3.49
1930	Pipgras	4.11
1931	Gomez	2.63
1932	Ruffing	3.09
1933	Gomez	3.18
1934	Gomez*	2.33
1935	Ruffing	3.12
1936	Pearson	3.71
1937	Gomez*	2.33
1938	Ruffing	3.32
1939	Ruffing	2.94
1940	Russo	3.29
1941	Russo	3.09
1942	Bonham	2.27
1943	Chandler*	1.64
1944	Borowy	2.63
1945	Bonham	3.28
1946	Chandler	2.10
1947	Shea	3.07
1948	Shea	3.41
1949	Lopat	3.27
1950	Lopat	3.47
1951	Lopat	2.91
1952	Reynolds*	2.07
1953	Lopat*	2.43
1954	Ford	2.82
1955	Ford	2.62
1956	Ford*	2.47
1957	Shantz*	2.45
1958	Ford*	2.01
1959	Ditmar	2.90
1960	Ditmar	3.06
1961	Stafford	2.68
1962	Ford	2.90
1963	Bouton	2.53
1964	Ford	2.13
1965	Stottlemyre	2.63
1966	Peterson	3.31
1967	Downing	2.63
1968	Bahnsen	2.06
1969	Peterson	2.55
1970	Peterson	2.91
1971	Stottlemyre	2.87
1972	Kline	2.40
1973	Medich	2.95
1974	Dobson	3.07
1975	Hunter	2.58
1976	Figueroa	3.01
1977	Guidry	2.82
1978	Guidry*	1.74
1979	Guidry*	2.78
1980	May*	2.46
1981	Righetti*	2.05
1982	John	3.69
1983	Guidry	3.42
1984	Niekro	3.09
1985	Guidry	3.27
1986	Rasmussen	3.88
1987	Rhoden	3.86
1988	Rhoden	4.29
1989	Hawkins	4.80
1990	Leary	4.11
1991	Sanderson	3.81
1992	M. Perez	2.87
1993	Key	3.00
1994	Key	3.27
1995	Cone	3.82
1996	PETTITTE	3.87
1997	Cone	2.82
1998	Wells	3.49
1999	Cone	3.44
2000	Clemens	3.70
2001	Mussina	3.15
2002	Wells	3.75
2003	Mussina	3.40
2004	Lieber	4.33
2005	Johnson	3.79
2006	Mussina	3.51
2007	Wang	3.70
2008	Mussina	3.37
2009	SABATHIA	3.37

*** Denotes Tied or Led League**

Year-by-Year Games Played Leaders

Year	CATCHER Leader	C	FIRST BASE Leader	1B	SECOND BASE Leader	2B	THIRD BASE Leader	3B
1903	Beville	75	Ganzel	129	Williams	104	Conroy	123
1904	McGuire	97	Ganzel	118	Williams	146	Conroy	110
1905	Kleinow	83	Chase	122	Williams	129	Yeager	90
1906	Kleinow	95	Chase	150	Williams	139	LaPorte	114
1907	Kleinow	86	Chase	121	Williams	139	Moriarty	91
1908	Kleinow	89	Chase	98	Niles	85	Conroy	119
1909	Kleinow	77	Chase	118	LaPorte	83	Austin	111
1910	Sweeney	78	Chase	130	LaPorte	79	Austin	133
1911	Blair	84	Chase	124	Gardner	101	Hartzell	124
1912	Sweeney	108	Chase	121	Simmons	88	Hartzell	56
1913	Sweeney	112	Knight	50	Hartzell	81	Midkiff	76
1914	Sweeney	78	Mullen	93	Boone	90	Maisel	148
1915	Nunamaker	77	Pipp	134	Boone	134	Maisel	134
1916	Nunamaker	79	Pipp	148	Gedeon	122	Baker	96
1917	Nunamaker	91	Pipp	155	Maisel	100	Baker	146
1918	Hannah	88	Pipp	91	Pratt	126	Baker	126
1919	Ruel	81	Pipp	140	Pratt	140	Baker	141
1920	Ruel	80	Pipp	153	Pratt	154	Ward	114
1921	Schang	132	Pipp	153	Ward	123	Baker	83
1922	Schang	119	Pipp	152	Ward	152	Baker	60
1923	Schang	81	Pipp	144	Ward	152	Dugan	146
1924	Schang	106	Pipp	153	Ward	120	Dugan	148
1925	Bengough	94	Gehrig	114	Ward	113	Dugan	96
1926	Collins	100	Gehrig	155	Lazzeri	149	Dugan	122
1927	Collins	89	Gehrig	155	Lazzeri	113	Dugan	111
1928	Grabowski	75	Gehrig	154	Lazzeri	110	Dugan	91
1929	Dickey	127	Gehrig	154	Lazzeri	147	Robertson	77
1930	Dickey	101	Gehrig	153	Lazzeri	77	Chapman	91
1931	Dickey	125	Gehrig	154	Lazzeri	90	Sewell	121
1932	Dickey	108	Gehrig	155	Lazzeri	133	Sewell	122
1933	Dickey	127	Gehrig	152	Lazzeri	138	Sewell	131
1934	Dickey	104	Gehrig	153	Lazzeri	92	Saltzgaver	84
1935	Dickey	118	Gehrig	149	Lazzeri	118	Rolfe	136
1936	Dickey	107	Gehrig	155	Lazzeri	148	Rolfe	133
1937	Dickey	137	Gehrig	157	Lazzeri	125	Rolfe	154
1938	Dickey	126	Gehrig	157	Gordon	126	Rolfe	151
1939	Dickey	126	Dahlgren	144	Gordon	151	Rolfe	152
1940	Dickey	102	Dahlgren	155	Gordon	155	Rolfe	138
1941	Dickey	104	Sturm	124	Gordon	131	Rolfe	131
1942	Dickey	80	Hassett	132	Gordon	147	Crosetti	62
1943	Dickey	71	Etten	154	Gordon	152	Johnson	155
1944	Garback	85	Etten	154	Stirnweiss	154	Grimes	97
1945	Garback	59	Etten	152	Stirnweiss	152	Grimes	141
1946	Robinson	95	Etten	84	Gordon	108	Stirnweiss	79
1947	Robinson	74	McQuinn	142	Stirnweiss	148	Johnson	132
1948	Niarhos	82	McQuinn	90	Stirnweiss	141	Johnson	118
1949	Berra	109	Henrich	52	Coleman	122	Brown	86
1950	Berra	148	Collins	99	Coleman	152	Johnson	100
1951	Berra	141	Collins	114	Coleman	102	Brown	90
1952	Berra	140	Collins	119	Martin	107	McDougald	117
1953	Berra	133	Collins	113	Martin	146	McDougald	136
1954	Berra	149	Collins	117	McDougald	92	Carey	120
1955	Berra	145	Skowron	74	McDougald	126	Carey	135
1956	Berra	135	Skowron	120	Martin	105	Carey	131
1957	Berra	121	Skowron	115	Richardson	93	Carey	81
1958	Berra	88	Skowron	118	McDougald	115	Carey	99
1959	Berra	116	Skowron	72	Richardson	109	Lopez	76
1960	Howard	91	Skowron	142	Richardson	141	Boyer	99
1961	Howard	111	Skowron	149	Richardson	161	Boyer	141
1962	Howard	129	Skowron	135	Richardson	161	Boyer	157
1963	Howard	132	Pepitone	143	Richardson	150	Boyer	141
1964	Howard	146	Pepitone	155	Richardson	157	Boyer	123
1965	Howard	95	Pepitone	115	Richardson	158	Boyer	147
1966	Howard	100	Pepitone	119	Richardson	147	Boyer	85
1967	Gibbs	99	Mantle	131	Clarke	140	Smith	115
1968	Gibbs	121	Mantle	131	Clarke	139	Cox	132
1969	Gibbs	66	Pepitone	132	Clarke	156	Kenney	83
1970	Munson	125	Cater	131	Clarke	157	Kenney	135
1971	Munson	117	Cater	78	Clarke	156	Kenney	109
1972	Munson	132	Blomberg	95	Clarke	143	Sanchez	68
1973	Munson	142	F. Alou	67	Clarke	147	Nettles	157
1974	Munson	137	Chambliss	106	Alomar	76	Nettles	154
1975	Munson	130	Chambliss	147	Alomar	150	Nettles	157
1976	Munson	121	Chambliss	155	Randolph	124	Nettles	158
1977	Munson	136	Chambliss	157	Randolph	147	Nettles	156
1978	Munson	125	Chambliss	155	Randolph	134	Nettles	159
1979	Munson	88	Chambliss	134	Randolph	153	Nettles	144
1980	Cerone	147	Watson	104	Randolph	138	Nettles	88
1981	Cerone	69	Watson	50	Randolph	93	Nettles	97
1982	Cerone	89	Mayberry	64	Randolph	143	Nettles	122
1983	Wynegar	94	Griffey	100	Randolph	104	Nettles	129
1984	Wynegar	126	Mattingly	133	Randolph	142	Harrah	74
1985	Wynegar	96	Mattingly	159	Randolph	143	Pagliarulo	134
1986	Wynegar	57	Mattingly	160	Randolph	139	Pagliarulo	143
1987	Cerone	111	Mattingly	140	Randolph	119	Pagliarulo	147
1988	Slaught	94	Mattingly	143	Randolph	110	Pagliarulo	124
1989	Slaught	105	Mattingly	145	Sax	158	Pagliarulo	69
1990	Geren	107	Mattingly	89	Sax	154	Velarde	74
1991	Nokes	130	Mattingly	127	Sax	149	P. Kelly	80
1992	Nokes	111	Mattingly	143	P. Kelly	101	Hayes	139
1993	Stanley	122	Mattingly	130	P. Kelly	125	Boggs	134
1994	Stanley	72	Mattingly	97	P. Kelly	93	Boggs	93
1995	Stanley	107	Mattingly	125	P. Kelly	87	Boggs	117
1996	Girardi	110	Martinez	152	Duncan	98	Boggs	123
1997	Girardi	109	Martinez	147	Sojo	51	Hayes	89
1998	POSADA	85	Martinez	139	Knoblauch	149	Brosius	147
1999	POSADA	98	Martinez	151	Knoblauch	150	Brosius	130
2000	POSADA	136	Martinez	149	Knoblauch	82	Brosius	133
2001	POSADA	127	Martinez	146	Soriano	156	Brosius	120
2002	POSADA	131	Giambi	92	Soriano	154	Ventura	130
2003	POSADA	131	Giambi	85	Soriano	154	Ventura	76
2004	POSADA	126	Clark	64	Cairo	96	RODRIGUEZ	155
2005	POSADA	133	Martinez	122	CANO	131	RODRIGUEZ	161
2006	POSADA	134	Phillips	94	CANO	118	RODRIGUEZ	151
2007	POSADA	138	Mientkiewicz	70	CANO	159	RODRIGUEZ	154
2008	Molina	97	Giambi	113	CANO	159	RODRIGUEZ	131
2009	POSADA	100	TEIXEIRA	152	CANO	161	RODRIGUEZ	116

Year-by-Year Games Played Leaders

Year	SHORTSTOP Leader	SS	DESIGNATED HITTER Leader	DH	OUTFIELD Leader	OF	OUTFIELD Leader	OF	OUTFIELD Leader	OF
1903	Elberfeld	90			Keeler	128	Davis	102	McFarland	103
1904	Elberfeld	122			Keeler	142	Anderson	112	Dougherty	106
1905	Elberfeld	108			Keeler	139	Fultz	122	Dougherty	108
1906	Elberfeld	98			Keeler	152	Hoffman	98	Conroy	97
1907	Elberfeld	118			Hoffman	135	Keeler	107	Conroy	100
1908	Ball	130			Hemphill	142	Keeler	88	Stahl	67
1909	Knight	78			Engle	134	Demmitt	109	Keeler	95
1910	Knight	79			Cree	134	Wolter	130	Hemphill	94
1911	Knight	82			Cree	137	Daniels	120	Wolter	113
1912	Martin	64			Daniels	131	Zinn	106	Hartzell	55
1913	Peckinpaugh	93			Cree	144	Wolter	121	Daniels	87
1914	Peckinpaugh	157			Hartzell	128	Cook	126	Cree	76
1915	Peckinpaugh	142			Cook	131	High	117	Hartzell	107
1916	Peckinpaugh	146			Magee	128	High	109	Gilhooley	57
1917	Peckinpaugh	148			Miller	112	Hendry	107	High	100
1918	Peckinpaugh	122			Gilhooley	111	Bodie	90	Miller	62
1919	Peckinpaugh	121			Lewis	141	Bodie	134	Vick	100
1920	Peckinpaugh	137			Ruth	139	Bodie	129	Lewis	99
1921	Peckinpaugh	147			Ruth	152	Meusel	147	Miller	56
1922	Scott	154			Witt	138	Meusel	121	Ruth	110
1923	Scott	152			Ruth	148	Witt	144	Meusel	121
1924	Scott	153			Ruth	152	Witt	143	Meusel	143
1925	Wanninger	111			Combs	149	Combs	150	Ruth	98
1926	Koenig	141			Ruth	149	Combs	145	Meusel	107
1927	Koenig	122			Combs	152	Ruth	151	Meusel	131
1928	Koenig	125			Ruth	154	Meusel	131	Meusel	131
1929	Durocher	93			Combs	141	Ruth	133	Meusel	96
1930	Lary	113			Ruth	144	Combs	135	Rice	87
1931	Lary	155			Ruth	142	Chapman	137	Combs	129
1932	Crosetti	83			Chapman	149	Combs	138	Ruth	127
1933	Crosetti	133			Chapman	147	Ruth	132	Combs	104
1934	Crosetti	119			Chapman	149	Ruth	111	Byrd	104
1935	Crosetti	87			Chapman	138	Selkirk	127	Hill	94
1936	Crosetti	151			DiMaggio	138	Selkirk	135	Powell	84
1937	Crosetti	147			DiMaggio	150	Hoag	99	Powell	94
1938	Crosetti	157			DiMaggio	145	Henrich	130	Selkirk	95
1939	Crosetti	152			Selkirk	124	DiMaggio	117	Keller	105
1940	Crosetti	145			Keller	136	DiMaggio	130	Selkirk	111
1941	Rizzuto	128			Henrich	139	DiMaggio	139	Keller	137
1942	Rizzuto	144			DiMaggio	154	Keller	152	Henrich	119
1943	Crosetti	90			Keller	141	Lindell	122	Metheny	91
1944	Milosevich	91			Lindell	149	Metheny	132	Martin	80
1945	Crosetti	126			Metheny	128	Martin	102	Stainback	83
1946	Rizzuto	125			Keller	149	DiMaggio	131	Henrich	111
1947	Rizzuto	151			DiMaggio	139	Henrich	132	Lindell	118
1948	Rizzuto	128			DiMaggio	152	Henrich	102	Lindell	79
1949	Rizzuto	152			Mapes	108	Woodling	98	Bauer	95
1950	Rizzuto	155			DiMaggio	137	Woodling	118	Bauer	110
1951	Rizzuto	144			Woodling	116	DiMaggio	113	Bauer	107
1952	Rizzuto	152			Mantle	141	Bauer	139	Woodling	118
1953	Rizzuto	133			Bauer	126	Mantle	121	Woodling	119
1954	Rizzuto	126			Mantle	144	Noren	116	Bauer	108
1955	Hunter	98			Mantle	145	Bauer	133	Noren	126
1956	McDougald	92			Bauer	146	Mantle	144	Howard	65
1957	McDougald	121			Mantle	139	Bauer	135	Howard	71
1958	Kubek	134			Mantle	150	Siebern	133	Bauer	123
1959	Kubek	67			Mantle	143	Bauer	111	Siebern	93
1960	Kubek	136			Mantle	150	Maris	131	Lopez	106
1961	Kubek	145			Maris	160	Mantle	150	Berra	87
1962	Tresh	111			Maris	154	Mantle	117	Lopez	84
1963	Kubek	132			Tresh	144	Lopez	124	Reed	89
1964	Kubek	99			Tresh	146	Maris	137	Mantle	132
1965	Kubek	93			Tresh	154	Mantle	108	Moschitto	89
1966	Clarke	63			Mantle	97	Maris	95	Tresh	84
1967	Amaro	123			Pepitone	123	Tresh	118	Whitaker	114
1968	Tresh	119			White	154	Robinson	98	Kosco	95
1969	Michael	118			White	126	Murcer	118	Woods	67
1970	Michael	123			White	161	Murcer	155	Blefary	79
1971	Michael	136			White	145	Murcer	143	F. Alou	80
1972	Michael	121			White	155	Murcer	151	Callison	74
1973	Michael	128	Hart	106	White	162	Murcer	160	M. Alou	85
1974	Mason	152	Blomberg	58	Murcer	156	Maddox	135	Piniella	130
1975	Mason	93	Herrmann	35	White	135	Bonds	129	Maddox	55
1976	Stanley	110	May	81	White	156	Rivers	136	Gamble	104
1977	Dent	157	May	51	Rivers	136	White	135	Jackson	127
1978	Dent	123	Johnson	39	Rivers	138	Jackson	104	Piniella	103
1979	Dent	141	Spencer	71	Jackson	125	Piniella	112	Murcer	70
1980	Dent	141	Soderholm	51	Brown	131	Piniella	104	Jackson	94
1981	Dent	73	Murcer	33	Winfield	102	Mumphrey	79	Jackson	61
1982	Smalley	93	Gamble	74	Winfield	135	Griffey	125	Mumphrey	123
1983	Smalley	90	Baylor	136	Winfield	151	Kemp	101	Mumphrey	83
1984	Meacham	96	Baylor	127	Winfield	140	Moreno	108	Griffey	82
1985	Meacham	155	Baylor	140	Winfield	152	Henderson	141	Griffey	110
1986	Meacham, Tolleson	56	Easler	129	Henderson	146	Winfield	145	Pasqua	81
1987	Tolleson	118	Kittle	49	Winfield	145	Ward	94	Pasqua	74
1988	Santana	148	Clark	112	Winfield	141	Henderson	136	Washington	117
1989	Espinoza	146	Balboni	82	R. Kelly	137	Barfield	129	Hall	75
1990	Espinoza	150	Balboni	72	R. Kelly	160	Barfield	151	Azocar	57
1991	Espinoza	147	Maas	109	R. Kelly	125	Hall	120	B. Williams	85
1992	Stankiewicz	81	Maas	62	R. Kelly	146	Hall	136	Tartabull	69
1993	Owen	96	Tartabull	88	B. Williams	139	O'Neill	138	James	103
1994	Gallego	72	Tartabull	78	B. Williams	107	O'Neill	99	Polonia	84
1995	Fernandez	103	Sierra	46	B. Williams	144	O'Neill	121	G. Williams	92
1996	JETER	156	Sierra	61	O'Neill	146	B. Williams	140	G. Williams	117
1997	JETER	159	Fielder	88	O'Neill	145	B. Williams	127	Curtis	92
1998	JETER	148	Strawberry	79	O'Neill	148	B. Williams	123	Curtis	121
1999	JETER	158	Davis	127	B. Williams	153	O'Neill	150	Ledee	68
2000	JETER	148	Spencer	33	O'Neill	139	B. Williams	136	Justice	57
2001	JETER	150	Justice	86	B. Williams	144	O'Neill	127	Knoblauch	104
2002	JETER	156	Giambi	63	B. Williams	147	Ron. White	105	Mondesi	59
2003	JETER	118	Giambi	69	Matsui	156	B. Williams	113	Mondesi	95
2004	JETER	154	Sierra	54	Matsui	160	Sheffield	136	B. Williams	93
2005	JETER	157	Giambi	59	Matsui	143	Sheffield	131	B. Williams	112
2006	JETER	150	Giambi	70	Damon	131	Cabrera	116	B. Williams	91
2007	JETER	155	Giambi	57	Abreu	157	Cabrera	131	Matsui	112
2008	JETER	148	Matsui	66	Abreu	150	Cabrera	117	Damon	87
2009	JETER	150	Matsui	118	Damon	132	SWISHER	130	Cabrera	103

Top 20 Career Batting Leaders

Special thanks to the *Elias Sports Bureau*

Games

1.	Mantle	2401
2.	Gehrig	2164
3.	**JETER**	**2138**
4.	Berra	2116
5.	Ruth	2084
6.	B. Williams	2076
7.	White	1881
8.	Dickey	1789
9.	Mattingly	1785
10.	DiMaggio	1736
11.	Randolph	1694
12.	Crosetti	1683
13.	Rizzuto	1661
14.	Lazzeri	1659
15.	**POSADA**	**1594**
16.	Nettles	1535
17.	Howard	1492
18.	Pipp	1488
19.	Combs	1456
20.	Munson	1423

At-Bats

	Player	AB
1.	**JETER**	**8659**
2.	Mantle	8102
3.	Gehrig	8001
4.	B. Williams	7869
5.	Berra	7546
6.	Ruth	7215
7.	Mattingly	7003
8.	DiMaggio	6821
9.	White	6650
10.	Dickey	6304
11.	Randolph	6303
12.	Crosetti	6276
13.	Lazzeri	6096
14.	Rizzuto	5816
15.	Combs	5752
16.	Pipp	5594
17.	Nettles	5519
18.	Richardson	5386
19.	**POSADA**	**5365**
20.	Munson	5344

Runs

1.	Ruth	1959
2.	Gehrig	1888
3.	Mantle	1677
4.	**JETER**	**1574**
5.	DiMaggio	1390
6.	B. Williams	1366
7.	Combs	1186
8.	Berra	1174
9.	Randolph	1027
10.	Mattingly	1007
11.	Crosetti	1006
12.	White	964
13.	Lazzeri	952
14.	Rolfe	942
15.	Dickey	931
16.	Henrich	901
17.	Rizzuto	878
18.	Pipp	820
19.	**POSADA**	**817**
20.	Bauer	792

Hits

1.	**JETER**	**2747**
2.	Gehrig	2721
3.	Ruth	2518
4.	Mantle	2415
5.	B. Williams	2336
6.	DiMaggio	2214
7.	Mattingly	2153
8.	Berra	2148
9.	Dickey	1969
10.	Combs	1866
11.	White	1803
12.	Lazzeri	1784
13.	Randolph	1731
14.	Rizzuto	1588
15.	Pipp	1577
16.	Meusel	1565
17.	Munson	1558
18.	Crosetti	1541
19.	**POSADA**	**1488**
20.	Richardson	1432

Doubles

	Player	2B
1.	Gehrig	534
2.	B. Williams	449
3.	Mattingly	442
4.	**JETER**	**438**
5.	Ruth	424
6.	DiMaggio	389
7.	Mantle	344
8.	Dickey	343
9.	**POSADA**	**342**
10.	Meusel	339
11.	Lazzeri	327
12.	Berra	321
13.	Combs	309
14.	O'Neill	304
15.	White	300
16.	Henrich	269
17.	Crosetti	260
18.	Pipp	259
	Randolph	259
20.	Rolfe	257

Triples

	Player	3B
1.	Gehrig	163
2.	Combs	154
3.	DiMaggio	131
4.	Pipp	121
5.	Lazzeri	115
6.	Ruth	106
7.	J. Williams	87
8.	Meusel	86
9.	Henrich	73
10.	Dickey	72
	Mantle	72
12.	Keller	69
13.	Rolfe	67
14.	Stirnweiss	66
15.	Crosetti	65
16.	Chapman	64
17.	Cree	62
	Rizzuto	62
19.	Conroy	59
20.	Randolph	58
	JETER	**58**

Home Runs

	Player	HR
1.	Ruth	659
2.	Mantle	536
3.	Gehrig	493
4.	DiMaggio	361
5.	Berra	358
6.	B. Williams	287
7.	Nettles	250
8.	**POSADA**	**243**
9.	**RODRIGUEZ**	**238**
10.	**JETER**	**224**
11.	Mattingly	222
12.	Giambi	209
13.	Winfield	205
14.	Maris	203
15.	Dickey	202
16.	Martinez	192
17.	O'Neill	185
18.	Keller	184
19.	Henrich	183
20.	Murcer	175

RBI (since 1920)

1.	Gehrig	1996
2.	Ruth	1976
3.	DiMaggio	1537
4.	Mantle	1509
5.	Berra	1430
6.	B. Williams	1257
7.	Dickey	1210
8.	Lazzeri	1159
9.	Mattingly	1099
10.	**JETER**	**1068**
11.	Meusel	1013
12.	**POSADA**	**964**
13.	O'Neill	858
14.	Nettles	834
15.	Winfield	818
16.	Henrich	795
17.	White	758
18.	Martinez	739
19.	Howard	733
20.	Keller	723

Batting Average (min. 500g)

1.	Ruth	.349
2.	Gehrig	.340
3.	DiMaggio	.325
4.	Combs	.324
5.	**JETER**	**.317**
6.	Boggs	.313
7.	Dickey	.312
8.	Meusel	.311
9.	Mattingly	.307
10.	**CANO**	**.306**
11.	Chapman	.305
12.	O'Neill	.303
13.	**RODRIGUEZ**	**.300**
14.	Mantle	.298
15.	B. Williams	.297
16.	Schang	.296
17.	Piniella	.295
18.	Keeler	.294
19.	Skowron	.294
20.	Cree	.293

Stolen Bases

	Player	SB
1.	Henderson	326
2.	**JETER**	**305**
3.	Randolph	251
4.	Chase	248
5.	White	232
6.	Chapman	184
	Conroy	184
8.	Maisel	183
9.	Mantle	153
10.	Clarke	151
	R. Kelly	151
12.	Rizzuto	149
13.	Lazzeri	147
	B. Williams	147
15.	Daniels	145
16.	Peckinpaugh	143
17.	Meusel	134
18.	Cree	132
19.	Stirnweiss	130
20.	Soriano	121

Single-Season Leaders by Position

P	No.	Player	Year
HR	5	Ruffing	1936
RBI	22	Ruffing	1936, 1941
AVG	.339	Ruffing	1935

C	No.	Player	Year
HR	30	Berra	1952, 1956
	30	Posada	2003
RBI	133	Dickey	1937
AVG	.362	Dickey	1936

1B	No.	Player	Year
HR	49	Gehrig	1934, 1936
RBI	184	Gehrig	1931
AVG	.379	Gehrig	1930

2B	No.	Player	Year
HR	39	Soriano	2002
RBI	114	Lazzeri	1926
AVG	.354	Lazzeri	1929

3B	No.	Player	Year
HR	54	RODRIGUEZ	2007
RBI	156	RODRIGUEZ	2007
AVG	.342	Boggs	1994

SS	No.	Player	Year
HR	24	JETER	1999
RBI	107	Lary	1931
AVG	.349	JETER	1999

OF	No.	Player	Year
HR	61	Maris	1961
RBI	170	Ruth	1921
AVG	.394	Ruth	1923

** Played at least 75% of games at that position*

Top 20 Career Pitching Leaders

Games Pitched

1.	**RIVERA**	**917**
2.	Righetti	522
3.	Ford, W.	498
4.	Stanton	456
5.	Ruffing	426
6.	Lyle	420
7.	Shawkey	415
8.	**PETTITTE**	**384**
9.	Murphy	383
10.	Guidry	368
11.	Gomez	367
12.	Hoyt	365
13.	Stottlemyre	360
14.	Pennock	346
15.	Nelson	331
16.	Gossage	319
17.	Hamilton	311
18.	Reynolds	295
19.	Peterson	288
20.	Page	278
	Mendoza	278

Wins

1.	Ford, W.	236
2.	Ruffing	231
3.	**PETTITTE**	**192**
4.	Gomez	189
5.	Guidry	170
6.	Shawkey	168
7.	Stottlemyre	164
8.	Pennock	162
9.	Hoyt	157
10.	Reynolds	131
11.	Chesbro	128
12.	Mussina	123
13.	Raschi	120
14.	Lopat	113
15.	Chandler	109
	Peterson	109
17.	Caldwell	95
18.	Murphy	93
	Pipgras	93
20.	John	91

Strikeouts

1.	Ford, W.	1956
2.	Guidry	1778
3.	**PETTITTE**	**1722**
4.	Ruffing	1526
5.	Gomez	1468
6.	Mussina	1278
7.	Stottlemyre	1260
8.	Shawkey	1166
9.	Downing	1028
10.	Clemens	1014
11.	**RIVERA**	**1006**
12.	Reynolds	967
13.	Righetti	940
14.	Chesbro	913
15.	Turley	909
16.	Peterson	891
17.	Cone	888
18.	Raschi	832
19.	Caldwell	803
20.	Hoyt	709

Complete Games

1.	Ruffing	261
2.	Gomez	173
3.	Chesbro	168
4.	Pennock	164
	Shawkey	164
6.	Ford, W.	156
	Hoyt	156
8.	Stottlemyre	152
9.	Caldwell	150
10.	Chandler	109
11.	Warhop	105
12.	Orth	102
13.	Ford, R.	100
14.	Raschi	99
15.	Reynolds	96
16.	Guidry	95
17.	Bonham	91
	Lopat	91
	Mays	91
20.	Fisher	88

Games Started

1.	Ford, W.	438
2.	Ruffing	391
3.	**PETTITTE**	**375**
4.	Stottlemyre	356
5.	Guidry	323
6.	Gomez	319
7.	Hoyt	276
8.	Shawkey	274
9.	Pennock	268
10.	Peterson	265
11.	Mussina	248
12.	Chesbro	227
13.	Reynolds	209
14.	Raschi	207
15.	John	203
16.	Lopat	202
17.	Caldwell	196
18.	Chandler	184
19.	Downing	175
	Turley	175

Win Pct. (min. 100 decisions)

1.	Chandler	.717
2.	Raschi	.706
3.	Ford, W.	.690
4.	Reynolds	.686
5.	Mays	.669
6.	Clemens	.664
7.	Lopat	.657
8.	Gomez	.652
9.	Guidry	.651
10.	Ruffing	.651
11.	Byrne	.643
	Pennock	.643
13.	**PETTITTE**	**.638**
14.	Murphy	.637
15.	Mussina	.631
16.	Bush	.620
17.	Hoyt	.616
18.	Cone	.615
19.	Figueroa	.614
20.	Bonham	.612

Shutouts

1.	Ford, W.	45
2.	Stottlemyre	40
	Ruffing	40
4.	Gomez	28
5.	Reynolds	27
6.	Chandler	26
	Guidry	26
	Shawkey	26
9.	Raschi	24
10.	Turley	21
11.	Lopat	20
12.	Pennock	19
13.	Chesbro	18
	Peterson	18
15.	Bonham	17
	Caldwell	17
17.	Hoyt	15
18.	Orth	14
	Pipgras	14
	Terry	14

ERA (Since 1913, min. 800.0 IP)

1.	**RIVERA**	**2.25**
2.	Fisher	2.60
3.	Caldwell	2.70
4.	Bonham	2.73
5.	Mogridge	2.74
6.	Ford, W.	2.74
7.	Chandler	2.84
8.	Stottlemyre	2.97
9.	Peterson	3.10
10.	Bahnsen	3.11
11.	Righetti	3.11
12.	Shawkey	3.12
13.	May, R.	3.12
14.	Shocker	3.16
15.	Lopat	3.19
16.	Downing	3.23
17.	Mays	3.25
18.	Guidry	3.29
19.	Reynolds	3.31
20.	Gomez	3.34

Earned runs became an official AL statistic in 1913.

Innings

1.	Ford, W.	3171.0
2.	Ruffing	3168.0
3.	Stottlemyre	2662.0
4.	Gomez	2497.0
5.	Shawkey	2493.0
6.	**PETTITTE**	**2406.2**
7.	Guidry	2393.0
8.	Hoyt	2274.0
9.	Pennock	2201.0
10.	Chesbro	1950.0
11.	Peterson	1856.0
12.	Caldwell	1714.0
13.	Reynolds	1700.0
14.	Mussina	1553.0
15.	Raschi	1538.0
16.	Lopat	1497.0
17.	Chandler	1485.0
18.	Warhop	1412.0
19.	Fisher	1386.0
20.	John	1366.0

Year-by-Year Save Leaders

Saves became an official statistic in 1969

Year	Pitcher	W	S
1969	Aker	8	11
1970	McDaniel	9	29
1971	McDaniel	5	4
	Aker	4	4
1972	Lyle	9	*35
1973	Lyle	5	27
1974	Lyle	9	15
1975	Martinez	1	8
1976	Lyle	7	23
1977	Lyle	13	26
1978	Gossage	10	*27
1979	Gossage	5	18
1980	Gossage	6	*33
1981	Gossage	3	20
1982	Gossage	4	30
1983	Gossage	13	22
1984	Righetti	5	31
1985	Righetti	12	29
1986	Righetti	8	*46
1987	Righetti	8	31
1988	Righetti	5	25
1989	Righetti	2	25
1990	Righetti	1	36
1991	Farr	5	23
1992	Farr	2	30
1993	Farr	2	25
1994	Howe	3	15
1995	Wetteland	1	31
1996	Wetteland	2	43
1997	RIVERA	6	43
1998	RIVERA	3	36
1999	RIVERA	4	*45
2000	RIVERA	7	36
2001	RIVERA	4	*50
2002	RIVERA	1	28
2003	RIVERA	5	40
2004	RIVERA	4	*53
2005	RIVERA	7	43
2006	RIVERA	5	34
2007	RIVERA	3	30
2008	RIVERA	6	39
2009	RIVERA	3	44

***Denotes League Leader**

Saves (Since 1969)

1.	**RIVERA**	**526**
2.	Righetti	224
3.	Gossage	151
4.	Lyle	141
5.	Farr	78
6.	Wetteland	74
7.	McDaniel	48
8.	Aker	31
	Howe	31
10.	Tidrow	23
11.	Davis	22
12.	Guetterman	21
13.	Fisher	20
14.	Mendoza	16
15.	Stanton	15
16.	Karsay	12
	Frazier	12
	Guante	12
19.	Stoddard	11
	Wickman	11

Top 10 Single-Season Leaders

BATTING

At-Bats
1. Soriano .....696...2002
2. Richardson..692...1962
3. Clarke.......686...1970
4. Soriano .....682...2003
5. Richardson..679...1964
6. Mattingly ...677...1986
7. Richardson..664...1965
8. Richardson..662...1961
9. Crosetti .....656...1939
10. JETER...... 654.. 1997
JETER...... 654.. 2005

Runs Scored
1. Ruth ....177...1921
2. Gehrig ......167...1936
3. Ruth ....163...1928
Gehrig ......163...1931
5. Ruth ....158...1920
Ruth ....158...1927
7. Ruth ....151...1923
DiMaggio ...151...1937
9. Ruth ....150...1930
10. Gehrig ......149...1927
Ruth ....149...1931

Hits
1. Mattingly ...238...1986
2. Combs......231...1927
3. Gehrig ......220...1930
4. JETER...... 219.. 1999
5. Gehrig ......218...1927
6. DiMaggio ...215...1937
7. JETER...... 214.. 2006
8. Rolfe........213...1939
9. JETER...... 212.. 2009
10. Gehrig ......211...1931
Mattingly ...211...1985

Doubles
1. Mattingly ...53 1986
2. Gehrig 52 1927
3. Soriano 51 2002
4. Mattingly ...48 1985
CANO...... 48... 2009
6. Gehrig 47 1926
Meusel......47 1927
Gehrig 47 1928
9. Rolfe........46 1939
10. Ruth 45 1923
Meusel......45 1928
Matsui 45 2005

Triples
1. Combs......23 1927
2. Cree 22 1911
Combs......22 1930
Stirnweiss...22 1945
5. Combs......21 1928
6. Gehrig 20 1926
7. Pipp 19 1924
8. Gehrig 18 1927
9. Gehrig 17 1930
10. 7 tied 16

Home Runs
1. Maris........61 1961
2. Ruth 60 1927
3. Ruth 59 1921
4. Ruth 54 1920
Ruth 54 1928
Mantle 54 1961
RODRIGUEZ.. 54... 2007
8. Mantle......52 1956
9. Ruth 49 1930
Gehrig 49 1934
Gehrig 49 1936

Runs Batted In
1. Gehrig ......184...1931
2. Gehrig ......175...1927
3. Gehrig ......174...1930
4. Ruth ....171...1921
5. DiMaggio ...167...1937
6. Gehrig ......165...1934
7. Ruth ....164...1927
8. Ruth ....162...1931
9. Gehrig ......159...1937
10. RODRIGUEZ.. 156...2007

Total Bases
1. Ruth ....457...1921
2. Gehrig ......447...1927
3. Gehrig ......419...1930
4. DiMaggio ...418...1937
5. Ruth ....417...1927
6. Gehrig ......410...1931
7. Gehrig ......409...1934
8. Gehrig ......403...1936
9. Ruth ....399...1923
10. Ruth ....391...1924

Stolen Bases
1. Henderson..93 1988
2. Henderson..87 1986
3. Henderson..80 1985
4. Maisel.......74 1914
5. Chapman ...61 1931
6. Stirnweiss...55 1944
7. Maisel.......51 1915
8. Cree 48 1911
9. Fultz 44 1905
10. 4 tied 43

Walks
1. Ruth ....170...1923
2. Ruth ....150...1920
3. Mantle......146...1957
4. Ruth ....145...1921
Ruth ....144...1926
6. Ruth ....142...1924
7. Ruth ....137...1927
Ruth ....137...1928
9. Ruth ....136...1930
10. Gehrig ......132...1935

Strikeouts (Batter)
1. Soriano .....157...2002
2. Tartabull ....156...1993
3. POSADA... 151.. 2000
4. Barfield .....150...1990
5. R. Kelly......148...1990
6. POSADA... 143.. 2002
7. Clark........141...1988
8. Giambi......140...2003
9. RODRIGUEZ.. 139.. 2005
RODRIGUEZ.. 139.. 2006

Batting Avg. (min. 500 PA)
1. Ruth ....394..1923
2. DiMaggio ....381..1939
3. Gehrig ....379..1930
4. Ruth ....378..1924
5. Ruth ....377..1921
6. Ruth ....376..1920
7. Gehrig ....374..1928
8. Gehrig ....373..1927
9. Ruth ....373..1931
10. Ruth ....372..1926

Hitting Streaks
1. DiMaggio ...56 1941
2. Chase.......33 1907
3. Peckinpaugh..29 1919
Combs......29 1931
Gordon 29 1942
6. Ruth 26 1921
7. JETER...... 25... 2006
8. Mattingly ...24 1986
9. DiMaggio ...23 1940
10. DiMaggio ...22 1937

PITCHING

Games Pitched
1. Quantrill 86 2004
2. Proctor......83 2006
3. Gordon 80 2004
4. Stanton 79 2002
Gordon 79 2005
6. Karsay 78 2002
7. Nelson 77 1997
Vizcaino.....77 2007
9. Stanton 76 2001
10. Righetti 74 1985
Righetti 74 1986
RIVERA .... 74... 2004

Complete Games
1. Chesbro.....48 1904
2. Powell 38 1904
3. Orth 36 1906
4. Chesbro.....33 1903
5. Caldwell 31 1915
6. R. Ford 30 1912
Mays........30 1921
Hunter.......30 1975
9. R. Ford 29 1910
10. Orth 26 1905
R. Ford 26 1911
Mays........26 1920

Wins
1. Chesbro.....41 1904
2. Orth 27 1906
Mays........27 1921
4. R.Ford.......26 1910
Mays........26 1920
Bush 26 1922
Gomez......26 1934
8. W. Ford......25 1961
Guidry 25 1978
10. 4 tied 24

Shutouts
1. Guidry ......9......1978
2. R. Ford ......8......1910
W. Ford......8......1964
4. Reynolds....7......1951
W. Ford......7......1958
Stottlemyre .7......1971
Stottlemyre .7......1972
Hunter ......7......1975
9. 14 tied 6

Strikeouts (Pitcher)
1. Guidry ......248...1978
2. Chesbro.....239...1904
3. Cone........222...1997
4. M. Perez.....218...1992
5. Downing....217...1964
6. Mussina.....214...2001
7. Clemens ....213...2001
8. Johnson.....211...2005
9. Turley ....210...1955
10 R. Ford ......209...1910
W. Ford......209...1961
Cone........209...1998

ERA (min. 1.0IP/per team game)
1. Chandler....1.64...1943
2. Guidry ....1.74...1978
3. Caldwell ....1.94...1914
4. W. Ford......2.01...1958
5. Cullop ....2.05...1916
6. Bahnsen ....2.06...1968
7. Reynolds....2.07...1952
8. Chandler....2.10...1946
9. Fisher ....2.11...1915
10. W. Ford......2.13...1964
Since earned runs became an official AL statistic in 1913.

Saves
1. RIVERA .... 53... 2004
2. RIVERA .... 50... 2001
3. Righetti 46 1986
4. RIVERA .... 45... 1999
5. RIVERA .... 44... 2009
6. Wetteland...43 1996
RIVERA .... 43... 1997
RIVERA .... 43... 2005
9. RIVERA .... 40... 2003
10. RIVERA .... 39... 2008

All-Time Club Records

Single-Season Club Records

Most Wins

Season	114	1998
Home	65^	1961
Road	54	1939
Month	28	Aug. 1938
Consecutive	19	1947
Consecutive, home	18	1942
Consecutive, road	15	1953
Shutout	24	1951
1-0	6	1908, 1968

Fewest Wins

Season	50	1912
Home	27	1913
Road	19	1912

Most Losses

Season	103	1908
Home	47	1908, 1913
Road	58	1912
Month	24	July 1908
Consecutive	13	1913
Consecutive, home	17	1913
Consecutive, road	12	1908
Shutout	27	1914
1-0	9	1914

Fewest Losses

Season	44	1927
Home	15^	1932
Road	20+	1939

Miscellaneous

Most games	164**	1964, 1968
Fewest games	107	1981
Consecutive extra-inning games	4	1992 (5/19-23)
Longest 1-0 game won	15 inn	vs. PHI, 7/4/25, G1
Longest 1-0 game lost	14 inn	at BOS, 9/24/69
Most players used	51	2005, 2008
Fewest players used	25	1923, 1927
Most pitchers used	28	2005, 2007
Fewest pitchers used	8	1922, 1923

Longest Games in Club History (Innings)

Inn.	Opponent	Date, Result
22	at Detroit	6/24/62, a 9-7 win
20	vs. Boston	8/29/67 (G2), a 4-3 win
19 (3x)	vs. Cleveland	5/24/18, a 3-2 loss
	vs. Detroit	8/23/68 (G2), a 3-3 tie
	vs. Minnesota	8/25/76, a 5-4 win
18 (6x)	vs. Chicago	6/25/1903, a 6-6 tie
	at Boston	9/5/27, a 12-11 loss
	at Chicago	8/21/33, a 3-3 tie
	vs. Boston	4/16/67, a 7-6 win
	at Washington	4/22/70, a 2-1 loss
	vs. Detroit	9/11/88, a 5-4 win
17	at Detroit	last on 6/1/2003, a 10-9 win
16	vs. Oakland	last on 8/9/02, a 3-2 loss

Single-Season Batting Records

Most at-bats	5717	2007
Most runs	1067^	1931
Fewest runs	459	1908
Most hits	1683	1930
Fewest hits	1136	1903
Batting avg (High)	.309	1930
Batting avg (Low)	.214	1968
Most singles	1237	1988
Most doubles	327	2006
Most triples	110	1930
Most home runs	244	2009
Consecutive games with a HR	25 (40 HR total)	1941
Grand slams	10	1987
Pinch hit home runs	10	1961
Total bases	2703	1936, 2009
Runs batted in	995^	1936
Most bases on balls	766	1932
Most hit by pitch	81	2003
Fewest hit by pitch	14	1969
Most stolen bases	289	1910
Fewest stolen bases	24	1948
Most caught stealing	82	1920
Fewest caught stealing	18	1961, 1964
Most strikeouts	1171	2002
Fewest strikeouts	420	1924
Highest slugging pct.	.489	1927
Lowest slugging pct.	.287	1914
Most GIDP	153	1996
Fewest GIDP	91	1963
Most left on base	1258	1996
Fewest left on base	1010	1920
Double-digit HR hitters	10	1998
Most .300 hitters	6	1930, 1931, 1936 (min 300 AB)
Most "walk-off" wins	17	1943

Single-Season Pitching Records

Lowest ERA (since 1913)	2.66	1917
Highest ERA (since 1913)	4.88	1930
Innings pitched	1506.2	1964
Complete games	123	1904
Fewest complete games	1**	2004, 2007, 2008
Most shutouts	24	1951
Consecutive shutouts	4	1932
Consecutive shutout innings	40	1932
Fewest shutouts	2	1994
Most saves (since 1969)	59	2004
Fewest hits allowed	1143	1919
Most hits allowed	1566	1930
Fewest home runs allowed	13	1907
Most home runs allowed	182	2004
Fewest runs allowed	507	1942
Most runs allowed	898	1930
Fewest earned runs allowed	394	1904
Most earned runs allowed	753	2000
Fewest bases on balls	245	1903
Most bases on balls	812	1949
Fewest strikeouts	431	1927
Most strikeouts	1266+	2001

KEY TO SYMBOLS

^ ML record (since 1900)
** tied for ML record
+ AL record
# tied for AL record

Single-Season Fielding Records

Highest fielding pct. ... .986 ... 1995, 2008
Lowest fielding pct. ... .939 ... 1912
Fewest errors ... 72 ... 1981
Fewest errors, non-abbr. season ... 83 ... 2008
Most errors ... 386 ... 1912
Most errorless games ... 99 ... 2007
Consecutive errorless games ... 18^ ... 2009 (5/14-6/1)
Most putouts ... 4520^ ... 1964
Fewest putouts ... 3993 ... 1935
Most assists ... 2086 ... 1904
Fewest assists ... 1487 ... 2000
Most double plays ... 214 ... 1956
Fewest double plays ... 81 ... 1912
Consective games, DP turned ... 19 (27 DPs) ... 1992
Most passed balls ... 32 ... 1913
Fewest passed balls ... 0^ ... 1931
Most chances ... 6584 ... 1916
Fewest chances ... 5551 ... 1935

Single-Game/Inning Batting Records

Most runs
Game, 9 innings, home ... 22 ... 7/26/31 vs. CWS (G2)
Game, 9 innings, road ... 25 ... 5/24/36 at PHI
Game, both teams ... 33 (3x) ... 5/3/12 at PHI
5/22/30 at PHI (G2)
6/3/32 at PHI
Game, both teams, home ... 31 ... 6/21/2005 vs. TB
Game, opponent, home ... 22 (2x) ... 8/31/2004 vs. CLE
4/18/2009 vs. CLE
Game, opponent, road ... 24 ... 7/29/28 at CLE
Shutout game ... 21 ... 8/13/39 at PHI
Shutout game, opponent ... 22 ... 8/31/2004 vs. CLE
Two consecutive games ... 40 ... 15 in G2 on 5/23/36
and 25 on 5/24/36 at CLE
Three consecutive games ... 52 ...
12 in G1 on 5/23/36 at PHI
15 in G2 on 5/23/36 at PHI
and 25 on 5/24/36 at PHI
Consecutive games scoring 10 or more ... 5 ... 6/12-17/30
Inning ... 14 ... 7/6/20 at WAS (5th)
Start of game, no outs ... 8 ... 4/24/60 vs. BAL
9/25/90 vs. BAL
Largest margin of victory ... 23 ... 5/24/36 at PHI (25-2)
Largest margin of victory, home ... 20 ... 7/4/27 vs. WAS (21-1)
7/24/99 vs. CLE (21-1 win)
Largest margin of defeat ... 22 ... 8/31/04 vs. CLE (22-0)

Most hits
Game, 9 innings ... 30 ... 9/28/23 at BOS
Game, both teams ... 45# ... 9/29/28 at DET
Consecutive, start of game ... 8** ... 9/25/90 vs. BAL
Most singles ... 22 ... 8/12/53 at WAS
Most doubles ... 10 ... 4/12/88 at TOR
and 6/5/2003 at CIN
Most triples ... 5 ... 5/1/34 at WAS
Most extra-base hits, game ... 12 ... 6/5/2003 at CIN
Most extra-base hits, inning ... 7 ... 5/3/51 vs. SLB

Most home runs
Game ... 8 ... 6/28/39 at PHI (G1)
7/31/07 vs. CWS
Game, both teams ... 11 ... 6/23/50 at DET
(NYY-6 HR, DET-5 HR)
Game, vs. one pitcher ... 6 ... off Tommy Thomas,
6/27/36 at STL
Inning ... 4 (2x) ... 6/30/77 at TOR
6/21/2005 vs. TB
Inning, with 2 outs ... 3 (2x) ... 6/28/39 at PHI (3rd)
6/21/2005 vs. TB (8th)
Consecutive ... 3 (11x) ... last on 5/20/2009
vs. Baltimore - Swisher, Cano, Cabrera
Start of game ... 2 (5x) ...
4/27/55 vs. CWS, Bauer and Carey;
7/30/99 at BOS, Knoblauch and Jeter;
4/6/2003 at TB, Soriano and Johnson;
6/28/2003 at NYM, Soriano and Jeter;
9/23/2005 vs. TOR, Jeter and Cano
Most "walk-off" HR in a season ... 7 ... 2009

Most grand slams
Game ... 2** (3x) ... 5/24/36 vs. PHI
6/29/87 at TOR
9/14/99 at TOR
Inning ... 1 ... (Many times)

Most bases on balls
Game ... 16 ... 6/23/15 at PHI
Game, vs. one pitcher ... 9 (11x) ... last: Josh Beckett,
8/19/06 at BOS

Most strikeouts
Game ... 17 ... 9/10/99 vs. BOS
(all vs. Pedro Martinez)

Most stolen bases
Game ... 15^ ... 9/28/11 vs. SLB
Game, both clubs ... 15# ... NY 15, SLB 0, 9/28/11
Game, steals of home ... 3** ... 4/17/15 vs. PHI

Most GIDP
Game ... 5 (3x) ... last on 9/27/68 at BOS

Most LOB
Game, 9 innings ... 20^ ... 9/21/56 at BOS
Game, extra innings ... 23 ... 9/5/27 at BOS (G1)

Single-Game/Inning Club Pitching Records

Most runs allowed
Game ... 24 ... 7/29/28 at CLE (24-6)
Game, home ... 22 (2x) ...
8/31/2004 vs. CLE (22-0)
4/18/2009 vs. CLE (22-4)
Inning ... 14 ... 4/18/2009 vs. CLE (2nd)
Two consecutive games ... 33 ... 9 on 7/28/28 at CLE
and 24 on 7/29/28 at CLE

Most hits allowed
Game ... 28 ... 9/29/28 at DET
Game, home ... 27 ... 5/28/05 vs. BOS

Most home runs allowed
Game ... 7 ... 7/4/2003 vs. BOS
Inning ... 4 (4x) ... 6/17/77 at BOS
5/2/92 vs. MIN
8/21/2005 at CWS
4/22/2007 at BOS

Most strikeouts
Most strikeouts, game ... 18 ... 6/17/78 vs. CAL

Most base on balls
Most bases on balls, game ... 17 ... 9/11/49 vs. WAS
Most bases on balls, inning ... 11 ... 9/11/49 vs. WAS (3rd)

Most wild pitches
Most wild pitches, game ... 5 ... 6/24/94 vs. CLE

Single-Game Club Miscellaneous

Longest game, time	7:00	6/24/62 at DET (22 inn.)
Longest game, time, 9 innings	4:45^	8/18/06 at BOS
Largest deficit overcome	9 (4x)	last on 5/16/06 vs. TEX
Largest lead blown	9 (2x)	last on 7/28/31 vs. CWS

Single-Game/Inning Club Fielding Records

Most errors

Game	10	6/12/1907 vs. DET
Inning (since Divisional Play began in 1969)	5	Stottlemyre, Clarke, Pepitone, Murcer (2) on 5/9/69 at OAK

Individual Single-Game/Inning Pitching Records

Runs allowed, game	13 (3x)	Jack Warhop, 7/31/11 vs. CWS
		Ray Caldwell, 10/3/13 at PHI
		Carl Mays, 7/17/23 at CLE
Hits allowed, game	21	Jack Quinn, 6/29/12 at BOS
HRs allowed, game	5 (5x)	Joe Ostrowski, 6/22/50 at CLE
		John Cumberland, 5/24/70 at CLE
		Ron Guidry, 9/17/85 at DET
		Jeff Weaver, 7/21/2002 vs. BOS
		David Wells, 7/4/2003 vs. BOS
HRs allowed, inning	4 (4x)	Catfish Hunter, 6/17/77 at BOS (1st)
		Scott Sanderson, 5/2/92 vs. MIN (5th)
		Randy Johnson, 8/21/2005 at CWS (4th)
		Chase Wright, 4/22/2007 at BOS (3rd), all consecutive tying ML record
Most strikeouts, game, LH	18	Ron Guidry, 6/17/78 vs. CAL
Most strikeouts, game, RH	16	David Cone, 6/23/97 at DET
Most strikeouts, inning	3	Many pitchers
Most strikeouts, relief	11	Steve Hamilton, 5/11/63 at BAL
Consecutive strikeouts	8	Ron Davis, 5/4/81 at CAL
Most bases on balls, game	13	Tommy Byrne, 6/8/49 at DET
Balks, game	#4	Vic Raschi, 5/3/50 vs. CWS

Individual Single-Game Batting Records

Most at-bats	**11	Bobby Richardson, 6/24/62 at DET (22 inn.)
Most runs	5 (16x)	last by Johnny Damon, 4/29/2006 vs. TB
Most hits	#6 (3x)	Myril Hoag (6-for-6), 6/6/34 at BOS
		Gerald Williams (6-for-8), 5/1/96 at BAL, 15 innings
		Johnny Damon (6-for-6), 6/7/08 vs. KC
Most singles	** 6	Myril Hoag, 6/6/34 at BOS
Most doubles	**4 (2x)	Johnny Lindell, 8/17/44 vs. CLE
		Jim Mason, 7/8/74 at TEX
Most triples	**3 (3x)	Hal Chase, 8/30/06 vs. WAS
		Earle Combs, 9/22/27 vs. DET
		Joe DiMaggio, 8/27/38 vs. CLE (G1)
Most home runs	**4	Lou Gehrig (consecutive), 6/3/32 at PHI
Most grand slams	**2	Tony Lazzeri, 5/24/36 at PHI
Most total bases	#16	Lou Gehrig, 6/3/32 at PHI
Most RBI	+11	Tony Lazzeri, 5/24/36 at PHI
Most sacrifice flies	**3 (2x)	Bob Meusel, 9/15/26 at CLE
		Don Mattingly, 5/3/86 vs. TEX
Most stolen bases	4 (18x)	last, Tony Womack, 5/15/2005 at OAK
Most caught stealing	3 (2x)	Fritz Maisel, 4/26/16 vs. BOS
		Lee Magee, 6/29/18 at PHI
Most bases on balls	5 (7x)	last, Mark Teixeira, 4/25/09 at BOS
Most strikeouts	**5 (4x)	Johnny Broaca, 6/25/34 vs. CWS
		Bernie Williams, 8/1/91 vs. MIN
		Andy Phillips, 5/2/2005 at TB
		Melky Cabrera, 7/7/2007 vs. LAA
Most grounded into DPs	3 (3x)	Eddie Robinson, 5/30/55 at WAS
		Jim Leyritz, 7/4/90 at KC
		Matt Nokes, 5/3/92 vs. MIN

Individual Single-Season Pitching Records

Most wins, RHP .... 41+ ...... Jack Chesbro, 1904
Most wins, LHP.................. 26 .... Lefty Gomez, 1934
Most consecutive wins, RHP ..... 16# .... Roger Clemens, 2001
Most consecutive wins, LHP ...... 14 .... Whitey Ford, 1961
Most shutouts .... 9 .... Ron Guidry, 1978
Most shutouts lost .... 7 .... Bill Zuber, 1945
Lowest ERA, RHP .... 1.64 .....Spud Chandler, 1943
Lowest ERA, LHP .... 1.74 .... Ron Guidry, 1978
Highest winning pct............. .893 .... Ron Guidry, 1978
Most losses, RHP .... 22 .... Joe Lake, 1908
Most losses, LHP .... 17 ..... Herb Pennock, 1921
Consecutive losses, RHP........... 9 (2x) ...... Bill Hogg, 1908
Thad Tillotson, 1967
Consecutive losses, LHP .... 11 ..George Mogridge, 1916
Most innings pitched, RHP .... 454.0 ...... Jack Chesbro, 1904
Most innings pitched, LHP..... 286.0 ..... Herb Pennock, 1924
Most saves, RHP.................. 53 .... Mariano Rivera, 2004
Most saves, LHP.................. 46 ...... Dave Righetti, 1986
Most games, RHP .... 86 ...... Paul Quantrill, 2004
Most games, LHP.................. 79 ...... Mike Stanton, 2002
Most games started .... 51^ ...... Jack Chesbro, 1904
Most complete games .... 48^ ...... Jack Chesbro, 1904
Most strikeouts, RHP .... 239 ...... Jack Chesbro, 1904
Most strikeouts, LHP .... 248 .... Ron Guidry, 1978
Most bases on balls, RHP .... 177 .... Bob Turley, 1955
Most bases on balls, LHP .... 179 ......Tommy Byrne, 1949
Most hits allowed .... 337 ...... Jack Chesbro, 1904
Most runs allowed .... 165 .... Russ Ford, 1912
Most earned runs allowed .... 127 .... Sam Jones, 1925
Most home runs allowed, RHP .... 40 .... Ralph Terry, 1962
Most home runs allowed, LHP .... 32 .... Randy Johnson, 2005
Most hit batsmen .... 26 .... Jack Warhop, 1909
Most wild pitches .... 23 .... Tim Leary, 1990

Individual Single-Season Batting Records

Games.......................... 163 ...... Hideki Matsui, 2003
Most at-bats .... 696 .... Alfonso Soriano, 2002
Highest batting average, RH..... .381 ...... Joe DiMaggio, 1939
Highest batting average, LH..... .394 .... Babe Ruth, 1923
Highest batting average, SH..... .365 ..... Mickey Mantle, 1957
Most Hits, RH .... 219 .... Derek Jeter, 1999
Most Hits, LH.................... 238 ..... Don Mattingly, 1986
Most Hits, SH .... 204 .... Bernie Williams, 2002
Consecutive games hit safely.... 56^ ...... Joe DiMaggio, 1941
Most runs..................... 177^ .... Babe Ruth, 1921
Consecutive games, run scored.. 18^ .... Red Rolfe, 1939
Most singles .... 171 .... Steve Sax, 1989
Most doubles .... 53 ..... Don Mattingly, 1986
Most triples...................... 23 .... Earle Combs, 1927
Most home runs, RH............... 54 .... Alex Rodriguez, 2007
Most home runs, LH............ 61+ .... Roger Maris, 1961
Most home runs, SH............ 54^ ..... Mickey Mantle, 1961
Most HR, home, LH (Polo Grounds)... 32 .... Babe Ruth, 1921
Most HR, home, RH (Polo Grounds)... 14 .... Bob Meusel, 1921
Most HR, home, LH (Orig. Yankee Stad.)... 30 .... Lou Gehrig, 1934
Roger Maris, 1961
Most HR, home, RH (Orig. Yankee Stad.)... 26 .... Alex Rodriguez, 2005, '07
Most HR, home, LH (Yankee Stad.).... 17 .... Johnny Damon, 2009
Most HR, home, RH (Yankee Stad.) ... 18 .... Alex Rodriguez, 2009
Most home runs, home, SH....... 27 ..... Mickey Mantle, 1956
Most home runs, road, RH........ 28 .... A. Rodriguez, 2007
Most home runs, road, LH .... 32# .... Babe Ruth, 1927
Most home runs, road, SH .... 30 ..... Mickey Mantle, 1961
Most home runs, month.......... 17 ... Babe Ruth, Sept., 1927
Most home runs, rookie, RH ...... 29 ...... Joe DiMaggio, 1936
Most home runs, rookie, LH ...... 21 .... Kevin Maas, 1990
Most home runs, rookie, SH ...... 20 .... Tom Tresh, 1962
Consecutive games with HR ..... 8** ..... Don Mattingly, 1987
Most grand slams .... 6** ..... Don Mattingly, 1987
Most RBI, RH .... 167 ..... Joe DiMaggio, 1937
Most RBI, LH .... 184+ .... Lou Gehrig, 1931
Most RBI, SH .... 130 ..... Mickey Mantle, 1956
Consecutive games with RBI...... 11 .... Babe Ruth, 1931
Most extra-base hits............ 119^ .... Babe Ruth, 1921
Most total bases .... 457^ .... Babe Ruth, 1921
Highest slugging pct. .... .847+ .... Babe Ruth, 1920
Most strikeouts, RH .... 157 .... Alfonso Soriano, 2002
Most strikeouts, LH.............. 133 .... Reggie Jackson, 1978
Most strikeouts, SH.............. 151 ...... Jorge Posada, 2000
Most bases on balls, RH .... 119 .... Willie Randolph, 1980
Most bases on balls, LH........ 170+ .... Babe Ruth, 1923
Most bases on balls, SH.......... 146 ..... Mickey Mantle, 1957
Most sacrifice hits .... 42 .... Willie Keeler, 1905
Most sacrifice flies............... 17# .... Roy White, 1971
Most stolen bases .... 93 ... Rickey Henderson, 1988
Most caught stealing.............. 23 ..... Ben Chapman, 1931
Most hit by pitch.................. 24 .... Don Baylor, 1985
Most grounded into DP .... 30 ...... Dave Winfield, 1983
Fewest grounded into DP .... 2 (2x) . Mickey Mantle, 1961
Mickey Rivers, 1977

Note: Records in "fewest" categories are based on full seasons and do not include 1918, 1981 and 1994.

KEY TO SYMBOLS

^ ML record (since 1900) — **tied for ML record
+ AL record — #tied for AL record

Yankees Rawlings Gold Glove Winners by Year

Award given since 1957

Year	NAME, POS	Year	NAME, POS
1957	Bobby Shantz, P	1984	Ron Guidry, P
1958	Bobby Shantz, P		Dave Winfield, OF
	Norm Siebern, OF	1985	Ron Guidry, P
1959	Bobby Shantz, P		Don Mattingly, 1B
1960	Bobby Shantz, P		Dave Winfield, OF
	Roger Maris, OF	1986	Ron Guidry, P
1961	Bobby Richardson, 2B		Don Mattingly, 1B
1962	Bobby Richardson, 2B	1987	Don Mattingly, 1B
	Mickey Mantle, OF		Dave Winfield, OF
1963	Elston Howard, C	1988	Don Mattingly, 1B
	Bobby Richardson, 2B	1989	Don Mattingly, 1B
1964	Elston Howard, C	1991	Don Mattingly, 1B
	Bobby Richardson, 2B	1992	Don Mattingly, 1B
1965	Joe Pepitone, 1B	1993	Don Mattingly, 1B
	Bobby Richardson, 2B	1994	Don Mattingly, 1B
	Tom Tresh, OF		Wade Boggs, 3B
1966	Joe Pepitone, 1B	1995	Wade Boggs, 3B
1969	Joe Pepitone, 1B	1997	Bernie Williams, OF
1972	Bobby Murcer, OF	1998	Bernie Williams, OF
1973	Thurman Munson, C	1999	Scott Brosius, 3B
1974	Thurman Munson, C		Bernie Williams, OF
1975	Thurman Munson, C	2000	Bernie Williams, OF
1977	Graig Nettles, 3B	2001	Mike Mussina, P
1978	Chris Chambliss, 1B	2003	Mike Mussina, P
	Graig Nettles, 3B	2004	DEREK JETER, SS
1982	Ron Guidry, P	2005	DEREK JETER, SS
	Dave Winfield, OF	2006	DEREK JETER, SS
1983	Ron Guidry, P	2008	Mike Mussina, P
	Dave Winfield, OF	2009	DEREK JETER, SS
			MARK TEIXEIRA, 1B

Yankees Rawlings Gold Glove Winners by Position

Pos.	Winner (Years)
P	Bobby Shantz (1957-60); Ron Guidry (1982-86); Mike Mussina (2001; '03, '08)
C	Elston Howard (1963-64); Thurman Munson (1973-75)
1B	Joe Pepitone (1965-66, '69); Chris Chambliss (1978); Don Mattingly (1985-89; '91-94); Mark Teixeira (2009)
2B	Bobby Richardson (1961-65)
3B	Graig Nettles (1977-78); Wade Boggs (1994-95); Scott Brosius (1999)
SS	Derek Jeter (2004-06; '09)
OF	Norm Siebern (1958); Roger Maris (1960); Mickey Mantle (1962); Tom Tresh (1965); Bobby Murcer (1972); Dave Winfield (1982-85, '87); Bernie Williams (1997-2002)

Yankees 20-Game Winners

Year	Pitcher	W	L
1903	Jack Chesbro	21	15
1904	Jack Chesbro	41	12
	Jack Powell	23	19
1906	Al Orth	27	17
	Jack Chesbro	24	16
1910	Russell Ford	26	6
1911	Russell Ford	22	11
1916	Bob Shawkey	24	14
1919	Bob Shawkey	20	11
1920	Carl Mays	26	11
	Bob Shawkey	20	13
1921	Carl Mays	27	9
1922	Joe Bush	26	7
	Bob Shawkey	20	12
1923	Sad Sam Jones	21	8
1924	Herb Pennock	21	9
1926	Herb Pennock	23	11
1927	Waite Hoyt	22	7
1928	George Pipgras	24	13
	Waite Hoyt	23	7
1931	Lefty Gomez	21	9
1932	Lefty Gomez	24	7
1934	Lefty Gomez	26	5
1936	Red Ruffing	20	12
1937	Lefty Gomez	21	11
	Red Ruffing	20	7
1938	Red Ruffing	21	7
1939	Red Ruffing	21	7
1942	Ernie Bonham	21	5
1943	Spud Chandler	20	4
1946	Spud Chandler	20	8
1949	Vic Raschi	21	10
1950	Vic Raschi	21	8
1951	Eddie Lopat	21	9
	Vic Raschi	21	10
1952	Allie Reynolds	20	8
1954	Bob Grim	20	6
1958	Bob Turley	21	7
1961	Whitey Ford	25	4
1962	Ralph Terry	23	12
1963	Whitey Ford	24	7
	Jim Bouton	21	7
1965	Mel Stottlemyre	20	9
1968	Mel Stottlemyre	21	12
1969	Mel Stottlemyre	20	14
1970	Fritz Peterson	20	11
1975	Catfish Hunter	23	14
1978	Ron Guidry	25	3
	Ed Figueroa	20	9
1979	Tommy John	21	9
1980	Tommy John	22	9
1983	Ron Guidry	21	9
1985	Ron Guidry	22	6
1996	Andy Pettitte	21	8
1998	David Cone	20	7
2001	Roger Clemens	20	3
2003	Andy Pettitte	21	8
2008	Mike Mussina	20	9

Mel Stottlemyre

Yankees Free Agent Signings

Player	Date
C. Hunter	12/31/74
D. Gullett	11/18/76
R. Jackson	11/29/76
R. Gossage	11/22/77
R. Eastwick	12/9/77
L. Tiant	11/13/78
T. John	11/22/78
R. May	11/8/79
B. Watson	11/8/79
D. Winfield	12/15/80
B. Castro	2/15/81
R. Guidry	12/15/81
D. Collins	12/23/81
D. Baylor	12/1/82
S. Kemp	12/9/82
B. Shirley	12/15/82
D. Murray	11/21/83
P. Niekro	1/6/84
E. Whitson	12/27/84
J. Niekro	1/8/86
P. Niekro	1/8/86
B. Wynegar	1/8/86
A. Holland	2/6/86
T. John	5/2/86
R. Scurry	12/5/86
C. Washington	12/11/86
L. Sakata	12/16/86
G. Ward	12/24/86
T. John	1/8/87
W. Tolleson	1/8/87
W. Randolph	1/8/87
B. Shirley	1/28/87
R. Cerone	2/13/87
R. Guidry	5/1/87
D. Righetti	12/23/87
J. Clark	1/6/88
J. Candelaria	1/18/88
J. Cruz	2/25/88
S. Sax	11/23/88
D. LaPoint	12/3/88
A. Hawkins	12/8/88
J. Quirk	12/20/88
R. Guidry	2/3/89
T. John	2/13/89
P. Perez	11/21/89
M. Hall	11/30/89
R. Cerone	12/22/89
D. Garcia	12/22/89
T. Leary	11/19/90
S. Farr	11/26/90
D. Tartabull	1/6/92
S. Owen	12/4/92
S. Howe	12/8/92
J. Key	12/10/92
W. Boggs	12/15/92
L. Polonia	12/20/93
D. Pall	1/18/94
S. Bankhead	11/1/94
T. Fernandez	12/14/94
W. Boggs	12/5/95
M. Duncan	12/11/95
D. Cone	12/21/95
K. Rogers	1/4/96
D. Gooden	10/16/96
M. Stanton	12/11/96
D. Wells	12/19/96
M. Whiten	1/9/97
D. Sveum	11/25/97
C. Davis	12/10/97
D. Holmes	12/22/97
O. Hernandez	3/7/98
S. Brosius	11/10/98
B. Williams	11/25/98
M. Stanton	11/29/99
D. Cone	12/6/99
A. Watson	12/7/99
P. O'Neill	11/16/00
J. Oliver	11/21/00
M. Mussina	11/30/00
L. Sojo	12/7/00
H. Rodriguez	2/16/01
S. Karsay	12/7/01
J. Giambi	12/13/01
Rond. White	12/17/01
S. Hitchcock	12/18/01
A. Castillo	12/21/01
D. Wells	1/10/02
R. Rivera	2/14/02
B. Rivera	11/21/02
C. Latham	12/4/02
R. Ventura	12/6/02
C. Widger	12/7/02
C. Hammond	12/12/02
T. Zeile	12/18/02
H. Matsui	12/19/02
J. Contreras	12/24/02
R. Clemens	12/30/02
E. Wilson	12/2/03
F. Heredia	12/3/03
R. Sierra	12/8/03
J. Flaherty	12/15/03
G. Sheffield	12/17/03
M. Cairo	12/19/03
P. Quantrill	12/22/03
T. Gordon	12/23/03
K. Lofton	12/23/03
T. Clark	1/13/04
T. Womack	12/21/04
C. Pavano	12/22/04
J. Wright	12/29/04
T. Martinez	12/31/04
R. Sanchez	2/16/05
K. Stinnett	11/30/05
K. Farnsworth	12/2/05
M. Myers	12/15/05
B. Williams	12/22/05
J. Damon	12/23/05
O. Dotel	12/29/05
M. Cairo	1/5/06
S. Ponson	7/14/06
M. Mussina	11/27/06
A. PETTITTE	12/20/06
D. Mientkiewicz	1/5/07
M. Cairo	1/26/07
S. Patterson	11/20/07
J. POSADA	11/29/07
J. Molina	12/3/07
A. PETTITTE	12/12/07
A. RODRIGUEZ	12/13/07
M. RIVERA	12/17/07
L. Hawkins	12/27/07
R. Sexson	7/18/08
C. SABATHIA	12/18/08
A. BURNETT	12/18/08
M. TEIXEIRA	1/6/09
A. PETTITTE	1/26/09
A. PETTITTE	12/9/09
N. JOHNSON	12/23/09
R. WINN	2/8/10

AL Most Valuable Players

YEAR	PLAYER	AGE	POS	G	AB	R	H	2B	3B	HR	RBI	BA	E
1923	Babe Ruth	28	OF	152	520	151*	205	45	13	41*†	130*	.394	11
1927	Lou Gehrig	23	1B	155*†	584	149	218	52*	18	47	175*	.373	15
1936	Lou Gehrig	32	1B	155†	579	167*	205	37	7	49*	152	.354	9
1939	Joe DiMaggio	24	OF	120	462	108	176	32	6	30	126	.381*	5
1941	Joe DiMaggio	26	OF	139	541	122	193	43	11	30	125*	.357	9
1942	Joe Gordon	27	2B	147	538	88	173	29	4	18	103	.322	28
1947	Joe DiMaggio	32	OF	141	534	97	168	31	10	20	97	.315	1
1950	Phil Rizzuto	32	SS	155	617	125	200	36	7	7	66	.324	14
1951	Yogi Berra	25	C	141	547	92	161	19	4	27	88	.294	13
1954	Yogi Berra	28	C	151	584	88	179	28	6	22	125	.307	8
1955	Yogi Berra	29	C	147	541	84	147	20	3	27	108	.272	13
1956	Mickey Mantle	24	OF	150	533	132*	188	22	5	52*	130*	.353*	4
1957	Mickey Mantle	25	OF	144	474	121*	173	28	6	34	94	.365	7
1960	Roger Maris	25	OF	136	499	98	141	18	7	39	112	.283	4
1961	Roger Maris	26	OF	161	590	132*†	159	16	4	61*	141†	.269	9
1962	Mickey Mantle	30	OF	123	377	96	121	15	1	30	89	.321	5
1963	Elston Howard	34	C	135	487	75	140	21	6	28	85	.287	5
1976	Thurman Munson	28	C	152	616	79	186	27	1	17	105	.302	14
1985	Don Mattingly	23	1B	159	652	107	211	48*	3	35	145*	.324	7
2005	ALEX RODRIGUEZ	29	3B	162*†	605	124	194	29	1	48	130	.321	12
2007	ALEX RODRIGUEZ	31	3B	158	583	143*	183	31	0	54*	156*	.314	13

YEAR	PITCHER	AGE	POS	G	GS	IP	W	L	PCT.	SV	H	R	ER	SO	BB	ERA
1943	Spud Chandler	35	RHP	30	30	253.0	20†	4	.833*	0	197	62	46	134	54	1.64*

Cy Young Awards

YEAR	PITCHER	AGE	POS	G	GS	IP	W	L	PCT.	SV	H	R	ER	SO	BB	ERA
1958	Bob Turley	27	RHP	33	31	245.1	21	7	.750*	1	178	82	81	168	128*	2.97
1961	Whitey Ford	32	LHP	39	39*	283.0*	25*	4	.862*	0	242	108	101	209	92	3.21
1977	Sparky Lyle	32	LHP	72	0	137.0	13	5	.722	26	131	41	33	68	33	2.17
1978	Ron Guidry	27	LHP	35	35	273.2	25*	3	.893*	0	187	61	53	248	72	1.74*
2001	Roger Clemens	38	RHP	33	33	220.1	20	3	.870*	0	205	94	86	213	72	3.51

AL Rookie of the Year Awards

YEAR	PLAYER	AGE	POS	G	AB	R	H	2B	3B	HR	RBI	BA	E
1951	Gil McDougald	22	INF	131	402	72	123	23	4	14	63	.306	14
1957	Tony Kubek	21	INF-OF	127	431	56	128	21	3	3	39	.297	20
1962	Tom Tresh	24	INF-OF	157	622	94	178	26	5	20	93	.286	20
1970	Thurman Munson	22	C	132	453	59	137	25	4	6	53	.302	8
1996	DEREK JETER	21	SS	157	582	104	183	25	6	10	78	.314	22

YEAR	PITCHER	AGE	POS	G	GS	IP	W	L	PCT.	SV	H	R	ER	SO	BB	ERA
1954	Bob Grim	24	RHP	37	20	199.0	20	6	.769	0	175	78	72	108	85	3.26
1968	Stan Bahnsen	23	RHP	37	34	267.1	17	12	.586	0	216	72	61	162	68	2.05
1981	Dave Righetti	22	LHP	15	15	105.1	8	4	.667	0	75	25	24	89	38	2.05

AL Triple Crown Winners

YEAR	PLAYER	AGE	POS	G	AB	R	H	2B	3B	HR	RBI	BA
1934	Lou Gehrig	30	1B	154*†	579	128	210	40	6	49*	165*	.363*
1956	Mickey Mantle	24	OF	150	533	132*	188	22	5	52*	130*	.353*

AL Batting Champions

YEAR	PLAYER	AGE	POS	AVG.	G	AB	R	H	2B	3B	HR	RBI	E
1924	Babe Ruth	29	OF	.378	153	529	143*	200	39	7	46*	121	14
1934	Lou Gehrig	31	1B	.363	154*†	579	128	210	40	6	49*	165*	8
1939	Joe DiMaggio	24	OF	.381	120	462	108	176	32	6	30	126	5
1940	Joe DiMaggio	25	OF	.352	132	508	93	179	28	9	31	133	8
1945	Snuffy Stirnweiss	26	2B	.309	152	632	107	195	32	22*	10	64	29
1956	Mickey Mantle	24	OF	.353	150	533	132*	188	22	5	52*	130*	4
1984	Don Mattingly	23	1B	.343	153	603	91	207	44*	2	23	110	7
1994	Paul O'Neill	31	OF	.359	103	368	68	132	25	1	21	83	1
1998	Bernie Williams	29	OF	.339	128	499	101	169	30	5	26	97	3

AL Home Run Champions

YEAR	YANKEE	G	AB	HR
1916	Wally Pipp	151	545	12*†
1917	Wally Pipp	155	587	9
1920	Babe Ruth	142	458	54*
1921	Babe Ruth	152	541	59*
1923	Babe Ruth	152	520	41*†
1924	Babe Ruth	153	529	46*
1925	Bob Meusel	156	624	33
1926	Babe Ruth	152	495	47*
1927	Babe Ruth	151	540	60*
1928	Babe Ruth	154	536	54*
1929	Babe Ruth	135	499	46*
1930	Babe Ruth	145	518	49
1931	Babe Ruth	145	534	46*
	Lou Gehrig	155	619	46*
1934	Lou Gehrig	154	579	49*
1936	Lou Gehrig	155	579	49*
1937	Joe DiMaggio	151	621	46*
1944	Nick Etten	154	573	22
1948	Joe DiMaggio	153	594	39
1955	Mickey Mantle	147	517	37
1956	Mickey Mantle	150	533	52*
1958	Mickey Mantle	150	519	42
1960	Mickey Mantle	153	527	40
1961	Roger Maris	161	590	61*
1976	Graig Nettles	158	583	32
1980	Reggie Jackson	143	514	41
2005	Alex Rodriguez	162	605	48
2007	Alex Rodriguez	158	583	54*
2009	Mark Teixeira	156	609	39†

AL RBI Champions

YEAR	YANKEE	G	AB	RBI
1920	Babe Ruth	142	458	137*
1921	Babe Ruth	152	541	171*
1923	Babe Ruth	152	520	131*
1925	Bob Meusel	156	624	138
1926	Babe Ruth	152	495	146*
1927	Lou Gehrig	155	584	175*
1928	Babe Ruth	154	536	142*†
	Lou Gehrig	154	562	142*†
1930	Lou Gehrig	154	581	174
1931	Lou Gehrig (AL RBI record)	155	619	184*
1934	Lou Gehrig	154	579	165*
1941	Joe DiMaggio	139	541	125*
1945	Nick Etten	152	565	111
1948	Joe DiMaggio	153	594	155*
1956	Mickey Mantle	150	533	130*
1960	Roger Maris	136	499	112
1961	Roger Maris	161	590	141†
1985	Don Mattingly	159	652	145*
2007	Alex Rodriguez	158	583	156*
2009	Mark Teixeira	156	609	122

Lou Gehrig

AL Runs Leaders

1920	Babe Ruth	158*
1921	Babe Ruth	177*
1923	Babe Ruth	151*
1924	Babe Ruth	143*
1926	Babe Ruth	139*
1927	Babe Ruth	158*
1928	Babe Ruth	163*
1931	Lou Gehrig	163*
1933	Lou Gehrig	138*
1935	Lou Gehrig	125
1936	Lou Gehrig	167*
1937	Joe DiMaggio	151*
1939	Red Rolfe	139*
1944	Snuffy Stirnweiss	125*
1945	Snuffy Stirnweiss	107
1948	Tommy Henrich	138*
1954	Mickey Mantle	128*
1956	Mickey Mantle	132*
1957	Mickey Mantle	121*
1958	Mickey Mantle	127*
1960	Mickey Mantle	119*
1961	Mickey Mantle	132*
1972	Bobby Murcer	102
1976	Roy White	104
1985	Rickey Henderson	146*
1986	Rickey Henderson	130*
1998	Derek Jeter	127
2002	Alfonso Soriano	128*
2005	Alex Rodriguez	124
2007	Alex Rodriguez	143*

AL Hits Leaders

1927	Earl Combs	231
1931	Lou Gehrig	211
1939	Red Rolfe	213*
1944	Snuffy Stirnweiss	205*
1962	Bobby Richardson	209
1984	Don Mattingly	207
1986	Don Mattingly	238
1999	Derek Jeter	219
2002	Alfonso Soriano	209

AL Doubles Leaders

1927	Lou Gehrig	52*
1928	Lou Gehrig	47
1939	Red Rolfe	46
1984	Don Mattingly	44*
1985	Don Mattingly	48*
1986	Don Mattingly	53*

Don Mattingly

AL Triples Leaders

1924	Wally Pipp	19
1926	Lou Gehrig	20
1927	Earl Combs	23*
1928	Earl Combs	21*
1930	Earl Combs	22
1934	Ben Chapman	13
1936	Joe DiMaggio	15*†
	Red Rolfe	15*†
1943	Johnny Lindell	12†
1944	Johnny Lindell	16†
	Snuffy Stirnweiss	16†
1945	Snuffy Stirnweiss	22*
1947	Tommy Henrich	13
1948	Tommy Henrich	14
1955	Andy Carey	11†
	Mickey Mantle	11†
1957	Hank Bauer	9†
	Gil McDougald	9†

AL Stolen Bases Leaders

1914	Fritz Maisel	74*
1931	Ben Chapman	61*
1932	Ben Chapman	38*
1933	Ben Chapman	27*
1938	Frank Crosetti	27*
1944	Snuffy Stirnweiss	44*
1945	Snuffy Stirnweiss	33*
1985	Rickey Henderson	80
1986	Rickey Henderson	87
1988	Rickey Henderson	93*
2002	Alfonso Soriano	41

200-Hit Seasons

AL leaders noted in *italics* / ML leaders noted with *

YEAR	YANKEE	AVG	AB	H
1921	Babe Ruth	.377	541	204
1923	Babe Ruth	.394	520	205
1924	Babe Ruth	_.378_	529	200
1925	Earle Combs	.342	593	203
1927	Earle Combs	.356	_648*_	_231_
1927	Lou Gehrig	.373	584	218
1928	Lou Gehrig	.374	562	210
1929	Earle Combs	.345	586	202
1930	Lou Gehrig	.379	581	220
1931	Lou Gehrig	.341	619	_211_
1932	Lou Gehrig	.349	596	208
1934	Lou Gehrig	_.363*_	579	210
1936	Joe DiMaggio	.323	637	206
1936	Lou Gehrig	.354	579	205
1937	Joe DiMaggio	.346	621	215
1937	Lou Gehrig	.351	569	200
1939	Red Rolfe	.329	648	_213*_
1944	Snuffy Stirnweiss	.319	643	_205*_
1950	Phil Rizzuto	.324	617	200
1962	Bobby Richardson	.302	_692_	_209_
1984	Don Mattingly	_.343_	603	_207_
1985	Don Mattingly	.324	652	211
1986	Don Mattingly	.352	677	_238*_
1989	Steve Sax	.315	651	205
1998	Derek Jeter	.324	626	203
1999	Derek Jeter	.349	627	_219*_
1999	Bernie Williams	.342	591	202
2000	Derek Jeter	.339	593	201
2002	Alfonso Soriano	.300	_696*_	_209*_
2002	Bernie Williams	.333	612	204
2005	Derek Jeter	.309	654	202
2006	Derek Jeter	.343	623	214
2007	Derek Jeter	.322	639	206
2009	Derek Jeter	.334	634	212
2009	Robinson Cano	.320	637	204

AL Wins Leaders

1904	Jack Chesbro	(Modern Era Record) 41*
1906	Al Orth	27*†
1921	Carl Mays	27*†
1927	Waite Hoyt	22†
1928	George Pipgras	24†
1934	Lefty Gomez	26
1937	Lefty Gomez	21
1938	Red Ruffing	21
1943	Spud Chandler	20†
1955	Whitey Ford	18†
1958	Bob Turley	21
1961	Whitey Ford	25*
1962	Ralph Terry	23
1963	Whitey Ford	24
1975	Catfish Hunter	23*†
1978	Ron Guidry	25*
1985	Ron Guidry	22
1994	Jimmy Key	17*
1996	Andy Pettitte	21
1998	David Cone	20*†
2006	Chien-Ming Wang	19*†
2009	CC Sabathia	19*†

AL Games Leaders

1904	Jack Chesbro	55*
1906	Jack Chesbro	49*
1918	George Mogridge	45*†
1921	Carl Mays	49*
1948	Joe Page	55
1949	Joe Page	60*
1961	Luis Arroyo	65*†
1977	Sparky Lyle	72
1994	Bob Wickman	53
2004	Paul Quantrill	86
2006	Scott Proctor	83

AL Innings Pitched Leaders

1904	Jack Chesbro	455.0*
1906	Al Orth	339.0
1921	Carl Mays	336.0*
1925	Herb Pennock	276.0
1928	George Pipgras	302.0
1934	Lefty Gomez	282.0
1961	Whitey Ford	283.0*
1962	Ralph Terry	299.0
1963	Whitey Ford	269.0
1965	Mel Stottlemyre	291.0
1975	Catfish Hunter	328.0*

AL Strikeouts Leaders

1932	Red Ruffing	190
1933	Lefty Gomez	163
1934	Lefty Gomez	158
1937	Lefty Gomez	194*
1951	Vic Raschi	164*†
1952	Allie Reynolds	160
1964	Al Downing	217

AL ERA Leaders

1927	Waite Hoyt	2.64
1934	Lefty Gomez	2.33*
1937	Lefty Gomez	2.33
1943	Spud Chandler	1.64*
1947	Spud Chandler	2.46
1952	Allie Reynolds	2.07*
1953	Ed Lopat	2.43*
1956	Whitey Ford	2.47*
1957	Bobby Shantz	2.45*
1958	Whitey Ford	2.01*
1978	Ron Guidry	1.74*
1979	Ron Guidry	2.78*
1980	Rudy May	2.47*

* indicates Major League leader,
† indicates tied for AL or ML lead

Yankees Outstanding Batting Feats (Regular Season)

Four Home Runs, One Game
Lou Gehrig................6/3/32 at PHI

Three Home Runs, One Game
(24 times by 18 players)
Tony Lazzeri............6/8/27 vs. CWS
5/24/36 at PHI
Lou Gehrig..............6/23/27 at BOS
5/4/29 at CWS
5/22/30 at PHI
Babe Ruth...............5/21/30 at PHI
Ben Chapman............7/9/32 vs. DET (G2)
Joe DiMaggio...........6/13/37 at STL
5/23/48 at CLE
9/10/50 at WAS
Bill Dickey..............7/26/39 vs. STL
Charlie Keller...........7/28/40 at CWS
Johnny Mize............9/15/50 at DET
Mickey Mantle..........5/13/55 vs. DET
Tom Tresh...............6/6/65 vs. CWS
Bobby Murcer...........6/24/70 vs. CLE
7/13/73 vs. KC
Cliff Johnson............6/30/77 at TOR
Mike Stanley............8/10/95 vs. CLE
Paul O'Neill.............8/31/95 vs. CAL
Darryl Strawberry.......8/6/96 vs. CWS
Tino Martinez.............4/2/97 at SEA
Tony Clark..............8/28/04 at TOR
Alex Rodriguez.........4/26/05 VS. LAA

Also accomplished three times in World Series play (by Babe Ruth, 10/6/26 at STL, 10/9/28 at STL; by Reggie Jackson, 10/18/77 vs. LAD).

Home Run, First Major League At-Bat
John Miller..............9/11/66 at BOS
Marcus Thames.........6/10/02 vs. ARI
Andy Phillips............9/26/04 at BOS

Home Run, First Two Major League Games
Joe Lefebvre.........5/22/80 & 5/23/80

Two Home Runs, One Inning
Joe DiMaggio..........6/24/36 at CWS
Joe Pepitone............5/23/62 vs. KC
Cliff Johnson............6/30/77 at TOR
Alex Rodriguez...........9/5/07 vs. SEA
Alex Rodriguez............10/4/09 at TB

Home Runs, First Two Plate Appearances (or At-Bats) With the Yankees
Cody Ransom.........8/7/08 vs. KC and
8/22/08 at BAL

Four Consecutive Home Runs
Lou Gehrig................6/3/32 at PHI
John Blanchard...........7/21-7/26/61
Mickey Mantle.............. 7/4-7/6/62
Bobby Murcer......6/24/70 vs. CLE (DH)
(all but Murcer were consec. PAs)

Two Consecutive Pinch-Hit HRs
Ray Caldwell......................1915
Charlie Keller.....................1948
John Blanchard...................1961
Ray Barker........................1965

Switch-Hitting HR, One Game
Mickey Mantle................10 times:
8/12/64 vs. CWS
5/6/62 vs. WAS (G2)
4/26/61 at DET
9/15/59 vs. CWS
7/28/58 at KC
6/12/57 at CWS
6/1/56 vs. DET (G2)
5/18/56 at CWS
8/15/55 at BAL (G2)
5/13/55 vs. DET (1RH, 2LH)

Jorge Posada..................8 times:
9/4/07 vs. SEA
8/1/07 vs. CWS
5/24/05 vs. DET
3/31/04 vs. TB (at Tokyo)
6/28/02 vs. NYM
4/23/00 at TOR
7/10/99 at NYM
8/23/98 at TEX

Bernie Williams................8 times:
5/17/02 vs. MIN
6/30/01 vs. TB
5/17/00 at CWS
4/23/00 at TOR
5/4/99 at MilN
9/4/98 at CWS
9/12/96 at DET
6/6/94 at TEX

Also two times in post-season play (on 10/6/95 at SEA; and 10/5/96 at TEX)

Roy White.......................5 times
Tom Tresh.......................3 times
Nick Swisher....................3 times
Mark Teixeira....................3 times
Melky Cabrera...................1 time
Tony Clark.......................1 time
Ruben Sierra.....................1 time
Roy Smalley......................1 time

Switch-Hit Home Runs by Teammates, One Game
Bernie Williams and Jorge Posada each hit home runs from both sides of the plate on 4/23/00 in a 10-7 win at Toronto, the only time in Major League history that two players have hit switch-hit home runs in the same game.

Switch-hit HR in 2009
According to *Elias*, the 2009 season marked the first time in Baseball history a team had three different players homer from both sides of the plate in a single game within the same season (Cabrera, Swisher and Teixeira)...it marked the second time the Yankees have recorded three sets of switch-hit HR in the same season (also in 2000: Bernie Williams twice and Jorge Posada once).

According to the *Elias Sports Bureau*, three AL players have hit three sets of switch-hit homers in a single season: Mark Teixeira (2009 w/ NYY), Nick Swisher (2009 w/ NYY and 2007 w/ Oakland) and Tony Clark (1998 w/ Detroit).

Most Back-to-Back Home Runs, Single Season
1. Johnny Damon/Mark Teixeira.... 6 (2009)
2. Gary Sheffield/Alex Rodriguez... 5 (2005)
   Lou Gehrig/Joe DiMaggio....... 5 (1936)
   Lou Gehrig/Babe Ruth.......... 5 (1927)

Most Yankees With At Least 25HR, Single Season
5................ 2009 (Robinson Cano, Hideki Matsui, Alex Rodriguez, Nick Swisher, Mark Teixeira)
4.......1938 (Bill Dickey, Joe DiMaggio, Lou Gehrig, Joe Gordon)

Multi-HR Game by Two Yankees in Same Game
7/11/09 at Los Angeles-AL (Alex Rodriguez-2, Eric Hinske-2)

Birthday Grand Slam
Hideki Matsui................6/12/2008
First Yankee to ever hit a grand slam on his birthday

Most RBI, Single Inning
Alex Rodriguez..........7, 10/4/09 at TB
(American League record)

Going Glass: On July 2, 2009, Seattle's Russell Branyan became the first and only player to hit a home run off the glass-facing of the Mohegan Sun Sports Bar in centerfield of Yankee Stadium with a two-run homer in Seattle's 8-4 victory against the Yankees.

No-Hitters

Regular Season (10)

1917	*George Mogridge, at Boston, April 24	2-1
1923	Sad Sam Jones, at Philadelphia, September 4	2-0
1938	Monte Pearson, vs. Cleveland, August 27 (G2)	13-0
1951	Allie Reynolds, at Cleveland, July 12 (night)	1-0
	Allie Reynolds, vs. Boston, September 28 (G1)	8-0
1983	*Dave Righetti, vs. Boston, July 4	4-0
1993	*Jim Abbott, vs. Cleveland, September 4	4-0
1996	Dwight Gooden, vs. Seattle, May 14	2-0
1998	*+ David Wells, vs. Minnesota, May 17	4-0
1999	+ David Cone, vs. Montreal, July 18	6-0

Post Season (1)

1956	+Don Larsen, vs. Brooklyn, October 8 (Game Five of the World Series; remains the only perfect game in Series history)	2-0

No-Hitters vs. Yankees (7)

1908	Cy Young, for Boston at New York, June 30	8-0
1916	Rube Foster, for Boston at Boston, June 21	2-0
1919	Ray Caldwell, for Cleveland at New York, September 10 (G1)	3-0
1946	Bob Feller, for Cleveland at New York, April 30	1-0
1952	Virgil Trucks, for Detroit at New York, August 25	1-0
1958	Hoyt Wilhelm, for Baltimore at Baltimore, September 20	1-0
2003	Six pitchers, for Houston at New York, June 11 (Oswalt, Munro, Saarloos, Lidge, Dotel, Wagner)	8-0

*** Lefthanded pitcher** **+ Perfect Game**

Don Larsen and Yogi Berra

Cone's Perfect Game

On July 18, 1999, David Cone tossed only the 15th perfect game in Baseball history (since 1901) on a day Don Larsen was on hand to throw out the game's ceremonial first pitch. It came only one season after David Wells accomplished the feat and gave the Yankees a record three perfect games in their history, including Don Larsen in the 1956 World Series. Prior to Wells' and Cone's, perfect games had only been pitched in consecutive seasons once (by Jim Bunning of the Phillies in 1964 and the Dodgers' Sandy Koufax in 1965) and never by pitchers from the same team. Yankee Stadium also became the only park to host as many as three perfect games (Dodger Stadium was the site of perfect games by Koufax in 1965 and Montreal's Dennis Martinez in 1991).

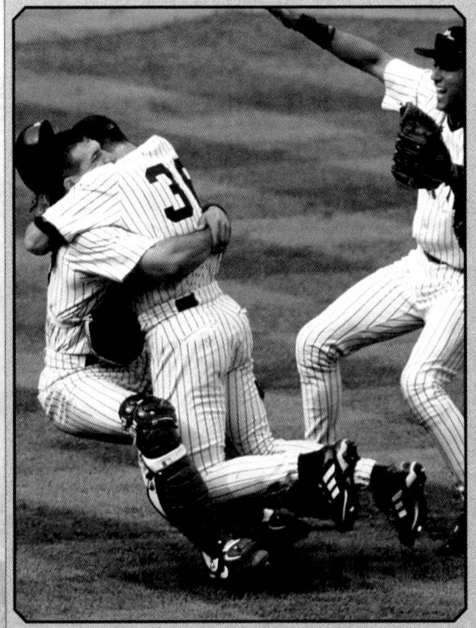

David Cone celebrates with Joe Girardi.

Yankees One-Hit Games

Mike Mussina

The most-recent one-hitter by a Yankees pitcher was thrown by Ted Lilly on 4/27/02 at Seattle (Lilly became the first Yankee pitcher ever to lose a one-hitter in the regular season)...the Yankees' last complete-game one-hit win was by Mike Mussina on 9/2/01 vs. the Boston Red Sox at Fenway Park in a 1-0 Yankees' victory...it was Mussina's fourth career complete game one-hitter...he retired 26 consecutive batters before Carl Everett singled with two outs in the ninth...it was the first complete-game one-hitter by a Yankee since Jimmy Key on 4/27/93 at California in a 5-0 Yankee win...the Yankees last authored a combined one-hitter on 6/30/06 vs. the Mets at Yankee Stadium, when five pitchers, led by Mike Mussina (also Ron Villone, Scott Proctor, Kyle Farnsworth and Mariano Rivera), limited the Mets to a sixth-inning single by Endy Chavez off Villone in a 2-0 victory...Roger Clemens still holds the all-time record for fewest hits allowed in an AL or NL Championship Series complete game with his one-hit, 15K performance in the Yankees' 5-0 ALCS Game 4 win at Seattle on 10/14/00.

Bob Turley and Whitey Ford each hurled three CG one-hitters for New York and both men participated in a fourth...Bob Shawkey, Rip Collins, Lefty Gomez, Vic Raschi and Floyd Bevens each threw two, with one of Bevens' coming in Game Four of the 1947 World Series vs. Brooklyn...Bevens was one out from a no-hitter when the pinch-hitter Cookie Lavagetto doubled in two runs to give the Dodgers a 3-2 victory...it was the last game Bevens and Lavagetto ever played in the Majors.

The Yankees were last held to one hit on 6/30/07 at Yankee Stadium by Oakland Athletics' RHP Chad Gaudin and RHP Rich Harden...the last starter to throw a one-hitter against the Yankees was RHP Mike Maroth on 7/16/04 at Detroit...Joe Wood, Earl Hamilton and Nolan Ryan are the only three men with a pair of one-hitters against the Yankees with both of Hamilton's coming in 1913...Hoyt Wilhelm, who no-hit the Yankees in 1958, also tossed a one-hitter against them in 1959.

Yankees Grand Slams

The Yankees hit three grand slams in 2009...on 4/28/09 at Detroit, Jose Molina became the first player since Oakland's Sal Bando to hit a grand slam and a sacrifice bunt in the same inning...Robinson Cano hit his second career grand slam on 9/28/09 vs. Kansas City...on the season's final day (10/4/09) at Tampa Bay, Alex Rodriguez hit a grand slam and a three-run home run in the sixth inning, becoming the first AL player ever to drive in seven runs in an inning...according to the *Elias Sports Bureau*, three Yankees have hit extra-inning grand slams in the last 25 years: Bobby Abreu (9/24/08 at Toronto, 10th inning), Tino Martinez (5/1/96 at Baltimore, 15th inning) and Jason Giambi (5/17/02 vs. Minnesota, 14th inning)...Alex Rodriguez's ninth-inning, walk-off slam off Baltimore's Chris Ray on 4/7/07 at Yankee Stadium was the eighth time in franchise history that the Yankees won a game with a walk-off grand slam...on 5/17/02 vs. the Minnesota Twins, Jason Giambi became only the 21st player in Major League history—and the second Yankee—to hit a last-inning grand slam to take a team to sudden victory when trailing by three runs (Babe Ruth did it on 9/25/25, hitting a one-out grand slam off Chicago's Sarge Connally in the 10th inning of New York's 6-5 win)...on 9/14/99 at Toronto, Bernie Williams and Paul O'Neill hit grand slams in the seventh and eighth innings respectively, the only time in franchise history that players have hit grand slams in consecutive innings...it was also only the third time in franchise history that the Yankees had two grand slams in the same game (also Tony Lazzeri on 5/24/36 at Philadelphia; and Dave Winfield and Don Mattingly on 6/29/87 at Toronto)...in 1998, Shane Spencer led the club with three grand slams (most ever by a Yankees rookie)...he also became the first Yankees rookie to hit at least two slams in one season since Yogi Berra in 1947...the Yankees gave up nine grand slams in 2000, the most in franchise history (surpassing eight in 1995)...the Yankees hit a franchise-record 10 grand slams in 1987, tying the Major League mark (since exceeded)...Don Mattingly hit a Major League-record six of the 10 grand slams that season (since tied by Travis Hafner, 2006)...four pitchers have hit grand slams for the Yankees - Red Ruffing (1933), Spud Chandler (1940), Don Larsen (1956) and Mel Stottlemyre (1965).

Career Leaders	No.
Lou Gehrig	23
Joe DiMaggio	13
Babe Ruth	12
Bernie Williams	11
Yogi Berra	9
Mickey Mantle	9
Bill Dickey	8
Tony Lazzeri	8
ALEX RODRIGUEZ	8
Charlie Keller	7
Tino Martinez	7
JORGE POSADA	7
Jason Giambi	6
Hideki Matsui	6
Don Mattingly	6
Mike Stanley	6

Season Leaders	No.	Year
Don Mattingly	6	1987
Tommy Henrich	4	1948
Lou Gehrig	4	1934
Joe DiMaggio	3	1937
Lou Gehrig	3	1931
Jorge Posada	3	2001
Alex Rodriguez	3	2007
Babe Ruth	3	1931
Ruben Sierra	3	2004
Shane Spencer	3	1998
Mike Stanley	3	1993

Pinch-Hit Grand Slams

2 .. 21 times by 17 players, last by Jorge Posada on 6/6/01 vs. Baltimore

Most by Club, Season

10 ... 1987
9 ... 1998, 2003, 2004
7 ... 1940, 1948, 1980, 1999, 2005, 2008
6 ... 1927, 1929, 1930, 1931, 1932, 1935, 1937, 1962, 2000, 2001, 2002

Most Allowed, Season

9 ... 2000
8 ... 1995
7 ... 2007, 2008
6 ... 1998, 1991, 1990, 1984, 1959, 1935

Yankees Pinch-Hit Home Runs

The Yankees hit three pinch-hit home runs in 2009, including two by Jorge Posada and one by Hideki Matsui...he became the 17th Yankee over the last 50 years to collect multiple pinch-hit homers in the same season...the Yankees recorded five pinch-hit home runs in 2004, their highest single-season total since they also hit five in 1994...in 1998, the Yankees hit two pinch-hit home runs, both ninth-inning grand slams by Darryl Strawberry (on 5/2 at Kansas City and 8/4 at Oakland, G2)...the Yankees franchise has 249 pinch-hit home runs, including 21 pinch-hit grand slams...Dion James' home run on 5/2/92 vs. Minnesota (off Gary Wayne) was the 200th pinch-hit home run in franchise history.

Career Leaders	No.
Y. Berra	9
B. Cerv	8
M. Mantle	7
B. Murcer	7
J. Blanchard	6
J. Mize	5
M. Skowron	5

Season Leaders	No.	Season
J. Blanchard	4	1961
K. Phelps	3	1989
D. Pasqua	3	1987
B. Murcer	3	1981
R. Barker	3	1965
B. Cerv	3	1961
J. Mize	3	1953
T. Henrich	3	1950

Club	Season
10	1961
8	1954
7	1986, 1960, 1953
6	1990, 1987, 1980, 1966, 1959

Yankees to Hit for the Cycle

Eleven Yankees have hit for the cycle (single, double, triple, and home run in the same game), on 15 occasions in franchise history. The last to do so was Melky Cabrera in an 8/2/09 win at Chicago-AL. He became the fourth Yankees centerfielder to hit for the cycle (also Joe DiMaggio twice, Mickey Mantle and Bobby Murcer) and the third switch-hitter to do so in club history, joining Tony Fernandez and Mantle. Only Bob Meusel (three), Lou Gehrig (two) and Joe DiMaggio (two) have hit for the cycle multiple times as a Yankee. The last player to hit for the cycle vs. New York was Detroit's Travis Fryman on 7/28/93 at Tiger Stadium. It was the first cycle vs. the Yankees since the L.A. Angels' Jim Fregosi did it on 7/28/64.

Player	Date
Bert Daniels (OF)	July 25, 1912 vs. Chicago
Bob Meusel (OF)	May 7, 1921 at Washington
Bob Meusel (OF)	July 3, 1922 at Philadelphia
Bob Meusel (OF)	July 26, 1928 at Detroit
Tony Lazzeri (2B)	June 3, 1932 at Philadelphia
Lou Gehrig (1B)	June 25, 1934 vs. Chicago
Joe DiMaggio (OF)	July 9, 1937 vs. Washington
Lou Gehrig (1B)	Aug. 1, 1937 vs. St. Louis
Buddy Rosar (C)	July 19, 1940 vs. Cleveland
Joe Gordon (2B)	Sept. 8, 1940 at Boston
Joe DiMaggio (OF)	May 20, 1948 at Chicago
Mickey Mantle (OF)	July 23, 1957 vs. Chicago
Bobby Murcer (OF)	Aug. 29, 1972 vs. Texas (G1)
Tony Fernandez (SS)	Sept. 3, 1995 vs. Oakland
Melky Cabrera (OF)	Aug. 2, 2009 at Chicago-AL

Yankees All-Star Game Selections

Casey Stengel managed more All-Star teams (10) than anyone else.

1933 Chapman*, lf
Dickey, c
Gehrig*, 1b
Gomez†, p
Lazzeri, 2b
Ruth*, rf
1934 Chapman, of
Dickey*, c
Gehrig*, 1b
Gomez†, p
Ruffing, p
Ruth*, rf
1935 Chapman, of
Gehrig*, 1b
Gomez†, p
1936 Crosetti, ss
Dickey, c
DiMaggio*, rf
Gehrig*, 1b
Gomez, p
Pearson, p
Selkirk, of
McCarthy, mgr
1937 Dickey*, c
DiMaggio*, rf
Gehrig, 1b
Gomez†, p
Murphy, p
Rolfe*, 3b
McCarthy, mgr
1938 Dickey*, c
DiMaggio*, rf
Gehrig, 1b
Gomez†, p
Rolfe, 3b
Ruffing, p
McCarthy, mgr
1939 Crosetti, ss
Dickey*, c
DiMaggio*, cf
Gehrig, 1b
Gomez, p
Gordon*, 2b
Murphy, p
Rolfe, 3b
Ruffing, p
Selkirk*, lf
McCarthy, mgr
1940 Dickey*, c
DiMaggio*, cf
Gordon*, 2b
Keller*, rf
Pearson, p
Rolfe, 3b
Ruffing†, p
McCarthy, mgr
1941 Dickey*, c
DiMaggio*, cf
Gordon, 2b
Keller, of
Ruffing, p
Russo, p
1942 Bonham, p
Chandler†, p
Dickey, c
DiMaggio*, cf
Gordon*, 2b
Henrich*, rf
Rizzuto, ss
Rosar, c
Ruffing, p
McCarthy, mgr
1943 Bonham, p
Chandler, p
Dickey, c
Gordon, 2b
Keller, of
Lindell, of
McCarthy, mgr
1944 Borowy†, p
Hemsley, c
Page, p
McCarthy, mgr
1945 No game due to World War II travel restrictions
1946 Chandler, p
Dickey, c
DiMaggio*, cf
Gordon, 2b
Keller*, rf
Stirnweiss, 3b
1947 Chandler, p
DiMaggio*, cf
Henrich, of
Johnson, 3b
McQuinn*, 1b
Page, p
Robinson, c
Shea, p
Keller, of
1948 Berra, c
DiMaggio*, of
Henrich†, rf
McQuinn, 1b
Page, p
Raschi, p
Harris, mgr
1949 Berra, c
DiMaggio*, cf
Henrich, of
Raschi, p
Reynolds, p
1950 Berra*, c
Byrne, p
Coleman, 2b
DiMaggio, of
Henrich, 1b
Raschi†, p
Reynolds, p
Rizzuto*, ss
Stengel, mgr
1951 Berra*, c
DiMaggio, of
Lopat, p
Rizzuto, ss
Stengel, mgr
1952 Bauer*, rf
Berra*, c
Mantle, of
Raschi†, p
Reynolds, p
Rizzuto, ss
McDougald, 2b
Stengel, mgr
1953 Bauer*, rf
Berra*, c
Mantle*, cf
Mize, 1b
Reynolds, p
Rizzuto, ss
Sain, p
Stengel, mgr
1954 Bauer, of
Berra*, c
Ford†, p
Mantle*, cf
Noren, of
Reynolds, p
Stengel, mgr
1955 Berra*, c
Ford, p
Mantle, of
Turley, p
1956 Berra*, c
Ford, p
Kucks, p
Mantle*, cf
Martin, 2b
McDougald, ss
Stengel, mgr
1957 Berra*, c
Grim, p
Howard, c
Mantle*, cf
McDougald, ss
Richardson, 2b
Shantz, p
Skowron, 1b
Stengel, mgr
1958 Berra, c
Duren, p
Ford, p
Howard, c
Kubek, inf
Mantle*, cf
McDougald, 2b
Skowron, 1b
Turley†, p
Stengel, mgr
1959 Berra3, c
Duren3, p
Ford1, p
Mantle3, of
McDougald3, ss
Richardson2, 2b
Skowron*3, 1b
Howard2, c
Kubek3, ss
Stengel, mgr
1960 Berra*3, c
Coates3, p
Ford†3, p
Howard3, c
Mantle*3, cf
Maris*3, rf
Skowron*3, 1b
1961 Arroyo2, p
Berra3, of
Ford3, p
Howard3, c
Kubek*3, ss
Mantle*3, cf
Maris*3, rf
Skowron2, 1b
1962 Berra2, c
Howard3, c
Mantle*3, rf
Maris*3, cf
Richardson3, 2b
Terry3, p
Tresh3, ss
Houk2, mgr
1963 Bouton, p
Howard, c
Mantle, of
Pepitone*, 1b
Richardson, 2b
Tresh, of
1964 Ford, p
Howard*, c
Mantle*, cf
Pepitone, 1b
Richardson, 2b
1965 Howard, c
Mantle, of
Pepitone, 1b
Richardson, 2b
Stottlemyre, p
1966 Richardson, 2b
Stottlemyre, p.
1967 Downing, p
Mantle, 1b
1968 Mantle, 1b
Stottlemyre, p
1969 Stottlemyre†, p
1970 Peterson, p
Stottlemyre, p
White, of
1971 Munson, c
Murcer*, cf
1972 Murcer*, cf
1973 Lyle, p
Munson, c
Murcer*, lf
1974 Munson*, c
Murcer*, cf
1975 Bonds*, cf
Hunter, p
Munson*, c
Nettles*, 3b
1976 Chambliss, 1b
Hunter, p
Lyle, p
Munson*, c
Randolph, 2b
Rivers, of
1977 Jackson*, rf
Lyle, p
Munson, c
Nettles, 3b
Randolph*, 2b
Martin, mgr
1978 Gossage, p
Guidry, p
Jackson*, of
Nettles, 3b
Martin, mgr

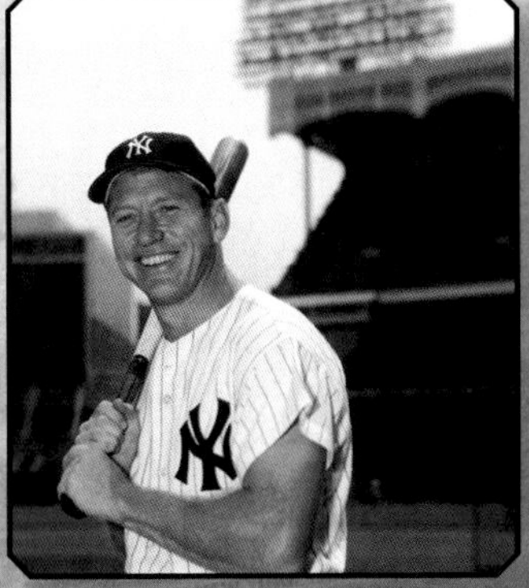

*** - Selected as starter** **† - Started, but not elected** **1 - On team for first game only**
2 - On team for second game only **3 - On team for both games**

Yankees All-Star Game Selections

1979	Guidry, p
	Jackson, of
	John, p
	Nettles, 3b
1980	Dent*, ss
	Gossage, p
	Jackson*, rf
	John, p
	Nettles*, 3b
	Randolph*, 2b
1981	Davis, p
	Dent*, ss
	Gossage, p
	Jackson*, rf
	Randolph*, 2b
	Winfield*, cf
1982	Gossage, p
	Guidry, p
	Winfield, of
1983	Guidry, p
	Winfield*, rf
1984	P. Niekro, p
	Mattingly, 1b
	Winfield*, lf
1985	Henderson*, cf
	Mattingly, 1b
	Winfield*, rf
1986	Henderson*, lf
	Mattingly, 1b
	Righetti, p
	Winfield*, rf
1987	Henderson*, cf
	Mattingly*, 1b
	Randolph*, 2b
	Righetti, p
	Winfield*, rf
1988	Henderson*, cf
	Mattingly, 1b
	Winfield*, rf
1989	Mattingly, 1b
	Sax, 2b
1990	Sax, 2b
1991	Sanderson, p
1992	R. Kelly, of
1993	Boggs*, 3b
	Key, p
1994	Boggs*, 3b
	Key*, p
	O'Neill, of
1995	Boggs*, 3b
	O'Neill, of
	Stanley, c
	Showalter, mgr.
1996	Boggs*, 3b
	PETTITTE, P
	Wetteland, p
1997	Cone, p
	Martinez*, 1b
	O'Neill†, of
	RIVERA, p
	B. Williams, of
	Torre, mgr.
1998	Brosius, 3b
	JETER, ss
	O'Neill, of
	Wells*, p
	B. Williams, of
1999	Cone, p
	JETER, ss
	RIVERA, p
	B. Williams, of
	Torre, mgr.
2000	JETER†, ss
	POSADA, c
	RIVERA, p
	B. Williams*, of
	Torre, mgr.
2001	Clemens†, p
	JETER, ss
	PETTITTE, P
	POSADA, c
	RIVERA, p
	Stanton, p
	B. Williams, of
	Torre, mgr.
2002	Giambi*, 1b
	JETER, ss
	POSADA*; c
	RIVERA, p
	Soriano*, 2b
	Ventura, 3b
	Torre, mgr.
2003	Clemens, p
	Giambi, 1b
	Matsui*, cf
	POSADA*, c
	Soriano*, 2b
2004	Giambi*; lb
	Gordon; p
	JETER*; ss
	Matsui; of
	RIVERA, p
	RODRIGUEZ*; 3b
	Sheffield, of
	VAZQUEZ, p
	Torre, mgr.
2005	RODRIGUEZ*, 3b
	RIVERA, p
	Sheffield, of
2006	RODRIGUEZ*, 3b
	JETER*, ss
	CANO, 2b
	RIVERA, p
2007	JETER*, ss
	POSADA, c
	RODRIGUEZ*, 3b
2008	JETER*, ss
	RIVERA, p
	RODRIGUEZ*, 3b
2009	JETER*, ss
	RIVERA, p
	TEIXEIRA*, 1b

*** - Selected as starter**
† - Started, but not elected
1 - On team for first game only
2 - On team for second game only
3 - On team for both games

Yankees All-Stars by Total Selections

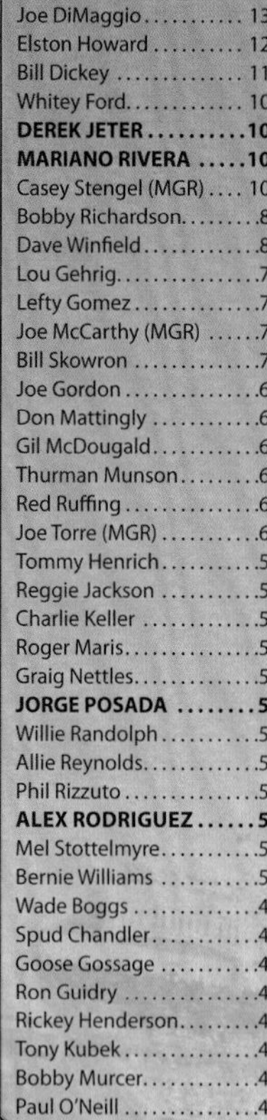

Mickey Mantle	20
Yogi Berra	18
Joe DiMaggio	13
Elston Howard	12
Bill Dickey	11
Whitey Ford	10
DEREK JETER	**10**
MARIANO RIVERA	**10**
Casey Stengel (MGR)	10
Bobby Richardson	8
Dave Winfield	8
Lou Gehrig	7
Lefty Gomez	7
Joe McCarthy (MGR)	7
Bill Skowron	7
Joe Gordon	6
Don Mattingly	6
Gil McDougald	6
Thurman Munson	6
Red Ruffing	6
Joe Torre (MGR)	6
Tommy Henrich	5
Reggie Jackson	5
Charlie Keller	5
Roger Maris	5
Graig Nettles	5
JORGE POSADA	**5**
Willie Randolph	5
Allie Reynolds	5
Phil Rizzuto	5
ALEX RODRIGUEZ	**5**
Mel Stottelmyre	5
Bernie Williams	5
Wade Boggs	4
Spud Chandler	4
Goose Gossage	4
Ron Guidry	4
Rickey Henderson	4
Tony Kubek	4
Bobby Murcer	4
Paul O'Neill	4
Vic Raschi	4
Red Rolfe	4
Hank Bauer	3
Ben Chapman	3
Ryne Duren	3
Jason Giambi	3
Sparky Lyle	3
Billy Martin	3 (2 as Mgr)
Joe Page	3
Joe Pepitone	3
Tom Tresh	3
Ernie Bonham	2
Roger Clemens	2
Jim Coates	2
David Cone	2
Frank Crosetti	2
Bucky Dent	2
Ralph Houk (MGR)	2
Catfish Hunter	2
Tommy John	2
Jimmy Key	2
Hideki Matsui	2
George McQuinn	2
John Murphy	2
Monte Pearson	2
ANDY PETTITTE	**2**
Dave Righetti	2
Babe Ruth	2
Steve Sax	2
George Selkirk	2
Gary Sheffield	2
Alfonso Soriano	2
Ralph Terry	2
Bob Turley	2
Luis Arroyo	1
Bobby Bonds	1
Hank Borowy	1
Jim Bouton	1
Scott Brosius	1
Tommy Byrne	1
ROBINSON CANO	**1**
Chris Chambliss	1
Jerry Coleman	1
Ron Davis	1
Al Downing	1
Tom Gordon	1
Bob Grim	1
Bucky Harris (MGR)	1
Rollie Hemsley	1
Billy Johnson	1
Roberto Kelly	1
Johnny Kucks	1
Tony Lazzeri	1
Bob Lemon (MGR)	1
Johnny Lindell	1
Eddie Lopat	1
Tino Martinez	1
Johnny Mize	1
Phil Neikro	1
Irving Noren	1
Fritz Peterson	1
Mickey Rivers	1
Aaron Robinson	1
Buddy Rosar	1
Marius Russo	1
Johnny Sain	1
Scott Sanderson	1
Bobby Shantz	1
Spec Shea	1
Buck Showalter (MGR)	1
Mike Stanley	1
Mike Stanton	1
Snuffy Stirnweiss	1
MARK TEIXEIRA	**1**
JAVIER VAZQUEZ	**1**
Robin Ventura	1
David Wells	1
John Wetteland	1
Roy White	1

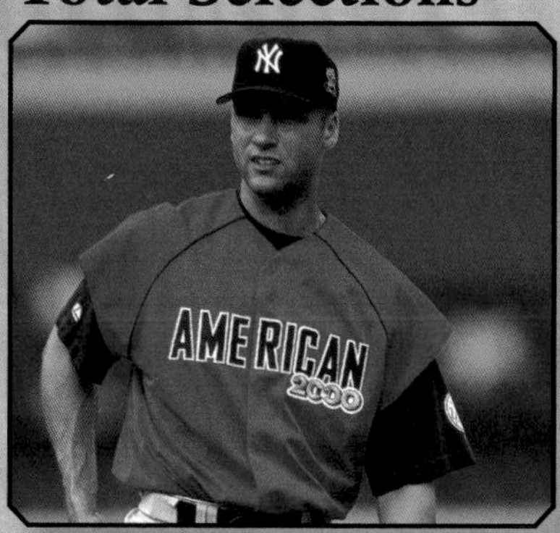

Derek Jeter is the only Yankees All-Star to take home MVP honors, doing so in the 2000 Midsummer Classic (3-for-3, double, 2RBI)

Previous Yankee Stadium All-Star Games

The Yankees have hosted four All-Star Games, including the 2008 Midsummer Classic in Yankee Stadium's final season. The Stadium also hosted the All-Star Game in 1977 (48th), 1960 (29th) and 1939 (seventh). Only Cleveland's old Municipal Stadium hosted as many All-Star Games as Yankee Stadium. Overall, New York City has hosted eight MLB All-Star Games, the highest total in Major League history, with the Polo Grounds (1934 and 1942), Ebbets Field (1949) and Shea Stadium (1964) also serving as host sites. The 2008 game marked the first time the Midsummer Classic was held in the host team's final season at its ballpark.

Since the game originated in 1933, the Yankees have had the most All-Star players (113) and the highest total All-Star selections (358) of any Major League Baseball franchise. Mickey Mantle owns the most All-Star selections in club history, having been named to 20 All-Star teams, fourth-most all-time, and Yankees pitcher Lefty Gomez is the only pitcher in All-Star Game history to earn three wins, having made five career All-Star starts. Joe DiMaggio (13 career All-Star nods) and Tom Tresh (three career All-Star selections), own the distinction as the only Yankees rookies to start for the American League (1936 and 1962, respectively). Of the 80 All-Star Games, a Yankees Manager has skippered the American League team 28 times (35%). Currently, third baseman Alex Rodriguez leads the team with 12 career trips to the Midsummer Classic, followed by shortstop Derek Jeter and closer Mariano Rivera with 10 All-Star appearances apiece. According to the *Elias Sports Bureau*, Jeter and Rivera are the only players to be named to the All-Star squad with their current team at least 10 times. Jeter holds the distinction as the only All-Star MVP in club history, taking home the honor in 2000 after going 3-for-3 with 1 double and 2RBI in the AL's 6-3 win at Atlanta's Turner Field. He became just the fourth shortstop to earn the award. Rodriguez led the Majors in All-Star balloting in 2007 and 2008.

Seventh All-Star Game

American League 3, National League 1
July 11, 1939, Yankee Stadium

Yankee Stadium was chosen to host the 1939 All-Star Game due to the World's Fair which was being held at Flushing-Meadows in Queens during the 1939 season. The Cubs' Gabby Hartnett managed the National League squad while Yankees skipper Joe McCarthy led the American League team, which featured 10 Yankees All-Stars, six of whom were starters. Yankees centerfielder Joe DiMaggio was 1-for-4 in the game, hitting a solo home run. Lou Gehrig, who announced his retirement in May of 1939, was an honorary member of the AL squad.

All-Star Team	1	2	3	4	5	6	7	8	9	R	H	E
National League	0	0	1	0	0	0	0	0	0	1	7	1
American League	0	0	0	2	1	0	0	0	x	3	6	1

Winning Pitcher: Tommy Bridges
Losing Pitcher: Bill Lee

48th All-Star Game

National League 7, American League 5
July 19, 1977, Yankee Stadium

Showcasing its renovation, Yankee Stadium hosted the All-Star Game on July 19, 1977, in a game dedicated to Jackie Robinson. With the Yankees defending their 1976 pennant, Billy Martin managed the AL team on his home field. The National League won its sixth consecutive All-Star Game, part of the Senior Circuit's 11-game win streak. Joe Morgan opened the game with a home run off Jim Palmer as the NL squad scored four first-inning runs. Yankees outfielder Reggie Jackson and second baseman Willie Randolph were AL starters. National League Manager Sparky Anderson described the game's final score by saying, "the only reason we're here is to kick the living hell out of those guys."

All-Star Team	1	2	3	4	5	6	7	8	9	R	H	E
National League	4	0	1	0	0	0	0	2	0	7	9	1
American League	0	0	0	0	0	2	1	0	2	5	8	0

Winning Pitcher: Don Sutton
Losing Pitcher: Jim Palmer

29th All-Star Game

National League 6, American League 0
July 13, 1960 (Game #2), Yankee Stadium

Yankee Stadium was the host site for baseball's second All-Star Game in three days in 1960. The National League completed the All-Star sweep with a 6-0 win, having won Game 1 on July 11 in Kansas City, marking the only year that both All-Star games were won by the same team. Yankees hurler Whitey Ford was the starting pitcher for the AL squad, while fellow Yankees Yogi Berra (catcher), Mickey Mantle (left field), Roger Maris (centerfield) and Bill Skowron (first base) all appeared in the starting lineup. The National League used six different pitchers to combine on the shutout effort and hit an All-Star record-tying four home runs, including one by Willie Mays. The 38,000 fans who attended the game witnessed Ted Williams in his final All-Star appearance.

All-Star Team	1	2	3	4	5	6	7	8	9	R	H	E
National League	0	2	1	0	0	0	1	0	2	6	10	0
American League	0	0	0	0	0	0	0	0	0	0	8	0

Winning Pitcher: Vern Law
Losing Pitcher: Whitey Ford

79th All-Star Game

American League 4, National League 3
July 15, 2008, Yankee Stadium

In the final Midsummer Classic at the original Yankee Stadium, the American League emerged with a 4-3 win in 15 innings as Texas' Michael Young brought home Minnesota's Justin Morneau with a "walk-off" sacrifice fly. The 4-hour, 50-minute contest was the longest All-Star Game time-wise and tied for the longest ASG in innings (also 1967 at Anaheim, 2-1 NL win). It was the AL's 12th straight All-Star Game victory and ensured American League homefield advantage in the World Series. SS Derek Jeter started and recorded the game's first hit in the first inning. RHP Mariano Rivera pitched 1.2 scoreless innings. Yankees Manager Joe Girardi joined the AL coaching staff as did Yankees Head Athletic Trainer Gene Monahan, who made his fourth All-Star Game appearance (also 1977, '86 and '92). Pregame ceremonies included 49 Hall of Famers, marking one of the largest gatherings of living baseball HOFers ever. The festivities were highlighted by Yankees Principal Owner/Chairperson George Steinbrenner, who delivered baseballs to the ceremonial first pitch participants (Reggie Jackson, Whitey Ford, Yogi Berra and Goose Gossage).

All-Star Team	1 2 3	4 5 6	7 8 9	10 11 12	13 14 15	R	H	E
National League	0 0 0	0 1 1	0 1 0	0 0 0	0 0 0	3	13	4
American League	0 0 0	0 0 0	2 1 0	0 0 0	0 0 1	4	14	1

Winning Pitcher: Scott Kazmir
Losing Pitcher: Brad Lidge

Yankees Postseason Results

1921 WORLD SERIES

Marked the Yankees' first ever World Series appearance in Baseball's last nine-game Fall Classic...Waite Hoyt went 2-1 despite not allowing an earned run in 27.0IP (18H, 11BB) over three starts...is tied with Christy Mathewson (1903) for the most Series IP without allowing an ER...lost, 1-0, in the Game 8 clincher, tossing a complete game while allowing an unearned run in the first inning...Carl Mays went 1-2 with a 1.73 ERA (26.0IP, 5ER) in his three starts, setting a still-standing record for the most innings pitched in a single postseason without allowing a walk...Babe Ruth hit the first of his 15 career World Series home runs in a losing effort in Game 4.

New York Yankees (AL) **3**
New York Giants (NL) **5**

1922 WORLD SERIES

The Yankees went 0-4-1 against the Giants, marking just one of three times in 39 World Series appearances that the Yankees have been held without a win (were swept in 1963 vs. Los Angeles and 1976 vs. Cincinnati)...hit just .203 as a team...Game 2 marked the Yankees' only tie in 219 overall World Series games (130-88-1).

New York Yankees (AL) **0**
New York Giants (NL) **4**

1923 WORLD SERIES

Won the first World Series in franchise history in the inaugural season of the original Yankee Stadium...their Game 2 win snapped a nine-game World Series winless streak dating to 1921 (0-8-1)...scored five runs in the eighth inning of the Game 6 clincher to win, 6-4...Babe Ruth and Bob Meusel led the Yankees in HR (3) and RBI (8), respectively.

New York Yankees (AL) **4**
New York Giants (NL) **2**

1926 WORLD SERIES

Series is most remembered for Game 7, which featured Pete Alexander's bases-loaded, seventh-inning strikeout of Tony Lazzeri, and Babe Ruth making the final out of the series attempting to steal second base...Ruth became the first player to hit 3HR in a single World Series game (Game 4 at St. Louis) and four total home runs in a World Series.

St. Louis Cardinals (NL) **4**
New York Yankees (AL) **3**

1927 WORLD SERIES

The Murderers' Row Yankees became the first AL team to sweep a Series...Babe Ruth had a Series-high 7RBI and his 2HR were the only homers of the Series...Herb Pennock was perfect through his first 22 batters of Game 3 before a Pie Traynor single...Yankees completed the sweep on a ninth-inning wild pitch from Pirates pitcher Johnny Miljus in Game 4...marked the first of eight consecutive winning World Series for the franchise.

New York Yankees (AL) **4**
Pittsburgh Pirates (NL) **0**

1928 WORLD SERIES

The Yankees' win marked their first back-to-back titles...was the sixth and last Series for manager Miller Huggins, who died during the 1929 season...used only three pitchers in the entire Series as each earned complete-game wins (Waite Hoyt in Games 1 and 4; George Pipgras in Game 2 and Tom Zachary in Game 3)...Lou Gehrig led the Yankees with 4HR and 9RBI...Babe Ruth tied his own record with three home runs in Game 4 at St. Louis.

St. Louis Cardinals (NL) **0**
New York Yankees (AL) **4**

1932 WORLD SERIES

Swept the Cubs to run their World Series winning streak to 12 games...was the first of Manager Joe McCarthy's eight Series appearances and seven titles with the club...Babe Ruth hit his "called shot" in the fifth inning of Game 3...he and Gehrig each hit 2HR in the game...the Yankees outscored the Cubs 37-19 in the Series...Gehrig batted .529 (9-for-17) with 9R, 3HR and 8RBI...was Ruth's last World Series with the Yankees.

Chicago Cubs (NL) **0**
New York Yankees (AL) **4**

1936 WORLD SERIES

The Yankees' victory was the first of four consecutive titles...had their 12-game World Series winning streak snapped with a Game 1 loss...the Yankees' 18-4 Game 2 win still marks the most runs scored by one team in a Series game...Bill Dickey and Tony Lazzeri (grand slam) each had 5RBI in the game...rookie Joe DiMaggio batted .346 (9-for-26) with 3RBI in the Series.

New York Yankees (AL) **4**
New York Giants (NL) **2**

1937 WORLD SERIES

The Yankees defeated the Giants for the second year in a row...Yankees pitchers posted a 2.45 ERA (44.0, 12ER) in the Series...Lefty Gomez recorded complete-game wins in Game 1 and in the Game 5 clincher...George Selkirk led the Yankees with 5R and 6RBI.

New York Giants (NL) **1**
New York Yankees (AL) **4**

1938 WORLD SERIES

The Yankees ran their all-time World Series mark vs. the Cubs to 8-0...became the first team to win three consecutive Series...middle infielders Joe Gordon and Frank Crosetti each drove in a team-high 6R...used just four pitchers, who sported a combined 1.75 ERA (36.0IP, 7ER)...Red Ruffing recorded complete-game wins in Game 1 and 4, tallying a 1.50 ERA in the Series (18.0IP, 3ER).

New York Yankees (AL) **4**
Chicago Cubs (NL) **0**

1939 WORLD SERIES

The Yankees won the last of four consecutive World Series with their second straight sweep...were led by Charlie Keller, who batted .438 (7-for-16) with 8R, 3HR and 6RBI...the Yankees hit just .206 (27-for-131) as a team...Yankees pitching compiled a 1.22 ERA, holding the Reds to just four extra-base hits (0HR) in the Series...Game 4 was won in the 10th inning on "Lombardi's Snooze" as Joe DiMaggio scored past dazed Cincinnati catcher Ernie Lombardi, who had just suffered a home plate collision with Charlie Keller.

Cincinnati Reds (NL) **0**
New York Yankees (AL) **4**

1941 WORLD SERIES

Marked the first World Series meeting between the Yankees and Dodgers...Game 4 featured the famous passed ball by Dodgers catcher Mickey Owen, which would have been the final out of the game and evened the Series at 2-2...the Yankees went on to score 4R with two out in the ninth to win, 7-4, at Ebbets Field...in the Game 5 clincher, Tiny Bonham tossed a complete game (1ER, 5H) and Tommy Henrich hit a solo homer...Joe Gordon (.500, 1HR, 5RBI) and Charlie Keller (.389, 5RBI) paced Yankees hitters...capped a run of 32 wins in 36 World Series games dating to 1927.

Brooklyn Dodgers (NL) **1**
New York Yankees (AL) **4**

1942 WORLD SERIES

The Yankees won Game 1 behind Red Ruffing but lost the next four games...marked the Yankees' first losing World Series since falling in seven games to the Cards in 1926...Joe DiMaggio went 7-for-21 (.333) and Phil Rizzuto went 8-for-21 (.381), while Charlie Keller led the Yankees with 2HR and 5RBI.

New York Yankees (AL) **1**
St. Louis Cardinals (NL) **4**

1943 WORLD SERIES

The Yankees reversed the prior year's result, winning in five games...right-hander Spud Chandler was dominant, allowing just 1ER over 18.0IP for complete-game wins in Games 1 and 5...Bill Dickey's two-run homer in the Game 5 clincher marked the only runs of the game...Yankees Joe DiMaggio, Tommy Henrich, Phil Rizzuto, George Selkirk, Red Ruffing and Buddy Hassett were all serving in the military and did not appear in the Series...marked the seventh and final World Series title in eight appearances under manager Joe McCarthy.

St. Louis Cardinals (NL) **1**
New York Yankees (AL) **4**

1947 WORLD SERIES

The Yankees were piloted by Bucky Harris in his only World Series managing the team...in Game 4, Yankees pitcher Bill Bevens lost both his no-hit bid and the game with two outs in the bottom of the ninth as pinch-hitter Cookie Lavagetto doubled home two runs for a 3-2 Brooklyn win...Spec Shea recorded two wins and Johnny Lindell batted .500 (9-for-18) with 7RBI.

Brooklyn Dodgers (NL) **3**
New York Yankees (AL) **4**

1949 WORLD SERIES

Marked the first of five straight World Series championships...was the first of 10 World Series appearances in a 12-year stretch under manager Casey Stengel (won seven)...Allie Reynolds allowed just 2H, winning Game 1, 1-0, over Don Newcombe on Tommy Henrich's leadoff homer in the bottom of the ninth...also pitched 3.1 scoreless innings to close out Game 4...Commissioner Happy Chandler ordered lights turned on during Game 5, marking the first time a World Series game was finished under electric light.

Brooklyn Dodgers (NL) **1**
New York Yankees (AL) **4**

1950 WORLD SERIES

Yankees pitchers allowed just 5R (3ER) all Series, tallying a 0.73 combined ERA in 37.0IP...each of the first three games were decided by one run, including a 1-0 victory behind Vic Raschi in Game 1 and a 2-1, 10-inning win behind Allie Reynolds in Game 2...Whitey Ford earned the first of his record 10 career World Series wins in the Game 4 clincher as Reynolds came out of the bullpen to strike out the final batter of the game with two runners on base.

New York Yankees (AL) **4**
Philadelphia Phillies (NL) **0**

1951 WORLD SERIES

The Yankees defeated the Giants in Joe DiMaggio's final World Series...Willie Mays and Mickey Mantle made their Series debuts, both in their rookie seasons...in Game 2, Mantle seriously injured his right knee after getting his cleat caught in a drainpipe, ending his Series...Ed Lopat allowed just 1ER in 18.0IP, notching wins in Games 2 and 5.

New York Giants (NL) **2**
New York Yankees (AL) **4**

1952 WORLD SERIES

Led by Mickey Mantle (.345, 5R, 2HR), Johnny Mize (.400, 3HR, 6RBI) and Gene Woodling (.348), the Yankees won in seven games...Allie Reynolds and Vic Raschi each recorded a pair of victories...the Yankees slugged 10HR in the Series...in Game 7, second baseman Billy Martin made a game-saving catch on a two-out, seventh-inning, based-loaded pop-up from Jackie Robinson to preserve the win.

New York Yankees (AL) **4**
Brooklyn Dodgers (NL) **3**

1953 WORLD SERIES

The Yankees won their all-time record fifth consecutive title...Billy Martin batted .500 (12-for-24) with 2HR and 8RBI...still shares the all-time mark for hits in a six-game World Series...Mickey Mantle won Game 2 with a two-run homer in the eighth inning...added a grand slam in the Game 5 win...Martin drove in the winning run in the Game 6 clincher with a single in the bottom of the ninth.

Brooklyn Dodgers (NL) **2**
New York Yankees (AL) **4**

1955 WORLD SERIES

Marked the Yankees' first Series loss to the Dodgers after five successive wins (1941, '47, '49, '52, '53)...is the only time the Dodgers triumphed over the Yankees before relocating to Los Angeles in 1958...Brooklyn's Johnny Podres tossed an eight-hit, 2-0, shutout in the Game 7 clincher at Yankee Stadium...with two on in the sixth, Yogi Berra's slicing line drive was famously caught by Brooklyn's Sandy Amoros, who then doubled off Gil McDougald to kill off a potential rally.

Brooklyn Dodgers (NL) **4**
New York Yankees (AL) **3**

1956 WORLD SERIES

Lost the first two games in Brooklyn, then came back to win in seven...was highlighted by Don Larsen's Game 5 perfect game caught by Yogi Berra, the only no-hitter in postseason history...Larsen didn't know he was pitching until he got to the park that day...had lasted only 1.2 innings in his Game 2 start, (4R, 0ER, 1H, 4BB)...Berra led the Yankees with a .360 (9-for-25) batting average, 3HR and a then-record 10 RBI...the Yankees hit 12HR, the second-highest total in Series history (San Francisco 14HR in 2002).

New York Yankees (AL) **4**
Brooklyn Dodgers (NL) **3**

1957 WORLD SERIES

The Yankees dropped their second seven-game World Series in three years in their first-ever meeting against Milwaukee...the Braves' Lew Burdette won Games 2, 5 and 7, the latter two on seven-hit shutouts...second baseman Jerry Coleman batted .364 (8-for-22) with 2 doubles and 2RBI in a losing effort.

Milwaukee Braves (NL) **4**
New York Yankees (AL) **3**

1958 WORLD SERIES

The Yankees came back from 2-0- and 3-1-game deficits to win in seven...after getting bombed for 4ER in just 0.1IP in his Game 2 start, Yankees pitcher Bob Turley recorded wins in Game 5 (five-hit shutout) and Game 7 (6.2IP in relief of Don Larsen)...the Series win meant the Yankees had defeated each of the eight modern NL teams (since 1900) in a World Series...Hank Bauer batted .323 (10-for-31) with 4HR, making him just one of four Yankees in franchise history to hit as many homers in a single Series (also Ruth 4HR in 1926; Gehrig 4HR in 1928; and Reggie Jackson 5HR in 1977)...was held hitless in Game 4, snapping an all-time Major League best 17-game World Series hitting streak.

New York Yankees (AL) **4**
Milwaukee Braves (NL) **3**

1960 WORLD SERIES

Despite outscoring Pittsburgh 55-27 and setting still-standing World Series marks in runs scored and team batting average (.338), the Yankees lost the decisive Game 7, 10-9, on Bill Maseroski's ninth-inning walk-off homer off Ralph Terry...marked Casey Stengel's final game as Yankees manager...Bobby Richardson batted .367 (11-for-30) and recorded a still-standing record 12RBI, becoming the only player in Baseball history to win the World Series MVP Award on a losing team...Whitey Ford tossed complete game shutouts in Games 3 and 6, allowing just 11H and 2BB in 18.0 Series IP.

New York Yankees (AL) **3**
Pittsburgh Pirates (NL) **4**

1961 WORLD SERIES

With the Series tied 1-1, the Yankees won Game 3 on a game-tying solo homer by Johnny Blanchard in the eighth and Roger Maris' game-winning solo shot in the ninth...outscored Cincinnati 20-5 in the final two games...manager Ralph Houk became the third Yankees skipper to win the World Series with the Yankees in his first season with the club...Hector Lopez led the Yankees with 7RBI in just 9AB...Whitey Ford pitched 14.0 scoreless inning, notching wins in Games 1 and 4.

Cincinnati Reds (NL) **1**
New York Yankees (AL) **4**

1962 WORLD SERIES

The Yankees clinched a tight seven-game Series on a 1-0, four-hit, Game 7 shutout from Ralph Terry...scored their only run when Tony Kubek grounded into a fifth-inning double play...Terry allowed just 17H and 5ER in 25.0 Series IP, taking home the MVP Award...the teams combined for just 41 total runs in a Series that stretched over 13 days due to rainouts.

New York Yankees (AL) **4**
San Francisco Giants (NL) **3**

1963 WORLD SERIES

The Yankees were swept despite allowing just 12 overall runs, marking just one of two four-game Series exits in franchise history (also 1976 vs. Cincinnati)...scored just four runs and batted .171 over the four games, marking the third and four-lowest all-time totals, respectively, by any team in a World Series.

Los Angeles Dodgers (NL) **4**
New York Yankees (AL) **0**

1964 WORLD SERIES

The Yankees' seven-game loss marked Mickey Mantle's final World Series...batted .333 (8-for-24) with 3HR, giving him a record 18HR for his career...Jim Bouton won both of his starts, allowing just 3ER in 17.1IP...Bobby Richardson batted .406 (13-for-32), setting an all-time record for hits in a Series (since tied by Lou Brock in 1968 and Marty Barrett in 1986).

New York Yankees (AL) **3**
St. Louis Cardinals (NL) **4**

1976 CHAMPIONSHIP SERIES

Chris Chambliss batted .524 (11-for-21) with 2HR and 8RBI, including the Series-winning "walk-off" home run off the Royals' Mark Littell in Game 5.

Kansas City Royals (AL)	**2**
New York Yankees (AL)	**3**

1976 WORLD SERIES

Marked the Yankees' first World Series appearance after a 11-year drought...was the first Series appearance under the majority ownership of George M. Steinbrenner...also was the club's first Series following the 1974-75 remodeling of the original Yankee Stadium...was the second and last time the Yankees have been swept in a Series...Thurman Munson led the Yankees, batting .529 (9-for-17) with 2R and 2RBI.

New York Yankees (AL)	**0**
Cincinnati Reds (NL)	**4**

1977 CHAMPIONSHIP SERIES

Sparky Lyle appeared in four of the five games and recorded wins in relief in Game 4 (5.1IP, 2H, 0R, 0BB, 1K) and Game 5 (1.1IP, 1H, 0R, 1K)...Yankees scored 1R in the eighth and 3R in the ninth to win the Game 5 clincher, 5-3.

New York Yankees (AL)	**3**
Kansas City Royals (AL)	**2**

1977 WORLD SERIES

The Yankees snapped a 14-season championship drought, defeating the Dodgers in six games...in the Game 6 clincher, Reggie Jackson joined Babe Ruth (twice) as the only players to hit 3HR in a single World Series game...batted .450 (9-for-20) overall with 10R (tied for most all-time), 5HR (tied for most all-time) and 8RBI, taking home the Series MVP...Mike Torrez won both of his starts, tossing complete-game wins in Games 3 and 6.

Los Angeles Dodgers (NL)	**2**
New York Yankees (AL)	**4**

1978 CHAMPIONSHIP SERIES

Reggie Jackson led the Yankees in batting .462 (6-for-13), HR (2) and RBI (6)...Ron Guidry (8.0IP, 1ER) and Goose Gossage (1.0IP, 0ER) pitched the Yankees to a Game 4 win.

Kansas City Royals (AL)	**1**
New York Yankees (AL)	**3**

1978 WORLD SERIES

The Yankees defeated the Dodgers for the second consecutive year, 4-games-to-2...Series cemented Graig Nettles' reputation for defensive excellence...Bucky Dent won the MVP, batting .417 (10-for-24) with 7RBI...second baseman Brian Doyle, filling in for the injured Willie Randolph, batted .438 (7-for-16) with 4R...Catfish Hunter allowed just 2ER in 7.0IP in recording the win in the Game 6 clincher at Los Angeles.

New York Yankees (AL)	**4**
Los Angeles Dodgers (NL)	**2**

1980 CHAMPIONSHIP SERIES

The Yankees' scored just two runs in each game, marking the only time in franchise history the Yankees have been swept in the ALCS or ALDS.

Kansas City Royals (AL)	**3**
New York Yankees (AL)	**0**

1981 DIVISION SERIES

The Yankees almost squandered a 2-games-to-none lead but defeated Milwaukee behind two wins from Dave Righetti (one as a starter, one as a reliever)...Oscar Gamble went 6-for-10 with 2HR and 4RBI.

Milwaukee Brewers (AL)	**2**
New York Yankees (AL)	**3**

1981 CHAMPIONSHIP SERIES

The Yankees outscored Oakland 20-4 in their only ALCS sweep in franchise history...Graig Nettles drove in three runs in each game, batting .500 (6-for-12) with 1HR.

New York Yankees (AL)	**3**
Oakland Athletics (AL)	**0**

1981 WORLD SERIES

After winning the first two games of the Series, the Yankees dropped the next four, falling to 8-3 in their World Series appearances vs. the Dodgers...pitcher George Frazier became the first pitcher to lose three games in a best-of-seven World Series...future GM Bob Watson led the club with 7RBI.

Los Angeles Dodgers (NL)	**4**
New York Yankees (AL)	**2**

1995 DIVISION SERIES

The Yankees snapped a 13-year playoff drought...Don Mattingly batted .417 (10-for-24) with 1HR and 6RBI in his only career postseason series...won first two games at home before dropping three straight in Seattle...won Game 2, 7-5, on Jim Leyritz's 15th-inning "walk-off" homer in the longest postseason game in franchise history...after throwing 135 pitches in a Game 1 win, David Cone threw 147 pitches in a Game 5 no-decision, tying Philadephia's Curt Schilling (1993 WS Game 5 vs. TOR) for the most pitches thrown in a postseason game since Britt Burns' 150 in ALCS Game 4 in 1983 (w/ CWS vs. BAL).

New York Yankees (AL)	**2**
Seattle Mariners (AL)	**3**

1996 DIVISION SERIES

The Yankees bullpen recorded wins in Games 2, 3 and 4, allowing just 1ER in 19.2IP over the series.

Texas Rangers (AL)	**1**
New York Yankees (AL)	**3**

1996 CHAMPIONSHIP SERIES

Down, 4-3, going into the bottom of the eighth inning of Game 1, the Yankees tied the score on Derek Jeter's disputed home run to right...Bernie Williams (9-for-19) batted .474 with 6R, 2HR and 6RBI, earning ALCS MVP honors.

Baltimore Orioles (AL) 1
New York Yankees (AL) 4

1996 WORLD SERIES

The Yankees snapped a 17-year World Championship drought, coming back from a 2-games-to-none deficit...Manager Joe Torre won in his first year at the helm...club came back from a 6-0 deficit in Game 4, with Jim Leyritz knotting the score at 6-6 with a three-run, eighth inning homer...Andy Pettitte outdueled John Smoltz, 1-0, in Game 5...Jimmy Key defeated Greg Maddux in the Game 6 clincher...John Wetteland saved each of the Yankees' victories, earning MVP honors.

Atlanta Braves (NL) 2
New York Yankees (AL) 4

1997 DIVISION SERIES

The Yankees' Game 1 win featured the first-ever back-to-back-to-back postseason homers (Tim Raines, Derek Jeter and Paul O'Neill)...O'Neill finished the series with a .421 batting average (8-for-19), 2HR and 7RBI, including a grand slam in Game 3...Mariano Rivera suffered a blown save in Game 4, on Sandy Alomar, Jr.'s eighth-inning solo home run...would not allow another run in his next 23 postseason appearances, spanning 33.1IP.

New York Yankees (AL) 2
Cleveland Indians (AL) 3

1998 DIVISION SERIES

The Yankees outscored Texas, 9-1, in the series, behind wins from David Wells, Andy Pettitte and David Cone...outfielder Shane Spencer recorded 4RBI in the series, including a three-run homer in Game 3.

Texas Rangers (AL) 0
New York Yankees (AL) 3

1998 CHAMPIONSHIP SERIES

The Yankees won the final three games of the series, taking the series in six...their Game 4 win featured 7.0 scoreless IP from starter Orlando Hernandez...David Wells earned series MVP honors with wins in Games 1 and 5.

Cleveland Indians (AL) 2
New York Yankees (AL) 4

1998 WORLD SERIES

The Yankees swept the Padres to finish with a 125-50 overall record (including the postseason), setting the all-time mark for most wins in a season...trailing 5-2, in Game 1 at Yankee Stadium, Chuck Knoblauch's three-run home run tied the game and Tino Martinez's grand slam put the Yankees ahead in the seventh...also came back from a 3-0 deficit after six innings in Game 3 with Series MVP Scott Brosius hitting a leadoff homer in the seventh and a three-run homer in the eighth...Mariano Rivera notched three saves, marking his highest total in a single World Series.

San Diego Padres (NL) 0
New York Yankees (AL) 4

1999 DIVISION SERIES

The Yankees defeated the Rangers in the ALDS for the third time in three attempts over a four-year stretch...outscored them 14-1 in the series...in Game 1, Orlando Hernandez limited Texas to 2H over 8.0 scoreless IP and Bernie Williams drove in six runs, tying Bobby Richardson (1960 World Series, Game 3) for the most in a single postseason game franchise history.

Texas Rangers (AL) 0
New York Yankees (AL) 3

1999 CHAMPIONSHIP SERIES

The Yankees won their first-ever postseason meeting vs. Boston...Bernie Williams won Game 1 with a 10th-inning walk-off home run...the club had a 12-game postseason winning streak snapped in a Game 3 loss...Derek Jeter led the Yankees with a .350 (7-for-20) batting average.

Boston Red Sox (AL) 1
New York Yankees (AL) 4

1999 WORLD SERIES

The Yankees recorded their second straight World Series sweep...Orlando Hernandez allowed just 1R on 1H in 7.0IP (10K), recording the Game 1 win...David Cone followed with 7.0 scoreless innings on 1H in Game 2...Chad Curtis hit a 10th-inning walk-off homer in Game 3...the Game 4 win extended the Yankees' World Series winning streak to 12 games.

Atlanta Braves (NL) 0
New York Yankees (AL) 4

2000 DIVISION SERIES

Dropped Game 1 of a postseason series for the first time since the 1996 World Series, snapping a winning streak of seven such games...also lost Game 4 at Yankee Stadium, snapping their home postseason winning streak at 10 games...Andy Pettitte and Mariano Rivera shut out the A's, 4-0, in Game 2...the Yankees scored 6R in the first inning of the deciding Game 5 in Oakland to provide the margin of victory in a 7-5 win.

New York Yankees (AL) 3
Oakland Athletics (AL) 2

2000 CHAMPIONSHIP SERIES

The Yankees scored 19 of their 31 total runs in the series in the seventh-inning-or-later, including three come-from-behind victories...MVP David Justice hit 2HR and had a series-best 8RBI...Bernie Williams hit .435 (10-for-23)...Roger Clemens struck out 15 batters while tossing a 1H, 2BB complete-game shutout in Game 4 at Seattle.

Seattle Mariners (AL) 2
New York Yankees (AL) 4

2000 WORLD SERIES

Marked the first "Subway Series" since the Yankees-Dodgers matchup in 1956...the Yankees won Games 1 and 5 in their last at-bat, winning on a 12th-inning single from Jose Vizcaino and a ninth-inning Luis Sojo single, respectively...Derek Jeter was named Series MVP, batting .409 (9-for-22) with 6R and 2 solo HR, including one on the first pitch of Game 4.

New York Mets (NL) 1
New York Yankees (AL) 4

2001 DIVISION SERIES

Postseason began less than a month after the attacks of 9/11...the Yankees won three straight after losing Games 1 and 2...were held to just two hits in Game 3 at Oakland but won, 1-0, behind Mike Mussina (7.0IP), Mariano Rivera (2.0IP) and Jorge Posada's fifth-inning solo home run...the game also featured Derek Jeter's famous "Flip Play," which nailed Jeremy Giambi at the plate in the seventh.

Oakland Athletics (AL) 2
New York Yankees (AL) 3

2001 CHAMPIONSHIP SERIES

The Yankees defeated a Seattle club that won a record 116 games during the regular season...Andy Pettitte was named Series MVP going 2-0 with a 2.51 ERA...Game 4 ended on Alfonso Soriano's two-run walk-off homer in the ninth...Bernie Williams homered in three consecutive games (Games 3-5).

New York Yankees (AL) 4
Seattle Mariners (AL) 1

2001 WORLD SERIES

All games were won by the home team in one of the most thrilling World Series of all time...President George W. Bush threw out the ceremonial first pitch prior Game 3 at Yankee Stadium...the Yankees came back from two-run deficits with two outs in the ninth vs. Arizona's Byung-Hyun Kim in both Games 4 and 5...Tino Martinez tied Game 4 with a two-run home run and Derek Jeter earned the nickname, "Mr. November," with a solo HR to win it in the 10th...Scott Brosius hit a two-run homer to tie Game 5 before Alfonso Soriano won the game with an RBI-single in the 12th...despite taking a 2-1 lead on a Soriano solo homer in the eighth inning of Game 7, the Yankees lost the Series after allowing two runs in the ninth.

New York Yankees (AL) 3
Arizona Diamondbacks (NL) 4

2002 DIVISION SERIES

The Yankees had their Division Series winning streak snapped at four, losing their first DS since 1997 vs. Cleveland...Derek Jeter batted .500 (8-for-16) with 2HR and 3RBI.

Anaheim Angels (AL) 3
New York Yankees (AL) 1

2003 DIVISION SERIES

The Yankees held Minnesota to just six runs in four games, including one run in each of Games 2-4...Derek Jeter batted .429 (6-for-14) with 1HR.

Minnesota Twins (AL) 1
New York Yankees (AL) 3

2003 CHAMPIONSHIP SERIES

Defined by the final game, the Series was won on Aaron Boone's first pitch leadoff home run off Tim Wakefield in the bottom of the 11th inning of Game 7...in the contest, the Yankees got 5ER off Boston starter Pedro Martinez...Mike Mussina made his first-ever relief appearance, getting a strikeout and double play with two on and no outs in the fourth to keep the Yankees in the game...tossed 3.0 scoreless IP on two days' rest...Jason Giambi hit solo homers in the fifth and seventh...club scored three runs in the eighth to tie the game, 5-5.

Boston Red Sox (AL) 3
New York Yankees (AL) 4

2003 WORLD SERIES

The Yankees outscored Florida, 21-17, in defeat...Andy Pettitte allowed just 3R (1ER) in 15.2IP over two starts, including a win in Game 2 and a loss in the decisive Game 6...Bernie Williams batted .400 (10-for-25) with 5R, 2HR and 5RBI.

Florida Marlins (NL) 4
New York Yankees (AL) 2

2004 DIVISION SERIES

The Yankees defeated Minnesota in the ALDS for the second straight season...won Game 2 scoring twice in the 12th inning and Game 4 with one run in the 11th...Alex Rodriguez batted .421 (8-for-19) with 1HR and 3RBI.

Minnesota Twins (AL) 1
New York Yankees (AL) 3

2004 CHAMPIONSHIP SERIES

The Yankees lost their first-ever postseason series after being up 3-games-to-none...scored 19 runs in their Game 3 win, marking the most ever by one team in an ALCS game...Hideki Matsui batted .412 (14-for-34) with 6 doubles, 1 triple, 2HR and 10RBI in the series, establishing the all-time mark for extra-base hits in a postseason series and the ALCS marks for hits, total bases and doubles.

Boston Red Sox (AL) 4
New York Yankees (AL) 3

2005 DIVISION SERIES

Mariano Rivera saved both of the Yankees' victories...Derek Jeter tied for the team lead in both RBI (5) and runs scored (4).

New York Yankees (AL) 2
Los Angeles Angels of Anaheim (AL) 3

2006 DIVISION SERIES

Chien-Ming Wang recorded his first career postseason win in Game 1...Derek Jeter (8-for-16) and Jorge Posada (7-for-14) each batted .500, combining for 15 of the team's 33 overall hits in the series.

Detroit Tigers (AL) 3
New York Yankees (AL) 1

2007 DIVISION SERIES

The Yankees were outhit, .315 to .228, in the series...the Yankees' 2-1, 11-inning loss in Game 2 featured the unusual postseason debut of Joba Chamberlain, who allowed the go-ahead run in the eighth on 2BB, 2WP and 1HP while "midges" descended on the pitcher's mound.

New York Yankees (AL) 1
Cleveland Indians (AL) 3

2009 DIVISION SERIES

The Yankees swept the Minnesota Twins, marking their third ALDS sweep all time (1998 and '99 vs. Texas) and fourth "best-of-five" series sweep (also '81 ALCS vs. Oakland)...came back to win in all three contests, and out-homered the Twins, 6-0...Yankees starters combined to allow just 3ER in 19.0IP (1.42 ERA), with 21K and only three extra-base hits.

Minnesota Twins (AL) 0
New York Yankees (AL) 3

2009 CHAMPIONSHIP SERIES

The Yankees earned their 11th ALCS victory and 40th AL title...hit 8HR and drew 38BB over the six games, while holding the Majors' second-highest scoring team to an average of 3.2R/G...CC Sabathia earned ALCS MVP honors after going 2-0 with a 1.13 ERA (16.0IP, 2ER) in two starts...3B Alex Rodriguez batted a team-high .429 (9-for-21) with 6R, 3HR, 6RBI and 8BB.

Los Angeles Angels (AL) 2
New York Yankees (AL) 4

2009 WORLD SERIES

The Yankees won their unprecedented 27th World Championship and first since 2000...after dropping Game 1 at home, the Yankees won the next three contests to take a commanding lead in the Series...Hideki Matsui (.615 avg., 3HR, 8RBI) was the unanimous World Series MVP, marking the first time a Japanese-born player earned the honor...had 6RBI in the Game 6 clincher, tying Bobby Richardson's World Series single-game record.

Philadelphia Phillies (NL) 2
New York Yankees (AL) 4

Postseason Honors

ALCS MVP

YEAR	PLAYER	AGE	POS	G	AB	R	H	2B	3B	HR	RBI	BA
1981	Graig Nettles	37	3B	3	12	2	6	2	0	1	9	.500
1996	Bernie Williams	28	CF	5	19	6	9	3	0	2	6	.474
2000	David Justice	34	LF	6	26	4	6	2	0	2	8	.231

YEAR	PITCHER	AGE	POS	G	GS	IP	W	L	SV	H	R	ER	SO	BB	ERA
1998	David Wells	35	LHP	2	2	15.2	2	0	0	12	5	5	18	2	2.87
1999	Orlando Hernandez	30	RHP	2	2	15.0	1	0	0	12	4	3	13	6	1.80
2001	Andy Pettitte	29	LHP	2	2	14.1	2	0	0	11	4	4	8	2	2.51
2003	Mariano Rivera	33	RHP	4	0	8.0	1	0	2	5	1	1	6	0	1.13
2009	CC Sabathia	29	LHP	2	2	16.0	2	0	0	9	2	2	12	3	1.13

World Series MVP

YEAR	PLAYER	AGE	POS	G	AB	R	H	2B	3B	HR	RBI	BA
1960	Bobby Richardson	25	2B	7	30	8	11	2	2	1	12	.367
1977	Reggie Jackson	31	RF	6	20	10	9	1	0	5	8	.450
1978	Bucky Dent	26	SS	6	24	3	10	1	0	0	7	.417
1998	Scott Brosius	32	3B	4	17	3	8	0	0	2	6	.471
2000	Derek Jeter	26	SS	5	22	6	9	2	1	2	2	.409
2009	Hideki Matsui	35	DH	6	13	3	8	1	0	3	8	.615

YEAR	PITCHER	AGE	POS	G	GS	IP	W	L	SV	H	R	ER	SO	BB	ERA
1956	Don Larsen	27	RHP	2	2	10.2	1	0	0	1	4	0	7	4	0.00
1958	Bob Turley	28	RHP	4	2	16.1	2	1	1	10	5	5	13	7	2.76
1961	Whitey Ford	32	LHP	2	2	14.0	2	0	0	6	0	0	7	1	0.00
1962	Ralph Terry	26	RHP	3	3	25.0	2	1	0	17	5	5	16	2	1.80
1996	John Wetteland	30	RHP	5	0	4.1	0	0	4	4	1	1	6	1	2.08
1999	Mariano Rivera	29	RHP	3	0	4.2	1	0	2	3	0	0	3	1	0.00

Yankee STADIUM

The 2009 season marked a new era for the winningest team in modern Baseball history as the New York Yankees moved their grand stage next door with the opening of Yankee Stadium. Located directly across the street from the site of the original, the new Stadium's architecture is a celebration of the spirit and tradition of the franchise. While firmly rooted in the past, the Stadium has a vision toward the future, incorporating the best in technology and state-of-the-art guest services.

All of the Stadium's modern amenities exist within the framework of classic elements of the original, most notably the instantly recognizable frieze that again circles the grandstand. Among the countless fan-friendly elements, massive video boards give Yankees fans more information than ever before, and concessions have been placed on concourses that allow for continuous viewing of the game.

Yankee Stadium, as a living museum, has been designed to set the standard—much like the team has done with its 27 World Championships.

The current Yankee Stadium [L] and the original Yankee Stadium in 2008.

THE STADIUM SITE

The Yankees are proud to play in the Bronx, which is home to approximately 1.4 million residents and is one of the five boroughs that make up New York City.

The Stadium sits on former parkland from Macombs Dam Park and Mullaly Park, with the Stadium grounds bounded by Jerome Avenue to the west, River Avenue to the east, and 161st Street to the south. The northern edge of the site is located between 162nd Street and 164th Street. In a nod to tradition, the footprint of the original Stadium has been replicated in the new Stadium.

Yankee Stadium is the fourth permanent home of the New York Yankees, following Hilltop Park (1903-12), the Polo Grounds (1913-22), and the original Yankee Stadium (1923-73, '76-2008). The Yankees also played two full seasons at Shea Stadium (1974-75) in Queens when the original Stadium underwent remodeling.

Gate 4 at Yankee Stadium

HOMAGE TO THE ORIGINAL STADIUM

The current Yankee Stadium evokes the spirit of the original, while restoring many of the lost treasures from before the renovations of 1974-75.

The signature frieze once again outlines the top of the Stadium bowl. As in the past, it is attached to a roof that extends into the Stadium, covering the top rows of the Grandstand.

Monument Park has been relocated to its original position in center field, albeit behind the fence, unlike before the renovation when the monuments were on the playing field. All plaques, monuments and tribute displays for the 16 Yankees who have had their numbers retired are on display for fans, who may visit Monument Park prior to all home games.

On the Main Level, near Gate 6, the Yankees Museum—a museum within a museum—tells the story of baseball and the Yankees franchise through various displays of artifacts and memorabilia. Items include a "Ball Wall" with hundreds of signed baseballs from Yankees greats, Thurman Munson's locker from the original Yankee Stadium and a replica of a locker from the Yankees clubhouse in the current Stadium. On game days, fans are welcome in the museum from the time the gates open until one hour after the game ends. On non-game days, visitors can enjoy the museum as part of Yankee Stadium tours.

Statue of Yogi Berra in the New York Yankees Museum

Babe Ruth Plaza, located on the south side of the Stadium in between Gates 4 and 6, honors the man proverbially credited with building the original House that Ruth Built. Through a series of storyboards displayed on light posts, the Babe's life story is recounted throughout the plaza.

INNOVATIVE ARCHITECTURE AND MODERN AMENITIES

One of the goals in building Yankee Stadium was to bring fans closer to the action in a facility more attuned to modern needs and expectations. The new building is 63 percent larger than the original Stadium with about 500,000 square feet of additional space.

Improved sight lines, wider concourses and the installation of nearly 1,400 high-definition video monitors throughout the Stadium all ensure guests won't miss a minute of on-field action while in their seats or at concession stands. In addition to the live game broadcast, these centrally controlled Internet protocol monitors can also provide up-to-the-moment news, scores, weather, traffic information and safety updates.

The Great Hall stretches from Gate 4 to Gate 6.

The Great Hall is a 31,000-square-foot space located between the Stadium's exterior wall and the interior of the Stadium. Spanning from Gate 4 to Gate 6, it is covered overhead but has massive open-air archways, which help support the Yankees' "green initiative." It is home to large banners bearing the images of past Yankees greats from Babe Ruth and Lou Gehrig to more modern stars such as Don Mattingly and Paul O'Neill. A 24-foot-high-by-36-foot-wide 10mm true high-definition video board and a 5-foot-by-383-foot LED ribbon board immediately greet guests who enter through this portion of the Stadium.

The audio/visual experience at Yankee Stadium is highlighted by a 59-foot-high-by-101-foot-long 16mm true high-definition centerfield video board, which is flanked by two smaller video boards that display day-of-game lineups and out-of-town scores. Additionally, the entire length of the Terrace Level is spanned by a 3-foot-high, 1,279-foot long full-color LED ribbon board. A distributed sound system optimizes speaker placement for audio quality vastly superior to that in the original Stadium. The entire Stadium is built with a future-proof infrastructure designed by Cisco Systems that is easily adaptable to new technologies.

A 7,000-square-foot state-of-the-art banquet and conference center is designed to meet the needs of guests who wish to host business functions in the ballpark.

URBAN PLANNING

The site for Yankee Stadium was in part selected for its proximity to mass transit. Like the original Stadium, it is served at the 161st Street/Yankee Stadium subway stop by the No. 4, B and D trains.

Metro-North offers train service to Yankee Stadium from anywhere in its service territory. For more information, call the MTA at (212) 532-4900 or visit www.mta.info.

As in previous years, Yankee Stadium is accessible by ferry service (800-53-FERRY) and New York City Transit bus lines (718-330-1234).

Babe Ruth Plaza facilitates pedestrian movement outside Yankee Stadium.

Pedestrian access points are located at Yankee Stadium's four gates: Gate 2 on Jerome Avenue and 164th Street; Gate 4 at Jerome Avenue and 161st Street; Gate 6 at River Avenue and 161st Street and Gate 8 at River Avenue, south of 164th Street.

RETAIL & FOOD OPTIONS

There are three distinct retail stores in Yankee Stadium—the 5,825-square-foot Home Plate Store in the Great Hall near Gate 4, which houses the largest selection of Yankees merchandise and memorabilia; the New Era Yankee Stadium Flagship Store on the Main Level, which sells caps and other Yankees merchandise; and the Great Hall Store at Gate 6, which sells various items and is open year-round.

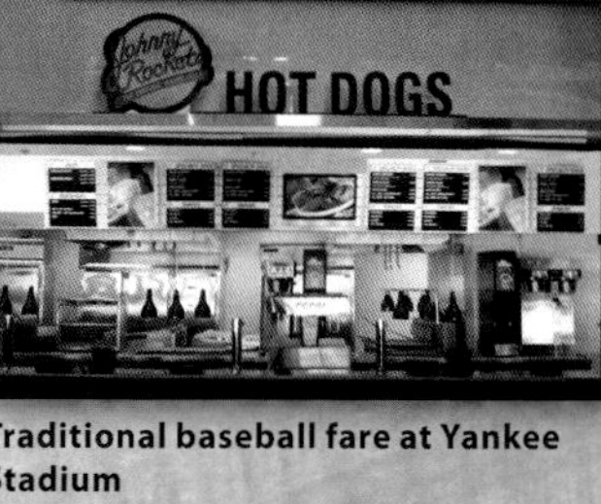

Traditional baseball fare at Yankee Stadium

Yankee Stadium is home to two premier dining establishments. The iconic Hard Rock Cafe is open year-round and houses music memorabilia and Yankees-related pieces in a 7,000 square-foot restaurant at Gate 6, and the newly created NYY Steak, located above the Hard Rock Cafe, offers an upscale dining experience.

More casual fare can be found at a New York-themed food court located on the third-base side of the Field Level concourse.

Membership restaurants include the Audi Yankees Club on the H&R Block Suite Level and the Mohegan Sun Sports Bar above Monument Park in center field.

DISABLED SERVICES

Yankee Stadium strives to provide an accessible environment for all of its guests. Wheelchair accessible and aisle transfer seats are available at various price points and locations, and include the Yankees' Premium Offerings seat locations.

There are two dedicated open-captioning video boards for guests who are deaf or have hearing impairments: one in left field, just below Section 233B, and one in right field, just below Section 206. Captioning is also provided on the right-center field televisions, the high-definition video board in the Great Hall, high-definition video monitors throughout Yankee Stadium and on the video board in the New York Yankees Museum presented by Bank of America.

The Yankees extend their appreciation to those who participated in periodic outreach meetings led by United Spinal Association, which helped build a Stadium that Acting U.S. Attorney for the Southern District of New York Lev Dassin called, "a model of accessibility to people with disabilities."

YANKEE STADIUM FIRSTS

STARTING LINE-UPS (on 4/16/09 vs. Cleveland)

YANKEES:	INDIANS:
Derek Jeter-SS	Grady Sizemore-CF
Johnny Damon-LF	Mark DeRosa-3B
Mark Teixeira-1B	Victor Martinez-1B
Nick Swisher-RF	Jhonny Peralta-SS
Jorge Posada-C	Shin-Soo Choo-DH
Robinson Cano-2B	Ben Francisco-RF
Hideki Matsui-DH	Kelly Shoppach-C
Cody Ransom-3B	Tony Graffanino-2B
Brett Gardner-CF	Trevor Crowe-LF
CC Sabathia-P	Cliff Lee-P

BATTING

First Out: Cleveland's Grady Sizemore, first-inning ground out to first base on 4/16/09

Hit: Johnny Damon first-inning single to center on 4/16/09 vs. Cleveland

Home Run: Jorge Posada, fifth-inning, solo-home run to center off Cliff Lee on 4/16/09 vs. Cleveland

Run Scored: Cleveland's Ben Francisco in the fourth inning on 4/16/09

Run Batted In: Cleveland's Kelly Shoppach in the fourth inning on 4/16/09

Stolen Base: Johnny Damon in the first inning on 4/17/09 vs. Cleveland

PITCHING

Pitch (Result): CC Sabathia to Cleveland's Grady Sizemore in the first inning on 4/16/09 (ball)

Win: Cleveland's Cliff Lee on 4/16/09 (10-2 Cleveland victory)

Save: Mariano Rivera on 4/17/09 vs. Cleveland

Strikeout: CC Sabathia on 4/16/09 vs. Cleveland (Victor Martinez, swinging, first inning)

GAMES

Exhibition Game: April 3, 2009 vs. the Chicago Cubs (7-4 Yankees victory)

Regular Season Game: April 16, 2009 vs. the Cleveland Indians (10-2 Indians victory)

OTHER

Star-Spangled Banner Performer: Kelly Clarkson

God Bless America Singer: Ronan Tynan

Ceremonial First Pitch: 4/16/09 vs. Cleveland, Yogi Berra

YANKEE STADIUM TIMELINE

JUNE 15, 2005 – The Yankees announce plans for a new Yankee Stadium to be constructed on parkland north of 161st Street – adjacent to the original Stadium's longtime site.

AUGUST 16, 2006 – The Yankees break ground for Yankee Stadium at a ceremony featuring George M. Steinbrenner, New York Governor George Pataki, New York City Mayor Michael Bloomberg, Bronx Borough President Adolfo Carrion and Commissioner Bud Selig.

OCTOBER 2006 – The first concrete is poured.

DECEMBER 2007 – The first piece of frieze is put in place.

DECEMBER 2007 – The Stadium is considered 50 percent completed.

JANUARY 14-15, 2008 – Limestone Panels containing "YANKEE STADIUM" gold lettering are installed above Gate 4.

MARCH 29, 2008 – Eagle medallions inspired by those on the 1923 Stadium are lifted into place above Gate 4.

APRIL 2008 – Frieze installation is completed.

MAY 1, 2008 – A "topping off" ceremony is held to commemorate the completion of Yankee Stadium's steel structure.

MAY 2008 – The foul poles are installed, along with the first seats.

JUNE 18, 2008 – The Yankees hold their first press conference at the new Yankee Stadium, announcing a long-term agreement with Seminole Hard Rock Entertainment to open a Hard Rock Cafe near Gate 6. In addition, the Yankees introduce the newly-branded NYY Steak, a prime steakhouse to be located in Yankee Stadium.

SEPTEMBER 19, 2008 – The massive, blue, backlit "YANKEE STADIUM" lettering above Gate 4 is hoisted and installed.

OCTOBER 15, 2008 – The first sections of sod are laid.

OCTOBER 2008 – Lighting in the interior bowl is tested for the first time.

NOVEMBER 8, 2008 – Yankees executives and former players, including Scott Brosius, David Cone, Paul O' Neill and Jeff Nelson, along with 60 local Bronx high school youth groups remove home plate, the pitcher's rubber and pails of dirt from the original Stadium and install them in the new Yankee Stadium. The participating Bronx youth groups—Youth Force 2020, led by Turner Construction Company, and the ACE Mentor Program at Yankee Stadium, guided by Tishman Speyer—took part in Yankees-sponsored after-school programs relating to the construction and engineering of the new Yankee Stadium.

JANUARY 23, 2009 – The front office moves in, bringing World Series trophies from 1977 and 2000 to the new building.

FEBRUARY 2009 – Plaques and monuments are placed in the new Monument Park.

APRIL 3-4, 2009 – The first exhibition games are played vs. the Chicago Cubs.

APRIL 16, 2009 – The home opener is played vs. the Cleveland Indians.

Yankee Stadium by the Numbers

THE STRUCTURE

Location: In the Bronx, bounded by 164th St. (north); 161st St. (south); Jerome Ave. (west); River Ave. (east)
Mailing address: Yankee Stadium, One East 161st Street, Bronx, NY 10451
Switchboard phone number: (718) 293-4300
Architect: Populous (formerly HOK Sport)
Construction: Turner Construction
Developer: Tishman Speyer
Square footage: approximately 1.3 million square feet
Distance around the building: 4,755 linear feet
Size of entire site: 634,335 square feet or 14.56 acres
Number of gates: Four (Gates 2, 4, 6 and 8)
Height at highest point: The top of the frieze is 134 feet, 7 inches above Field Level.
Internet bandwidth: 135 megabits
Light bulbs (number of): 20,000
Main centerfield video board size: 59-feet-by-101-feet
Ribbon board ringing the Terrace Level: 3-feet-by-1,279-feet
Great Hall size: 31,000 square feet
Great Hall LED ribbon board: 5-feet-by-383-feet
Great Hall high-definition video board: 24-feet-by-36-feet
Number of player flags in the Great Hall: 10 double-sided
Seating Capacity: 50,287

FIELD

Surface: Kentucky bluegrass grown at DeLea Sod Farms in Pilesgrove, N.J.
Acreage: 3.14 acres, including the bullpens
Dimensions: LF 318'; LC 399'; CF 408'; RC 385'; RF 314'
Outfield walls height: From left-field foul pole, wall is 8-feet, 6-inches high until the Yankees bullpen, where it gradually descends to 8 feet at the right-field foul pole.
Distance from the plate to the backstop: 52 feet, 4 inches
Yankees bullpen size: averages approximately 82 feet wide by 32 feet deep
Opponents bullpen size: averages approximately 85 feet wide by 30 feet deep
Distance of batter's eye glass to home plate: 432 feet away and 19 feet off the ground
Height of Bleachers Café above the field: 37 feet
Infield foundation: Sand-based
Feet below street level: approximately 8 feet on average
Drainage pipe length: 14,000 linear feet
Irrigation pipe: 17,100 linear feet
Irrigation heads: 116
Distance from first base or third base to the nearest spectator: 43 feet
Concourse (average width): 32 feet
Foul poles height: 90 feet

MATERIALS

Concrete: approximately 45,000 cubic yards
Excavation: approximately 363,000 cubic yards
Rebar: approximately 4,000 tons
Structural steel: approximately 11,800 tons in over 30,000 pieces
Piles driven: 1,675 piles averaging 80 feet long
Stone: Indiana Limestone and Deer Isle Granite
Frieze: approximately 1,400 feet long with 300 tons of structural steel
Doors: 1,300
Gallons of paint: 15,000
Length of electrical wire: 946 miles (*The distance from Yankee Stadium to George M. Steinbrenner Field in Tampa is approximately 1,012 miles*)
Length of Ethernet cable (CAT 6A): 227 miles
Power required to turn on sports lighting: 3,500 KVA
Power required to turn on video board: 2,000 KVA

IN THE BUILDING

Ticket windows: 26 Total, including 19 by Gate 4, four by the Bleachers and three in-Stadium
Concessions (fixed): 25
Concessions (moveable): more than 100
Total concessions points of sale: approximately 444
Retail locations (fixed): approximately 10
Retail locations (moveable): approximately 46
Total retail points of sale: 86
Width of seats: 19 inches to 24 inches
Width of aisles: 4 feet
Legroom in front of seats: 33 inches to 39 inches
Number of elevators: 16 (two each at Gates 2, 4, 6 and 8 and eight in the Great Hall)
Stairways: 30
Pedestrian ramps: 2 (at Gates 2 and 6)
Video monitors: approximately 1,400 flat-panel, high-definition monitors
Cup holders: approximately 45,000
Toilet fixtures: approximately 878
Men's fixtures ratio in non-premium seating: approximately 1 fixture per 78 men (based on 50% male / 50% female attendance)
Women's fixtures ratio in non-premium seating: approximately 1 fixture per 75 women (based on 50% male / 50% female attendance)
Family bathooms: 12
Yankees clubhouse dressing area: 3,344 square feet
Visitors clubhouse dressing area: 1,496 square feet

Yankee Stadium Map

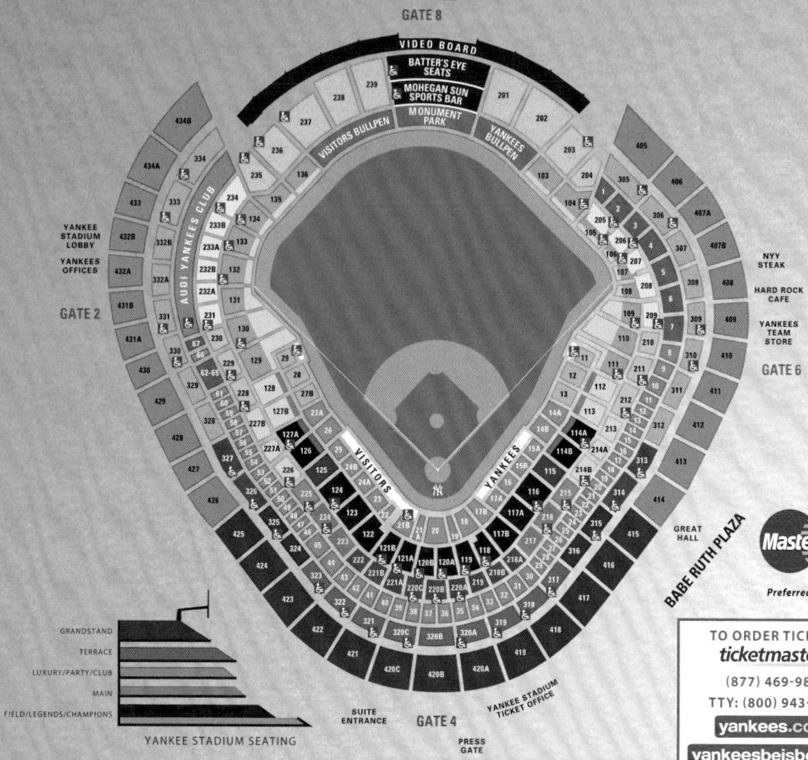

GATE 8

VIDEO BOARD

BATTER'S EYE SEATS

MOHEGAN SUN SPORTS BAR

MONUMENT PARK

VISITORS BULLPEN

YANKEES BULLPEN

AUDI YANKEES CLUB

YANKEE STADIUM LOBBY

YANKEES OFFICES

GATE 2

NYY STEAK

HARD ROCK CAFE

YANKEES TEAM STORE

GATE 6

GREAT HALL

BABE RUTH PLAZA

VISITORS

YANKEES

SUITE ENTRANCE

GATE 4

PRESS GATE

YANKEE STADIUM TICKET OFFICE

GRANDSTAND

TERRACE

LUXURY/PARTY/CLUB

MAIN

FIELD/LEGENDS/CHAMPIONS

YANKEE STADIUM SEATING

MasterCard

Preferred by

TO ORDER TICKETS:

ticketmaster®

(877) 469-9849

TTY: (800) 943-4327

yankees.com

yankeesbeisbol.com

ALCOHOL-FREE SEATING

Sections 407A and 433

ATMs presented by Bank of America

Great Hall: Adjacent to the Guest Services Booth near Gate 6

Field Level: Section 127B-128

Main Level: Section 214A and 222

Terrace/Grandstand Level: Sections 313, 320C and 330-331

Bleachers: Section 239

AUDI YANKEES CLUB

H&R Block Suite Level

Audi

BUDWEISER HALL OF FAME LOUNGE

H&R Block Suite Level

Budweiser

ELEVATORS

Yankee Stadium's 16 public elevators are located in the Great Hall and throughout Yankee Stadium.

ESCALATORS

Escalators are located near Gates 4 and 6.

FAMILY RESTROOMS

Field Level: Sections 106, 124 and 130

Delta SKY360° Suite: Section 221B

Main Level: Sections 219, 227A and 234

Terrace/Grandstand Level: Sections 311, 316, 327 and 333

Bleachers: Section 201

FIRST AID

Field Level: Section 128

Main Level: Section 221

Terrace/Grandstand Level: Section 320C

GREAT HALL

The Great Hall is located along Babe Ruth Plaza between the exterior wall and the interior of Yankee Stadium between Gates 4 and 6.

GUEST SERVICES BOOTHS

Great Hall: Near Gate 6

Field Level: Section 128

Terrace/Grandstand Level: Section 320C

HARD ROCK CAFE YANKEE STADIUM

(open year-round)

Great Hall at Gate 6

Hard Rock Cafe Yankee Stadium

H&R BLOCK SUITE LOUNGE

H&R Block Suite Level

Tommy Bahama's BAR

Great Hall, near Gate 4

MERCHANDISE STORES

Yankees Team Store-Home Plate: Great Hall, near Gate 4

Yankees Team Store-Great Hall: Great Hall at Gate 6

5TH & OCEAN

New York Yankees Women's Team Store: Section 114A

New Era: Yankee Stadium: Main Level, behind home plate

MOHEGAN SUN SPORTS BAR

Mohegan Sun a world at play

Center field above Monument Park

NYY STEAK

(Open year-round)

Above Hard Rock Cafe at Gate 6

RAMPS

Adjacent to Gates 2 and 6

YANKEES-STEINER COLLECTIBLES STORE

Field Level: Section 114B

NOTICE: All persons specifically consent to and are subject to metal detector and physical pat-down inspections prior to entry. Any person or property that could affect the safety of Yankee Stadium occupants/property shall be denied entry.

WARNING: During all batting practices, fielding practices, warm-ups and the course of the game experience, hard hit baseballs and bats and fragments thereof may be thrown or hit into the stands, concourses and concessions areas. For everyone's safety, please stay alert and be aware of your surroundings. Any guest who is concerned with his or her seat location should contact any guest services representative for an alternate seat location.

SEATING CATEGORY	ADVANCE PRICE	GAME-DAY PRICE
FIELD*	$300	$300
FIELD	$275	$300
FIELD	$250	$275
FIELD**	$235	$250
FIELD	$200	$225
FIELD	$125	$150
FIELD	$90	$95
MAIN	$150	$175
MAIN	$125	$150
MAIN	$90	$95
MAIN	$75	$80
MAIN	$55	$60
TERRACE†	$80	$85
TERRACE††	$70	$75
TERRACE††	$48	$50
GRANDSTAND	$29	$30
GRANDSTAND	$22	$23
BLEACHERS§	$14/$5§§	$14/$5§§
BATTER'S EYE SEATS	$125	$135
MOHEGAN SUN SPORTS BAR	$90	$95
AUDI YANKEES CLUB	$140#	$150#

YANKEES PREMIUM	
LEGENDS SUITE	For more information on Full- and Partial-Season Yankees Premium, please visit yankees.com, call (718) 508-3955 or e-mail premium@yankees.com.
CHAMPIONS SUITE	
DELTA SKY360° SUITE	
LUXURY SUITES	
PARTY CITY PARTY SUITES/ CLUB SUITE (62-65)	
JIM BEAM SUITE##	

Please note that the backstop netting is located approximately between Sections 117B and 122.

*Wheelchair accessible seating in Sections 116 and 124 is $275 for advance price and $300 for game-day price.

**Wheelchair accessible seating in Sections 114A and 127A is $125 for advance price and $150 for game-day price.

†Wheelchair accessible seating in Sections 315, 317-319, 321-323 and 325 is $29 for advance price and $30 for game-day price.

††Wheelchair accessible seating in Sections 305, 306, 309, 310, 313, 314, 326, 327, 330, 331, 333 and 334 is $22 for advance price and $23 for game-day price.

§Wheelchair accessible seating in the Bleachers is $5 for advance and game-day price.

§§Designated seats in Sections 201 and 239 are considered obstructed and sold for $5.

Includes food and non-alcoholic beverages.

##Wheelchair accessible seating in the Jim Beam Suite is located in Sections 320A and 320C

The game-day ticket price is effective as of 12:01 a.m. on the day the game initially is scheduled to be played.

Be advised that the Yankees reserve the right to take appropriate action against individuals who fraudulently obtain wheelchair accessible and companion seats, including, without limitation, ejection and legal action.

Getting to Yankee Stadium

Yankee Stadium, One East 161st Street, Bronx, NY 10451

Yankee Stadium is accessible from the Major Deegan Expy. (Interstate 87) at the following exits:

- Northbound I-87: Exit 3 (Grand Concourse and E. 138th St.), Exit 4 (E. 149th St.) and Exit 5 (E. 161st St.)
- Southbound I-87: Exit 6 (E. 153rd St. and River Ave.) and Exit 5 (E. 161st St.)

BY CAR

For directions from points other than those listed below, visit www.yankees.com.

MANHATTAN

From East Side: FDR Drive north to Exit 18 (Willis Ave. Bridge). Cross bridge. Follow signs for Major Deegan (I-87) north.

From West Side: Henry Hudson Pkwy. (Route 9A) north to Exit 14. Follow Cross Bronx Expy. (I-95 north) to Major Deegan (I-87) south.

BROOKLYN/QUEENS

Brooklyn-Queens Expy.: Take BQE (I-278) east to RFK Bridge (formerly Triboro Bridge). Cross bridge. Follow signs for Bronx and Major Deegan (I-87) north.

LONG ISLAND

From Throgs Neck or Whitestone Bridge:

- **Option 1:** Follow signs for I-95 south, which becomes westbound Cross Bronx Expy. Proceed to Major Deegan (I-87) south.
- **Option 2:** Follow signs for westbound Bruckner Expy. (I-278). From Bruckner, take exit for Major Deegan (I-87) north.

From RFK Bridge (formerly Triboro Bridge): Once over bridge, follow signs for Bronx and Major Deegan (I-87) north.

WESTCHESTER

From Bronx River Pkwy. or Hutchinson River Pkwy.: Take Cross County Pkwy. west to I-87 south, which becomes Major Deegan.

NEW JERSEY/GEORGE WASHINGTON BRIDGE

- **Option 1:** Take eastbound Cross Bronx Expy. (I-95 north). Exit for Major Deegan (I-87) south.
- **Option 2:** Take eastbound Cross Bronx Expy. (I-95 north). Use Exit 2A (Jerome Avenue). Make right off exit and continue on Jerome Avenue to Yankee Stadium.
- **Option 3:** Take Exit 2 (Harlem River Drive). Once on Harlem River Drive south, take Exit 23 toward W. 155th St. At first light, turn left onto W. 155th St. Cross Macombs Dam Bridge. Yankee Stadium is ahead.

CONNECTICUT

From Merritt Pkwy.: Merritt Pkwy. becomes Hutchinson River Pkwy. Proceed to westbound Cross County Pkwy., then to I-87 south, which becomes Major Deegan.

The Yankees urge guests to use public transportation.

BY SUBWAY

The Yankee Stadium subway stop is on E. 161st St. and River Ave. The No. 4 train and B and D trains make stops there. For more information, call (718) 330-1234 or visit www.mta.info.

BY TRAIN

Metro-North offers train service to Yankee Stadium from anywhere in its service territory. For more information, call the MTA at (212) 532-4900 or visit www.mta.info.

BY BUS

The Bx6 and Bx13 buses stop at 161st St. and River Ave. The Bx1 bus stops at 161st St. and Grand Concourse — a short walk from Yankee Stadium. For information, call (718) 330-1234 or visit www.mta.info.

BY FERRY

For information, call (800) 53-FERRY (533-3779) or visit www.nywaterway.com.

History of Original Yankee Stadium

One year after changing the course of Baseball history with the purchase of Babe Ruth from the Boston Red Sox, the Yankees made another acquisition that would forever alter the way the game was watched.

On February 5, 1921, the Yankees issued a press release announcing the purchase of 10 acres of property in the west Bronx. The land, purchased from the estate of William Waldorf Astor for $675,000, sat directly across the Harlem River from the Manhattan-situated Polo Grounds, which the Yankees had been unhappily sharing with their landlord, the New York Giants of the National League, since 1913.

The relationship between the clubs crumbled after the 1920 season when the Yankees' attendance—boosted by their new slugging sensation—doubled to almost 1.3 million, approximately 25 percent more than that of the Giants. In 1921, the Giants asked the Yankees to vacate the Polo Grounds as soon as possible. With their departure from the Polo Grounds now inevitable, Yankees co-owners Jacob Ruppert and Tillinghast l'Hommedieu Huston set out to build a spectacular ballpark of their own, Baseball's first triple-decked structure. With an advertised capacity of 70,000, it would also be the first to be labeled a "stadium."

Original plans by the architect—the Osborn Engineering Company of Cleveland, Ohio—had the Stadium triple-decked and roofed all the way around. An early press release, in fact, described the Yankees' new home as a field enclosed with towering embattlements rendering the events inside "impenetrable to all human eyes, save those of aviators." But the initial grand design was quickly scaled back with the triple-decked grandstand not reaching either foul pole. Contrary to the owners' wishes, the action would be visible from the elevated trains that passed by the outfield, as well as from the buildings that would spring up across River Avenue. Fortunately, a purely decorative element survived the project's early downsizing and would become the park's most recognizable feature. A 15-foot-high copper frieze would adorn the front of the roof, which covered much of the Stadium's third deck. It would give Yankee Stadium a stately dignity that no park has possessed—either before or since.

The new stadium would favor left-handed power with the right-field foul pole only 295 feet from home plate (though the right-field fence would shoot out to 429 feet in right-center). The left-field pole measured only 281 feet from the plate, but right-handed hitters would be neutralized by a 395-foot left field and a whopping 460 feet to left-center. The new stadium would also be patron-friendly, boasting an unheard of "eight toilet rooms for men and as many for women scattered throughout the stands and bleachers." (After the Stadium was remodeled 50 years later, it included more than 50 restrooms.) The club's executive offices would be moved from Midtown Manhattan and relocated between the main and mezzanine decks with an electric elevator connecting them with the main entrance.

The construction contract was awarded to New York's White Construction Company on May 5, 1922, with the edict that the job be completed "at a definite price" of $2.5 million by Opening Day 1923. Incredibly, it was. In only 284 working days, Yankee Stadium was ready for its inaugural game on April 18, 1923 vs. the Boston Red Sox.

An announced crowd of 74,200 fans packed Yankee Stadium while thousands more milled around outside after the fire department finally ordered the gates closed. Before the game began, John Philip Sousa and the Seventh Regiment Band led both clubs to the flagpole in deep center field, where the American flag and the Yankees' 1922 pennant were raised. Appropriately, Ruth christened his new home with a three-run homer to cap a four-run third inning as the Yankees coasted to a 4-1 win.

Yankee Stadium in the 1920s

Because it was widely recognized that Ruth's tremendous drawing power made the new stadium possible, *New York Evening Telegram* sportswriter Fred Lieb dubbed it "The House That Ruth Built." Later that season, the Stadium hosted the first of 37 World Series, as the Yankees won their first World Championship, defeating their former landlord, the Giants. Of course, as the original Stadium became the stage for a staggering 26 world titles, it would also become known as "The Home of Champions."

In its early years, when wooden bleachers surrounded the outfield, a grass slope rose toward the outfield walls from foul pole to foul pole. Outfielders, especially Ruth in right, routinely backed up the small hill to pull down fly balls. Advertising signs lined the tops of the bleachers except in right-center, where a lone manually operated wooden scoreboard was large enough to record 12 innings for games played by every club in the two major leagues. Over the years, the board would be replaced by more modern models. The Yankees, in fact, would unveil Baseball's first electronic message board in 1959.

By 1928, the Stadium was ready for its first major face-lift. The triple-decked grandstand in left field was extended beyond the foul pole to its current termination point, and several rows of box seats were removed in order to extend the left-field foul pole distance to 301 feet. The right-field grandstand was extended in 1937, allowing for "upper-deck" home runs in both directions. With the grandstand expansion, the remaining wooden bleachers were replaced with a concrete structure, and the distance to center field dropped from 490 feet to a still-distant 461 feet.

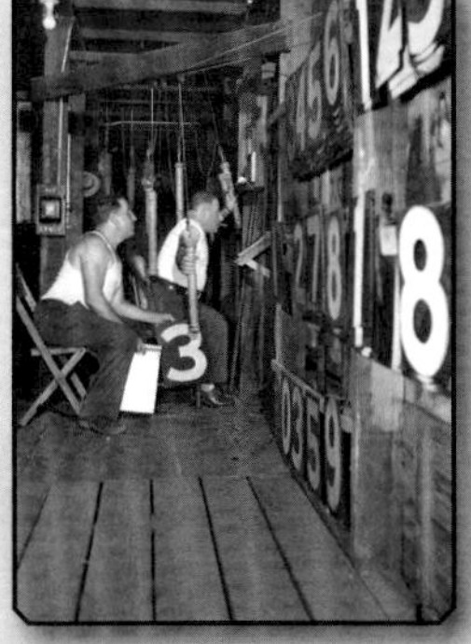
The original manual scoreboard

In 1932, the Yankees began their tradition of commemorating their heroes with monuments or plaques when they dedicated a monument to Manager Miller Huggins, who had died suddenly during the 1929 season. Five more monuments have since been added (one each for Lou Gehrig, Ruth, Mickey Mantle and Joe DiMaggio and one to honor the victims and heroes of the terrorists attacks of September 11, 2001) along with numerous plaques. For years, existing monuments were in the field of play in deep center field, and outfielders occasionally had to work around them to retrieve baseballs hit to that part of the park.

Except for the addition of lights in 1946, the look of Yankee Stadium remained relatively the same until the winter of 1966-67. Then, under the direction of the Yankees' new owner, CBS, the 44-year-old facility received a $1.5 million modernization, most of which was spent on 90 tons of paint. The brown concrete exterior was painted white as was the timeworn greenish copper frieze. Also, all of the grandstand seats went from green to blue, a color scheme that would be retained when the Stadium was completely remodeled after the 1973 season.

On August 8, 1972, after years of debate about the future of the aging ballpark, the Yankees signed a 30-year lease with the City of New York, which called for Yankee Stadium to be completely modernized in time for the 1976 season. After completing the Stadium's 50th-anniversary season in 1973, the Yankees moved to Shea Stadium for two seasons while the majority of the Stadium was torn down and rebuilt.

The most striking change of the modernization was the removal of the numerous obstructive steel columns that supported the second and third decks, as well as the roof. By "cantilevering" the upper decks and lowering the playing field while increasing the slope of the lower stands, sight lines for fans were dramatically improved. Capacity was reduced from 65,010 in 1973 to 54,028 upon reopening as wider plastic seats replaced wooden seats.

Of course, with the removal of the original roof, the Stadium almost lost its most-recognizable feature: the copper frieze. However, an innovative design concept included an exact replica of the frieze atop the new 560-foot-long scoreboard wall, which stretched across the rear of the bleachers. The board also included Baseball's first "telescreen," which could provide instant replays of the action by employing a then-incredible "nine shades of gray."

Yankee Stadium's exterior changed dramatically, too, as three escalator towers were added, one at

The original Yankee Stadium, shown during construction, was completed in only 284 working days.

each of the Stadium's three entrances. With seven additional rows of seats added to the upper deck, the already grand Stadium received an even more majestic look. A 138-foot Louisville Slugger-shaped smokestack, commonly called "The Bat," was added outside the Stadium near the home-plate entrance.

The renovated Stadium also saw the mammoth fence distances in left and center field greatly reduced as "Death Valley" in left-center was brought in from 457 feet to 430 feet, and straightaway center field was slimmed from 463 feet to 417 feet. Subsequent alterations prior to the 1985 and 1988 seasons have brought fences in to the configuration that remains today.

The remodeled Yankee Stadium opened on April 15, 1976—with the Yankees topping Minnesota, 11-4. Like its predecessor, it hosted the World Series in its inaugural season. In fact, the remodeled Stadium hosted the Fall Classic in its first three seasons, as the Yankees followed their 1976 Series loss to Cincinnati by winning back-to-back World Series titles in 1977 and 1978 over the Dodgers.

As one of the world's most prestigious addresses, Yankee Stadium has also been the home for scores of other sports, entertainment and cultural events. While the Yankees were on the road or in the offseason, the Stadium opened its gates to college and pro football, soccer, political assemblies, religious conventions, concerts and even the circus.

Boxing immediately found a home at Yankee Stadium with Benny Leonard winning a 15-round decision over Lou Tendler for the lightweight title just three months after the gates opened on July 23, 1923. When Muhammad Ali stopped Ken Norton on September 28, 1976, it marked the 30th championship fight at the Stadium. All previous title bouts had taken place between 1923 and 1959–perhaps none more memorable than the June 22, 1938, heavyweight championship match between Joe Louis and Germany's Max Schmeling. After suffering a knockout loss in the initial non-title encounter at the Stadium two years earlier, Louis—now the heavyweight champ—avenged his defeat with a stunning first-round KO in the rematch.

Football also became an immediate fixture at Yankee Stadium with the 1923 Army-Navy game inaugurating a rich history of collegiate and later professional football matchups. On November 12, 1928, with Notre Dame and Army locked in a scoreless game at halftime, the legendary Knute Rockne made his famous "Win One for the Gipper" pep talk, and the Fighting Irish went on to defeat the Cadets, 12-6.

The New York football Giants also called Yankee Stadium home from 1956 through 1973 and on December 28, 1958, played in what is widely recognized as "The Greatest Game Ever Played." With the NFL championship at stake, a crowd of 64,185 watched the Baltimore Colts tie the game, 17-17, on a Steve Myrha field goal with seven seconds left. Eight minutes into professional football's first-ever "sudden-death" overtime period, the Colts' Alan Ameche crashed into the end zone from the 1-yard line, ending a contest that would help establish pro football as a major sport.

The Stadium was also an important stop for religious conventions, especially those of the Jehovah's Witnesses. In 1950, the group began holding conventions at the Stadium, including one that drew 123,707 people on August 8, 1958—the largest single-day event in Stadium history. On October 4, 1965—with the Yankees out of the World Series for only the third time in 17 years—the Stadium held the first-ever Papal Mass in the United States as Pope Paul VI celebrated Mass before a crowd in excess of 80,000. Pope John Paul II also celebrated Mass at Yankee Stadium on October 2, 1979, during his tour of the United States.

On August 16, 2006, a groundbreaking ceremony was held for a new Yankee Stadium to be ready for the 2009 season. The location chosen for the new building was the north side of 161st Street and River Avenue in the Bronx, directly across the street from the site of the original Stadium.

As part of its final season in 2008, Yankee Stadium hosted a third papal visit on April 20 from Pope Benedict XVI, NYU's commencement ceremony on May 14 (believed to be the first ever college commencement in Stadium history) and a 15-inning 4-3 AL victory in the 2008 All-Star Game on July 15 (the fourth at Yankee Stadium, joining Midsummer Classics in 1939, 1960-Game 2, and 1977).

The building took its final bow on September 21, when the Yankees played the last game in Stadium history. Gates opened at 1:00 p.m., allowing approximately 13,000 fans the opportunity to visit Monument Park and walk around the warning track. With a national Sunday night audience watching on television, all-time Yankees greats, along with the evening's starting lineup, took their positions in the field before Julia Ruth Stevens, daughter of Babe Ruth, tossed out the ceremonial first pitch. Fittingly, the game ended in a Yankees victory, this one over the Baltimore Orioles, 7-3. After the final out, the club assembled by the pitcher's mound at the side of captain Derek Jeter. Over the PA, he thanked the crowd for their years of support, while reminding everyone of the new memories soon to be made.

In the bottom of the seventh inning of the Yankees' final home game on September 21, 2008, a taped valedictory was given on the Yankee Stadium video board by longtime public address announcer Bob Sheppard, who was unable to say goodbye in person as he continued to recover at home from an illness that had kept him away from the Stadium for the entire season. His appearance on screen brought a reverential hush to the crowd as everyone recognized they were about to hear the most perfect of all couplings perhaps for the last time—Bob Sheppard's voice reverberating in the original Yankee Stadium. He said the following:

***"Farewell, old Yankee Stadium, farewell.
What a wonderful story you can tell.
DiMaggio, Mantle, Gehrig and Ruth,
A baseball cathedral in truth."***

Yankees Attendance Records

Yankees All-Time Attendance Records (Regular Season)

Largest Single-Season Home Attendance (2008) ... 4,298,543
Largest Single-Season Road Attendance (2004) ... 3,308,666
Largest Single-Season Combined Home-Road Attendance (2006) ... 7,325,051
Largest Crowd in Baseball History (Exhibition Game for Roy Campanella - NYY vs. LAD, at the L.A. Coliseum, 5/7/1959) ... 93,103
Most Consecutive Seasons with 4 Million Attendance in Baseball History: ... 4 (2005-2008)

2009 Regular Season Attendance

HOME
Largest Night Game Attendance (vs. Boston, 8/6/09) ... 49,005
Largest Day Game Attendance (vs. Boston, 9/26/09) ... 48,809

ROAD
Largest Night Game Attendance (at Atlanta, 6/25/09) ... 47,508
Largest Day Game Attendance (at Texas, 5/25/09) ... 48,914

OVERALL
Yankees Home Attendance (81 games, 81 dates) ... 3,719,358
Yankees Road Attendance (81 games, 81 dates) ... 2,793,058
Yankees Total Attendance (162 games, 162 dates) ... 6,512,416

POSTSEASON
Largest Single-Game Home Attendance (World Series Game 6 vs. Philadelphia, 11/4/09) ... 50,315

Remodeled Original Yankee Stadium 1976-2008 (Regular Season)

Largest Single-Game Home Attendance, Day (vs. Oakland, 4/10/1998, Opening Day) ... 56,717
Largest Single-Game Home Attendance, Night (vs. N.Y. Mets, 6/17/1997) ... 56,253
Largest Day Doubleheader Home Attendance (vs. Detroit, 10/4/1980) ... 55,410
Largest Twi-Night Doubleheader Attendance (vs. Baltimore, 9/10/1983) ... 55,605
Largest Weekday/Day/Non-Opening Day Crowd (vs. N.Y. Mets, Wed., 6/18/1997) ... 56,278
Largest Opening Day Home Attendance (vs. Oakland, 4/10/1998) ... 56,717
Largest Old-Timers' Day Attendance (vs. Chicago-AL, 7/25/1998) ... 55,642
Largest Home Series Attendance, three-game series (vs. N.Y. Mets, 6/4-6/1999) ... 168,404
Largest Home Series Attendance, all series (vs. Boston, 9/16-17/2006, 4 games, 2 day-night DH) ... 220,481
Largest Single-Season Home Attendance (2008) ... 4,298,543

Top 10 Crowds at Remodeled Yankee Stadium (1976-2008)

	Opponent	Date / Game	Attendance
1.	vs. Texas	10/7/99, ALDS Game 2	57,485
2.	vs. Cleveland	9/30/97, ALDS Game 1	57,398
3.	vs. Texas	9/29/98, ALDS Game 1	57,362
4.	vs. Texas	9/30/98, ALDS Game 2	57,360
	vs. Cleveland	10/2/97, ALDS Game 2	57,360
6.	vs. Texas	10/1/96, ALDS Game 1	57,205
7.	vs. Boston	10/13/99, ALCS Game 1	57,181
8.	vs. Boston	10/14/99, ALCS Game 2	57,180
9.	vs. Seattle	10/3/95, ALDS Game 1	57,178
10.	vs. Texas	10/2/96, ALDS Game 2	57,156

Note: They are all postseason games.

Top 10 Regular Season Crowds at Remodeled Yankee Stadium (1976-2008)

	Opponent	Date	Attendance
1.	vs. Oakland	4/10/98, Opening Day	56,717
2.	vs. Oakland	4/11/97, Opening Day	56,710
3.	vs. Texas	4/4/94, Opening Day	56,706
4.	vs. Kansas City	4/12/93, Opening Day	56,704
5.	vs. Detroit	4/9/99, Opening Day	56,583
6.	vs. Boston	4/7/92, Opening Day	56,572
7.	vs. Kansas City	4/9/96, Opening Day	56,329
8.	vs. N.Y. Mets	6/6/99	56,294
9.	vs. N.Y. Mets	6/18/97	56,278
10.	vs. N.Y. Mets	6/17/97	56,253

Pre-Remodeled Original Yankee Stadium, 1923-1973 (Regular Season)

Please note: Official Attendance Records are not available prior to 1938.
Largest Single-Game Home Attendance, Day (vs. Boston, 9/26/1948) ... 69,755*
Largest Single-Game Home Attendance, Night (vs. Boston, 5/26/1947) ... 74,747
Largest Doubleheader Home Attendance (vs. Boston, 5/30/1938) ... 81,841
Largest Opening Day Home Attendance (vs. Washington, 4/19/1946) ... 54,826*
Largest Old-Timers' Day Attendance (vs. Boston, 8/9/1958) ... 67,916
Largest Home Series Attendance, all series (vs. Cleveland 6/11-13, 4 games, DH on 6/12) ... 186,151
Largest Single-Season Total Attendance ... 2,373,901 (1948)
*According to published reports, the Stadium's first Opening Day (vs. Boston, 4/18/23) had an estimated attendance of 74,200.

Home Ballparks

TOTAL ATTENDANCE
Hilltop Park (1903-12, 10 seasons, 168th St. & Broadway, Manhattan) ... 3,451,542
Polo Grounds (1913-22, 10 seasons, 157th St. & 8th Avenue, Manhattan) ... 6,220,031
Pre-Remodeled Original Yankee Stadium (1923-73, 51 seasons, 161st St. & River Avenue, Bronx) ... 64,333,705
Shea Stadium (1974-75, 2 seasons, 126th St. & Roosevelt Avenue, Queens) ... 2,561,123
Remodeled Original Yankee Stadium (1976-2008, 33 seasons, 161st St. & River Avenue, Bronx) ... 87,625,300*
Yankee Stadium (2009, 1 season, One East 161st St., Bronx, NY) ... 3,719,358
TOTAL ... 167,911,059
*Game vs. Anaheim on 4/15/1998 was played at Shea Stadium when Yankee Stadium was closed by the City of New York after an expansion joint fell on 4/13/1998.

Original Yankee Stadium Information

Original Yankee Stadium Dimensions

Field	Distances/Dates	Distances/Dates	Distances/Dates	Distances/Dates	Distances/Dates
Left Field Foul Pole:	281 Ft. (1923-27)	301 Ft. (1928-73)	312 Ft. (1976-84)	312 Ft. (1985-87)	318 Ft. (1988-2008)
Left Field:	395 Ft. (1923-27)	402 Ft. (1928-73)	387 Ft. (1976-84)	379 Ft. (1985-87)	NA
Left-center Field:	460 Ft. (1923-36)	457 Ft. (1937-73)	430 Ft. (1976-84)	411 Ft. (1985-87)	399 Ft. (1988-2008)
Center Field:*	461 Ft. (1937-66)	463 Ft. (1967-73)	417 Ft. (1976-84)	410 Ft. (1985-87)	408 Ft. (1988-2008)
Right-center Field:	429 Ft. (1923-36)	407 Ft. (1937-73)	385 Ft. (1976-84)	385 Ft. (1985-87)	385 Ft. (1988-2008)
Right Field:	370 Ft. (1923-36)	344 Ft. (1937-73)	353 Ft. (1976-84)	353 Ft. (1985-87)	NA
Right-field Foul Pole:	295 Ft. (1923-38)	296 Ft. (1939-73)	310 Ft. (1976-84)	310 Ft. (1985-87)	314 Ft. (1988-2008)

* 490 Ft. (1923-36)

Original Yankee Stadium Firsts and Lasts

FIRSTS

Game: April 18, 1923 (4-1 win over Boston Red Sox)
Ceremonial First Pitch: N.Y. Governor Al Smith
Pitch: Bob Shawkey (ball)
Victory: April 18, 1923 (4-1 over Boston)
Loss: April 22, 1923 (4-3 to Washington)
Batter: Boston's Chick Fewster (grounded to short)
Yankee Batter: Whitey Witt
Hit: Boston's George Burns (April 18, 2nd-inning single)
Yankee Hit: Aaron Ward (April 18, 3rd-inning single)
Run: Bob Shawkey (April 18, on Joe Dugan's single in 3rd)
Home Run: Babe Ruth (April 18, three-run homer in 3rd)
Error: Babe Ruth (April 18, dropped fly ball in 5th)

PRE-REMODELING LASTS

Game: September 30, 1973 (8-5 loss to Detroit Tigers)
Attendance: 32,969
Batter: Mike Hegan (flied out to CF)
Home Run: Duke Sims (September 30 off Detroit's Fred Holdsworth)
Pitch: Detroit's John Hiller
Victory: September 29, 1973 (3-0 over Detroit Tigers)
NYY Winning Pitcher: Doc Medich (September 29, 3-0 CG over Detroit)

REMODELED YANKEE STADIUM LASTS

Game September 21, 2008 (7-3 win over Baltimore)
Ceremonial First Pitch Julia Ruth Stevens (daughter of Babe Ruth)
Pitch Mariano Rivera to Baltimore's Brian Roberts
Batter Baltimore's Brian Roberts (9th-inning ground out to first base)
Yankees Batter Derek Jeter (8th-inning ground out to third base)
Hit Jason Giambi (7th-inning single to left on Sept. 21, 2008)
Run Brett Gardner (7th inning on Sept. 21, 2008)
Home Run Jose Molina (4th-inning, two-run homer to left off Chris Waters on Sept. 21, 2008)
Error Baltimore's Brandon Fahey (misplayed grounder in 7th on Sept. 21, 2008)
Winning Pitcher Andy Pettitte on Sept. 21, 2008 vs. Baltimore (7-3 Yankees victory)
Strikeout Joba Chamberlain (Baltimore's Aubrey Huff on Sept. 21, 2008 in the 7th inning)
Star-Spangled Banner Performer: United States Army Field Band
God Bless America Singer: Ronan Tynan
Final Two Songs Played over PA: "Good Night Sweetheart" played by organist Ed Alstrom in memory of Eddie Layton, followed by "New York, New York" sung by Frank Sinatra

The Yankees posted an all-time regular season record of 4,133-2,430-17 at the original Yankee Stadium.

ORIGINAL YANKEE STADIUM LEADERS (1923-2008)

Most Career Games
1 Mickey Mantle 1,213
2 Lou Gehrig 1,080
3 Yogi Berra 1,068
4 Bernie Williams 1,039
5 Derek Jeter 1,004

Most Career Hits
1 Derek Jeter 1,274
2 Lou Gehrig 1,269
3 Mickey Mantle 1,211
4 Bernie Williams 1,123
5 Joe DiMaggio 1,060

Most Career Home Runs
1 Mickey Mantle 266
2 Babe Ruth 259
3 Lou Gehrig 251
4 Yogi Berra 210
5 Joe DiMaggio 148

Most Career RBI
1 Lou Gehrig 949
2 Babe Ruth 777
3 Mickey Mantle 744
4 Yogi Berra 727
5 Joe DiMaggio 720

Most Career Wins
1 Red Ruffing 126
2 Whitey Ford 120
3 Lefty Gomez 112
4 Ron Guidry 99
5 Andy Pettitte 94

Best Career ERA (500+ innings)
1 Fritz Peterson 2.52
2 Whitey Ford 2.57
3 Mariano Rivera 2.61
4 Spud Chandler 2.62
5 Stan Bahnsen 2.65

Most Career Strikeouts
1 Ron Guidry 969
2 Andy Pettitte 816
3 Whitey Ford 748
4 Roger Clemens 710
5 Mike Mussina 701

Most Career Saves (since 1969)
1 Mariano Rivera 230
2 Dave Righetti 111
3 Goose Gossage 70
4 Sparky Lyle 63
5 Steve Farr 45

Most Career Managerial Wins
1 Joe McCarthy 809
2 Joe Torre 614
3 Casey Stengel 604
4 Ralph Houk 550
5 Miller Huggins 339

Other Events at Yankee Stadium

Championship Fights
(unless otherwise noted)

DATE	WINNER/LOSER
7/23/23	Leonard dec Tendler
6/26/24	Greb dec Moore
5/30/25	Berlenbach dec McTigue
9/11/25	Berlenbach KO Slattery
9/25/25	Walker dec Slade
6/10/26	Berlenbach dec Stribling
7/21/27	Dempsey KO Sharkey (first $1 million non-title fight)
6/26/28	Tunney KO Heeney
7/18/29	Loughran dec Braddock
6/12/30	Schmeling DQ (foul) Sharkey
7/17/30	Singer KO Mandell
8/30/37	Louis dec Farr
6/22/38	Louis KO Schmeling
6/28/39	Louis KO Galento
8/22/39	Ambers dec Armstrong
6/28/40	Louis KO Godoy
6/19/46	Louis KO Conn
9/18/46	Louis KO Mauriello
9/27/46	Zale KO Graziano
6/25/48	Louis KO Walcott
9/23/48	Williams KO Flores
8/10/49	Charles KO Lesnevich
9/27/50	Charles dec Louis
9/8/50	Saddler KO Pep
6/25/52	Maxim KO Robinson
6/17/54	Marciano dec Charles
9/17/54	Marciano KO Charles
9/21/55	Marciano KO Moore
9/23/57	Basilio dec Robinson
6/26/59	Johansson KO Patterson
9/28/76	Ali dec Norton

Professional Football

1926	New York Yankees (AFL)
1927-28	New York Yankees (NFL)
1936-37	New York Yankees (AFL)
1940	New York Yankees (AFL)
1946-49	New York Yankees (AAFC)
1950-51	New York Yanks (NFL)
1956-73	New York Giants (NFL); all-time regular season record at Yankee Stadium, 66-49-6. All-time postseason record at Yankee Stadium, 2-2.
1976	New York Jets (NFL) exhibition games

Notable Games:

12/30/56	New York Giants 47 - Chicago Bears 7; NFL Championship Game, Giants win third title in team history.
12/28/58	Baltimore Colts 23 - New York Giants 17 (OT); "The Greatest Game Ever Played," NFL Championship Game, first OT game in NFL history.
12/30/62	Green Bay Packers 16 - New York Giants 7; NFL Championship Game
12/10/72	Miami Dolphins 23 - New York Giants 13; Dolphins improve to 13-0 en route to perfect 17-0 season.

College Football

1923-46	Fordham vs. NYU series
1923-48	NYU uses Stadium as a secondary home field
1925-46	Army vs. Notre Dame at the Stadium (also played in 1969)
1930-31	Army vs. Navy played at the Stadium
1968-'73; '76-87	Grambling played 18 times

Notable Games:

11/12/28	Notre Dame 12 - Army 6, scoreless at halftime, Knute Rockne gives his famous "win one for the Gipper" speech in the locker room
11/9/46	Notre Dame 0 - Army 0 in battle featuring four Heisman Trophy winners (Doc Blanchard-1945, Glenn Davis-1946, Johnny Lujack-1947 and Leon Hart-1949)
12/15/62	Gotham Bowl, Nebraska 36 - Miami 34

Notable Team Records in Yankee Stadium Games:

Army	17-17-4 in 38 games
Fordham	13-5-1 in 19 games
Notre Dame	15-6-3 in 24 games
NYU	52-40-4 in 96 games

Soccer

6/28/31	Exhibition: Glasgow Celtic 4, New York Yankees 1 (of the American Soccer League)
9/16/34	Charity match: Jewish All-Stars 3 - Irish All-Stars 0
9/27/36	Macabees of Palestine 6 - NY State All-Stars 0
11/8/36	ASL All-Stars 4 - Macabees of Palestine 1
5/4/47	Hapoel of Palestine 2 - U.S. All-Stars 0 (61,000 tickets sold)
1952	American Soccer League games
6/15/52	Tottenham Hotspur 7 - Manchester United 1
6/8/53	International Soccer Friendly: England 6 - United States 3
6/14/53	Liverpool 1 - Young Boys Club of Switzerland 1
4/29/56	Israel Olympic Team 2 - ASL All-Stars 1
9/5/66	Santos 4 - Inter Milan 1
1967	New York Skyliners a.k.a. Cerro of Uruguay (United Soccer Association)
1967-68	New York Generals (NPSL)
8/26/67	Inter Milan 1 - Santos 0
10/15/67	Israel National Team 3 - ASL All-Stars 1
6/21/68	Santos 4 - Napoli 2
7/12/68	New York Generals 5 - Santos 3
8/21/68	Real Madrid 4 - New York Generals 1
9/1/68	Santos 1 - Benfica 1
5/30/69	Barcelona 3 - Juventus 2
6/27/69	Inter Milan 2 (PK win) - Sparta Prague 2 A.C. Milan 4 - Panathinaikos 0
6/29/69	A.C. Milan 6 - Inter Milan 4
1971, 1976	New York Cosmos (NASL), including Pele
5/28/76	USA Bicentennial Cup, England 3 - Italy 2, Att: 40,650

Other Performers and Events

7/20/57	Rev. Billy Graham preaches.
12/7/57	Cardinal Spellman celebrates Mass.
8/8/58	A Jehovah's Witnesses convention draws a single-day Stadium record 123,707 people.
10/4/65	Pope Paul VI celebrates Mass.
10/2/79	Pope John Paul II celebrates Mass.
5/1/86	Cardinal O'Connor officiates at World Youth Assembly.
6/21/90	Nelson Mandela welcomed with a huge celebration.
6/22/90	Billy Joel performs first of two dates in succession.
8/29/92	U2 performs first of two dates in succession.
6/10/94	Pink Floyd performs first of two dates in succession.
6/25/94	Closing ceremonies for the 1994 Unity Games.
4/25/99	Paul Simon sings "Mrs. Robinson" while standing in center field on the day Joe DiMaggio's Monument is dedicated.
9/23/01	"A Prayer for America" service held for those lost on September 11, 2001.
3/10/06	Baseball reporter Ed Lucas marries Allison Pheifle in the first on-field wedding in Stadium history.
4/20/08	Pope Benedict XVI celebrates Mass.
5/14/08	New York University holds commencement.

Previous Homes of the Yankees

Hilltop Park

American League Park (commonly known as Hilltop Park) was the Yankees' first home. Hastily constructed in just six weeks on one of the highest points in Upper Manhattan, the all-wooden ballpark sat on a block bounded by Broadway, 165th Street, Fort Washington Avenue and 168th Street, in close proximity to the New York Giants' 155th Street home, the Polo Grounds. The first game at Hilltop Park was played on April 30, 1903—a 6-2 win over Washington, started by Hall of Famer Jack Chesbro.

The ballpark had a covered grandstand ringing the infield from first base to third base and uncovered bleachers running up the foul lines. There was seating for approximately 15,000 people, but as was the case in many ballparks of that time, it could accommodate overflow crowds both in the outfield and along foul ground in the infield, occasionally bringing capacity up toward 25,000.

Hilltop Park (above/below) served as the Yankees' first home. It was built in just six weeks and was located near Broadway and 168th Street in Upper Manhattan.

When a fire ravaged the Polo Grounds on April 14, 1911, the Yankees allowed the Giants to play their home games at Hilltop Park until the Polo Grounds could be rebuilt. From April 15 through May 30, the Giants put together a 20-8 record at their temporary home.

The Yankees were successful in their 10 years at Hilltop Park, compiling a 398-342 all-time record there. The club's final game at the structure came on October 5, 1912—an 8-6 win vs. Washington. After the Yankees' lease at Hilltop Park expired at the end of the season, they decided to leave the rickety ballpark to become renters at the Polo Grounds, where the Giants became their landlords. The move, unthinkable years earlier, was facilitated by the Yankees' post-fire hospitality.

In 1914, Hilltop Park was torn down. Currently, its former location is the site of Columbia-Presbyterian Medical Center.

Polo Grounds

The Yankees called the Polo Grounds home from 1913 through 1922, sharing the park with the New York Giants. Located on West 157th Street and Eighth Avenue in Upper Manhattan, the Polo Grounds was overlooked by a promontory called Coogan's Bluff to the west. To the east was the Harlem River—on the other side of which Yankee Stadium was built in 1923.

The Polo Grounds was constructed with straight sides, and the outfield fences by the foul poles ran parallel to each other and away from home plate. The foul poles in left and right were approximately 277 and 258 feet away from the plate, respectively, while left-center, center and right fields were all in the range of 445-483 feet away from home.

The Polo Grounds, located on West 157th Street and Eighth Avenue in Upper Manhattan, served as the home of the Yankees from 1913-22.

The Yankees compiled a 416-338 all-time regular season record at the uniquely-shaped facility, winning the first two pennants in franchise history while tenants in 1921 and 1922. The club lost both of those World Series to the NL Champion Giants—5 games to 3 in 1921 and 4 games to none with one tie in 1922—in Fall Classics played entirely at the Polo Grounds.

The American Leaguers were welcome tenants as long as they remained less popular than the Giants. But with Babe Ruth's arrival in 1920 and the team's subsequent success, the dynamic quickly changed. After the Yankees started outdrawing the Giants in their own park in 1920 and 1921, the National Leaguers asked the Pinstripers to vacate to a new facility as soon as possible. The 1922 season marked their final season in Manhattan before their April 18, 1923, Yankee Stadium debut in the Bronx.

The Polo Grounds remained home to the Giants until they moved to San Francisco in 1958. It stood empty until 1962 when the Mets arrived to play two seasons there before moving into Shea Stadium. In 1964, the Polo Grounds was demolished. Apartment buildings called the Polo Grounds Towers occupy the site today.

Monument Park

Since 1932, the New York Yankees have honored their all-time greats with the dedication of monuments and plaques in Yankee Stadium. The tradition continues in the current Stadium in Monument Park, located behind the outfield fence in center field.

The first monument was dedicated on May 30, 1932, to the memory of Miller Huggins, who died suddenly in 1929. The diminutive manager guided the Yankees to six American League pennants and three World Championships in his 11-plus seasons.

The first plaque was placed on the center-field wall in April 1940, a tribute to Jacob Ruppert, the former owner who built Yankee Stadium and brought the tradition of winning to the Yankees.

Two more monuments followed: in 1941 for Lou Gehrig and in 1949 for Babe Ruth. Later plaques were placed in center field for General Manager Ed Barrow (1954) and two great Yankees center fielders, Joe DiMaggio and Mickey Mantle (1969). After his death, Mantle's plaque was removed and replaced by a fourth monument in his honor on August 25, 1996. On April 25, 1999, DiMaggio—who passed away less than two months earlier—was honored with the Stadium's fifth monument. (The two plaques which previously honored DiMaggio and Mantle were donated by the Yankees to the Yogi Berra Museum and Learning Center in Montclair, N.J.).

Monument Park is located just behind the centerfield fence and is accessible to all fans.

Originally, the monuments and plaques were part of the playing field. The monuments and flagpole were located in straight-away center field on the warning track approximately 10 feet in front of the wall. Sometimes long hits and fly balls forced fielders to go behind the monuments to retrieve the baseball.

One tradition of Yankee Stadium before it was remodeled was the policy of allowing fans to exit through the center-field gates via the warning track, where they could pause and reflect on the achievements of these honored legends. After Yankee Stadium was remodeled in 1974 and 1975, the monuments and plaques were relocated to an area off the field between the Yankees' and visitors' bullpens. Additionally, fans were no longer allowed to exit via the warning track, and viewing Monument Park was only possible at a great distance.

In 1976, two more plaques were added to memorialize managers Joe McCarthy and Casey Stengel. In the 1980s, plaques were dedicated to Yankees greats Thurman Munson (1980), Elston Howard and Roger Maris (1984), Phil Rizzuto (1985), Billy Martin (1986), Whitey Ford and Lefty Gomez (1987), Yogi Berra and Bill Dickey (1988), and Allie Reynolds (1989). Two recent plaques were dedicated to non-uniformed Yankees legends: the "Voice of the Yankees," Mel Allen (1998); and the "Voice of Yankee Stadium," public-address announcer Bob Sheppard (2000). Yankees greats Don Mattingly (1997), Reggie Jackson (2002), Ron Guidry (2003) and Red Ruffing (2004) are the most recent Bombers to be honored with plaques in Monument Park. Plaques commemorating the visits of Pope Paul VI in 1965 and Pope John Paul II in 1979 were dedicated by the Knights of Columbus, and a plaque commemorating the New York Yankees' interlocking "NY" insignia was added to the park in 2001. The most recent plaque was dedicated in 2008 following the visit of Pope Benedict XVI.

In 1985, after the left-center-field fence of the original Stadium was moved in, the Yankees were able to open Monument Park for up-close fan viewing. By 1988, long lines and increased fan interest caused the Yankees to move the fence in further and expand the area. A special walkway was added with an exhibit honoring those Yankees who have had their uniform numbers retired.

In a pregame ceremony on Sept. 11, 2002, the Yankees dedicated a monument in remembrance of the victims and heroes of the 9/11 tragedy. It was the sixth monument dedicated in Yankee Stadium and the first to non-Yankees personnel.

In all, there are six monuments (five for Yankees players or managers and one to commemorate 9/11) and 24 plaques (16 Yankees players or managers, two for Yankees owner/executives, two for public-address/broadcasting personnel, three for papal visit commemorations and one related to the Yankees insignia) in Monument Park.

Monument Park prior to the final game at Original Yankee Stadium on September 21, 2008.

Monument Park Monuments

(In order of dedication)

MILLER JAMES HUGGINS

MANAGER OF NEW YORK YANKEES, 1918-1929
PENNANT WINNERS, 1921-22-23...1926-27-28
WORLD CHAMPIONS, 1923, 1927 AND 1928

AS A TRIBUTE TO A SPLENDID CHARACTER
WHO MADE PRICELESS CONTRIBUTION TO BASEBALL
AND ON THIS FIELD BROUGHT GLORY TO THE
NEW YORK CLUB OF THE AMERICAN LEAGUE

THIS MEMORIAL IS ERECTED BY
COL. JACOB RUPPERT
AND
BASEBALL WRITERS OF NEW YORK

MAY 30, 1932

HENRY LOUIS GEHRIG

JUNE 19TH 1903 - JUNE 2ND 1941
A MAN, A GENTLEMAN
AND
A GREAT BALL PLAYER
WHOSE AMAZING RECORD
OF 2130 CONSECUTIVE GAMES
SHOULD STAND FOR ALL TIME.

THIS MEMORIAL IS A TRIBUTE
FROM THE
YANKEE PLAYERS
TO THEIR BELOVED CAPTAIN AND TEAM MATE

JULY THE FOURTH
1941

GEORGE HERMAN "BABE" RUTH

1895 - 1948
A GREAT BALL PLAYER
A GREAT MAN
A GREAT AMERICAN

ERECTED BY
THE YANKEES
AND
THE NEW YORK BASEBALL WRITERS

APRIL 19, 1949

MICKEY MANTLE

"A GREAT TEAMMATE"
1931-1995
536 HOME RUNS

WINNER OF TRIPLE CROWN	1956
MOST WORLD SERIES HOMERS	18
SELECTED TO THE ALL STAR GAME	20 TIMES
WON MVP AWARD	1956, 1957 + 1962
ELECTED TO HALL OF FAME	1974

A MAGNIFICENT YANKEE
WHO LEFT A LEGACY OF
UNEQUALED COURAGE

DEDICATED BY
THE NEW YORK YANKEES
AUGUST 25, 1996

JOSEPH PAUL DIMAGGIO

"THE YANKEE CLIPPER"
1914 - 1999
RECOGNIZED AS BASEBALL'S
"GREATEST LIVING PLAYER"

LIFETIME BATTING AVERAGE	.325
WON MVP AWARD	1939, 1941, 1947
SELECTED TO ALL-STAR GAME	13 TIMES
AMERICAN LEAGUE BATTING TITLE	1939, 1940
ELECTED TO HALL OF FAME	1955

SET ONE OF BASEBALL'S MOST ENDURING RECORDS,
56-GAME HITTING STREAK
MAY 15 TO JULY 16, 1941

LED THE YANKEES TO AN INCREDIBLE NINE WORLD
CHAMPIONSHIPS
IN HIS 13-YEAR CAREER

A BASEBALL LEGEND AND
AN AMERICAN ICON
"HE HAS PASSED, BUT HE WILL NEVER LEAVE US"

DEDICATED BY
THE NEW YORK YANKEES,
APRIL 25, 1999

SEPTEMBER 11, 2001 TRIBUTE

We Remember
On September 11, 2001, despicable acts of terrorism were perpetrated on our country.

In tribute to the eternal spirit of the innocent victims of these crimes and to the selfless courage shown by both public servants and private citizens, we dedicate this plaque.

These valiant souls, with unfettered resolve, exemplify the true character of this great nation. Their unity and resilience during this time of distress defined American heroism for future generations.

Dedicated by the New York Yankees
September 11, 2002

Monument Park Plaques

(In order of dedication)

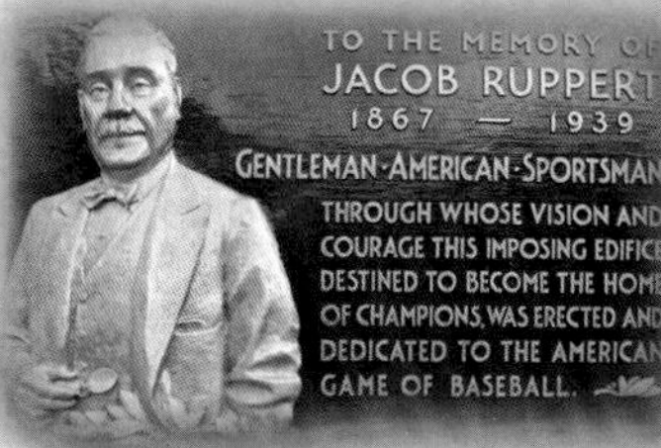

JACOB RUPPERT

TO THE MEMORY OF
JACOB RUPPERT
1867-1939
GENTLEMAN - AMERICAN - SPORTSMAN
THROUGH WHOSE VISION AND
COURAGE THIS IMPOSING EDIFICE,
DESTINED TO BECOME THE HOME
OF CHAMPIONS, WAS ERECTED AND
DEDICATED TO THE AMERICAN
GAME OF BASEBALL.

EDWARD GRANT BARROW

1868-1953
MOULDER OF A TRADITION OF VICTORY
UNDER WHOSE GUIDANCE THE YANKEES WON
FOURTEEN AMERICAN LEAGUE PENNANTS AND
TEN WORLD CHAMPIONSHIPS AND BROUGHT
TO THIS FIELD SOME OF THE GREATEST
BASEBALL STARS OF ALL TIME
THIS MEMORIAL IS A TRIBUTE FROM THOSE
WHO SEEK TO CARRY ON HIS GREAT WORKS
ERECTED APRIL 15, 1954

POPE PAUL VI

IN COMMEMORATION
OF THE SOLEMN MASS
FOR PEACE OFFERED
BY HIS
HOLINESS POPE PAUL VI
OCTOBER 4, 1965
HERE IN YANKEE STADIUM
GIFT OF
KNIGHTS OF COLUMBUS

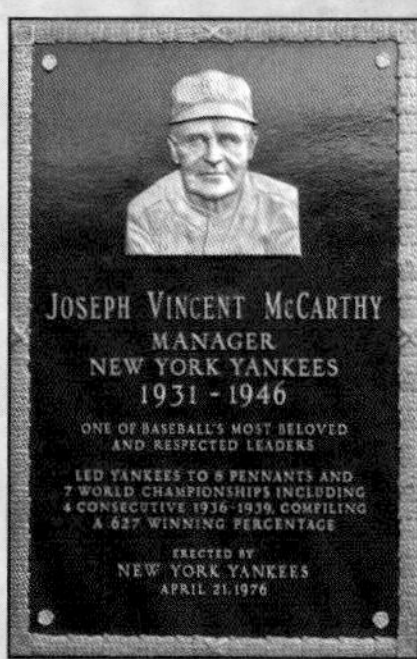

JOSEPH VINCENT McCARTHY

MANAGER
NEW YORK YANKEES
1931-1946
ONE OF BASEBALL'S MOST BELOVED
AND RESPECTED LEADERS
LED YANKEES TO 8 PENNANTS AND
7 WORLD CHAMPIONSHIPS INCLUDING
4 CONSECUTIVE 1936-1939, COMPILING
A .627 WINNING PERCENTAGE

ERECTED BY
NEW YORK YANKEES
APRIL 21, 1976

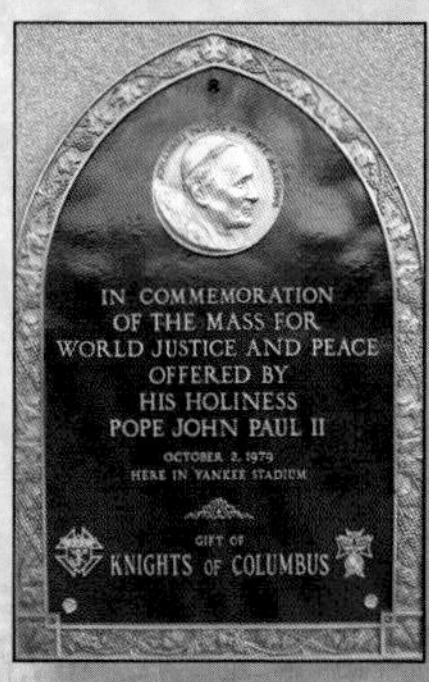

CHARLES DILLON "CASEY" STENGEL

1890-1975

BRIGHTENED BASEBALL FOR OVER 50 YEARS

WITH SPIRIT OF ETERNAL YOUTH
YANKEE MANAGER 1949-1960 WINNING
10 PENNANTS AND 7 WORLD CHAMPIONSHIPS
INCLUDING A RECORD 5 CONSECUTIVE
1949-1953

ERECTED BY
NEW YORK YANKEES
JULY 30, 1976

POPE JOHN PAUL II

IN COMMEMORATION
OF THE MASS FOR
WORLD JUSTICE AND PEACE
OFFERED BY
HIS HOLINESS
POPE JOHN PAUL II
OCTOBER 2, 1979
HERE IN YANKEE STADIUM
GIFT OF
KNIGHTS OF COLUMBUS

THURMAN MUNSON

NEW YORK YANKEES
JUNE 7, 1947-AUGUST 2, 1979
YANKEE CAPTAIN

"OUR CAPTAIN AND LEADER HAS NOT
LEFT US-
TODAY, TOMORROW, THIS YEAR, NEXT...
OUR ENDEAVORS WILL REFLECT OUR
LOVE AND ADMIRATION FOR HIM."

ERECTED BY
THE NEW YORK YANKEES
SEPTEMBER 20, 1980

Monument Park Plaques

ELSTON GENE HOWARD
1929-1980

"A MAN OF GREAT GENTLENESS AND DIGNITY"
ONE OF ALL-TIME YANKEE GREATS
AMERICAN LEAGUE MVP IN 1963
WINNER OF TWO GOLD GLOVES
A FITTING LEADER TO BE FIRST BLACK PLAYER
TO WEAR THE YANKEE UNIFORM
"IF INDEED, HUMILITY IS A TRADEMARK
OF MANY GREAT MEN–ELSTON HOWARD WAS
ONE OF THE TRULY GREAT YANKEES"

ERECTED BY
NEW YORK YANKEES
JUNE 21, 1984

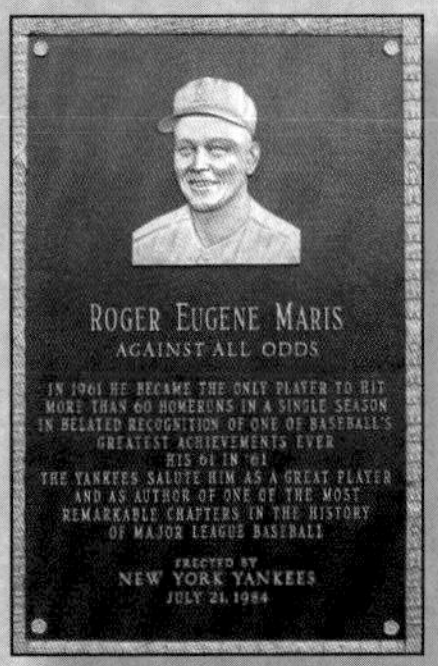

ROGER EUGENE MARIS
AGAINST ALL ODDS

IN 1961 HE BECAME THE ONLY PLAYER TO HIT
MORE THAN 60 HOMERUNS IN A SINGLE SEASON
IN BELATED RECOGNITION OF ONE OF BASEBALL'S
GREATEST ACHIEVEMENTS EVER
HIS 61 IN '61
THE YANKEES SALUTE HIM AS A GREAT PLAYER
AND AS AUTHOR OF ONE OF THE MOST
REMARKABLE CHAPTERS IN THE HISTORY
OF MAJOR LEAGUE BASEBALL

ERECTED BY
NEW YORK YANKEES
JULY 21, 1984

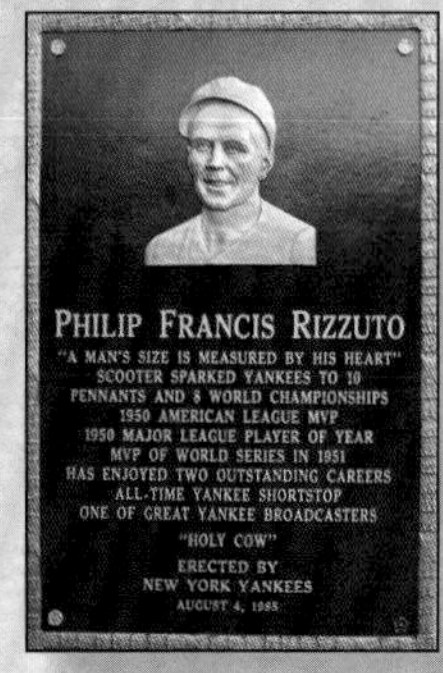

PHILIP FRANCIS RIZZUTO

"A MAN'S SIZE IS MEASURED BY HIS HEART"
SCOOTER SPARKED YANKEES TO 10
PENNANTS AND 8 WORLD CHAMPIONSHIPS
1950 AMERICAN LEAGUE MVP
1950 MAJOR LEAGUE PLAYER OF THE YEAR
MVP OF WORLD SERIES IN 1951
HAS ENJOYED TWO OUTSTANDING CAREERS
ALL-TIME YANKEE SHORTSTOP
ONE OF GREAT YANKEE BROADCASTERS
"HOLY COW"

ERECTED BY
NEW YORK YANKEES
AUGUST 4, 1985

ALFRED MANUEL "BILLY" MARTIN
CASEY'S BOY

A YANKEE FOREVER
A MAN WHO KNEW ONLY ONE WAY TO PLAY-TO WIN
AS A PLAYER FOR CASEY STENGEL HE THRIVED ON
PRESSURE, DELIVERING THE KEY PLAY OR HIT.
MVP OF 1953 WORLD SERIES, SETTING RECORD FOR
MOST HITS IN SIX-GAME SERIES WITH 12.
LATER AS MANAGER HE BECAME
ONE OF THE GREATEST YANKEE MANAGERS.

ERECTED BY
NEW YORK YANKEES
AUGUST 10, 1986

EDWARD "WHITEY" FORD
"CHAIRMAN OF THE BOARD"
NEW YORK YANKEES 1950, 1953-67

LED YANKEES TO 11 PENNANTS AND SIX WORLD
CHAMPIONSHIPS LEADS ALL YANKEE PITCHERS
IN GAMES, INNINGS, WINS, STRIKEOUTS AND
SHUTOUTS CY YOUNG AWARD WINNER IN 1961
HOLDS MANY WORLD SERIES RECORDS INCLUDING
33 2/3 CONSECUTIVE SCORELESS INNINGS

ERECTED BY
NEW YORK YANKEES
AUGUST 2, 1987

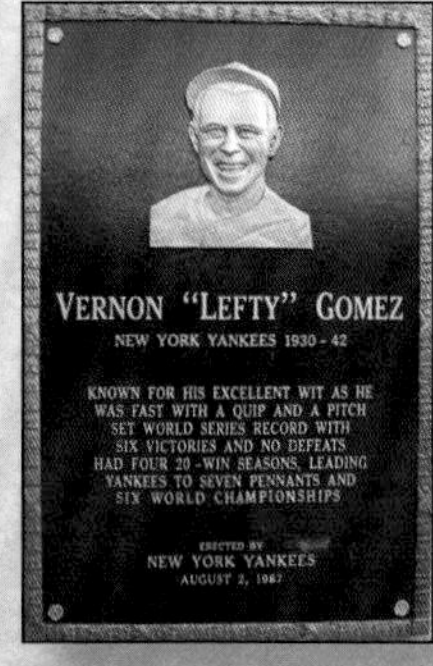

VERNON "LEFTY" GOMEZ
NEW YORK YANKEES 1930-42

KNOWN FOR HIS EXCELLENT WIT AS HE
WAS FAST WITH A QUIP AND A PITCH
SET WORLD SERIES RECORD WITH
SIX VICTORES AND NO DEFEATS
HAD FOUR 20-WIN SEASONS, LEADING
YANKEES TO SEVEN PENNANTS AND
SIX WORLD CHAMPIONSHIPS

ERECTED BY
NEW YORK YANKEES
AUGUST 2, 1987

Monument Park Plaques

WILLIAM MALCOLM "BILL" DICKEY
1928-1943, 1946
YANKEE COACH 1949-1957

ELECTED TO THE HALL OF FAME IN 1954
NAMED TO THE A.L. ALL-STAR TEAM 11 TIMES
HAD A .313 LIFETIME AVG.
HIT OVER .300 IN 11 SEASONS
CAUGHT MORE THAN 100 GAMES
IN 13 CONSECUTIVE SEASONS
LED THE YANKEES TO 8 PENNANTS
AND 7 WORLD CHAMPIONSHIPS
FIRST IN THE LINE OF
GREAT YANKEE CATCHERS
THE EPITOME OF YANKEE PRIDE

ERECTED BY
NEW YORK YANKEES
AUGUST 21, 1988

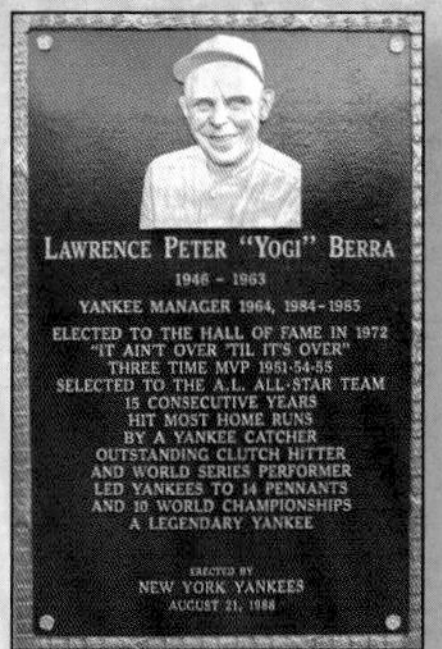

LAWRENCE PETER "YOGI" BERRA
1946-1963
YANKEE MANAGER 1964, 1984-1985

ELECTED TO THE HALL OF FAME IN 1972
"IT AIN'T OVER 'TIL IT'S OVER"
THREE TIME MVP 1951-54-55
SELECTED TO THE A.L. ALL-STAR TEAM
15 CONSECUTIVE YEARS
HIT MOST HOME RUNS
BY A YANKEE CATCHER
OUTSTANDING CLUTCH HITTER
AND WORLD SERIES PERFORMER
LED YANKEES TO 14 PENNANTS
AND 10 WORLD CHAMPIONSHIPS
A LEGENDARY YANKEE

ERECTED BY
NEW YORK YANKEES
AUGUST 21, 1988

ALLIE PIERCE REYNOLDS
"SUPERCHIEF"

NEW YORK YANKEES 1947-1954
ONE OF THE YANKEES' GREATEST
RIGHT-HANDED PITCHERS
HURLED TWO NO-HITTERS IN 1951
STARRED ON FIVE STRAIGHT
WORLD CHAMPIONS 1949-1953
FIVE-TIME ALL-STAR
.686 YANKEE WINNING PERCENTAGE

ERECTED BY
NEW YORK YANKEES
AUGUST 26, 1989

DONALD ARTHUR MATTINGLY
"DONNIE BASEBALL'
1982-1995

AMERICAN LEAGUE BATTING CHAMPION 1984
AMERICAN LEAGUE MVP (145 RBI) 1985
NINE-TIME GOLD GLOVE WINNER
SIX-TIME AMERICAN LEAGUE ALL-STAR
SET RECORDS FOR MOST GRAND SLAMS IN A SEASON (6) 1987
MAJOR LEAGUE RECORD FOR MOST HOME RUNS IN SEVEN CONSECUTIVE GAMES (9) AND EIGHT CONSECUTIVE GAMES (10) 1987
10TH PLAYER IN TEAM HISTORY TO BE NAMED CAPTAIN 1991

A HUMBLE MAN OF GRACE AND DIGNITY.
A CAPTAIN WHO LED BY EXAMPLE.
PROUD OF THE PINSTRIPE TRADITION
AND DEDICATED TO THE PURSUIT OF EXCELLENCE,
A YANKEE FOREVER

DEDICATED BY
THE NEW YORK YANKEES
AUGUST 31, 1997

MEL ALLEN
"THE VOICE OF THE YANKEES"
1939-1964

WITH HIS WARM PERSONALITY AND SIGNATURE GREETING "HELLO THERE, EVERYBODY," HE SHAPED BASEBALL BROADCASTING BY CHARISMATICALLY BRINGING THE EXCITEMENT AND DRAMA OF YANKEES BASEBALL TO GENERATIONS OF FANS. HE MADE PET PHRASES SUCH AS "GOING, GOING, GONE!" A PART OF OUR LANGUAGE AND CULTURE.

A YANKEE INSTITUTION, A NATIONAL TREASURE.

"HOW ABOUT THAT?"

DEDICATED BY
THE NEW YORK YANKEES
JULY 25, 1998

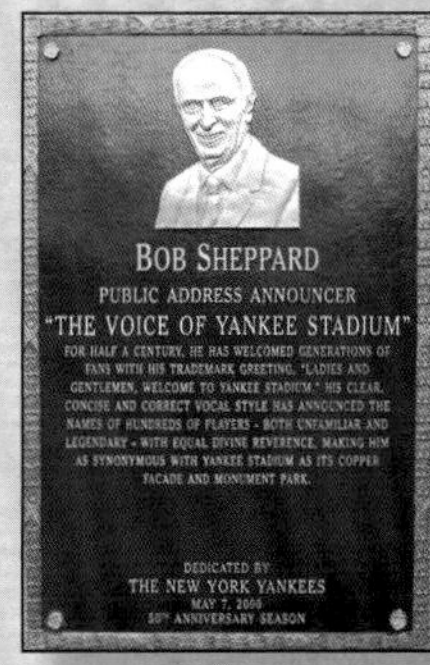

BOB SHEPPARD
PUBLIC ADDRESS ANNOUNCER
"THE VOICE OF YANKEE STADIUM"

FOR HALF A CENTURY, HE HAS WELCOMED GENERATIONS OF FANS WITH HIS TRADEMARK GREETING, "LADIES AND GENTLEMEN, WELCOME TO YANKEE STADIUM." HIS CLEAR, CONCISE AND CORRECT VOCAL STYLE HAS ANNOUNCED THE NAMES OF HUNDREDS OF PLAYERS - BOTH UNFAMILIAR AND LEGENDARY - WITH EQUAL DIVINE REVERENCE, MAKING HIM AS SYNONYMOUS WITH YANKEE STADIUM AS ITS COPPER FACADE AND MONUMENT PARK.

DEDICATED BY
THE NEW YORK YANKEES
MAY 7, 2000
50TH ANNIVERSARY SEASON

Monument Park Plaques

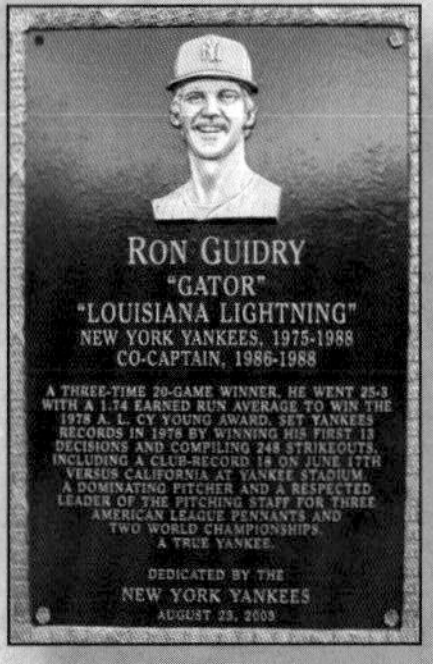

REGGIE JACKSON

"MR. OCTOBER"
NEW YORK YANKEES
1977-1981

ONE OF THE MOST COLORFUL AND EXCITING PLAYERS OF HIS ERA

A PROLIFIC POWER HITTER WHO THRIVED IN PRESSURE SITUATIONS

IN FIVE YEARS IN PINSTRIPES, HELPED LEAD THE YANKEES TO FOUR DIVISION TITLES, THREE AMERICAN LEAGUE PENNANTS AND TWO WORLD CHAMPIONSHIPS

AT HIS BEST IN OCTOBER, BELTED FOUR HOME RUNS ON FOUR CONSECUTIVE SWINGS IN THE 1977 WORLD SERIES–INCLUDING THREE IN GAME SIX AT YANKEE STADIUM

INDUCTED INTO THE BASEBALL HALL OF FAME IN 1993

DEDICATED BY
THE NEW YORK YANKEES
JULY 6, 2002

RON GUIDRY

"GATOR"
"LOUISIANA LIGHTNING"
NEW YORK YANKEES, 1975-1988
CO-CAPTAIN, 1986-1988

A THREE-TIME 20-GAME WINNER, HE WENT 25-3 WITH A 1.74 EARNED RUN AVERAGE TO WIN THE 1978 A.L. CY YOUNG AWARD. SET YANKEES RECORDS IN 1978 BY WINNING HIS FIRST 13 DECISIONS AND COMPILING 248 STRIKEOUTS, INCLUDING A CLUB-RECORD 18 ON JUNE 17TH VERSUS CALIFORNIA AT YANKEE STADIUM. A DOMINATING PITCHER AND A RESPECTED LEADER OF THE PITCHING STAFF FOR THREE AMERICAN LEAGUE PENNANTS AND TWO WORLD CHAMPIONSHIPS. A TRUE YANKEE.

DEDICATED BY
THE NEW YORK YANKEES
AUGUST 23, 2003

CHARLES HERBERT "RED" RUFFING

New York Yankees
1930-1942
1945-1946
U.S. ARMY AIR DIVISION
1943-1945

THE YANKEES' ALL-TIME LEADER IN WINS BY A RIGHT-HANDED PITCHER WITH 231. THE ONLY PITCHER IN FRANCHISE HISTORY TO COMPILE FOUR CONSECUTIVE 20-WIN SEASONS, FROM 1936-1939, WHEN HE LED THE YANKEES TO FOUR STRAIGHT WORLD CHAMPIONSHIPS. A DURABLE PITCHER, HE HOLDS THE YANKEES' RECORD FOR MOST COMPLETE GAMES WITH 261. ONE OF THE GREATEST HITTING PITCHERS OF ALL TIME, HE BATTED .300 OR BETTER IN EIGHT SEASONS.
INDUCTED INTO THE BASEBALL HALL OF FAME IN 1967

DEDICATED BY
THE NEW YORK YANKEES
JULY 10, 2004

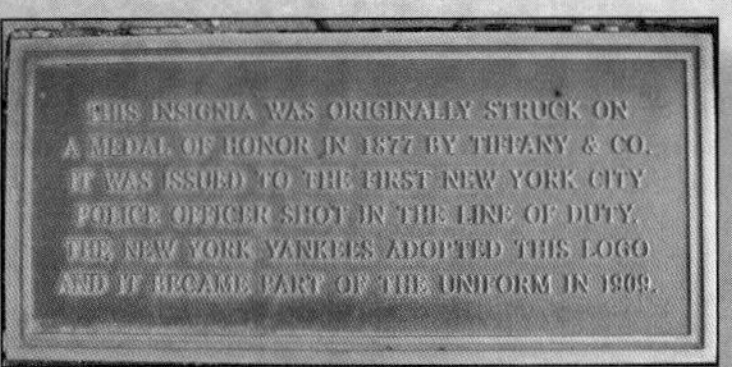

NEW YORK YANKEES INSIGNIA

THIS INSIGNIA WAS ORGINALLY STRUCK ON A MEDAL OF HONOR IN 1877 BY TIFFANY & CO. IT WAS ISSUED TO THE FIRST NEW YORK CITY POLICE OFFICER SHOT IN THE LINE OF DUTY. THE NEW YORK YANKEES ADOPTED THIS LOGO AND IT BECAME PART OF THE UNIFORM IN 1909.

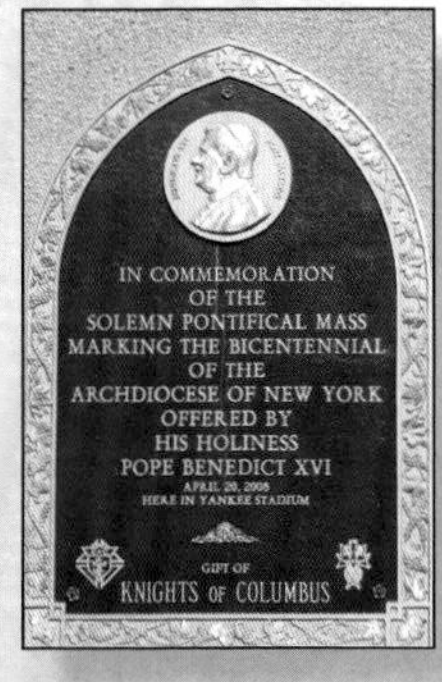

POPE BENEDICT XVI

IN COMMEMORATION
OF THE
SOLEMN PONTIFICAL MASS
MARKING THE BICENTENNIAL
OF THE
ARCHDIOCESE OF NEW YORK
OFFERED BY
HIS HOLINESS
POPE BENEDICT XVI
APRIL 20, 2008
HERE IN YANKEE STADIUM
GIFT OF
KNIGHTS OF COLUMBUS

RHP Zach McAllister was named the 2009 Kevin Lawn Award winner as the organization's Minor League Pitcher of the Year after going 7-5 with a 2.23 ERA (121.0IP, 30ER) with the Double-A Trenton Thunder last season

2010 Player Development & Scouting Directory

EXECUTIVE

Mark Newman .... Senior Vice President, Baseball Operations
Billy Connors .... Vice President, Player Personnel

PLAYER DEVELOPMENT

Pat Roessler .... Director of Player Development
Eric Schmitt .... Assistant Director, Baseball Operations

PROFESSIONAL SCOUTING

Billy Eppler .... Senior Director, Pro Personnel
Will Kuntz .... Assistant, Pro Scouting
Ron Brand .... Professional Scout (Plano, Tex.)
Joe Caro .... Professional Scout (Tampa, Fla.)
Jay Darnell .... Professional Scout (San Diego, Calif.)
Gary Denbo .... Professional Scout (Tampa, Fla.)
Bill Emslie .... Professional Scout (Tampa, Fla.)
Dan Freed .... Professional Scout (Lexington, Ill.)
Jalal Leach .... Professional Scout (Sacramento, Calif.)
Bill Livesey .... Professional Scout (St. Petersburg, Fla.)
Bill Mele .... Professional Scout (Boston, Mass.)
Tim Naehring .... Professional Scout (Cincinnati, Ohio)
Greg Orr .... Professional Scout (Sacramento, Calif.)
Kevin Reese .... Professional Scout (Sterling, Va.)
Rick Williams .... Professional Scout (Tampa, Fla.)
Tom Wilson .... Professional Scout (Lake Havasu, Ariz.)
Bob Miske .... Part-time Professional Scout (Amherst, N.Y.)

AMATEUR SCOUTING

Damon Oppenheimer .... Vice President, Amateur Scouting
John Kremer .... Assistant Director, Amateur Scouting
Tim Kelly .... National Crosschecker
Kendall Carter .... National Crosschecker
Brian Barber .... National Crosschecker
Mark Batchko .... Kansas, North Texas, Oklahoma
Steve Boros .... South Texas (not including El Paso)
Andy Cannizaro .... Arkansas, Louisiana, Mississippi
Jeff Deardorff .... Central and South Florida (excluding Miami/Ft. Lauderdale)
Mike Gibbons .... Central Canada, Indiana, Kentucky, Michigan, Ohio, W. Virginia
Matt Hyde .... Conn., Maine, Mass., New Hampshire, N.Y. State, Penn., Rhode Island, Vermont, Quebec
Dave Keith .... Southern California (Orange County)
Steve Kmetko .... Arizona, Colorado, New Mexico, Utah, El Paso
Steve Lemke .... Illinois, Iowa, Kansas, Minn., Missouri, Nebraska, N. Dakota, S. Dakota, Wisconsin
Scott Lovekamp .... Maryland, North Carolina, Virginia, Wash. D.C.
Carlos Marti .... Miami, Puerto Rico
Tim McIntosh .... Northern California, Northern Nevada (Reno)
Darryl Monroe .... Georgia, S. Carolina
Jeff Patterson .... Inland Empire, Las Vegas
Cesar Presbott .... Delaware, New Jersey, New York City
Dennis Twombley .... California (North L.A. to Fresno), Hawaii
D.J. Svihlik .... Alabama, Tennessee, Florida Panhandle
Mike Thurman .... Alaska, Idaho, Montana, Oregon, Washington, Wyoming, British Columbia

INTERNATIONAL SCOUTING

Pat McMahon .... Coordinator of International Player Development
Donny Rowland .... Director, International Scouting
Alex Cotto .... Assistant Director, International Operations
Joel Lithgow .... Director, Latin Baseball Academy
Aniuska Sanchez .... Manager, Latin Baseball Academy
Victor Mata .... International Scouting Supervisor, Dominican Republic
Ricardo Finol .... International Scouting Supervisor, Venezuela
Argenis Paulino .... Scouting Development Coach (Dominican Republic)
Jonnathan Saturria .... Scouting Development Coach (Dominican Republic)
Angel Ovalles .... Dominican Republic
Juan Rosario .... Dominican Republic
Jose Sabino .... Dominican Republic
Raymond Sanchez .... Dominican Republic
Alan Atacho .... Venezuela
Darwin Bracho .... Venezuela
Jose Gavidea .... Venezuela
Cesar Suarez .... Venezuela
Chairon Isenia .... Curacao
Carlos Levy .... Panama
Edgar Rodriguez .... Nicaragua
Luis Sierra .... Columbia
Lee Sigmen .... Mexico
Jason Lee .... Korea
Ken Su .... Pacific Rim
John Wadsworth .... Australia
Doug Skiles .... Europe

Player Development Staff

NARDI CONTRERAS - ROVING PITCHING COORDINATOR

BORN: 9/19/51 in Tampa, Fla. • RESIDES: Lutz, Fla.

COACHING CAREER: Enters his sixth season as the Yankees' roving pitching coordinator...will be his 40th year in professional baseball and his 28th as a coach...prior to rejoining the Yankees organization in 2005, served as the pitching coach for the rookie-level Princeton Devil Rays in the 2004 season after spending seven years as a Major League pitching coach with the Chicago White Sox (1998-2002), Seattle Mariners (1997) and Yankees (1995)...began his coaching career in the White Sox organization in 1982 and made stops within the minor league systems of the Atlanta Braves, Montreal Expos, Yankees and Arizona Diamondbacks before being promoted to the Yankees' Major League squad in 1995...**PLAYING CAREER:** Pitched for 13 seasons in the minor leagues, compiling a 69-72 career record and 3.86 ERA...appeared in eight Major League games with the White Sox in 1980 (0-0, 5.93 ERA)...**PERSONAL:** Graduated from Tampa Catholic High School in 1969, where he was named the "Most Valuable Athlete"...later graduated from Hillsborough Community College.

JAMES ROWSON - ROVING HITTING COORDINATOR

BORN: 9/12/76 in Mount Vernon, N.Y. • RESIDES: Spring Hill, Fla.

COACHING CAREER: Begins his third season as the Yankees' roving hitting coordinator...will be his fifth season in the organization after spending two seasons (2006-07) as the hitting coach at Single-A Tampa...previously served four seasons in the Angels organization as the hitting coach at Single-A Rancho Cucamonga (2004-05), Single-A Cedar Rapids (2003) and rookie-level Provo (2002)...**PLAYING CAREER:** Originally drafted by the Seattle Mariners out of Mount St. Michael High School in the Bronx ...played minor league ball with the Mariners, Yankees and White Sox...**PERSONAL:** Is married to Maria with two daughters, Katiria and Kiana.

JODY REED - DEFENSIVE COORDINATOR

BORN: 7/26/62 in Tampa, Fla. • RESIDES: Brandon, Fla.

COACHING CAREER: Begins his second season as defensive coordinator...served the previous two seasons as manager of the Gulf Coast Yankees (2007-08), guiding the club to the GCL title in 2007 and earning league "Manager of the Year" honors in his managerial debut...**PLAYING CAREER:** Enjoyed an 11-year Major League career from 1987-97 with the Boston Red Sox, Los Angeles Dodgers, Milwaukee Brewers, San Diego Padres and Detroit Tigers...led the American League with 45 doubles and ranked 10th among all AL hitters with 173 hits in 1990 with Boston...played college baseball for Florida State University...**PERSONAL:** With wife Michelle, has two daughters, Jessica and Kassidy...founded the "Jody Reed Baseball School," helping kids develop the physical and mental skills needed to prepare for a future in baseball.

JACK HUBBARD - ROVING OUTFIELD INSTRUCTOR

BORN: 10/4/50 in Chestertown, Md. • RESIDES: Trinity, Fla.

COACHING CAREER: Returns for a sixth season as a roving outfield instructor in the Yankees organization...previously served as the first base coach for the Triple-A Columbus Clippers in 2004...began his career with the Milwaukee Brewers as a scouting supervisor for the state of Florida...a former Physical Education teacher, he spent more than 10 years as a minor league instructor and coach, special assignment scout, professional scout, and director of player development...worked in various capacities with several teams including the St. Louis Cardinals, Toronto Blue Jays and the Chicago White Sox...**PERSONAL:** Is a graduate of the University of Baltimore with a bachelor of science degree in marketing.

JULIO MOSQUERA - ROVING CATCHING INSTRUCTOR

BORN: 1/29/72 in Panama City, Panama • RESIDES: Tarpon Springs, Fla.

COACHING CAREER: Enters his fifth season as the roving catching instructor with the Yankees...joined the Yankees player development staff in 2005 after playing professionally for 15 years...**PLAYING CAREER:** Signed by the Toronto Blue Jays as a non-drafted free agent in 1991 and played parts of 15 seasons within the minor league systems of the Blue Jays, Tampa Bay Devil Rays, Yankees, Texas Rangers, Seattle Mariners and Milwaukee Brewers...made his Major League debut on 8/17/96 with Toronto and appeared in 12 career Major League games across three seasons (1996, 1997, 2005)...**PERSONAL:** Lives with wife Jennifer and their two children, Dayana and Julio, Jr. in Tarpon Springs, Fla.

MARK LITTLEFIELD - HEAD ATHLETIC TRAINER

BORN: 11/27/67 in Portland, Maine • RESIDES: Tampa, Fla.

Begins his 19th season in the Yankees organization, his 17th as head athletic trainer...served as trainer for the Single-A Oneonta Yankees in 1991-92...graduated from Portland High School (Maine) in 1986...earned a bachelor of science degree from the University of South Carolina in physical education/athletic training...joined the Yankees as a minor league athletic trainer in 1991...married to his wife, Cara, and has a son, R.J., and daughter, Alexis.

MIKE WICKLAND - STRENGTH AND CONDITIONING COORDINATOR

BORN: 7/24/77 in Bridgeport, W.V. • RESIDES: Tampa, Fla.

Enters his third season as the Yankees' strength and conditioning coordinator with the player development staff...is his ninth consecutive season in the organization, having served for six seasons as the head trainer at Single-A Tampa (2002-07) and spending a season as the trainer with Single-A Greensboro in 2001...graduated from the University of North Carolina at Greensboro with a bachelor's degree in exercise and sports science in 1999...was an athletic trainer at UNC-Greensboro during his four years there.

Additional Player Development Staff

JAVIER ALVIDREZ - ASSISTANT STRENGTH & CONDITIONING COORDINATOR
BORN: 7/14/75 in El Paso, Tex. • RESIDES: El Paso, Tex.

Returns for his third season in the Yankees' player development staff as the assistant strength and conditioning coordinator...served for seven seasons (2000-06) as a trainer in the Oakland organization, including the last three at Double-A Midland of the Texas League...graduated from New Mexico State University.

DAVID HAYS - PLAYER DEVELOPMENT EQUIPMENT MANAGER
BORN: 2/21/49 in Herrin, Ill. • RESIDES: Lutz, Fla.

Enters his 22nd season as the Yankees' player development equipment manager and clubhouse supervisor...prior to joining the Yankees, taught in the Southwestern (Ill.) school system for 14 years and also coached baseball and basketball...was a member of the 1989 Eastern League Diamond Diplomacy team that toured the Soviet Union...graduated from Southern Illinois University with a bachelor of arts degree in education...married (Lissa) with two sons, Christopher and Michael.

CHRIS ROOT - PLAYER DEVELOPMENT CLUBHOUSE MANAGER
BORN: 5/22/69 in Cleveland, Ohio • RESIDES: Tampa, Fla.

Enters his eighth season in the Yankees organization and his sixth consecutive season as the Yankees' player development clubhouse manager in Tampa...previously worked in the Boston Red Sox system...prior to joining the Tampa staff, served as the clubhouse manager for the Eastern League's Trenton Thunder...graduated from High Point University with a bachelor of arts degree in Sports Management...married (Adina).

Yankees Roots

There are currently 28 players on opposing teams' active 40-man rosters that came through the Yankees' system (either drafted or originally signed as a non-drafted free agent by the Yankees).

Manny Acosta (Atlanta) ....Signed by the Yankees as a non-drafted free agent on January 6, 1998
Joaquin Arias (Texas)..................................... Signed by the Yankees as a non-drafted free agent on July 21, 2001
John Axford (Milwaukee)............................. Signed by the Yankees as a non-drafted free agent on August 11, 2006
Justin Berg (Chicago–NL)......................... Selected by the Yankees in the 43rd round of the 2003 First-Year Player Draft
Melky Cabrera (Atlanta) ....Signed by the Yankees as a non-drafted free agent on November 13, 2001
Randy Choate (Tampa Bay)......................Selected by the Yankees in the fifth round of the 1997 First-Year Player Draft
Tyler Clippard (Washington)....................Selected by the Yankees in the ninth round of the 2003 First-Year Player Draft
Phil Coke (Detroit) .... Selected by the Yankees in the 26th round of the 2002 First-Year Player Draft
Mike Dunn (Atlanta)............................. Selected by the Yankees in the 33rd round of the 2004 First-Year Player Draft
Randy Flores (Colorado).........................Selected by the Yankees in the ninth round of the 1997 First-Year Player Draft
Cristian Guzman (Washington) .... Signed by the Yankees as a non-drafted free agent on August 24, 1994
Sean Henn (Toronto)............................ Selected by the Yankees in the 26th round of the 2000 First-Year Player Draft
Austin Jackson (Detroit)...................... Selected by the Yankees in the eighth round of the 2005 First-Year Player Draft
Ian Kennedy (Arizona)...............Selected by the Yankees in the first round (21st overall) of the 2006 First-Year Player Draft
Zach Kroenke (Arizona).........................Selected by the Yankees in the fifth round of the 2005 First-Year Player Draft
Wilton Lopez (Houston) ....Signed by the Yankees as a non-drafted free agent on April 30, 2002
Mike Lowell (Boston)............................ Selected by the Yankees in the 20th round of the 1995 First-Year Player Draft
Jeff Marquez (Chicago–AL) .... Selected by the Yankees in Comp. Rd-A (41st overall) of the 2004 First-Year Player Draft
Hideki Matsui (Los Angeles–AL) .... Signed by the Yankees as a free agent on January 14, 2003
Dan McCutchen (Pittsburgh) .... Selected by the Yankees in the 13th round of the 2006 First-Year Player Draft
Carlos Monasterios (Los Angeles–NL) Signed by the Yankees as a non-drafted free agent on September 19, 2004
Dioner Navarro (Tampa Bay).......................... Signed by the Yankees as a non-drafted free agent on August 21, 2000
Juan Rivera (Los Angeles–AL)............................Signed by the Yankees as a non-drafted free agent on April 12, 1996
Jesus Sanchez (Philadelphia) ....Signed by the Yankees as a non-drafted free agent on July 2, 2004
Omir Santos (New York–NL) ....Selected by the Yankees in the 21st round of the 2001 First-Year Player Draft
Alfonso Soriano (Chicago–NL)............. Signed by the Yankees as a non-drafted free agent (Japan) on September 29, 1998
Jose Tabata (Pittsburgh).............................. Signed by the Yankees as a non-drafted free agent on August 12, 2004
Jose Valdez (Houston)................................ Signed by the Yankees as a non-drafted free agent on October 5, 2000

***Rosters as of 1/25/10**

Yankees Around the Globe

As the game of Baseball continues to grow on a global scale, "America's Pastime" has become infused with talent from all four corners of the world.

The New York Yankees, as one of the most recognized brands in the world, are dedicated to making meaningful and lasting footprints throughout the international Baseball community.

Twenty eight percent of players on Major League rosters on Opening Day 2009 were born outside the United States. For the Yankees, the total was 46.2 percent, with 12 of the Yankees' 26 players on the team's Opening Day roster (including one on the disabled list) having been born in a foreign country. Among American League clubs, only the Mariners (15) had more foreign-born players on their Opening Day roster. The Yankees' 2009 Major League Opening Day roster was composed of players from seven different nations (Dominican Republic, Japan, Panama, Puerto Rico, Taiwan, United States and Venezuela).

The Yankees' brand transcends international borders as fans show their pride around the globe.

Signing and developing exceptional talent from around the globe has become a trademark of the Yankees organization. Some of the club's acquisitions include the American League's all-time saves leader and Panama native Mariano Rivera, five-time All-Star Jorge Posada of Puerto Rico, two-time All-Star Hideki Matsui from Japan, 2006 Cy Young Award runner-up Chien-Ming Wang from Taiwan and 2006 All-Star Robinson Cano of the Dominican Republic.

At the minor league level, the organization has signed two Chinese minor leaguers, two players from the Israel Baseball League, Cuban-born Juan Miranda and top minor league talent from Australia, Brazil, Mexico and Nicaragua. In addition, the Yankees field two Dominican Summer League teams and operate a state-of-the-art Latin Baseball Academy in the Dominican Republic.

The Latin Béisbol Academy

For the vast majority of the Yankees' Latin American prospects, the Latin Béisbol Academy is the starting point for their professional careers.

Constructed in Boca Chica, Dominican Republic, the Yankees built their academy from scratch, allowing player development personnel to manage every detail of the project, from the trainer's room to the clubhouses to the classrooms. The end result is a four-building, four-field complex with the capacity to house up to 110 players. There is also a small apartment building for coaches and instructors. The academy, which officially opened in June 2005 and was completed in the spring of 2006, has a campus feel to it that is not lost on the ballplayers, many of whom are spending time away from their families for the first time.

Previously, the Yankees had leased a variety of facilities in Latin America for scouting and player development use, but it became apparent that it was necessary to find and develop their own facility.

"We've never had as many fields or batting cages," said Mark Newman, Yankees Senior Vice President of Baseball Operations. "We've never had this level of control over player nutrition or this kind of strength and conditioning facility. All of these things enhance our player development efforts. Already, we've seen the physical, mental, emotional and fundamental maturation of players at a more rapid rate, and we should see it to a greater degree in the future."

As a dedicated investor in Latin American talent, the Yankees make every effort to enhance the instruction the players receive off the field. The complex is staffed with educators who teach American customs and provide one-on-one tutoring sessions. To further these goals, the Yankees created a partnership with Iberoamerican University (UNIBE) in Santo Domingo, a private institution that brings a group of 12 college professors to the academy. The professors teach everything from basic Spanish to three different levels of English, in addition to leading lectures on subjects such as conflict resolution and financial literacy.

The Yankees also arrange for past and present Major League stars, such as Mariano Rivera, Robinson Cano and Reggie Jackson, to be guest lecturers for the prospects. In November 2007, Yankees Manager Joe Girardi visited the Béisbol Academy and spoke to the coaching staff and 55 Latin players, including eight players from the 2006 and 2007 drafts. He also dined with the Yankees' senior Latin staff and watched a Dominican Instructional League game.

> **"The Latin Béisbol Academy was built to instruct, enhance and further develop the inherent skills in young, aspiring baseball players from all parts of Central and South America."**
>
> ~ Yankees Chief International Officer, Executive Vice President Felix Lopez

The players and staff are active in local community events as well, hosting annual instructional clinics in the Dominican Republic, Nicaragua and Venezuela. In addition, the Yankees' Latin complex has hosted several R.B.I. (Reviving Baseball in the Inner City) tournament games and joined the Yankees organization in the 2007 donation of $65,000 in food and cash to hurricane damaged areas in the Dominican Republic and Nicaragua. The Yankees have also adopted an orphanage in the Dominican town of La Romana, supplying it with food, money and clothing.

The Yankees field two Dominican Summer League teams and have reached the playoffs in four of the last five years (2005-07, '09), taking home back-to-back titles in 2005 and 2006. With the hard work and dedication of the Yankees Player Development staff, the organization looks forward to the future, when these young players can be a part of a World Championship in the Bronx.

Partners in Japan

During the 2002 season, the Yankees entered into a working agreement with the Yomiuri Giants, winners of 21 Japan Series Championships. Pursuant to the agreement, the teams consented to share baseball information, ideas and strategies. Also in 2002, the Yankees pursued and signed three-time Central League MVP Hideki Matsui. A nine-time Japanese League All-Star and three-time home run champion, Matsui became the first bonafide power hitter to make the transition from Japan to the Major Leagues.

In 2004, the Yankees traveled to Tokyo to open the regular season against the Tampa Bay Devil Rays. The historic trip marked the 70th anniversary of Babe Ruth and Lou Gehrig's 1934 All-Star tour of Japan. It also recognized the anniversary of the founding of the Yomiuri Giants franchise, Japan's oldest professional baseball team. The two-game series was just the second-ever Major League season opener to take place in Japan. At the time, the two games were the highest-rated televised Major League games in Japan's history.

Yankees Teach in Taiwan

In January 2009, the Yankees joined the Chinese Taipei Baseball Association under the auspices of Major League Baseball in holding a clinic for high school pitchers, catchers and coaches at the National Taiwan Sport University's Taoyuan Campus in Taipei, Taiwan. It marked the Yankees' first-ever large-scale outreach in Taiwan and represented the club's initiative in cultivating baseball talent and increasing brand recognition in Asia and the greater international community.

The five-day clinic focused on pitching and catching fundamentals and philosophy. Taiwanese participants included approximately 40 pitchers, 10 catchers and 20 coaches, all from the high school level. The Chinese Taipei Baseball Association oversees all amateur baseball in Taiwan and organizes their Olympic and World Baseball Classic teams.

Yankees and Chinese Baseball Association Reach Memorandum of Understanding

The New York Yankees and the Chinese Baseball Association (CBA) held a press conference in Beijing, China, on January 29, 2007, to announce a Memorandum of Understanding that for the first time formalized a strategic alliance between a Major League Baseball club and the Chinese Baseball Association. More recently, during the Yankees' 2009 World Series trophy tour, club officials met with the CBA in Beijing on February 3, 2010, to further the cooperation agreement between the two entities.

The agreement, subject to Major League Baseball's rules, regulations and agreements pertaining to the People's Republic of China, states that the Yankees will provide the CBA with guidance in training baseball players, including sending coaches, player development staff, scouting and training personnel to China to assist the CBA. The partnership also allows the CBA to send staff to the Yankees' facilities in the United States in furtherance of those goals.

Yankees Team President Randy Levine and General Manager Brian Cashman established a working agreement with the Chinese Baseball Association on Jan. 29, 2007.

During their 2007 trip, the Yankees were represented in Beijing by team President Randy Levine, Senior Vice President and General Manager Brian Cashman, Vice President and Assistant General Manager Jean Afterman, and Vice President of Corporate Sales and Sponsorship Michael Tusiani. Beijing Womei Advertising Company Limited and Sportscorp China, headed by President and Managing Director Marc Ganis and Managing Director Kenneth Huang, coordinated the meetings and were instrumental in the Yankees' involvement in China.

"This agreement marks another milestone in Baseball's international evolution," Levine said. "We are excited to begin working alongside our friends in the Chinese Baseball Association, and they will receive our full support throughout this exciting process. The Yankees brand is recognized around the world, and this unprecedented opportunity allows us to further integrate the Yankees name and our proud history of success into Baseball's global landscape."

"It is a great honor to be a part of this unique and exciting opportunity," Cashman said. "Throughout China's history it's easy to see their passion for sports and their determination to excel in all athletic fields. With that belief in excellence, we are proud to begin work with the Chinese Baseball Association, and we will provide all of our available tools and resources to help develop and cultivate their baseball program from the ground up."

The CBA was represented by Chairman Hu Jianguo, Secretary General Shen Wei and Deputy Secretary General Tian Yuan.

On June 16, 2007, the Yankees announced the signings of catcher Zhenwang Zhang and left-handed pitcher Kai Liu to minor league contracts, marking the first-ever acquisition by a Major League organization of Chinese baseball players. The two minor leaguers were introduced at a press conference at Yankee Stadium on July 6, 2007, and then reported to the Yankees Complex in Tampa, Fla., to begin their workouts. Both players were members of the Chinese National team that competed in the 2008 Olympics in Beijing.

Yankees Championship Trophy Tour of the Dominican Republic, Japan and China

Following their championship season, the Yankees embarked on a world tour with their 2009 World Series Trophy, traveling to the Dominican Republic and Asia.

The Yankees' 2009 championship trophy (left) visited the MLB Café in Tokyo, Japan, on Feb. 1, 2010. It was displayed alongside the Yomiuri Giants' 2009 Championship trophy (right) in the first-ever instance of the two titles being side-by-side.

Led by Chief International Officer and Executive Vice President Felix Lopez, a Yankees contingent took the championship trophy to the Dominican Republic for a three-day tour from Jan. 7-9. On the first night, the Yankees and the trophy went to the National Palace for a ceremony with Dominican Republic President Dr. Leonel Fernández. Lopez was joined by bench coach Tony Pena, and players Robinson Cano, Damaso Marte, Francisco Cervelli and Edwar Ramirez as well as by several Yankees minor leaguers. The next day, the Yankees visited the U.S. Embassy and the National Police Headquarters. That evening prior to the Dominican Winter League playoff game between the Licey Tigers and Escogido Lions at Quisqueya Stadium in Santo Domingo, Lopez threw out the ceremonial first pitch, and the Yankees displayed the trophy for fans in attendance. In their final day in the D.R., the Yankees placed the trophy on display for residents of the town of Casa de Campo. In the evening, Lopez tossed the ceremonial first pitch at a game between La Romano and Escogido, and the Yankees again displayed the trophy for fans.

Three weeks later, a Yankees delegation including Team President Randy Levine, Senior Vice President and General Manager Brian Cashman, Vice President and Assistant General Manager Jean Afterman and Senior Vice President of Corporate Sales and Sponsorships Michael Tusiani, took the trophy on a six-day tour to Tokyo, Beijing and Hong Kong from Jan. 31 through Feb. 5.

Chinese youth players were on hand to see the trophy during a press conference with the Chinese Baseball Association on Feb. 3, 2010.

Upon arriving at Tokyo's Narita Airport, Levine and Cashman addressed the media to mark this first-ever occasion of a Yankees World Series trophy being brought to Asia. The next day, another historic moment took place at the MLB Café in Tokyo as the Yankees' 2009 World Series trophy was displayed alongside the Yomiuri Giants' 2009 Japan Series championship trophy in the first-ever instance of the two titles being side-by-side. The Yankees' delegation was joined by Yomiuri Giants owner Takuo Takihana and MLB Asia Vice President Jim Small for an exchange of gifts and a brief press conference. The trophies then remained on display for fans to enjoy throughout the evening.

From there, the trophy traveled to China, where fans in Beijing and Hong Kong had their first opportunity to gaze at Major League Baseball's grandest prize. The trophy tour in China was organized by QSL Sports, which has been active in the promotion of Baseball in the People's Republic of China (PRC) and operates the China Youth Baseball League together with the Chinese Baseball Association. The events in China were hosted by QSL Sports, New World Department Stores (one of the largest owners and operators of department stores in China), and K11, the "World's First Art Mall," which integrates elements of art, culture and nature, while elevating the shopping experience.

On Feb. 3, Yankees officials met with the CBA in Beijing to further the cooperation agreement between the two entities, after which the groups held a joint press conference at the Kunlun Hotel. Later that evening, the championship trophy made its first public appearance in China at the New World Department Store, where media and fans were treated to traditional Chinese performances and ceremonies. Particpants included the full Yankees delegation, CBA officials, New World representatives and the Beijing Yankees youth baseball team, which is part of MLB's "Play Ball" youth baseball program in China.

Hong Kong marked the final stop on the Asian tour. On Feb. 5, Yankees officials addressed the media and greeted fans at the Hyatt Regency hotel adjacent to the recently-opened K11 Mall. The next morning, the trophy was introduced to players and fans during the opening ceremony for Phoenix Cup 2010, Hong Kong's International Women's Baseball Tournament. Yankees Vice President and Assistant General Manager Jean Afterman addressed the players, stressing dedication and perseverance as the means toward achieving great things.

The Yankees thank their partner Delta Air Lines for ensuring the safe transportation of the World Series trophy and appreciate the efforts of Sportscorp China, led by president Marc Ganis.

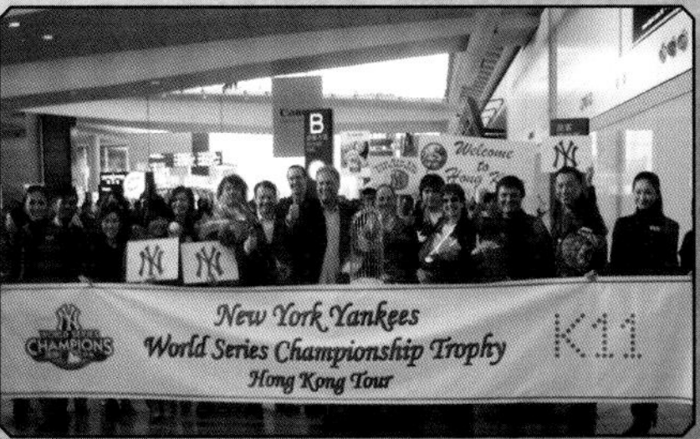

The Yankees received a warm greeting from their Hong Kong fans on Feb. 4, 2010, when they became the first Major League team to step foot in the Chinese city.

New York Yankees 2009 First-Year Player Draft

RD	SEL	PLAYER	POS	HT	WT	B	T	DOB	SCHOOL (STATE)
1	**#29**	**Slade Heathcott**	**OF**	**6'1"**	**190**	**L**	**L**	**9/28/90**	**Texas HS (TX)**
2	**#76**	**John Murphy**	**C**	**5'10"**	**170**	**R**	**R**	**5/13/91**	**The Pendleton School (FL)**
3		(no pick)							
4	**#135**	**Adam Warren**	**RHP**	**6'3"**	**215**	**R**	**R**	**8/25/87**	**University of North Carolina**
5	**#165**	**Caleb Cotham**	**RHP**	**6'3"**	**215**	**R**	**R**	**11/6/87**	**Vanderbilt University**
6	**#195**	**Robert Lyerly**	**3B**	**6'1"**	**205**	**L**	**R**	**7/23/87**	**UNC Charlotte**
7	**#225**	**Sean Black**	**RHP**	**6'4"**	**205**	**R**	**R**	**4/23/88**	**Seton Hall University**
8	**#255**	**Samuel Elam**	**LHP**	**6'4"**	**220**	**L**	**L**	**6/16/87**	**Univ. of Notre Dame**
9	**#285**	**Gavin Brooks**	**LHP**	**6'3"**	**220**	**L**	**L**	**10/27/87**	**UCLA**
10	#315	Tyler Lyons	LHP	6'2"	205	S	L	2/21/88	Oklahoma St. University
11	**#345**	**Neil Medchill**	**OF**	**6'3"**	**170**	**L**	**R**	**6/25/87**	**Oklahoma St. University**
12	**#375**	**Brett Gerritse**	**RHP**	**6'4"**	**220**	**R**	**R**	**3/4/91**	**Pacifica HS (CA)**
13	**#405**	**Deangelo Mack**	**OF**	**5'10"**	**185**	**L**	**L**	**11/19/86**	**University of South Carolina**
14	**#435**	**Graham Stoneburner**	**RHP**	**6'1"**	**190**	**R**	**R**	**9/29/87**	**Clemson University**
15	**#465**	**Shane Greene**	**RHP**	**6'4"**	**210**	**R**	**R**	**11/17/88**	**Daytona Beach CC (FL)**
16	**#495**	**Bryan Mitchell**	**RHP**	**6'2"**	**175**	**L**	**R**	**4/19/91**	**Rockingham County HS (NC)**
17	#525	Chad Thompson	RHP	6'8"	205	R	R	2/6/91	El Toro HS (CA)
18	**#555**	**Hector Rabago**	**C**	**5'10"**	**180**	**R**	**R**	**8/24/88**	**University of Southern California**
19	**#585**	**Luke Murton**	**1B**	**6'4"**	**235**	**R**	**R**	**5/21/86**	**Georgia Tech**
20	#615	Thomas Keeling	LHP	6'3"	184	L	L	3/30/88	Oklahoma St. University
21	**#645**	**Joseph Talerico**	**OF**	**6'0"**	**195**	**R**	**R**	**10/21/88**	**Brookdale CC (NJ)**
22	#675	Richard Soignier	SS	6'0"	187	R	R	8/16/85	University of Louisiana-Monroe
23	**#705**	**Kevin Mahoney**	**3B**	**6'0"**	**205**	**L**	**R**	**5/11/87**	**Canisius College (NY)**
24	**#735**	**Isaac Harrow**	**2B**	**5'11"**	**185**	**R**	**R**	**1/25/87**	**Appalachian St. Univ. (NC)**
25	**#765**	**Shaeffer Hall**	**LHP**	**6'0"**	**180**	**R**	**L**	**10/2/87**	**University of Kansas**
26	#795	Stephen Bruno	SS	5'9"	168	R	R	11/17/90	Gloucester Catholic HS (NJ)
27	**#825**	**Jeffrey Farnham**	**C**	**6'1"**	**195**	**R**	**R**	**8/30/87**	**New Mexico St. University**
28	#855	Aaron Meade	LHP	6'3"	190	S	L	5/2/88	Missouri St. University
29	#885	Scott Matyas	RHP	6'4"	220	R	R	1/18/88	University of Minnesota
30	#915	Kyle McKenzie	RHP	6'1"	175	L	R	9/13/90	Thayer Academy HS (MA)
31	**#945**	**Judd Golson**	**OF**	**6'0"**	**180**	**L**	**R**	**12/6/90**	**Mountain Brook HS (AL)**
32	#975	John Ebert	1B	6'0"	215	R	R	10/16/87	University of South Carolina
33	#1005	Andrew Aplin	OF	6'0"	190	L	L	3/21/91	Vanden HS (CA)
34	#1035	Jacob Petricka	RHP	6'5"	195	R	R	6/5/88	Indiana St. University
35	#1065	Brett Bruening	RHP	6'6"	210	R	R	12/30/88	Grayson County College (TX)
36	#1095	Kyle Ottoson	LHP	6'3"	150	L	L	7/11/90	South Mountain CC (AZ)
37	**#1125**	**Justin Milo**	**OF**	**5'8"**	**180**	**L**	**R**	**2/23/87**	**Univ. of Vermont**
38	#1155	Adam Bailey	OF	6'1"	195	L	L	3/6/88	Univ. of Nebraska
39	#1185	Cody Stiles	RHP	6'1"	185	R	R	3/17/91	Taravella HS (FL)
40	**#1215**	**Ben Watkins**	**RHP**	**6'3"**	**225**	**R**	**R**	**3/11/87**	**University of Pittsburgh-Johnstown**
41	**#1245**	**Mariel Checo**	**RHP**	**6'3"**	**190**	**R**	**R**	**10/16/89**	**Norman Thomas HS (NY)**
42	#1275	Daniel Black	SS	6'2"	170	L	R	8/19/88	Feather River College (CA)
43	**#1305**	**Isaiah Brown**	**OF**	**6'0"**	**165**	**R**	**R**	**10/16/89**	**Paradise Valley CC (AZ)**
44	**#1335**	**Evan DeLuca**	**LHP**	**6'1"**	**195**	**L**	**L**	**3/9/91**	**Immaculata HS (NJ)**
45	#1365	Jeremy Baltz	OF	6'3"	195	R	R	9/17/90	Vestal HS (NY)
46	#1395	Anthony Plagman	1B	6'2"	220	L	L	8/14/87	Georgia Tech
47	#1425	Shane Brown	C	5'11"	197	R	R	1/11/88	University Central Florida
48	#1455	Patrick White	OF	6'1"	185	L	L	2/25/86	West Virginia University
49	#1485	Xavier Esquivel	RHP	5'10"	195	R	R	9/5/88	Loyola Marymount University
50	#1515	Stephen Kaupang	1B	6'5"	235	R	R	1/20/89	Cypress College (CA)

Bold=Signed

New York Yankees No. 1 Draft Choices

Year	Round	Pick	Name	Pos	School/Hometown	w/NYY in Majors
2009	1	29	Slade Heathcott	OF	Texas HS (TX)	-
2008	1	28	Gerritt Cole	RHP	Orange Lutheran HS (CA)	Did not sign
2007	1	30	Andrew Brackman	RHP	North Carolina St.	-
2006	1	21	Ian Kennedy	RHP	University of Southern California	2007-2009
2005	1	17	Carl (C.J.) Henry	SS	Putnam City HS (OK)	-
2004	1	23	Phil Hughes	RHP	Foothill HS (CA)	2007-present
2003	1	27	Eric Duncan	3B	Seton Hall Prep (NJ)	-
2002	2	71	Brandon Weeden	RHP	Santa Fe HS (NM)	-
2001	1	23	John-Ford Griffin	OF	Florida State University	-
	1	34	Bronson K. Sardinha	INF	Kamehameha HS (HI)	2007
	1	42	Jon S. Skaggs	RHP	Rice University	-
2000	1	28	David Parrish	C	University of Michigan	-
1999	1	27	David Walling	RHP	University of Arkansas	-
1998	1	24	Andrew Brown	OF	Richmond H.S. (Ind)	-
	1	43	Mark Prior	RHP	University H.S. (S.D.)	-
1997	1	24	Tyrell Godwin	OF	East Bladen H.S. (NC)	-
	1	40	Ryan Bradley	RHP	Arizona State University	1998
1996	1	20	Eric Milton	LHP	University of Maryland	-
1995	1	27	Shea Morenz	RF	University of Texas	-
1994	1	24	Brian Buchanan	OF	University of Virginia	-
1993	1	13	Matt Drews	RHP	Sarasota H.S. (FL)	-
1992	1	6	Derek Jeter	SS	Kalamazoo Cent. H.S. (MI)	1995-present
1991	1	1	Brien Taylor	LHP	East Carteret H.S. (NC)	-
1990	1	10	Carl Everett	OF	Hillsborough H.S. (FL)	-
1989	2	42	Andy Fox	3B	Christian Bros. H.S. (CA)	1995-97
1988	4	105	Todd Malone	LHP	Casa Robles H.S. (CA)	-
1987	3	81	Bill DaCosta	RHP	New York Tech	-
1986	2	25	Rich Scheid	LHP	Seton Hall University (NJ)	-
1985	1	27	Rick Balabon	RHP	Berwyn, PA	-
1984	1	22	Jeff Pries	RHP	U.C.L.A.	-
1983	4	13	Mitch Lyden	C	Beaverton, OR	-
1982	2	8	Tim Birtsas	LHP	Michigan St. University	-
	2	22	Bo Jackson	SS	Bessemer, AL	-
1981	2	26	John Elway	OF	Stanford University	-
1980	3	22	Billy Cannon	SS	Baton Rouge, LA	-
1979	2	25	Todd Demeter	INF	Oklahoma City, OK	-
1978	1	18	Rex Hudler	SS	Fresno, CA	1984-85
	1	24	Matt Winters	OF	Williamsville, NY	-
	1	26	Brian Ryder	RHP	Shrewsbury, MA	-
1977	1	23	Steve Taylor	RHP	University of Delaware	-
1976	1	16	Pat Tabler	OF	Cincinnati, OH	-
1975	1	19	James McDonald	1B	Los Angeles, CA	-
1974	1	12	Dennis Sherrill	SS	Miami, FL	1978, '80
1973	1	13	Doug Heinold	RHP	Victoria, TX	-
1972	1	14	Scott McGregor	LHP	El Segundo, CA	-
1971	1	19	Terry Whitfield	OF	Blythe, CA	1974-76
1970	1	12	Dave Cheadle	LHP	Ashevill, NC	-
1969	1	11	Charlie Spikes	OF	Bogalusa, LA	1972
1968	1	4	Thurman Munson	C	Kent State University	1969-79
1967	1	1	Ron Blomberg	1B	Atlanta, GA	1969, '71-77
1966	1	10	Jim Lyttle	OF	Florida St. University	1969-71
1965	1	19	Bill Burbach	RHP	Dickeyville, WI	1969-71

Growing Up Yankee

Twenty-two players on the Yankees active 40-man roster entering the 2010 season were either drafted or originally signed as a non-drafted free agent by the Yankees (as of Feb. 1).

Andrew Brackman	Selected in the first round (30th overall) of the 2007 First-Year Player Draft
Robinson Cano	Signed as a non-drafted free agent on January 5, 2001
Francisco Cervelli	Signed as a non-drafted free agent on March 1, 2003
Reegie Corona	Signed by the Yankees as a non-drafted free agent on July 2, 2003
Joba Chamberlain	Selected in Compensation Round A (41st overall) of the 2006 First-Year Player Draft
Wlkin De La Rosa	Signed as a non-drafted free agent on November 15, 2001
Christian Garcia	Selected in the third round of the 2004 First-Year Player Draft
Brett Gardner	Selected in the third round of the 2005 First-Year Player Draft
Phil Hughes	Selected in the first round (23rd overall) of the 2004 First-Year Player Draft
Derek Jeter	Selected in the first round (sixth overall) of the 1992 First-Year Player Draft
Nick Johnson	Selected in the third round of the 1996 First-Year Player Draft
Mark Melancon	Selected in the ninth round of the 2006 First-Year Player Draft
Juan Miranda	Signed as a non-drafted free agent on December 22, 2006
Hector Noesi	Signed by the Yankees as a non-drafted free agent on December 3, 2004
Ivan Nova	Signed by the Yankees as a non-drafted free agent on July 15, 2004
Eduardo Nunez	Signed by the Yankees as a non-drafted free agent on February 25, 2004
Ramiro Pena	Signed as a non-drafted free agent on February 18, 2005
Andy Pettitte	Selected in the 22nd round of the 1990 First-Year Player Draft
Jorge Posada	Selected in the 24th round of the 1990 First-Year Player Draft
David Robertson	Selected in the 17th round of the 2006 First-Year Player Draft
Mariano Rivera	Signed as a non-drafted free agent on February 17, 1990
Kevin Russo	Selected in the 20th round of the 2006 First-Year Player Draft

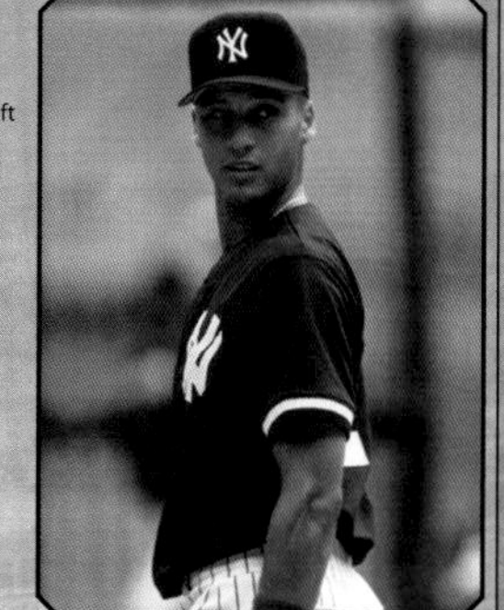

2009 Organizational Summary

AAA	Scranton/Wilkes-Barre Yankees	International League	81-60 (.574)
AA	Trenton Thunder	Eastern League	69-72 (.489)
A	Tampa	Florida State League	77-56 (.579)
A	Charleston	South Atlantic League	74-65 (.532)
Short-A	Staten Island	New York-Penn League	47-29 (.618)
R	GCL Yankees	Gulf Coast League	33-27 (.550)

WINNING BASEBALL: Yankees affiliates combined for a 459-369 (.554) record in 2009, finishing the regular season with the second-best record and winning percentage in all of baseball...in fact, Yankees farm clubs have combined for a winning record in each of the last 20 seasons (1990-2009).

CHAMPIONS: The **Single-A Tampa Yankees** (77-56) and **Short-Season Single-A Staten Island Yankees** (47-29) each won their league's titles, making the Yankees the only organization to bring home multiple titles in 2009...for Tampa, it was their fourth Florida State League championship in franchise history...marked their first appearance in the playoffs since 2004...Staten Island brought home the New York-Penn League trophy for the fifth time in the team's 11-year existence...marked the 17th time that a Yankees affiliate won the NYPL championship...the **Triple-A Scranton/Wilkes-Barre Yankees** won their fourth consecutive International League North Division title, making them the first team in the history of the league to accomplish the feat...advanced to the Governor's Cup Championship round, but lost the series, three-games-to-none, to the Durham Bulls.

2009 Draft Summary: With their first-round pick (29th selection) in the 2009 First-Year Player Draft, the Yankees selected **OF Slade Heathcott** out of Texas High School...was ranked as the 72nd-best prospect (18th-best high school position player) in the draft by *Baseball America* and rated by the publication as the 10th-best prospect in the state of Texas this season...the Yankees selected **catcher John Murphy** with their second round pick (76th overall) out of Pendleton High School in Bradenton, Fla...*Baseball America* rated him as the fifth-best catcher among the 2009 draft class...the Yankees drafted a total of 24 pitchers, four catchers, 10 infielders and 11 outfielders...36 of those drafted were out of college...signed 27 of their picks, including their top eight and 14 of their top 15 selections.

DSL YANKEES: The Dominican Summer League Yankees 2 completed the 2009 season with a 47-23 record, winners of the Boca Chica Baseball City Division...dropped a best-of-three first round series to the DSL Twins two-games-to-one...the Dominican Summer League Yankees 1 finished 31-37, tied for fifth in the Boca Chica North Division...**INF Reymond Nunez** and **OF Kelvin Duran**, both of the DSL Yankees 2, were each selected to the DSL All-Star team...Nunez hit .296 (66-for-223) with 23 extra-base hits (12 doubles, 1 triple, 10HR) in 59G in 2009...led the team with 57 RBI, tying for the league-lead in the category...Duran batted .302 (44-for-195) with a league-best 12 triples in 62G...tied for third in the DSL in runs scored (59).

The Tampa Yankees posted a 77-56 regular season record and captured the fourth Florida State League title in franchise history.

ORGANIZATIONAL LEADERS

Batting Average

Kevin Russo	SWB	.326
Eduardo Nunez	SWB	.322
Deangelo Mack	STA	.306
Daniel Brewer	TAM	.306
Jimmy Paredes	STA	.302

HR

Shelley Duncan	SWB	30
Melky Mesa	CHA	20
Juan Miranda	SWB	19
Jesus Montero	TRE	17
John Rodriguez	SWB	14
Neil Medchill	STA	14

RBI

Shelley Duncan	SWB	99
Juan Miranda	SWB	82
David Adams	TAM	75
Brandon Laird	TAM	75
Melky Mesa	CHA	74

SB

Abraham Almonte	CHA	36
Austin Jackson	SWB	24
Raymond Kruml	CHA	23
Jimmy Paredes	STA	23
Daniel Brewer	TAM	22

ERA

Jose A. Ramirez	STA	1.41
Zach McAllister	SWB	2.23
David Phelps	TAM	2.38
D.J. Mitchell	TAM	2.63
Nik Turley	STA	2.82

Wins

David Phelps	TAM	13
D.J. Mitchell	TAM	12
Lance Pendleton	TRE	12
Kei Igawa	SWB	10
4 others tied		9

Strikeouts

Lance Pendleton	TRE	130
D.J. Mitchell	TAM	125
David Phelps	TAM	122
Hector Noesi	TAM	118
Jeremy Bleich	TRE	116

Saves

Jonathan Hovis	TAM	22
Pat Venditte	TAM	22
Jonathan Ortiz	TAM	17
Jonathan Albaladejo	SWB	11
Julian Arballo	GCL	11

Scranton/Wilkes-Barre Yankees (AAA)

AFFILIATE SINCE 2007
International League – PNC Field
Office Address: 235 Montage Mountain Road, Moosic, PA 18507
Telephone: (570) 969-2255. **Fax:** (570) 963-6564
Website: www.swbyankees.com
Executive Vice President and General Manager: Jeremy Ruby
Director of Broadcasting and Media Relations: Mike Vander Woude
2009 Record, finish: 81-60, First in North Division

DAVE MILEY - MANAGER

BORN: 4/3/62 in Tampa, Fla. • **RESIDES:** Covington, Ky.

COACHING CAREER: Returns for his fifth season as the Yankees' Triple-A Manager...has guided the SWB Yankees to the IL North Division title in each of the last three seasons, compiling an IL-best 253-175 (.591) mark combined over the last three seasons and recording the league's best record in both 2007 and 2008, winning the league title in 2008 and finishing as runner-up in 2009...named 2007 IL "Manager of the Year"...owns 23 seasons of minor league managerial experience with a record of 1,437-1,089 (.569), including 16 winning seasons...ranks fifth among active minor league managers in wins...joined the Yankees organization in 2006 after spending 26 seasons with the Cincinnati Reds as a player, coach and manager...took over as manager of the Reds on 7/28/03, replacing Bob Boone...was named *Baseball America*'s NL "Manager of the Year" for the first half of the 2004 season...also spent time on the Major League staff in 1993 as bench coach under manager Tony Perez...served as the organization's assistant minor league field coordinator in 1994...spent three-plus seasons as manager at Triple-A Louisville from 2000-03, where he went 296-245 (.547) and established franchise records for wins (296) and games managed (541)...in 2001, guided Louisville to its first IL championship...also had managerial assignments with Triple-A Indianapolis (1996-99), Double-A Chattanooga (1992, '95), Triple-A Nashville (1992), Single-A Charleston (1991), Single-A Cedar Rapids (1989-90) and Single-A Greensboro (1988)...coached at Double-A Vermont in 1997...began his coaching career in 1986, splitting the season at Single-A Tampa and Single-A Sarasota...**PLAYING CAREER:** Signed with the Reds in 1980 as a catcher and played in seven minor league seasons (1980-86)...in 403 minor league games, hit .238 with 16HR, 172RBI and 13SB...**PERSONAL:** Attended Chamberlain High School in Tampa, Fla., where he played football and baseball...was a second-team all-conference defensive end.

CODY MILEY SCHOLARSHIP FUND: In 2008, a scholarship fund was established for Cody Miley, the 17-year-old son of Scranton/Wilkes-Barre Manager Dave Miley, who was killed in a car accident in August of that year...the Cody Miley Memorial Art Scholarship Fund is awarded each year to a deserving and needy student from Chamberlain High School in Tampa.

SCOTT ALDRED – PITCHING COACH

BORN: 6/12/68 in Flint, Mich. • **RESIDES:** Fenton, Mich.

COACHING CAREER: Begins his second season as pitching coach with Scranton/Wilkes-Barre...guided a staff that led the IL in ERA (3.32) and shutouts (16) in 2009...is his fifth year as a professional coach, after spending the prior two seasons (2007-08) as pitching coach with Double-A Trenton and one season (2006) at Single-A Charleston in the same role...his 2007 staff had a 3.18 ERA, second-lowest among all full-season minor league clubs and struck out 1,159 batters, second-most among all Double-A clubs...led the Charleston pitching staff to the second-best ERA in the South Atlantic League (3.20) in 2006...**PLAYING CAREER:** Originally drafted by the Detroit Tigers in 1987...appeared in 229 games over an 11-year Major League career, posting a 20-39 record with a 6.02 ERA with six different teams (Detroit, 1990-92, '96; Colorado, 1993; Montreal, 1993; Minnesota, 1996-97; Tampa Bay, 1998-99 and Philadephia, 1999-2000)...**PERSONAL:** Married to Stacy with three daughters: Lindsey, Courtney and Kiley.

BUTCH WYNEGAR – HITTING COACH

BORN: 3/14/56 in York, Pa. • **RESIDES:** Longwood, Fla.

COACHING CAREER: Enters his fourth season with the Yankees organization as hitting coach at Triple-A Scranton/Wilkes-Barre...under his guidance in 2007, SWB led the IL in runs scored...spent his previous four years as the batting coach for the Milwaukee Brewers...guided the Brewers' offense to 196HR in 2003, tying for third-most among NL teams...under his direction, the Brewers established a franchise record with 327 doubles in 2005...prior to joining the Brewers, served as a coach in the Texas organization from 1995-2002...spent part of the 1999 season as the Rangers' Major League bullpen coach...**PLAYING CAREER:** Played 13 ML seasons with Minnesota (1976-82), the Yankees (1982-86) and California (1987-88)...was named the 1976 *Sporting News* "AL Rookie of the Year" and became the youngest player at the time to appear in an All-Star Game (20 yrs, 212 days)...while with the Yankees, caught Dave Righetti's no-hitter on 7/4/83 and Phil Niekro's 300th career win on 10/1/85...**PERSONAL:** Full name is Harold Delano Wynegar, Jr...married (Debbie) with one son (Mark)...graduated from Red Lion High School in York, Penn.

AARON LEDESMA - COACH

BORN: 9/12/1976 in Union City, Calif. • **RESIDES:** Spring Hill, Fla.

COACHING CAREER: Begins his third season as a professional coach, second with Scranton/Wilkes-Barre...made his coaching debut with Single-A Tampa in 2008...led SWB to the IL's second-best fielding percentage in 2009 (.980)...**PLAYING CAREER:** Originally drafted by the New York Mets in the second round of the 1990 First-Year Player Draft...batted .296 with 38 doubles, 4 triples, 2HR and 76RBI in 284 career Major League games over parts of five seasons with the Mets, Baltimore, Tampa Bay and Colorado...**PERSONAL:** Graduated from James Logan (Calif.) HS where he hit .488 as a senior...earned Junior College All-American honors at Chabot College in 1990...is married to Kersten with a son, Samuel (11).

DARREN LONDON - TRAINER

BORN: 12/26/66 in Sherman Station, Maine • **RESIDES:** Hilliard, Ohio

Enters his 21st consecutive season in the Yankees organization, 18th with the Triple-A affiliate...was honored as the 2006 IL "Athletic Trainer of the Year," as selected by the Professional Baseball Athletic Trainers Society (PBATS)...began his career in 1989 with Single-A Prince William where he worked for two seasons...was named trainer at Single-A Ft. Lauderdale in 1991 and moved to Double-A Albany in 1992...**PERSONAL:** Graduated from the University of Maine-Orono, where he earned a BS in physical education with a coaching minor.

LEE TRESSEL - STRENGTH AND CONDITIONING COACH

BORN: 5/6/81 in Cleveland, Ohio • **RESIDES:** Tampa, Fla.

Returns as SWB's strength and conditioning coach in 2010...served as the assistant strength and conditioning coordinator at the Yankees' minor league complex in Tampa, Fla in 2007 before joining Double-A Trenton's staff in 2008...served for three seasons (2004-06) as an assistant in the Yankees' baseball operations department under General Manager Brian Cashman...graduated from Baldwin Wallace College in Berea, Ohio, in 2003 with a degree in sports management and business.

2009 Scranton/Wilkes-Barre Yankees (AAA)

BATTERS	AVG	G	AB	R	H	2B	3B	HR	RBI	BB	SO	SB	CS	OBP	SLG	E
Bernier, Doug	.181	79	227	33	41	9	2	0	20	34	71	1	0	.305	.238	5
Berroa, Angel	.316	14	57	7	18	4	0	2	13	4	7	0	2	.365	.491	2
Cash, Kevin	.221	23	68	7	15	1	0	2	9	9	23	0	0	.312	.324	1
Cervelli, Francisco	.275	21	69	7	19	5	0	1	7	3	13	0	2	.311	.391	3
#Corona, Reegie	.200	44	160	13	32	7	0	3	14	9	20	4	0	.241	.300	8
*Curtis, Colin	.235	70	251	29	59	10	0	6	29	24	46	1	2	.302	.347	3
de Caster, Yurendell	.301	53	186	23	56	12	0	5	21	13	28	3	0	.369	.446	2
*Duncan, Eric	.204	95	323	35	66	12	1	4	24	16	69	1	0	.242	.285	11
Duncan, Shelley	.277	123	452	85	125	30	1	30	99	64	94	2	0	.370	.546	2
*Gardner, Brett	.091	4	11	3	1	0	0	0	0	5	1	3	0	.375	.091	0
#Guzman, Freddy	.286	6	21	7	6	0	1	0	1	5	5	7	0	.423	.381	0
#Guzman, Freddy	.224	88	308	39	69	7	4	2	14	23	49	41	7	.276	.292	2
Jackson, Austin	.300	132	504	67	151	23	9	4	65	40	123	24	4	.354	.405	2
Leone, Justin	.178	55	185	17	33	11	0	4	28	21	59	2	0	.259	.303	11
#Linden, Todd	.312	60	237	43	74	17	5	7	42	27	61	5	0	.381	.515	2
#Malec, Chris	.226	19	62	8	14	1	0	1	13	6	10	1	0	.300	.290	1
#Mendoza, Carlos	.222	3	9	1	2	1	0	0	1	1	3	0	0	.300	.333	1
*Miranda, Juan	.290	122	438	74	127	30	2	19	82	55	101	1	0	.369	.498	10
Molina, Jose	.250	2	4	0	1	1	0	0	1	1	0	0	0	.400	.500	0
Nady, Xavier	.200	2	5	0	1	1	0	0	0	1	1	0	0	.333	.400	0
Nunez, Luis	.214	25	70	11	15	2	0	0	4	4	7	2	1	.257	.243	2
#Pena, Ramiro	.231	43	156	18	36	9	0	2	9	18	28	5	1	.310	.327	2
Peterson, Brian	.176	6	17	3	3	1	0	0	1	4	7	0	0	.333	.235	1
Peterson, Brian	.143	20	49	6	7	2	0	1	3	13	19	0	0	.333	.245	3
Pilittere, P.J.	.244	28	86	8	21	6	0	1	9	3	9	0	0	.272	.349	2
Ransom, Cody	.240	31	96	24	23	7	1	3	16	19	22	0	0	.367	.427	6
*Robnett, Richie	.000	2	2	0	0	0	0	0	0	0	0	0	0	.000	.000	0
*Rodriguez, John	.261	93	322	47	84	18	2	14	59	37	85	0	2	.352	.460	1
Russo, Kevin	.326	90	353	51	115	18	2	5	31	42	55	13	7	.397	.431	12
Stewart, Chris	.280	78	232	33	65	11	0	1	18	25	29	1	1	.375	.341	5
Team Total	**.261**	**141**	**4603**	**654**	**1203**	**247**	**26**	**114**	**616**	**490**	**977**	**76**	**22**	**.337**	**.401**	**102**

PITCHERS	W-L	ERA	G	GS	CG	SHO	SV	IP	H	R	ER	HR	HB	BB	SO	WP
Aceves, Alfredo	2-0	3.80	4	4	0	0	0	23.2	18	11	10	3	1	5	18	0
Albaladejo, Jonathan	3-0	1.75	27	0	0	0	11	36.0	25	8	7	4	0	3	26	1
Arbiso, Cory	0-0	6.00	1	1	0	0	0	6.0	4	4	4	1	0	4	1	0
Bruney, Brian	0-0	9.00	1	1	0	0	0	1.0	2	1	1	0	0	0	1	0
Bush, Paul	2-2	4.86	7	2	0	0	0	16.2	13	10	9	1	0	7	20	1
Claggett, Anthony	7-7	3.07	39	5	0	0	4	82.0	78	32	28	6	3	32	43	3
Cox, J.B.	0-1	7.08	12	1	0	0	1	20.1	29	18	16	2	2	9	11	4
*Dunn, Michael	1-0	2.25	12	0	0	0	0	20.0	17	5	5	1	1	14	23	1
*Fossum, Casey	3-3	3.38	10	10	0	0	0	50.2	50	24	19	7	1	16	43	4
*Fossum, Casey	3-3	2.92	12	12	0	0	0	61.2	55	25	20	7	1	21	55	6
Hacker, Eric	0-1	7.88	3	3	0	0	0	16.0	19	14	14	3	2	4	12	0
Hirsh, Jason	4-0	1.35	6	6	0	0	0	26.2	24	4	4	2	0	6	21	0
Hughes, Phil	3-0	1.86	3	3	0	0	0	19.1	17	4	4	2	0	3	19	0
*Igawa, Kei	10-8	4.15	26	26	1	0	0	145.1	165	75	67	21	5	40	105	2
Jackson, Steven	0-0	1.88	7	1	0	0	1	14.1	16	3	3	1	0	3	8	0
Johnson, Jason	2-2	5.50	7	7	0	0	0	37.2	49	27	23	4	1	16	14	1
Kennedy, Ian	1-0	1.59	4	4	0	0	0	22.2	18	5	4	0	0	7	25	1
Kontos, George	3-4	3.35	9	9	1	0	0	51.0	44	24	19	6	2	21	39	2
*Kroenke, Zachary	7-1	1.99	36	2	0	0	4	72.1	54	24	16	4	0	30	55	3
*Marte, Damaso	0-1	2.45	11	0	0	0	0	11.0	10	3	3	2	0	4	9	0
Melancon, Mark	4-0	2.89	32	0	0	0	3	53.0	37	22	17	3	6	11	54	5
Mitre, Sergio	3-1	2.40	7	7	0	0	0	45.0	40	13	12	3	3	5	35	1
Nova, Ivan	1-4	5.10	12	12	1	0	0	67.0	72	39	38	4	3	28	43	4
Ortiz, Russ	2-1	1.59	3	3	0	0	0	17.0	14	4	3	1	0	8	12	2
Prihoda, Luke	1-0	1.69	2	0	0	0	0	5.1	5	1	1	0	0	1	4	0
Ramirez, Edwar	1-5	3.18	29	0	0	0	4	51.0	39	19	18	3	0	16	62	8
Robertson, David	0-3	1.84	8	0	0	0	2	14.2	10	7	3	0	0	6	25	0
Sanchez, Humberto	2-0	0.00	3	0	0	0	0	5.0	2	0	0	0	0	4	6	0
Sanchez, Romulo	5-5	4.04	19	13	0	0	0	64.2	66	31	29	3	5	34	64	8
Sanchez, Romulo	6-5	4.09	29	13	0	0	0	77.0	77	37	35	4	6	39	79	8
Sanit, Amaury	0-3	4.13	19	0	0	0	0	24.0	27	12	11	2	1	7	13	1
Stephens, Jason	1-1	5.40	3	1	0	0	0	6.2	7	9	4	2	0	5	8	0
Tomko, Brett	1-0	0.64	10	0	0	0	4	14.0	8	1	1	1	0	4	17	0
Towers, Josh	7-6	2.74	19	18	0	0	0	101.2	89	32	31	13	4	24	55	1
Towers, Josh	7-6	3.05	20	18	0	0	0	103.1	95	36	35	13	4	24	55	1
Valdez, Jose	2-1	4.19	9	0	0	0	0	19.1	23	9	9	2	0	10	18	2
Wang, Chien-Ming	1-0	0.00	2	2	1	1	0	13.0	7	0	0	0	0	3	7	0
Whelan, Kevin	0-0	2.84	14	0	0	0	1	12.2	7	4	4	0	0	13	22	0
Williams, Jeff	0-0	0.00	1	0	0	0	0	2.0	0	0	0	0	0	0	0	0
Wordekemper, Eric	2-0	4.32	10	0	0	0	1	16.2	19	8	8	2	0	2	12	0
Team Total	**81-60**	**3.32**	**141**	**141**	**4**	**16**	**36**	**1205.1**	**1124**	**507**	**445**	**109**	**40**	**405**	**950**	**55**

KEY: *- Lefthanded hitter/pitcher, # - switch hitter

Trenton Thunder (AA)

AFFILIATE SINCE 2003
Eastern League – Mercer County Waterfront Park
Office Address: One Thunder Rd., Trenton, NJ 08611
Telephone: (609) 394-3300. **Fax:** (609) 394-9666
Website: www.trentonthunder.com
General Manager, Chief Operating Officer: Will Smith
Director of Public Relations: Bill Cook
2009 Record, finish: 69-72, Third in North Division

TONY FRANKLIN - MANAGER

BORN: 6/9/50 in Portland, Maine • **RESIDES:** Los Angeles, Calif.

COACHING CAREER: Returns for his fourth season as Manager of the Thunder…joined Ozzie Smith's staff as a coach at the 2009 All-Star Futures Game…led the club to back-to-back Eastern League championships in 2007 and '08 in his first two seasons with the team…were the franchise's first titles in its 14-year history…also compiled the EL's best regular season record each of the two seasons…owns an 842-771 (.522) career managerial record over 14 seasons…also managed in the Arizona Fall League in 2007, leading the Peoria Javelinas to a 17-15 record…prior to joining the Yankees organization in 2007, spent most of the previous 11 years as the minor league infield instructor for the San Diego Padres…his managerial career began with the White Sox organization at Single-A Geneva of the NY-Penn League from 1982-85…managed at rookie-level Wytheville (1986) before taking over the helm of the Single-A Sarasota White Sox from 1987-89…served as manager for Double-A Birmingham from 1990-91, guiding the Barons to the 1991 SL Championship Series…led Single-A South Bend to the Midwest League title in 1993…also served as the interim manager with Triple-A Las Vegas in 2000…**PERSONAL:** Married to Haiba with three children: Derrick, Wayne and Shelby…was honored by San Diego in 1997 with the Jack Krol Award for Outstanding Minor League Instruction in the Padres organization…was honored at the 11th Annual Black Executive Awards on 2/26/09 in Trenton…managed former Heisman Trophy winner Bo Jackson for four rehab games while with Birmingham in 1991.

TOMMY PHELPS – PITCHING COACH

BORN: 3/7/74 in Seoul, S. Korea • **RESIDES:** Valrico, Fla.

COACHING CAREER: Begins his second season with the Thunder after serving as the Yankees' minor league rehabilitation coach in 2008…**PLAYING CAREER:** Pitched for 14 seasons from 1993-2006 with Montreal (1993-99), Detroit (2000-01), Florida (2002-04), Milwaukee (2005) and Yankees (2006) organizations…appeared in 75 combined Major League games (11 starts) with the Marlins and Brewers, posting a 4-5 record with one save and a 4.34 ERA…went 2-3 with a 4.00 ERA in 27 games (seven starts) for the 2003 World Series champion Marlins…the right-hander pitched in 330 career minor league games (199 starts), going 84-72 with five saves and a 4.14 ERA…**PERSONAL:** Full name is Thomas Allen Phelps…graduated from Robinson High School in Tampa, Fla. in 1992.

FRANK MENECHINO – HITTING COACH

BORN: 1/7/71 in Staten Island, N.Y. • **RESIDES:** Staten Island, N.Y.

COACHING CAREER: Returns for his second season as the Thunder's hitting coach after making his professional coaching debut in 2009…**PLAYING CAREER:** Played in 450 Major League games over parts of seven seasons with Oakland (1999-2004) and Toronto (2004-05), batting .240 with 58 doubles, 36HR and 149RBI…originally drafted by Chicago-AL in the 45th round of the 1993 First-Year Player Draft, was a minor league Rule 5 selection by Oakland in 1997…the infielder also spent time in the Cincinnati (2006), Yankees (2006), Colorado (2007) and San Diego (2007) organizations…played for Team Italy in the 2006 World Baseball Classic and played in the Italian Baseball League in 2008…**PERSONAL:** Graduated from Wagner High School in Staten Island…played ball at the University of Alabama.

VICTOR VALENCIA – COACH

BORN: 5/30/77 in Maracay, Venezuela • **RESIDES:** Maracay, Venezuela

COACHING CAREER: Enters his third season of coaching after making his debut with short-season Single-A Staten Island in 2008…**PLAYING CAREER:** Was signed by the Yankees as a non-drafted free agent in 1993 and played 10 seasons of minor league baseball in the Yankees (1995-2000), Cincinnati (2001), Texas (2002), Cleveland (2003-04) and Toronto (2004) systems…the catcher combined for a .224 career average with 120 doubles, 114HR and 395RBI in 885 games…named the best defensive catcher in the Eastern League by *Baseball America* following the 1999 season…played with Newark in the independent Atlantic League in 2006.

TIM LENTYCH - TRAINER

BORN: 9/3/78 in South Bend, Ind. • **RESIDES:** Tampa, Fla.

Begins his third season as the Thunder's trainer and his seventh year in the Yankees organization…named the 2009 "Athletic Trainer of the Year" in the EL…spent three seasons as the trainer with Single-A Charleston from 2005-07 after making his pro debut as the trainer for short-season Single-A Staten Island in 2004…earned his bachelor's degree in applied sciences and technology with a concentration in athletic training from Ball State University in 2001 and a master's degree from the University of Tennessee in 2004…previously worked as an athletic training intern with the Baltimore Orioles in 2001.

JASON MEREDITH - STRENGTH AND CONDITIONING COACH

BORN: 6/5/83 in Tampa, Fla. • **RESIDES:** Tampa, Fla.

Begins his first year with Trenton's staff…has a BS in Exercise Sport Science/Athletic Training from Iowa State University and a MS in Applied Physiology and Kinesiology from University of Florida… spent 2009 with Reading in the Phillies organization.

2009 Trenton Thunder (AA)

BATTERS	AVG	G	AB	R	H	2B	3B	HR	RBI	BB	SO	SB	CS	OBP	SLG	E
#Anson, Kyle	.227	57	163	23	37	9	0	2	24	36	33	1	0	.374	.319	8
Baker, Ryan J.	.125	8	16	0	2	0	0	0	0	2	3	0	0	.222	.125	0
Cervelli, Francisco	.190	16	58	8	11	1	0	2	7	6	13	0	0	.266	.310	5
*Cooper, James	.240	81	258	42	62	12	3	1	31	22	27	2	2	.326	.322	1
#Corona, Reegie	.287	85	307	56	88	21	2	3	26	56	50	12	4	.397	.397	8
*Curtis, Colin	.268	56	213	28	57	14	4	1	19	20	37	7	0	.343	.385	1
*Cusick, Matthew	.240	28	96	9	23	4	0	0	9	10	16	0	1	.324	.281	0
*Fortenberry, Seth	.160	38	125	12	20	6	3	0	8	15	40	5	1	.259	.256	1
Gil, Jose	.194	12	36	2	7	2	0	2	4	0	7	0	0	.194	.417	1
Gonzalez, Edwar	.232	115	413	46	96	26	1	4	37	30	93	7	3	.296	.329	5
Hall, Noah	.245	59	200	29	49	7	3	3	33	21	23	5	2	.320	.355	0
*Krum, Austin	.234	77	290	43	68	14	5	2	24	36	68	11	2	.321	.338	4
#Malec, Chris	.279	117	430	42	120	23	2	8	56	42	63	0	1	.351	.398	6
#Mendoza, Carlos	.286	7	14	2	4	1	0	0	1	0	3	0	0	.286	.357	0
Molina, Jose	.000	3	7	0	0	0	0	0	0	2	4	0	0	.300	.000	0
Montero, Jesus	.317	44	167	19	53	10	0	9	33	14	21	0	0	.370	.539	0
Nunez, Eduardo	.322	123	497	70	160	26	1	9	55	22	63	19	7	.349	.433	33
Pilittere, P.J.	.198	27	96	5	19	3	0	0	8	7	8	0	0	.260	.229	0
*Robnett, Richie	.269	46	156	15	42	11	2	2	12	12	36	2	2	.321	.404	1
*Rye, Jack	.111	3	9	0	1	1	0	0	0	2	3	0	0	.333	.222	0
*Santana, Francisco	.000	5	7	2	0	0	0	0	0	0	2	0	0	.000	.000	0
*Smith, Kevin	.247	48	158	19	39	7	1	2	14	10	44	0	1	.296	.342	5
*Snyder, Justin	.195	94	262	25	51	9	0	3	29	29	49	1	2	.279	.263	9
Vazquez, Jorge	.329	57	225	30	74	15	1	13	56	8	45	0	0	.357	.578	8
#Vechionacci, Marcos	.213	122	422	44	90	18	1	10	43	35	113	0	0	.278	.332	20
Team Total	**.254**	**141**	**4625**	**571**	**1173**	**240**	**29**	**76**	**529**	**437**	**864**	**72**	**28**	**.324**	**.367**	**125**

PITCHERS	W-L	ERA	G	GS	CG	SHO	SV	IP	H	R	ER	HR	HB	BB	SO	WP
*Arias, Wilkins	5-4	3.65	48	2	0	0	0	61.2	53	26	25	4	2	22	66	3
Bartleski, Philip	0-1	12.00	2	0	0	0	0	3.0	6	4	4	0	0	1	3	0
*Bleich, Jeremy	3-6	6.65	13	13	0	0	0	65.0	84	54	48	6	6	34	60	5
Bruney, Brian	0-0	0.00	1	1	0	0	0	1.0	0	0	0	0	0	0	0	0
Bush, Paul	1-1	1.33	5	5	0	0	0	20.1	8	3	3	1	1	11	23	1
Castillo, Noel	0-0	11.25	6	0	0	0	0	8.0	11	10	10	1	2	10	12	2
Cox, J.B.	0-2	8.31	5	0	0	0	0	4.1	5	4	4	1	0	6	4	1
*De La Rosa, Wilkin	4-5	3.48	16	16	0	0	0	82.2	67	37	32	11	2	41	77	4
Duff, Grant	4-2	3.22	21	0	0	0	1	36.1	30	15	13	1	2	16	37	4
*Dunn, Michael	3-3	3.71	26	0	0	0	2	53.1	41	23	22	3	2	32	76	0
Garcia, Christian	2-0	0.71	5	5	0	0	0	25.1	15	3	2	1	1	17	24	1
Hacker, Eric	1-1	4.11	3	3	0	0	0	15.1	16	10	7	0	0	7	8	2
Horne, Alan	0-3	11.15	5	4	0	0	0	15.1	25	21	19	3	1	16	13	2
Hovis, Jonathan	0-1	4.91	2	0	0	0	0	3.2	4	3	2	1	2	1	4	0
Johnson, Jason	0-2	14.54	2	2	0	0	0	8.2	20	14	14	3	0	4	8	2
Kontos, George	1-1	2.66	4	4	0	0	0	20.1	19	7	6	0	2	9	24	5
McAllister, Zach	7-5	2.23	22	22	0	0	0	121.0	98	39	30	4	7	33	96	0
Mendoza, Carlos	0-0	0.00	1	0	0	0	0	1.0	0	0	0	0	0	0	0	0
Nova, Ivan	5-4	2.36	12	12	0	0	0	72.1	65	27	19	3	2	31	47	5
Olbrychowski, Adam	0-0	0.00	1	0	0	0	0	1.0	2	0	0	0	0	0	0	0
Pendleton, Lance	1-3	4.47	8	8	0	0	0	44.1	40	25	22	4	2	15	43	1
Pope, Ryan	5-12	4.78	26	25	0	0	0	141.1	155	91	75	7	8	34	106	4
Sanchez, Humberto	2-0	3.72	12	0	0	0	1	19.1	13	11	8	3	0	8	19	0
Sanit, Amaury	1-2	2.95	21	0	0	0	10	21.1	13	7	7	1	0	8	18	2
Schmidt, Josh	8-4	1.61	46	5	0	0	0	83.2	57	16	15	2	5	38	96	4
Stephens, Jason	1-1	2.98	13	8	0	0	0	45.1	40	17	15	3	2	14	21	2
Texeira, Kanekoa	9-6	2.84	41	6	0	0	2	101.1	90	39	32	7	2	43	88	7
Valdez, Jose	1-1	3.05	34	0	0	0	10	38.1	32	17	13	2	3	23	42	13
Whelan, Kevin	4-0	2.63	30	0	0	0	2	54.2	38	17	16	1	1	28	63	5
Wordekemper, Eric	1-2	3.00	28	0	0	0	1	42.0	31	15	14	3	3	13	32	0
Team Total	**69-72**	**3.54**	**141**	**141**	**0**	**15**	**29**	**1211.1**	**1078**	**555**	**476**	**76**	**58**	**515**	**1110**	**75**

KEY: *- Lefthanded hitter/pitcher, # - switch hitter

Tampa Yankees (A)

AFFILIATE SINCE 1994
Florida State League – George M. Steinbrenner Field
Office Address: One Steinbrenner Dr., Tampa, FL 33614
Telephone: (813) 875-7753. **Fax**: (813) 673-3174
Web Site: www.steinbrennerfield.com
General Manager: Vance Smith
2009 Record, finish: Florida State League Champions
30-37, Fifth in North Division (1st Half)
47-19, First in North Division (2nd Half)

TORRE TYSON – MANAGER

BORN: 12/31/75 in Tampa, Fla. • **RESIDES:** Columbia, Mo.

COACHING CAREER: Begins his first season as Tampa's Manager…served the previous three years as Single-A Charleston's skipper, leaving as the RiverDogs' all-time winningest manager with 232 career victories…had served the two previous seasons as Charleston's hitting coach (2005-06)…was selected as a coach for the South Atlantic League's All-Star game each of the last two years (2008-09) and joined the Yankees' Major League staff in September 2008…is his seventh season as a professional instructor/coach, having previously worked as a coach with short-season Single-A Staten Island in 2004…**PLAYING CAREER:** Began his professional baseball career in 1998 when he signed with the Boston Red Sox as a non-drafted free agent…after spending almost two seasons in the Boston farm system, joined the Yankees in 2000 and spent time with Single-A Greensboro, Single-A Tampa and Double-A Norwich…**PERSONAL:** He and his wife, Jennifer, have a son, Tagger, and a daughter, Taryn…graduated from John Borroughs High School (Mo.) in 1994…played baseball at the University of Missouri…is the son of former Major League infielder Mike Tyson.

GREG PAVLIK - PITCHING COACH

BORN: 3/10/50 in Washington, D.C. • **RESIDES:** Tierra Verde, Fla.

COACHING CAREER: Begins his ninth consecutive season as the pitching coach for the Tampa Yankees after serving in the same capacity for the Triple-A Columbus Clippers in 2001…his 2009 staff tied for the fourth-lowest ERA (3.46) and walked the fourth-fewest batters (369)…guided a 2008 staff that led the FSL in shutouts (13) and ranked second in strikeouts (996) and third in ERA (3.53)…in 2004, helped lead the Tampa pitching staff to the Florida State League Championship…prior to joining the coaching ranks in 2001, spent four years as the roving pitching instructor for the Yankees organization from 1997-2000…before joining the Yankees, spent 26 seasons in the New York Mets organization…began his coaching career in 1977 as a pitching instructor for Single-A Tidewater…coached for the Mets at the Major League level from 1985-86, 1988-91 and again from 1994-96…**PLAYING CAREER:** Was the Mets' second pick in the secondary phase of the January 1971 free-agent draft…in 1971, tied for the Appalachian League lead in victories and ranked sixth in ERA and was named to the league's All-Star team…in 1973, finished eighth in the California League in ERA…won a career-high nine games for Triple-A Victoria of the Texas League in 1976…**PERSONAL:** Graduated from Thomas Edison High School in Alexandria, Va. in 1968…attended the University of North Carolina.

JULIUS MATOS – HITTING COACH

BORN:12/12/74 in New York, N.Y. • **RESIDES:** Racine, Wisc.

COACHING CAREER: Begins his second season as hitting coach with Tampa after making his professional coaching debut in 2008 as a coach with the Trenton Thunder…guided the T-Yanks to the third-highest batting average in 2009 anchored by FSL "Player of the Year" Austin Romine…**PLAYING CAREER:** Had a 13-year professional playing career in the Cleveland (1994-95), Arizona (1998-99), San Diego (2000-02, '06), Kansas City (2003), Toronto (2004, '05) and Montreal (2004) organizations…also played in the Independent Northern League with Thunder Bay in 1995 and Sioux City in 1996…saw Major League action with the Padres in 2002 and the Royals in 2003, combining to bat .244 (59-for-242) with 4 doubles, 4HR and 26RBI in 104 games…was originally selected by Cleveland in the 16th round of the 1994 First-Year Player Draft.

DEREK SHUMPERT – COACH

BORN: 9/30/75 in St. Louis, Mo. • **RESIDES:** St. Louis, Mo.

COACHING CAREER: Begins his first season with Tampa having served for two years as hitting coach with the GCL Yankees… coached with the Houston Miracle 18 and under baseball team for two seasons (2000-01)…**PLAYING CAREER:** Selected by the Yankees in the 10th round of the 1993 First-Year Player Draft…played seven seasons in the Yankees minor league system, batting .238 with 76 doubles, 23 triples, 17HR, 160RBI and 84SB in 588 career minor league games…from 2002-07, played in the Australian Baseball League, winning three championships…also played with the Australian National team, capturing the Claxton Shield National Championship in 2006…**PERSONAL:** Graduated from St. Thomas Aquinas-Mercy High School in Missouri where he played baseball, basketball and football…he and his wife, Anielle, have two daughters, Jade and Allanah.

KRIS RUSSELL - TRAINER

BORN: 7/11/80 in St. Petersburg, Fla. • **RESIDES:** Tarpon Springs, Fla.

Begins his third season as a trainer at Tampa…spent the previous four seasons in the Tampa Bay organization (2004-07)…a St. Petersburg, Fla., native, Russell graduated from the University of South Florida with a degree in athletic training in 2004…while at USF, he worked with the football, basketball, baseball and men's soccer teams.

JAY SIGNORELLI - STRENGTH AND CONDITIONING COACH

BORN: 5/27/78 in Bradenton, Fla. • **RESIDES:** Nashville, Tenn.

Enters his third season as strength and conditioning coordinator with Single-A Tampa…spent prior two seasons in the Diamondbacks system at short-season Single-A Yakima in 2007 and Single-A Lancaster in 2006…prior to his work with Major League organizations, worked at the International Performance Institute at the IMG Academy as well as Velocity Sports Performance…graduated from Tennessee Wesleyan with a bachelors degree in exercise science…was a pitcher in college, also playing at Manatee Community College and Florida Southern…was selected by the Yankees in the 32nd round 1998 First-Year Player Draft but did not sign…is a member of the National Strength and Conditioning Association…he and his wife, Julia, have a son, Brody.

2009 Tampa Yankees (A)

BATTERS	AVG	G	AB	R	H	2B	3B	HR	RBI	BB	SO	SB	CS	OBP	SLG	E
Adams, David	.281	65	231	37	65	17	6	7	41	26	39	3	4	.360	.498	5
Baisley, Brian	.170	33	106	8	18	3	0	0	6	9	37	2	0	.261	.198	4
*Baldridge, Tommy	.204	17	49	6	10	2	0	0	0	3	8	2	0	.250	.245	1
Brewer, Daniel	.290	59	224	32	65	7	3	4	29	22	46	13	3	.359	.402	0
*Cusick, Matthew	.313	63	217	27	68	14	3	1	17	25	23	5	3	.384	.419	7
*Fortenberry, Seth	.175	59	189	18	33	7	2	6	27	20	58	3	0	.265	.328	1
Fryer, Eric	.250	59	224	34	56	11	2	2	24	27	43	11	5	.333	.344	4
Gil, Jose	.208	29	96	10	20	4	0	0	8	5	24	0	0	.248	.250	3
*Hilligoss, Mitch	.233	51	163	15	38	7	2	0	14	11	25	5	2	.282	.301	5
#Ibarra, Walter	.265	74	234	38	62	10	1	0	16	10	23	11	5	.294	.316	12
*Krum, Austin	.272	53	191	32	52	7	3	0	14	35	43	7	4	.395	.340	1
Laird, Brandon	.266	124	451	53	120	20	4	13	75	39	75	1	1	.329	.415	16
#Landoni, Emerson	.185	10	27	0	5	0	0	0	3	5	4	0	1	.333	.185	1
Maruszak, Addison	.148	24	81	8	12	1	0	0	4	7	14	2	3	.222	.160	5
Montero, Jesus	.356	48	180	26	64	15	1	8	37	14	26	0	0	.406	.583	2
Nunez, Luis	.304	49	158	23	48	10	3	3	23	14	16	4	5	.362	.462	9
Romine, Austin	.276	118	442	61	122	28	3	13	72	29	78	11	5	.322	.441	10
Rufino, Wady	.235	40	136	16	32	8	0	1	9	8	39	2	2	.295	.316	5
*Rye, Jack	.256	75	238	31	61	13	5	1	21	40	42	7	11	.365	.366	2
*Smith, Kevin	.317	63	218	30	69	15	2	1	29	19	48	4	0	.370	.417	0
Strausbaugh, Steve	.500	1	4	0	2	0	0	0	0	0	1	0	0	.500	.500	-
*Sublett, Damon	.270	114	397	68	107	24	11	4	41	65	93	11	7	.376	.416	11
Team Total	**.265**	**133**	**4257**	**573**	**1129**	**223**	**51**	**64**	**510**	**433**	**806**	**104**	**61**	**.337**	**.387**	**123**

PITCHERS	W-L	ERA	G	GS	CG	SHO	SV	IP	H	R	ER	HR	HB	BB	SO	WP
*Banuelos, Manuel	0-0	0.00	1	0	0	0	0	1.0	0	0	0	0	0	0	2	0
Bartleski, Philip	4-1	2.86	16	0	0	0	1	28.1	23	9	9	2	3	8	30	0
Betances, Dellin	2-5	5.48	11	11	0	0	0	44.1	48	29	27	2	2	27	44	3
*Bleich, Jeremy	6-4	3.40	14	14	0	0	0	79.1	79	34	30	4	0	22	56	6
Castillo, Noel	3-2	2.91	31	2	0	0	2	58.2	52	24	19	1	8	31	56	5
*De La Rosa, Wilkin	1-0	1.29	3	3	0	0	0	14.0	9	2	2	0	0	4	17	1
Duff, Grant	0-1	3.82	24	1	0	0	1	35.1	35	17	15	2	1	11	26	2
Heredia, Jairo	2-2	6.91	4	4	1	1	0	14.1	25	14	11	2	0	5	10	3
Heyer, Craig	4-3	3.11	30	6	0	0	1	72.1	73	30	25	1	1	9	29	2
Hovis, Jonathan	2-2	3.38	44	0	0	0	22	48.0	44	19	18	2	0	13	41	1
*Lare, Trenton	0-0	9.00	1	0	0	0	0	2.0	2	2	2	1	0	0	2	0
Marte, Ronny	1-0	1.93	2	0	0	0	0	4.2	3	1	1	0	0	2	3	0
Mitchell, D.J.	8-6	2.87	19	18	1	0	0	103.1	93	41	33	1	8	38	83	10
Mitre, Sergio	1-0	1.93	2	2	0	0	0	9.1	10	6	2	0	1	2	8	1
Noesi, Hector	3-0	3.92	9	9	0	0	0	41.1	34	18	18	3	1	4	40	2
Nolte, Charles	1-1	5.34	15	0	0	0	0	32.0	43	23	19	2	0	11	14	5
Norton, Tim	2-1	2.75	23	0	0	0	0	36.0	31	12	11	1	3	9	30	0
Nunez, Luis	0-0	0.00	1	0	0	0	0	1.0	0	0	0	0	0	2	0	0
Olbrychowski, Adam	3-2	2.73	32	2	0	0	0	62.2	55	23	19	3	2	43	52	3
Ortiz, Jonathan	3-3	4.67	24	0	0	0	8	27.0	35	16	14	3	0	7	36	2
Pendleton, Lance	11-5	2.58	20	18	0	0	0	104.2	101	43	30	1	5	31	87	3
Phelps, David	3-1	1.17	7	7	0	0	0	38.1	34	9	5	1	0	6	32	2
Ramirez, Jose A.	0-0	0.00	1	0	0	0	0	3.0	1	0	0	0	0	0	2	0
Rulon, Brad	3-0	3.47	14	0	0	0	2	23.1	18	10	9	2	0	13	22	0
Sanchez, Humberto	0-1	4.76	9	3	0	0	0	11.1	7	7	6	1	1	4	11	1
Sanit, Amaury	0-0	0.00	4	0	0	0	0	6.0	5	0	0	0	0	0	5	0
Smith, Kevin	0-0	0.00	1	0	0	0	0	1.2	0	0	0	0	0	1	0	0
Stephens, Jason	3-4	4.50	11	8	0	0	0	50.0	55	27	25	3	3	13	39	0
Venditte, Pat	2-0	2.21	21	0	0	0	2	36.2	37	11	9	1	0	9	47	0
Zink, Ryan	9-12	5.07	26	25	0	0	0	135.0	157	87	76	10	7	44	95	6
Team Total	**77-56**	**3.46**	**133**	**133**	**2**	**10**	**39**	**1125.0**	**1109**	**514**	**433**	**49**	**46**	**369**	**919**	**58**

KEY: *- Lefthanded hitter/pitcher, # - switch hitter

Charleston RiverDogs (A)

AFFILIATE SINCE 2005
South Atlantic League – Joseph P. Riley, Jr. Ballpark
Office Address: 360 Fishburne Street, Charleston, SC 29403
Telephone: (843) 723-7241. **Fax:** (843) 723-2641
Web site: www.riverdogs.com
Executive Vice President & General Manager: Dave Echols
Media Contact: Danny Reed
2009 Record, finish: 39-31, Second in Southern Division (1st Half)
35-34, Third in Southern Division (2nd Half)

GREG COLBRUNN – MANAGER

BORN: 7/26/69 in Fontana, Calif. • **RESIDES:** Mt. Pleasant, S.C.

COACHING CAREER: Enters his first season as Charleston's manager...served the previous three years as the club's hitting coach...guided the 2008 RiverDogs to the SAL's second-highest average (.256) and second-most runs scored (705)...**PLAYING CAREER:** Selected by the Montreal Expos in the sixth round of the 1987 First-Year Player Draft...played in 992 Major League games over 13 seasons for the Expos (1992-93), Florida Marlins (1994-96), Minnesota Twins (1997), Atlanta Braves (1997,'98), Colorado Rockies (1998), Arizona Diamondbacks (1998-2002,'04) and Seattle Mariners (2003)...was a member of the Diamondbacks' World Series Championship squad in 2001...**PERSONAL:** With wife, Erika and daughters, Danielle and Kelsey Paige, makes home in nearby Mount Pleasant, S.C...graduated in 1987 from Fontana High School (Calif.), earning All-State honors in baseball and All-Conference honors in football...turned down a baseball scholarship to Stanford in order to sign with Montreal.

JEFF WARE – PITCHING COACH

BORN: 11/11/70 in Norfolk, Va. • **RESIDES:** Palm Harbor, Fla.

COACHING CAREER: Enters his third season as pitching coach with Charleston, having served the same role with short-season Single-A Staten Island in 2007...his 2008 staff ranked second in the SAL in ERA (3.41), strikeouts (1,123) and shutouts (12)...spent the 2006 season as the pitching coach for the North Shore Spirit in the Can-Am League, guiding the Spirit pitching staff to a league-best 58 wins and a 2.78 combined ERA...**PLAYING CAREER:** Selected by the Toronto Blue Jays in the first round of the 1991 First-Year Player Draft (35th overall), made stops in the Milwaukee Brewers, Anaheim Angels, Chicago White Sox and Blue Jays organizations...appeared in 18 Major League games with the Blue Jays over two seasons (1995-96), going 3-6 with a 7.47 ERA...was a member of Team USA in the Pan-American Games, winning a bronze medal in 1991...**PERSONAL:** Went 22-9 in three seasons at Old Dominion University in Virginia...graduate of First Colonial High School in Virginia Beach.

JUSTIN TURNER – HITTING COACH

BORN: 12/19/79 in Indianapolis, Ind. • **RESIDES:** Lake Wales, Fla.

COACHING CAREER: Makes his professional coaching debut with the RiverDogs in 2010...**PLAYING CAREER:** Originally selected by the Angels in the eighth round of the 2001 First-Year Player Draft, the former infielder played four seasons of minor league ball in the Angels and Red Sox systems...**PERSONAL:** Played ball at Warner Robbins College in Florida.

CARLOS MENDOZA – COACH

BORN: 11/27/79 in Barquisimeto, Venezuela • **RESIDES:** Barquisimeto, Venezuela

COACHING CAREER: Joins Charleston after making his coaching debut with Staten Island in 2009...**PLAYING CAREER:** Originally signed by San Francisco as a non-drafted free agent in 1996, the utility infielder played 13 seasons of minor league baseball in the Giants and Yankees organizations as well as three years for the Independant Pensacola Pelicans...the switch-hitter owned .232 average with 97 doubles, 15 triples, 19HR and 200RBI in 705 career minor league games...he also had two brief Major League appearances, with the Mets in 1997 and the Rockies in 2000, appearing in 28 combined games.

SCOTT DiFRANCISCO - TRAINER

BORN: 10/8/84 in Hanover, N.H. • **RESIDES:** Thetford, Vt.

Returns for his third season as Charleston's trainer...completed an internship with Mark Littlefield at the Yankees Tampa complex during the 2006 Gulf Coast League season...graduated from Ball State University with a Bachelor of Science in athletic training...was also the head manager for the Ball State men's basketball team.

KAZ MANABE – STRENGTH AND CONDITIONING COACH

BORN: 9/13/72 in Iwakuni, Japan • **RESIDES:** Iwakuni, Japan

Begins his second season with Charleston and in the Yankees organization...spent the 2008 season in the same role with Single-A Beloit in the Twins organization...following his graduation from Hiroshima University in Japan, Manabe worked as a personal trainer before coming to California State University, Northridge to earn his Masters degree in Kinesiology.

2009 Charleston RiverDogs (A)

BATTERS	AVG	G	AB	R	H	2B	3B	HR	RBI	BB	SO	SB	CS	OBP	SLG	E
Abeita, Mitch	.225	74	249	28	56	12	1	4	32	31	58	1	0	.322	.329	8
Adams, David	.290	67	259	32	75	23	2	0	34	35	49	8	4	.385	.394	9
#Almonte, Abraham	.280	115	440	63	123	14	10	5	56	35	81	36	5	.333	.391	6
Angelini, Carmen	.197	33	132	18	26	5	0	1	8	8	32	6	1	.255	.258	18
Baisley, Brian	.339	29	109	12	37	12	0	2	23	12	31	0	0	.402	.505	2
*Baldridge, Tommy	.184	42	125	13	23	3	0	1	8	8	19	3	0	.233	.232	2
Brewer, Daniel	.323	58	201	38	65	18	3	2	25	33	49	9	5	.429	.473	4
Farnham, Jeffrey	.323	20	62	13	20	6	0	1	10	5	13	0	1	.389	.468	2
French, Neall	.238	64	210	25	50	6	1	2	22	29	70	0	0	.344	.305	2
*Grote, Taylor	.232	113	418	54	97	22	0	4	42	48	139	8	3	.311	.313	6
#Ibarra, Walter	.241	12	29	2	7	0	0	0	3	2	10	1	0	.290	.241	6
*Joseph, Corban	.300	100	380	39	114	17	8	4	57	49	61	8	5	.381	.418	18
*Kruml, Raymond	.246	100	382	53	94	15	4	2	35	26	100	23	5	.297	.322	5
*Lassiter, Garrison	.260	74	265	25	69	12	1	2	29	22	74	3	0	.330	.336	22
Lyon, Mike	.236	54	165	15	39	6	1	2	10	17	55	3	1	.319	.321	5
Maruszak, Addison	.263	64	217	29	57	4	1	2	20	32	44	6	1	.367	.318	14
Mesa, Melky	.225	133	497	76	112	24	7	20	74	51	168	18	6	.309	.423	7
Pirela, Jose	.295	97	404	65	119	23	6	0	46	37	65	9	8	.354	.381	17
*Weems, Chase	.260	55	173	19	45	10	1	1	14	15	55	0	0	.317	.347	3
Team Total	**.260**	**139**	**4717**	**619**	**1228**	**232**	**46**	**55**	**548**	**495**	**1173**	**142**	**45**	**.337**	**.364**	**175**

PITCHERS	W	ERA	G	GS	CG	SHO	SV	IP	H	R	ER	HR	HB	BB	SO	WP
Arbiso, Cory	4-7	4.85	30	10	0	0	1	91.0	109	58	49	8	3	14	62	1
*Banuelos, Manuel	9-5	2.67	25	19	0	0	0	108.0	88	40	32	4	8	28	104	13
Barreda, Manuel	1-0	13.50	2	0	0	0	0	2.2	1	4	4	0	0	4	2	0
Braboy, Brandon	4-5	3.97	33	9	0	0	1	93.0	83	51	41	8	8	24	77	12
Brackman, Andrew	2-12	5.91	29	19	0	0	0	106.2	106	79	70	8	10	76	103	26
Erickson, Casey	3-3	2.25	21	3	0	0	0	44.0	51	14	11	0	2	13	37	3
Flannery, Ryan	0-0	10.13	6	0	0	0	0	5.1	12	7	6	0	0	1	10	0
Heidler, Paul	0-0	4.50	2	0	0	0	0	4.0	5	3	2	1	0	3	4	0
Heredia, Jairo	1-1	2.37	4	4	0	0	0	19.0	14	6	5	1	1	1	17	0
Horne, Alan	0-1	5.50	3	3	0	0	0	18.0	17	12	11	1	2	11	13	6
Kapala, Daniel	6-2	2.64	38	4	0	0	2	95.1	84	36	28	2	9	26	50	7
*Lare, Trenton	2-3	2.76	7	7	0	0	0	42.1	36	16	13	0	1	7	35	4
Marquez, Dickson	1-0	0.00	2	0	0	0	0	4.0	1	0	0	0	0	0	4	0
Marshall, Brett	3-6	5.56	17	17	0	0	0	87.1	98	67	54	7	9	37	60	8
Mitchell, D.J.	4-1	1.95	6	6	0	0	0	37.0	31	16	8	1	1	6	42	5
Noesi, Hector	3-4	2.38	17	11	0	0	0	75.2	62	24	20	3	0	11	78	0
Nolte, Charles	4-3	5.26	22	2	0	0	1	51.1	59	31	30	5	2	17	39	12
Ortiz, Jonathan	0-1	1.26	24	0	0	0	9	28.2	21	6	4	1	2	3	40	3
*Patterson, Garrett	0-0	20.25	1	0	0	0	0	1.1	5	4	3	0	0	1	1	1
Patterson, Paul	0-0	1.59	2	1	0	0	0	5.2	8	1	1	0	0	1	4	1
Phelps, David	10-3	2.80	19	19	0	0	0	112.2	117	48	35	9	4	25	90	5
Prihoda, Luke	3-0	3.10	12	0	0	0	2	20.1	21	7	7	1	0	0	23	1
Rodriguez, Wilton	1-0	6.75	2	2	0	0	0	9.1	11	8	7	1	1	2	8	2
Rulon, Brad	4-1	1.18	29	0	0	0	1	53.1	35	11	7	2	2	12	58	6
Smith, Brett	0-1	3.00	3	3	0	0	0	15.0	11	8	5	0	2	9	3	3
Tatis, Gabriel	3-2	5.68	15	0	0	0	0	25.1	25	16	16	2	2	16	20	3
Venditte, Pat	2-2	1.47	28	0	0	0	20	30.2	24	8	5	1	0	2	40	0
*Walker, Edwin	2-0	0.78	14	0	0	0	1	23.0	14	2	2	0	0	4	20	0
Williams, Jeff	2-2	3.66	13	0	0	0	3	19.2	21	8	8	2	2	4	18	0
Team Total	**74-65**	**3.54**	**139**	**139**	**0**	**12**	**41**	**1229.2**	**1170**	**591**	**484**	**68**	**71**	**358**	**1062**	**122**

KEY: *- Lefthanded hitter/pitcher, # - switch hitter

Staten Island Yankees (Short-Season A)

AFFILIATE SINCE 1999
New York-Penn League – Richmond County Bank Ballpark at St. George
Office Address: 75 Richmond Terrace, Staten Island, NY 10301
Telephone: (718) 720-9265. **Fax:** (718) 273-5763
Website: www.siyanks.com
Executive VP, General Manager: Jane Rogers
Media Contact: John McCutchan
2009 Record, finish: 47-29, First in the McNamara Division, NYPL Champions

JOSH PAUL - MANAGER

BORN: 5/19/75 in Evanston, Ill. • **RESIDES:** Naperville, Ill.

COACHING CAREER: Returns for his second season Manager of the Staten Island Yankees, after guiding the club to their fifth title in 2009...**PLAYING CAREER**: Was a career .244 batter with 35 doubles, 10HR and 73RBI in 321 games across nine seasons with Chicago-AL (1999-2003), Chicago-NL (2003), Los Angeles-AL (2004-05) and Tampa Bay (2006-07), appearing in all but nine games at catcher...played the 2008 season at Triple-A Round Rock before being released in June...was originally drafted by the White Sox in the second round of the 1996 First-Year Player Draft...saw action as a defensive replacement in three postseason games, one in the 2000 Division Series vs. Seattle, and two contests in the 2005 playoffs vs. the Yankees (Division Series) and at Chicago-AL (ALCS)...**PERSONAL:** Played collegiately at Vanderbilt where he was named All-SEC as a sophomore...was inducted into the Cape Cod Hall of Fame on 11/4/06, honoring his achievement as the only player in the league's history to win the batting title, MVP and Outstanding Pro Prospect Award in the same season (1995 with Cotuit)...is writing a book on the mental game of baseball.

PAT DANEKER – PITCHING COACH

BORN: 1/14/76 in Williamsport, Pa. • **RESIDES:** Voorhees, N.J.

COACHING CAREER: Enters his third season as Staten Island's pitching coach...his 2009 staff led the league in ERA (2.53), tied for tops in shutouts (12) and ranked second in wins (47)...in 2008, his staff compiled the most wins (49) and the second-lowest ERA (2.98) in the NYPL...**PLAYING CAREER:** Selected by Chicago (AL) in the fifth round of the 1997 First-Year Player Draft...saw his lone Major League action with the White Sox in 2000, pitching in three games (2GS) with a 4.20 ERA without earning a decision...played for five seasons in the White Sox (1997-2000), Toronto (2000-01) and Chicago Cubs (2001) organizations before joining the independent Atlantic League from 2002-06 where he pitched for Camden, Pennsylvania, Somerset and Newark...compiled a career minor league record of 65-94 with a 5.27 ERA in 237 games (207 starts)...**PERSONAL:** Graduated from Loyalsock High School (Pa.) and played baseball at the University of Virginia where he was named a Mizuno Freshman All-American...ranked fourth in school history in innings pitched (280.1), tied for fourth in games started (40), sixth in strikeouts (213) and fifth in complete games (15)...selected by the Boston Red Sox in the 40th round of 1997 First-Year Player Draft but chose to attend college...married Bree in 2007.

TY HAWKINS - HITTING COACH

BORN: 11/8/67 in Point Pleasant, N.J. • **RESIDES:** Brielle, N.J.

COACHING CAREER: Returns for his fifth consecutive season as the hitting coach in Staten Island...has led the Yankees to the second-best batting average in the NYPL in each of the last three seasons, hitting an NYPL-most 52HR in 2009...guided the 2006 Staten Island offense to a league-best .267 average and 365R en route to the club's second consecutive NY-Penn League Championship...also fulfilled coaching duties with Double-A Trenton (2005), Single-A Tampa (2004), Single-A Battle Creek (2003), Single-A Greensboro (2002) and the Gulf Coast Yankees (1999-2001)...before joining the Yankees organization, coached at Vanderbilt University and the University of Illinois...**PLAYING CAREER:** Played baseball at Old Dominion University, helping his team advance to the NCAA Regionals in 1990...graduated with a Bachelor of Science degree from ODU in that year as well...**PERSONAL:** Married to Jennifer with two children, Brier and Ty Bayley.

JUSTIN POPE - COACH

BORN: 11/8/79 in West Palm Beach, Fla. • **RESIDES:** Lake Worth, Fla.

COACHING CAREER: Makes his coaching debut with Staten Island in 2010...**PLAYING CAREER:** Originally selected by St. Louis in the first round (28th overall) of the 2001 First-Year Player Draft, played for eight season in the minors, going 38-34 with a 3.24 ERA in 66 games (6GS)... was acquired by the Yankees in 2003 as part of the trade that sent LHP Sterling Hitchcock to the Cardinals, making stops in Single-A, Double-A and Triple-A... pitched his final season in 2008 with Philadelphia's Double-A Reading...**PERSONAL:** Played baseball at the University of Central Florida where he was named First-Team All-American.

LEE MEYER - TRAINER

BORN: 12/27/83 in Marinette, Wisc.

Begins his first season in the Yankees organization... received his undergraduate degree in Athletic Training from the University of Wisconsin–Stevens Point in May 2008, while also holding a minor in Spanish... is currently working towards his Master's Degree in Sports Management at Minnesota State University, Mankato... previously worked as an Athletic Training Intern with the Colorado Rockies and Pittsburgh Pirates as well as the NFL's Indianapolis Colts.

Organizational Accomplishments

The Yankees are one of only two organizations whose minor-league affiliates posted a winning record in every season since 1990 (also the Cleveland Indians)...the Yankees were named the "Organization of the Year" in 1998 by *Baseball America* and in 1999 by *USA Today*.

2009 Staten Island Yankees (Short-Season A)

BATTERS	AVG	G	AB	R	H	2B	3B	HR	RBI	BB	SO	SB	CS	OBP	SLG	E
Afenir, Buck	.167	5	12	0	2	2	0	0	2	2	1	0	0	.333	.333	0
#Almonte, Zoilo	.274	69	259	43	71	20	1	7	39	31	58	15	7	.355	.440	3
Angelini, Carmen	.190	59	200	18	38	5	1	3	14	15	34	3	2	.253	.270	11
Baker, Ryan J.	.241	10	29	3	7	1	0	2	6	3	8	0	0	.313	.483	1
Castro, Kelvin	.212	65	217	24	46	11	5	2	27	13	62	6	4	.265	.336	19
Gross, Chad	.145	21	55	4	8	2	1	1	4	4	32	2	0	.203	.273	3
Higashioka, Kyle	.253	60	217	24	55	11	0	2	32	26	31	0	1	.333	.332	5
#Landoni, Emerson	.237	27	76	8	18	1	1	0	9	8	14	4	1	.318	.276	9
*Lyerly, Robert	.268	20	71	8	19	8	0	0	7	2	16	0	2	.307	.380	7
Lyon, Mike	.217	20	69	10	15	5	0	1	7	8	19	0	0	.308	.333	3
*Mack, Deangelo	.306	66	232	27	71	19	4	7	41	21	44	2	4	.372	.513	2
*Medchill, Neil	.278	62	216	42	60	13	2	14	41	24	66	7	2	.350	.551	1
*Milo, Justin	.253	25	75	13	19	5	0	1	12	22	23	4	0	.429	.360	1
Murton, Luke	.295	69	237	45	70	17	1	8	35	23	61	4	0	.374	.477	9
#Paredes, Jimmy	.302	54	205	36	62	8	4	2	17	10	30	23	9	.336	.410	12
Rabago, Hector	.216	34	111	10	24	2	0	1	5	13	16	3	2	.326	.261	3
*Santana, Francisco	.236	40	140	17	33	6	1	1	10	10	29	5	4	.289	.314	1
Team Total	**.255**	**76**	**2421**	**332**	**618**	**136**	**21**	**52**	**308**	**235**	**544**	**78**	**38**	**.328**	**.393**	**104**

PITCHERS	W	ERA	G	GS	CG	SHO	SV	IP	H	R	ER	HR	HB	BB	SO	WP
Arbiso, Cory	0-1	1.17	2	1	0	0	0	7.2	6	3	1	0	1	0	6	1
Bailey, Griffin	3-2	1.49	32	0	0	0	2	48.1	35	13	8	1	1	14	28	6
Bartleski, Philip	0-0	0.00	2	0	0	0	0	4.0	1	0	0	0	1	0	7	0
Black, Sean	6-0	1.62	10	10	0	0	0	50.0	30	14	9	2	1	9	34	0
*Brooks, Gavin	5-1	0.62	30	0	0	0	3	43.1	27	8	3	1	1	24	48	1
Cotham, Caleb	0-1	4.50	2	2	0	0	0	6.0	5	3	3	1	0	3	8	0
*Elam, Sam	0-0	23.62	3	0	0	0	0	2.2	1	7	7	0	2	11	2	5
Flannery, Ryan	4-2	1.45	34	0	0	0	6	43.1	32	10	7	0	1	12	41	0
*Hall, Shaeffer	0-0	1.86	2	2	0	0	0	9.2	9	2	2	0	2	0	11	1
*Lare, Trenton	3-2	1.07	6	6	0	0	0	33.2	20	9	4	3	1	3	38	0
Marte, Ronny	6-3	4.24	31	0	0	0	7	40.1	36	25	19	2	1	13	45	4
Miller, Dan	0-0	4.15	6	0	0	0	0	8.2	9	4	4	0	1	2	9	0
Patterson, Paul	1-1	5.64	14	0	0	0	0	22.1	28	17	14	1	2	6	16	1
Perez, Kelvin	3-2	2.06	13	9	0	0	0	52.1	50	24	12	0	2	24	48	3
Richardson, Matthew	0-3	6.56	9	9	0	0	0	35.2	45	31	26	2	0	23	30	2
*Rondon, Francisco	3-2	2.32	11	11	0	0	0	54.1	38	22	14	2	3	33	48	3
Solbach, Michael	2-3	3.92	24	2	0	0	1	39.0	40	27	17	2	4	22	34	6
Stoneburner, Graham	0-0	0.00	1	0	0	0	0	1.0	1	0	0	0	0	0	2	0
Vizcaino, Arodys	2-4	2.13	10	10	0	0	0	42.1	34	18	10	2	1	15	52	2
Warren, Adam	4-2	1.43	12	12	0	0	0	56.2	49	12	9	1	0	10	50	3
Watkins, Benjamin	5-0	2.47	25	2	0	0	0	47.1	38	16	13	0	4	11	43	3
Team Total	**47-29**	**2.53**	**76**	**76**	**0**	**12**	**19**	**648.2**	**534**	**265**	**182**	**20**	**29**	**235**	**600**	**41**

KEY: *- Lefthanded hitter/pitcher, # - switch hitter

Gulf Coast Yankees (Rookie)

AFFILIATE SINCE 1990
Gulf Coast League – Yankees Complex
Office Address: 3102 N. Himes Ave, Tampa, FL 33607
Telephone: (813) 875-7569. **Fax:** (813) 873-2302
General Manager: Eric Schmidt
2009 Record, finish: 33-27, First place, North Division

TOM SLATER – MANAGER

BORN: 4/6/68 in Charlottesville, Va. • **RESIDES:** Auburn, Ala.

COACHING CAREER: Returns for his second season as Manager with the GCL Yankees after leading the club to a first-place finish in the North Division in 2009 in his pro coaching debut...spent his previous four seasons (2005-08) as the head coach at Auburn University, going 115-113 and seeing 15 of his players drafted by Major League clubs over the four-year span...was his second stint with the Tigers, having served as an assistant coach there from 1995-2000...prior to taking over as head coach at Auburn, spent one season (2004) as an assistant coach at the University of Florida under Pat McMahon and three years (2001-03) as the head coach at Virginia Military Institute, earning Southern Conference "Coach of the Year" in 2003...began his coaching career in 1991 as an assistant coach at St. Christopher's School in Richmond, Va., then served as an assistant at Marshall in 1992 and VMI from 1993-94...was the hitting coach and third base coach for the 2006 USA National Team that won the gold medal...**PERSONAL:** With wife Beth, has two children, Julia and Jack...graduated from VMI in 1990 where he was a four-year starter, ending his career ranked in the top five in RBI, total bases, runs scored and doubles...was part of the 1988 Southern Conference Northern Division championship team.

CARLOS CHANTRES – PITCHING COACH

BORN: 4/1/76 in Miami, Fla. • **RESIDES:** Miami, Fla.

COACHING CAREER: Returns for his fourth season as pitching coach with the GCL club and fifth season in the Yankees organization after spending the 2006 campaign as the pitching coach for the NY-Penn League champion Staten Island Yankees...his staff led all rookie-level teams with a 2.72 ERA in 2007 with a GCL-best 42-17 regular season record and a league-low .228 opponents batting average...**PLAYING CAREER:** Played parts of 11 professional seasons in the systems of the Chicago White Sox, Tampa Bay Devil Rays, St. Louis Cardinals and Philadelphia Phillies, going 80-88 with a 4.01 ERA in 291 games (233 starts)...**PERSONAL:** Is married to Melisa with two daughters, Nina and Lia...selected in the 12th round of the 1994 draft by the Chicago White Sox out of Christopher Columbus High School in Miami, Fla.

DAN BORRELL – PITCHING COACH

BORN: 1/24/79 in Landsdale, Penn. • **RESIDES:** Wichita, Kan.

COACHING CAREER: Enters his second season as a rehabilitation pitching coach in the GCL...**PLAYING CAREER:** Selected by the Yankees in the second round of the 2000 First-Year Player Draft, played nine minor league seasons with the Yankees (2000-06) and Oakland (2007-08)...the left-hander compiled a career record of 39-35 with a 3.49 ERA in 138 games (130 starts)...split the 2008 season between the Athletics' Double-A Midland and Triple-A Sacramento squads, before landing on the disabled list in June for the remainder of the season with a left elbow strain...**PERSONAL:** Pitched at Wake Forest.

JULIO VINAS – HITTING COACH

BORN: 2/14/73 in Miami, Fla. • **RESIDES:** Miramar, Fla.

COACHING CAREER: Enters his first season as a coach with the GCL club...has spent the last eight seasons (2002-09) in the Orioles system as a coach, hitting instructor and field coordinator...**PLAYING CAREER:** Played 11 seasons in the minors, batting .264 with 84HR and 504RBI with five different organizations (Chicago-AL, Baltimore, Los Angeles-NL, Cleveland and Boston)...was originally selected in 33rd round of the 1991 First-Year Player Draft by the White Sox...**PERSONAL:** Graduated from Miami American HS, where he earned All-America and All-State honors in baseball...hit .556 as a senior, establishing a Florida state record.

DANILO VALIENTE - COACH

BORN: 1/13/66 in Havana, Cuba. • **RESIDES:** Tampa, Fla.

COACHING CAREER: Enters his second season as a coach with the GCL Yankees...is his fourth season in the Yankees organization, serving as a coach with Single-A Tampa from 2007-08...**PERSONAL:** A native of Cuba, Valiente managed and coached for 15 seasons with the Cuban professional team, Industriales...served as a third base coach and hitting instructor with the Cuban National team...also served as a coach with Cuba's mid-superior league where future Major Leaguers Jose Contreras, Orlando Hernandez and Kendry Morales played for him...won the league championship in 1997.

GREG SPRATT – TRAINER

BORN: 7/8/65 in Lexington, Ky. • **RESIDES:** Plant City, Fla.

Returns for his fourth consecutive season as the athletic trainer for the Yankees' Gulf Coast squad after rejoining the Yankees organization in 2007...previously served with the Yankees for parts of 16 seasons beginning in 1990...was selected Eastern League "Trainer of the Year" in 1995...began with Oneonta in 1990 and moved to Greensboro in 1991, where he was the All-Star trainer for the Northern Division squad...was voted "Trainer of the Year" in 1992 by the Professional Baseball Athletic Trainers Society...earned a bachelor's degree from the University of Louisville...was the trainer for the National Champion Louisville Cardinals and the U.S. Pan American basketball team in 1986...received a master's degree in sports medicine from Ohio University.

2009 Gulf Coast Yankees (Rookie)

BATTERS	AVG	G	AB	R	H	2B	3B	HR	RBI	BB	SO	SB	CS	OBP	SLG	E
Afenir, Buck	.400	6	15	3	6	4	0	1	5	0	5	0	0	.400	.867	1
#Arcia, Francisco	.247	31	97	10	24	7	0	2	13	11	16	0	0	.330	.381	1
Brown, Isaiah	.167	20	36	5	6	1	0	1	4	8	14	2	1	.354	.278	1
Cervelli, Francisco	.167	2	6	1	1	0	0	0	0	1	0	0	0	.286	.167	1
*Delaney, Mitchell	.178	40	101	8	18	6	1	3	15	17	41	0	1	.311	.347	4
De Leon, Kelvin	.269	56	201	28	54	13	0	7	31	16	61	5	1	.330	.438	3
Farnham, Jeffrey	.167	5	12	0	2	1	0	0	2	1	3	1	0	.231	.250	0
*Flores, Ramon	.196	51	158	14	31	5	1	0	14	22	35	7	5	.303	.241	4
*Golsan, Judd	.224	39	98	16	22	3	0	0	5	13	34	4	2	.330	.255	1
Harrow, Issac	.186	30	86	7	16	4	1	1	8	10	25	0	1	.268	.291	3
*Heathcott, Zachary	.100	3	10	0	1	0	0	0	0	1	2	0	0	.182	.100	0
#Landoni, Emerson	.000	1	3	0	0	0	0	0	0	0	0	0	0	.000	.000	0
*Lassiter, Garrison	.500	1	2	1	1	0	0	0	1	1	0	0	0	.500	.500	0
Liccien, Jhorge	.100	29	80	6	8	0	0	0	1	7	18	0	0	.182	.100	5
*Mahoney, Kevin	.226	57	190	28	43	17	1	6	30	24	70	3	2	.330	.421	8
*Milo, Justin	.267	7	15	2	4	1	0	1	3	4	2	2	0	.450	.533	1
Mojica, Jose	.278	55	198	18	55	11	2	1	22	10	20	4	1	.321	.369	15
#Murphy, John	.333	9	33	4	11	2	0	1	7	3	8	0	0	.405	.485	0
*Smith, Christopher	.091	17	44	5	4	1	0	1	1	8	17	1	0	.259	.182	2
*Sosa, Eduardo	.200	49	165	24	33	7	1	2	14	16	47	11	4	.280	.291	4
Tabares, Yunior	.230	30	87	9	20	3	1	0	6	7	21	0	0	.292	.287	2
Toussen, Jose	.223	58	202	27	45	12	1	2	15	27	36	8	3	.316	.322	14
Team Total	**.220**	**60**	**1839**	**216**	**405**	**98**	**9**	**29**	**197**	**207**	**475**	**48**	**21**	**.309**	**.331**	**72**

PITCHERS	W-L	ERA	G	GS	CG	SHO	SV	IP	H	R	ER	HR	HB	BB	SO	WP
Acosta, Ryan	0-0	0.00	1	0	0	0	0	1.0	1	0	0	0	0	0	1	0
Arballo, Julian	0-3	2.81	20	0	0	0	11	25.2	24	9	8	0	4	17	26	3
Barreda, Manuel	0-1	1.93	14	0	0	0	2	23.1	10	7	5	0	5	7	25	1
Bartleski, Philip	0-0	4.50	1	0	0	0	0	2.0	2	1	1	0	0	1	0	0
Checo, Mariel	1-1	8.40	10	0	0	0	0	15.0	14	15	14	1	0	14	14	3
Cotham, Caleb	0-0	0.00	1	1	0	0	0	2.0	2	0	0	0	0	0	5	0
*Elam, Sam	0-2	6.75	7	0	0	0	0	5.1	5	7	4	0	2	10	8	3
Gerritse, Brett	0-1	3.93	6	5	0	0	0	18.1	15	11	8	0	1	7	20	1
Gil, Daniel	4-3	3.00	13	7	0	0	0	45.0	41	21	15	3	2	10	31	2
Greene, Shane	1-2	5.87	13	0	0	0	0	23.0	30	19	15	2	5	6	20	4
Heidler, Paul	3-1	2.16	13	0	0	0	0	16.2	15	4	4	1	1	8	13	0
Heredia, Jairo	0-0	1.80	2	2	0	0	0	5.0	3	2	1	0	0	2	5	0
Horne, Alan	4-0	2.86	6	5	0	0	0	28.1	23	9	9	2	1	10	22	6
Marquez, Dickson	1-3	1.86	20	0	0	0	1	29.0	19	9	6	1	1	2	21	1
*Marte, Damaso	0-0	4.50	2	2	0	0	0	2.0	2	1	1	0	0	0	2	0
Martinez, Alejandro	1-0	0.00	2	0	0	0	0	3.1	3	1	0	0	0	0	6	0
Miller, Dan	1-0	2.25	15	0	0	0	1	20.0	13	5	5	0	0	9	12	3
O'Brien, Michael	2-4	5.09	11	8	0	0	0	46.0	51	33	26	1	2	9	44	0
Patterson, Paul	0-0	0.00	1	0	0	0	0	2.0	1	0	0	0	0	0	0	0
Perez, Kelvin	2-0	1.50	2	0	0	0	0	6.0	4	1	1	0	0	3	8	1
Ramirez, Jose A.	6-0	1.48	11	10	0	0	0	61.0	33	12	10	5	3	16	53	0
Richardson, Matthew	3-0	0.64	5	4	0	0	0	28.0	20	2	2	0	2	1	21	1
Rodriguez, Wilton	0-1	3.32	8	2	0	0	1	19.0	15	8	7	3	2	2	18	0
Smith, Brett	0-2	6.75	4	4	0	0	0	12.0	15	9	9	2	0	6	10	1
Tatis, Gabriel	2-0	0.84	6	0	0	0	3	10.2	10	2	1	1	0	1	14	2
*Turley, Nik	2-3	2.82	11	10	0	0	0	54.1	45	21	17	1	6	23	46	9
Team Total	**33-27**	**3.00**	**60**	**60**	**0**	**5**	**19**	**504.0**	**416**	**209**	**168**	**23**	**37**	**164**	**445**	**41**

KEY: *- Lefthanded hitter/pitcher, # - switch hitter

Dominican Summer League Yankees

The Latin Béisbol Academy • One Yankee Way • Boca Chica, Dominican Republic

PAT McMAHON – COORDINATOR OF INTERNATIONAL PLAYER DEVELOPMENT

BORN: 5/28/53 in Lakawanna, N.Y. • **RESIDES:** Jacksonville, Fla.

COACHING CAREER: Begins his first season in his new position of Coordinator of International Player Development in his third season with the Yankees organization...prior to joining the Yankees in 2007, served for seven seasons (2001-07) as the Head Coach with the University of Florida where he earned the Collegiate Baseball Foundation's "National Coach of the Year" and Southeastern Conference "Coach of the Year" Awards in 2005 after guiding the Gators to a second-place finish in the College World Series...owns a career coaching record of 555-287-1 with Old Dominion (1990-94), Mississippi State (1997-2000) and Florida...also managed the 2001 USA Baseball team that played in tournaments in the United States, Japan and Taiwan...**PERSONAL:** Married (Cheri) with daughter Logan and son J. Wells...is one of eight siblings.

JOEL LITHGOW - LATIN AMERICAN ACADEMY DIRECTOR

BORN: 12/4/78 in Santo Domingo, D.R. • **RESIDES:** Santo Domingo, D.R.

Enters his first full season as the Operations Director of the DSL Yankees Latin Beisbol Academy...as director, supervises the Yankees' entire Dominican baseball development program...responsibilities include overseeing scouting, player signings and ensuring proper maintenance of all baseball-related facilities...also aids in coordinating community events, such as skill-building baseball clinics, in the Dominican...prior to joining the Yankees organization, worked as an attorney in the Department of Investigations for Major League Baseball in the Dominican Republic...he is a graduate of the Pontifica Universidad Catolica Madre y Maestra.

CARLOS MENDEZ MOTA - MANAGER, DSL 1

BORN: 1/10/67 in San Cristobal, D.R. • **RESIDES:** Haina, D.R.

COACHING CAREER: Enters his ninth season as a coach or manager in the Yankees player development system...prior to joining the Yankees in 2002, served as a coach in the Arizona Diamondbacks system from 2000-01...began his career in player development with the St. Paul Saints of the independent Northern League as a player/coach...**PLAYING CAREER:** Played for 12 seasons in the minor leagues as a catcher...was signed by Cleveland as a non-drafted free agent in 1986 and played in the Indians system through the 1989 season...played four seasons in independent leagues from 1996-1999...**PERSONAL:** Married (Runalina Medina) with two children: Carlos and Dahiana...played baseball at San Marcos High School in Haina.

WILFRIDO CORDOBA - PITCHING COACH, DSL 1

BORN: 8/11/57 in Panama City, Panama • **RESIDES:** Panama City, Panama

COACHING CAREER: Begins his 10th season as a pitching coach with the Yankees player development system in the Dominican Republic...has served as an instructor within the Yankees organization since 1991...**PLAYING CAREER:** Played five professional seasons in the Pittsburgh Pirates organization from 1981-85...was signed by the Pirates as a non-drafted free agent on 4/2/81...also played one year of professional baseball in Mexico...**PERSONAL:** Married to Magdalena with five children: Maira, Marleen, Keyla, Wilfredo and Maria...played high school baseball in Panama City and won MVP honors as an amateur.

FREDDIE TIBERCIO – HITTING COACH, DSL 1

BORN: 6/24/61 in Santo Domingo, D.R. • **RESIDES:** Santo Domingo, D.R.

COACHING CAREER: Will be his 14th season working with the Yankees organization...his offense ranked second in the DSL in batting average (.272) in 2009, and tied for third in home runs (30)...**PLAYING CAREER:** Played professional baseball for 16 seasons...logged nine seasons within the Atlanta Braves and Detroit Tigers systems...also spent six seasons playing in Taiwan and played for one year in Mexico...**PERSONAL:** Married (Arlette Correa) with three sons - Frederick, Cristofer and Bryan.

RAFAEL JIMENEZ – COACH, DSL 1

BORN: 3/26/64 in Azua, D.R. • **RESIDES:** Azua, D.R.

COACHING CAREER: Enters his 17th year as a coach in the Yankees player development system...worked for three years as a scout for the Yankees from 1990-92 before shifting roles into an on-field instructor...served as an infield instructor and field coordinator since 1993...**PERSONAL:** Married (Yisa Marte Vargas) with two daughters, Denisse Ysamar and Yalisa...attended Universidad O&M after graduating from Liceo Roman B. de Astro High School in Azua.

MANUEL LUIS ROJAS - TRAINER, DSL 1

BORN: 6/13/71 in San Cristobal, D.R. • **RESIDES:** Villa Mella, D.R.

Enters his ninth season as a trainer in the Yankees player development system...began his professional training career with the Tampa Bay organization, where he worked for six years before joining the Yankees...**PLAYING CAREER:** Played professional baseball with the Montreal Expos organization from 1989-91...**PERSONAL:** Married (Glenys Cruz Pinales) with one son, Junior...graduated from Liceo Aras Nacionales in Villa Mella.

RAUL DOMINGUEZ - MANAGER, DSL 2

BORN: 7/25/81 in Panama City, Panama • **RESIDES:** Panama City, Panama

COACHING CAREER: Returns for his second season as Manager of the DSL 2 team after guiding the club to a first place finish in the Boca Chica Division in 2009...began his coaching career in 2008 with the DSL 2 squad after spending 2007 as the Yankees' tryout scout in the Dominican Republic...**PLAYING CAREER:** Signed by the Yankees as a non-drafted free agent in 2001, he played four minor league seasons as an outfielder with the DSL and GCL clubs.

JOSE DURAN - PITCHING COACH, DSL 2

BORN: 5/19/64 in Santo Domingo, D.R. • **RESIDES:** Santo Domingo, D.R.

COACHING CAREER: Enters his seventh season as a coach in the Yankees organization...has served as a professional pitching coach since he made his coaching debut with the Florida Marlins in 1994...prior to joining the Yankees, spent two years as a special instructor with the Cincinnati Reds and parts of two seasons with the Los Angeles Dodgers organization...**PLAYING CAREER:** Played professionally in the Los Angeles Dodgers system from 1984-88...**PERSONAL:** Married (Sandra Garcia) with four children: Darwin, Alexandra, Erika and Alby...graduated from San Francisco de Asis High School in Santo Domingo.

ROY GOMEZ - HITTING COACH, DSL 2

BORN: 1/7/85 in Santo Domingo, D.R. • **RESIDES:** Santo Domingo, D.R.

COACHING CAREER: Returns for his second year as hitting coach of the Dominican Summer League Yankees 2...**PLAYING CAREER:** Played for five years in the Yankees organization with the Tampa, Staten Island, Gulf Coast League and Dominican Summer League Yankees after being signed as a non-drafted free agent on 11/26/03...compiled a .271 batting average with 40 doubles, 9HR and 99RBI in 259 combined games.

SONDER ENCARNACION - COACH, DSL 2

BORN: 4/28/77 in San Cristobal, D.R. • **RESIDES:** San Cristobal, D.R.

Enters his sixth season of coaching in the Yankees system with the Dominican Summer League entries...the former infielder signed with Seattle in 1995 and played three seasons for the Mariners' Dominican Summer League team.

ANTONIO GARCIA – TRAINER, DSL 2

BORN: 7/20/69 in Maracaibo, Venezuela • **RESIDES:** Maracaibo, Venezuela

Enters his fifth season with the Yankees Player Development System...prior to joining the Yankees, served for six years as a trainer in the Dominican Republic for the Texas Rangers organization.

RAUDO BAEZ - CLUBHOUSE/EQUIPMENT MANAGER

BORN: 4/5/70 in San Cristobal, D.R. • **RESIDES:** Palenque, D.R.

Enters his ninth season with the Yankees player development system in the Dominican Republic...**PERSONAL:** Married (Jovanna) with one son, Raudy...graduated from Padre Borbon High School in Palenque.

Tony Dimel - Head Groundskeeper
Pat Maturine - Assistant Head Groundskeeper
Jose Guillen - Assistant Equipment Manager
Ambiorix Osuna - Assistant Clubhouse Attendant
Luis Morillo - Strength and Conditioning Coach

U.S. MILITARY ALL-STAR BASEBALL TEAM VISITS YANKEES' LATIN BÉISBOL ACADEMY IN THE DOMINICAN REPUBLIC

On April 24, 2008, the U.S. Military Baseball Team paid a visit to the Yankees' Latin Béisbol Academy in Boca Chica, Dominican Republic to join Yankees players for a workout as part of their Armed Forces' "Baseball Diplomacy" program in conjunction with the United States Embassy, the Dominican Armed Forces and National Police Sporting Club, and the Dominican Baseball Federation. Following the training session, coaches from the academy joined U.S. military players at Ensanche Luperon, in Santo Domingo, to give a baseball clinic to local children. In return, the Yankees sent coaches and scouts to participate in a clinic on April 26, 2008 at the Olympic Center, also in Santo Domingo.

Minor League Players, Non-Roster Invitees

ABEITA, Mitch – C

HT: 6-0; **WT:** 190; **B:** R; **T:** R; **BORN:** 4/7/86 in Oakcliff, Tex.; **RESIDES:** Duncanville, Tex.; **COLLEGE:** University of Nebraska; **OBTAINED:** Selected by the Yankees in the 19th round of the 2008 First-Year Player Draft; **M.L. SVC:** 0.000; **CAREER NOTES: 2009**: Batted .225 with 12 doubles, 4HR and 32RBI in 74 games with Single-A Charleston...threw out 28-of-109 base runners attempting to steal (25.7%)...**2008:** Made his professional debut, batting .250 with 10 doubles, 1HR and 19RBI in 53 games with short-season Single-A Staten Island...ranked fourth among catchers in the NYPL with a 40.7% caught-stealing rate (22-for-54)...hit .167 (1-for-6) with 1HR in two postseason games...**PERSONAL:** Last name is pronounced "Uh-bay-tuh"...attended the University of Nebraska where he majored in sociology...batted .337 with 45R, 7 doubles, 10HR and 49RBI in 56 games during his senior year, recording more walks (43) than strikeouts (29)...earned an All-Big 12 honorable mention in 2007...was named to the Big 12 Commissioner's Honor Roll in Fall 2007...also attended North Central Texas College in Duncanville, Tex.

YEAR	CLUB	CLASS	AVG	G	AB	R	H	2B	3B	HR	RBI	SH	SF	HP	BB	SO	SB	CS	E	SLUG	OBP
2008	Staten Island	SS-A	.250	53	172	21	43	10	2	1	19	1	1	3	25	45	0	0	6	.349	.353
2009	Charleston	A	.225	74	249	28	56	12	1	4	32	2	1	5	31	58	1	0	8	.329	.322
Minor League Totals			**.235**	**127**	**421**	**49**	**99**	**22**	**3**	**5**	**51**	**3**	**2**	**8**	**56**	**103**	**1**	**0**	**14**	**.337**	**.335**

ACOSTA, Ryan – RHP

HT: 6-2; **WT:** 170; **B:** R; **T:** R; **BORN:** 11/4/88 in Lubbock, Tex.; **RESIDES:** Safety Harbor, Fla.; **OBTAINED:** Signed by the Yankees as a free agent on 8/21/09; **M.L. SVC:** 0.000; **CAREER NOTES: 2009:** Was released during spring training and signed a minor league contract with Kansas City before being released two weeks later on 5/6...signed with the Yankees on 8/21 and pitched in one game with the GCL Yankees, tossing 1.0 scoreless inning...**2008:** Combined to go 1-1 with a 4.42 ERA in 11 games (eight starts) with Single Peoria and Rookie-level Mesa...missed the final two months of the season with right elbow tendinitis...**2007:** Split his first professional season with Mesa and Single-A Boise, going 0-2 with a 3.00 ERA in six combined games (four starts)...**PERSONAL:** His father, Oscar, played in the Phillies farm system for three years and was a coach with the Cubs (2000-01) and Rangers (2002), was a minor league manager with the Yankees...was originally selected by the Cubs in the 12th round of the 2007 First-Year Player Draft out of Clearwater Central Catholic HS where he was named an Under Armour-All American and Rawlings All-American.

YEAR	CLUB	CLASS	W-L	ERA	G	GS	CG	SHO	SV	IP	H	R	ER	HR	HB	BB	SO	WP	BK
2007	AZL Cubs	R	0-0	3.00	3	1	0	0	0	6.0	5	2	2	0	0	3	6	0	0
	Boise	SS-A	0-2	3.00	3	3	0	0	0	12.0	9	4	4	2	1	3	8	0	0
2008	Peoria	A	1-1	4.19	8	8	0	0	0	34.1	45	25	16	7	2	9	25	3	0
	AZL Cubs	R	0-0	6.23	3	0	0	0	0	4.1	4	3	3	1	0	1	5	0	0
2009	GCL Yankees	R	0-0	0.00	1	0	0	0	0	1.0	1	0	0	0	0	0	1	0	0
Minor League Totals			**1-3**	**3.90**	**18**	**12**	**0**	**0**	**0**	**57.2**	**64**	**34**	**25**	**10**	**3**	**16**	**45**	**3**	**0**

ADAMS, David – INF

HT: 6-2; **WT:** 205; **B:** R; **T:** R; **BORN:** 5/15/87 in Margate, Fla.; **RESIDES:** Margate, Fla.; **COLLEGE:** University of Virginia; **OBTAINED:** Selected by the Yankees in the third round of the 2008 First-Year Player Draft; **M.L. SVC:** 0.000; **CAREER NOTES: 2009**: Combined to hit .286 with 69R, 40 doubles, 8 triples, 7HR and 75RBI in 132 games with Single-A Charleston and Single-A Tampa...tied for third among all Yankees minor leaguers in RBI...began the season with Charleston, batting .290 with 23 doubles and 34RBI in 67 games...tied for second on the team in doubles...was promoted to Tampa on 6/25, where he batted .281 with 17 doubles, 6 triples, 7HR and 41RBI in 65 games...ranked second on the team in triples and tied for third in RBI...**2008:** Made his professional debut, batting .257 with 45R, 19 doubles, 4HR and 31RBI in 67 games with short-season Single-A Staten Island...batted .333 (3-for-9) with 1RBI in two postseason games...**PERSONAL:** Full name is David Lee Adams...attended the University of Virginia where he batted .286 with 48R, 11 doubles, 6HR and 51RBI in 61 games his junior year...successfully stole a base in 16-of-19 attempts (84.2%)...was a career .325 batter in college, scoring 150 runs with 30 doubles, 16HR and 143RBI in 183 games...was named to the 2008 Third-Team Louisville Slugger Preseason All-America squad and the Wallace Award Watch List...was also named co-team captain...finished his junior season with 84 hits, tied for sixth-most in school history for a single season...was one of *Baseball America's* Top 30 prospects (No. 27) from the Cape Cod League in 2007 after hitting .302 for Falmouth...led the league in doubles (14), ranked second in hits (51) and triples (3) and placed ninth in batting average...was named Second Team *Baseball America* Freshman All-American, a Louisville Slugger Freshman All-American and earned a spot on *Baseball America's* Fab 50 list for top freshman in 2006...attended Grandview Prep (Fla.) where he played for his father, Dale, and was a four-year letter-winner in baseball...was named team captain and MVP in his senior year...was rated the No. 19 prospect by *Baseball America* in 2005...named a scholar athlete each year from 2002-05...also lettered three years in football...was drafted by the Tigers in the 21st round of the 2005 First-Year Player Draft but chose to attend college.

YEAR	CLUB	CLASS	AVG	G	AB	R	H	2B	3B	HR	RBI	SH	SF	HP	BB	SO	SB	CS	E	SLUG	OBP
2008	Staten Island	SS-A	.257	67	257	45	66	19	2	4	31	0	2	6	32	57	8	2	8	.393	.350
2009	Charleston	A	.290	67	259	32	75	23	2	0	34	0	3	7	35	49	8	4	9	.394	.385
	Tampa	A	.281	65	231	37	65	17	6	7	41	1	3	4	26	39	3	4	5	.498	.360
Minor League Totals			**.276**	**199**	**747**	**114**	**206**	**59**	**10**	**11**	**106**	**1**	**8**	**17**	**93**	**145**	**19**	**10**	**22**	**.426**	**.365**

AFENIR, Buck – C

HT: 6-1; **WT:** 205; **B:** R; **T:** R; **BORN:** 5/3/87 in Escondido, Calif.; **RESIDES:** Escondido, Calif.; **COLLEGE:** University of Kansas; **OBTAINED:** Signed by the Yankees as a non-drafted free-agent on 6/15/09; **M.L. SVC:** 0.000; **CAREER NOTES: 2009:** Made his professional debut and combined to hit .296 with 6 doubles and 7RBI in 11 games with the GCL and Staten Island Yankees...batted .400 (6-for-15) with 4 doubles, and 1HR in six games in the GCL before being transferred to Staten Island on 8/8 where he appeared in five games...**PERSONAL:** Full name is Matthew Tye Afenir...is the son of former Major League catcher Troy Afenir...named All-Section "Athlete of the Year" as a senior at Escondido High School.

YEAR	CLUB	CLASS	AVG	G	AB	R	H	2B	3B	HR	RBI	SH	SF	HP	BB	SO	SB	CS	E	SLUG	OBP
2009	GCL Yankees	R	.400	6	15	3	6	4	0	1	5	0	0	0	0	5	0	0	1	.867	.400
	Staten Island	SS-A	.167	5	12	0	2	2	0	0	2	0	0	1	2	1	0	0	0	.333	.333
Minor League Totals			**.296**	**11**	**27**	**3**	**8**	**6**	**0**	**1**	**7**	**0**	**0**	**1**	**2**	**6**	**0**	**0**	**1**	**.630**	**.367**

ALCANTARA, Jorge – INF

HT: 6-1; **WT:** 195; **B:** R; **T:** R; **BORN:** 8/9/91 in Cristo Rey, D.R.; **RESIDES:** Cristo Rey, D.R.; **OBTAINED:** Signed by the Yankees as a non-drafted free agent on 7/11/09; **M.L. SVC:** 0.000; **CAREER NOTES: 2009:** Made his professional debut with the DSL Yankees 1, batting .250 with 11R, 2 doubles, 1HR and 9RBI in 22 games...appeared in games at 3B and SS.

YEAR	CLUB	CLASS	AVG	G	AB	R	H	2B	3B	HR	RBI	SH	SF	HP	BB	SO	SB	CS	E	SLUG	OBP
2009	DSL Yankees 1	R	.250	22	72	11	18	2	1	1	9	0	2	1	10	20	5	1	9	.347	.341

ALMONTE, Abraham – OF

HT: 5-9; **WT:** 170; **B:** S; **T:** R; **BORN:** 6/27/89 in Santo Domingo, D.R.; **RESIDES:** Santo Domingo, D.R.; **OBTAINED:** Signed by the Yankees as a non-drafted free agent on 7/2/05; **M.L. SVC:** 0.000; **CAREER NOTES: 2009:** Batted .280 (123-for-440) with 14 doubles, 10 triples, 5HR and 56RBI in 115 games with Single-A Charleston, establishing career highs in hits, triples and RBI...recorded a career-high 26-game hitting streak from 8/6-9/4, batting .405 (45-for-111) with 12 extra-base hits (six doubles, three triples, 3HR) over the stretch...was the longest hitting streak recorded in the South Atlantic League in 2009...**2008:** Hit .228 with 61R, 20 doubles, 7 triples, 8HR and 46RBI in 115 games with Single-A Charleston...led the team and ranked second among Yankees farmhands with 29SB...began the season with a seven-game hitting streak, batting .400 (12-for-30) over the span...was placed on the disabled list from 5/9-29 with a left hamstring strain...was named to the South Atlantic League midseason All-Star team...appeared in three games for the Leones del Escogido of the Dominican Baseball League following the season...**2007:** Batted .288 with 29R and 16RBI in 49 games with the GCL Yankees...led the team in runs, walks (21) and stolen bases (8)...fashioned a nine-game hitting streak from 7/31-8/11...**2006:** Made his professional debut in 2006, batting .254 in 63 games played with the Yankees' Dominican Summer League 1 squad (25 games at 2B)...led the league in stolen bases (36), ranked fourth in home runs (8) and ranked fifth among all Dominican Summer League players with 51 runs scored.

YEAR	CLUB	CLASS	AVG	G	AB	R	H	2B	3B	HR	RBI	SH	SF	HP	BB	SO	SB	CS	E	SLUG	OBP
2006	DSL Yankees 1	R	.254	63	209	51	53	11	3	8	26	1	0	0	55	45	36	14	13	.450	.409
2007	GCL Yankees	R	.288	49	160	29	46	4	3	3	16	2	1	1	21	34	8	9	3	.406	.372
2008	Charleston	A	.228	115	443	61	101	20	7	8	46	3	1	1	47	101	29	10	7	.359	.303
2009	Charleston	A	.280	115	440	63	123	14	10	5	56	4	3	2	35	81	36	5	6	.391	.333
Minor League Totals			**.258**	**342**	**1252**	**204**	**323**	**49**	**23**	**24**	**144**	**10**	**5**	**4**	**158**	**261**	**109**	**38**	**29**	**.391**	**.342**

ALMONTE, Zoilo – OF

HT: 5-11; **WT:** 165; **B:** S; **T:** R; **BORN:** 6/10/89 in Santo Domingo, D.R.; **RESIDES:** Santo Domingo, D.R.; **OBTAINED:** Signed by the Yankees as a non-drafted free agent on 7/2/05; **M.L. SVC:** 0.000; **CAREER NOTES: 2009:** Played the entire season at short-season Single-A Staten Island and hit .274 with 20 doubles, 7HR and 39RBI in 69 games...tied for third in the New York-Penn League in doubles, ranked fourth in AB (259) and tied for fourth in extra-base hits (28)...was named to the league's midseason All-Star team...hit .333 (8-for-24) with a team-high five extra-base hits and 5RBI during the NYPL playoffs...**2008:** Batted .239 with 7 doubles, 5HR and 20RBI in 57 games with the GCL Yankees, leading the club in homers...played in the second-most games in the GCL...grounded into eight double plays, tied for most in the league...hit .486 (18-for-37) when leading off an inning...**2007:** Batted .268 with 25R, 11 doubles and 24RBI in 50 games with the GCL Yankees...**2006:** Made his professional debut with the Yankees DSL 1 squad, batting .219 in 53 games played...hit the Yankees' only grand slam of the season on 8/23 vs. the Diamondbacks.

YEAR	CLUB	CLASS	AVG	G	AB	R	H	2B	3B	HR	RBI	SH	SF	HP	BB	SO	SB	CS	E	SLUG	OBP
2006	DSL Yankees 1	R	.219	53	192	28	42	6	3	6	36	0	1	1	28	52	4	3	4	.375	.320
2007	GCL Yankees	R	.268	50	190	25	51	11	2	3	24	3	1	2	9	35	2	2	1	.395	.307
2008	GCL Yankees	R	.239	57	180	24	43	7	1	5	20	1	4	2	13	35	3	0	1	.372	.291
2009	Staten Island	SS-A	.274	69	259	43	71	20	1	7	39	1	1	2	31	58	15	7	3	.440	.355
Minor League Totals			**.252**	**229**	**821**	**120**	**207**	**44**	**7**	**21**	**119**	**5**	**7**	**7**	**81**	**180**	**24**	**12**	**9**	**.400**	**.322**

ALVAREZ, Isaias – RHP

HT: 6-2; **WT:** 175; **B:** R; **T:** R; **BORN:** 12/9/89 in Bonao, D.R.; **RESIDES:** Bonao, D.R.; **OBTAINED:** Signed as a non-drafted free agent on 6/18/08; **M.L. SVC:** 0.000; **CAREER NOTES: 2009:** Appeared in 16 games in relief with DSL Yankees 1, posting a 1-2 record and a 4.63 ERA...earned his first save on 8/5, tossing 4.0 scoreless innings to close out the game...**2008:** Made his professional debut with the DSL Yankees 1, going 1-3 with a 3.57 ERA in 10 games (four starts).

YEAR	CLUB	CLASS	W-L	ERA	G	GS	CG	SHO	SV	IP	H	R	ER	HR	HB	BB	SO	WP	BK
2008	DSL Yankees 1	R	1-3	3.57	10	4	0	0	0	22.2	23	15	9	0	2	17	12	7	0
2009	DSL Yankees 1	R	1-2	4.63	16	0	0	0	1	35.0	43	24	18	4	3	13	17	9	0
Minor League Totals			**2-5**	**4.21**	**26**	**4**	**0**	**0**	**1**	**57.2**	**66**	**39**	**27**	**4**	**5**	**30**	**29**	**16**	**0**

ANGELINI, Carmen – INF

HT: 6-2; **WT:** 185; **B:** R; **T:** R; **BORN:** 9/22/88 in Lake Charles, La.; **RESIDES:** Lake Charles, La.; **OBTAINED:** Selected by the Yankees in the 10th round of the 2007 First-Year Player Draft; **M.L. SVC:** 0.000; **CAREER NOTES: 2009:** Split the season with Single-A Charleston and short-season Single-A Staten Island, batting .193 with 10 doubles, 4HR and 22RBI...**2008:** Batted .236 with 14 doubles, 4HR and 46RBI in 134 games with Charleston...**2007:** Made his professional debut, playing in one game for the GCL Yankees and going 0-for-1 as a pinch-hitter...**PERSONAL:** Was selected out of A.M. Barbe High School (La.)...hit .433 with 58R, 14 doubles, 8 triples, 6HR and 52RBI in 40 games during his senior year, setting a school record in triples...also stole 38 bases in 42 attempts (90.5%).

YEAR	CLUB	CLASS	AVG	G	AB	R	H	2B	3B	HR	RBI	SH	SF	HP	BB	SO	SB	CS	E	SLUG	OBP
2007	GCL Yankees	R	.000	1	1	0	0	0	0	0	0	0	0	0	0	1	0	0	0	.000	.000
2008	Charleston	A	.236	134	474	64	112	14	1	4	46	1	3	4	42	99	17	6	42	.295	.302
2009	Charleston	A	.197	33	132	18	26	5	0	1	8	1	2	3	8	21	6	1	18	.258	.255
	Staten Island	SS-A	.190	59	200	18	38	5	1	3	14	1	0	2	15	34	3	2	11	.270	.253
Minor League Totals			**.218**	**227**	**807**	**100**	**176**	**24**	**2**	**8**	**68**	**3**	**5**	**9**	**65**	**166**	**26**	**9**	**71**	**.283**	**.282**

ANSON, Kyle – C

HT: 6-0; **WT:** 200; **B:** S; **T:** R; **BORN:** 4/21/83 in El Paso, Tex.; **RESIDES:** San Marcos, Tex.; **COLLEGE:** Texas State University; **OBTAINED:** Selected in the 10th round of the 2005 First-Year Player Draft; **M.L. SVC:** 0.000; **CAREER NOTES: 2009**: Batted .227 with 9 doubles and 24RBI in 57 games for Double-A Trenton...walked (36) more times than he struck out (33) for the fourth time in his four minor league seasons...went 2-for-5 with 1HR and a season-high 5RBI on 7/3 at Erie...missed time on the disabled list from 8/3-22 with right shoulder tendinitis...**2008:** Batted .241 with 11 doubles, 4HR and 25RBI in 68 games with Single-A Tampa...was placed on the disabled list from 6/3-7/11 with a right ankle sprain...made a seven-game rehab assignment with the GCL Yankees, batting .111...landed on the D.L. for the final two weeks of the season with a bruised left thumb...caught 36.0% of potential basestealers (27-for-75)...was charged with an FSL-high 13 passed balls...**2007**: In his first season as a catcher, batted .272 with 40R, 17 doubles and 44RBI in 98 games with Single-A Charleston...ranked second in the South Atlantic League with a 40.4% caught-stealing rate (42-for-104)...was placed on the D.L. from 4/13-5/3 with a right hamstring strain...recorded a 10-game hitting streak from 7/15-25...**2006:** Missed the entire season while on the disabled list with an injured left calf muscle...**2005:** Signed with the Yankees on 6/12 and joined the short-season Single-A Staten Island Yankees...appeared in 37 games and posted a .252 batting average, helping the Yankees advance to the NY-Penn League Championship...**PERSONAL:** Graduated from Texas State University prior to joining the Yankees organization in 2005...following his junior season, was named to the All-Southland Conference Second Team after finishing third on the team with a .292 batting average...played for two years at El Paso JC...following his second season, was named an All-Conference and All-Region third baseman...was also named an All-Conference third baseman his first year at El Paso...led his team to a Region 14 Championship his first year at El Paso and was named Team MVP in 2002 and 2003.

YEAR	CLUB	CLASS	AVG	G	AB	R	H	2B	3B	HR	RBI	SH	SF	HP	BB	SO	SB	CS	E	SLUG	OBP
2005	Staten Island	SS-A	.252	37	131	24	33	7	0	0	10	3	1	3	27	26	7	2	1	.305	.389
2006									Did Not Play - Injured												
2007	Charleston	A	.272	98	334	40	91	17	0	4	44	1	4	2	49	48	5	1	12	.359	.365
2008	Tampa	A	.241	68	224	27	54	11	1	4	25	2	1	1	44	35	1	3	5	.353	.367
	GCL Yankees	R	.111	7	18	0	2	0	0	0	2	0	0	1	3	5	0	0	0	.111	.273
2009	Trenton	AA	.227	57	163	23	37	9	0	2	24	0	3	4	36	33	1	0	8	.319	.693
Minor League Totals			**.249**	**267**	**870**	**114**	**217**	**44**	**1**	**10**	**105**	**6**	**9**	**11**	**159**	**147**	**14**	**6**	**26**	**.337**	**.369**

ARBALLO, Julian – RHP

HT: 6-0; **WT:** 225; **B:** R; **T:** R; **BORN:** 10/9/87 in El Centro, Calif.; **RESIDES:** El Centro, Calif.; **COLLEGE:** California Baptist University; **OBTAINED:** Signed by the Yankees as a free agent on 6/14/09; **M.L. SVC:** 0.000; **CAREER NOTES: 2009:** Made his professional debut with the GCL Yankees, going 0-3 with a 2.81 ERA and a team-high 11 saves...ranked second in the GCL in saves and games finished (17).

YEAR	CLUB	CLASS	W-L	ERA	G	GS	CG	SHO	SV	IP	H	R	ER	HR	HB	BB	SO	WP	BK
2009	GCL Yankees	R	0-3	2.81	20	0	0	0	11	25.2	24	9	8	0	4	17	26	3	0

ARBISO, Cory – RHP

HT: 6-3; **WT:** 210; **B:** R; **T:** R; **BORN:** 4/21/86 in LaMirada, Calif.; **RESIDES:** LaMirada, Calif.; **COLLEGE:** Cal State Fullerton; **OBTAINED:** Selected by the Yankees in the 22nd round of the 2008 First-Year Player Draft; **M.L. SVC:** 0.000; **CAREER NOTES: 2009**: Combined at three levels (Single-A Charleston, Single-A Staten Island and Triple-A Scranton/Wilkes-Barre) to go 4-8 with a 4.64 ERA in 33 appearances (12 starts)...**2008:** Made his professional debut, going 0-2 with a 4.18 ERA in eight appearances (seven starts) with short-season Single-A Staten Island...was placed on the disabled list from 7/2-8/10 with a sprained left ankle...made one postseason relief appearance with Staten Island, tossing 1.2 scoreless innings (2H, 1BB, 1K)...**PERSONAL:** Full name is Cory Edward Arbiso...has a twin brother, Casey...attended California State University at Fullerton, going 12-3 with a 4.46 ERA in 16 starts during his senior year, leading the team in wins.

YEAR	CLUB	CLASS	W-L	ERA	G	GS	CG	SHO	SV	IP	H	R	ER	HR	HB	BB	SO	WP	BK
2008	Staten Island	SS-A	0-2	4.18	8	7	0	0	0	28.0	33	17	13	2	0	4	20	0	0
2009	Charleston	A	4-7	4.85	30	10	0	0	1	91.0	109	58	49	8	3	14	62	1	0
	Staten Island	SS-A	0-1	1.17	2	1	0	0	0	7.2	6	3	1	0	1	0	6	1	0
	Scranton/WB	AAA	0-0	6.00	1	1	0	0	0	6.0	4	4	4	1	0	4	1	0	0
Minor League Totals			**4-10**	**4.55**	**41**	**19**	**0**	**0**	**1**	**132.2**	**152**	**82**	**67**	**11**	**4**	**14**	**62**	**2**	**0**

ARCIA, Francisco – C

HT: 6-0; **WT:** 155; **B:** S; **T:** R; **BORN:** 9/14/89 Maiquetia, Venezuela; **RESIDES:** Catia La Mar, Venezuela; **OBTAINED:** Signed by the Yankees as a non-drafted free agent on 7/2/06; **M.L. SVC:** 0.000; **CAREER NOTES: 2009:** Played his second straight season with the GCL Yankees, hitting .247 and catching 12-of-37 stolen base attempts (32.4%)...**2008:** Hit .128 with 1HR in 22 games with the GCL Yankees...**2007**: Batted .269 with 26R and 21RBI in 47 games with the DSL Yankees 2.

YEAR	CLUB	CLASS	AVG	G	AB	R	H	2B	3B	HR	RBI	SH	SF	HP	BB	SO	SB	CS	E	SLUG	OBP
2007	DSL Yankees 2	R	.269	47	156	26	42	11	4	3	21	1	1	10	25	35	5	2	9	.449	.401
2008	GCL Yankees	R	.128	22	47	5	6	1	0	1	2	1	1	2	2	6	0	1	2	.213	.192
2009	GCL Yankees	R	.247	31	97	10	24	7	0	2	13	0	2	2	11	16	0	0	1	.381	.330
Minor League Totals			**.240**	**100**	**300**	**41**	**72**	**19**	**4**	**6**	**36**	**2**	**4**	**14**	**38**	**57**	**5**	**3**	**12**	**.390**	**.348**

ARIAS, Gian – INF

HT: 5-11; **WT:** 179; **B:** S; **T:** R; **BORN:** 10/6/91 in Santo Domingo, D.R.; **RESIDES:** Santo Domingo, D.R.; **OBTAINED:** Signed by the Yankees as a non-drafted free agent on 7/2/08; **M.L. SVC:** 0.000; **CAREER NOTES: 2009:** Made his professional debut with DSL Yankees 2, batting .227 with 47R, 7 doubles, 2 triples and 26RBI in 62 games...drew a team-high 48BB.

YEAR	CLUB	CLASS	AVG	G	AB	R	H	2B	3B	HR	RBI	SH	SF	HP	BB	SO	SB	CS	E	SLUG	OBP
2009	DSL Yankees 2	R	.227	62	225	47	51	7	2	0	26	4	6	5	48	49	7	5	18	.276	.366

ARIAS, Justo – RHP

HT: 6-2; **WT:** 145; **B:** R; **T:** R; **BORN:** 10/29/88 in Sabana Grande, D.R.; **RESIDES:** Sabana Grande, D.R.; **OBTAINED:** Signed as a non-drafted free agent on 7/2/05; **M.L. SVC:** 0.000; **CAREER NOTES: 2009:** Made five relief appearances with the DSL Yankees 2 and went 1-0 with a 7.20 ERA in 5.0IP...**2008:** Went 5-4 with a 3.18 ERA in 20 games (one start) with the DSL Yankees 2...**2007**: Was 4-3 with a 4.57 ERA in 13 games (seven starts) with the DSL Yankees 2...**2006:** Appeared in 10 games and made one start with the Yankees' Dominican Summer League 1 squad, posting a 2-0 record with a 7.23 ERA.

YEAR	CLUB	CLASS	W-L	ERA	G	GS	CG	SHO	SV	IP	H	R	ER	HR	HB	BB	SO	WP	BK
2006	DSL Yankees 1	R	2-0	7.23	10	1	0	0	0	18.2	30	15	15	2	1	5	17	5	0
2007	DSL Yankees 2	R	4-3	4.57	13	7	0	0	0	43.1	48	32	22	3	6	14	33	1	0
2008	DSL Yankees 2	R	5-4	3.18	20	1	0	0	3	45.1	32	16	16	2	5	9	38	8	0
2009	DSL Yankees 2	R	1-0	7.20	5	0	0	0	0	5.0	9	4	4	1	0	1	5	1	0
Minor League Totals			**12-7**	**4.57**	**48**	**9**	**0**	**0**	**3**	**112.1**	**119**	**67**	**57**	**8**	**12**	**29**	**93**	**15**	**0**

ARIAS, Wilkins – LHP

NON-ROSTER INVITEE

HT: 6-1; **WT:** 150; **B:** L; **T:** L; **BORN:** 11/4/80 in San Cristobal, D.R.; **RESIDES:** San Cristobal, D.R.; **OBTAINED:** Signed by the Yankees as a non-drafted free agent on 6/7/05; **M.L. SVC:** 0.000; **CAREER NOTES: 2009:** Spent the season with Double-A Trenton, going 5-4 with a 3.65 ERA in 48 appearances (two starts)...held left-handed batters to a .183 (20-for-109) batting average with 1HR...following the season, pitched for the Aguilas Cibaenas of the Dominican Winter League, going 2-1 with one save and a 4.76 ERA in 26 relief outings...**2008:** Appeared in 40 combined games with Single-A Tampa and Trenton, going 4-0 with a 3.34 ERA...surrendered just 2HR in 62.0IP...threw more than 1.0 inning in 23 of his 40 outings...limited lefthanders to a .141 average (9-for-64, 0HR)...collected his first save since 2006 on 5/13 vs. Lakeland (1.0IP, 2H)...allowed just 3ER over his final 14 appearances (22.1IP, 1.21 ERA) with Tampa before being promoted on 7/27 for his first Double-A action...did not allow a run in the month of June (8G, 13.0IP)...**2007:** Was 6-3 with a 4.59 ERA in 41 relief appearances with Single-A Tampa...**2006:** Went 9-6 with a 3.01 ERA in 31 games (22 starts) with Single-A Charleston, leading the staff in wins...finished the season tied for sixth among all South Atlantic League pitchers in ERA...was named SAL "Pitcher of the Week" on 8/21...finished the season with a 28.0-consecutive-inning scoreless streak...his 3.01 ERA also ranked eighth among all Yankees minor leaguers...**2005:** In his first professional season, posted a 3-3 record with a 1.40 ERA in 11 games (seven starts) with the Yankees' Dominican Summer League 1 squad.

YEAR	CLUB	CLASS	W-L	ERA	G	GS	CG	SHO	SV	IP	H	R	ER	HR	HB	BB	SO	WP	BK
2005	DSL Yankees 1	R	3-3	1.40	11	7	0	0	0	45.0	27	10	7	1	1	10	56	1	0
2006	Charleston	A	9-6	3.01	31	22	1	0	2	140.2	118	50	47	9	4	53	114	2	0
2007	Tampa	A	6-3	4.59	41	0	0	0	0	68.2	70	37	35	4	2	29	60	6	0
2008	Tampa	A	4-0	2.61	29	0	0	0	1	48.1	46	16	14	1	2	14	64	3	1
	Trenton	AA	0-0	5.93	11	0	0	0	0	13.2	14	9	9	1	1	11	16	1	0
2009	Trenton	AA	5-4	3.65	48	2	0	0	0	61.2	53	26	25	4	2	22	66	3	0
Minor League Totals			**27-16**	**3.26**	**171**	**31**	**1**	**0**	**3**	**378.0**	**328**	**148**	**137**	**20**	**12**	**139**	**376**	**16**	**1**

ARON, Nathan – OF

HT: 6-1; **WT**: 187; **B**: R; **T**: R; **BORN**: 5/15/91 in Melbourne, Australia; **RESIDES**: Dingley Village, Australia; **OBTAINED**: Signed by the Yankees as a non-drafted free agent on 1/17/08; **M.L. SVC**: 0.000; **CAREER NOTES**: Will be making his professional debut in 2010...**PERSONAL:** Was signed at the age of 16 after being spotted during the under-18 national championship in Canberra, Australia, where he was teammates with fellow signee Kyle Perkins.

YEAR	CLUB	CLASS	AVG	G	AB	R	H	2B	3B	HR	RBI	SH	SF	HP	BB	SO	SB	CS	E	SLUG	OBP
NO PROFESSIONAL RECORD																					

BAILEY, Griffin – RHP

HT: 6-5; **WT:** 220; **B:** R; **T:** R; **BORN:** 9/19/84 in Lexington, Ky.; **RESIDES:** Lexington, Ky.; **COLLEGE:** Louisville; **OBTAINED:** Signed by the Yankees as a free agent on 6/18/09; **M.L. SVC:** 0.000; **CAREER NOTES: 2009:** Signed with the Yankees on 6/18 after being purchased from Sioux City of the Independent League...pitched in 32 games in relief for short-season Single-A Staten Island, going 3-2 with a 1.49 ERA...did not allow an earned run over 19 consecutive appearances from 7/9-8/25 (26.2IP)...ranked second in the NYPL in appearances...**2008:** Spent the season with Independent Southern Illinois, making a league-high 47 relief appearances and posting a 5-5 record and a 2.79 ERA...**2007:** Released from the Astros organization on 6/1 and signed with Southern Illinois...appeared in 15 games (eight starts) with the Miners, going 2-4 with a 6.27 ERA...**2006:** Made his professional debut with rookie-level Greeneville, going 0-1 with a 4.50 ERA in five games...**PERSONAL:** Attended Lexington Catholic High School where he was a member of the state championship team as a freshman in 1999...originally signed by Houston as a non-drafted free agent on 7/7/06.

YEAR	CLUB	CLASS	W-L	ERA	G	GS	CG	SHO	SV	IP	H	R	ER	HR	HB	BB	SO	WP	BK
2006	Greeneville	R	0-1	4.50	5	0	0	0	0	8.0	11	7	4	0	0	5	6	2	0
2007	Southern Ill.	IND	2-4	6.27	15	8	0	0	0	56.0	67	44	39	8	11	23	45	2	0
2008	Southern Ill.	IND	5-5	2.79	47	0	0	0	6	58.0	58	23	18	5	5	10	44	4	0
2009	Staten Island	SS-A	3-2	1.49	32	0	0	0	2	48.1	35	13	8	1	1	14	28	6	1
Minor League Totals			**3-3**	**1.92**	**37**	**0**	**0**	**0**	**2**	**56.1**	**46**	**20**	**12**	**1**	**1**	**19**	**34**	**8**	**1**

BAKER, Ryan – C

HT: 5-9; **WT:** 205; **B:** R; **T:** R; **BORN:** 11/9/84 in Portland, Maine; **RESIDES:** Portland, Maine; **M.L. SVC:** 0.000; **OBTAINED:** Signed by the Yankees as a non-drafted free agent on 6/12/08; **CAREER NOTES: 2009**: Combined to bat .200 with 1 double, 2HR and 6RBI in 18 games with short-season Single-A Staten Island and Double-A Trenton...began the season with Staten Island, batting .241 with 1 double, 2HR and 6RBI in 10 games...hit his first career HR and recorded his first professional RBI on 7/15 at Mahoning Valley...five of his six RBI on the season came on 7/22 vs. Jamestown...in eight games with Trenton, batted .125 with 2BB...was placed on the disabled list on 8/27 with a right ankle contusion, where he remained for the rest of the season...**2008:** Made his professional debut, combining to bat .100 (2-for-20) in 12 games with the GCL Yankees and Single-A Tampa.

YEAR	CLUB	CLASS	AVG	G	AB	R	H	2B	3B	HR	RBI	SH	SF	HP	BB	SO	SB	CS	E	SLUG	OBP
2008	GCL Yankees	R	.077	10	13	0	1	0	0	0	0	0	0	0	0	6	0	0	1	.077	.077
	Tampa	A	.143	2	7	0	1	0	0	0	0	0	0	0	0	1	0	0	0	.143	.143
2009	Staten Island	SS-A	.241	10	29	3	7	1	0	2	6	0	0	0	3	8	0	0	1	.483	.313
	Trenton	AA	.125	8	16	0	2	0	0	0	0	0	0	0	2	3	0	0	0	.125	.222
Minor League Totals			**.169**	**30**	**65**	**3**	**11**	**1**	**0**	**2**	**6**	**0**	**0**	**0**	**5**	**17**	**0**	**0**	**2**	**.277**	**.229**

BANUELOS, Manuel – LHP

HT: 5-10; **WT:** 155; **B:** L; **T:** L: **BORN:** 3/13/91 in Monterrey, Mexico; **RESIDES:** Durango, Mexico; **OBTAINED:** Signed by the Yankees as a non-drafted free agent on 3/30/08; **M.L. SVC:** 0.000; **CAREER NOTES: 2009**: Went 9-5 with a 2.67 ERA in 25 games (19 starts) with Single-A Charleston...began the season as a starter and allowed 2ER or less in 14 of his 19 starts...moved to the bullpen in August where he went 1-0 with a 1.64 ERA (11.0IP, 2ER) in six relief appearances with the RiverDogs...was transferred to Single-A Tampa on 9/14 and made one appearance out of the bullpen, recording 2K in 1.0IP...was selected to the World Team in the 2009 Futures Game during All-Star Weekend at St. Louis' Busch Stadium, but did not play...**2008:** Made his professional debut, going 4-1 with a 2.57 ERA in 12 appearances (three starts) with the GCL Yankees.

YEAR	CLUB	CLASS	W-L	ERA	G	GS	CG	SHO	SV	IP	H	R	ER	HR	HB	BB	SO	WP	BK
2008	GCL Yankees	R	4-1	2.57	12	3	0	0	0	42.0	32	14	12	3	6	13	37	2	1
2009	Charleston	A	9-5	2.67	25	19	0	0	0	108.0	88	40	32	4	8	28	104	13	5
	Tampa	A	0-0	0.00	1	0	0	0	0	1.0	0	0	0	0	0	0	2	0	0
Minor League Totals			**13-6**	**2.62**	**38**	**22**	**0**	**0**	**0**	**151.0**	**120**	**54**	**44**	**7**	**14**	**41**	**143**	**15**	**6**

BARREDA, Manuel – RHP

HT: 5-11; **WT:** 165; **B:** R; **T:** R; **BORN:** 10/8/88 in Sahuarita, Ariz.; **RESIDES:** Amado, Ariz.; **OBTAINED:** Selected by the Yankees in the 12th round of the 2007 First-Year Player Draft; **M.L. SVC:** 0.000; **CAREER NOTES: 2009:** Opened the season with the GCL Yankees and went 0-1 with a 1.93 ERA in 14 relief appearances, 13 of which were scoreless...his .123 opponents batting average was second-lowest among GCL relievers...promoted to Single-A Charleston on 9/2 and appeared in two games, allowing 4ER in 2.2IP...**2008:** Appeared in six games (two starts) with the GCL Yankees, recording one save and a 2.65 ERA...had season cut short after undergoing season-ending elbow surgery on 7/28...**2007:** Made his professional debut, going 5-0 with a 3.00 ERA in 11 games (three starts) with the GCL Yankees...tossed a season-high 6.1 scoreless innings in relief in 8/7 win at the GCL Tigers (2H, 1BB, 5K)...recorded at least 2K in each of his 11 appearances...**PERSONAL:** Attended Sahuarita High School (Ariz.) before being drafted by the Yankees in 2007.

YEAR	CLUB	CLASS	W-L	ERA	G	GS	CG	SHO	SV	IP	H	R	ER	HR	HB	BB	SO	WP	BK
2007	GCL Yankees	R	5-0	3.00	11	3	0	0	1	39.0	30	20	13	3	3	15	44	3	0
2008	GCL Yankees	R	0-0	2.65	6	2	0	0	1	17.0	15	6	5	1	0	8	14	2	0
2009	GCL Yankees	R	0-1	1.93	14	0	0	0	2	23.1	10	7	5	0	5	7	25	1	0
	Charleston	A	1-0	13.50	2	0	0	0	0	2.2	1	4	4	0	0	4	2	0	0
Minor League Totals			**6-1**	**2.96**	**33**	**5**	**0**	**0**	**4**	**82.0**	**56**	**37**	**27**	**4**	**8**	**34**	**85**	**6**	**0**

BARTLESKI, Philip – RHP

HT: 6-7; **WT:** 240; **B:** R; **T:** R; **BORN:** 4/22/83 in Lynchburg, Va.; **RESIDES:** Charlottesville, Va.; **COLLEGE:** Oklahoma City University; **OBTAINED:** Signed by the Yankees as a non-drafted free agent on 5/23/07; **M.L. SVC:** 0.000; **CAREER NOTES: 2009**: Combined to go 4-2 with a 3.38 ERA in 21 relief appearances with the GCL Yankees, Single-A Staten Island, Single-A Tampa and Double-A Trenton...spent the majority of the season with Tampa, going 4-1 with a 2.86 ERA in 16 appearances out of the bullpen, holding the opposition without an earned run in 13 of the 16 outings...opponents combined to hit just .225 (32-for-142) off of him during the year...**2008:** Made 29 relief appearances with Single-A Tampa, going 2-1 with one save and a 1.64 ERA...opponents batted just .179 (34-for-190, 2HR)...allowed runs in only five outings...threw a season-high 3.0IP five times, including four straight appearances from 6/1-17...**2007:** Made his professional debut, going 1-1 with a 4.03 ERA in 13 appearances with short-season Single-A Staten Island...was placed on the D.L. from 8/30-9/16 with a right elbow strain.

YEAR	CLUB	CLASS	W-L	ERA	G	GS	CG	SHO	SV	IP	H	R	ER	HR	HB	BB	SO	WP	BK
2007	Staten Island	SS-A	1-1	4.03	13	0	0	0	1	22.1	22	14	10	0	4	8	19	1	0
2008	Tampa	A	2-1	1.64	29	0	0	0	1	55.0	34	10	10	2	1	26	60	1	0
2009	GCL Yankees	R	0-0	4.50	1	0	0	0	0	2.0	2	1	1	0	0	1	0	0	0
	Staten Island	SS-A	0-0	0.00	2	0	0	0	0	4.0	1	0	0	0	1	0	7	0	0
	Tampa	A	4-1	2.86	16	0	0	0	1	28.1	23	9	9	2	3	8	30	0	0
	Trenton	AA	0-1	12.00	2	0	0	0	0	3.0	6	4	4	0	0	1	3	0	0
Minor League Totals			**7-4**	**2.67**	**63**	**0**	**0**	**0**	**3**	**114.2**	**88**	**38**	**34**	**4**	**9**	**44**	**119**	**2**	**0**

BAUTISTA, Rony – LHP

HT: 6-7; **WT**: 200; **B**: L; **T**: L; **BORN**: 9/17/91 in San Juan, D.R.; **RESIDES**: San Juan, D.R.; **OBTAINED**: Signed by the Yankees as a non-drafted free agent on 11/4/09; **M.L. SVC**: 0.000; **CAREER NOTES**: Will be making his professional debut in 2010.

YEAR	CLUB	CLASS	W-L	ERA	G	GS	CG	SHO	SV	IP	H	R	ER	HR	HB	BB	SO	WP	BK
NO PROFESSIONAL RECORD																			

BEARD, Edwin – OF

HT: 6-3; **WT:** 190; **B:** R; **T:** R; **BORN:** 8/31/89 in Moca, D.R.; **RESIDES:** Moca, D.R.; **OBTAINED:** Signed by the Yankees as a non-drafted free agent on 7/2/07; **M.L. SVC:** 0.000; **CAREER NOTES: 2009**: Appeared in a career-high 55 games with the DSL Yankees 1 and batted .290 (63-for-217) with 9 doubles, 2HR and 26 RBI...hit .331 (56-for-169) against right-handed pitching with nine doubles and 2HR...**2008:** Made his professional debut with the DSL Yankees 1, batting .211 with 1HR and 1RBI in 19 games.

YEAR	CLUB	CLASS	AVG	G	AB	R	H	2B	3B	HR	RBI	SH	SF	HP	BB	SO	SB	CS	E	SLUG	OBP
2008	DSL Yankees 1	R	.211	19	38	14	8	2	0	1	1	1	0	3	11	13	3	1	0	.342	.423
2009	DSL Yankees 1	R	.290	55	217	30	63	9	1	2	26	0	2	7	24	44	8	3	7	.369	.376
Minor League Totals			**.278**	**74**	**255**	**44**	**71**	**11**	**1**	**3**	**27**	**1**	**2**	**10**	**35**	**57**	**11**	**4**	**7**	**.365**	**.384**

BERIGUETE, Victor – RHP

HT: 6-1; **WT:** 185; **B:** R; **T:** R; **BORN:** 11/6/88 in Santo Domingo, D.R.; **RESIDES:** Santo Domingo, D.R.; **OBTAINED:** Signed by the Yankees as a non-drafted free agent on 11/2/07; **M.L. SVC:** 0.000; **CAREER NOTES: 2009:** Went 2-3 with a 3.56 ERA in a team-high-tying 11 starts with the DSL Yankees 1, issuing just 10BB in 43.0IP...held opponents to a .217 batting average...**2008:** Made his professional debut with the DSL Yankees 2, posting a 2-1 record with a 4.50 ERA in 10 games (nine starts).

YEAR	CLUB	CLASS	W-L	ERA	G	GS	CG	SHO	SV	IP	H	R	ER	HR	HB	BB	SO	WP	BK
2008	DSL Yankees 2	R	2-1	4.50	10	9	0	0	0	34.0	43	19	17	3	3	9	10	2	0
2009	DSL Yankees 1	R	2-3	3.56	11	11	0	0	0	43.0	36	27	17	2	2	10	31	2	0
Minor League Totals			**4-4**	**3.97**	**21**	**20**	**0**	**0**	**0**	**77.0**	**79**	**46**	**34**	**5**	**5**	**19**	**41**	**4**	**0**

BETANCES, Dellin – RHP

HT: 6-8; **WT:** 215; **B:** R; **T:** R; **BORN:** 3/23/88 in New York, N.Y.; **RESIDES:** New York, N.Y.; **OBTAINED:** Selected by the Yankees in the eighth round of the 2006 First-Year Player Draft ; **M.L. SVC:** 0.000; **CAREER NOTES: 2009**: Went 2-5 with a 5.48 ERA in 11 starts with Single-A Tampa, recording 44K in 44.1IP...threw 5.0IP or more in six of his 11 starts...was placed on the disabled list on 6/25 with elbow inflammation and missed the remainder of the season...**2008:** Went 9-4 with a 3.67 ERA in 22 starts for Single-A Charleston...ranked second among Yankees minor league pitchers with 141 strikeouts...led the RiverDogs staff in wins (9) and strikeouts (135)...tied for fifth in the South Atlantic League, averaging 10.5K/9.0IP...held opponents to a .208 batting average, eighth-best among all minor league starters...was placed on the disabled list on 5/27 with right shoulder inflammation...began a rehab assignment with the GCL Yankees on 6/20, going 0-1 with a 8.53 ERA in three appearances (two starts)...was returned from rehab and reinstated from the D.L. on 7/4...struck out a career-high 12 batters on 8/16 at Lakeland...following the season, was ranked by *Baseball America* as the fifth-best prospect in the Yankees' organization...**2007:** Was 1-2 with a 3.60 ERA in six starts with short-season Single-A Staten Island before being placed on the disabled from 7/21 with right elbow inflammation, missing the remainder of the season...struck out 29 batters in 25.0IP and recorded at least 3K in each of his six appearances...**2006:** Made his professional debut with the Yankees Gulf Coast squad, appearing in seven games and holding opponents to just three earned runs in 23.1 innings pitched...also limited hitters to a .173 batting average...following the season, was ranked as the Yankees' third-best prospect, according to *Baseball America*...**PERSONAL:** As a senior at Grand Street Campus High School in Brooklyn, set a school record with 20 strikeouts in a single game...became the first player from New York City to be honored as an Aflac All-American in 2005...during the 2005 regular season, posted a 6-0 record with a 0.22 ERA, allowing just 1ER while recording 100K in 41.2IP.

YEAR	CLUB	CLASS	W-L	ERA	G	GS	CG	SHO	SV	IP	H	R	ER	HR	HB	BB	SO	WP	BK
2006	GCL Yankees	R	0-1	1.16	7	7	0	0	0	23.1	14	5	3	1	1	7	27	2	1
2007	Staten Island	SS-A	1-2	3.60	6	6	0	0	0	25.0	24	11	10	0	2	17	29	3	1
2008	Charleston	A	9-4	3.67	22	22	0	0	0	115.1	87	57	47	9	11	59	135	9	3
	GCL Yankees	R	0-1	8.53	3	2	0	0	0	6.1	13	7	6	0	0	3	6	2	0
2009	Tampa	A	2-5	5.48	11	11	0	0	0	44.1	48	29	27	2	2	27	44	3	0
Minor League Totals			**12-13**	**3.91**	**49**	**48**	**0**	**0**	**0**	**214.1**	**186**	**109**	**93**	**12**	**16**	**113**	**241**	**19**	**5**

BLACK, Sean – RHP

HT: 6-3; **WT:** 185; **B:** R; **T:** R; **BORN:** 4/23/88 in Mt. Laurel, N.J.; **RESIDES:** South Orange, N.J.; **COLLEGE:** Seton Hall; **OBTAINED:** Selected by the Yankees in the seventh round of the 2009 First-Year Player Draft; **M.L. SVC:** 0.000; **CAREER NOTES: 2009:** Went 6-0 with a 1.62 ERA in 10 starts with short-season Single-A Staten Island in his first professional action...tied for the team lead in wins...named NYPL "Pitcher of the Week" for the period of 8/10-17, going 2-0 and allowing only 2ER in 11.0IP over two starts...included was 6.0 innings of no-hit ball on 8/13 vs. Auburn (2BB, 8K)...**PERSONAL:** Attended Seton Hall University where as a junior in 2009 was named the school's "Junior Male Athlete of the Year" and was a member of the All-New Jersey College Baseball Association First Team and All-Big East Second Team...was drafted by Washington in 2006 but chose to attend college.

YEAR	CLUB	CLASS	W-L	ERA	G	GS	CG	SHO	SV	IP	H	R	ER	HR	HB	BB	SO	WP	BK
2009	Staten Island	SS-A	6-0	1.62	10	10	0	0	0	50.0	30	14	9	2	1	9	34	0	0

BLEICH, Jeremy – LHP

NON-ROSTER INVITEE

HT: 6-2; **WT:** 185; **B:** L; **T:** L; **BORN:** 6/18/87 in Metairie, La.; **RESIDES:** Metairie, La.; **COLLEGE:** Stanford University; **OBTAINED:** Selected by the Yankees in Compensation Round A (44th overall) of the 2008 First-Year Player Draft.; **M.L. SVC:** 0.000; **CAREER NOTES:** Enters the season ranked as the Yankees' ninth-best prospect by *Baseball America*...**2009**: Combined to go 9-10 with a 4.86 ERA in 27 starts with Single-A Tampa and Double-A Trenton...ranked fifth among all Yankees minor leaguers with 116K...began the season with Tampa, going 6-4 with a 3.40 ERA in 14 starts...won his final three decisions with Tampa, holding his opponents to 1ER in 18.1IP (15H, 2R, 3BB, 13K)...was promoted to Trenton on 6/30, going 3-6 with a 6.65 ERA in 13 starts...**2008:** Made his professional debut with short-season Single-A Staten Island, making one start and allowing 2H and 2ER in 3.0IP (4K, 1HR)...made one postseason relief appearance for Staten Island, tossing 4.0 scoreless innings (2H, 4K)...pitched for the Waikiki BeachBoys in the Hawaiian Winter Baseball League following the season, going 3-2 with a 1.77 ERA in seven starts (35.2IP, 29H, 10R, 7ER, 12BB, 33K, 1HR)...**PERSONAL:** Full name is Jeremy Michael Bleich...attended Stanford University, where he went 3-3 with a 2.09 ERA during his junior year in 2008, allowing just 11ER in 47.1IP and leading the team in ERA (min. 5G)...missed eight weeks of the season (March through mid-May) with a strained ligament in his left elbow...started the opening game of the 2008 College World Series vs. Florida State, recording a no-decision despite allowing 1ER while striking out a season-high seven batters in 5.0IP...his sixth-inning leadoff HR allowed to FSU's Dennis Quinn on his 89th and final pitch of the game snapped a 25.2-inning stretch without allowing an earned run...faced fellow Yankees-draftee Jack Rye in the game, with Rye going 0-for-3 with 1K...earned Cape Cod League All-Star honors while playing for the Wareham Gatemen in 2006...was on the U.S.A. Junior National Team in 2005.

YEAR	CLUB	CLASS	W-L	ERA	G	GS	CG	SHO	SV	IP	H	R	ER	HR	HB	BB	SO	WP	BK
2008	Staten Island	SS-A	0-0	6.00	1	1	0	0	0	3.0	2	2	2	1	1	0	4	0	0
2009	Tampa	A	6-4	3.40	14	14	0	0	0	79.1	79	34	30	4	0	22	56	6	0
	Trenton	AA	3-6	6.65	13	13	0	0	0	65.0	84	54	48	6	6	34	60	5	0
Minor League Totals			**9-10**	**4.89**	**28**	**28**	**0**	**0**	**0**	**147.1**	**165**	**90**	**80**	**11**	**7**	**56**	**120**	**11**	**0**

BRABOY, Brandon – RHP

HT: 6-0; **WT:** 195; **B:** R; **T:** R; **BORN:** 10/31/85 in Kevil, Ky.; **RESIDES:** Kevil, Ky.; **COLLEGE:** University of Indianapolis; **OBTAINED:** Selected by the Yankees in the 18th round of the 2008 First-Year Player Draft; **M.L. SVC:** 0.000; **CAREER NOTES: 2009**: Went 4-5 with a 3.97 ERA in 33 games (nine starts) with Single-A Charleston...went 2-3 as a reliever with one save and a 4.01 ERA (49.1IP, 22ER) in 24 appearances out of the bullpen...shifted to the starting rotation in July and made nine consecutive starts to end the campaign, going 2-2 with a 3.92 ERA (43.2IP, 19ER)...threw 5.0IP or more in five of his nine starts...**2008:** Made his professional debut with short-season Single-A Staten Island, going 2-1 with a 3.21 ERA in 10 starts...was named the New York-Penn League's "Pitcher of the Week" for the period of 7/21-27, going 1-0 with a 0.00 ERA in two starts (11.0IP, 5H, 1R, 0ER, 3BB, 10K)...was placed on the disabled list on 8/7 for the remainder of the season with right shoulder tendinitis...**PERSONAL:** Attended the University of Indianapolis, going 8-3 with a 3.61 ERA and four complete games in 14 appearances (13 starts) during his junior year...named All-Region and team MVP in baseball and basketball as a senior at Heath (Ky.) High School.

YEAR	CLUB	CLASS	W-L	ERA	G	GS	CG	SHO	SV	IP	H	R	ER	HR	HB	BB	SO	WP	BK
2008	Staten Island	SS-A	2-1	3.21	10	10	0	0	0	42.0	42	20	15	2	4	18	31	2	0
2009	Charleston	A	4-5	3.97	33	9	0	0	1	93.0	83	51	41	8	8	24	77	12	2
Minor League Totals			**6-6**	**3.73**	**43**	**19**	**0**	**0**	**1**	**135.0**	**125**	**71**	**56**	**10**	**12**	**42**	**108**	**14**	**2**

BRAVO, Wilfi – RHP

HT: 6-1; **WT:** 155; **B:** R; **T:** R; **BORN:** 2/26/89 in Santo Domingo, D.R.; **RESIDES:** Santo Domingo, D.R.; **OBTAINED:** Signed by the Yankees as a non-drafted free agent on 6/1/07; **M.L. SVC:** 0.000; **CAREER NOTES: 2009:** Went 1-3 with five saves and a 5.13 ERA in 13 relief appearances with the DSL Yankees 1...led the team in saves...**2008:** Appeared in 18 games (one start) with the DSL Yankees 1 and went 2-2 with a 2.36 ERA...was a perfect 7-for-7 in save opportunities...limited opponents to 1ER or less in all but two if his 18 appearances...**2007:** Made his professional debut, going 1-2 with a 4.11 ERA in 19G (one start) with the DSL Yankees 2.

YEAR	CLUB	CLASS	W-L	ERA	G	GS	CG	SHO	SV	IP	H	R	ER	HR	HB	BB	SO	WP	BK
2007	DSL Yankees 2	R	1-2	4.11	19	1	0	0	0	35.0	37	23	16	3	3	17	23	6	0
2008	DSL Yankees 1	R	2-2	2.36	18	1	0	0	7	45.2	39	17	12	0	3	17	30	4	0
2009	DSL Yankees 1	R	1-3	5.13	13	0	0	0	5	26.1	26	17	15	1	1	12	18	1	0
Minor League Totals			**4-7**	**3.62**	**50**	**2**	**0**	**0**	**12**	**107.0**	**102**	**57**	**43**	**4**	**7**	**46**	**71**	**11**	**0**

BREWER, Daniel – OF

HT: 6-0; **WT:** 185; **B:** R; **T:** R; **BORN:** 7/19/87 in Brookfield, Ill.; **RESIDES:** Batavia, Ill.; **COLLEGE:** Bradley University; **OBTAINED:** Selected by the Yankees in the eighth round of the 2008 First-Year Player Draft; **M.L. SVC:** 0.000; **CAREER NOTES: 2009**: Combined to hit .306 with 70R, 25 doubles, 6HR and 54RBI in 117 games with Single-A Charleston and Single-A Tampa...tied for third among all Yankees minor leaguers in batting average and ranked fifth in stolen bases (22)...began the season with Charleston, batting .323 with 38R, 18 doubles, 2HR and 25RBI in 58 games...was promoted to Tampa on 6/25 and hit .290 with 32R, 7 doubles, 4HR and 29RBI in 59 games...**2008:** Made his professional debut, batting .296 with 29R, 19 doubles, 3HR and 40RBI in 66 games with short-season Single-A Staten Island...tied for fourth among Yankees minor leaguers in batting average...hit .381 (43-for-113) with 12 doubles and 17RBI in 31 road games...batted .571 (4-for-7) with 1 double and 9RBI with the bases loaded...hit .111 (1-for-9) with 2RBI in two postseason games...**PERSONAL:** Attended Bradley University where he majored in business with an emphasis in marketing...was named to the Brooks Wallace Award Preseason Watch List prior to his junior year and batted .341 (63-for-185) with 51R, 15 doubles, 6HR and 36RBI in 53 games...was named First-Team All-MVC as an outfielder, becoming the fourth Brave since 1973 to earn the honor...became the first player in school history with at least 20 career homers and 40 stolen bases...was a career .333 (197-for-592) batter with 142R, 47 doubles, 21HR and 101RBI in 163 games at Bradley, tying for fourth all-time with nine triples and ranking seventh in runs, doubles and stolen bases (47), while placing ninth in total bases (325)...was a Cape Cod League All-Star in 2007...attended Lyons Township High School where he played football and baseball for four seasons and wrestled for three years...was a three-time all-conference performer in baseball, batting .460 with 13HR and 57RBI during his senior year.

YEAR	CLUB	CLASS	AVG	G	AB	R	H	2B	3B	HR	RBI	SH	SF	HP	BB	SO	SB	CS	E	SLUG	OBP
2008	Staten Island	SS-A	.296	66	230	29	68	19	1	3	40	1	2	8	21	65	10	1	2	.426	.372
2009	Charleston	A	.323	58	201	38	65	18	3	2	25	1	1	5	33	49	9	5	4	.473	.429
	Tampa	A	.290	59	224	32	65	7	3	4	29	2	2	3	22	46	13	3	0	.402	.359
Minor League Totals			**.302**	**183**	**655**	**99**	**198**	**44**	**7**	**9**	**94**	**4**	**5**	**16**	**76**	**160**	**32**	**9**	**6**	**.432**	**.386**

BROOKS, Gavin – LHP

HT: 6-3; **WT:** 220; **B:** L; **T:** L; **BORN:** 10/27/87 in Vista, Calif.; **RESIDES:** Los Angeles, Calif.; **COLLEGE:** UCLA; **OBTAINED:** Selected by the Yankees in the ninth round of the 2009 First-Year Player Draft; **M.L. SVC:** 0.000; **CAREER NOTES: 2009:** Made 30 appearances in relief for short-season Single-A Staten Island in his first professional season, going 5-1 with a 0.62 ERA...struck out 48 batters in 43.1IP and held opponents scoreless in 25 of his outings...did not allow an earned run over his first 12 appearances (14.2IP, 10H, 3R, 11BB, 18K)...ranked fourth in the NYPL in appearances...made five postseason appearances for the NYPL champs, going 1-1 with a 1.29 ERA (7.0IP, 1ER)...**PERSONAL:** Drafted out of UCLA where he recorded a team-high eight saves as a Junior and earned All-Pac 10 honorable mention...graduated from Rancho Buena Vista HS (Calif.), earning AFLAC All-American honors in 2005 as a junior and the school's "Male Athlete of the Year" as a senior in 2006.

YEAR	CLUB	CLASS	W-L	ERA	G	GS	CG	SHO	SV	IP	H	R	ER	HR	HB	BB	SO	WP	BK
2009	Staten Island	SS-A	5-1	0.62	30	0	0	0	3	43.1	27	8	3	1	1	24	48	1	0

BROWN, Isaiah – OF

HT: 6-0; **WT:** 160; **B:** R; **T:** R; **BORN:** 10/16/89 in Phoenix, Ariz.; **RESIDES:** Glendale, Ariz.; **COLLEGE:** Paradise Valley CC; **OBTAINED:** Selected by the Yankees in the 43rd round of the 2009 First-Year Player Draft; **M.L. SVC:** 0.000; **CAREER NOTES: 2009:** Played in 20 games with the GCL Yankees in his first professional season, batting .167.

YEAR	CLUB	CLASS	AVG	G	AB	R	H	2B	3B	HR	RBI	SH	SF	HB	BB	SO	SB	CS	E	SLUG	OBP
2009	GCL Yankees	R	.167	20	36	5	6	1	0	1	4	0	1	3	8	14	2	1	1	.278	.354

BUSH, Paul – RHP

HT: 6-1; **WT:** 195; **B:** R; **T:** R; **BORN:** 10/5/79 in Titusville, Fla.; **RESIDES:** Titusville, Fla.; **COLLEGE:** Georgia Southwestern; **OBTAINED:** Signed by the Yankees as a free agent on 5/29/09; **M.L. SVC:** 0.000; **CAREER NOTES: 2009:** Was signed by the Yankees on 5/29 and reported to Triple-A Scranton/Wilkes-Barre...went 2-2 with a 4.86 ERA in seven games (two starts) before being transferred to Double-A Trenton on 7/31...made just five starts (1-1, 1.33ERA) over the remaining two months in between two stints on the disabled list (7/31-8/11 with a bruised middle finger and 8/22 through the end of the season with right elbow tendinitis)...**2008:** Completed rehab from "Tommy John" surgery and appeared in 17 combined games (three starts) with the GCL Braves and Double-A Mississippi, going 0-2 with a 2.67 ERA...**2007:** Underwent season-ending surgery after making only six appearances, all in relief...**2006:** Combined to go 5-9 with a 4.38 ERA in 37 games (10 starts) with Double-A Mississippi and Triple-A Richmond...was promoted to Richmond on 6/17 for the remainder of the season...tossed four straight scoreless outtings (6/20-29) in his first Triple-A action...pitched in eight games (five starts) for the Leones del Caracas of the Venezuelan Winter League and recorded a 1-2 record with a 3.57 ERA...went to spring training with the Braves (3G, 0-0, 10.38ERA, 4K)...**2005:** Split the season between Single-A Myrtle Beach and Mississippi, going 3-3 with five saves and a 2.36 ERA in 37 games (eight starts) and held opponents to a .193 batting average (eighth-lowest among Atlanta farmhands...posted the fifth-lowest ERA among Braves minor leaguers...earned his first career save on 4/20 vs. Winston-Salem...struck out 52 batters in 52.2IP in his Doule-A debut...went 3-1 with a 6.66 ERA in seven games (six starts with Pheonix in the Arizona Fall League following the season...**2004:** Pitched his second straight season with Myrtle Beach, posting a 5-3 record and a 3.56 ERA in 24 games (four starts)...**2003:** Made 34 appearances (two starts) with Myrtle Beach, going 4-4 with a 3.63 ERA...allowed just 2ER and struck out 22 batters over the final two months of the season (21.0IP)...ranked second in the Myrtle Beach bullpen with 64K...**2002:** Made his professional debut with rookie-level Danville, going 4-1 with a 2.35 ERA...led team relievers with 48K...**PERSONAL:** Full name is Paul David Bush...was originally selected by the Atlanta Braves in the 24th round of the 2002 First-Year Player Draft

YEAR	CLUB	CLASS	W-L	ERA	G	GS	CG	SHO	SV	IP	H	R	ER	HR	HB	BB	SO	WP	BK
2002	Danville	R	4-1	2.35	20	2	0	0	0	46.0	39	19	12	2	1	14	48	0	0
2003	Myrtle Beach	A	4-4	3.63	34	2	0	0	0	62.0	49	32	25	7	1	30	64	1	0
2004	Myrtle Beach	A	5-3	3.56	24	4	0	0	0	65.2	58	27	26	7	3	25	78	4	1
2005	Myrtle Beach	A	1-3	2.32	18	3	0	0	4	42.2	36	16	11	3	1	13	40	3	0
	Mississippi	AA	2-0	2.39	19	5	0	0	1	52.2	29	17	14	2	3	22	52	2	0
2006	Mississippi	AA	5-5	4.91	20	6	0	0	0	58.2	62	36	32	8	6	23	60	2	0
	Richmond	AAA	0-4	3.60	17	4	0	0	0	40.0	29	17	16	3	3	16	36	1	0
2007	Richmond	AAA	1-0	1.74	5	0	0	0	1	10.1	5	2	2	0	2	5	10	1	0
	Mississippi	AA	0-0	0.00	1	0	0	0	0	1.0	1	0	0	0	0	0	2	0	0
2008	GCL Braves	R	0-1	1.74	5	3	0	0	0	10.1	5	3	2	0	3	2	13	0	0
	Mississippi	AA	0-1	3.24	12	0	0	0	0	16.2	10	6	6	2	4	7	21	2	0
2009	Scranton/WB	AAA	2-2	4.86	7	2	0	0	0	16.2	13	10	9	1	0	7	20	1	0
	Trenton	AAA	1-1	1.33	5	5	0	0	0	20.1	8	3	3	1	1	11	23	1	0
Minor League Totals			**25-25**	**3.21**	**187**	**36**	**0**	**0**	**6**	**443.0**	**344**	**188**	**158**	**36**	**28**	**175**	**467**	**18**	**1**

CABRERA, Cristofer – RHP

HT: 6-0; **WT**: 180; **B**: R; **T**: R; **BORN**: 12/25/92 in Altamira, Puerto Plata, D.R.; **RESIDES**: Altamira, Puerto Plata, D.R.; **OBTAINED**: Signed by the Yankees as a non-drafted free agent on 7/2/09; **M.L. SVC**: 0.000; **CAREER NOTES**: Will be making his professional debut in 2010.

YEAR	CLUB	CLASS	W-L	ERA	G	GS	CG	SHO	SV	IP	H	R	ER	HR	HB	BB	SO	WP	BK
NO PROFESSIONAL RECORD																			

CALDERON, Yeicok – OF

HT: 6-2; **WT:** 185; **B:** L; **T:** L; **BORN:** 12/23/91 in La Romana, D.R.; **RESIDES:** La Romana, D.R.; **OBTAINED:** Signed by the Yankees as a non-drafted free agent on 7/2/08; **M.L. SVC:** 0.000; **CAREER NOTES: 2009:** Made his professional debut with the DSL Yankees 1, batting .321 with 38R, 5 doubles, 2 triples, 3HR, 27RBI and 9SB...ranked eighth in the league in batting average...hit safely in 10 straight games from 7/6-16, batting .526 (20-for-38) with 13R and 8BB over the stretch.

YEAR	CLUB	CLASS	AVG	G	AB	R	H	2B	3B	HR	RBI	SH	SF	HP	BB	SO	SB	CS	E	SLUG	OBP
2009	DSL Yankees 1	R	.321	55	193	38	62	5	2	3	27	0	4	6	38	45	9	1	8	.415	.440

CANELA, Erick - RHP

HT: 6-1; **WT:** 155; **B:** R; **T:** R; **BORN:** 10/2/90 in Villa Vazquez, D.R.; **RESIDES:** Villa Vazquez, D.R.; **OBTAINED:** Signed by the Yankees as a non-drafted free agent on 6/6/09; **M.L. SVC:** 0.000; **CAREER NOTES: 2009:** Went 3-1 with a 4.22 ERA in 16 games (eight starts) with the DSL Yankees 1...did not earn a win in any of his eight starts but pitched to a 3.52 ERA, while going 3-0 with a 5.40 mark and 27K in 18.1IP in his eight relief outings.

YEAR	CLUB	CLASS	W-L	ERA	G	GS	CG	SHO	SV	IP	H	R	ER	HR	HB	BB	SO	WP	BK
2009	DSL Yankees 1	R	3-1	4.22	16	8	0	0	0	49.0	46	34	23	2	6	34	54	15	0

CASTILLO, Ali - INF

HT: 5-10; **WT:** 165; **B:** R; **T:** R; **BORN:** 6/19/89 in Maracaibo, Venezuela; **RESIDES:** Maracaibo, Venezuela; **OBTAINED:** Signed by the Yankees as a non-drafted free agent on 10/10/07; **M.L. SVC:** 0.000; **CAREER NOTES: 2009:** Batted .319 with 40R, 13 doubles, 9 triples, 1HR, 27RBI and 10SB in 52 games...drew 24BB with only 14K...was caught stealing just once...ranked fifth in the league in slugging (.503) and 10th in average, and tied for the team lead in triples...had the fifth-most PA/K (15.14)...led all DSL third basemen with a .955 fielding percentage (9E, 198TC)...**2008:** In his professional debut, hit .288 with 10 doubles, 4 triples and 36RBI in 68 games for the DSL Yankees 1...fashioned a 15-game hitting streak from 7/22-8/9, batting .369 (24-for-65) with 11R, 3 doubles and 11RBI over the stretch.

YEAR	CLUB	CLASS	AVG	G	AB	R	H	2B	3B	HR	RBI	SH	SF	HP	BB	SO	SB	CS	E	SLUG	OBP
2008	DSL Yankees 1	R	.288	68	243	42	70	10	4	1	36	2	0	7	27	25	8	10	14	.374	.375
2009	DSL Yankees 1	R	.319	51	185	40	59	13	9	1	27	0	2	1	24	14	10	1	9	.503	.396
Minor League Totals			**.301**	**119**	**428**	**82**	**129**	**23**	**13**	**2**	**63**	**2**	**2**	**8**	**51**	**39**	**18**	**11**	**23**	**.430**	**.384**

CASTILLO, Noel - RHP

HT: 6-1; **WT:** 160; **B:** R; **T:** R; **BORN:** 10/05/83 in San Pedro de Macoris, D.R.; **RESIDES:** San Pedro de Macoris, D.R.; **OBTAINED:** Signed by the Yankees as a non-drafted free agent on 9/16/04; **M.L. SVC:** 0.000; **CAREER NOTES: 2009**: Combined to go 3-2 with a 3.92 ERA in 37 appearances (two starts) with Single-A Tampa and Double-A Trenton...began the season with Tampa, going 3-2 with a 2.91 ERA in 31 appearances (two starts)...combined to toss 6.0 scoreless innings in his only two starts on 8/11 at Daytona and 8/18 (Game 2) vs. Daytona (4H, 2BB, 4K)...appeared in six games with Trenton from 4/25-5/13, allowing 10ER in 8.0IP (11.25 ERA) without recording a decision...following the season, pitched in three game for the Estrellas de Oriente of the Dominican Winter League...**2008:** Combined to go 8-8 with a 3.79 ERA in 26 appearances (22 starts) with Single-A Charleston and Single-A Tampa...ranked fourth among Yankees minor league pitchers in strikeouts (126)...struck out a season-high eight batters three times (4/5 at Rome, 5/18 vs. Asheville and 6/8 at Savannah)...was placed on the disabled list from 7/18-26 with a right oblique muscle strain...tossed a rain-shortened complete-game on 8/14 at Delmarva and recorded the loss, for his first career CG (5.2IP, 10H, 4ER, 1BB, 6K)...was promoted to Tampa on 8/30 and made the start that day at Fort Myers, allowing 6H and 1ER in 6.0IP (2BB, 7K)...**2007:** Was 6-3 with two saves and a 1.88 ERA in 13G (seven starts) with the GCL Yankees...ranked eighth in the minors, fourth in the GCL and led all Yankees minor league pitchers in ERA...did not allow a run in back-to-back starts on 8/3 and 8/9 (11.0IP)...struck out at least one batter in each of his 13 appearances and allowed only one home run during the season...**2006:** Made 14 appearances (10 starts) for the Yankees' Dominican Summer League 1 team, posting a 3-1 record with a 2.67 ERA...held opposing hitters to a .202 batting average and limited right-handed batters to just .188...**2005:** In first professional season, posted a 2-0 record with a 0.69 ERA in four games with the Yankees' Dominican Summer League 1 squad.

YEAR	CLUB	CLASS	W-L	ERA	G	GS	CG	SHO	SV	IP	H	R	ER	HR	HB	BB	SO	WP	BK
2005	DSL Yankees 1	R	2-0	0.69	4	0	0	0	0	13.0	11	2	1	0	2	1	5	0	0
2006	DSL Yankees 1	R	3-1	2.67	14	10	0	0	0	54.0	40	20	16	2	6	8	43	2	0
2007	GCL Yankees	R	6-3	1.88	13	7	0	0	2	52.2	53	17	11	1	7	7	51	2	0
2008	Charleston	A	7-8	3.90	25	21	1	0	0	127.0	115	64	55	6	6	44	119	8	2
	Tampa	A	1-0	1.50	1	1	0	0	0	6.0	6	1	1	0	1	2	7	0	0
2009	Tampa	A	3-2	2.91	31	2	0	0	2	58.2	52	24	19	1	8	31	56	5	0
	Trenton	AA	0-0	11.25	6	0	0	0	0	8.0	11	10	10	1	2	10	12	2	0
Minor League Totals			**22-14**	**3.18**	**94**	**41**	**1**	**0**	**4**	**319.1**	**288**	**138**	**113**	**11**	**32**	**103**	**293**	**19**	**2**

CASTRO, Kelvin - INF

HT: 6-3; **WT:** 164; **B:** R; **T:** R; **BORN:** 12/14/87 in San Pedro, D.R.; **RESIDES:** San Pedro, D.R.; **OBTAINED:** Signed by the Yankees as a non-drafted free agent on 1/28/06; **M.L. SVC:** 0.000; **CAREER NOTES: 2009:** Spent the entire season with short-season Single-A Staten Island, batting .212 with a career-high 11 doubles, 5 triples, 2HR and 27RBI...**2008:** Was limited to 15 combined games with the GCL Yankees and Staten Island after beginning the season on the disabled list with a strained muscle in his back...**2007:** Batted .277 with 25R, 10 doubles and 22RBI in 49 games for the GCL Yankees...**2006:** Made professional debut with the DSL Yankees 2, batting .183 in 65 games at shortstop...among DSL shortstops, led the league in games, total chances (353), putouts (108), assists (214) and double plays (35).

YEAR	CLUB	CLASS	AVG	G	AB	R	H	2B	3B	HR	RBI	SH	SF	HB	BB	SO	SB	CS	E	SLUG	OBP
2006	DSL Yankees 2	R	.183	65	246	41	45	8	0	6	30	4	2	4	28	68	9	4	31	.289	.275
2007	GCL Yankees	R	.277	49	177	25	49	10	3	1	22	3	0	2	6	42	6	1	11	.384	.308
2008	GCL Yankees	R	.286	6	14	3	4	1	0	0	0	2	0	0	1	2	0	0	1	.357	.333
	Staten Island	SS-A	.000	9	26	2	0	0	0	0	1	0	0	0	1	11	0	0	5	.000	.037
2009	Staten Island	SS-A	.212	65	217	24	46	11	5	2	27	2	1	3	13	62	6	4	19	.336	.265
Minor League Totals			**.212**	**194**	**680**	**95**	**144**	**30**	**8**	**9**	**80**	**12**	**3**	**9**	**49**	**185**	**21**	**9**	**67**	**.319**	**.273**

CHECO, Mariel – RHP

HT: 6-3; **WT**: 190; **B**: R; **T**: R; **BORN**: 10/16/89 in New York, N.Y.; **RESIDES**: New York, N.Y.; **OBTAINED**: Selected by the Yankees in the 41st round of the 2009 First-Year Player Draft; **M.L. SVC**: 0.000; **CAREER NOTES**: **2009**: Made his professional debut, going 1-1 with an 8.40 ERA in 10 appearances out of the bullpen with the GCL Yankees…recorded 14K in 15.0IP.

YEAR	CLUB	CLASS	W-L	ERA	G	GS	CG	SHO	SV	IP	H	R	ER	HR	HB	BB	SO	WP	BK
2009	GCL Yankees	R	1-1	8.40	10	0	0	0	0	15.0	14	15	14	1	0	14	14	3	0

COOPER, James – OF

HT: 5-10; **WT:** 190; **B:** L; **T:** R; **BORN:** 2/18/84 in Los Angeles, Calif.; **RESIDES:** Los Angeles, Calif.; **COLLEGE:** Loyola Marymount University; **OBTAINED:** Selected by the Yankees in the ninth round of the 2005 First-Year Player Draft; **M.L. SVC:** 0.000; **CAREER NOTES: 2009**: Spent the entire season with Double-A Trenton, batting .240 with 12 doubles, 3 triples, 1HR and 31RBI in 81 games…hit .292 (21-for-72, 1HR) against left-handed pitchers and .220 (41-for-186, 0HR) off righties…missed nearly two months on the disabled list with a right oblique muscle strain from 6/10-7/18…**2008:** Combined to bat .279 with 20 doubles, 1HR and 39RBI in 118 games with Single-A Tampa and Double-A Trenton…reached the Double-A level for the first time following a 7/2 promotion…hit .232 with 5 doubles and 17RBI in 52 games with Trenton, including a 12-game hitting streak from 7/24-8/5…also appeared in two postseason games for the Eastern League champions, going 3-for-5 with 1 double and 1RBI…opened the year at Tampa where he hit .311 with 15 doubles, 1HR and 22RBI in 66 games…batted a team-high .396 (21-for-53) in April with seven multi-hit games…hit safely in his final 10 games with Tampa and 19 of his final 22…did not commit an error on the season, playing at all three outfield positions…**2007:** Combined to hit .279 with 42R, 17 doubles, 5 triples, 5HR and 25RBI in 87 games with Single-A Tampa and Single-A Charleston…was transferred from Tampa to Charleston on 6/22…**2006:** Played in a combined 57 games with Single-A Charleston and short-season Single-A Staten Island, posting a .234 batting average…began the season with Charleston and played in nine games before being transferred to Staten Island…played in 22 games with Staten Island before being transferred back to Charleston on 7/24…played the remainder of the season with the RiverDogs…**2005:** Made professional debut with Staten Island, batting .247 with 1HR and 34RBI in 64 games…ranked fifth in the NY-Penn League, averaging a strikeout every 10.56AB…**PERSONAL:** Full name is James William Cooper…was a three-year starter at Loyola Marymount University in Los Angeles prior to being drafted by the Yankees in 2005…lettered in football and baseball at Santa Monica High School…was the Bay League's "Most Outstanding Player" as a senior…set a school record for career touchdowns and set a state baseball record, hitting a home run in six consecutive games.

YEAR	CLUB	CLASS	AVG	G	AB	R	H	2B	3B	HR	RBI	SH	SF	HP	BB	SO	SB	CS	E	SLUG	OBP
2005	Staten Island	SS-A	.247	64	243	30	60	7	3	1	34	3	2	10	27	27	5	9	0	.313	.344
2006	Charleston	A	.211	35	90	8	19	3	0	1	8	1	1	5	6	17	0	0	1	.278	.294
	Staten Island	SS-A	.260	22	77	10	20	5	1	0	10	1	1	5	6	8	3	1	0	.351	.348
2007	Tampa	A	.259	32	108	11	28	4	2	3	10	0	0	2	7	17	0	1	1	.417	.316
	Charleston	A	.291	57	189	31	55	13	3	2	15	1	1	10	19	28	8	4	2	.423	.384
2008	Tampa	A	.311	66	241	32	75	15	1	1	22	1	3	15	19	25	7	3	0	.394	.392
	Trenton	AA	.232	52	168	13	39	5	1	0	17	0	1	3	22	28	3	3	0	.372	.330
2009	Trenton	AA	.240	81	258	42	62	12	3	1	31	1	0	11	22	27	2	2	1	.322	.326
Minor League Totals			**.261**	**409**	**1374**	**177**	**358**	**64**	**14**	**9**	**147**	**8**	**9**	**61**	**128**	**177**	**28**	**23**	**5**	**.347**	**.348**

COTHAM, Caleb – RHP

HT: 6-3; **WT:** 215; **B:** R; **T:** R; **BORN:** 11/6/87 in Mt. Juliet, Tenn.; **RESIDES:** Mt. Juliet, Tenn.; **COLLEGE:** Vanderbilt; **OBTAINED:** Selected by the Yankees in the fifth round of the 2009 First-Year Player Draft; **M.L. SVC:** 0.000; **CAREER NOTES: 2009:** Made three combined starts with the GCL Yankees and short-season Single-A Staten Island, going 0-1 with a 3.38 ERA and 13K in 8.0IP…**PERSONAL:** Was a two-year captain of the Mt. Juliet High School baseball team…was also his high school junior class president and a member of the National Junior Honors Society.

YEAR	CLUB	CLASS	W-L	ERA	G	GS	CG	SHO	SV	IP	H	R	ER	HR	HB	BB	SO	WP	BK
2009	GCL Yankees	R	0-0	0.00	1	1	0	0	0	2.0	2	0	0	0	0	0	5	0	0
	Staten Island	SS-A	0-1	4.50	2	2	0	0	0	6.0	5	3	3	1	0	3	8	0	0
Minor League Totals			**0-1**	**3.38**	**3**	**3**	**0**	**0**	**0**	**8.0**	**7**	**3**	**3**	**1**	**0**	**3**	**13**	**0**	**0**

COX, J.B. – RHP

HT: 6-3; **WT:** 205; **B:** L; **T:** R; **BORN:** 5/13/84 in Bay City, Tex.; **RESIDES:** Austin, Tex.; **COLLEGE:** University of Texas; **OBTAINED:** Selected in the second round of the 2005 First-Year Player Draft; **M.L. SVC:** 0.000; **CAREER NOTES: 2009**: Combined to go 0-3 with a 7.30 ERA in 17 appearances (one start) with Triple-A Scranton/Wilkes-Barre and Double-A Trenton…made his first professional start on 5/25 with Scranton/WB, recording the loss after allowing 6H and 5ER in 2.1IP (2BB)…was placed on the disabled list on 5/27 with right shoulder inflammation…reinstated from the D.L. on 6/12 and transferred to Trenton, where he made five relief appearances, going 0-2 with an 8.31 ERA before being placed on the disabled list for a second time on 6/26 with right shoulder inflammation and missing the remainder of the season…**2008:** Combined at three levels (Single-A Tampa, Double-A Trenton and Triple-A Scranton/Wilkes-Barre) to go 5-4 with a 4.07 ERA in 39 relief appearances…held right-handers to a .198 average (18-for-91, 2HR)…joined Scranton/WB on 5/13 and did not allow a run in his first nine outings (10.1IP)…**2007:** Spent the season on the disabled list after having right elbow surgery on 3/27…entered the 2007 season ranked as the eighth-best prospect in the Yankees organization by *Baseball America* and as having the "best slider" among all Yankees farmhands…**2006:** Posted a 6-2 record with a 1.75 ERA and three saves in 41 relief appearances for Double-A Trenton…did not allow a run in 15 consecutive appearances from 6/8-7/23 (22.0IP)…was selected to be a member of Team USA at the COPABE Olympic Qualifying Tournament in Cuba in August…appeared in three games for Team USA and allowed one run in 5.2IP with one walk and six strikeouts to help lead the US to a first-place finish and automatic berth in the 2008 Olympics in Berlin…**2005:** In first professional season, went 1-2 with a 2.60 ERA in 16 games for the Single-A Tampa Yankees…held opposing hitters to a .206 batting average…**PERSONAL:** Full name is James Brent Cox…played baseball at the University of Texas and helped guide the Longhorns to the National Championship in 2005, leading the club with a 1.72 ERA and 19 saves in 42 appearances…following the season, was named to the 2005 College World Series All-Tournament Team…was honored as the first-ever winner of the National Collegiate Baseball Writers' Association (NCBWA) "Stopper of the Year" Award, given to the top relief pitcher in collegiate baseball…was a 2005 first-team All-Big 12 selection and second-team All-American after tying the UT record with 19 saves in a single season…previously named to the 2004 Big-12 All-Conference Team, ranking third with a 2.12 ERA in 37 appearance…also named to the Big-12 All-Conference Team in 2003.

YEAR	CLUB	CLASS	W-L	ERA	G	GS	CG	SHO	SV	IP	H	R	ER	HR	HB	BB	SO	WP	BK
2005	Tampa	A	1-2	2.60	16	0	0	0	0	27.2	20	9	8	1	3	5	27	1	0
2006	Trenton	AA	6-2	1.75	41	0	0	0	3	77.0	54	21	15	2	2	24	60	2	1
2007			Did Not Pitch - Injured																
2008	Tampa	A	0-0	3.00	6	0	0	0	1	6.0	8	2	2	0	0	2	2	0	0
	Trenton	AA	0-0	1.35	5	0	0	0	1	6.2	3	1	1	0	0	2	6	0	0
	Scranton/WB	AAA	5-4	4.75	28	0	0	0	0	36.0	30	21	19	3	2	17	16	1	0
2009	Scranton/WB	AAA	0-1	7.08	12	1	0	0	1	20.1	29	18	16	2	2	9	11	4	0
	Trenton	AA	0-2	8.31	5	0	0	0	0	4.1	5	4	4	1	0	6	4	1	0
Minor League Totals			**12-11**	**3.29**	**113**	**1**	**0**	**0**	**6**	**178.0**	**149**	**76**	**65**	**9**	**9**	**65**	**126**	**10**	**1**

CROUSSETT, Melvin – LHP

HT: 6-1; **WT:** 170; **B:** L; **T:** L; **BORN:** 12/28/88 in Santo Domingo, D.R.; **RESIDES:** Santo Domingo, D.R.; **OBTAINED:** Signed by the Yankees as a non-drafted free agent on 6/4/07; **M.L. SVC:** 0.000; **CAREER NOTES: 2009:** Made a team-high 22 relief appearances with the DSL Yankees 2, going 1-1 with 13 saves (in 14 chances) and a 1.61 ERA...struck out 45 batters in 28.0IP...ranked second in the league in saves...struck out at least one batter in all but one outing and held opponents to a .173 average (17-for-98)...**2008:** Went 4-2 with a 0.64 ERA in 17 relief appearances with the DSL Yankees 2, leading the team in ERA and ranking fourth on the staff in strikeouts...recorded 47K in 28.1IP, including a 7K performance in a 6/11 save vs. the DSL Diamondbacks (3.0IP, 1H)...**2007:** Made his professional debut in 2007, going 2-2 with two saves and a 1.42 ERA in 17 relief appearances with the DSL Yankees 2...struck out seven batters in 3.2IP in 8/14 loss at the DSL Devil Rays.

YEAR	CLUB	CLASS	W-L	ERA	G	GS	CG	SHO	SV	IP	H	R	ER	HR	HB	BB	SO	WP	BK
2007	DSL Yankees 2	R	2-2	1.42	17	0	0	0	2	38.0	22	10	6	0	2	25	55	10	2
2008	DSL Yankees 2	R	2-0	0.64	17	0	0	0	9	28.1	12	2	2	1	1	9	47	1	0
2009	DSL Yankees 2	R	1-1	1.61	22	0	0	0	13	28.0	17	5	5	0	0	14	45	1	0
Minor League Totals			**5-3**	**1.24**	**56**	**0**	**0**	**0**	**24**	**94.1**	**51**	**17**	**13**	**1**	**3**	**48**	**147**	**12**	**2**

CRUZ, Dawerd – RHP

HT: 6-1; **WT:** 170; **B:** R; **T:** R; **BORN:** 12/7/88 in San Pedro de Macoris, D.R.; **RESIDES:** San Pedro de Macoris, D.R.; **OBTAINED:** Signed by the Yankees as a non-drafted free agent on 12/12/07; **M.L. SVC:** 0.000; **CAREER NOTES: 2009:** Went 6-2 with one save and a 3.48 ERA in 16 games (one start) with the DSL Yankees 2...tied for the team lead in wins...**2008:** In his professional debut with the DSL Yankees 2, went 1-0 with a 4.11 ERA in 11 appearances out of the bullpen.

YEAR	CLUB	CLASS	W-L	ERA	G	GS	CG	SHO	SV	IP	H	R	ER	HR	HB	BB	SO	WP	BK
2008	DSL Yankees 2	R	1-0	4.11	11	0	0	0	0	15.1	15	8	7	0	4	8	9	3	0
2009	DSL Yankees 2	R	6-2	3.48	16	1	0	0	1	31.0	25	14	12	2	6	15	29	5	0
Minor League Totals			**7-2**	**3.69**	**27**	**1**	**0**	**0**	**1**	**46.1**	**40**	**22**	**19**	**2**	**10**	**23**	**38**	**8**	**0**

CURTIS, Colin – OF

NON-ROSTER INVITEE

HT: 6-1; **WT:** 200; **B:** L; **T:** L; **BORN:** 2/1/85 in Issaquah, Wash.; **RESIDES:** Sammamish, Wash.; **COLLEGE:** Arizona State University; **OBTAINED:** Selected in the fourth round of the 2006 First-Year Player Draft; **M.L. SVC:** 0.000; **CAREER NOTES: 2009**: Combined to bat .250 with 24 doubles, 7HR and 48RBI in 126 games with Double-A Trenton and Triple-A Scranton/Wilkes-Barre, setting a career-high in doubles...began the season with Trenton, where he hit .268 with 14 doubles, 1HR and 19RBI in 56 games...fashioned a season-high 13-game hitting streak from 4/13-28, batting .408 (20-for-49) with 6R, 7 doubles, 1 triple and 4RBI over the stretch...collected a career-high five hits on 5/26 at New Britain, going 5-for-5 with 3R and 1BB...was promoted to Scranton/WB on 6/22 where he batted .235 with 10 doubles, 6HR and 29RBI in 70 games...recorded his first career multi-homer game on 7/25 vs. Toledo...following the season, played for Surprise in the Arizona Fall League, batting .397 (31-for-78) with 19R, 7 doubles, 2 triples, 5HR and 18RBI in 20 games and leading the AFL in slugging (.731)...**2008:** Batted .255 with 20 doubles, 3 triples, 10HR and 71RBI in 132 games with Double-A Trenton, setting career highs in games, runs (68), home runs and RBI...hit in 13 straight games from 4/15-30, batting .373 (19-for-51) with 5 doubles over the stretch...**2007:** Combined to hit .270 with 69R, 19 doubles and 41RBI in 126 games with Single-A Tampa and Double-A Trenton...fashioned a 14-game hitting streak from 5/23-6/7 and hit in 22-of-23 games from 5/23-6/18...was transferred from Tampa to Trenton on 6/22...**2006:** Made professional debut after earning All-Pac-10 honors at Arizona State University...played in three games with Gulf Coast Yankees before being promoted to short-season Single-A Staten Island...with Staten Island, batted .302 in 44 games and helped lead the Yankees to their second straight NY-Penn League Championship...combined to bat .311 with 28 runs scored in his first professional season...**PERSONAL:** Earned All-Pac-10 Honorable Mention in 2004 and 2005 at Arizona State...was named to the College World Series All-Tournament Team in 2005...wore No. 9 during college career in honor of Roger Maris.

YEAR	CLUB	CLASS	AVG	G	AB	R	H	2B	3B	HR	RBI	SH	SF	HB	BB	SO	SB	CS	E	SLUG	OBP
2006	GCL Yankees	R	.500	3	8	3	4	2	0	1	4	0	0	1	1	0	1	0	0	1.125	.600
	Staten Island	SS-A	.302	44	159	25	48	9	2	1	18	0	2	4	12	19	4	5	1	.403	.362
2007	Tampa	A	.298	65	245	37	73	9	2	5	26	3	1	3	29	43	4	4	2	.412	.378
	Trenton	AA	.242	61	240	32	58	10	1	3	15	0	2	3	17	47	1	1	1	.329	.298
2008	Trenton	AA	.255	132	495	68	126	20	3	10	71	2	7	3	55	86	6	3	6	.368	.329
2009	Trenton	AA	.268	56	213	28	57	14	4	1	19	1	1	5	20	37	7	0	1	.385	.343
	Scranton/WB	AAA	.235	70	251	29	59	10	0	6	29	1	2	1	24	46	1	2	3	.347	.302
Minor League Totals			**.264**	**431**	**1611**	**222**	**425**	**74**	**12**	**27**	**182**	**7**	**15**	**20**	**158**	**278**	**24**	**15**	**14**	**.375**	**.334**

CUSICK, Matt – INF

HT: 5-11; **WT:** 195; **B:** L; **T:** R; **BORN:** 5/5/86 in San Dimas, Calif.; **RESIDES:** Mission Viejo, Calif.; **COLLEGE:** University of Southern California; **OBTAINED:** Acquired by the Yankees from the Houston Astros on 7/30/08 in exchange for RHP LaTroy Hawkins and cash considerations; **M.L. SVC:** 0.000; **CAREER NOTES: 2009**: Combined to bat .291 with 36R, 18 doubles, 1HR and 26RBI in 91 games with Single-A Tampa and Double-A Trenton...began the season with Tampa, batting .313 with 14 doubles and 17RBI in 63 games...hit his only HR of the season on 5/8 at Dunedin...was promoted to Trenton on 8/7 where he appeared in 28 games...**2008:** Combined to hit .278 with 23 doubles, 9HR and 40RBI in 101 games with Single-A Lexington and Single-A Tampa...began the season with Lexington, batting .285 in 94 games before being traded to the Yankees on 7/30...recorded a 10-game hitting streak from 4/20-5/1, batting .425 (17-for-40) with 3 doubles, 1HR and 7RBI...was placed on the disabled list from 8/3-23 with a muscle strain in his back...**2007:** Hit .306 (68-for-222) with 42R, 68H, 14 doubles and 35RBI in 61 games with Single-A Tri-City...recorded 38 walks while striking out just 25 times...led the team in batting average and runs scored...was named to the NYPL All-Star team...**PERSONAL:** Full name is Matthew Stephen Cusick...was originally selected by the Astros in the 10th round of the 2007 First-Year Player Draft...batted .369 with 4HR and 35RBI as a senior in 2006, starting every Trojans game at 3B...earned all-Pac 10 honors, ranking second on the team in batting average...played with the Brewster Whitecaps in the Cape Cod League in 2006, earning All-League honors and a spot in the All-Star Game...attended Santa Margaraita (Calif.) High School, earning all-conference honors three times...named to the *Orange County Register* All-County First Team as a senior...played in the 1997 Little League World Series for South Mission Viejo.

YEAR	CLUB	CLASS	AVG	G	AB	R	H	2B	3B	HR	RBI	SH	SF	HP	BB	SO	SB	CS	E	SLUG	OBP
2007	Tri-City	A	.306	61	222	42	68	14	4	3	35	3	2	8	38	25	5	1	4	.446	.422
2008	Lexington	A	.285	94	351	55	100	23	6	9	38	4	4	1	40	43	8	1	15	.462	.356
	Tampa	A	.174	7	23	1	4	0	0	0	2	0	0	1	2	2	0	0	0	.174	.269
2009	Tampa	A	.313	63	217	27	68	14	3	1	17	8	2	1	25	23	5	3	7	.419	.384
	Trenton	AA	.240	28	96	9	23	4	0	0	9	5	0	2	10	16	0	1	0	.281	.324
Minor League Totals			**.289**	**253**	**909**	**134**	**263**	**55**	**13**	**13**	**101**	**20**	**8**	**13**	**115**	**109**	**18**	**6**	**26**	**.421**	**.374**

DE LA ROSA, Elio – INF

HT: 6-0; **WT:** 185; **B:** R; **T:** R; **BORN:** 4/18/91 in Bani, D.R.; **RESIDES:** Bani, D.R.; **OBTAINED:** Signed by the Yankees as a non-drafted free agent on 7/2/07; **M.L. SVC:** 0.000; **CAREER NOTES: 2009:** Batted .226 with 9 doubles, 1 triple, 4HR and 21RBI in 53 games with the DSL Yankees 2...**2008:** In his professional debut, batted .134 with 3 doubles and 12 RBI in 32 games with the DSL Yankees 2.

YEAR	CLUB	CLASS	AVG	G	AB	R	H	2B	3B	HR	RBI	SH	SF	HB	BB	SO	SB	CS	E	SLUG	OBP
2008	DSL Yankees 2	R	.134	32	119	9	16	3	0	0	12	0	1	0	5	35	1	0	13	.160	.168
2009	DSL Yankees 2	R	.226	53	195	26	44	9	1	4	21	1	1	6	9	55	3	3	16	.344	.280
Minor League Totals			**.191**	**85**	**314**	**35**	**60**	**12**	**1**	**4**	**33**	**1**	**2**	**6**	**14**	**90**	**4**	**3**	**29**	**.274**	**.238**

DE LEON, Kelvin – OF

HT: 6-3; **WT:** 190; **B:** R; **T:** R; **BORN:** 10/29/90 in Boca Chica, D.R.; **RESIDES:** Boca Chica, D.R.; **OBTAINED:** Signed by the Yankees as a non-drafted free agent on 7/2/07; **M.L. SVC:** 0.000; **CAREER NOTES: 2009:** Batted .269 with 13 doubles, 7HR and 31RBI in 56 games with the GCL Yankees...led the team in HR and RBI and ranked third in the GCL in homers...following the season, named by *Baseball America* as the second-best prospect in the GCL in 2009...**2008:** In his first professional season, batted .289 with 9HR and 43RBI in 63 games with the DSL Yankees 2...recorded 27 extra-base hits in 235AB (16 doubles, 2 triples, 9HR)...did not go more than two consecutive games without recording at least 1H until the last three games of the season.

YEAR	CLUB	CLASS	AVG	G	AB	R	H	2B	3B	HR	RBI	SH	SF	HB	BB	SO	SB	CS	E	SLUG	OBP
2008	DSL Yankees 2	R	.289	63	235	43	68	16	2	9	43	0	2	10	34	74	8	3	4	.489	.399
2009	GCL Yankees	R	.269	56	201	28	54	13	0	7	31	0	1	3	16	61	5	1	3	.438	.330
Minor League Totals			**.280**	**19**	**436**	**71**	**122**	**29**	**2**	**16**	**74**	**0**	**3**	**13**	**50**	**135**	**13**	**4**	**7**	**.466**	**.369**

DE LEON, Nestor – LHP

HT: 6-2; **WT:** 200; **B:** R; **T:** R; **BORN:** 6/22/89 in Azua, Dominican Republic; **RESIDES:** Azua, Dominican Republic; **OBTAINED:** Signed by the Yankees as a non-drafted free agent on 6/6/09; **M.L. SVC:** 0.000; **CAREER NOTES:** Will be making his professional debut in 2010.

YEAR	CLUB	CLASS	W-L	ERA	G	GS	CG	SHO	SV	IP	H	R	ER	HR	HB	BB	SO	WP	BK
NO PROFESSIONAL STATS																			

DeLUCA, Evan – LHP

HT: 6-1; **WT**: 195; **B:** L; **T**: L; **BORN**: 3/9/91 in Whitehouse Station, N.J.; **RESIDES**: Whitehouse Station, N.J.; **OBTAINED**: Selected by the Yankees in the 44th round of the 2009 First-Year Player Draft; **M.L. SVC**: 0.000; **CAREER NOTES**: Will be making his professional debut in 2010...**PERSONAL**: Graduated from Immaculata High School.

YEAR	CLUB	CLASS	W-L	ERA	G	GS	CG	SHO	SV	IP	H	R	ER	HR	HB	BB	SO	WP	BK
NO PROFESSIONAL RECORD																			

DUFF, Grant – RHP **NON-ROSTER INVITEE**

HT: 6-6; **WT:** 210; **B:** R; **T:** R; **BORN:** 12/19/82 in Milton, Fla.; **RESIDES:** Mammoth Lakes, Calif.; **COLLEGE:** College of the Sequoias (Calif.); **OBTAINED:** Selected by the Yankees in the 31st round of the 2004 First-Year Player Draft; **M.L. SVC:** 0.000; **CAREER NOTES: 2009**: Combined to go 4-3 with two saves and a 3.52 ERA in 45 appearances (one start) with Single-A Tampa and Double-A Trenton (71.2IP, 28ER)...began the season with Tampa, before being promoted to Trenton on 7/8, where he went 4-2 with one save and a 3.22 ERA in 21 relief appearances (36.1IP, 13ER)...following the season, pitched for the Surprise Rafters of the Arizona Fall League, earning two saves without recording a decision in 10 relief appearances (2.89 ERA, 9.1IP, 7H, 3ER)...**2008:** Went 3-6 with two saves and a 4.30 ERA in 30 appearances (eight starts) with Single-A Tampa...struck out a season-high six batters on 6/9 at St. Lucie, while tossing a season-high 6.1 innings on 6/19 at Lakeland...recorded a career-high five straight losing decisions from 5/10-7/6...was placed on the disabled list from 8/21 through the remainder of the season with a left knee strain...**2007:** Was 14-8 with a 3.82 ERA in 27 starts with Single-A Charleston...tied for fourth in the South Atlantic League in starts and tied for fifth with a career-high and team-high 14 wins...tied for second among all Yankees minor leaguers in wins and ranked third in strikeouts...had two career-high four-game winning streaks (4/22-5/9 and 6/16-7/8)...recorded at least 1K in 26 of his 27 appearances...was placed on the D.L. from 7/30-8/8 with a right thigh contusion...**2006:** Ranked third among all Yankees' minor-league pitchers with a 1.97 combined ERA, posting a 5-4 record in 14 games with the Gulf Coast League Yankees and short-season Single-A Staten Island...spent majority of season with the Gulf Coast Yankees, posting a 5-1 record with a 1.14 ERA in 11 games (eight starts)...led all Gulf Coast League pitchers in ERA and strikeouts (59) and ranked second in the league in wins...made three starts with Class-A Staten Island and went 0-3 with a 5.25 ERA...**2005:** In his first professional season, went 0-1 with a 6.48 ERA in four games (two starts) with the Gulf Coast Yankees...appeared in only four games before being placed on the disabled list with a fractured right foot...**PERSONAL:** Was selected by the Yankees in the 30th round of the 2003 First-Year Player Draft but elected to attend the College of the Sequoias in Visalia, Calif., where he graduated from in May 2005.

YEAR	CLUB	CLASS	W-L	ERA	G	GS	CG	SHO	SV	IP	H	R	ER	HR	HB	BB	SO	WP	BK
2005	GCL Yankees	R	0-1	6.48	4	2	0	0	0	8.1	7	12	6	1	0	8	9	2	0
2006	GCL Yankees	R	5-1	1.14	11	8	0	0	0	47.1	26	12	6	2	1	17	59	4	0
	Staten Island	SS-A	0-3	5.25	3	3	0	0	0	12.0	10	9	7	0	1	11	8	1	0
2007	Charleston	A	14-8	3.82	27	27	0	0	0	139.0	135	71	59	15	5	80	82	13	0
2008	Tampa	A	3-6	4.30	30	8	0	0	2	81.2	73	42	39	2	9	35	64	10	0
2009	Tampa	A	0-1	3.82	24	1	0	0	1	35.1	35	17	15	2	1	11	26	2	0
	Trenton	AA	4-2	3.22	21	0	0	0	1	36.1	30	15	13	1	2	16	37	4	0
Minor League Totals			**26-22**	**3.63**	**120**	**49**	**0**	**0**	**4**	**360.0**	**316**	**178**	**145**	**23**	**19**	**178**	**285**	**36**	**0**

DURAN, Francisco – C

HT: 6-2; **WT:** 185; **B:** R; **T:** R; **BORN:** 10/3/91 in San Francisco de Aci, Venezuela; **RESIDES:** San Francisco de Aci, Venezuela; **OBTAINED:** Signed by the Yankees as a non-drafted free agent on 2/13/09; **M.L. SVC:** 0.000; **CAREER NOTES: 2009:** Made his professional debut with the DSL Yankees 1 and batted .250 (39-for-156) with 5 doubles, 2 triples and 23RBI in 40 games.

YEAR	CLUB	CLASS	AVG	G	AB	R	H	2B	3B	HR	RBI	SH	SF	HP	BB	SO	SB	CS	E	SLUG	OBP
2009	DSL Yankees 1	R	.250	40	156	22	39	5	2	1	23	1	1	1	6	45	3	1	4	.327	.280

DURAN, Kelvin– OF

HT: 5-11; **WT:** 165; **B:** L; **T:** L; **BORN:** 11/10/90 in Santo Domingo, D.R.; **RESIDES:** Sabana Perdida, D.R.; **OBTAINED:** Signed by the Yankees as a non-drafted free agent on 4/17/08; **M.L. SVC:** 0.000; **CAREER NOTES: 2009**: Hit .302 with 59R, 9 doubles, 12 triples, 3HR and 39RBI in 62 games with the DSL Yankees 2...led the DSL in triples, tied for third in runs scored and tied for fourth in total bases (121)...**2008:** Made his professional debut, hitting .278 with 10R, 2 triples and 5RBI in nine games with the DSL Yankees 1.

YEAR	CLUB	CLASS	AVG	G	AB	R	H	2B	3B	HR	RBI	SH	SF	HP	BB	SO	SB	CS	E	SLUG	OBP
2008	DSL Yankees 1	R	.278	9	36	10	10	0	2	0	5	1	0	0	6	11	2	0	0	.389	.381
2009	DSL Yankees 2	R	.302	62	262	59	79	9	12	3	39	1	2	2	26	45	28	7	6	.462	.366
Minor League Totals			**.299**	**71**	**298**	**69**	**89**	**9**	**14**	**3**	**44**	**2**	**2**	**2**	**32**	**56**	**30**	**7**	**6**	**.453**	**.368**

ELAM, Sam – LHP

HT: 6-4; **WT:** 220; **B:** L; **T:** L; **BORN:** 6/16/87 in Mesquite, Tex.; **RESIDES:** Mesquite, Tex.; **COLLEGE:** Notre Dame ; **OBTAINED:** Selected by the Yankees in the eighth round of the 2009 First-Year Player Draft; **M.L. SVC:** 0.000; **CAREER NOTES: 2009:** Split his first professional season between short-season Single-A Staten Island and the GCL Yankees, combining to go 0-2 with a 12.38 ERA...**PERSONAL:** Graduated from Poteet HS (IN)...was drafted by the Rockies in the 23rd round in 2008 but returned to college.

YEAR	CLUB	CLASS	W-L	ERA	G	GS	CG	SHO	SV	IP	H	R	ER	HR	HB	BB	SO	WP	BK
2009	Staten Island	SS-A	0-0	23.62	3	0	0	0	0	2.2	1	7	7	0	2	11	2	5	0
	GCL Yankees	R	0-2	6.75	7	0	0	0	0	5.1	5	7	4	0	2	10	8	3	0
Minor League Totals			**0-2**	**12.38**	**10**	**0**	**0**	**0**	**0**	**8.0**	**6**	**14**	**11**	**0**	**4**	**21**	**10**	**8**	**0**

EUSEBIO, Wilkinson – RHP

HT: 6-2; **WT:** 178; **B:** R; **T:** R; **BORN:** 9/26/90 in San Pedro, D.R.; **RESIDES:** San Pedro, D.R.; **OBTAINED:** Signed by the Yankees as a non-drafted free agent on 10/10/07; **M.L. SVC:** 0.000; **CAREER NOTES: 2009**: Went 0-2 with a 10.59 ERA in 17 relief appearances with the DSL Yankees 2...**2008:** Made his professional debut, going 4-5 with a 5.27 ERA in 16 games (four starts) with the DSL Yankees 2...in his first career game, struck out seven batters in a 6/2 win vs. the DSL Diamondbacks (4.0IP, 3H, 1R, 1HR).

YEAR	CLUB	CLASS	W-L	ERA	G	GS	CG	SHO	SV	IP	H	R	ER	HR	HB	BB	SO	WP	BK
2008	DSL Yankees 2	R	4-5	5.27	16	4	0	0	0	41.0	43	28	24	2	1	17	34	5	0
2009	DSL Yankees 2	R	0-2	10.59	17	0	0	0	0	17.0	25	23	20	3	3	14	15	3	0
Minor League Totals			**4-7**	**6.83**	**33**	**4**	**0**	**0**	**0**	**58.0**	**68**	**51**	**44**	**5**	**4**	**31**	**49**	**8**	**0**

FARNHAM, Jeffrey – C

HT: 6-1; **WT:** 195; **B:** R; **T:** R; **BORN:** 8/30/87 in Las Vegas, Nev.; **RESIDES:** Las Vegas, Nev.; **COLLEGE:** New Mexico State University; **OBTAINED:** Selected by the Yankees in the 27th round of the 2009 First-Year Player Draft; **M.L. SVC:** 0.000; **CAREER NOTES: 2009:** Opened the season in the Gulf Coast League, playing in five games before being promoted to Single-A Charleston on 7/23…batted .323 with 13R, 6 doubles, 1HR and 10RBI in 20 games with the RiverDogs…threw out 11-of-34 (32.4%) potential base stealers with Charleston…**PERSONAL:** Graduated from Faith Lutheran High School (NV) where he was a member of the State Championship team in 2003, '04 and '05…was a first-team All-State catcher in 2004 and 2005…played two seasons at Allen Hancock Junior College before transferring to New Mexico State where he earned All-Western State Conference honors as a sophomore.

YEAR	CLUB	CLASS	AVG	G	AB	R	H	2B	3B	HR	RBI	SH	SF	HB	BB	SO	SB	CS	E	SLUG	OBP
2009	GCL Yankees	R	.167	5	12	0	2	1	0	0	2	0	0	0	1	3	1	0	0	250	.231
	Charleston	A	.323	20	62	13	20	6	0	1	10	0	2	3	5	13	0	1	2	.468	.389
Minor League Totals			**.297**	**25**	**74**	**13**	**22**	**7**	**0**	**1**	**12**	**0**	**2**	**3**	**6**	**16**	**1**	**1**	**2**	**.432**	**.365**

FELIX, Anderson – INF

HT: 6-0; **WT:** 155; **B:** S; **T:** R; **BORN:** 5/11/92 in Santo Domingo, D.R.; **RESIDES:** Boca Chica, D.R.; **OBTAINED:** Signed by the Yankees as a non-drafted free agent on 7/2/08; **M.L. SVC:** 0.000; **CAREER NOTES: 2009**: Made his professional debut and hit .254 with 5 doubles, 3 triples, 1HR and 16RBI in 40 games with the DSL Yankees 2.

YEAR	CLUB	CLASS	AVG	G	AB	R	H	2B	3B	HR	RBI	SH	SF	HP	BB	SO	SB	CS	E	SLUG	OBP
2009	DSL Yankees 2	R	.254	40	142	35	36	5	3	1	16	0	0	1	21	36	7	2	11	.352	.354

FLANNERY, Ryan – RHP

HT: 6-3; **WT:** 245; **B:** R; **T:** R; **BORN:** 1/6/86 in Carlstadt, N.J.; **RESIDES:** Carlstadt, N.J.; **OBTAINED:** Signed by the Yankees as a non-drafted free agent on 6/9/08; **M.L. SVC:** 0.000; **CAREER NOTES: 2009:** Combined to go 4-2 with six saves and a 2.40 ERA in 40 appearances with Single-A Charleston and short-season Single-A Staten Island…held opponents without an earned run in 34 of his 40 outings…led the New York-Penn League in appearances…**2008:** Made his professional debut, going 2-1 with a 0.86 ERA in 15 games with the GCL Yankees…ranked fifth in the GCL with seven saves…allowed runs in just two of his 15 appearances out of the bullpen…held opponents to a .164 batting average (12-for-73).

YEAR	CLUB	CLASS	W-L	ERA	G	GS	CG	SHO	SV	IP	H	R	ER	HR	HB	BB	SO	WP	BK
2008	GCL Yankees	R	2-1	0.86	15	0	0	0	7	21.0	12	3	2	0	3	0	16	0	1
2009	Charleston	A	0-0	10.13	6	0	0	0	0	5.1	12	7	6	0	0	1	10	0	0
	Staten Island	SS-A	4-2	1.45	34	0	0	0	6	43.1	32	10	7	0	1	12	41	0	0
Minor League Totals			**6-3**	**1.94**	**55**	**0**	**0**	**0**	**13**	**69.2**	**56**	**20**	**15**	**0**	**4**	**13**	**67**	**0**	**1**

FLORES, Ramon – OF

HT: 5-10; **WT:** 150; **B:** L; **T:** L; **BORN:** 3/26/92 in Barinas, Venezuela; **RESIDES:** Barinas, Venezuela; **OBTAINED:** Signed by the Yankees as a non-drafted free agent on 7/4/08; **M.L. SVC:** 0.000; **CAREER NOTES: 2009**: Made his professional debut and combined to hit .208 with five doubles, four triples and 19RBI in 62 combined games with the DSL Yankees 2 and the GCL Yankees…began the season in the DSL before being transferred to the GCL on 6/12, where he batted .196 with five doubles and 14RBI in 51 games.

YEAR	CLUB	CLASS	AVG	G	AB	R	H	2B	3B	HR	RBI	SH	SF	HP	BB	SO	SB	CS	E	SLUG	OBP
2009	DSL Yankees 2	R	.256	11	39	8	10	0	3	1	5	0	1	1	11	5	0	1	2	.487	.423
	GCL Yankees	R	.196	51	158	14	31	5	1	0	14	2	2	3	22	35	7	5	4	.241	.303
Minor League Totals			**.208**	**62**	**197**	**22**	**41**	**5**	**4**	**1**	**19**	**2**	**3**	**4**	**33**	**40**	**7**	**6**	**6**	**.289**	**.329**

FORTENBERRY, Seth – OF

HT: 6-2; **WT:** 175; **B:** L; **T:** L; **BORN:** 9/1/83 in Waco, Tex.; **RESIDES:** Waco, Tex.; **COLLEGE:** Baylor University; **OBTAINED:** Selected by the Yankees in the 11th round of the 2006 First-Year Player Draft; **M.L. SVC:** 0.000; **CAREER NOTES: 2009**: Combined to bat .169 with 30R, 13 doubles, 5 triples, 6HR and 35RBI in 97 games with Double-A Trenton and Single-A Tampa…**2008:** Appeared in 119 games with Single-A Tampa, batting .263 with 18 doubles, 7 triples, 12HR and 46RBI…led the team in home runs and walks (64), drawing the third-most free passes in the Florida State League…also struck out 125 times, ranking fifth in the FSL…hit for the cycle on 6/6 vs. Palm Beach, going 4-for-5 with 1RBI…missed most of spring training with a jammed left wrist…following the season, was tabbed as having the best outfield arm in the organization by *Baseball America*…**2007:** Hit .255 with 97R, 23 doubles, 4 triples, 18HR and 87RBI with Single-A Charleston…was the only RiverDog to play in all 140 games (138GS), leading South Atlantic League outfielders with a .996 fielding percentage (1E, 246TC)…ranked third in the league with a team-best 97R and led the team in home runs, RBI, walks (73) and tied for the team lead in triples…placed second among all Yankees farmhands in home runs and RBI…following the season, was ranked by *Baseball America* as having the "Best Outfield Arm" among all Yankees minor leaguers…**2006:** Made professional debut with short-season Single-A Staten Island, batting .268 in 67 games played (all in OF)…**PERSONAL:** Full name is Jeffrey Seth Fortenberry…graduated from Baylor University where he was honored in 2005 with the NCAA Waco Regional All-Tournament Team and the Spring Award for Academic Excellence and was a seven-time Big 12 Conference Commissioner's Honor Roll member…was named the fifth-best pro prospect in the Jayhawk League by *Baseball America*…was a four-letter winner at Midway High School in Waco, Tex., (also lettered in football, basketball and track)…was named first-team all-district and honorable mention all-state as an outfielder in 2000…was an all-district selection in 2001 and 2002 and earned all-state honors in 2001…can complete a Rubik's Cube in less than three minutes.

YEAR	CLUB	CLASS	AVG	G	AB	R	H	2B	3B	HR	RBI	SH	SF	HB	BB	SO	SB	CS	E	SLUG	OBP
2006	Staten Island	SS-A	.268	67	254	34	68	11	5	4	25	2	2	7	24	65	12	5	6	.398	.345
2007	Charleston	A	.255	140	505	97	129	23	4	18	87	0	6	11	73	137	25	8	1	.424	.358
2008	Tampa	A	.263	119	399	50	105	18	7	12	46	6	2	6	64	125	9	5	2	.434	.372
2009	Trenton	AA	.160	38	125	12	20	6	3	0	8	1	1	2	15	40	5	1	1	.256	.259
	Tampa	A	.175	59	189	18	33	7	2	6	27	1	2	4	20	58	3	0	1	.328	.265
Minor League Totals			**.241**	**423**	**1472**	**211**	**365**	**65**	**21**	**40**	**193**	**10**	**13**	**30**	**196**	**425**	**54**	**19**	**11**	**.395**	**.340**

FRENCH, Neall – INF

HT: 6-3; **WT:** 210; **B:** R; **T:** R; **BORN:** 8/5/83 in Bay Village, Ohio; **RESIDES:** Bay Village, Ohio; **COLLEGE:** University of Cincinnati; **OBTAINED:** Signed by the Yankees as a non-drafted free agent on 2/14/08; **M.L. SVC:** 0.000; **CAREER NOTES: 2009**: Hit .238 with 6 doubles, 1 triple, 2HR and 22RBI in 64 games with Single-A Charleston…recorded a career-high 15-game hitting streak from 7/19 to 8/15, batting .302 (16-for-53) with 1 double, 1HR and 9RBI over the stretch…committed only 2 errors in 44 games at first base (.995 fielding percentage)…**2008:** Made his professional debut, hitting .345 with 4 doubles, 3HR and 15RBI in 35 games with the GCL Yankees…led the team in batting average but did not have enough at-bats to qualify among league leaders…**PERSONAL:** Was with the Florence Freedom of the Independent Frontier League in 2009 before being signed by the Yankees…attended the University of Cincinnati, batting .343 (69-for-201) with 36R, 14 doubles, 11HR and 65RBI over 55 games during his senior year…played for the Delaware Cows of the Great Lakes Summer Collegiate League in the summer of 2005 and '06…was named to the league's All-Star team in 2005…played at Triton Community College during his sophomore year…spent his freshman year at Grand Rapids Community College where he was named a junior college All-American and participated in the World Series All-Tournament team in 2003…set school and conference records for batting average, on-base percentage and slugging percentage at Grand Rapids, leading the team to a national championship…was selected by the Indians in the 38th round of the 2003 First-Year Player Draft after his freshman year, but decided to return to college…attended St. Ignatius High School (Ohio).

YEAR	CLUB	CLASS	AVG	G	AB	R	H	2B	3B	HR	RBI	SH	SF	HP	BB	SO	SB	CS	E	SLUG	OBP
2008	GCL Yankees	R	.345	35	84	15	29	4	0	3	15	1	1	4	10	13	2	1	2	.500	.434
2009	Charleston	A	.238	64	210	25	50	6	1	2	22	1	0	5	29	70	0	0	2	.305	.344
Minor League Totals			**.269**	**99**	**294**	**40**	**79**	**10**	**1**	**5**	**37**	**2**	**1**	**9**	**39**	**83**	**2**	**1**	**4**	**.361**	**.370**

FRIAS, Joel – RHP

HT: 5'10"; **WT:** 145; **B:** R; **T:** R; **BORN:** 3/12/90 in Las Tablas, Panama; **RESIDES:** Las Tablas, Panama; **OBTAINED:** Signed by the Yankees as a non-drafted free agent on 12/4/09; **M.L. SVC:** 0.000; **CAREER NOTES:** Will be making his professional debut in 2010.

YEAR	CLUB	CLASS	W-L	ERA	G	GS	CG	SHO	SV	IP	H	R	ER	HR	HB	BB	SO	WP	BK
NO PROFESSIONAL RECORD																			

FULGENCIO, Edwin – OF

HT: 6-2; **WT:** 190; **B:** R; **T:** R; **BORN:** 7/22/91 in Santo Domingo, D.R.; **RESIDES:** Santo Domingo, D.R.; **OBTAINED:** Signed by the Yankees as a non-drafted free agent on 10/18/08; **M.L. SVC:** 0.000; **CAREER NOTES: 2009**: Made his professional debut with the DSL Yankees 1 and hit .172 with 4HR and 17RBI in 53 games…15 of his 31H went for extra-bases (9 doubles, 2 triples, 4HR).

YEAR	CLUB	CLASS	AVG	G	AB	R	H	2B	3B	HR	RBI	SH	SF	HP	BB	SO	SB	CS	E	SLUG	OBP
2009	DSL Yankees 1	R	.172	53	180	28	31	9	2	4	17	0	0	4	32	95	3	1	5	.311	.310

GARCE, Harold – RHP

HT: 6-4; **WT:** 205; **B:** R; **T:** R; **BORN:** 11/28/85 in Santo Domingo, D.R.; **RESIDES:** Santo Domingo, D.R.; **OBTAINED:** Signed by the Yankees as a non-drafted free agent on 11/21/07; **M.L. SVC:** 0.000; **CAREER NOTES: 2009:** Went 2-3 with a 3.80 ERA in 13 games (nine starts) with the DSL Yankees 1…recorded a season-high 7K in 4.0IP in a 7/28 victory over the DSL Blue Jays (4H, 2ER, 2BB)…**2008:** Made his professional debut with the DSL Yankees 1, going 0-7 with a 7.65 ERA in 17 games (eight starts)…opponents combined for a .200 batting average against (26-for-130).

YEAR	CLUB	CLASS	W-L	ERA	G	GS	CG	SHO	SV	IP	H	R	ER	HR	HB	BB	SO	WP	BK
2008	DSL Yankees 1	R	0-7	7.65	17	8	0	0	0	37.2	26	45	32	2	6	84	32	21	0
2009	DSL Yankees 1	R	2-3	3.80	13	9	0	0	0	47.1	39	29	20	0	6	32	37	21	1
Minor League Totals			**2-10**	**5.51**	**30**	**17**	**0**	**0**	**0**	**85.0**	**65**	**74**	**52**	**2**	**12**	**116**	**69**	**42**	**1**

GARCIA, Charlyn – RHP

HT: 6-1; **WT:** 164; **B:** R; **T:** R; **BORN:** 6/9/86 in Sabana Grande, D.R.; **RESIDES:** Sabana Grande, D.R.; **OBTAINED:** Signed by the Yankees as a non-drafted free agent on 5/11/07; **M.L. SVC:** 0.000; **CAREER NOTES: 2009:** Appeared in 13 games (11 starts) with the DSL Yankees 1 and went 1-2 with a 4.20 ERA…recorded 47K and allowed just 1HR in 49.1IP…**2008:** Appeared in 19 games (eight starts) with the DSL Yankees 2, going 3-2 with a 4.27 ERA…did not allow 1ER in his final four relief outings (8.2IP)…**2007:** Made his professional debut, going 1-1 with a 5.73 ERA in six appearances (three starts) with the DSL Yankees.

YEAR	CLUB	CLASS	W-L	ERA	G	GS	CG	SHO	SV	IP	H	R	ER	HR	HB	BB	SO	WP	BK
2007	DSL Yankees 1	R	1-1	5.73	6	3	0	0	0	11.0	11	14	7	0	3	16	10	6	0
2008	DSL Yankees 2	R	2-1	3.82	13	5	0	0	0	35.1	31	24	15	1	2	31	28	6	0
2009	DSL Yankees 1	R	1-2	4.20	13	11	0	0	0	49.1	48	31	23	1	9	24	47	8	2
Minor League Totals			**4-4**	**4.23**	**32**	**19**	**0**	**0**	**0**	**95.2**	**90**	**69**	**45**	**2**	**14**	**71**	**85**	**20**	**2**

GERRITSE, Brett – RHP

HT: 6-4; **WT:** 220; **B:** R; **T:** R; **BORN:** 3/4/91 in Cypress, Calif.; **RESIDES:** Cypress, Calif.; **OBTAINED:** Selected by the Yankees in the 12th round of the 2009 First-Year Player Draft; **M.L. SVC:** 0.000; **CAREER NOTES: 2009**: Made his professional debut, going 0-1 with a 3.93 ERA in six games (five starts) with the GCL Yankees…recorded 20K in 18.1IP…**PERSONAL:** Graduated from Pacifica High School.

YEAR	CLUB	CLASS	W-L	ERA	G	GS	CG	SHO	SV	IP	H	R	ER	HR	HB	BB	SO	WP	BK
2009	GCL Yankees	R	0-1	3.93	6	5	0	0	0	18.1	15	11	8	0	1	7	20	1	0

GIL, Francisco Daniel – RHP

HT: 6-3; **WT:** 187; **B:** R; **T:** R; **BORN:** 4/24/89 in Agua Prieta, Mexico; **RESIDES:** Agua Prieta, Mexico; **OBTAINED:** Signed by the Yankees as a non-drafted free agent on 12/21/05; **M.L. SVC:** 0.000; **CAREER NOTES: 2009:** Missed the entire season, recovering from "Tommy John" surgery...**2008:** Underwent surgery on his right elbow on 5/8 and missed the remainder of the season...**2007:** Went 2-1 with a 6.00 ERA in five games (one start) with the GCL Yankees...struck out 12 batters while walking just four in 15.0IP...was placed on the disabled list on 8/24 with a right knee sprain, ending his season...**2006:** Posted a 1-2 record with a 3.26 ERA in nine games (seven starts) with the Yankees DSL 1 squad...allowed only 27 hits in 30.1IP.

YEAR	CLUB	CLASS	W-L	ERA	G	GS	CG	SHO	SV	IP	H	R	ER	HR	HB	BB	SO	WP	BK
2006	DSL Yankees 1	R	1-2	3.26	9	7	0	0	0	30.1	27	12	11	0	2	8	27	3	1
2007	GCL Yankees	R	2-1	6.00	5	1	0	0	0	15.0	18	12	10	0	1	4	12	3	0
2008							Did Not Play - Injured												
2009							Did Not Play - Injured												
Minor League Totals			**3-3**	**4.17**	**14**	**8**	**0**	**0**	**0**	**45.1**	**45**	**24**	**21**	**0**	**3**	**12**	**39**	**6**	**1**

GIL, Jose – C

HT: 6-0; **WT:** 170; **B:** S; **T:** R; **BORN:** 9/4/86 in Barcelona, Venezuela; **RESIDES:** Barcelona, Venezuela; **OBTAINED:** Signed by the Yankees as a non-drafted free agent on 7/2/03; **M.L. SVC:** 0.000; **CAREER NOTES: 2009**: Batted .205 with six doubles, 2HR and 12RBI in 41 combined games with Double-A Trenton and Single-A Tampa...combined to catch 35.4% of potential base stealers (17-of-48)...**2008:** Batted .243 with 17 doubles, 1HR and 25RBI in 73 games with Single-A Tampa, matching his career high in doubles...caught 39.7 percent of potential basestealers (25-of-63)...**2007:** Combined to hit .234 with 40R, 21 doubles, 12HR and 50RBI in 100 games with Single-A Charleston and short-season Single-A Staten Island...caught 33.7 percent of potential base stealers (29-of-86), third-best caught stealing rate in the New York-Penn League...**2006:** Combined to bat .229 with 2HR and 21RBI in 56 games with Single-A Charleston and Staten Island...**2005:** Batted .279 with 11 doubles, one home run and 20RBI in 41 games with the Gulf Coast Yankees...batted .301 (22-for-73) in 22 road games and posted a .294 (15-for-51) average with runners in scoring position...helped lead the Yankees to the GCL Championship for the second straight season...**2004:** In first professional season, batted .223 in 45 games with the Yankees DSL 2 squad.

YEAR	CLUB	CLASS	AVG	G	AB	R	H	2B	3B	HR	RBI	SH	SF	HP	BB	SO	SB	CS	E	SLUG	OBP
2004	DSL Yankees 2	R	.223	45	148	10	33	10	0	0	17	1	1	0	14	22	1	0	--	.291	.288
2005	GCL Yankees	R	.279	41	140	21	39	11	0	1	20	0	0	0	19	18	1	1	4	.379	.364
2006	Charleston	A	.189	22	74	5	14	1	0	0	6	0	1	1	4	15	0	0	4	.203	.238
	Staten Island	SS-A	.257	34	105	10	27	4	0	2	15	1	1	0	17	16	0	0	5	.352	.358
2007	Charleston	A	.221	42	136	14	30	4	0	5	13	1	1	0	10	32	0	1	5	.360	.272
	Staten Island	SS-A	.242	58	198	26	48	17	0	7	37	6	2	3	12	41	4	3	9	.434	.293
2008	Tampa	A	.240	73	246	17	59	17	0	1	25	4	2	4	14	41	8	4	4	.321	.289
2009	Trenton	AA	.194	12	36	2	7	2	0	2	4	1	0	0	0	7	0	0	1	.417	.194
	Tampa	A	.208	29	96	10	20	4	0	0	8	3	0	0	5	24	0	0	3	.250	.248
Minor League Totals			**.235**	**356**	**1179**	**115**	**277**	**70**	**0**	**18**	**145**	**17**	**10**	**9**	**95**	**216**	**14**	**9**	**31**	**.340**	**.295**

GOLSAN, Judd – OF

HT: 6-1; **WT**: 185; **B**: L; **T**: R; **BORN**: 12/6/90 in Birmingham, Ala.; **RESIDES**: Birmingham, Ala.; **OBTAINED**: Selected by the Yankees in the 31st round of the 2009 First-Year Player Draft; **M.L. SVC**: 0.000; **CAREER NOTES**: **2009**: Made his professional debut and batted .224 with three doubles and five RBI in 39 games with the GCL Yankees.

YEAR	CLUB	CLASS	AVG	G	AB	R	H	2B	3B	HR	RBI	SH	SF	HP	BB	SO	SB	CS	E	SLUG	OBP
2009	GCL Yankees	R	.224	39	98	16	22	3	0	0	5	0	1	3	13	34	4	2	1	.255	.330

GONZALEZ, Edwar – OF

HT: 5-10; **WT:** 200; **B:** R; **T:** R; **BORN:** 1/1/83 in Maracaibo, Venezuela; **RESIDES:** Miami, Fla.; **COLLEGE:** Seminole JC (Okla.); **OBTAINED:** Signed by the Yankees as a non-drafted free agent on 6/12/02; **M.L. SVC:** 0.000; **CAREER NOTES: 2009:** Batted .232 with 46R, 26 doubles, 4HR and 37RBI in 115 games with Double-A Trenton, tying for the team lead in doubles... missed time from 4/25-5/14 on the disabled list with a left oblique strain... opened the year batting .326 (14-for-43) prior to the injury...had seven outfield assists...following the season, appeared in 39 games with the Lara Cardinals in the Venezuelan Winter League (.268, 3 doubles, 1HR and 11RBI)...**2008:** Hit a combined .292 with 41 doubles, 20HR and 85RBI in 131 games with Single-A Tampa and Double-A Trenton...opened year at Tampa before being promoted on 5/3...recorded his first career multi-homer game and tied his career high with 6RBI on 4/6 at Sarasota...had his second two-homer game of the year on 4/22 at Clearwater...collected 9RBI in his first seven games at the Double-A level...hit .422 (27-for-64) over his final 17 games of the season...also appeared in five postseason games with the Eastern League champions, going 4-for-17 (.235) with 2RBI...played winter ball with the Cardenales de Lara of the Venezuelan League, batting .355 with 5 doubles, 4HR and 11RBI in 29 games...**2007:** Hit .259 with 64R, 27 doubles, 5 triples, 9HR and 26RBI in 131 games with Single-A Tampa...led the team in hits, doubles and RBI...recorded an 11-game hitting streak from 8/3-12, batting .333 (12-for-36) with 6R during the stretch...fashioned a 10-game hitting streak from 8/16-25, hitting .400 (16-for-40) with 8R and 6RBI during the span...played for the Cardenales de Lara of the Venezuelan Winter League, batting .261 (18-for-69) with 5R, 4 doubles, 1HR and 9RBI in 31 games...**2006:** Played in 99 games with Single-A Tampa, batting .260 with 10HR and 43 RBI...missed a month of action from 4/20-5/20 while on the disabled list with a sprained left ankle...recorded a career-high 18 stolen bases...**2005:** Batted .286 with 10HR and 52RBI in 89 games for the Single-A Charleston RiverDogs...**2004:** Split time between Single-A Battle Creek and Staten Island, combining to hit .222 with 3RBI and 17RBI...**2003:** Batted .229 in 61 games with the Staten Island Yankees...**2002:** In first professional season, batted .275 with 1HR and 8RBI in 19 games for the Gulf Coast Yankees.

YEAR	CLUB	CLASS	AVG	G	AB	R	H	2B	3B	HR	RBI	SH	SF	HP	BB	SO	SB	CS	E	SLUG	OBP
2002	GCL Yankees	R	.275	19	51	7	14	2	1	1	8	0	1	1	0	11	0	0	0	.412	.283
2003	Staten Island	SS-A	.229	61	231	25	53	12	3	2	22	1	1	5	10	72	4	0	4	.333	.275
2004	Battle Creek	A	.214	14	28	4	6	2	1	0	4	0	0	1	1	10	0	2	0	.357	.267
	Staten Island	SS-A	.223	33	130	18	29	6	1	3	14	1	0	3	7	27	1	0	2	.354	.279
2005	Charleston	A	.286	89	294	36	84	12	4	10	52	0	3	5	11	54	6	4	4	.456	.319
2006	Tampa	A	.260	99	384	58	100	19	4	10	43	0	2	5	23	81	18	6	1	.409	.309
2007	Tampa	A	.259	131	518	64	134	27	5	9	68	0	3	5	27	89	13	8	5	.382	.300
2008	Tampa	A	.279	27	111	18	31	11	1	6	18	0	1	2	5	18	3	1	1	.559	.319
	Trenton	AA	.295	104	396	58	117	31	0	14	67	0	5	5	20	74	8	5	2	.480	.333
2009	Trenton	AA	.232	115	413	46	96	26	1	4	37	0	4	9	30	93	7	3	5	.329	.296
Minor League Totals			**.260**	**692**	**2556**	**334**	**664**	**148**	**21**	**59**	**333**	**2**	**20**	**41**	**134**	**529**	**60**	**29**	**24**	**.403**	**.305**

GONZALEZ, Felipe – RHP

HT: 6-2; **WT:** 165; **B:** R; **T:** R; **BORN:** 8/15/91 in Guadalupe, Mexico.; **RESIDES:** Guadalupe, Mexico; **OBTAINED:** Signed as a non-drafted free agent on 2/16/08; **M.L. SVC:** 0.000; **CAREER NOTES: 2009**: Made two relief appearances for the DSL Yankees 2 and went 0-1, not allowing an earned run in 1.0IP...**2008:** Made his professional debut with the DSL Yankees 1, going 2-1 with a 8.79 ERA in seven relief appearances.

YEAR	CLUB	CLASS	W-L	ERA	G	GS	CG	SHO	SV	IP	H	R	ER	HR	HB	BB	SO	WP	BK
2008	DSL Yankees 1	R	2-1	8.79	7	0	0	0	0	14.1	24	17	14	3	2	2	10	1	0
2009	DSL Yankees 2	R	0-1	0.00	2	0	0	0	0	1.0	3	6	0	0	0	1	0	1	0
Minor League Totals			**2-2**	**8.22**	**9**	**0**	**0**	**0**	**0**	**15.1**	**27**	**23**	**14**	**3**	**2**	**3**	**10**	**2**	**0**

GORECKI, Reid – OF

NON-ROSTER INVITEE

HT: 6-1; **WT:** 176; **B:** R; **T:** R; **BORN:** 12/22/80 in Queens, N.Y.; **RESIDES:** East Rockaway, N.J.; **COLLEGE:** University of Delaware; **OBTAINED:** Signed as a free agent on 12/22/09; **M.L. SVC:** 0.049; **CAREER NOTES: 2009**: Saw his first big league action, batting .200 with 6R and 3RBI in 31 games with Atlanta...had his contract purchased from Triple-A Gwinnett and made his Major League debut on 8/17 vs. Arizona, entering the game as a defensive replacement in LF (did not bat)...collected his first Major League hit with a ninth-inning RBI single off Sean Green on 8/19 at New York-NL...began the season with Gwinnett, batting .286 with 27 doubles, 9HR and 49RBI in 106 games, setting a career high in doubles...following the season, played for Mayos de Navojoa of the Mexican Pacific Winter League, hitting .250 (47-for-188) with 17SB in 53 games in the outfield...**2008**: Signed with the Braves on 5/2 and was assigned to Double-A Mississippi on 5/10 where he batted .292 with 51R, 9 doubles, 10HR and 43RBI in 63 games...missed a month on the disabled list from 5/19-6/11 with a left hamstring strain...was named the Southern League "Hitter of the Week" for the period ending on 5/18, batting .423 (11-for-26) over the stretch...reached base safely via hit or walk in 15 straight games from 5/10-6/18...was promoted to Triple-A Richmond on 7/4 where he played in four games, batting .538 with 1RBI before being optioned back to Mississippi on 7/10...was placed back on the disabled list from 8/22 through the end of the season with a right hamstring strain...was activated for the playoffs and hit .158 with 3R...following the season, played for Mayos de Navojoa of the Mexican Pacific Winter League, batting .226 with 11 doubles, 2 triples, 4HR, 27RBI, 52BB and 19SB...**2007**: Split time between Double-A Springfield and the GCL Cardinals...in 10 games with the GCL Cardinals, hit .313 with 5 doubles and 5RBI...hit .237 in 24 games with Springfield with just one extra-base hit...had 8RBI and 20K with just 18H...**2006**: Combined to hit 17HR for Double-A Springfield and Triple-A Memphis, ranking sixth among all Cardinals minor leaguers...nine of his homers and 18 of his extra-base hits came in 24 April games...had an 11-game hitting streak from 4/9-20, batting .383 (18-for-47) during the span...**2005**: Combined to hit .244 (96-for-393) in 110 games with Single-A Palm Beach and Double-A Springfield...hit the game-tying home run in the top of the ninth inning in Game 5 of the Florida State League Championship as Palm Beach defeated Lakeland, 5-4, in 10 innings to clinch the League title...**2004**: Was named the Cardinals Minor League "Player of the Year," combining to bat .280 with 75R, 26 doubles, 8HR and 48RBI in 125 games with Single-A Palm Beach and Double-A Tennessee...ranked second in the FSL with 74R...following the season, played for Mesa in the Arizona Fall League, ranking sixth with a .363 (37-for-102) batting average in 26 games...**2003**: Hit .267 with 19 doubles, 15HR and 61RBI in 128 games for Single-A Peoria...batted .356 in June with 6HR and 21RBI...fashioned a 15-game hitting streak from 6/22-7/1 with 10 multi-hit games to raise his batting average from .251 to .296...**2002**: Batted .281 with 55R, 8 doubles, 13 triples and 52RBI in 73 games for Single-A New Jersey...was selected to *Baseball America's* New York-Penn League All-Star team...led the league in runs scored and triples, ranked third in total bases (135) and RBI and ranked fourth in extra-base hits (29)...tripled in five straight games—hitting six triples total—from 8/29-9/1, also recording an RBI in each game...**PERSONAL**: Full name is Reid Evan Gorecki...attended the University of Delaware...selected by the Cardinals in the 13th round of the 2002 First-Year Player Draft.

YEAR	CLUB	CLASS	AVG	G	AB	R	H	2B	3B	HR	RBI	SH	SF	HP	BB	SO	SB	CS	E	SLUG	OBP
2002	New Jersey	A	.281	73	274	55	77	8	13	8	52	1	7	2	20	57	22	11	3	.493	.327
2003	Peoria	A	.267	128	480	77	128	19	8	15	61	4	4	3	51	90	23	11	13	.433	.338
2004	Palm Beach	A	.277	118	440	74	122	23	3	8	47	7	8	2	46	80	23	9	9	.398	.343
	Tennessee	AA	.320	7	25	1	8	3	0	0	1	0	0	0	2	3	1	0	0	.440	.370
2005	Springfield	AA	.182	46	159	12	29	6	0	3	16	4	1	0	18	38	1	3	2	.277	.264
	Palm Beach	A	.286	64	234	38	67	18	2	6	41	2	4	3	32	55	24	7	0	.457	.374
2006	Springfield	AA	.251	85	327	56	82	21	2	16	51	7	2	3	42	80	17	9	5	.474	.340
	Memphis	AAA	.162	21	74	7	12	4	0	1	9	1	2	1	9	21	3	3	1	.257	.256
2007	GCL Cardinals	R	.313	10	32	7	10	5	0	0	5	0	0	0	4	4	4	0	0	.469	.389
	Springfield	AA	.237	24	76	9	18	1	0	0	8	0	0	0	11	20	3	2	2	.250	.333
2008	Richmond	AAA	.538	4	13	2	7	0	0	0	1	0	0	0	2	4	1	1	1	.538	.600
	Mississippi	AA	.292	63	240	51	70	9	0	10	43	1	2	3	31	47	16	4	4	.454	.377
2009	Gwinnett	AAA	.286	106	371	57	106	27	6	9	49	3	3	5	34	73	14	7	8	.464	.351
	ATLANTA	MAJ	.200	31	25	6	5	0	0	0	3	0	1	0	1	12	1	0	1	.200	.222
Minor League Totals			**.268**	**749**	**2745**	**446**	**736**	**144**	**34**	**76**	**384**	**30**	**33**	**22**	**302**	**572**	**152**	**67**	**48**	**.428**	**.342**
Major League Totals			**.200**	**31**	**25**	**6**	**5**	**0**	**0**	**0**	**3**	**0**	**1**	**0**	**1**	**12**	**1**	**0**	**1**	**.200**	**.222**

GREENE, Shane – RHP

HT: 6-4; **WT:** 210; **B:** R; **T:** R; **BORN:** 11/17/88 in Clermont, Fla.; **RESIDES:** Clermont, Fla.; **COLLEGE:** Daytona State College; **OBTAINED:** Selected by the Yankees in the 15th round of the 2009 First-Year Player Draft; **M.L. SVC:** 0.000; **CAREER NOTES: 2009:** Made 13 appearances with the GCL Yankees in first professional season, going 1-2 with a 5.87 ERA and 20K in 23.0IP.

YEAR	CLUB	CLASS	W-L	ERA	G	GS	CG	SHO	SV	IP	H	R	ER	HR	HB	BB	SO	WP	BK
2009	GCL Yankees	R	1-2	5.87	13	0	0	0	0	23.0	30	19	15	2	5	6	20	4	0

GROTE, Taylor David – OF

HT: 6-2; **WT:** 195; **B:** L; **T:** R; **BORN:** 12/5/88 in The Woodlands, Tex.; **RESIDES:** The Woodlands, Tex.; **OBTAINED:** Signed by the Yankees as a non-drafted free agent on 8/14/07; **M.L. SVC:** 0.000; **CAREER NOTES: 2009:** With Single-A Charleston, hit .232 with 22 doubles, 4HR and 42RBI…hit safely in 12 of his first 13 games of the season…**2008:** Batted .223 with 6 doubles, 3HR and 20RBI in 56 games with short-season Single-A Staten Island…ranked fourth in the NYPL with 73K…**2007:** Appeared in only one game with the Gulf Coast Yankees in his professional debut, going 0-for-1 with 1BB on 8/24.

YEAR	CLUB	CLASS	AVG	G	AB	R	H	2B	3B	HR	RBI	SH	SF	HB	BB	SO	SB	CS	E	SLUG	OBP
2007	GCL Yankees	R	.000	1	1	0	0	0	0	0	0	0	0	0	1	0	0	0	0	.000	.500
2008	Staten Island	SS-A	.223	56	188	23	42	6	1	3	20	0	1	0	24	73	2	2	4	.314	.310
2009	Charleston	A	.232	113	418	54	97	22	0	4	42	0	3	1	48	139	8	3	6	.313	.311
Minor League Totals			**.229**	**170**	**607**	**77**	**139**	**28**	**1**	**7**	**62**	**0**	**4**	**1**	**73**	**212**	**10**	**5**	**10**	**.313**	**.311**

GUZMAN, Miguel – INF

HT: 5-11; **WT:** 167; **B:** S; **T:** R; **BORN:** 7/18/90 in Paya Bani, D.R.; **RESIDES:** Paya Bani, D.R.; **OBTAINED:** Signed by the Yankees as a non-drafted free agent on 5/7/09; **M.L. SVC:** 0.000; **CAREER NOTES: 2009:** Made his professional debut, batting .250 with two doubles and 5RBI in 15 games with the DSL Yankees 1…recorded 4SB in five attempts.

YEAR	CLUB	CLASS	AVG	G	AB	R	H	2B	3B	HR	RBI	SH	SF	HP	BB	SO	SB	CS	E	SLUG	OBP
2009	DSL Yankees 1	R	.250	15	36	6	9	2	0	0	5	0	0	0	8	15	4	1	3	.306	.386

HALL, Shaeffer – LHP

HT: 6-0; **WT:** 180; **B:** R; **T:** L; **BORN:** 10/2/87 in Independence, Mo.; **RESIDES:** Lee's Summit, Mo.; **COLLEGE:** Kansas; **OBTAINED:** Selected by the Yankees in the 25th round of the 2009 First-Year Player Draft; **M.L. SVC:** 0.000; **CAREER NOTES: 2009:** Made two starts with short-season Single-A Staten Island, striking out 11 batters in 9.2IP…**PERSONAL:** Full name is William Shaeffer Hall…graduated from Lee's Summit West HS (MO), earning the 2006 *Kansas City Star* "All-Metro Player of the Year" award and First Team All-State by the Missouri Sportswriters and Missouri Coaches…was selected by Texas in the 28th round of the 2006 First-Year Player Draft and Cleveland in the 23rd round in 2007…attended Jefferson College before transferring to Kansas.

YEAR	CLUB	CLASS	W-L	ERA	G	GS	CG	SHO	SV	IP	H	R	ER	HR	HB	BB	SO	WP	BK
2009	Staten Island	SS-A	0-0	1.86	2	2	0	0	0	9.2	9	2	2	0	2	0	11	1	0

HARROW, Isaac – INF

HT: 5-11; **WT:** 185; **B:** R; **T:** R; **BORN:** 1/25/87 in Hickory, N.C.; **RESIDES:** Taylorsville, N.C.; **COLLEGE:** Appalachian State University; **OBTAINED:** Selected by the Yankees in the 24th round of the 2009 First-Year Player Draft; **M.L. SVC:** 0.000; **CAREER NOTES: 2009:** In his first professional season, batted .186 with 4 doubles, 1 triple, 1HR and 8RBI in 30 games with the GCL Yankees…**PERSONAL:** Attended Appalachian State University, where in 2009 he set single-season school records with 75RBI, 163 total bases and 6 triples…has a degree in construction management.

YEAR	CLUB	CLASS	AVG	G	AB	R	H	2B	3B	HR	RBI	SH	SF	HP	BB	SO	SB	CS	E	SLUG	OBP
2009	GCL Yankees	R	.186	30	86	7	16	4	1	1	8	0	1	0	10	25	0	1	3	.291	.268

HEATHCOTT, Slade – OF

HT: 6-1; **WT:** 190; **B:** L; **T:** L; **BORN:** 9/28/90 in Texarkana, Ark.; **RESIDES:** Texarkana, Ark.; **OBTAINED:** Selected by the Yankees in the first round (29th overall) of the 2009 First-Year Player Draft; **M.L. SVC:** 0.000; **CAREER NOTES: 2009:** Appeared in three games with the GCL Yankees, going 1-for-10…named the Yankees' fourth-best prospect by *Baseball America* following the season…**PERSONAL:** Full name is Zachary Heathcott…graduated from Texas High School where he was a third-team All-State selection and named first-team All-District as a senior…was an AFLAC All-American selection as a left-handed pitcher in 2008, while also playing outfield at various events, including the Perfect Game National Showcase and the Area Code Games…ranked as the 72nd-best prospect (18th-best high school position player) in the draft by *Baseball America* and rated by the publication as the 10th-best prospect in the state of Texas in 2009.

YEAR	CLUB	CLASS	AVG	G	AB	R	H	2B	3B	HR	RBI	SH	SF	HP	BB	SO	SB	CS	E	SLUG	OBP
2009	GCL Yankees	R	.100	3	10	0	1	0	0	0	0	0	0	0	1	2	0	0	0	.100	.182

HEIDLER, Paul – RHP

HT: 6-2; **WT:** 195; **B:** R; **T:** R; **BORN:** 11/12/86 in Farmville, Va.; **RESIDES:** Farmville, Va.; **COLLEGE:** Longwood University; **OBTAINED:** Signed by the Yankees as a non-drafted free agent on 6/16/09; **M.L. SVC:** 0.000; **CAREER NOTES: 2009:** Spent the majority of his first professional season with the GCL Yankees, going 3-1 with a 2.16 ERA in 13 relief appearances… was promoted to Single-A Charleston on 9/2 and made two appearances with the RiverDogs (0-0, 4.50 ERA)… **PERSONAL:** Played three seasons in the outfield prior to converting to pitcher his senior year.

YEAR	CLUB	CLASS	W-L	ERA	G	GS	CG	SHO	SV	IP	H	R	ER	HR	HB	BB	SO	WP	BK
2009	GCL Yankees	R	3-1	2.16	13	0	0	0	0	16.2	15	4	4	1	1	8	13	0	0
	Charleston	A	0-0	4.50	2	0	0	0	0	4.0	5	3	2	1	0	3	4	0	0
Minor League Totals			**3-1**	**2.61**	**15**	**0**	**0**	**0**	**0**	**20.2**	**20**	**7**	**6**	**2**	**1**	**11**	**17**	**0**	**0**

HEREDIA, Jairo – RHP

HT: 6-1; **WT:** 189; **B:** R; **T:** R; **BORN:** 10/8/89 in Santo Domingo, D.R.; **RESIDES:** Santo Domingo, D.R.; **OBTAINED:** Signed by the Yankees as a non-drafted free agent on 7/2/06; **M.L. SVC:** 0.000; **CAREER NOTES: 2009:** Went 3-3 with a 3.99 ERA in 10 combined starts with the GCL Yankees, Single-A Charleston and Single-A Tampa...was placed on the disabled list on 4/9 with right shoulder inflammation...did not record a decision in two rehab starts with the GCL Yankees, allowing 3H and 1ER in 5.0IP (2R, 2BB, 5K)...reinstated from the DL on 7/21 and made four starts with Charleston, going 1-1 with a 2.37 ERA...was transferred to Tampa on 8/17 where he went 2-2 with a 6.91 ERA in four starts...named the Florida State League "Pitcher of the Week" on 8/24 after earning two wins and combining to allow just 1ER in 12.0IP over two starts (14H, 4BB, 5K)...**2008:** Went 6-7 with a 3.25 ERA in 21 starts with Single-A Charleston...was placed on the disabled list from 4/21-5/23 with right elbow tendinitis...tossed a career-high 7.0 innings on 6/30 vs. Savannah...was named the SAL's "Pitcher of the Week" for the period of 6/30-7/6, going 2-0 with a 0.00 ERA in two starts, allowing just 5H and striking out 11 batters in 13.1IP (2R, 2BB)...struck out a career-high-tying eight batters in 5.1IP on 7/27 vs. Hickory...allowed just 1HR over his final 11 starts of the season (60.0IP) after giving up 6HR over his first 10 starts (52.1IP)...**2007:** Made his professional debut with the GCL Yankees, going 2-2 with a 2.72 ERA in 11 games (six starts)...led the GCL staff with 52 strikeouts, while walking just 11 batters in 46.1IP...recorded a career-high 8K in back-to-back starts on 7/10 and 7/18.

YEAR	CLUB	CLASS	W-L	ERA	G	GS	CG	SHO	SV	IP	H	R	ER	HR	HB	BB	SO	WP	BK
2007	GCL Yankees	R	2-2	2.72	11	6	0	0	0	46.1	39	15	14	4	3	11	52	1	0
2008	Charleston	A	6-7	3.25	21	21	0	0	0	102.1	99	58	37	7	5	43	95	4	1
2009	GCL Yankees	R	0-0	1.80	2	2	0	0	0	5.0	3	2	1	0	0	2	5	0	0
	Charleston	A	1-1	2.37	4	4	0	0	0	19.0	14	6	5	1	1	1	17	0	0
	Tampa	A	2-2	6.91	4	4	1	1	0	14.1	25	14	11	2	0	5	10	3	1
Minor League Totals			**11-12**	**3.27**	**42**	**37**	**1**	**1**	**0**	**187.0**	**180**	**95**	**68**	**14**	**9**	**62**	**179**	**8**	**2**

HEREDIA, Juan – LHP

HT: 6-3; **WT:** 160; **B:** L; **T:** L; **BORN:** 1/20/89 in San Pedro de Macoris, D.R.; **RESIDES:** San Pedro de Macoris, D.R.; **OBTAINED:** Signed by the Yankees as a non-drafted free agent on 4/18/08; **M.L. SVC:** 0.000; **CAREER NOTES: 2009:** Allowed just 3R/2ER in 13 starts (57.0IP) with the DSL Yankees 2, posting a 0.32 ERA...fell just shy of qualifying for the league's lowest ERA...did not allow a run until his seventh start of the season, opening the year with 27.0 consecutive scoreless innings...limited opponents to a .179 batting average (34-for-190), holding the opposition to 3H or less in eight starts...**2008:** Made his professional debut, posting a record of 5-3 with a 3.35 ERA in 15 games (six starts) with the DSL Yankees 2...recorded at least 6K in six of his 15 appearances, including three straight outings from 7/4-15.

YEAR	CLUB	CLASS	W-L	ERA	G	GS	CG	SHO	SV	IP	H	R	ER	HR	HB	BB	SO	WP	BK
2008	DSL Yankees 2	R	5-3	3.35	15	6	0	0	0	48.1	34	22	18	1	7	18	58	6	1
2009	DSL Yankees 2	R	2-0	0.32	13	13	0	0	0	57.0	34	3	2	0	3	20	63	5	1
Minor League Totals			**7-3**	**1.71**	**28**	**19**	**0**	**0**	**0**	**105.1**	**68**	**25**	**20**	**1**	**10**	**38**	**121**	**11**	**2**

HERRERA, Javier – OF

HT: 5-11; **WT**: 191; **B**: R; **T**: R; **BORN**: 4/9/85 in Caracas, Venezuela; **RESIDES**: Caracas, Venezuela; **OBTAINED**: Signed by the Yankees as a free agent on 12/15/09; **M.L. SVC**: 0.000; **CAREER NOTES**: **2009**: Played in one game for Double-A Midland (4/9), suffering a left hand fracture...was released from the Oakland organization on 5/19...following the season, played for the Cardenales de Lara of the Venezuelan Winter League, batting .311 (14-for-45) with 8R, 3 doubles, 2HR and 6RBI in 22 games...**2008**: Hit .267 with 9HR and 36RBI in 61 games with Double-A Midland after spending the first two-and-a-half months on the disabled list with a strained left hamstring...hit in every spot in the lineup except cleanup...following the season, was named the "Best Defensive Outfielder" and as having the Athletics' "Best Outfield Arm" by *Baseball America*...**2007**: Began the year at Single-A Stockton and was transferred to Double-A Midland on 7/4 before his season ended early on 7/25 with a strained right hamstring...combined to bat .269 with 12HR and 52RBI in 82 games...hit a career-high 22 doubles...batted .285 off right-handed pitching and .206 off left-handers...**2006**: Missed the season after going on the disabled list on 4/6 with an injury to the ulnar collateral ligament in his right elbow and undergoing "Tommy John" surgery...attended spring training with the A's and went 2-for-10 (.200) with 1 double and 1RBI in six games before being optioned to Sacramento on 3/13...following the season, was named the A's sixth-best prospect by *Baseball America*...**2005**: Spent nearly the entire season at Single-A Kane County, where he batted .275 with 13HR and 62RBI in 94 games...was named to the Midwest League Postseason All-Star team and was named as the A's second-best prospect by *Baseball America* following the season...also had a five-game stint with Triple-A Sacramento from 5/21-27, going 5-for-12 (.417) with 1HR and 3RBI...hit .280 with 14HR and 65RBI in 99 games overall...had career highs in nearly every offensive category, including games, at-bats (372), runs (75), hits (104), HR, RBI, walks (48) and stolen bases (27)...led the A's farm system in stolen bases...hit 12 of his 14HR off right-handed pitchers...batted .500 (7-for-14) with 1HR and 21RBI with the bases loaded (grand slam came on 5/4 at Dayton)...played on the World Team in the All-Star Futures Game at Comerica Park on 7/10, going 1-for-1 with 1RBI...recorded a season-high 6RBI on 7/19 vs. Wisconsin and had 23RBI in 26 games in July...batted .265 with 3HR and 12RBI in 53 games with Caracas in the Venezuelan Winter League...**2004**: Spent the entire season at Single-A Vancouver and was named Northwest League MVP after batting .331 with 12HR and 47RBI in 65 games...ranked second in the Northwest League in hits (87) and stolen bases (23), third in slugging (.555), tied for third in triples (4), fourth in batting average and tied for fourth in extra-base hits (31)...had career highs in average, slugging and on-base percentage (.392)...led the team in average, hits, doubles (15), triples, home runs, stolen bases and total bases (146)...went 4-for-12 (.333) with 2 doubles, 1HR and 4RBI in three playoff games for the Canadians...was named as the A's second-best prospect by *Baseball America* following the season...**2003**: Appeared in just 17 games for the A's affiliate in the Arizona Rookie League, batting .230 with 2HR and 13RBI...appeared in 14 games in CF and two in LF...**2002**: Played for the A's affiliate in the Dominican Summer League and batted .286 with 5HR and 47RBI in 65 games...had a career-high five triples...**PERSONAL**: Full name is Javier Armando Herrera...was originally signed by the Athletics as a non-drafted free agent on 7/27/01.

YEAR	CLUB	CLASS	AVG	G	AB	R	H	2B	3B	HR	RBI	SH	SF	HP	BB	SO	SB	CS	E	SLUG	OBP
2002	DSL Athletics	R	.286	65	227	40	65	14	5	5	47	2	2	4	23	56	21	4	-	.458	.359
2003	AZL Athletics	R	.230	17	61	12	14	3	1	2	13	0	0	2	7	19	3	1	0	.410	.329
2004	Vancouver	A	.331	65	263	50	87	15	4	12	47	0	2	4	24	59	23	1	4	.555	.392
2005	Sacramento	AAA	.417	5	12	5	5	1	0	1	3	0	0	2	1	1	1	0	0	.750	.533
	Kane County	A	.275	94	360	70	99	18	2	13	62	0	3	12	47	110	26	5	8	.444	.374
2006							Did Not Play-Injured														
2007	Stockton	A	.274	62	252	45	69	17	0	9	39	0	2	6	19	60	11	7	3	.448	.337
	Midland	AA	.254	20	71	13	18	5	0	3	13	0	1	3	4	13	1	0	1	.451	.316
2008	Midland	AA	.267	61	255	44	68	13	2	9	36	2	0	2	22	71	8	4	2	.439	.330
2009	Midland	AA	.000	1	2	0	0	0	0	0	0	0	0	0	0	0	0	0	1	.000	.000
Minor League Totals			**.283**	**390**	**1503**	**279**	**425**	**86**	**14**	**54**	**260**	**4**	**10**	**35**	**147**	**389**	**94**	**22**	**19**	**.466**	**.358**

HEYER, Craig – RHP

HT: 6-3; **WT:** 195; **B:** R; **T:** R; **BORN:** 11/15/85 in Scottsdale, Ariz.; **RESIDES:** Scottsdale, Ariz.; **COLLEGE:** University of Nevada-Las Vegas; **OBTAINED:** Selected by the Yankees in the 22nd round of the 2007 First-Year Player Draft; **M.L. SVC:** 0.000; **CAREER NOTES: 2009:** Spent the season with Single-A Tampa, going 4-3 with one save and a 3.11 ERA in 30 appearances (six starts)...held left-handed batters to a .231 (34-for-147, 1HR) batting average, while right handers hit .302 (39-for-129, 0HR)...made all of his starts over his final seven appearances of the season (7/13-8/12)...was placed on the disabled list on 8/21 with a right hand fracture, missing the remainder of the season...**2008:** Went 7-1 with one save and a 2.08 ERA in 41 appearances (one start) with Single-A Charleston...tossed a season-high 3.2 innings on 6/23 vs. Rome...made his only start of the season on 8/12 at Delmarva, allowing 5H and 2ER in 3.0IP (3K)...recorded his first professional loss on 8/26 vs. Savannah after winning his first 12 career decisions (five in 2007 and first seven in 2008)...**2007:** Made his professional debut with short-season Single-A Staten Island, going 5-0 with a 3.20 ERA in 17 games (one start)...recorded the win in three consecutive relief appearances from 7/31-8/7, allowing 1ER in 11.1IP...**PERSONAL:** Attended the Community College of Southern Nevada before transferring to UNLV in 2006...earned all-state honors in 2003 and 2004 at Coronado (Ariz.) High School.

YEAR	CLUB	CLASS	W-L	ERA	G	GS	CG	SHO	SV	IP	H	R	ER	HR	HB	BB	SO	WP	BK
2007	Staten Island	SS-A	5-0	3.20	17	1	0	0	0	50.2	59	20	18	4	2	13	25	0	1
2008	Charleston	A	7-1	2.08	41	1	0	0	1	86.1	78	25	20	3	2	15	51	4	0
2009	Tampa	A	4-3	3.11	30	6	0	0	1	72.1	73	30	25	1	1	9	29	2	0
Minor League Totals			**16-4**	**2.71**	**88**	**8**	**0**	**0**	**2**	**209.1**	**210**	**75**	**63**	**8**	**5**	**37**	**105**	**6**	**1**

HIGASHIOKA, Kyle – C

NON-ROSTER INVITEE

HT: 6-1; **WT:** 190; **B:** R; **T:** R; **BORN:** 4/20/90 in Huntington Beach, Calif.; **RESIDES:** Huntington Beach, Calif.; **OBTAINED:** Selected by the Yankees in the seventh round of the 2008 First-Year Player Draft; **M.L. SVC:** 0.000; **CAREER NOTES: 2009:** Batted .253 with 11 doubles, 2HR and 32RBI in 60 games with short-season Single-A Staten Island...led all league catchers in games (57), chances (497) and putouts (451) and ranked fifth in caught stealing percentage (25.3, 19-for-75)...**2008:** Made his professional debut, appearing in 18 games with the GCL Yankees and making 14 starts behind the plate...hit .261 with 1 double, 1HR and 3RBI...**PERSONAL:** Graduated from Edison (Calif.) High School where he batted .382 with 7HR and 31RBI in his senior season and earned All-County honors...was selected as the starting catcher for the 2008 Orange County All-Star South team...was the 2006 All-Sunset League "Rookie of the Year."

YEAR	CLUB	CLASS	AVG	G	AB	R	H	2B	3B	HR	RBI	SH	SF	HP	BB	SO	SB	CS	E	SLUG	OBP
2008	GCL Yankees	R	.261	18	46	5	12	1	0	1	3	0	1	1	2	8	0	0	0	.348	.300
2009	Staten Island	SS-A	.253	60	217	24	55	11	0	2	32	1	2	1	26	31	0	1	5	.332	.333
Minor League Totals			**.255**	**78**	**263**	**29**	**67**	**12**	**0**	**3**	**35**	**1**	**3**	**2**	**28**	**39**	**0**	**1**	**5**	**.335**	**.328**

HIRSH, Jason – RHP

NON-ROSTER INVITEE

HT: 6-8; **WT**: 250; **B**: R; **T**: R; **BORN**: 2/20/82 in Santa Monica, Calif.; **RESIDES**: Burbank, Calif.; **COLLEGE**: Cal Lutheran University; **OBTAINED**: Acquired by the Yankees on 7/29/09 from the Colorado Rockies in exchange for a player to be named later or cash considerations; **M.L. SVC**: 1.153; **CAREER NOTES**: Owns a career 8-11 record with a 5.32 ERA in parts of three Major League seasons with Houston (2006) and Colorado (2007-08)...has made 32 Major League appearances (29 starts), allowing 166H and 98ER in 165.2IP (110K, 74BB)...**2009**: Combined to go 10-7 with a 5.55 ERA in 26 appearances (22 starts) with Triple-A Colorado Springs and Triple-A Scranton/Wilkes-Barre...began the season with Colorado Springs, going 6-7 with a 6.66 ERA (101.1IP, 75ER) in 20 appearances (16 starts) before a mid-season trade to the Yankees on 7/29...went undefeated in six starts with Scranton/WB, going 4-0 with a 1.35 ERA (26.2IP, 4ER)...made his final start of the season on 9/5 at Rochester, facing only two batters before suffering an injury fielding a ball in the first inning (0.1IP, 1H)...was placed on the disabled list on 9/6 through the end of the season with plantar fasciitis of his right heel...**2008**: Did not record a decision in four appearances (one start) with Colorado, allowing 8ER in 8.2IP (8.31 ERA)...made his first career relief appearance in his season debut on 9/3 vs. San Francisco, tossing a perfect ninth inning (1.0IP)...in three relief outings, had a 10.38 ERA (4.1IP, 5ER)...made his only start of the season on 9/26 at Arizona—his first start since 8/7/07 vs. Milwaukee—and recorded a no-decision, tossing 4.1 innings and allowing 3ER with 2BB and 4K...began the season on the 15-day disabled list with a strained right shoulder and was transferred to the 60-day D.L. on 5/11...made three rehab starts with Triple-A Colorado Springs from 5/30-6/10, allowing 5ER in 12.1IP (3.65 ERA) without recording a decision...was reinstated from the disabled list on 6/12 and optioned to Colorado Springs where he spent the majority of the season...in 18 overall appearances (17 starts), went 4-4 with a 5.80 ERA (99.1IP, 115H, 64ER)...recorded more walks (52) than strikeouts (51) and allowed 16HR...tossed at least 6.0 innings in seven consecutive starts from 7/23-8/24...**2007**: Entered the season ranked by *Baseball America* as the third-best prospect in the Rockies organization...went 5-7 with a 4.81 ERA in 19 starts for Colorado (112.1IP, 60ER), with the Rockies going 10-9 in his starts...received fewer than three runs of support in 10 of his 19 starts...among NL rookies, tied for third in games started, ranked seventh in strikeouts (75) and tied for ninth in wins...tossed a 9.0-inning complete game on 6/10 at Baltimore, becoming one of only seven Major League rookies to toss a CG that season and just the 15th rookie pitcher to toss a complete game for the Rockies in franchise history...made his Rockies debut in the Padres' home opener on 4/6 at San Diego, earning the win after allowing just 1ER in 6.2IP and striking out a career-high-tying eight batters (also 8/2/07 at Florida)...tossed 6.0 shutout innings in 7/2 win vs. New York-NL before leaving the game early after spraining his right ankle on the basepaths...hit a two-run single off Tom Glavine earlier in the game for just his second career hit and first RBI...was placed on the 15-day disabled list with the injury from 7/3-8/1...made three rehab starts for Colorado Springs...made his final start of the season—and just his second his being reinstated from the disabled list—on 8/7 vs. Milwaukee, earning the win despite being struck in the right leg by a line drive off the Brewers' second batter of the game (J.J. Hardy)...remained in the game to earn the win (6.0IP, 3H, 2ER), but underwent X-rays the following day which revealed a fractured right fibula...was placed on the D.L. again on 8/9 (retroactive to 8/8)...was transferred to the 60-day disabled list on 9/4, missing the remainder of the season...**2006**: Saw his first big league action, going 3-4 with a 6.04 ERA (44.2IP, 30ER) in nine starts for Houston after his recall on 8/12...made his Major League debut that night vs. San Diego, taking the loss after allowing 7H and 4ER in 4.0IP...earned his first Major League win in his next start on 8/17 at Milwaukee (5.1IP, 3ER)...entered the season ranked by *Baseball America* as the Astros' top prospect and was listed by the publication as having the "Best Control" in both the PCL and Houston organization...began the season with Triple-A Round Rock, going 13-2 with a 2.10 ERA (137.1IP, 32ER) in 23 starts for the Express while posting a career high in wins and leading the PCL in ERA and wins...was selected as the U.S. team's starting pitcher in the Futures Game on 7/9 in Pittsburgh (1.0IP, 1H, 1K) and was a mid-season All-Star...tossed 1.0 inning of relief for the PCL squad in the Triple-A All-Star game vs. the IL on 7/12 in Toledo...compiled a Houston franchise-record 12-game winning streak to end his Triple-A stint and had a 1.19 ERA (113.2IP, 15ER) over his final 18 starts...set a club record with a 46.2-inning stretch without allowing an earned run from 6/13-7/27...struck out a career-high 12 batters on 6/24 vs. Nashville...was named the PCL's "Pitcher of the Year" following the season, becoming the only pitcher to earn the distinction in both the PCL and Texas Leagues...was also named to the *Baseball America* Triple-A All-Star team following the season, while being rated by the publication as the ninth-best PCL prospect after posting the third-lowest qualifying ERA in the league's history (trailed only Chris Codiroli's 1.90 ERA for Tacoma in 1982 and Peter Mikkelson's 1.91 ERA for Tulsa in 1968)...**2005**: Was named Texas League "Pitcher of the Year" in his Double-A debut, going 13-8 with a 2.87 ERA (172.1IP, 55ER) in 29 starts for Corpus Christi...named to the league's midseason and postseason All-Star squads, as well as a Double-A All-Star and the league's "Pitcher of the Year" by *Baseball America*...the publication also tabbed him as having the "Best Breaking Pitch" in the Texas League...tossed 2.0 shutout innings of relief in the Texas League All-Star Game on 6/21 at Frisco...named the Corpus Christi MVP and the club's "Pitcher of the Month" in April and July...led the league with 165K and ranked second in ERA and innings pitched...named the league's "Pitcher of the Week" three times...**2004**: Went 11-7 with a 4.01 ERA (130.1IP, 58ER) in 26 games (23 starts) for Single-A Salem in his first full professional season...led Salem and ranked fourth in the Carolina League in wins...struck out a season-high 10 batters in 6.0IP on 8/30 at Winston-Salem...**2003**: Made his professional debut with Single-A Tri-City, going 3-1 with a 1.95 ERA (32.1IP, 7ER) in 10 appearances (eight starts)...all 7ER allowed came in his lone loss in the first game of a doubleheader on 8/8 at Lowell...finished the season with a 17.0-inning scoreless stretch over his final four outings...was rated as the Astros' eighth-best prospect by *Baseball America* following the season...**PERSONAL**: Full name is Jason Michael Hirsh...married wife, Pamela, in November 2007...attended Cal Lutheran University in Thousand Oaks, Calif., where he earned all-conference and all-region honors...went to St. Francis High School in La Canada, Calif...younger brother, Matthew, was selected by the Astros in the 30th round of the 2005 First-Year Player Draft...Jason was originally selected as the Astros first pick (second round) in the 2003 First-Year Player Draft.

YEAR	CLUB	CLASS	W-L	ERA	G	GS	CG	SHO	SV	IP	H	R	ER	HR	HB	BB	SO	WP	BK
2003	Tri-City	A	3-1	1.95	10	8	0	0	0	32.1	22	10	7	0	2	7	33	1	0
2004	Salem	A	11-7	4.01	26	23	0	0	0	130.1	128	66	58	8	9	5	96	5	0
2005	Corpus Christi	AA	13-8	2.87	29	29	1	1	0	172.1	137	63	55	12	12	42	65	7	1
2006	Round Rock	AAA	13-2	2.10	23	23	1	1	0	137.1	94	37	32	5	8	5	118	2	0
	HOUSTON	MAJ	3-4	6.04	9	9	0	0	0	44.2	48	32	30	11	3	22	29	4	0
2007	COLORADO	MAJ	5-7	4.81	19	19	1	0	0	112.1	103	63	60	18	2	48	75	5	1
	Colo. Springs	AAA	1-2	4.85	3	3	0	0	0	13.0	16	8	7	1	1	4	7	0	0
2008	Colo. Springs	AAA	4-4	5.80	18	17	0	0	0	99.1	115	66	64	16	3	52	51	5	0
	COLORADO	MAJ	0-0	8.31	4	1	0	0	0	8.2	15	10	8	3	0	4	6	0	0
2009	Colo. Springs	AAA	6-7	6.66	20	16	0	0	0	101.1	130	78	75	14	3	35	59	6	1
	Scranton/WB	AAA	4-0	1.35	6	6	0	0	0	26.2	24	4	4	2	0	6	21	0	0
Minor League Totals			**55-31**	**3.81**	**135**	**125**	**2**	**2**	**0**	**712.2**	**666**	**332**	**302**	**58**	**38**	**254**	**550**	**26**	**2**
Major League Totals			**8-11**	**5.32**	**32**	**29**	**1**	**0**	**0**	**165.2**	**166**	**105**	**98**	**32**	**5**	**74**	**110**	**9**	**1**

HORNE, Alan – RHP

HT: 6-4; **WT:** 195; **B:** R; **T:** R; **BORN:** 1/05/83 in Marianna, Fla.; **RESIDES:** Marianna, Fla.; **COLLEGE:** University of Florida; **OBTAINED:** Selected by the Yankees in the 11th round in the 2005 draft; **M.L. SVC:** 0.000; **CAREER NOTES: 2009**: began the season on the disabled list to continue rehabbing his shoulder injury from 2008...was reinstated from the D.L. on 4/30 and assigned to Trenton where he went 0-3 with an 11.15 ERA in five appearances (four starts)...was placed on the disabled list for a second time from 5/13-6/2 with a left hamstring strain...made two appearances (one start) with the Thunder before being placed back on the D.L. for a third stint on 6/8 with a left hamstring strain...began a rehab assignment with the GCL Yankees on 7/23, going 4-0 with a 2.86 ERA in six appearances (five starts)...was reinstated from the disabled list on 8/25 and assigned to Charleston where he went 0-1 with a 5.50 ERA in three starts...**2008:** Combined to go 2-4 with an 8.77 ERA in 11 starts with Triple-A Scranton/Wilkes-Barre and Single-A Tampa...began the season with Scranton/WB, going 2-3 with a 5.63 ERA in eight starts (32.0IP, 20ER)...was placed on the disabled list twice with Scranton/WB (4/11-6/8 with a right biceps strain and 7/2-28 with a cracked fingernail)...was transferred to Tampa on 7/31 where he went 0-1 with a 23.14 ERA in three starts (7.0IP, 18ER)...made two D.L. stints while with Tampa (8/4-17 with a right shoulder strain and 8/23-9/17 with right shoulder inflammation)...**2007:** Went 12-4 with a 3.11 ERA in 27 starts for Double-A Trenton...was named Eastern League "Pitcher of the Year" after leading the league in ERA, strikeouts (165) and a .750 winning percentage while ranking fourth in innings pitched (153.1)...ranked first among all Yankees farmhands in strikeouts and fourth in ERA...was named to the Eastern League midseason All-Star team and was selected as the EL's top right-handed starter on the postseason All-Star squad...had six or more strikeouts in 21 of his 27 starts...from 6/13-7/31, recorded a career-high five game winning streak, tossing 51.2 innings and allowing 11ER, while striking out 49 batters during the nine-game span...following the season, was ranked by *Baseball America* as the Yankees' fifth-best prospect...**2006:** Made professional debut with Single-A Tampa, posting a 6-9 record with a 4.84 ERA...ranked third in the Florida State League with 122K and 61BB...ranked fourth among all Yankees minor-league pitchers in strikeouts...**PERSONAL:** Full name is William Alan Horne...led the 2005 University of Florida team with 10 wins and 108K...helped lead the Gators to the finals of the College World Series...previously played at Chipola Junior College in 2004 and was selected in the 30th round of the 2004 draft by the Anaheim Angels (did not sign)...played baseball at Ole Miss in 2002 and 2003 before undergoing "Tommy John" surgery on his right elbow in 2003...was ranked No. 6 on *Baseball America's* list of the nation's top 50 sophomores prior to the 2003 season and also rated as the SEC's No. 2 prospect for the 2004 Major League Baseball Draft...also listed as one of the top players to watch in the SEC by *Collegiate Baseball*...earned honorable mention Freshman All-America honors from *Collegiate Baseball* in 2002...helped lead Marianna (Fla.) High School to four consecutive appearances in the state 3A Final Four, including a state title his junior year...was originally drafted in the first round by the Cleveland Indians with the 27th overall pick in the 2001 First-Year Player Draft but did not sign...was a Louisville Slugger "National Player of the Year" finalist and a three-time all-state honoree.

YEAR	CLUB	CLASS	W-L	ERA	G	GS	CG	SHO	SV	IP	H	R	ER	HR	HB	BB	SO	WP	BK
2006	Tampa	A	6-9	4.84	28	26	0	0	0	122.2	105	72	66	10	6	61	122	7	1
2007	Trenton	AA	12-4	3.11	27	27	0	0	0	153.1	149	68	53	10	11	57	165	7	2
2008	Scranton/WB	AAA	2-3	5.63	8	8	0	0	0	32.0	35	25	20	2	3	22	24	0	1
	Tampa	A	0-1	23.14	3	3	0	0	0	7.0	21	18	18	3	1	5	6	3	0
2009	Trenton	AA	0-3	11.15	5	4	0	0	0	15.1	25	21	19	3	1	16	13	2	0
	GCL Yankees	R	4-0	2.86	6	5	0	0	0	28.1	23	9	9	2	1	10	22	6	0
	Charleston	A	0-1	5.50	3	3	0	0	0	18.0	17	12	11	1	2	11	13	6	0
Minor League Totals			**24-21**	**4.68**	**80**	**76**	**0**	**0**	**0**	**376.2**	**375**	**225**	**196**	**32**	**25**	**182**	**365**	**31**	**4**

HOVIS, Jonathan – RHP

HT: 5-11; **WT:** 185; **B:** R; **T:** R; **BORN:** 12/27/83 in Florence, S.C.; **RESIDES:** Gastonia, N.C.; **COLLEGE:** University of North Carolina; **OBTAINED:** Signed by the Yankees as a non-drafted free agent on 7/3/06; **M.L. SVC:** 0.000; **CAREER NOTES: 2009**: Combined to go 2-3 with 22 saves and a 3.48 ERA in 46 relief appearances with Single-A Tampa and Double-A Trenton…led all Yankees minor leaguers in saves…began the season with Tampa, posting a 2-2 record with 22 saves and a 3.38 ERA in 44 relief outings…led the league in saves and led the team in appearances…recorded a save in both opportunities in the postseason, allowing just 1H with 3K in 2.0IP…was named to the Florida State League postseason All-Star team…also made two relief appearances for Trenton from 5/10-19, going 0-1 with a 4.91 ERA…**2008:** Limited to 21 games with Single-A Tampa due to a pair of injuries (right forearm strain, 5/4-6/6 and right triceps tendinitis, 7/23-end of season)…went 2-0 with 10 saves (in 11 opportunities) and a 1.14 ERA…walked just three batters while striking out 24 batters in 23.2IP and held opponents to a .155 batting average (13-for-84, 2HR)…did not allow a run over his final 15 outings (17.1IP)…**2007:** Was 4-5 with 30 saves and a 1.69 ERA in a team-high 55 relief appearances with Single-A Charleston…struck out 56 batters while walking just 11…led the South Atlantic League in saves and ranked eighth overall in the minor leagues…also ranked third in the league in appearances…placed second among all Yankees minor leaguers in saves…pitched in relief in the SAL midseason All-Star Game (0.2IP, 1K)…**2006:** Made professional debut with short-season Single-A Staten Island, posting a 5-1 record with a team-best 1.73 ERA in 25 relief appearances…held opponents to a .200 batting average (25-for-125) while limiting right-handed hitters to just .187 (14-for-75)…**PERSONAL:** Full name is Jonathan William Hovis…was named pre-season All-Atlantic Coast Conference entering his senior season…ranked second in the ACC with 9.44K/9.0IP and ranked fifth with a 2.51 ERA in 2005…was a member of the ACC Academic Honor Roll and earned Dean's List status at UNC Chapel Hill.

YEAR	CLUB	CLASS	W-L	ERA	G	GS	CG	SHO	SV	IP	H	R	ER	HR	HB	BB	SO	WP	BK
2006	Staten Island	SS-A	5-1	1.73	25	0	0	0	0	36.1	25	10	7	0	2	13	30	1	0
2007	Charleston	A	4-5	1.69	55	0	0	0	30	64.0	49	17	12	2	2	11	56	3	0
2008	Tampa	A	2-0	1.14	21	0	0	0	10	23.2	13	3	3	2	0	3	24	1	0
2009	Tampa	A	2-2	3.38	44	0	0	0	22	48.0	44	19	18	2	0	13	41	1	0
	Trenton	AA	0-1	4.91	2	0	0	0	0	3.2	4	3	2	1	2	1	4	0	0
Minor League Totals			**13-9**	**2.15**	**147**	**0**	**0**	**0**	**62**	**175.2**	**135**	**52**	**42**	**7**	**6**	**41**	**155**	**6**	**0**

IBARRA, Walter – INF

HT: 5-11; **WT:** 150; **B:** S; **T:** R; **BORN:** 11/1/87 in Los Mochis Sinola, Mexico; **RESIDES:** Monterrey, Mexico; **OBTAINED:** Signed by the Yankees as a non-drafted free agent on 8/23/05; **M.L. SVC:** 0.000; **CAREER NOTES: 2009**: Hit .262 (69-for-263) with 10 doubles, one triple and 19RBI in 86 combined games with Single-A Charleston and Single-A Tampa…following the season, appeared in 34 games with the Naranjeros de Hermosillo of the Mexican Winter League and hit .250 (16-for-64) with one double and 4RBI…**2008:** Combined to bat .224 with 28R, 12 doubles, 4HR and 24RBI in 57 games with Single-A Charleston, short-season Single-A Staten Island and Double-A Trenton…began the season with Charleston, batting .198 in 27 games before being transferred to Staten Island on 6/27…in 12 games with Staten Island, batted .224…was promoted to Trenton on 7/12 where he hit .268…missed time from 8/7-12 to be with his wife for the birth of their child…sprained his left ankle on 8/24 vs. Reading and was placed on the disabled list the following day…remained on the D.L. through the end of the season…played for the Naranjeros de Hermosillo of the Mexican Pacific League following the season…**2007:** Split time between the GCL Yankees and Single-A Tampa…in 16 games with GCL, hit .205 (8-for-39) with 6R and 4RBI…batted .179 (5-for-28) with 5R and 1 double in 10 games for Tampa…**2006:** Made professional debut with the Gulf Coast Yankees, batting .264 in 24 games played (19 at SS, five at 2B).

YEAR	CLUB	CLASS	AVG	G	AB	R	H	2B	3B	HR	RBI	SH	SF	HP	BB	SO	SB	CS	E	SLUG	OBP
2006	GCL Yankees	R	.264	24	72	4	19	2	0	0	7	1	0	1	12	8	3	2	5	.292	.376
2007	Tampa	A	.179	10	28	5	5	1	0	0	0	0	0	0	2	9	1	0	1	.214	.233
	GCL Yankees	R	.205	16	39	6	8	2	0	0	4	0	1	2	4	8	0	1	2	.256	.304
2008	Charleston	A	.198	27	91	13	18	6	1	1	13	0	0	0	6	16	1	0	4	.319	.247
	Staten Island	SS-A	.224	12	49	10	11	3	0	2	6	1	0	0	2	7	2	1	5	.408	.255
	Trenton	AA	.268	18	56	5	15	3	0	1	5	1	0	1	2	8	0	2	4	.375	.305
2009	Charleston	A	.241	12	29	2	7	0	0	0	3	1	0	0	2	10	1	0	6	.241	.290
	Tampa	A	.265	74	234	38	62	10	1	0	16	2	3	1	10	23	11	5	12	.316	.294
Minor League Totals			**.242**	**193**	**598**	**83**	**145**	**27**	**2**	**4**	**54**	**6**	**4**	**5**	**40**	**89**	**19**	**11**	**39**	**.314**	**.294**

IGAWA, Kei – LHP

NON-ROSTER INVITEE

HT: 6-1; **WT:** 212; **B:** L; **T:** L; **BORN:** 7/13/79 in Ibaraki, Japan; **RESIDES:** Ibaraki, Japan; **OBTAINED:** Signed through the MLB/Japanese posting system on 12/27/06…signed a five-year contract that runs through 2011; **M.L. SVC:** 0.095; **CAREER NOTES: 2009**: Went 10-8 with a 4.15 ERA in 26 starts for Triple-A Scranton/Wilkes-Barre, leading the team in both wins and games started and ranking fourth among all Yankees minor leaguers in wins…set the record for most career wins in Scranton/WB history (29)…owned a 7-3 record with a 2.72 ERA (76.0IP, 23ER) in 13 home starts, compared to a 3-5 mark with a 5.71 ERA in 13 starts on the road (69.1IP, 44ER)…struck out a season-high eight batters twice (6/16 vs. Toledo and 7/16 vs. Gwinnett)…made two postseason appearances (one start) for the International League runner-ups, going 0-2 with a 10.29 ERA (7.0IP, 8ER)…**2008:** Was 0-1 with a 13.50 ERA in two games (one start) over two stints with the Yankees (5/9-15; 6/27-28)…recalled from Triple-A Scranton/Wilkes-Barre and started on 5/9 at Detroit, making his only start of the season and recording the loss in a 6-5 Tigers victory (3.0IP, 6ER, 11H)…recalled a second time from Scranton/WB prior to Game 2 of a split-stadium doubleheader on 6/27 vs. the Mets…made his only relief appearance of the season in the 9-0 Yankees victory at Shea Stadium (1.0IP, 2H)…was optioned back to Scranton/WB the following day…earned Scranton/WB's "Pitcher of the Year" Award, appearing in 26 games (24 starts) and going 14-6 with a 3.45 ERA…led the team in wins, starts, innings pitched (156.1IP) and strikeouts (117)…tied for second in the International League in wins and ranked fourth in ERA…made two starts in the IL playoffs, going 1-0 with a 1.35 ERA for the IL champions…**2007:** Was 2-3 with a 6.25 ERA in 14 games (12 starts) over three stints with the Yankees (4/2-5/7; 6/22-7/27; 9/9-9/30)…made Opening Day roster and started on 4/7 vs. Baltimore in his Major League debut, allowing 7ER in 5.0IP and recording a no-decision in a 10-7 Yankees victory…earned his first Major League win on 4/18 vs. Cleveland in his third career start (6.0IP, 5H, 2ER, 1BB, 5K)…was optioned to Single-A Tampa on 5/7 after going 2-1 with a 7.63 ERA in six games (5GS) with the Yankees…went 1-1 in two starts at Tampa, allowing 7H and 2ER in 9.0IP…was transferred to Triple-A Scranton/Wilkes-Barre on 5/29…overall with Scranton/WB, was 5-4 with a 3.69 ERA (68.1IP, 68H, 30R, 28ER, 15BB, 71K, 10HR) in 11 starts…in his only minor league postseason start, recorded a no-decision in Scranton/Wilkes-Barre's 6-4 Game 2 victory on 9/6 in the first round of the International League playoffs at Richmond (5.0IP, 6H, 2ER, 2BB, 4K)…received the 2007 James P. Dawson Award for "Most Outstanding

Rookie in Spring Training" from the New York chapter of the BBWAA on 3/31 at Steinbrenner Field (formerly Legends Field)...in six Grapefruit League starts, posted a 2-0 record with a 3.13 ERA and a team-high 22 strikeouts...**JAPANESE PLAYING CAREER**: Played with the Hanshin Tigers of the Central League from 1998-2006...was selected to the Central League All-Star Team in three consecutive seasons from 2001-03...led the Central League in strikeouts in 2002, 2004 and 2006...in 2003, helped lead Hanshin to the pennant with a league-leading 20 victories and a 2.80 ERA...was named the Central League's "Most Valuable Player" and was honored as the co-winner of the prestigious Sawamura Award, given to the top pitcher in Japanese baseball each year...was also named to the Best Nine following the season, recognizing the top player at each of the nine baseball positions in the Japan League...tossed a no-hitter on 10/4/04 at Hiroshima in a 1-0 Hanshin victory...won at least 13 games in five consecutive seasons (2002-06)...played in the 2006 Major League Baseball Japan All-Star Series...made one start for the Japanese All-Stars vs. the U.S. Major League All-Star Team on 11/7, allowing 2ER—including a David Wright home run—in 6.0IP (5H, 6BB, 4K)...was posted by the Hanshin Tigers on 11/16...on 11/29, the New York Yankees posted the highest bid and gained exclusive negotiating rights for a 30-day window...**PERSONAL**: Name is pronounced "KAY Ee-GAH-wah"...was originally selected by the Hanshin Tigers out of Mito Shogyo High School...enjoys playing shogi (Japanese chess)...according to the *Elias Sports Bureau*, was the 39th Japanese-born player in Major League history, the 26th Japanese-born pitcher and just the eighth to debut as a starter.

YEAR	CLUB	CLASS	W-L	ERA	G	GS	CG	SHO	SV	IP	H	R	ER	HR	HB	BB	SO	WP	BK
1999	Hanshin	JAP	1-1	6.46	7	3	0	0	0	15.1	23	11	11	1	1	13	14	0	0
2000	Hanshin	JAP	1-3	4.35	9	5	0	0	0	39.1	36	19	19	5	0	19	37	7	0
2001	Hanshin	JAP	9-13	2.67	29	28	3	2	0	192.0	174	76	57	11	3	53	206	8	0
2002	Hanshin	JAP	14-9	2.49	31	29	8	4	1	209.2	163	63	58	15	7	53	206	8	0
2003	Hanshin	JAP	20-5	2.80	29	29	8	2	0	206.0	184	72	64	15	3	58	179	5	0
2004	Hanshin	JAP	14-11	3.73	29	29	6	3	0	200.1	190	95	83	29	6	54	228	5	0
2005	Hanshin	JAP	13-9	3.86	27	27	2	1	0	172.1	199	91	74	23	1	60	145	4	0
2006	Hanshin	JAP	14-9	2.97	29	29	8	3	0	209.0	180	77	69	17	6	49	194	4	0
2007	YANKEES	MAJ	2-3	6.25	14	12	0	0	0	67.2	76	48	47	15	4	37	53	5	1
	Tampa	A	1-1	2.00	2	2	0	0	0	9.0	7	4	2	0	0	3	6	0	0
	Scranton/WB	AAA	5-4	3.69	11	11	0	0	0	68.1	68	30	28	10	2	15	71	0	1
2008	Scranton/WB	AAA	14-6	3.45	26	24	2	0	0	156.1	141	65	60	15	4	45	117	5	0
	YANKEES	MAJ	0-1	13.50	2	1	0	0	0	4.0	13	6	6	0	0	0	0	0	0
2009	Scranton/WB	AAA	10-8	4.15	26	26	1	0	0	145.1	165	75	67	21	5	40	105	2	0
Japanese League Totals			**86-60**	**3.15**	**190**	**179**	**35**	**15**	**1**	**1244.0**	**1149**	**504**	**435**	**116**	**27**	**395**	**1174**	**39**	**0**
Minor League Totals			**30-19**	**3.73**	**65**	**63**	**3**	**0**	**0**	**379.0**	**381**	**174**	**157**	**46**	**11**	**103**	**299**	**7**	**1**
Major League Totals			**2-4**	**6.66**	**16**	**13**	**0**	**0**	**0**	**71.2**	**89**	**54**	**53**	**15**	**4**	**37**	**53**	**5**	**1**

JIMENEZ, Antonio – RHP

HT: 6-0; **WT:** 175; **B:** R; **T:** R; **BORN:** 3/1/91 in Yuguate, D.R.; **RESIDES:** Yuguate, D.R.; **OBTAINED:** Signed by the Yankees as a non-drafted free agent on 6/6/09; **M.L. SVC:** 0.000; **CAREER NOTES: 2009:** Made his professional debut and went 4-2 with a 5.58 ERA in 18 games (one start) with the DSL Yankees 1...did not allow an earned run in seven of his last 10 relief appearances.

YEAR	CLUB	CLASS	W-L	ERA	G	GS	CG	SHO	SV	IP	H	R	ER	HR	HB	BB	SO	WP	BK
2009	DSL Yankees 1	R	4-2	5.58	18	1	0	0	1	30.2	26	32	19	1	4	35	27	12	1

JIMENEZ, Warlin – RHP

HT: 6-0; **WT:** 165; **B:** R; **T:** R; **BORN:** 10/26/88 in Baharona, D.R.; **RESIDES:** Boca Chica, D.R.; **OBTAINED:** Signed by the Yankees as a non-drafted free agent on 11/21/07; **M.L. SVC:** 0.000; **CAREER NOTES: 2009:** Posted a 2-1 record with a 2.51 ERA in nine games (six starts) with the DSL Yankees 1...worked to a 1.16 ERA (23.1IP, 3ER) as a starter, allowing just 1ER over his final four starts of the year (20.0IP, 17H, 5R, 1ER, 3BB, 19K, 1HR)...**2008:** In his professional debut, went 2-2 with a 4.50 ERA in 12 games (five starts) with the DSL Yankees 1...was 2-0 with a 3.80 ERA and recorded 11K in 21.1IP as a reliever.

YEAR	CLUB	CLASS	W-L	ERA	G	GS	CG	SHO	SV	IP	H	R	ER	HR	HB	BB	SO	WP	BK
2008	DSL Yankees 1	R	2-2	4.50	12	5	0	0	0	34.0	38	27	17	1	4	14	14	2	0
2009	DSL Yankees 1	R	2-1	2.51	9	6	0	0	0	28.2	24	12	8	0	2	11	22	2	0
Minor League Totals			**4-3**	**3.59**	**21**	**11**	**0**	**0**	**0**	**62.2**	**62**	**39**	**25**	**1**	**6**	**25**	**36**	**4**	**0**

JOSEPH, Corban – INF

HT: 6-0; **WT:** 168; **B:** L; **T:** R; **BORN:** 10/28/88 in Franklin, Tenn.; **RESIDES:** Franklin, Tenn.; **OBTAINED:** Selected by the Yankees in the fourth round of the 2008 First-Year Player Draft; **M.L. SVC:** 0.000; **CAREER NOTES: 2009**: Batted .300 with 29 extra-base hits (17 doubles, 8 triples, 4HR) and 57RBI in 100 games with Single-A Charleston...ranked fifth in the SAL in average...began the season by recording a hit in 12 consecutive contests from 5/11-5/23, batting .308 (16-for-52) with 4 doubles and 1 triple over the stretch...was named the South Atlantic League's "Player of the Month" in July after hitting .410 (43-for-105) during the month with 13 multi-hit games...was selected to the SAL's postseason All-Star team as the league's top third baseman...**2008:** Made his professional debut, batting .277 with 25R, 15 doubles, 2HR and 18RBI in 49 games with the GCL Yankees...led team in doubles, tying for third-most in the GCL, and runs...reached base safely in a team-high 18 straight games from 7/11 through the end of the season...**PERSONAL:** Batted .510 with 15HR and 58RBI in his senior season at Franklin (Tenn.) High School and was named Midstate "Player of the Year"...his brother, Caleb, was drafted in 2008 by Baltimore.

YEAR	CLUB	CLASS	AVG	G	AB	R	H	2B	3B	HR	RBI	SH	SF	HP	BB	SO	SB	CS	E	SLUG	OBP
2008	GCL Yankees	R	.277	49	159	25	44	15	2	2	18	2	1	1	20	24	2	5	8	.434	.359
2009	Charleston	A	.300	100	380	39	114	17	8	4	57	0	4	3	49	61	8	5	18	.418	.381
Minor League Totals			**.293**	**149**	**539**	**64**	**158**	**32**	**10**	**6**	**75**	**2**	**5**	**4**	**69**	**85**	**10**	**10**	**26**	**.423**	**.374**

KAPALA, Dan – RHP

HT: 6-5; **WT:** 220; **B:** R; **T:** R; **BORN:** 9/6/85 in Royal Oak, Mich.; **RESIDES:** Royal Oak, Mich.; **COLLEGE:** Notre Dame; **OBTAINED:** Selected by the Yankees in the 46th round of the 2007 First-Year Player Draft; **M.L. SVC:** 0.000; **CAREER NOTES: 2009**: Went 6-2 with a 2.64 ERA in 38 appearances (four starts) with Single-A Charleston…was 4-0 in 19 appearances out of the bullpen prior to the All-Star break, allowing 12ER in 42.1IP (2.55 ERA)…made four starts after the break and went 1-1 with a 0.82 ERA (22.0IP, 2ER), holding the opposition scoreless in three of those four outings with a .213 batting average (17-for-80)…**2008:** Combined to go 2-2 with one save and a 1.91 ERA in 17 relief appearances with the GCL Yankees, Single-A Charleston and short-season Single-A Staten Island…held right-handed batters to a .143 (8-for-56) batting average…recorded his first professional save on 6/25 vs. the GCL Phillies, tossing 1.0 perfect inning…earned his first career win on 7/13 at Tri-City (w/ Staten Island)**…2007:** Made his professional debut with short-season Single-A Staten Island, posting a 3.94 ERA with no decisions in 10 relief appearances…**PERSONAL:** Full name is Daniel Joseph Kapala…attended Notre Dame where he posted a career record of 9-13 with a 3.26 ERA…played with the Falmouth Commodores of the Cape Cod League in the summer of 2005…was the Gatorade Michigan "Player of the Year" as a senior at Shrine Catholic High School…ranked by *Baseball America* as the No. 2 prep prospect in Michigan in 2003…was a two-year letter winner in football.

YEAR	CLUB	CLASS	W-L	ERA	G	GS	CG	SHO	SV	IP	H	R	ER	HR	HB	BB	SO	WP	BK
2007	Staten Island	SS-A	0-0	3.94	10	0	0	0	0	16.0	16	10	7	1	2	6	10	2	0
2008	GCL Yankees	R	0-0	0.00	1	0	0	0	1	1.0	0	0	0	0	0	0	0	0	0
	Charleston	A	0-0	0.00	1	0	0	0	0	1.2	4	2	0	0	0	1	0	0	0
	Staten Island	SS-A	2-2	2.10	15	0	0	0	0	25.2	16	9	6	0	4	9	18	2	1
2009	Charleston	A	6-2	2.64	38	4	0	0	2	95.1	84	36	24	2	9	26	50	7	1
Minor League Totals			**8-4**	**2.64**	**65**	**4**	**0**	**0**	**3**	**139.2**	**120**	**57**	**41**	**3**	**15**	**42**	**78**	**11**	**2**

KONTOS, George – RHP

HT: 6-3; **WT:** 215; **B:** R; **T:** R; **BORN:** 6/12/85 in Lincolnwood, Ill.; **RESIDES:** Lincolnwood, Ill.; **COLLEGE:** Northwestern University; **OBTAINED:** Selected by the Yankees in the fifth round of the 2006 First-Year Player Draft; **M.L. SVC:** 0.000; **CAREER NOTES: 2009**: Combined to go 4-5 with a 3.15 ERA in 13 starts with Double-A Trenton and Triple-A Scranton/Wilkes-Barre…began the season with Trenton, going 1-1 with a 2.66 ERA in four starts before being promoted to Scranton/WB on 5/4…in nine starts with Scranton/WB, went 3-4 with a 3.35 ERA…tossed his first career complete game on 6/6 at Charlotte, recording the loss despite allowing just 4H and 2ER in 8.0IP (3R, 2BB, 5K)…was 3-1 with a 2.25 ERA (28.0IP, 7ER) in his first five starts with Scranton/WB, but went 0-3 with a 4.70 ERA (23.0IP, 12ER) over his final four starts…was placed on the disabled list on 6/26 with a right biceps strain, missing the remainder of the season…**2008:** Made a team-high 27 starts for Double-A Trenton, going 6-11 with a 3.68 ERA and leading the team in strikeouts (152) and innings pitched (151.2)…held opponents to a .239 batting average, including a .212 (67-for-316) mark vs. lefthanders…led all Yankees minor leaguers and ranked third in the Eastern League in strikeouts…named EL "Pitcher of the Week" for the period ending 8/3…**2007:** Went 4-6 with a 4.02 ERA in 19 appearances (17GS) with Single-A Tampa…recorded a career-high 11K in 6.1IP on 4/17 vs. Clearwater…was placed on the disabled list from 4/19-6/13 with a right shoulder contusion…following the season, pitched for the Honolulu Sharks of the Hawaiian Winter Baseball League, going 3-4 with a 3.71 ERA in eight appearances (seven starts), tossing 34.0IP and allowing 34H, 16R, 14ER, 10BB and 1HR while striking out 42 batters…**2006:** Made professional debut with short-season Single-A Staten Island, going 7-3 with a 2.64 ERA in 14 starts…ranked third among all NY-Penn League pitchers with 82K…won seven consecutive decisions from 7/8-8/17…following the season, was named to the *Baseball America* Minor League Short-Season All-Star Team…**PERSONAL:** Full name is George Nicholas Kontos…at Northwestern University in 2006, started the most games of any Wildcat pitcher (16) and ranked second in the Big Ten with 84 strikeouts…at Niles West (Ill.) High School was a three-year varsity baseball and golf letterwinner…also lettered in basketball…was honored as the 2003 Illinois state baseball Gatorade "Player of the Year"…also earned first-team all-state by the Illinois Coaches Association and *Chicago Sun-Times* and was the Central Suburban "Player of the Year."

YEAR	CLUB	CLASS	W-L	ERA	G	GS	CG	SHO	SV	IP	H	R	ER	HR	HB	BB	SO	WP	BK
2006	Staten Island	SS-A	7-3	2.64	14	14	0	0	0	78.1	64	25	23	3	2	19	82	3	0
2007	Tampa	A	4-6	4.02	19	17	0	0	0	94.0	95	51	42	15	0	30	101	6	0
2008	Trenton	AA	6-11	3.68	27	27	0	0	0	151.2	134	76	62	14	4	57	152	2	0
2009	Trenton	AA	1-1	2.66	4	4	0	0	0	20.1	19	7	6	0	2	9	24	5	0
	Scranton/WB	AAA	3-4	3.35	9	9	1	0	0	51.0	44	24	19	6	2	21	39	2	0
Minor League Totals			**21-25**	**3.46**	**73**	**71**	**1**	**0**	**0**	**395.1**	**356**	**183**	**152**	**38**	**10**	**136**	**398**	**18**	**0**

KRUM, Austin – OF

HT: 5-9; **WT:** 175; **B:** L; **T:** L; **BORN:** 1/19/86 in Highlands Ranch, Colo.; **RESIDES:** McGregor, Tex.; **COLLEGE:** Dallas Baptist University; **OBTAINED:** Selected by the Yankees in the ninth round of the 2007 First-Year Player Draft; **M.L. SVC:** 0.000; **CAREER NOTES: 2009**: Combined to bat .249 with 75R, 21 doubles, 8 triples, 2HR and 38RBI in 130 games with Single-A Tampa and Double-A Trenton…began the season with Tampa, hitting .272 with 32R, 7 doubles and 14RBI in 53 games…was promoted to Trenton on 6/16, where he hit .234 with 43R, 14 doubles, 2HR and 24RBI in 77 games…**2008:** Batted .272 with 74R, 21 doubles, 6 triples, 8HR and 67RBI in 131 games with Single-A Charleston…ranked third on the team in RBI and stolen bases (12)…hit .339 (20-for-59) with 4 doubles, 2 triples and 1HR with RISP and two outs, driving in 28 runs…recorded an 11-game hitting streak from 7/28-8/7, batting .500 (19-for-38) with 2 doubles, 1 triple, 3HR and 9RBI…**2007:** Made his professional debut with short-season Single-A Staten Island, batting .238 with 32R, 14 doubles, 4 triples, 1HR and 22RBI in 60 games…recorded a career-high nine-game hitting streak from 8/29-9/5, batting .543 (19-for-35) with 5R, 4 doubles, 1 triple, 1HR and 10RBI during the stretch…in those nine games, recorded three-hits five times, including in each of the first four games of the streak…**PERSONAL:** Was a two-year starter at Dallas Baptist University (.356, 22 doubles, 18HR, 78RBI, and 38SB in 45 attempts)…led team in average in 2006 and hits in 2007…was invited to try out for the 2006 USA Baseball team.

YEAR	CLUB	CLASS	AVG	G	AB	R	H	2B	3B	HR	RBI	SH	SF	HB	BB	SO	SB	CS	E	SLUG	OBP
2007	Staten Island	SS-A	.238	60	202	32	48	14	4	1	22	2	1	4	16	44	11	5	1	.361	.305
2008	Charleston	A	.272	131	459	74	125	21	6	8	67	3	4	7	55	92	12	7	10	.397	.356
2009	Tampa	A	.272	53	191	32	52	7	3	0	14	1	2	5	35	43	7	4	1	.340	.395
	Trenton	AA	.234	77	290	43	68	14	5	2	24	5	6	4	36	68	11	2	4	.338	.321
Minor League Totals			**.257**	**321**	**1142**	**181**	**293**	**56**	**18**	**11**	**127**	**11**	**13**	**20**	**142**	**247**	**41**	**18**	**16**	**.366**	**.345**

KRUML, Ray – OF

HT: 6-0; **WT:** 185; **B:** L; **T:** R; **BORN:** 8/5/85 in Lisle, Ill.; **RESIDES:** Lisle, Ill.; **COLLEGE:** University of South Alabama; **OBTAINED:** Selected by the Yankees in the 11th round of the 2008 First-Year Player Draft; **M.L. SVC:** 0.000; **CAREER NOTES: 2009**: Hit .246 with 15 doubles, 4 triples, 2HR and 35RBI in 100 games with Single-A Charleston…stole 23 bases in 28 attempts…**2008:** Made his professional debut with short-season Single-A Staten Island, batting .294 with 42R, 15 doubles and 24RBI in 65 games…batted .286 (2-for-7) with 2R, 2BB and 1SB in two postseason games…**PERSONAL:** Attended the University of South Alabama, earning second-team All-Sun Belt Conference honors during his senior year…batted .350 with 68R, 21 doubles, 8HR and 45RBI in 57 games as a senior, leading the team in batting average and successfully stealing a base in 31 of his 36 attempts (86.1%)…also attended Indian Hills Community College where he lettered in both of his two seasons there…went to St. Francis High School (Ill.) where he was named an all-conference, all-city, all-area, all-state and the conference "Player of the Year" in baseball during his senior year…batted .420 during his team's regional championship season in 2003…was also all-conference and all-city selection in football…was selected in the 35th round of the 2005 First-Year Player Draft by Arizona but did not sign.

YEAR	CLUB	CLASS	AVG	G	AB	R	H	2B	3B	HR	RBI	SH	SF	HP	BB	SO	SB	CS	E	SLUG	OBP
2008	Staten Island	SS-A	.294	65	231	42	68	15	2	0	24	1	2	4	16	65	13	4	5	.377	.348
2009	Charleston	A	.246	100	382	53	94	15	4	2	35	1	3	3	26	100	23	5	5	.322	.297
Minor League Totals			**.264**	**165**	**613**	**95**	**162**	**30**	**6**	**2**	**59**	**2**	**5**	**7**	**42**	**165**	**36**	**9**	**10**	**.343**	**.316**

KUO, Fu-Lin – INF

HT: 5-11; **WT:** 187; **B:** R; **T:** R; **BORN:** 1/57/91 in Tainan City, Taiwan; **RESIDES:** Tainan City, Taiwan; **OBTAINED:** Signed by the Yankees as a free agent on 12/1/09; **M.L. SVC:** 0.000; **CAREER NOTES:** Will make his professional debut in 2010…**PERSONAL:** Graduated from Nan-Ying High School in Tainan City…was a member of the 2008 IBAF Taiwanese youth national team.

YEAR	CLUB	CLASS	AVG	G	AB	R	H	2B	3B	HR	RBI	SH	SF	HB	BB	SO	SB	CS	E	SLUG	OBP
NO PROFESSIONAL RECORD																					

LAIRD, Brandon – INF

NON-ROSTER INVITEE

HT: 6-1; **WT:** 215; **B:** R; **T:** R; **BORN:** 9/11/87 in Cypress, Calif.; **RESIDES:** Garden Grove, Calif.; **COLLEGE:** Cypress College; **OBTAINED:** Selected by the Yankees in the 27th round of the 2007 First-Year Player Draft; **M.L. SVC:** 0.000; **CAREER NOTES: 2009**: Batted .266 with 20 doubles, 13HR and 75RBI in 124 games with Single-A Tampa, setting a career high in games played…tied for third among all Yankees minor leaguers and led the Florida State League in RBI…led the team with 8RBI in seven playoff games for the FSL-champion Yankees…was named to the FSL postseason All-Star team…following the season, played for Surprise in the Arizona Fall League, batting .333 (30-for-90) with 18R, 9 doubles, 6HR and 24RBI in 22 games and was named to the AFL top prospects team…**2008:** Hit .273 with 71R, 31 doubles, 23HR and 86RBI in 122 games with Single-A Charleston…led all Yankees farmhands in homers and ranked second in RBI…split time between 1B and 3B, batting .310 (98-for-316) with 60R, 23 doubles, 20HR and 73RBI as a first baseman and .171 (22-for-129) with 9R, 6 doubles, 3HR and 11RBI as a third baseman…hit .333 (20-for-60) with 4HR and 26RBI with RISP and two outs…was placed on the disabled list from 5/7-19 with a left hamstring strain…batted .324 (34-for-105) with 24R, 7 doubles,11HR and 37RBI during the month of August…**2007:** Made his professional debut with the GCL Yankees, hitting .339 with 27R, 14 doubles, 8HR and 29RBI in 45 games…ranked third among all Yankees farmhands in batting average…was named to the GCL postseason All-Star team…recorded an eight-game hitting streak from 8/10-17, batting .567 (17-for-30) with 7R, 5 doubles, 3HR and 8RBI during the stretch, including five multi-hit games…collected a career-high four hits on 8/17 at the GCL Blue Jays, going 4-for-5 with 1 double, 1HR and 1RBI…**PERSONAL:** Is the younger brother of Detroit Tigers catcher Gerald Laird…was a two-year starter at Cypress College in California…played in 106 of 107 games combined over both seasons…in 2007, he led his team in every major offensive category (average, run, hits, doubles, home runs and RBI)…named Orange County "Player of the Year" as a senior at La Quinta High School where he helped his team win the CIF Championship, playing games at Angel Stadium of Anaheim…was named to the Los Angeles Times' 2005 All-Star team…played on USA Baseball's junior national team in the summer of 2005…selected by Cleveland in the 27th round of the 2005 First-Year Player Draft but did not sign, opting to attend school…participated in the Gene Autry R.B.I. (Reviving Baseball in the Inner City) program.

YEAR	CLUB	CLASS	AVG	G	AB	R	H	2B	3B	HR	RBI	SH	SF	HB	BB	SO	SB	CS	E	SLUG	OBP
2007	GCL Yankees	R	.339	45	168	27	57	14	1	8	29	1	1	2	6	26	0	0	7	.577	.367
2008	Charleston	A	.273	122	454	71	124	31	1	23	86	0	7	5	40	86	1	0	12	.498	.334
2009	Tampa	A	.266	124	451	53	120	20	4	13	75	0	5	6	39	75	1	1	16	.415	.329
Minor League Totals			**.281**	**291**	**1073**	**151**	**301**	**65**	**6**	**44**	**190**	**1**	**13**	**13**	**85**	**187**	**2**	**1**	**35**	**.475**	**.337**

LANDONI, Emerson Jose – INF

HT: 5-11; **WT:** 170; **B:** S; **T:** R; **BORN:** 2/19/89 in Maracay, Venezuela; **RESIDES:** El Tigrito, Venezuela; **OBTAINED:** Signed by the Yankees as a free agent on 10/18/07; **M.L. SVC:** 0.000; **CAREER NOTES: 2009:** Played at three different levels, combining to bat .217 with 1 double, 1 triple and 12RBI…**2008:** Hit .310 (31-for-100) with 15R, 1HR and 8RBI in 36 games with the GCL Yankees…hit his first home run on 8/11 at the GCL Phillies…signed by Florida as a non-drafted free agent on 12/1/05 and played with their Venezuelan Summer League team in 2006, appearing in games at 2B, 3B and SS…did not play in 2007 after he was released by the Marlins on 5/18/07.

YEAR	CLUB	CLASS	AVG	G	AB	R	H	2B	3B	HR	RBI	SH	SF	HB	BB	SO	SB	CS	E	SLUG	OBP
2006	VSL Marlins	R	.263	62	198	25	52	7	1	0	18	5	1	9	25	48	6	5	25	.308	.369
2007								Did Not Play													
2008	GCL Yankees	R	.310	36	100	15	31	2	2	1	8	1	0	2	9	18	2	1	5	.400	.378
2009	Tampa	A	.185	10	27	0	5	0	0	0	3	1	0	1	5	4	0	1	1	.185	.333
	Staten Island	SS-A	.237	27	76	8	18	1	1	0	9	2	0	1	8	14	4	1	9	.276	318
	GCL Yankees	R	.000	1	3	0	0	0	0	0	1	0	0	0	0	0	0	0	0	.000	.000
Minor League Totals			**.262**	**136**	**404**	**48**	**106**	**10**	**4**	**1**	**38**	**10**	**1**	**13**	**47**	**84**	**12**	**8**	**40**	**.314**	**.357**

LARE, Trent - LHP

HT: 6-4; **WT:** 195; **B:** L; **T:** L; **BORN:** 8/29/84 in Edgerton, Kan.; **RESIDES:** Edgerton, Kan.; **COLLEGE:** Emporia State University; **OBTAINED:** Signed by the Yankees as a minor league free agent on 6/18/09; **M.L. SVC:** 0.000; **CAREER NOTES: 2009:** Combined to go 5-5 with a 2.19 ERA in 14 appearances (13 starts) with short-season Single-A Staten Island, Single-A Charleston and Single-A Tampa...struck out 75 batters while walking just 10...began the season with Staten Island, going 3-2 with a 1.07 ERA in six starts...did not allow an earned run in four of those six outings...was transferred to Single-A Charleston on 7/21 and went 2-3 with a 2.76 ERA in seven starts...tossed a season-high 7.2IP on 8/24 at Augusta (4H, 1R, 0ER, 1BB, 8K)...was transferred to Tampa on 8/31, allowing 2ER in 2.0IP in one relief appearance (9.00 ERA)...**2008:** Pitched for the Kalamazoo Kings of the independent Frontier League, going 8-5 with a 4.13 ERA in 21 appearances (19 starts)...**2007:** Went 5-4 with a 3.17 ERA in 12 games (11 starts) for the independent Kalamazoo Kings...**PERSONAL:** Full name is Trenton Lare...graduated Emporia State University where he went 9-3 with a 3.00 ERA in 13 starts (78.0IP, 26ER), earning second team All-MIAA recognition as a senior...was also named to the All-Central Region's Second Team...led the team with 74K...prior to ESU, attended Coffeyville Community College and Oklahoma State University.

YEAR	CLUB	CLASS	W-L	ERA	G	GS	CG	SHO	SV	IP	H	R	ER	HR	HB	BB	SO	WP	BK
2009	Staten Island	SS-A	3-2	1.07	6	6	0	0	0	33.2	20	9	4	3	1	3	38	0	0
	Charleston	A	2-3	2.76	7	7	0	0	0	42.1	36	16	13	0	1	7	35	4	0
	Tampa	A	0-0	9.00	1	0	0	0	0	2.0	2	2	2	1	0	0	2	0	0
Minor League Totals			**5-5**	**2.19**	**14**	**13**	**0**	**0**	**0**	**78.0**	**58**	**27**	**19**	**4**	**2**	**10**	**75**	**4**	**0**

LASSITER, Garrison Lane – INF

HT: 6-1; **WT:** 185; **B:** L; **T:** R; **BORN:** 12/22/89 in High Point, N.C.; **RESIDES:** Tampa, Fla.; **OBTAINED:** Signed by the Yankees as a non-drafted free agent on 8/15/08; **M.L. SVC:** 0.000; **CAREER NOTES: 2009:** Spent the season with Single-A Charleston, batting .260 with 12 doubles, 1 triple, 2HR and 29RBI in 74 games...was on the disabled list from 5/6-6/8 with a right shoulder strain...played in one rehab game with the GCL Yankees...**2008:** Made his professional debut with the GCL Yankees, batting .261 with 6H and 2RBI in six games.

YEAR	CLUB	CLASS	AVG	G	AB	R	H	2B	3B	HR	RBI	SH	SF	HP	BB	SO	SB	CS	E	SLUG	OBP
2008	GCL Yankees	R	.261	6	23	2	6	0	0	0	2	0	0	0	1	6	1	0	4	.261	.292
2009	Charleston	A	.260	74	265	25	69	12	1	2	29	3	1	6	22	74	3	0	22	.336	.330
	GCL Yankees	R	.500	1	2	1	1	0	0	0	1	0	1	0	1	0	0	0	0	.500	.500
Minor League Totals			**.262**	**81**	**290**	**28**	**76**	**12**	**1**	**2**	**32**	**3**	**2**	**6**	**24**	**80**	**4**	**0**	**26**	**.331**	**.329**

LEONORA, Ericson – OF

HT: 5-11; **WT:** 174; **B:** R; **T:** R; **BORN:** 8/25/92 in Punto Fijo, Venezuela; **RESIDES:** Punto Fijo, Venezuela; **OBTAINED:** Signed by the Yankees as a non-drafted free agent on 8/25/08; **M.L. SVC:** 0.000; **CAREER NOTES: 2009**: Made his professional debut and batted .286 with 25 extra-base hits (12 doubles, nine triples, 4HR) and 39RBI in 61 games with the DSL Yankees 1...recorded a career-high 12-game hitting streak from 7/9–24, hitting .393 (22-for-56) with three doubles, two triples and 1HR over the stretch.

YEAR	CLUB	CLASS	AVG	G	AB	R	H	2B	3B	HR	RBI	SH	SF	HP	BB	SO	SB	CS	E	SLUG	OBP
2009	DSL Yankees 1	R	.286	61	259	40	74	12	9	4	39	0	4	1	18	66	15	8	7	.448	.330

LICCIEN, Jhorge Ramon – C

HT: 6-0; **WT:** 165; **B:** R; **T:** R; **BORN:** 10/10/90 in Tucupita, Venezuela; **RESIDES:** Barrana del Orinoco, Venezuela; **OBTAINED:** Signed as a non-drafted free agent on 7/2/07; **M.L. SVC:** 0.000; **CAREER NOTES: 2009**: Appeared in 29 games with the DSL Yankees 2 and hit .100 with 7BB...**2008:** Batted .274 with 3HR and 22RBI in 56 games in his professional debut with the DSL Yankees 2...recorded an 11-game hitting streak from 7/1-7/18...committed just one error in 46 appearances at catcher.

YEAR	CLUB	CLASS	AVG	G	AB	R	H	2B	3B	HR	RBI	SH	SF	HB	BB	SO	SB	CS	E	SLUG	OBP
2008	DSL Yankees 2	R	.274	56	215	39	59	14	0	3	22	0	0	1	15	33	5	3	1	.381	.325
2009	DSL Yankees 2	R	.100	29	80	6	8	0	0	0	1	2	0	1	7	18	0	0	5	.100	.182
Minor League Totals			**.227**	**85**	**295**	**45**	**67**	**14**	**0**	**3**	**23**	**2**	**0**	**2**	**22**	**51**	**5**	**3**	**6**	**.305**	**.285**

LIU, Kai – LHP

HT: 5-10; **WT:** 180; **B:** L; **T:** L; **BORN:** 10/11/87 in Guangdong, China; **RESIDES:** Guangzhou, China; **OBTAINED:** Signed by the Yankees as a non-drafted free agent on 6/16/07; **M.L. SVC:** 0.000; **CAREER NOTES:** Began playing baseball in 2000 for the Guangdong Province team...was chosen to participate as a member of the People's Republic of China National Team and was a member of the 2008 Olympic Team...made two relief appearances for Team China in the 2009 World Baseball Classic, allowing 5ER in 1.1IP...along with C Zhenwang Zhang, were the first members of Chinese Baseball to sign with a Major League team in accordance with the Yankees and Chinese Baseball Association's Memorandum of Understanding signed in January 2007...**2007:**Was introduced at a press conference at Yankee Stadium on 7/6/07 and then reported to the Yankees complex in Tampa.

YEAR	CLUB	CLASS	W-L	ERA	G	GS	CG	SHO	SV	IP	H	R	ER	HR	HB	BB	SO	WP	BK

NO PROFESSIONAL RECORD

LOCKWOOD, Trent – INF

HT: 6-4"; **WT**: 235; **B**: L; **T**: L; **BORN**: 5/5/86 in Waco, Tex.; **RESIDES**: San Antonio, Tex.; **COLLEGE**: University of Texas-San Antonio; **OBTAINED**: Signed by the Yankees as a non-drafted free agent on 10/5/09; **M.L. SVC**: 0.000; **CAREER NOTES**: Will be making his professional debut in 2010...**PERSONAL**: Was undrafted out of college, playing his first two professional seasons in the Independent leagues.

YEAR	CLUB	CLASS	AVG	G	AB	R	H	2B	3B	HR	RBI	SH	SF	HP	BB	SO	SB	CS	E	SLUG	OBP

NO PROFESSIONAL RECORD

LOPEZ, Daniel – OF

HT: 6-2; **WT**: 175; **B**: R; **T**: R; **BORN**: 1/17/92 in Santiago, D.R.; **RESIDES**: Santiago, D.R.; **OBTAINED**: Signed by the Yankees as a non-drafted free agent on 7/13/09; **M.L. SVC**: 0.000; **CAREER NOTES**: **2009**: Made his professional debut, batting .259 with 2 doubles, 2 triples and 7RBI in 18 games with the DSL Yankees 2.

YEAR	CLUB	CLASS	AVG	G	AB	R	H	2B	3B	HR	RBI	SH	SF	HP	BB	SO	SB	CS	E	SLUG	OBP
2009	DSL Yankees 2	R	.259	18	54	16	14	2	2	0	7	1	0	8	4	19	2	1	3	.370	.394

LOPEZ, Jerison – INF

HT: 5-11; **WT**: 177; **B**: R; **T**: R; **BORN**: 8/24/91 in San Pedro de Macoris, D.R.; **RESIDES**: San Pedro de Macoris, D.R.; **OBTAINED**: Signed by the Yankees as a non-drafted free agent on 4/22/09; **M.L. SVC**: 0.000; **CAREER NOTES**: **2009**: Made his professional debut, hitting .238 with 8 doubles, 3 triples, 3HR and 33 RBI in 58 games with the DSL Yankees 1...recorded 15 multi-hit games.

YEAR	CLUB	CLASS	AVG	G	AB	R	H	2B	3B	HR	RBI	SH	SF	HP	BB	SO	SB	CS	E	SLUG	OBP
2009	DSL Yankees 1	R	.238	58	252	51	60	8	4	3	33	2	1	3	23	55	10	2	15	.337	.308

LYERLY, Robert – INF

HT: 6-2; **WT:** 200; **B:** L; **T:** R; **BORN:** 7/23/87 in Indian Trail, N.C.; **RESIDES:** Indian Trail, N.C.; **COLLEGE:** UNC-Charlotte; **OBTAINED:** Selected by the Yankees in the sixth round of the 2009 First-Year Player Draft; **M.L. SVC:** 0.000; **CAREER NOTES: 2009:** Made his professional debut with the short-season Single-A Staten Island Yankees, batting .268 with 8 doubles and 7RBI and appearing in games at 1B (two) and 3B (18).

YEAR	CLUB	CLASS	AVG	G	AB	R	H	2B	3B	HR	RBI	SH	SF	HP	BB	SO	SB	CS	E	SLUG	OBP
2009	Staten Island	SS-A	.268	20	71	8	19	8	0	0	7	1	0	2	2	16	0	2	7	.380	.307

LYON, Mike – INF

HT: 6-2; **WT:** 220; **B:** R; **T:** R; **BORN:** 8/13/86 in Plainville, Mass.; **RESIDES:** Plainville, Mass.; **COLLEGE:** Northeastern University; **OBTAINED:** Selected by the Yankees in the 24th round of the 2008 First-Year Player Draft; **M.L. SVC:** 0.000; **CAREER NOTES: 2009**: Combined to hit .231 with 25R, 3HR and 17RBI in 74 games with Single-A Charleston and short-season Single-A Staten Island...began the season with Charleston, batting .236 with 2HR and 10RBI in 54 games...was transferred to Staten Island on 8/2 where he hit .217 with 1HR and 7RBI in 20 games...**2008:** Made his professional debut, batting .268 with 32R, 11 doubles, 6HR and 27RBI in 61 games with short-season Single-A Staten Island...was selected to the New York-Penn League's midseason All-Star team after batting .288 (46-for-160) with 11 doubles and 21RBI before the break...hit .125 (1-for-8) with 1HR in two postseason games...**PERSONAL:** Attended Northeastern University as a mechanical engineering major...hit .357 with 49R, 19 doubles, 14HR and 46RBI in 52 games during his senior year as co-team captain...set a single-season school record in total bases (138) and extra-base hits (36) while tying the Husky record in doubles...led the team in runs and slugging percentage (.693), tied for first in triples (3) and ranked second in homers, RBI and on-base percentage (.444)...finished his college career as the school's all-time leader with 89 extra-base hits, ranking second with 50 doubles, third in home runs (32), sixth in hits (192) and ninth in RBI (114)...enjoys playing the guitar and listening to music.

YEAR	CLUB	CLASS	AVG	G	AB	R	H	2B	3B	HR	RBI	SH	SF	HP	BB	SO	SB	CS	E	SLUG	OBP
2008	Staten Island	SS-A	.268	61	205	32	55	11	2	6	27	0	2	2	29	54	6	0	14	.429	.361
2009	Charleston	A	.236	54	165	15	39	6	5	2	10	0	0	3	17	55	3	1	5	.321	.319
	Staten Island	SS-A	.217	20	69	10	15	5	0	1	7	1	0	1	8	19	0	0	3	.333	.308
Minor League Totals			**.248**	**135**	**439**	**57**	**109**	**22**	**3**	**9**	**44**	**1**	**2**	**6**	**54**	**128**	**9**	**1**	**22**	**.374**	**.337**

MACK, DeAngelo – OF

HT: 5-10; **WT:** 190; **B:** L; **T:** L; **BORN:** 11/19/86 in West Columbia, S.C.; **RESIDES:** West Columbia, S.C.; **COLLEGE:** University of South Carolina; **OBTAINED:** Selected by the Yankees in the 13th round of the 2009 First-Year Player Draft **M.L. SVC:** 0.000; **CAREER NOTES: 2009:** Made his professional debut with short-season Single-A Staten Island, batting .306 with 19 doubles, 4 triples, 7HR and 41RBI in 66 games...ranked second in the NYPL in extra-base hits (30), tied for third in total bases (119), placed fifth in slugging (.513) and sixth in average and was a member of the midseason All-Star team...**PERSONAL:** Selected as a Second-Team All-SEC in 2009 with USC...graduated from Airport HS (SC) where he was an All-State selection his junior and senior seasons.

YEAR	CLUB	CLASS	AVG	G	AB	R	H	2B	3B	HR	RBI	SH	SF	HP	BB	SO	SB	CS	E	SLUG	OBP
2009	Staten Island	SS-A	.306	66	232	27	71	19	4	7	41	1	1	4	21	44	2	4	2	.513	.372

MAHONEY, Kevin – INF

HT: 6-1; **WT:** 205; **B:** L; **T:** R; **BORN:** 5/11/87 in Miller Place, N.Y.; **RESIDES:** Coram, N.Y.; **COLLEGE:** Canisius College; **OBTAINED:** Selected by the Yankees in the 23rd round of the 2009 First-Year Player Draft; **M.L. SVC:** 0.000; **CAREER NOTES: 2009:** Made his professional debut with the GCL Yankees, batting .226 with 17 doubles, 6HR and 30RBI in 57 games...played the second-most games in the GCL, tied for second in the league in doubles, tied for fourth in extra-base hits (24)...led all league third basemen with a .954 fielding percentage (8E, 173TC)...hit a grand slam on 8/3 at the GCL Phillies...**PERSONAL:** While at Canisius, selected as the 2009 MAAC "Player of the Year," 2008 Rawlings "Coastal Plains Offensive Player of the Year"...left as the school's all-time career leader in runs (202), hits (317) and RBI (130)...lettered in football, basketball and baseball at Miller Place High School...named All-State, All-County and league MVP as a senior in 2005.

YEAR	CLUB	CLASS	AVG	G	AB	R	H	2B	3B	HR	RBI	SH	SF	HP	BB	SO	SB	CS	E	SLUG	OBP
2009	GCL Yankees	R	.226	57	190	28	43	17	1	6	30	5	3	7	24	70	3	2	8	.421	.330

MALEC, Chris – INF

HT: 5-11; **WT:** 195; **B:** S; **T:** R; **BORN:** 8/28/82 in Laguna Niguel, Calif.; **RESIDES:** Laguna Niguel, Calif.; **COLLEGE:** University of California-Santa Barbara; **OBTAINED:** Selected by the Yankees in the 16th round of the 2005 First-Year Player Draft; **M.L. SVC:** 0.000; **CAREER NOTES: 2009**: Combined to bat .272 with 24 doubles, 9HR and 69RBI in 136 games with Double-A Trenton and Triple-A Scranton/Wilkes-Barre…began the season with Trenton, batting .279 with 8HR and 56RBI in two stints overall…tied for the team lead in RBI…**2008:** Played the entire season at Double-A Trenton, batting .291 with 28 doubles, 3 triples, 5HR and 52RBI in 119 games…played primarily at 1B and 3B, but made three starts at DH, one start at 2B and appeared as a defensive replacement in LF twice…named to the Eastern League's midseason All-Star team…**2007:** Split the season between Single-A Charleston and Single-A Tampa, combining to bat .316 with 64R, 28 doubles, 9HR and 79RBI in 137 games…ranked fourth among all Yankees farmhands in RBI and fifth in batting average…walked 69 times while striking out just 48…recorded 42 multi-hit games with Charleston and Tampa…was placed on the D.L. from 9/6-16 with a left hamstring strain…**2006:** Split the season between Single-A Charleston and Single-A Tampa, combining to bat .229 in 99 games…began the season with Charleston and batted .262 in 36 games (29 at 3B)…in 63 games with Tampa, batted .205…**2005:** Made professional debut with the Gulf Coast Yankees, batting .384 with 1HR and 14RBI in 21 games…**PERSONAL:** Graduated from UC Santa Barbara with a degree in Law & Society prior to joining the Yankees in 2005…was named to the First Team All-Big West following the 2004 season…played shortstop at Santa Margarita (Calif.) High School…was named All-Sierra League, All-County *Orange County Register* and All-County *Los Angeles Times* as a senior.

YEAR	CLUB	CLASS	AVG	G	AB	R	H	2B	3B	HR	RBI	SH	SF	HP	BB	SO	SB	CS	E	SLG	OBP
2005	GCL Yankees	R	.384	21	73	16	28	4	0	1	14	0	1	1	7	4	1	1	3	.479	.439
2006	Charleston	A	.262	36	130	15	34	4	0	1	14	1	2	1	6	0	14	0	4	.315	.295
	Tampa	A	.205	63	176	25	36	6	1	0	19	2	2	7	32	19	2	1	10	.250	.346
2007	Charleston	A	.308	70	227	33	70	11	1	4	38	0	6	11	42	27	7	3	7	.419	.430
	Tampa	A	.323	67	229	31	74	17	1	5	41	0	1	6	27	21	4	4	5	.472	.407
2008	Trenton	AA	.291	119	405	65	118	28	3	5	52	0	2	12	68	57	0	2	20	.412	.407
2009	Trenton	AA	.279	117	430	42	120	23	2	8	56	0	4	8	42	63	0	1	6	.398	.351
	Scranton/WB	AAA	.226	19	62	8	14	1	0	1	13	0	1	1	6	10	1	0	1	.290	.300
Minor League Totals			**.285**	**512**	**1732**	**235**	**494**	**94**	**8**	**25**	**247**	**3**	**19**	**47**	**230**	**215**	**15**	**13**	**56**	**.392**	**.380**

MARCANO, Juan Alberto – LHP

HT: 6-1; **WT:** 145; **B:** L; **T:** L; **BORN:** 8/24/90 in Porlamar, Venezuela; **RESIDES:** Porlamar, Venezuela; **OBTAINED:** Signed by the Yankees as a non-drafted free agent on 10/4/06; **M.L. SVC:** 0.000; **CAREER NOTES: 2009**: Went 2-1 with a 2.20 ERA in 12 games (11 starts) with the DSL Yankees 1…as a starter, was 1-1 with a 1.98 ERA, recording 63K and allowing just 9ER in 41.0IP…was 1-0 with a 4.50 ERA (2ER, 4.0IP) as a reliever…**2008:** Was 2-1 with a 2.75 ERA in 11 games (eight starts) with the DSL Yankees 1…opponents combined for a .179 batting average against…**2007:** Made his professional debut with the DSL Yankees 2, going 0-2 with a 1.37 ERA in seven appearances (5GS)…struck out 23 batters in 19.2IP, including 4K in each of his first three starts.

YEAR	CLUB	CLASS	W-L	ERA	G	GS	CG	SHO	SV	IP	H	R	ER	HR	HB	BB	SO	WP	BK
2007	DSL Yankees 2	R	0-2	1.37	7	5	0	0	0	19.2	10	6	3	0	3	6	23	4	0
2008	DSL Yankees 1	R	2-1	2.75	11	8	0	0	0	36.0	22	13	11	1	4	23	45	5	0
2009	DSL Yankees 1	R	2-1	2.20	12	11	0	0	0	45.0	27	13	11	1	3	20	70	5	0
Minor League Totals			**4-4**	**2.24**	**30**	**24**	**0**	**0**	**0**	**100.2**	**59**	**32**	**25**	**2**	**10**	**49**	**138**	**14**	**0**

MARQUEZ, Dickson – RHP

HT: 6-2; **WT:** 170; **B:** R; **T:** R; **BORN:** 4/19/86 in San Cristobal, D.R.; **RESIDES:** San Cristobal, D.R.; **OBTAINED:** Signed by the Yankees as a non-drafted free agent on 2/2/06; **M.L. SVC:** 0.000; **CAREER NOTES: 2009:** Pitched the majority of the season with the GCL Yankees, going 1-3 with a 1.86 ERA in a team-high-tying 20 appearances…allowed second-fewest baserunners per 9.0IP among GCL relievers (6.83)…promoted to Single-A Charleston on 9/3 and made two appearances with the RiverDogs, tossing 4.0 scoreless innings…**2008:** Appeared in 12 games (six starts) with the GCL Yankees, going 5-2 with a 6.03 ERA…**2007:** Was 2-3 with two saves and a 3.66 ERA in 11 appearances (four starts) with the Gulf Coast Yankees…struck out 45 batters while walking only 11 in 44.0IP…**2006:** Made professional debut with the Yankees DSL 1 team, going 2-0 with a 2.42 ERA in seven games (five starts)…limited opposing hitters to a .198 batting average.

YEAR	CLUB	CLASS	W-L	ERA	G	GS	CG	SHO	SV	IP	H	R	ER	HR	HB	BB	SO	WP	BK
2006	DSL Yankees 1	R	2-0	2.42	7	5	0	0	0	26.0	20	9	7	2	1	3	26	2	0
2007	GCL Yankees	R	2-3	2.66	11	4	0	0	2	44.0	37	18	13	3	4	11	45	3	0
2008	GCL Yankees	R	5-2	6.03	12	6	0	0	0	37.1	57	30	25	3	2	4	18	2	1
2009	GCL Yankees	R	1-3	1.86	20	0	0	0	1	29.0	19	9	6	1	1	2	21	1	2
	Charleston	A	1-0	0.00	2	0	0	0	0	4.0	1	0	0	0	0	0	4	0	0
Minor League Totals			**11-8**	**3.27**	**52**	**15**	**0**	**0**	**3**	**140.1**	**134**	**66**	**51**	**9**	**8**	**20**	**114**	**8**	**3**

MARSHALL, Brett – RHP

HT: 6-1; **WT:** 195; **B:** R; **T:** R; **BORN:** 3/22/90 in Highlands, Tex.; **RESIDES:** Highlands, Tex.; **OBTAINED:** Selected in the sixth round of the 2008 First-Year Player Draft; **M.L. SVC:** 0.000; **CAREER NOTES: 2009:** Went 3-6 with a 5.56 ERA in 17 starts with Single-A Charleston…held lefthanders to a .231 batting average…season was cut short on 7/17 when he was placed on disabled list for the remainder of the season with right elbow tendinitis…**2008:** Made his professional debut with the GCL Yankees, holding opponents to only one unearned run and two hits in three starts (6.0IP)…**PERSONAL:** Graduated from Ross Sterling (Tex.) High School…named the 2008 All-Greater Houston "Player of the Year" by the *Houston Chronicle*…went 10-2 with a 2.27 ERA and 116 strikeouts as a senior…also served as the cleanup hitter, batting .440 with 10HR and 49RBI…signed a letter of intent at Rice University…has a brother (Chris) who serves in the Army.

YEAR	CLUB	CLASS	W-L	ERA	G	GS	CG	SHO	SV	IP	H	R	ER	HR	HB	BB	SO	WP	BK
2008	GCL Yankees	R	0-0	0.00	3	3	0	0	0	6.0	2	1	0	0	0	2	8	1	0
2009	Charleston	A	3-6	5.56	17	17	0	0	0	87.1	98	67	54	7	9	37	60	8	0
Minor League Totals			**3-6**	**5.21**	**20**	**20**	**0**	**0**	**0**	**93.1**	**100**	**68**	**54**	**7**	**9**	**39**	**68**	**9**	**0**

MARTE, Joel – RHP

HT: 6-0; **WT:** 201; **B:** R; **T:** R; **BORN:** 1/18/88 in Santiago, D.R.; **RESIDES:** Santiago, D.R.; **OBTAINED:** Signed by the Yankees as a non-drafted free agent on 6/1/07; **M.L. SVC:** 0.000; **CAREER NOTES: 2009**: Made 20 relief appearances with the DSL Yankees 2, going 4-2 with a 3.89 ERA...recorded 43K in 39.1IP and threw 2.0IP or more in nine of his 20 outings...**2008:** Appeared in 15 games (nine starts) with the DSL Yankees 1, going 1-4 with a 3.02 ERA...allowed 2ER or less in eight of his nine starts...**2007:** Made his professional debut with the DSL Yankees 1, going 5-2 with a 4.04 ERA in 14 appearances (six starts)...struck out 58 batters in only 49.0IP, including a career-high 8K in 7/28 win vs. the DSL Blue Jays (4.0IP).

YEAR	CLUB	CLASS	W-L	ERA	G	GS	CG	SHO	SV	IP	H	R	ER	HR	HB	BB	SO	WP	BK
2007	DSL Yankees 1	R	5-2	4.04	14	6	0	0	0	49.0	39	27	22	1	5	23	58	7	0
2008	DSL Yankees 1	R	1-4	3.02	15	9	0	0	0	53.2	51	37	18	0	9	26	41	8	1
2009	DSL Yankees 2	R	4-2	3.89	20	0	0	0	2	39.1	44	36	17	3	4	13	43	9	0
Minor League Totals			**10-8**	**3.61**	**49**	**15**	**0**	**0**	**2**	**142.0**	**134**	**100**	**57**	**4**	**18**	**62**	**142**	**24**	**1**

MARTE, Ronny – RHP

HT: 6-1; **WT:** 173; **B:** R; **T:** R; **BORN:** 2/26/86 in Las Guaras, D.R.; **RESIDES:** San Pedro de Macoris, D.R.; **OBTAINED:** Signed by the Yankees as a non-drafted free agent on 7/22/04; **M.L. SVC:** 0.000; **CAREER NOTES: 2009:** Opened the season with Single-A Tampa, making two relief appearances before being transferred to short-season Staten Island for the remainder of the season...ranked third in the New York-Penn League in appearances (31), converting seven of 10 save opportunities...**2008:** Combined to go 4-2 with one save and a 3.53 ERA in 18 appearances (two starts) with the GCL Yankees and Tampa...began the season with the GCL Yankees, going 3-1 with one save and a 2.60 ERA in 14 appearances (one start), striking out 26 batters in 27.2IP (5BB)...recorded his first professional save on 7/11 at the GCL Braves...made four appearances with Tampa (one start), going 1-1 with a 6.75 ERA...**2007:** Went 2-1 with a 4.14 ERA in 12 appearances (eight starts) with the DSL Yankees 1...tossed a season-high 6.2 innings in 8/20 (Game 2) win vs. the DSL Reds, allowing 3H (4K)...**2006:** Made 18 relief appearances for the DSL Yankees 1 and posted a 3-1 record with a 3.34 ERA...**2005:** In sophomore campaign, posted a 2-1 record with a 4.22 ERA in 10 games with the Yankees' Dominican Summer League 1 squad...**2004:** Made professional debut with the DSL Yankees 2, posting an 0-6 record with an 8.63 ERA.

YEAR	CLUB	CLASS	W-L	ERA	G	GS	CG	SHO	SV	IP	H	R	ER	HR	HB	BB	SO	WP	BK
2004	DSL Yankees 2	R	0-6	8.63	10	7	0	0	0	32.1	49	38	31	3	2	16	16	6	0
2005	DSL Yankees 1	R	2-1	4.22	10	5	0	0	0	32.0	37	16	15	3	2	7	21	5	0
2006	DSL Yankees 1	R	3-1	3.34	18	0	0	0	0	29.2	32	15	11	0	4	9	17	3	0
2007	DSL Yankees 1	R	2-1	4.24	12	8	0	0	0	46.2	48	30	22	2	1	12	36	10	0
2008	GCL Yankees	R	3-1	2.60	14	1	0	0	1	27.2	25	13	8	1	1	5	26	1	1
	Tampa	A	1-1	6.75	4	1	0	0	0	8.0	11	7	6	1	0	2	5	2	0
2009	Tampa	A	1-0	1.93	2	0	0	0	0	4.2	3	1	1	0	0	2	3	0	0
	Staten Island	SS-A	6-3	4.24	31	0	0	0	7	40.1	36	25	19	2	1	13	45	4	1
Minor League Totals			**18-14**	**4.59**	**101**	**22**	**0**	**0**	**8**	**221.1**	**241**	**145**	**113**	**12**	**11**	**66**	**169**	**31**	**2**

MARTINEZ, Richard Jesus – RHP

HT: 6-1; **WT:** 185; **B:** R; **T:** R; **BORN:** 7/19/88 in Turmero, Venezuela; **RESIDES:** Turmero, Venezuela; **OBTAINED:** Signed by the Yankees as a non-drafted free agent on 11/18/05; **M.L. SVC:** 0.000; **CAREER NOTES: 2009:** Missed the season after undergoing an appendectomy on 6/22...**2008:** Was 0-3 with a 4.50 ERA in six relief appearances for the GCL Yankees...**2007:** Was 2-3 with a 4.67 ERA in 13 appearances (eight starts) with the DSL Yankees 1...tossed 3.2 hitless innings in his first appearance of the season on 6/6 at the DSL Diamondbacks (4BB, 4K)...**2006:** Made professional debut with the DSL Yankees 1, going 3-4 with a 4.72 ERA in 14 games (nine starts).

YEAR	CLUB	CLASS	W-L	ERA	G	GS	CG	SHO	SV	IP	H	R	ER	HR	HB	BB	SO	WP	BK
2006	DSL Yankees 1	R	3-4	4.72	14	9	0	0	0	47.2	51	31	25	3	7	24	34	4	1
2007	DSL Yankees 1	R	2-3	4.67	13	8	0	0	0	44.1	42	31	23	4	4	25	41	4	0
2008	GCL Yankees	R	0-3	4.50	6	0	0	0	0	14.0	16	10	7	2	0	4	11	5	0
2009							Did Not Pitch - Injured												
Minor League Totals			**5-10**	**4.67**	**33**	**17**	**0**	**0**	**0**	**106.0**	**109**	**72**	**55**	**9**	**11**	**53**	**86**	**13**	**1**

MARUSZAK, Addison – INF

HT: 6-1; **WT:** 190; **B:** R; **T:** R; **BORN:** 12/21/86 in Pinellas Park, Fla.; **RESIDES:** Pinellas Park, Fla.; **COLLEGE:** University of South Florida; **OBTAINED:** Selected by the Yankees in the 17th round of the 2008 First-Year Player Draft; **M.L. SVC:** 0.000; **CAREER NOTES: 2009**: Combined to hit .232 with 5 doubles, 1 triple, 2HR and 24RBI in 88 games with Single-A Tampa and Single-A Charleston...**2008:** Made his professional debut, batting .317 with 30R, 9 doubles, 6HR and 25RBI in 44 games with short-season Single-A Staten Island...hit safely in 34 of his 44 games, never going more than two consecutive games without a hit...was named to the New York-Penn League midseason All-Star team...hit .341 (14-for-41, 6HR) off right-handed pitching and .310 (39-for-126, 0HR) off lefties...was placed on the disabled list from 6/27-7/9 with a sprained right knee and again from 8/19-9/5 with a right hip contusion...recorded a 10-game hitting streak from 8/1-11, batting .405 (17-for-42) with 11R, 2 doubles, 2 triples, 1HR and 6RBI...hit .556 (5-for-9) with 1 double and 3RBI in two postseason games...**PERSONAL:** Full name is Addison John Maruszak...attended the University of South Florida where he majored in pre-business administration...hit .364 with 55R, 12 doubles, 6HR and 32RBI in 58 games during his junior year, ranking second on the team in batting average (33BB, 20K)...played for the Bourne Braves of the Cape Cod League in 2007, batting .278 with 14R, 1HR, 17RBI and 4SB...was named Big East "Rookie of the Year" and a Louisville Slugger Freshman All-American in 2006...attended St. Petersburg Catholic High School where he was a four-year letter-winner...was named team captain during his senior year...graduated sixth in his class.

YEAR	CLUB	CLASS	AVG	G	AB	R	H	2B	3B	HR	RBI	SH	SF	HP	BB	SO	SB	CS	E	SLUG	OBP
2008	Staten Island	SS-A	.317	44	167	30	53	9	2	6	25	1	1	1	14	25	5	1	6	.503	.372
2009	Tampa	A	.148	24	81	8	12	1	0	0	4	2	1	1	7	14	2	3	5	.160	.222
	Charleston	A	.263	64	217	29	57	4	1	2	20	1	4	6	32	44	6	1	14	.318	.367
Minor League Totals			**.262**	**132**	**465**	**67**	**122**	**14**	**3**	**8**	**49**	**4**	**6**	**8**	**53**	**83**	**13**	**5**	**25**	**.357**	**.344**

McALLISTER, Zach – RHP

NON-ROSTER INVITEE

HT: 6-5; **WT:** 230; **B:** R; **T:** R; **BORN:** 12/8/87 in Chillicothe, Ill.; **RESIDES:** Chillicothe, Ill.; **OBTAINED:** Selected by the Yankees in the third round of the 2006 First-Year Player Draft; **M.L. SVC:** 0.000; **CAREER NOTES:** Enters the season ranked by *Baseball America* as the fifth-best prospect and as having the "Best Control" in the Yankees organization...**2009**: Went 7-5 with a league-leading 2.23 ERA in 22 starts with Double-A Trenton (121.0IP, 98H, 30ER, 33BB, 96K), earning Yankees Minor League "Pitcher of the Year"...ranked second among all Yankees minor leaguers in ERA, trailing only Jose Ramirez (1.41)...held opponents to a .220 batting average (98-for-446) with 4HR...was 4-0 on the road with a 1.98 ERA, allowing just 11ER in 50.0IP away from Waterfront Park...named to the midseason All-Star team...missed more than three weeks from 7/16-8/8 on the disabled list with right shoulder inflammation...struck out a season-high 11 batters in just 4.2IP on 8/19 vs. Erie...**2008:** Went 14-9 with a 2.09 ERA in 25 combined games (24 starts) between Single-A Charleston and Single-A Tampa, striking out 115 batters while walking only 21...led all Yankees minor leaguers in ERA and tied for most wins...placed seventh among all full-season minor leaguers in ERA...opened the year at Charleston before being promoted to Tampa on 5/30...tied for most wins on the Tampa staff (8)...drew a decision in 23 of his 24 starts and held his opponents scoreless nine times...credited with his first career complete game and shutout on 7/26 vs. Dunedin in Game 1 of a doubleheader, throwing 7.0 scoreless innings and allowing only 3H with 4K...named Florida State League "Pitcher of the Week" for the effort...earned his first career save on 8/17 at Lakeland, throwing 4.0 scoreless innings of relief...held opponents to 2ER over his final 31.0IP (0.58 ERA)...placed on the disabled list for the final two weeks of the season with a left ankle strain...following the season, was selected as the organization's sixth-best prospect by *Baseball America* as well as the 20th-best prospect in the FSL...**2007:** Was 4-6 with a 5.17 ERA in 16 appearances (15 starts) with short-season Single-A Staten Island...ranked third in the New York-Penn League with 75K and struck out a career-high 10 batters on 7/11 vs. Auburn...was named to the NYPL North All-Star team...**2006:** Made professional debut with the Yankees' Gulf Coast League squad, posting a 5-2 record with a 3.09 ERA...ranked second among all GCL pitchers in wins...**PERSONAL:** Went 12-1 with a 1.04 ERA and 116K at Illinois Valley Central High School...also hit .486 with 13 doubles, 6HR and 38RBI...earned First-Team All-State honors from *Illinois Prep Baseball Report*, *Chicago Tribune* and Illinois High School Baseball Coaches Association...is the son of Diamondbacks' scout Steve McAllister.

YEAR	CLUB	CLASS	W-L	ERA	G	GS	CG	SHO	SV	IP	H	R	ER	HR	HB	BB	SO	WP	BK
2006	GCL Yankees	R	5-2	3.09	11	1	0	0	0	35.0	35	14	12	1	1	12	28	3	0
2007	Staten Island	SS-A	4-6	5.17	16	15	0	0	0	71.1	80	42	41	3	2	28	75	2	0
2008	Charleston	A	6-3	2.45	10	10	0	0	0	62.1	59	28	17	3	2	8	53	3	0
	Tampa	A	8-6	1.83	15	14	1	1	1	88.2	74	24	18	6	4	13	62	2	0
2009	Trenton	AA	7-5	2.23	22	22	0	0	0	121.0	98	39	30	4	7	33	96	0	1
Minor League Totals			**30-22**	**2.81**	**74**	**62**	**1**	**1**	**1**	**378.1**	**346**	**147**	**118**	**17**	**16**	**94**	**314**	**10**	**1**

MEDCHILL, Neil – OF

HT: 6-3; **WT:** 210; **B:** L; **T:** R; **BORN:** 6/25/87 in Oxford, Mich.; **RESIDES:** Henderson, Nev.; **COLLEGE:** Oklahoma State University; **OBTAINED:** Selected by the Yankees in the 11th round of the 2009 First-Year Player Draft; **M.L. SVC:** 0.000; **CAREER NOTES: 2009:** Made his professional debut, hitting .278 with 13 doubles, 14HR and 41RBI in 62 games with short-season Single-A Staten Island...finished the season ranked first in the New York-Penn League in HR and slugging (.551) and third in extra-base hits (29)...awarded the NYPL "Player of the Week" on 7/20 and was named to the league's midseason All-Star team...**PERSONAL:** Attended Chandler-Gilbert Community College for two years before transferring to OSU, and was a National Junior College All-American as a freshman, becoming the first baseball to earn the honor in the school's history...was previously drafted by the Los Angeles Angels in 2005 (30th round) and New York Mets in 2008 (33rd round)...graduated from Lake Orion High School (MI) where he played baseball and basketball and earned first-team all-state as a senior.

YEAR	CLUB	CLASS	AVG	G	AB	R	H	2B	3B	HR	RBI	SH	SF	HP	BB	SO	SB	CS	E	SLUG	OBP
2009	Staten Island	SS-A	.278	62	216	42	60	13	2	14	41	1	2	1	24	66	7	2	1	.551	.350

MEJIA, Edison – RHP

HT: 6-1; **WT:** 185; **B:** R; **T:** R; **BORN:** 7/2/90 in Bienvenido, D.R.; **RESIDES:** Bienvenido, D.R.; **OBTAINED:** Signed by the Yankees as a non-drafted free agent on 6/18/08; **M.L. SVC:** 0.000; **CAREER NOTES: 2009:** Went 0-3 with a 4.50 ERA in 12 games (eight starts) with the DSL Yankees 2...**2008:** In his professional debut, went 1-1 with a 2.90 ERA in 10 games (five starts) with the DSL Yankees 1.

YEAR	CLUB	CLASS	W-L	ERA	G	GS	CG	SHO	SV	IP	H	R	ER	HR	HB	BB	SO	WP	BK
2008	DSL Yankees 1	R	1-1	2.90	10	5	0	0	0	31.0	20	21	10	0	5	13	19	7	0
2009	DSL Yankees 2	R	0-3	4.50	12	8	0	0	0	38.0	45	24	19	2	3	14	24	2	0
Minor League Totals			**1-4**	**3.78**	**22**	**13**	**0**	**0**	**0**	**69.0**	**65**	**45**	**29**	**2**	**8**	**27**	**43**	**9**	**0**

MESA, Melky – OF

HT: 6-1; **WT:** 165; **B:** R; **T:** R; **BORN:** 1/31/87 in Bajos de Haina, D.R.; **RESIDES:** Bajos de Haina, D.R.; **OBTAINED:** Signed by the Yankees as a non-drafted free agent on 7/2/03; **M.L. SVC:** 0.000; **CAREER NOTES: 2009**: Hit .225 with 24 doubles, 7 triples, 20HR and 74RBI in 133 games with Single-A Charleston...finished the season tied for fourth in the league in HR and ranked fifth in runs (76)...was the lone RiverDogs player to be selected to both the South Atlantic League's midseason and postseason All-Star teams...was also awarded the league's "Player of the Week" honor on 6/29...tabbed by *Baseball America* as the Yankees' "fastest baserunner," "best athlete" and "best outfield arm"...**2008:** Batted .221 with 19R, 5 doubles, 2 triples, 7HR and 23RBI in 46 games with short-season Single-A Staten Island...led the team in homers...over half (14) of his 27 hits went for extra-bases...**2007:** Batted .235 with 27R, 10 doubles, 3HR and 13RBI in 49 games with the GCL Yankees..**2006:** Batted .207 in 40 games with the Gulf Coast League Yankees, appearing in 39 games in the OF...**2005:** Appeared in eight games with the DSL Yankees 1, batting .304...**2004:** In first professional season, batted .146 with 3HR and 10RBI in 49 games for the Yankees' DSL 2 squad...**PERSONAL:** Full name is Melquisedec Mesa.

YEAR	CLUB	CLASS	AVG	G	AB	R	H	2B	3B	HR	RBI	SH	SF	HP	BB	SO	SB	CS	E	SLUG	OBP
2004	DSL Yankees 2	R	.146	49	144	13	21	5	0	3	10	0	1	15	12	67	2	2	0	.243	.279
2005	DSL Yankees 1	R	.304	8	23	3	7	2	0	2	6	0	0	1	3	7	1	0	0	.652	.407
2006	GCL Yankees	R	.207	40	145	20	30	7	2	3	22	1	1	1	11	45	3	3	2	.345	.266
2007	GCL Yankees	R	.235	49	153	27	36	10	2	3	13	2	1	4	9	55	5	3	4	.386	.293
2008	Staten Island	SS-A	.221	46	122	19	27	5	2	7	23	1	0	1	4	38	4	1	1	.467	.252
2009	Charleston	A	.225	133	497	76	112	24	7	20	74	0	5	11	51	168	18	6	7	.423	.309
Minor League Totals			**.217**	**333**	**1107**	**161**	**240**	**55**	**13**	**40**	**154**	**4**	**8**	**34**	**93**	**387**	**34**	**15**	**14**	**.398**	**.295**

MILLER, Dan – RHP

HT: 6-3; **WT:** 220; **B:** R; **T:** R; **BORN:** 7/7/86 in Clearwater, Fla.; **RESIDES:** Pinellas Park, Fla.; **OBTAINED:** Signed by the Yankees as a free agent on 5/11/09; **M.L. SVC:** 0.000; **CAREER NOTES: 2009:** Signed by the Yankees to a minor league contract on 5/11 and reported to the GCL Yankees...went 1-0 with a 2.25 ERA in 15 appearances before being promoted to short-season Single-A Staten Island on 8/22 where he made six outings (0-0, 4.15 ERA)...opened the season with 12 consecutive scoreless appearances (19.1IP)...**2008:** Combined at three stops (GCL Blue Jays, Single-A Dunedin and short-season Single-A Auburn) to go 0-1 with a 4.78 ERA in 20 relief appearances...was released following the season...was originally signed by the Blue Jays as a non-drafted free agent.

YEAR	CLUB	CLASS	W-L	ERA	G	GS	CG	SHO	SV	IP	H	R	ER	HR	HB	BB	SO	WP	BK
2008	GCL Blue Jays	R	0-1	2.28	17	0	0	0	2	27.2	24	13	7	1	0	11	15	0	0
	Dunedin	A	0-0	27.00	1	0	0	0	0	0.1	1	1	1	0	0	1	0	0	0
	Auburn	SS-A	0-0	6.75	2	0	0	0	0	4.0	6	5	3	0	0	2	5	1	0
2009	GCL Yankees	R	1-0	2.25	15	0	0	0	1	20.0	13	5	5	0	0	9	12	3	0
	Staten Island	SS-A	0-0	4.15	6	0	0	0	0	8.2	9	4	4	0	1	2	9	0	0
Minor League Totals			**1-1**	**2.97**	**41**	**0**	**0**	**0**	**3**	**60.2**	**53**	**28**	**20**	**1**	**1**	**25**	**41**	**4**	**0**

MILO, Justin – OF

HT: 5-8; **WT:** 180; **B:** L; **T:** R; **BORN:** 2/23/87 in Edina, Minn.; **RESIDES:** Edina, Minn.; **COLLEGE:** University of Vermont; **OBTAINED:** Selected by the Yankees in the 37th round of the 2009 First-Year Player Draft **M.L. SVC:** 0.000; **CAREER NOTES: 2009:** Opened the season with the GCL Yankees, batting .267 in seven games before being promoted to short-season Single-A Staten Island on 7/11...hit a two-run home run in his first professional AB on 6/29 at the GCL Phillies...did not get caught in six stolen base attempts...**PERSONAL:** Remains a member of the University of Vermont's hockey team.

YEAR	CLUB	CLASS	AVG	G	AB	R	H	2B	3B	HR	RBI	SH	SF	HP	BB	SO	SB	CS	E	SLUG	OBP
2009	GCL Yankees	R	.267	7	15	2	4	1	0	1	3	0	0	1	4	2	2	0	1	.533	.450
	Staten Island	SS-A	.253	25	75	13	19	5	0	1	12	1	0	1	22	23	4	0	1	.360	.429
Minor League Totals			**.256**	**32**	**90**	**15**	**23**	**6**	**0**	**2**	**15**	**1**	**0**	**2**	**26**	**25**	**6**	**0**	**3**	**.389**	**.432**

MITCHELL, Bryan – RHP

HT: 6-2; **WT**: 175; **B**: L; **T**: R; **BORN**: 4/19/91 in Pensacola, Fla.; **RESIDES**: Pensacola, Fla.; **OBTAINED**: Selected by the Yankees in the 16th round of the 2009 First-Year Player Draft; **M.L. SVC**: 0.000; **CAREER NOTES**: Will be making his professional debut in 2010.

YEAR	CLUB	CLASS	W-L	ERA	G	GS	CG	SHO	SV	IP	H	R	ER	HR	HB	BB	SO	WP	BK
NO PROFESSIONAL RECORD																			

MITCHELL, D.J. – RHP

NON-ROSTER INVITEE

HT: 6-2; **WT:** 165; **B:** R; **T:** R; **BORN:** 5/13/87 in Winston-Salem, N.C.; **RESIDES:** Rural Hall, N.C.; **COLLEGE:** Clemson University; **OBTAINED:** Selected by the Yankees in the 10th round of the 2008 First-Year Player Draft; **M.L. SVC:** 0.000; **CAREER NOTES: 2009**: Made his professional debut, combining to go 12-7 with a 2.63 ERA in 25 appearances (24 starts) for Single-A Charleston and Single-A Tampa...ranked second among all Yankees minor leaguers in strikeouts (125), tied for second in wins and ranked fourth in ERA...began the season with Charleston, going 4-1 with a 1.95 ERA in six starts...won each of his first four decisions from 4/10-5/1...was transferred to Tampa on 5/13 where he remained for the rest of the season, going 8-6 with a 2.87 ERA in 19 appearances (18 starts)...tossed his first career complete game on 6/18 vs. Palm Beach, taking the loss after allowing 7H and 5ER in 7.0IP (2BB, 7K)...**2008:** Was placed on the 60-day disabled list on 8/19 with a right oblique muscle strain before appearing in a game...**PERSONAL:** Full name is William Douglas Mitchell, Jr...attended Clemson University where he went 6-5 with a 3.47 ERA in 20 appearances (14 starts) while leading all team starters in ERA and tying for the team-lead in games started (98.2IP, 97H, 49R, 38ER, 40BB, 106K, 5HR) in 2008...made the transition from position player to pitcher during the 2007 season...played for the Bourne Braves of the Cape Cod League in 2007, going 1-2 with a 1.47 ERA in eight starts (49.0IP, 36H, 8ER, 23BB, 58K)...appeared in *Sports Illustrated's* "Faces in the Crowd" edition on 9/3/07 for leading the Cape Cod League in strikeouts...attended North Forsyth Senior High School (N.C.) where he was a three-time all-conference pick...also lettered four times in baseball and twice in basketball.

YEAR	CLUB	CLASS	W-L	ERA	G	GS	CG	SHO	SV	IP	H	R	ER	HR	HB	BB	SO	WP	BK
2008					Did Not Pitch - Injured														
2009	Charleston	A	4-1	1.95	6	6	0	0	0	37.0	31	16	8	1	1	6	42	5	0
	Tampa	A	8-6	2.87	19	18	1	0	0	103.1	93	41	33	1	8	38	83	10	1
Minor League Totals			**12-7**	**2.63**	**25**	**24**	**1**	**0**	**0**	**140.1**	**124**	**57**	**41**	**2**	**9**	**44**	**125**	**15**	**1**

MOJICA, Deivi – RHP

HT: 6-1; **WT:** 165; **B:** R; **T:** R; **BORN:** 1/19/90 in San Cristobal, D.R.; **RESIDES:** San Cristobal, D.R.; **OBTAINED:** Signed by the Yankees as a non-drafted free agent on 6/19/08; **M.L. SVC:** 0.000; **CAREER NOTES: 2009:** Went 2-4 with a 3.17 ERA in 14 games (11 starts) with the DSL Yankees 2, striking out 64 batters in 59.2IP...held the opposition to 3ER or less in each of his starts...**2008:** In his professional debut with the DSL Yankees 1, was 1-4 with a 5.45 ERA in 12 games (six starts).

YEAR	CLUB	CLASS	W-L	ERA	G	GS	CG	SHO	SV	IP	H	R	ER	HR	HB	BB	SO	WP	BK
2008	DSL Yankees 1	R	1-4	5.45	12	6	0	0	0	38.0	61	32	23	3	0	11	24	6	1
2009	DSL Yankees 2	R	2-4	3.17	14	11	0	0	0	59.2	68	29	21	1	1	11	64	11	2
Minor League Totals			**3-8**	**4.05**	**26**	**17**	**0**	**0**	**0**	**97.2**	**129**	**61**	**44**	**4**	**1**	**22**	**88**	**17**	**3**

MOJICA, Jose – INF

HT: 6-0; **WT:** 145; **B:** R; **T:** R; **BORN:** 12/26/88 in Bani, D.R.; **RESIDES:** Bani, D.R.; **OBTAINED:** Signed by the Yankees as a non-drafted free agent on 7/2/07; **M.L. SVC:** 0.000; **CAREER NOTES: 2009:** Made his professional debut, batting .278 with 18R, 11 doubles, 2 triples, 1HR and 22RBI in 55 games with the GCL Yankees.

YEAR	CLUB	CLASS	AVG	G	AB	R	H	2B	3B	HR	RBI	SH	SF	HP	BB	SO	SB	CS	E	SLUG	OBP
2009	GCL Yankees	R	.278	55	198	18	55	11	2	1	22	1	1	3	10	20	4	1	15	.369	.321

MONTERO, Jesus Alejandro – C — NON-ROSTER INVITEE

HT: 6-4; **WT:** 225; **B:** R; **T:** R; **BORN:** 11/28/89 in Guacara, Venezuela; **RESIDES:** Guacara, Venezuela; **OBTAINED:** Signed by the Yankees as a non-drafted free agent on 10/17/06; **M.L. SVC:** 0.000; **CAREER NOTES:** Enters the 2010 season ranked by *Baseball America* as the Yankees' top prospect and the fifth-best prospect in all of Baseball (top catcher)...was also tabbed by the publication as the organization's "Best Hitter for Average" and "Best Power Hitter"...also named the organization's top prospect by *The Sporting News*...**2009**: Combined to bat .337 (117-for-347) with 45R, 25 doubles, 17HR and 70RBI in 92 games with Single-A Tampa and Double-A Trenton, ranking fourth among all Yankees minor leaguers in home runs...was named to the midseason All-Star teams with both Tampa and Trenton...began the season with Tampa, batting .356 with 8HR and 37RBI in 48 games...was promoted to Trenton on 6/3 where he hit .317 with 9HR and 33RBI in 44 games...homered in four straight games from 6/28-7/2, including 2HR on 6/30 at Erie...appeared for the World Team in the 2009 Futures Game during All-Star Weekend at St. Louis' Busch Stadium on 7/12...was removed defensively in the third inning on 8/1 at Altoona after being hit by a pitch while behind the plate, fracturing his middle finger...was placed on the disabled list on 8/2 through the end of the season with the injury...**2008:** Hit .326 with 86R, 34 doubles, 17HR and 87RBI in 132 games with Single-A Charleston...owned the eighth-most hits (171) among all minor leaguers and most among any catcher in 2008...led the Yankees organization in batting average, runs, hits and RBI, while ranking fourth in home runs...was named the seventh-best prospect in the South Atlantic League by *Baseball America*...led the SAL and ranked third among all Single-A batters in hits and led all SAL catchers with a .993 fielding percentage (4E, 588TC)...was selected to the midseason All-Star team and the South Atlantic League's postseason All-Star team as the league's top catcher...went 1-for-2 and caught the final four innings in the All-Star Futures Game at Yankee Stadium, playing for the World Team...participated in the SAL All-Star Home Run Derby, totaling 11 homers for a second-place finish...hit .360 (95-for-264) with 49R, 15 doubles, 8HR and 39RBI in 64 road games...recorded a career-high 15-game hitting streak from 7/29-8/13, batting .414 (24-for-58) with 5 doubles, 4HR and 11RBI...attended spring training with the Yankees as a non-roster invitee, hitting a solo-homer in his only at-bat...was named by *Baseball America* as the second-best prospect in the Yankees' system following the season, as well as the organization's "Best Power Hitter"...**2007:** Made his professional debut with the GCL Yankees, batting .280 with 3HR and 19RBI in 33 games...was rated the Yankees' top catching prospect (sixth overall) and the organization's "Best Power Hitter" by *Baseball America*...committed just 1E in 182TC as catcher...went 2-for-5 on 8/31 at the GCL Dodgers, with a game-tying home run to lead the Yankees in the decisive Game 3 win in the GCL Championship.

YEAR	CLUB	CLASS	AVG	G	AB	R	H	2B	3B	HR	RBI	SH	SF	HP	BB	SO	SB	CS	E	SLUG	OBP
2007	GCL Yankees	R	.280	33	107	13	30	6	0	3	19	0	1	3	12	18	0	0	1	.421	.366
2008	Charleston	A	.326	132	525	86	171	34	1	17	87	0	1	6	37	83	2	1	4	.491	.376
2009	Tampa	A	.356	48	180	26	64	15	1	8	37	1	1	2	14	26	0	0	2	.583	.406
	Trenton	AA	.317	44	167	19	53	10	0	9	33	0	0	0	14	21	0	0	0	.539	.370
Minor League Totals			**.325**	**257**	**979**	**144**	**318**	**65**	**2**	**37**	**176**	**1**	**3**	**11**	**14**	**148**	**2**	**1**	**7**	**.509**	**.379**

MORILLO, Ronald Enrique – INF

HT: 5-11; **WT:** 155; **B:** R; **T:** R; **BORN:** 1/15/90 in Maracaibo, Venezuela; **RESIDES:** Maracaibo, Venezuela; **OBTAINED:** Signed by the Yankees as a non-drafted free agent on 10/10/07; **M.L. SVC:** 0.000; **CAREER NOTES: 2009:** Hit .257 with 22R, 9RBI and 5SB in 39 games with the DSL Yankees, appearing in games at 1B, 3B, SS and LF...**2008:** Made his professional debut with the DSL Yankees 1, hitting .183 with 3HR and 27RBI in 57 games.

YEAR	CLUB	CLASS	AVG	G	AB	R	H	2B	3B	HR	RBI	SH	SF	HP	BB	SO	SB	CS	E	SLUG	OBP
2008	DSL Yankees 1	R	.183	57	208	28	38	5	0	3	27	1	1	9	24	51	7	5	21	.250	.293
2009	DSL Yankees 1	R	.257	39	105	22	27	3	1	1	9	1	0	2	26	33	5	1	10	.333	.414
Minor League Totals			**.208**	**96**	**313**	**50**	**65**	**8**	**1**	**4**	**36**	**2**	**1**	**11**	**50**	**84**	**12**	**6**	**31**	**.278**	**.336**

MORONTA, Eladio – OF

HT: 5-11; **WT:** 175; **B:** R; **T:** R; **BORN:** 12/16/88 in Azua, Dominican Republic; **RESIDES:** Azua, Dominican Republic; **OBTAINED:** Signed by the Yankees as a non-drafted free agent on 11/17/09; **M.L. SVC:** 0.000; **CAREER NOTES:** Will be making his professional debut in 2010.

YEAR	CLUB	CLASS	AVG	G	AB	R	H	2B	3B	HR	RBI	SH	SF	HP	BB	SO	SB	CS	E	SLUG	OBP
NO PROFESSIONAL STATS																					

MURPHY, J.R. – C

HT: 5-10; **WT:** 170; **B:** S; **T:** R; **BORN:** 5/13/91 in Bradenton, Fla.; **RESIDES:** Bradenton, Fla.; **OBTAINED:** Selected by the Yankees in the second round of the 2009 First-Year Player Draft; **M.L. SVC:** 0.000; **CAREER NOTES: 2009:** Played in nine game with the GCL Yankees in his professional debut, hitting safely in eight of the contests...following the season, was selected as the Yankees' eighth-best prospect by *Baseball America* and their best "pure hitter" from the draft...also tabbed as the organization's sixth-best prospect by *Baseball Digest*...**PERSONAL:** Attended the IMG Academy in Bradenton, Fla...Rated by *Baseball America* as fifth-best catcher among the 2009 draft class and as having the second-best "strike-zone judgment" among high school players.

YEAR	CLUB	CLASS	AVG	G	AB	R	H	2B	3B	HR	RBI	SH	SF	HP	BB	SO	SB	CS	E	SLUG	OBP
2009	GCL Yankees	R	.333	9	33	4	11	2	0	1	7	0	0	1	3	8	0	0	0	.485	.405

MURTON, Luke – INF

HT: 6-4; **WT:** 222; **B:** R; **T:** R; **BORN:** 5/21/86 in McDonough, Ga.; **RESIDES:** McDonough, Ga.; **COLLEGE:** Georgia Tech; **OBTAINED:** Selected by the Yankees in the 19th round of the 2009 First-Year Player Draft; **M.L. SVC:** 0.000; **CAREER NOTES: 2009:** Played his first professional season with the short-season Single-A Staten Island Yankees, batting .295 with 45R, 17 doubles, 8HR and 35RBI in 69 games...made 68 starts at 1B, recording the most total chances (683), putouts (613) and assists (61) and tying for the most errors (9) among NYPL first basemen...tied for second in the league in home runs...**PERSONAL:** Is the brother of Major Leaguer Matt Murton...graduated from Eagle's Landing High School (GA), earning Henry County "Player of the Year" honors as a senior...selected by the Yankees in the 40th round of the 2007 First-Year Player Draft but returned to school.

YEAR	CLUB	CLASS	AVG	G	AB	R	H	2B	3B	HR	RBI	SH	SF	HP	BB	SO	SB	CS	E	SLUG	OBP
2009	Staten Island	SS-A	.295	69	237	45	70	17	1	8	35	1	2	8	23	61	4	0	9	.477	.374

NOLTE, Charles – RHP

HT: 6-3; **WT:** 200; **B:** R; **T:** R; **BORN:** 3/19/86 in La Jolla, Calif.; **RESIDES:** San Diego, Calif.; **COLLEGE:** San Diego State University; **OBTAINED:** Acquired from the Minnesota Twins in exchange for cash considerations on 3/28/09; **M.L. SVC:** 0.000; **CAREER NOTES: 2009**: Acquired by the Yankees in late March, split the season between Single-A Charleston and Single-A Tampa, combining to go 5-4 with a 5.29 ERA...held right-handed hitters to a .206 batting average (26-for-126) while with the RiverDogs, and recorded 10K in 8.0IP as a starter...**2008**: Pitched the entire season with Single-A Beloit, going 4-3 with one save and a 2.05 ERA in a team-high 44 relief appearances...30 of his outings were more than 1.0IP...**2007**: In his professional debut, went 3-0 with a 1.85 ERA in 14 relief appearances with the GCL Twins...ranked fifth among league relievers with a .193 opponents batting average...**PERSONAL**: Graduated from Serra High School (CA) where he played baseball and football...was originally selected by the Twins in the 24th round of the 2007 First-Year Player Draft.

YEAR	CLUB	CLASS	W-L	ERA	G	GS	CG	SHO	SV	IP	H	R	ER	HR	HB	BB	SO	WP	BK
2007	GCL Twins	R	3-0	1.85	14	0	0	0	0	24.1	17	7	5	0	5	11	22	3	0
2008	Beloit	A	4-3	2.05	44	0	0	0	1	70.1	63	26	16	1	10	35	71	11	2
2009	Tampa	A	1-1	5.34	15	0	0	0	0	32.0	43	23	19	2	0	11	14	5	1
	Charleston	A	4-3	5.26	22	2	0	0	0	51.1	59	31	30	5	2	17	38	12	0
Minor League Totals			**12-7**	**3.54**	**95**	**2**	**0**	**0**	**3**	**178.0**	**182**	**87**	**70**	**8**	**17**	**74**	**150**	**31**	**3**

NORTON, Timothy – RHP

HT: 6-5; **WT:** 230; **B:** R; **T:** R; **BORN:** 5/23/83 in Franklin, Mass.; **RESIDES:** Franklin, Mass.; **COLLEGE:** University of Connecticut; **OBTAINED:** Selected in the seventh round of the 2006 First-Year Player Draft; **M.L. SVC:** 0.000; **CAREER NOTES: 2009**: Went 2-1 with a 2.75 ERA in 23 appearances out of the bullpen with Single-A Tampa...did not allow an earned run in 18 of his 23 relief appearances...tossed at least 2.0 innings in 11 outings...recorded 30K and held right-handed hitters to a .195 batting average...was placed on the DL on 8/5 with right shoulder inflammation for the remainder of the season...**2008:** Missed the season on the disabled list, recovering from rotator cuff surgery...**2007:** Was limited to five starts with Single-A Charleston, going 1-3 with a 3.71 ERA...was placed on the disabled list on 4/27 through the end of the season with a right shoulder strain...underwent surgery on his right rotator cuff on 5/10...**2006:** Made 15 starts for short-season Single-A Staten Island, posting a 3-3 record with a 2.60 ERA and 83K in 72.2IP...led all NY-Penn League pitchers with his 15 starts and ranked second in the league in strikeouts...was named the NY-Penn League "Pitcher of the Week" for the week of 9/4...helped lead the Yankees to their second consecutive NY-Penn League Championship...**PERSONAL:** Drafted by the Yankees out of the University of Connecticut, where he was a 2006 Pre-Season All-Big East selection and led the Huskies with a 2.04 ERA...recorded 226 career strikeouts at UConn, ranking second on the Connecticut all-time list...following the season was named All-Big East First Team and All-New England First Team.

YEAR	CLUB	CLASS	W-L	ERA	G	GS	CG	SHO	SV	IP	H	R	ER	HR	HB	BB	SO	WP	BK
2006	Staten Island	SS-A	3-3	2.60	15	15	0	0	0	72.2	60	29	21	1	7	14	83	9	2
2007	Charleston	A	1-3	3.71	5	5	0	0	0	26.2	28	14	11	0	1	8	32	2	1
2008							Did Not Pitch - Injured												
2009	Tampa	AA	2-1	2.75	23	0	0	0	0	36.0	31	12	11	1	3	9	30	0	0
Minor League Totals			**6-7**	**2.86**	**43**	**20**	**0**	**0**	**0**	**135.1**	**119**	**55**	**43**	**2**	**10**	**31**	**145**	**11**	**3**

NUNEZ, Luis – INF

HT: 5-11; **WT:** 160; **B:** R; **T:** R; **BORN:** 11/21/86 in Maracaibo, Venezuela; **RESIDES:** Maracaibo, Venezuela; **OBTAINED:** Signed by the Yankees as a non-drafted free agent on 11/12/03; **M.L. SVC:** 0.000; **CAREER NOTES: 2009**: Combined to hit .276 with 34R, 12 doubles, 3 triples, 3HR and 27RBI in 74 games with Single-A Tampa and Triple-A Scranton/Wilkes-Barre...began the season with Tampa, batting .304 with 23R, 10 doubles, 3HR and 23RBI in 49 games...made one relief outing—the first pitching appearance of his career—in 8/29 loss vs. Brevard County, tossing a scoreless ninth inning in the 9-2 loss (1.0IP, 2BB)...also appeared for Scranton/WB, hitting .214 with 11R, 2 doubles and 4RBI in 25 games...following the season, played for the Aguilas del Zulia of the Venezuelan Winter League, batting .289 (13-for-45) with 2R, 3 doubles and 7RBI in 15 games...**2008:** Batted .280 with 17 doubles, 3HR and 40RBI in 110 games with Single-A Tampa...appeared in games at 1B, 2B, 3B, SS, LF and DH...collected a career-high five hits on 8/10 at Clearwater...hit his first career grand slam on 8/31 at Fort Myers...hit .346 (37-for-107) with 20RBI in August, including a .407 mark (33-for-81) over his final 20 games...promoted to Triple-A Scranton/Wilkes-Barre from 6/14-19, appearing in three games and going 3-for-9 (.333)...played with Zulia in the Venezuelan Winter League...**2007:** Combined to hit .235 (71-for-302) with 17 doubles, 2HR and 27RBI in 89 games with short-season Single-A Staten Island, Single-A Charleston and Single-A Tampa...**2006:** Played in 16 games and batted .279 with Single-A Tampa before being placed on the disabled list on 6/11 with a strained right hamstring, missing the remainder of the season...**2005:** Batted .230 in 42 games with the Gulf Coast League Yankees...helped lead the Yankees to the GCL Championship...**2004:** Made his professional debut with the DSL Yankees 1, posting a .249 batting average with 7 doubles and 33 RBI in 63 games.

YEAR	CLUB	CLASS	AVG	G	AB	R	H	2B	3B	HR	RBI	SH	SF	HP	BB	SO	SB	CS	E	SLUG	OBP
2004	DSL Yankees 1	R	.249	63	229	27	57	7	1	0	33	1	2	5	13	23	5	4	–	.288	.301
2005	GCL Yankees	R	.230	42	126	16	29	3	2	0	23	4	3	0	6	15	2	3	10	.286	.259
2006	Tampa	A	.279	16	43	7	12	2	0	1	1	3	0	0	4	5	3	2	2	.395	.340
2007	Tampa	A	.267	12	45	5	12	3	0	0	2	1	0	0	0	8	1	0	3	.333	.267
	Charleston	A	.224	43	134	11	30	7	2	1	12	1	1	0	7	20	0	0	3	.328	.261
	Staten Island	SS-A	.236	34	123	19	29	7	2	1	13	3	2	1	10	8	5	2	9	.350	.294
2008	Tampa	A	.280	110	415	49	116	17	2	3	40	7	4	1	25	40	16	6	16	.352	.319
	Scranton/WB	AAA	.333	3	9	0	3	0	0	0	1	0	0	0	0	1	0	0	1	.333	.333
2009	Tampa	A	.304	49	158	23	48	10	3	3	23	2	3	2	14	16	4	5	9	.462	.362
	Scranton/WB	AAA	.214	25	70	11	15	2	0	0	4	01	0	0	4	7	2	1	2	.243	.257
Minor League Totals			**.260**	**398**	**1357**	**168**	**353**	**59**	**12**	**9**	**152**	**23**	**15**	**9**	**83**	**145**	**39**	**23**	**55**	**.341**	**.304**

NUNEZ, Reymond – INF

HT: 6-4; **WT:** 210; **B:** R; **T:** R; **BORN:** 9/25/90 in Santo Domingo, D.R.; **RESIDES:** Santo Domingo, D.R.; **OBTAINED:** Signed by the Yankees as a non-drafted free agent on 11/21/07; **M.L. SVC:** 0.000; **CAREER NOTES: 2009**: Hit .296 with 12 doubles, 1 triple and 10HR in 59 games with the DSL Yankees 2...recorded a career-high 13-game hitting streak from 7/1-17, batting .455 (25-for-55) with 4HR and 23RBI over the stretch...**2008:** Made his professional debut with the DSL Yankees 2, batting .230 with 8 doubles, 2HR and 41RBI in 65 games.

YEAR	CLUB	CLASS	AVG	G	AB	R	H	2B	3B	HR	RBI	SH	SF	HP	BB	SO	SB	CS	E	SLUG	OBP
2008	DSL Yankees 2	R	.230	65	256	25	59	8	2	2	41	1	0	4	19	73	0	3	10	.301	.294
2009	DSL Yankees 2	R	.296	59	223	32	66	12	1	10	57	0	3	9	21	44	2	2	11	.493	.375
Minor League Totals			**.261**	**124**	**479**	**57**	**125**	**20**	**3**	**12**	**98**	**1**	**3**	**13**	**40**	**117**	**2**	**5**	**21**	**.390**	**.333**

O'BRIEN, Michael – RHP

HT: 5-11; **WT:** 195; **B:** R; **T:** R; **BORN:** 3/3/90 in Salem, Va.; **RESIDES:** Roanoke, Va.; **OBTAINED:** Selected by the Yankees in the ninth round of the 2008 First-Year Player Draft; **M.L. SVC:** 0.000; **CAREER NOTES: 2009:** Spent his second straight season with the GCL Yankees, going 2-4 with a 5.09 ERA in 11 games (eight starts)...**2008:** Made his professional debut with the GCL Yankees, going 1-0 with a 5.00 ERA in six games (two starts)...**PERSONAL:** Graduated from Hidden Valley (Va.) High School...named the 2008 Timesland "Player of the Year," after going 11-1 with a 0.69 ERA and 142 strikeouts in 81.0IP as a senior...also named the Virginia High School Coaches Association's "Player of the Year"...has been diagnosed as a Type 1 diabetic...hosts baseball clinics in Roanoke in the offseason...bypassed a scholarship offer from Winthrop.

YEAR	CLUB	CLASS	W-L	ERA	G	GS	CG	SHO	SV	IP	H	R	ER	HR	HB	BB	SO	WP	BK
2008	GCL Yankees	R	1-0	5.00	6	2	0	0	0	18.0	26	14	10	1	4	4	14	1	0
2009	GCL Yankees	R	2-4	5.09	11	8	0	0	0	46.0	51	33	26	1	2	9	44	0	0
Minor League Totals			**3-4**	**5.06**	**17**	**10**	**0**	**0**	**0**	**64.0**	**77**	**47**	**36**	**2**	**6**	**13**	**58**	**1**	**0**

OLBRYCHOWSKI, Adam – RHP

HT: 6-3; **WT:** 180; **B:** R; **T:** R; **BORN:** 9/7/86 in Los Angeles, Calif.; **RESIDES:** Calabasas, Calif.; **COLLEGE:** Pepperdine University; **OBTAINED:** Selected by the Yankees in the fifth round of the 2007 First-Year Player Draft; **M.L. SVC:** 0.000; **CAREER NOTES: 2009**: Went 3-2 with a 2.73 ERA in 32 games (two starts) with Single-A Tampa...made two relief appearances during the postseason with the FSL champs, allowing 1ER in 4.0IP (2.25 ERA)...did not record a decision as a starter, despite allowing a combined 2ER in 7.2IP over two starts (2.35 ERA)...was transferred to Double-A Trenton on 9/5, where he made one scoreless appearance out of the bullpen, allowing 2H in 1.0IP...**2008:** Went 7-8 with one save and a 5.13 ERA in 22 appearances (19 starts) with Single-A Charleston...was placed on the disabled list from 5/5-22 with a right elbow strain...recorded his first professional save on 5/27 at Augusta...had a second stint on the D.L. from 6/30-7/20 with right elbow inflammation...recorded a season-high 9K on 8/13 at Delmarva...**2007:** Made 13 starts with short-season Single-A Staten Island, going 3-5 with a 4.47 ERA in his professional debut...did not allow a run in each of his first two starts (5.2IP, 1H)...began the season 0-4 with a 4.93 ERA over his first nine starts leading up to the All-Star break...won three of his final four starts following the break (3-1, 3.60 ERA)...**PERSONAL:** Played three seasons at Pepperdine, posting a career record of 9-8 with a 3.62 ERA...named all West Coast Conference in 2007, ranking fifth in the conference in ERA (2.90).

YEAR	CLUB	CLASS	W-L	ERA	G	GS	CG	SHO	SV	IP	H	R	ER	HR	HB	BB	SO	WP	BK
2007	Staten Island	SS-A	3-5	4.47	13	13	0	0	0	58.1	51	34	29	4	1	33	51	6	0
2008	Charleston	A	7-8	5.13	22	19	0	0	1	98.1	112	69	56	9	5	41	72	4	0
2009	Tampa	A	3-2	2.73	32	2	0	0	0	62.2	55	23	19	3	2	43	52	3	1
	Trenton	AA	0-0	0.00	1	0	0	0	0	1.0	2	0	0	0	0	0	0	0	0
Minor League Totals			**13-15**	**4.25**	**68**	**34**	**0**	**0**	**1**	**220.1**	**220**	**126**	**104**	**16**	**8**	**117**	**175**	**13**	**1**

OROZCO, Jamiel – INF

HT: 5-11; **WT**: 156; **B**: R; **T**: R; **BORN**: 1/29/93 in Santo Domingo, D.R.; **RESIDES**: Santo Domingo, D.R.; **OBTAINED**: Signed by the Yankees as a non-drafted free agent on 11/4/09; **M.L. SVC**: 0.000; **CAREER NOTES**: Will be making his professional debut in 2010.

YEAR	CLUB	CLASS	AVG	G	AB	R	H	2B	3B	HR	RBI	SH	SF	HP	BB	SO	SB	CS	E	SLUG	OBP
NO PROFESSIONAL RECORD																					

ORTIZ, Jonathan Alexander – RHP

HT: 5-10; **WT:** 170; **B:** R; **T:** R; **BORN:** 10/29/85 in Bani, D.R.; **RESIDES:** Bani, D.R.; **OBTAINED:** Signed by the Yankees as a non-drafted free agent on 8/19/04; **M.L. SVC:** 0.000; **CAREER NOTES: 2009**: Combined at Single-A Charleston and Single-A Tampa to go 3-4 with 17 saves and a 2.91 ERA in 48 appearances out of the bullpen...began the season at Charleston and went 0-1 with nine saves and a 1.26 ERA, allowing just 4ER in 28.2IP and striking out 40 batters with only 3BB...promoted to Tampa on 8/12 where he went 3-3 with eight saves and a 4.67 ERA (27.0IP, 14ER)...was the lone Tampa hurler to be selected to the Florida State League's midseason All-Star team...made six relief appearances with the Tigres del Licey of the Dominican Winter League, allowing just 4H in 4.0IP (0R, 1BB, 3K)...**2008:** Went 4-2 with 33 saves (in 38 opportunities) and a 2.03 ERA in 57 relief appearances with Single-A Charleston...led the South Atlantic League and all Yankees' farmhands in saves, while ranking 11th among all minor league pitchers with a 12.63K/9.0IP ratio...also led the league in appearances en route to being named the "Best Reliever" in the SAL by *Baseball America*...was selected to the midseason SAL All-Star team, recording 20 saves and a 1.85 ERA in 30 pre-All-Star relief outings...allowed an earned run in just 11 of his appearances...suffered the loss on 5/17 vs. Ashville, recording his first defeat since the 2004 season...pitched in one game with Licey in the Dominican Winter League (1.0IP, 1HP, 2K)...**2007:** Pitched at three different levels (Single-A Tampa, GCL Yankees and short-season Single-A Staten Island), working exclusively as a reliever and combining to post 15 saves with a 5-0 record and a 1.93 ERA...ranked second among all minor leaguers, averaging 14.60 strikeouts per 9.0IP and ranked 10th with a .160 opponents batting average...held opponents hitless in 17 of 26 relief appearances...opened the year at Tampa and pitched in two games before he was transferred to the GCL Yankees where he did not allow a run three appearances (3.0IP), converting both his save chances...promoted to Staten Island on 7/10 where he ranked fourth in the New York-Penn League with 13 saves...earned the win or save in 18 of his 21 appearances with Staten Island, converting 13-of-15 save opportunities (86.7%)...named NYPL "Pitcher of the Week" for 7/30-8/6...did not allow a run over his final 10 outings (2-0, six saves, 12.0IP)...**2006:** Posted a combined 4-0 record with a 0.71 ERA (4ER, 51.0IP) in 18 games (seven starts) with the Yankees' Dominican Summer League teams...limited opposing hitters to a .138 batting average (24-for-174)...after three professional seasons, owned a 13-1 record with a 1.31 ERA...**2005:** Appeared in 25 games for the Yankees' DSL 1 squad, posting a 5-0 record with a 1.03 ERA and 58 strikeouts...**2004:** Made professional debut in the Dominican Summer League, appearing in 10 games and notching a 4-1 record with a 2.27 ERA.

YEAR	CLUB	CLASS	W-L	ERA	G	GS	CG	SHO	SV	IP	H	R	ER	HR	HB	BB	SO	WP	BK
2004	DSL Yankees 1	R	4-1	2.27	10	7	0	0	0	47.2	40	15	12	0	5	6	42	4	0
2005	DSL Yankees 1	R	5-0	1.03	25	0	0	0	13	52.2	26	7	6	1	7	4	58	1	0
2006	DSL Yankees 1	R	1-0	0.64	10	0	0	0	7	14.0	5	1	1	0	2	3	17	0	0
	DSL Yankees 2	R	3-0	0.73	8	7	0	0	0	37.0	19	4	3	1	1	4	40	1	0
2007	Tampa	A	0-0	3.86	2	0	0	0	0	4.2	3	2	2	0	1	1	9	0	0
	GCL Yankees	R	0-0	0.00	3	0	0	0	2	3.0	0	0	0	0	0	0	5	0	0
	Staten Island	SS-A	5-0	1.80	21	0	0	0	13	25.0	14	5	5	1	1	8	39	0	0
2008	Charleston	A	4-2	2.03	57	0	0	0	33	62.0	48	21	14	2	5	13	87	3	1
2009	Charleston	A	0-1	1.26	24	0	0	0	9	28.2	21	6	4	1	2	3	40	3	1
	Tampa	A	3-3	4.67	24	0	0	0	8	27.0	36	16	14	3	0	7	36	2	0
Minor League Totals			**25-7**	**1.82**	**184**	**14**	**0**	**0**	**85**	**301.2**	**211**	**77**	**61**	**9**	**24**	**49**	**373**	**14**	**2**

PALOMO, Jesus Alberto – C

HT: 5-11; **WT:** 170; **B:** R; **T:** R; **BORN:** 12/15/89 in Maturin, Venezuela; **RESIDES:** Maturin, Venezuela; **OBTAINED:** Signed by the Yankees as a non-drafted free agent on 1/20/07; **M.L. SVC:** 0.000; **CAREER NOTES: 2009:** Batted .263 in 23 games with the DSL Yankees 2...caught 17-of-41 (41.5%) of stolen base attempts...**2008:** Appeared in 37 games with the DSL Yankees 2, batting .215 with six doubles and 6RBI...**2007:** Made his professional debut with the DSL Yankees 2, batting .176 with 1 double, 1HR and 4RBI.

YEAR	CLUB	CLASS	AVG	G	AB	R	H	2B	3B	HR	RBI	SH	SF	HP	BB	SO	SB	CS	E	SLUG	OBP
2007	DSL Yankees 2	R	.176	23	51	4	9	1	0	1	4	0	0	1	6	24	0	0	6	.255	.276
2008	DSL Yankees 2	R	.215	37	93	19	20	6	1	1	6	0	0	7	17	31	1	2	5	.333	.376
2009	DSL Yankees 2	R	.263	23	80	11	21	1	2	1	7	1	0	3	6	26	2	0	6	.363	.337
Minor League Totals			**.223**	**83**	**224**	**34**	**50**	**8**	**3**	**3**	**17**	**1**	**0**	**11**	**29**	**81**	**3**	**2**	**17**	**.326**	**.341**

PARACHE, Luis – INF

HT: 5-9; **WT:** 170; **B:** L; **T:** R; **BORN:** 8/4/89 in New York, N.Y.; **RESIDES:** Santo Domingo, D.R.; **OBTAINED:** Signed by the Yankees as a non-drafted free agent on 4/18/07; **M.L. SVC:** 0.000; **CAREER NOTES: 2009**: Batted .275 with 5 triples and 14RBI in 36 games with the DSL Yankees 2...**2008:** Batted .290 with 4HR and 43RBI in 69 games with the DSL Yankees 1...did not go more than two consecutive games without recording at least 1H...**2007:** Made his professional debut with the DSL Yankees 2, batting .246 with 8 doubles, 2 triples, 1HR and 9RBI...from 8/3-15, four of his seven hits went for doubles.

YEAR	CLUB	CLASS	AVG	G	AB	R	H	2B	3B	HR	RBI	SH	SF	HP	BB	SO	SB	CS	E	SLUG	OBP
2007	DSL Yankees 2	R	.246	45	118	15	29	8	1	1	9	1	3	0	13	21	1	1	10	.356	.313
2008	DSL Yankees 1	R	.290	69	272	47	79	16	6	4	43	1	4	4	28	30	7	2	16	.438	.360
2009	DSL Yankees 2	R	.275	36	102	20	28	3	5	0	14	1	2	2	8	7	4	0	8	.402	.333
Minor League Totals			**.276**	**150**	**492**	**82**	**136**	**27**	**12**	**5**	**66**	**3**	**9**	**6**	**49**	**58**	**12**	**3**	**34**	**.411**	**.344**

PAREDES, Jimmy – INF

HT: 6-1; **WT:** 178; **B:** S; **T:** R; **BORN:** 11/25/88 in Haina, D.R.; **RESIDES:** Santo Domingo, D.R.; **OBTAINED:** Signed by the Yankees as a non-drafted free agent on 7/2/06; **M.L. SVC:** 0.000; **CAREER NOTES: 2009:** Batted .302 with 8 doubles, 4 triples, 2HR, 7RBI and 23SB with short-season Single-A Staten Island...ranked fifth in the NYPL in stolen bases and eighth in average...earned NYPL All-Star Game MVP honors after going 1-for-2 with the game-winning two-run home run...following the season, was named by *Baseball America* as the 14th-best prospect in the NYPL in 2009...**2008:** Played in 47 games with the GCL Yankees, appearing at 3B, SS and DH, and batting .280 with 9 doubles, 2 triples, 1HR and 15RBI...led the team with 45H and 6SB...collected a career-high 5H on 7/19 vs. Bluefield, going 5-for-5 with 2R and 1RBI, one of only four 5-hit games in the GCL in 2008...**2007:** Hit .259 with 14 doubles, 4 triples, 2HR and 42RBI with the DSL Yankees 1 in his professional debut...led the team in RBI, ranked second with 69H and tied for second in doubles...recorded a season-high 5RBI on 7/9 at the DSL Diamondbacks, going 3-for-6 with 1HR...compiled a 14-game hitting streak from 7/31-8/17, batting .328 (19-for-58) with 12RBI over the stretch.

YEAR	CLUB	CLASS	AVG	G	AB	R	H	2B	3B	HR	RBI	SH	SF	HP	BB	SO	SB	CS	E	SLUG	OBP
2007	DSL Yankees 1	R	.259	64	266	31	69	14	4	2	42	0	4	6	6	44	5	4	34	.365	.287
2008	GCL Yankees	R	.280	47	161	23	45	9	2	1	15	1	1	4	8	20	6	0	13	.379	.328
2009	Staten Island	SS-A	.302	54	205	36	62	8	4	2	17	1	3	2	10	30	23	9	12	.410	.336
Minor League Totals			**.278**	**165**	**632**	**90**	**176**	**31**	**10**	**5**	**74**	**2**	**8**	**12**	**24**	**94**	**34**	**13**	**59**	**.383**	**.314**

PATTERSON, Garrett – LHP

HT: 6-2; **WT:** 220; **B:** L; **T:** L; **BORN:** 5/11/82 in McAlester, Okla.; **RESIDES:** McAlester, Okla.; **COLLEGE:** University of Oklahoma; **OBTAINED:** Selected by the Yankees in the seventh round of the 2005 First-Year Player Draft; **M.L. SVC:** 0.000; **CAREER NOTES: 2009**: Began the season on the disabled list before appearing in only one game with Single-A Charleston, allowing 4R in 1.1IP in relief (5H, 3ER, 1BB, 1K)...was placed back on the D.L. with left shoulder inflammation on 7/3 through the remainder of the season...**2008:** Missed the entire season on the disabled list with a left foot fracture...**2007:** Played for most of the season with Single-A Charleston, going 1-5 with a 6.29 ERA in 29 appearances (five starts)...tossed 2.0 or more innings in 10 of his 24 relief outings, including a season-high 3.2 in his season debut on 4/9 vs. Ashville...promoted to Single-A Tampa on 8/30 and made one relief appearance on 9/2 in Tampa's season finale, earning the win (2.0IP, 1H, 1ER, 1HR)...**2006:** Went 2-5 with a 4.50 ERA in 14 games (12 starts) with Single-A Charleston...**2005:** In first professional season, posted a 1-2 record with a 3.71 ERA in 17 games (11 starts) for the NY-Penn League Champion Staten Island Yankees...ranked fifth among all NY-Penn League pitchers with 71 strikeouts...**PERSONAL:** Posted a 6-3 record in his senior season at the University of Oklahoma in 2005, one year after undergoing elbow surgery...graduated from McAlester (Okla.) High School and was a key member of two state championships and four regional titles...earned first team All-State honors by The Oklahoman and first team all-area and all-conference accolades as a senior...received one of 40 invitations to the U.S. Junior National Team Trials following his senior year...member of the Oklahoma Junior Sunbelt team that won the AAU National Championship in the summer of 2000...was selected in the 11th round of the 2001 First-Year Player Draft by the Anaheim Angels but did not sign.

YEAR	CLUB	CLASS	W-L	ERA	G	GS	CG	SHO	SV	IP	H	R	ER	HR	HB	BB	SO	WP	BK
2005	Staten Island	SS-A	1-2	3.71	17	11	0	0	0	51.0	37	22	21	1	1	38	71	9	0
2006	Charleston	A	2-5	4.50	14	12	0	0	0	50.0	47	40	25	3	5	37	39	4	0
2007	Charleston	A	1-5	6.29	29	5	0	0	2	54.1	61	45	38	6	3	36	37	9	0
	Tampa	A	1-0	4.50	1	0	0	0	0	2.0	2	1	1	1	0	1	0	0	0
2008	Did Not Pitch – Injured																		
2009	Charleston	A	0-0	20.25	1	0	0	0	0	1.1	5	4	3	0	0	1	1	1	0
Minor League Totals			**5-12**	**4.99**	**62**	**28**	**0**	**0**	**2**	**158.2**	**152**	**112**	**88**	**11**	**9**	**113**	**148**	**23**	**0**

PENA, Henry – OF

HT: 6-0; **WT:** 180; **B:** L; **T:** R; **BORN:** 10/26/90 in Bani, D.R.; **RESIDES:** Bani, D.R.; **OBTAINED:** Signed by the Yankees as a non-drafted free agent on 7/2/07; **M.L. SVC:** 0.000; **CAREER NOTES: 2009**: In 57 games with the DSL Yankees 2, batted .315 with 23 extra-base hits (15 doubles, four triples, 4HR) and 36RBI...recorded a career-high 4H in back-to-back games from 8/4–8/5, going 8-for-9 with 2 doubles and 6RBI in the two contests...**2008:** Made his professional debut, hitting .167 with 14 doubles, 1HR and 17RBI in 51 games with the DSL Yankees 2.

YEAR	CLUB	CLASS	AVG	G	AB	R	H	2B	3B	HR	RBI	SH	SF	HP	BB	SO	SB	CS	E	SLUG	OBP
2008	DSL Yankees 2	R	.167	51	192	22	32	14	0	1	17	0	0	1	32	64	1	3	2	.255	.289
2009	DSL Yankees 2	R	.315	57	197	44	62	15	4	4	36	1	2	2	42	57	5	2	1	.492	.436
Minor League Totals			**.242**	**108**	**389**	**66**	**94**	**29**	**4**	**5**	**53**	**1**	**2**	**3**	**74**	**121**	**6**	**5**	**3**	**.375**	**.365**

PENA, Jose – RHP

HT: 6-0; **WT**: 160; **B**: R; **T**: R; **BORN**: 3/22/91 in Guayubin, D.R.; **RESIDES**: Guayubin, D.R.; **OBTAINED**: Signed by the Yankees as a non-drafted free agent on 7/11/09; **M.L. SVC**: 0.000; **CAREER NOTES**: **2009**: Made his professional debut with the DSL Yankees 2 and went 2-0 with a 1.42 ERA in five relief appearances, striking out 11 batters in 12.2IP...threw 2.0IP or more in each of his five outings.

YEAR	CLUB	CLASS	W-L	ERA	G	GS	CG	SHO	SV	IP	H	R	ER	HR	HB	BB	SO	WP	BK
2009	DSL Yankees 2	R	2-0	1.42	5	0	0	0	1	12.2	6	2	2	0	0	4	11	1	0

PENDLETON, Lance – RHP

HT: 6-3; **WT:** 195; **B:** L; **T:** R; **BORN:** 9/10/83 in Houston, Tex.; **RESIDES:** Kingwood, Tex.; **COLLEGE:** Rice University; **OBTAINED:** Selected by the Yankees in the fourth round of the 2005 First-Year Player Draft; **M.L. SVC:** 0.000; **CAREER NOTES: 2009**: Combined to go 12-8 with a 3.14 ERA in 28 appearances (26 starts) with Single-A Tampa and Double-A Trenton...led all Yankees minor leaguers in strikeouts (130) and tied for second in wins...began the season with Tampa, going 11-5 with a 2.58 ERA in 20 appearances (18 starts)...did not allow an earned run over four consecutive starts from 6/15-7/3 (21.1IP)...was named to the FSL postseason All-Star team...was promoted to Trenton on 7/31 and went 1-3 with a 4.47 ERA in eight starts...**2008:** Went 7-9 with a 3.52 ERA in 28 appearances (23 starts) with Single-A Charleston...struck out a season-high eight batters three times (5/17 vs. Asheville, 6/11 at Rome and 8/9 vs. Rome)...began the season as a reliever, going 1-0 with a 3.38 ERA in five appearances...had a 34.2-inning scoreless stretch from 5/6-6/1...during the six-start stretch, allowed just 12H and 13BB, while striking out 28 batters...was named to the SAL midseason All-Star team...**2007:** Appeared in eight games (six starts) with the GCL Yankees, posting a 4.61 ERA with no decisions...did not begin the season until 7/26 as he began rehabilitation from an elbow injury...**2006:** Missed the entire season while on the disabled list with a right elbow injury...**2005:** In first professional season, posted a 1-0 record with a 2.33 ERA in nine games (six starts) with short-season Single-A Staten Island before being placed on the disabled list on 8/26 with tendinitis in his right elbow...**PERSONAL:** Helped lead Rice University to the College World Series in 2004...posted a 5-3 record with a 3.69 ERA in his senior season with the Owls...was named to the Minute Maid College Classic All-Tournament team for the second consecutive year in 2005...graduated from Kingwood (Texas) High School, where he was named to the Texas High School Baseball Coaches Association All-State Team as a senior outfielder in 2002.

YEAR	CLUB	CLASS	W-L	ERA	G	GS	CG	SHO	SV	IP	H	R	ER	HR	HB	BB	SO	WP	BK
2005	Staten Island	SS-A	1-0	2.33	9	6	0	0	0	27.0	27	11	7	1	1	13	23	2	1
2006	Did Not Pitch - Injured																		
2007	GCL Yankees	R	0-0	4.61	8	6	0	0	0	13.2	14	7	7	1	1	6	16	2	0
2008	Charleston	A	7-9	3.52	28	23	0	0	0	128.0	136	62	50	3	6	46	119	15	1
2009	Tampa	A	11-5	2.58	20	18	0	0	0	104.2	101	43	30	1	5	31	87	3	1
	Trenton	AA	1-3	4.47	8	8	0	0	0	44.1	40	25	22	4	2	15	43	1	0
Minor League Totals			**20-17**	**3.29**	**73**	**61**	**0**	**0**	**0**	**317.2**	**318**	**148**	**116**	**10**	**15**	**111**	**288**	**23**	**3**

PEREZ, Kelvin – RHP

HT: 6-1; **WT:** 140; **B:** R; **T:** R; **BORN:** 10/10/85 in Manoguallavo, D.R.; **RESIDES:** Manoguallavo, D.R.; **OBTAINED:** Signed by the Yankees as a non-drafted free agent on 3/16/05; **M.L. SVC:** 0.000; **CAREER NOTES: 2009:** Went 5-2 with a 2.01 ERA in 15 combined games (two starts) with the GCL Yankees and short-season Single-A Staten Island...started and won his lone postseason game, tossing 5.0 scoreless innings to clinch the first round of the NYPL playoffs...**2008:** Opened the season on the disabled list, recovering from right elbow surgery performed on 8/17/07...began year on a rehab assignment with the GCL Yankees, going 0-2 with a 4.08 ERA in eight games (one start) before being promoted to Single-A Tampa for his final appearance of the season...**2007:** Joined the GCL Yankees, going 5-3 with a 2.84 ERA in 11 games (five starts), striking out 32 with nine walks...was 3-1 with a 1.77 ERA in six relief appearances and 2-2 with a 4.08 ERA in his five starts...held opponents scoreless in five consecutive outings from 6/26-7/17, going 4-0 and holding opponents to a .153 average (19.0IP, 10H, 2BB, 14K)...struck out a career-high seven batters in a 5.0-inning start on 8/11 vs. the GCL Phillies to earn the win...**2006:** Made 14 appearances (nine starts) with the Yankees DSL 1 squad, posting a 7-2 record with a 3.18 ERA and 52K in 51.0IP...held opponents to a .205 batting average...helped lead the squad to their second consecutive Dominican Summer League championship...**2005:** In first professional season, posted a 1-3 record with a 5.42 ERA in 12 games (five starts) for the Yankees' DSL 2 squad.

YEAR	CLUB	CLASS	W-L	ERA	G	GS	CG	SHO	SV	IP	H	R	ER	HR	HB	BB	SO	WP	BK
2005	DSL Yankees 2	R	1-3	5.42	12	5	0	0	0	36.1	33	32	22	5	5	28	26	5	3
2006	DSL Yankees 1	R	7-2	3.18	14	9	0	0	0	51.0	41	25	18	2	1	18	52	7	0
2007	GCL Yankees	R	5-3	2.84	11	5	0	0	0	38.0	32	15	12	2	4	9	32	2	1
2008	GCL Yankees	R	0-2	4.08	8	1	0	0	0	17.2	15	8	8	0	5	7	19	1	0
	Tampa	A	0-0	9.00	1	0	0	0	0	1.0	3	1	1	0	0	3	0	1	0
2009	GCL Yankees	R	2-0	1.50	2	0	0	0	0	6.0	4	1	1	0	0	3	8	1	0
	Staten Island	SS-A	3-2	2.06	13	9	0	0	0	52.1	50	24	12	0	2	24	48	3	0
Minor League Totals			**18-12**	**3.29**	**61**	**29**	**0**	**0**	**0**	**202.1**	**178**	**106**	**74**	**9**	**17**	**92**	**185**	**20**	**4**

PERKINS, Kyle – C

HT: 6-0; **WT:** 195; **B:** R; **T:** R; **BORN:** 6/28/89 in Canberra, Australia; **RESIDES:** Macquarie, Australia; **OBTAINED:** Signed by the Yankees as a free agent on 1/26/08; **M.L. SVC:** 0.000; **CAREER NOTES:** Will be making his professional debut in 2010...**PERSONAL:** Was signed at the age of 16 after being spotted during the under-18 national championship in Canberra, Australia, where he was teammates with fellow signee Nathan Aron.

YEAR	CLUB	CLASS	AVG	G	AB	R	H	2B	3B	HR	RBI	SH	SF	HP	BB	SO	SB	CS	E	SLUG	OBP
NO PROFESSIONAL STATS																					

PHELPS, David – RHP

HT: 6-3; **WT:** 185; **B:** R; **T:** R; **BORN:** 10/9/86 in St. Louis, Mo.; **RESIDES:** Hazelwood, Mo.; **COLLEGE:** Notre Dame; **OBTAINED:** Selected by the Yankees in the 14th round of the 2008 First-Year Player Draft; **M.L. SVC:** 0.000; **CAREER NOTES: 2009**: Combined to go 13-4 with a 2.38 ERA in 26 starts with Single-A Charleston and Single-A Tampa...ranked third among all Yankees minor leaguers in ERA and strikeouts (122)...was promoted to Tampa on 7/21, going 3-1 with a 1.17 ERA in seven starts...allowed 1ER in the first inning of his first start with Tampa on 7/24 and then held opponents scoreless over the next 18.1 innings before allowing 1ER in the second inning of his fourth start on 8/9...**2008:** Made his professional debut, going 8-2 with a 2.72 ERA in 15 starts with short-season Single-A Staten Island (72.2IP, 67H, 28R, 22ER, 18BB, 52K, 4HR)...tied for second in the New York-Penn League in wins and ranked fourth in the league in ERA, earning a spot on the league's midseason All-Star roster...tied for fourth among Yankees farmhands in ERA...went 6-0 with a 2.75 ERA in eight road starts...won each of his final six decisions of the season over his last nine starts...made one postseason start for Staten Island, going 0-1 with a 33.75 ERA (1.1IP, 5H, 8R, 5ER, 2BB, 1K)...**PERSONAL:** Full name is David Edward Phelps...attended the University of Notre Dame where he majored in political science and computer applications...went 5-5 with a 4.65 ERA in his junior year in 2008, allowing 102H and 48ER while leading the team in games started (14), innings pitched (93.0) and strikeouts (75)...was named to the 2008 Preseason Watch List for the Brooks Wallace national "Player of the Year" award, as well as earning pre-season First Team All-Big East honors in 2007 and '08...became the second Notre Dame pitcher in school history to strike out at least 100 batters (102) and record an ERA under 2.00 (1.88) in the same season in 2007 (also Aaron Heilman)...attended Hazelwood West High School (Mo.) where he went 14-4 with a 2.96 ERA in 27 appearances (17 starts), striking out 172 batters in 109.2IP...was named a top prospect in Missouri among 2005 prep seniors by *Baseball America* after setting a school record with a 30.0-inning scoreless stretch that season...was a team captain, all-conference and all-metro performer in 2004 and '05.

YEAR	CLUB	CLASS	W-L	ERA	G	GS	CG	SHO	SV	IP	H	R	ER	HR	HB	BB	SO	WP	BK
2008	Staten Island	SS-A	8-2	2.72	15	15	0	0	0	72.2	67	28	22	4	1	18	52	1	1
2009	Charleston	A	10-3	2.80	19	19	0	0	0	112.2	117	48	35	9	4	25	90	5	2
	Tampa	A	3-1	1.17	7	7	0	0	0	38.1	34	9	5	1	0	6	32	2	0
Minor League Totals			**21-6**	**2.49**	**41**	**41**	**0**	**0**	**0**	**223.2**	**218**	**85**	**62**	**14**	**5**	**49**	**174**	**8**	**3**

PILITTERE, P.J. – C

NON-ROSTER INVITEE

HT: 6-0; **WT:** 215; **B:** R; **T:** R; **BORN:** 11/23/81 in Galesburg, Ill.; **RESIDES:** Walnut, Calif.; **COLLEGE:** Cal State Fullerton; **OBTAINED:** Selected by the Yankees in the 13th round of the 2004 First-Year Player Draft; **M.L. SVC:** 0.000; **CAREER NOTES: 2009**: Combined to bat .220 with 1HR and 17RBI in 55 games with Triple-A Scranton/Wilkes-Barre and Double-A Trenton...had three stints on the disabled list with a left thumb sprain (4/9-16), right oblique muscle strain (6/1-13) and a sprained right ankle (7/24-31)...began the season with Scranton/WB, batting .244 in 28 games...was transferred to Trenton on 8/2, where he remained through the end of the season...**2008:** Hit .277 with 15 doubles, 3HR and 48RBI in 97 games with Double-A Trenton...hit .336 (38-for-113, 0HR) off left-handed pitching and .251 (63-for-251, 3HR) off righties...struck out just once every 11.38AB, leading the EL and 11th overall in the minors (32K, 392PA)...ranked fifth among qualifying EL catchers with a 21.3% caught stealing rate (17-of-80)...named to the EL midseason All-Star team...**2007:** Batted .261 with 16 doubles, 2HR and 34RBI in 100 games with Double-A Trenton...led all Eastern League catchers with a .995 fielding percentage (4E, 844TC) and 97 games played...also appeared in two games at 1B...was a .372 hitter when leading off an inning (27-for-79)...**2006:** Batted .302 with 5HR and 38RBI in 87 games with Single-A Tampa...led all Florida State League catchers with a .998 fielding percentage, committing just one error in 587 total chances...in 12 games with the Peoria Saguaros in the Arizona Fall League, batted .394 (13-for-33) with 8RBI...**2005:** In second season with short-season Single-A Staten Island, batted .250 with 4HR and 25RBI in 53 games played...**2004:** Made professional debut with short-season Single-A Staten Island...batted .215 in 34 games for the Yankees...**PERSONAL:** Full name is Peter John Pilittere...was named team captain at Cal State Fullerton in 2004, helping lead his team to the College World Series...batted .351 with 18 doubles, 4HR and 49RBI in 69 games during his senior season...graduated from Bishop Amat High School in Walnut, Calif...was honored with first-team All-Del Rey League and honorable mention All-San Gabriel Valley recognitions...was the starting catcher in the 1999 San Gabriel Valley All-Star Game.

YEAR	CLUB	CLASS	AVG	G	AB	R	H	2B	3B	HR	RBI	SH	SF	HP	BB	SO	SB	CS	E	SLUG	OBP
2004	Staten Island	SS-A	.215	34	121	9	26	6	0	0	11	1	0	3	3	18	1	1	1	.264	.252
2005	Staten Island	SS-A	.250	53	176	18	44	11	0	4	25	3	4	8	12	17	0	0	5	.381	.320
2006	Tampa	A	.302	87	291	39	88	14	2	5	38	5	2	5	20	24	3	2	1	.416	.355
2007	Trenton	AA	.261	100	348	43	91	16	2	2	34	1	7	6	26	42	0	1	4	.336	.318
2008	Trenton	AA	.277	97	364	46	101	15	1	3	48	1	4	3	20	32	0	1	6	.349	.317
2009	Scranton/WB	AAA	.244	28	86	8	21	6	0	1	9	1	2	1	3	9	0	0	2	.349	.272
	Trenton	AA	.198	27	96	5	19	3	0	0	8	0	0	1	7	8	0	0	0	.229	.260
Minor League Totals			**.263**	**426**	**1482**	**168**	**390**	**71**	**5**	**15**	**173**	**12**	**19**	**27**	**91**	**150**	**4**	**5**	**19**	**.348**	**.314**

PIRELA, Jose Manuel – INF

HT: 6-1; **WT:** 180; **B:** R; **T:** R; **BORN:** 11/21/89 in Valera, Venezuela; **RESIDES:** Bobures, Venezuela; **OBTAINED:** Signed by the Yankees as a non-drafted free agent on 7/2/06; **M.L. SVC:** 0.000; **CAREER NOTES: 2009**: Hit .295 with 29 extra-base hits (23 doubles, 6 triples) and 46RBI in 97 games with Single-A Charleston…recorded multiple hits in six of seven games from 7/23–8/1, batting .516 (16-for-31) with two doubles, one triple and 4RBI over the stretch…**2008:** Appeared in 35 games with the GCL Yankees, batting .234 with 4 doubles, 1 triple and 10RBI…**2007:** Made his professional debut with the DSL Yankees 1, batting .273 with 7 doubles, 3 triples, 4HR, 29RBI and 15SB in 65 games…ranked second on the team in stolen bases and third in runs (44).

YEAR	CLUB	CLASS	AVG	G	AB	R	H	2B	3B	HR	RBI	SH	SF	HP	BB	SO	SB	CS	E	SLUG	OBP
2007	DSL Yankees 1	R	.273	65	238	44	65	7	3	4	29	0	6	5	34	36	15	5	29	.378	.367
2008	GCL Yankees	R	.234	35	141	19	33	4	1	0	10	0	1	3	8	19	4	2	3	.277	.288
2009	Charleston	A	.295	97	404	65	119	23	6	0	46	4	1	1	37	65	9	8	17	.381	.354
Minor League Totals			**.277**	**197**	**783**	**128**	**217**	**34**	**10**	**4**	**85**	**4**	**8**	**9**	**79**	**120**	**28**	**15**	**49**	**.361**	**.347**

POPE, Ryan – RHP

NON-ROSTER INVITEE

HT: 6-3; **WT:** 190; **B:** R; **T:** R; **BORN:** 5/21/86 in Bradenton, Fla.; **RESIDES:** Bradenton, Fla.; **COLLEGE:** Savannah College of Arts and Design; **OBTAINED:** Selected by the Yankees in the third round of the 2007 First-Year Player Draft; **M.L. SVC:** 0.000; **CAREER NOTES: 2009**: Spent the season with Trenton, going 5-12 with a 4.78 ERA in 26 appearances (25 starts)…recorded 106K with only 34BB…made his only relief appearance of the season—the second of his career—on 6/13 vs. Binghamton, allowing 9H and 4ER in 4.2IP (1K, 1HR)…**2008:** Made 20 starts with Single-A Tampa, going 7-7 with a 4.15 ERA…missed over a month on the disabled list from 5/25-7/2 with a right groin strain…made two rehab appearances (one start) with the GCL Yankees…went 4-4 with a 2.81 ERA prior to the injury and 3-3 with a 5.47 ERA after returning to the rotation…named to the Florida State League midseason All-Star team…credited with his first career complete game on 7/18 at Jupiter, recording the win in the 7.0-inning Game 1 of a doubleheader…**2007:** Made 10 starts for short-season Single-A Staten Island, going 3-0 with a 2.49 ERA and 46 strikeouts in 43.1IP in his first professional season…held the opposition to 2ER or less in nine starts and did not allow an earned run in four of his starts…tossed 3.0 scoreless innings in his debut vs. Vermont…**PERSONAL:** Full name is Ryan Joseph Pope…became the first player ever drafted out of the Savannah College of Art and Design…set a school single-season record in 2007 with a 1.15 ERA, ranking third among all NAIA pitchers…also ranked third among NAIA hurlers in opponents batting average (.162) and 11th in strikeouts per 9.0IP (10.76)…threw the school's second no-hitter on 1/27/07 in the season opener against Tennessee Temple University…holds school career records in starts (42), wins (24), strikeouts (284), complete games (32), innings pitched (289.1) and ERA (2.36)…was named 2007 "Player of the Year" for the Florida Sun Conference and the NAIA Region XIV and earned the SCAD "Male Athlete of the Year" Award in 2006 and '07…named to the 2007 NAIA All-American first team as well as the Rawlings NAIA Gold Glove team.

YEAR	CLUB	CLASS	W-L	ERA	G	GS	CG	SHO	SV	IP	H	R	ER	HR	HB	BB	SO	WP	BK
2007	Staten Island	SS-A	3-0	2.49	10	10	0	0	0	43.1	41	16	12	2	1	10	46	1	0
2008	Tampa	A	7-7	4.15	20	20	1	0	0	104.0	114	57	48	8	4	22	72	2	0
	GCL Yankees	R	0-0	6.43	2	1	0	0	0	7.0	7	5	5	1	1	1	4	0	0
2009	Trenton	AA	5-12	4.78	26	25	0	0	0	141.1	155	91	75	7	8	34	106	4	1
Minor League Totals			**15-19**	**4.26**	**58**	**56**	**1**	**0**	**0**	**295.2**	**317**	**169**	**140**	**18**	**14**	**67**	**228**	**7**	**1**

PRIHODA, Luke – RHP

HT: 6-5; **WT:** 233; **B:** R; **T:** R; **BORN:** 8/10/84 in Weimar, Tex.; **RESIDES:** Weimar, Tex.; **COLLEGE:** Sam Houston State; **OBTAINED:** Signed by the Yankees as a free agent on 7/8/09; **M.L. SVC:** 0.000; **CAREER NOTES: 2009**: Signed by the Yankees in July, was limited to 14 combined relief appearances with Single-A Charleston and Triple-A Scranton/Wilkes-Barre (4-0, two saves, 2.81 ERA) after a short stint (7/23-8/1) on the disabled list with right shoulder inflammation…was named the South Atlantic League's "Pitcher of the Week" on 8/31, after going 2-0 with one save in three relief appearances (5.0IP, 2H, 0R, 7K)…opened the season with Grand Prairie in the Independent League, going 3-1 with three saves and a 1.89 ERA…**2008**: Spent the season with Edinburg of the Independent United League, going 3-0 with a team-high-tying nine saves and a 3.18 ERA in 37 appearances…was released by Arizona in spring training…**2007**: Made his professional debut with rookie-level Missoula, allowing 38R in 37.2IP…**PERSONAL**: Originally drafted by the Arizona Diamondbacks in the 24th round of the 2007 First-year Player Draft…attended Sam Houston State University where he was named the 2007 "Stopper of the Year" by the National Collegiate Baseball Writers Association after leading the nation with 18 saves…also earned the Southland Conference "Pitcher of the Year" Award.

YEAR	CLUB	CLASS	W-L	ERA	G	GS	CG	SHO	SV	IP	H	R	ER	HR	HB	BB	SO	WP	BK
2007	Missoula	R	3-2	7.88	22	0	0	0	1	37.2	58	38	33	10	3	9	25	4	1
2008	Edinburg	IND	3-0	3.18	37	0	0	0	0	39.1	30	15	14	1	5	8	49	2	0
2009	Grand Prairie	IND	3-1	1.89	21	0	0	0	3	38.0	29	11	8	1	2	6	27	2	0
	Charleston	A	3-0	3.10	12	0	0	0	2	20.1	21	7	7	1	0	0	23	1	0
	Scranton/WB	AAA	1-0	1.69	2	0	0	0	0	5.1	5	1	1	0	0	1	4	0	0
Minor League Totals			**7-2**	**5.83**	**36**	**0**	**0**	**0**	**3**	**63.1**	**84**	**46**	**41**	**11**	**3**	**10**	**52**	**5**	**1**

QUINTANA, Jose – LHP

HT: 6-0; **WT:** 172; **B:** R; **T:** L; **BORN:** 1/24/89 in Arjona, Colombia; **RESIDES:** Barranquilla, Colombia.; **OBTAINED:** Signed by the Yankees as a free agent on 3/10/08; **M.L. SVC:** 0.000; **CAREER NOTES: 2009**: Went 2-1 with a 2.32 ERA in 14 games with the DSL Yankees 2...led all DSL Yankees pitchers with 80K (in 50.1IP)...struck out six or more batters in eight of his 11 starts...**2008:** Posted a record of 3-2 with a 1.96 ERA in 15 games (12 starts) with the DSL Yankees 2...recorded a career-high 10K in an 8/2 no-decision vs. the DSL Twins (5.1IP, 2H, 1HB, 1WP)...**2007:** Did not pitch during the regular season...**2006:** Was 0-1 with an 8.44 ERA in 3G with the VSL Mets.

YEAR	CLUB	CLASS	W-L	ERA	G	GS	CG	SHO	SV	IP	H	R	ER	HR	HB	BB	SO	WP	BK
2006	VSL Mets	R	0-1	8.44	3	0	0	0	0	5.1	6	7	5	0	2	8	5	0	0
2007							Did Not Pitch												
2008	DSL Yankees 2	R	3-2	1.96	15	12	0	0	0	55.0	36	17	12	0	5	24	76	5	0
2009	DSL Yankees 2	R	2-1	2.32	14	14	0	0	0	50.1	25	17	13	0	3	37	80	6	1
Minor League Totals			**5-4**	**2.44**	**32**	**26**	**0**	**0**	**0**	**110.2**	**67**	**41**	**30**	**0**	**10**	**69**	**161**	**11**	**1**

RABAGO, Hector – C/INF

HT: 5-10; **WT:** 185; **B:** R; **T:** R; **BORN:** 8/24/88 in Riverside, Calif.; **RESIDES:** Riverside, Calif.; **COLLEGE:** University of Southern California; **OBTAINED:** Selected by the Yankees in the 18th round of the 2009 First-Year Player Draft; **M.L. SVC:** 0.000; **CAREER NOTES: 2009:** Played entire season with short-season Single-A Staten Island, appearing in games at catcher, second base, third base and shortstop...**PERSONAL:** Named the *Los Angeles Times'* "Player of the Year" for the Inland Empire area as a junior in 2005...played infield and pitched with USC.

YEAR	CLUB	CLASS	AVG	G	AB	R	H	2B	3B	HR	RBI	SH	SF	HP	BB	SO	SB	CS	E	SLUG	OBP
2009	Staten Island	SS-A	.216	34	111	10	24	2	0	1	5	2	0	5	13	16	3	2	3	.261	.326

RAMIREZ, Alcibiades – C

HT: 5-11; **WT:** 165; **B:** S; **T:** R; **BORN:** 1/27/89 in Panama City, Panama; **RESIDES:** Panama City, Panama; **OBTAINED:** Signed by the Yankees as a non-drafted free agent on 1/7/07; **M.L. SVC:** 0.000; **CAREER NOTES: 2009:** Appeared in 11 games with the DSL Yankees 2 and hit .150 (3-for-20) with 1 double and 3RBI...**2008**: Posted a .286 batting average in four games with the DSL Yankees 2...**2007:** Made his professional debut with the DSL Yankees 2, batting .111 in five games.

YEAR	CLUB	CLASS	AVG	G	AB	R	H	2B	3B	HR	RBI	SH	SF	HB	BB	SO	SB	CS	E	SLUG	OBP
2007	DSL Yankees 2	R	.111	5	9	1	1	0	0	0	1	0	0	0	1	4	0	0	0	.111	.200
2008	DSL Yankees 2	R	.286	4	7	1	2	1	0	0	1	0	0	1	1	3	0	0	1	.429	.444
2009	DSL Yankees 2	R	.150	11	20	4	3	1	0	0	3	0	0	0	4	7	0	0	2	.200	.292
Minor League Totals			**.167**	**20**	**36**	**6**	**6**	**2**	**0**	**0**	**5**	**0**	**0**	**1**	**6**	**14**	**0**	**0**	**3**	**.222**	**.302**

RAMIREZ, Jose Altagracia – RHP

HT: 6-1; **WT:** 155; **B:** R; **T:** R; **BORN:** 1/21/90 in Yaguate, D.R.; **RESIDES:** Yaguate, D.R.; **OBTAINED:** Signed by the Yankees as a free agent on 6/10/07; **M.L. SVC:** 0.000; **CAREER NOTES: 2009:** Earned milb.com's "Short-Season Starting Pitcher of the Year" award...went 6-0 with a 1.48 ERA in 11 games (10 starts) with the GCL Yankees...was promoted to Single-A Tampa on 9/5 where he made one relief appearance, tossing 3.0 scoreless innings...tied for third in the GCL in wins and ranked eighth in ERA and strikeouts (53)...had the lowest opponents average (.159) and allowed the fewest baserunners per 9.0IP (7.23) among GCL starters...**2008:** In his first professional season, posted an 0-3 record and 4.15 ERA in 12 games (10 starts) for the Dominican Summer League Yankees 2...tossed a season-high 5.0 innings in 8/9 win vs. the DSL Reds (6H, 3ER, 1BB, 2K, 1HR).

YEAR	CLUB	CLASS	W-L	ERA	G	GS	CG	SHO	SV	IP	H	R	ER	HR	HB	BB	SO	WP	BK
2008	DSL Yankees 2	R	0-3	4.15	12	10	0	0	0	39.0	35	23	18	2	9	18	39	6	1
2009	GCL Yankees	R	6-0	1.48	11	10	0	0	0	61.0	33	12	10	5	3	16	53	0	0
	Tampa	A	0-0	0.00	1	0	0	0	0	3.0	1	0	0	0	0	0	2	0	0
Minor League Totals			**6-3**	**2.45**	**24**	**20**	**0**	**0**	**0**	**103.0**	**69**	**35**	**28**	**7**	**12**	**34**	**94**	**6**	**1**

RAMIREZ, Jose Miguel – RHP

HT: 6-1; **WT:** 160; **B:** R; **T:** R; **BORN:** 10/29/88 in Santo Domingo, D.R.; **RESIDES:** Santo Domingo, D.R.; **OBTAINED:** Signed by the Yankees as a free agent on 6/14/07; **M.L. SVC:** 0.000; **CAREER NOTES: 2009:** Made 19 relief appearances with the DSL Yankees 2, going 1-0 with three saves and a 2.84 ERA...closed out the season with six straight scoreless outings (6.2IP, 4H, 2BB, 9K, 1HR)...**2008:** Was 1-2 with a 6.32 ERA in 24 games (four starts) with the DSL Yankees 1...recorded a career-high 4K twice (6/5 at DSL Dodgers and 7/7 vs. DSL Red Sox)...**2007:** Made his professional debut with the DSL Yankees 2, making seven relief appearances and posting a 6.43 ERA with no record.

YEAR	CLUB	CLASS	W-L	ERA	G	GS	CG	SHO	SV	IP	H	R	ER	HR	HB	BB	SO	WP	BK
2007	DSL Yankees 2	R	0-0	6.43	7	0	0	0	0	14.0	16	14	10	1	0	8	8	7	0
2008	DSL Yankees 1	R	1-2	6.28	17	4	0	0	0	43.0	58	41	30	2	3	35	29	7	2
2009	DSL Yankees 2	R	1-0	2.84	19	0	0	0	3	25.1	17	12	8	1	2	10	25	7	0
Minor League Totals			**2-2**	**5.25**	**43**	**4**	**0**	**0**	**3**	**82.1**	**91**	**67**	**48**	**4**	**5**	**53**	**62**	**21**	**2**

RAMOS, Abraham – INF

HT: 5-10; **WT:** 150; **B:** R; **T:** R; **BORN:** 8/3/92 in Santiago-Ixcuintla, Mexico; **RESIDES:** Santiago-Ixcuintla, Mexico; **OBTAINED:** Signed by the Yankees as a non-drafted free agent on 9/8/08; **M.L. SVC:** 0.000; **CAREER NOTES: 2009**: Made his professional debut with the DSL Yankees 1 and hit .182 (8-for-44) with 2RBI and 1SB...three of his eight hits went for extra bases (3 doubles).

YEAR	CLUB	CLASS	AVG	G	AB	R	H	2B	3B	HR	RBI	SH	SF	HP	BB	SO	SB	CS	E	SLUG	OBP
2009	DSL Yankees 1	R	.182	15	44	7	8	3	0	0	2	0	0	0	4	8	1	0	7	.250	.250

REYES, Yobanny – RHP

HT: 6-0; **WT:** 165; **B:** R; **T:** R; **BORN:** 11/29/88 in Villa Gonzalez, Venezuela; **RESIDES:** Santiago, D.R.; **OBTAINED:** Signed by the Yankees as a non-drafted free agent on 2/25/06; **M.L. SVC:** 0.000; **CAREER NOTES: 2009**: Appeared in 11 games (one start) with the DSL Yankees 2, going 2-1 with a 3.54 ERA in 20.1IP...held right-handed batters to a .200 batting average (11-for-55)...**2008:** Made his professional debut with the DSL Yankees 2, going 2-0 with a 5.64 ERA in 14 games...recorded his first career save on 7/17 vs. the DSL Cubs 1, allowing 1H in 2.0IP (1K, 1HB).

YEAR	CLUB	CLASS	W-L	ERA	G	GS	CG	SHO	SV	IP	H	R	ER	HR	HB	BB	SO	WP	BK
2008	DSL Yankees 2	R	2-0	5.64	14	0	0	0	1	22.1	20	15	14	2	2	20	17	2	0
2009	DSL Yankees 2	R	2-1	3.54	11	1	0	0	0	20.1	19	11	8	1	0	9	13	3	0
Minor League Totals			**4-1**	**4.64**	**25**	**1**	**0**	**0**	**1**	**42.2**	**39**	**26**	**22**	**3**	**2**	**29**	**30**	**5**	**0**

REYNOSO, Victor – OF

HT: 6-3; **WT:** 190; **B:** R; **T:** R; **BORN:** 10/31/91 in San Pedro de Macoris, D.R.; **RESIDES:** San Pedro de Macoris, D.R.; **OBTAINED:** Signed by the Yankees as a non-drafted free agent on 9/29/08; **M.L. SVC:** 0.000; **CAREER NOTES: 2009:** Made his professional debut with the DSL Yankees 2, batting .269 with 18 doubles, 6HR and 51RBI in 62 games...tied for most games played on the team and ranked second in RBI.

YEAR	CLUB	CLASS	AVG	G	AB	R	H	2B	3B	HR	RBI	SH	SF	HP	BB	SO	SB	CS	E	SLUG	OBP
2009	DSL Yankees 2	R	.269	62	234	38	63	18	2	6	51	0	5	8	11	61	5	3	6	.440	.318

RICHARDSON, Matthew – RHP

HT: 6-1; **WT:** 175; **B:** R; **T:** R; **BORN:** 5/28/90 in Lake Mary, Fla.; **RESIDES:** Lake Mary, Fla.; **OBTAINED:** Signed by the Yankees as a non-drafted free agent on 6/20/08; **M.L. SVC:** 0.000; **CAREER NOTES: 2009:** Split the season between the GCL Yankees and short-season Single-A Staten Island, going 3-3 with a 3.96 ERA in 14 games (13 starts)...did not allow a run over three straight starts from 6/29-7/10 with the GCL Yankees (16.0IP, 10H, 1BB, 14K, 1HP)...**2008:** Made his professional debut, going 0-1 with a 3.86 ERA in six appearances (four starts) with the GCL Yankees...recorded 17K in 14.0IP.

YEAR	CLUB	CLASS	W-L	ERA	G	GS	CG	SHO	SV	IP	H	R	ER	HR	HB	BB	SO	WP	BK
2008	GCL Yankees	R	0-1	3.86	6	4	0	0	0	14.0	12	6	6	2	1	6	17	2	0
2009	GCL Yankees	R	3-0	0.64	5	4	0	0	0	28.0	20	2	2	0	2	1	21	1	0
	Staten Island	SS-A	0-3	6.56	9	9	0	0	0	35.2	45	31	26	2	0	23	30	2	0
Minor League Totals			**3-4**	**3.94**	**20**	**17**	**0**	**0**	**0**	**77.2**	**77**	**39**	**34**	**4**	**3**	**30**	**68**	**5**	**0**

RING, Royce – LHP

NON-ROSTER INVITEE

HT: 6-0; **WT:** 220; **B:** L; **T:** L; **BORN:** 12/21/80 in La Mesa, Calif.; **RESIDES:** La Mesa, Calif.; **COLLEGE:** San Diego State University; **OBTAINED:** Signed by the Yankees as a free agent on 1/5/10; **M.L. SVC:** 1.132; **CAREER NOTES:** Owns a 3-3 record with a 4.93 ERA in 94 relief appearances over parts of four Major League seasons with the Mets (2005-06), San Diego (2007) and Atlanta (2007-08)...**2009**: Spent the entire season with Triple-A Memphis, going 5-2 with four saves and a 3.04 ERA in 51 relief outings...ranked second on the team in appearances...held lefthanders to a .208 (15-for-72, 1HR) batting average...posted an 11.12 ERA with no decisions in seven spring training relief appearances with St. Louis...signed with the Cardinals as a free agent on 1/6/09...**2008**: Began the season with the Braves, going 2-1 with an 8.46 ERA in 42 relief appearances...faced only Pittsburgh's Adam LaRoche in each of his first three appearances of the season (3/31-4/3), striking him out each time...according to the *Elias Sports Bureau*, became the first pitcher since 1900 to play in three consecutive games and face the same lone batter while also striking him out each time...allowed just 1R (0ER) in June, spanning 11 games and 6.1IP...recorded a 21.94 ERA in 10 July games (5.1IP, 13ER)...over his final eight appearances with Atlanta (7/19-8/1), recorded a 31.50 ERA (4.0IP, 14ER) with a .536 opponents batting average...the 14ER allowed were twice as many as he allowed over 34 appearances from 3/31-7/6...was designated for assignment on 8/2 and assigned to Triple-A Richmond where he went 0-1 with a 3.00 ERA in 11 games...**2007**: Was acquired by the Padres along with RHP Heath Bell in exchange for OF Ben Johnson and RHP Jon Adkins on 11/15/06...went 1-0 with a 3.60 ERA in 15 relief appearances with San Diego...nine of his first 10 appearances with the Padres were scoreless, before allowing runs in four of his last five Padre games (7/13-22)...was 4-0 with a 1.99 ERA in 27 outings with Triple-A Portland...was traded to the Braves in exchange for LHPs Wilfredo Ledezma and Will Startup on 7/31/07...did not allow a run in 11 relief appearances (5.0IP) with Atlanta after having his contract purchased on 9/1, holding opponents to 2H and 3BB (4K)...also saw time with Triple-A Richmond following the trade, going 1-2 with a 5.68 ERA in 15 relief outings...**2006**: Posted a 2.13 ERA in 11 relief appearances with the Mets without recording a decision...nine of his 11 outings were scoreless...held left-handed batters to a .118 (2-for-17) batting average, while right-handers hit .190 (4-for-21)...began the season with Triple-A Norfolk, going 2-2 with 11 saves and a 2.97 ERA in 36 games...28 of his 36 appearances were scoreless...set a Norfolk record with a 26.2-inning scoreless stretch from 4/19-7/8, spanning 22 appearances...named to the Triple-A All-Star Game and pitched 1.0 scoreless inning for the IL on 7/12 in the IL's 6-0 shutout of the PCL in Toledo...**2005**: Was signed to a Major League contract on 4/26 and made a career-high 15 appearances for the Mets, going 0-2 with a 5.06 ERA...11 of his 15 outings were scoreless...made his Major League debut on 4/29 at Washington and retired his only batter faced...**2004**: Combined to go 5-3 with a 3.69 ERA in 48 relief appearances with Triple-A Norfolk and Double-A Birmingham...**2003**: Split the season between Double-A Birmingham and Double-A Binghamton, combining to go 4-4 with 26 saves and a 2.20 ERA in 54 relief appearances...averaged 9.7K/9.0IP (57.1IP, 62K)...began the season with Birmingham, going 1-4 with a 2.52 ERA in 36 appearances...did not allow a run in 20 straight outings from 4/11-5/31 (24.1IP)...was traded to New York-NL along with RHP Edwin Almonte and INF Andrew Salvo in exchange for INF Roberto Alomar on 7/1/03...went 3-0 with a 1.66 ERA in 18 appearances with Binghamton...was selected to the All-Star Futures Game at U.S. Cellular Field and earned a save (0.1IP) in the United States' 3-2 win vs. the World Team...**2002**: Appeared in 21 games for Single-A Winston-Salem, going 2-0 with a 3.91 ERA...was named the 10th-best prospect in the White Sox organization by *Baseball America*...began the season at rookie-level Phoenix, tossing 5.0 scoreless innings...made his professional debut on 6/25...**PERSONAL**: Graduated from Monte Vista High School (Calif.) where he won his team's "Most Valuable Pitcher" award as a senior, while also playing RF and batting cleanup...was selected by Cleveland in the 41st round of the 1999 First-Year Player Draft, but did not sign and instead chose to attend San Diego State University...went 5-1 with a 1.85 ERA and a school-record 17 saves in his junior year (2002), leading his team in appearances (36) and games finished (34), and ranking second in ERA and opponent batting average (.205)...holds the school career saves record with 26...was a third-team All-American and First-Team All-Mountain West Conference selection...was a member of the United States qualifying team which played in Panama City in 2003 to qualify for the 2004 Summer Olympics in Athens, Greece...his cousin is former White Sox pitcher Bill Simas...was selected by Chicago-AL in the first round (18th overall pick) of the 2002 First-Year Player Draft.

YEAR	CLUB	CLASS	W-L	ERA	G	GS	CG	SHO	SV	IP	H	R	ER	HR	HB	BB	SO	WP	BK
2002	AZL White Sox	R	0-0	0.00	3	0	0	0	0	5.0	2	0	0	0	0	0	9	0	0
	Winston-Salem	A	2-0	3.91	21	0	0	0	5	23.0	20	11	10	2	0	11	22	1	0
2003	Birmingham	AA	1-4	2.52	36	0	0	0	19	35.2	33	11	10	1	3	14	44	3	0
	Binghamton	AA	3-0	1.66	18	0	0	0	7	21.2	13	4	4	2	1	11	18	1	0
2004	Norfolk	AAA	3-1	3.63	29	0	0	0	0	34.2	37	15	14	5	0	12	22	1	0
	Binghamton	AA	2-2	3.77	19	0	0	0	2	28.2	25	13	12	5	1	11	23	0	0
2005	NEW YORK-NL	MAJ	0-2	5.06	15	0	0	0	0	10.2	10	6	6	0	0	10	8	0	0
	Norfolk	AAA	3-0	3.26	33	0	0	0	2	38.2	34	16	14	2	3	13	26	2	0
2006	Norfolk	AAA	2-2	2.97	36	0	0	0	11	39.1	30	14	13	2	3	15	40	1	1
	NEW YORK-NL	MAJ	0-0	2.13	11	0	0	0	0	12.2	7	3	3	2	0	3	8	0	0
2007	SAN DIEGO	MAJ	1-0	3.60	15	0	0	0	0	15.0	11	8	6	1	0	14	17	2	0
	Portland	AAA	4-0	1.99	27	0	0	0	1	31.2	22	8	7	0	0	11	44	1	0
	Richmond	AAA	1-2	5.68	15	0	0	0	1	12.2	17	9	8	2	1	7	14	1	0
	ATLANTA	MAJ	0-0	0.00	11	0	0	0	0	5.0	2	0	0	0	0	3	4	0	0
2008	ATLANTA	MAJ	2-1	8.46	42	0	0	0	0	22.1	32	25	21	2	2	10	16	0	1
	Richmond	AAA	0-1	3.00	11	0	0	0	0	9.0	5	3	3	0	0	7	7	2	0
2009	Memphis	AAA	5-2	3.04	51	0	0	0	4	47.1	44	18	16	4	2	15	38	1	0
Minor League Totals			**26-14**	**3.05**	**299**	**0**	**0**	**0**	**52**	**327.1**	**282**	**122**	**111**	**25**	**14**	**127**	**307**	**14**	**1**
Major League Totals			**3-3**	**4.93**	**94**	**0**	**0**	**0**	**0**	**65.2**	**62**	**42**	**36**	**5**	**2**	**40**	**53**	**2**	**1**

RIVERA, Mike – C — NON-ROSTER INVITEE

HT: 6-1; **WT**: 236; **B**: R; **T**: R; **BORN**: 9/8/76 in Rio Piedras, P.R.; **RESIDES**: Kissimmee, Fla.; **COLLEGE**: Troy State University; **OBTAINED**: Signed by the Yankees as a free agent on 12/22/09; **M.L. SVC**: 3.081; **CAREER NOTES**: Owns a career .244 batting average with 13HR and 69RBI in 181 games over parts of seven Major League seasons with Detroit (2001-02), San Diego (2003) and Milwaukee (2006-09)...**2009**: Batted .228 with 2HR and 14RBI in 41 games with Milwaukee, making 31 starts at C...the team went 19-12 in games he started, despite being 80-82 overall...Brewers pitchers had a 4.38 ERA in games he caught (271.0IP, 132ER) and a 4.83 ERA overall...threw out five of 23 potential basestealers (21.7%) without committing an error...was placed on the 15-day disabled list from 4/29-5/13 with a sprained left ankle...suffered the injury on 4/28 vs. Pittsburgh on a play at the plate (was slid into by Brian Bixler)...recorded his first career two-homer game and a career-high 5RBI on 8/13 vs. San Diego...**2008**: Batted .306 with 1HR and 14RBI in 21 games for Milwaukee...made 15 starts (13 at C, two at 1B)...his starts at 1B were the first of his career...hit only home run of the season on 4/30 at Chicago-NL...**2007**: Spent most of the season with Triple-A Nashville, batting .215 with 19HR and 61RBI in 96 games...had his contract purchased by Milwaukee on 9/4...in 11 games with the Brewers, hit .231 with 2HR and 3RBI...made his only start on 9/29 vs. San Diego...**2006**: Began the season with Triple-A Nashville, batting .296 with 10HR and 46RBI in 60 games...was named to the Pacific Coast League All-Star team...had his contract purchased by Milwaukee on 7/6 and hit .268 with 6HR and 24RBI in 46 games (39GS at C) for the Brewers...threw out eight of 47 potential basestealers (17.0%)...made his Brewers debut on 7/7 vs. Chicago-NL and homered off Ryan Dempster in his final at-bat (1-for-4, 1RBI)...started each of the final 10 games of the season, batting .333 (12-for-36) with 6 doubles, 1HR and 10RBI over the stretch...collected his first career three-hit game on 9/22 vs. San Francisco, going 3-for-5 with 1R, 2 doubles and 3RBI...**2005**: Signed a minor league contract with Detroit on 1/6...was released by the Tigers on 4/4 and signed a minor league contract with Milwaukee on 5/17...spent the season with Triple-A Nashville, where he batted .285 with 16HR and 43RBI in 60 games...**2004**: Began the year with the White Sox organization, batting .100 with 2RBI in 11 games at Triple-A Charlotte...was claimed off waivers by Oakland on 4/22 and assigned to Triple-A Sacramento, where he hit .224 with 5HR and 20RBI in 49 games...hit safely in 12-of-13 games from 7/10-8/15, batting .455 (20-for-44) with 4HR and 11RBI over the stretch...**2003**: Began the season at Triple-A Portland before being recalled by San Diego on 4/17...batted .170 with 1HR and 2RBI in 19 games with the Padres before being optioned to Portland on 5/23...in 13 games with Portland, hit .160 with 2RBI...was claimed off waivers by the White Sox on 6/9 and assigned to Triple-A Charlotte, where he batted .310 with 12HR and 52RBI in 68 games...**2002**: Was the Tigers' Opening Day catcher, going 2-for-4 with 1R and 1RBI on 4/2 at Tampa Bay...batted .227 with 1HR and 11RBI in 39 games over two stints with Detroit (4/2-5/25 and 9/7-end)...hit his first Major League home run on 4/4 at Tampa Bay, a solo shot off Jorge Sosa...played in 74 games with Triple-A Toledo, batting .249 with 20HR and 53RBI...was traded to San Diego in exchange for OF Gene Kingsale on 11/15...**2001**: Was named the Tigers' co-Minor League Player of the Year (with teammate Eric Munson) after batting .289 with 33HR and 101RBI in 112 games at Double-A Erie...led the Eastern League in HR and ranked second in slugging percentage (.578) and RBI...was named to both the Eastern League's midseason and postseason All-Star teams...was named the "Best Power Prospect" and 15th-best prospect in the Eastern League by *Baseball America*...was named the Eastern League "Player of the Week" for the period from 4/5-15, batting .500 (15-for-30) with 5HR and 18RBI during the span...was selected to play in the All-Star Futures Game at Safeco Field in Seattle...had his contract purchased by Detroit on 9/10, appearing in four games for the Tigers...made his Major League debut on 9/18 at Minnesota, entering the game defensively and going 0-for-1...recorded his first Major League hit on 9/27 at Kansas City with a single off Mike MacDougal...**2000**: Batted .254 with 13HR and 63RBI in 107 games between Single-A Lakeland (64 games), Triple-A Toledo (four games) and Double-A Jacksonville (39 games)...was named the Florida State League "Player of the Week" for the period from 4/17-23, batting .526 (10-for-19) with 2HR and 10RBI...was named the Topps FSL "Minor League Player of the Month" in June, hitting .390 with 6HR and 28RBI...**1999**: Spent most of the season at Single-A Lakeland, batting .278 with 14HR and 72RBI in 104 games, leading the team in home runs and RBI...was named to both the Florida State League's midseason and postseason All-Star teams and hit a two-run HR in the FSL All-Star Game...**1998**: Batted .275 with 9HR and 67RBI in 108 games with Single-A West Michigan...tied for fifth in the Midwest League in doubles (34)...was named the "Best Defensive Catcher" in the Midwest League by league managers in *Baseball America's* "Best Tools" survey...**1997**: Made his professional debut, batting .286 with 10HR and 36RBI in 47 games with the GCL Tigers...led the Gulf Coast League in HR and ranked among league leaders in slugging percentage (second, .565), RBI (third), extra-base hits (third, 21) and total bases (fourth, 87)...named to the GCL All-Star team...**PERSONAL**: Full name is Michael Rene Rivera...is married to Izaly with one son, Michael Jr...attended Troy State University...appeared in the movie "For the Love of the Game"...was originally signed by the Tigers as a non-drafted free agent on 1/20/97.

YEAR	CLUB	CLASS	AVG	G	AB	R	H	2B	3B	HR	RBI	SH	SF	HP	BB	SO	SB	CS	E	SLUG	OBP
1997	GCL Tigers	R	.286	47	154	34	44	9	2	10	36	0	2	3	18	25	0	0	1	.565	.367
1998	West Michigan	A	.275	108	403	40	111	34	3	9	67	1	5	2	15	68	0	2	10	.442	.301
1999	Jacksonville	AA	.174	7	23	3	4	1	0	2	6	0	0	0	2	5	0	0	8	.478	.240
	Lakeland	A	.278	104	370	44	103	20	2	14	72	0	8	3	20	59	1	1	0	.457	.314
2000	Lakeland	A	.292	64	243	30	71	19	4	11	53	0	2	1	16	45	2	0	6	.539	.336
	Toledo	AAA	.231	4	13	0	3	3	0	0	1	0	0	0	0	2	0	0	1	.462	.231
	Jacksonville	AA	.193	39	150	10	29	8	1	2	9	0	1	0	7	30	0	0	8	.300	.228
2001	Erie	AA	.289	112	415	76	120	19	1	33	101	0	4	10	44	96	2	2	10	.578	.368
	DETROIT	MAJ	.333	4	12	2	4	2	0	0	1	0	0	0	0	2	0	0	2	.500	.333
2002	Toledo	AAA	.249	74	265	43	66	11	1	20	53	0	2	3	35	64	0	1	2	.525	.341
	DETROIT	MAJ	.227	39	132	11	30	8	1	1	11	0	1	1	4	35	0	0	3	.326	.254
2003	SAN DIEGO	MAJ	.170	19	53	2	9	1	0	1	2	0	0	0	5	11	0	0	1	.245	.241
	Portland	AAA	.160	13	50	0	8	1	0	0	2	0	0	0	1	21	0	1	2	.180	.176
	Charlotte	AAA	.310	68	245	38	76	11	0	12	52	0	1	9	16	50	0	1	2	.502	.373
2004	Charlotte	AAA	.100	11	40	3	4	0	1	0	2	0	1	1	3	12	0	0	2	.150	.178
	Sacramento	AAA	.224	49	170	12	38	7	2	5	20	1	3	0	10	34	1	1	7	.376	.262
2005	Nashville	AAA	.285	60	214	34	61	12	1	16	43	0	2	3	9	37	3	1	6	.575	.320
2006	Nashville	AAA	.296	60	213	30	63	11	0	10	46	0	6	4	13	40	3	3	6	.488	.339
	MILWAUKEE	MAJ	.268	46	142	16	38	9	0	6	24	1	2	3	10	21	0	0	4	.458	.325
2007	Nashville	AAA	.215	96	349	37	75	15	0	19	61	0	5	4	24	71	5	5	4	.421	.270
	MILWAUKEE	MAJ	.231	11	13	2	3	0	0	2	3	1	0	0	1	3	0	0	0	.692	.286
2008	MILWAUKEE	MAJ	.306	21	62	8	19	5	0	1	14	0	0	1	6	10	2	0	3	.435	.377
2009	Nashville	AAA	.231	3	13	1	3	1	0	0	3	0	0	0	0	5	0	0	0	.308	.231
	MILWAUKEE	MAJ	.228	41	114	10	26	7	0	2	14	0	1	2	15	32	1	0	1	.342	.326
Minor League Totals			**.264**	**919**	**3330**	**435**	**879**	**182**	**18**	**163**	**627**	**2**	**42**	**43**	**233**	**664**	**17**	**18**	**76**	**.476**	**.317**
Major League Totals			**.244**	**181**	**528**	**51**	**129**	**32**	**1**	**13**	**69**	**2**	**4**	**7**	**41**	**114**	**3**	**0**	**13**	**.383**	**.305**

RODINO, Manuel Alfonso – RHP

HT: 6-3; **WT:** 190; **B:** R; **T:** R; **BORN:** 3/7/90 in Santa Barbara de Zulia, Venezuela; **RESIDES:** Santa Barbara de Zulia, Venezuela; **OBTAINED:** Signed by the Yankees as a non-drafted free agent on 12/4/07; **M.L. SVC:** 0.000; **CAREER NOTES: 2009:** Appeared in 18 games in relief for the DSL Yankees 2, going 6-1 with a 3.94 ERA…tied for the team lead in wins…11 of the outings were at least 2.0IP…**2008:** Made his professional debut with the DSL Yankees 1, going 2-1 with a 6.00 ERA in 18 games (two starts).

YEAR	CLUB	CLASS	W-L	ERA	G	GS	CG	SHO	SV	IP	H	R	ER	HR	HB	BB	SO	WP	BK
2008	DSL Yankees 1	R	2-1	6.00	18	2	0	0	1	36.0	46	28	24	2	2	24	23	5	1
2009	DSL Yankees 2	R	6-1	3.94	18	0	0	0	2	32.0	34	21	14	5	2	8	32	1	0
Minor League Totals			**8-2**	**5.03**	**36**	**2**	**0**	**0**	**3**	**68.0**	**80**	**49**	**38**	**7**	**4**	**32**	**55**	**6**	**1**

RODRIGUEZ, Josue Daniel – C

HT: 6-0; **WT:** 165; **B:** R; **T:** R; **BORN:** 10/2/90 in Maracaibo, Venezuela; **RESIDES:** Maracaibo, Venezuela; **OBTAINED:** Signed by the Yankees as a non-drafted free agent on 7/2/07; **M.L. SVC:** 0.000; **CAREER NOTES: 2009:** Went 8-for-16 with 3 doubles and 1 triple in 10 games with the DSL Yankees 1…**2008:** Made his professional debut, batting .279 with 8R and 13RBI in 27 games with the DSL Yankees 1…hit .323 against right-handed pitchers, including 3 doubles, 1 triple and 12RBI.

YEAR	CLUB	CLASS	AVG	G	AB	R	H	2B	3B	HR	RBI	SH	SF	HP	BB	SO	SB	CS	E	SLUG	OBP
2008	DSL Yankees 1	R	.279	27	86	8	24	3	1	0	13	0	1	4	7	25	1	1	5	.337	.357
2009	DSL Yankees 1	R	.500	10	16	5	8	3	1	0	3	0	0	1	2	3	0	1	2	.813	.579
Minor League Totals			**.314**	**37**	**102**	**13**	**32**	**6**	**2**	**0**	**16**	**0**	**1**	**5**	**9**	**28**	**1**	**2**	**7**	**.412**	**.393**

RODRIGUEZ, Keny Jose – INF

HT: 6-1; **WT:** 170; **B:** R; **T:** R; **BORN:** 2/25/90 in Tucupita, Venezuela; **RESIDES:** Barrana del Orinoco, Venezuela; **OBTAINED:** Signed by the Yankees as a non-drafted free agent on 9/15/07; **M.L. SVC:** 0.000; **CAREER NOTES: 2009:** Batted .333 with 23R, 6 doubles and 10RBI in 40 games with the DSL Yankees 2…drew 20BB with only 15K…appeared primarily at 2B, committing just 2E in 25G (.975 fielding %)…batted in seven different spots in the lineup…**2008:** Made his professional debut, hitting .226 with seven doubles, 14RBI and nine stolen bases in 55 games with the DSL Yankees 2.

YEAR	CLUB	CLASS	AVG	G	AB	R	H	2B	3B	HR	RBI	SH	SF	HP	BB	SO	SB	CS	E	SLUG	OBP
2008	DSL Yankees 2	R	.226	55	155	26	35	7	1	1	14	0	1	6	32	29	9	2	7	.303	.376
2009	DSL Yankees 2	R	.333	40	96	23	32	6	0	0	10	1	0	0	20	15	5	4	4	.396	.448
Minor League Totals			**.267**	**95**	**251**	**49**	**67**	**13**	**1**	**1**	**24**	**1**	**1**	**6**	**52**	**44**	**14**	**6**	**11**	**.339**	**.403**

RODRIGUEZ, Ramon – RHP

HT: 6-1; **WT**: 170; **B**: R; **T**: R; **BORN**: 7/23/91 in Callejon Los Cocos, D.R.; **RESIDES**: Callejon Los Cocos, D.R.; **OBTAINED**: Signed by the Yankees as a non-drafted free agent on 6/6/09; **M.L. SVC**: 0.000; **CAREER NOTES**: **2009**: Made his professional debut, going 2-2 with a 6.31 ERA in 15 games with the DSL Yankees 1.

YEAR	CLUB	CLASS	W-L	ERA	G	GS	CG	SHO	SV	IP	H	R	ER	HR	HB	BB	SO	WP	BK
2009	DSL Yankees 1	R	2-2	6.31	15	0	0	0	0	25.2	32	28	18	2	2	21	21	9	0

RODRIGUEZ, Wilton – RHP

HT: 6-3; **WT:** 195; **B:** R; **T:** R; **BORN:** 11/6/90 in Haina, D.R.; **RESIDES:** Haina, D.R.; **OBTAINED:** Signed by the Yankees as a non-drafted free agent on 6/19/08; **M.L. SVC:** 0.000; **CAREER NOTES: 2009:** Spent the majority of the season with the GCL Yankees, going 0-1 with a 3.32 ERA in eight games (two starts), striking out 18 batters in 19.0IP...was promoted to Single-A Charleston on 9/3 and made two start with the RiverDogs (1-0, 6.75 ERA), winning his Single-A debut on 9/3 vs. Savannah...**2008:** Made his professional debut, going 0-2 with a 6.75 ERA in 10 games (five starts) with the DSL Yankees 1.

YEAR	CLUB	CLASS	W-L	ERA	G	GS	CG	SHO	SV	IP	H	R	ER	HR	HB	BB	SO	WP	BK
2008	DSL Yankees 1	R	0-2	6.75	10	5	0	0	0	20.0	25	18	15	1	2	14	13	8	0
2009	GCL Yankees	R	0-1	3.32	8	2	0	0	1	19.0	15	8	7	3	2	2	18	0	0
	Charleston	A	1-0	6.75	2	2	0	0	0	9.1	11	8	7	1	1	2	8	2	1
Minor League Totals			**1-3**	**5.40**	**20**	**9**	**0**	**0**	**1**	**48.1**	**51**	**34**	**29**	**5**	**5**	**18**	**39**	**10**	**1**

ROMINE, Austin – C

NON-ROSTER INVITEE

HT: 6-1; **WT:** 195; **B:** R; **T:** R; **BORN:** 11/22/88 in Lake Forest, Calif.; **RESIDES:** Lake Forest, Calif.; **OBTAINED:** Selected by the Yankees in the second round of the 2007 First-Year Player Draft; **M.L. SVC:** 0.000; **CAREER NOTES:** Enters the 2010 season ranked by *Baseball America* as the Yankees' second-best prospect...**2009:** Was named the Yankees "Minor League Player of the Year" and Topps Florida State League "Player of the Year," batting .276 with 28 doubles, 13HR and 72RBI in 118 games for Single-A Tampa...tied his career high in hits (122) and established career highs in doubles and RBI...led the team in hits and doubles, tied for the team lead in homers, and ranked second in games played, runs scored and RBI...ranked fourth in the league in RBI and tied for fourth in both doubles and extra-base hits (44)...did not go more than three straight games without recording a hit and went hitless in three straight contests just once (both games of a doubleheader on 4/15 and 4/16)...was named to the midseason and postseason FSL All-Star teams...following the season, played in four games for the Surprise Rafters of the Arizona Fall League, batting .400 (6-for-15) with 2R and 2RBI...**2008:** Batted .300 with 66R, 24 doubles, 10HR and 49RBI in 104 games with Single-A Charleston...ranked second on the team and third among Yankees minor leaguers in batting average...recorded 35 multi-hit games, including 12 games with at least 3H and four contests with four hits...batted .517 (15-for-29) with six multi-hit contests from 4/12-20...was placed on the D.L. from 4/23-5/22 with a right groin strain...played for the Waikiki BeachBoys in the Hawaii Winter Baseball League after the season, hitting .208 (11-for-53) with 8R, 4 doubles and 4RBI in 17 games...was named by *Baseball America* as the fourth-best prospect in the Yankees organization following the season...attended spring training as a non-roster invitee, but did not appear in a game...**2007:** Made his professional debut, appearing in one game–the season finale–with the GCL Yankees, going 1-for-2 with 1RBI as the DH...doubled in his first at-bat...after signing, reported to the Dominican Republic to take part in an instructional league...**PERSONAL:** Full name is Austin Allen Romine...rated by *Baseball America* as having the third-best arm strength among high school catchers in the 2007 draft...is the son of former Major League outfielder Kevin Romine (Boston, 1985-1991) and his brother, Andrew, was the Los Angeles Angels' fifth-round pick in the 2007 draft.

YEAR	CLUB	CLASS	AVG	G	AB	R	H	2B	3B	HR	RBI	SH	SF	HB	BB	SO	SB	CS	E	SLUG	OBP
2007	GCL Yankees	R	.500	1	2	2	1	1	0	0	1	0	0	0	1	1	0	0	0	1.000	.667
2008	Charleston	A	.300	104	407	66	122	24	1	10	49	0	1	3	25	56	3	0	6	.437	.344
2009	Tampa	A	.276	118	442	61	122	28	3	13	72	0	6	4	29	78	11	5	10	.441	.322
Minor League Totals			**.288**	**223**	**851**	**129**	**245**	**53**	**4**	**23**	**122**	**0**	**7**	**7**	**55**	**135**	**14**	**5**	**16**	**.441**	**.334**

RONDON, Francisco – LHP

HT: 6-1; **WT:** 160; **B:** L; **T:** L; **BORN:** 4/19/88 in Santo Domingo, D.R.; **RESIDES:** Santo Domingo, D.R.; **OBTAINED:** Signed as a non-drafted free agent on 2/25/06; **M.L. SVC:** 0.000; **CAREER NOTES: 2009:** Made 11 starts with short-season Single-A Staten Island, going 3-2 with a 2.32 ERA...was named to the NYPL midseason All-Star team...**2008:** Appeared in nine games (four starts) with the GCL Yankees, going 2-1 with a 3.22 ERA...recorded 34K in 36.1IP...**2007:** Went 4-1 with a 3.65 ERA in 13 appearances (eight starts) with the DSL Yankees 1 team...all four wins came as a reliever, pitching to a 1.42 ERA out of the bullpen and holding opponents to a .194 batting average...was 0-1 with a 5.33 ERA in his eight starts with a .263 opponents average...all of his relief appearances were 3.0-or-more innings...**2006:** Made his professional debut with the Yankees' DSL 2 team, posting a 1-3 record with a 3.09 ERA...held opponents to a .195 batting average.

YEAR	CLUB	CLASS	W-L	ERA	G	GS	CG	SHO	SV	IP	H	R	ER	HR	HB	BB	SO	WP	BK
2006	DSL Yankees 2	R	1-3	3.09	14	8	0	0	1	43.2	32	20	15	1	2	24	27	11	2
2007	DSL Yankees 1	R	4-1	3.65	13	8	0	0	0	44.1	38	21	18	0	2	32	45	7	0
2008	GCL Yankees	R	2-1	3.22	9	4	0	0	0	36.1	31	17	13	4	2	13	34	1	0
2009	Staten Island	SS-A	3-2	2.32	11	11	0	0	0	54.1	38	22	14	2	3	33	48	3	1
Minor League Totals			**10-7**	**3.02**	**47**	**31**	**0**	**0**	**1**	**178.2**	**139**	**80**	**60**	**7**	**9**	**102**	**154**	**22**	**3**

ROSARIO, Jose – INF

HT: 5-11; **WT**: 160; **B**: R; **T**: R; **BORN**: 11/29/91 in Villa Mella, D.R.; **RESIDES**: Villa Mella, D.R.; **OBTAINED**: Signed by the Yankees as a non-drafted free agent on 6/30/09; **M.L. SVC**: 0.000; **CAREER NOTES**: **2009**: Made his professional debut, hitting .253 (19-for-75) with 4 doubles and 6RBI in 23 games with the DSL Yankees 1.

YEAR	CLUB	CLASS	AVG	G	AB	R	H	2B	3B	HR	RBI	SH	SF	HP	BB	SO	SB	CS	E	SLUG	OBP
2009	DSL Yankees 1	R	.253	23	75	13	19	4	0	0	6	1	0	0	14	23	3	3	10	.307	.371

ROSARIO, Melvin – OF

HT: 6-3; **WT**: 177; **B**: R; **T**: R; **BORN**: 11/2/90 in San Pedro de Macoris, D.R.; **RESIDES**: San Pedro de Macoris, D.R.; **OBTAINED**: Signed by the Yankees as a non-drafted free agent on 5/14/09; **M.L. SVC**: 0.000; **CAREER NOTES**: **2009**: Made his professional debut with the DSL Yankees 1 and hit .297 with 16 doubles, 3HR and 36RBI in 51 games...went hitless in consecutive games only once (three straight 6/8–6/10).

YEAR	CLUB	CLASS	AVG	G	AB	R	H	2B	3B	HR	RBI	SH	SF	HP	BB	SO	SB	CS	E	SLUG	OBP
2009	DSL Yankees 1	R	.297	51	212	33	63	16	0	3	36	1	2	4	17	32	10	5	4	.415	.357

RULON, Brad – RHP

HT: 5-11; **WT:** 190; **B:** L; **T:** R; **BORN:** 6/22/86 in Columbus, Ga.; **RESIDES:** Columbus, Ga.; **COLLEGE:** Georgia Tech; **OBTAINED:** Selected by the Yankees in the 34th round of the 2008 First-Year Player Draft; **M.L. SVC:** 0.000; **CAREER NOTES: 2009**: Combined to go 7-1 with three saves and a 1.88 ERA in 43 relief appearances with Single-A Charleston and Single-A Tampa…won his final seven decisions of the season…began the season with Charleston, going 4-1 with a 1.18 ERA in 29 relief outings…tossed a season-high 4.0 scoreless innings on 7/6 at Asheville (2H, 4K)…was transferred to Tampa on 7/22, where he went 3-0 with a 3.47 ERA in 14 relief appearances…**2008:** Made his professional debut, going 2-0 with four saves and a 0.41 ERA in 28 relief appearances with short-season Single-A Staten Island…led the team in ERA and ranked second in appearances and strikeouts (68)…ended the season with a 15.1-inning scoreless stretch…made one postseason relief appearance, allowing 1H and 1ER in 2.0IP (1BB, 4K, 1HR)…**PERSONAL:** Full name is Bradley Michael Rulon…attended Georgia Tech, majoring in management…went 3-1 with seven saves and a 4.15 ERA in a team-leading 34 relief appearances during his senior year in 2008…was named to the 2006 ACC Honor Roll and the Academic All-ACC Baseball Team, leading all Georgia Tech pitchers in ERA (2.20) and appearances (39), while going 5-0 with two saves…attended Columbus (Ga.) High School, lettering in baseball four times…led Columbus to the Georgia AAAA State Championship in 2004…his team was ranked No. 2 in the nation by *USA Today* and No. 5 by *Baseball America*…also lettered two years in football as a placekicker…brother, Ben, played in the Tampa Bay Rays organization.

YEAR	CLUB	CLASS	W-L	ERA	G	GS	CG	SHO	SV	IP	H	R	ER	HR	HB	BB	SO	WP	BK
2008	Staten Island	SS-A	2-0	0.41	28	0	0	0	4	44.0	21	2	2	1	0	20	68	5	0
2009	Charleston	A	4-1	1.18	29	0	0	0	1	53.1	35	11	7	2	2	12	58	6	0
	Tampa	A	3-0	3.47	14	0	0	0	2	23.1	18	10	9	2	0	13	22	0	0
Minor League Totals			**9-1**	**1.34**	**71**	**0**	**0**	**0**	**7**	**120.2**	**74**	**23**	**18**	**5**	**2**	**45**	**148**	**11**	**0**

RYE, Jack – OF

HT: 6-1; **WT:** 200; **B:** L; **T:** L; **BORN:** 3/8/86 in Irvine, Calif.; **RESIDES:** South Miami, Fla.; **COLLEGE:** Florida State University; **OBTAINED:** Selected by the Yankees in the 13th round of the 2008 First-Year Player Draft; **M.L. SVC:** 0.000; **CAREER NOTES: 2009**: Combined to hit .241 with 31R, 14 doubles, 1HR and 21RBI in 78 games with Single-A Tampa and Double-A Trenton…began the season with Tampa, batting .256 with 31R, 13 doubles, 1HR and 21RBI in 75 games…hit his only home run of the season on 6/22 at Clearwater…recorded a season-high four hits on 8/16 at Clearwater and 9/2 vs. Dunedin…**2008:** Made his professional debut with short-season Single-A Staten Island, batting .276 with 26R, 10 doubles, 2HR and 17RBI in 49 games…recorded a career high in hits on 8/14 at State College, going 4-for-5 with 3R, 2 doubles and 1RBI…ended the season with an eight-game hitting streak, including six multi-hit contests, to raise his average from .236 to .276 (14-for-30, .467 during the stretch)…went hitless in his only postseason game with Staten Island (0-for-4)…**PERSONAL:** Attended Florida State University, where he was named baseball team captain during his senior year…left FSU ranked fifth in school history in hits (312), seventh in walks (162) and tied for 10th in doubles (57)…recorded more walks than strikeouts in each of his four seasons, totaling 162BB and 107K…batted .371 with 48R, 15 doubles, 7HR and 52RBI as the team's primary No. 4 hitter in 2008, ranking sixth in the ACC in OBP (.478), seventh in walks (47) and eighth in batting average…was named to the 2006 and 2008 All-ACC Academic Team and was a four-time member of the ACC Academic Honor Roll…majored in real estate…attended Woodbridge High School (Calif.)…hit over .400 all four years en route to being named first team all-league four times and second team All-Southern California once…won the "Big Stick Award" in the Mickey Mantle World Series…hobbies include surfing and snowboarding.

YEAR	CLUB	CLASS	AVG	G	AB	R	H	2B	3B	HR	RBI	SH	SF	HP	BB	SO	SB	CS	E	SLUG	OBP
2008	Staten Island	SS-A	.276	49	170	26	47	10	1	2	17	1	2	0	18	31	3	3	4	.382	.342
2009	Tampa	A	.256	75	238	31	61	13	4	1	21	5	2	2	40	42	7	11	2	.366	.365
	Trenton	AA	.111	3	9	0	1	1	0	0	0	0	0	1	2	3	0	0	0	.222	.333
Minor League Totals			**.261**	**127**	**417**	**57**	**109**	**24**	**6**	**3**	**38**	**6**	**4**	**3**	**60**	**76**	**10**	**14**	**6**	**.369**	**.355**

SANCHEZ, Anthony – RHP

HT: 6-4; **WT:** 185; **B:** R; **T:** R; **BORN:** 7/3/91 in Puerto Cabello, Venezuela.; **RESIDES:** Puerto, Venezuela; **OBTAINED:** Signed by the Yankees as a non-drafted free agent on 2/9/09; **M.L. SVC:** 0.000; **CAREER NOTES: 2009:** Made his professional debut with the DSL Yankees 1, going 2-3 with a 11.12 ERA in 11.1IP out of the bullpen.

YEAR	CLUB	CLASS	W-L	ERA	G	GS	CG	SHO	SV	IP	H	R	ER	HR	HB	BB	SO	WP	BK
2009	DSL Yankees 1	R	2-3	11.12	11	0	0	0	0	11.1	13	16	14	2	3	15	6	10	0

SANCHEZ, Gary – C

HT: 6-2; **WT:** 195; **B:** R; **T:** R; **BORN:** 12/2/92 in Santo Domingo, D.R.; **RESIDES:** Santo Domingo, D.R.; **OBTAINED:** Signed by the Yankees as a non-drafted free agent on 7/2/09; **M.L. SVC:** 0.000; **CAREER NOTES:** Will be making his professional debut in 2010.

YEAR	CLUB	CLASS	AVG	G	AB	R	H	2B	3B	HR	RBI	SH	SF	HP	BB	SO	SB	CS	E	SLUG	OBP
NO PROFESSIONAL RECORD																					

SANIT, Amaury - RHP **NON-ROSTER INVITEE**

HT: 5-8; **WT:** 205; **B:** R; **T:** R; **BORN:** 7/4/79 in Havana, Cuba; **RESIDES:** San Jose, Costa Rica; **OBTAINED:** Signed by the Yankees as a non-drafted free agent on 8/9/08; **M.L. SVC:** 0.000; **CAREER NOTES: 2009**: Combined to go 1-5 with 10 saves and a 3.16 ERA in 44 relief appearances with Single-A Tampa, Double-A Trenton and Triple-A Scranton/Wilkes-Barre...began the season with Tampa, making four scoreless relief appearances (6.0IP) before being transferred to Trenton on 4/25...went 1-2 with a 2.95 ERA in 21 relief appearances with the Thunder, converting 10 of his 12 save opportunities...was promoted to Scranton/WB on 7/8 and went 0-3 with a 4.13 ERA in 19 relief appearances...made two relief appearances for the International League runner-ups, allowing 4H and 2ER in 3.0IP (6.00 ERA) without recording a decision...following the season, made six relief appearances for the Indios de Mayaguez of the Puerto Rican Winter League, going 1-0 with one save and an 8.31 ERA (4.1IP, 9H, 4ER)...**2008:** Made his professional debut with the DSL Yankees, recording one save without allowing a run in two relief appearances (0.00 ERA, 2.0IP, 1H, 2K)...pitched for the Tigres del Licey in the Dominican Baseball League following the season, recording a 5.19 ERA in seven relief appearances.

YEAR	CLUB	CLASS	W-L	ERA	G	GS	CG	SHO	SV	IP	H	R	ER	HR	HB	BB	SO	WP	BK
2008	DSL Yankees 2	R	0-0	0.00	2	0	0	0	1	2.0	1	0	0	0	0	0	2	0	0
2009	Tampa	A	0-0	0.00	4	0	0	0	0	6.0	5	0	0	0	0	0	5	0	0
	Trenton	AA	1-2	2.95	21	0	0	0	10	21.1	13	7	7	1	0	8	18	2	0
	Scranton/WB	AAA	0-3	4.13	19	0	0	0	0	24.0	27	12	11	2	1	7	13	1	0
Minor League Totals			**1-5**	**3.04**	**46**	**0**	**0**	**0**	**11**	**53.1**	**46**	**19**	**18**	**3**	**1**	**15**	**38**	**3**	**0**

SANTANA, Francisco – OF

HT: 5-10; **WT:** 170; **B:** L; **T:** L; **BORN:** 6/18/88 in Higuey, D.R.; **RESIDES:** Higuey, D.R.; **OBTAINED:** Signed by the Yankees as a non-drafted free agent on 6/15/06; **M.L. SVC:** 0.000; **CAREER NOTES: 2009:** Played the season at short-season Single-A Staten Island, batting .236 with 6 doubles, 1 triple, 1HR and 10RBI in 40 games in CF...was transferred to Double-A Trenton from 8/12-29, going hitless in 7AB over five games...**2008:** Batted .307 with 10 doubles, 8 triples, 6HR and 38RBI in 52 games with the DSL Yankees 1...tied for third in the DSL in triples. **2007:** Hit .264 with 11 doubles, 7 triples, 3HR and 25RBI for the DSL Yankees 2...tied for second in the league in triples...was 4-for-10 (.400) with 9RBI with the bases loaded...drove in a career-high 5R on 7/11 vs. the DSL Blue Jays 2, going 4-for-5 with 1 double and 1 triple...**2006:** In his first professional season, batted a combined .118 in 31 games with both of the Yankees' Dominican Summer League teams.

YEAR	CLUB	CLASS	AVG	G	AB	R	H	2B	3B	HR	RBI	SH	SF	HB	BB	SO	SB	CS	E	SLUG	OBP
2006	DSL Yankees 1	R	.140	21	57	8	8	1	0	0	4	2	0	0	5	13	1	0	0	.158	.210
	DSL Yankees 2	R	.071	10	28	4	2	0	0	0	0	0	0	1	2	9	0	0	2	.071	.161
2007	DSL Yankees 2	R	.264	51	197	29	52	11	7	3	25	2	1	2	14	38	6	2	4	.437	.318
2008	DSL Yankees 1	R	.307	52	225	41	69	10	8	6	38	0	3	1	27	38	19	2	2	.502	.379
2009	Staten Island	SS-A	.236	40	140	17	33	6	1	1	10	1	1	1	10	29	5	4	1	.314	.289
	Trenton	AA	.000	5	7	2	0	0	0	0	0	0	0	0	0	2	0	0	0	.000	.000
Minor League Totals			**.251**	**179**	**654**	**101**	**164**	**28**	**16**	**10**	**77**	**5**	**5**	**5**	**58**	**129**	**31**	**8**	**9**	**.388**	**.314**

SANTANA, Gabriel – RHP

HT: 6-2; **WT**: 170; **B**: R; **T**: R; **BORN**: 11/9/89 in Santo Domingo, D.R.; **RESIDES**: Santo Domingo, D.R.; **OBTAINED**: Signed by the Yankees as a non-drafted free agent on 8/1/09; **M.L. SVC**: 0.000; **CAREER NOTES**: 2009: Made his professional debut with the DSL Yankees 1 and did not record a decision, allowing 5ER in 1.2 IP in two relief appearances (27.00 ERA).

YEAR	CLUB	CLASS	W-L	ERA	G	GS	CG	SHO	SV	IP	H	R	ER	HR	HB	BB	SO	WP	BK
2009	DSL Yankees 1	R	0-0	27.00	2	0	0	0	0	1.2	3	5	5	0	0	5	1	3	1

SANTANA, Ravel – OF

HT: 6-2; **WT:** 160; **B:** R; **T:** R; **BORN:** 5/1/92 in San Pedro de Macoris, D.R.; **RESIDES:** San Pedro de Macoris, D.R.; **OBTAINED:** Signed by the Yankees as a non-drafted free agent on 11/17/08; **M.L. SVC:** 0.000; **CAREER NOTES: 2009**: Made his professional debut, hitting a combined .234 (39-for-167) with 8 doubles, 1 triple and 5HR in 50 games with both DSL entries.

YEAR	CLUB	CLASS	AVG	G	AB	R	H	2B	3B	HR	RBI	SH	SF	HP	BB	SO	SB	CS	E	SLUG	OBP
2009	DSL Yankees 1	R	.207	7	29	4	6	2	1	0	3	0	0	1	4	8	1	0	0	.345	.324
	DSL Yankees 2	R	.239	43	138	27	33	6	0	5	25	0	3	6	22	35	7	3	5	.391	.361
Minor League Totals			**.234**	**50**	**167**	**31**	**39**	**8**	**1**	**5**	**28**	**0**	**3**	**7**	**26**	**43**	**8**	**3**	**5**	**.383**	**.355**

SCHMIDT, Josh – RHP

HT: 6-4; **WT:** 175; **B:** R; **T:** R; **BORN:** 11/14/82 in Sierra Madre, Calif.; **RESIDES:** Sierra Madre, Calif.; **COLLEGE:** University of the Pacific; **OBTAINED:** Selected by the Yankees in the 15th round of the 2005 First-Year Player Draft; **M.L. SVC:** 0.000; **CAREER NOTES: 2009**: Went 8-4 with a 1.61 ERA in 46 appearances (five starts) for Double-A Trenton...as a starter, went 1-0 and allowed only 4ER in 21.0IP (1.71 ERA)...was 7-4 as a reliever, recording 77K in 41 appearances out of the bullpen...34 of his 46 appearances were scoreless, including 32 of his 41 relief outings...was named to the mid-season All-Star team...made his first career start on 6/1 vs. Bowie (5.0IP, 2H, 0ER, 1BB, 3K), recording the win in his longest outing since a 3.2-inning relief appearance on 8/5/06 w/ Tampa vs. Palm Beach...also marked the longest outing of his career, later matched on 9/2 at Portland...following the season, pitched for the Aguilas del Zulia in the Venezuelan Winter League...**2008:** Made 38 combined relief appearances with Single-A Tampa and Double-A Trenton, going 1-3 with 16 saves and a 2.57 ERA...ranked third in the organization in saves...struck out 49 batters in 49.0IP and held opponents to a .233 batting average (41-for-176)...began season at Trenton before being transferred to Tampa on 5/20 for the remainder of the season...allowed only 1ER over his final 10 games (12.1IP)...**2007:** Went 6-1 with three saves and a 2.79 ERA in 39 relief appearances with Single-A Tampa, leading Yankees relievers in wins, strikeouts (92) and opponents average (.214)...ranked second overall among FSL relievers, averaging 12.24 K/9.0IP and third in opponents average...held opponents to a .214 batting average, including a .196 mark against right-handers...was 2-0 with a 4.40 ERA prior to the All-Star break and 4-1 with a 1.46 ERA after the break...did not allow a run over his final seven outings (11.1IP) and allowed only 1ER over his final 11 appearances of the season (18.0IP)...**2006:** Appeared in 39 games with the Tampa Yankees, posting a 4-4 record with one save and a 4.24 ERA...**2005:** Made professional debut with the short-season Single-A Staten Island Yankees, posting a 5-1 record with a 0.27 ERA and 47 strikeouts in 26 games (33.0IP, 1ER)...was named the NY-Penn League Rolaids "Relief Man of the Year"...ranked second among all NYPL pitchers with 13 saves and third in games pitched (26)...**PERSONAL:** Graduated from the University of the Pacific in Stockton, Calif. with a degree in communications...led the Tigers pitching staff in his senior season, posting a 6-4 record with a 1.79 ERA in a school-record 36 appearances out of the bullpen...also established a school record with 11 saves during the season...transferred to Pacific in 2003 after two years at Citrus College in Glendora, Calif...helped lead his team to the Western States Conference (WSC) title in 2003...and was named to the All-WSC Second Team...graduated from La Salle High School in Pasadena, Calif. in 2001 and led the Lancers to the state playoffs during each of his final three years there.

YEAR	CLUB	CLASS	W-L	ERA	G	GS	CG	SHO	SV	IP	H	R	ER	HR	HB	BB	SO	WP	BK
2005	Staten Island	SS-A	5-1	0.27	26	0	0	0	13	33.0	14	1	1	0	1	8	47	1	1
2006	Tampa	A	4-4	2.94	39	0	0	0	1	68.0	56	37	32	4	8	31	66	2	0
2007	Tampa	A	6-1	2.79	39	0	0	0	3	67.2	54	24	21	3	3	28	92	2	0
2008	Trenton	AA	1-1	3.09	8	0	0	0	0	11.2	11	7	4	2	2	7	8	0	0
	Tampa	A	0-2	2.41	30	0	0	0	16	37.1	30	10	10	1	4	14	41	1	0
2009	Trenton	AA	8-4	1.61	46	5	0	0	0	83.2	57	16	15	2	5	38	96	4	1
Minor League Totals			**24-13**	**2.48**	**188**	**5**	**0**	**0**	**33**	**301.1**	**222**	**95**	**83**	**12**	**23**	**126**	**350**	**10**	**2**

SEGOVIA, Zack – RHP — NON-ROSTER INVITEE

HT: 6-2; **WT:** 244; **B:** R; **T:** R; **BORN:** 4/11/83 in Dallas, Tex.; **RESIDES:** Safety Harbor, Fla.; **OBTAINED:** Signed by the Yankees as a free agent on 1/5/10; **M.L. SVC:** 0.035; **CAREER NOTES: 2009:** Had his contract purchased by the Nationals on 9/8 and went 1-0 with a 7.84 ERA in eight relief appearances at the Major League level...tossed at least 1.0 inning in six of those appearances...earned his first Major League win on 10/3 at Atlanta...combined to go 3-5 with six saves and a 3.24 ERA in 51 appearances (three starts) with Double-A Harrisburg and Triple-A Syracuse...following the season, pitched for the Leones del Escogido of the Dominican Baseball League, going 2-0 with six saves and a 0.71 ERA in 12 relief appearances (12.2IP, 1ER)...**2008:** Combined at six different stops to go 8-7 with a 5.78 ERA in 25 games (19 starts) with Double-A Reading, Single-A Clearwater, the GCL Nationals, Single-A Hagerstown, Single-A Potomac and Double-A Harrisburg...began the season in the Phillies organization before being released on 6/12...was signed as a free agent by Washington on 6/18 and placed on the disabled list on 6/22 with a right shoulder strain...immediately began a rehab assignment, going 1-0 with a 4.50 ERA in two appearances (one start) with the GCL Nationals before being reinstated from the D.L. on 6/30...**2007:** Made his first Opening Day roster, appearing with the Phillies...made his Major League debut on 4/8 at Florida, starting and recording the loss (5.0IP, 8H, 5ER, 1BB, 2K, 1HR)...was his only Major League appearance in 2007...was optioned to Triple-A Ottawa following the start, where he went 1-9 with a 6.05 ERA in 13 starts before being transferred to Double-A Reading in June...went 5-3 with a 4.84 ERA in 10 starts with Reading, tossing at least 6.0 innings in seven of those starts (including each of his first five)...was designated for assignment on 8/10 and outrighted to Reading on 8/13...in 23 overall minor league starts, went 6-12 with a 5.53 ERA...had right shoulder surgery on 9/19...**2006:** Combined to go 16-6 with a 2.82 ERA in 24 appearances (23 starts) with Single-A Clearwater and Double-A Reading...tied for second in wins among all minor league pitchers...tossed a seven-hit shutout on 7/4 w/ Reading vs. Altoona (9.0IP, 3BB, 5K)...won Eastern League "Pitcher of the Week" honors on 8/5, going 2-0 with a 1.20 ERA...tied for the EL lead in complete games (3) and ranked fifth with 1.93BB/9.0IP...pitch for Team USA in the Olympic qualifier from 8/12-9/20 in Cuba, going 2-0...was leading all professional pitchers with 16 wins when he joined Team USA...following the season, pitched for Peoria in the Arizona Fall League...**2005:** Spent the season with Single-A Clearwater, going 4-14 with a 5.54 ERA...allowed 3R in 4.1IP on 4/9 vs. Dunedin in his first appearance since 8/30/03...lost five consecutive starts from 5/21-6/16...**2004:** Missed the entire season recovering from "Tommy John" surgery on his right elbow, performed in October 2003 by Dr. James Andrews...**2003:** Opened the season with Single-A Lakewood, going 1-5 with a 3.99 ERA...was placed on the disabled list on 5/29 with a right elbow strain...had two separate rehab stints with the GCL Phillies before making one appearance with Lakewood on 8/30...**2002:** Made his professional debut with the GCL Phillies going 3-2 with a 2.10 ERA in eight starts...did not allow a home run in 34.1IP...held opponents to a .174 batting average...earned the win in relief in the clinching game of the GCL championship...following the season, was ranked by *Baseball America* as the 14th-best prospect in the GCL and the 10th-best prospect in the Phillies organization...**PERSONAL:** Full name is Zachary Ernest Segovia...graduated from Forney High School (Tex.)...pitched for the U.S. Junior National Team in the summer of 2001, striking out 15 batters in 8.0IP for Team USA (0ER)...was originally selected by the Phillies in the second round of the 2002 First-Year Player Draft.

YEAR	CLUB	CLASS	W-L	ERA	G	GS	CG	SHO	SV	IP	H	R	ER	HR	HB	BB	SO	WP	BK
2002	GCL Phillies	R	3-2	2.10	8	8	0	0	0	34.1	21	11	8	0	3	3	30	1	0
2003	GCL Phillies	R	0-1	4.00	5	4	0	0	0	9.0	8	5	4	0	1	0	6	0	0
	Lakewood	A	1-5	3.99	11	10	0	0	0	49.2	63	25	22	2	2	14	27	2	0
2004					Did Not Pitch - Injured														
2005	Clearwater	A	4-14	5.54	27	27	0	0	0	144.2	168	98	89	18	17	48	83	9	1
2006	Clearwater	A	5-1	2.19	7	7	0	0	0	49.1	39	14	12	2	5	12	41	1	0
	Reading	AA	11-5	3.11	17	16	3	1	0	107.0	90	45	37	8	8	24	75	5	0
2007	PHILLIES	MAJ	0-1	9.00	1	1	0	0	0	5.0	8	5	5	1	0	1	2	0	0
	Ottawa	AAA	1-9	6.05	13	13	1	0	0	77.1	99	55	52	8	2	28	22	4	0
	Reading	AA	5-3	4.84	10	10	0	0	0	57.2	65	34	31	4	5	22	30	1	0
2008	Reading	AA	0-1	14.40	4	1	0	0	0	5.0	7	9	8	1	0	6	1	1	0
	Clearwater	A	1-3	5.35	7	7	0	0	0	38.2	50	26	23	6	0	12	32	0	0
	GCL Nationals	R	1-0	4.50	2	1	0	0	0	6.0	5	3	3	0	1	1	6	1	0
	Hagerstown	A	0-1	7.20	1	1	0	0	0	5.0	8	4	4	0	1	0	3	0	0
	Potomac	A	2-1	2.70	3	3	0	0	0	16.2	17	8	5	2	2	3	13	0	0
	Harrisburg	AA	4-1	6.45	8	6	0	0	0	37.2	50	29	27	5	1	14	24	1	0
2009	Harrisburg	AA	1-3	3.68	24	3	0	0	1	44.0	57	19	18	2	3	19	39	1	0
	Syracuse	AAA	2-2	2.54	27	0	0	0	5	28.1	18	8	8	1	4	8	27	0	0
	WASHINGTON	MAJ	1-0	7.84	8	0	0	0	0	10.1	11	10	9	1	0	6	4	1	0
Minor League Totals			**41-51**	**4.45**	**174**	**117**	**4**	**1**	**6**	**710.1**	**765**	**393**	**351**	**59**	**55**	**214**	**459**	**27**	**1**
Major League Totals			**1-1**	**8.22**	**9**	**1**	**0**	**0**	**0**	**15.1**	**19**	**15**	**14**	**2**	**0**	**7**	**6**	**1**	**0**

SHIVE, Andy – RHP

HT: 6-5; **WT:** 225; **B:** R; **T:** R; **BORN:** 11/5/85 in Bakersfield, Calif.; **RESIDES:** Bakersfield, Calif.; **COLLEGE:** Azusa Pacific University; **OBTAINED:** Selected by the Yankees in the 35th round of the 2008 First-Year Player Draft; **M.L. SVC:** 0.000; **CAREER NOTES: 2009:** Underwent "Tommy John" surgery on 4/27 and missed the season...**2008:** Made his professional debut, going 9-2 with a 1.96 ERA in 22 appearances (one start) with short-season Single-A Staten Island...led the league in wins, all coming in relief...won each of his final nine decisions over his last 17 appearances of the season, beginning 6/27...pitched to a 1.27 ERA (35.1IP, 5ER) over the stretch, allowing runs in just four of the outings...named to the New York-Penn League All-Star staff...made his first professional start on 8/4 at Brooklyn, allowing 5H and 1ER in 3.2IP (1BB, 5K)...**PERSONAL:** Attended Azusa Pacific University, going 6-2 with a 3.95 ERA over 12 appearances (10 starts) during his senior year in 2008.

YEAR	CLUB	CLASS	W-L	ERA	G	GS	CG	SHO	SV	IP	H	R	ER	HR	HB	BB	SO	WP	BK
2008	Staten Island	SS-A	9-2	1.96	22	1	0	0	0	46.0	42	13	10	0	2	17	50	1	0
2009						Did Not Pitch - Injured													
Minor League Totals			**9-2**	**1.96**	**22**	**1**	**0**	**0**	**0**	**46.0**	**42**	**13**	**10**	**0**	**2**	**17**	**50**	**1**	**0**

SMITH, Kevin – INF

HT: 6-1; **WT:** 215; **B:** L; **T:** R; **BORN:** 1/15/84 in Whittier, Calif.; **RESIDES:** La Mirada, Calif.; **COLLEGE:** University of Oklahoma; **OBTAINED:** Selected by the Yankees in the 39th round of the 2006 First-Year Player Draft; **M.L. SVC:** 0.000; **CAREER NOTES: 2009**: Combined to hit .287 with 49R, 22 doubles, 3HR and 43RBI in 109 games with Double-A Trenton and Single-A Tampa ...was transferred to Tampa on 6/20 where he hit .317 with 30R, 15 doubles, 1HR and 29RBI in 63 games...recorded six multi-hit contests in a seven-game span from 7/13-22, batting .406 (13-for-32) with 6R, 1 double, 1 triple and 6RBI during the stretch...made his second career relief appearance on 8/29 vs. Brevard County, tossing 1.2 scoreless innings (1BB) in the 9-2 loss...**2008:** Spent the season at Single-A Tampa, batting .290 with 35 doubles, 5HR and 62RBI in 124 games...led the team in games, average, hits (129), doubles and RBI...ranked second in the Florida State League in doubles and ninth in average...led all FSL first basemen with a .994 fielding percentage (6E, 1,060TC)...**2007:** With Single-A Charleston, batted .297 with 12 doubles, 3 triples, 8HR and 52RBI in 83 games at 1B, 3B and DH...hit .315 (8-for-254) against right-handers and .190 (8-for-42) vs. lefties...was named South Atlantic League "Player of the Week" for the period of 7/15-21, hitting .478 (11-for-23) with 7R, 5 doubles, 1 triple, 1HR, 5RBI and 7BB...**2006:** In first professional season, batted .277 in 43 games with the short-season Single-A Staten Island Yankees...made an emergency pitching appearance on 8/23 at Aberdeen, allowing 4ER in 1.0IP...**PERSONAL:** Full name is Kevin Daniel Smith...received All-Big 12 honorable mention in 2005 at Oklahoma...at Cypress CC, garnered Southern California All-America and first team All-Orange Empire Conference honors in 2004 before transferring...was a three-year letterman at La Mirada High School and was named to first team all-league three straight years...earned state tournament MVP honors after batting .539 (7-for-13) with three doubles and 7RBI over four games...previously drafted by the Yankees in 2003.

YEAR	CLUB	CLASS	AVG	G	AB	R	H	2B	3B	HR	RBI	SH	SF	HB	BB	SO	SB	CS	E	SLUG	OBP
2006	Staten Island	SS-A	.277	43	155	28	43	12	1	2	21	0	3	3	5	30	1	0	0	.406	.307
2007	Charleston	A	.297	83	296	43	88	23	3	8	52	0	1	5	35	58	1	1	2	.476	.380
2008	Tampa	A	.290	124	445	51	129	35	1	5	62	0	4	2	32	93	7	5	6	.407	.337
2009	Trenton	AA	.247	48	158	19	39	7	1	2	14	0	0	1	10	44	0	1	5	.342	.296
	Tampa	A	.317	63	218	30	69	15	2	1	29	1	4	2	19	48	4	0	0	.417	.370
Minor League Totals			**.289**	**361**	**1272**	**171**	**368**	**92**	**8**	**18**	**178**	**1**	**12**	**13**	**101**	**273**	**13**	**7**	**13**	**.417**	**.345**

SNYDER, Justin – INF

HT: 5-9; **WT:** 190; **B:** L; **T:** R; **BORN:** 4/8/86 in El Cajon, Calif.; **RESIDES:** El Cajon, Calif.; **COLLEGE:** University of San Diego; **OBTAINED:** Selected by the Yankees in the 21st round of the 2007 First-Year Player Draft; **M.L. SVC:** 0.000; **CAREER NOTES: 2009**: Spent the season with Double-A Trenton, batting .195 with 25R, 9 doubles, 3HR and 29RBI in 94 games...made just nine errors after making 27E the previous season...**2008:** Batted .288 with 33 doubles, 7HR and 59RBI in 132 games with Single-A Tampa...led the team with 68BB, ranking third in the South Atlantic League...named to the midseason All-Star Team...led all SAL second basemen in games (124), total chances (634), putouts (216), assists (393) and double plays (77)...also saw time at 1B, 3B, SS, CF and DH...collected 12H in 17AB over a four-game stretch from 7/18-21...**2007:** Made his professional debut with short-season Single-A Staten Island, batting .335 with 20 doubles, 1 triple, 5HR and 40RBI in 73 games...saw time at 2B, 3B, SS, CF and DH...led the New York-Penn League in runs (68), hits (87) and on-base percentage (.459), ranked second in walks (58), tied for third with a team-high 20 doubles and fifth with a team-high .335 average...scored at least one run in each of his first six games and 23 of his first 28 games (27R total)...compiled a 10-game hitting streak from 7/9-20 with seven multi-hit games during the span (.488, 20-for-41, 2HR, 12RBI)...on 8/6 vs. Hudson Valley, hit a two-out, two-run "walk-off" home run in the bottom of the ninth inning...started at 3B in the NYPL All-Star Game on 8/14 in Fishkill...named the starting shortstop on *Baseball America's* Short-Season All-Star Team...**PERSONAL:** Full name is Justin Richard Snyder...played three seasons at University of San Diego, batting .326 with 44 doubles, 11HR, 100RBI, 112BB and 86K in his college career...led the Toreros in batting (.352) and doubles (21) in 2007, recording the second-most hits (89) and doubles in a single-season in school history...lettered in baseball and football at El Capitan (Calif.) High School...won back-to-back baseball conference championships as a junior and senior, garnering prep All-American honors in senior season.

YEAR	CLUB	CLASS	AVG	G	AB	R	H	2B	3B	HR	RBI	SH	SF	HB	BB	SO	SB	CS	E	SLUG	OBP
2007	Staten Island	SS-A	.335	73	260	68	87	20	1	5	40	0	5	6	58	50	10	10	13	.477	.459
2008	Charleston	A	.288	132	504	77	145	33	3	7	59	4	6	2	68	95	7	1	27	.407	.371
2009	Trenton	AA	.195	94	262	25	51	9	0	3	29	4	1	2	29	49	1	2	9	.263	.279
Minor League Totals			**.276**	**299**	**1026**	**170**	**283**	**62**	**4**	**15**	**128**	**8**	**12**	**10**	**155**	**194**	**18**	**13**	**49**	**.388**	**.372**

SOLBACH, Michael – RHP

HT: 6-3; **WT:** 185; **B:** R; **T:** R; **BORN:** 7/31/85 in Lynchburg, Va.; **RESIDES:** Aldic, Va.; **COLLEGE:** Liberty University; **OBTAINED:** Signed by the Yankees as a free-agent on 8/8/07; **M.L. SVC:** 0.000; **CAREER NOTES: 2009:** Went 2-3 with a 3.92 ERA in 24 games (two starts) with short-season Single-A Staten Island...allowed just 1ER in each of his two starts...earned his first save in his only chance of the season on 7/18 vs. State College, tossing 1.0 scoreless innings...**2008:** Made his professional debut, combining for a 1.29 ERA in five appearances (one start) with the GCL Yankees and Single-A Tampa...opened the season on the disabled list with a right elbow strain...made four scoreless relief rehab appearances at the GCL Yankees before being activated and assigned to Tampa on 8/29...made one start with Tampa, allowing 1ER in 2.0IP...**PERSONAL:** Full name is Michael Thomas Solbach...played baseball for three years at Liberty University, going 22-10 with a 4.03 ERA...tied for fifth-most career wins in school history...originally selected by the Arizona Diamondbacks in the 19th round of the 2007 First-Year Player Draft but his contract was voided...was also selected by the Diamondbacks in the 48th round of the 2006 First-Year Player Draft.

YEAR	CLUB	CLASS	W-L	ERA	G	GS	CG	SHO	SV	IP	H	R	ER	HR	HB	BB	SO	WP	BK
2008	GCL Yankees	R	0-0	0.00	4	0	0	0	0	5.0	5	0	0	0	0	2	6	1	0
	Tampa	A	0-0	4.50	1	1	0	0	0	2.0	1	1	1	0	0	0	0	0	0
2009	Staten Island	SS-A	2-3	3.92	24	2	0	0	1	39.0	40	27	17	2	4	22	34	6	2
Minor League Totals			**2-3**	**3.52**	**29**	**3**	**0**	**0**	**1**	**46.0**	**46**	**28**	**18**	**2**	**4**	**24**	**40**	**7**	**2**

SOSA, Eduardo Jose – OF

HT: 5-11; **WT:** 155; **B:** L; **T:** L; **BORN:** 3/14/91 in Bolivar, Venezuela; **RESIDES:** Bolivar, Venezuela; **OBTAINED:** Signed by the Yankees as a non-drafted free agent on 7/2/07; **M.L. SVC:** 0.000; **CAREER NOTES: 2009**: Hit .200 with 2HR and 14RBI in 49 games with the GCL Yankees...**2008:** In his first professional season, hit .315 with 18 doubles, 4HR and 37RBI in 63 games with the DSL Yankees 2...finished the season tied for third in the DSL with 80H...recorded at least 1H in 25 of his first 27G (.358, 39-for-109)...batted .319 (68-for-213) against right-handed pitchers, including 25 extra-base hits (17 doubles, five triples, 3HR).

YEAR	CLUB	CLASS	AVG	G	AB	R	H	2B	3B	HR	RBI	SH	SF	HP	BB	SO	SB	CS	E	SLUG	OBP
2008	DSL Yankees 2	R	.315	63	254	48	80	18	5	4	37	0	2	6	34	54	30	8	1	.472	.405
2009	GCL Yankees	R	.200	49	165	24	33	7	1	2	14	1	2	3	16	47	11	4	4	.291	.280
Minor League Totals			**.270**	**112**	**419**	**72**	**113**	**25**	**6**	**6**	**51**	**1**	**4**	**9**	**50**	**101**	**41**	**12**	**5**	**.401**	**.357**

STONEBURNER, Graham – RHP

HT: 6-1; **WT:** 190; **B:** R; **T:** R; **BORN:** 9/29/87 in Richmond, Va.; **RESIDES:** Richmond, Va.; **COLLEGE:** Clemson University; **OBTAINED:** Selected by the Yankees in the 14th round of the 2009 First-Year Player Draft; **M.L. SVC:** 0.000; **CAREER NOTES: 2009:** Made just one relief appearance with short-season Single-A Staten Island, tossing 1.0 scoreless inning and striking out two.

YEAR	CLUB	CLASS	W-L	ERA	G	GS	CG	SHO	SV	IP	H	R	ER	HR	HB	BB	SO	WP	BK
2009	Staten Island	SS-A	0-0	0.00	1	0	0	0	0	1.0	1	0	0	0	0	0	2	0	0

SUBLETT, Damon – OF

HT: 6-1; **WT:** 190; **B:** L; **T:** R; **BORN:** 9/22/85 in Wichita, Kan.; **RESIDES:** Wichita, Kan.; **COLLEGE:** Wichita State University; **OBTAINED:** Selected by the Yankees in the seventh round of the 2007 First-Year Player Draft; **M.L. SVC:** 0.000; **CAREER NOTES: 2009**: Spent the season with Single-A Tampa, batting .270 with 68R, 24 doubles, 11 triples, 4HR and 41RBI in 114 games...led the team in triples, ranked second in doubles, tied for third in RBI and ranked third in hits (107)...switched positions from second base to the outfield on 6/16, seeing time in center field and left field...made just two errors as an outfielder (both coming in Game 2 of a doubleheader on 7/10 vs. Daytona), while making 9E as an infielder...**2008:** Was limited to 42 games with Single-A Tampa, batting .263 with 22R, 6 doubles, 2HR and 11RBI before being placed on the disabled list on 5/30 for the remainder of the season with a sprained left ankle...played for the Waikiki BeachBoys in the Hawaii Winter Baseball League following the season, batting .253 (19-for-75) with 15R, 6 doubles, 2HR and 18RBI in 20 games...**2007:** Made his professional debut with short-season Single-A Staten Island, batting .326 with 19 doubles, 3 triples, 8HR, 5RBI and 10SB in 68 games at 2B and DH...led the New York-Penn League in RBI and sacrifice flies (9), ranked second in slugging percentage (.531), tied for third in extra-base hits (30), fourth in walks (43) and on-base percentage (.426) and fifth in total bases (127)...his average ranked sixth in the league and led all minor league second baseman...led the team with 8HR...played in 65 games at 2B and was involved in 40 double plays, both ranking second among league second basemen...batted .280 (49-for-175) in prior to the All-Star break then hit at a .453 clip following the break (29-for-64)...batted from the third spot in the lineup the entire season and was a .379 hitter when leading off an inning (11-for-29, 3 doubles, 7BB)...was 4-for-7 (.571) with the bases loaded, including his first career grand slam on 7/17 at Mahoning Valley...hit safely in a season-high 10 straight games from 7/3-17...played ball with the Harwich Mariners of the Cape Cod League in the summer of 2006 and was invited to play in the Team USA trials...**PERSONAL:** Full name is Damon Alexander Sublett...studied psychology at Wichita State...played on the baseball team for three seasons, appearing primarily at 2B but also pitching in relief...as a sophomore in 2006, was named the Joe Carter Missouri Valley Conference "Player of the Year" and a semi-finalist for the Dick Howser Trophy after leading the conference in batting average (.394) and ranking third in home runs (10)...was named MVC "Freshman of the Year" in 2005 and first team Freshman All-American...was an All-State selection in 2002 and 2004 with Northwest (Kan.) High School.

YEAR	CLUB	CLASS	AVG	G	AB	R	H	2B	3B	HR	RBI	SH	SF	HB	BB	SO	SB	CS	E	SLUG	OBP
2007	Staten Island	SS-A	.326	68	239	43	78	19	3	8	53	4	9	5	43	47	10	4	8	.531	.426
2008	Tampa	A	.263	42	160	22	42	6	3	2	11	1	1	2	24	44	3	1	12	.375	.364
2009	Tampa	A	.270	114	397	68	107	24	11	4	41	5	2	4	65	93	11	7	11	.416	.376
Minor League Totals			**.285**	**224**	**796**	**133**	**227**	**49**	**17**	**14**	**105**	**10**	**12**	**11**	**132**	**184**	**24**	**12**	**31**	**.442**	**.389**

SUTTLE, Bradley – INF

HT: 6-2; **WT:** 215; **B:** S; **T:** R; **BORN:** 1/24/86 in Boerne, Tex.; **RESIDES:** Boerne, Tex.; **COLLEGE:** University of Texas; **OBTAINED:** Selected by the Yankees in the fourth round of the 2007 First-Year Player Draft; **M.L. SVC:** 0.000; **CAREER NOTES: 2009:** Missed the entire season on the disabled list rehabbing from shoulder surgery performed on 9/30/08...**2008:** Batted .271 with 63R, 23 doubles, 11HR and 44RBI in 96 games with Single-A Charleston...was placed on the disabled list from 4/13-24 with a left hip flexor strain...appeared in four games (going 2-for-12) before being placed back on the disabled list until 6/1 with the same injury...following the season, was named the South Atlantic League's "Best Defensive Third Baseman" in *Baseball America's* Best Tools Survey, as well as the publication's 10th-best prospect in the organization and the Yankees' "Best Hitter for Average"...**2007:** Appeared in three games with the GCL Yankees, batting .125 (1-for-8) with 1RBI in his first professional action...entered the 2007 draft ranked as the 34th-best prospect and fifth-best third baseman by *Baseball America* as well as the top pure hitter in college...**PERSONAL:** Played two seasons at the University of Texas, earning All-American honors in 2007 as well as first team All-Big 12 and a spot on the COSIDA Academic All-American team...was the Longhorns' 2007 co-MVP after ranking second on the squad in batting average (.359), hits (84), home runs (12) and RBI (68)...also named an ABCA/Rawlings All-American second team...entered the year one of the top 50 players on the Dick Howser watch list...was named to the 2006 Freshman All-American first team.

YEAR	CLUB	CLASS	AVG	G	AB	R	H	2B	3B	HR	RBI	SH	SF	HB	BB	SO	SB	CS	E	SLUG	OBP
2007	GCL Yankees	R	.125	3	8	1	1	0	0	0	1	0	0	0	1	2	0	0	1	.125	.222
2008	Charleston	A	.271	96	377	63	102	23	7	11	44	0	4	2	45	93	2	1	17	.456	.348
2009										Did Not Pitch – Injured											
Minor League Totals			**.268**	**99**	**385**	**64**	**103**	**23**	**7**	**11**	**45**	**0**	**4**	**2**	**46**	**95**	**2**	**1**	**18**	**.449**	**.346**

TALERICO, Joseph – OF

HT: 6-0; **WT:** 195; **B:** R; **T:** R; **BORN:** 11/13/89 in El Ceybo, D.R.; **RESIDES:** La Romana, D.R.; **COLLEGE:** Brookdale CC; **OBTAINED:** Selected by the Yankees in the 21st round of the 2009 First-Year Player Draft; **M.L. SVC:** 0.000; **CAREER NOTES:** Will be making his professional debut in 2010.

YEAR	CLUB	CLASS	AVG	G	AB	R	H	2B	3B	HR	RBI	SH	SF	HP	BB	SO	SB	CS	E	SLUG	OBP
NO PROFESSIONAL STATS																					

TAPIA, Erick – LHP

HT: 6-1; **WT:** 193; **B:** L; **T:** L; **BORN:** 9/6/87 in Santo Domingo, D.R.; **RESIDES:** Santo Domingo, D.R.; **OBTAINED:** Signed by the Yankees as a non-drafted free agent on 11/23/05; **M.L. SVC:** 0.000; **CAREER NOTES: 2009**: Made 13 starts with the DSL Yankees 2, going 3-1 with a 1.36 ERA...held opponents without an earned run in nine of his 13 outings...**2008:** Appeared in 11 games (seven starts) for the DSL Yankees 2, going 1-0 with a 4.58 ERA...opponents batted .237 (32-for-135), including a .111 (2-for-18) batting average from left-handed hitters...**2007:** Made his professional debut with the DSL Yankees 1, going 1-2 with a 5.06 ERA in 11 appearances (seven starts)...was 1-1 with a 2.70 ERA in his seven starts and 0-1 with an 11.42 ERA in 11 relief appearances...did not allow a first-inning run...did not allow an earned run in his first four starts (13.0IP).

YEAR	CLUB	CLASS	W-L	ERA	G	GS	CG	SHO	SV	IP	H	R	ER	HR	HB	BB	SO	WP	BK
2007	DSL Yankees 1	R	1-2	5.06	11	7	0	0	0	32.0	39	25	18	0	2	28	21	1	1
2008	DSL Yankees 2	R	1-0	4.58	11	7	0	0	0	37.1	32	20	19	0	5	17	30	3	0
2009	DSL Yankees 2	R	3-1	1.36	13	13	0	0	0	53.0	33	11	8	1	0	13	42	3	1
Minor League Totals			**5-3**	**3.31**	**35**	**27**	**0**	**0**	**0**	**122.1**	**104**	**56**	**45**	**1**	**7**	**58**	**93**	**7**	**2**

TATIS, Gabriel – RHP

HT: 6-0; **WT:** 180; **B:** R; **T:** R; **BORN:** 5/18/85 in Santo Domingo, D.R.; **RESIDES:** Santo Domingo, D.R.; **OBTAINED:** Signed by the Yankees as a non-drafted free agent on 2/21/06; **M.L. SVC:** 0.000; **CAREER NOTES: 2009:** Went 5-2 with a 4.25 ERA in 21 combined relief appearances between GCL Yankees and Single-A Charleston...opened the season with the GCL squad, allowing 1ER in six relief appearances before being promoted to Charleston on 7/15 where he made 15 relief outings (3-2, 5.68 ERA)...allowed just 1ER over his final four appearances (9.0IP)...**2008:** Appeared in 11 games out of the bullpen with the GCL Yankees and went 1-2 with a 3.71 ERA in 17.0IP...**2007:** Combined at both DSL teams to go 2-1 with a 2.53 ERA in 20 relief appearances...did not allow a home run in 32.0IP...**2006:** In first professional season, posted an 0-2 record and 6.00 ERA in eight games (three starts) for the DSL Yankees 2.

YEAR	CLUB	CLASS	W-L	ERA	G	GS	CG	SHO	SV	IP	H	R	ER	HR	HB	BB	SO	WP	BK
2006	DSL Yankees 2	R	0-2	6.00	8	3	0	0	0	21.0	23	15	14	1	1	12	17	3	0
2007	DSL Yankees 2	R	1-1	3.14	8	0	0	0	0	14.1	10	6	5	0	1	3	17	2	0
	DSL Yankees 1	R	1-0	2.04	12	0	0	0	1	17.2	19	5	4	0	2	9	16	3	0
2008	GCL Yankees	R	1-2	3.71	11	0	0	0	0	17.0	20	16	7	1	0	12	18	2	0
2009	GCL Yankees	R	2-0	0.84	6	0	0	0	3	10.2	10	2	1	1	0	1	14	2	2
	Charleston	A	3-2	5.68	15	0	0	0	0	25.1	25	16	16	2	2	16	20	3	0
Minor League Totals			**8-7**	**3.99**	**60**	**3**	**0**	**0**	**4**	**106.0**	**107**	**60**	**47**	**5**	**6**	**53**	**102**	**15**	**2**

TAVERAS, Damian – INF/C

HT: 6-1; **WT:** 180; **B:** R; **T:** R; **BORN:** 11/28/89 in Santo Domingo, D.R.; **RESIDES:** Santo Domingo, D.R.; **OBTAINED:** Signed by the Yankees as a non-drafted free agent on 7/29/06; **M.L. SVC:** 0.000; **CAREER NOTES: 2009**: Batted .396 with 13 doubles, 2HR and 22RBI in 30 games with the DSL Yankees 1...hit safely in 25 of his 30 contests...**2008:** Batted .229 with 24R and 19RBI in 43 games with the DSL Yankees 1...recorded 12 extra-base hits (9 doubles, 2 triples and 1HR)...**2007:** Made his professional debut with the DSL Yankees 2, hitting .207 with 22R and 16RBI in 55 games.

YEAR	CLUB	CLASS	AVG	G	AB	R	H	2B	3B	HR	RBI	SH	SF	HP	BB	SO	SB	CS	E	SLUG	OBP
2007	DSL Yankees 2	R	.207	55	193	22	40	6	1	1	16	0	1	6	22	50	0	2	31	.264	.306
2008	DSL Yankees 1	R	.229	43	166	24	38	9	2	1	19	0	0	7	19	38	4	2	10	.325	.333
2009	DSL Yankees 1	R	.396	30	106	17	42	13	0	2	22	1	2	6	12	16	1	3	10	.575	.476
Minor League Totals			**.258**	**128**	**465**	**63**	**120**	**28**	**3**	**4**	**57**	**1**	**3**	**19**	**53**	**104**	**5**	**7**	**51**	**.357**	**.356**

TEJEDA, Isaias – C

HT: 6-1; **WT**: 195; **B**: R; **T**: R; **BORN**: 10/28/91 in Santo Domingo, D.R.; **RESIDES**: Santo Domingo, D.R.; **OBTAINED**: Signed by the Yankees as a non-drafted free agent on 9/3/09; **M.L. SVC**: 0.000; **CAREER NOTES**: Will be making his professional debut in 2010.

YEAR CLUB	CLASS	AVG	G	AB	R	H	2B	3B	HR	RBI	SH	SF	HP	BB	SO	SB	CS	E	SLUG	OBP
NO PROFESSIONAL RECORD																				

THAMES, Marcus– OF

NON-ROSTER INVITEE

HT: 6-2; **WT:** 220; **B:** R; **T:** R; **BORN:** 3/6/77 in Louisville, Miss.; **RESIDES:** Starkville, Miss.; **COLLEGE:** East Central Community College (Miss.); **OBTAINED:** Signed by the Yankees as a free agent on 2/8/10; **M.L. SVC:** 5.108; **CAREER NOTES:** Owns a career .243 (376-for-1,529) batting average with 75 doubles, 101HR and 261RBI in 522 games over parts of eight Major League seasons with the Yankees (2002), Rangers (2003) and Tigers (2004-09)...since 2006, has averaged 1HR every 14.52AB, marking the fourth-best ratio in the American League over the stretch (min. 1,100AB)...in his career, has made 252 appearances in LF (219 starts), 67 in RF (47 starts) and 44 at 1B (34 starts)...**2009:** Batted .252 with 13HR and 36RBI in 87 games with Detroit (55G/50GS at DH, 20G/17GS in LF and 2G/0GS at 1B)...hit .272 (34-for-125) with 9HR in 38 games prior to the All-Star break and .233 (31-for-133) with 4HR in 49 games following the break...was placed on the 15-day disabled list from 4/19-6/7 with a left rib cage strain...in 12 rehab games with Triple-A Toledo, hit .245 with 2HR and 6RBI...recorded his eighth career multi-homer game on 6/19 vs. Milwaukee, going 2-for-4 with 2HR and 4RBI...established a career high with four hits on 7/12 vs. Cleveland, going 4-for-4 with 3R, 1 double and 1RBI...hit his 100th career home run on 8/9 vs. Minnesota, a fourth-inning solo-HR off Scott Baker...**2008:** Hit .241 with 12 doubles, 25HR and 56RBI in 103 games with the Tigers...ranked second on the team in homers...recorded three multi-HR games (all 2HR)—5/28 at Los Angeles-AL, 6/16 at San Francisco and 9/5 at Minnesota...recorded eight straight home runs (accounting for all of his hits) from 6/7-17, marking the longest such streak in the Majors since St. Louis' Mark McGwire (11 straight HR in 2001)—credit: *Elias*...homered in five straight games from 6/13-17 to match a Tigers record, homering six times during the span...was named Tigers "Player of the Month" for June after batting .306 (22-for-72) with 3 doubles, 10HR and 16RBI in 22 games, ranking second in the AL in home runs during the month...hit his sixth career grand slam on 9/14 at Chicago-AL...**2007:** Hit .242 with 15 doubles, 18HR and 54RBI in 86 games with Detroit...batted .310 (27-for-87) off left-handed pitchers and .209 (38-for-182) off righthanders...hit .265 (49-for-185) with 17HR in 64 games before the All-Star Break...hit .206 (27-for-131) with 8HR in 39 games after the break...batted .315 (23-for-73) with RISP and .400 (4-for-5) with 2HR and 13RBI with the bases loaded...made his first career appearance at 1B on 4/11 at Baltimore...hit his third career grand slam and tied a career high with 5RBI on 7/6 vs. Boston...was placed on the 15-day disabled list from 7/19-8/9 with a left hamstring pull...hit the fourth grand slam of his career in his second game back from the D.L...**2006:** Hit a career-high 26HR, batting .256 with 20 doubles and 60RBI in 110 games with Detroit...batted .297 (60-for-202) in 61 pre-All-Star games and .199 (29-for-146) after the break...hit safely in a career-high 11 straight games from 6/8-18, batting .318 (14-for-44) with 3 doubles, 4HR and 7RBI during the stretch...was named Tigers "Player of the Month" for June after batting .309 (30-for-97) with 18R, 8 doubles, 8HR and 20RBI in 26 games, tying for fourth in the AL in homers during the month...tied his career high with 5RBI on 7/16 vs. Kansas City...batted .238 (5-for-21) in eight postseason games...**2005:** Hit .196 with 7HR and 16RBI in 38 games with Detroit...was recalled from Triple-A Toledo on 4/9 and started in LF that night vs. Cleveland, going 1-for-4 with a third-inning grand slam off Jake Westbrook, the second grand slam of his career...hit .056 (1-for-18) with 10K over a seven-game stretch from 5/25-6/12, including a career-high 4K on 6/12 at Colorado...was optioned back to Toledo on 6/14...was recalled again on 9/16...batted .340 with 22HR and 56RBI in 73 overall games with Toledo...was named the International League "Player of the Week" for the period from 7/4-10, batting .539 (14-for-26) with 12R, 4HR and 13RBI in seven games...batted .407 (11-for-27) with 3HR and 10RBI during the International League playoffs...**2004:** Began the season with Triple-A Toledo, batting .329 with 21 doubles, 24HR and 59RBI in 64 games...was named TOPPS International League "Player of the Month" and Tigers "Minor League Player of the Month" for May, batting .343 (34-for-99) with 25R, 10 doubles, 9HR and 27RBI in 27 games, tying for second in the league in RBI and ranking third in homers...had his contract purchased by Detroit on 6/22...at the time of his promotion, was leading the IL in home runs (24), runs scored (57), extra-base hits (46), RBI (59) and slugging percentage (.735)...in 61 games with the Tigers, batted .255 with 12 doubles, 10HR and 33RBI...drove in a career-high five runs on 7/25 at Chicago-AL, hitting his first career grand slam off Mike Jackson...recorded his first career multi-homer game on 10/2 vs. Tampa Bay, becoming the 11th Tigers player to reach double digits in home runs in 2004 to establish a Major League record...was signed by the Tigers as a minor league free agent on 12/7/03...**2003:** Combined to bat .273 with 19 doubles, 4HR and 35RBI in 70 games with Triple-A Columbus and Triple-A Oklahoma...began the season with Columbus, batting .278 with 15 doubles, 2HR and 28RBI in 52 games...was traded from the Yankees to the Texas Rangers in exchange for Ruben Sierra on 6/6/03 and assigned to Oklahoma...in 18 games, hit .258 with 3 doubles, 2HR and 7RBI...was recalled by the Rangers on 7/16...homered in his Rangers debut on 7/17 at Tampa Bay...jammed his right shoulder making a diving catch on 8/23 at Chicago-AL...appeared in only 11 games through the end of the season due to the injury, batting .150 (3-for-20)...did not have an at-bat after 9/7...**2002:** Hit .207 with 13HR and 45RBI in 107 games with Triple-A Columbus...was recalled by the Yankees on 6/10 and made his Major League debut that day vs. Arizona, starting in RF...hit a two-run home run off Randy Johnson in his first Major League at-bat...was optioned back to Columbus for the remainder of the season on 6/27...**2001:** Batted .321 with 43 doubles, 31HR and 97RBI in 139 games with Double-A Norwich...earned Eastern League All-Star honors and was named co-winner of the Yankees' Kevin Lawn Award as the organization's minor league "Player of the Year"...led the EL in runs scored (114), total bases (311), extra-base hits (78), doubles, on-base percentage (.410) and slugging percentage (.598)...finished second in the league in batting average, hits (167) and home runs and third in RBI...tied for the lead among all minor leaguers in extra-base hits and finished third in runs scored and total bases...established a Norwich single-season record in home runs...named EL "Player of the Week" from 7/2-8, hitting .355 (11-for-31) with 9R, 5 doubles, 5HR and 12RBI...was selected to *Baseball America*'s Double-A All-Star team...following the season, played for Peoria in the Arizona Fall League...was named the seventh-best prospect in the Yankees organization and eighth-best prospect in the Eastern League by *Baseball America* following the season...**2000:** Hit .241 with 30 doubles, 15HR and 79RBI in 131 games with Double-A Norwich, ranking second among all Yankees minor leaguers in RBI...**1999:** Combined to bat .237 with 18 doubles, 15HR and 64RBI in 120 games with Double-A Norwich and Single-A Tampa...following the season, hit .361 with 18R, 10 doubles, 4HR and 19RBI for Rancho Cucamonga in the California Fall League...**1998:** Hit .284 with 18 doubles, 11HR and 59RBI in 122 games with Single-A Tampa...batted .269 (7-for-26) with 1 double, 2HR and 4RBI in seven playoff games...**1997:** Made his professional debut, combining to bat .341 with 18 doubles, 7HR and 38RBI in 61 games with the GCL Yankees and Single-A Greensboro...made his debut with the GCL Yankees, batting .344 in 57 games...was selected to the Gulf Coast League's postseason All-Star squad after leading the league in runs scored (51), total bases (113), extra-base hits (28), doubles 17) and slugging percentage (.579)...hit .227 (5-for-22) with 2 doubles and 2RBI in six postseason games with Greensboro...**PERSONAL:** Full name is Marcus Markey Thames...he and his wife Danna have two daughters, Deja (13) and Jade (2)...actively participated with Play Baseball Detroit, Tigers Dreams Come True and the Detroit Tigers Autographed Memorabilia Donation Program while with the Tigers...supports Gloves for Kids...has also sponsored youth baseball teams during the annual Negro Leagues Weekend...was originally selected by the Yankees in the 30th round of the 1996 First-Year Player Draft.

YEAR	CLUB	CLASS	AVG	G	AB	R	H	2B	3B	HR	RBI	SH	SF	HP	BB	SO	SB	CS	E	SLUG	OBP
1997	GCL Yankees	R	.344	57	195	51	67	17	4	7	36	1	4	3	16	26	6	4	2	.579	.394
	Greensboro	A	.313	4	16	2	5	1	0	0	2	0	0	0	0	3	1	0	0	.375	.313
1998	Tampa	A	.284	122	457	62	130	18	3	11	59	1	5	8	24	78	13	6	9	.409	.328
1999	Norwich	AA	.225	51	182	25	41	6	2	4	26	1	2	3	22	40	0	1	7	.346	.316
	Tampa	A	.244	69	266	47	65	12	4	11	38	1	2	3	33	58	3	0	3	.444	.332
2000	Norwich	AA	.241	131	474	72	114	30	2	15	79	0	8	4	50	89	1	5	9	.407	.313
2001	Norwich	AA	.321	139	520	114	167	43	4	31	97	0	3	7	73	101	10	4	8	.598	.410
2002	Columbus	AAA	.207	107	386	51	80	21	3	13	45	0	2	7	43	71	5	4	5	.378	.297
	YANKEES	MAJ	.231	7	13	2	3	1	0	1	2	0	0	0	0	4	0	0	0	.538	.231
2003	Columbus	AAA	.278	52	194	26	54	15	2	2	28	0	5	1	17	48	3	4	3	.407	.332
	Oklahoma	AAA	.258	18	66	9	17	4	0	2	7	0	0	0	8	12	1	0	1	.409	.338
	TEXAS	MAJ	.205	30	73	12	15	2	0	1	4	0	1	2	8	18	0	1	0	.274	.298
2004	Toledo	AAA	.329	64	234	57	77	21	1	24	59	1	4	2	33	40	4	1	2	.735	.410
	DETROIT	MAJ	.255	61	165	24	42	12	0	10	33	0	1	2	16	42	0	1	0	.509	.326
2005	Toledo	AAA	.340	73	265	53	90	18	3	22	56	0	5	3	41	59	4	1	2	.679	.427
	DETROIT	MAJ	.196	38	107	11	21	2	0	7	16	0	1	1	9	38	0	0	1	.411	.263
2006	DETROIT	MAJ	.256	110	348	61	89	20	2	26	60	0	1	4	37	92	1	1	2	.549	.333
2007	Toledo	AAA	.375	2	8	2	3	0	0	1	2	0	0	0	0	1	0	0	0	.750	.375
	DETROIT	MAJ	.242	86	269	37	65	15	0	18	54	0	1	1	13	72	2	1	4	.498	.278
2008	DETROIT	MAJ	.241	103	316	50	76	12	0	25	56	0	2	0	24	95	0	3	5	.516	.292
2009	Toledo	AAA	.245	12	49	6	12	0	0	2	6	0	0	0	5	14	0	0	0	.367	.315
	DETROIT	MAJ	.252	87	258	33	65	11	1	13	36	0	6	1	29	72	0	2	0	.453	.323
Minor League Totals			**.278**	**901**	**3312**	**577**	**922**	**206**	**28**	**145**	**540**	**5**	**40**	**41**	**365**	**640**	**51**	**30**	**51**	**.489**	**.353**
Major League Totals			**.243**	**522**	**1549**	**230**	**376**	**75**	**3**	**101**	**261**	**0**	**13**	**11**	**136**	**433**	**3**	**9**	**12**	**.491**	**.306**

TOLENTINO, Israel – RHP

HT: 6-4; **WT:** 190; **B:** R; **T:** R; **BORN:** 1/11/88 in Monte Plata, D.R.; **RESIDES:** Monte Plata, D.R.; **OBTAINED:** Signed by the Yankees as a non-drafted free agent on 11/2/07; **M.L. SVC:** 0.000; **CAREER NOTES: 2009:** Made 13 appearances (11 starts) with the DSL Yankees 1 and went 1-2 with a 4.76 ERA in 45.1P…recorded a career-high 6K twice, on 6/27 at the DSL Rangers 1 and on 8/6 at the DSL Mets…**2008:** Made his professional debut with the DSL Yankees 2, going 0-0 with a 13.50 ERA in six games…did not allow more than 1H in five of his six relief appearances.

YEAR	CLUB	CLASS	W-L	ERA	G	GS	CG	SHO	SV	IP	H	R	ER	HR	HB	BB	SO	WP	BK
2008	DSL Yankees 2	R	0-0	13.50	6	0	0	0	0	4.2	4	8	7	1	2	9	3	3	0
2009	DSL Yankees 1	R	1-2	4.76	13	11	0	0	0	45.1	35	35	24	0	11	36	37	18	0
Minor League Totals			**1-2**	**5.58**	**19**	**11**	**0**	**0**	**0**	**50.0**	**39**	**43**	**31**	**1**	**13**	**45**	**40**	**21**	**0**

TOUSSEN, Jose – INF

HT: 6-1; **WT:** 156; **B:** R; **T:** R; **BORN:** 11/13/89 in El Ceybo, D.R.; **RESIDES:** La Romana, D.R.; **OBTAINED:** Signed by the Yankees as a non-drafted free agent on 7/2/06; **M.L. SVC:** 0.000; **CAREER NOTES: 2009:** Played the entire season with the GCL Yankees, hitting .223 with 12 doubles, 1 triple, 2HR and 15RBI and leading the league with 58 games played…**2008:** Batted .269 with 41R, 12 doubles and 23RBI in 65 games with the DSL Yankee's 2…recorded the most putouts (123) among all league shortstops…**2007:** Batted .235 with 12 doubles, 4 triples, 3HR and 31RBI in 62 games with the DSL Yankees 2 in his professional debut…was 3-for-5 in his first pro game on 7/2 at the DSL Giants…hit a grand slam on 7/16 vs. the DSL Giants.

YEAR	CLUB	CLASS	AVG	G	AB	R	H	2B	3B	HR	RBI	SH	SF	HP	BB	SO	SB	CS	E	SLUG	OBP
2007	DSL Yankees 2	R	.235	62	255	23	60	12	4	3	31	0	0	4	17	72	2	4	33	.349	.293
2008	DSL Yankees 2	R	.269	65	234	41	63	12	1	0	23	1	0	6	34	45	16	7	20	.329	.376
2009	GCL Yankees	R	.223	58	202	27	45	12	1	2	15	0	5	3	27	36	8	3	2	.322	.316
Minor League Totals			**.243**	**185**	**691**	**91**	**168**	**36**	**6**	**5**	**69**	**1**	**5**	**13**	**78**	**153**	**26**	**14**	**55**	**.334**	**.329**

TURLEY, Nik – LHP

HT: 6-4; **WT:** 195; **B:** L; **T:** L; **BORN:** 9/11/89 in La Canada, Calif.; **RESIDES:** La Canada, Calif.; **OBTAINED:** Selected by the Yankees in the 50th round of the 2008 First-Year Player Draft; **M.L. SVC:** 0.000; **CAREER NOTES: 2009:** Pitched for the second straight season with the GCL Yankees, going 2-3 with a 2.82 ERA in 11 games (10 starts)…**2008:** Made his professional debut with the GCL Yankees, going 2-1 with a 1.13 ERA in four games (one start)…**PERSONAL:** Graduated from Harvard-Westlake (Calif.) High School and had signed a letter of intent with Brigham Young University.

YEAR	CLUB	CLASS	W-L	ERA	G	GS	CG	SHO	SV	IP	H	R	ER	HR	HB	BB	SO	WP	BK
2008	GCL Yankees	R	2-1	1.13	4	1	0	0	0	8.0	6	1	1	0	1	0	13	0	0
2009	GCL Yankees	R	2-3	2.82	11	10	0	0	0	54.1	45	21	17	1	6	23	46	9	1
Minor League Totals			**4-4**	**2.60**	**15**	**11**	**0**	**0**	**0**	**62.1**	**51**	**22**	**18**	**1**	**7**	**23**	**59**	**9**	**1**

URENA, Carlos – OF/C

HT: 6-1; **WT:** 183; **B:** R; **T:** R; **BORN:** 11/17/89 in Santo Domingo, D.R.; **RESIDES:** Santo Domingo, D.R.; **OBTAINED:** Signed by the Yankees as a non-drafted free agent on 7/2/06; **M.L. SVC:** 0.000; **CAREER NOTES: 2009:** Hit .159 with 3HR and 12RBI in 30 games with the DSL Yankees 1…batted .346 (9-for-26) with 2HR and 7RBI vs. lefthanders…**2008:** Hit .375 with 6R and 8RBI in six games with the DSL Yankees 2…**2007:** Combined to hit .237 with a 9 doubles, 2 triples, 8HR and 32RBI with the two Yankees DSL teams in his professional debut…tied for third in the league in home runs…hit safely in each of his first eight games to begin his career (.345, 10-for-29)…homered in each of his first two games with the DSL 2 team on 7/20 and 7/23, combining in both games to 4-for-9 with 5R, 2HR and 7RBI.

YEAR	CLUB	CLASS	AVG	G	AB	R	H	2B	3B	HR	RBI	SH	SF	HP	BB	SO	SB	CS	E	SLUG	OBP
2007	DSL Yankees 1	R	.225	28	102	18	23	6	0	4	15	0	5	3	8	34	1	0	3	.402	.288
	DSL Yankees 2	R	.250	24	88	11	22	3	2	4	17	0	0	5	3	25	2	0	4	.466	.313
2008	DSL Yankees 2	R	.375	6	24	6	9	2	1	1	8	0	1	1	1	4	0	0	1	.667	.407
2009	DSL Yankees 1	R	.159	30	113	15	18	4	0	3	12	0	2	4	15	37	0	0	4	.274	.276
Minor League Totals			**.220**	**88**	**327**	**50**	**72**	**15**	**3**	**12**	**52**	**0**	**8**	**13**	**27**	**100**	**3**	**0**	**12**	**.394**	**.299**

VALERA, Jackson – INF/C

HT: 6-1; **WT:** 175; **B:** R; **T:** R; **BORN:** 4/8/92 in Valencia, Venezuela; **RESIDES:** Valencia, Venezuela; **OBTAINED:** Signed by the Yankees as a non-drafted free agent on 7/4/08; **M.L. SVC:** 0.000; **CAREER NOTES: 2009**: Made his professional debut and hit .217 with 7 doubles, 2HR and 23RBI in 53 games with the DSL Yankees 2.

YEAR	CLUB	CLASS	AVG	G	AB	R	H	2B	3B	HR	RBI	SH	SF	HP	BB	SO	SB	CS	E	SLUG	OBP
2009	DSL Yankees 2	R	.217	53	184	31	40	7	0	2	23	2	3	6	24	26	0	0	2	.288	.323

VARGAS, Cesar – RHP

HT: 6-1; **WT:** 160; **B:** R; **T:** R; **BORN:** 12/30/91 in Puebla, Mexico; **RESIDES:** Puebla, Mexico; **OBTAINED:** Signed by the Yankees as a non-drafted free agent on 2/9/09; **M.L. SVC:** 0.000; **CAREER NOTES: 2009:** In his professional debut, made 16 relief appearances with the DSL Yankees 1, going 2-1 with three saves and a 3.50 ERA.

YEAR	CLUB	CLASS	W-L	ERA	G	GS	CG	SHO	SV	IP	H	R	ER	HR	HB	BB	SO	WP	BK
2009	DSL Yankees 1	R	2-1	3.50	16	0	0	0	3	36.0	39	23	14	0	6	11	30	10	0

VAZQUEZ, Jorge – INF

NON-ROSTER INVITEE

HT: 6-0; **WT:** 225; **B:** R; **T:** R; **BORN:** 3/15/82 in Culiacan, Mexico; **RESIDES:** Culiacan, Mexico; **OBTAINED:** Signed by the Yankees as a free agent on 12/7/08; **M.L. SVC:** 0.000; **CAREER NOTES: 2009:** Made his Double-A debut, batting .329 with 13HR and 56RBI in 57 games for Trenton...hit .352 (57-for-162) with 12 of his 13HR off right-handed pitching...went 2-for-4 with 1HR and a season-high-tying 4RBI (also 5/6 at Bowie and 5/8 vs. Binghamton) in his first game on 4/23 vs. New Britain...was placed on the disabled list from 7/17 for the remainder of the season with a left wrist sprain...following the season, played for the Tomateros de Culiacan...played for Mexico in the World Baseball Classic prior to the season, batting .294 (5-for-17) with 5R, 1 double, 1HR and 5RBI in five games (4GS at DH)...**PERSONAL:** Was a 10-year veteran of the Mexican League, recording at least a .300 average and 15HR in each of his final five seasons there (2004-08)...led the league in slugging percentage (.796) and ranked second in homers (33) in 2005...also led the league in slugging (.739) in 2006...was a member of the 2000 and '01 Mexican League championship teams...**2008:** Played for the Tigres de Quintana Roo of the Mexican League, batting .339 with 30R, 7 doubles, 18HR and 59RBI in 56 games...hit safely in 17 straight games from 5/18-6/11, batting .431 (31-for-72) with 1 double, 10HR and 25RBI during the stretch, including a career-high 3HR and 5RBI on 6/7 at Saltillo...recorded a hit in 25-of-26 games from 5/18-7/2 (Game 1), going 43-for-109 (.394) over the span...played for the Tomateros de Culiacan of the Mexican Pacific League, following the season, leading the league in slugging percentage (.636), ranking second in batting average (.348), homers (15) and extra-base hits (.27), placing third in on-base percentage (.416) and ranking fifth in RBI (46).

YEAR	CLUB	CLASS	AVG	G	AB	R	H	2B	3B	HR	RBI	SH	SF	HP	BB	SO	SB	CS	E	SLUG	OBP
1999	Tigres	MEX	.000	3	4	0	0	0	0	0	0	0	0	0	0	2	0	0	0	.000	.000
2000	Tigres	MEX	.242	41	66	9	16	2	0	2	9	0	0	2	3	20	0	0	5	.364	.296
2001	Tigres	MEX	.284	91	232	35	66	11	0	5	24	1	1	6	14	55	0	1	15	.397	.340
2002	Tigres	MEX	.275	67	189	29	52	10	0	10	35	3	2	3	4	50	0	0	3	.487	.298
2003	Tigres	MEX	.279	80	247	35	69	11	1	14	60	0	5	1	19	65	2	1	16	.502	.327
2004	Tigres	MEX	.329	85	289	43	95	8	2	21	61	0	2	5	17	62	0	3	--	.588	.374
2005	Tigres	MEX	.379	71	285	61	108	20	0	33	96	0	2	4	14	55	1	2	2	.796	.413
2006	Tigres	MEX	.359	75	284	61	102	15	0	31	98	0	4	7	25	46	0	1	8	.739	.419
2007	Tigres	MEX	.323	58	223	45	72	12	0	17	49	0	2	5	18	60	0	0	2	.605	.383
2008	Tigres	MEX	.339	56	224	30	76	7	0	18	59	0	0	2	20	45	1	0	3	.612	.398
2009	Trenton	AA	.329	57	225	30	74	15	1	13	56	0	2	3	8	45	0	0	8	.578	.357
Mexican League Totals			**.321**	**627**	**2043**	**348**	**656**	**96**	**3**	**151**	**491**	**4**	**18**	**35**	**134**	**460**	**4**	**8**	**53**	**.593**	**.370**
Minor League Totals			**.329**	**57**	**225**	**30**	**74**	**15**	**1**	**13**	**56**	**0**	**2**	**3**	**8**	**45**	**0**	**0**	**8**	**.578**	**.357**

VECHIONACCI, Marcos – INF

HT: 6-2; **WT:** 170; **B:** S; **T:** R; **BORN:** 8/7/86 in Valencia, Venezuela; **RESIDES:** Valencia, Venezuela; **OBTAINED:** Signed as a non-drafted free agent on 8/26/02; **M.L. SVC:** 0.000; **CAREER NOTES: 2009:** Batted .213 with 18 doubles, 10HR and 43RBi in 122 games... set a career high in HR after hitting 18 home runs in 514 career games entering the season... recorded his first two-homer game on 6/19 at Binghamton, driving in four runs... hit .328 (39-for-119) with 6HR off left-handers and .168 (51-for-303) with 4HR against righties... following the season, batted .260 in 37 games with Magallanes in the Venezuelan Winter League... **2008:** Was limited to just 17 games with Double-A Trenton, before suffering a strained right quadriceps muscle that put him on the disabled list from 4/21 through the remainder of the season... played in a seven-game rehab stint with short-season Single-A Staten Island... rated as having the organization's best infield arm by Baseball America following the season... **2007:** Played the entire season with Single-A Tampa, batting .266 with 23 doubles, 2HR and 39RBI in 108 games... joined Double-A Trenton for the final two games of the regular season and the playoffs where he hit .242 with 2 doubles in eight games... connected for a grand slam on 8/3 vs. Clearwater in Game 1 of a doubleheader... hit in a season-high 11 straight games 8/5-16 (.475, 19-for-40)... following the season, he joined Magallanes in the Venezuelan Winter League where he hit .286 (30-for-105) in 41 games... was rated as having the "Best Infield Arm" in the Yankees' player development system by *Baseball America* for the second straight season... **2006:** With Single-A Tampa and Single-A Charleston, combined to bat .235 in 134 games... in 36 games with the Tampa Yankees, collected a .178 batting average... in 98 games with Charleston, batted .255 and recorded a career-highs 55 walks... in 12 games with Navegentes of the Venezuelan Winter League, batted .292 (7-for-24) with 1HR and 5RBI... **2005:** Played in 128 games with Single-A Charleston, batting .252 with 26 doubles and 62RBI... ranked third in the South Atlantic League in triples (8), fifth in runs scored (83), and fifth in at-bats (503)... **2004:** Began the season with Single-A Tampa and played in one game before being transferred to the Gulf Coast League... with the GCL Yankees, batted .336 in 36 games... made a brief stint with short-season Single-A Staten Island, playing in 19 games and batting .292 from 7/4-8/2... **2003:** Made professional debut with the Yankees' Dominican Summer League 1 team, batting .300 with 2HR and 30RBI in 62 games played.

YEAR	CLUB	CLASS	AVG	G	AB	R	H	2B	3B	HR	RBI	SH	SF	HP	BB	SO	SB	CS	E	SLUG	OBP
2003	DSL Yankees 1	R	.300	62	200	28	60	10	4	2	30	1	4	3	37	22	4	1	--	.420	.410
2004	Tampa	A	.250	1	4	1	1	0	0	0	0	0	0	0	0	0	0	0	0	.250	.250
	GCL Yankees	R	.336	36	131	24	44	9	1	4	22	0	0	0	12	19	5	3	6	.511	.392
	Staten Island	SS-A	.292	19	72	13	21	5	0	0	8	0	0	1	11	13	0	0	4	.361	.393
2005	Charleston	A	.252	128	503	83	127	26	8	2	62	3	5	4	43	83	16	2	22	.348	.314
2006	Tampa	A	.178	36	135	15	24	3	1	1	15	0	2	1	11	29	1	2	11	.237	.242
	Charleston	A	.255	98	368	56	94	15	6	7	44	0	2	4	55	52	7	4	12	.386	.357
2007	Tampa	A	.266	108	391	44	104	23	5	2	39	1	3	1	36	69	11	6	13	.366	.327
	Trenton	AA	.111	2	9	0	1	1	0	0	0	0	0	0	0	4	0	0	0	.222	.111
2008	Trenton	AA	.302	17	53	8	16	5	0	0	8	1	1	0	8	11	0	0	3	.396	.387
	Staten Island	SS-A	.440	7	25	2	11	1	0	0	7	0	0	0	0	2	0	0	1	.480	.440
2009	Trenton	AA	.213	122	422	44	90	18	1	10	43	0	3	4	35	113	0	0	20	.332	.278
Minor League Totals			**.256**	**636**	**2313**	**318**	**593**	**116**	**26**	**28**	**278**	**6**	**20**	**18**	**248**	**417**	**44**	**18**	**128**	**.365**	**.331**

VENDITTE, Pat – SP

HT: 6-1; **WT:** 180; **B:** R; **T:** S; **BORN:** 6/30/85 in Omaha, Neb.; **RESIDES:** Omaha, Neb.; **COLLEGE:** Creighton University; **OBTAINED:** Selected by the Yankees in the 20th round of the 2008 First-Year Player Draft; **M.L. SVC:** 0.000; **CAREER NOTES: 2009**: Combined to go 4-2 with 22 saves and a 1.87 ERA (67.1IP 14ER) in 49 relief appearances with Single-A Charleston and Single-A Tampa…recorded 87K and allowed just 11BB…led the RiverDogs with 20 saves and was named to the South Atlantic League's midseason All-Star team before being promoted to Tampa on 6/27…went 2-0 with two saves and a 2.21 ERA with Tampa…made five postseason relief appearances for the Florida State League champions, going 1-0 with a 1.69 ERA (5.1IP, 1ER)…appeared in seven games for the Aguilas del Zulia of the Venezuelan Winter League and went 1-0 with a 4.82 ERA (9.1IP, 11H, 6R, 5ER, 3BB, 7K, 2HR)…**2008:** Went 1-0 with a 0.83 ERA in 30 relief appearances with short-season Single-A Staten Island, converting each of his 23 save opportunities…led the league in saves and ranked second in appearances…owned the most saves among all short-season relievers…ranked second among all Yankees farmhands in saves…was named to the New York-Penn League midseason All-Star team…held opponents to a .117 batting average, with left-handers batting .089 (4-for-45, 1HR) and righties hitting .136 (9-for-66, 1HR)…allowed an earned run in just two of his outings (7/12 at Tri-City – 1ER and 7/21 vs. Brooklyn – 2ER)…held opponents hitless in 21 of his 30 appearances…did not allow an earned run over his final 17 regular season appearances (19.1IP)…made one postseason relief appearance, tossing 1.0 scoreless inning (1H)…was named MiLB's "Best Short-Season Reliever of the Year" at the close of the season…**PERSONAL:** Full name is Patrick Michael Venditte…is the only ambidextrous pitcher in professional baseball…uses a six-finger glove with two thumb holes…is a natural right-hander, but has thrown with both arms since the age of three…caused the Professional Baseball Umpire Corporation (PBUC) to create a new rule regarding ambidextrous pitchers on 7/2/08, that stated that a "pitcher must visually indicate to the umpire, batter and runner(s) which way he will begin pitching to the batter"…attended Creighton University where he majored in marketing…went 9-3 with seven saves and a 3.34 ERA in 37 appearances (one start) during his senior year in 2008…led the team in wins, innings pitched, saves, strikeouts and opponents batting average (.207)…was named second-team preseason All-American by the NCBWA and Collegiate Baseball in 2008 and was selected to the Brooks Wallace Watch List…earned All-America honors from *Baseball America* and Collegiate Baseball in 2007…was also named the MVC Tournament Most Outstanding Player and Collegiate Baseball's national "Player of the Week" after leading Creighton to its first-ever tournament title…attended Central High School (Neb.) where he was named All-Nebraska second team, team MVP and a Lincoln Journal Star Academic All-Star during his senior year…lettered twice in baseball…was previously drafted by the Yankees in the 45th round of the 2007 First-Year Player Draft, but chose to finish his senior year of college.

YEAR	CLUB	CLASS	W-L	ERA	G	GS	CG	SHO	SV	IP	H	R	ER	HR	HB	BB	SO	WP	BK
2008	Staten Island	SS-A	1-0	0.83	30	0	0	0	23	32.2	13	5	3	2	0	10	42	1	0
2009	Charleston	A	2-2	1.47	28	0	0	0	20	30.2	24	8	5	1	0	2	40	0	0
	Tampa	A	2-0	2.21	21	0	0	0	2	36.2	37	11	9	1	0	9	47	0	0
Minor League Totals			**5-2**	**1.53**	**79**	**0**	**0**	**0**	**45**	**100.0**	**74**	**24**	**17**	**4**	**0**	**21**	**129**	**1**	**0**

WARREN, Adam – RHP

HT: 6-1; **WT:** 200; **B:** R; **T:** R; **BORN:** 8/25/87 in Birmingham, Ala.; **RESIDES:** New Bern, N.C.; **COLLEGE:** University of North Carolina; **OBTAINED:** Selected by the Yankees in the fourth round of the 2009 First-Year Player Draft; **M.L. SVC:** 0.000; **CAREER NOTES: 2009:** Made his professional debut, going 4-2 with a 1.43 ERA (56.2IP, 9ER) in 12 starts with short-season Single-A Staten Island…allowed 1ER or less in 10 of his 12 starts…earned NYPL "Pitcher of the Week" honors twice and was named to the NYPL midseason All-Star team…made two starts in the playoffs for the NYPL Champions, going 1-0 with a 1.69 ERA…led all postseason pitchers with 15K and tied for the league lead in innings pitched (10.2)…**PERSONAL:** Graduated from North Carolina with a degree in business administration…went 32-4 with a 3.42 ERA and 240K in 65 games (49 starts) in his collegiate career…left school with the second-most wins by a Tar Heel and tied with Scott Bankhead for the school's highest winning percentage (.889)…won his first 19 games at UNC, marking the longest since Bankhead won 20 straight from 1983-84…graduated fifth in his class from New Bern High School (NC) where he earned all-state honors as a junior in 2004 and was selected as the *New Bern Sun Journal* "Baseball Player of the Year."

YEAR	CLUB	CLASS	W-L	ERA	G	GS	CG	SHO	SV	IP	H	R	ER	HR	HB	BB	SO	WP	BK
2009	Staten Island	SS-A	4-2	1.43	12	12	0	0	0	56.2	49	12	9	1	0	10	50	3	0

WATKINS, Benjamin – RHP

HT: 6-3; **WT:** 225; **B:** R; **T:** R; **BORN:** 3/11/87 in Johnstown, Penn.; **RESIDES:** Johnstown, Penn.; **COLLEGE:** University of Pittsburgh-Johnstown; **OBTAINED:** Selected by the Yankees in the 40th round of the 2009 First-Year Player Draft; **M.L. SVC:** 0.000; **CAREER NOTES: 2009:** Went 5-0 with a 2.47 ERA in 25 games (two starts) with short-season Single-A Staten Island in his first professional season…held opponents to a .210 batting average, including a .167 mark vs. right-handers…made back-to-back starts (8/26 and 8/31) and did not allow an earned run in either outing (10.0IP, 4H, 1R, 1BB, 9K)…tossed 5.0 scoreless innings of relief and earned the win in the SI Yankees' championship-clinching game on 9/16 vs. Mahoning Valley…**PERSONAL:** Selected as the 2008-09 Atlantic Region Male Scholar-Athlete of the Year, *ESPN The Magazine* Academic All-American and West Virginia Intercollegiate Athletic Conference Male Scholar-Athlete in 2009…also named WVIAC "Pitcher of the Year" after leading Division II and setting a WVIAC record with a 0.84 ERA in 2009.

YEAR	CLUB	CLASS	W-L	ERA	G	GS	CG	SHO	SV	IP	H	R	ER	HR	HB	BB	SO	WP	BK
2009	Staten Island	SS-A	5-0	2.47	25	2	0	0	0	47.1	38	16	13	0	4	11	43	3	0

WEBER, Jon - OF

NON-ROSTER INVITEE

HT: 5-10; **WT:** 190; **B:** L; **T:** L; **BORN:** 1/20/78 in Lakewood, Calif.; **RESIDES:** Lakewood, Calif.; **COLLEGE:** Texas Tech; **OBTAINED:** Signed by the Yankees as a free agent on 12/4/09; **M.L. SVC:** 0.000; **CAREER NOTES: 2009:** Attended spring training as a non-roster invitee with the Rays and spent the season with Triple-A Durham where he batted .302 with 14HR and 69RBI in 117 games…led the team in hits (136) and doubles (46), ranked third in runs (63) and RBI and ranked fourth in homers…following the season, played for Mazatlan of the Mexican Winter League…**2008:** Entered spring training with the Rays as a non-roster invitee and played the entire season with Triple-A Durham, appearing in 108 games…played mostly LF and RF, but saw action in four games in CF and one at 1B…batted everywhere in the lineup except cleanup…hit .309 (58-for-188) on the road and just .224 (45-for-206) at home…played winter ball in Mexico for Mazatlan, appearing at all three outfield positions over 45 games…**2007:** Hit .265 with 3HR and 21RBI over 39 games for Triple-A Durham after being acquired from the Texas Rangers on 7/17 in exchange for cash considerations…was released by the Diamondbacks organization in spring training and signed with the Fargo-Moorhead RedHawks of the independent Northern League, where he played from 2002-03…appeared in 16 games there before being sold to the Rangers on 6/3…joined Single-A Bakersfield, batting .356 with 34R, 14 doubles, 5HR and 25RBI…played for the Caneros de los Mochis in the Mexican League over the winter…**2006:** Began the season with Triple-A Las Vegas and hit .258 in 82 games before being released on 7/16…signed with Arizona on 7/20 and played for Triple-A Tucson, batting .321 with 5HR in 46 games…helped the Sidewinders capture the PCL Championship…hit .319 (9-for-29) in seven postseason games, including a game-tying, two-run single in the title-clinching game…played in the Mexican Winter League, Venezuelan Winter League and the Caribbean Series following the season…**2005:** Signed a minor league contract with the Dodgers on 11/1/04…spent the entire season with Double-A Jacksonville, batting .300 in 117 games…ranked eighth in the Southern League in batting average…**2004:** Split the season between Double-A Midland and Triple-A Sacramento…combined to hit a career-high 17HR…**2003:** Began the season with Fargo-Moorhead of the Independent Northern League…had his contract purchased by Oakland on 7/24…hit .361 for Single-A Modesto with 7HR in 35 games…**2002:** Played the entire season with Fargo-Moorhead, ranking among league leaders in several offensive categories…**2001:** Was a Frontier League All-Star with the Independent Canton Crocodiles…led the league in HR (18), triples (7) and games played (84), while finishing among league leaders in total bases, RBI and slugging percentage…**2000:** Batted .221 in 108 games in his first full season in the minors with Single-A Clinton…was released by Cincinnati on 9/27…**1999:** Played for Billings of the Rookie-level Pioneer League in his first professional season…**PERSONAL:** Full name is Jonathan Brian Weber…played at Texas Tech and as a junior, batted .356 with 13HR and 84RBI…led the Big 12 with eight triples…attended Lakewood (Calif.) High School…was originally signed by the Reds as a non-drafted free agent on 8/2/99.

YEAR	CLUB	CLASS	AVG	G	AB	R	H	2B	3B	HR	RBI	SH	SF	HP	BB	SO	SB	CS	E	SLUG	OBP
1999	Billings	R	.238	22	80	16	19	6	0	5	17	0	0	0	16	15	1	1	2	.500	.365
2000	Clinton	A	.221	108	321	60	71	14	2	6	34	4	2	5	50	50	8	6	8	.333	.333
2001	Canton	IND	.307	84	329	60	101	15	7	18	69	0	7	7	37	51	16	3	3	.559	.382
2002	Fargo-Moorehead	IND	.296	90	365	69	108	30	3	13	52	2	2	4	31	70	11	2	4	.501	.356
2003	Fargo-Moorehead	IND	.309	52	204	46	63	8	1	11	48	0	0	3	31	28	14	3	4	.520	.408
	Modesto	A	.361	35	147	28	53	10	4	7	38	0	6	3	9	26	2	0	0	.626	.394
2004	Sacramento	AAA	.341	19	44	9	15	4	0	2	12	0	0	0	3	9	0	0	-	.568	.383
	Midland	AA	.280	111	421	64	118	24	5	15	68	2	7	6	46	102	10	5	-	.468	.354
2005	Jacksonville	AA	.300	117	450	81	135	27	5	11	68	2	1	5	45	78	10	6	7	.456	.369
2006	Las Vegas	AAA	.258	82	260	39	67	18	1	2	31	2	1	3	27	39	9	3	2	.358	.333
	Tucson	AAA	.321	46	168	26	54	18	0	5	27	1	3	1	15	23	1	1	3	.518	.374
2007	Fargo-Moorehead	IND	.283	16	60	10	17	5	0	1	10	0	1	1	8	8	2	2	1	.417	.371
	Bakersfield	A	.356	37	149	34	53	14	0	5	25	0	1	1	15	15	9	5	1	.550	.416
	Durham	AAA	.265	39	136	20	36	5	2	3	21	0	3	1	21	24	0	0	2	.397	.360
2008	Durham	AAA	.265	108	389	58	103	24	4	13	51	2	5	3	40	99	11	6	5	.447	.334
2009	Durham	AAA	.302	117	451	63	136	46	0	14	69	0	5	6	56	98	3	7	4	.497	.382
Minor League Totals			**.285**	**841**	**3016**	**498**	**860**	**210**	**23**	**88**	**461**	**13**	**34**	**34**	**343**	**578**	**64**	**40**	**34**	**.458**	**.361**

WHELAN, Kevin – RHP

NON-ROSTER INVITEE

HT: 6-0; **WT:** 200; **B:** R; **T:** R; **BORN:** 1/8/84 in Kerrville, Tex.; **RESIDES:** Kerrville, Tex.; **OBTAINED:** Acquired by the Yankees from the Detroit Tigers on 11/10/06 along with RHPs Humberto Sanchez and Anthony Claggett in exchange for OF Gary Sheffield; **M.L. SVC:** 0.000; **CAREER NOTES: 2009**: Combined to go 4-0 with three saves and a 2.67 ERA in 44 relief appearances (67.1IP, 20ER) with Double-A Trenton and Triple-A Scranton/Wilkes-Barre, allowing just 1HR…began the season with Trenton, going 4-0 with two saves and a 2.63 ERA in 30 relief outings…was promoted to Scranton/WB on 7/21 where he had one save and a 2.84 ERA in 14 relief appearances without recording a decision…made two postseason appearances out of the bullpen for the International League runner-ups, earning one save and tossing 2.2 scoreless innings (1H, 4BB, 6K)…**2008:** Posted a 1-0 record with two saves and a 4.50 ERA in 24 combined appearances between Single-A Tampa and Double-A Trenton…struck out 46 batters in 38.0IP…opened the season on the disabled list with a right forearm strain (4/3-5/13)…missed four games (6/9-12) for the birth of his child…also missed another month from 6/24-7/30 with a right elbow strain…held left-handed batters to a .098 batting average (5-for-51, 0HR)…made two postseason appearances for the Eastern League champions, allowing 4ER in 2.1IP…pitched with the Peoria Javelinas in the Arizona Fall League, holding opponents scoreless in nine of his 11 outings…**2007:** Combined at Single-A Tampa and Double-A Trenton to go 6-2 with a 2.62 ERA in 38 appearances (eight starts) in his first season with the Yankees organization…overall, held opponents to a .162 batting average with right-handers batting just .133 off him…began season with Trenton, was transferred to Tampa on 6/11, then returned to Trenton on 7/23…appeared in a starting role for the first time with Tampa, making seven starts (2-0, 1.93 ERA, 12BB, 28K) and holding opponents scoreless four times…was named Florida State League "Pitcher of the Week" for the period ending 7/8 (1-0, 10.0IP, 2H, 0ER, 3BB, 8K)…began the season with five straight scoreless outings, converting on all three save opportunities (9.0IP, 5H, 4BB, 11K)…following the season, appeared in three games with the Peoria Javelinas of the Arizona Fall League (0-0, 12.00 ERA)…**2006:** Ranked third among all Detroit Tigers' minor-league pitchers with 27 saves in 2006, going 4-1 with a 2.67 ERA in 51 games for the Single-A Lakeland Tigers…limited opposing hitters to a .178 batting average (33-for-185) and held right-handed hitters to a .158 average (18-for-114)…ranked second among all Florida State League pitchers with 46 games finished, ranked third in the league in saves and ranked fourth with 51 games pitched…**2005:** Selected as the Tigers Minor League "Pitcher of the Month" for August after posting a 0.84 ERA (10.2IP, 1ER), nine saves and 20 strikeouts in 11 appearances for short-season Single-A West Michigan…named the 10th-best prospect in the Tigers organization and 18th-best prospect in the New York-Penn League following the season by *Baseball America*…selected to the publication's all-star squad for players drafted out of college…**PERSONAL:** Pitched for three seasons at Texas A&M…compiled a 4-1 record with four saves and a 2.90 ERA (40K) in 19 games in 2005…also saw time at catcher in 2004 as a sophomore…finished 0-2 with a 4.15 ERA in 10 games as a pitcher and hit .233 (10-for-43) with 1HR and 4RBI behind the plate…tabbed as a 2004 Second-Team Summer All-American by *Baseball America* after earning Cape Cod League All-Star honors for Wareham, finishing 2-2 with a 0.42 ERA, 11 saves and 31K in 18 games…named the 10th-best prospect overall in the Cape Cod League by *Baseball America*…batted .245 with 1HR and 6RBI as a freshman catcher…named the eighth-best prospect in the Jayhawk League during the summer by *Baseball America* after pitching for Liberal High School.

YR	CLUB	CLASS	W-L	ERA	G	GS	CG	SHO	SV	IP	H	R	ER	HR	HB	BB	SO	WP	BK
2005	Oneonta	SS-A	1-1	2.25	11	0	0	0	4	12.0	2	4	3	1	1	6	19	2	1
	W. Michigan	A	0-1	0.73	14	0	0	0	11	12.1	4	1	1	0	0	2	22	1	0
2006	Lakeland	A	4-1	2.67	51	0	0	0	27	54.0	33	20	16	1	1	29	69	4	0
2007	Trenton	AA	4-2	2.98	31	1	0	0	4	54.1	34	18	18	2	2	42	68	8	1
	Tampa	A	2-0	1.93	7	7	0	0	0	28.0	11	6	6	2	0	12	28	2	0
2008	Tampa	A	1-0	4.67	9	0	0	0	1	17.1	11	9	9	0	0	14	19	2	0
	Trenton	AA	2-0	4.35	15	0	0	0	1	20.2	13	10	10	2	0	15	27	7	0
2009	Trenton	AA	4-0	2.63	30	0	0	0	2	54.2	38	17	16	1	1	28	63	5	0
	Scranton/WB	AAA	0-0	2.84	14	0	0	0	1	12.2	7	4	4	0	0	13	22	0	0
Minor League Totals			**18-4**	**2.81**	**182**	**8**	**0**	**0**	**51**	**266.0**	**153**	**89**	**83**	**9**	**5**	**161**	**337**	**31**	**2**

WINFREE, David – OF

NON-ROSTER INVITEE

HT: 6-3; **WT**: 231; **B**: R; **T**: R; **BORN**: 8/5/85 in Virginia Beach, Va.; **RESIDES**: Virginia Beach, Va.; **OBTAINED**: Signed by the Yankees as a free agent on 1/5/10; **M.L. SVC**: 0.000; **CAREER NOTES**: **2009**: Spent the season with Triple-A Rochester, batting .273 with 48R, 14HR, 61RBI and a career-high-tying 31 doubles in 116 games...led the team in doubles, ranked second in HR and RBI and ranked third in hits...attended spring training as a non-roster invitee with Minnesota, batting .344 (11-for-32) in 23 games...**2008**: Hit .252 with 27 doubles, 19HR and 87RBI in 126 games for Double-A New Britain...led the club in HR and ranked third in the Eastern League in RBI...homered in three straight games from 8/15-17...was named the Twins' "Player of the Month" for August...**2007**: Batted .267 with 27 doubles, 12HR and 51RBI in 123 games with Double-A New Britain...led the team with 5 triples...following the season, played for Phoenix in the Arizona Fall League...**2006**: Hit .276 with 43R, 13 doubles, 13HR and 48RBI in 67 games with Single-A Ft. Myers...missed time on the disabled list from 4/12-7/1 with a right thumb contusion...**2005**: Batted .294 with 31 doubles, 16HR and 101RBI in 135 games with Single-A Beloit, establishing career highs in doubles and RBI...led all Twins minor leaguers and the Midwest League in RBI...also led the league in at-bats (562), hits (165) and total bases (254) and ranked second in games and fifth in extra-base hits (52)...recorded a season-high 12-game hitting streak from 6/27-7/8, going 21-for-58 (.362)...was named to the Midwest League Postseason All-Star team and received the Sherry Robertson Award winner as the Twins' "Minor League Player of the Year"...also named as the 14th-best prospect in the Midwest League by *Baseball America*...**2004**: Hit .286 with 31R, 8HR and 37RBI in 59 games with short-season Single-A Elizabethton...ranked second on the team in HR and RBI and third in runs and hits (62)...**2003**: Made his professional debut with the GCL Twins, batting .129 in 23 games...**PERSONAL**: Full name is David Lynn Winfree, Jr...graduated from First Colonial High School (Va.) in 2003 where he also played football...was originally selected by the Twins in the 13th round of the 2003 First-Year Player Draft.

YEAR	CLUB	CLASS	AVG	G	AB	R	H	2B	3B	HR	RBI	SH	SF	HP	BB	SO	SB	CS	E	SLUG	OBP
2003	GCL Twins	R	.129	23	70	4	9	1	2	0	3	0	0	1	2	16	0	0	3	.200	.164
2004	Elizabethton	SS-A	.286	59	217	31	62	8	0	8	37	0	2	4	18	51	1	1	18	.433	.349
2005	Beloit	A	.294	135	562	80	165	31	5	16	101	0	6	11	22	93	3	2	34	.452	.329
2006	Fort Myers	A	.276	67	261	43	72	13	2	13	48	0	4	3	19	59	2	0	11	.490	.328
	GCL Twins	R	.200	4	15	2	3	1	0	0	1	0	0	0	1	4	0	0	0	.267	.250
2007	New Britain	AA	.267	123	460	57	123	27	5	12	51	0	2	2	26	106	0	0	17	.426	.308
2008	New Britain	AA	.252	126	453	59	114	27	3	19	87	0	3	5	41	87	2	3	2	.450	.319
2009	Rochester	AAA	.273	116	422	48	115	31	3	14	61	0	5	2	28	88	0	2	8	.460	.317
Minor League Totals			**.270**	**653**	**2460**	**324**	**663**	**139**	**20**	**82**	**389**	**0**	**22**	**28**	**157**	**504**	**8**	**8**	**93**	**.442**	**.318**

WORDEKEMPER, Eric – RHP

HT: 6-1; **WT:** 200; **B:** R; **T:** R; **BORN:** 8/8/83 in Storm Lake, Iowa; **RESIDES:** Storm Lake, Iowa; **COLLEGE:** Creighton University; **OBTAINED:** Selected by the Yankees in the 46th round of the 2005 First-Year Player Draft; **M.L. SVC:** 0.000; **CAREER NOTES: 2009**: Combined to go 3-2 with a 3.38 ERA in 38 relief appearances with Double-A Trenton and Triple-A Scranton/Wilkes-Barre...began the season with Trenton, going 1-2 with a 3.00 ERA in 28 relief outings...held right-handed batters to a .171 (14-for-82, 0HR) batting average, while left-handers hit .243 (17-for-70, 3HR)...went 2-0 with a 4.32 ERA in 10 relief appearances with Scranton/WB...went 0-1 with a 3.86 ERA in two postseason relief appearances for the International League runner-ups, allowing 3H and 1ER in 2.1IP (2K)...following the season, earned one save while pitching for the Aguilas del Zulia of the Venezuelan Winter League, making five appearances (one start) and allowing 12H and 9ER in 8.1IP (9.72 ERA, 10R, 5BB, 3K)...**2008:** Appeared in 33 games (one start) for Double-A Trenton, going 3-2 with six saves and a 3.93 ERA...landed on the disabled list from 7/29-8/14 with a muscle strain in his left ribcage...had not allowed an earned run in seven July appearances prior to the injury (12.1IP)...was activated and assigned to Single-A Tampa where he made two relief appearances, allowing four runs (2ER) in 1.2IP...**2007:** Was 2-0 with 33 saves and a 0.57 ERA in 43 relief appearances for Single-A Tampa, leading the team in ERA, saves and games...was named the Florida State League's "Most Valuable Pitcher" after leading the league in saves and earned a spot on the league's mid- and postseason All-Star teams as well as the Topps Class-A All-Star team...appeared in one game with Double-A Trenton on 9/2, throwing a scoreless inning to earn the save...appeared in one postseason game with Trenton, throwing a scoreless inning in the Thunder's Division Series win at Portland on 9/8...his organization-high 34 combined saves were the fifth-most in the minors...allowed an earned run in just three of his 44 appearances in 2007, finishing the season with 28 consecutive outings without allowing an earned run (from 5/31 on)...with Tampa, struck out 34 batters with only 11 walks and held opponents to a .223 batting average, converting 33-of-35 save opportunities...did not allow a home run all season...following the season, pitched with the Peoria Javelinas of the Arizona Fall League, going 1-0 with one save and a 2.89 ERA...**2006:** With Single-A Charleston, posted a 4-3 record with a 1.81 ERA...appeared in one game with Triple-A Columbus on 9/3 at Toledo, retiring all six batters faced (2K)...**2005:** Made professional debut with the Gulf Coast Yankees, going 2-0 with a 2.12 ERA in nine games (five starts)...was promoted to short-season Single-A Staten Island on 8/28 and made two starts, going 0-2 with a 4.50 ERA...**PERSONAL:** Played baseball at Creighton University before being drafted by the Yankees in 2005...was given All-MVC Conference Honorable Mention following the 2004 season...graduated from St. Mary's HS in Storm Lake, Iowa, where he participated in four years of baseball and three years of basketball and track...won the Bob Feller Award as a senior for "Pitcher of the Year" in Iowa after going 11-2 with three saves and 180K with just 14BB in 83.0IP...was named to the all-conference team all four seasons...chosen as a first-team all-state player his junior and senior seasons and a second-team selection as a sophomore and freshman...voted the team MVP his sophomore through senior seasons and named the area "Athlete of the Year" his junior year.

YEAR	CLUB	CLASS	W-L	ERA	G	GS	CG	SHO	SV	IP	H	R	ER	HR	HB	BB	SO	WP	BK
2005	GCL Yankees	R	2-0	2.12	9	5	0	0	0	29.2	28	7	7	2	2	1	24	0	0
	Staten Island	SS-A	0-2	4.50	2	2	0	0	0	10.0	15	5	5	1	0	2	3	1	0
2006	Charleston	A	4-3	1.81	39	4	0	0	7	79.2	62	24	16	3	6	21	69	4	0
	Columbus	AAA	0-0	0.00	1	0	0	0	0	2.0	0	0	0	0	0	0	2	0	0
2007	Tampa	A	2-0	0.57	43	0	0	0	33	47.0	39	5	3	0	0	11	34	1	0
	Trenton	AA	0-0	0.00	1	0	0	0	1	1.0	0	0	0	0	0	0	1	0	0
2008	Trenton	AA	3-2	3.93	33	1	0	0	6	50.1	59	25	22	6	1	26	46	2	0
	Tampa	A	0-0	10.80	2	0	0	0	0	1.2	5	4	2	0	0	0	0	0	0
2009	Trenton	AA	1-2	3.00	28	0	0	0	1	42.0	31	15	14	3	3	13	32	0	0
	Scranton/WB	AAA	2-0	4.32	10	0	0	0	1	16.2	19	8	8	2	0	2	12	0	0
Minor League Totals			**14-9**	**2.48**	**168**	**12**	**0**	**0**	**49**	**280.0**	**258**	**93**	**77**	**17**	**12**	**76**	**223**	**8**	**0**

ZHANG, Zhenwang – C

HT: 6-1; **WT**: 170; **B**: R; **T**: R; **BORN**: 3/1/88 in Tianjin, China; **RESIDES**: Tianjin, China; **OBTAINED**: Signed by the Yankees as a non-drafted free agent on 6/16/07; **M.L. SVC**: 0.000; **CAREER NOTES**: Appeared in three games for Team China in the 2009 World Baseball Classic and went hitless in 6AB...along with LHP Kai Liu, were the first members of Chinese Baseball to sign with a Major League team in accordance with the Yankees and Chinese Baseball Association's Memorandum of Understanding signed in January 2007...along with LHP Kai Liu, was introduced at a press conference at Yankee Stadium on 7/6/07 and then reported to the Yankees complex in Tampa.

YEAR	CLUB	CLASS	AVG	G	AB	R	H	2B	3B	HR	RBI	SH	SF	HP	BB	SO	SB	CS	E	SLUG	OBP
NO PROFESSIONAL RECORD																					

ZINK, Ryan – RHP

HT: 6-4; **WT:** 210; **B:** R; **T:** R; **BORN:** 4/1/85 in Madison, Wisc.; **RESIDES:** Madison, Wisc.; **COLLEGE:** University of Illinois-Chicago; **OBTAINED:** Selected by the Yankees in the 17th round of the 2007 First-Year Player Draft; **M.L. SVC:** 0.000; **CAREER NOTES: 2009**: Spent the season with Single-A Tampa, going 9-12 with a 5.07 ERA in 26 appearances (25 starts)...ranked second on the team in wins...made his only relief appearance of the season on 6/14, allowing 4H and 1ER in 4.2IP (3R, 4BB, 5K)...struck out a season-high seven batters on three occasions (5/15 vs. Dunedin, 8/10 at Clearwater and 8/22 vs. Lakeland)...**2008:** Went 3-2 with one save and a 2.42 ERA in 25 appearances (four starts) with Single-A Charleston...held right-handed batters to a .175 average (20-for-114)...was placed on the disabled list from 5/5-21 with a left oblique muscle strain...began the season in the bullpen, going 2-2 with a 3.55 ERA...moved into the rotation on 8/17, and in four starts through the end of the season went 1-0 with a 0.47 ERA, holding his opponents scoreless in three of those appearances (19.0IP, 9H, 1ER, 4BB, 15K, 1HR)...**2007:** Made his professional debut with short-season Single-A Staten Island, going 6-1 with one save and a 3.23 ERA in 15 appearances (five starts)...was 3-0 with a 2.39 ERA in 10 relief appearances and 3-1 with a 4.29 ERA in his five starts...converted his lone save chance on 7/12 vs. Auburn...did not allow a run over his final four outings (9.2IP)...**PERSONAL:** Played ball at the University of Illinois-Chicago, finishing his three-year career there with a 24-12 record and a 3.32 ERA...at the time he left, ranked second in school history in career wins and strikeouts (228) and fifth in ERA...threw 8.0 innings of one-hit ball vs. Long Beach State (ranked No. 16 in the country) in the NCAA Regional, leading UIC to the 4-1 upset win–the program's first-ever NCAA postseason win...missed the 2006 season after undergoing "Tommy John" surgery...was a 2005 All-Horizon League second team selection after leading his team with 74 strikeouts and setting a UIC single-season record with 119.0IP...as a freshman, led the Horizon League with 95.1IP and six complete games, earning Louisville Slugger All-Freshman honors and a spot on the All-Horizon League first team and Horizon League All-Newcomer Team...majored in education/history at UIC...drafted out of La Follette (Wisc.) High School by Milwaukee in the 47th round of the 2003 First-Year Player Draft...was the 2003 Wisconsin Gatorade "Player of the Year" and named Wisconsin's top draft prospect by *Baseball America*...named the city, conference and state "Player of the Year" as a senior...participated in the Northwoods League in both 2004 and '07.

YEAR	CLUB	CLASS	W-L	ERA	G	GS	CG	SHO	SV	IP	H	R	ER	HR	HB	BB	SO	WP	BK
2007	Staten Island	SS-A	6-1	3.23	15	5	0	0	1	47.1	45	19	17	2	2	22	39	2	0
2008	Charleston	A	3-2	2.42	25	4	0	0	1	52.0	43	16	14	3	2	14	43	5	0
2009	Tampa	A	9-12	5.07	26	25	0	0	0	135.0	157	87	76	10	7	44	95	6	1
Minor League Totals			**18-15**	**4.11**	**66**	**34**	**0**	**0**	**2**	**234.1**	**245**	**122**	**107**	**15**	**11**	**80**	**177**	**13**	**1**

Home Runs in First At-Bat with the Yankees

Since 1961 (expansion era)

Player	Date
John A. Miller	9/11/1966
Graig Nettles	4/6/1973*
Jimmy Wynn	4/7/1977
Barry Foote	4/28/1981
Glenallen Hill	7/24/2000
Ron Coomer	4/6/2002
Marcus Thames	6/10/2002
Todd Zeile	4/2/2003
Bubba Crosby	4/9/2004
Andy Phillips	9/26/2004
Nick Green	7/2/2006*
Wilson Betemit	8/2/2007
Cody Ransom	8/17/2008**

* All players except Nettles and Green homered in their first plate appearance as a Yankee.

** Ransom also homered in his second plate appearance (and AB) with the Yankees, becoming the first Yankee ever to accomplish the feat.

New York Yankees™ MEDIA

Yankees General Manager Brian Cashman [at C] answers questions from the New York and Boston media.

New York Yankees

Media Relations Department
Yankee Stadium • One East 161st Street • Bronx, NY 10451
Switchboard: (718) 293-4300
Media Relations: (718) 579-4460
Fax: (718) 293-8414
E-mail: media@yankees.com, credentials@yankees.com
Web site: www.yankees.com, www.yankeesbeisbol.com

Jason Zillo – Director, Media Relations and Publicity
Jason Latimer – Manager, Media Relations and Publicity
Michael Margolis – Manager, Media Relations and Publicity
Lauren Moran – Coordinator, Media Relations and Publicity
Connie Schwab – Coordinator, Media Relations and Publicity
Kenny Leandry – Assistant, Media Relations and Publicity
Germania-Dolores Hernandez – Administrative Assistant

Media Services for Yankees Games

The New York Yankees Media Relations staff welcomes you to Yankee Stadium. Please see below for helpful information and guidelines for the 2010 season. Contact us with any questions or concerns you may have. We look forward to working with you.

ADMISSION TO STADIUM/CREDENTIAL PICK-UP: All media must enter Yankee Stadium via the Press Gate, adjacent to Gate 4. The Press Gate opens five hours prior to game time. BBWAA cards, MLB-issued passes or credentials issued by the New York Yankees are necessary for admittance. NO OTHER CREDENTIAL WILL BE HONORED. All bags are subject to search upon entry. Photo ID will be required.

ADMISSION TO FIELD AND DUGOUTS: Entrance to the field and dugouts can be accessed through the tunnel on the Service Level adjacent to the Yankees clubhouse (only during regular clubhouse hours) as well as the outfield side of the Visitor's clubhouse on the Service Level. Take the press elevator or stairs from the Press Gate to the Service Level and follow the concourse to the first or third base side. The field is closed to media at the conclusion of the visiting team's batting practice.

CLUBHOUSES: The Yankees Clubhouse is open to those with BBWAA cards, MLB-issued passes or applicable credentials issued by the New York Yankees. NO OTHER CREDENTIAL WILL BE HONORED. The Clubhouse is open from three and a half hours prior to the game until one hour before game time. At times, certain additional restrictions may be imposed. Private corridors inside the clubhouse, including the trainer's room, player's lounge, weight room, etc. are CLOSED TO MEDIA AT ALL TIMES. Visiting clubhouse is governed by the visiting club.

CREDENTIAL QUESTIONS: Please direct questions to Connie Schwab or Dolores Hernandez in the Yankees Media Relations office at credentials@yankees.com or (718) 579-4460.

DAILY CREDENTIALS: All requests for 2010 single-game regular season media credentials for games played at Yankee Stadium may be made online at https://credentials.mlb.com. The online application is the only acceptable method for requesting single-game regular season media credentials for games played at Yankee Stadium. Applications must be completed by a Sports Editor or Sports Director and require at least 24 hours notice.

ELEVATOR TO PRESS BOX: The Field Level entrance is directly behind the Press Gate between Gate 4 and the Great Hall. A staircase adjacent to the press elevator also provides route to the Service, Field and Press Box Levels. Entrance on the Service Level is near the Legends Suite Club on the first base side.

FIELD: All media, with BBWAA cards or applicable credentials issued by the New York Yankees, are permitted on the field in designated areas during pre-game practice. FOR SAFETY PURPOSES, ALL MEDIA MUST LEAVE THE FIELD ONCE THE BATTING CAGE IS REMOVED. DUGOUTS ARE TO BE CLEARED ONE-HALF HOUR PRIOR TO ALL GAMES. PLEASE DISPLAY PASSES AT ALL TIMES.

INTERNET: Wireless internet is available throughout all working media areas. Please see a Yankees Media Relations representative for login instructions.

INTERVIEW REQUESTS: To schedule interviews requiring special arrangements, please e-mail your request to media@yankees.com.

MEDIA GUIDES: Please see a member of the Yankees Media Relations department.

NO AUTOGRAPHS: ANY MEMBER OF THE MEDIA REQUESTING AUTOGRAPHS WHILE CREDENTIALED WILL HAVE THEIR CREDENTIAL REVOKED.

Departamento de las Relaciones de Prensa
Yankee Stadium • One East 161st Street • Bronx, NY 10451
Centralita de Teléfonos: (718) 293-4300
Medios de Prensa: (718) 579-4460 • **Fax:** (718) 293-8414
Correo Electrónico: media@yankees.com, credentials@yankees.com
Página de Internet: www.yankees.com, www.yankeesbeisbol.com

Jason Zillo – Director, Relaciones de Prensa y Publicidad
Jason Latimer – Gerente, Relaciones de Prensa y Publicidad
Michael Margolis – Gerente, Relaciones de Prensa y Publicidad
Lauren Moran – Coordinadora, Relaciones de Prensa y Publicidad
Connie Schwab – Coordinadora, Relaciones de Prensa y Publicidad
Kenny Leandry – Asistente, Relaciones de Prensa y Publicidad
Germania- Dolores Hernandez – Asistente de Administración

Servicios a los medios de comunicación durante Los Juegos

El departamento de prensa de los Yankees de Nueva York quisiera darle la bienvenida al Yankee Stadium. Por favor vea abajo las pautas para la temporada del 2010. Póngase en contacto con nosotros con cualquier pregunta o preocupación que usted pueda tener. Deseamos tener el placer de trabajar con usted este año.

ADMISIÓN AL ESTADIO/ ENTREGA DE CREDENCIALES: Todos los medios deben de entrar por la entrada de la prensa (Press Gate), adyacente a la entrada número 4 del estadio (Gate 4). La entrada de la prensa (Press Gate) abre cinco horas antes del inicio del juego. Las tarjetas BBWAA, los pases distribuidos por MLB o las credenciales repartidas por los Yankees de Nueva York son necesarios para entrar. NO SE HONRARÁ NINGUNA OTRA CREDENCIAL. Todas las bolsas están sujetas a ser revisadas a la entrada. Identificación de foto será requerida.

ADMISIÓN AL TERRENO Y A LAS TRINCHERAS: La entrada al terreno y a las trincheras está accesible por el túnel ubicado en el Service Level adyacente al clubhouse de los Yankees (solamente durante las horas que el clubhouse esté abierto) y también por la parte del jardín ubicado en el lado del clubhouse de los visitantes en el Service Level. Desde la entrada de prensa, tome el ascensor o escalera al Service Level y siga el pasillo hacia la primera o tercera base. El terreno cierra a la prensa al concluir la práctica de bateo del equipo visitante.

CLUBHOUSES: El clubhouse de los Yankees es accesible por aquellos que tengan las tarjetas BBWAA, los pases distribuidos por MLB o las credenciales repartidas por los Yankees de Nueva York. NO SE HONRARÁ NINGUNA OTRA CREDENCIAL. El Clubhouse abre tres horas y media antes del juego y cierra una hora antes del inicio del juego. Ocasionalmente, ciertas restricciones adicionales pueden ser impuestas. CORREDORES PRIVADOS DENTRO DEL CLUBHOUSE, INCLUYENDO EL CUARTO DEL ENTRENADOR, EL SALÓN DE LOS JUGADORES Y EL GIMNASIO ESTÁN SIEMPRE CERRADOS PARA LA PRENSA. El clubhouse de los visitantes es gobernado por el equipo visitante.

PREGUNTAS SOBRE CREDENCIALES: Por favor de dirigir cualquier pregunta a Connie Schwab o a Germania-Dolores Hernandez, del departamento de relaciones de prensa de los Yankees, vía correo electrónico a credentials@yankees.com o al número de teléfono (718) 579-4460.

CREDENCIALES POR JUEGO INDIVIDUAL: Solicitudes de credenciales por juego individual en el Yankee Stadium deben ser sometidas vía la página web de *Major League Baseball (MLB)* en https://credentials.mlb.com. La solicitud vía el internet es el único método aceptable para el pedido de credenciales para juegos individuales durante la temporada 2010. Dichos pedidos solo pueden ser hechos por un director o editor de deportes y deben ser recibidas con un mínimo de 24-horas de aviso.

ASCENSOR AL PALCO DE PRENSA: La entrada Field Level está ubicada directamente detrás de la entrada de la prensa (Press Gate), entre la entrada número 4 (Gate 4) del estadio y el Great Hall. Una escalera al lado del elevador de la prensa también provee ruta a los niveles Service, Field y Press Box. La entrada en el Service Level está cerca del Legends Suite Club, que está localizado por la parte de la primera base del estadio.

EL TERRENO: Toda la prensa con tarjetas BBWAA o con credenciales con terreno asignado distribuidos por los Yankees de Nueva York, son permitidos en el terreno en áreas designadas durante la práctica de bateo. CON PROPOSITOS DE SEGURIDAD, TODA LA PRENSA DEBE IRSE DEL TERRENO UNA VEZ QUE LA JAULA DE BATEO ES RETIRADA DEL TERRENO. LAS TRINCHERAS DEBEN SER DESALOJADAS MEDIA HORA ANTES DE CADA JUEGO. POR FAVOR MANTENGAN SUS CREDENCIALES VISIBLES SIEMPRE.

INTERNET: El internet inalámbrico está disponible en todas las areas de trabajo para los medios. Por favor comunicárselo a un representante del departamento de prensa de los Yankees de Nueva York para que lo atienda.

SOLICITUD PARA ENTREVISTAS: Entrevistas que requieran arreglos especiales. Envíelo por escrito vía correo-electrónico a media@yankees.com.

GUIAS DE PRENSA: Por favor comunicárselo a un representante del departamento de prensa de los Yankees de Nueva York para que lo atienda.

NO AUTOGRAFOS: TODOS LOS MIENBRO DE MEDIOS DE COMUNICACIÓN QUE SOLICITE UN AUTOGRAFO Y HAYA ADQUIRIDO ADMISION VIA UN CREDENCIAL, ESTE SE LE SERA REVOCADO.

NOTAS, RECORDS, ETC.: Las estadísticas y notas de prensa están disponible en la sesión principal y en el salón laborar de la prensa antes del juego, Hojas de jugadas por jugadas y las notas post- juego están disponible en la sesión principal de la prensa al final del juego.

Useful New York Telephone Numbers

AIRLINES		TAXI COMPANIES	AUTO RENTALS
Air Canada.... (888) 247-2262	American... (800) 433-7300	City Ride...... (718) 706-6666	Avis .... (800) 331-1212
Continental... (800) 523-3273	Delta .... (800) 221-1212	Coast to Coast (718) 439-3810	Budget ..... (800) 527-0700
USAir......... (800) 428-4322	United...... (800) 241-6522	Partners ...... (516) 741-1515	Hertz....... (800) 654-3131
Jet Blue....... (800) 538-2583			

HOTELS

Grand Hyatt	42nd St. at Grand Central bet. Lex and Park	(212) 883-1234
Hilton	650 Terrace Ave, Hasbrouck Hts., NJ	(201) 288-6100
Hilton New York and Towers	Ave. of Americas/6th Ave. bet. 53rd and 54th	(212) 586-7000
Hotel Edison	228 W. 47th St. bet. Broadway and 8th Ave.	(212) 840-5000
Marriott Marquis	1535 Broadway	(212) 398-1900
Park Central	870 7th Ave. bet. 55th and 56th	(212) 247-8000
Sheraton New York	811 7th Ave. at 53rd St.	(212) 581-1000
Sheraton–Manhattan	790 7th Ave. at 51st St.	(212) 581-3300
Waldorf Astoria	301 Park Ave.	(212) 355-3000

RESTAURANTS

Artisanal	2 Park Avenue	(212) 725-8585
Aureole	34 E. 62st St. between Madison and Park Ave.	(212) 319-1660
Ben Benson's	123 W. 52nd St. between 6th and 7th Ave.	(212) 581-8888
Carmine's	200 W. 44th St. between Broadway and 8th Ave.	(212) 221-3800
Elaine's	1703 2nd Ave. between 88th and 89th St.	(212) 534-8103
Gallagher's Steak House	228 W. 52nd St. between Broadway and 8th Ave.	(212) 245-5336
Hard Rock Cafe	Yankee Stadium	(646) 977-8888
Il Fornaio	132A Mulberry St. between Grand and Hester St.	(212) 226-8306
Il Vagabondo	351 E. 62nd St. between 1st and 2nd Ave.	(212) 832-9221
Mesa Grill	102 Fifth Ave. between 15th and 16th St.	(212) 807-7400
Mickey Mantle's	42 Central Park South between 5th and 6th Ave.	(212) 688-7777
Monte's	97 MacDougal St.	(212) 228-9194
NYY Steak	Yankee Stadium	(646) 977-8325
Palm	837 Second Ave. between 44th and 45th St.	(212) 687-2953
Peter Luger Steak House	178 Broadway, Brooklyn	(718) 387-7400
TAO	42 E. 58th Street	(212) 888-2288
Union Square Café	21 E. 16th St. bet. Union Square West and 5th Ave.	(212) 243-4020
Yolanda's Restaurant	292 E. 149th St., Bronx	(718) 993-2709

MEDIA INFORMATION, continued

NOTES, RECORDS, ETC.: Statistics and press notes are available in the press box and press conference room prior to games. Postgame box scores and notes are available in the press box after games.

PARKING: Media are encouraged to park in the Ruppert Plaza Garage, located on the corner of Jerome Ave. and the Macombs Dam Bridge ramp, directly across the street from the Press Gate. The garage will open six hours prior to the start of the game and remain open at least three hours after the last pitch.

PHOTO REQUESTS: Please e-mail media@yankees.com.

PHOTOGRAPHERS: Photographers will not be permitted on the field during games and have no access to the clubhouse. All photographers work from assigned locations. NO ROVING PHOTO PASSES WILL BE ISSUED.

PREGAME AND POSTGAME TV INTERVIEWS: Available upon request whenever possible. Please notify a Yankees Media Relations representative so assistance can be provided.

PRESS BOX: Take the press elevator or stairs to Main Level. Doors open by the TV and radio booths. The press box, working press room and media dining room will be to the left of the elevator. Please sit in assigned seats. If no seat is assigned, please ask a Yankees Media Relations representative for assistance.

PRESS CONFERENCE ROOM: Take the press elevator or stairs down to the Service Level. The Press Conference Room is on the first base side, opposite of the Yankees clubhouse.

PRESS DINING: Sheppard's Place is open to those with BBWAA cards, MLB-issued passes or applicable credentials issued by the New York Yankees. Entrance is through the Press Box, behind the working press box. Meals are served starting 2 hours and 30 minutes prior to game time and will remain open through the sixth inning.

TELEPHONE ASSISTANCE: For assistance with ordered telephone lines, please call a Yankee Global Technology representative at 646-977-TECH.

TELEVISION CREWS: Crews are not permitted on field during games. LIVE TRANSMISSION IS NOT PERMITTED DURING GAMES FOR NON-RIGHTSHOLDERS. NO ROVING TV CREW PASSES WILL BE ISSUED.

WORKING PRESS ROOMS: Both Print and Audio Workrooms are located behind the working press box. The Photographers workroom is on the Service Level across from the Visitors' clubhouse on the third base side.

Roving in the stands and concourses is prohibited. Likewise, Field Level access during the game is limited to the first and third base photo boxes.

ESTACIONAMIENTO: Los medios de prensa deben de estacionarse en el garaje *Ruppert Plaza*, localizado en la esquina de la avenida Jerome y el *Macombs Dam Bridge*, al otro lado de la entrada número 4 del estadio. El garaje estará abierto seis horas antes del principio del juego y hasta tres horas después del último lanzamiento.

SOLICITUD PARA FOTOGRAFIAS: Por favor envié un correo electrónico a media@yankees.com. **NO FOTOGRAFIAS:** Fotógrafos no serán permitidos al terreno durante juegos y no tienen admisión al clubhouse. Fotógrafos laboran en puntos asignados. NO SE LE OTORGARA ADMISION A FOTOGRAFOS PARA VAGAR.

ENTREVISTAS TELEVISIVAS PRE Y POST-JUEGO: SE PUEDEN OBTERNER CON SOLICITUD PREVIA CUANDO SEA POSIBLE. Por favor comunicárselo a un representante del departamento de prensa de los Yankees de Nueva York para que lo atienda.

PALCO PRINCIPAL DE PRENSA: Tome el ascensor de prensa o las escaleras hacia el Main Level. Las puertas del ascensor abren cerca de las salas de televisión y radio. El palco principal de la prensa y el comedor están localizados a la izquierda del ascensor. Por favor tomen los asientos asignados. Si no se le asigno un asiento, por favor pregunte a un representante del departamento de prensa de los Yankees.

SALA DE CONFERENCIAS DE PRENSA: Tome el elevador de prensa o las escaleras hacia abajo para el Service Level. Tome una derecha el salón laborar de prensa se encuentra al mismo lado de la primera base, y al otro lado del clubhouse de los Yankees.

COMEDOR DE PRENSA: El comedor de prensa está abierto para aquellos con tarjetas de admisión del BBWAA, pases de admisión de las grandes ligas o los credenciales con comedor asignado por los New York Yankees. La entrada está localizada en el palco de prensa, detrás del espacio laborar de la prensa. Las comidas serán servidas dos horas y medias antes del juego y se mantendrá abierto hasta la sexta entrada.

ASISTENCIA TELEFONICA: Asistencia para ordenar líneas telefónicas, por favor llame a un representante de Yankees Global Technology a 646-977-TECH.

EQUIPO DE TRABAJADORES DE TELEVISION: Ningún miembro del equipo tendrá admisión al terreno durante el juego. TRAMISION EN VIVO NO SERA PERMITIDA DURANTE LOS JUEGOS A NINGUNA PERSONA QE NO TENGA DERECHOS RESERVADOS. . NO SE LE OBTORGARAN PASES PARA VAGAR A NINGUN MIEMBRO DEL EQUIPO DE TELEVISION.

SALA LABORAR DE PRENSA: Las salas laborares de la prensa escritas y de la prensa audiovisual están localizadas detrás de la sesión principal de la prensa. El salón laborar de los fotógrafos esta en el Service Level al cruzar el CLUBHOUSE de los visitantes en el lado de la tercera base.

VAGAR POR LAS ALCOVAS Y LOS PASILLO ES PROIVIDO. AL IGUAL, ACESO AL TERRENO DURANTE EL JUEGO ES LIMITADO A LAS SECIONES FOTOGRAFICAS DE PRIMERA Y TERCERA BASE.

Major League Baseball PR Directory

Club	Contact	Office Number	Fax
Commissioner's Office	Richard Levin Pat Courtney	(212) 931-7878	(212) 949-5654
Club Relations	Phyllis Merhige Katy Feeney	(212) 931-7800	(212) 949-5409
AMERICAN LEAGUE			
Baltimore	Monica Barlow Jeff Lantz	(410) 685-9800	(410) 547-6272
Boston	Pam Ganley Leah Tobin	(617) 226-6613	(617) 226-6416
Chicago	Scott Reifert Bob Beghtol	(312) 674-1000	(312) 674-5116
Cleveland	Bart Swain Jeff Sibel	(216) 420-4380	(216) 420-4396
Detroit	Brian Britten Rick Thompson	(313) 471-2000	(313) 471-2138
Kansas City	Mike Swanson David Holtzman	(816) 921-8000	(816) 921-5775
Los Angeles	Tim Mead Eric Kay	(714) 940-2014	(714) 940-2205
Minnesota	Mike Herman Dustin Morse	(612) 659-3400	(612) 659-4029
New York	Jason Zillo Jason Latimer Michael Margolis	(718) 579-4460	(718) 293-8414
Oakland	Bob Rose Mike Selleck	(510) 638-4900	(510) 562-1633
Seattle	Tim Hevly Jeff Evans	(206) 346-4000	(206) 346-4400
Tampa Bay	Rick Vaughn Chris Costello	(727) 825-3242	(727) 825-3111
Texas	John Blake Rich Rice	(817) 273-5222	(817) 273-5110
Toronto	Jay Stenhouse Mal Romanin	(416) 341-1000	(416) 341-1250
NATIONAL LEAGUE			
Arizona	Mike McNally Lynita Johnson	(602) 462-6519	(602) 462-6527
Atlanta	Brad Hainje Adrienne Midgley Jim Misudek	(404) 522-7630	(404) 614-1391
Chicago	Peter Chase Jason Carr	(773) 404-4191	(773) 404-4129
Cincinnati	Rob Butcher Larry Herms Jamie Ramsey	(513) 765-7800	(513) 765-7180
Colorado	Jay Alves Charlie Hepp	(303) 292-0200	(303) 312-2319
Florida	Matt Roebuck Marty Sewell	(305) 626-7492	(305) 626-7302
Houston	Jay Lucas Sally Gunter	(713) 259-8900	(713) 259-8981
Los Angeles	Josh Rawitch Joe Jareck Mark Rogoff	(323) 224-1301	(323) 224-1459
Milwaukee	Tyler Barnes Mike Vassallo	(414) 902-4500	(414) 902-4053
New York	Jay Horwitz Shannon Forde	(718) 639-3619	(718) 639-3619
Philadelphia	Greg Casterioto Kevin Gregg	(215) 463-6000	(215) 389-3050
Pittsburgh	Jim Trdinich Dan Hart	(412) 323-5000	(412) 325-4413
St. Louis	Brian Bartow Jim Anderson Melody Yount	(314) 345-9600	(314) 345-9530
San Diego	Warren Miller Bret Picciolo	(619) 795-5265	(619) 795-5266
San Francisco	Staci Slaughter Jim Moorehead	(415) 972-2448	(415) 947-2800
Washington	John Dever Mike Gazda	(202) 640-7000	(202) 640-7437

Yankees Broadcasters

Michael Kay

Now in his ninth season as the play-by-play announcer for the YES Network and WWOR-TV, Michael Kay immerses himself in all things New York in order to provide his listeners and viewers with original opinions and the most exclusive, up-to-the-minute Yankees information. Additionally, Kay is the host of YES' CenterStage and YESterday's series, hosts his own radio talk show on ESPN 1050 AM in New York and is a frequest contributor to ESPN's Emmy Award-winning Sports Reporters. In 2008, he handled play-by-play duties for ESPN Radio Network's coverage of the American League Divisional Series.

A 21-time Emmy Award nominee and three-time Emmy winner, Kay signed a multi-year extension with the YES Network in 2008 to remain as the club's lead play-by-play voice as well as host on a variety of YES Network programs.

Before joining the YES Network, Kay worked at the MSG Network from 1989-2001 as a Yankees reporter. In 1992, he added the assignment of Knicks locker room reporter to his responsibilities and continued in that role through the 1998-99 season.

In addition to his television work, the Bronx, N.Y., native also worked as a Yankees analyst on WABC Radio from 1992-2002. Kay was a winner with Bob Goldscholl (WBBR) for "Best Sports Reporter" at the 2000 New York Metro Achievement in Radio Awards. After the Yankees' World Series victories in 1996, 1998, 2000 and 2009, Kay and John Sterling were asked by New York City's Mayor to host the post-parade victory celebration at City Hall.

In 1998, Kay also began co-hosting *Sports Talk with John Sterling and Michael Kay*, an MSG-produced nightly sports radio call-in show which aired on WABC Radio during the winter months. During the baseball season, Kay and Sterling hosted *Yankee Talk* which aired 90 minutes prior to all weekend Yankees games.

Shortly after graduating from Fordham University in 1982 with a B.A. in Communications, Kay became one of the hot sports reporters in New York City with a style that combined great reporting skills with quality writing. While at Fordham, he honed his skills working for the school newspaper and radio station, working at Sports Phone and as the public address announcer for the New York Pro Summer Basketball League. In 1982, Kay landed a job as a general assignment writer for the *New York Post*. Two years later he began covering college basketball (1984-85) and then the New Jersey Nets, whom he covered for two seasons before becoming the newspaper's general basketball writer. In 1987, he moved to baseball where he served as his paper's Yankees beat reporter. While he was in that position, he got his first television job with MSG Network as host of the "Hot Stove League" segment of MSG's Sports Night. Kay moved from the *Post* to the *New York Daily News* in 1989, where he covered the Yankees until 1992, when he made the jump to radio. With the move, he became the first newspaper reporter in any sport to make the jump into the broadcast booth full-time, performing both play-by-play and analysis.

Kay was given the Dick Young Award for Excellence in Sports Media by the New York Pro Baseball Scouts in 1995. He was also a part of the Yankees/MSG Production team that was nominated for New York Emmy Awards for six consecutive years. In 1998, he was on the MSG team that won for "Outstanding Live Sports Coverage–Series". In 1996 and '97, he was a member of the MSG team that won New York Emmys for "Outstanding Live Sports Coverage–Single Program" for Dwight Gooden's no-hitter and "The Battle for New York: Yankees vs. Mets".

Kay resides in Hartsdale, N.Y., and is active with the Alzheimer's Association in memory of his mother, Rose, who passed away from the disease in 2006. For the past two years, Kay has joined Joe Girardi for the "Remember When, Remember Now" banquet at the Grand Central Oyster Bar to benefit Girardi's Catch 25 Foundation and Alzheimer's research.

Ken Singleton

Former Major Leaguer Ken Singleton enters his ninth season as a game analyst and announcer for YES Network broadcasts of the New York Yankees. Known on the diamond as a consistent power hitter, Singleton has proven to be equally as reliable since joining the radio and television broadcast booths.

Prior to joining YES, Singleton divided his time calling play-by-play and providing commentary at the MSG Network. In 1998, he was part of MSG's production team that won four New York Emmys for its Yankees coverage.

Singleton joined the MSG Network in 1997 from The Sports Network (TSN), where he served as analyst for the Montreal Expos from 1985-96. From 1991-96, he also called play-by-play and served as analyst for CIQ Radio, the Expos' flagship radio network. In 1996 and '97, he was named by FOX Sports as a lead analyst for Saturday afternoon baseball broadcasts. In 1997 and '98, he worked as an analyst for Major League Baseball International.

Singleton enjoyed a 15-year Major League career with the New York Mets, Montreal Expos and Baltimore Orioles, batting .282 with 317 doubles and 246HR. He is one of only six players in Baseball history to hit 35 or more home runs in a season as a switch-hitter. He also ranks among the all-time leaders in most Baltimore offensive categories, including homers, RBI and total bases. During his career, Singleton was named to the American League All-Star team in 1977, '79, and '81. He was named Most Valuable Oriole in 1975, '77, and '79 and was a member of the Orioles' 1983 World Championship team. He was the 1982 recipient of Major League Baseball's Roberto Clemente Award, honoring Singleton's contributions both on and off the field.

A native New Yorker, Singleton played both baseball and basketball in high school, and also played baseball in the Bronx Federation League at Macombs Dam Park on the current site of Yankee Stadium. After getting a scholarship to play basketball at Hofstra University and playing baseball as well for one year, Singleton was drafted by the Mets in 1967.

He enjoys golf and reading historical novels and lives with his wife Suzanne in Sparks, Md. He also has three sons and a daughter.

BATTING PRACTICE SCHEDULE AT YANKEE STADIUM

Start Time	1:05	4:05	7:05	8:05
Yankees Hit	10:40-11:40	1:40-2:40	4:40-5:40	5:40-6:40
Visitors Hit	11:40-12:40	2:40-3:20	5:40-6:20	6:40-7:20
Yankees Infield	12:20-12:30	3:20-3:30	6:20-6:30	7:20-7:30
Visitors Infield	12:30-12:40	3:30-3:40	6:30-6:40	7:30-7:40

Yankees Broadcasters

John Flaherty

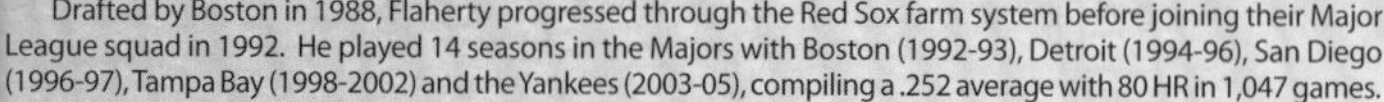

Former Yankees catcher John Flaherty enters his fifth season as a field reporter, studio analyst and game analyst for YES Network telecasts in 2010.

Drafted by Boston in 1988, Flaherty progressed through the Red Sox farm system before joining their Major League squad in 1992. He played 14 seasons in the Majors with Boston (1992-93), Detroit (1994-96), San Diego (1996-97), Tampa Bay (1998-2002) and the Yankees (2003-05), compiling a .252 average with 80 HR in 1,047 games.

Flaherty brought his knowledge of the game and his veteran style of leadership to the Yankees clubhouse when he signed as a free agent in 2003. Though he played in 134 games with the Yankees across three seasons, he may be long remembered for his dramatic pinch-hit, "walk-off" single that defeated the Boston Red Sox in the 13th inning of a 5-4 victory on 7/1/04.

Flaherty is a New York City native and a graduate of George Washington University. On May 15, 2009, he was awarded an honorary Doctorate of Humane Letters from St. Thomas Aquinas College in Sparkill, N.Y.

Kimberly Jones

Kimberly Jones returns for her sixth season as a Yankees pregame and postgame clubhouse reporter. She is also a contributor to YES Network's "This Week in Football" and "Yankees Hot Stove" shows, as well as occasionally hosting talk shows on WFAN-AM 660 in New York.

Jones previously spent four-and-a-half years at the *Star-Ledger* (Newark, N.J.), where she covered the New York Giants for three seasons and was the NFL columnist for one. For the 2005 NFL season, she continued to contribute as the *Star-Ledger's* Sunday NFL notes columnist and also appeared as an NFL contributor on *Out of Bounds* on CN8, The Comcast Network.

Prior to moving to New Jersey, Jones worked at the *Central Daily Times* (State College, Pa.), where she was the beat writer for Penn State football and men's basketball.

Jones graduated from Penn State with a B.A. in Journalism and an M.S. in Exercise and Sport Science. Following graduation, she completed a one-year internship in the communications department of the Big Ten Conference in suburban Chicago. A native of Dallastown, Pa., she currently resides in Bergen County, N.J.

Al Leiter

Entering his fifth year with the YES Network, former Yankees pitcher Al Leiter has established himself as an outstanding color commentator, providing viewers with insight gained from his 19 years as a player in the Major Leagues. Prior to signing with YES, Leiter had worked as a postseason game analyst for FOX Sports and ESPN.

Originally drafted by the Yankees in 1984, Leiter played parts of 19 professional seasons with the Yankees (1987-89, 2005), Toronto Blue Jays (1989-95), Florida Marlins (1996-97, 2005) and New York Mets (1998-2004). A two-time All-Star (1996, 2000), he was a part of two world championship teams (Toronto in 1993 and Florida in 1997) and became the first pitcher in history to record a victory against all 30 Major League teams. On 5/11/96, Leiter tossed the first no-hitter in Marlins history in an 11-0 win vs. Colorado.

Leiter returned to the Yankees in a trade with the Marlins on 7/16/05. His start vs. the Boston Red Sox on 7/17 at Fenway Park marked a span of 16 years and 82 days between Yankees starts (first since 4/26/89 vs. Kansas City), the longest gap between starts by a Yankees pitcher in franchise history.

A native of Bayville, N.J., Leiter has been nearly as busy off the field as he was on it. Since 1996, he has donated more than $1.5 million to various charities in the New York area and South Florida. In 2000, he was honored by Major League Baseball with the Roberto Clemente Award for his contribution to the community and in 2002, he was appointed to the board of directors of the Twin Towers Fund in New York City. He was named the March of Dimes "Sportsman of the Year" in 2003 and the John V. Mara "Sportsman of the Year" in 2004 by the Catholic Youth Organization. With his wife, Lori, he created "Leiter's Landing," a charitable organization committed to the betterment of youth through education, health care and social and community service. Leiter has also been the recipient of numerous other awards and honors as a result of his charity work, including the 2008 "Breakthrough Spirit Award" at the Children's Cancer and Blood Foundation gala in New York City.

Paul O'Neill

Paul O'Neill returns for his ninth consecutive season in broadcast television in 2010, serving as a game analyst for the YES Network.

The gritty and revered five-time All-Star outfielder played 17 years in the Major Leagues, spending his final nine seasons in pinstripes. He appeared in six World Series, winning five titles, including four with the Yankees (1996, '98-2000).

Affectionately known as a "warrior" to most Yankees followers, O'Neill began his Major League career in 1985 with the Cincinnati Reds and earned the first of his five World Series championships in 1990. He joined the Yankees in 1993 after eight seasons with the Reds, and in 1994 claimed the American League batting title with a .359 average. From July 1995 to May 1997, he played in 235 consecutive games in right field without making an error. In 2001, at the age of 38, O'Neill became the oldest player in Major League history to steal 20 bases and hit 20 home runs in the same season.

He lives in his native Cincinnati with his wife, Nevalee, and their three children: Andrew, Aaron and Alexandra. He was named the "Father of the Year" in June 2008 by the National Father's Day Council at its 67th Annual Father of the Year dinner in New York.

Bill Boland
Senior Producer

John Moore
Director

Bob Lorenz
Studio Anchor

Nancy Newman
Studio Host

Chris Shearn
Studio Host

Yankees Broadcasters

John Sterling

"Yankees win! Theeeeeee Yankees win!"

If anything has become synonymous with the Yankees' run of success over recent years, it is John Sterling's memorable conclusion to so many Yankees victories. As the radio voice to 162 games a year, plus preseason and postseason, he has called 3,476 games (3,333 regular season/143 postseason) over the last 21 seasons, without missing even one, making him one of the most recognized—and imitated voices—in all of New York sports.

Sterling joined the Yankees broadcast team in 1989 from Atlanta's TBS and WSB Radio, where he called Hawks basketball (1981-89) and Braves games (1982-87). It marked a return to the town where he first achieved fame, hosting a talk show on WMCA from 1971-78, and calling the Nets (1975-80, and as a fill-in, in 1997) and Islanders (1975-78) for WMCA ,WVNJ, WWOR-TV and SportsChannel.

Sterling also previously broadcasted Morgan State Football (eight years) and Washington Bullets basketball in 1981. In addition to his seven years at WMCA and a year at WSB in Atlanta, he has also hosted talk shows on WFAN and WABC in New York. He has not missed a broadcast since the fall of 1981.

As the host of the YES Network's acclaimed *Yankeeography* series, Sterling has won a total of nine Emmy Awards since 2003. He has also been honored by the New Jersey Sportswriters Association with its Radio-TV Excellence Award (1999), and was the winner of the 2001 Whitney Radio Jimmy Cannon Award. In addition, his call of a Jason Giambi home run on WCBS radio in 2002 was voted the "Best Baseball Call" of the year in a poll conducted by MLB.com. In 2002, Sterling was also honored by the NY Air Awards for being a part of the best play-by-play team on radio.

When he's not in the booth, Sterling serves as a master of on-field ceremonies for major Yankees events. He is also well known for his emcee work at City Hall (with his former longtime radio partner Michael Kay) at "Key to the City" ceremonies following Yankees World Series victories.

Sterling enjoys attending Broadway shows and boasts an extensive knowledge of the lyrics to many American pop standards. In 2007, he embarked on his own Broadway venture in a cabaret show titled "Baseball and Broadway" in which he both served as emcee and sang alongside broadway talent.

For the past 17 years, he has been a spokesman for the Leukemia Society of America. He enjoys reading, movies and swimming. He lives in Bergen County, N.J., and is the proud father of four children: daughter Abigail and triplets, Veronica, Bradford and Derek.

Suzyn Waldman

Award-winning journalist Suzyn Waldman begins her 24th season either covering or broadcasting the New York Yankees. She joined John Sterling in the radio booth in 2005 as the Yankees' color commentator on WCBS-AM radio, becoming the first woman to hold a full-time position as a Major League broadcaster.

Waldman has spent more than two decades overcoming all the obstacles that go along with being a female sports broadcaster and has risen to the top of her profession. In 2006, she became a permanent part of the "Women in Baseball" exhibit at the Hall of Fame in Cooperstown, and in 2009, her World Series Game 6 scorecard was added to the Hall of Fame's collection, commemorating her being the first female radio broadcaster to call game action in the World Series.

In 1987, Waldman became the first female voice heard on WFAN-AM in New York, the first all-sports radio station in the country. She was a mainstay on that station for almost 15 years, creating the job of the radio beat reporter, covering both the New York Yankees and New York Knicks. Her news-breaking reports, exclusive interviews and always original and controversial opinions won her countless journalism awards. Her accolades include the "International Radio Award" for her live and emotional reporting from the upper deck of Candlestick Park during the 1989 San Francisco earthquake, the 1996 "NY Sportscaster of the Year" Award from the National Sportscasters & Sportswriters and the 1999 "Star Award" for radio from the American Women in Radio and TV. Waldman became a popular talk show host at WFAN and co-hosted the coveted midday slot until leaving WFAN in 2002 to join the YES Network.

The word "first" invariably precedes the name of Suzyn Waldman in every facet of her television and radio career. The first woman to work on a nationally-televised baseball broadcast, Waldman added another first, being the first woman to provide play-by-play for a Major League team, when she started broadcasting New York Yankees games for WPIX, MSG Network and WNYW/FOX5 in the mid 1990s. The first woman ever to host an NBA pre-and post-game show, Suzyn worked in that capacity for the NY Knicks on WFAN, provided play-by-play for the WNBA on Lifetime TV and was an analyst on St. John's basketball games for MSG and WFAN.

She has been honored by countless organizations, including the Thurman Munson Foundation, the March of Dimes, the B'nai B'rith, the Jimmy Fund of Boston and the US Federal Women's Program. In 2006, she received the first Women's Global Health Award from the Albert Einstein College of Medicine at the United Nations. She is a tireless motivational speaker at schools and cancer centers around the country, encouraging young women to pursue their dreams despite any pitfalls they may encounter.

Waldman's life and accomplishments have been the subject of hundreds of magazine and newspaper articles, and chapters in children's and motivational books. She has been profiled on the *Today Show, CBS Evening News with Dan Rather,* ABC's *20/20* and NBC's *Dateline*.

A native Bostonian with a degree in Economics from Boston's prestigious Simmons College, Suzyn spent 15 years on the Broadway Musical Stage and performed in countless night clubs around the world. She is proudest of her two years starring opposite Richard Kiley in *Man of La Mancha*. She lives in Westchester with her German Shepherds, Gatsby and A.J.

Yankees en Español

For the 14th consecutive season, the Yankees – in conjunction with WCBS radio – will provide Spanish radio and SAP (second audio programming) for game broadcasts.

Beto Villa

Beto Villa, a native of Caracas, Venezuela, has broadcast Yankees games since the beginning of the club's Spanish radio network in 1997, becoming one of the most recognized voices in baseball. The 2010 season will mark Villa's 14th season as the "Spanish voice of the New York Yankees." His famous home run call: "*¡La bola va atrás, se va, se va, se va, se vaaaaaaaaaa...se fue de cuadrangular...jonrón de...!*" has made him very popular in the tri-state area and around the world.

Beto provides Spanish listeners with thorough and thoughtful Yankees coverage. He treasures his pages and pages of statistics of Latin American ballplayers, which he uses during his radiocasts. After beginning his career in 1981, he has had the opportunity to broadcast both the Major League World Series and the Caribbean World Series. He is currently the Senior Editor of Latinobaseball.com, a Web site covering Latin American players in the Majors and Winter Leagues. Beto has a daughter, Margarita.

Francisco Rivera

Since 1995, Francisco Rivera has been involved in baseball as a color commentator and play-by-play announcer, including the five years in the Yankees' broadcast booth. A native of Morovis, Puerto Rico, he covered the Philadelphia Phillies for "Radio Tropical" from 1995 to 1998 and worked the American League Championship Series in 2003 and 2004 for ESPN. Rivera received his Bachelors Degree in Spanish Literature from Rutgers University and graduated from Miguel Angel Torres School of Communications in Manhattan, a school affiliated with Cambridge University, in 1978. He was one of the pioneers of the talk show WADO Deportivo where he worked until 2003, Rivera began his communications career covering NBA basketball for WADO.

Felix DeJesus

Felix DeJesus, a native New Yorker, enters his fifth season as a back-up commentator for the New York Yankees. He also serves as a Yankees correspondent for WCBS, writes for Latinobaseball.com and is one of the co-hosts of "El Mundo de Las Grandes Ligas," an internet show on MLB Radio.

DeJesus has been involved with the Hispanic market since 1993 when he became the color commentator for the NHL's Florida Panthers. He has worked in all areas of broadcasting, television, radio and the Internet. From 1998 to 2004, he covered Major League Baseball on television for XTRA Innings in New York. He covered the Caribbean World Series in 2002 for New York's Radio Unica 1660 AM and served as one of the play-by-play voices for the international broadcast of the 2007 Caribbean Series. He has also worked for FOX Sports, ESPN International and CNN. In 1999, he became the first announcer to broadcast in SAP for NBC News. DeJesus has also served the last four years as the Spanish language translator for Showtime Championship Boxing.

DeJesus graduated from Fordham University in 1988 with a degree in Economics and currently resides in the tri-state area. He and his wife, Melissa, have two sons, Christopher and Brendan.

Carlos Silva

Carlos Silva, a native of Caracas, Venezuela, enters his fifth season producing and engineering Yankees games for WCBS Radio 880 AM. The 2010 season will mark his 10th year working on Yankees radio broadcasts and his 21st overall season in baseball. Silva has also worked for ESPN Radio and Phillies Spanish radio as well the NBA's Orlando Magic.

In the offseason, he resides in Tampa, Fla., with his wife, Teresa, and his children Leslie (23), Kimberly (20) and Matthew (10).

New York Yankees Broadcast Teams - Radio & TV

1939 (WABC) Arch McDonald, Garnett Marks and Mel Allen
1940 (WABC) Mel Allen and J. C. Flippen
1941 No games broadcast
1942 (WOR) Mel Allen and Connie Desmond
1943 No games broadcast
1944 (WINS) Don Dunphy and Bill Slater
1945 (WINS) Bill Slater and Al Helfer
1946 (WINS) Mel Allen and Russ Hodges
1947 (WINS) Mel Allen and Russ Hodges
1948 (WINS) Mel Allen and Russ Hodges
1949 (WINS radio, Dumont TV) Mel Allen and Curt Gowdy
1950 (WINS radio, Dumont TV) Mel Allen and Curt Gowdy
1951 (WINS radio, WPIX TV) Mel Allen and Art Gleeson
1952 (WINS radio, WPIX TV) Mel Allen, Art Gleeson and Bill Crowley
1953 (WINS radio, WPIX TV) Mel Allen, Jim Woods and Joe E. Brown
1954 (WINS radio, WPIX TV) Mel Allen, Jim Woods and Red Barber
1955 (WINS radio, WPIX TV) Mel Allen, Jim Woods and Red Barber
1956 (WINS radio, WPIX TV) Mel Allen, Jim Woods and Red Barber
1957 (WINS radio, WPIX TV) Mel Allen, Red Barber and Phil Rizzuto
1958 (WMGM radio, WPIX TV) Mel Allen, Red Barber and Phil Rizzuto
1959 (WMGM radio, WPIX TV) Mel Allen, Red Barber and Phil Rizzuto
1960 (WMGM radio, WPIX TV) Mel Allen, Red Barber and Phil Rizzuto
1961 (WCBS radio, WPIX TV) Mel Allen, Red Barber and Phil Rizzuto
1962 (WCBS radio, WPIX TV) Mel Allen, Red Barber and Phil Rizzuto
1963 (WCBS radio, WPIX TV) Mel Allen, Red Barber, Phil Rizzuto and Jerry Coleman
1964 (WCBS radio, WPIX TV) Mel Allen, Red Barber, Phil Rizzuto and Jerry Coleman
1965 (WCBS radio, WPIX TV) Red Barber, Phil Rizzuto, Jerry Coleman and Joe Garagiola
1966 (WCBS radio, WPIX TV) Red Barber, Phil Rizzuto, Joe Garagiola and Jerry Coleman
1967 (WHN radio, WPIX TV) Phil Rizzuto, Jerry Coleman and Joe Garagiola
1968 (WHN radio, WPIX TV) Phil Rizzuto, Jerry Coleman and Frank Messer
1969 (WHN radio, WPIX TV) Phil Rizzuto, Jerry Coleman, Frank Messer and Whitey Ford
1970 (WHN radio, WPIX TV) Phil Rizzuto, Frank Messer, Whitey Ford and Bob Gamere
1971 (WMCA radio, WPIX TV) Phil Rizzuto, Frank Messer, Bill White and Whitey Ford
1972 (WMCA radio, WPIX TV) Phil Rizzuto, Frank Messer and Bill White
1973 (WMCA radio, WPIX TV) Phil Rizzuto, Frank Messer and Bill White
1974 (WMCA radio, WPIX TV) Phil Rizzuto, Frank Messer and Bill White
1975 (WMCA radio, WPIX TV) Phil Rizzuto, Frank Messer, Bill White and Dom Valentino
1976 (WMCA radio, WPIX TV) Phil Rizzuto, Frank Messer and Bill White
1977 (WMCA radio, WPIX TV) Phil Rizzuto, Frank Messer and Bill White
1978 (WINS radio, WPIX TV) Phil Rizzuto, Frank Messer, Bill White, Mel Allen and Fran Healy
1979 (WINS radio, WPIX TV, Sports Channel) Phil Rizzuto, Frank Messer, Bill White, Mel Allen and Fran Healy
1980 (WINS radio, WPIX TV, Sports Channel) Phil Rizzuto, Frank Messer, Bill White, Mel Allen and Fran Healy
1981 (WABC radio, WPIX TV, Sports Channel) Phil Rizzuto, Frank Messer, Bill White, Mel Allen and Fran Healy
1982 (WABC radio, WPIX TV, Sports Channel) Phil Rizzuto, Frank Messer, Bill White, Mel Allen and John Gordon
1983 (WABC radio, WPIX TV, Sports Channel) Mel Allen, Phil Rizzuto, Frank Messer, Bill White and John Gordon
1984 (WABC radio, WPIX TV, Sports Channel) Mel Allen, Phil Rizzuto, Frank Messer, Bill White and John Gordon
1985 (WABC radio, WPIX TV, Sports Channel) Phil Rizzuto, Bill White, Frank Messer, Mel Allen, Mickey Mantle, John Gordon and Spencer Ross
1986 (WABC radio, WPIX TV, Sports Channel) Phil Rizzuto, Bill White, Jim Kaat, Billy Martin, Mel Allen, Mickey Mantle, John Gordon, Spencer Ross and Bobby Murcer
1987 (WABC radio, WPIX TV, Sports Channel) Phil Rizzuto, Bill White, Billy Martin, Ken "Hawk" Harrelson, Bobby Murcer, Mickey Mantle, Spencer Ross, Hank Greenwald and Tommy Hutton
1988 (WABC radio, WPIX TV, Sports Channel) Phil Rizzuto, Bill White, Ken "Hawk" Harrelson, Hank Greenwald, Bobby Murcer, Mickey Mantle, Ed Randall and Tommy Hutton
1989 (WABC radio, WPIX TV, MSG NETWORK) Phil Rizzuto, George Grande, Tom Seaver, Tommy Hutton, Bobby Murcer, Lou Piniella, Greg Gumbel, Michael Kay, John Sterling and Jay Johnstone
1990 (WABC radio, WPIX TV, MSG NETWORK) Phil Rizzuto, George Grande, Tom Seaver, Dewayne Staats, Tony Kubek, Al Trautwig, Michael Kay, John Sterling and Jay Johnstone

1967 Yankees broadcast team (from left): Jerry Coleman, Phil Rizzuto and Joe Garagiola

1991 (WABC radio, WPIX TV, MSG NETWORK) Phil Rizzuto, Bobby Murcer, Tom Seaver, Dewayne Staats, Tony Kubek, Al Trautwig, Michael Kay, John Sterling and Joe Angel
1992 (WABC radio, WPIX TV, MSG NETWORK) Phil Rizzuto, Bobby Murcer, Tom Seaver, Dewayne Staats, Tony Kubek, Al Trautwig, John Sterling and Michael Kay
1993 (WABC radio, WPIX TV, MSG NETWORK) Phil Rizzuto, Bobby Murcer, Tom Seaver, Dewayne Staats, Tony Kubek, Al Trautwig, John Sterling and Michael Kay
1994 (WABC radio, WPIX TV, MSG NETWORK) Phil Rizzuto, Dewayne Staats, Tony Kubek, Al Trautwig, John Sterling and Michael Kay
1995 (WABC radio, WPIX TV, MSG NETWORK) Phil Rizzuto, Bobby Murcer, Paul Olden, Dave Cohen, Jim Kaat, Al Trautwig, Steve Palermo, John Sterling and Michael Kay
1996 (WABC radio, WPIX TV, MSG NETWORK) Phil Rizzuto, Bobby Murcer, Rick Cerone, Paul Olden, Dave Cohen, Jim Kaat, Al Trautwig, Steve Palermo, John Sterling and Michael Kay
1997 (WABC radio, WPIX TV, MSG NETWORK) Jim Kaat, Ken Singleton, Bobby Murcer, Al Trautwig, Michael Kay, Rick Cerone, Steve Palermo, Suzyn Waldman, John Sterling and Michael Kay
1998 (WABC radio, WPIX TV, MSG NETWORK) Bobby Murcer, Jim Kaat, Ken Singleton, Bobby Murcer, Al Trautwig, Tommy John, Suzyn Waldman, John Sterling and Michael Kay
1999 (WABC radio, WNYW TV, MSG NETWORK) Tim McCarver, Bobby Murcer, Jim Kaat, Ken Singleton, Al Trautwig, Suzyn Waldman, John Sterling and Michael Kay
2000 (WABC radio, WNYW TV, MSG Network) Tim McCarver, Bobby Murcer, Jim Kaat, Ken Singleton, Al Trautwig, Suzyn Waldman, John Sterling and Michael Kay
2001 (WABC radio, WNYW TV, MSG NETWORK) Tim McCarver, Bobby Murcer, Jim Kaat, Ken Singleton, Al Trautwig, Suzyn Waldman, John Sterling and Michael Kay
2002 (WCBS radio, WCBS TV, YES NETWORK) Fred Hickman, Jim Kaat, Michael Kay, Bobby Murcer, Paul O'Neill, Ken Singleton, Suzyn Waldman, Charley Steiner and John Sterling
2003 (WCBS radio, WCBS TV, YES NETWORK) Fred Hickman, Jim Kaat, Michael Kay, Bobby Murcer, Paul O'Neill, Ken Singleton, Suzyn Waldman, Charley Steiner and John Sterling
2004 (WCBS radio, WCBS TV, YES NETWORK) Joe Girardi, Fred Hickman, Jim Kaat, Michael Kay, Bobby Murcer, Paul O'Neill, Ken Singleton, Suzyn Waldman, Charley Steiner and John Sterling
2005 (WCBS radio, WWOR TV, YES NETWORK) Jim Kaat, Michael Kay, Bobby Murcer, Paul O'Neill, Ken Singleton, Suzyn Waldman and John Sterling
2006 (WCBS radio, WWOR TV, YES NETWORK) Kimberly Jones, David Justice, Jim Kaat, Michael Kay, Bobby Murcer, Paul O'Neill, Ken Singleton, Suzyn Waldman and John Sterling
2007 (WCBS radio, WWOR TV, YES NETWORK) Michael Kay, Ken Singleton, Bobby Murcer, David Justice, Joe Girardi, John Flaherty, Kimberly Jones, Paul O'Neill, Al Leiter , Suzyn Waldman and John Sterling
2008 (WCBS radio, WWOR TV, YES NETWORK) Michael Kay, Ken Singleton, Bobby Murcer, David Cone, John Flaherty, Kimberly Jones, Paul O'Neill, Al Leiter, Suzyn Waldman and John Sterling
2009 (WCBS radio, WWOR TV, YES NETWORK) Michael Kay, Ken Singleton, David Cone, John Flaherty, Kimberly Jones, Paul O'Neill, Al Leiter, Suzyn Waldman and John Sterling
2010 (WCBS radio, WWOR TV, YES NETWORK) Michael Kay, Ken Singleton, John Flaherty, Kimberly Jones, Paul O'Neill, Al Leiter, Suzyn Waldman and John Sterling

(rightsholders in parenthesis)

George M. Steinbrenner Field

This year marks the 15th season the Yankees will play their spring training games at George M. Steinbrenner Field in Tampa, Fla. The complex has also served as the home of the Single-A Tampa Yankees of the Florida State League since it opened in 1996. The field's dimensions are an exact replica of Yankee Stadium in the Bronx, measuring 318 feet down the left line, 408 feet to center field and 314 feet down the right field line. In 2008, the addition of the *Tampa Tribune* Deck in right field expanded the Stadium's capacity to 11,076, making it the largest spring training facility in the Grapefruit League.

Fans will also notice another link to the Bronx with a replica of the Yankees' retired numbers placards greeting the Yankees faithful as they enter the complex.

Originally opened in 1996 as Legends Field, the complex was renamed after the Yankees' Principal Owner and Chairman prior to the Yankees' March 27, 2008, spring training game against the Pittsburgh Pirates. On February 14, 2008, Hal and Hank Steinbrenner announced that the New York Yankees would rename the facility George M. Steinbrenner Field. The name change followed two unanimous resolutions recommending and supporting the change from the Hillsborough County Commission and the Tampa City Council.

"I am humbled and flattered to have this outstanding and totally unexpected honor conferred on me. I extend my thanks to the Tampa City Council and to the Hillsborough County Commissioners for passing resolutions suggesting and recommending the change. I also thank my family for supporting the renaming of the stadium and for everything they have done for so many years that helped bring about this great day," George M. Steinbrenner said at the time the resolution was passed.

The resolution passed by the Tampa City Council on February 7, 2008, endorsed the naming of Legends Field after George M. Steinbrenner by citing his many charitable donations on behalf of youth activities, hospitals and the arts. The resolution passed by the Board of the Hillsborough County Commissioners on February 6, 2008, urged the Yankees to honor George M. Steinbrenner by renaming Legends Field in recognition of his numerous extraordinary contributions to the area.

STADIUM CAPACITY

Total Seating	11,076
Rooms To Go Luxury Suites	13 suites, 290 seats
Field Box Seats	161
Bright House Networks Dugout Club	104
Tampa Tribune Deck	539
Reserved Seats	9,982

FIRST GAME: 3/1/96 vs. Cleveland
LARGEST CROWD: 11,079 – 3/21/08 vs. the Tampa Bay Rays

STADIUM DIMENSIONS*

Left Field foul line	318 feet
Center Field	408 feet
Right Field foul line	314 feet

* Identical to Yankee Stadium

Spring Training Records Since 1962

Year	Record	Year	Record	Year	Record
1962	17-10	1978	10-13	1994	12-15-1
1963	12-17-1	1979	7-18	1995	11-18/4-8
1964	12-16	1980	10-8-1	1996	16-15
1965	12-18	1981	13-13-1	1997	20-11
1966	17-11	1982	9-16	1998	15-12
1967	13-17	1983	16-8	1999	14-19
1968	14-14-1	1984	10-16	2000	13-20
1969	16-9	1985	15-12	2001	9-20
1970	18-9	1986	17-11	2002	20-14
1971	8-23	1987	14-15	2003	15-13
1972	11-15-1	1988	22-10	2004	13-9
1973	18-11	1989	16-15	2005	14-15
1974	14-14-1	1990	5-9	2006	15-16
1975	14-17	1991	19-12	2007	14-13-3
1976	10-7	1992	17-14	2008	14-12-2
1977	11-13	1993	20-12	2009	24-10-1

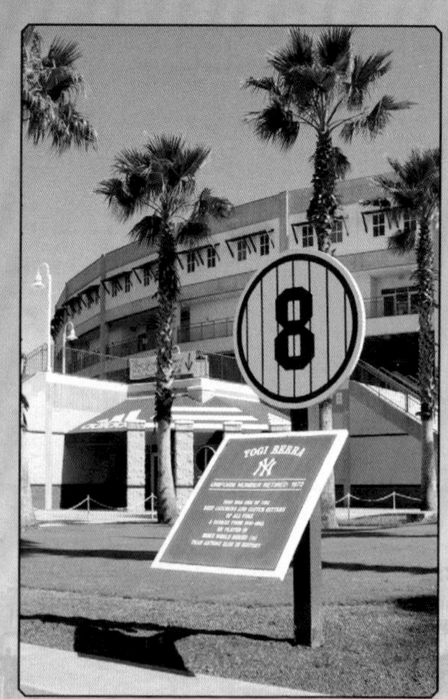

2010 Yankees Spring Training Schedule

Day/date	Opponent	Site	Time	TV/RADIO
Wed., Mar. 3	**Pittsburgh**	**GMS Field**	**1:05 p.m.**	**YES**
Thur., Mar. 4	Philadelphia	at Clearwater	1:05 p.m.	
Fri., Mar. 5	**Tampa Bay**	**GMS Field**	**1:05 p.m.**	**YES**
Sat., Mar. 6	**Toronto**	**GMS Field**	**1:05 p.m.**	**MY9/WCBS**
Sun., Mar. 7	Minnesota	at Ft. Myers	1:05 p.m.	
Mon., Mar. 8	**Philadelphia (ss)**	**GMS Field**	**1:05 p.m.**	**YES**
	Pittsburgh (ss)	at Bradenton	1:05 p.m.	
Tue., Mar. 9	**Pittsburgh**	**GMS Field**	**1:05 p.m.**	**YES**
Wed., Mar. 10	Detroit	at Lakeland	1:05 p.m.	
Thur., Mar. 11	**Atlanta**	**GMS Field**	**7:05 p.m.**	**YES/WCBS**
Fri., Mar. 12	Washington	at Viera	1:05 p.m.	
Sat., Mar. 13	**Baltimore (ss)**	**GMS Field**	**1:05 p.m.**	**MY9/WCBS**
	Detroit (ss)	at Lakeland	1:05 p.m.	
Sun., Mar. 14	Pittsburgh	at Bradenton	1:05 p.m.	
Mon., Mar. 15	Off Day			
Tue., Mar. 16	**Houston**	**GMS Field**	**7:05 p.m.**	
Wed., Mar. 17	Philadelphia	at Clearwater	1:05 p.m.	
Thur., Mar. 18	**Tampa Bay**	**GMS Field**	**7:05 p.m.**	**YES/WCBS**
Fri., Mar. 19	**Detroit (ss)**	**GMS Field**	**1:05 p.m.**	**YES**
	Tampa Bay (ss)	at Port Charlotte	7:05 p.m.	
Sat., Mar. 20	Houston	at Kissimmee	1:05 p.m.	
Sun., Mar. 21	**Detroit**	**GMS Field**	**1:05 p.m.**	**YES/WCBS**
Mon., Mar. 22	Philadelphia	at Clearwater	1:05 p.m.	YES
Tue., Mar. 23	Off Day			
Wed., Mar. 24	**Washington**	**GMS Field**	**7:05 p.m.**	
Thur., Mar. 25	Baltimore	at Sarasota	1:05 p.m.	
Fri., Mar. 26	**Philadelphia**	**GMS Field**	**7:05 p.m.**	**WCBS**
Sat., Mar. 27	Detroit	at Lakeland	1:05 p.m.	
Sun., Mar. 28	**Detroit**	**GMS Field**	**1:05 p.m.**	**YES/WCBS**
Mon., Mar. 29	Baltimore	at Sarasota	7:05 p.m.	
Tue., Mar. 30	**Toronto (ss)**	**GMS Field**	**7:05 p.m.**	**YES/WCBS**
	Atlanta (ss)	at Lake Buena Vista	1:05 p.m.	
Wed., Mar. 31	**Minnesota**	**GMS Field**	**1:05 p.m.**	**YES**
Thur., Apr. 1	Toronto	at Dunedin	1:05 p.m.	
Fri., Apr. 2	**Baltimore**	**GMS Field**	**1:05 p.m.**	**YES**
Sat., Apr. 3	**Yankees Future Stars**	**GMS Field**	**1:05 p.m.**	**YES**

Bold=Home Games ss=Split Squad *All Times Eastern and Subject to Change*

1966 Spring Training (L-R): Clete Boyer, Bobby Murcer, Bobby Richardson and Joe Pepitone.

2009 SPRING TRAINING ATTENDANCE

Home Attendance at GMS Field in Tampa, FL (16 dates, 10,557 average) 168,905
Road Attendance (17 dates/7,648 average) 130,015
Overall Attendance (33 dates/9,058 average) 298,920

SPRING TRAINING ATTENDANCE SINCE 1996

Year	Attendance
1996	173,247
1997	172,092
1998	149,496
1999	164,015
2000	153,385
2001	173,107
2002	172,544
2003	162,890
2004	122,374
2005	152,640
2006	152,024
2007	154,590
2008	139,496
2009	168,905

Yankees All-Time Spring Training Sites

Year	Location
1903-04	Atlanta, GA
1905	Montgomery, AL
1906	Birmingham, AL
1907-08	Atlanta, GA
1909	Macon, GA
1910-11	Athens, GA
1912	Atlanta, GA
1913	Hamilton, Bermuda
1914	Houston, TX
1915	Savannah, GA
1916-18	Macon, GA
1919-20	Jacksonville, FL
1921	Shreveport, LA
1922-24	New Orleans, LA
1925-42	St. Petersburg, FL
1943	Asbury Park, NJ
1944-45	Atlantic City, NJ
1946-50	St. Petersburg, FL
1951	Phoenix, AZ
1952-61	St. Petersburg, FL
1962-95	Ft. Lauderdale, FL
1996-present	Tampa, FL

2010 New York Yankees Schedule

APRIL

SUN	MON	TUE	WED	THU	FRI	SAT
				1	2	3
4 BOS 8:05 YES	5	6 BOS 7:10 YES	7 BOS 7:10 YES	8	9 TB 7:10 YES	10 TB 3:05 FOX
11 TB 1:40 YES	12	13 LAA 1:05 YES	14 LAA 1:05 YES	15 LAA 7:05 MY9	16 TEX 7:05 YES	17 TEX 1:05 YES
18 TEX 1:05 YES	19	20 OAK 10:05 YES	21 OAK 10:05 YES	22 OAK 3:35 YES	23 LAA 10:05 YES	24 LAA 4:05 FOX
25 LAA 3:35 YES	26	27 BAL 7:05 MY9	28 BAL 7:05 YES	29 BAL 7:05 YES	30 CWS 7:05 YES	

MAY

SUN	MON	TUE	WED	THU	FRI	SAT
						1 CWS 1:05 YES
2 CWS 1:05 YES	3 BAL 7:05 YES	4 BAL 7:05 YES	5 BAL 1:05 YES	6	7 BOS 7:10 YES	8 BOS 3:05 FOX
9 BOS 8:05 ESPN	10 DET 7:05 YES	11 DET 7:05 MY9	12 DET 7:05 YES	13 DET 1:05 YES	14 MIN 7:05 YES	15 MIN 1:05 YES
16 MIN 1:05 YES	17 BOS 7:05 YES	18 BOS 7:05 MY9	19 TB 7:05 YES	20 TB 7:05 MY9	21 NYM 7:10 YES	22 NYM 7:05 FOX
23 NYM 8:05 ESPN	24	25 MIN 8:10 MY9	26 MIN 8:10 YES	27 MIN 8:10 YES	28 CLE 7:05 YES	29 CLE 1:05 YES
30 CLE 1:05 YES	31 CLE 1:05 YES					

yankees.com

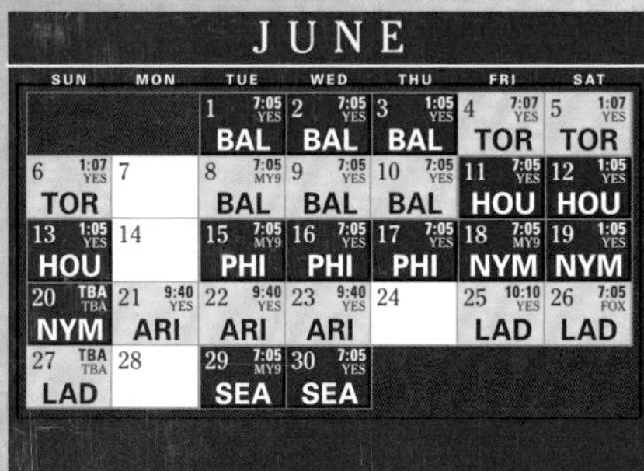

JUNE

SUN	MON	TUE	WED	THU	FRI	SAT
		1 BAL 7:05 YES	2 BAL 7:05 YES	3 BAL 1:05 YES	4 TOR 7:07 YES	5 TOR 1:07 YES
6 TOR 1:07 YES	7	8 BAL 7:05 MY9	9 BAL 7:05 YES	10 BAL 7:05 YES	11 HOU 7:05 YES	12 HOU 1:05 YES
13 HOU 1:05 YES	14	15 PHI 7:05 MY9	16 PHI 7:05 YES	17 PHI 7:05 YES	18 NYM 7:05 MY9	19 NYM 1:05 YES
20 NYM TBA TBA	21 ARI 9:40 YES	22 ARI 9:40 YES	23 ARI 9:40 YES	24	25 LAD 10:10 YES	26 LAD 7:05 FOX
27 LAD TBA TBA	28	29 SEA 7:05 MY9	30 SEA 7:05 YES			

JULY

SUN	MON	TUE	WED	THU	FRI	SAT
				1 SEA 1:05 YES	2 TOR 1:05 YES	3 TOR 1:05 YES
4 TOR 1:05 YES	5 OAK 10:05 YES	6 OAK 10:05 YES	7 OAK 10:05 YES	8 SEA 10:10 YES	9 SEA 10:10 YES	10 SEA 10:10 YES
11 SEA 4:10 YES	12	13 ALL-STAR GAME	14	15	16 TB 7:05 MY9	17 TB 4:05 FOX
18 TB 1:05 YES	19	20 LAA 7:05 MY9	21 LAA 1:05 YES	22 KC 7:05 YES	23 KC 7:05 YES	24 KC 1:05 YES
25 KC 1:05 YES	26 CLE 7:05 YES	27 CLE 7:05 MY9	28 CLE 7:05 YES	29 CLE 7:05 YES	30 TB 7:10 YES	31 TB 7:10 YES

OLD-TIMERS' DAY IS JULY 17
CEREMONIES BEGIN AT 2:00 PM ON YES

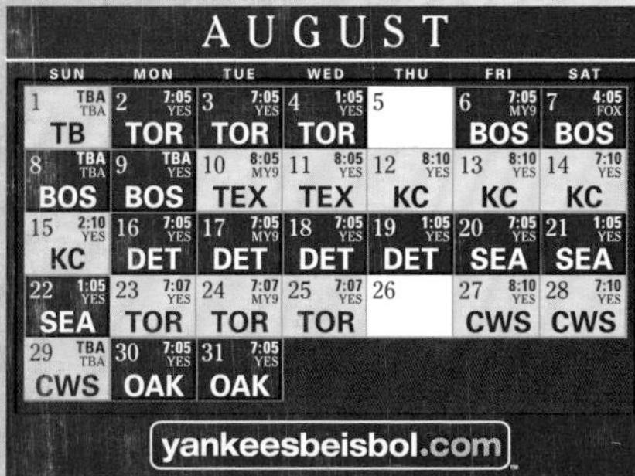

AUGUST

SUN	MON	TUE	WED	THU	FRI	SAT
1 TB TBA TBA	2 TOR 7:05 YES	3 TOR 7:05 YES	4 TOR 1:05 YES	5	6 BOS 7:05 MY9	7 BOS 4:05 FOX
8 BOS TBA TBA	9 BOS TBA YES	10 TEX 8:05 MY9	11 TEX 8:05 YES	12 KC 8:10 YES	13 KC 8:10 YES	14 KC 7:10 YES
15 KC 2:10 YES	16 DET 7:05 YES	17 DET 7:05 MY9	18 DET 7:05 YES	19 DET 1:05 MY9	20 SEA 7:05 YES	21 SEA 1:05 YES
22 SEA 1:05 YES	23 TOR 7:07 YES	24 TOR 7:07 MY9	25 TOR 7:07 YES	26	27 CWS 8:10 YES	28 CWS 7:10 YES
29 CWS TBA TBA	30 OAK 7:05 YES	31 OAK 7:05 YES				

yankeesbeisbol.com

SEPT./OCT.

SUN	MON	TUE	WED	THU	FRI	SAT
			1 OAK 7:05 YES	2 OAK 1:05 YES	3 TOR 1:05 YES	4 TOR 1:05 YES
5 TOR TBA TBA	6 BAL 1:05 YES	7 BAL 7:05 YES	8 BAL 1:05 YES	9	10 TEX 8:05 YES	11 TEX 8:05 YES
12 TEX TBA TBA	13 TB 7:10 YES	14 TB 7:10 MY9	15 TB 7:10 YES	16	17 BAL 7:05 YES	18 BAL 7:05 YES
19 BAL 1:35 YES	20 TB 7:05 YES	21 TB 7:05 MY9	22 TB 7:05 YES	23 TB 7:05 YES	24 BOS 7:05 YES	25 BOS TBA TBA
26 BOS TBA TBA	27 TOR 7:07 YES	28 TOR 7:07 MY9	29 TOR 7:07 YES	30	1 BOS 7:10 MY9	2 BOS TBA TBA
3 BOS 1:35 YES						

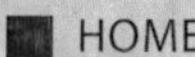 HOME 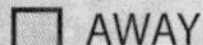 AWAY

ALL GAMES ARE EASTERN TIME

FOR YANKEES TICKET INFORMATION, PLEASE VISIT YANKEES.COM OR CALL (718) 293-6000

Game times listed as TBA are subject to determination by Major League Baseball and its television partners.

All seat locations are subject to availability.

Time, opponent, date and team rosters and lineups, including the Yankees' roster and lineup, are subject to change.

Tickets may not be used by the ticket holder/licensee or anyone else other than the Yankees for advertising, promotion or other commercial purposes, including, without limitation, contests, auctions, sweepstakes and giveaways.

NOTICE: All persons specifically consent to and are subject to metal detector and physical pat-down inspections prior to entry. Any person or property that could affect the safety of Yankee Stadium occupants/property shall be denied entry.

WARNING: During all batting practices, fielding practices, warm-ups and the course of the game experience, hard hit baseballs and bats and fragments thereof may be thrown or hit into the stands, concourses and concessions areas. For everyone's safety, please stay alert and be aware of your surroundings. Any guest who is concerned with his or her seat location should contact any guest services representative for an alternate seat location.

Be advised that the Yankees reserve the right to take appropriate action against individuals who fraudulently obtain wheelchair accessible and companion seats, including, without limitation, ejection and legal action.

Distribution of promotional items is for fans in attendance only, while supplies last. Promotion dates, items and distribution are subject to change and/or cancellation.